The Papers of
HENRY CLAY

The Papers of
HENRY CLAY

James F. Hopkins, *Editor*

Mary W. M. Hargreaves, *Associate Editor*

Wayne Cutler *and* Burton Milward, *Assistant Editors*

VOLUME 4

SECRETARY OF STATE

1825

THE UNIVERSITY PRESS OF KENTUCKY

Printed in the United States of America

"My ambition is that we may enter a new and larger era of service to humanity."

Dedicated to the memory of
JOSIAH KIRBY LILLY
1861-1948
President of Eli Lilly and Company
Founder of Lilly Endowment, Inc.

Whose wisdom and foresight were
devoted to the service of
education, religion, and
public welfare

PREFACE

Selection of documents for *The Papers of Henry Clay* during the period of Clay's service as Secretary of State has presented very different problems from those encountered in preparation of the previous volumes in the series. As originally contemplated, the volumes were not to have included materials identified with Clay's professional duties. Since his personal correspondence at this time became inextricably interlocked with comments upon foreign affairs, such an approach was quickly rejected. For the same reason, a separate calendaring of official correspondence also proved unsatisfactory. Yet the availability of many of the papers as published Congressional documents suggested that full reproduction was not now necessary. The editors have accordingly provided summaries of most of the official correspondence, both incoming and outgoing —summaries which, it is hoped, will fulfill not only the basic purpose of these volumes in illuminating Clay's role but also the needs of those who seek guidance to related subjects more fully developed in the original manuscripts.

Where Clay's personal contribution as author was significant, the official documents have been reproduced in full, either from the version received by the addressee or from the letterbook copy, which constituted the official Department record. Files of the foreign service posts, though generally preferable for their inclusion of the signed instructions, as received, are broken; for this reason they were not filmed by the National Archives until the more complete letterbook series was made available. Since this volume and the succeeding one went to press, the post papers (RG84) have been cataloged and the Clay documents reproduced. No items have been found which were not included in the letterbooks, here cited. Where Clay's original draft versions have been available, they have been collated to the final form and annotations supplied, if noteworthy, to indicate the possibility that revisions were made in deference to the views of colleagues. As in previous volumes of the series, Clay's personal correspondence, incoming and outgoing, has generally been published in full.

Two categories of the official correspondence have impressed the editors as warranting more consideration than might have been anticipated—the consular files and the letters of application and recommendation for office or for publication of the laws. Since both are voluminous, they have been presented in summary. Neither has been extensively published heretofore, and neither has been generally consulted by scholars. Yet during the period when diplomatic and commercial ties with the Latin-American states were newly developing, the consular reports proved highly interesting, particularly in relation to the role of Clay as Secretary of State. And at a time when old party affiliations were rapidly shifting, the correspondence in relation to patronage distribution reveals much that is pertinent to Clay's position as political leader. When first made available to this project through the cooperation of the National Historical Publications Commission, the letters of application and recommendation for office were filmed as a special project; and, for the most part, they have been so identified in our source listing. Subsequently, they have been reproduced as one of the regular collections available on microfilm from the National Archives. Where, in some instances, the latter file has proved more complete than that originally consulted, the revised series has been utilized and so indicated. Since both series are organized chronologically under the name of the applicant or individual recommended, the dual forms of citation should not occasion serious difficulties for those who would consult the manuscript record.

Official correspondence sent to the Secretary of State without designation by name or, during the first weeks of the administration, even when addressed to John Quincy Adams has been defined as Clay's if it was dated after he assumed his duties. Clerical correspondence has generally been omitted, though notation has been given when replies to published letters were written at the Secretary's direction.

Numerous categories of documents clearly identifiable with the office rather than with Clay have also been excluded. These encompass most ceremonial communications, requests for and grants of exequaturs and other diplomatic courtesies, shipping reports and financial accounts from consular or diplomatic officers, accounts for publication of the laws, formal signature of laws and commissions of appointment, correspondence relating to filing of State laws, certification of patents, pardons, passports, and naturalization, transmittal of court orders to Federal judicial officers, requests for authentication of documents and for transmittal of mail via diplomatic pouch, notices of the sailing of vessels, and offers to transmit public mail. The range and volume of such papers, nevertheless, should be recognized as adding a very considerable burden to Clay's duties as Secretary of State.

During the prolonged interval since publication of earlier volumes in this series, the editors have incurred deep obligations.

First they would express apologies to those whose interest in the forthcoming papers has been so long deferred. Among these, Lilly Endowment, Inc., claims particular consideration, for its basic funding permitted initiation of the Clay Papers Project. Throughout the development of the undertaking the National Historical Publications Commission and its executive directors, first, Dr. Philip M. Hamer and, subsequently, Dr. Oliver Wendell Holmes, have extended encouragement and support, by making available microfilm copies of State Department records, by providing supplementary funds for secretarial and research assistance, and, in two instances, by assigning editorial trainees under the Commission's fellowship program. To those young scholars, Peter T. Harsted and Paul J. Woehrmann, who interrupted teaching careers for a year of postdoctoral training in the frequently exacting chores of editorial assistants, the Clay Papers Project conveys special thanks. The editors acknowledge with sincere appreciation the services of the staff of the National Historical Publications Commission, and particularly those of Miss F. Helen Beach, now retired, in searching the records of the National Archives for the major files of Clay's official correspondence.

The cooperation of the University of Kentucky Research Foundation and the executive committee of the Project has given a sustaining direction for which the editors are also grateful. With sorrow they here note the recent loss of a long-time friend and counselor, Dr. Albert D. Kirwan, who served most recently as chairman of the executive committee and for many years as director of the Research Foundation. For all these and many more who have assisted in this undertaking—typists, graduate assistants, encouraging colleagues, and librarians of many institutions—the editors voice the hope that their efforts will have proved fruitful.

J. F. H.
M.W.H.

SYMBOLS

The following symbols are used to describe the nature of the originals of documents copied from manuscript sources.

AD	Autograph Document
AD draft	Autograph Document, draft
ADS	Autograph Document Signed
AE	Autograph Endorsement
AEI	Autograph Endorsement Initialed
AES	Autograph Endorsement Signed
AL	Autograph Letter
AL draft	Autograph Letter, draft
ALI draft	Autograph Letter Initialed, draft
ALS	Autograph Letter Signed
AN	Autograph Note
ANS	Autograph Note Signed
Copy	Copy not by writer (indicated "true" if so certified)
D	Document
DI	Document Initialed
DS	Document Signed
ES	Endorsement Signed
L draft	Letter, draft
LS	Letter Signed
N	Note
N draft	Note, draft

The following, from the *Symbols Used in the National Union Catalog of the Library of Congress* (8th ed., rev.; Washington, 1960), indicate the location of the original documents in institutional libraries of the United States.

CSmH	Henry E. Huntington Library and Museum, San Marino, California
CtY	Yale University, New Haven, Connecticut
DLC	United States Library of Congress, Washington, D.C.
DLC-HC	Library of Congress, Henry Clay Collection
DLC-TJC	Library of Congress, Thomas J. Clay Collection

DNA	United States National Archives Library, Washington, D.C. Following the symbol for this depository, the letters A. and R. mean Applications and Recommendations; M, Microcopy; P. and D. of L., Publication and Distribution of the Laws; R, Reel; and RG, Record Group.
ICHi	Chicago Historical Society, Chicago, Illinois
ICU	University of Chicago, Chicago, Illinois
IEN	Northwestern University, Evanston, Illinois
InU	Indiana University, Bloomington, Indiana
KyHi	Kentucky Historical Society, Frankfort, Kentucky
KyLoF	Filson Club, Louisville, Kentucky
KyLxT	Transylvania University, Lexington, Kentucky
KyU	University of Kentucky, Lexington, Kentucky
MH	Harvard University, Cambridge, Massachusetts
MHi	Massachusetts Historical Society, Boston, Massachusetts
MiU-C	University of Michigan, William L. Clements Library, Ann Arbor, Michigan
NBuHi	Buffalo Historical Society, Buffalo, New York
NHi	New York Historical Society, New York City
NN-A	American Geographical Society, New York
NNC	Columbia University, New York
NNPM	Pierpont Morgan Library, New York City
NRU	University of Rochester, Rochester, New York
NUtHi	Oneida Historical Society, Utica, New York
NcD	Duke University, Durham, North Carolina
NcU	University of North Carolina, Chapel Hill, North Carolina
NhD	Dartmouth College, Hanover, New Hampshire
NjP	Princeton University, Princeton, New Jersey
OCHP	Historical and Philosophical Society of Ohio, Cincinnati, Ohio
OClWHi	Western Reserve Historical Society, Cleveland, Ohio
OHi	Ohio Historical Society, Columbus, Ohio
PHi	Historical Society of Pennsylvania, Philadelphia, Pennsylvania
PPL-R	Library Company of Philadelphia, Ridgeway Branch, Philadelphia, Pennsylvania
ScHi	South Carolina Historical Society, Charleston, South Carolina
THi	Tennessee Historical Society, Nashville, Tennessee
TxU	University of Texas, Austin, Texas
ViU	University of Virginia, Charlottesville, Virginia

The Papers of
HENRY CLAY

Remarks and Toast at Public Dinner

[January 1, 1825]

Mr. Clay, wished, in a parting glass, to propose a sentiment for which he anticipated a cordial reception from both their illustrious guests, and from every other gentleman present. It had indeed been, as it was impossible it should not be, on this pleasing occasion, alluded to in the toasts prepared with so much judgment and taste by the excellent Committee of arrangement,[1] and which had already received, as they merited, unqualified approbation. But the sentiment deserved repetition—he hoped, without arrogance, that he might say a distinct and emphatic expression from him. Whilst we are enjoying, in peace plenty and safety, the blessings of those free institutions which the valor and the patriotism of our sires and their gallant companions now present have established, and freely and gratefully indulging in our Revolutionary recollections, can we forget that our neighbours and friends, on the same Continent, are now struggling to achieve that freedom and independence which here happily was so successfully vindicated? In their behalf no Foreign nation, no generous and disinterested La Fayette has risen unaided, they have sustained their glorious cause alone, conscious of its righteousness, and with no other helps than those which their courage, their morasses, and their Andes have supplied. If the monarch of miserable Spain[2] had ever displayed any extraordinary moral fitness—if he possessed any superior wisdom, for governing—if, situated beyond the Atlantic, within his contracted European Peninsula, all mankind was not obliged to confess the folly and the presumption of his vain effort to regain his lost dominion over the greater part of America, we might moderate our sympathies, and feel a less lively interest in the final issue of the War. But wretched Spain, governed itself by foreign force—infatuated monarch, yet to cherish the impracticable hope of maintaining a rule in the new world for which he is utterly incompetent in the old— He would not longer detain the Company. He proposed

Genl Bolivar, the Washington of South America, and the Republic of Colombia

AD draft. DLC-HC (DNA, M212, R5). Published in Washington *Daily National Intelligencer*, January 3, 1825; Lexington *Kentucky Reporter*, February 7, 1825; *Niles' Weekly Register*, XXVII (January 8, 1825), 291-92. Clay presented this salute after the regular toasts had been offered, near the end of a dinner given by members of both Houses of Congress in honor of Lafayette. Attended by 200 guests, the banquet was held at Williamson's "Mansion House" (or "Mansion Hotel") on Pennsylvania Avenue in Washington. Williamson not further identified.

John Quincy Adams, who sat next to Clay, reported that the latter commented that "he should be glad to have with me soon some confidential conversation upon public affairs. I said I should be happy to have it whenever it might suit his convenience." Adams, *Memoirs*, VI, 457. See below, Clay to Adams, January 9, 1825.

1 Composed of Robert Y. Hayne, Richard M. Johnson, and Elijah Hunt Mills, of the Senate, and James Hamilton, Jr., Stephen Van Rensselaer, and Duncan McArthur, of the House of Representatives.

2 Ferdinand VII. See above, III, 313n, 498n, 606-607; below, Nelson to Clay, April 26, 1825, note.

Account with Samuel Redd

Lexington 1st January. 1825

H. Clay Esqr. To Saml Redd

Dr

May 31st	Charg d in Specie.	
	Repairing the mouldings on the Dorr of Your Carrige [*sic*]	0 50
	A new roof cover made of Russia Sheeting puting it on & painting it	3 ....
	New wooden mouldings around the Top to receive the plated mouldings of the body.—	0 75
	puting new Sprigs in the plated mouldings for the Top, Cleaning the mouldings & puting them on—	1 ....
	A new Sett of fellows in one of the hind wheels & eight new Spokes—	3 75
	Cuting welding & puting on one tyre & fourteen new tyre nails	1 25
	Wedging Boxes in the wheels	0 37½
	Two new Bolts for the carriage	0 50
	One large Iron washer for front wheel & two new nuts for old bolts	0 50
	Repairing the raising pieces that Supports the board behind	1 ....
	10 yds of Rattinitte for the inside curtains & Roof lining at 5/3 p yd	8 75
	25 yds of fringe at 12½ Cents p yd	3 12½
	Making & puting up inside roof & curtains	2 50
	18 plated nails for inside curtains at 25/100 [*sic*]	0 37½
	eight new plated knobs for outside curtains	0 37½
	A new pr of Footman holders & Tassels	4 ....
	Furnishing materials & Stringing two real Venitian Blinds & one mock Venitian Blind	2 ....
	A new piece of Leather over the pole pin	0 12½
	Mending one of the long Braces with new leather	1 ....

Cleaning oyling & Varnishing the long Braces Check Braces Footboard Braces pole Braces & Swingletree Braces	1	50
Cleaning oyling & Varnishing the curtains for the body	0	75
Puting piece leather on the pole to make it fit the futchels	0	37½
Painting ornamenting Varnishing & Polishing Body & Painting & Varnishing the carriage & Wheels	35	....
2 new Britchbands with plated Buckles for the harness	5	....
2 new pads for Do	2	....
one new throat Latch with two plated Buckles	0	50
	$80	00

Amount Brt over	$80	00
Two new Brow Bands for the Bridles—	0	50
A new howsing Strap & a new Strap for Belly band,	0	25
Mending one howsing tug with new leather & Mending collar & putting on a new plated buckle at the Top	0	37½
Mending Bridle in Sundry places & one new gag Strap	0	62½
Cleaning oyling & Varnishing the harness	2	....
A new key for the Boot	0	12½
A new pole hook for the end of the pole two new Bolts for Do	1	50

June 18th

Piecing four Traces for your Tandum Harness with new leather, two feet long each	4	....
Mending one trace in another place with new leather	0	25
A new Belly band & new plated Buckle	0	50
4 new loops on hame tugs & Sewing them where they were ript	0	50
Mending two pads & one back band	0	37½
One half of the long reins for the Tandum harness made new	3	....
One collar nearly new	1	75
Cleaning oyling & Varnishing Tandum Harness	2	....
One large Iron clip on Double Tree for the Tandum Horses to Draw By	0	50

June 25th.

2 new hame straps with plated Buckles & a new Buckle & strap for the pole hook	0	75
A new hinge for the dorr of your light carriage new Screws & puting it on	0	62½

July 2nd.

Mending curtains for your light carriage & puting on new leather patches	0	50
four new loops for the harness & one new plated Dee, & a new Strap for Belly Band	0	62½

One new clip for the hame two new Rivits & puting it on	0 37½
Mending one collar & puting on a new cap	0 37½
Acct for 1824 as p Bill Rend., herwith [*sic*]	$101 50
	14
	$115 50

[Endorsement][1]
Amount brought up $115.50
By bal. due H.C on a/c of 1823
    in Commths notes—$11.75   5:87½
                           109:62½
Received the above sum of $109:62½ in full this 4h. July 1825
Note The wood delivered by Mr. Hawkins[2] in the fall 1823 has been settled at 20 Cords. If it were more I am to account for it. SAML REDD

D. DLC-TJC (DNA, M212, R16).   1 ES, in Clay's hand.   2 Francis Hawkins.

From James Cowan

Dear Sir   Lexington Jany 1st, 1825

Your attention & time has generally been so faithfully and generously bestowed on business coming from the West that I feel somewhat unwilling to trouble you with mine. However as I have no acquaintances in Congress whose general acquaintance with the Lawyers from the different Sea port towns is as extensive as your own, you must excuse this intrusion on your time, and oblige your friend very much by employing a Lawyer of integrity who lives in the town or City, wherever the Frigate John Adams[1] is stationed, to sue (and hold to bail if practicable.) the Obligee *Hugh N. Page*[2] to the inclosed Note for $540 with interest from 1815.

Mr Page is a Lieutenant in the navy, & is attached to the John Adams. His Parents live near Winchester Virginia,[3] are wealthy and respectable as I am told. He is a nephew of the late Wm Briant.[4]

If upon inquiry you find that the John Adams is stationed in any American Port, you will be so good as to enclose the note to some Lawyer of your acquaintance at the place— If the John Adams is at sea and it is uncertain when or where she will be in port, you will then (if you deem it expedient) prevail on some Lawyer at Washington (to be confided in) to take charge of the Note, who may probably be able to stop a portion of Lieutenant Page's pay at the proper Office or hold him to bail, if he ever comes to Washington.

You may well imagine the general regret, common to all your Western friends, at the result of the late Presidential election. But however much on your own account, they may regret it, yet so

far as the general welfare of the United States is concerned, they
have cause of congratulation that your exertions will be continued
in the councils of the Nations [*sic*], where in my opinion an honest,
firm and undeviating patriotic spirit will be more needed than at
any period since our separation from England— Whether the bonds
of Union which have been thrown around us by our Forefathers,
in the various guards, checks & balances introduced into their
improvements on the republican system of government, will or
will not be burst asunder by those convulsions produced by local
causes, interests, lawless ambition, prejudice & passion, is yet to be
tried. Nor do I believe the time is far distant, so far as it relates
to Kentucky. You have no doubt learnt through the medium of
the Newspaper & other wise the "fantastic tricks" which our Legislature have been & are now playing "before high Heaven"   And
if the "Angels have not wept" I am sure that every true patriot,
every man who loves Justice, law & order, every friend to Kentuckys
honor & future prosperity will weep over the ruins of her Constitution prostrated by a prostituted Legislature. If there is not a
redeeming spirit in the powers of the General Government it is
in vain that we boast of Governments superior to those of the
Petty States of Greece & Rome.

The Legislature have passed a law to place the Judiciary, so far
as they can place it, under the entire control of the Legislature.[5]
Are not the Legislature in a state of rebellion against the government? Have they not invaded and violently trampled on one
coordinate Branch of Government?

Is not the Congress of the United States bound & solemnly
pledged in the Constitution of the U. S. to guarantee to each
State a republican *form* of Government. If the General Government has no power to bring a rebellious State to anchor it must
be most obvious from the case of Kentucky that it should possess
the power. One great object in organizing the Government of
the U. S. was to keep the States in their proper Spheres to regulate
their Centrifugal and centripetal tendencies, and to *compel* them,
"sic utere tuo, non alienum laedas" so to exercise their own
rights, as not to encroach on the rights of others; to move in their
proper Orbits.

My dear Sir, you hold the fate of Kentucky in your hands. You
can impress on the Supreme Court of this Union, the absolute
necessity of marching straight up to the *relief questions* from
Kentucky now before them,[6] and of deciding fully and at large all
the questions involved in the cases, without resorting to "go bys"
or hiding behind technicallites [*sic*]   The firmness of the Judicial
Tribunals is the Sheet Anchor of the Nation, their temporizing

policy & timidity its ruin, and their own certain degradation. The
Mandate of the Supreme Court on all the relief laws of Kentucky
ought to be in Kentucky early next Spring so as to bring the new
relief Court to issue and let it be decided at once whether Kentucky can set up for herself, or whether the laws of the Union
shall prevail.

The old Court of Appeals in their response to the Legislature
say that they are bound as honest men to disregard the law repealing
the Court of Appeals as clearly unconstitutional and that they will
"remain on the forlorn hope to the last hour of official existence"[7]
From which it is inferrable that they will not succumb— They
have adjourned to meet again on the 4th Monday of this month,
by which time the *relief Court* will be organized. Have, or have
not, Congress the power of interfering to settle this matter? It
seems to me that the Government of the U. S cannot be so imperfect
as not to provide for such a case. The importance of this subject I
offer as an apology for boring you with this long letter   Your Friend

JAS. COWAN

ALS. DLC-HC (DNA, M212, R1). Addressed to Clay at Washington. MS. badly
faded.
1 The *John Adams,* a corvette, not a frigate, then attached to the West Indian
squadron, had sailed from Philadelphia for Thompson's Island (Key West) in November and returned to Norfolk in March.
2 Hugh Nelson Page, born in North End, Gloucester (now Middlesex) County,
Virginia, in 1788, had entered the United States Navy as a midshipman in 1811, had
served with distinction during the War of 1812, and remained in the service until
his retirement in 1855.
3 John Page, of Caroline County, Virginia, had married Elizabeth Burwell, of King's
Mills, York County, Virginia, in 1764. He had died in 1789, and she, in 1811. Hugh
Nelson Page was the youngest of their fifteen children.
4 Not identified. Peyton Randolph Page, a much older brother of Hugh, had
married Elizabeth Schona, widow of a William Bryan, around 1801.
5 See above, III, 902.   6 See above, III, 261n, 349n.
7 "The Response of the Judges of the Court of Appeals, to the Preamble, Resolutions
and Address. . . ," December 9, 1824, in Ky. H. of Reps., *Journal . . . 1824-1825,* p. 348.
The old court judges were John Boyle, Benjamin Mills, and William Owsley.

From Robert Scott

Dr. Sir,   Lexington 3 Jany 1825—
Your favors of the 7 & 16th. Ulto.[1] have been received in due
course.—

I have recd. a letter from Thos. B. Reed Esqr. of Natchez,
acknowledging the receipt of Colo. Butler's Note, and also a
letter from the latter to the former stating his motives for refusing
payment— I enclose herewith a copy of the first and the letter of
Colo B.[2]

From these letters you will see there are difficulties in the way,
but notwithstandg I have requested Mr. Reed to bring suit leaving
it optional with himself in what court to institute it—

I have recd. also a letter from the Messrs. Henderson's[3] of Natchez of 29th. Novr.— in which they state that they had not been able to dispose of our Bale Rope— unless 5 Coils @ $5\frac{3}{4}$c. except at a great sacrifice from 3 to 4c.   they say it is good—but Smaller than what the planters wish it—and there was a large supply of thicker rope in market—I know it was heavier than Morrison & Bruce had been in the habit of making theirs—

On last week Hawkins[4] left the farm & Car[5] [*sic*], the New Overseer came on it— Parker[6] has paid the interest on his Note & I deposited it in Bank to your credit— Warfield[7] has not yet paid the interest on his, but promises in a few days— In case he fails I think you directed suit to be brought on his Note—please say in your next— To day I paid Mrs. Clay 200$ more in Coms. Notes—and [she][8] informed me she stil [*sic*] had some of what I paid her before.[9]

In two or three days will forward the Accounts for last month[10]— Very respectfully Your Hble Servt.   Robt. Scott
The Honble H. Clay

ALS. KyLxT.   1 Neither letter found.
2 Cf. above, III, 628. The enclosures not found.   3 John Henderson and Sons.
4 Francis Hawkins.
5 John H. Kerr, who had married a Fayette County girl two years earlier.
6 Alexander Parker.   7 Dr. Walter Warfield.   8 MS. torn.
9 See above, III, 889.   10 See below, Scott to Clay, January 7, 1825.

To John C. Calhoun

Washington Jany 4. 1825
Hon J. C. Calhoun Secy of the Dept. of War
Sir

We beg leave to recommend for a place as a Cadet in the Military Academy at West Point *Robert Holley* of Lyons in the County of Wayne in the State of New York

We are Sir Respectfully Yr Obdt Servt
Henry R. Storrs
S V Rensselaer
H. Clay

ALS by Storrs, signed also by Van Rensselaer and Clay. DNA, RG94, U. S. Military Academy, Cadet Applications, 1824/324. Cf. above, III, 904-905.

Inventory of Livestock and Farming Implements at "Ashland"

Jany 5th. 1825

66 Head Cattle
28 Head of Horses

    6 Mules
  190 Head of Hogs
  112 Head of Sheep
    8 Ploughes & 5 Harrows
    7 Axes—2 Waggons 3 Carts & 6 Setts Geer— 5 Hemp brakes
    7 Hemp Hooks
    3 pr Stretchers
    5 Clevis's & One Wheat Fan

AD by Robert Scott. DLC-TJC (DNA, M212, R16). Endorsed by Scott on verso: "List of Stock &c. deld. by [Francis] Hawkins to Carr [*i.e.*, John H. Kerr] 5 Jany. 1825—"

Check to Pishey Thompson

7 Jan. 1825

Pay to Pishey Thompson or order nineteen dollars and 65 Cents, balance of his account.   H. CLAY
Cashr. of the Off. of Dt. & Dt. Washington[1]—

ADS. DLC-TJC (DNA, M212, R16). Thompson was a Washington, District of Columbia, author and bookseller.   [1] Richard Smith.

From Robert Scott

Dr. Sir,   Lexington, 7 Jany 1825
On the 3rd. inst. I wrote you enclosing the letter of Thos. B. Reed Esqr. on the subject of Colo. Butlers Note—

Herewith are your Accounts Current with the estate of Colo. Morrison for the last month[1]— By them you will perceive that collections have been very inconsiderable— The purchasers at the Sale all promise payment very soon— If they fail will bring suits on their Notes to the March Court—

I have been Solicited to enquire of you, if you would lease your Hotel establishment,[2] including the Stable, for the term of 3 or 5 Years, to be occupied as a public house—and if you would at what rent—to take it as it is, or repair it— It is a Mr. Edwards[3] formerly of Russellsville who wishes to get it—

I was out at the farm[4] yesterday— Mr. Carr[5] was spreading hemp— We have nothing new I beleive [*sic*]—at least nothing but what our papers will give you— Our Legislature have carried on with a high hand this sessession [*sic*] It is supposed they will adjourn some time next week— Aunt Morrison and family are well—

Very respectfully Yr Hble Servt   ROBT. SCOTT
The Honble H. Clay—

ALS. KyLxT.
[1] Private accounts not found. For the executor's accounts, see below, *ca.* June 13, 1825 (the monthly accounts, ADS by Scott, may be found in KyLxT).
[2] The Kentucky Hotel.   [3] Not identified.   [4] "Ashland."   [5] John H. Kerr.

To Francis Preston Blair

My dear Sir.   Washington 8th Jan. 1824 [*i.e.*, 1825]
I sent you by this days Mail Lord Byrons conversations[1] which notwithstanding Mr Walshes[2] unfavorable opinion of them, I think you will find often piquant, and worth upon the whole an attentive perusal. Besides the literary & critical interest which they possess they will have the effect of diminishing, though not entirely removing, the odium brought[3] upon himself by his conduct to his wife[4]—

My position in relation to the friends of the three returned candidates is singular enough and often to me very amusing. In the first place they all beleive [*sic*] that my friends have the power of deciding the question, and that I have the power of controling my friends. Acting upon this supposition in the same hour, I am sometimes touched gently on the shoulder by a friend (for example) of Genel. Jackson, who will thus address me. "My dear Sir, all our[5] dependence is on you; don't disappoint us; you know our partiality was for you next to the Hero; and how much we want a western President— Immediately after a friend of Mr. Crawford will accost me[6] "The hopes of the Republican party are concentrated on you   For God's sake preserve it— If you had been returned instead of Mr. Crawford every man of us would have supported you to the last hour. We consider him & you as the only genuine Republican Candidates." Next a friend of Mr. Adams comes "with tears in his eyes."[7] "Sir Mr Adams has always had the greatest respect for you, & admiration for[8] your talents— There is no station to which they[9] are not equal— Most undoubtedly you were the second choice of New England. And I pray you to consider seriously whether the public good & your own future interests do not point most distinctly to the choice which you ought to make—" How can one withstand all this distinterested homage & kindness? Really the friends of all the three Gentlemen are so very courteous, and affectionate, that I sometimes almost wish that it was in my power to accomodate [*sic*] each of them. But that being impossible we are beginning to think seriously of the choice which we must finally make. I will tell you then, that I believe the contest will be limited to Mr. Adams & Genl. Jackson; Mr. Crawford's personal condition precludes the choice of him; if there were no other objection to his election. As to the only alternative which is presented to us, it is sufficiently painful, & I consider whatever choice we may make will be only a choice of evils— To both those[10] Gentlemen there are strong personal objections— The principal difference between them is that in the election of Mr Adams we shall not by the example inflict any wound upon the character of our institutions; but I should much fear hereafter, if not during the present generation, that the election of the General would give to the Military Spirit a Stimulus and a confidence that might lead to the most pernicious results— I shall therefore with great regret, on account of the dilemma in which the people have placed us, support Mr Adams— My friends are generally so inclined. what has great weight with me is the decided preference which a majority of the delegation from Ohio has for him over the[11] Genl. Jackson— If therefore Kentucky were to vote for the Genl. it would probably only have the effect of dividing our friends, without defeating ultimately the election of Mr Adams. Three of the four States, favorable to Mr. Crawford are believed to prefer Mr. Adams to[12] the General. Virginia is one of them—

I am inclined to think that nearly three-fourths of our delegation have yeilded [sic] to the influence of these views, and will vote for Mr Adams— My friends entertain the belief that their kind wishes[13] will, in the end, be more likely to be accomplished by so bestowing their votes— I have however most earnestly entreated them to throw me out of their consideration in bringing their Judgements to a final conclusion and to look, & be guided solely by the public good— If I know my self that alone has determined me— Your representative[14] is inclined to concur with us in these sentiments and views; and if they should meet your approbation, as I know that[15] he has great respect for your Opinions, I would be glad if you would by the return mail address a letter to him to strengthen him in his inclination. Be pleased to show this letter to Crittenden[16] alone. I remain faithy. Your friend   H CLAY

Copy. DLC-HC (DNA, M212, R1). Endorsed by Clay: "This is a true copy—" Another version, attested by Blair as "a true copy" (KyHi), differs from this only in punctuation, capitalization, spelling, and the instances noted below. Blair also noted: "The original is misdated it should be Jany 8. 1825."

The letter was first published in its entirety, from a copy of the Blair copy, in Richmond *Whig*, October 7, 1844, reprinted in Washington *Daily National Intelligencer*, October 10, 1844, and widely recopied. It had been summarized, with quoted passages, by Amos Kendall, in Washington *United States Telegraph*, July 21, 1828 (*United States Telegraph-Extra*, I [July 26, 1828], 315), and by him interpreted as significant proof of the charge that Clay's support had been given to John Quincy Adams for the Presidency in return for a promise of appointment as Secretary of State. It is included, without the first paragraph, in Colton (ed.), *Private Correspondence of Henry Clay*, 109-10.

1 After the death of Lord Byron (George Gordon Byron, sixth Baron Byron) in April, 1824, Thomas Medwin had published the *Journal of the Conversations of Lord Byron: Noted during a Residence with His Lordship at Pisa in the Years 1821 and 1822* (London, 1824). An edition had been published in New York later in the year.

2 Robert Walsh, Jr.

3 This word preceded by "which he" in Blair's true copy.

4 On January 2, 1815, Byron had married Anna Isabella Milbanke, who had left him slightly more than a year later.

5 This word given as "my" in Blair's true copy.

6 This word interlined subsequently in unidentified hand.

7 Cf. above, III, 187n.   8 "Of" in Blair's true copy.

9 "You" in Blair's true copy.   10 "Of those" in Blair's true copy.

11 This word omitted in Blair's true copy.

12 Last three words interlined subsequently in unidentified hand.
13 This word followed by "towards me" in Blair's true copy.
14 David White, of New Castle, who represented the Sixth Kentucky District, composed of Shelby, Henry, Franklin, Owen, and Gallatin Counties.
15 This word not in Blair's true copy.   16 John J. Crittenden.

To John Quincy Adams

9 Jan. 25.

Mr. Clay's Compliments. to Mr. Adams, and, if he be not engaged, Mr. C. will call this evening at six O Clock to see him on an affair of business.

[Endorsement]¹

Mr Adams, with his respectful Compliments to Mr Clay, will be happy to see him this Evening at 6. O'Clock. Sunday 9. Jany 1825.

AN. MHi-Adams Papers. Addressed: "The Honble J. Q. Adams, Present." Cf. above, Remarks, January 1, 1825, note.
1 AE by Adams. Reporting this interview, Adams noted: "Mr. Clay came at six, and spent the evening with me in a long conversation explanatory of the past and prospective of the future. He said that the time was drawing near when the choice must be made in the House of Representatives of a President from the three candidates presented by the electoral colleges; that he had been much urged and solicited with regard to the part in that transaction that he should take, and had not been five minutes landed at his lodgings before he had been applied to by a friend of Mr. Crawford's, in a manner so gross that it had disgusted him; that some of my friends also, disclaiming, indeed, to have any authority from me, had repeatedly applied to him, directly or indirectly, urging considerations personal to himself as motives to his cause. He had thought it best to reserve for some time his determination to himself: first, to give a decent time for his own funeral solemnities as a candidate; and, secondly, to prepare and predispose all his friends to a state of neutrality between the three candidates who would be before the House, so that they might be free ultimately to take that course which might be most conducive to the public interest. The time had now come at which he might be explicit in his communication with me, and he had for that purpose asked this confidential interview. He wished me, as far as I might think proper, to satisfy him with regard to some principles of great public importance, but without any personal considerations for himself. In the question to come before the House between General Jackson, Mr. Crawford, and myself, he had no hesitation in saying that his preference would be for me." Adams, *Memoirs*, VI, 464-65.

From William T. Barry

My Dear Sir   Frankfort 10th. January 1825

I have received yours of the 22nd. Ult.¹ As soon as it was known that you would be left out of the House of Representatives, the sentiment in favour of Genl. Jackson grew strong. the disposition to express a preference for him over Mr. Adams too powerful to be resisted. Resolutions expressive of this have passed both houses of our Legislature.² The proceedings will be seen in the papers. You stand on an eminence that overlooks the whole nation,   in the survey you will take of its great interests, you can best decide on the proper course to be pursued in the approaching contest, suggestions of mine could hardly be useful, I will only remark that Mr. Adams is more unpopular in this State, than I had supposed him to be, altho' my views in relation to his standing have ever been unfavorable.

We are pleased to learn of the determination of Genl. Lafayette to visit the west, it is particularly gratifying to know that he will accompany you & it is presumed other members of our delegation.[3] It is expected that the Govr.[4] will be advised in due time of your approach, in order that arrangements may be made for the reception. It was the intention of the Govr. to have communicated the invitation thro' you, but upon reflection, it was thought that the more regular channel was our Senators, the more immediate representatives of the State. I am pleased to inform you of a resolution that has just passed the Senate, & which will undoubtedly pass the H. of R. directing the Govr. to employ M. H. Jouett to paint the Portrait of Genl. Lafayette, to be placed in our capital [*sic*].[5] It is cause of pride that native genius is employed to assist in perpetuating the fame of the illustrious man, that the Nation so much delights to honour. The act will be a new and interesting evidence of devotion; whilst it reflects honour on the State & rewards genius. We flatter ourselves that Jouett will not suffer by comparison with other artists; and if he should chance to excell, the reputation of our State will be raised by the triumph of his genius. Would it not be well & promotive of Jouetts interest for him to go on & paint the portrait at Washington?[6] It would introduce him as an artist to the public, in an interesting & imposeing [*sic*] attitude, stimulate his genius, and probably in this way improve highly the work that he has to perform.

The Legislature will adjourn this week. It has been an animated Session, to[o] much characterized by violent debate & personal reflections, which unhappily does not subside as it approaches the close. The bitterness of party is without example. It is hoped that when the members return home, cool reflection will calm the violence of feeling that has been excited by the discussions here. The great body of the people remain queit [*sic*] & will continue so, unless disturbed by political partizans. Very sincerely & truely Your friend & Sert.   W. T. BARRY
Honbe. H. Clay   Washington

ALS. DLC-HC (DNA, M212, R1).
1 Not found.   2 See above, III, 901-902.
3 Cf. above, III, 856n. Members of Congress and of the Kentucky Legislature were components of the procession which honored the general upon his arrival at Frankfort, May 14.
4 Joseph Desha. The invitation had been extended by resolution of the State legislature approved November 17, 1824. Ky. Gen. Assy., *Acts . . . 1824-1825*, pp. 215-17.
5 The resolution was formally approved January 12, 1825. *Ibid.*, 229-30. The

portrait still hangs in the old State Capitol at Frankfort. Drawn full length, it was reportedly based as to body lineament on a painting by the artist, Ary Scheffer, born in Holland but long resident in Paris, who had presented the work to the United States Congress on the occasion of Lafayette's visit to that body (above, III, 893-94; below, Clay to Brown, March 29, 1825). Jouett sketched the head and facial detail from life when the general visited Lexington in May. Lexington *Kentucky Reporter*, May 23, 1825.

6 Jouett did not reach Washington in time to see Lafayette before the latter's departure on his tour of the South, which began on February 23.

From John Boyle

Dear Sir   Jany 10th 1825

Inclosed is a paper[1] containing the suggestions I have to make in answer to Mr Websters argument before the Supreme court on the constitutional question.depending in that court.[2] I am sorry I had not bestowed my attention earlier upon the subject.that I might have rendered the answers I have given to Mr. Websters argument more perfect & satisfactory,   I may have misconceived his argument— & no doubt I have not stated it in its most imposing aspect. But what ever shape it may assume I am perfectly convinced that the principles I have suggested are the true answer to it. You may think otherwise & when you shall find an answer to it upon other principles which are correct I will readily acknowledge my error.

Fearful that what I have said in the inclosed paper might not be worth decyphering in my hierogly hical [*sic*] hand writing I have had it copied as you will see in a more legible hand.

Before I returned from Frankfort your son Tom[3] had gone to Lexington to spend his Christmas & he has not yet got home. I have been however looking for him every day, & when he gets back I will take care he shall not take such an other trip shortly

I am with great respect & esteem Your Friend   JOHN BOYLE
The Honbl. H Clay Esqr

ALS. DLC-HC (DNA, M212, R1).
1 See below, this date.
2 Probably relating to the case of Ogden *vs.* Saunders, first argued before the United States Supreme Court at the February Term, 1824, when, as members of opposing counsel, Daniel Webster had attacked and Clay had defended the validity of bankrupt or insolvent laws passed by various States. The cause was continued until the January Term, 1827, when (without Clay's participation) it was re-argued. The decision then reached by the Court was adverse to Webster's position. 25 *U. S.* (12 Wheaton) 213-368.
3 Thomas Hart Clay, who read law under Judge Boyle until the fall of this year.

From J[ohn] B[oyle]

Dear Sir   [January 10, 1825]

I have not forgotten the promise which I made you last summer of giving you my ideas in writing, in answer to the argument said to be used before the supreme Court of the U. S. at their last term, to prove that a law of a State, which discharges a debtor from his contract, on condition of his giving up his effects in compliance with the requisitions of the Law, was, in its operation upon a contract made after its passage, a violation of that clause of the constitution of the U. S., which declares that "no State shall pass any law impairing the obligations of contracts."

When I made this promise, I had no very distinct view of the subject, but confident that the argument was fallacious, and unsound, I expected, a little time for reflection would suggest the reasoning, necessary to prove it so, and time sufficient for that purpose has elapsed, but various circumstances, which I need not mention, have occur'd to prevent any portion of it from being bestowed by me upon the subject. What I shall now say, therefore, must be view'd rather as loose and disjointed suggestions, than as a regular and logical discourse upon the subject.

[Approximately ten manuscript pages here present argument upholding the authority of States to enact bankruptcy laws.]

respectfully   J B

DI. KyU-Thomas Hart Papers.

Check to John Davis

11 Jan. 1825

Pay to John Davis or order One hundred & seventy five dollars.

H CLAY

Cash. of the Off. of Dt. & Dt. Washn.[1]

ADS. DLC-TJC (DNA, M212, R16). Cf. above, III, 531n.
[1] Richard Smith.

From Martin Duralde (Jr.)

Dr. Sir,   New Orleans 12th. January 1825

You wrote to Mr. Cox[1] last year that you would accept the procurations of Individuals of this State having claims on the General Government. Inclosed I take the liberty of sending you two, one from the heirs of the widow Dupré and one from heirs of Solomon Provost.[2] The heirs of the widow Dupré Say that all the papers concerning their Claims, which Mr. Fromentin[3] took to Washington, were left with Mr. Wm. Blendley[4] & the heirs of Provost Say that their papers are in the hands of Messrs. Law & Wallach,[5] attorneys in Washington.

I am authorised by these claiments [sic] to offer you ten per

Cent on the moneis [*sic*] you may collect for them. They are all my neighbours in the Country. They are plain and honest farmers. I have promised them that I would interest myself in their behalf. If your business will not permit you to attend to their claims you will confer a particular favor on me by intrusting them to a zelous [*sic*] person.

The Claims of the heirs of Dupré amounted at first to nearly $18,000 but they have only received $6202. .94 of it, which is the amount of Materials furnished for the purpose of building a Fort, the balance being the amount of damages occasioned by our own troops.

I have delivered to Mr. Whittlesey[6] the last papers you sent me concerning Col. Morrison's[7] business. He must have written to you and geven [*sic*] you his opinion[8].

I am happy to be able to tell you that we succeded [*sic*] on monday last, to reelect Josiah S. Johnston a Senator to Congress by a majority of five votes over Mr. Levingston.[9] The opposition was great and we had nearly as much intrigue on this occasion as we had on a former one,[10] but we were more fortunate this time.

We have received the returns of the Presidential election from all the States & your friends here regret very much to see that for the want of the votes of this State you have been left out of the House. The friends of Mr. Crawford must be now convinced of their folly. They are the cause of what has happened. Gel. Jackson I presume will be our next President.

Mr. Erwin has at last obtained a Judgment against Flood's estate.[11] He and his wife are both well. They stayed with us when they first arrived but since the arrival of Mrs. Yatman,[12] Mr. Es Sister, they have moved to town.[13] Mrs. Erwin is more fond of her husband than any Lady I ever saw.— They appear to be quite happy.

Our last child[14] is labouring under a very Severe cold which has geven [*sic*] us a great deal of uneasiness. Since a day or two he seems to be doing better. The rest of the family is well. Susan[15] will [wr]ite to you in a few days.

I am with due respect Dr. Sir, Your Obt. Servt.   M. DURALDE

ALS. DLC-TJC (DNA, M212, R13). MS. torn. Addressed to Clay.
1 Probably Nathaniel Cox. Letter not found.
2 The plantation of Augustin Dupré (or Duprès), who had been appointed a justice of the peace of Plaquemine Parish in 1808 and elected mayor of New Orleans in 1814, was near General Andrew Jackson's lines during the Battle of New Orleans. By act of May 29, 1830, Congress approved an appropriation of $8,995 to the heirs of Dupré's widow in compensation for damage to buildings and fences while the property was under military occupation "during the late war." 6 *U.S. Stat.*, 438.
   Under act of May 7, 1822 (6 *U.S. Stat.*, 273), Solomon Prevost, appointed a justice of the peace of New Orleans in 1807, had been awarded $1,966, in full settlement of his losses during the same conflict.

3 Eligius Fromentin.   4 Not identified.

5 Probably Edmund Law and Richard Wallach. Law had resigned his appointment as judge of the Circuit Court of East Florida and returned to Washington in 1823. Wallach was a distinguished lawyer, active in community affairs of the District.

6 Chauncey Whittelsey, at this time residing and practicing law in New Orleans.

7 James Morrison.   8 No letter found.

9 Edward Livingston, who continued as a member of the United States House of Representatives.

10 Possibly a reference to the recent presidential election in Louisiana. See above, III, 900.

11 Suit not found. It apparently dealt with a claim by James Erwin against the estate of Dr. William Flood, a Virginian who had served as a major of militia and port physician of New Orleans during the Territorial period.

12 Jane Erwin Yeatman, wife of Thomas Yeatman, a Nashville commission merchant and banker, later prominent as an iron manufacturer.

13 Mr. and Mrs. James Erwin were now residents of New Orleans.

14 Henry Clay Duralde, born in 1824.   15 Mrs. Duralde.

To Josiah Stoddard Johnston

To remind   Friday 14 Jan. [1825].

Mr. Clay expects the pleasure of the Company of Mr Johnson at dinner tomorrow at 4 OClock—

AN. PHi. Addressed: "The Honble Josiah S. Johnson [sic] Of the Senate." Endorsed, in Johnston's hand: "1825."

From Peter B. Porter

Dear Sir,   Black Rock Jany 14th. 1825

I have received your favour of the 26th. Ult. and thank you for the interest you are taking in favour of Mr Holley, whose situation is such as to demand the sympathy & kindness of all his friends.

I learnt, some time ago, & with a good deal of mortification the result of the election in Louisiana;[1] but I confess that I was not altogether disappointed, for I had anticipated that the same confident and bullying policy which was pursued by the friends of Genl. Jackson at the north, would be extended also to that State, & with more probability of success.

Three or four days before the appointment of our Elector [sic] an Express arrived at Albany from Ohio, under whip & spur, bringing a letter from Caleb Atwater of Circleville to Dewit [sic] Clinton headed "Glorious News" and announcing the election of the Jackson ticket in that State by a majority of 4,000! I was told by a Gentleman who was at Columbus at the time of the Canvas [sic], that similar letters were dispatched from there to Indiana & Illinois, some three or four days before so as to reach their respective destinations at the commencement of the elections—and all these accompanied by strong solicitations to your friends to give up your cause as hopeless. My regret at the loss of Louisiana after knowing the state of the vote in the other States, was a good deal chastened by the reflection, that if you had succeeded there, it would have brought you into the house where Mr Crawford now is, with so lean a vote compared with the other two candidates, as to have greatly diminished your chance of ultimate success; such a defeat there would have rendered your situation much more mortifying than it is at present. I was disappointed at the result of the election in this State, although my calculations had never been very sanguine. I intended to have given you a full history of all the manoeuvring [*sic*] at Albany, but it would be a tedious, &, under present circumstances, an uninteresting story, & I will omit it untill I see you. Had Young succeeded[2] we should have given you the entire vote of the State without any difficulty. But he was prostrated and with him, for a time, the whole Republican party, by the selfish & petty fogging course of Van Buren[3] & his friends. Clintons success gave him some influence in this question & it was all exerted against you. Then a few Clintonian members from this part of the State who were warm advocates of yours & had attended all our meetings were persuaded as soon as the result of the election was known, to vote for the Adams ticket— Not that Clinton was in favour of Adams, but they would not vote for Jackson; & he was less afraid of Adams than of you. The 4 Electors (Crawford men) last chosen, did not succeed by the honest supporters of that ticket nor by your friends but by the aid of some half a dozen of Mr. Clinton's partizans, & with an understanding that if their votes would elect Jackson, by the College he should have them—otherwise to go to Crawford. The grand mistake in the policy of your friends in this State was, in not closing at once with the offer made by the Adams men to divide the ticket equally. Many of us were fully impressed with the propriety of this course, but we could not bring a sufficient number into the measure, while it was practicable.— But I perceive that I am going into the details I promised to avoid, & will stop.

As you are now hors du combat, who is to be the next President? I know not what your views may be, but I have no hesitation in expressing my own—not however with any expectation that they will have any weight with you.

Toward Mr Crawford personally, I have no other feelings than those of respect. But I confess that I was never an admirer of the *company he keeps.* I know not how it has happened but he has been the nucleus around which all the radicalism or jacobinism of the country when sent to Washington has instinctively gathered. The public policy, moreover, which local interest & feeling would naturally lead him, & in fact have led him to pursue, is not such as I admire, or as is adapted to the interests of this part of the country.

While I respect Genl. Jackson for his military qualifications, I doubt whether he has political information & experience that fit him for the office— But my great objection to him is that he is by nature a *Tyrant*— I mean no *unworthy* imputation, for I believe him to be a man of the purest honor & integrity, but his habits as well as his native disposition have always been to consider the law, & his own notions of justice as synonimous. As watchfull republicans I should think we were committing, to say the least of it, a great indiscretion, in placing the whole military & civil power of the country in such hands.

In point of strictly executive qualifications Mr Adams falls perhaps as far short of the proper mark as Genl. J. goes beyond it. But he is certainly a splendid Cabinet Minister, & I believe an honest politician. In peace I think his administration would be respectable, & even in war our hazards would not be great. I confess I should prefer him even though my views were not to extend beyond four years, but I think that his election would be most propitious to your elevation four years hence. Give the presidency this time to the north and the people will naturally look to the west for a successor. Clinton is preparing for the next election, & his policy is to have Jackson elected now, & by a strict concert with him which I believe already exists, pave the way to his own elevation. I hope that in four years more the people of New York will better understand their own interests & your merrits [*sic*].   Yours truly & respectfully   P. B. PORTER

Please give my respects to your friend Mr Vance, & present him my thanks for his able & eloquent speech in favour of the Niagara Sufferers.[4] Mrs P. & Mrs. Breckenridge[5] beg to be kindly remembered to you. I should be pleased to hear from you when you have leasure

ALS. DLC-HC (DNA, M212, R1). Addressed to Clay at Washington.

1 See above, III, 900.

2 DeWitt Clinton had defeated Samuel Young by a large margin in the New York gubernatorial election of November, 1824.

3 Martin Van Buren.

4 Early in the current Session, the Congress had taken up a bill "authorizing payment for property lost or destroyed by the enemy during the late war," in which debate the discussion had centered on the ravages on the Niagara frontier (cf. above, II, 270-72, 275n, 563-64). Joseph Vance had spoken, in Committee of the Whole, on December 30. The measure, in the form of "An Act further to amend the act . . . passed ninth April, one thousand eight hundred and sixteen," became law on March 3, 1825. *Register of Debates*, 18 Cong., 2 Sess., 9-10, 101-105; 4 *U. S. Stat.*, 123.

5 Mrs. Porter; Mrs. John Breckinridge.

To Josephus B. Stuart

Dr Sir   Washn. 15h. Jan. 1825

I duly recd. your letter of the 8h. inst.[1] On the question to which

it principally relates there is much uncertainty prevailing here; and I do not believe that any one can, with any degree of probability, affirm what will be the issue of it. Many states are supposed to be doubtful, and your own among the number. With respect to my friends generally and myself all that I can venture now to assure you is that we are looking at the subject with an anxious desire to make that decision which will best promote the public interest. The truth is that anticipations, as to the final result, vary from day to day, and according to the wishes of individuals who make them. The most that may be safely now said is that either Mr Adams or Genl. Jackson will probably be elected, but which it would be extremely hazardous to designate. I will add that the Kentucky delegation I believe feels perfectly free to vote, as its own judgment shall dictate, notwithstanding the recent request of the K. Legislature.[2]   I am Yr's with high regard   H CLAY
Dr. J. B. Stuart.

ALS. NcD.   [1] Not found.   [2] See above, III, 901-902n.

To George Thompson

Dr. Sir: Washington, 15th Jan. 1825
I received your kind letter[1] respecting Gen'l La Fayette and will take some opportunity to communicate your message to him. He appears to delight in all Revolutionary recollections, and especially in the society of his companions in arms. As he will be in Kentucky in the Spring, I hope you will both live to meet and embrace each other. We have passed a law for his benefit[2] which I doubt not will be approved by our Constituents. It conforms pretty much to the ideas expressed in your letter.

As we have to make a President this session, we shall do but little else. It is by no means certain who will be chosen. All I think that can be safely affirmed is that it will be Mr. Adams or Gen'l Jackson.

Be pleased to give my kind regards to your son[3] and believe me, Faithfully your friend,   H. CLAY.
Col. Geo. Thompson.

Kentucky State Historical Society, *Register*, XXXIII (1935), 128. Addressed: "Col. Geo. Thompson, Senior, Shawnee Springs, Harrodsburg, Ky."
[1] Not found.   [2] See above, III, 899, 900.   [3] George C. Thompson.

Speech on Cumberland Road

[January 17, 1825]
Mr. CLAY, (Speaker,) rose, and observed, that, from his attachment to that system of internal policy, of which the measure

now before the committee formed a part, he had entertained a wish to offer to their consideration some views in relation to it which had forcibly impressed his own mind; but had he anticipated the state of expectation which it would be needless for him to affect not to perceive, or that debilitated state in which he now appeared before the committee, he should have contented himself with giving his silent vote in favor of the bill.

The object proposed, he said, involved a question which had often been debated in that House, and the general views of which were already so familiar to the minds of those whom he addressed, that he despaired of adding any thing to that knowledge of it which they already possessed. Indeed, he considered the views of policy which he held on this subject as having been vindicated and maintained by the votes of the House at the last session.[1] Yet he would say thus much: that he considered the question, as to the existence and the exercise of a power in the General Government to carry into effect a system of internal improvements, as amounting to the question whether the union of these states should be preserved or not—a question which involved the dearest hopes and brightest prospects of our country. As to the opinion, that the carrying on of these improvements belonged to the states in their individual and separate character, it might as well be expected that the states should perform any other duty which appertained to the General Government. You have no more right, observed Mr. C. to ask the individual states to make internal improvements *for the general welfare,* than you have to ask them to make war for the general welfare, or to build fortifications for the general defence, because some of them may happen to have a peculiar local interest in either. They are no more bound to do any one of the duties which pertain to the General Government, than to do any other one of the duties which pertain to it. Sir, it is our province, not theirs. It is, indeed, true, that the interests of the whole and of one of the parts may be coincident, and sometimes to a very remarkable degree—nay, to such a degree as may induce a State Government to undertake a duty which more properly belongs to Congress. But such cases are rare, and such an effect has seldom happened. One instance, indeed, may be pointed out—that of the great Canal in the state of New York. When that state applied to this House for aid in her great and spirited undertaking, it was my opinion that she ought to receive it[2]—and it is now my opinion that, for what she has advanced in the completion of that noble enterprise, she has at this hour a just claim upon the General Government. But cases of this kind always will be rare—it is vain to expect that any state will feel a sufficient interest in any object or improvement (unless such as are purely local in their character) as to induce her to make an appropriation of her individual resources for its accomplishment.

With these preliminary observations on the great policy of measures of the kind of that now proposed, he would go on to inquire in the first place, is the object in the present bill of sufficient magnitude to authorize an application to it of the resources of the nation? To answer this inquiry, the object must be considered, not as standing isolated and alone—but as constituting one link in the great chain of the Internal Improvement of the Union. What, said he, is the actual state of the facts? There now exists from the city of Baltimore to Wheeling, in the state of Virginia, an uninterrupted line of turnpike road, extending to a total distance of two hundred and seventy miles; and there also exists a like line of road from this city to the same place, with the exception of one small gap between Montgomery Court House and Fredericktown. Taking its origin at the foot of the Alleghany Mountains, the Cumberland Road extends to the Eastern Bank of the Ohio a distance of *one hundred and thirty-five miles*. Of this distance eighty-five miles lie in Pennsylvania, thirty or thirty-five in Maryland, and the residue in Virginia—the entire work, from one end to the other, and through its whole extent, lying exclusively in the states East of the Ohio river. The proposition now presented to the committee is to extend this road from the West bank of that river to Zanesville, in the state of Ohio, a distance of *eighty miles*. If the proposition shall meet with the favor of Congress, the whole length of road from Baltimore to Zanesville will be 350 miles.

Mr. C. then remarked on the character of the country through which the contemplated road is to pass, which he described as containing a succession of hills, some of which might perhaps have been called mountains, but for the altitude of the neighboring Alleghanies—and which continue as far west as the Muskingum River, on the bank of which Zanesville is situated. There, or a little to the west of it, commences a level plain of an alluvial character, extending from the Muskingum to the Mississippi, a distance of four hundred and twenty miles.

The present proposition, Mr. C. said, was to be considered in reference, first, to what had been done, and second, to what remained to be done. The proposed part of the road must be viewed, first, in respect to one termination of the entire line which is at Cumberland, and then in respect to the other termination of it, which he trusted would one day be on the Missouri. It must also be viewed in reference to that branch of it, which he hoped, at no distant day, would pass through Kentucky and

Tennessee, to Natchez and New Orleans, intersecting the great road, now proposed from the latter place to this city.[3] It must be remembered, said he, that it is a part of a road which is to traverse nine States and two Territories; so that whether we look to the right or to the left, we find the interests of nine entire States and two Territories, all concentrated in the present design.

Here Mr. C. wished to be permitted to state one fact with which, perhaps, but few members of the committee were acquainted. A distinguished member of the other House had lately travelled in company with the Delegate from Florida,[4] now on this floor, over the very route which was contemplated in this bill for the road proposed. They had found it, though somewhat hilly, free from any mountainous obstructions, and abounding in all the materials which would be required for construction.

Mr. C. next proceeded to inquire, whether the object, such as he had now described it, was not justly entitled to be considered a national object. Look, said he, at the effect produced upon the convenience of the whole country, from what has been already done. The usual space of time formerly required to go from Baltimore to Wheeling, was from eight to ten days—the time now occupied is three days. The effect of such a saving of time would readily be conceived. To this consideration might be added the advantage resulting from the investment of so much capital, and the expenditure of so much public money, in a region of country where both were so much needed. Settlements had been multiplied—buildings of all kinds erected—villages had sprung up as if by enchantment; and, to use the language of one of the gentlemen who had ably advocated the bill, the road resembled one continued street, almost the whole way from Cumberland to Wheeling.[5] The effect had been a great addition to the value of property, and an important increase of the wealth of three states through which this great public work had been constructed.

It has been called, by some gentlemen, a Western road, but how could it be a Western road, when not one foot of it lay within any one of the Western states, but the entire road, in all its parts, lay wholly in the Eastern states? The direct benefit, and much that was collateral, was felt by the three Eastern states where the road lay; the only benefit to the Western states was a mere right of way. All they enjoyed in the road was the right to pass over it to visit their brethren in the East, and to come to this Metropolis to mingle their counsels with their fellow citizens of the South and East—important benefits no doubt—but not such as ought to designate this road as a Western road. In fact, Mr. C. said, it was neither an Eastern nor a Western road, but partly the one and partly the other. The benefits derived from it were strictly mutual.

Mr. C. asked, if the United States were not under a positive obligation to extend this road? What was the history of this undertaking? It arose out of a compact between the United States and the state of Ohio, at the time that state was admitted into the Union, by which two per cent. of the nett proceeds of the sales of the public lands was to be applied to the making of a road leading to the state of Ohio.[6] A similar provision was also made in the compacts, by which Indiana, Illinois, Missouri, Mississippi, and, he believed, Alabama, were admitted as states.[7] It had been contended by some gentlemen, that the construction of the Cumberland road was a fulfilment of this compact on the part of the United States. This, said Mr. C. I deny utterly. I grant, indeed, that it is a fulfilment of the compact with the state of Ohio. The United States covenanted to make a road leading to that state. They have done so; and Ohio has no right to demand that the road should be carried one foot further. But the case is entirely different with the states beyond Ohio. They have a right, under their respective compacts, to demand a road which shall terminate at their limits—a road which shall be brought *up to* the boundary line of those states respectively. It is very true, that Congress may begin the road wherever they please, but it must terminate *at* the state *to* which Congress had covenanted that the road shall lead.

Am I not, said Mr. CLAY, arguing a question which is too plain to be illustrated? Can it be said, that Government has made a road to Missouri, when it has made a road which no where approaches Missouri within 500 miles? or, that it has made a road *to* the other Western states, when it has made one to a point 250, 300, or 500 miles from them? Gentlemen say, that a road has been made in that direction. It might as well be said, that the making of Pennsylvania avenue, in this city, was a fulfilment of the contract, or that the Government might begin a road in the remotest part of the East, and end it there, provided it had a western direction. He repeated, Government was not bound to spend more than the two per cent. under the contract—but the road must end *at* the limit of the states with whom the compact was made.

And here, said Mr. C. let me ask my worthy friend from Mississippi, (Mr. RANKIN,[8]) whether he would consider a road ending at Wheeling as a road *to* Mississippi, because it leads, though obliquely, toward that state? I am sure he would not. He would say Congress had fulfilled its bargain only when the road terminated *at* the Mississippi.

It has been said, that the provision which pledges the two per cent. fund of the several Western states for defraying the expense of the Cumberland road, had been inserted in all the former bills on that subject. I admit this, said Mr. C. but I should never have given my consent to its insertion, had I not thought that it was understood and agreed upon, as a part of the plan, that Congress should go on with the road, and carry it to all the states whose funds have been thus pledged.

On the question of the utility of the present undertaking, Mr. C. trusted he need say no more. He was happy, he said, to find that the worthy gentleman from Virginia, (Mr. P. P. BARBOUR,) who, to his great regret, could not, with his views of the constitution, support the bill, had declared, with that honorable frankness for which he was so eminently distinguished, that, apart from that view of the question, he should be in favor of the measure now proposed.[9]

Mr. C. thought that the principle of preservation itself afforded sufficient argument in support of the measure now under consideration. He knew, indeed, that all questions which glanced at the union of the states, and the possibility of its severance, should be touched lightly, and with a cautious hand. But, if they were not to be discussed in that august assembly, where might they be? I, said Mr. CLAY, am not one of those who are in favor of covering our eyes, and concealing from ourselves the dangers to which we may be exposed. Danger, of whatever kind, is best guarded against when it is deliberately contemplated, and fully understood. It is not to be averted by shutting our eyes and ears against the possibility of its approach. Happily, there exist among us many great and powerful principles of cohesion—a common origin—common language—a common law—common liberty—common recollection of national glory. But, asked Mr. C. have we not seen, in at least one instance in history,[10] that all these have not been strong enough to prevent a total and lasting separation. And, though causes of the opposite kind may not in our case go all the length of producing this, yet they operate on every natural tendency to separation. That such tendencies do exist, will not be denied by any candid and reflecting man, and they call on us to look far a-head, and to prevent if possible, the disastrous evil which they threaten. Among the causes which go to increase the tendencies to separation, in such a system as ours, may be enumerated the lofty mountains which separates [sic] different parts of our country—the extended space over which our population and government are spread, together with the different scenes to which commercial pursuits lead the citizens of different districts of the Union. Some of these are, indeed, beyond human control, but the effect of many of them may be, in a certain degree, corrected, if not wholly removed. The mountains may be cut through: we will teach the lofty Alleghany to bow its proud head to the interest and repose of our country. As to space and distance, they are terms wholly relative, and they have relation as much to the facility of intercourse as to actual distance of place. It will be the business of wise legislation, to correct the evils to which a sparse population exposes us. We have already seen what may be effected. A distance which formerly consumed nine days, (and in this I speak from personal knowledge, having passed the route in all conditions of the road,) can now be done in three. Wheeling is thus six days' travel nearer to Washington. So is St. Louis. So is every place West of Wheeling. If two places are twenty miles apart, and two other places are eighty miles asunder, and yet the distance between both occupies but one day, the two latter places, for every practical purpose, are as near to each other as the two former. And is it not the solemn duty of this House, to strengthen, by every means in its power, the principles of cohesion which bind us together—to perpetuate the union of these states, and to weaken and diminish, to the utmost of its ability, whatever has an opposite tendency? Can the imagination of man conceive a policy better calculated than that of which the present measure forms a part, to bring the opposite extremities of our country together—to bind its various parts to each other, and to multiply and strengthen the various and innumerable ties of commercial, social, and literary intercourse—in a word, to make of the various and wide-spread population of these confederated Republics one united people? It is true, that no efforts of the Government can altogether remove one effect of our local situation, which causes one part of our country to find its commercial vent in one ocean, and another in another. Yet, even this may be in part corrected, and one great advantage attending the proposed national highway—the formation of a part of which is contemplated in the present bill— will be its effect upon the commerce of the country. And here, said Mr. C. let me state one fact. If, at this moment, the alternative were presented to me, of a total exclusion of my state from all use of the Mississippi river for commercial purposes, or the same exclusion from the Atlantic states, I would, without hesitation, prefer the former, and I believe that the commerce, that now passes the mountains from the West, to seek its outlet on the Atlantic coast, is of greater value than that which passes down the Mississippi to the Gulf of Mexico—and this will be increasingly the case, if, as I hope, we are to have several different outlets like that which is now proposed. I beg gentlemen not to be alarmed.

It is not my intention to ask for any further appropriations for
this purpose, at least for some time to come, but we shall live,
I hope, as a nation, as long as any other nation. I speak not of the
works of one year, or of twenty years, but of those to which we
may look forward, should our present state of peace continue.
An appropriation of half a million of dollars annually would not
be felt by a country like this, and yet it would effect every object
which the friends of internal improvement propose to themselves
or to this House.

But it may be said, Why should the General Government make
a road for the state of Ohio? Sir, if this were a road for the benefit
of Ohio, I would not ask an appropriation of a single dollar. Ohio
has no such peculiar interest in this measure as would ever induce
her to undertake to make this road. It is not a state road, but a
national road, that is contemplated. It is not the duty of the
state, it is your duty to make it. The route for the road passes
through one of the poorest parts of the state of Ohio. Indeed, for
sixty miles, it runs through as poor a country as I ever saw. Let
me ask of the gentleman from Pennsylvania, Had this argument
been used with respect to the Cumberland Road, would Pennsylvania have made that part of the road which now passes through
her territory? Or would Maryland or Virginia have made what
passes through theirs? No, sir! So far from it, that I am well
satisfied, if that road were destroyed to-morrow, a part of the
population of these states would heartily rejoice.[11] The resources
of Ohio are scanty, and she will not do that which you ought to
do. Ohio will certainly be benefitted by this road, just as Pennsylvania, Virginia, and Maryland, are now benefitted by the Cumberland road. But these incidental advantages, resulting to Ohio,
are not to deter you from performing your duty to the Union, any
more than the incidental benefits of a fortification in any particular
state should prevent the General Government from making the
fortification.

Without troubling the committee with any further observations
on the first branch of the subject, Mr. C. trusted he was authorized
to say, that the present is an object of such importance as to be
worthy of the application of the national resources.

He then proceeded to the second branch of the subject, and
inquired, is this object a fit one to be pursued *at this time?* As
an objection, it had been said,[12] that this was an anticipation of a
part of the *system* of Internal Improvement devised at the last
session, and that the execution of that system ought not to be begun
till the whole has been considered. But, in the first place, said Mr.
C. I do not know that any general system of internal improvement

has as yet been devised. The act of the last session was intended merely to collect information, but did not give any authority to use or apply it in any general system of measures; and, if gentlemen are to wait till all the objects which may be proposed go on together, I will venture to say that the system of internal improvements will be postponed indefinitely. If any thing is to be done, we must select some object on which to begin. But, even on gentlemen's own ground, I contend that this measure is not in the least inconsistent with the act of last session. What was the object of that act? To obtain facts and collect information respecting objects of improvements where that knowledge was not yet obtained. But, with respect to this object, the information is obtained, the facts are known. Surveys and estimates have been made. The length of the road proposed by this bill is eighty miles. Its estimated cost is 450,000 dollars. The work is already begun—it is still in progress. A momentary pause has indeed taken place, but it is ready to proceed, and to be continued on the other side of the Ohio, as it has been finished on this side.

But we have been told that it is to be the policy of the next administration to pay the public debt; that it must be paid with as much expedition as is at all practicable, and that no part of the public resources are to be diverted to any other object.[13] Sir, there is no member of this House more desirous to see the national debt paid than I am. I never was one of those who believe that a public debt is a public blessing. I have always considered it as a mortgage, dragging on our finances, and one which it was our duty to foreclose and pay off as soon as possible. Yet, we have also other duties. There are, indeed, some debts which we may not devolve on posterity—debts which spring from wasteful and ambitious wars—debts which have their origin in national luxury and extravagance. But there are debts of another description, which I feel no hesitation in devolving on posterity. I refer to a debt which carries the benefit with the burden. When we bequeath both together, posterity cannot equitably reproach our memory, because, while they bear the burden, they cannot but recollect that they are, at the same time, enjoying the benefit. But, sir, is there any proposition before you to create a national debt for internal improvements? What is the scheme proposed in the report lately laid before this House, by the officer who presides with so much ability over the Department of the Treasury, and which has received the approbation of the Committee of Ways and Means of this House? That officer tells you, that the public debt may be completely extinguished in ten years; that, by the year 1835, the last dollar of it will have been paid, and that all [sic] this time there will remain in the Treasury a surplus of three millions, applicable to any object within the constitutional powers of the General Government.[14] The present bill cannot, therefore, be rejected from any want of means to carry it into effect. There is another view of the subject, not, indeed, contained in any public document, and which ought not to be, since it has not that entire degree of certainty which ought to accompany all documentary information. What is your source of revenue? It is consumption. And what are the sources of consumption? Population and wealth. Then, in a course of ten years, starting on any given tariff of duties, the increase of population will occasion an increase of the revenue of 40 per cent. at a ratio of four per cent. per annum. These truths are sufficiently obvious. It is said, indeed, that the policy that has been adopted for the encouragement of industry will diminish the revenue. But, when that subject was under consideration last session, I endeavored to show and I now repeat, that this cannot be the case.[15] Different years will vary. In some, the revenue may fall short, but the redundance of others will supply the deficiency. The measure of our export trade will always be the measure of our imports, and the measure of our imports will be the measure of our revenue. I hope, therefore, that the policy which was, at the last session, fixed upon,[16] will ever be adhered to by this nation, as long as the course pursued by foreign nations shall render it necessary. On the whole, I think that gentlemen may calm their fears about the extent of the public debt. That debt is melting away before us faster, perhaps, than for some of our financial interests, it might be wished. We have the prospect that it will be extinguished in ten years, and when we have paid this, we shall have fulfilled the whole of our duty in that respect.

But, if we are invited to the present measure by the abundance of our means, are we not less so by a variety of other considerations? One of these is the cheapness of labor, greater, perhaps, at this time than ever before. Some gentlemen, indeed, spoke in the language of alarm about the vast expense of the Cumberland road. But, it must be remembered, that there were peculiar causes to produce that effect. The general aspect of the times, when it was constructed; the nature of the materials which were required for it; the difficulty in some cases of obtaining them; and the unnecessary number and extravagant price, of the bridges on that road, several of which cost forty thousand dollars each, and which are so numerous, that, upon one single creek, in a course of ten miles, there are eleven bridges, some of which cost $20,000 a-piece. These, indeed, are beautiful specimens of architecture, surpassed by nothing which I ever saw, unless it be the bridge of Jena at

Paris: but they have been also very costly. Under the circumstances, this was certainly a useless expense. I pledge myself, however, said Mr. C. that if Congress shall grant the one hundred and fifty thousand dollars estimated as the total expense of the road from Wheeling to Zanesville, nothing more shall be asked for bridges, or any other expenses, on that road.

An additional consideration in favor of this measure, Mr. C. said, was to be found in the pecuniary distresses of the West, which would in part be alleviated by the expenditure of the public money in that quarter, and which was certainly entitled to the parental consideration of this body.

Its being, then, a national object—an object which has been commenced—an object due by compact to the Western states—all these considerations united to call for the passage of the present bill.

As to commencing a general system of internal improvement, said he, if gentlemen can shew us any road beginning at the heart of the confederacy, of equal national importance, I for one, will heartily support it; but I believe there is not another object in which all these considerations unite. Why pause for what we do not want? For plans, estimates, and surveys, which we have already got? Why pause in prosecuting this object, more than in another— (the Delaware and Chesapeake Canal) a bill which I was delighted to see pass the committee to its third reading; and which I cannot doubt will continue its progress through the House with a still increasing majority.[17] It has been said by some gentlemen in conversation, though not of a confidential kind, that the West ought not to have this bill, until other portions of this Union receive a simultaneous benefit. But I can assure gentlemen, there is no danger of undue appropriation in favor of the West. In a late report from the Department of War, a document consistent with the high character of that Department, and which bore the impress of the mind of its author, rapid yet correct, we are informed what objects are indicated by the Secretary of War, as more immediately calling for the attention of the General Government. They are only four. The canal to unite the Potomac with the Ohio, the canal round the Falls at Louisville, the canal round the Muscle Shoals, and the Cumberland Road.[18] It is possible that for some, at least, of these objects, the National resources will never be appealed to. The state which I in part represent, said Mr. C., lately passed a bill through one branch of the Legislature, to cut the canal round the Falls at Louisville, entirely from the state resources, and it is highly probable that that bill will pass the other House, and become a law.[19] The number of objects, then, claiming immediate attention will be reduced to three. Of these

the Cumberland road is certainly not a Western object, any more
than the canal uniting the Ohio and Potomac.[20] That canal is not
located in the West, nor, on the other hand, is it exclusively an
Eastern improvement. Like the National road, it is neither an
Eastern nor a Western object, but one which belongs to the whole
nation, and is calculated, in its effects, to cement the East and the
West in bonds of an affectionate kind. Let me advert to one other
topic, to which I refer, not for the purpose of exciting, but of
allaying jealousy. It is to the small comparative amount of the
public expenditures beyond the mountains. I do not say an
equivalent is to be given to the West for the vast sums expended
on this side upon the navy, fortifications, &c. No such thing. I
know the disproportion results from local circumstances, not in the
control of Government. Yet, am I wrong to say, that it forms an
equitable consideration which addresses itself strongly to the feeling, to the justice, and to the generosity of Congress; all which
cannot but induce them to correct, as far as possible, such a state
of things, and make the balance of public benefits more equal
whenever the opportunity is presented to them? I may ask with
confidence, has the West ever acted on this narrow policy? Did it
ever hesitate when the public wants required its aid? Did you
ask for navies?—The moneys for building and equipping them
were freely granted; and here I must be permitted to say, that,
when the navy was friendless and forlorn, and I well knew that
my vote in its favor would be no sooner given than denounced,
anticipating the triumphs which have since wreathed with laurels
the national brow, I personally risked every thing in giving my
vote in favor of it.[21] No, sir, there was no hesitation ever manifested
by the West, in granting any appropriation, the object of which
is clearly shewn to be the public good. Enquiry, it is true, is
sometimes called for, but as soon as gentlemen from the West
are convinced that the object is a good one, they give without
hesitation. Do you call for war? A war to protect commerce? What
was the conduct of the West? No seamen sprang from her bosom.
They were dear to her indeed, as the sons of our own common
country. Yes [sic], they were not peculiarly hers—her interest in them
was collateral, not direct—sympathetic, not selfish. The West rushed
manfully on—but what they bore, what they suffered, and what
they did, it does not belong to me here to say.

With respect to the hon. member from South Carolina, (Mr.
McDUFFIE,) whom I was delighted, on a former occasion, to
find co-operating with the friends of internal improvement, I
must say that my delight was only equalled by the regret I now
feel at his opposition to the present bill.[22] He tells us that the
West is filled with emigrants from the Eastern states; that her

inhabitants are but one part of the same family, spread on the eastern and western side of the mountains; that all the various and fond recollections which belong to the birth-place of these emigrants, constitute so many ties and safeguards to cement the common union. But, need I remind that gentleman, that other generations are hereafter to spring up—generations who will find the tombs of their ancestry, not upon the shores of the Atlantic, but in the valley of the Mississippi and the Ohio. On them no such ties will exert their power—no such recollections spread their healing influence. Is it not then the duty of the General Government to bind our population by other and more lasting ties? And, after all, what is it that is asked from Congress, not only at this session, but at all future sessions, for these eighty miles of the great National highway? Less than the cost of a single frigate—not twice the sum which will build those ten sloops of war which are now called for, and which I apprehend will be required for the defence of our commerce against the depredations of piracy[23]—this is all that is asked. Yet we are told of the ravenous voracity of the West! Will Pennsylvania decline an appeal, not to her generosity, but to her justice? Is it fair—is it generous—is it just—after she has enjoyed the expenditure of more than a million of the public money, on the Cumberland road—after houses have sprung up, and villages been formed, and settlements multiplied upon her soil, in consequence of that expenditure—I ask, is it generous, to say, the moment the road leaves the limit of that territory, that she will oppose its farther progress? But, if neither justice nor generosity will prevail with her, let me remind her delegation of the *interest* of that state. What is this road but an extension of the road from Philadelphia to Pittsburg? And whither will its branches lead but to Bedford, to Carlisle, and downward, from thence, through all the neighboring towns? Sir, I do hope that the gentleman from Pennsylvania will not oppose this bill.[24] I know, indeed, that there did once exist a prejudice against the Cumberland road, in one city of that state;[25] but I feel satisfied that ere now the good sense which so eminently distinguishes that city, has prevailed against the prejudice arising from a local interest, by which, for a moment, it was clouded. May I not appeal to the whole House? We have a great trust—we have also a great duty to perform. Let us lend our hearty co-operation for the common good of those who sent us.

What shall we, from the West, say to our constituents when we return home, and they ask us, what have you done for the Cumberland road? Must we answer, "No money, no money." If they can ask us what was done for the Delaware and Chesapeake canal, must we say, "O! there was some money for that—about twice the sum we asked for the Cumberland road?" Sir, we are men, and we have the feelings of men. But I will not longer detain the committee on an object so simple and a proposition so self-evident as the expediency of this measure. Let me rather anticipate your parental kindness—your paternal feelings, in promoting a design so intimately connected, I will say, with the safety and the best interests of our country.[26]

Register of Debates, 18 Cong., 2 Sess., 231-39. Debate on "the bill for the continuation of the Cumberland road" had begun in Committee of the Whole on January 12 and had continued on the following day, when the discussion had centered on a motion by Philemon Beecher to fill the blank for an appropriation with the figure, $150,000. Proceedings on the latter date had ended when Clay "rose, and, expressing a desire of presenting to the committee his views on the general subject, requested, as the hour was late, the indulgence that the committee would rise." When the House, in Committee of the Whole, returned to consideration of Beecher's motion, Clay immediately took the floor.

1 In connection with the bill for surveys for roads and canals. See above, III, 633n.

2 By act of April 8, 1811, the New York Legislature had appointed commissioners empowered to apply to Congress for cooperation and aid in opening a canal system between the Great Lakes and the Hudson River. The commissioners had submitted a memorial to this effect, presented to the United States House of Representatives on December 23, 1811, and to the Senate the following day. In a special message of December 23, President Madison had called the attention of Congress to "the signal advantages to be derived to the United States from a general system of internal communication and conveyance," particularly in connection "with arrangements and exertions for the general security. . . ." The matter had been referred to committee; but that body, while approving the concept of aid by the General Government to effect such improvements, had reported it "improper, at the present time, to grant that effectual aid . . . to which they are so well entitled." Annals of Cong., 12 Cong., 1 Sess., XXIII, 87, 569, 1078; XXIV, 2167.

3 President Monroe had stated, in his message to Congress, December 7, 1824, that a survey of a route from Washington to New Orleans, in accordance with the provision for road surveys under the act of April 30, 1824 (see above, III, 568-69, 592n, 593n, 626n, 633n), was to begin "early in the next season." Register of Debates, 18 Cong., 2 Sess. Appendix, 5.

4 Senator Andrew Jackson; Delegate Richard K. Call.

5 See speech by William McLean, of Ohio, January 13. Register of Debates, 18 Cong., 2 Sess., 202. McLean, a brother of John McLean, had been born in Mason County, Kentucky, had studied and practiced law in Cincinnati, and served in Congress from 1823 to 1829.

6 See above, II, 188n.

7 3 U. S. Stat., 290 (April 19, 1816), 349 (March 1, 1817), 430 (April 18, 1818), 491 (March 2, 1819), 547 (March 6, 1820).

8 Christopher Rankin.   9 Register of Debates, 18 Cong., 2 Sess., 209.

10 The American Revolution.   11 See above, III, 575, 593n.

12 By Christopher Rankin, on January 13. Register of Debates, 18 Cong., 2 Sess., 199-201.

13 George McDuffie, speaking in opposition to the bill on January 13, had said: "It appeared very clear that, for at least ten years to come, all the surplus revenue of this country would be exhausted in paying the public debt—and, from the character and well known wishes of the nation, he presumed that it must be the great object of the next administration to pay that debt." Ibid., 212.

14 [William H. Crawford], "Report from the Secretary of the Treasury, on the State of the Finances, January 3, 1825," Senate Docs., 18 Cong., 2 Sess., no. 8, p. 13.

15 See above, III, 707-709.   16 See above, III, 756n.

17 The bill, authorizing a subscription of stock in the Chesapeake and Delaware Canal Company, had been ordered to a third reading by a margin of only three votes (86 to 83). On the question of its final passage in the House, January 21, it was approved by a vote of 113 to 74. It became law on March 3, 1825. Register of Debates, 18 Cong., 2 Sess., 223-24, 333-34; 4 U. S. Stat., 124; and above, III, 593n.

18 John C. Calhoun to the President of the United States, December 3, 1824, in Senate Docs., 18 Cong., 2 Sess., no. 1, p. 61.

The Muscle Shoals Canal, the only one of these projects not discussed more fully elsewhere in this speech, was given Federal support under act of May 23, 1828, as amended February 12, 1831, wherein Congress granted the State of Alabama 400,000 acres of certain relinquished public lands in that State for use in improvement of navigation and construction of a canal at the shoals in the Tennessee River. *4 U. S. Stat.*, 290, 441. The canal was completed by 1836 but still failed to solve the problems of hazardous river navigation. The system was abandoned within a few years, and more comprehensive works were not attempted until much later.

[19] In his message to the legislature Governor Joseph Desha had recommended that construction of a canal around the falls of the Ohio be undertaken with public funds. Both House and Senate committees had endorsed this recommendation, but legislation to carry it into effect had been tabled in the Senate and defeated in the House. Instead, an act to incorporate the Louisville and Portland Canal Company for construction of the works with private funds had been approved January 12, 1825, efforts in the Senate to amend the measure to provide for State financing of the company having also been defeated. *Ky. H. of Reps., Journal . . . 1824-1825*, pp. 146, 520-21, 522, 539, 582; *Ky. Sen., Journal . . . 1824-1825*, pp. 271-78, 344, 413-17, 431; *Ky. Gen. Assy., Acts . . . 1824-1825*, pp. 167-73.

The Federal Government later, under acts of May 13, 1826, and March 2, 1829, was authorized to purchase 2,350 shares of stock in the corporation at prices not to exceed $100 a share; and by virtue of stock payments in lieu of interest returns, this financial involvement in support of the canal was considerably increased. *4 U. S. Stat.*, 162, 352; "Report on the Louisville and Portland Canal," *House Misc. Docs.*, 40 Cong., 2 Sess., no. 83 (February 28, 1868), p. 5. Navigation of the canal was opened in 1829.

[20] See above, III, 593n.   [21] See above, I, 618-27n.

[22] At the previous Session of Congress McDuffie had spoken in support of the bill to provide surveys for roads and canals. *Annals of Cong.*, 18 Cong., 1 Sess., XLI, 1371-88.

[23] Early in the current Session the House had rejected a motion to go into Committee of the Whole on a bill to authorize construction of ten sloops of war. On January 10 the Senate had begun consideration of "A Bill for the Suppression of Piracy in the West Indies," one provision of which was the addition of "a number of sloops of war" to the naval force of the United States. As finally enacted, the measure authorized the building of a maximum of ten of these vessels. *4 U. S. Stat.*, 131 (March 3, 1825).

[24] Samuel Breck subsequently offered a substitute bill, by way of amendment, which would have permitted the Federal Government to subscribe to twenty per cent of the stock of a company if incorporated by the State of Ohio for construction of the road from a point opposite Wheeling to Zanesville. This amendment was defeated. *Register of Debates*, 18 Cong., 2 Sess., 239-40 (January 17, 1825).

[25] See above, III, 593n.

[26] Following this speech the appropriation was fixed at $150,000, and the bill, with amendments, was enacted. The measure provided not only for construction of the road "from the town of Canton, in the state of Ohio, on the right bank of the Ohio river, opposite the town of Wheeling, to the Muskingum river, at Zanesville, in said state," but also for completion of surveys authorized under an act of May 25, 1820 (*3 U. S. Stat.*, 604-605), which had projected extension of the route from Wheeling to "a point on the left bank of the Mississippi river . . . between St. Louis and the mouth of the Illinois river, . . . the said road to be on a straight line, or as nearly so as, having a due regard to the condition and situation of the ground and water-courses over which the same shall be laid out, shall be deemed expedient and practicable." The new law further extended this route "to the permanent seat of government of the state of Missouri" and delineated its course by requiring that it "shall pass by the seat of government of the states of Ohio, Indiana, and Illinois. . . ." *4 U. S. Stat.*, 128 (March 3, 1825).

Check to Robert Blair Campbell

21 Jan. 1825

Pay to Rob. Campbell or order Two hundred and thirty dollars. Cashr. of the Off. of Dt. & Dt. Washn[1]—   H CLAY

ADS. DLC-TJC (DNA, M212, R16). Endorsed on verso: "R B Campbell." Campbell, a member of the United States House of Representatives from South Carolina (1823-1825, 1834-1837), later moved successively to Alabama, to Texas, and to London, England. He was United States consul at Havana, 1842-1850, and at London, 1854-1861.

[1] Richard Smith.

To George William Featherstonhaugh

My dear Sir   Washn. 21 Jan. 1825

I ought earlier to have acknowledged the receipt of your very friendly letter of the 30h. Ulto.[1] under date at Albany. Of the difficulties which my friends had to encounter, in relation to the choice of Electors by your State, as detailed in your letter I entertain no doubt. Your account is corroborated by that which I have received from other highly respectable sources. I never had, I assure you, the smallest doubt of the zeal fidelity and discretion of my friends; and to you, my dear Sir, who have given me such disinterested, generous and efficient support, I feel an extent of obligation which I cannot express.

There is but one alternative, in the discharge of the duty which has devolved on the H. of R., as it appears to me, and that is to select Mr. Adams or Genl. Jackson. To say nothing more of Mr. Crawford, his personal condition is, in my mind, an insuperable objection to him. That alternative is far from being agreeable. We must however meet it, with a determination to make for our Country the best choice we can under actual circumstances. As I am at present advised, I think the preponderating considerations are on the side of Mr. Adams. I cannot but fear that the election of Genl. Jackson, when we look at the cause which would produce it, and the principles by which it has been supported, would be a precedent fraught with much danger to the character and security of our institutions.

I thank you for the two volumes of Agricultural transactions which you kindly sent me by your member.[2] Do you know of any Bologna Hemp seed in your State?

I am very desirous to visit the interior of your State. I had once, some years ago, fixed upon a summer for that gratification, but I was prevented from enjoying it by the situation of Mrs. Clay, arising out of a mutual fault. I hope I shall be able in the course of no very distant period to pay you my respects, and there is no one in N. York whom I shall see with more satisfaction than yourself.

I am faithfully and Cordially Yr. ob. Servt.   H. CLAY
G. W. Featherstonhaugh Esqr.

ALS. CSmH. Addressed to "Duanesburgh New York." Featherstonhaugh, an Englishman who had settled in New York, was later (1834-1835) employed by the United States War Department to make a geological survey of a part of the West. He served as Commissioner for the British Government to settle the boundary between the United States and Canada under the terms of the Webster-Ashburton Treaty (1842) and subsequently became a British consul in France. He published numerous works, mainly geological and travel accounts, among which the best known is *Excursion through the Slave States, from Washington on the Potomac to the Frontier of Mexico; with Sketches of Popular Manners and Geological Notices* (2 vols., London, 1844).

[1] Not found.   [2] Lewis Eaton, who resided in Duanesburg.

From Amos Kendall

FRANKFORT, Jan. 21st, 1825.

Dear Sir:—Our Legislature is gone, but have left us no repose. We have a prospect of a contest more embittered than ever.[1] I regret it, and would gladly escape from it; but the fates seem to order it otherwise. I may mistake; but I think the legislature will be sustained. The excitement is among those opposed to removing the judges by any means.

As I informed you,[2] the resolutions requesting you to vote for Jackson passed, and you have doubtless received them. Jackson is my second choice, all circumstances being equal between him and Adams. But if our interest in the west can be promoted by any other arrangement, I shall be content. At any rate, let us have a President. I would sooner vote for any of the three than have a Vicegerent for four years. Do what you think best—the Argus will not complain, because it has faith that you will do nothing to compromit the interests of the western country, or the nation.

Sincerely your friend,   AMOS KENDALL.

Frankfort *Argus of Western America,* July 2, 1828. Published also in Washington *United States Telegraph,* July 19, 1828; *United States Telegraph-Extra,* I (July 26, 1828), 308-309, 322.
[1] See above, III, 902n; Cowan to Clay, January 1, 1825.
[2] Cf. above, III, 901-902.

To Walter Dun

Dear Sir   Washn. 22d. Jan. 1825

I duly received your letter of the 10h. inst[1] and thank you for your friendly communication of the condition of a tract of land in Ohio, which you suppose to belong to the Estate of the late Col. Morrison.[2] I expect it has been assigned to some of the legatees who ought to take care of the affair of taxes; but I have written to my agent at home,[3] with directions to do what may be proper.

Your suggestions in respect to the Military district[4] shall receive due consideration; but I apprehend it would be difficult to prevail upon Congress to substitute other lands for those which were reserved for the satisfaction of Virginia Military warrants, however equitable it may be.

I cannot express my very great obligations to my Ohio friends for their firm and faithful support of me for the Presidency. As the event has not realized their kind expectations and wishes, all that remains for me is to acquiesce, as I do most entirely, in the public decision. In the selection which has devolved on the H. of

R. we have great difficulty; but I must confess that the preponderating considerations appear to me to be rather on the side of Mr.
Adams, as a choice which is least likely to prove injurious to the
public interests or to establish a precedent fraught with future
mischief.   With great regard I am faithfly Yrs   H. CLAY
Walter Dun Esq.

ALS. Ross County Historical Society, Chillicothe, Ohio.   1 Not found.
2 James Morrison.   3 Robert Scott; letter not found.
4 See above, I, 654n; III, 8n-9n.

From Percival Butler

Hon H Clay   Versailles Jan 22d 1825
Dear Sir
Apprised of the arduousness of your publick duties and your
untiring devotion to the discharge of them, it was with difficulty
I persuaded myself to trouble you with an office of private friend-
ship.
You are acquainted with the decree of the court in the case of
Edwards and wife against Wilson Tandy & others foreclosing the
mortgage and ordering a sale of the property purchased by Mrs
Russell of James Huges [sic] the mortgagor[1]—under that decree a
sale has taken place and the property has been (by Wickliff[2] [sic]
instructions) purchased for the benefit of the mortgagee at $3450
By this decision Mrs Russell will be ultimately liable to the last
purchaser (unless it can be otherwise accomodated [sic]) for the
price paid by her immediate alienee with the interest & charges for
improvements which, after the deduction for rents, will be at
least double the present value of the property. Thus she is
compelled either to secure to the last purchaser the title to the
property or become responsible upon her warranty for double its
value. Mr Wickliff availing, himself of this dilemma has purchased
in the property; hoping thereby to extort from her any amount
short of her liability to the last alienee— Now this is surely unworthy of a man who wishes to be esteemed liberal honourable
& just— and degrading when pactised [sic] upon one whom he has
affected to befriend. His duty to his client did not require him to
avail himself of the fraud of the Brother, to gratify the cupidity of
the sister. He may be excused for resorting to chicane to obtain
his ends at the bar; but here his duty as counsel terminates, and he
cannot (the circumstances of the case considered) be justified for
descending to tricks to sell the property above its intrinsick worth—
But this is foreign from my object in adressing [sic] you: Which is
to request that you will as soon as you can possibly make it convenient, see Mr Nurse[3] (who I am informed is atty in fact for

Edwards with unlimited discretion) and endeavour to purchase of him the premises in question at a fair price. he may may [*sic*] assume the price they sold at as a criterion of their value, (it is certainly an evidence that no one would give more). or he may let them be valued by disinterested gentlemen in Lexington and Mrs R will abide their award. I am informed that Edwards needs money and his agent is anxious to sell   you may stimulate that anxiety by remarking upon the probability of compromise between Mrs R and the tenant in possession, and in good faith assure him that from the low price and little demand for houses in Lexington at present, if he lets pass this chance of sale he may be bedeviled with bad tenants and run the risk of conflagration for many years before another presents itself

I have made these suggestions as to the plan to be pursued in the attempt to purchase to save you trouble in thinking of the matter. regard them as mere hints which you will weigh at their worth, whilst you exercise your own sound judgement and discretion in the affair

If you should succeed in negotiating a purchase, you may bind Mrs. R to pay *$2500* in hand—and obtain for the balance the longest time you can— upon being notified of your success, you will receive my check for $500 on the U S Bk Pha, and your check for 2000 on Lex payable in 60 days will be punctually, paid or any other plan of payment you may agree upon will be punctiliously complied.[4] I hope you will feel no distrust in binding yourself for the fulfillment of the terms you may agree upon— be assured that Mrs R is prepared to fulfil what she through me has requested you to engage for her, and your exertions in this business will be gratefully acknowled [*sic*] by her and not forgotten by your Friend & humble St   P BUTLER

P S If a valuation is agreed upon Messrs J Tilford Gratz[5] J C Richardson and J M McCalla or any of them would do   P B

[Marginal note on last page]

I addressed by private hand on the 18th Decr[6] but presume you did not get my letter, I having recd no answer

ALS. DLC-HC (DNA, M212, R1). Butler, a lawyer, had resided in Fayette County before moving to Woodford and had represented both counties in the Kentucky House of Representatives (the former in 1820, the latter in 1821 and 1822). He later settled in Louisville, where he was an eminent member of the bar, and represented that city in the State legislature.

[1] See above, III, 135, 136n. The Wilson here mentioned could have been either James or Robert, both of whom were among the defendants in this case.

[2] Robert Wickliffe.   [3] Probably Joseph Nourse.

[4] Clay apparently failed in this mission. A kinsman of Mrs. Russell subsequently claimed to have paid Wickliffe $10,000 in full discharge of her liability under the decree. Amended bill, filed April 28, 1849, in Todd's Heirs *vs.* Wickliffe, Fayette Circuit Court.

[5] Benjamin Gratz.   [6] Not found.

To James Brown

My dear Sir   Washington 23 Jan. 1825

I had heard, with much regret, prior to the receipt of your letter of the 12th. Nov.[1] which has just come to hand, of your serious indisposition and confinement. I am rejoiced to find that your health has improved, and that you have assurances of its complete restoration. My own was better the last year throughout than it was during that which preceded it; but I yet am some times too distinctly reminded that my complaint has not finally taken leave of me. During the present year I hope, however, entirely to subdue it. Our Kentucky friends were generally well at my last dates. Mrs. Clay did not accompany me here as I wished. Her long absence from society, and the too rigorous economy to which she thinks herself bound to subject herself opposed [sic], in her view, obstacles to her accompanying me which I could not overcome. I am beginning to reap some of the fruits of her frugality; and of my professional success, by gradually emerging from the weight of debt which bore us down. I have paid off my Astor bond,[2] and no longer am afflicted by fears of the condition in which I should leave my family, if I were cut off suddenly. Two years more of such prosperity as I have enjoyed during those two which are past would find me liberated from debt. My purchase of Kentucky bank paper is likely to realize all my anticipations,[3] and if I had as I wished extended that operation I should even now consider myself as freed from pecuniary difficulties.

The papers will have informed you of the results so far of the Presidential contest. In spite of all the discouragements which all the friends of the other Candidates industriously contributed to throw around my cause, *accident* alone prevented my return to the H. of R. and, as is generally now believed, my election. In the actual position in which I find myself, my friends have probably the power of controlling the ultimate result. Those of the three Candidates returned make to us the strongest professions &c &c. We are endeavoring to form the best judgment we can of the existing state of things, and our resolution will be dictated exclusively by public considerations and public duty. Looking to these we regard the contest as now limited to two in fact although it embraces three in form. Mr. Crawford's personal condition, to say nothing more, seems to us to put him out of the question. Between the other two we are inclined to select Mr. Adams, as a choice of evils. The probability is that he will be elected; but, as throughout this whole affair, all calculations appear to have been most completely baffled, we may yet be disappointed in that result. I will not trouble you with details, especially as those of day [*sic*] may be varied by tomorrow.

Genl La Fayette has filled our papers and engrossed all our Conversations. His arrival among us, by diverting the public from too intense devotion to the affair of the Presidency, ha[s][4] had good effect, altho' it doubtless contributed, in the military and other parades to which it gave rise, to the unexpected advancement of the interests of one of the Candidates. We have passed for the Generals benefit an act creditable to the gratitude of the nation and comfortable to him.[5] It has made him very happy.

There is an eddy in Congress produced by the termination of one and the commencement of a new administration. The Session will pass off without being characterized by any great national measure; for such I do not call the continuation of the Cumberland road, which has been authorized by a vote of the H. of R., nor the business of the pirates, now under consideration, important as both of them undoubtedly are[6]—

I can tell you nothing of the formation of the new Cabinet. I believe that, if I choose to go into it, I can enter in *any* situation that I may please. This opinion is formed from circumstances, not from assurances to which I should not listen, but which I should instantly check if attempted to be made. Feeling really great indifference about any office, resting upon the will of one man, I do not know that I should accept the first place in the Cabinet, if offered.

I sent to Mrs Clay the letter of Mrs. Brown, to whom be pleased to present my affectionate regards and believe me Faithfully Yr friend   H CLAY
James Brown Esq.

ALS. DLC-HC (DNA, M212, R1).   1 Not found.
2 See above, III, 857, 874, 886-87.
3 See above, III, 519, 525-27, 549-50, 671-72, 810.   4 MS. torn.
5 See above, III, 899, 900.   6 See above, Speech, January 17, 1825, and notes.

To Peter B. Porter

My dear General   Washn. 23d. Jan. 1825
I have this moment received your letter of the 14h. inst. I agree with you in thinking it unprofitable and unnecessary to review the circumstances by which I lost the vote of your state and am placed, by adverse causes elsewhere, in my present position. The important enquiry should be what are the duties now incident to that position? And I am happy to find that, by a similar train of reasoning, we have brought our minds to the same conclusion.

Whatever objections exist against Mr. Adams (and they are many and strong) I believe he is the best choice we can now make. I shall support him. I think he will be elected, but of that there is not entire certainty.

I congratulate you on the passage of the Niagara bil[l.][1] Altho' I was prevented from taking a part in the discussion, I was not indifferent as to its passage, and believe I rendered some service in promoting that object. Mr. Tracey[2] ascribed even more to me than I am disposed to admit.

Give my respects to Mrs. B. and to Mrs. P.[3] and believe me, my dear General, always Your friend   H. CLAY
Genl. P. B. Porter.

ALS. NBuHi.   [1] MS. torn.   [2] Albert H. Tracy. Reference not found.
[3] Mrs. John Breckinridge; Mrs. Porter.

To Littleton Dennis Teackle

Sir   Washn. 24 Jan. 1825
I received the letter which you did me the honor to write me on the 11h. inst. with the bill which accompanied it;[1] and I shall express with great frankness my opinion upon the project which it proposes. I do not think it will succeed. The emission of paper, founded upon any other basis than that of specie, cannot I think, under any conceivable circumstances, be attended with success. The paper must depreciate. If in funding it, as is proposed, the interest were payable in *specie* it might give it a temporary support. But then the value of the paper, as a circulating medium, would be tested by its being thrown out of circulation, and would depend upon the rate of specie interest which the funded debt bore. It would, on that contingency, be rapidly funded. So that it would come to the question, whether it would be desirable to create any given amount of stock, bearing a rate of three or four per Cent. I have not time to give you at large the reasons of the opinion which I entertain. Our paper bank in Kentucky[2] has so far disappointed the hopes of the public that every body is tired of it and desirous to get back, as soon as we can, to a specie circulation. With all the precautions which you could employ, the public would be ultimately defrauded in the execution of your plan. There would be false values upon and false conveyances of property; and in winding up the concern great losses, which society would not be compensated for by the accruing interest. I could not say more without writing an essay.

With great respect I am Yr. ob. Servt.   H. CLAY
Littleton Dennis Teackle Esq.

ALS. ViU-U. B. Quinby Manuscripts. Addressed to Annapolis, Maryland, where Teackle had recently removed from Princess Anne, in Somerset County, on the Eastern Shore. Having come to Maryland from Virginia at the turn of the century, he had for many years served as president of the Bank of Somerset and was prominent in financial and manufacturing activities.
1 Neither the letter nor the enclosure has been found.
2 Bank of the Commonwealth.

From Francis Preston Blair

My Dear Sir　　　　　　　　　　　　Frankfort Jany 24. 1825

I received your letter of 8th this night & the "conversations of Lord Byron" by the previous Mail. I thank you for the pleasure which I have derived from them—

I had anticipated (even before a letter from Letcher[1] which hinted at it, had been received) that our Representative might brought [sic] by Bibb[2] into his leading strings, patticularly [sic] as he furnishd [sic] with a strong hold upon him in our Legislative Resolutions[3]— Both Crittenden[4] & myself therefore wrote him emancipating letters. I spoke to Thos Bryan[5] our newsmonger, who gives Davy[6] all the advices, to tell him better about the Sentiments of his immediate Constituents— He showed me the letter after it was written—it was just such as I would have dictated— I send off one from John Logan[7] which I have procured from him because I thought he might have a sort of Special influence on him— This I put in the mail with this scrawl— Dudley & Kendall[8] promised me to write to him to the same purpose & he should be told that Charles Allen[9] another Senator in his District voted against the Resolutions I have no doubt that Adams is the safest Choice & therefore the best— Mrs Blair tells me to thank you over again for the Books which you were so good as to forward— Your friends are well except the Judges[10] of whom I would tell you more if I had time to do anything, but acknowledge my obligations to you & that I am Sir Yr Mo Ob st.　　　　　　　　F P. BLAIR

ALS. DLC-HC (DNA, M212, R1). Addressed to Clay at Washington.
1 Robert P. Letcher.　　2 George M. Bibb.　　3 See above, III, 901-902 and note.
4 John J. Crittenden.　　5 Of Frankfort.　　6 David White (Jr.).
7 Brother of William and Benjamin (the younger) Logan. John Logan, a lawyer, represented Shelby County in the Kentucky Legislature from 1815 through 1818 and in 1825. He died January 6, 1826.
8 Either Peter or Jephthah Dudley; Amos Kendall.　　9 Charles H. Allen.
10 Probably a reference to the judges of the old court. Cf. above, III, 902n; Cowan to Clay, January 1, 1825.

From Nicholas Biddle

Dear Sir,　　　　　　Bank of the United States—Jany. 25th. 1825

I have the pleasure of inclosing two letters from Mr Jones, one

of the 27th. ulto & the other of the 4th inst[1] and will thank you at your first leisure, to consider the proposition contained in them, to obtain an assignment of the judgment of the U.S. against Jesse Hunt,[2] and give me your views in relation to it. This case appears to present one of those attempts to evade the payment to the Bank by secret & fraudulent conveyances, from which a Court of Chancery might afford relief. The extent & the probability of that relief you can best estimate—but in the mean time it may be worth reflection whether by succeeding to the claim of the government we may not protect the property which that claim may be made the pretext for sacrificing. You will have the goodness when you have no further occasion for these original letters to return them to me, & to believe me With great respect very truly Yrs
Honble Henry Clay. Washington Cola.   N BIDDLE Prest.

ALS. DLC-TJC (DNA, M212, R13).
[1] George W. Jones. Letters not found. Cf. below, Clay to Biddle, January 31, 1825.
[2] See above, III, 389n.

Remarks on the Judicial System

[January 26, 1825]
Mr. CLAY observed that he had not been aware of the intention of his colleague to call up the resolution at this time. He had, however, no objections to it. He now rose chiefly for the purpose of presenting an inquiry to the chairman of the Committee on the Judiciary.[1] The whole House, as well as that gentleman, were perfectly aware that some alteration was requisite in the Judicial system of the United States, so as to make it comprise all parts of the Union, and to extend it to those six or seven states,[2] which are at present out of the pale of its benefits. He had hoped that the House would have received, before now, a bill for that purpose from the Judiciary Committee—a bill that should either go to alter the whole system, or, if that was not to be done, at least to extend it in its present form to all the states.[3] He should be glad to know whether there was any probability of such report being made. If any new Judges were to be added to the present number of those on the bench of the Supreme Court, it would require the blank to be differently filled. If there was any probability that such a report would soon be presented, he should advise his colleagues to defer the consideration of the present subject until the House should have the bill before it, which the committee might report.
[Daniel Webster called attention to the bill on this subject, reported by him at the last Session, "which was now on the Order Book" and which he was eager to call up. He agreed with critics

of the existing judicial system but hoped that Letcher's "resolutions might not be further discussed, till the general subject of the judiciary should be considered."]

Mr. CLAY observed, in reply, that he was not unaware that the bill referred to had been reported at the last session, and now lay on the table. But, as he had observed no movement with respect to it, he had begun to fear, that it was intended to suffer it to lie there. He was glad to learn that it was to be called up. There was not a case of more crying injustice to be found in the Union, than that presented by the present organization of the Judiciary system of the United States. Seven, (and indeed he might say nine,) states were cut off from the enjoyment of its benefits. There was, to be sure, one Judge to hold circuits in all these states; but the task was vastly beyond the strength of any individual, and the constitution of the present Judge[4] was suffering under the burden. Two states were occasionally favored by the presence of the Judge; the remaining seven had no aid whatever from the United States Courts. He was confident, he said, that gentlemen would agree with him in the sentiment, that the principle of representation was not more important in legislation itself, than in the administration of justice. In the present state of things, the Judges of the Supreme Court know as little about the local laws of some of the Western and Southern states, as if they did not belong to the confederacy. Of the great variety of different codes existing in those states, not one was represented on the bench of the Supreme Court, and the people of the West had certainly a right to expect that if Congress did not approve the present system, they would alter it, or if they did approve it, that they would then extend its operations to the Western states. Mr. C. closed with observing, that, important as the bill was, which had this day been ordered to its third reading, the object of which was to punish crimes against the United States,[5] it was not more important nor more necessary, than that which went to secure the administration of justice by the Courts of the United States, throughout nine states of this Union.[6]

Register of Debates, 18 Cong., 2 Sess., 369-70. Earlier in the day, on motion of Robert P. Letcher, the House in Committee of the Whole had taken up the resolutions, introduced by Letcher at the preceding Session, concerning the authority of the United States Supreme Court in cases involving the validity of State constitutions and laws (see above, III, 746, 753-56).

1 Daniel Webster.

2 Indiana, Illinois, Missouri, Alabama, Mississippi, and Louisiana, for which States an act of February 19, 1831 (4 *U. S. Stat.*, 444), ultimately assigned circuit court jurisdiction to the district courts. Clay here counted Tennessee as a seventh State and, below, included Ohio and Kentucky in referring to the nine States which lacked adequate service under the Federal judicial system.

3 See above, III, 551n.   4 Thomas Todd.

5 The bill was enacted. 4 *U. S. Stat.*, 115-23 (March 3, 1825).

6 Letcher agreed to postponement of consideration of his resolutions, and the Committee rose. The House did not return to this subject during the Session.

To John Quincy Adams

Thursday morning [January 27, 1825].
Mr. Clay's Compliments to Mr. Adams, and he will call to see
him this evening at six OClock, if he should be disengaged.

AN. MHi-Adams Papers. Addressed on attached sheet: "The Honble J. Q. Adams."
Endorsed on verso by Adams: "Clay—H. 27. Jany 1825."
Upon receipt of this note Adams sent word to Clay that he "had company to
dine with me this evening, but would see him at any other time that would suit
his convenience, at my house or at his lodgings." Clay called on the evening of
January 29 and sat "a couple of hours, discussing all the prospects and probabilities
of the Presidential election." Adams, *Memoirs*, VI, 480, 483.

From Philander Chase

VERY DEAR SIR:—   *Worthington, Jan.* 27, 1825.
Your kind letter, in answer to mine of the 14th of October,
dated at Washington the 14th of Dec. last,[1] was duly received.

That you condescend to become the umpire in the matter alluded
to commands my respect and grateful consideration, and I firmly
trust your name will prove as serviceable in the *progress* as it
was in the beginning of our seminary's prosperity. My English
correspondents continue to increase in number and zeal.

The legislature of Ohio have granted us a charter.[2] We are
allowed to conduct our affairs in our own way, and hold to the
amount of twenty thousand dollars annual income. The Bishops
are to be members of our corporation, and have a visitatorial power.
What severe reflections will these auspicious tidings bring on all
who reported me as a schismatical and scheming fugitive, un-
supported by my own state and people!

The place where our seminary will be fixed will not be known
till the next June convention.[3] In the mean time I am faithfully
and gratefully yours,   P. CHASE.

Extract. Chase, *Reminiscences*, I, 463-64.   [1] Not found.
[2] Ohio, *Laws, 1824-1825 (Local Laws)*, XXIII, 12 (app. December 29, 1824).
[3] "The Convocation of the Protestant Episcopal Church for the Diocese of Ohio,
which met at Columbus on the 7th" of June, 1826, resolved unanimously "to locate
the Theological Seminary on the land purchased for that purpose . . . by Bishop
Chase. . . ." Washington *Daily National Intelligencer*, July 3, 1826. Construction of
the buildings at Gambier Hill, Ohio, was not completed until 1828. In the interim
classes were begun on Chase's farm at Worthington.

To Nicholas Biddle

Sir   Washington 28h. Jan. 1825.
I beg leave to introduce to your acquaintance Mr. Houston,[1] who
will present you this letter. He is a gentleman of great respectability
whose integrity and veracity are entirely to be relied on. The

executor of the late Genl. M. D. Hardin,[2] he goes to Philadelphia with the view of endeavoring to effect some accommodation in the payment of a large debt due from his testator to the Bank of the U. S., at its Lexington office. The very great esteem which I felt for Genl. Hardin, and the interest which I take in the welfare of his family induce me strongly to wish that the Board may see fit to afford to the estate some indulgence in the payment of this debt. Nevertheless it is my duty to say, what I am sure Mr. Huston would himself not fail to communicate, that the Bank can coerce payment of this debt, not however without great if not ruinous sacrifices to the Estate. Should the Board feel disposed to yield any accommodation, among the objects which will be offered, I should recommend the acceptance of the Bridge stock.[3] In the value of that stock I have high confidence. The removal of the seat of Government from Frankfort, which would certainly somewhat diminish that value, I do not believe will happen.[4]

I am with great respect Your ob. Servant   H. CLAY
Nicholas Biddle Esq &c &c &c

ALS. KyLoF.
[1] Felix Huston, born and reared in the Green River district of Kentucky, was at this time practicing law in Frankfort. He later removed to Natchez, Mississippi, where he became a planter, lawyer, and member of the State legislature. In 1836 he led a force of volunteers in the struggle for Texan independence and there attained the rank of major general. Upon his return to Mississippi in 1840 he resumed the practice of law.
[2] Who had died October 8, 1823.
[3] The Frankfort Bridge Company, incorporated in 1810, built the first permanent bridge across the Kentucky River at Frankfort. Under the act of incorporation a stock issue had been authorized not to exceed $30,000. This had been extended by another $20,000 under legislation of 1816. Ky. Gen. Assy., *Acts, 1809-1810*, ch. CXLV, p. 86; *1812-1816*, ch. CCCXXIII, p. 530.
[4] Cf. above, III, 878-79 and note, 880-81 and note.

To Francis T. Brooke

Washington 28th. Jany. 1825
My Dear Sir: My position, in regard to the Presidential election, is highly critical, & such as to leave me no path on which I can move without censure; I have pursued, in regard to it, the rule which I always observe in the discharge of my public duty. I have interrogated my conscience as to what I ought to do, & that faithful guide tells me that I ought to vote for Mr. Adams. I shall fulfill its injunctions. Mr. Crawford's state of health, & the circumstances under which he presents himself to the house, appear to me to be conclusive against him. As a friend of liberty, & to the permanence of our institutions, I cannot consent, in this early stage of their existence, by contributing to the election of a military chieftain, to give the strongest guarranty that this republic will march in

the fatal road which has conducted every other republic to ruin. I owe to our friendship this frank exposition of my intentions. I am, & shall continue to be, assailed by all the abuse, which partizan zeal, malignity, & rivalry can invent. I shall risk, without emotion, these effusions of malice, & remain unshaken in my purpose. What is a public man worth, if he will not expose himself, on fit occasions, for the good of his country?—

As to the result of the election, I cannot speak with absolute certainty; but there is every reason to believe that we shall avoid the dangerous precedent to which I allude.

Be pleased to give my respects to Mr. . . . . . . & believe me always your cordial friend   H. CLAY[1]
The Honorable F. Brooke—

Copy by Brooke. DLC-TJC (DNA, M212, R13). Published in Washington *Daily National Intelligencer,* February 12, 1825 (republished, March 28, 1828), reprinted from Richmond *Enquirer,* February 8, 1825; *Niles' Weekly Register,* XXVII (February 19, 1825), 386; Lexington *Kentucky Reporter,* February 28, 1825 (republished, April 2, 1828); Lexington *Kentucky Gazette,* March 3, 1825.

1 An answer to this letter, by way of a communication from Andrew Jackson to Samuel Swartwout, dated February 23, 1825, was published in the Washington *Daily National Intelligencer,* March 9, 1825, reprinted from the New York *National Advocate.* In it Jackson commented on the use "of the epithet 'military chieftain.'" Then he spoke of Clay:

"Mr. Clay has never risked himself for his country. He has never sacrificed his repose, nor made an effort to repel an invading foe; of course 'his conscience' assured him it was altogether wrong in any other man to lead his countrymen to battle and victory. He who fights, and fights successfully, must, according to his standard, be held up as 'a military chieftain.' Even Washington, could he appear again among us, might be so considered, because he dared to be a virtuous and successful soldier—a correct man, and an honest statesman."

Again referring to Clay, Jackson continued: "To him, thank God, I am in no wise responsible. There is a purer tribunal to which I would in preference refer myself—to the judgment of an enlightened, patriotic, and uncorrupted people. To that tribunal I would rather appeal, whence is derived whatever of reputation either he or I may possess. By a reference, there, it will be ascertained that I did not solicit the office of President; it was the frank and flattering call of the freemen of this country, not mine, which placed my name before the nation. When they failed in their colleges to make a choice, no one beheld me seeking, through art or management, to entice any Representative in Congress from a conscientious responsibility to his own, or the wishes of his constituents. No midnight taper burnt by me; no secret conclaves were held, nor cabals entered into, to persuade any one to a violation of pledges given, or of instructions received. By me no plans were concerted to impair the pure principles of our republican institution, nor to prostrate that fundamental maxim which maintains the supremacy of the people's will. On the contrary, having never, in any manner, either before the people or Congress, interfered in the slightest degree with the question, *my* conscience stands void of offence, and will go quietly with me, regardless of the insinuations of those who, through management, may seek an influence not sanctioned by integrity and merit.

"Demagogues, I am persuaded, have, in times past, done more injury to the cause of freedom, and the rights of man, than ever did a military Chieftain; and, in our country, at least in times of peace, should be much more feared."

To Francis Preston Blair

My Dear Blair,   Washington 29. Jany. 1825.
I received this morning your very agreeable favor of the 17th

Inst.[1] A letter from you is always refreshing, and I wish that I could entitle myself to expect them more frequently, by more punctuality & diligence, on my part, in our correspond[ence].[2] — — My last letter[3] informed you of the unction that was unceasingly applied to me by all the returned Candidates for the Presidency, or rather their friends. Since then I have avowed my intention to support Mr Adams, under actual circumstances, and thereupon the oil has been instantly transformed into vinegar. The friends of (   ) (The devil knows who else for I think if he does not preside in their councils he must be quite conversant with them)[4] have turned upon me and with the most amiable unanimity agree to vituperate me. I am a deserter from Democracy: A Giant at intrigue; have sold the West—sold myself—defeating Genl Jacksons election to leave open the Western pretentions that I may hereafter fill them myself—blasting all my fair prospects &c &c &c To these are added a thousand other of the most gentle and kind and agreeable epithets and things in the world. — — — — who are themselves straining every nerve to elect Jackson that the claims of the West may be satisfied and I be thereby pretermitted, are accusing me of acting on their own principles. The Knaves cannot comprehend how a man can be honest.[5] They cannot conceive that I should have solemnly interrogated my Conscience and asked it to tell me seriously what I ought to do? that it should have enjoined me not to establish the dangerous precedent of elevating, in this early stage of the Republic, a Military Chieftain, merely because he has won a great victory? that it should have told me that a public man is undeserving his station who will not regardless of aspersions and calumnies, risk himself for his country? I am afraid that you will think me moved by these abuses. Be not deceived. I assure you that I never in my whole life felt more perfect composure, more entire confidence in the resolutions of my judgment and a more unshakeable determination to march up to my duty. And, my Dear Sir, is there an intelligent and unbiased man who must not sooner or later, concur with me? Mr Adams, you know well, I should never have selected, if at liberty to draw from the whole mass of our citizens for a President. But there is no danger in his elevation now or in time to come. Not so of his competitor, of whom I cannot believe that killing 2500 Englishmen at N. Orleans qualifies for the various, difficult and complicated duties of the Chief Magistracy.   I perceive that I am unconsciously writing a sort of defence, which you may possibly think imp[lies][6] guilt. What will be the result? you will ask with curiosity, if not anxiety. I think Mr Adams must be elected. Such is the prevailing opinion. Still I shall not consider the matter as certain until the election is over. With my

best respects to Mrs Blair and to Mr Crittenden,[7] I remain truly
Your friend   H. CLAY
F. P. Blair Esqr.

Copy. KyHi. Endorsed (ES): "The above is a true extract from so much of Mr.
Clays letter of the above date as speaks of the presidential Election with the omission
of the names of individuals. F. P. Blair—" A copy from this copy may be found in
DLC-HC (DNA, M212, R1). The letter was first published from a copy of the Blair
copy, in Richmond *Whig*, October 7, 1844, reprinted in Washington *Daily National
Intelligencer*, October 10, 1844, and widely recopied.
  [1] Not found.   [2] MS. torn.   [3] Above, January 8, 1825.
  [4] This parenthetical comment interlined in same hand.
  [5] This sentence interlined in same hand.
  [6] MS. torn.   [7] John J. Crittenden.

To Gales and Seaton

Gent.   30 Jan. 1825
  I will thank you to inform me if you will publish the inclosed
article in your paper of tomorrow   Yr. ob. Servt.   H. CLAY
[Enclosure]

A. Card.

  I have seen, without any other emotion than that of ineffable
contempt, the abuse which has been poured out upon me by a
scurrillous paper issued in this City[1] and by other kindred prints
and persons, in regard to the Presidential election. The editor[2]
of one of those prints, ushered forth in Philadelphia, called the
Columbian Observer, for which I do not subscribe, and which
I have not ordered, has had the impudence to transmit to me his
vile paper of the 28h. instant. In that number is inserted a letter,
purporting to have been written from this City, on the 25th. instant,
by a member of the H. of R. belonging to the Pennsylvania Delegation.[3] I believe it to be a forgery; but, if it be genuine, I pronounce
the member, whoever he may be, a base and infamous calumniator,
a dastard and a liar; and if he dare unveil himself and avow his
name I will hold him responsible, as I here admit myself to be,
to all the laws which govern and regulate the conduct of men
of honor.   H. CLAY
                                                          31 January 1825.

ALS. MHi-Adams Papers. Addressed on attached sheet: "Mess. Gales & Seaton
Present." The "Card," with minor editorial changes, was published in Washington
Daily National Intelligencer, January 31, 1825; it was republished in most contemporary
newspapers.
  [1] See, e.g., *Washington Gazette*, January 21, 27-29, 1825.
  [2] Stephen Simpson.
  [3] The letter, reprinted in Washington *Daily National Intelligencer*, February 4,
1825, professing to reveal "one of the most disgraceful transactions that ever covered
with infamy the Republican Ranks," accused Clay of giving his support to Adams
in return for an appointment as Secretary of State, "should this unholy coalition
prevail." See below, Kremer to Clay, *ca.* February 3, 1825.

To Nicholas Biddle

Dear Sir   Washington 31 January 1825

I duly received your letter under date the 25h. instant with two letters inclosed from Mr. Jones, the agent of the Bank of the U. States, one dated the 27h. Ulto. and the other the 4h. instant; and I have considered the recommendation which he makes of procuring from the Government of the U. States an assignment of its Judgments against Jesse Hunt.

Mr. Jones's letters, supposing him not to be mistaken in the alleged connivance of the Atto. of the U. States,[1] and his co-operation with Mr. Hunt, disclose a most nefarious attempt to perpetrate a gross fraud upon the creditors of the latter, including the Bank; and it is certainly very desirable to prevent the consummation of it. I am inclined however to think that the course which Mr. Jones has already adopted, of attending the sales advertized under the Government executions, and thereby preventing unjust sacrifices of the debtor's estate, a better one than that would be of obtaining an assignment of the Judgments. If the Government would transfer them (which I presume is doubtful) it would only be upon the payment of the full amount of what remains to be paid upon them. This would consequently require an advance of the clear amount of that balance, with the hazard, whatever it may be of ultimate reimbursement. Supposing the Bank now to be the assignee of the Judgments, enforcing their execution, the debtor would through himself and his friends take care that whatever property was sold should bring something like its real value. Instead of the facilities which are now afforded to the operation of the executions, whilst they are under the friendly direction of the U.S. Attorney, every obstacle would be thrown in the way, when they should be under the adverse control of the Bank. In fact the transfer would only transpose the Bank and the Debtor. Now, the Bank is interested in the property not being sacrificed under the executions, and he is interested in its sacrifice. After the transfer, the Bank would be interested in the sacrifice, with the view to the payment of other debts, and he that it should not be. And he would then as the Bank may now prevent the sacrifice. If the Government would place the collection of its debt, under the control of the Bank, it would be well to obtain such control; but I take it for granted it would not be given.

Upon the supposition of the existence of the alleged combination and confederacy, a Court of Chancery upon proper application to it, or the Court on its common law side would doubtless interpose and prevent the abuse of its process. The difficulty, I apprehend, however, in either case would be to make out by proof the necessary facts. For there are many things which we may suspect or believe, of which it would be extremely difficult, if not impracticable, to adduce competent proof.

Upon the whole I am induced to believe that, for the present, the safer and better plan is for Mr. Jones to attend future sales of Mr. Hunt's property and prevent its fraudulent sacrifice. That course appears so far to have been attended with success.

If nevertheless you should prefer an assignment of the judgments, or the acquisition of a control over their execution, and will signify your request to me, I will make application to the Secretary of the Treasury[2] accordingly.

It may also be worthy of consideration whether the Executive should not be applied to in order that the necessary corrective should be employed with the Attorney of the U. S.

I return Mr. Jones's letters.

I have the honor to be with great respect Your obedient Servant

H. CLAY

Nicholas Biddle Esqr. &c. &c. &c.

ALS. KyU.
1 Joseph S. Benham, born in Connecticut, Cincinnati attorney at law, appointed to the government post in 1823 and reappointed in 1827.
2 William H. Crawford.

From Robert Scott

Dr. Sir,   Lexington 2d. Feby 1825

Your favor of 20th. Ulto.[1] came to hand to day—

Doctr. Warfield[2] has not yet paid the interest on his Note—tho' I have not given him an oppy. of forgetting that circumstance and shall continue reminding him of it until the interest shall be paid— Confidentially—that connexion are I believe [sic] much pressed for money— I have been informed that Majr. Parker[3] has mortgaged all his property but did not enquire to whom— I would not therefore be surprized if a stoppage or blow up should take place ere long— However this is principally surmise as I have not collected certain data sufficient to enable me to form a positive opinion.—

The land in Ohio, to which you refer I think indeed am pretty certain was disposed of by Colo. Morrison— However I have written to Genl. Taylor,[4] who will doubtless inform me whether it is so or not— I will attend to it—

Herewith is the Accts of Colo. Morrison's estate with you for the last month[5]— From them you will see no collection of consequence has been made during the month— You will see by them also that I have paid Mr Gibson's[6] Acct.— He and others it is true are indebted to the estate for a road, but as that could not be finally setled [sic] until your return— The Acct. being of pretty old standing and as he took ½ in Comths. Notes,[7] I believed it best to pay it— By the Comths. Note Acct you will observe also what I have paid for repairing the fence of the lot where Mr. Mason[8] lives—the amt of course will greatly exceed your expectations On examining the fence I found it so old and rotten, that I was compelled to have a great part of it made anew (or to suffer the lot to become common with the adjoining ones— I believed it best to have the fence made complete and had it done— I have had a cross fence made in front of the house.   this might have been dispensed with, but Mr Mason has promised (and doubtless will perform his promise) to plant the space in trees and shrubery [sic], which will render the place more desirable and comfortable in appearance at least— In addition to this he has had Some old fence put up about the Stable at his own expense—

I have seen those indebted for purchases at C Farm in Octr. 1823[9] and informed them that suits would be brot. on their Notes to the March Court if not paid very soon and they have said it would not be necessary to resort to that alternative as they would certainly prevent it by making payment—

Mr. Foster[10] (Tailor) wishes to rent your corner brik [sic] House on Short and Market Streets—including that part lately occupied by Mr. Breckenridge & Curry[11]— His object is for his shop and family Could he get it provided the other tenants would relinquish their leases—and if he could at what price? On computation I find your rents for that property are 600$. He says he will give 500$. I suppose nothing will be done in the matter until your return, but have been frequently pressed and now make the inquiry— Curry's time is out the first of March and suppose [sic] he will not want it longer as he will not be able to go on and if Mr. F. can get the property would be glad to take possession of that part when C shall give it up—I have issued a Warrt. of distress vs Curry— Mrs Blanton has paid me a part of her quarters rent[12]—

Among the papers which you have with you belonging to the estate is an acct. against Colo. Jno. McPherson[13]— Should you present it for payment add 50c. which I have since paid—a fee bill—

We are all well—as are I believe all your domestic affairs—

                    Respectfully Yr. obt. Servt.   ROBT. SCOTT
The Honble H— Clay

ALS. KyLxT.   1 Not found. Cf. above, Clay to Dun, January 22, 1825.
2 Dr. Walter Warfield.   3 Alexander Parker.   4 James Taylor.
5 Private account not found. For the executor's accounts, see below, ca. June 13, 1825 (the monthly accounts, ADS by Scott, may be found in KyLxT).
6 William Gibson, blacksmith, who owned a farm southeast of "Ashland" and adjacent to the Morrison "Carlisle Farm." William was a brother of James Gibson.

7 Notes of the Bank of the Commonwealth.

8 John T. Mason, who, after suffering financial reverses, had given up his home on the Richmond Road in 1819 and moved to Mount Sterling, Kentucky. He had only recently returned to Lexington, apparently as a tenant in the "Large Brick house and ground" on High Street bought by Morrison from James and David Maccoun.

9 See above, III, 488-89, 774.   10 Hugh Foster.

11 Robert J. Breckinridge; Thomas Curry.

12 Mrs. K. H. Blanton, who with Mrs. Henrietta Warren was residing in Clay's house at the corner of Short and Market Streets. The rental agreement has not been found.

13 Of Frederick, Maryland, a veteran of the Revolutionary War, for a time a member of the State legislature, one of the judges of the orphans' court (1813-1819), iron manufacturer, and large landowner. He was an active proponent of internal improvements.

To [John Quincy Adams]

Feb. 3 1825.

The subscribers, understand that Mr Rd. H Mosby. is willing to accept the appointment of attorney for the District of Florida, shortly to be filled.— Mr. Mosby was born in Virginia, & has for the last five or six years, resided & practised law in the West[1]— We take pleasure in recommending him to the President[2] as a man of high charactr [sic] & honor, & qualifd for the station to be filled.—

<blockquote>
AND: STEVENSON   J. T. JOHNSON

ARTHUR SMITH[3]   H. CLAY
</blockquote>

ADS by Stevenson, signed also by Smith, Johnson, and Clay. MHi-Adams Papers, Letters Received (MR467).

1 His residence in the West not located. A son of Wade Mosby, he was living in Petersburg, Virginia, by the summer of 1825.

2 James Monroe.

3 Of Smithfield, Virginia; a member of the United States House of Representatives, 1821-1825.

From George Kremer

[ca. February 3, 1825]

ANOTHER CARD.

GEORGE KREMER, of the House of Representatives, tenders his respects to the Honorable "H. Clay," and informs him, that, by reference to the Editor of the Columbian Observer, he may ascertain the name of the writer of a letter of the 25th ult. which, it seems, has afforded so much concern to "H. Clay:" in the mean time, George Kremer holds himself ready to prove, to the satisfaction of unprejudiced minds, enough to satisfy them of the accuracy of the statements which are contained in that letter, to the extent that they concern the course and conduct of "H. Clay." Being a Representative of the People, he will not fear to "cry aloud and spare not," when their rights and privileges are at stake.

Washington *Daily National Intelligencer,* February 3, 1825. Published widely in contemporary newspapers. See above, Clay to Gales and Seaton, January 30, 1825, and enclosure. On Kremer's authorship, cf. below, Address, March 26, 1825; Eaton to Clay, March 28, 31, 1825; Clay to Eaton, March 30, April 1, 1825.

Appeal to the House

[February 3, 1825]

The SPEAKER rose, and observed, that he requested the indulgence of the House for a few moments, while he asked its attention to a subject in which he felt himself deeply concerned. A note had appeared this morning in the National Intelligencer, under the name, and with the authority, as he presumed, of a member of this House from Pennsylvania, (Mr. Kremer,) which adopted as his own, a previous letter published in another print, containing serious and injurious imputations against him, and which the author avowed his readiness to substantiate by proof.[1] These charges implicated his conduct in regard to the pending Presidential election; and the respectability of the station which the member holds, who thus openly prefers them, and that of the people whom he represents, entitled them to grave attention. It might be, indeed, worthy of consideration, whether the character and dignity of the House itself, did not require a full investigation of them, and an impartial decision on their truth. For, if they were true; if he were capable and base enough, to betray the solemn trust which the constitution had confided to him; if, yielding to personal views and considerations, he could compromit the highest interests of his country, the House would be scandalized by his continuance to occupy the chair with which he had been so long honored in presiding at its deliberations, and he merited instantaneous expulsion. Without, however, presuming to indicate what the House might conceive it ought to do, on account of its own purity and honor, he hoped that he should be allowed, respectfully, to solicit, in behalf of himself, an inquiry into the truth of the charges to which he referred. Standing in the relations to the House, which both the member from Pennsylvania and himself did, it appeared to him, that here was the proper place to institute the inquiry, in order that, if guilty, here the proper punishment might be applied, and if innocent, that here his character and conduct may be vindicated. He anxiously hoped, therefore, that the House would be pleased to direct an investigation to be made into the truth of the charges. Emanating from the source which they did, this was the *only* notice which he could take of them. If the House should think proper to raise a committee, he trusted that some other than the ordinary mode pursued by the practice and rules of the House would be adopted to appoint the committee.[2]

U. S. H. of Reps., *Journal*, 18 Cong., 2 Sess., 198. Published also in *Register of Debates*, 18 Cong., 2 Sess., 440-41, and in most contemporary American newspapers.

1 See above, Clay to Gales and Seaton, January 30, 1825, enclosure; Kremer to Clay, *ca*. February 3, 1825.

2 At the conclusion of his remarks, Clay called John W. Taylor to the chair in his place. John Forsyth now rose and expressed hopes that the Speaker's address would be entered on the journal of the House, that the document to which Clay had referred would be laid on the table, and that both address and document "would be referred to a committee of nine members, to be chosen by ballot." George Kremer declared that "if, upon an investigation being instituted, it should appear that he had not sufficient reason to justify the statements he had made, he trusted he should receive the marked reprobation which had been suggested by the Speaker.— Let it fall where it might, Mr. K. said, he was willing to meet the inquiry, and abide the result." After some discussion of the propriety of considering the matter and of the method of procedure to be followed, the House ordered Clay's address to be entered on the journal and postponed further action. On the following day, after lengthy debate, Forsyth's motion was adopted, referring Clay's statement to a special committee; and another motion by Forsyth, to select the committee by ballot, also carried.

According to the report of the special committee, submitted by Philip P. Barbour on February 9, Kremer was invited to offer any evidence or explanation he wished in relation to his charges and "replied that he would make a communication to the committee." In his "communication," a skillfully worded letter dated February 8, he declined to appear before the committee, whose jurisdiction he refused to recognize on constitutional grounds. Further, though considering himself "justified, as the writer of the letter," he felt "bound by prudence and duty, not to appear in the character of an accuser of the Speaker upon charges not . . . [his] own, but those which he [Clay] has requested to be investigated." Referring to the "deep excitement" attending the presidential election and "the unequal contest between an humble member on the floor, and the Speaker of the House," Kremer ended by stating: "the issue should be left before the American people, or the ordinary tribunals of the country; and I therefore protest against the proceedings in this view, as well as against the power of the House to exercise jurisdiction over me, as being equally calculated to restrain the exercise of my just rights, in an unconstitutional manner."

Barbour's report concluded: "In this posture of the case, the committee can take no further steps. They are aware that it is competent to the House to invest them with power to send for persons and papers, and by that means, to enable them to make any investigation which might be thought necessary; and if they knew any reason for such investigation, they would have asked to be clothed with the proper power; but not having, themselves, any such knowledge, they have felt it to be their duty only to lay before the House the communication which they have received."

The report and letter, after being read, were, on Barbour's motion, "ordered to lie on the table, with the accompanying papers, and to be printed." No further action was reported. *Register of Debates*, 18 Cong., 2 Sess., 441-44, 463-86, 522-25.

To ....

WASHINGTON, FEBRUARY 4, 1825

MY DEAR SIR: I have received, and read with all the attention due to our ancient and unbroken friendship, your letter of the 2d inst.[1] You state that the conviction has been forced upon the Richmond public, by the papers which are daily received from this City, that "I have gone over to the party of Mr. Adams *with a view to constitute a part of his Cabinet.*" Do you believe it? Then you ought not to respect me. Do you wish me to deny it? Then you cannot respect me. What do you desire? That I should vote for

Mr. Crawford? I cannot. For Gen. Jackson? I will not. I shall pursue the course which my conscience dictates, regardless of all imputations and all consequences. I love the State which gave me birth more than she loves me. Personally, I would make any sacrifices to evince this attachment. But I have public duties to perform which comprehend a consideration of her peculiar interest and wishes, and those of the rest of the Confederacy. Those I shall perform. In doing so, I may incur, unfortunately, her displeasure. Be it so. I cannot help it. The quiet of my conscience is of more importance to me than the good opinion of even Virginia, highly as I do and ever must respect it. Your faithful friend, H. CLAY.

Washington *Daily National Intelligencer*, April 28, 1828, reprinted from the Richmond *Constitutional Whig*. Published also in Lexington *Kentucky Reporter*, May 7, 1828; *Niles' Weekly Register*, XXXIV (July 5, 1828), 312. Reportedly sent to a member of the Virginia Legislature. 1 Not found.

To Francis T. Brooke

My dear Sir,   Washington 4th Feb: 1825

I received your obliging letter of the 1st. instant.[1] Altho' my letter[2] to which it is an answer was not intended for publication, I would rather that it should be published and speak for itself, than that its contents should appear through the medium of Mr. Ritchie's[3] representation of them. With regard to its publication, you will be pleased to do as you may think proper. All that I feel anxious about is that the public should not receive an impression that it was my intention that it should be published.

My condition at this moment is most peculiar. The batteries of some of the friends of every man who would now be President, or who four or eight years hence would be President, are directed against me, with only the exception of those of Mr. Adams. Some of the friends of Gen: Jackson, Mr. Crawford, Mr. Calhoun and Mr. Clinton, with very different ultimate ends agree for the present to unite in assailing me. The object now is on the part of Mr. Crawford and Gen: Jackson to drive me from the course which my deliberate judgment points out, and for the future, on the part of Mr. Clinton and Mr. Calhoun, to remove me as an obstacle to their elevation. They all have yet to learn my character if they suppose it possible to make me swerve from my duty, by any species of intimidation or denunciation. But I did not expect that my old friend Ritchie would join in the general cry. He ought to recollect that he is struggling for a man, I for the country.—he to elevate an unfortunate Gentleman worn down by disease, I, to preserve our youthful institutions from the bane which has destroyed all the republics of the old world.— I might have expected from the patriotism of Thomas Ritchie, that he would have surrendered his personal predilections, and joined with me in the effort to save us from a precedent fraught with the most pernicious consequences. I am so far disappointed: I say it with mortification and regret. But all attempts to make me unite with him; to induce me to give up the defence of our institutions, that we may elect a sick Gentleman who has also been rejected by the great body of the Nation, are vain and utterly fruitless.— Mr. Ritchie ought to awake, should be himself again, and love Rome more than Cesar [*sic*].

I observe what you kindly tell me about the future cabinet: My dear Sir, I want no office. When have I shewn an avidity for office? In rejecting the mission to Russia, and the department of war under one administration?[4] In rejecting the same department, the mission to England, or any other foreign mission under the succeeding administration?[5] If Mr. Adams is elected, I know not who will be his Cabinet; I know not whether I shall be offered a place in it or not. If there should be an offer, I shall decide upon it, when it may be made according to my sense of duty. But do you not perceive that this denunciation of me by anticipation, is a part of the common system between the discordant confederates which I have above described? Most certainly, if an office should be offered to me under the new administration, and I should be induced to think that I ought to accept it, I shall not be deterred from accepting it, either by the denunciations of open or secret enemies, or the hypocrisy of pretended friends.

With great respect I am faithfully your friend   H. CLAY.
The Hon: Francis Brooke.

Copy. DLC-TJC (DNA, M212, R13). Published in Washington *Daily National Intelligencer*, March 28, 1828; Lexington *Kentucky Reporter*, April 2, 1828; *Niles' Weekly Register*, XXXIV (July 5, 1828), 312. Endorsed: "I do certify that the preceding is a true copy of the original letter from Mr. Clay to Mr. Brooke, of the date which it bears above. W. C. C. Claiborne."   1 Not found.
2 Above, January 28, 1825.
3 Thomas Ritchie, in *Richmond Enquirer*, February 8, 1825.
4 See above, II, 88-89, 226, 233.   5 See above, II, 391n.

From Lafayette

GENTLEMEN.   WASHINGTON, FEB. 4TH, 1825.
I have been highly gratified by the honour, which the citizens of Fayette County and Lexington have, in their much valued kindness, conferred upon me, and of which you have been pleased, in most flattering terms, to become the organs.[1] It has ever been my intention to visit the Western part of the Union, and particularly

the State of Kentucky. But I could not, until lately, fix the time when I will begin a journey to the Southern States and New Orleans, which will bring me up to Lexington sometime in the next Spring. I with regret foresee, that in this tour of five thousand miles, my passage must be rapid, as I will not leave Washington before the anniversary of the 22d of this month, and must be at Boston on the 17th of June, for the inauguration and laying the Corner Stone of the Bunker's Hill Monument, an engagement which will be approved of in a state, the first settlers of which have adopted the name of Lexington. One of you, gentlemen, my friend Mr. Clay, will be, before my departure, more particularly informed of my expectations as to the dates of this long Southern and Western Tour; but I could not longer delay the expression of my respectful affectionate gratitude to the citizens of Fayette county and Lexington, and particularly to you, gentlemen, whom I beg to accept the assurance of my highest regard.   LA FAYETTE.
The Hon. HENRY CLAY, &c.

Lexington *Kentucky Reporter,* April 25, 1825.
[1] Cf. above, III, 855-56. The letter of invitation has not been found.

From Robert Oliver and Others

Sir   Balto [Feby] 4th. 1825
    The Bearer Mr Saml J. Donaldson[1] is Authorized by the Creditors of the late Saml & Robt Purviance to proceed to Washington & receive from you the Money in your hands as Trustee for said Estate, and we hereby Guaranty that he will deposit the Amount in the Chan[cery] Office of Maryland to be applied under the direction of the Chancello[r].
    Mr Donaldson is also Authorized so far as the Creditors have that Power to Make Arrangements with you for Closing Your Agenc[y] in relation to this Estate, and any Plan agreed on between you will be acceptable to the Creditors and receive their Sanction.
                We are Sir Yr Obt Servts   ROBERT OLIVER

T Smith Assee   J. Carey[6]
  of Hans Morrison[2]   James Purviance[7] Exer.
John Nicholson[3]   Robert Purviance—
Rossiter Scott[4]   John Purviance
Robert Casey for   Saml Moale
  Elizabeth Casey Exx.   Atty for Ellen Moale
  of John Hammond[5]   exx of Jno Moale[8]
                                        a creditor—

[Hen]ry Clay Esq

[Endorsement on verso][9]
Recd. Five thousand dollars on a/c. of the within   16 Feb. 1825
                    H. CLAY   SAML J. DONALDSON

LS, in Samuel J. Donaldson's hand. DLC-TJC (DNA, M212, R13). MS. torn. Oliver was surviving partner of the firm Robert and John Oliver, Baltimore merchants and financiers.   1 Baltimore lawyer.

2 Smith not identified; Morrison was probably of Mississippi, where he had been commissioned a captain of the United States Army in 1813.

3 Of Baltimore, probably a former officer of the United States Navy who had served as a captain of "Sea Fencibles" during the War of 1812.

4 A Quaker, reared near Gunpowder, Carroll County, Maryland.

5 Hammond, who had served as an officer in the Continental Army during the Revolutionary War, had been proprietor of extensive wharves at Fell's Point in Baltimore and had been one of the town commissioners in 1789. In 1795 he had married Elizabeth Anderson, also of Baltimore, who, following his death in 1811, had become the wife of Robert Casey.

6 Probably James Carey, who had settled in Baltimore and engaged in mercantile business since shortly after the close of the Revolution. He had been a member of the city council around the turn of the century and had been one of those active in organizing the Bank of Maryland, which he still served as president.

7 Of Baltimore, having represented that district in the Maryland Assembly (1802).

8 Ellen North Moale, born and throughout her life resident in Baltimore, died the next month. John Moale, her deceased husband, had been a merchant and had held numerous local public offices—long a Baltimore town commissioner; member of the Provincial Assembly (1767), of the pre-Revolutionary Baltimore committee of correspondence (1774), and of the Annapolis Convention (1775); and for many years thereafter presiding judge of the county court. He had died in 1798.

9 AES, in Clay's hand, signed also by Donaldson.

To Horace Holley

Dear Sir   Washington 5h Feb. 1825

I recd. your favor of the 16h. Ulto.[1] The transmission to you of the same documents, in triplicate, was a mistake, and was not intended. It is one easily committed, considering the multitude of documents published by the order of Congress. I thank you for the information contained in your letter respecting the state of the College. I hope another year the number in the Academical classes and Preparatory department will be increased. The success is very encouraging of the Medical class.[2]

The final result of the P. election is near at hand. At a distance you will be deceived as to the state of excitement here. It is by no means as great as you may imagine.

I congratulate you on the recent marriage of your daughter.[3] I hope that all parties will find it a happy union. With my best respects to Mrs. Holley, I am faithfully Your ob. Servt.   H. CLAY
The Revd. Mr. Holley.

ALS. CSmH.   1 Not found.

2 Two hundred thirty four students, the largest number in any year to this date, were enrolled in the Medical Department at Transylvania University during the session of 1824-1825.

3 Harriette Williman Holley, only daughter of Horace Holley, had married, January 8, 1825, William Moses Brand, son of John Brand.

To [Thomas I.] Wharton

Dear Sir   Washington 5 Feb. 1825.
I recd. your letter[1] of the   respecting the Kentucky books. I cannot take upon myself to advise any disposition of them. The recent burning of the Capitol at Frankfort[2] I know caused a considerable destruction of books, and perhaps some of those under your care may even be wanted in Kentucky. Who is the present Secretary of state I have not heard. Mr. Barry, the late Secretary, has been appointed to the Bench.[3] A letter to our mutual friend Blair[4] would obtain for you the necessary directions.

On the other interesting topic to which your letter refers I regret that I cannot give you any authority to contradict the rumor which you state 'as prevailing, in regard to the person for whom I am likely to' vote. Most certainly that person would not be the object of my choice, if I were left free to select from among the Citizens of the U.S. the person who should be their chief Magistrate. But that is not the state of the case; and restricted as we are to the three returned Candidates, after the best consideration which I have been able to give to the matter, it does appear to me that I ought to vote for Mr. Adams. I need not say to you how highly gratifying it would have been to me if I could have been spared from performing the painful duty which lies before me. But that I cannot escape. I have therefore conscientiously sought to know what I ought to do, and believing that I have ascertained it, I shall march up to my duty, regardless of all consequences.

My friends at a distance appear to be much divided, and give me advise [sic] of the most opposite character. Indeed I could not comply with their wishes unless, at the same time, I were to vote for all three of the Candidates.

I pray you to communicate my respectful compliments to Mrs. Wharton[5] and believe me Faithfy Your friend   H. CLAY
Mr. Wharton.

ALS. PHi.   1 Not found.
2 See above, III, 878-79n.
3 After passage of the act reorganizing the Kentucky Court of Appeals (see above, III, 902), William T. Barry, who had become secretary of state in the fall of 1824, had been appointed chief justice (January 10, 1825). James C. Pickett, a native of Virginia, an officer of United States Artillery during the War of 1812, a lawyer of Mason County, Kentucky, briefly editor of the Maysville *Eagle*, and member of the Kentucky Legislature in 1822, was appointed secretary of state in February, 1825, and held this office until 1828. Pickett subsequently held numerous political and diplomatic appointments—as Secretary of Legation at Colombia, 1829 to 1833; Commissioner of the Patent Office, 1834; Fourth Auditor of the Treasury, 1835 to 1838; Chargé d'Affaires to the Peru-Bolivian Confederation, 1838; and Chargé to Peru, 1838 to 1845. He was a son of Colonel John Pickett and son-in-law of Governor Joseph Desha.
4 Francis Preston Blair.
5 The former Arabella Griffith, of Philadelphia.

From Tucker and Carter

NEW-YORK, FEB. 5th, 1825.

SIR.—Presuming that it will not be unacceptable to you, to be informed of the state of our Hemp market and of its future prospects, we beg leave to state, that owing to the late inundation at St. Petersburgh, in Russia, by which a considerable quantity of hemp has been either wholly destroyed or greatly injured, and moreover from the unusually small supply at present in the United States—hemp has advanced in price here and in our other ports.

The whole quantity in this place is not more than 1000 tons, old and new.— To the eastward of this, they have 1600 to 1800 tons, of old and new, and the ports to the south have very little indeed. Our next sales will probably be at $200 per ton, for clean new St. Petersburgh hemp—at which price it is now held, and we think that it will maintain that price, at least until August next, and perhaps go much higher. We are strengthened in this belief, by the fact, that at the latest London quotations, hemp cannot be imported thence into the United States, to cost less than 225 to $230, per ton, and it was rising there.

This is certainly favorable to the growers of hemp in this country, and we sincerely hope, that you will be able to get yours to market in the spring, or quite early in the summer, when water-rotted, or such as that received through Mr. Smedes,[1] will, without doubt, be in demand and bring a good price; and even dew-rotted will in our opinion, do better this season than for many years past, especially if in well spun yarns—in which state we should recommend all the hemp raised in Kentucky to be sent to market; the rough parts of the hemp could be taken out at home, for coarse purposes, such as bale rope, &c. &c.— The yarns could be secured from damage by covering the reels with tarpauling [sic], and there would be a saving in the transportation, equal perhaps to the expense of spinning.

We are very desirous that it should be known in Kentucky, that no prejudice exists here against American hemp, if water-rotted or prepared as your's has been—but that on the contrary, if the hemp be also as well-cleaned as foreign hemp, and have [sic] grown thick, consequently being fine fibred, and not long coarse hemp, it would have a preference here, at the same price, over any imported hemp.

We have for many years dealt largely in hemp, and manufactured cordage upon an extensive scale, and we rejoice at the efforts which you are making to bring our hemp to a competition with that of foreign growth. You may rely upon our best disposition, and exertions too, to aid you in so laudable an endeavour. We shall be happy to receive your own hemp, and still more gratified to make you profitable and satisfactory returns—and if any of your friends are disposed to send theirs also to us, they may freely command our best services.

The following statement will afford you some guide as to probable prices. When Russia clean hemp is scarce, and will bring $200 per ton, then we consider dew rotted Kentucky, well cleaned, as being worth about $150, and water rotted $200, or as much as Russia.

Dew Rotted Yarns worth 8 cents per lb.

Water Rotted, do   — 10 to 10½ do

Hemp well cleaned out by Smedes' Machine, worth as much as Russia or thereabouts—and the yarns from the same, at a cent, or a cent and a half more than the hemp.

We have the honor to be, Very respectfully, Sir, Your most ob't Servants,   TUCKER & CARTER.
Hon. H. Clay.

Lexington *Kentucky Reporter*, February 21, 1825.
1 Abraham K. Smedes. See above, III, 735n.

To [Thomas Smith]

                                                    H. of R. 7th Feb., '25.
Will you be good enough to publish the inclosed[1] in the Reporter?   Yours, &c.   H. Clay.

Lexington *Kentucky Reporter*, February 21, 1825.
1 The letter above, Tucker and Carter to Clay, February 5, 1825.

To James Taylor

Dear Sir   H. of R. 7 Feb. 1825
I take pleasure in introducing to your acquaintance Mr. W. Bell and Mr. Jas. Hansborough,[1] who will deliver you this letter. Altho' I have not the satisfaction of personally knowing them, they have been mentioned to me in a manner which authorizes me to present them to you as gentlemen of great respectability and to request your kind attention to them.

                    With great respect I am Yr. ob. Servt.   H. Clay
Genl. James Taylor—

ALS. NNC.
1 Both of Virginia. Hansborough was married in Lunenburg County in 1830.

From Nicholas Biddle

Dear Sir,   Bank of the U. States Feby. 9th 1825

Your favor of the 31st ulto was duly received. I am very reluctant to draw your attention from the important occupations which at the present moment naturally engross so much of your time, but I am anxious to close if possible the transaction which forms the subject of the inclosed paper[1] and it is so familiar to you that you can readily give your opinion of it. The sum in question is small—but if it be clearly due to the Bank, I should not be disposed to yield it from any unwillingness to encounter either the opposition or the expence which may attend the enforcement of the just rights of the institution. Have the goodness at your leisure, to give me your advice on this point. And in the mean time, believe me to be with great respect & regard Very truly yrs

N BIDDLE   Prest.

Honble Henry Clay   Speaker of the H of R.
Washington Cola.

ALS. DLC-HC (DNA, M212, R1).

[1] An extract of a letter from Abraham Claypool, cashier of the Chillicothe branch of the Bank of the United States, to Thomas Wilson, cashier of the parent institution, January 17, 1825, stating that a conditional settlement of the case, Bank of the United States *vs.* Osborn and Others, had been made by acceptance of $2,000 from the State auditor (see above, III, 647n). The "conditional" feature of the transaction had resulted from an interpretation by the auditor that interest on this sum was chargeable only from July 16, 1824, the date of the final decree of the circuit court. To this interpretation the solicitor of the bank had agreed, but Claypool raises the question whether interest should not be charged from the date of the decree of restitution, in September, 1821. See above, III, 111-15.

To Francis T. Brooke

My dear Sir   Washington 10h. Feb. 1825

I recd. your letters of the 6h. and 8h. inst.[1] In the former was inclosed a ten dollar note, about which not one word was contained in your letter. Was it inclosed by mistake? Or did you intend that I should apply it to some object for you? Be pleased to instruct me.

The "long agony" was terminated yesterday, and Mr. Adams was elected on the first ballot.[2] Exertions to defeat or even to delay the result, of the most strenuous kind, were made up to the last moment. Without refering to the issue of the election, the manner in which the whole scenic [*sic*] was exhibited in the H. of R. was creditable to our institutions and to our Country.

I have not yet recd. the Enquirer in which my letter has been published.[3] It did not arrive to day. With great regard I am faithfly & Cordially Your Friend   H. CLAY

The Honble Francis Brooke.

ALS. KyU.   1 Neither letter has been found.

2 On February 9 the "President of the Senate, in the presence of both Houses of Congress, [had] proceeded to open the certificates of the electors of the several states"; announced that, of the 261 votes for President, Andrew Jackson had received 99, John Quincy Adams, 84, William H. Crawford, 41, and Henry Clay, 37; and declared that, since none of the candidates had received a majority of the electoral votes, "it therefore devolved upon the House of Representatives of the United States to choose a President of the United States . . . from the three highest on the list of those voted for by the electors. . . ." After the vote for Vice President had also been announced and John C. Calhoun had been declared winner of that contest, the Senate had retired to its own chamber.

The House had then divided into State delegations and proceeded to the election of a President. The tellers for the various delegations had reported the votes of 13 States for John Quincy Adams, those of 7 States for Andrew Jackson, and those of 4 States for William H. Crawford. "The Speaker [had] again announced the state of the votes to the House, and declared, 'That JOHN QUINCY ADAMS of Massachusetts, having received a majority of the votes of all the states of this Union, was duly elected President of the United States for four years, to commence on the fourth of March, 1825.'" U. S. H. of Reps., *Journal*, 18 Cong., 2 Sess., 220-22.

3 The letter to Brooke, January 28, 1825, had been published in the *Richmond Enquirer*, February 8, 1825.

To John Quincy Adams

Dr Sir   11h. Feb. 25

I should be glad to have the opportunity of an early interview with you, this evening, if you are not engaged, or on sunday evening, at such hour as may be most convenient.

                    I am respectfully Yr. ob. Servt   H. CLAY

Honble Mr. Adams.

[Endorsement on same sheet][1]

Dear Sir

I shall be happy to see you this Evening at half past six if it will suit your convenience.[2]   J.Q.A.

                                        Friday 11. Feby 1825.

ALS. MHi-Adams Papers.   1 AEI.

2 According to Adams, Clay arrived at the appointed time, "and we had a conversation of about an hour. I then offered him the nomination to the Department of State.

"He said he would take it into consideration, and answer me as soon as he should have time to consult his friends.

"I desired him to take his own time; but he promised if anything should occur requiring that he should hasten his answer, he would, upon my giving him notice of it, answer immediately. He made light of the threatened opposition, and thought all the projects of that nature which have been announced were mere ebullitions of disappointment at the issue of the election, which would soon be abandoned. He said that as to his affair with Kremer, if Kremer had gone before the committee, he (Clay) could have proved something very much like a conspiracy against himself. He would have proved that Kremer had disclaimed in the most explicit terms to several persons his having intended any imputation against Clay, and declared his readiness to sign a paper to that effect, from which he had been dissuaded by [Samuel D.] Ingham, [James] Buchanan, and [George] McDuffie." Adams, *Memoirs*, VI, 508-509.

From Francis Preston Blair

My dear Sir   Frankfort: Feby. 11. 1825.

I received your letter of the 29: by the last mail & I assert that notwithstanding the seal of reprobation you have set upon the fate of my party in this world & the world to come, it gave me very great delight— There are certain points in our home politics which I hope I shall have the pleasure shortly to dispute with you in person, & as I am sensible I have all the advantages which grow out of the subject on my side, I anticipate the satisfaction of driving you to extremities—

Is it possible that Wickliffe is considered orthodox or eloquent on your side of the mountains? Is he read abroad, whom nobody will hear at home?[1] I cannot but beleive [sic] that it is the horrid tragedy of which he speaks, that has caught attention, & the monstrous opprobrium with which he would brand his state has made patient readers of those whose habitual love of scandal has there found a new feild [sic] to root in— There is scarcely one word of truth in the whole speech— There never was a case in which a change of venue was more necessary for the interest, excitement & violent feelings produced in the vicinity was so great, that I doubt very much whether a legal Jury could have been impannelled there to try the case— All the designs which Wickliffes suspicions imputed as the motives which actuated those who voted for measure [sic], proved to be the mere fabrication of his brain— There was no attempt to evade a fair trial— Trimble[2] did not sit— Roper[3] of the opposite party was invited to preside— he accepted and afterwards threw the duty on Shannon[4]— The commonwealths Atto:[5] was a political opponent of the Governors— all the officers did their duty most rigidly, & the Jury was acknowledged on all hands to be intelligent, impartial & independent— I am sure I do not differ from you in opinion as it regards the propriety of the verdict rendered— Nor do I think that we should form a different Judgement of Wickliffe's conduct if you knew all the circumstances— Was it not unmanly to wring the heart of a father by false suppositions, & suggestions who already labored under the weight of an affliction, so dreadful? Was it not against the spirit of our humane laws, as a Legislator to take advantage of his position to prejudice the whole community against a miserable wretch loaded with guilt & shackles? How mean to strike at a poor devil in his dungeon!— Was it not shameful to attempt to stain a whole party, (because of a difference about the responsibility of Judges), with the blood of this horrible Murder, & to tarnish the reputation of the country by propagating a beleif, that the public were not only disposed to tolerate, but to sanction the deed, by screening the culprit? Whatever others may think of the speech, I hold it in every way inexcusable, the effusion of morbid feelings acted on by the horrors of a spectral imagination—

You will perceive by the late papers that I have been appointed Clerk to the new court of Appeals & you will catch a glimpse of the accidental causes which put me into the station[6]— I may well say with Shakespeare's Malvolio "that some are born great, some atcheive greatness, but I have it thrust upon me"— I assure you my advancement was as unexpected, as it was welcome— Indeed I was one of the first to recommend Mr Sneed to the new court, & when the old court met in Frankfort & compelled him to choose between the two tribunals I most anxiously advised him against serving his old Masters, although I thought I should profit by it— & to the last, I refused to be considered as willing to accept, if the new court preferred Mr Sneed to other candidates, with the exception of myself— I know it will be said that the place was given to me, as a reward for the party zeal I may have manifested, but I attribute my good luck, (if in the present state of uncertainty it can be so considered) to an inclination to propitiate influential persons in the opposition to the new state of things—for when it was found that Sneed was out of the question Crittenden[7] & all the rest of the Bar young & old—even Judge Todd[8] (who by the way let me tell is mending) all desired that the fortune might fall on one who needed it so much as I did— Let me tell you too that remote as you were, I have no doubt but that the kind sentiments you have manifested for me, proved a preponderating weight in my scale— Indeed Barry[9] told me that he employed it as an argument to the other Judges[10] (who were indisposed to my appointment because I opposed them) that although it would not change any opinion you had formed in respect to the questions connected with the court, yet that it would soften your feelings toward them individually.— In this however I fear he gave me credit for more influence than I have, much more I am sure than I deserve, & yet you see by the details I give you of my affairs, how greatly I overvalue my importance with you— Mrs Blair still holds out a shew, of support to her old opinions, but she intimates now & then "how extremely amiable it is to acquiesce as a wife in the opinions of a husband particularly in political affairs &c &c" Indeed I really suspect you are about to lose a proselyte— She has felt so severely the oppression of debt & the humiliations of poverty, that to invite her to take sides with a party whose success must renew those ills, will be something like inviting an unfortunate person relieved from the rack to make another experiment of its powers—

I recd. letters from Moore,[11] by which I find that all the letters I wrote to him with a view to release him from the influence of the Jackson instructions[12] have been thrown away— Being well acquainted with him, I addressed him as a pragmatical little body who would use what I wrote to influence the other members with whom I was not so well acquainted— From his replies I find I was deceived in his feelings towards you, & in my influence over him— He has as much of Jackson in him, as so small a man can hold— His letters however furnish me with one fact, which I mean to use to prepare the public mind to expect the vote of our delegation against Jackson— It appears from them that Jackson has determined to frown upon the future hopes of Kentucky should he be elected president.— Under such circumstances I shall rejoice in his defeat, & doubt not, it will reconcile the State to Adams' elevation— pardon my long letter & measure my love by it, for you see it holds out to the very end   Yr. mo. ob. st   F. P. Blair

LS. DLC-HC (DNA, M212, R1).

1 Robert Wickliffe, who at the preceding Session of the Kentucky Legislature had been defeated in a motion for public printing of his protest against the resolutions condemning the Green-Biddle decision (see above, III, 393n; Ky. H. of Reps., *Journal, 1823-1824,* pp. 397-426), on November 30 had delivered a lengthy attack, widely publicized (see Lexington *Kentucky Reporter,* December 27, 1824; March 21, 1825; Washington *Daily National Journal,* January 28, 1825; Washington *Gazette,* February 12, 1825), against proposed legislation authorizing a change of venue for trial of Isaac B. Desha, a resident of Fleming County, Kentucky, son of Governor Joseph Desha. Young Desha was accused of robbing and murdering Francis Baker, a lawyer and editor of Natchez, Mississippi, who had been crossing Kentucky en route to his native State, New Jersey. Following enactment of the measure permitting removal of the trial from Fleming County, where Governor Desha was not politically popular, to Harrison, where he was (Ky. Gen. Assy., *Acts, 1824-1825,* pp. 25-27, December 4, 1824), the young man had, nevertheless, been found guilty. The proceedings had thereafter been ruled a mistrial, on grounds that the jury had been contaminated and intimidated and that the verdict was not in accordance with the evidence.

At a subsequent trial, in February, 1826, Desha was again found guilty. Shortly before the date set for his execution, he attempted suicide, by cutting his windpipe, but recovered and was eventually pardoned by Governor Desha a few months before the close of his administration, in 1827. The son soon afterward went to New Orleans, and from there to Texas, whence it was reported that he was again indicted for murder of a fellow traveler and did commit suicide in prison, at San Felipe de Austin, pending trial. Letter of Thomas M. Duke, from San Felipe, September 23, 1828, in Lexington *Kentucky Reporter,* December 3, 1828.

2 John Trimble, of Harrison County, Kentucky, brother of Robert Trimble, had as a young man served about two years as secretary to the Governor of Indiana Territory, had returned to Kentucky and studied law under George Nicholas, had practiced at Paris from 1807 to 1816, had been appointed circuit judge, and thereupon had removed to Cynthiana. Earlier in 1825 he had resigned his judgeship and, on January 10, had been appointed by Governor Desha to the new court of appeals. He was later a member of the State legislature for several terms.

3 William P. Roper, circuit judge for the district composed of Bracken, Fleming, Greenup, Lewis, and Mason Counties, had at first agreed to sit, then, a day or two before the trial, had declined.

4 George Shannon, recently re-commissioned circuit judge for the district composed of Bourbon, Clark, Estill, and Madison Counties, after a legislative inquiry into

charges of "judicial arrogance." The reappointment and its support by the Governor and his adherents contributed to angry criticism of Shannon's decision to grant a second trial. He was burned in effigy in both Harrison and Bourbon Counties. Frankfort *Argus of Western America,* February 9, 1825.

5 William K. Wall, born in Washington County, Pennsylvania, and brought as a child to Harrison County, Kentucky, had studied law under Richard M. Johnson, had been licensed to practice in 1809, and had located in Cynthiana. After service in the War of 1812, he had been a member of the Kentucky House of Representatives, 1814 to 1818, and Commonwealth attorney for Harrison County since 1820. He retained the latter post until 1843 and later became a State senator from 1846 to 1850.

6 No appointment of clerk for the new court had been made until its first sitting, which had been delayed by the engagement of William T. Barry in Harrison Circuit Court, as counsel for Desha, until the week after the regular meeting of the old court. Achilles Sneed, the incumbent clerk, had not attended the latter session but had sent a deputy. His position relative to the new court had remained in doubt until it convened—only two days before then he had written to one of the judges, stating his wish to be made the clerk and his promise to "act as your Clerk only." The latter body, however, deeming his recent recognition of the old court's authority as incompatible with service to the new, had named Blair to the post. Frankfort *Argus of Western America,* February 9, 1825.   7 John J. Crittenden.

8 Thomas Todd.   9 William T. Barry.

10 Besides Barry and Trimble, the judges of the new court were James Haggin and Benjamin W. Patton. Haggin, a native of Mercer County, Kentucky, had moved to Lexington in 1810 and engaged in the practice of law. Acclaimed as an expert on land law, he held no public office other than this court appointment. Patton, born in Clark County, Kentucky, was practicing law in Hopkinsville when appointed to the bench. Though young, he died on February 11, 1825, and was succeeded on the court by Rezin H. Davidge, a native of Baltimore County, Maryland, who had settled at Russellville, Kentucky, in early manhood and was now a resident of Hopkinsville. Davidge had been appointed the first Commonwealth attorney of the Logan County Circuit, in 1803, and later, in 1831, was named to the bench of the newly established circuit court for the Sixteenth District, covering the "Purchase" area. He subsequently resided briefly in Livingston County and at Princeton, Kentucky, but returned to spend the bulk of his life at Hopkinsville.

11 Thomas P. Moore.   21 See above, III, 901-902n.

To Francis T. Brooke

My dear Sir   (Confidential)   H. of R. 14h. Feb. 1825
I return the 10$.[1]

Southard[2] remains in the Navy Dept. I am offered that of the State, but have not yet decided. The others not yet determined on.[3] Crawford retires.

What shall I do?   In haste Yr friend   H. CLAY
The Honble F. Brooke.

ALS. NcD.   1 See above, Clay to Brooke, February 10, 1825.
2 Samuel L. Southard.   3 See below, Commission, March 7, 1825, note.

From John J. Crittenden

Hon. H. Clay,   Frankfort, Feby. 15, 1825—
Dear Sir

We are all waiting with breathless impatience to know the result of the presidential election. It was rumored here a few days past, that a coalition had been formed between Jackson &

Crawford; that New York, Virginia, &c., had fallen into its ranks; that it was bearing on irresistibly & triumphantly; & that you & Adams were its destined victims. The mail of last night, however, brought no Confirmation of this terrible rising, & we are all settling down again into the opinion, which has for some time prevailed here, that Adams is to be the president.

I have seen the abuse that has been heaped upon you in some of the Newspapers, & your card in the Intelligencer.[1] I confess that I feel some apprehension for you. There are about you a thousand desperadoes, political & military, following at the heels of leaders, & living upon expectations, that would think it a most honorable service to fasten a quarrel upon Mr. Clay, & shoot him. And this card of yours, evincing such a spontaneous & uncalculating spirit, of gallantry, will be a signal, I fear, for some of these fellows to gather about you, & to endeavor to provoke you to some extremity. For God's sake, be upon your guard, at least as it respects these subalterns. As for the abuse there has been heaped upon you, you may safely regard it as the idle wind that passes by.[2] I expected to hear you vilified. You occupy too lofty & imposing a stand to escape. You prefer Mr. Adams under existing circumstances, & for that you are calumniated. And so it would equally have been had you announced your preference for either of the other competitors.

If, notwithstanding your support of Adams, Jackson should be elected, that circumstance would certainly embolden your comparatively few adversaries in this state, & enable them for a little while to excite some petty clamor against you. But no such thing can displace you from the hold you have on the pride & affections of Kentucky. If Adams is elected, & you will accept a station in his cabinet, all will be quieted in a moment. This is my view.—

I think I can see the policy which dictates the charges which are now made against you, "of going over to Mr. Adams," of having "made your bargain," with him, & of a thousand other horrible conspiracies, &c. It is intended to intimidate you, if possible, from the acceptance of the department of State, which they think Mr. Adams must tender to you, & where they tremble to see you. They wish to obstruct your passage to it by heaping up the way with all the falsehood & calumny they can create & invent. This is the real secret of the whole business, as I think. Whether I am right or wrong, I trust you will hold on your course unshaken & unaltered by all the calumny, calumny [sic], falsehood, & scandal of your enemies. It will not be long before it will all recoil on themselves. I think it is due to yourself, to your friends here, & to the expectations & wishes of the State, that you should accept the office of Secretary of State, if it should be offered to you. Some few of your friends think your present station the more elevated & commanding one, & of course that you should retain it. Whatever may be its nominal elevation, its practical importance & power is not to be compared with that of the department of State. The Chair of the house of representatives is undoubtedly a very high & lofty station, but all its honors & advantages are of the abstract, fruitless kind, & I am now convinced, that no man will live to see the incumbent of that Chair transferred at once to the presidency. You best know, [h]owever, what course to pursue. That it may be a prosperous & happy one is the earnest wish of yours &c,

J. J. CRITTENDEN

Copy. DLC-John J. Crittenden Papers (DNA, M212, R20).
1 See above, Clay to Gales and Seaton, January 30, 1825.
2 Cf. Shakespeare, *Julius Caesar*, Act IV, Sc. 3, line 66.

Promissory Note to Samuel J. Donaldson

$5175.96   Washington Feby 16th 1825
    In Two Years after date I promise to pay Saml J. Donaldson or order Five Thousand One Hu[ndred] Seventy five Dollars & ninety Six Cents for Value re[ceived.]
[Endorsement on verso][1]
Paid in a check[2] on Off. B. U. S. at Washn. 19 Feb. 1827.

H CLAY

    D (signature removed), in Donaldson's hand. DLC-TJC (DNA, M212, R16). See below, Agreement, this date.
    1 AES. This endorsement follows two others which have been omitted by the editors: the first, by Donaldson, his signature; the second, by George T. Dunbar, cashier of the Commercial and Farmers Bank, of Baltimore, an assignment of the note to Richard Smith.   2 Not found.

Agreement with Samuel J. Donaldson

[February 16, 1825]
    An Agreement made this 16th day of Feb 1825 between H Clay and Saml J. Donaldson acting in behalf of the Creditors of Saml & Robert Purviance.
    The parties have agreed to Settle the agency and Trust of the Said Clay so far as they can settle it in the Business of Saml and Robert Purviance in Kentucky, according to an account which is hereto annexed Marked A. By that account the Said Clay Stands Chargeable with the Sum of Twenty thousand five Hundred and twenty Seven Dollars and 89 Cents, of which he has this day paid five thousand dollars,[1] and given three Notes each for the Sum of five thousand One Hundred and Seventy five Dollars and 96 Cents, one payable one year, another two years, and the third three years from the date.[2]

The Said Clay is, Upon the request of the Said Donaldson to Execute a Mortgage[3] Upon real Estate in Lexington or its vicinity sufficient to Guaranty the payment of the Said Notes in the Judgment of the Cashr of the Off. of Discount and Deposit at Lexington. Upon the payment of the Said Notes the Said Clays responsibility on account of any pecuniary Transactions or Sales of Land Made by him in his agency and trust aforesaid is to be Considered Closed and terminated.

The Said Clay is to Convey the lands bought in by him for the Trust and which he did not Subsequently Sell in Such Manner as the Chancellor of Maryland May hereafter direct, or as May hereafter be agreed upon. If the said Clay Shall have Omitted in the Said Account Marked A to Charge himself with any lands bought in by him for the trust and which he Subsequently Sold he is to be hereafter Charged with the Amount for which Such Omitted Lands Sold with Interest.

Witness the Seals of the parties   H CLAY [LS]

                        SAML J. DONALDSON [LS]

                        for Crs of S. & R Purviance

A

The paper referred to as the account, in our agreement of the 16 Feb 1825   H CLAY

                                  SAML J. DONALDSON

Dr H Clay   To the Trustees of the Messrs Purviances

To gross amount of Sales Made the 6h Octr 1811 upon a credit of Six Months according to the first report of the Comrs—		$20787.—[4]
Credit by Ten per Cent for Services incident to the Sales Making conveyances, Collections &c &c	2078.70	
By fee in the Suit in Chy to foreclose the Mortgage—	100.00	
By Cash paid Comrs for their Services	10.00	
By Do paid the Cryer	5.00	
By Do. paid the Printer for Advertizing	5.00	
By Amount of purchases made in behalf of the Trust by H Clay See report	2300.00	4498.70
		16288.30
To Interest thereon from 6 April 1812 to the 6 Feby 1825 at Six per Cent		12542.53
By Cash paid 12 Feby 1814	$5000.00[5]	
„ Exchange between Lexn & Balto	100.00	
Int on the whole Until 6 Feby 1825	3361.75	
By Cash paid 28 Augt 1817 including Exchange	4590.00[6]	
Int on Do Until 6 Feby 1825	2058.52—	15110.27
		13720.56

To gross amt. of Sales Made
2d Octr. 1813[7] Six Mos. Credit $10719.50
Credit By Ten per Cent
for Services &c $1071.90
By Cash paid Comrs
Cryer & Printer[8]   19.00
„ Amt of Purchases for Trust   5570.00
„ Fees in Cross Suits in
Chancery & Court of Appeals   200.00
„ Costs in Circuit Court
Moale vs Purviance[9]   39.00
„ Costs in Fayette Circuit
vs Hopkins[10]   75.00
„ Court of Appeals vs Same   41.77
„ Taxes & Postage   11.19—   7027.86—   3691.64
To Int on $3691.64 from 2 Apl. 1814
Until 6 Feby 1815   2401.65

To Amt of Sales of 2237 Acres of land
sold to Clarkson & Kendricks[11] $575.00   19813.85
„ Int on Do from 26 Decr 1816
Until 6 Feby 1825   249.79
                                                        764.79

By Cash paid to W. Prentiss $50.00[12]
& Int from 8 Novr 1824   50.75
                                                        714.04—   714.04
                                                                      $20527.89
                    By Cash paid 16 Feby 1825   5000.00
                                                                      $15527.89

Copy. DLC-TJC (DNA, M212, R16).
[1] See above, Oliver and others to Clay, February 4, 1825, endorsement.
[2] Only the second (see above, this date) of the three notes has been found.
[3] Not found.   [4] Cf. above, I, 811-12.
[5] Cf. above, *ibid.*, 868.   [6] Cf. above, II, 375-76.
[7] Cf. above, I, 827-28.   [8] See above, *ibid.*, 830.
[9] See above, *ibid.*, 494n.   [10] See above, II, 325-27n.
[11] Probably of Bourbon County, Kentucky; individuals not identified.
[12] See above, III, 882.

Note of Introduction for Felix Huston

Washington City 16 Feb. 1825
I do hereby Certify and make known that the bearer hereof Mr. Felix Huston is a native and highly respectable Citizen of the State of Kentucky, one of the States of the North American Union; that his connexions are among the most eminent and highly esteemed in that State; & that he is a member of its Bar, and has practised his profession for some time with great promise of success and attaining eminence. Fired with a laudable zeal for the establishment of Grecian Liberty, Mr. Huston has determined to dedicate

himself to that noble cause. I have great pleasure in recommending him as a man of honor and gallantry to all good men.

H. CLAY

ANS. NRU.

From Samuel J. Donaldson

Dr Sir   Feb 16th. 1825

In Compliance with my promise, I Send a Copy of the agreement Executed by You & myself toDay[1] together with the account annexed thereto.   Very respectfully Yr Obt servt

H Clay Esq   SAML J. DONALDSON

ALS. DLC-TJC (DNA, M212, R16).   1 Above.

To John Quincy Adams

Thursday morning [February 17, 1825]

Mr. Clay presents his Compliments to Mr. Adams, and would be happy to have the honor to wait upon him, at such hour this evening as may best suit his convenience, and which he will be pleased by a line to indicate. Should Mr. Adams engagements prevent him from receiving Mr. Clay this evening, he would call on that of tomorrow, if agreeable.

[Endorsement][1]

Mr Adams will be happy to see Mr Clay this Evening at 9. O'Clock.

Thursday 17. Feby.

AN. MHi-Adams Papers.   1 AE by Adams.

To Nicholas Biddle

Dear Sir   Washington 18h. Feb. 1825

I received your favor of the 9h. instant, and hope you will have the goodness to excuse the delay which has arisen in the transmission of my answer.

The decree, in the case refered to by you, does not in terms direct the payment of any interest, nor am I aware of any law of the State of Ohio which attaches, as a necessary incident to such a decree, the obligation, on the part of the defendant, to pay interest. The arrangement by which interest has been agreed to be paid from the 16h. of July last, the day when the decree of the Supreme Court was entered at Columbus as the decree of the Circuit Court, grows out of my consent to forbear enforcing the decree until the meeting

of the Legislature of Ohio. The payment of that interest is equitable and just; but I do not think that the Bank can lawfully demand any interest prior to the 16h. of July. It appears to me therefore that the settlement of that affair has been right and ought to be acquiesced in.   I am with great respect faithfy Yr. ob. Servt.
Nicholas Biddle Esqr.   H. CLAY

ALS. PHi.

To Francis T. Brooke

My dear Sir   (Confidential)   Washn. 18h. Feb. 1825
    When the subject of the offer of the Department of State to me was first opened to my Congressional friends there existed among them some diversity of opinion as to the propriety of my accepting it. On the one hand it was said that, if I took it, that fact would be treated as conclusive evidence of the imputations which have been made against me;[1] that the H. of R. was my theatre; that the administration would want me there, if it should prove itself worthy of support, more than in the Cabinet; and that my own section would not like to see me translated from the Legislative Hall to the Executive departments. On the other hand it was urged that, whether I accepted or declined the office, I should not escape severe animadversion; that, in the latter contingency, it would be said that the patriotic Mr. Kremer, by an exposure of the corrupt arrangement, had prevented its consummation; that the very object of propagating the calumny would be accomplished; that, conscious of my own purity of intentions, I ought not to give the weight of a feather to Mr. Kremer's affair; that there would be much difficulty in filling the administration without me; that either of the other Candidates, if he had been elected, would have made me the same offer; that it would be said of me that, after having contributed to the election of a President, I thought so ill of him that I would not take the first place under him; that he was now the Constitutional Head of the Government, and as such I ought to regard him, dismissing any personal objections which I might have heretofore had to him; that I had perhaps remained long enough in the H. of R.; and that my own section could not be dissatisfied with seeing me placed where, if I should prove myself possessed of the requisite attainments, my services might have a more extended usefulness.
    On mature consideration, those of my friends who were originally averse from my entering the office, changed their opinion, and I believe they were finally unanimous in thinking that I ought not to

hesitate in taking upon myself its duties. Those of Mr. Adams, especially in New England, were alike unanimous and indeed extremely urgent in their solicitations. Several of Mr. Crawfords friends (Mr. McLane of Delaware Mr. Forsythe, Mr. Mangum[2] &c &c) and also some of those of Genl. Jackson in Pennsylvania have expressed to me their strong convictions that I ought to accept. The opposition to my acceptance is limited chiefly to the violent of Mr. Calhouns friends, and to some of those of Mr. Crawford and Genl. Jackson.

From the first I determined to throw myself into the hands of my friends; and, if they advised me to decline the office, not to accept it; but if they thought it was my duty and for the public interest to go into it, to do so. I have an unaffected repugnance to any Executive employment, and my rejection of the offer, if it were in conformity to their deliberate judgment, would have been more compatible with my feelings than its acceptance.

But as their advice to me is to accept, I have resolved accordingly; and I have just communicated my final determination to Mr. Adams.[3] I am not yet at liberty to communicate the names of the persons who will fill the other vacant departments; but I will say to you that they will be Republicans. I entertain a strong belief, and sanguine hopes, that the administration will be conducted upon principles which will entitle it to liberal and general support. An opposition is talked of here; but I regard that as the ebullition of the moment, the natural offspring of chagrin and disappointment. There are elements for faction; none for opposition. Opposition to what? to measures and principles which are yet to be developed! Opposition may follow, it cannot precede, the unknown measures of administration, without meriting the denomination of faction. Mr. Adams is on his trial. Hear him and then decide. This is the rational sentiment of every candid and impartial mind. He would not have been my President, if I had been allowed to range at large among the great mass of our Citizens to select a President; but I was not so allowed, & circumscribed as I was, I thought that, under all circumstances, he was the best choice that I could practically make.

I received your kind letter of the 16h. instant[4] and I am happy to find that your better judgment points to the course which I am about to take. I hope that on further reflection, my other Richmond friends will probably unite in sentiment with you.

This is not written for publication in whole or in part; but I request you to shew it to Mr Call, Mr. Leigh and Mr. Ritchie,[5] who will have the goodness to regard it in the same confidential light.

I am, my dear Sir, Your affte friend

The Honble F. Brooke.   H. CLAY

ALS. KyU.
[1] See above, Clay to Gales and Seaton, January 30, 1825; Appeal, February 3, 1825.
[2] Louis McLane; John Forsyth; Willie Person Mangum. Mangum, a Representative from North Carolina, had been graduated from the University of North Carolina in 1815, had studied law and established himself as an attorney at Red Mountain, North Carolina, had served in the State legislature and as a judge, and from 1823 to 1826 was a member of the United States House of Representatives. He served in the United States Senate from 1840 to 1853.
[3] Cf. above, Clay to Adams, February 17, 1825. No journal entries are available for this period in Adams' Diary.
[4] Not found.
[5] Daniel Call; Benjamin W. Leigh; Thomas Ritchie.

To Robert Walsh, Jr.

{CONFIDENTIAL.}　　　　WASHINGTON, 18th Feb. '25.

DEAR SIR: I thank you for your prompt attention to the paragraph which I sent you, and for your friendly letter.[1]

You did not like my Kremer Card.[2] I was not surprised, but hear me. I was assailed from all quarters. The cannon of every man who would now, or four or eight years hence, be President, (except that of Mr. A.,[3]) was directed against me. I heard it all, and saw every movement. I should have disregarded it, whilst the attack assumed the ordinary form of anonymous or even editorial commentary. But when a person was so far designated as to be elected to be a *member* of the H. of R. belonging to the *Pennsylvania* delegation, it assumed a tangible shape. A crisis arose in my poor affairs. Silence and criminality would have been the same. And it seemed to me that I was called upon to take a step even of apparent rashness. I ought to have omitted the last sentence in the Card; but as to the rest, I yet approve of it. And still the reason, the philosophy, the religion of no man more decidedly condemns duelling than, I hope I may say, mine does. The corrective of that pernicious practice must be found in communities, not in individuals, at least in such humble ones as I am. When the public shall cease to stamp with dishonor the man who tamely submits to injurious imputations, duels will cease. I hope the sequel of that affair was more satisfactory to the northern public.

I have consented to go into the department of state, after much deliberation. They will abuse me for it. They would have abused me more if I had declined it. I shall carry into it zeal and industry only. The other departments which are vacant by Mr. Calhoun's election to the V. P., and Mr. Crawford's retirement,[4] remain to be filled, but I am not at liberty to indicate their probable incumbents.[5]

An opposition is threatened; but there is no danger of any, unless the course of the Administration shall furnish just occasion for it, which we shall strive to prevent. What is now threatened, is the offspring of chagrin and disappointment. What will they oppose?

If we go right, that will not, is it [*sic*] to be hoped, make them go wrong. An impartial trial and a just verdict are all that is demanded, and that the country will render, whatever the hopes of faction may inspire. I am, with great regard, Faithfully yours,
ROBERT WALSH, JR., ESQ.   H. CLAY.

Mallory, *Life and Speeches of the Hon. Henry Clay*, II, 637-38.
[1] Neither the "paragraph" nor the letter has been found.
[2] See above, Clay to Gales and Seaton, January 30, 1825.
[3] John Quincy Adams.
[4] John C. Calhoun; William H. Crawford.
[5] See below, Commission, March 7, 1825, note.

From William Creighton, Jr.

My dear Sir: Chillicothe Feby. 19 1825
I was gratified to learn by the mail of this morning that the long agony is over, and particularly that the contest was terminated on the first ballot.[1] A protracted ballot could not have failed to produce great excitement both within and without. Here there is entire acquiescence. The inflammable materials artificially excited in Pennsylvania & New York will soon spend themselves.

Thinking it probable in the event of Mr. Adams' election you might be invited to the administration, the question propounded in your letter of the 7th Inst:[2] is one on which I have thought a great deal this winter, and have endeavoured with the feeble lights I possess to view it in all its ulterior bearings. Necessarilly [*sic*] ignorant of many circumstances that may exist at Washington that may have a bearing pro or con. My opinion is, if the offer is made you ought to accept   This opinion is formed regardless of the scurrility and abuse that the election has given rise to. If a man would suffer himself to be driven from his purpose by means like these he would always be at the mercy of the profligate and unprincipled. In the expression of this opinion it is taken for granted that Mr. Adams will pursue a liberal policy and embrace within its scope the great leading policy that you have been advocating. By uniting with such an administration you could not be charged by the most fastidious with a dereliction of principle for place.

I could not in the compass of a letter detail my views for the opinion expressed, and therefore shall not attempt it.

Should the invitation be given, your friends in Ohio will acquiesce in whatever decision you make.

Will our friend Cheves[3] be invited to the Treasury?
                             Your friend   W CREIGHTON JUN

ALS. NcD.   [1] See above, Clay to Brooke, February 10, 1825.
[2] Not found.   [3] Langdon Cheves. See below, Commission, March 7, 1825, note.

From Amos Kendall

Dear Sir,   Frankfort Feb. 19th 1825

The course which has been taken by yourself and a majority of the Kentucky delegation,[1] has created considerable excitement in this quarter. Some justify, some condemn and some palliate; but the general impression is certainly unfavorable to you. My impression is, that much will be said for a while and that it will be made to operate on some of the elections; but that there will not be any thing like a general attack upon you. There are some who are for going all lengths, and I have frequently been advised that I must quit you and give you up "to a reprobate mind." But I have uniformly answered, that there are relations in life which men cannot forget or disregard; that I have been an inmate of your family, was treated with kindness when friendless and a stranger,[2] and that could I [. . .][3] descend to injure the feelings or destroy the hopes of that family, I should feel myself guilty of petit treason. It is true, I owe no obligations to you on that score; but I cannot separate you from Mrs. Clay whose kindness I never shall return by an attempt to destroy the popularity and hopes of her husband. Yet I cannot promise, that nothing shall be said on the subject in the Argus.[4] I consider a newspaper, in some degree as public property, at least an avenue through which a community has a right to make its feelings known. Whatever may be written, be advised, that it shall not receive form, aid or polish from my pen. I have had a frank conversation with Maj. Barry[5] on the subject, and I am happy that his views correspond with my own. Although he hoped you would vote for Jackson, he can see no public good to be answered by assailing you. In Harrodsburg and even in Lexington, threats have been made to submit you to the fiery ordeal of burning in effigy, a mode of punishing refractory witnesses, judges, governors and statesmen now quite the rage in Kentucky; but for our own sakes as well as yours, measures have been taken which, I presume, will prevent it. We wish this mode of proceeding to be left wholly to our political enemies, that when they have progressed a little further with it, we may roll back the odium which it must excite with a force which will overwhelm them.

In Desha's case[6] I think public feeling is recoiling. Before the trial, I thought him guilty; but a portion of the evidence and many circumstances have brought my mind to a pause. The means used to procure his conviction are base beyond the power of my pen to paint, and the use intended to be made of it was baser still. I was shocked at hearing of the eulogies bestowed on Wickliffe's speech at Washington. He will be roughly handled or I mistake the signs of

the times. Would it not shock you, should this young man be condemned and executed while his father holds the pardoning power?
Should he be condemned, I am confident, such will be the result!
I believe his father, although convinced of his innocence, has come
to a resolute determination not to pardon him, after he shall have
had a fair trial. But I doubt whether a trial can be had until the
next session of the Legislature. The office of Judge in that District
is vacant and no man hereafter appointed by the governor will sit.[7]
Nor can it be presumed, that any other Judge will sit in the case
after the treatment received by judge Shannon.

You doubtless hear much of public meetings, reaction &c. &c. in
Kentucky. Unless I am deceived, it is all wind. The *people* have
little concern in these preconcerted affairs, and look on them with
almost perfect indifference. The only county in which the *real*
public sentiment has been sufficiently expressed to insure a change,
is Green, and there the change is in favor of the new order of
things.[8] In fact, nothing can yet be determined as to the final result.

I thank you for your kind intentions relative to myself. If I
delighted in power, I should remain at the post I now hold; for
I could not expect in any other situation to have the same influence. But such are not my feelings. My soul pants for a peaceful
and quiet life, aloof from all broils and all controversies. Before the
loss of my wife,[9] I looked forward with delight to the period when
I could establish myself in the country and retire from my public
post to the pleasures of domestic life. That prospect is all blasted,
but I have been prosecuting the improvements which I had then
commenced. Her death deprived me of a large portion of the means
on which I depended, and I cannot borrow here without giving an
interest which my prospects will not justify. I cannot, therefore,
complete my plan at present, and am compelled, from sheer necessity, to remain at this vile business, make great men who never
thank me, new enmities which I neither wish nor deserve, get praised
as a patriot, & cursed as a knave, with but a miserable compensation
either for my favors or my labors. Thank God, I am under no obligations to any man or any party—I have avoided incurring them—
and therefore nothing will prevent my embracing the first opportunity to make an honorable retreat from this battle ground. I
should be content to fix myself on my little farm, could I complete
my improvements, or I should like a residence in some peaceful
vocation in any eastern city, or I would not shrink from any public
duty, although I do not covet public employment. However, you
owe me nothing and I ask nothing. Should any opportunity occur
which you could turn thus to my advantage, it would be a relief
measure which I would suffer no judge to declare *unconstitutional*

with impunity. Till something more agreeable to my feelings offers, I shall manfully support the party whose side[10] I have espoused, because, in the main, I prefer their principles.

Your friend &c   AMOS KENDALL

ALS. DLC-HC (DNA, M212, R1). Addressed: "Henry Clay Esq Speaker House of Reps. Washington."
   [1] The Kentucky delegation had determined, by a vote of eight to four, to support Adams for the Presidency. Those taking this position were: David Trimble, Francis Johnson, Thomas Metcalfe, Robert P. Letcher, Richard A. Buckner, Philip Thompson, David White, and Clay. Those in opposition, all Jackson adherents, were Robert P. Henry, John T. Johnson, Thomas P. Moore, and Charles A. Wickliffe.
   Buckner, born in Fauquier County, Virginia, had moved to Green County, Kentucky, in 1803, had studied law, had begun practice at Greensburg in 1811, had served in the Kentucky Legislature in 1813 and 1815, and was a member of Congress from 1823 to 1829. Defeated for re-election in 1828, he held appointment as an associate justice of the court of appeals briefly in 1829. Unsuccessful as Whig candidate for Governor in 1832, he returned to the Kentucky House of Representatives from 1837 to 1839, was appointed a State circuit judge in 1845, and held that post until his death two years later.
   [2] See above, II, 54n.
   [3] MS. faded; one or two words missing.
   [4] Frankfort *Argus of Western America*. Kendall's comment, in the issue of February 23, 1825, was as follows: "Adams is President. And what do you intend to say about it, asks this one and that one? *Nothing at all*. We have lost both our first and second choice; but we are too busy just now to march off in search of new adversaries and new adventures. So we shall leave our delegation and their constituents to make their own explanations without our interference one way or the other."
   [5] William T. Barry.
   [6] See above, Blair to Clay, February 11, 1825, and note.
   [7] John Trimble was succeeded as circuit judge by Henry O. Brown, member of the house of representatives for Harrison County, who assumed his new duties at the regular term in March, 1825, and presided at the second trial of Isaac Desha the following year.
   [8] Shortly after passage of the legislation establishing the new court (above, III, 902 and note), numerous protest meetings had been organized—in Washington, Garrard (including representatives from Lincoln and Mercer), Whitley, Madison, Shelby, Scott, Bourbon, Harrison, Bracken, Estill, Henry, Mason, Woodford, Fleming, and Grayson counties, as well as in the towns of Louisville and Lexington. Several of these had been countered by meetings endorsing the change, and Green County sentiment was cited particularly for such a stand. Frankfort *Argus of Western America*, February 23, 1825, quoting recent mail.
   [9] The former Mary B. Woolfolk, of Jefferson County, Kentucky. She had died October 13, 1823.
   [10] MS. torn; possibly one or two words missing.

From [Daniel Drake]

Dear Sir   Lexington February 20h. 1825

When you shall have, or have not, glanced your eye into Mr. Bests little book,[1] with this transmitted to you, please to forward it to our common friend, Dr. Godman,[2] for whom it is designed.

We have had the misfortune to lose Profr Brown.[3] He delivered a final valedictory to the class on friday and will send in his resignation perhaps tomorrow. I did all in my power to prevent such a consummation; and greatly fear that we shall suffer from it, by a diminution in our future classes.

As it is of great importance that a chair so fundamental as that of

Theory & practice of Medicine, should not be suffered to remain vacant for any considerable length of time; and as it is probable that our Trustees will not fill it in your absence, I hope you will be here by the first monday of April, that an election may then be held.[4] On the early and judicious selection of a successor for Prof. B. much of the prosperity of our school, in future, must depend. We have a class of 234 pupils. Mr. Mathews[5] I am happy to say fulfills the expectations under which he was elected. For the last 3 weeks he has been indisposed; but is now convalescent.

I am of course delighted with the final result of the Presidential election. It is agreeable to your friends that *you* should, at last, have given them the best man of the three returned to the House; and it is something that he who defeated your election, should himself be defeated. The Kremer, and McDuffie? [sic][6] Conspiracy is perfectly consonant with the whole system of operations & expedients, by which the return to the House, of the Tennessee Candidate,[7] was effected. His friends here are in a state of equal irritation and dismay. The former, at least, will soon subside. Decisive blows do not in general produce lingering effects. I have no doubt that all the Mississippi states except Ten. will sustain you in the great act of Umpirage which you have so daringly performed.

We have much speculation here on the questions whether you will be invited to a seat in the new Cabinet; and, if so, whether you will accept it.

I consider the latter a great political question, involving the interests of the American System and of the states of the Interior; and am happy in believing, that your own sagacity, aided by that of the congregated friends of those two important interests, will be likely to enable you to make a correct decision. If your friends in Congress advise the step and promise to sustain you in it, I cannot doubt that it will prove in the end to be sound policy for yourself personally and for the great interests which you are destined still to represent. I consider the contest for the next presidency as now established between yourself and one other gentleman only, and every step which is taken

AL (incomplete). DLC-HC (DNA, M212, R1).

[1] Robert Best (ed.), *Tables of Chemical Equivalents, Incompatible Substances, and Poisons and Antidotes; with an Explanatory Introduction* (Lexington, Ky., 1825).

[2] John D. Godman.

[3] Samuel Brown.

[4] Drake, who was serving as professor of *materia medica* and medical botany, himself took over Brown's courses, while Dr. Charles Wilkins Short was hired for Drake's former position. The new instructor, son of Peyton Short and nephew of Dr. Frederick Ridgely, had been born in Woodford County, Kentucky, graduated from Transylvania with honors in 1810, and, after beginning the study of medicine under Dr. Ridgely, had completed his training at the Medical School of the University of Pennsylvania in 1815. He had been practicing medicine and conducting botanical re-

search at Hopkinsville, Kentucky, when he accepted the post at Transylvania. He succeeded Drake as dean of the Medical Department from 1827 to 1837, when he transferred to the Medical Institute in Louisville, 1838 to 1848.
5 Thomas J. Matthews.
6 George Kremer; George McDuffie.
7 Andrew Jackson.

From Amos Kendall

FRANKFORT, Feb. 20th, 1825.

DEAR SIR:—Since the enclosed was written,[1] we have received
the news of the result of the Presidential election. It creates very
little sensation here. In Frankfort, probably half or nearly so, approve the course of our representation. Jackson's original friends
are loud in their complaints, and several who were for you join them.
I think in some sections of the country, there will be a considerable
stir; but if the Administration is prudent it will die away. I speak
of Kentucky only. There is much inquiry whether you will be
offered or will accept the Secretaryship of State, and much diversity
of opinion as to what you ought to do if it is offered. It seems to
me, that no man here can tell what you ought to do; because it is
impossible for us to know all the circumstances.

Is there not a probability that Jackson may be elected by the
people at the end of four years? Will not Clinton[2] unite his interest
with Jackson's with the expectation that he will succeed him in the
Presidency, and will not such a combination be too powerful to
withstand? Will not Adams for his own safety, retain Crawford,
and thereby conciliate his interest? I know nothing of these matters; but on viewing at this distance, the posture of men and parties,
ideas indicated by these queries, have flitted through my mind.

Your friend, &c.   AMOS KENDALL.

Frankfort *Argus of Western America,* July 2, 1828. Published also in Washington
United States Telegraph, July 19, 1828; *United States Telegraph-Extra,* I (July 26,
1828), 309.
1 Above, February 19, 1825.   2 DeWitt Clinton.

To James Erwin

Dr Sir   Washn. 24 Feb. 1825

I recd. your letter of the 15h. Jan.[1] with the bill inclosed for
$5200. drawn by Commodore S. G. Pitot,[2] requesting me to put it
in a train for collection. I have sent it to Mr. Palacios,[3] the Consul
General of Colombia, a very particular friend of mine and a worthy
and highly esteemed gentleman, whose letter I transmit to you
inclosed. It will be some time before the fate of it is known, which
I will take care to apprize you of.

I have not time to inform you of all the late public events, of which you will, through the papers, receive a full account. Kremer[4] is an old vulgar gross drinking half dutchman half irishman, of whom I could make nothing, and whose affair has, for the present, passed off. The Department of State is offered to me, and I have determined to accept it. I shall be much abused, and I should have been more if I had declined it. My present intention is to be in Kentucky during the greater part of the month of May and until about the 10h. of June. I shall then wish to bring my family here. I should be rejoiced to meet my daughters there and Mr. Duralde[5] and yourself.

I have given a letter[6] of introduction to the girls to Genl. La Fayette. Tell them both that they must be very courteous and affectionate to him. Give my love to Anne. Yr's Affectionately
James Erwin Esqr.   H. CLAY

ALS. THi.   1 Not found.   2 Not identified.
3 Leandro Palacios, who had taken up this post in the spring of 1823, after holding appointment as agent for Colombia in France in 1821.
4 George Kremer.
5 Anne Brown Clay Erwin; Susan Hart Clay Duralde; Martin Duralde (Jr.).
6 Not found. Cf. below, Clay to Bledsoe and others, April 7, 1825.

To Hubbard Taylor

Dear Sir   Washn. 25 Feb. 25
I recd. and thank you for your letter of the 22d Ulto.[1] You will have heard of the event of the P. question. I am greatly flattered by the confidence reposed in me by my Clarke[2] friends and yourself, to vote according to my best judgment. That I have done, and shall be happy if in that instance I obtain their approbation. I have that of my deliberate convictions.

I am offered and shall accept the Dept. of State. They will abuse me for it; but they would have abused me more, and I think with more reason, if I had declined it. I hope to see my friends in May or June.   Your's faithfy.   H. CLAY
H. Taylor Esq.

ALS. TxU.   1 Not found.   2 Clark County, Kentucky.

APPLICATIONS, RECOMMENDATIONS   February 25, 1825

L[EVI] W. SIBLEY, Rochester (New York), urges transfer of the appointment for publication of the laws from "Mr. O[ran]. Follett, the printer of the 'Spirit of the Times' at Batavia" to himself as proprietor of the Rochester *Monroe Republican*. ALS. DNA, RG59, P. and D. of L. Addressed to Clay as Secretary of State. The printing contract for the Nineteenth Congress, First Session, was awarded to Sibley, partner of Derick Sibley as proprietor of the *Monroe Republican*. Follett had established the *Spirit of the Times* in 1819.

To George W. Featherstonhaugh

My dear Sir   Washington 26 Feb. 1825

I recognize in your letter of the 20h. inst.[1] a new proof which I duly appreciate of your friendly regard of me. Personally I do not know Mr. Lockwood.[2] He became my unsolicited correspondent, and I saw in his letters marks of zeal and intelligence, and integrity. I regret if I have been deceived in him; but I do not think that he has any letter from me, which, being properly interpreted by its contents and circumstances, can do me any injury. Such a correspondent, if he be unworthy, is one of the misfortunes of public life. What can one do but to answer civilly and kindly letters which breathe nothing but disinterested zeal and devotion?

I have accepted the Department of State, if the appointmt. shd. be confirmed. I hesitated, but finally concluded that they would abuse me at any rate, and more if I declined than if I accepted.

Mr. Adams, I am persuaded, will strive, by the wisdom and prudence of his measures, to deprive opposition of all just cause of complaint. A fair trial and an impartial decision are all that is asked.   Your's faithfly.   H. CLAY

G. W. Featherstonhaugh Esqr.

ALS. CSmH.   1 Not found.   2 Ralph I. Lockwood.

From Samuel J. Donaldson

Dr Sir   Balto Feby 26h 1825

On my return to Baltimore, the arrangements made by you & myself[1] were Submitted to those who were principally interested in the Estate of Messrs Saml & Robt Purviance which, I am happy to add were approved of by them.

On Consultation with Messrs Jno Purviance & Moale,[2] we have thought it Expedient, that for the purpose of relieving yourself from this Trust, you Should address a Petition to "The Hon Theodorick Bland Chancellor of Maryland" praying to be discharged from it & Stating the reasons which make it inconvenient for you further to attend to it. This Petition you Can send to me & one on behalf of the Creditors will be prepared here, Shewing their Consent to your Withdrawing from the Trust & praying for the appointment of another Trustee in your place. I have been named as your Successor, & if appointed shall advise you of it when you Can Convey to me the Lands purchased by you for the Trust and Which you have not Since Sold.   this perhaps had better be done in Kentucky, and you Can at the Same time Execute the Mortgage as agreed on at Washington & have them recorded according to the Laws of Your State.

In writing, Oblige me by mentioning the name of Some person, who would be a Suitable Agent in Kentucky for the Sale of the residue of the Lands, & if in possession of any papers Shewing the Quantity or locality of them I will thank you to forward them. You were good Enough to Offer me in one of our interviews, Copies of the Reports of Sales made by the Comrs under the Decree in the Case of Moale Trustee vs Purviance, which I then declined taking Supposing they Could be readily had here. In this I was mistaken & should be glad to have them if not wanted by you.

Copies of our Agreement & the Account were addressed to you under Cover which Mr Handy[3] promised to Send to you. If they have not been received (by mentioning it when you write) others Shall be prepared & forwarded. I am Sir very respectfully yours
Henry Clay Esq   SAML J. DONALDSON

ALS. DLC-TJC (DNA, M212, R13).
[1] See above, Agreement, February 16, 1825.   [2] Samuel Moale.
[3] Not identified. The family was prominent on the Maryland peninsula.

From John Binns

Dr. Sir   Phila. Feby 27—1825.

I wrote to Mr. Markley[1] yesterday on a subject which shall occupy this letter and I requested him to ask you for what information you could furnish. Further reflections induce me to write you directly and thus open two sources of information. I know that immediately on the adjournment of Congress an attack will be opened, on the Admistration [sic] of Mr. Adams, in this State from every press, which can be commanded by Ingham, Kremer[2] & Co. I need not say how important it is that this attack should be met promptly with all the facts and all the ability which can be mustered. If this be not done, the presses of the State will be enlisted and public opinion influenced so decidedly that it may hereafter be difficult indeed to divert them into other channels. If I have the materials I will instantly repel the attack and what I write will at once find its way into nearly one half the papers and thus we shall ensure a hearing which I trust is all we shall want. I have already taken some pains so to impress the Govr.[3] and our State Admn. as to make them feel that they have an interest in turning the current agst Kremer inasmuch as some of Genl. Jackson's original friends seriously contemplate runing [sic] Kremer, on Jackson's interest as the next Govr. of Pena. You will at once perceive how much this intention on the one side and the consequent resistance on the other will tend to embark feeling & zeal in the question which in the first instance will only appear to be an attack by Kremer on you although in truth it will involve so many other interests and feelings.

I learn from Washington that McDuffie[4] & Ingham wrote Kremers letter, that in the copy made by Kremer and sent to the Committee[5] he had misspelled many words and that the corrections of the spelling were in the hand writing of Mc.Duffie. As that letter is in possession of the Come. and you have several friends on it, nothing can be more easy than to have the letter examined and every thing worth noting carefully & correctly noted down and forwarded. As the house will soon adjourn the sooner this and all other information, can be obtained & forwarded the better. Yrs Truly & Respectfully
H. Clay Esqr   JOHN BINNS.

ALS. DLC-HC (DNA, M212, R1).
[1] Philip Swenk Markley, of Norristown, Pennsylvania, a member of the United States House of Representatives, 1823 to 1827.
[2] Samuel D. Ingham; George Kremer.
[3] John A. Shulze.   [4] George McDuffie.
[5] See above, Appeal, February 3, 1825, note.

To [John Quincy Adams]

House of Representatives;
Washington City, March 1st, 1825.

The undersigned having understood, that Mr. Jeremy Robinson has been in the service of the Government, and has rendered important services in South America,[1] and being impressed with a favourable opinion of the capacity and integrity of this gentleman, as well as of his thorough knowledge of the character of the people of Spanish and Portuguese America, and with the course of events in those countries, beg leave to recommend him to the President of the United States[2] for any diplomatic, or other, appointment, in the public service, for which his experience, and qualifications, fit him.[3]—

Copy. DLC-Jeremy Robinson Papers (DNA, M212, R22).
[1] In 1817 Robinson had been appointed agent for commerce and seamen in Lima, Callao, and other places in South America.
[2] James Monroe.
[3] Signed by Clay and thirty-six other members of Congress.
Robinson was nominated by President John Quincy Adams, on March 8, 1825, for the post of consul of the United States at Rio de Janeiro, Brazil; the nomination was confirmed the following day. Cf. below, Clay to Silsbee, April 21, 1825, note. Born at Boxford, Massachusetts, Robinson at this date resided in Virginia.

To Samuel Smith

Dear Sir   H. of R. 1 Mar. 25.

I received your note[1] respecting our friend Mr. Hughes, towards whom I retain, with unabated force, the kind dispositions which I have ever cherished. On the details of the appointments to which you refer I have had as yet but little conversation with Mr. Adams; but if in the arrangements which may be made for the public service any thing can be done (as I am inclined to think there may be) to promote his ease and comfort, and at the same time the public interest, be assured of my sincere desire to embrace the opportunity of effecting an object which would be so agreeable to me[2]—

With great regard I am faithfy Yrs   H. CLAY
The Honble Genl Smith

ALS. DLC-Samuel Smith Papers (DNA, M212, R22).
[1] Not found.
[2] On March 5 Christopher Hughes (Jr.) was nominated Chargé d'Affaires to the Netherlands; the proposed appointment was confirmed on March 7. Following the death of Hughes' father (see below, Oliver to Clay, March 12, 1825, note), the son had dropped the "Jr.," which had heretofore been attached, somewhat irregularly, to his signature.

APPLICATIONS, RECOMMENDATIONS   [*ca.* March 1, 1825]

T. L. F. HIGGINS, "Washington City," solicits a clerkship. States that he resided in Maryland "till a few days ago." ALS. DNA, RG59, A. and R. (MR2). Dated "March 1825." Cover addressed to Clay. Higgins, not further identified, received no appointment.

Remarks on Bill to Establish Navy Yard

[March 2, 1825]

Cited in *Register of Debates*, 18 Cong., 2 Sess., 738. The House, in Committee of the Whole at an evening session, had taken up a bill from the Senate, providing for the establishment of a navy yard at Pensacola. Clay participated in the debate, his remarks not recorded; and, after the bill had been changed to authorize location of the navy yard at any point "on the coast of Florida, in the gulf of Mexico," he spoke in its support. The measure was passed and, with Senate concurrence in the amendment, was enacted on March 3, 1825. 4 *U. S. Stat.*, 127.

Resolution of Thanks
from the House of Representatives

[March 3, 1825]

Resolved, That the thanks of this House be presented to the Honorable Henry Clay, for the able, impartial, and dignified manner, in which he has presided over its deliberations, and performed the arduous and important duties of the chair during the present session of Congress

AD by Philip S. Markley. DNA, RG233, HR 18A-B4. Published in U.S. H. of Reps., *Journal*, 18 Cong., 2 Sess., 309; *Register of Debates*, 18 Cong., 2 Sess., 739.

Remarks on Adjourning the House of Representatives

[March 3, 1825]

GENTLEMEN: For the honorable testimony which you have been pleased this day to express to my official conduct in this highly distinguished station, I pray you to accept my profound acknowledgments. Near fourteen years, with but two comparatively short intervals, the arduous duties of the chair have been assigned to me. In that long period, of peace and of war, causes, from without and within, of great public excitement, have, occasionally, divided our councils, disturbed our harmony, and threatened our safety. Happily, however, past dangers, which appeared to encompass us, were dispelled, as I anxiously hope those of the present will be, in a spirit of mutual forbearance, moderation, and wisdom. The debates in this House, to which those causes gave rise, were sometimes ardent and animated; but amidst all the heats and agitations produced by our temporary divisions, it has been my happy fortune to experience, in an unexampled degree, the kindness, the confidence, and the affectionate attachment of the members of the House. Of the numerous decisions which I have been called upon to pronounce from this place, on questions often suddenly started and of much difficulty, it has so happened, from the generous support given me, that not one of them has ever been reversed by the House. I advert to this fact, not in a vain spirit of exultation, but as furnishing a powerful motive for undissembled gratitude.

In retiring, perhaps for ever, from a situation with which so large a portion of my life has been associated, I shall continually revert, during the remainder of it, with unceasing respect and gratitude, to this great theatre of our public action, and with the firm belief that the public interests and the liberty of our beloved country will be safely guarded hereafter, as they have been heretofore, by enlightened patriotism.

Gentlemen: In retiring to your respective families and constituents, I beg all of you, without exception, to carry with you my fervent prayers for the continuation of your lives, your health, and your happiness.

U. S. H. of Reps., *Journal*, 18 Cong., 2 Sess., 314. Published also in *Register of Debates*, 18 Cong., 2 Sess., 739-40.

To Francis T. Brooke

My dear Sir   Washn. 4 Mar. 1825

I have the gratification to tell you that all my information from the West bespeaks a satisfied state of the public mind, in relation to the result of the late election. In Ohio the approbation of it is enthusiastic. In K. too the expression of public opinion evinces general acquiescence.

I transmit to you inclosed two letters which are from Crittenden and Creighton,[1] two of the most discreet men in Ohio & K. Be pleased to shew them to Mr. Pleasants.[2]   Yr. friend   H. CLAY

ALS. KyU. Addressed on attached sheet: "The Honble Francis Brooke   Richmond Va."
[1] See above, Crittenden to Clay, February 15, 1825; Creighton to Clay, February 19, 1825.   [2] Probably John H. Pleasants.

To [John Quincy Adams]

Dear Sir   4 O'Clock 5 Mar. 25—

My cold or influenza has obliged me to confine myself today to my room, and a great part of it to my bed, and to take medicine. I should otherwise have called to see you.

Will you have the goodness to peruse, at your leisure, the inclosed letter from Mr. Rochester,[1] one of the most intelligent members of the N. York delegation in the H. of R. in the 17h. Congress, and now one of the Judges of the Superior Courts of that State? His venerable father,[2] whose name has been confered [sic] on one of the most flourishing villages in the Western part of N. York, of which he is an inhabitant, is one of the purest and best men I ever knew. The son is worthy of the sire. I am Your ob. Servant

H. CLAY.

ALS. MHi-Adams Papers, Letters Received (MR468).
[1] William B. Rochester; letter not found.
[2] Nathaniel Rochester.

To [James Barbour]

Sir   Washn. 5 Mar. 1825

The name of the soldier, for whose release Mr. Letcher[1] had the goodness to apply at my instance some days ago is Joseph Parkinson[2] of the 4h. Company of Artillery commanded by Capt. Morris[3] and stationed at St. Augustine. His sister[4] is willing to refund bounty &c. and conform to any other reasonable condition. I have the honor to be Your obedient Servt.   H. CLAY
The Honble Secy of War.

ALS. DNA, RG94, Letters Received, 1825, no. 5. Endorsed on cover: "Adjt Gl. apply the rule in similar cases. By order   C[hristopher]. V[an de Venter, a native of New York, Chief Clerk in the War Department]."
For Barbour's appointment to the Cabinet, see below, Commission, March 7, 1825, note.   [1] Robert P. Letcher.
[2] Probably of Mercer County, Kentucky.

3 William Walton Morris, born at Ballston Springs, New York, and graduated from the United States Military Academy in 1820, had been raised to the rank of first lieutenant in 1823 and assigned to the Fourth Artillery in July, 1824; but he did not attain the permanent rank of captain until 1836. He remained on Army duty until his death in 1865, with the permanent rank of colonel, brevetted a major general.

4 Not identified.

INSTRUCTIONS AND DISPATCHES March 5, 1825

From RICHARD RUSH, London, no. 423. Encloses copies of correspondence with William Huskisson, member of Parliament and (from 1823 to 1827) president of the Board of Trade, relating to inquiries made by the United States consul at Liverpool (James Maury); reports further conversation with Huskisson, in which the latter has warned that if a recent recommendation by the Treasury Department to Congress be enacted so as "to discriminate between citizens of the United States and foreigners in the collection of duties upon our imports, by continuing to give credits on bond to the former, but to demand immediate payment from the latter," Great Britain would deem it "at variance with the spirit of the subsisting treaty between the two countries and . . . she would have to meet it by some measure of counteraction." ALS. DNA, RG59, Dip. Disp., Great Britain, vol. 32 (M30, R28). Addressed to Secretary of State; received April 19.

The enclosed correspondence concerns the interpretation of regulations on tonnage duties with respect to vessels carrying passengers and baggage, only, or in ballast, Huskisson assuming a liberal position which absolved such vessels from duty. His accompanying protest related to a letter from William H. Crawford to Clay, as Speaker of the House of Representatives, on December 14, 1824, in which the Secretary of the Treasury, answering a House resolution of inquiry about the losses incurred on credits extended for importation duties, had argued against "abolishing or curtailing the credits now given for duties" but had perceived "no sufficient reason . . . [for] continuing it [a credit] to foreigners, who are not domiciliated in the republic. A discrimination, in this respect, between citizens of the United States and others," he had commented, "would tend to confine the commerce of the nation to its own citizens, and would aid in restraining the practice of shipping merchandise to this country, upon consignment, for foreign account, which has hitherto been found to interfere with the interests of our own regular merchants." *House Docs.*, 18 Cong., 2 Sess., no. 13, p. 3.

APPLICATIONS, RECOMMENDATIONS March 5, 1825

ROBERT P. LETCHER, Washington, recommends Joseph Duncan for appointment as register of the land office in Illinois. LS. DNA, RG59, A. and R. (MR2). Duncan, born in Paris, Kentucky, had served in the War of 1812 and, in 1818, had moved to Illinois, where he became a farmer in Jackson County. He had been a justice of the peace (1821-1823), was a member of the State legislature (1824-1826), and, as a Jackson Democrat, became a member of Congress (1827-1834) and Governor of Illinois (1834-1838). He did not receive the Federal appointment here sought for him.

DUTEE J. PEARCE, Washington, recommends Richard Fitzpatrick, of Key West, as United States marshal in Florida. ALS. *Ibid.* (MR2). Pearce, of Newport, Rhode Island, elected a member of the United States House of Representatives for the term beginning March 4, 1825, served in Congress until March 3, 1837. He had been State attorney general from 1819 until 1825 and, on January 3, 1825, had been appointed Federal district attorney for the District of Rhode Island. Fitzpatrick, not further identified, received no appointment.

INSTRUCTIONS AND DISPATCHES   March 6, 1825

From CHARLES SAVAGE, Guatemala (City). Announces his arrival on February 22, after a voyage from Boston of five months, involving "two partial shipwrecks"; his accreditation on March 5; and the probability of delay in supplying the information requested "in relation to the American commerce in this Republic." ALS. DNA, RG59, Cons. Disp., Guatemala, vol. 1 (M-T337, R1). Addressed to Secretary of State; received May 27.

Commission as Secretary of State

[March 7, 1825]

John Quincy Adams, President of the United States of America.

To all who shall see these presents, Greeting:

Know Ye, That reposing special Trust and Confidence in the Patriotism, Integrity and Abilities of Henry Clay, of Kentucky, I have nominated and by and with the advice and Consent of the Senate, do appoint him Secretary of State; and do authorize and empower him to execute and fulfil the duties of that Office according to law; and to Have and to Hold the said Office, with all the powers, privileges and emoluments to the same of right appertaining unto him the said Henry Clay, during the pleasure of the President of the United States for the time being.

> In Testimony whereof, I have caused these Letters to be made patent, and the Seal of the United States to be hereunto affixed.
>
> Given under my hand at the City of Washington the Seventh day of March A.D. 1825; and of the Independence of the United States of America, the Forty Ninth.
>
> JOHN QUINCY ADAMS.

DS. DLC-HC (DNA, M212, R1). President Adams had sent to the Senate on March 5 a list of nominations to three Cabinet posts (Clay, Secretary of State; Richard Rush, Secretary of the Treasury; and James Barbour, Secretary of War) and various other offices. The only evidence of opposition to these appointments came in the vote, March 7, confirming Clay as Secretary of State by a tally of twenty-seven to fourteen. Andrew Jackson had been among those opposing the nomination.

Pending the return of Rush from England, Samuel L. Southard was appointed acting Secretary of the Treasury, in addition to continuing his duties as Secretary of the Navy.

From Francis Preston Blair

My dear Sir   Frankfort March 7. 1825

Your letter of the 19 to Kendall[1] brought the first certain intelli-

gence of your determination to accept the appointment of secy. of
State. I rejoice most sincerely that you so determined— I wrote to
white[2] some time since, that it was decidedly my opinion that you
should accept on your account, that of your friends & your country—
I rejoice to find that I was but uniting my voice to that of your
other friends. The Jackson party among us are quite vociferous—
reiterate the Kremer[3] abuse, & seem to consider that your acceptance of the Office of Secretary, a greater outrage, than even
defeating the election of General Jackson. As it regards themselves,
I really beleive [sic] they think rightly. For the latter only prevented the General for the present, the first circumstance will I
greatly hope cut off his [prospects][4] forever. Your friends here all
concur in the wish to see you Secretary of State, & I have no doubt
but the great mass of those throughout the State who preferred
Jackson next to yourself will feel that they & the Country have
more than an equivalent in your appointment for the loss of the
election in the house, on the part of the Western Candidate— All
attacks here on the administration with which you have connected
yourself will be easily made to recoil on the assailants. Your present
Situation & future prospects are advantages in which the whole
West participate & of which it will make the most by cherishing
your popularity. I have remarked an attempt in the Washington
Gazette to alienate from you the majority here opposed to the late
Judges[5]— From certain indices afforded by the peice [sic] although
it is an editorial article, I am convinced that it is the production
of some sinister Kentucky enemy of yours— From such hands we
might expect such attempts; but I was astonished at the paragraph
by which your note to Judge Brooks [sic] was ushered to the
public[6]— Is it possible that Judge Brooks could have written it?
If he did he is mistaken as to facts for when some of the relief party
were persuaded from bringing forward the resolutions they were
at last introduced by one of the pillars of "the temple of liberty"
as the Judge would call him—one of the Judge party & was supported by most of them[7]—

Now that you are loaded with the correspondence of half the
world, I fear that you will feel the idle letters of your friends an
irksome addition. Yet you must allow me now & then the privilege
to indulge the vanity I feel in being remembered by you & to
bring my self to your recollection by a letter that shall reach you
on a holy day— An anniversary congratulation I shall consider
as a right[8]—

When do you expect to return to Kentucky? We want some
occasion such as your return or the arrival of LaFayette[9] to call
us off awhile from from [sic] party strife— Your men of order, have
become the most outrageous fellows in the world— They threaten

on the first Monday in April to arm themselves with the orders of
the ex-Court & to punish the iniquities of the whole Judge breaking
crew, by laying pains & penalties on a certain poor Clerk of your
acquaintance.[10] As I have got into the courts allow me to ask to
whom you will leave your professional mantle in Kentucky? Is
not Crittenden[11] the ablest & worthiest to bear it? The Bank of
the United States I think owes him some favors, for to my certain
knowledge he has presented it with several gratuities on behalf of
some of its insolvent debtors— I should be pleased to see his
profession made profitable for during the term of your presidency
I should be glad to see him enabled to go into the counsels of his
country that he might add to the glory & lustre of his state— I am
sorry Rush[12] is appointed secretary of the Treasury

Do command in any thing in which I can be serviceable to you—
The marks of your confidence & kindness have been many to me,
& every time you shall put in my power to be grateful will confer
a new obligation— In haste Your affectionate friend

F. P. BLAIR

ALS. DLC-HC (DNA, M212, R1).
1 Amos Kendall; letter not found.
2 David White, Jr.   3 George Kremer.   4 Word not clear.
5 John Boyle, Benjamin Mills, and William Owsley. An editorial had asserted that
Clay had rallied support for Adams with "the assurance . . . that the defeat of Gen.
Jackson was essential to ensure the triumph of the judge party in Kentucky." *Washington Gazette*, February 14, 1825. Reference is here made to the supporters of the
old court. Cf. above, III, 902n.
6 The note "To the Editors of the Richmond Enquirer," prefacing a request for
publication of Clay's letter to Francis T. Brooke, January 28, 1825, spoke of Clay's
decision "to vote for Mr. Adams, in the face of instructions from a dominant party
in Kentucky; a party who have prophaned the temple of their liberty, by putting
down their constitution. . . ." Reprinted in Lexington *Kentucky Gazette*, March 3,
1825.
7 John Jordan Crittenden had introduced the resolutions (see above, III, 901-902)
in the Kentucky House of Representatives on December 24. The votes in their
support had been decisive and had included members of both the relief and antirelief forces. Ky. H. of Reps., *Journal, 1824–1825*, pp. 455, 496-98.
8 Probably a reference to their shared birthday anniversary, April 12.
9 See above, Barry to Clay, January 10, 1825, note.
10 See above, III, 902 and note. The judges of the old court at the April term
decided against undertaking measures to regain their records from Blair, who with
other officers of the new court had been indicted on February 7, in Franklin Circuit
Court, for seizing the papers from the office of Achilles Sneed. Rejecting "the singular
spectacle of those clothed with the garb of peace officers of the country, warring
against each other and applying and resisting physical force, and thus endangering
the peace and good order of society," the old court called upon the electorate in the
approaching August contest to render a verdict upon the actions of the preceding
legislature. Apart from continuances and interlocutory decrees, judicial actions of this
court were suspended until October. The judges' statement was published in Lexington
Kentucky Reporter, April 5, 1825.
11 John J. Crittenden. Cf. below, Clay to Todd, March 27, 1825.
12 Richard Rush.

MISCELLANEOUS LETTERS   March 7, 1825

From P[ETER] A. BROWNE, corresponding secretary of the Franklin Institute of
the State of Pennsylvania for the Promotion of the Mechanic Arts, Philadelphia.

Protesting against the refusal of employees of the Patent Office to release for publication the specifications of patented inventions prior to expiration of the patent, charges that these officers are ignorant of the law, partial, and inconsistent in their application of the regulations. LS. DNA, RG59, Misc. Letters (M179, R62).

APPLICATIONS, RECOMMENDATIONS March 7, 1825

JAMES DEWOLF, Washington, transmits a letter from George McKinley (not identified; the letter not found), urging the propriety of appointing a commercial agent for the United States to reside at Puerto Plata, Santo Domingo; recommends McKinley for the post should an appointment be made. LS. DNA, RG59, A. and R. (MR1). No commercial agent was named for this port, and no appointment was given to McKinley.

To Nicholas Biddle

Dear Sir   Washington 8h. March 1825

As I am about to enter upon the duties of an office which will put it out of my power to render the services any longer to the Bank, which I have heretofore performed as its Counsel, in the States of Ohio and Kentucky, I think it right to apprize you of the termination of that relation from this day. It is my intention to be in Kentucky, during the sitting of the Court in May, at which time I will do any thing in my power to enable my successor[1] to complete whatever professional business, confided to my care, remains to be finished. In the mean time I will take pleasure, by correspondence, with the Bank or with its officers and agents, in those two states, to afford any information or assistance that I may be capable of rendering.

I have drawn in favor of the office here for $2000 upon the Bank $1500 of that sum being the residue of my compensation for the year terminating on the 31st. Decr. last and $500 on account of what has since accrued. I have the honor to be with great respect Your obedient Servant   H. CLAY

Nicholas Biddle Esqr. &c. &c. &c.

ALS. PHi. Endorsed: "recd March 10. 1825."
[1] Cf. below, Clay to Todd, March 27, 1825.

INSTRUCTIONS AND DISPATCHES March 8, 1825

From HUGH NELSON, Madrid, no. [53]. Encloses copies of documents relating to the practice of "exacting bonds from American Shipmasters entering the ports of Spain with goods in transit," to "the outrage" suffered by the Secretary of Legation on his way to Paris with dispatches for the American Government, to "a demand made at Cadiz, for the tonnage duty on the Brig Dick [of New York] entering that port in distress," and to an attempt at Barcelona to exact from American vessels a double payment of duty. Reports on the ill health of the King (Ferdinand VII). Notes that English recognition of the South American States has made a deep impression, that Spain desires a rupture between the continental powers and Great Britain, that "something is in preparation between France and Spain," that "Mr Heredia the new Minister to the United States has not yet left," and that the government is compiling evidence to use in pressing claims "which they pretend to set up for injuries sustained by naval equipments in the ports of the United States." LS. DNA, RG59, Dip. Disp., Spain, vol. 24 (M31, R26). Addressed to Secretary of State; received May 6.

The Secretary of Legation (since 1822), John James Appleton, of Massachusetts, en route from Madrid to the United States with diplomatic dispatches, had been requested by the French gendarmerie at Buitrago to surrender his passport and, upon his refusal, had been arrested.

Notice of the British Cabinet's decision to recognize Buenos Aires, Mexico, and Colombia as independent states had been transmitted to the Spanish Foreign Minister on December 31, 1824 (see below, Brown to Secretary of State, March 22, 1825) and to the London representatives of the continental powers during the next month; it had been announced publicly in Parliament on February 7, 1825. The first formal act of recognition was accorded in the exchange of ratifications of a commercial treaty with the Government of Buenos Aires, on May 11, 1825, the treaty having been signed the preceding February 2. Harold Temperley, *The Foreign Policy of Canning, 1822-1827* . . . (London, 1925), 147, 151, 499.

The Chevalier José de Heredia, whose appointment had been announced in November, 1824, did not assume his post; Hilario de Rivas y Salmon, former Secretary of Legation, who had performed the duties as Chargé d'Affaires since 1821, continued until he was relieved by Francisco Tacon, as Minister Resident, in July, 1827. Tacon in 1825 was serving as a commissioner for the Spanish Government in London.

From RICHARD RUSH, London, no. 424. Encloses a copy of a note of March 5 from (George) Canning, British Foreign Secretary (1822–1827; Prime Minister, 1827, when he died), in reply to Rush's note of February 25, relative to the St. Petersburg Convention (see above, III, 736n). ALS. DNA, RG59, Dip. Disp., Great Britain, vol. 32 (M30, R28). Addressed to Secretary of State. Canning's note explains that in view of the British Government's "earnest desire . . . to act up both to the letter and spirit of the 3rd article of the convention," he will present Rush's "renewed representation" to the Board of Admiralty. The third article of the convention provided that, after the average value of the slaves had been fixed, the commissioners were to constitute a board to examine claims and the British Government was "to cause to be produced before the Commission, as material towards ascertaining facts, all the evidence of which His Majesty's Government may be in possession . . . of the number of Slaves carried away." Miller (ed.), *Treaties. . .* , III, 98-99.

Rush's note to Canning on February 25 had protested against the stand taken by the British Commissioner, (George) Jackson, who had contended that the reproduction of certain documents requested from the British archives for presentation to the board by the American claimants "would take so much time as to defeat, probably, the object of the application," the documents "being so voluminous that they could not or would not be transmitted identically." DNA, RG59, Dip. Disp., Great Britain, vol. 32 (M30, R28).

MISCELLANEOUS LETTERS   March 8, 1825

From WILLIAM P. DUVAL, Washington City. Endorses a claim by Thomas

Murphy for compensation for services as clerk to the Governor of Florida. ALS. DNA, RG59, Misc. Letters (M179, R62). Published in Carter (ed.), *Territorial Papers. . .* , XXIII, 211-12. Murphy not further identified.

APPLICATIONS, RECOMMENDATIONS   March 8, 1825

JOHN BARNEY, Baltimore, recommends John Pendleton Kennedy for the mission to Sweden. ALS. DNA, RG59, A. and R. (MR1). Barney, son of Joshua Barney, was a member of Congress from Maryland (1825-1829). Kennedy, son of John Kennedy of Baltimore, was a lawyer and former member of the Maryland Legislature; he later became a Congressman (1838-1839, 1841-1845), Secretary of the Navy (1852-1853), and a well known author.

J[EREMY] ROBINSON encloses a copy of a note sent to the President because, at the time he wrote it, there was no acting Secretary of State. ALS. *Ibid.* (MR3). In the enclosure, dated March 7, Robinson solicits appointment as Chargé to Peru. Cf. above, Clay and others to Adams, March 1, 1825, note; below, Clay to Silsbee, April 21, 1825, note.

SAMUEL SMITH, Washington, stating a belief that it would give Clay "pleasure to do an Act of kindness to Mr. Jefferson," recommends appointment of Thomas Jefferson's grandnephew, Dabney Carr, who is also Smith's nephew, as successor to Christopher Hughes. ALS. DNA, RG59, A. and R. (MR1). Dabney Smith Carr, born in Albemarle County, Virginia, had begun a business career in Smith's employ. The young man founded the Baltimore *Republican and Commercial Advertiser* in support of Andrew Jackson in 1827, was appointed naval officer for the port of Baltimore in 1829, and in 1843 became Minister to Turkey.

From Alexander Armstrong and Samuel Potts

Hon. Henry Clay—   St. Clairsville, O, March 9, 1825.

Sir, Mr. Patterson,[1] late Representative in Congress from this District, has returned home, and informs that there are two Candidates before the Executive for the appointment of Superintendant of the Road from Wheeling towards Zanesville. One a gentleman living near Harpers Ferry, and the other a Citizen of Wheeling: and that Mr. Ruggles[2] and Mr. Patterson had signed the recommendation of the latter.

The intelligence that our immediate Representatives had united in the recommendation of Mr. M Lure[3] of Wheeling, was received here with general astonishment. We should suppose that a moments consideration would have satisfied them that a Superintendant from abroad would be much more acceptable here, than any man resident at Wheeling. It was sufficiently obvious, that the proximity of Wheeling to this place, added to the circulation of Cash there, occasioned by the construction of the Road east of the Ohio, and the throng of strangers from navigation and the use of the Cumberland Road, operated for some years to affect severely the business and property on this side the river. In fact a large proportion of the business of this county was transacted at Wheeling for two or three years. The last year or two has witnessed a considerable check to this unnatural course of business. There is no longer a general monopoly of the business of this county at Wheeling. The prospect of an appropriation for the road, which might operate to some extent in equalizing matters between the two places, was always regarded with much interest. But if a Superintendant should be appointed at Wheeling, he can make his deposits there; he can pay contractors in checks on Wheeling, he can supply the wants of the hands on the road by remittances of merchandize and country fabrics from that place; and by throwing us again under the power of Wheeling he can prevent us from obtaining a fair participation of the advantages which have heretofore been enjoyed in a higher degree (from more extravagant expenditures) in the neighbourhood of the Road east of the Ohio. Wheeling in particular has reaped decisive advantages from that Road. By the appointment of a Superintendant at Wheeling, the power will be vested in his hands, (and the people there have acquired skill in the use of advantages) to draw to that place most of the profits of the expenditure for the construction of the Road on this side of the River. This is called a Western Road, and is to be made in a Western State. But will a Wheeling Superintendant manage the business so as to dispense the benefits of the expenditu[re] in Ohio, or will he endeavour to secure as much to Virginia as may be?

It may, then, be readily seen, how much more desirable it would be, to have a Superintendant from abroad, who would have no rival interest to support. Any foreigner of the proper character ought to have been preferred by our Representatives. They have improperly, and inconsiderately as we suppose, yielded to the solicitations in favour of Mr. M Lure; and we should be glad to have it understood at head quarters, that this act of theirs is wholly disapproved at home.

There exists here a good deal of concern on this subject. It is a matter of public interest; and being so, we tru[st] you will forgive our intrusion upon your notice in relation to it. It may be that the appointment is still undeterm[in]ed—that you are not committed respecting it, and that you may be consulted on the subject by the proper Department. We would fain hope that the propriety of selecting a Super[in]tendant, whose local feelings and interests would not be in direct opposition to those of this section of Ohio, and whose management would not be suspected of having an eye to any local considerations, may be taken into Consideration; and that the gentleman from the east of the Mountains may be preferred. Your known sentiments in favour of *securing* to the Western States a reasonable participation in the public expenditures, lead us to believe that our objections against the appointment from Wheeling, will be regarded by you as possessing some weight.

On another subject, allow us the pleasure of expressing our feelings. We would use the opportunity afforded by this communication to say, that the course pursued by yourself and friends in the Delegations of Ohio, Kentucky and Missouri, in the recent election of President, has our decided and unqualified approbation. Having had the honour of being taken into notice by the friends of "an American System," at the Meeting held in Columbus last Summer, which formed the Clay Ticket in Ohio,[4] (one of us being called to act as Secretary at that meeting, and the other appointed by that meeting the Standing Committee for the County of Belmont,) we would say for ourselves and the considerate persons with whom we are in the habit of associating, that the support of Mr. Adams by the states above mentioned, appears to have been in the highest degree judicious. We presume the friends of Mr. Adams Mr Crawford and Gen Jackson, upon repeated ballottings would have tenaciously adhered to them. If O. K. & Missouri had went for Jackson (waving [*sic*] all objections against him) they could not have elected him. If they had went for Cra[wford][5] they could not have carried him. And it seems that if [there] had been 20 or 30 ballottings these three states must have went for Adams in the end in order to effect an election.[6] How much more dignified, and creditable to the government, to avoid the excitement resulting from reiterated ballottings, and go at once as it was obvious those states must eventually go?

We are with sincere regard Yours   ALEXR. ARMSTRONG
                                                  SAM POTTS

ALS by Armstrong, signed also by Potts, both of St. Clairsville, Ohio. DNA, RG59, Misc. Letters (M179, R62).   1 John Patterson.

2 Benjamin Ruggles, born and educated at law in Connecticut, had begun practice in Marietta, Ohio, in 1807, but shortly thereafter had removed to St. Clairsville, where he had been president judge of the court of common pleas (1810-1815) until elected to the United States Senate (1815-1833).

3 John McLure received the post of superintendent of repairs for the Cumberland Road; but Caspar W. Wever, of Washington County, Maryland, had been nominated on March 8, and confirmed on the date of this letter, as construction superintendent for the extension of the road west to Zanesville. Wever, a former member of the Maryland Legislature, resigned from service under the Federal Government in 1828, to become the first superintendent of construction for the Baltimore and Ohio Railroad. In 1832 and 1833, as an expert on macadamized roads, he supervised the paving of Pennsylvania Avenue in Washington, District of Columbia.

4 See above, III, 798-99n.

5 Hole in MS. obscures this and the next bracketed word.

6 See above, Clay to Brooke, February 10, 1825, note.

From Robert Scott

Dr. Sir,   Lexington 9th. March 1825
Herewith are the Accounts of Colo. Morrison's estate with you

as its executor for the month of February[1]— By them you will perceive that very little has been collected during that period.—

Since their date, Jno. Hart[2] has paid his Note—in a day or two the Clarks[3] will pay the bal. of theirs—that of George & Hawkins[4] I left in Versailles for the purpose of having suit brought on it in time to obtain judgment at their Court for the present month, unless they should prevent it by payment— I expect they have paid at least a part of it— Atcheson[5] I have sued and doubtless will have to bring suit on the Note of Browns.[6]

Dr. Warfield[7] has not yet paid the interest on his Note— I have apprized him that I would bring suit on it in time to obtain Judgment at our March Court, unless payment of the interest should be made in time to prevent it—and have been assured that the interest would be paid within that period— I have not heard anything further from Mr Reed of Natchez since I wrote you on the subject of Butler's debt[8]— When a decision shall be rendered in the case of Ogden vs Sanders from the Orleans Circuit,[9] I will thank you to inform me, and what the decision is, as the estate of Colo. Morrison, as well as myself are interested in it—

It appears you have accepted of the appointment of Secretary of State— Of course you will not be much with us for some time to come— Individually, many of your friends will regret it; but when public good is taken into veiw [sic]—they approve of your acceptance— There are a few malcontents amongst the Jacksonians, but am confident not to such extent as to effect [sic] your public standing— Let them growl— they cannot injure you—

Confidential—I beg you if you can effect it, to procure some appointment for Mr. J.W.E.,[10] as it seems to be reduced to a certainty that he never will have energy enough to do any thing in a professional way—I have not been informed, but feel pretty confident it would be very agreeable to his Aunt[11] and other connexions—

Aunt Morrison and family are well—

very respectfully Yr. obt Servt   ROBT. SCOTT

The Honble H. Clay   Congress

ALS. KyLxT.

[1] See below, *ca.* June 13, 1825 (monthly accounts, ADS by Scott, may be found in KyLxT).

[2] John Hart, Sr., who, with the subsequent debtors listed in this paragraph, owed the estate for purchases made at the sale at "Carlisle Farm" in October, 1823 (above, III, 488-89, 774n).

[3] John (probably not the Lexington carpenter) and A. (probably Alexander) Clark, of the Tate's Creek Road, near Lexington.

[4] See above, III, 503.

[5] Hamilton Atchison, whose debt for stock purchases amounted to $138.00.

[6] Samuel M. Brown, of Fayette County, later a post office agent at New Orleans, who had already paid part of his note and completed payment on June 9, 1825. He was the son of Joshua and Margaret Brown.

7 Walter Warfield.
8 See above, III, 628; Scott to Clay, January 3, 1825.
9 See above, Boyle to Clay, January 10, 1825, note.
10 Joseph William Edmiston, a young lawyer, graduated from Yale University and, with a master's degree in 1824, from Transylvania University. He later moved to Washington, Alabama, where he died in October, 1829.
11 Mrs. James Morrison.

MISCELLANEOUS LETTERS   March 9, 1825

From JOHN BOYER, Reading, Pennsylvania. Asks for information concerning the law for payment of Niagara claims. ALS. DNA, RG59, Misc. Letters (M179, R62). See above, Porter to Clay, January 14, 1825, note.

APPLICATIONS, RECOMMENDATIONS   March 9, 1825

JAMES NOBLE, Washington, recommends Vincent Masi for a clerkship in the State Department. ALS. DNA, RG59, A. and R. (MR3). Masi, a music teacher and dancing master, for several years had operated a dance hall, offering cotillion parties, in Washington. He did not receive an appointment in the Government.

JOSEPH VANCE, Baltimore, recommends Jonah Baldwin, of Springfield, Clark County, Ohio, as a commissioner to lay out the road from Detroit to Chicago. ALS. *Ibid.* (MR1). Under an act approved March 3, 1825, the President had been authorized to appoint three commissioners to "explore, survey, and mark, in the most eligible course" such a road. 4 *U. S. Stat.*, 135. Baldwin was appointed one of the three.

LEWIS WILLIAMS, Washington, recommends Vincent Masi for a clerkship. ALS. DNA, RG59, A. and R. (MR3).

Circular

Department of State, Washington, 10th. March, 1825.
To the Foreign Ministers residing in the United States.

The Undersigned has the honour of notifying the Foreign Ministers accredited to the Government of the United States, that, having been appointed Secretary of State, he has entered upon the discharge of the duties of that Office, and will be happy to receive from them such communications as they may think proper to address to him in that capacity.

He avails himself, with pleasure, of the opportunity afforded him of requesting the Minister of His   Majesty the King of to accept the assurance of his distinguished Consideration.

HENRY CLAY.

Copy. DNA, RG59, Notes to Foreign Ministers and Consuls, vol. 3, p. 202 (M38, R3). Formal acknowledgments of the receipt of this circular, and felicitations upon the appointment, were received by Clay on March 11 from Antonio José Cañaz (see below, that date); the Baron Durand de Mareuil (LS. DNA, RG59, Notes from French Legation, vol. 9 [M53, R7]); José Silvester Rebello (LS. DNA, RG59, Notes from

Brazilian Legation, vol. 1 [M49, R1]); José Maria Salazar (LS. DNA, RG59, Notes
from Colombian Legation, vol. 1 [M51, R2]); and the Baron Tuyll (LS. DNA, RG59,
Notes from Russian Legation, vol. 1 [M39, R1]); on March 12 from Pablo Obregón
(LS. DNA, RG59, Notes from Mexican Legation, vol. 1 [M54, R1]); and Hilario de
Rivas y Salmon (LS. DNA, RG59, Notes from Spanish Legation, vol. 8 [M59, R11]);
on March 14 from Peter Pedersen (see below, that date).

From Nicholas Biddle

Dear Sir   Philada. March 10th 1825.

As my occupation brings me into some familiarity with the trade
between the United States and Mexico, and renders our intercourse
with that Country an object of peculiar attention, I take the liberty
of bringing to your notice a circumstance in relation to it, which
has recently excited some uneasiness here. Our Merchants have
hitherto found in Mexico a valuable market for our domestic
cotton goods, which have in consequence been sent there in considerable quantities. Not long since as one of the exporters assured
me there were shipped from Philada. in the course of three weeks
more than $140.000 worth of these articles all of American and the
greater part of Philadelphia manufacture and the trade appeared so
promising, that prepartions [sic] were made for carrying it on
upon a much larger scale. A vessel however has within a few days
arrived from Alvarado, with intelligence, that the Custom House
of that place has demanded double the duty hitherto paid.—that the
Americans had refused to pay it, but had sent an appeal to the Government at Mexico, and that until the decision was known the
goods were placed in depot ready to be reshipped to the U. S. in case
the double duty should be exacted, as the article would not bear the
additional charge on it. This sudden increase of duty on American
manufactures is ascribed by our Merchants to the ascendancy of
the English interest—and they believe, though they do not know
the fact that an equal duty is not charged on English goods of the
same description. This last consideration is however of great importance. It would certainly be unfortunate if this growing branch
of commerce were destroyed by excessive duties, yet if these be general and applicable to all similar fabrics it is a cause rather of
regret than complaint. But a distinction to the disadvantage of this
Country is equally injurious and insidious, and it would be very
hard indeed if England after a tardy acknowledgment of an independence which we were the first to proclaim should be able thus
early to infuse into the legislation of Mexico any jealousy of our
commerce. The late Mexican papers which I have seen, contain no
act of the Congress on that subject, and the arrivals from Alvarado
which are daily expected will probably bring some more satisfactory
information. In the meantime I have thought it right to state to

you the fact that American vessels, with American manufactures were according to the last accounts awaiting the decision of the Mexican Government on a charge of duties on those manufactures double that heretofore paid, and which if enforced must put an end to the exportation of those goods to Mexico. It will be for your consideration how far this state of things may require any explanations from Mr Obregon[1] or any instructions to Mr Poinsett.[2] The gentlemen aggrieved had actually prepared a memorial to the Government on this subject, but on considering it last evening some difference of opinion arose as to the introduction of other causes of complaint against the Mexican Government to which some persons present objected, and the memorial was not adopted. It is however too important in a national point of view to be neglected, and I therefore promised two of our most respectable merchants, who have more than $70.000 of goods affected by this change of duty that I would present the object to your attention. If any apology be needed for this trouble you will I am sure readily find it in my solicitude for the public interests with which you are now so conspicuously charged and in the consideration and regard with which I am Yours   N BIDDLE
Hon: Henry Clay   Secretary of State   Washington

Copy. DLC-Nicholas Biddle Papers, President's Letter Book, 216-17 (DNA, M212, R20).
1 Pablo Obregón, Mexican Minister to the United States, who had arrived in this country in the fall of 1824.
2 Joel R. Poinsett, appointed on March 8, 1825, as Minister to Mexico.

INSTRUCTIONS AND DISPATCHES   March 10, 1825

To RICHARD RUSH, no. 1. Informs him of his appointment as Secretary of the Treasury and requests his return to the United States no later than June. Encloses "Letters of recredence, to be used on . . . taking leave; when . . . [he is to] assure the British Government that the President is animated with a sincere desire to to [sic] maintain, and, if possible, to give fresh vigour, to the amicable relations which happily exist between the two Governments." This communication is being carried by George S. Watkins, as special messenger. Copy. DNA, RG59, Dip. Instr., vol. 10, pp. 224-25 (M77, R5). Another version, ALS draft, may be found in DCL-HC (DNA, M212, R7). Watkins was appointed a clerk in the State Department May 8, 1827, and held that post until discharged by the Jackson administration, effective May 1, 1829. His name was inserted in this document in place of that of Edward Wyer, crossed out. See below, Clay to Adams, March 11, 1825.

From ROBERT MONROE HARRISON, Antigua. Reports condemnation of the brig *Liberty* of Kennebunk (Maine) at this place on February 7 and the requirement that full tonnage be paid on it despite the fact that it had been forced into harbor "by distress of weather, and in a sinking state. . . ." ALS. DNA, RG59, Cons. Disp., Antiqua, vol. 1 (M-T327, R1). Addressed to John Quincy Adams, Secretary of State; received April 25. Harrison, a Virginian and former naval officer (1799-1801), had held posts as United States consul on the islands of St. Thomas (appointed in 1816) and St. Bartholomew (appointed in 1821) before assuming the same position for the islands of St. Christopher and Antigua in 1823. He returned to the consular office at St. Bartholomew from 1827 to 1831, when he was transferred to Kingston, Jamaica, where he died in 1858.

MISCELLANEOUS LETTERS   March 10, 1825

From MATHEW CAREY, RICHARD PETERS, JR., and JOSEPH HEMPHILL, on behalf of the Pennsylvania Society for the Promotion of Internal Improvements, Philadelphia. Ask Clay for a letter of introduction for William Strickland, who goes to Europe as agent of the Society to study canals, railways, roads, and bridges. Attested by Gerard Ralston, corresponding secretary. LS. DNA, RG59, Misc. Letters (M179, R62). Peters, son of Judge Richard Peters, was solicitor of Philadelphia County before succeeding Henry Wheaton as United States Supreme Court Reporter, in 1827. His numerous compilations and other works include *Reports of Cases in the Supreme Court of the United States, 1828 to 1842* (16 vols., 1828-1842). Strickland, an artist, engineer, and architect, is best remembered for his work in the field of Greek Revival architecture. His early training had been under Benjamin H. Latrobe.

APPLICATIONS, RECOMMENDATIONS   March 10, 1825

JAMES WILLIAMS, "Stafford near Port Deposit," Maryland, solicits appointment as receiver or register of public lands in East Florida. ALS. DNA, RG59, A. and R. (MR1). Williams, formerly a prominent merchant of Baltimore, did not receive an appointment. On March 16 Daniel Brent replied that he had been directed by the Secretary to state "that it is not the present purpose of the Executive to open a Land Office in East Florida or make appointments for such an Office immediately. . . ." Copy, in DNA, RG59, Dom. Letters, vol. 21, pp. 5-6 (M40, R19).

To [John Quincy Adams]

Dear Sir   11 Mar. 1825.

Mr. Wyer declines being messenger to England,[1] and has given publicity, I understand, in the City, to the offer and to the fact of his declining it.

Dr. Watkins[2] would be gratified if his son George S. was designated for that service. Altho' I have not thought it very necessary to send the despatch to Mr. Rush,[3] by a special messenger, perhaps the facts that, in a former instance, that was done, and the *publicity* given in this to what was contemplated might make it expedient. If you think so, I should be glad if Dr. Watkins's son could be employed on the occasion.   Your obedient Servant

The President.   H. CLAY

ALS. MHi-Adams Papers, Letters Received (MR468).
[1] See above, Clay to Rush, March 10, 1825, note.
[2] Tobias Watkins.   [3] Above, March 10, 1825.

From Nicholas Biddle

Dear Sir,   Bank of the United States March 11. 1825
    Your letter of the 8th inst. is received. Though prepared to anticipate the contents of it, and already apprized by you personally that your services would not be required after the present year, I cannot see without regret the dissolution of your professional connection with the Bank. I have long known & appreciated your services, & have uniformly borne a willing testimony, that the remuneration for them, liberal as it was designed to be, has been amply earned. To myself individually, it has been a source of great satisfaction to repose with such entire reliance on your abilities & judgment in managing the important concerns entrusted to you. These sentiments are shared by all who have been charged with the administration of the Bank—and I am accordingly instructed, by an unanimous vote of the Board this day, to convey to you the expression of their entire satisfaction at the able & faithful manner in which you have uniformly discharged your professional duties to the institution. Wishing you the same success in the new & brilliant career on which you are entering, I remain,
                With great respect Yrs   N BIDDLE   Prest.
Honble Henry Clay   Secretary of State   Washington Cola.

ALS. DLC-HC (DNA, M212, R1).

From Antonio José Cañaz

Washington Marzo 11 de 1825.
Legon. del centro de america
Honorl. Sor. Henry Clay Secretario de Estado.
Por la nota[1] con que el Sr. Clay me favo recio el dia de ayer, he tenido la pura satisfaccion de saber que se haya posesionado del alto destino de Secretario de Estado de este Supremo Gobierno para que fue nombrado.
    Si toda la Union debe prometerse las conciderables ventajas que producira el sabis desempeño de tan importante negociado digno de las acreditadas manos del Sr. Clay, la America toda del sur i del centro que ha visto en él el amigo de su independencia, debe penetrarse de gozo i congratularse al verlo elevado al destino a que lo llamó su merito.
    Yo le felicito cordialmente en nombre de la america del centro que tengo el honor de representar; i me lisonjeo con la satisfaccion de que en lo sucsesivo [sic] los negocios entre esta nacion i la de Guatemala serán inmediatamente attendidos por la direccion i tino del Sor. Clay, quien se sevirá aceptar la particular consideracion con quele ofrece sus respectos.   ANTONIO JOSE CANAZ

LS, with trans. in State Department file. DNA, RG59, Notes from Central American Legation, vol. 1 (M-T34, R1). Cañaz, who had been a deputy from San Vicente in the General Congress of El Salvador during 1822, had arrived in the United States late in December, 1824, as the first Minister Plenipotentiary from the Federation (or United Provinces) of Central America. This state, from 1821 to 1823 a part of Mexico, had declared its independence by action of assembly in Guatemala City, on July 1, 1823. The unstable union disintegrated in 1838. Cañaz remained in the United States until the summer of 1826, when, because of ill health, he returned home. He subsequently held a variety of governmental offices, including the position of Chief of State for El Salvador from 1839 to 1840, following the breakup of the Federation.

1 See above, March 10, 1825.

INSTRUCTIONS AND DISPATCHES   March 11, 1825

From CONDY RAGUET, Rio de Janeiro. States that (Thomas) Cochrane, upon his arrival at Maranham (Maranhão) in November, had found a civil war underway between two factions, both "under the Imperial flag." Notes the desire of the Brazilian "Government to assume the rank of a naval power," the success of Brazil's application for a foreign loan, and indications of a revival of freedom of the press. Cites anticipation that the arrival of Charles Stuart will mean adjustment of affairs between Brazil and Portugal. Speculates that a commercial treaty between Great Britain and Brazil would mean exclusive advantages to the former country and abolition of the slave trade; reports local news that a treaty has been signed between Britain and the Government of Buenos Aires. Discusses the effect upon Brazil of news of the defeat of the (Spanish) Royalist army in Peru. Transmits copies of Raguet's representations to the Brazilian authorities concerning imprisonment of an American, James Hude Rodgers (Rogers), for participation in the rebellion at Pernambuco, and seizure of two American vessels, the *Spermo* and the *Exchange*. ALS. DNA, RG59, Cons. Disp., Rio de Janeiro, vol. 2 (M-T172, R3). Addressed to Secretary of State; received May 2. Raguet, United States consul at Rio de Janeiro since 1822, was a native of Philadelphia. He had engaged in mercantile business, fought in the War of 1812, practiced law, served briefly in the Pennsylvania Senate, and published a study on money. Returning to the United States in 1827, he was later editor of newspapers in Philadelphia and Washington and author of books and articles on currency, banking, and free trade, which established his reputation as an economist.

Cochrane, named Marquis of Maranham upon assumption of his duties as commander of the Brazilian Navy, had undertaken in the fall of 1824 to put down rebellion, centering at Pernambuco, in the northern provinces. He remained in this area until late in the spring, when, upon the ground that his crew was sickly, he set sail for the North Atlantic and, in June, arrived off England. The Brazilian Minister, to whom he there presented a request for supplies, complained that Cochrane had deserted the service and stolen the vessel. As the admiral remained in England, his crew was ordered to return without him. In November Cochrane finally submitted his resignation.

Sir Charles Stuart (created Baron Stuart de Rothesay in 1828), who had begun his diplomatic career as British Chargé d'Affaires at Madrid in 1808, had served as British Ambassador to Paris from 1815 until the autumn of 1824. In the spring of 1825 he served as mediator in the settlement by which Portugal recognized the independence of Brazil (which had been asserted at San Paulo on September 7, 1822) and the establishment of Dom Pedro, eldest son and heir to John VI of Portugal, as the constitutional Emperor of Brazil. Under the terms of the treaty, dated August 29, 1825, John first assumed the title Emperor of Brazil, then renounced the throne in favor of his son, while the Brazilian

Government undertook to pay some £2,000,000 as compensation to Portugal.

A treaty of friendship, navigation, and commerce between Great Britain and the United Provinces of Río de la Plata, concluded February 19, 1825, had provided for reciprocity of most-favored-nation arrangements, with the British conceding these privileges in respect to both their "dominions in Europe, and other parts of the world," and with mutual concession of freedom of worship. The United Provinces agreed, however, to prohibit those subject to their jurisdiction, "in the most effectual manner, and by the most solemn laws, from taking any part in the" slave traffic. *Annual Register, 1825,* "Public Documents," 84-87. On the treaty between Great Britain and Brazil, see below, Raguet to Clay, October 26, 1825, note.

Defeat of the Spanish Royalists in Peru at Junín, in August, and at Ayacucho, in December, 1824, had virtually terminated the Latin-American war for independence.

James Hude Rodgers (Rogers), of New York, who had been serving as a warrant officer in the Brazilian Navy, had been convicted and sentenced to death for participation on the side of the Brazilian natives against the Portuguese supporters of the Imperial Government at Pernambuco. His case having been recommended by the court to the mercy of the Emperor, clemency was denied on March 16 and the young man was executed.

The *Spermo,* of New York, had been seized in August, 1824, while in the harbor of Pernambuco, when Brazilian authorities had reimposed a blockade without advance notice. The claim was finally settled in full by the Brazilian Government under a convention negotiated in 1849. The *Exchange,* of Boston, had been taken ten miles off the coast of Brazil, in November, 1824, and claimed as a prize because she was carrying gunpowder not included in the manifest. A lower court at Bahia had ordered return of the vessel, with damages, but the case was under appeal.

MISCELLANEOUS LETTERS   March 11, 1825

From SAMUEL KEITH, Philadelphia. Requests Clay to urge (Richard C.) Anderson (Jr.) to obtain payment of a claim on Colombia "for an unwarrantable Capture, of the Cargo of the Schooner Minerva. . . ." LS. DNA, RG76, Misc. Claims, Colombia. Keith signs as president of the Delaware Insurance Company. See below, Anderson to Secretary of State, March 18, 1825.

The *Minerva* had been captured by a Venezuelan vessel near Santiago, Cuba, in June, 1820, on the ground that the cargo was Spanish. The schooner had subsequently been ordered released, with freight charges to be paid for the cargo from the proceeds of its sale. Neither order had been carried out.

APPLICATIONS, RECOMMENDATIONS   March 11, 1825

PHILIP J. BARZIZA, Williamsburg, Virginia, congratulates Clay upon his elevation to the office of Secretary of State and solicits "the appointment of Consul at Tangiers on the Coast of Barbary if vaccant [*sic*] or to any port of South America." He is a citizen of the United States and can obtain recommendations from the Virginia delegation in both houses of Congress and from Thomas Jefferson. The letter continues:

"At Sight of my name it is probable you will not hold me a total stranger; But least the multiplicity of your occupations might have obbliterated [*sic*] me from your memory; Permit me to remind you of a Young Man, who in the Spring of the year 1815 had the honor to be introduced to you in London, and who at that time asked your advice on certain claims to Landed, and personal Estate of his Ancestors in Virginia.

"Well, and greatfully do I remember your kind reception, and the promptitude with which you favored me with your friendly Counsil [*sic*]. I have been however contrary to the opinions of Eminent Lawyers in this state, frustrated in my hopes; and hafter [*sic*] ten years of an expensive Law suit I find myself with a Large family in a Situation different from what I had expected and my abbandoned [*sic*] pretensions in Europe ensured.

"I am induced therefore to be an applicant for office as well for the means of Support, as from a desire to devote some part of my Life to the Service of the country of my Ancestors, and of my adoption."

ALS. DNA, RG59, A. and R. (MR1). Barziza, son of Count Philip J. Barziza, of Venice, was through his mother a descendant of the Ludwell family of Virginia. Young Barziza had settled in Williamsburg around 1816. He did not receive a Federal appointment. In a note dated March 16, 1825, Daniel Brent, at Clay's direction, acknowledged receipt of the young man's letter and informed him "that the United States now have, as they have long had, a Consul residing at Tangier [see below, Salmon to Clay, March 16, 1825, note]—[and] with respect to an appointment in South America . . . that there is no vacancy, known to this Department, worth the acceptance of any one." Copy. DNA, RG59, Dom. Letters, vol. 21, p. 8 (M40, R19).

WILLIAM DRAYTON, Charleston, South Carolina, asks for appointment to a consulship in France or England. ALS. DNA, RG59, Misc. Letters (M179, R62). Drayton, who had been an officer in the War of 1812, was judge of the city court of Charleston. Later in the year he was elected to succeed Joel R. Poinsett in Congress, where he served until 1833. He then moved to Philadelphia.

To Nicholas Biddle

Sir   Washington 12h. Mar. 1825

I received and thank you for your communication respecting the duty to which American Cotton fabrics are supposed to have been recently subjected in Mexico.[1] It has come to hand at the moment when I happen to be engaged in preparing instructions for our Minister lately appointed to that Republic,[2] and shall receive, as shall all other similar communications with which you may honor me, the particular attention of your obliged and Obedient Servant

Nicholas Biddle Esqr.   H. CLAY

ALS. DLC-Nicholas Biddle Papers (DNA, M212, R20). Endorsed: ". . . recd. March 16. 1825."
[1] See above, March 10, 1825.   [2] See below, Clay to Poinsett, March 26, 1825.

From N. C. Findlay

Sir,   Chambersbg[1] March 12th. 1825.

Accept of my good wishes on your being admitted one of the Cabinet of the Nation, hoping you may prove not only an honour to yourself, but usefull to the Nation at large, and the West in particular, as well as to act that part that will be agreeable to your friends, and be efficient in doing away the [*sic*] slander of your enemies— —Not knowing from the extensive patronage of the Office you have the honour to hold, but it may be in your power to bestow a Clerkship, which from my misfortunes in Ohio would be acceptable—and would hope that if you have it in your power, that you feel the disposition to confer one on me that would enable me to make *a genteel & honest support,* and should you grant me an appointment, it would be one I hope you would not regret, as well as one that would be acceptable to a number of *your political,* and *our* personal friends of OHio—

With good wishes and prayers for your health & happiness, Yr., friend
The Honble Henry Clay Secy of State   N., C. FINDLAY

P.S. Understanding that Genl. Harrison was still a candidate for Minister to Mexico, I thought it probable from your influence in his favour that he might be appointed, but it appears that he has not received the appointment[2]—   N. C. F—

ALS. DNA, RG59, A. and R. (MR2). Findlay, probably related to the politically prominent brothers, James, John, and William Findlay, did not receive an appointment.
[1] Pennsylvania.
[2] On the appointment of Joel R. Poinsett, instead of William Henry Harrison, see above, Biddle to Clay, March 10, 1825, note.

MISCELLANEOUS LETTERS   March 12, 1825

From THOMAS MORRIS, New York. Notes that his absence from this city has prevented earlier acknowledgment of the receipt of a letter from (John Quincy) Adams, dated February 3, giving notice of Morris' reappointment as marshal of the district, and states that the commission has been received from Judge (William P.) Van Ness. Congratulates Clay on his appointment "to the very important & distinguished Office in which" he has "recently been placed." Requests delivery of a letter to Morris' son, Robert, in Washington. ALS. DNA, RG59, A. and R. (MR1). Robert Morris, who had served as an ensign in the War of 1812, has not been further identified.

From ROBERT OLIVER, Baltimore. Encloses "an open letter" from Christopher Hughes, to which an early answer is requested. States that he (Oliver) and (Samuel) Smith think "Mr. Hughes presence here, is *now* necessary" and they hope he may be permitted to return home before assuming his new duties at Brussels. ALS. DNA, RG59, Dip. Disp., Sweden and Norway, vol. 4 (M45, R5). See below, Clay to Smith, March 17, 1825. Hughes' letter, dated November 18, 1824, and addressed to John Quincy Adams, as Secretary of State, reports that he has been informed of the death of his father (Christopher Hughes, Sr., Baltimore merchant) and requests leave from his post for six months.

APPLICATIONS, RECOMMENDATIONS   March 12, 1825

ROBERT ANDREWS, Philadelphia, solicits appointment as consul at Bordeaux. ALS. DNA, RG59, A. and R. (MR1). Andrews not further identified.

MISCELLANEOUS LETTERS   March 13, 1825

From ISRAEL THORNDIKE, Boston. Presents briefly his claim against the Russian Government in the case of the *Hector,* which had been captured by "a
Russian Frigate . . . in the gulph of Smyrna" in 1807. Requests Clay's attention
to the matter; notes that (Henry) Middleton "has never condescended to answer
any . . . Letters" relative to the claim; and asks Clay to inform (Daniel) Webster
"whether all the papers, respecting this vessel remain" in the State Department.
LS. DNA, RG76, Misc. Claims, Russia. Thorndike, born in Beverly, Massachusetts, had commanded several privateers during the American Revolution and,
from 1788 to 1814, had been a partner in a shipping firm engaged in the China
trade. Long active in Massachusetts politics, he had served thirteen terms in the
legislature, had been a member of the constitutional conventions of 1788 and
1820, and had been chosen a presidential elector in 1812 and 1816. He was
prominent also as a benefactor of Harvard University.

APPLICATIONS, RECOMMENDATIONS   March 13, 1825

O[THO] H. WILLIAMS, Hagerstown (Maryland), solicits some office for his
brother, John S. Williams. ALS. DNA, RG59, A. and R. (MR4). John S. Williams received no appointment but was nominated in February, 1829, to serve
as superintendent of the Cumberland Road from Canton to Zanesville, Ohio.

Settlement with James Smith, Jr.

[March 14, 1825]

Whereas H. Clay during past years has had many collections of
various persons to make for me in Kentucky and other parts of the
Western Country, and has made me, from time to time, sundry
payments on account thereof; and whereas I have agreed with him
to receive Two hundred & fifty dollars in full of all claims and
demands whatever which I have upon him on account of any such
collections, and moreover have agreed that the said sum shall be a
full satisfaction of whatever remains to be collected of any debts
or accounts heretofore put by me in his hands and especially what
may remain due to me from Woodson Wren of the State of Mississippi; all of which, when collected are to accrue to the exclusive
benefit of the said Clay. Now I do hereby acknowledge the receipt
of the said Sum of Two hundred & fifty dollars and do hereby
assign and transfer to the said Clay all such debts or balances as are
due from the said Woodson Wren and others as aforesaid to me, but
this assignment is without any sort of recourse upon me. Witness
my hand & seal this fourteenth[1] day of March 1825.
Witness Ed: E: Law.[2]   JAS SMITH JR {LS}

DS, in Clay's hand (exception noted). DLC-TJC (DNA, M212, R16).
[1] This word in Smith's hand.   [2] Not identified.

From Simon Gratz and Brother

Honle Henry Clay   Philadelphia March 14. 1825
Dear Sir
We have reinsured at the Pensy. fire Insurance Company the house occupied by the late Colo Morrison for Four thousand Dollars Premium & policy Twenty one Dollars—
Very Respectfully Your Obt Sevts   SIMON GRATZ & BROTHER

ALS. DLC-TJC (DNA, M212, R13).

DIPLOMATIC NOTES   March 14, 1825

From PETER PEDERSEN, Philadelphia. Acknowledges receipt of Clay's note of March 10; extends congratulations on his appointment as Secretary of State; and states that, if the Government of the United States be disposed to negotiate a commercial convention with Denmark, Pedersen now has full powers to sign one. ALS. DNA, RG59, Notes from Danish Legation, vol. 1 (M52, R1). Pedersen, who had served as consul general and Chargé d'Affaires to the United States *ad interim* from 1803 to 1815, remained as Minister Resident from 1815 to 1830.

MISCELLANEOUS LETTERS   March 14, 1825

From W[ILLIAM] BROWNE, Department of State, Washington. Outlines his duties as a clerk. ALS. DNA, RG59, Misc. Letters (M179, R62). Browne had been hired in October, 1823; he was discharged under the Jackson administration, in May, 1829.

From LANGDON CHEVES, Office of the Board of Commissioners under the Convention of St. Petersburg. Refers to a letter dated February 19, 1825, from Cheves to Clay's predecessor in office (John Quincy Adams), requesting instructions on a specific point; notes that Cheves on February 25 presented an argument in the case of John Couper of Georgia, supporting the claim for interest, a copy of the journal entry of which document is here enclosed; and encloses a copy of an argument submitted by (Edward) Livingston, also on February 25, on the same topic. ALS. DNA, RG76, G.B.9-Folder 8. True copy of the journal extract of the argument of Cheves, *ibid.*; the Livingston argument, not found.
   In his letter to Adams on February 19, Cheves had requested instruction regarding whether he should accede to the insistence of George Jackson, the British Commissioner, that the latter should "prescribe" the points of controversy to be brought before arbitration under Article 5 of the St. Petersburg Convention (see above, III, 736n; Rush to the Secretary of State, March 8, 1825; and below, Clay to King, May 10, 1825). The issue had arisen when the British Commissioner declined to submit the American claimants' demands for interest to such a determination. Copy, in DNA, RG76, Indemnity for Slaves.
   Couper (Cowper), born in Scotland, had emigrated to Georgia in 1792 and shortly thereafter settled on St. Simon's Island. He had listed 55 slaves as carried off by the British after the conclusion of the War of 1812.

From RICHARD FORREST. Similar in content to the letter from Browne to Clay, above, this date. ALS. DNA, RG59, Misc. Letters (M179, R62). Forrest, born in Maryland, had been attached to the State Department for nearly twenty years and retained his position until his death in October, 1828.

From GEORGE E. IRONSIDE. Similar in content to the letter from Browne to Clay, above, this date. Notes that the information is supplied in response to Clay's request (not found). ALS. *Ibid.* Ironside, an expert in the Spanish language, had been hired in November, 1820, and remained in the State Department until his death in May, 1827.

From JOSIAS W. KING. Similar in content to the letters from Browne to Clay and Ironside to Clay, above, this date. ALS. *Ibid.* King had been a clerk for the past decade and remained in the Department through the first years of the Jackson administration.

From ANDREW T. McCORMICK. Similar in content to the letter from Browne to Clay, above, this date. ALS. *Ibid.* Born in Ireland, McCormick had resided in Washington since 1796 and had been minister of the First Episcopal Congregation and clerk in the State Department since 1818. He remained with the Department for another decade.

From LINNAEUS SMITH. Similar in content to the letter from Browne to Clay, above, this date. ALS. *Ibid.* Smith had been hired in October, 1822, and remained with the State Department until the spring of 1829, when he became mentally deranged, reportedly from worry occasioned by the dismissals of the Jackson administration. Adams, *Memoirs,* VIII, 144, 147.

From WILLIAM THORNTON, Patent Office, Department of State. Presents his defense against the attack on his office by Peter A. Browne (see above, Browne to Clay, March 7, 1825) and requests Clay's ruling on the matter. ALS. DNA, RG59, Misc. Letters (M179, R62).

From TH[OMAS] L. THRUSTON. Similar in content to the letter from Browne to Clay, above, this date. ALS. *Ibid.* The date of the Thruston letter is supplied by the editors. Thruston had been hired in May, 1818, and was discharged under the Jackson administration, in April, 1829.

APPLICATIONS, RECOMMENDATIONS   March 14, 1825

WILLIAM H. BRISCOE, Chaptico, St. Mary's County, Maryland, pleads a previous acquaintance with Clay and membership of both Clay and himself in "the ancient society of free and accepted masons" as basis for his application for office in the State Department; states that he has already requested a "mutual friend the Hob. R. Neale" to write a letter of recommendation (below, March 15, 1825); and notes that other recommendations may be had from Doctor Joseph Kent, Charles F. Mercer, Henry Ashford, Judge (Gabriel) Duvall, and Briscoe's "half brother Edmund Key Esq. Judge of the Lower district Court of Maryland." ALS. DNA, RG59, A. and R. (MR1). Postmarked at Leonardtown, Maryland. Raphael Neale, of Leonardtown, had been a member of the United States House of Representatives from 1819 to 1825. Briscoe did not receive an appointment.

EDWARD B. BROOKING, Spring Grove, Georgia, though not acquainted personally with Clay, asks him to recommend a nephew, James Henry Brooking, who lives in or near Winchester, Kentucky, for "a cadetship in the Academy at West Point." ALS. DNA, RG59, Misc. Letters (M179, R62). Endorsed by Daniel Brent: "Referred respectfully to the Dept. of War— As soon as Circumstances will permit, it would be very agreeable to Mr Clay, if Mr. Barbour could give this young Gentleman a warrant at [sic] Cadet." Brooking, nevertheless, did not enter the Academy.

On March 31, Daniel Brent, at Clay's direction, acknowledged receipt of Brooking's letter, "which a little indisposition, with a pressure of other business of more urgency" prevented Clay from doing, informed Brooking of Clay's effort in the young man's behalf, but warned that it was "very doubtful whether his request can be complied with for some time. . . ." Copy in DNA, RG59, Dom. Letters, vol. 21, pp. 19-20 (M40, R19).

ZACHEUS FLINT, JR., Burlington, Otsego County, New York, solicits "a situation as Clk in one of the departments of Government" and names, as a reference, William G. Angel, Congressman from New York (1825-1827, 1829-1833), under whose direction Flint is reading law. ALS. DNA, RG59, A. and R. (MR2). Flint did not receive an appointment.

Draft by James Smith, Jr.

250 Dollars   Philada. March 15h. 1825
    At sight please pay to the Order of S & M Allens & Co.[1] Two hundred and Fifty Dollars— as advised by Yr. Friend
                                                          JAS SMITH JR
Honble. Henry Clay   City of Washington
[Endorsement on verso][2]
Pay the amt. of the within to the Cashr. of the Off. of Dt & Dt. of Washn.   H. Clay Exor of James Morrison
To the Cashr. Off. of D & Dt Washn.[3]

ADS. DLC-TJC (DNA, M212, R16). See above, Settlement, March 14, 1825. Endorsed on verso: "S & M Allen & Co."
    1 Founded by Solomon and Moses Allen in New York in 1815, as dealers in lottery tickets and exchange, but subsequently expanded with branches in most of the leading cities.   2 AES.   3 Richard Smith.

From Josephus B. Stuart

My dear Sir.   New York. 15th. March 1825.
    Since my return I have been solicited by the friends of most of the papers in this City, to reccommend [sic] each one of them to you as printers of the Laws & Notices of the U.S.:—the designation of which, it is understood belongs to you.

    Heretofore, I believe [sic], the National Advocate & New York American were the two designated by Mr. Adams—but when we got 2 Advocates,[1] & it was difficult to distinguish the real Simon Pure, the Navy Commissioners have directed their notices to be published in the *American & Commercial Advertizer*.[2] At first I thought it not worth while to trouble you with a line on this subject, but on consulting with Worth & Lynch,[3] they thought it best that you should know our opinion—which is *to let it remain where it now is:* at least for a time.—Early in May a meeting will be called in this City of the friends of the Administration as now formed; at which, measures will be adopted to organize committees in all the districts which shall insure the election of Republicans to our next Legislature who are friendly to the Administration. At this meeting we shall adopt a paper in this City.—

Your acceptance as Secretary gives almost universal satisfaction in this City.—

I think Mr. Clinton will go to London.[4]— The Ohio Commissioners are here, & will have no difficulty in getting money on fair terms.[5]— Yours with great regard   J, B, STUART. Honbl. H. Clay.

ALS. DNA, RG59, P. and D. of L.
[1] When political and financial difficulties forced sale of the "Establishment" of the New York *National Advocate*, edited by M. M. Noah, in December, 1824, he retained possession of the building and claimed continuation of editorial proprietorship. During the next year he issued a journal styled the *New York National Advocate* in competition with the former publication, now edited by Thomas Snowden.
[2] New York *Commercial Advertiser* (1797-1904).
[3] Gorham A. Worth, who around 1822 had left the service of the United States Bank and returned to his home city, Albany; probably General James Lynch, of New York City, a lawyer and a leading tariff advocate.
[4] On February 18 Adams had offered DeWitt Clinton the mission as United States Minister to Great Britain. Clinton had declined the appointment on February 25. Cf. below, Stuart to Clay, March 29, 1825, note.
[5] By act of February 4, 1825, the Ohio Legislature had authorized construction of canals from Lake Erie to the Ohio River by way of the Cuyahoga and Scioto Rivers (known as the Ohio and Erie Canal) and by way of the Maumee and Miami (the Miami and Erie Canal). Commissions were authorized to borrow up to $400,000 the first year and not over $600,000 in any succeeding year, at interest not to exceed six per cent, in exchange for stock certificates to mature at periods ranging from 1850 to 1875. John Kilbourn (comp.), *Public Documents Concerning the Ohio Canals* . . . (Columbus, 1828), 158-66 *passim.*

INSTRUCTIONS AND DISPATCHES   March 15, 1825

To the MINISTERS, CONSULS, and PUBLIC AGENTS OF THE UNITED STATES IN EUROPE, a circular. Written at the direction of the President, requests that "your friendly offices and every convenient facility" be extended to William Strickland. Copy. DNA, RG59, Dip. Instr., vol. 10, pp. 246-47 (M77, R5). Another version, AL draft, is located in DLC-HC (DNA, M212, R7). Cf. above, Carey and others to Clay, March 10, 1825.

MISCELLANEOUS LETTERS   March 15, 1825

From JOHN MARTIN BAKER. Outlines his duties as clerk in the State Department. ALS. DNA, RG59, Misc. Letters (M179, R62). Baker had been hired in October, 1822, and remained in the position until November, 1831.

From P[ETER] A. BROWNE. Requests reply to his letter of March 7. LS. *Ibid.*
On March 19, Daniel Brent, "by direction of the Secretary," acknowledged
receipt of Browne's letters of March 5 and 15 and promised attention to the
matter "as soon as more important duties will admit of." Copy, in DNA, RG59,
Dom. Letters, vol. 21, pp. 9-10 (M40, R19).

From WILLIAM SLADE, JR. Similar in content to the letter from Baker, above,
this date. ALS. DNA, RG59, Misc. Letters (M179, R62). Slade had practiced
law, edited a newspaper, and held office as county judge and secretary of state
in Vermont. He was a clerk in the Department of State from 1823 to 1829;
later a member of the United States House of Representatives (1831-1843)
and Governor of Vermont (1844-1846). He had compiled and published a
volume of *Vermont State Papers* (1823) and *The Laws of Vermont of a
Publick and Permanent Nature* (1825).

From WILLIAM C. SOMERVILLE. Sends his address as "Baltimore," pending his
departure for Sweden. ALS. DNA, RG59, Dip. Disp., Sweden and Norway,
vol. 4 (M45, R5). Somerville, a native of St. Mary's County, Maryland, who
had fought in the struggle for South American independence and traveled
extensively in Europe, had been appointed on March 9 as Chargé d'Affaires for
the United States in Sweden. His writings include *Letters from Paris, on the
Causes and Consequences of the French Revolution* (Baltimore, 1822).

From PETER W. SPROAT, Philadelphia. Notes that in August (1824) he sent
"J. Q. Adams several Documents relative to the dentention [*sic*] of the Morning
Star for indemnity"; sends "duplicates, as the others were mislaid or lost"; and
adds: "Please to give instructions." ALS. DNA, RG76, Misc. Claims, Spain.
An enclosure reveals that the detention of the vessel had occurred at Pernambuco
in February, 1818. Sproat not identified.
On March 19, Daniel Brent, "by direction of the Secretary," acknowledged
receipt of Sproat's letter. Copy, in DNA, RG59, Dom. Letters, vol. 21, p. 11
(M40, R19).

APPLICATIONS, RECOMMENDATIONS   March 15, 1825

ARCHIBALD BARD, Franklin County, Pennsylvania, recommends for "a clerkship
in a respectable office under the Government," his "neighbour," David Fullerton,
formerly a Pennsylvania Congressman (1819-1820); states that a further recommendation may be obtained from Matthew St. Clair Clarke; and assures Clay
"that notwithstanding the base and wicked conduct of that silley creature G
Kremer to arouse public feeling & the part taken by Genl. Jackson and his
partisans I have not a doubt but your appointment by our friend the President
is the most pleasing to the generall mass of the people that he could possibly
have made. . . ." ALS. DNA, RG59, A. and R. (MR2). Bard was several
times a member of the Pennsylvania Legislature, held a judicial position, and
filled other offices on a local level. Fullerton, who did not receive a Federal
appointment, became a member of the Pennsylvania Senate from 1827 to 1839.
In addition to his earlier statements (see above, Clay to Gales and Seaton,
January 30, 1825, note; Kremer to Clay, *ca.* February 3, 1825; Appeal, February
3, 1825, note), George Kremer had published in the *Washington Gazette* of
February 28, 1825, an address "To the Electors of the Ninth Congressional
District of the State of Pennsylvania," dated February 25. Referring to Clay's
acceptance of the Secretaryship of State, Kremer said: "Surely Mr. Clay must

have been compelled by some fatal madness to take this step, which lays open the motives of his conduct, and gives the seal of truth to the charges I have made against him."

RAPHAEL NEALE, Leonardtown, Maryland, recommends William H. Briscoe for an appointment. ALS. DNA, RG59, A and R. (MR1).

DAVID and SETH PAINE, editors of the *Portland Advertiser and Gazette of Maine,* apply for appointment as printers of the laws of the United States. ALS by David Paine. DNA, RG59, P. and D. of L. David Paine, born in Eastham, Massachusetts, had settled in Portland; he later removed to Athens, Pennsylvania. Seth was probably his son. The *Portland Gazette,* established in 1798, and the *Portland Advertiser,* begun in 1823, had been combined in January, 1825. The Paines did not obtain the contract for public printing.

J[OHN] S. WILLIAMS, "Highlands, near Baltimore," Maryland, applies "for some public employment, for which" he thinks himself "better adapted, than for turning the clods of sterile soil," and states that his "family connexions & the services rendered our Country by some of them, are perfectly familiar to" Clay. ALS. DNA, RG59, A. and R. (MR4). See above, O[tho] H. Williams to Clay, March 13, 1825, note; below, Kent to Clay, March 23, 1825.

From J[oseph] A[nderson]

The Honble Henry Clay, late Speaker &ca   16th March 1825
    Sir,
    Your account for paying compensation and mileage to the Members of the House of Representatives of the United States, at the 2d Session of the 18th Congress, including your own compensation & the Salary of the Chaplain, has been adjusted at the Treasury; and a balance of $12,698 60/100 found due from you to the United States.   With great respect   J. A.

Copy. DNA, RG217, Records of First Comptroller, Misc. Letters Sent, vol. 22, p. 323.

From Caleb Atwater

Sir,   Circleville March 16, 1825.
    On your arrival in this town from Columbus, immediately after the trial of the U. S. Bank case, against Ohio,[1] you remarked in my hearing, that "I wished to belong to your party, but you would not permit me to belong to it." From that day to this, I have not belonged to *your party* and the late election shows that my opposition was zealous, persevering and not without its effect, either in this, or the surrounding states. Before the period alluded to, when you drove me away from you, I had written and published a pamphlet[2] in a distant city, in your favor.

Since the late election (by the people) I have lain perfectly quiet, and propose to do so for some months to come, until I can ascertain what course the administration is about to pursue, after which time, I shall either support, or oppose it, with vigor, if not with effect.

It is quite probable that, placed as you now are, at the head of the government, (*in reality,*) my friendship or ill will, my support or opposition, are both alike to you. If so, burn this letter, without reading the remainder of it. If on the other hand, you do not feel, entirely indifferent on the subject, say so, and let me know, first, whether for supporting Gen. Jackson, I am to be proscribed? Whether Mr. Adams is to be the head of a party, or a president of the United States? Whether, the relations of members of congress, when entirely incapable, are to be appointed to office? Whether, men, who never attend to the duties of their offices, are to be continued in them? Whether, the Augean stable is to be cleansed? Whether, internal Improvements are to be encouraged by the General Government? And finally, what course will the present administration pursue, as to our foreign relations?

Nothing is further from my intentions, in what I have written, above, than a wish to say any thing to wound your feelings. You may think it strange that I write to you at all, but, it is done with a view to conciliation, if that can be brought about, in a fair and honorable manner, otherwise to proceed on with as fair and honorable an opposition.

The relation in which I stand to a great number of my fellow citizens, as it respects this administration, imposes on me, the necessity and propriety of addressing you this note. *This* is confidential and your answer, if you think it worth your attention, enough to write one I will consider and treat as such, under the solemn promise of a MASON[.]

And if you treat me as Mr. A[dams] did *more than once,* by not answ[ering] this, I shall not trouble you agai[n] in the same way, during life. Respectfully your's   CALEB ATWATER.
Hon. H. Clay Esqr   Secy of State.

I have not been able to obtain the Report on the National Armory, on the Western waters,[3] and would feel much obliged to you for a copy, provided you have one to spare to a *Jacksonian.*

ALS. DLC-HC (DNA, M212, R1). MS. torn.
[1] See above, III, 111-16.   [2] Not found.
[3] The "Report of the Commissioners Appointed under the Act of the Third of March, 1823, to Establish a National Armory on the Western Waters" had been transmitted by President Monroe to the United States House of Representatives on January 18, 1825. *House Docs.,* 18 Cong., 2 Sess., no. 55.

DIPLOMATIC NOTES   March 16, 1825

From SEVERIN LORICH, Philadelphia. Notes receipt of a dispatch from his Government, dated December 10, 1824, dealing with complaints which he has earlier presented to the State Department, in notes of July 25 and September 2, 1824, relating to duties imposed upon Swedish vessels and those from the Island of St. Bartholomew in ports of the United States. As evidence of Swedish desire to promote reciprocal trade, cites royal decree of December 9, 1824, rescinding a fine levied against J. Demming, master of the American ship *La Jaronne,* for filing an improper cargo manifest at a Swedish port. States that, under a decree of the Swedish Diet of 1812, the inhabitants of St. Bartholomew are exempt from Swedish legislative authority and that the commercial regulations of the island "differ materially from those of Sweden, foreign vessels being permitted to import the productions of their own and all other countries"; furthermore, that "the Treaty of 1816. between His Majesty and the Government of the United States has at S. Bartholomew been invariably so applied as to permit American vessels to import American as well as foreign productions, upon their paying duties and charges equal with those to which the vessels of the Island are subjected." Requests that under the terms of the act of Congress of January 7, 1824, vessels of St. Bartholomew, "importing from whatever country foreign as well as domestic productions into the United States, may enjoy the benefit of the equalisation of duties and charges." ALS. DNA, RG59, Notes from Swedish Legation, vol. 3 (M60, R2).

From the fall of 1824 to January 17, 1826, Lorich acted as Chargé d'Affaires during the absence of Baron Berndt Robert Gustaf Stackelberg, former Governor of the Island of St. Bartholomew, who held the diplomatic assignment to Washington from 1819 to 1832.

The above-mentioned act of Congress of January 7, 1824, suspended discriminating duties on foreign vessels in American ports in the case of shipping owned by citizens of certain designated governments, those of the Netherlands, Prussia, the Hanseatic cities of Hamburg, Lübeck, and Bremen, Oldenburg, Norway, Sardinia, and Russia, provided American vessels and cargoes should be exempt from discriminating duties in their ports. A similar lifting of such duties was authorized with respect to "goods, wares, and merchandise, imported into the United States. . . , so far as the same respects the produce or manufactures of the territories in Europe, or such produce and manufactures as can only be, or most usually are, first shipped from a port or place in the said territories in Europe. . . , the same being imported in vessels truly and wholly belonging to the subjects or citizens of each of the said nations, respectively, the vessels of each nation importing its own produce and manufactures as aforesaid." The measure also authorized the President to extend such suspension to any foreign nation, by proclamation, upon receipt of evidence that no discrimination was imposed by that country against the vessels and goods of citizens of the United States. 4 *U. S. Stat.,* 2-3; below, Clay to Anderson, September 16, 1825.

On the treaty of commerce of 1816 between the United States and the Kingdom of Sweden and Norway, see above, II, 427-28, note. Separate legislation, approved February 22, 1827, temporarily extended the exemptions under the act of January 7, 1824, with respect to Swedish and Norwegian vessels and those from the Island of St. Bartholomew. 4 *U. S. Stat.,* 206. The temporary nature of this arrangement was eliminated with completion of a new commercial treaty on July 4, 1827, which also specifically included the Island of St. Bartholomew. See below, Appleton to Clay, July 11, 1827.

From HILARIO DE RIVAS Y SALMON, Philadelphia. Complains of the conduct of the American consul in Tangier, "for sheltering and protecting the Revolutionary Spaniards, who, having escaped from Tarifa, had taken refuge in that place . . . and the said Consul not content with admitting them to his house and table, has had the effrontery to solicit from the Government of Morocco personal security for men so unnatural and perverse, giving for that purpose his security in the most positive terms." Transmits copies of the protest to, and answer of, Hugh Nelson, in Madrid, on this matter and requests the recall and punishment of the consul. LS. DNA, RG59, Notes from Spanish Legation, vol. 8 (M59, R11). John Mullowny, of Pennsylvania, United States consul at Tangier from 1820 until his death in 1831, had granted a request by Joseph Morena de Guerro, who held a commission as "Consul of Guatimala for Gibraltar," for the protection of the United States flag. Mullowny's action had been based on a belief, derived from a passage in President Monroe's last message to Congress, "that Guatimala is an independent nation." Mullowny to John Q. Adams, Secretary of State, March 4, 1825, in DNA, RG59, Cons. Disp., Tangier, vol. 4 (M-T61, R4).

INSTRUCTIONS AND DISPATCHES   March 16, 1825

From A[LEXANDER] BURTON, Cádiz. Transmits copy of an order closing the port of Cádiz, from June 1 through the summer (as had been done the previous year), to vessels "coming from the West Indies, the Gulf of Mexico, or other Countries exposed to Yellow Fever—this latter clause is intended to include all ports of the United States, south of Rhode-Island"; also encloses a copy of another order, ending the requirement that masters of foreign vessels give bond "for Merchandize on board of their vessels, in transit"; reports a growing scarcity of grain and a decision, not yet publicized, to open the port to foreign wheat and flour; and notes the activity of French troops in building up the defences of "this Isla." ALS. DNA, RG59, Cons. Disp., Cádiz, vol. 4 (M-T186, R4). Addressed to Secretary of State; received May 6. Burton, of Pennsylvania, was consul at Cádiz from 1824 to 1856. On the presence of French troops at Cádiz, see above, III, 313, n.4; below, Nelson to Secretary of State, April 26, 1825, note.

From RICHARD RUSH, no. 425. Acknowledges receipt of instructions of January 25, requesting documents relating to the State of Georgia from British archives. ALS. DNA, RG59, Dip. Disp., Great Britain, vol. 32 (M30, R28). Addressed to Secretary of State; received April 21. Authorized by the Legislature of Georgia to compile and publish documents connected with the history of that State, Joseph Vallence Bevan, of Savannah, had applied, through the Department of State, to the British Government "for all Provincial papers." Bevan to William Godwin, July 4, 1825, in Jack W. Marken (ed.), "Joseph Bevan and William Godwin," Georgia Historical Quarterly, XLIII (September, 1959), 316-17. Bevan died in 1830, before the work was completed.

MISCELLANEOUS LETTERS   March 16, 1825

To MATHEW CAREY, RICHARD PETERS, JR., and JOSEPH HOPKINSON [sic]. Encloses a general letter of introduction for William Strickland. Copy. DNA, RG59, Dom. Letters, vol. 21, p. 8 (M40, R19). Cf. above, Carey, Peters, and Hemphill to Clay, March 10, 1825; Clay to Ministers and others, March 15, 1825.

To JOHN VAWTER, Vernon (Indiana). Informs him that his commission as

"Marshal of the United States for the District of Indiana, has just been forwarded . . . to Mr. Parke, Judge of the said District. . . ." Copy. DNA, RG59,
Dom. Letters, vol. 21, pp. 6-7 (M40, R19). The commission was sent to Judge
Benjamin Parke on the same day. Copy. *Ibid.*, p. 6. Vawter acknowledged
receipt, May 10, 1825. ALS. DNA, RG59, Acceptances and Orders for Comms.
(M-T645, R2). Vawter, born in Virginia, had settled in Madison, Indiana, in
1807. He had been appointed a Federal marshal in 1810 and remained in that
post until 1829. Founder of the towns of Vernon and Morgantown, Indiana,
he was pastor of a Baptist Church at the former place from 1821 to 1848 and
sat in the State legislature from 1831 to 1836.

From N[ICHOLAS] BIDDLE, Philadelphia. Sends a copy of a letter from an un-
named "respectable merchant." ALS. DNA, RG59, Misc. Letters (M179, R62).
The enclosure, without signature, same source, reports an increase in Mexican
duties on "Domestick Goods" over 33 inches in width and interprets this change
as a "partial" duty, aimed against the United States. Cf. above, Biddle to Clay,
March 10, 1825; Clay to Biddle, March 12, 1825.

From C[ORNELIUS] P. VAN NESS, "Vermont Executive Department, Burlington."
Forwards a letter from Sir Francis Burton, Acting Governor of Canada (1824-
1825), and Van Ness' reply to it. ALS. DNA, RG59, Misc. Letters (M179, R62).
The enclosures, both copies, same source, present Sir Francis' application for
delivery to Canadian officials of two fugitives, deserters from the Canadian Army,
who have been imprisoned under civil suits for robbery brought in Vermont
by their Canadian officers, and Governor Van Ness' rejection of the request on
the ground that, under the Constitution and laws of the United States, he has
no authority to deliver any person to a foreign power.

To Samuel Smith

Dear Sir   Washn. 17h. Mar. 1825
    I recd. your letter of yesterday,[1] and thank you for your ob-
servations contained in it. You are mistaken however in supposing
that there is any want of *reciprocity* in the Colombian treaty in
respect to the Navigation of the two Countries.[2] The stipulation
on that subject is reciprocal, although it leaves each party to discriminate, in favor of its own, up to the point of the amount of
favor granted to any other nation. Consequently if Colombia
makes such a discrimination, in behalf of her navigation, so may
we, with the limit suggested. But in the instructions which I have
already prepared,[3] I have endeavored to get established a principle
of more practical equality. I think with you that the article concerning piracy has no great value, and may possibly be mischievous.
    I regret I did not see you when you called. Yr's faithfully
The Honble S. Smith.   H. CLAY
P.S. Mr Hughes will be allowed to return for a short time.[4]   H.C.

ALS. DLC-Samuel Smith Papers (DNA, M212, R22). Postmarked at Washington,
"Mar 16 [*sic*]." Endorsed: "Henry Clay   17 March 1825   Ansd. 18th." Answer not found.
    1 Not found.   2 See below, Clay to Salazar, March 21, 1825.

3 Clay sent no instructions on this subject to diplomatic agents of the United States in Colombia until the document below, September 16, 1825. He apparently referred to work on the instructions to Poinsett, below, March 26, 1825.

4 See above, Oliver to Clay, March 12, 1825.

To Samuel Smith

Dear Sir   Washn. 17 Mar. 1825

In reply to your letter of yesterday[1] I have to say that Mr. Hughes[2] will be allowed to return to the U.S., and I shall prepare as soon as possible the requisite permission and other despatches for him.[3] Perhaps he may be required to stop at Copenhagen, but without being long detained there.

Your determination of giving to the new administration a fair trial is liberal and all that could be expected. I do not apprehend any serious opposition, because it is not intended to lay any just foundation for it. If the Administration commit no intentional error, and faithfully discharge the public trust committed to it, why should there be any opposition? Your's faithfy and cordially

The Honble S. Smith.   H. CLAY

ALS. DLC-Samuel Smith Papers (DNA, M212, R22).   1 Not found.
2 See above, Oliver to Clay, March 12, 1825.
3 See below, Clay to Hughes (1), March 24, 1825.

INSTRUCTIONS AND DISPATCHES   March 17, 1825

From ALEXANDER H. EVERETT, Washington. Transmits documents relating to a private claim on the Netherlands, put into his hands since his return to the United States; encloses a copy of a letter requesting "Mr. Mertens of Brussels" to deliver to Christopher Hughes the archives of the Legation; and requests a letter of recall which he can forward to the Count de Reede, Foreign Minister of the Low Countries. ALS. DNA, RG59, Dip. Disp., Spain, vol. 24 (M31, R27). On March 9, 1825, Everett had been appointed Envoy Extraordinary and Minister Plenipotentiary to Spain. Mertens not further identified.

From JOHN WARNER, commercial agent, Havana. Encloses the court calendar which announces recognition of the French consul, states that Warner is attempting to secure release of seven American seamen imprisoned in Havana, and notes that the United States schooner *Shark* is providing convoy service twice a week for protection against pirates. LS. DNA, RG59, Cons. Disp., Havana, Cuba, vol. 3 (M-T20, R3). Warner, a resident of Delaware, had formerly held the position of United States consul at Puerto Rico. On the significance of the recognition accorded the French consul in Havana, see below, Robertson to Clay, April 20, 1825; Clay to Everett, April 27, 1825.

MISCELLANEOUS LETTERS   March 17, 1825

To [JOHN M. BAILHACHE,] the editor of the Chillicothe, Ohio, *Supporter.* Daniel Brent, at the direction of the Secretary of State, requests that this newspaper be sent regularly to the Department. Copy. DNA, RG59, Dom. Letters, vol. 21, p. 9 (M40, R19). After editing another Chillicothe newspaper for several years, Bailhache in 1815 had acquired the *Scioto Gazette*. In 1821 the latter journal had been merged with the *Supporter* (established in 1808), and the two appeared as the *Supporter and Scioto Gazette*.

On the same date Brent also wrote similar letters to [THOMAS SMITH,] the editor of the Lexington *Kentucky Reporter* and to [FRANCIS G. YANCEY,] the editor of the Petersburg, Virginia, *Intelligencer*. Copies of both letters in DNA, RG59, Dom. Letters, vol. 21, p. 9 (M40, R19). *The Intelligencer, and Petersburg Commercial Advertiser* was a continuation of the *Virginia Gazette, and Petersburg Intelligencer,* established in 1786, with the basic change in title dating from 1800; it remained in publication until 1860. Yancey was the editor from 1815 to 1828.

APPLICATIONS, RECOMMENDATIONS   March 17, 1825

ANDREW BODEN, Carlisle, Pennsylvania, acknowledges receipt of a letter from Clay dated March 11 (not found). Since "it was not convenient" for his wishes "to be realized in regard to the Indian agency," Boden applies for a clerkship in the State Department or other Washington office or for any government employment in the Western States. ALS. DNA, RG59, Misc. Letters (M179, R62). Boden received no appointment.

From Samuel Smith

Dear Sir/   Baltimore 18 March 1825

I may be mistaken in my construction of the treaty with Columbia [*sic*]— The senate appears to concurr [*sic*] with me in Opinion—and I thought Mr. Adams[1] did when I conversed with him on the subject and promised me that an explanation should be had on the subject with Salazar[2] & words more definite be used in what I thought he meant a seperate [*sic*] Convention— The sooner this shall be done the better— The English will be as anxious as we are on the subject— I dislike that a solemn treaty should depend on Construction.

I am well pleased that C. H.[3] will have leave of absence however short. I think a return from foreign Countries at proper periods useful to themselves and their Country— Do me the favour with as little delay as possible to send me Original and a Copy of his leave of return. that I may send them without delay. It takes from 60 to 75 days for a letter to go to him. It will take a month to prepare and another month before he Can reach Liverpool—as he will bring his family I wish him to avoid the Equinox.

The Enclosed is from a highly respectable merchant.[4] I sincerely wish you may find it Convenient to gratify him   If you do—send the Commission thro: me. and you will greatly Oblige Your Friend & Servant   S. SMITH

Copy. DNA, RG59, Misc. Letters (M179, R62). Cf. above, Clay to Smith, March
17, 1825 (1).   1 John Quincy Adams.
2 José Maria Salazar, who had arrived in the United States the preceding October
as Minister Plenipotentiary from the Republic of Colombia.
3 Christopher Hughes.
4 The enclosed letter, written by R. H. Douglass, Baltimore merchant, and addressed
to Smith, March 17, 1825, seeks the appointment of John L. McGregor, a native of
Charleston, South Carolina, now residing at Campeche, as United States consul in
Yucatan. McGregor was named consul at Campeche, but not until 1839.

From J. Wingate, Jr.

(Private)   State of Maine   Portland, March 18th. 1825
  Dr. Sir,
  Permit me to address you on the subject of the conversation, I
had the honor to hold with you in relation to the publication of the
laws of the U. States being given to the "Independent Statesman
and Main [sic] Republican"[1] instead of the "Eastern Argus."[2] The
ground on which the patronage of the general Government is
claimed for the "Statesman" is, that it has uniformly supported
the measures of the late Administration, and the Election of our
present most estimable Chief Magistrate— In doing which it has had
to repel, during the late Electioneering Campaign, the vituperative
assaults, made by the "Argus," not only upon Mr Adams, but also
upon those of our own Citizens, who had the honesty and independence to avow themselves the advocates of his Election.— In
fact the "Argus" has been the most personally abusive Paper,
printed in our Section of the Union—and its principal supporters
a set of political charlatans, who after it was ascertained there was
no hopes of their favorite candidate, for the Presidency, succeeding
became the ardent supporters of Genl Jackson. In short the course
pursued by that Paper has been marked by such a wanton profligacy
and baseness, that its claims to the patronage of the general Government, are nowise better or stronger than those of the Washington
City Gazette or Columbian Observer.[3] I think [it] would be considered a species of political suicide, in the present Administration,
to patronise and foster Papers of this discription [sic]. A cordial,
hearty and efficient support of the Administration can reasonably
be expected only from its friends, and such Papers as have defended
it and its measures "through good report and through evil report"—
from those who have sustained and upheld the Government because
they conscientiously believed, by so doing, they were promoting the
best interests of their Country. Whereas by giving its patronage
to men & Papers, that have been personally and politically opposed
to Administration [sic], it ought not and cannot expect any thing
in return, but a cold hollow hearted support, which would ultimately

do it more injury than benefit. Under these circumstances I cannot doubt you will give the publishing of the laws of the U. States to the "Statesman." As the laws of the last session of Congress are not yet published it is necessary and expedient, I presume, this appointment should be made in season to afford the Paper selected an opportunity to commence the publication of them as soon as practicable, I, therefore, confidently hope & expect you will be pleased to make an early decision in this case.

The Editor[4] of the New York Daily Advertiser, of the 15h. inst, in his remarks on Genl Jacksons letter to Mr Swartwout,[5] has in a very brief manner exhibited the opinions and views of the "Military Chieftain," in such a light as to satisfy eve[ry] honest Republican of the soundness & correctness of your objections to his being made President. The insidious attempt that is making, in this quarter of the Union to excite a hostility to you, by circulating the imbecile letters of Kremer,[6] and the egotistical and tyrannical sentiments of Genl Jackson, you may rest assured will produce a salutary effect, and the Actors in this political drama will be completely foiled in their calculations and expectations. And as soon as this temporary and unnatural excitment, which has been produced, on this occasion, shall have subsided, the course you have pursued will receive the unequivocal approbation of all honorable Men. I have the honor to be with Sentiments of Esteem & respect— Your obt St   J. WINGATE, JR
Hon Henry Clay   Secy of State   Washington City

ALS. DNA, RG59, P. and D. of L. MS. torn. Wingate not further identified.
1 This Portland newspaper ceased publication the following May but was succeeded by the Portland *American Patriot,* which received the contract for public printing in 1827 and 1828.
2 Published at this time by Thomas Todd and ———— Smith, not further identified.
3 Cf. above, Clay to Gales and Seaton, January 30, 1825, enclosure.
4 Theodore Dwight, Sr.
5 See above, Clay to Brooke, January 28, 1825, note.
6 See above, Bard to Clay, March 15, 1825, note.

INSTRUCTIONS AND DISPATCHES   March 18, 1825

From RICHARD C. ANDERSON, JR., Bogotá, no. 28. States that his departure has been delayed pending final adjustment of old claims against the Government of Colombia. Reports "successful settlement in the cases of the Schooner Liberty and Cargo, the Schooner Tiger and Cargo, the Cargo of the Brig America, the Minerva and Cargo [see above, Keith to Clay, March 11, 1825, note], and the Josephine and Cargo." He will, upon his arrival (in Washington), deposit in the Secretary's office the bills, received in payment, "drawn on the Colombian Consul General in the United States" (José Leandro Palacios). In regard to captures last summer, Colombia rejects the contention that Spanish goods under the United States flag are exempt from seizure. The claim in the case of the *Paloma* has also been rejected; Secretary (Pedro) Gual has offered to prepare a paper in explanation of the position, but Anderson has declined this formalization of the statement, with the hope that opportunity may arise for reopening the discussion. ALS. DNA, RG59, Dip. Disp., Colombia, vol. 3 (M-T33, R3). Addressed to J. Q. Adams, Secretary of State; received April 21. On Anderson's departure, see below, Watts to Secretary of State, April 8, 1825; Anderson to Clay, May 17, 1825. On the Colombian claims convention, which had been signed by Anderson and Pedro Gual, at Bogotá, on March 16, see Miller (ed.), *Treaties* . . . , III, 195-96.

The claims successfully negotiated all related to seizures by Venezuelan squadrons during the revolutionary action of the period from 1817 to 1820. The *Tiger,* sailing out of Salem, had been captured in July, 1817. The *Liberty,* the *America,* and the *Josephine* sailed out of Philadelphia. The first had been seized in the Orinoco River, in July, 1817. Military supplies, representing a part of the cargo of the *America,* had been confiscated and sold at Santa Marta in 1820. A Colombian court of appeals had upheld the claim of the owners, but the amount of collateral damages had been in controversy. The *Josephine* had been seized off La Guaira, in January, 1819.

The claims for damages during the summer of 1824 arose from the depredations of the Colombian privateer, *General Santander,* sailing under Captain John Chase, of Baltimore, with American officers and crew, which had seized three American vessels, the *Mechanic* (see below, Gracie to Clay, March 25, 1825), the *Midas,* and the *Ned,* on the ground that they transported Spanish property. Two additional American vessels, the *Junius,* of Baltimore, and the *Oris,* had been captured by other Colombian privateers later in the summer. The *Paloma* was a Spanish vessel, seized by Colombian privateers on the high seas between La Guaira and Cumana in July, 1818. The United States interest in the case related to the cargo of military supplies, owned by American citizens.

On May 30, 1825, Daniel Brent, "In the absence of the Secretary," sent to Thomas Wilson "the first of several sets of Exchange, at ninety days sight, drawn by the Government of Colombia on the 18th. day of March last upon Col. Jose Leandro Palacio [*sic*], its Consul General in the United States, in favour of Mr. Richard C. Anderson . . . , for the benefit of those entitled to the proceeds of them. . . ." One bill, for $21,750, with interest at six per cent from January 27, 1819, to March 18, 1825, was "to satisfy the claim of the Brig Josephine"; one, for $9,461.40, "to satisfy the claim of the Cargo of the Schooner Liberty, with interest as above from 5th. July 1817, to the date of the bill"; one for $20,000, "for the claim of the Schooner Minerva, Cargo, &c. with interest, from 27th. June 1820"; and one for $21,442, "for the claim of the Brig America's Cargo." Brent requested Wilson to procure acceptance of the bills and pay the proceeds to "the rightful Owners." Brent further requested, in a postscript, that Wilson obtain acceptance also of an enclosed "first and second of Exchange on Mr. [Manuel José] Hurtado, the Colombian Agent in London, at ninety days sight, for eighteen hundred and forty eight pounds, eight shillings and five pence, Sterling, to the order of Mr. Anderson . . . to answer the Claim for the Schooner Liberty. . . ." Copy, in DNA, RG59, Dom. Letters, vol. 21, pp. 73-75 (M40, R19). Hurtado, a member of the Colombian Senate, had been sent as his country's representative to Great Britain in 1824.

On May 30, Brent informed each of the following claimants of the action that had been taken: Joseph E. Read, Troy, Massachusetts, and Samuel Keith, relative to the *Minerva*; Daniel Smith and John Leamy, Philadelphia, the *Josephine*; John A. Leamy, Philadelphia, "the claim for the cargo of the Schooner Liberty"; Charles H. Baker and John "Reinhard [*i.e.,* Rianhard]," the *America*; and Joseph Peabody and Gideon Tucker, Salem, Massachusetts, "the Schooner Tyger [Tiger] and Cargo." Copies, in *ibid.*, pp. 75-78 (M40, R19).

Two days later, on June 1, Wilson informed Brent that the bills had "been accepted by Mr Palacio [*sic*]"; stated that, since the Bank could not assume the responsibility of disbursing the proceeds in the manner designated by Brent, "an officer of the Government" should be authorized to liquidate claims by drawing on the fund; and inquired concerning disposition of the proceeds, when collected, of the bill of exchange on Hurtado. ALS, in DNA, RG76, Misc. Claims, Colombia. Read and Smith have not been further identified.

John Leamy, president of the Insurance Company of the State of Pennsylvania, had been prominent as a merchant in Philadelphia as early as 1790. John A. Leamy was his son.

Baker and Rianhard have not been further identified.

Peabody, wealthy merchant shipper, owned a fleet of vessels trading in many parts of the world. Tucker had grown up in the business and had become Peabody's partner.

From CHARLES SAVAGE, Guatemala (City). Reports receipt of a file of the Government *Gazette* (of the Federation of Central America) for the last year, three copies of the constitution of the republic, and as many of a discourse recently delivered by "the president of the Executive"; transmits "a few of the last papers and one of each of the pamphlets" with this dispatch. ALS. DNA, RG59, Cons. Disp., Guatemala, vol. 1 (M-T337, R1). Addressed to Secretary of State; received August 4. Manuel José Arce (or De Arza) had been appointed President of the Regency by the Guatemalan Congress in June of 1823 and thus became the first President of the new Republic, organized as the Federation of Central America. On his earlier activities, see below, Clay to Miller, April 22, 1825, note. Arce remained in this office until he was overthrown in 1829.

MISCELLANEOUS LETTERS   March 18, 1825

To JOHN TUCKER MANSFIELD, "Consular Commercial Agent of the U. S. pro. tem. at Pernambuco [Brazil]." Encloses "evidence of . . . appointment, together with a copy of the printed Circular Instructions to Consuls." Copy. DNA, RG59, Cons. Instr., vol. 2, p. 346 (M78, R2). On March 19 Mansfield, writing from Salem (Massachusetts), acknowledged receipt of this letter, brought by Justice (Joseph) Story, and stated his intention of leaving for the post about April 10. ALS. DNA, RG59, Cons. Disp., Pernambuco, vol. 1 (M-T344, R1). This was an interim appointment, not confirmed until December 19. He remained in the position until 1836.

From JOHN A. LEAMY, Philadelphia. States that he was informed in 1823 of an offer by Colombia to pay his claim, resulting from "the capture and condemnation of Schr [*sic*] Liberty & Cargo . . . in 1817," but that he was told in 1824 that nothing could be found in (Richard C.) Anderson's correspondence relative to the matter. Wishes to know whether Anderson has written anything about it. ALS. DNA, RG76, Misc. Claims, Colombia. See above, Anderson to Secretary of State, this date.

From HENRY WHEATON, Washington. Seeks opinion on whether a claim of "Capt. Ordronnaux" (John Ordronaux) can be admitted to the list of American claims on France (see above, III, 154-55n, 313n). AL. DNA, RG59, Misc. Letters (M179, R62). Ordronaux, a native of France, naturalized a citizen of the United States, had commanded an American privateer during the War of 1812. His award on prize vessels taken into French ports had been attached by action of French tribunals under judgments requiring payment of obligations alleged to have been assumed by him in re-outfitting after his vessel had been disarmed at Cherbourg, following the peace agreement between France and England in the spring of 1814.

APPLICATIONS, RECOMMENDATIONS   March 18, 1825

WILLIAM D. FORD, Watertown (New York), seeks appointment as collector of customs at the port of Cape Vincent, Jefferson County, New York, in the place of John B. Esselstyne, (Essylstine, Esseltyne). ALS. DNA, RG 59, A. and R. (MR2). Esselstyne had been first appointed surveyor and inspector of revenue at this port in 1811; he had held this post jointly with the collector-ship since 1818. His appointment was renewed for an additional term at its expiration November 30, 1826.

GEORGE McCLURE, Albany, New York, recommends "Capt. Read" (Samuel C. Reid) as surveyor of the port of New York. ALS. *Ibid.* (MR3). See below, Savage to Clay, March 21, 1825.

ARCHIBALD McINTYRE, Albany, New York, observing that he, a State senator, is not personally acquainted with Clay but supported him "during the ardous [*sic*] Struggle Last fall," assures him that he has "lost no real friends in this State" and invites attention to "Captain Read" (Reid), "who goes to Washington for the purpose of obtaining the appointment of Marshal of the State of New York or Surveyor of that port—" ALS. DNA, RG59, A. and R. (MR3). See below, Savage to Clay, March 21, 1825.

From [Samuel L.] Southard

Washington 19 March 1825

Mr. Southard encloses for the consideration of the Secretary of State, a letter from Mr. Mc. Ilvaine,[1] requesting a title to a tract of land in New Jersey.—

[Endorsement][2]

Mr. Clay's Compliments to Mr Southard, and he returns the above mentioned letter which he has perused.   21 Mar.

AN. NjP-Samuel L. Southard Papers.
[1] Joseph McIlvaine, Burlington, New Jersey, lawyer, had been elected to the United States Senate in 1823 to fill Southard's unexpired term. The letter, addressed to Southard and dated March 1, 1825 (ALS), accompanies this document.
[2] AE.

INSTRUCTIONS AND DISPATCHES   March 19, 1825

From HEMAN ALLEN, Valparaiso, no. 13. Comments on the political in-stability in Chile and the unfavorable situation for settlement of the claims of United States citizens against the Republic. ALS. DNA, RG59, Dip. Disp., Chile, vol. 1 (M-T2, R1). Addressed to Secretary of State; received July 13. The

American claims generally stemmed from seizures of vessels and cargoes by the Chilean Navy and privateers in operations directed against trade with Spanish royalists.

From CHRISTOPHER HUGHES, Stockholm. Reports that he has been informed by the Marquis de Gabriac, French Minister in Sweden, that Spain will not break off relations with England over the latter's recognition of the new American States and that France has used her influence to dissuade the Emperor of Austria (Francis I) "from all hostile determinations." Discusses the formidable war preparations of the Turks and Greeks, a rumor of Britain's dissatisfaction with political events in Portugal, and the great importance to Swedish commercial classes of the "projected reduction of British duties on foreign iron." Notes that there has been no further progress in settlement of the claims of American citizens against either Sweden or Denmark. ALS. *Ibid.*, Sweden and Norway, vol. 4 (M45, R5). Addressed to Secretary of State; received May 14. The American claims against Sweden and Denmark grew out of seizures of vessels and their cargoes under application of the Continental System during the Napoleonic wars, those against Sweden, identified as the "Stralsund claims," arising out of enforcement of the restrictive decrees in Swedish Pomerania.

MISCELLANEOUS LETTERS   March 19, 1825

To NICHOLAS BIDDLE. Acknowledges receipt of Biddle's note (of March 16) and states that the instructions prepared for (Joel R.) Poinsett (below, March 26, 1825) have "directed his attention to that interesting object." ALS. DLC-Nicholas Biddle Papers (DNA, M212, R20).

To GEORGE IZARD, Philadelphia. Transmits his commission as Governor of the Territory of Arkansas. Copy. DNA, RG59, Dom. Letters, vol. 21, p. 10 (M40, R19). Published in Carter (ed.), *Territorial Papers. . .*, XX, 60. Izard had been nominated for the office by President Monroe on February 17, and the nomination had been confirmed on March 3; he acknowledged, on March 31, receipt of his commission and Clay's accompanying letter. ALS. DNA, RG59, Acceptances and Orders for Comms.

From LYDE GOODWIN, Baltimore. Calls "attention to the claims of certain individuals of this City on the government of Mexico, for supplies furnished to General [Francisco Xavier] Mina in the year 1816 . . . . by the Mexican Company of Baltimore"; requests that the American Minister to Mexico (Joel R. Poinsett) be instructed to press the matter; and notes that D (ennis) A. Smith, bearer of the letter and one of the claimants, can supply additional information. ALS. DNA, RG76, Mexican Claims Commissions.
   Goodwin had also outfitted privateers for service in the War of 1812. His company's claims on Mexico, amounting to $25,933, were not allowed under the Mexican Claims Convention of 1839. The Mexican Company of Baltimore, represented by David M. Perine and John Glenn, had claims amounting to $608,313.53 for "munitions of war" supplied to Mina. The commissioners under the Mexican Convention awarded the company $417,427.47. *House Docs.*, 27 Cong, 2 Sess., no. 291, p. 51. Perine was a distinguished lawyer, for many years clerk of court for Baltimore County, and active in civic affairs. Glenn, also a lawyer, later (1852-1853) became judge of the United States District Court of Maryland.

To José Maria Salazar

Don Jose Maria Salazar, Envoy Extraordinary,
and Minister Plenipotentiary from the
Republic of Colombia.

Sir,   Department of State   Washington 21. March 1825.

I have the honour to inform you that the President of the United States, by and with the advice and consent of the Senate, having ratified the "general Convention of Peace, Amity, Navigation and Commerce" concluded and signed at Bogota on the 3d. day of October 1824.[1] [sic] I shall be ready to exchange the ratification for that of your Government whenever you may be ready to make it.[2]

By the Constitution of the United States, as by that of the Republic of Colombia in respect to its Congress, the Senate is a component part with the Executive of the Treaty making power; and no Treaty is binding on them, to which the Senate does not give its Consent and advice. Each branch of the power acts independently of the other, and upon its own responsibility to the people and to the States, the common sources from which both derive all their authority. The Senate is as competent as the President to entertain and determine upon all the considerations which should be weighed in judging of the fitness and expediency of any Treaty. From this organization of the power instances may occur, in the progress of the Government, of its two branches entertaining different views of the effect upon the public interest, of the stipulations of a proposed Treaty. Any inconvenience which may arise from that cause are [sic] abundantly compensated by the Security to the public in the mutual action of those reciprocal checks. Of the value of that kind of security the framers of the Constitutions both of the United States and Colombia appear to have been fully sensible. These observations are called for by the communication which I have now the honour to make that an instance has occurred of such a difference of opinion between the late President of the United States and their Senate, in respect to the Convention for the complete suppression of the African slave trade which was concluded and signed at Bogota on the 10th. day of December 1824.[3] That Convention, having been submitted to the Senate for its consent and advice, after great deliberation, it has not thought proper to advise its ratification; and consequently, for the want of the concurrence of both parties, it cannot be considered as binding on either. In communicating this decision to your Government, I have to request that you will accompany it by assurances that it is not to be regarded as proceeding from any want of the most friendly feelings towards the Republic of Colombia, nor from any insensibility to the great moral duty under which all Christendom is placed of totally suppressing that abominable traffic.

I pray you, Sir, to accept the assurance of my distinguished Consideration.   HENRY CLAY.

Copy. DNA, RG59, Notes to Foreign Ministers and Consuls, vol. 3, pp. 202-204 (M38, R3). AL draft is located in CSmH.
[1] Miller (ed.), *Treaties* . . . , III, 163-85.
[2] The ratifications were exchanged in Washington on May 27, 1825, with Daniel Brent acting in the absence of Clay. *Ibid.*, 190.
[3] *American State Papers, Foreign Relations*, V, 733-35.

From R[obert] D. Richardson

Dear Sir,   The Retreat, East Baton Rouge, 21st, March 1825.

Your highly esteemed favour of the 20th. Ultimo,[1] was received in course by the Mail,—and I find myself placed under fresh obligations to you, for the kind solicitude which it expresses for my future welfare. I would greatly prefer the ambient air, which circulates freely throughout the district of Columbia, to the scorching rays of the matinal Sun, that we sensibly feel in this Southern latitude. If therefore, any clerkship can be conferred on me, by any one of my friends in Washington, by which I could obtain a decent support, and confer moderate education on my children; and at the same time, render some services to our common country, I will with pleasure repair to the city, altho' it would cost me a considerable sum for the transportation of my small family, and my baggage.

My neighbor, and friend, Mr. Gurley,[2] has not yet arrived; but his family and friends are anxiously looking out for the event of his return.

With best wishes for your prosperity, I remain, in sincerity, Your friend and very obedient servant,   R. D. RICHARDSON

ALS. DNA, RG59, A. and R. (MR3). Addressed to Clay at Washington.
[1] Not found.   [2] Henry H. Gurley.

From Henry R. Storrs

Dear Sir   Whitesborough March 21st. 1825.

I should have written to you from Albany had I not left there rather earlier than I expected. The election of Mr. Adams is generally approved of by the People of this State. The good sense and intelligence of the community is the basis on which their opinion rests. Their sectional feelings are gratified; and their confidence in the ability and integrity of Mr. Adams satisfies them that his administration will be founded on the interests of the nation and the steady support of our public institutions. The fact is that the great mass of the People of this State have never been excited to a very great degree on the question—and our local politics in a great measure overlaid the national question. It may also be generally considered as a truth that the People of this country cannot be brought to much excitement in relation to *men* merely. If they are well governed, they naturally rally round an administration which gives them good measures. For Mr. Crawford and Genl. Jackson there is scarcely sympathy left. The first was identified with the odious measures of our last Legislature[1] and the last has never had much hold on the feelings of this State. He was artificially made to appear to have had some strength but in reality had very little. Such is the popularity of the election of Mr. Adams that both political parties find themselves morally constrained to support it and neither can safely, whatever their personal wishes may be, venture to any opposition. Indeed the great leading object of both at Albany at this time is to endeavor to place the other in opposition to it, with the view to their own ascendancy at home—for the contest between them here is whether Mr. Clinton[2] shall be put down as Governor or not. The opposition to him consider that his election last fall (and there is much truth in it) was the effect of circumstances and not from his personal popularity—that there was combined in aid of his election all the topics of influence which had for some time been accumulating to render the then dominant power unpopular. The discordancy of the materials of which his strength in that election was composed has appeared most strikingly in the Legislature this winter. At Albany every thing is in confusion, except the opposition to Mr. C. and it is highly probable that the next legislature will present a majority against him in both branches of the legislature. There is a settled and implacable determination not only in the old Caucus party but with many of the Peoples party to destroy his political power as soon as they can accomplish it. Having the majority of the Senate against him he cannot effect any measures to strengthen his situation and they seem to understand in that body well the science which they practise. This state of things has rendered his declining the Mission to London[3] an important event—and the understanding that it is left open, and may yet be in his power to take, has created great solicitude among those who are opposed to him—lest he should accept it yet—for they consider (and with much reason) that should he accept he becomes more identified with the administration and of course more unassailable and is at the same time delivered from the chance of losing his moral power by a defeat at another election which should it so happen terminates his political life irrecoverably. It is also by them con-

strued and represented as having originated from secret hostility
to the administration as formed—and this is an impression which
may be perhaps considerably made. If it should prevail in the State
it is fatal to him. My own opinion of his declining is that he was
governed by the notion that *the administration was not to be permanent*—that he was led away by the notion that such was and
would be the opposition to it that it could not stand more than four
years and that he himself would accomplish his chief object at that
time. That he had made up his mind to decline such an offer even
before it was actually made, there can be no doubt. He received Mr.
Adams' letter by mail at evening—and on the same evening stated
his intention to decline—so that it is not possible that he could have
come to that conclusion in any *deliberate* reflection *after* the receipt
of the letter. A confidential friend of his, too, who had been in
Washington for some time (a Judge Hertell[4] of N York) left Washington three or four days after Mr. Adams was elected and went
directly to Albany. This gentleman was at W. very intimate with the
opposition to Mr. Adams from two quarters (since united) and
carried with him, doubtless, the impression that the new administration would be overturned. I believe that this is the real solution
of his motives in declining the place.—and I observed that in almost
every conversation where his friends were present, when I expressed
the opinion decidedly that it would be firmly sustained, that they
received it with *evident* doubt and with some *disappointment*. I did
not personally converse with him on the subject, tho' it seemed to
have been expected by some that I should have done so. I knew that
nothing which I should say would be received as it should have
been. He would have considered, whatever I might have said, as
rather intended for purposes adverse to *his* personal views hereafter;
and as coming with motives at least to be suspected by him. Besides
I could urge no other or farther considerations to induce him to
take the place than what his own confidential friends from Washington, who were in Albany with me, had urged already and which
to them were considered conclusive in favor of his accepting the
place. Had he been offered the State Dept. I do not doubt that it
would have been taken unless he would have considered that in
taking it he would have in honor been precluded from opposing
Mr. A. at four years. And this may be the solution also why in his
letter to Mr. A. he *virtually* declines *any place* under the administration—considering that by accepting any place he would honorarily
be placed *hors du combat*. His indiscreet and blabbing friends often
say openly that had he have gone to London Mr. A. & Mr. Clay
would have laid him on the shelf.

It is not however to be denied that as regards the party of Mr. C. *in the State* it is not for their interest that he should leave the State and more especially as Mr. Tallmadge[5] would be thus left in the Executive govt. who is known to be hostile to Mr. C. & his friends— and I find that Mr. Clintons letter to Mr. A. declining the offer[6] is made a great merit of, as being the offspring of motives altogether disinterested and patriotically regarding the State interest *alone*. If he does not take the place it is considered by his sagacious and well informed friends at Albany who regard his ulterior views as a great error in judgment.

There is a *settled determination* in the Senate not to meet any measures on the part of the Assembly which shall elect Judge Spencer to the Senate of the U. S. and the intimate friends of Mr. C. are of opinion I understand that they should adhere to Judge S. and let the choice go over to another Legislature. If so, Judge S. will never be elected.[7]

There is one view of the appointment of the successor of Mr. Rush[8] which very strongly creates solicitude in the part of Mr. C.'s friends. i.e.—that after the offer has been thus made to Mr. C. it may perhaps hereafter be offered to some one in the State who is not decidedly friendly to Mr. C. personally or intimately connected with his party feelings and views.—and indeed they cannot *claim* that it is to be conferred as a gift of theirs or with a view to the local politics of the State. The considerations growing out of such an alternative are indeed well calculated to alarm that interest and should have formed a conclusive reason in itself why Mr. C. should have at once accepted it.

I know that our State politics are difficult to be understood and have endeavored only to speak as much of them as may enable you to understand their bearing on the question relating to the offer to Mr. Clinton.   I am, Dr. Sir, Yrs truly

Hon. H. Clay   H R STORRS

ALS. DLC-HC (DNA, M212, R1).

1 See above, III, 401, 475-76, 776, 822, 848; Porter to Clay, January 14, 1825.

2 DeWitt Clinton.   3 See above, Stuart to Clay, March 15, 1825, note.

4 Thomas Hertell, later a member of the New York Legislature, identified with the movement for revision of women's rights under the State property laws.

5 James Tallmadge, Jr., now Lieutenant Governor of New York.

6 Dated February 25, 1825. ALS. MHi-Adams Papers, Letters Received, LXXIV, 189 (M467).

7 An effort on the part of the Clintonians to elect Ambrose Spencer to the United States Senate resulted in a deadlock in the New York Legislature that kept the seat vacant through 1825. Spencer, brother-in-law of DeWitt Clinton and father of John C. Spencer, had held several political offices in New York, had been a member of the supreme court of that State from 1804 to 1823 (chief justice, 1819-1823), and was mayor of Albany (1824-1825). He was later a member of Congress, 1829-1831.

8 Richard Rush.

INSTRUCTIONS AND DISPATCHES   March 21, 1825

From JAMES BROWN, Paris, "Private." Inquires whether his expenses to be incurred in attendance at the coronation of Charles X of France will be paid by the United States Government. LS. DNA, RG59, Dip. Disp., France, vol. 22 (M34, R25). Addressed to Secretary of State. Charles X had succeeded Louis XVIII upon the latter's death September 16, 1824.

From W[ILLIAM] TUDOR, Lima, no. 24. Reports the activities of French and British vessels at Chorrillos (near Lima) and a French demand for restitution of property and readmission of French citizens ordered out of the country; notes that the besiegers of Callao will soon open a heavier battery; outlines difficulties in trying to obtain official information concerning "a most infamous libel" written against Tudor by one Alsop, of Connecticut, a merchant at Lima (probably Richard Alsop); and states that reports of conditions in Upper Peru are contradictory. ALS. DNA, RG59, Cons. Disp., Lima, vol. 1 (M154, R1). Addressed to Secretary of State; received July 2. Published in Manning (arr.), *Diplomatic Correspondence . . . Latin-American States*, III, 1780-81.

Tudor, born in Boston and graduated from Harvard University, had been active in founding the Anthology Club (Boston), the Boston Atheneum, and the *North American Review*, the last of which he had served as the first editor (1815), and had filled several terms in the Massachusetts Legislature. He had been appointed consul to Lima in 1823 and continued in this post until his transfer to that of Chargé d'Affaires in Brazil, in June, 1827, where he died three years later. Besides editorial writings, Tudor had published *The Life of James Otis, of Massachusetts . . .* (Boston, 1823).

The patriot siege of the Spanish fortresses at Callao, invested soon after the fall of Ayacucho (above, Raguet to Secretary of State, March 11, 1825, note), continued until January, 1826 (see below, Allen to Clay, February 23, 1826).

MISCELLANEOUS LETTERS   March 21, 1825

From DANIEL WYNNE, New York. States his wish to delay departure until September, so that he may complete arrangements for establishing a commercial house in Santiago. ALS. DNA, RG59, Cons. Disp., Santiago, Cuba, vol. 1 (M-T55, R1). Wynne had been named in February, 1825, consul for the United States at Santiago de Chile. Daniel Brent informed him, on March 25, that the Secretary had no objection to his "remaining in the United States, till September. . . ." Copy, in DNA, RG59, Cons. Instr., vol. 2, p. 348 (M78, R2).

APPLICATIONS, RECOMMENDATIONS   March 21, 1825

LATHROP GEDERKIN and THOMAS ABORN recommend appointment of Thomas H. Roberts as public printer. LS. DNA, RG59, P. and D. of L. Undated; postmarked: "N. Albany Ind. March 22." Neither correspondent has been identified. On Roberts, see below, this date.

WILLIAM C. KEEN, Vevay, Indiana, publisher of the *Indiana Register*, applies for "the appointment of printer of the laws of the U.S. in the 3d congressional district of Indiana." A veteran of the War of 1812, during which he was wounded in service on board the *Lawrence*, on Lake Erie, Keen says he supported Clay during the recent presidential campaign and will support the Adams

administration, "so far as its measures may tend to promote the general good."
ALS. DNA, RG59, P. and D. of L. Keen had founded the *Indiana Register* in
1816, had surrendered ownership the following year, and, after the paper had
been discontinued, had revived it in 1824.

T[HOMAS] H. ROBERTS, New Albany, Indiana, states that he had established
in Louisville in the spring of 1824 a newspaper "in opposition to the two papers
then published in that place, both violently in favor of Genl Jackson for the
Presidency"; that he had "dared advocate the cause, of both" Adams and Clay
and, in consequence, had suffered bodily injury and property loss at the hands
of a mob on the night of September 5; and that, unable to obtain justice in
Louisville, he had moved across the Ohio River and had "commenced the publication of a small paper" in New Albany. Presents his application as "one of
the Printers to [*sic*] the laws of the Union, in the State of Indiana." Refers "to
the records of the Medical College of Baltimore" for information concerning
his character and notes that he is "a son of old Counsellor Roberts of Frankfort Ky (formerly of Baltimore Md)." ALS. DNA, RG59, P. and D. of L.
    Dr. Thomas Henry Roberts, both a medical doctor and a licensed preacher
of the Christian Society of the New Jerusalem, had established his paper, the
Microscope and General Advertiser, in Louisville in April, 1824, and had moved
it to New Albany in September, 1825. Soon thereafter it was succeeded by the
Indiana Recorder and Public Advertiser, with which Roberts was connected
until his death, April 6, 1827. His father, not identified.

JOHN SAVAGE, Albany, introduces "Captain Read [Samuel C. Reid]," who
wishes Clay's "aid and influence in procuring some appointment. . . ." ALS.
DNA, RG59, A. and R. (MR3). See above, II, 436, 437n. Reid received no
appointment.

INSTRUCTIONS AND DISPATCHES   March 22, 1825

From JAMES BROWN, Paris, "Private." Encloses copies of the answer, dated
January 21, 1825, by Dr. Francisco de Zea Bermudez, Spanish Minister of Foreign Affairs, to the note of December 31, 1824, from George Bosanquet, British
Chargé d'Affaires at Madrid, communicating the British decision to recognize
the independence of the Latin American Republics (above, Nelson to Secretary
of State, March 8, 1825); also of a note "by one of the diplomatic corps at
London, and addressed to one of the ministers of the continent," indicating
the reaction of Francis I, Emperor of Austria, to news of the British measure.
Reports the arrival of Prince Metternich in Paris but comments that his visit
is probably not occasioned by "the affairs of the late Spanish colonies." LS.
DNA, RG59, Dip. Disp., France, vol. 22 (M34, R25). Addressed to Secretary of
State; received April 25.
    Zea Bermudez had been appointed to head the Ministry on December 31,
1824, an action said "to have been almost forced upon Ferdinand [VII] by the
influence of France, and by the extreme difficulties in which the court found
itself placed." He was known as "a man of ability, of knowledge, and of
moderation in politics"; but he lacked personal influence, family connections, or
party support. He and his cabinet were dismissed the following October.
Annual Register, 1825, "History of Europe," 166, 173.
    Metternich had come to Paris in February because of the illness of his wife,
née Eleonore von Kaunitz. Though she had died on March 19, the Austrian
Chancellor remained in the French capital until the middle of April, using the

time to consolidate support for his views. The European diplomatic maneuvering of this period, however, centered less upon the problems of Spain than upon the conflict between Turkey and Greece (see below, Middleton to Clay, April 21, 1825).

MISCELLANEOUS LETTERS   March 22, 1825

To WILLIAM DRAYTON, Charleston, South Carolina. Offers, with authorization of the President, the consulate at Dublin, vacated by the death of "Mr. English." Copy. DNA, RG59, Dom. Letters, vol. 21, pp. 15-16 (M40, R19). Thomas English had been appointed consul at Dublin in 1816.

From Amos Kendall

Mount Pleasant,—near Frankfort   March 23d. 1825.

Dear Sir,

Yours of the 19th. ult. was duly received and shewn to Messrs Blair and Crittenden.[1] We have heard of your appointment and the opposition to it in the Senate.[2] If Jackson has before acted magnanimously since the election he has certainly forfeited all claim to that attribute by voting against your nomination. I presume there is more of spite in it against you than against Mr. Adams, and that the opposition are more desirous to destroy your future prospects than they are to disturb the present administration.

In some parts of this state there is a strong feeling of dissatisfaction at the vote of the Kentucky delegation and I fear your friends Trimble and F. Johnson[3] will have to meet a tempest. In this district there was some sensation; but it is dying away. White[4] is mingling freely with the people; they like him, and are easily induced to excuse him. But I must say I believe that more than three fourths of the people in his district would have instructed him to vote for Jackson.

An impression is abroad, that our local question was brought to bear on the presidential election and that you at Washington have acted in concert with the old Judges and their friends in Kentucky.[5] I put no confidence in this rumor; but it excites in some places a disposition to mingle the two subjects in our discussions. I am apprized of your opinion upon the late act of the Legislature,[6] but I have learnt nothing to make me believe you have pressed it any where improperly or with a view of putting up one party and another down in Kentucky. I hope I shall be pardoned in the suggestion that as little interference in our contentions as a free citizen can well submit to would seem to me to be prudent and necessary for you in the present situation both of us and yourself. If it were shewn that you were using your influence to crush the party with whom our fortunes are united here, how could such men as Blair and myself defend you or restrain that angry discussion to which many of our friends are inclined? Besides, suffer me to say that in the present state of public feeling here, even your voice would have little influence. Passion is taking the place of reason and you have little conception of the ferocious feelings by which many men, especially of the old Judge Party, are actuated. Violence on one side begets it on the other, and a degree of heat is rising which not only puts an end to all fair and honorable discussion, but actually endangers the public peace. You might do yourself and some of your friends much harm by an active interference and you can do neither any good.

I doubt not you are much deceived as to the true state of public opinion here. I am perfectly satisfied that the great mass of the people are settling down for and against the late act almost precisely as they were for and against removing the Judges, and that there will be little or no change of parties in favor of the old judges in the next Legislature. The whole parade of public meetings[7] is preconcerted and forced, and if they have made any impression it is vanishing almost as rapidly as it was made. Indeed, we have, I humbly think, the best materials for arguments, the ablest hands to put them together, and the popular side with the people. The anarchy attempted to be introduced by the disobedience of the Circuit Courts is more likely to end in the destruction of that system than in any serious change of public opinion.[8]

I have spent most of my time lately at my little farm where I now write and am much relieved when I can escape from town and the bustle of the political world. I am becoming much attached to my little place. I have on it an old saw mill and grist mill, a new two vat paper mill one vat of which is nearly ready to start, a dwelling house and out buildings. The death of Mrs. K. removed all her real property out of my disposal and much crippled the means on which I relied to build my paper mill. The more I live in the country the less inclination I have to mingle with the busy quarrelling world. Could I borrow money on a liberal credit to finish my improvements here which I could secure by a mortgage on the place and if required get my building insured, the value of which would be two or three times the amount I w[. . .][9] would abandon all local party politics to those who love quarrels better than I do, and spend the rest of life on this farm. I think I prefer this to any public or any other private employment. And now, sir, if you can tell me where I can borrow not less than $2000 nor more than $3000 in specie secured so as in no way to endanger the lender, on a credit of not less than two nor over four years, I believe you will do me the highest favor in your power.[10] If I had friends at the east I could soon get it in Philadelphia or New York; but I know nobody there. If I cannot make some such arrangement I shall from necessity have to stick to my printing office and my political discussions, which, if they bring no pleasure, will finally enable me to accomplish that which I would gladly compass at once.

Your friend   AMOS KENDALL

ALS. DLC-HC (DNA, M212, R1). Addressed to Clay at Washington. MS. faded.
[1] Francis Preston Blair; John J. Crittenden. Letter not found. Cf. above, Blair to Clay, March 7, 1825.
[2] See above, Commission, March 7, 1825, note.
[3] David Trimble; Francis Johnson.   [4] David White, Jr.
[5] Cf. above, Blair to Clay, March 7, 1825.   [6] See above, III, 896-97, 902 and note.
[7] See above, Kendall to Clay, February 19, 1825, note.
[8] During 1825 cases in two of the fifteen circuits of the Kentucky judicial system were sent on appeal exclusively to the old court; those in two others were sent exclusively to the new court; and those of the remaining eleven circuits were divided in their assignment. Arndt M. Stickles, *The Critical Court Struggle in Kentucky, 1819-1829* ([Bloomington, Ind.], 1929), 85-87. The confusion was heightened by contrary rulings on the constitutionality of the court legislation and by refusal of circuit judges to accept certifications—of legal papers and of lawyers' licensing—by appellate jurists of the opposing faction. See Lexington *Kentucky Reporter*, March 7, 14, 28; April 18, 1825; Lexington *Kentucky Gazette*, March 17, May 5, 1825; Frankfort *Argus of Western America*, April 27, 1825.
[9] MS. torn; one or two words missing.
[10] Cf. below, Kendall to Clay, July 8, 1826, and note.

DIPLOMATIC NOTES   March 23, 1825

From JOSE MARIA SALAZAR, Washington, no. 2. Acknowledges receipt of Clay's note of March 21 and expresses understanding of the system of government which occasions Senate refusal to concur in the convention respecting abolition of the slave trade. LS. DNA, RG59, Notes from Colombian Legation, vol. 1 (M51, R22).

INSTRUCTIONS AND DISPATCHES   March 23, 1825

From JAMES BROWN, Paris, no. 27. Encloses a copy of a letter which Brown addressed to (Ange-Hyacinthe-Maxence) the Baron de Damas, on March 18, explaining why the United States refuses to link discussion of the claims of American citizens on the French Government with the dispute on interpretation of the most favored nation clause in "the 8th. article of the Louisiana treaty of cession." LS. DNA, RG59, Dip. Disp., France, vol. 22 (M34, R25). Addressed to Secretary of State; received April 25. See above, III, 154n, 313n, 382, 383n. Damas, who, as a French emigré, had been trained in the Russian Army and after the restoration of the monarchy in France had attained the rank of lieutenant general in the forces of his native land, had fought with the expedition to Spain (cf. above, III, 313n), had become Minister of War (1823-1824), and now (1824-1828) served as Minister of Foreign Affairs.

MISCELLANEOUS LETTERS   March 23, 1825

To LEWIS CASS, Governor of Michigan Territory. Transmits a copy of a letter from Hugh Goodwin, Jr. Copy. DNA, RG59, Dom. Letters, vol. 21, pp. 12-13 (M40, R19). Cf. below, Clay to Goodwin, this date.

To HUGH GOODWIN, JR., Spotsylvania, Virginia. In reply to a letter (not found) asking that an effort be made to obtain information relative to Major Benjamin Graves, supposedly still a prisoner of Indians, states that Clay will transmit a copy of the request to Governor Lewis Cass of Michigan and urge him to use "every exertion to ascertain the fate of Major Graves, and to procure his liberation, if it be practicable." Copy. DNA, RG59, Dom. Letters, vol. 21, p. 13 (M40, R19). See above, II, 131-32, 139-40, 160; Clay to Cass, this date.

From THOMAS U. P. CHARLTON, Savannah. Having been disappointed in his hope to receive from President Monroe an appointment as Minister to Mexico and having been dismissed from "high Official Station" in Georgia because of his opposition to "the friends and pretentions of one of the Candidates for the Presidency," Charlton asks Clay to ascertain from Adams "any reason, any cause, any difficulty, which prevented Mr. Monroe from handing over to him" his letters and recommendations. He reminds Clay of "a transient personal acquaintance at Washington, through the introduction of . . . Mr: [William] Pinkney" and bases an apology for this letter upon the ground of "an intimacy with some friends whom" Clay esteems "—and, perhaps, above all, to the marriage of a branch of" Clay's "family to one of . . . [Charlton's] near relatives—" ALS. DNA, RG59, Misc. Letters (M179, R62). Charlton, a Savannah jurist and author, had served as a member of the Georgia Legislature (1801), attorney general of the State (1804-1808), and for many years as judge of the Eastern Circuit of Georgia. He had recently compiled the first volume of Georgia court decisions, *Report of Cases Argued and Determined in the Superior Courts of the Eastern District of the State of Georgia* (1824). The family relationship mentioned in his letter has not been identified.

From S[AMUEL] L. S[OUTHARD]. Transmits, "by order of the President . . . , several communications received from Commre. [Isaac] Hull which relate to transactions upon which instructions are to be given to our foreign diplomatic Agents." Asks that the documents be returned to the Navy Department and that Southard be informed, "Should it be thought necessary that any change should be made in the instructions of Commre. Hull, so far as relates to his intercourse with the Governments of South America. . . ." Copy. DNA, RG45, Executive Letter Books, vol. 1821-1831, p. 98.

APPLICATIONS, RECOMMENDATIONS   March 23, 1825

ABRAM BELL AND COMPANY, New York, recommends Isaac English to succeed his late brother, Thomas, as consul at Dublin. ALS. DNA, RG59, A. and R. (MR2). Cf. below, Maury to Clay, March 29, 1825.

JOSEPH KENT, "Rose Mount" (letter postmarked at Bladensburg, Maryland), encloses a letter from "Judge Buchanan" recommending John S. Williams, formerly of Hagerstown and presumed to be well known to Clay, for "some situation under the Govt."; notes his own long friendship with Williams, who "like many others who were engaged in commerce with small capital," was ruined financially at "about the close of the late war"; and adds that Williams' father "Coln. Eli [*sic*] Williams was a valuable man engaged through the most of a long life in the public service & his uncle Genl. Otho Williams acted as conspicuous a part as any officer of his grade during the revolutionary war"

and that "not one of the immediate relatives of Genl. Ws. hold [*sic*] an office
under the Genl. Govt." ALS. DNA, RG59, A. and R. (MR4). See above, Williams to Clay, March 13, 1825, note.

John Buchanan, chief judge of the Fifth Judicial District of Maryland and
an associate justice of the State court of appeals, became chief justice of the
latter court in July, 1824. Elie Williams, a veteran of the Revolutionary War,
who had died in 1823, had been clerk of the Washington County court,
Maryland, a member of the first commission to lay out the Cumberland Road,
and a promoter of the Chesapeake and Ohio Canal. His brother, Otho Holland Williams (1749-1794), after service in the Revolutionary War, had held
the office of collector of the port of Baltimore. Elie Williams' children included
Otho H. (the younger), John S., and Maria Sophia, the wife of John
Buchanan.

To Christopher Hughes

No. 1. Christopher Hughes, appointed chargé d'affaires of the
U.S. to the Netherlands.

Sir,   Department of State, Washington, 24. March 1825.

I have the honour to inform you that the President of the United-
States, by and with the advice and consent of the Senate, has ap-
pointed you Charge d'Affaires to the King of the Netherlands; and
to transmit herewith your Commission and a letter of introduction.
I also transmit a letter of recall to be presented on your taking leave.[1]
On that occasion, you will inform the Swedish Government that
Mr. Wm. C. Somerville has been appointed your Successor, and if
he shall not then have arrived, that no time will be unnecessarily
lost in his replacing you. You will also assure it of the desire of the
President to maintain in their full vigour the amicable relations
which are at present happily subsisting between the two Countries.

Your dispatch, under date the 18th. November 1824, forwarded
through Mr. Oliver,[2] has been received at the Department. The
President is unwilling to give countenance to the practice of the
return to the United-States of their foreign agents, during the
continuance of their Commissions, but under the peculiar circumstances of your case he consents to your return to the U. States,
as requested in that dispatch. With respect to the duration of your
absence from your foreign post, he is willing to extend it to the six
months which you solicit, if the public interest shall admit of it.
But as that may happen to require a speedier return, you must take
the indulgence which is given, subject to that contingency.

On your way to the United-States, the President directs you to
call at Copenhagen. Several Citizens of the United-States have just
claims upon the Danish Government founded upon illegal captures made of their vessels and property during the late wars in
Europe. These claims have been frequently urged upon the Danish

Government, and particularly by Mr. George W. Erving, special Minister sent to the Court of Denmark in the year 1811, and by Mr. John M. Forbes, then Consul General of the U.S. at Copenhagen, in the years 1817 and 1818. Mr. Erving's correspondence with Mr. Monroe,[3] then Secretary of State, and with Mr. Rosencrantz,[4] the Danish Minister of State of the Department of Foreign Affairs, will be found in the ninth volume of Wait's State Papers[5] from page 90 to 119 inclusive, now transmitted. It is expected that Mr. John Connell of Philadelphia, the agent of the claimants, will be at Copenhagen on your arrival there, supporting the claims before the Danish Government, and who will be able to supply any additional information that may be necessary. It is wished that you should afford to him any aid in your power; and particularly that you should address a Note to the Minister of Foreign Affairs stating the regret which the United-States feel at the great delay which has occurred in rendering justice to their Citizens who have these claims; the hope that the Danish Government will cause, without further procrastination, full and complete indemnity to be made to them; and the determination of the Government of the United-States not to abandon these claimants to the injustice under which they have so long suffered, but to persevere in the support of their just claims until full satisfaction is made. The President does not expect you to protract your continuance at Copenhagen for any considerable length of time, especially if there should be no favourable manifestations made of a disposition to allow and pay the claims. It is supposed that you will be able in the course of a period, not exceeding ten days or a fortnight, to ascertain what the probability of success may be, and if you find it unpromising you may not remain longer, but continue your voyage to the United-States. if you avail yourself of the permission to return which is given you[6] A letter of introduction to the Danish Minister of State of the Department of Foreign Affairs is herewith transmitted.[7]

I am, with great respect, Sir, your very humble and obedt. Servt.

H. Clay

LS. MiU-C. Endorsed: "Instructions. Original from Mr Clay." AL draft is located in DLC-HC (DNA, M212, R7); copy, in DNA, RG59, Dip. Instr., vol. 10, pp. 247-49 (M77, R5).

[1] Copies of the letters of recall and credence, both dated March 23, 1825, from Clay to the Ministers of Foreign Affairs of Sweden and Norway and of the Netherlands, respectively, are filed in DNA, RG59, Ceremonial Communications, II, 5-6.

[2] Robert Oliver.   [3] James Monroe.

[4] Niels Rosenkrantz, who had continued in that post until his death in January, 1824.

[5] Thomas B. Wait and Sons, Boston publishers, had issued three editions of *State Papers and Public Documents of the United States from the Accession of George Washington to the Presidency, Exhibiting a Complete View of Our Foreign Relations since That Time. . . .* The first, of three volumes (often considered as eight volumes, with five volumes already in print on the period from 1801 to 1815), had been published in 1815; the second, of ten volumes, in 1817; and the third, of twelve volumes, in 1819.

⁶ The last thirteen words interlined, in Clay's hand.

⁷ Dated March 24, 1825. Copy. DNA, RG59, Ceremonial Communications, II, 6-7. Clay writes that Hughes is sent to Denmark "for the purpose of rendering such aid as it may be in his power to give towards procuring a satisfactory adjustment of the well known and no less well founded claims of a numerous and valuable class of American Citizens upon the Government of His Majesty the King of Denmark, arising from circumstances connected with the late Wars in Europe, which claims have been heretofore often brought to the notice of the Danish Government and Indemnities to the Parties interested, requested from its justice, by this Government. . . ."

INSTRUCTIONS AND DISPATCHES   March 24, 1825

To CHRISTOPHER HUGHES, no. 2. Encloses an extract of a letter written June 28, 1818, by Secretary of State John Quincy Adams to George W. Campbell, concerning "the appointment of a Minister on the part of the United States, of equal rank with the Danish Minister residing here, to reside at Copenhagen," and the terms under which the United States consul on the Island of St. Thomas "should be permitted to hold and exercise the functions of that Office." Clay continues: "You will take an early opportunity to make known to the Minister of Foreign Affairs [Niels Rosenkrantz] that the views of this Government remain unchanged upon both these objects, and to invite his attention particularly to the last, by all the considerations referred to in the extract, and by the obvious necessity which continues to exist that the interests of the Citizens of the United States, resorting to the Island of St. Thomas, should be placed under the care of an authorised Agent of their Government." LS, "Duplicate." MiU-C. AL draft, in the hand of Daniel Brent, is located in DLC-HC (DNA, M212, R7); copy, in DNA, RG59, Dip. Instr., vol. 10, p. 249 (M77, R5).

MISCELLANEOUS LETTERS   March 24, 1825

To WILLIAM MILLER, Warrenton, North Carolina. Transmits his commission as Chargé d'Affaires to Guatemala (the Federation of Central America) and requests that he be ready to depart as soon as instructions are prepared, "which will be with all possible dispatch." Copy. DNA, RG59, Dip. Instr., vol. 10, p. 250 (M77, R5). AL draft, in the hand of Daniel Brent, in DLC-HC (DNA, M212, R7). Miller, a lawyer, member of the State legislature (1810-1814), and Governor of North Carolina (1814-1817), had been appointed on March 7. His acceptance, addressed to Clay, is dated March 28. DNA, RG59, Dip. Disp., Central America, vol. 1 (M219, R2). A copy of his commission, dated March 7, is located in DNA, RG59, Ceremonial Communications, vol. 2, p. 8; for his instructions, see below, Clay to Miller, April 22, 1825. He died at Key West in September, en route to his post.

From PETERS, POND AND COMPANY, Boston. Transmits "a copy of the protest of Capt Prentiss Crowell, which sets forth the particulars of his capture, & treatment during his detention at Porto rico [*sic*]"; expresses "a strong belief" that the Government (of the United States) "will restore to all of its citizens the amount of property thus wrongfully taken, and look to the government of Spain for redress. . . ." LS. DNA, RG76, Misc. Claims, Spain. The enclosure identifies Crowell as of Barnstable, Massachusetts, and his vessel as the brig *Sam*, captured by a privateer in 1822. The shipping firm, composed of John Peters and Sabin Pond, was ultimately, under a convention of 1834, awarded compensation in full for the loss of the *Sam* and for the wages of Captain Crowell. *Sen. Docs.*, 35 Cong., 2 Sess., no. 18, pp. 20, 21.

APPLICATIONS, RECOMMENDATIONS   March 24, 1825

CHRISTOPHER NEALE, Alexandria, asks that commissions be made out for Thomas Vowell, William Minor, and Neale as justices of the peace, to enable them "to receive security in a number of cases adjudicated before them, and now lying over to the prejudice of the Plaintiffs." ALS. DNA, RG59, A. and R. (MR1). All three had held these offices in Alexandria County since 1814; Minor and Neal continued in their posts for another decade. In August, 1824, Neale had also been named Brazilian vice-consul for Alexandria and the District of Columbia.

CHARLES JOHN STEEDMAN, Charleston, South Carolina, recalls having been introduced to Clay by (William) Lowndes; solicits, as joint owner of the Charleston *City Gazette and Commercial Daily Advertiser,* "the publication attached to the Department over which" Clay presides; characterizes his paper, "purely Republican" for nearly fifty years, as "the rallying point of the whole Republican Party in the State of South Carolina"; and cites John Gaillard and Langdon Cheves as references. ALS. DNA, RG59, P. and D. of L. Steedman was at various times sheriff of Charleston District, member of the South Carolina General Assembly, and naval officer at the Charleston customhouse. Cf. below, Haig to Clay, December 19, 1825.

DIPLOMATIC NOTES   March 25, 1825

To PETER PEDERSEN. States that Pedersen's note of March 14 has been submitted to the President, who has instructed Clay to say that the United States is willing to negotiate a convention which shall place commerce and navigation between this country and Denmark "on a basis of equality and reciprocity." Clay continues: "Owing to his recent entry upon the duties of his office, and the very great pressure of official business, he ["The undersigned Secretary of State"] must defer the consideration and discussion of the articles which should form the proposed Convention until a more distant day, of which he will apprize Mr. Pedersen. In the mean time he would receive and consider with great respect and attention any Communications on the Commerce and navigation of the two Countries which Mr. P. might think proper to make preparatory to the discussions on which it is proposed to enter." Copy. DNA, RG59, Notes to Foreign Ministers and Consuls, vol. 3, pp. 204-205 (M38, R3). AL draft is located in CSmH.

To the BARON DE TUYLL [VAN SEROOKSKERKEN], Russian Minister to the United States. Transmits the response of Bryant and Sturgis to an informal note from the Baron relating to their claim for indemnity. Copy. DNA, RG59, Notes to Foreign Ministers and Consuls, vol. 3, p. 304 (M38, R3). L draft is located in CSmH. Baron Tuyll had succeeded Pierre de Polética at this post in 1823. The partnership of John Bryant and William Sturgis, Boston merchants, formed in 1810 and lasting for fifty-three years, handled much of the United States trade with the Pacific Coast and the Orient during the period to 1840. Their claim on Russia related to the case of the *Pearl* (see below, Clay to Tuyll, April 19, 1825), expelled from the northwest coast of North America under a *ukase* of Czar Alexander I, in 1821, which had forbidden foreign vessels to approach within 100 Italian miles of that coast as far south as 51 degrees north latitude. The Russian *ukase* had evoked protest from the governments of both Britain and the United States.

INSTRUCTIONS AND DISPATCHES   March 25, 1825

From R[ICHARD] C. ANDERSON, JR., Bogotá, no. 29. Encloses copies of correspondence transmitting to him bills of exchange submitted in settlement of American claims against the Government of Colombia. ALS. DNA, RG59, Dip. Disp., Colombia, vol. 3 (M-T33, R3). Addressed to John Quincy Adams, Secretary of State; received May 22. Cf. above, Anderson to Adams, as Secretary of State, March 18, 1825.

From CHRISTOPHER HUGHES, Stockholm, no. 7. Notes the satisfaction of the commercial and governing classes of Sweden with the recent reduction in British duties on iron. The Government has intimated to the British Cabinet its willingness "to grant, to England, whatever equivalent in the relaxation of its commercial system, England may ask! England has only *to ask,* and she will *get!*" ALS. DNA, RG59, Dip. Disp., Sweden and Norway, vol. 4 (M45, R5). Addressed to Secretary of State; received May 21.

From CHRISTOPHER HUGHES [unnumbered]. Transmits copies of signed transcripts of oral communications to (George) Canning, from (Christoph Andreievich) Count von Lieven, the Russian Ambassador, on March 2, and from Prince (Paul Anthony) Esterhazy, Austrian Ambassador, on March 3, expressing the irritation of their governments over the British recognition of the Latin American Republics. Notes that the Baron Maltzahn, the Prussian Minister in London, expressed similar views. ALS. *Ibid.* Addressed to Secretary of State. See above, Nelson to Clay, March 8, 1825, note. Count Lieven, accorded the title of "Prince" in 1826, had risen to the rank of lieutenant general of the army in 1807, had been sent to Berlin as Russian Minister in 1810 and thence to London, in the same capacity, in 1812. He remained in the latter position until 1834.

From JOHN MULLOWNY, Tangier, no. 34. Reports receipt of a letter from Captain James Allen, III, and others, officers and crew of the ship *Oscar,* of New York, wrecked forty-eight hours out of Lisbon, who have reached Rabat; states that arrangements have been made to bring them to Tangier, whence they will be sent to Gibraltar. ALS. DNA, RG59, Cons. Disp., Tangier, vol. 4 (M-T61, R4). Addressed to John Quincy Adams, Secretary of State; received June 30.

MISCELLANEOUS LETTERS   March 25, 1825

To CORNELIUS P. VAN NESS. Notes that the letter from Van Ness of March 16, with its enclosures, has been submitted to the President. Clay continues: "I am instructed by the President to express his regret to your Excellency, that the request of the acting Governor of Canada cannot be complied with, under any authority now vested in the Executive Government of the United States— The stipulation between this and the British Government for the mutual delivery over of fugitives from justice being no longer in force, and the renewal of it by Treaty being at this time a subject of negotiation between the two Governments." Copy. DNA, RG59, Dom. Letters, vol. 21, pp. 16-17 (M40, R19).

From ARCHIBALD GRACIE, President of the Atlantic Insurance Company, New York. States that his firm had insured for $12,000 a part of the cargo of the schooner *Mechanic,* which, en route to Tampico with goods brought from Havana to Thompson's Island (Key West) and reshipped, had been seized by a Colombian privateer. Inquires whether the United States Government can get redress from Colombia for the cargo, condemned at Puerto Cabello as Spanish property, on the ground that it was protected by the American flag. ALS. DNA, RG59, Misc. Letters (M179, R62). The Atlantic Insurance Company had been organized in April, 1824, to deal in marine insurance. On the case of the *Mechanic,* see above, Anderson to Secretary of State, March 18, 1825.

From MARY PERRY, Boston, Massachusetts. Asks that the Department of State act for the relief of her son, William, who has been imprisoned in Havana, Cuba, for fifteen months, although acquitted of the charge against him. ALS. DNA, RG59, Misc. Letters (M179, R62).

On March 31, Daniel Brent at Clay's direction acknowledged receipt of Mrs. Perry's letter, reported the steps taken by the State Department "to attend to the case," and enclosed an extract from the most recently received correspondence on the subject, "dated the 10th. Instant, which explains the then situation of your Son and his fellow prisoners, and the measures which the Consul [John Warner] had taken in their behalf." Copy, DNA, RG59, Dom. Letters, vol. 21, pp. 20-21 (M40, R19). Mrs. Perry having again written to Clay in a letter dated September 6, 1825 (not found), she was informed by Daniel Brent, on September 12, 1825, that no further information had been received but that he saw "little reason . . . to doubt his release before this time." Copy. *Ibid.,* p. 148. Cf. below, Diamond to Clay, October 8, 1825; Clay to Rodney, October 29, 1825; Clay to Vives, November 14, 1825; Rodney to Clay, December 19, 1825; January 7, 1826; February 4, 1826.

From RICHARD PETERS, JR., on behalf of the Pennsylvania Society for the Promotion of Internal Improvement, Philadelphia. Thanks Clay for his letters introducing William Strickland to representatives of the United States in Europe. LS. DNA, RG59, Misc. Letters (M179, R62). See above, Clay to Ministers and others, March 15, 1825.

Address to the People of the Congressional District

Washington, 26th March, 1825.

The relations of your representative and of your neighbour in which I have so long stood, and in which I have experienced so many strong proofs of your confidence, attachment and friendship, having just been, the one terminated, and other suspended, I avail myself of the occasion on taking, I hope a temporary, leave of you, to express my unfeigned gratitude for all your favours, and to assure you that I shall cherish a fond and unceasing recollection of them. The extraordinary circumstances in which, during the late session of Congress, I have been placed, and the unmerited animadversions which I have brought upon myself, for an honest and faithful discharge of my public duty, form an additional motive for this appeal to your candour and justice. If, in the office which I have just left, I have abused your confidence and betrayed your interests, I cannot deserve your support in that on the duties of which I have now entered. On the contrary, should it appear that

I have been assailed without just cause, and that misguided zeal and interested passions have singled me out as a victim, I cannot doubt that I shall continue to find, in the enlightened tribunal of the public, that cheering countenance and impartial judgment, without which a public servant cannot possibly discharge with advantage the trust confided to him.

It is known to you, that my name had been presented, by the respectable states of Ohio, Kentucky, Louisiana and Missouri,[1] for the office of President, to the consideration of the American public, and that it had attracted some attention in other quarters of the Union. When, early in November last, I took my departure from the district to repair to this city, the issue of the Presidential election before the people was unknown. Events, however, had then so far transpired as to render it probable that there would be no election by the people, and that I should be excluded from the House of Representatives. It became, therefore, my duty to consider, and to make up an opinion on, the respective pretensions of the three gentlemen that might be returned, and at that early period I stated to Dr. Drake,[2] one of the Professors in the Medical School of Transylvania University, and to John J. Crittenden, Esq. of Frankfort, my determination to support Mr. Adams in preference to Gen. Jackson. I wrote to Charles Hammond, Esq. of Cincinnati, about the same time, and mentioned certain objections to the election of Mr. Crawford, (among which was that of his continued ill health,) that appeared to me almost insuperable.[3] During my journey hither, and up to near Christmas, it remained uncertain whether Mr. Crawford or I would be returned to the House of Representatives. Up to near Christmas, all our information made it highly probable that the vote of Louisiana would be given to me, and that I should consequently be returned, to the exclusion of Mr. Crawford. And, whilst that probability was strong, I communicated to Mr. Senator Johnston,[4] from Louisiana, my resolution not to allow my name, in consequence of the small number of votes by which it would be carried into the House, if I were returned, to constitute an obstacle, for one moment, to an election in the House of Representatives.

During the month of December, and the greater part of January, strong professions of high consideration, and of unbounded admiration of me, were made to my friends, in the greatest profusion, by some of the active friends of all the returned candidates. Every body professed to regret, after I was excluded from the House, that I had not been returned to it. I seemed to be the favourite of every body. Describing my situation to a distant friend, I said to him, "I am enjoying, whilst alive, the posthumous honors which are usually awarded to the venerated dead."[5] A person not acquainted with human nature would have been surprised, in listening to these praises, that the object of them had not been elected by general acclamation. None made more or warmer manifestations of these sentiments of esteem and admiration, than some of the friends of General Jackson. None were so reserved as those of Mr. Adams; under an opinion, (as I have learnt since the election,) which they early imbibed, that the western vote would be only influenced by its own sense of public duty; and that if its judgment pointed to any other than Mr. Adams, nothing which they could do would secure it to him. These professions and manifestations were taken by me for what they were worth. I knew that the sunbeams would quickly disappear, after my opinion should be ascertained, and that they would be succeeded by a storm; although I did not foresee exactly how it would burst upon my poor head. I found myself transformed from a candidate before the people, into an elector for the people. I deliberately examined the duties incident to this new attitude, and weighed all the facts before me, upon which my judgment was to be formed or reviewed. If the eagerness of any of the heated partisans of the respective candidates suggested a tardiness in the declaration of my intention, I believed that the new relation, in which I was placed to the subject, imposed on me an obligation to pay some respect to delicacy and decorum.

Meanwhile that very reserve supplied aliment to newspaper criticism. The critics could not comprehend how a man, standing as I had stood towards the other gentlemen, should be restrained, by a sense of propriety, from instantly fighting under the banners of one of them, against the others. Letters were issued from the manufactory at Washington, to come back, after performing long journeys, for Washington consumption. These letters imputed to "Mr. Clay and his friends a mysterious air, a portentous silence," &c.[6] From dark and distant hints the progress was easy to open and bitter denunciation. Anonymous letters,[7] full of menace and abuse, were almost daily poured in on me. Personal threats were communicated to me, through friendly organs, and I was kindly apprised of all the glories of village effigies which awaited me.[8] A systematic attack was simultaneously commenced upon me from Boston to Charleston, with an object, present and future, which it was impossible to mistake. No man but myself could know the nature, extent, and variety of means which were employed to awe and influence me. I bore them, I trust, as *your* representative ought to have borne them, and as became me. Then followed the letter, afterwards adopted as his own by Mr. Kremer, to the Columbian

Observer[9]— With its character and contents you are well acquainted. When I saw that letter, alleged to be written by a member of the very House over which I was presiding, who was so far designated as to be described as belonging to a particular delegation, by name, a member with whom I might be daily exchanging, at least on my part, friendly salutations, and who was possibly receiving from me constantly acts of courtesy and kindness, I felt I could no longer remain silent. A crisis appeared to me to have arisen in my public life. I issued my card. I ought not to have put in it the last paragraph, because, although it does not necessarily imply the resort to a personal combat, it admits of that construction; nor will I conceal that such a possible issue was within my contemplation. I owe it to the community to say, that whatever heretofore I may have done, or, by inevitable circumstances, might be forced to do, no man in it holds in deeper abhorrence than I do, that pernicious practice. Condemned as it must be by the judgment and philosophy, to say nothing of the religion, of every thinking man, it is an affair of feeling about which we cannot, although we should, reason. Its true corrective will be found when all shall unite, as all ought to unite, in its unqualified proscription.

A few days after the publication of my Card, "Another Card," under Mr. Kremer's name, was published in the Intelligencer.[10] The night before, as I was voluntarily informed, Mr. Eaton, a Senator from Tennessee, and the Biographer of Gen. Jackson[11] (who boarded in the end of this city opposite to that in which Mr. Kremer took up his abode, a distance of about two miles and an half) was closeted for some time with him. Mr. Kremer is entitled to great credit for having overcome all the disadvantages, incident to his early life and want of education, and forced his way to the honourable station of a member of the House of Representatives. Ardent in his attachment to the cause which he had espoused, Gen. Jackson is his idol, and of his blind zeal others have availed themselves, and have made him their dupe and their instrument. I do not pretend to know the object of Mr. Eaton's visit to him. I state the fact, as it was communicated to me, and leave you to judge. Mr. Kremer's card is composed with some care and no little art, and he is made to avow in it, though somewhat equivocally, that he is the author of the letter to the Columbian Observer. To Mr. Crowninshield,[12] a member from Massachusetts, formerly Secretary of the Navy, he declared that he was not the author of that letter. In his Card, he draws a clear line of separation between my friends and me, acquitting them, and undertaking to make good his charges, in that letter, only so far as I was concerned.

The purpose of this discrimination is obvious. At that time the election was undecided, and it was therefore as important to abstain from imputations against my friends, as it was politic to fix them upon me. If they could be made to believe that I had been perfidious, in the transport of their indignation, they might have been carried to the support of Gen. Jackson. I received the National Intelligencer, containing Mr. Kremer's card, at breakfast, (the usual time of its distribution,) on the morning of its publication. As soon as I read the card, I took my resolution. The terms of it clearly implied that it had not entered into his conception to have a personal affair with me; and I should have justly exposed myself to universal ridicule, if I had sought one with *him*. I determined to lay the matter before the House and respectfully to invite an investigation of my conduct. I accordingly made a communication to the House, on the same day, the motives for which I assigned. Mr. Kremer was in his place, and, when I sat down, rose and stated that he was prepared and willing to substantiate his charges against me.[13] This was his voluntary declaration, unprompted by his aiders and abettors, who had no opportunity of previous consultation with him on that point. Here was an issue publicly and solemnly joined, in which the accused invoked an inquiry into serious charges against him, and the accuser professed an ability and a willingness to establish them. A debate ensued, on the next day, which occupied the greater part of it, during which Mr. Kremer declared to Mr. Brent, of Louisiana, a friend of mine, and to Mr. Little, of Maryland, a friend of Gen. Jackson, as they have certified, "that he never intended to charge Mr. Clay with corruption or dishonor in his intended vote for Mr. Adams as President, or that he had transfered, or could transfer, the votes or interest of his friends; that he (Mr. Kremer) was among the last men in the nation to make such a charge *against Mr. Clay;* and that his letter was never intended to convey the idea given to it." Mr. Digges, a highly respectable inhabitant of this city, has certified to the same declarations of Mr. Kremer.[14]

A message was also conveyed to me, during the discussions, through a member of the House, to ascertain if I would be satisfied with an explanation which was put on paper and shown me, and which it was stated Mr. Kremer was willing, in his place, to make. I replied that the matter was in the possession of the House. I was afterwards told that Mr. Ingham, of Pennsylvania, got hold of that paper, put it in his pocket, and that he advised Mr. Kremer to take no step without the approbation of his friends.[15] Mr. Cook, of Illinois, moved an adjournment of the House, on informa-

tion which he received of the probability of Mr. K.'s making a
satisfactory atonement, on the next day, for the injury which he
had done me, which I have no doubt he would have made, if he
had been left to the impulses of his native honesty. The House
decided to refer my communication to a committee, and adjourned
until the next day to appoint it by ballot. In the mean time Mr.
Kremer had taken, I presume, or rather there had been forced
upon him, the advice of *his friends,* and I heard no more of the
apology. A committee was appointed of seven gentlemen, of whom,
not one was my political friend, but who were among the most
eminent members of the body.[17] I received no summons or
notification from the committee from its first organization to its
final dissolution, but Mr. Kremer was called upon by it to bring
forward his proofs. For one moment be pleased to stop here and
contemplate his posture, his relation to the House and to me,
and the high obligations under which he had voluntarily placed
himself. He was a member of one of the most august assemblies
upon earth, of which he was bound to defend the purity, or expose
the corruption, by every consideration which ought to influence
a patriot bosom. A most responsible and highly important constitutional duty was to be performed by that assembly. He had
chosen, in an anonymous letter, to bring against its presiding
officer charges, in respect to that duty, of the most flagitious
character. These charges comprehended delegations from several
highly respectable states. If true, that presiding officer merited
not merely to be dragged from the chair, but to be expelled the
House.— He challenges an investigation into his conduct, and Mr.
Kremer boldly accepts the challenge, and promises to sustain his
accusation. The committee, appointed by the House itself, with
the common consent of both parties, calls upon Mr. Kremer to
execute his pledge, publicly given in his proper place, and also
previously given in the public prints. Here is the theatre of the
alleged arrangements; this the vicinage in which the trial ought
to take place.— Every thing was here fresh in the recollection of
the witnesses, if there were any. Here all the proofs were concentrated. Mr. Kremer was stimulated by every motive which
could impel to action, by consistency of character; by duty to *his*
constituents—to his country; by that of redeeming his solemn
pledge; by his anxious wish for the success of his favourite, whose
interests could not fail to be advanced by supporting his atroiocus
[*sic*] charges. But Mr. Kremer had now the benefit of the advice
of his friends. He had no proofs, for the plainest of all reasons,
because there was no truth in his charges. They saw that to attempt,
to establish them, and to fail, as he must fail, in the attempt, might

lead to an exposure of the conspiracy, of what [sic] he was the organ. They advised therefore that he should make a retreat, and their adroitness suggested that, in an objection to that jurisdiction of the House, which had been admitted, and in the popular topics of the freedom of the press, *his* duty to his constituents, and the inequality in the condition of the Speaker of the House and a member on the floor, plausible means might be found to deceive the ignorant, and conceal his disgrace. A laboured communication was accordingly prepared by them, in Mr. Kremer's name, and transmitted to the committee, founded upon these suggestions. Thus the valiant champion, who had boldly stepped forward, and promised, as a Representative of *the* people, "to cry aloud and spare not," forgot all his gratuitous gallantry and boasted patriotism, and sunk at once into profound silence.

With these remarks, I will, for the present, leave him, and proceed to assign the reasons to you, to whom alone I admit myself to be officially responsible, for the vote which I gave on the Presidential election. The first inquiry which it behoved me to make was, as to the influence which ought to be exerted on my judgment, by the relative state of the electoral votes which the three returned candidates brought into the House, from the colleges. General Jackson obtained 99, Mr. Adams 84, and Mr. Crawford 41. Ought the fact of a plurality being given to one of the candidates to have any, and what weight? If the Constitution had intended that it should have been decisive, the Constitution would have made it decisive, and interdicted the exercise of any discretion on the part of the House of Representatives. The Constitution has not so ordained, but, on the contrary, it has provided, that "from the persons having the highest numbers, not exceeding three, on the list of those voted for as President, the H. of Representatives shall *choose,* immediately, by ballot, a President." Thus, a discretion is necessarily invested in the House; for choice implies examination, comparison, judgment.— The fact, therefore, that one of the three persons was the highest returned, not being, by the constitution of the country, conclusive upon the judgment of the House, it still remains to determine what is the true degree of weight belonging to it? It has been contended that it should operate, if not as an instruction, at least in the nature of one, and that in this form it should control the judgment of the House. But this is the same argument of conclusiveness, which the constitution does not enjoin, thrown into a different, but more imposing shape. Let me analyze it.— There are certain States, the aggregate of whose electoral votes conferred upon the highest returned candidate, indicates their wish that he should be the

President. Their votes amount in number to 99, out of 261
electoral votes of the whole Union. These 99 do not, and cannot,
of themselves, make the President. If the fact of particular states
giving 99 votes can, according to any received notions of the
doctrine of instruction, be regarded in that light, to whom are
those instructions to be considered addressed? According to that
doctrine, the people, who appoint, have the right to direct, by their
instructions, in certain cases, the course of the representative whom
they appoint. The States, therefore, who gave those 99 votes may,
in some sense, be understood thereby to have instructed *their*
representatives in the House to vote for the person on whom they
were bestowed, in the choice of a President. But most clearly the
representatives coming from other states which gave no part of
those 99 votes, cannot be considered as having been under any
obligation to surrender their judgments to those of the States which
gave the 99 votes. To contend that they are under such an obligation, would be to maintain that the people of one state have the
right to instruct the representatives from another state. It would
be to maintain a still more absurd proposition, that, in a case
where the representatives from a state did not hold themselves
instructed and bound by the will of that state, as indicated in
its electoral college, the representatives from another state were,
nevertheless, instructed and bound by that alien will. Thus, the
entire vote of North-Carolina, and a large majority of that of
Maryland, in their respective electoral colleges, were given to one
of the three returned candidates, for whom the delegation from
neither of those states voted.[18]— And yet the argument combatted
requires that the delegation from Kentucky, who do not represent
the people of North-Carolina nor Maryland, should be instructed
by, and give an effect to, the indicated will of the people of those
two states, when their own delegation paid no attention to it.
Doubtless, those delegations felt themselves authorized to look
into the actual composition of, and all other circumstances connected with, the majorities which gave the electoral votes, in their
respective states; and felt themselves justified, from a view of the
whole ground, to act upon their responsibility and according to
their best judgments, disregarding the electoral votes in their
states. And are the representatives from a different state not only
bound by the will of the people of a different commonwealth,
but forbidden to examine into the manner by which the expression
of that will was brought about—an examination which the immediate representatives themselves feel it their duty to make?

Is the fact, then, of a plurality to have no weight? Far from it.
Here are 24 communities, united under a common government.

The expression of the will of any one of them is entitled to the most respectful attention. It ought to be patiently heard and kindly regarded by the others; but it cannot be admitted to be conclusive upon them. The expression of the will of 99 out of 261 electors is entitled to very great attention, but that will cannot be considered as entitled to control the will of the 162 electors, who have manifested a different will. To give it such controlling influence, would be a subversion of the fundamental maxim of the Republic—that the majority should govern. The will of the 99 can neither be allowed rightfully to control the remaining 162, nor any one of the 162 electoral votes. It may be an argument, a persuasion, addressed to all, and to each of them, but it is binding and obligatory upon none. It follows, then, that the fact of a plurality was only one among the various considerations which the House was called upon to weigh, in making up its judgment. And the weight of the consideration ought to have been regulated by the extent of the plurality. As between General Jackson and Mr. Adams, the vote standing in the proportions of 99 to 84, it was entitled to less weight; as between the General and Mr. Crawford it was entitled to more, the vote being as 99 to 41. The concession may even be made that, upon the supposition of an equality of pretensions between competing candidates, the preponderance ought to be given to the fact of a plurality.

With these views of the relative state of the vote, with which the three returned candidates entered the House, I proceeded to examine the other considerations which belonged to the question. For Mr. Crawford, who barely entered the House, with only four votes more than one candidate not returned,[19] and upon whose case, therefore, the argument derived from the fact of plurality, operated with strong, though not decisive force, I have ever felt much personal regard. But I was called upon to perform a solemn public duty, in which my private feelings, whether of affection or aversion, were not to be indulged, but the good of my country only consulted. It appeared to me that the precarious state of that gentleman's health, although I participated with his best friends, in all their regrets and sympathies, on account of it, was conclusive against him, to say nothing of other considerations of a public nature which would have deserved examination, if, happily, in that respect, he had been differently circumstanced. He had been ill near eighteen months; and although I am aware that his actual condition was a fact depending upon evidence, and that the evidence in regard to it, which had been presented to the public, was not perfectly harmonious, I judged for myself upon what I saw and heard. He may, and I ardently hope, will, recover; but I did not think it became me to assist in committing the Executive administration of this great Republic on the doubtful contingency of the restoration to health of a gentleman who had been so long and so seriously afflicted. Moreover, if, under all the circumstances of his situation, his election had been desirable, I did not think it practicable. I believed, and yet believe, that if the votes of the Western States, given to Mr. Adams, had been conferred on Mr. Crawford, the effect would have been to protract in the House the decision of the contest, to the great agitation and distraction of the country, and, possibly, to defeat an election altogether[20]—the very worst result, I thought, that could happen. It appeared to me then, that sooner or later we must arrive at the only practical issue of the contest before us, and that was between Mr. Adams and General Jackson, and I thought that the earlier we got there, the better for the country and for the House.

In considering this only alternative, I was not unaware of your strong desire to have a Western President; but I thought that I knew enough of your patriotism, and magnanimity, displayed on so many occasions, to believe that you could rise above the mere gratification of sectional pride, if the common good of the whole required you to make the sacrifice of local partiality. I solemnly believed it did, and this brings me to the most important consideration which belonged to the whole subject—that arising out of the respective fitness of the only two real competitors, as it appeared to my best judgment. In speaking of Gen. Jackson, I am aware of the delicacy and respect which are justly due to that distinguished citizen. It is far from my purpose to attempt to disparage him. I could not do it if I were capable of making the attempt; but I shall nevertheless speak of him as becomes me, with truth. I did not believe him so competent to discharge the various, intricate, and complex duties of the office of Chief Magistrate, as his competitor. He has displayed great skill and bravery as a military commander; and his renown will endure as long as the means exist of preserving a recollection of human transactions. But to be qualified to discharge the duties of President of the United States, the incumbent must have more than mere military attainments—he must be a STATESMAN. An individual may be a gallant and successful general, an eminent lawyer, an eloquent divine, a learned physician, or an accomplished artist; and doubtless the union of all these characters in the person of a Chief Magistrate would be desirable; but no one of them, nor all combined, will qualify him to be President, unless he superadds that indispensable requisite of being a statesman. Far from meaning to say, that it is an objection to the elevation, to the chief magistracy, of any person,

that he is a military commander, if he unites the other qualifications, I only intend to say that, whatever may be the success or
splendor of his military achievements, if his qualification be *only*
military, that is an objection, and I think a decisive objection to
his election. If General Jackson has exhibited, either in the councils
of the Union, or in those of his own state, or in those of any other
state or territory, the qualities of a statesman, the evidence of the
fact has escaped my observation. It would be as painful as it is
unnecessary to recapitulate some of the incidents, which must be
fresh in your recollection, of his public life. But I was greatly
deceived in my judgment if they proved him to be endowed with
that prudence, temper, and discretion, which are necessary for
civil administration. It was in vain to remind me of the illustrious
example of Washington. There was, in that extraordinary person,
united a serenity of mind, a cool and collected wisdom, a cautious
and deliberate judgment, a perfect command of the passions, and
throughout his whole life, a familiarity and acquaintance with
business and civil transactions, which rarely characterize any human
being. No man was ever more deeply penetrated than he was, with
profound respect for the safe and necessary principle of the entire
subordination of the military to the civil authority. I hope I do
no injustice to General Jackson, when I say, that I could not
recognise, in his public conduct, those attainments for both civil
government and military command, which cotemporaries [*sic*] and
posterity have alike unanimously concurred in awarding as yet
only to the father of his country. I was sensible of the gratitude
which the people of this country justly feel towards Gen. Jackson
for his brilliant military services. But the impulses of public
gratitude should be controled [*sic*], it appeared to me, by reason
and discretion, and I was not prepared blindly to surrender myself
to the hazardous indulgence of a feeling, however amiable and
excellent that feeling may be when properly directed. It did not
seem to me to be wise or prudent, if, as I solemnly believed,
General Jackson's competency for the office was highly questionable, that he should be placed in a situation where neither his
fame nor the public interests would be advanced. General Jackson
himself would be the last man to recommend or vote for any one
for a place, for which he thought him unfit. I felt myself sustained
by his own reasoning, in his letter to Mr. Monroe, in which,
speaking of the qualifications of our venerable Shelby for the
Department of War, he remarked: "I am compelled to say to
you, that the acquirements of this worthy man are not competent
to the discharge of the multiplied duties of this Department, I
therefore hope he may not accept the appointment. I am fearful,

if he does, he will not add much splendor to his present well-earned standing as a public character."[21]   Such was my opinion of General Jackson, in reference to the Presidency. His convictions of Governor Shelby's unfitness, by the habits of his life, for the appointment of Secretary of War, were not more honest nor stronger than mine were of his own want of experience, and the necessary civil qualifications to discharge the duties of a President of the United States. In his elevation to this office, too, I thought, I perceived the establishment of a fearful precedent; and I am mistaken in all the warnings of instructive history, if I erred in my judgment. Undoubtedly there are other and many dangers to public liberty, besides that which proceeds from military idolatry, but I have yet to acquire the knowledge of it, if there be one more perilous or more frequent.

Whether Mr. Adams would or would not have been my choice of a President, if I had been left freely to select from the whole mass of American citizens, was not the question submitted to my decision. I had no such liberty: but I was circumscribed, in the selection I had to make, to one of the three gentlemen, whom the people themselves had thought proper to present to the House of Representatives. Whatever objections might be supposed to exist against him, still greater appeared to me to apply to his competitor. Of Mr. Adams, it is but truth and justice to say, that he is highly gifted, profoundly learned, and long and greatly experienced in public affairs, at home and abroad. Intimately conversant with the rise and progress of every negotiation with foreign powers, pending or concluded; personally acquainted with the capacity and attainments of most of the public men of this country, whom it might be proper to employ in the public service; extensively possessed of much of that valuable kind of information, which is to be acquired neither from books nor tradition, but which is the fruit of largely participating in public affairs; discreet and sagacious; he would enter on the duties of the office with great advantages. I saw in his election the establishment of no dangerous example. I saw in it, on the contrary, only conformity to the safe precedents which had been established in the instances of Mr. Jefferson, Mr. Madison, and Mr. Monroe, who had respectively filled the same office from which he was to be translated.

A collateral consideration of much weight was derived from the wishes of the Ohio delegation. A majority of it, during the progress of the session, made up their opinions to support Mr. Adams, and they were communicated to me. They said, "Ohio supported the candidate who was the choice of Kentucky. We failed in our common exertions to secure his election. Now, among those returned, we have a decided preference, and we think you ought to make some sacrifice to gratify us." Was not much due to our neighbour and friend?

I considered, with the greatest respect, the resolution of the General Assembly of Kentucky, requesting the delegation to vote for General Jackson.[22] That resolution, it is true, placed us in a peculiar situation. Whilst every other delegation, from every other state in the Union, was left by its Legislature entirely free to examine the pretensions of all the candidates, and to form its unbiased judgment, the General Assembly of Kentucky thought proper to interpose and to request the delegation to give its vote to one of the candidates, whom they were pleased to designate I felt a sincere desire to comply with a request emanating from a source so respectable, if I could have done so consistently with those paramount duties which I owed to you and to the country. But after full and anxious consideration, I found it incompatible with my best judgment of those duties to conform to the request of the General Assembly. The resolution asserts, that it was the wish of the people of Kentucky, that their delegation should vote for the General. It did not inform me by what means that body had arrived at a knowledge of the wish of the people. I knew that its members had repaired to Frankfort before I departed from home to come to Washington. I knew their attention was fixed on important local concerns, well entitled, by their magnitude, exclusively to engross it. No election, no general expression of the popular sentiment had occurred since that in November, when electors were chosen, and at that the people, by an overwhelming majority, had decided against General Jackson.[23] I could not see how such an expression *against* him, could be interpreted into that of a desire *for* his election. If, as is true, the candidate whom they preferred, were not returned to the House, it is equally true, that the *state* of the contest as it presented itself here to me, had never been considered, discussed, and decided by the people of Kentucky, in their collective capacity. What would have been their decision on this *new* state of the question, I might have undertaken to conjecture, but the certainty of any conclusion of fact, as to their opinion, at which I could arrive, was by no means equal to that certainty of conviction of my duty to which I was carried by the exertion of my best and most deliberate reflections. The letters from home, which some of the delegation received, expressed the most opposite opinions, and there were not wanting instances of letters from some of the very members who had voted for the resolution, advising a different course. I received from a highly respectable portion of my constituents a paper, instructing me as follows: "We, the under-

signed voters in the Congressional district, having viewed the instruction or request of the Legislature of Kentucky, on the subject
of choosing a President and Vice-President of the United States,
with regret, and the said request or instruction to our representative in Congress from this district, being without our knowledge
or consent; we for many reasons known to ourselves, connected with
so momentous an occasion, hereby *instruct* our representative in
Congress to vote on this occasion agreeable to his own judgment,
and by the best lights he may have on the subject, with, or without,
the consent of the Legislature of Kentucky."[24] This instruction
came both unexpected and unsolicited by me, and it was accompanied by letters assuring me, that it expressed the opinion of a
majority of my constituents.[25] I could not therefore regard the
resolution as conclusive evidence of your wishes.

Viewed as a mere request, as it purported to be, the General
Assembly doubtless had the power to make it. But then, with
great deference, I think it was worthy of serious consideration
whether the dignity of the General Assembly ought not to have
induced it to forbear addressing itself, not to another legislative
body, but to a small part of it, and requesting the members who
composed that part, in a case which the constitution had confided
to them, to vote according to the wishes of the General Assembly,
whether those wishes did or did not conform to their sense of
duty. I could not regard the resolution as an instruction; for, from
the origin of our State, its legislature has never assumed nor exercised the right to instruct the Representatives in Congress. I did
not recognise the right, therefore, of the Legislature to instruct
me.[26] I recognised that right only when exerted by you. That the
portion of the public servants who made up the General Assembly
have no right to instruct that portion of them who constituted the
Kentucky delegation in the House of Representatives, is a proposition too clear to be argued. The members of the General Assembly
would have been the first to behold as a presumptuous interposition,
any instruction, if the Kentucky delegation could have committed
the absurdity to issue, from this place, any instruction to them to
vote in a particular manner on any of the interesting subjects
which lately engaged their attention at Frankfort. And although
nothing is further from my intention than to impute either absurdity or presumption to the General Assembly, in the adoption
of the resolution referred to, I must say that the difference between
an instruction emanating from them to the delegation, and from
the delegation to them, is not in principle, but is to be found only
in the degree of superior importance which belongs to the General Assembly.

Entertaining these views of the election on which it was made my duty to vote, I felt myself bound, in the exercise of my best judgment, to prefer Mr. Adams; and I accordingly voted for him. I should have been highly gratified if it had not been my duty to vote on the occasion; but that was not my situation, and I did not choose to shrink from any responsibility which appertained to your Representative. Shortly after the election, it was rumored that Mr. Kremer was preparing a publication, and the preparations for it which were making excited much expectation. Accordingly, on the 26th [*sic*] of February, the address, under his name, to the "Electors of the ninth Congressional District of the State of Pennsylvania," made its appearance in the Washington City Gazette.[27] No member of the House, I am persuaded, believed that Mr. Kremer wrote one paragraph of that address, or of the plea, which was presented to the committee, to the jurisdiction of the House.[28] Those who counselled him, and composed both papers, and their purposes, were just as well known as the author of any report from a committee to the House. The first observation which is called for by the address is the *place* of its publication. That place was in this City, remote from the centre of Pennsylvania, near which Mr. Kremer's district is situated, and in a paper having but a very limited, if any, circulation in it. The *time* is also remarkable. The fact that the President intended to nominate me to the Senate for the office which I now hold, in the course of a few days, was then well known; and the publication of the address was, no doubt, made less with an intention to communicate information to the electors of the ninth Congressional District of Pennsylvania, than to affect the decision of the Senate on the intended nomination. Of the character and contents of that address of Messrs. George Kremer & Co. made up, as it is, of assertion without proof, of inferences without premises, and of careless, jocose, and quizzing conversations of some of my friends, to which I was no party, and of which I had never heard, it is not my intention to say much. It carried its own refutation, and the parties concerned saw its abortive nature the next day in the indignant countenance of every unprejudiced and honorable member. In his card, Mr. Kremer had been made to say, that he held himself ready "to *prove,* to the satisfaction of unprejudiced minds, enough to satisfy them of the accuracy of the statements which are contained in that letter, *to the extent that they concern the course of conduct of H. Clay."* The object for excluding my friends from this pledge has been noticed. But now the election was decided, and there no longer existed a motive for discriminating between them and me. Hence the only statements that are made, in the address, having the semblance of proof, relate rather to them than to me; and the design was, by establishing something like facts upon them, to make those facts re-act upon me.

Of the few topics of the address upon which I shall remark, the first is, the accusation, brought forward against me, of violating instructions. If the accusation were true, who was the party offended, and to whom was I amenable? If I violated any instructions, they must have been yours, since you only had the right to give them, and to you alone was I responsible. Without allowing hardly time for you to hear of my vote, without waiting to know what your judgment was of my conduct, George Kremer & Co. chose to arraign me before the American public as the violater [*sic*] of instructions which I was bound to obey. If, instead of being, as you are, and I hope always will be, vigilant observers of the conduct of your public agents, jealous of your rights, and competent to protect and defend them, you had been ignorant and culpably confiding, the gratuitous interposition, as your advocate, of the honorable George Kremer, of the ninth Congressional district in Pennsylvania, would have merited your most grateful acknowledgments. Even upon that supposition, his arraignment of me would have required for its support one small circumstance, which happens not to exist, and that is, the *fact* of your having actually instructed me to vote according to his pleasure.

The relations in which I stood to Mr. Adams constitute the next theme of the address, which I shall notice. I am described as having assumed "a position of peculiar and decided hostility to the election of Mr. Adams," and expressions towards him are attributed to me, which I never used. I am made also responsible for "pamphlets and essays of great ability," published by my friends in Kentucky, in the course of the canvass. The injustice of the principle of holding me thus answerable, may be tested by applying it to the case of General Jackson, in reference to publications issued, for example, from the Columbian Observer. That I was not in favour of the election of Mr. Adams, when the contest was before the people, is most certain. Neither was I in favour of that of Mr. Crawford or General Jackson. That I ever did any thing against Mr. Adams, or either of the other gentlemen, inconsistent with a fair and honorable competition, I utterly deny. My relations to Mr. Adams have been the subject of much misconception, if not misrepresentation. I have been stated to be under a public pledge to expose some nefarious conduct of that gentlemen, during the negotiation at Ghent; which would prove him to be entirely unworthy of public confidence; and that, with a knowledge of his perfidy, I, nevertheless, voted for him. If these imputations are well founded, I should, indeed, be a fit object for public censure; but if, on the contrary, it shall be found that others, inimical both to him and to me, have substituted their own interested wishes for my public promises, I trust that the indignation, which they would excite, will be turned from me. My letter, addressed to the Editors of the Intelligencer, under date of the 15th November, 1822,[29] is made the occasion for ascribing to me the promise and the pledge to make those treasonable disclosures on Mr. Adams. Let that letter speak for itself, and it will be seen how little justification there is for such an assertion. It adverts to the controversy which had arisen between Messrs. Adams and Russell, and then proceeds to state that, "in the course of the several publications, of which it has been the occasion, and, particularly, in the appendix to a pamphlet which had [sic] been recently published by the Hon. John Quincy Adams, I think there are some errors (no doubt *unintentional*) both as to matters of fact and matters of opinion, in regard to the trans-actions at Ghent, relating to the navigation of the Mississippi, and certain liberties claimed by the United States in the Fisheries, *and to the part which I bore in those transactions.* These important interests are now well secured"—"An account, therefore, of what occurred in the negociation at Ghent, on those *two* subjects, is not, perhaps, necessary to the present or future security of any of the rights of the nation, and is *only* interesting as appertaining to its *past* history. With these impressions, and being extremely unwilling to present myself, at any time, before the public, I had *almost* resolved to remain silent, and thus expose myself to the inference of an acquiescence in the correctness of all the statements made by both my colleagues; but I have, on more reflection, thought it may be expected of me, and be considered as a duty on my part, to contribute all in my power towards a full and faithful under-standing of the transactions referred to. Under this conviction, I will, at some future period, more propitious than the present to calm and dispassionate consideration, and when there can be no misinterpretation of motives, lay before the public a narrative of those transactions, as I understood them."

From even a careless perusal of that letter, it is apparent, that the only *two* subjects of the negociations at Ghent to which it refers, were the navigation of the Mississippi and certain fishing liberties; that the errors, which I had supposed were committed, applied to both Mr. Russell and Mr. Adams, though more particularly to the appendix of the latter; that they were unintentional; and they affected myself principally; that I deemed them of no public im-portance, as connected with the then, or future security of any of the rights of the nation, but only interesting to its past history;

that I doubted the necessity of my offering to the public any account of those transactions; and that the narrative which I promised was to be presented at a season of more calm, and when there could be no misinterpretation of motives. Although Mr. Adams believes otherwise, I yet think there are some unintentional errors, in the controversial papers between him and Mr. Russell. But I have reserved to myself an exclusive right of judging when I shall execute the promise which I have made, and I shall be neither quickened nor retarded in its performance, by the friendly anxieties of any of my opponents.

If injury accrue to any one by the delay in publishing the narrative, the public will not suffer by it. It is already known by the publication of the British and American projets, the protocols, and the correspondence between the respective plenipotentiaries, that the British government made at Ghent a demand of the navigation of the Mississippi, by an article in their projet nearly in the same words as those which were employed in the treaty of 1783; that a majority of the American commissioners was in favour of acceding to that demand, upon the condition that the British government would concede to us the same fishing liberties, within their jurisdiction, as were secured to us by the same treaty of 1783; and that both demands were finally abandoned. The fact of these mutual propositions was communicated by me to the American public in a speech which I delivered in the House of Representatives, on the 29th day of January, 1816.[30] Mr. Hopkinson[31] had arraigned the terms of the treaty of peace, and charged upon the War, and the Administration, the loss of the fishing liberties, within the British jurisdiction, which we enjoyed prior to the war. In vindicating, in my reply to him, the course of the government and the conditions of the peace, I stated:—

"When the British Commissioners demanded, in their projet, a renewal to Great Britain of the right to the navigation of the Mississippi, secured by the treaty of 1783, a bare majority of the American Commissioners offered to renew it, upon the condition that the liberties in question were renewed to us. He was not one of that majority. He would not trouble the Committee with his reasons for being opposed to the offer. A majority of his colleagues, *actuated he believed by the best motives,* made, however, the offer, and it was refused by the British Commissioners."

{See *Daily Nat. Intelligencer, of the 21st March, 1816.*} And what I thought of my colleagues of the majority, appears from the same extract. The spring after the termination of the negotiations at Ghent, I went to London, and there entered upon a new and highly important negotiation with two of them, (Messrs. Adams and Gallatin,) which resulted, on the 3d July, 1815, in the Commercial Convention,[32] which has been since made the basis of most of our commercial arrangements with foreign powers. Now, if I had discovered at Ghent, as has been asserted, that either of them was false and faithless to his country, would I have voluntarily commenced with them another negotiation? Further: there never has been a period, during our whole acquaintance, that Mr. Adams and I have not exchanged when we have met, friendly salutations, and the courtesies and hospitalities of social intercourse.

The address proceeds to characterize the support which I gave to Mr. Adams as *unnatural*. The authors of the address have not stated why it is unnatural, and we are therefore left to conjecture their meaning. Is it because Mr. Adams is from New-England, and I am a citizen of the West? If it be unnatural in the Western States to support a citizen of New-England, it must be equally unnatural in the New-England States to support a citizen of the West. And, on the same principle, the New-England States ought to be restrained from concurring in the election of a citizen in the Southern States, or the Southern States from co-operating in the election of a citizen of New-England. And, consequently, the support which the last three Presidents have derived from New-England, and that which the Vice-President recently received, has been most unnaturally given. The tendency of such reasoning would be to denationalize us, and to contract every part of the Union within the narrow selfish limits of its own section. It would be still worse: it would lead to the destruction of the Union itself. For if it be unnatural in one section to support a citizen in another, the Union itself must be unnatural; all our ties; all our glories; all that is animating in the past; all that is bright and cheering in the future, must be unnatural. Happily, such is the admirable texture of our Union, that the interests of all its parts are closely interwoven. If there are strong points of affinity between the South and the West, there are interests of not less, if not greater, strength and vigour, binding the West, and the North, and the East.

Before I close this address, it is my duty, which I proceed to perform with great regret, on account of the occasion which calls for it, to invite your attention to a letter addressed by Gen. Jackson to Mr. Swartwout, on the 23d Feb. last.[33] The names of both the General and myself had been before the American public, for its highest office. We had both been unsuccessful. The unfortunate have usually some sympathy for each other. For myself, I claim no merit for the cheerful acquiescence which I have given in a result by which I was excluded from the House. I have believed that the decision by the constituted authorities, in favour of others, has been founded upon a conviction of the superiority of their pretensions. It has been my habit, when an election is once decided, to forget, as soon as possible, all the irritating circumstances which attended the preceding canvass. If one be successful, he should be content with his success. If he have lost it, railing will do no good. I never gave General Jackson nor his friends any reason to believe that I would, in any contingency, support him. He had, as I thought, no public claim, and I will now add, no personal claim, if these ought to be ever considered, to my support. No one, therefore, ought to have been disappointed or chagrined that I did not vote for him. No more than I was neither surprised nor disappointed, that he did not, on a more recent occasion, feel it to be his duty to vote for me.[34] After commenting upon a particular phrase used in my letter to Judge Brooke, a calm reconsideration of which will, I think, satisfy any person that it was not employed in an offensive sense, if indeed it have an offensive sense, the General, in his letter to Mr Swartwout, proceeds to remark, "No one beheld me seeking through art or management to entice any representative in Congress from conscientious responsibility to his own, or the wishes of his constituents. No midnight taper burnt by me; no secret conclaves were held, nor cabals entered into to persuade any one to a violation of pledges given, or of instructions received. By me no plans were concerted to impair the pure principles of our republican institutions, nor to prostrate that fundamental maxim which maintains the supremacy of the people's will. On the contrary, having never in any manner before the people or Congress interfered in the slightest degree with the question, my conscience stands void of offence, and will go quietly with me, regardless of the insinuations of those who, through management, may seek an influence not sanctioned by integrity and merit."—I am not aware that this defence of himself was rendered necessary by any charges brought forward against the General. Certainly I never made any such charges against him. I will not suppose that in the passages cited, he intended to impute to me the misconduct which he describes; and yet, taking the whole context of his letter together, and coupling it with Mr. Kremer's address, it cannot be disguised that others may suppose he intended to refer to me. I am quite sure that if he did, he could not have formed those unfavourable opinions of me upon any personal observation of my conduct made by himself; for, a supposition that they were founded upon his own knowledge, would imply that my lodgings and my person had been subjected to a system of espionage wholly incompatible with the open, manly, and honourable conduct of a gallant soldier. If he designed any insinuations against me, I must believe that he made them upon the information of others, of whom I can only say, that they have deceived his credulity, and are entirely unworthy of all credit. I entered into no cabals; I held no secret conclaves; I enticed no man to violate pledges given or instructions received. The members from Ohio and from the other Western States, with whom I voted, were all of them as competent as I was to form an opinion on the pending election. The M'Arthurs and the Metcalfes,[35] and the other gentlemen from the West (some of whom have, if I have not, bravely "made an effort to repel an invading foe") are as incapable of dishonor as any men breathing; as disinterested, as unambitious, as exclusively devoted to the best interests of their country. It was quite as likely that I should be influenced by them, as that I could control their votes. Our object was not to impair, but to preserve from all danger, the purity of our republican institutions. And how I prostrated the maxim which maintains the supremacy of the people's will, I am entirely at a loss to comprehend. The illusions of the General's imagination deceive him. *The people* of the United States had never decided the election in his favour. If the people had *willed* his election, he would have been elected. It was because they had *not willed* his election, nor that of any other candidate, that the duty of making a choice devolved on the House of Representatives.

The General remarks: "Mr. Clay has never yet risked himself for his country. He has never sacrificed his repose, nor made an effort to repel an invading foe; *of course,* his conscience assured him it was altogether wrong in any other man to lead his countrymen to battle and victory." The logic of this conclusion is not very striking. Gen. Jackson fights better than he reasons. When have I failed to concur in awarding appropriate honours to those who on the sea or on the land have sustained the glory of our arms, if I could not always approve of the acts of some of them? It is true, that it has been my misfortune never to have repelled an invading foe, nor to have led my countrymen to victory. If I had, I should have left to others to proclaim and appreciate the deed. The General's destiny and mine have led us in different directions. In the civil employment of my country, to which I have been confined, I regret that the little service which I have been able to render it, falls far short of my wishes. But, why this denunciation of those who have not repelled an invading foe, or led our armies to victory? At the very moment when he is inveighing against an objection to the election to the Presidency, founded upon the exclusive military nature of his merits, does he not perceive that he is establishing its validity by proscribing every man who has not successfully fought the public enemy? And that, by such a general proscription, and the requirement of successful military service as the only condition of civil preferment, the inevitable effect would be the ultimate establishment of a Military Government?

If the contents of the letter to Mr. Swartwout were such as justly to excite surprise, there were other circumstances not calculated to diminish it. Of all the citizens of the United States, that gentleman is one of the last to whom it was necessary to address any vindication of Gen. Jackson. He had given abundant evidence of his entire devotion to the cause of the General. He was here after the election, and was one of a committee who invited the General to a public dinner, proposed to be given to him in this place. My letter to Judge Brooke was published in the papers of this City on the 12th of February. The General's note declining the invitation of Mr. Swartwout and others was published on the 14th in the National Journal.[36] The probability therefore is, that he did not leave this City until after he had a full opportunity to receive, in a personal interview with the General, any verbal observations upon it which he might have thought proper to make. The letter to Mr. Swartwout bears date the 23d of February. If received by him in New-York, it must have reached him, in the ordinary course of the mail, on the 25th or 26th. Whether intended or not as a "private communication," and not for the "public eye," as alleged by him, there is much probability in believing that its publication in New-York, on the 4th March, was then made, like Mr. Kremer's address, with the view to its arrival in this City in time to affect my nomination to the Senate. In point of fact, it reached here the day before the Senate acted on that nomination.

Fellow-citizens, I am sensible that generally a public officer had better abstain from any vindication of his conduct, and leave it to the candor and justice of his countrymen, under all its attending circumstances. Such has been the course which I have heretofore prescribed to myself. This is the first, as I hope it may be the last, occasion of my thus appearing before you. The separation which has just taken place between us, and the venom, if not the vigor, of the late onsets upon my public conduct, will, I hope, be allowed in this instance to form an adequate apology. It has been upwards of twenty years since I first entered the public service. Nearly three fourths of that time, with some intermissions, I have represented the same district in Congress, with but little variation in its form. During that long period, you have beheld our country passing through scenes of peace and war, of prosperity and adversity, and of party divisions, local and general, often greatly exasperated against each other. I have been an actor in most of those scenes. Throughout the whole of them you have clung to me with an affectionate confidence which has never been surpassed. I have found in your attachment, in every embarrassment in my public career, the greatest consolation, and the most encouraging support. I should regard the loss of it as one of the most afflicting public misfortunes which could befal [*sic*] me. That I have often misconceived your true interests is highly probable. That I have ever sacrificed them to the object of personal aggrandizement I utterly deny. And for the purity of my motives, however in other respects I may be unworthy to approach the Throne of Grace and Mercy, I appeal to the justice of my God, with all the confidence which can flow from a consciousness of perfect rectitude.

Your obedient servant,   H. CLAY.

Address, To the People of the Congressional District Composed of the Counties of Fayette, Woodford, and Clarke in Kentucky [Washington, 1825]. Published also in Washington *Daily National Journal*, March 28, 1825; widely reprinted in contemporary newspapers, including the Lexington *Kentucky Reporter*, April 11, 1825; Lexington *Kentucky Gazette*, April 21, 1825; and Frankfort *Argus of Western America*, May 4, 1825.

1 See above, III, 301n, 351, 415n. Members of the Legislature of Louisiana had endorsed Clay for the Presidency on March 15, 1823.

2 Daniel Drake.

3 None of these communications has been found, but cf. above, III, 901, 905, 906.

4 Josiah S. Johnston; letter not found.

5 Cf. above, III, 901.

6 Exact quotation not found. Cf. the letter signed "Hermes" in *Washington Gazette,* January 20, 1825; also the statements in George Kremer's letter of February 25 (see above, Wingate to Clay, March 18, 1825), that Clay had "enveloped himself in profound mystery from the beginning of the session until the 24th of January . . ." and, "after nearly two months of dubious silence and mysterious concealment," had accepted the Secretaryship. "Why this strange reserve and mystery on the part of Mr. Clay?" Kremer had asked. *Washington Gazette,* February 28, 1825.

7 Not found.

8 Report that Clay had been burnt in effigy at Pittsburgh on February 24 had been published in the *Washington Gazette* on February 25 [*sic*], 1825. The same journal on March 18 had noted a similar incident at Brownsville, Pennsylvania. Such actions at Rutledge and Knoxville, Tennessee, and Carlisle, Kentucky, were also widely publicized. Lexington *Kentucky Reporter*, March 18, 1825.

9 See above, Clay to Gales and Seaton, January 30, 1825, enclosure and note.

10 See above, Kremer to Clay, *ca.* February 3, 1825.

11 John Reid and John Henry Eaton, *The Life of Andrew Jackson, Major General in the Service of the United States: Comprising a History of the War in the South, from the Commencement of the Creek Campaign, to the Termination of Hostilities before New Orleans . . .* (Philadelphia, 1817). A second edition had appeared in 1824. Several later editions were published, with expanded text and varying title.

12 Benjamin W. Crowninshield.

13 See above, Appeal, February 3, 1825, and note.

14 The statement of William L. Brent, as here quoted, was dated February 25 and printed originally in the Washington *National Journal*, March 1, 1825, after Kremer had been requested to examine it for inaccuracies and to suggest alterations. The conversation between Kremer and Brent had reportedly occurred "at the fire-place, in the lobby of the House of Representatives." Peter Little, of Maryland, appended a statement that he "was present, and heard the observations, as above stated." Following publication of the statements of the Congressmen, Brent and Little, William Dudley Digges, who had also been among those present, testified: "I feel no hesitation in saying that Mr. Brent's statement in the paper of this day, is substantially correct." *Ibid.,* March 2, 1825.

15 Cf. above, Clay to Adams, February 11, 1825, note.

16 Daniel Pope Cook, in the course of the lengthy debate on John Forsyth's motion. See above, Appeal, February 3, 1825. Cook's proposal had been rejected.

17 The committee had been composed of Philip Pendleton Barbour, Daniel Webster,

Louis McLane, John W. Taylor, John Forsyth, Romulus Mitchell Saunders (of North Carolina), and Christopher Rankin.

18 The electoral vote of North Carolina had been given to Jackson (see above, III, 889n), but in the election by the House of Representatives that State's delegation had voted for Crawford. The electoral votes of Maryland had been divided (Jackson, 7; Adams, 3; Crawford, 1); in the House, the State's representatives had voted for Adams.

19 See above, Clay to Brooke, February 10, 1825, note.

20 Cf. above, Armstrong and Potts to Clay, March 9, 1825.

21 Clay quotes from a letter written by Jackson to James Monroe, March 18, 1817, in which the Tennesseean deplored the offer of the Secretaryship of War to Isaac Shelby (see above, II, 316-17n). Bassett (ed.), *Correspondence of Andrew Jackson*, II, 283. The Jackson-Monroe correspondence had been brought to light as a feature of the political campaign in the spring of 1824, when Walter Lowrie had forced publication of the documents to prove that Jackson had urged the appointment of Federalists in the Monroe Cabinet. Livermore, *The Twilight of Federalism*, 160-65.

22 See above, III, 902 and note.

23 In Kentucky, Clay had received 17,331 votes; Jackson, 6,455.

24 Not found; but see above, Clay to Taylor, February 25, 1825, also an editorial notice of such instruction in Lexington *Kentucky Reporter*, March 21, 1825.

25 Cf. above, Kendall to Clay, January 21, 1825; Crittenden to Clay, February 15, 1825; Drake to Clay, February 20, 1825; Clay to Taylor, February 25, 1825. See also Lexington *Kentucky Reporter*, January 3, 17, 1825.

26 For earlier statements of Clay's views on legislative instruction to United States Senators and Representatives, see above, II, 199-200, 216-17.

27 See above, Wingate to Clay, March 18, 1825, note.

28 See above, this document, pp. 148-49.

29 Above, III, 322-23.

30 See above, II, 144.

31 Joseph Hopkinson, whose statement followed, not preceded, Clay's remarks of that date.

32 See above, II, 57-59 *et passim*.

33 See above, Clay to Brooke, January 28, 1825, note.

34 Jackson had been among those Senators who voted in opposition to Clay's appointment as Secretary of State. See above, Commission, March 7, 1825, note.

35 Duncan McArthur; Thomas Metcalfe.

36 The invitation had been issued on February 10, for a dinner to be held at Williamson's Hotel on February 11. Jackson's reply had also been dated February 10. Both the invitation and the reply had been published in the Washington *Daily National Intelligencer* as early as February 12. For Swartwout's answer to this passage, see his letter addressed to the editors of the New York *American*, published without date in *Niles' Weekly Register*, XXVIII (April 16, 1825), 102.

To Joel R. Poinsett

Department of State. Washington 26 March 1825.

No. 1. Joel R. Poinsett appointed Envoy Extraordinary
and Minister Plenipotentiary to Mexico.

Sir,

The mission on which the President wishes you, with all practicable dispatch, to depart, would, at any time, be highly important, but possesses, at this moment, a peculiar interest. Every where, on this Continent, but on the side of the United Mexican States, the United States are touched by the Colonial Territories of some Sovereign Authority, fixed in Europe. You are the first Minister actually leaving the United States, to reside near a Sovereign Power established and exerted on this Continent, whose territories are co-terminous with our own. You will probably be the first Minister received by that Power from any foreign State, except from those which have recently sprung out of Spanish America. The United Mexican States, whether we regard their present posture, or recall to our recollection their ancient history, and fortunes, are entitled to high consideration. In point of population, position and resources, they must be allowed to rank among the first powers of America. In contemplating the progress in them, towards civilization, which the Aborigines had made at the Epoch of the Spanish invasion, and the incidents connected with the Spanish conquest which ensued, an irresistible interest is excited, which is not surpassed, if it be equalled, by that which is awakened in perusing the early history of any other part of America. But what gives, with the President, to your Mission, peculiar importance, at this time, is that it has, for its principal object, to lay, for the first time, the foundations of an intercourse of Amity Commerce, Navigation and Neighbourhood, which may exert a powerful influence, for a long period upon the prosperity of both States.

In more particularly inviting your attention to the objects which should engage it on your mission, I will, in the first place, refer you to the general instructions which were given by my predecessor, on the 27th. May, 1823, to Mr. Anderson, the Minister of the United States at Colombia, of which a copy is annexed, and which are to be considered as incorporated in these.[1] So far as they are applicable alike to the condition of Colombia and of Mexico, and shall not be varied in this or subsequent letters, you will view them as forming a guide for your conduct. In that letter of the 27th. of May, the principles which have regulated the course of this Goverment in respect to the contest between Spanish America and Spain, from its origin, are clearly stated, explained and vindicated; and the bases of those upon which it is desirable to place the future intercourse between the United States and the several Governments which have been established in Spanish America, are laid down;—so that, although that Letter was intended to furnish instructions for the American Minister deputed to one of those Governments only, it should be contemplated as unfolding a system of relations which it is expedient to establish with all of them.

From that letter, as well as from notorious public facts, it clearly appears that the people and the Government of the United States have alike, throughout all the stages of the struggle between Spain and her former Colonies, cherished the warmest feelings and the strongest sympathies towards the latter; that the establishment of their Independence and freedom has been anxiously desired; that the recognition of that Independence was made as early as it was possible, consistently with those just considerations of policy and

duty which this Government felt itself bound to entertain towards both parties;[2] and that, in point of fact, with the exception
of the act of the Portuguese Brazilian Government, to which it
was prompted by self interest, and which preceded that of the
United States only a few months,[3] this Government has been the
first to assume the responsibility and encounter the hazard of
recognizing the Governments which have been formed out of
Spanish America. If there ever were any ground for imputing tardiness to the United States in making that recognition, as it respects
other parts of what was formerly, Spanish America, there is not
the slightest pretext for such a suggestion in relation to Mexico.
For within a little more than a year after its independence was
proclaimed, the United States hastened to acknowledge it. They
have never claimed, and do not now claim, any peculiar favour
or concession to their commerce or navigation, as the consideration
of the liberal policy which they have observed towards those Governments. But the President does confidently expect that the priority of movement on our part, which has disconcerted plans which
the European Allies were contemplating against the independent
Governments, and which has, no doubt, tended to accelerate similar
acts of recognition by the European Powers, and especially that
of Great Britain, will form a powerful motive with our southern
neighbours, and particularly with Mexico, for denying to the Commerce and Navigation of those European States, any favours or
privileges which shall not be equally extended to us.[4]

In pursuance of the Instructions given to Mr. Anderson, a general Convention of Peace, Amity, Navigation, and Commerce was
concluded and signed at Bogota on the 3rd. of October 1824. Its
ratification has been consented to, and advised, by the Senate of the
United States; but the ratifications have not yet been exchanged
in consequence of the unavoidable delay which has arisen in the
transmission of its anticipated ratification on the part of Colombia,
to her Minister here.[5] A copy of that Convention will accompany
these instructions, and it will serve to assist you in the formation of
the treaty which it is expected you will be able to conclude at
Mexico.

The basis of the regulations of the Commerce and Navigation
of the United States and Colombia which that Convention as-
sumes, is that of extending to them, respectively, the rule of the
most favoured Nation. To that rule there are some objections, and
the President would therefore prefer, and you are accordingly instructed to endeavour to get substituted to it, that of placing the
Commerce and Navigation of the two Countries on the more
liberal footing of reciprocity between the resident Citizen and the

Foreigner, which is provided for by the Act of 7th. January, 1824,[6] passed since the instructions to Mr. Anderson were prepared. The rule of the most favoured Nation may not be, and scarcely ever is, equal in its operation between two contracting parties. It could only be equal if the measure of voluntary concession by each of them to the most favoured third Power were precisely the same; but as that rarely happens, by referring the Citizens of the two contracting Powers to such a rule, the fair competition between them, which ought always to be a primary object, is not secured, but, on the contrary, those who belong to the Nation which has shewn least liberality to other Nations, are enabled to engross almost the entire Commerce and Navigation carried on between the two contracting Powers. The rule of the most favoured Nation is not so simple as the proposed substitute. In order to ascertain the quantum of favour which, being granted to the Commerce & Navigation of one Nation, is claimed by another, in virtue of a treaty-stipulation embracing that principle, it is necessary that the claimant should be accurately informed of the actual state of the Commercial relations between the Nation on which the claim of equal favour is preferred, and all the rest of the Commercial world. A knowledge of those relations must be sometimes sought after in numerous treaties, statutes, orders, decrees, and other regulations, and is often of very difficult attainment. When acquired, it is not always very easy to distinguish between what was a voluntary grant, and that which was a concession by one party for an equivalent yielded by the other. Sometimes the equivalent for the alledged favour proceeding from the one party may be diffused throughout all the stipulations in the treaty by the other, and is to be extracted only after a careful view and comparison of the whole of them. Not unfrequently the equivalent may not even be clearly deducible from the instrument itself, conveying the supposed favour. Peculiar considerations may lead to the grant of what, on a first impression, might be conceived to be a voluntary favour, but which has really been founded upon a received equivalent; and these considerations may sometimes apply to the entire commerce and navigation of a Country, and at others to particular ports only. Examples of the latter description are to be found in the Louisiana treaty, (See Laws U. S. V. 1. P. 134) by the 7th. Article of which, in respect to New Orleans and other ports of that Province, privileges were secured for the space of twelve years to the ships of France and Spain, and their cargoes, exclusive of all other nations.[7] And by the 15th. Article of the Treaty with Spain which was signed on the 22nd. day of February, 1819,[8] (See 6th. vol. U. S. Laws p. 614) like exclusive privileges were secured to Spanish vessels and their cargoes, for the term of twelve years, in the ports of Pensacola and St. Augustine. From some or all of these causes it so happens that in the practical application of the rule of the most favoured Nation, perplexing and embarrassing discussions sometimes arise; and there are not wanting instances of such discussions in our own intercourse and correspondence with Foreign Powers. It is better to avoid sowing the seeds of all collissions [sic] and misunderstandings; and that desirable object the President thinks will be best accomplished by adopting a plain and familiar rule for the two parties themselves, instead of referring each of them to that complicated rule which may happen to exist between either and third parties. By placing the admission into the Ports of Mexico, of a vessel of the United States, and her cargo, being of their produce or manufacture, upon the same footing with the admission into those ports of a like cargo imported in a vessel owned by a resident citizen of Mexico, and vice versa, the simplicity which it is desirable the rule should possess, will be secured, and all causes of misunderstanding be prevented. The President does not anticipate that you will experience any difficulty in impressing upon the United Mexican Government the very great liberality which characterizes the Act of 7th. January, 1824, and in making it perceive the utility of engrafting on the treaty which you are expected to conclude, the principle of that act. It has been already embraced by several of the European Powers, and been mutually extended to the commerce and navigation between them and the United States.[9] He wishes it applied as extensively as practicable to all the commercial world; and he would see with regret that any of the Governments of America should be behind any European Power in acting on such a scale of enlightened liberality. Nevertheless if all your efforts should be unavailing to carry to the Mexican Government a conviction of the expediency of the proposed principle, and the propriety of treating on it, you are then at liberty to conclude a Convention, comprehending the rule for the regulation of the commerce and navigation of the two countries which was incorporated in the late Colombian Treaty. It is hardly necessary to remark that both principles leave the respective parties entirely free to impose such duties of impost and tonnage as they may think proper. A full power for negociating concerning matters of Commerce and navigation, accompanies these Instructions.[10]

You will bring to the notice of the Mexican Government, the Message of the late President of the United States, to their Congress, on the 2nd. December 1823, asserting certain important principles of intercontinental law in the relations of Europe and America.[11] The first principle asserted in that message is, that the American

Continents are not, henceforth, to be considered as subjects for future colonization by any European Powers. In the maintenance of that principle, all the Independent Governments of America have an interest, but that of the United States has probably the least. Whatever foundation may have existed three centuries ago, or even at a later period, when all this Continent was under European subjection, for the establishment of a rule founded on priority of discovery, and occupation, for apportioning among the Powers of Europe, parts of this Continent, none can be now admitted as applicable to its present condition. There is no disposition to disturb the Colonial possessions as they may now exist, of any of the European Powers; but it is against the establishment of new European Colonies upon this Continent, that the principle is directed. The Countries in which any such new establishments might be attempted are now open to the enterprise and commerce of all Americans. And the justice or propriety cannot be recognized, of arbitrarily limiting and circumscribing that enterprize and commerce, by the act of voluntarily planting a new Colony without the consent of America, under the auspices of foreign Powers belonging to another and a distant Continent. Europe would be indignant at any American attempt to plant a Colony on any part of her shores. And her justice must perceive in the rule contended for, only perfect reciprocity.

The other principle asserted in the message is that, whilst we do not desire to interfere, in Europe, with the political system of the allied Powers, we should regard as dangerous to our peace and safety, any attempt on their part, to extend their system to any portion of this Hemisphere. The political systems of the two Continents are essentially different. Each has an exclusive right to judge for itself what is best suited to its own condition, and most likely to promote its happiness, but neither has a right to enforce upon the other the establishment of its peculiar system. This principle was declared in the face of the world at a moment when there was reason to apprehend that the allied Powers were entertaining designs inimical to the freedom, if not the Independence of the new Governments. There is ground for believing that the declartion [sic] of it had considerable effect in preventing the maturity, if not in producing the abandonment, of all such designs. Both principles were laid down after much and anxious deliberation on the part of the late Administration. The President who then formed a part of it, continues entirely to coincide in both. And you will urge upon the Government of Mexico the utility and expediency of asserting the same principles on all proper occasions.

The final establishment of the limits between the territories of the United States, and those of the United Mexican States, is an interesting object to which you will direct your attention. By the third Article of the Treaty "of Amity, Settlement and limits between the United States of America and His Catholic Majesty," concluded and signed at Washington, on the 22nd. day of February, 1819, it is provided that "the boundary line between the two countries west of the Mississippi, shall begin on the Gulf of Mexico, at the mouth of the river Sabine, in the sea, continuing north, along the western bank of that river to the 32nd. degree of latitude; thence by a line due north, to the degree of latitude where it strikes the Rio Roxo of Natchitoches or *Red river;* then following the course of the Rio Roxo westward, to the degree of longitude, 100 west from London, and 23 from Washington; then crossing the said Red river, and running thence, by a line due north, to the river Arkansas; thence following the course of the southern bank of the Arkansas, to its source, in latitude 42 North; and thence by that parallel of latitude to the South sea. The whole being as laid down in Melish's map of the United States, published at Philadelphia, improved to the first of January, 1818. But if the source of the Arkansas river shall be found to fall north or south of latitude 42, then the line shall run from the said source, due south or north, as the case may be, till it meets the said parallel of latitude 42, and thence along the said parallel to the South sea. All the Islands in the Sabine and the said Red and Arkansas rivers, throughout the course thus described, to belong to the United States; but the use of the waters and the navigation of the Sabine to the sea, and of the said Rivers Roxo and Arkansas, throughout the extent of the said Boundary, on their respective banks, shall be common to the respective inhabitants of both Nations."

By the fourth Article, provision is made for the appointment by each of the contracting parties, of a commissioner and surveyor, to fix, with more precision the line described in the third, and to place the land-marks which shall designate exactly, the limits of both Nations; but it has not yet been carried into execution. That Treaty having been concluded when Mexico composed a part of the Dominions of Spain, is obligatory upon both the United States and Mexico. On the 15th. of February, 1824, Mr. Torrens, the Chargé d'Affaires from Mexico, near this Government, addressed a Note[12] to this Department (of which a copy is annexed) in which he declares the willingness of the Supreme Executive power of Mexico, to accede to the limits agreed upon in the third Article above mentioned; and its readiness to co-operate with the United States, in carrying into complete effect those two Articles.

Some difficulties may possibly hereafter arise between the two

countries from the line thus agreed upon, against which it would
be desirable now to guard, if practicable; and as the Government
of Mexico may be supposed not to have any disinclination to the
fixation of a new line which would prevent those difficulties, the
President wishes you to sound it on that subject; and to avail yourself of a favourable disposition, if you should find it, to effect that
object. The line of the Sabine approaches our great western Mart,
nearer than could be wished. Perhaps the Mexican Government
may not be unwilling to establish that of the Rio Brassos de dios,
or the Rio Colorado, or the Snow Mountains, or the Rio del Norte,
in lieu of it. By the agreed line, portions of both the Red river
and branches of the Arkansas, are thrown on the Mexican side, and
the navigation of both those rivers, as well as that of the Sabine
is made common to the respective inhabitants of the two Countries.
When the Countries adjacent to those waters shall come to be
thickly inhabited, collissions [sic] and misunderstandings may arise
from the community thus established in the use of their navigation,
which it would be well now to prevent. If the line were so altered
as to throw altogether on one side, Red river and Arkansas, and
their respective tributary streams, and the line on the Sabine were
removed further west, all causes of further collission would be
prevented. The Government of Mexico may have a motive for
such an alteration of the line as is here proposed, in the fact that it
would have the effect of placing the City of Mexico nearer the
centre of its territories. If the line were so changed, the greater
part, if not the whole of the powerful, warlike, and turbulent Indian
Nation of the Camanches [sic] would be thrown on the side of the
United States, and, as an equivalent for the proposed cession of
territory, they would stipulate to restrain, as far as practicable, the
Camanches from committing hostilities and depredations upon the
Territories and people, whether Indians or otherwise, of Mexico.

But if you shall find that the Mexican Government is unwilling
to alter the agreed line in the manner proposed, and that it insists
upon the execution of the third and fourth Articles of the Treaty
before mentioned, you are authorised to agree to the recognition
and establishment of the line as described in the third Article, and
to the demarcation of it forthwith as is stipulated in the fourth. But,
in that case, you will urge, not, however, as a sine qua non, the
insertion of an Article in the Treaty by which each party shall
undertake to restrain the Indians residing within his territories,
from committing hostilities upon the people, Indians, or territories,
of the other. The example of such an Article, which will, at the
same time, furnish a model for that which is proposed, is to be
found in the fifth Article of the Treaty of friendship, limits and

navigation between the United States of America, and the King of
Spain, which was signed at San Lorenzo el Real, the 27th. day of
October, 1795.[13] The hostilities which the President is desirous
to restrain, are afflicting to humanity when confined to the Indians
themselves; but they often affect, collaterally, peaceable citizens,
who are no parties to them, and their property.

Instances are beleived [sic] to have occurred, and others may
be expected more frequently, of escape by slaves from their owners,
in Louisiana, Missouri, and Arkansas, and their taking refuge in
the adjacent territories of Mexico. The pursuit after, and recaption
of, these slaves, which it would be difficult for this Government to
restrain, may lead to irritations, if not acts of violence. And as
their acquisition cannot be desired by Mexico, especially as the
fugitive may be supposed to be the most worthless part of that
unfortunate portion of our population, you are instructed to endeavour to get an Article inserted in the proposed Treaty, providing for the regular apprehension and surrender to their respective
proprietors, or their lawful agents, of any such fugitive slaves.

The victorious termination to which Genl. Bolivar has recently
brought the war in Peru,[14] liberates the Colombian arms from
any further employment against the forces of Spain in South
America. Those of Mexico have no Spanish force to encounter in
North America. In this state of the contest, it is to be hoped that
Spain, listening to wiser and better councils, and at last being made
sensible of what all America and Europe have long since seen, that
her dominion on this Continent is lost, will hasten, by a formal
pacification with the southern Nations, to put an end to a war
which she has not the ability any longer to wage. Such a pacific
disposition, it is presumed, will be cordially met by the Government of the United Mexican States; and you will avail yourself of
every fit occasion to strengthen it by friendly and frank representations of the desire of the President to see an honourable close of
the war. Nevertheless, peace may not be established, and the pride
of Spain may dissuade her from acceding to terms which a prudent
regard of her actual comparative weakness should render acceptable.
If the war be indefinitely protracted, to what object will the arms
of the new Governments be directed? It is not unlikely that they
may be turned upon the conquest of Cuba and Porto Rico, and that,
with that view, a combined operation will be concerted between
those of Colombia and Mexico. The United States cannot remain
indifferent to such a movement. Their commerce, their peace and
their safety are too intimately connected with the fortunes and
fate of the Island of Cuba to allow them to behold any change in its
condition and political relations without deep solicitude. They

are not disposed, themselves, to interfere with its present actual state; but they could not see, with indifference, any change that may be attempted in it. It commands, from its position, the Gulf of Mexico, and the valuable commerce of the United States, which must necessarily pass near its shores. In the hands of Spain, its ports are open, its cannon silent and harmless, and its possession guaranteed by the mutual jealousies and interests of the maritime powers of Europe. Under the dominion of any one of those powers other than Spain, and especially under that of Great Britain, the United States would have just cause of serious alarm. Nor could they see that dominion passing either to Mexico or Colombia without some apprehensions of the future. Neither of those two states has, or is likely shortly to acquire, the naval ability to maintain and protect Cuba, if its conquest could be achieved. The United States have no desire to aggrandize themselves by the acquisition of Cuba. And yet if that Island is to be made a dependence of any one of the American States, it is impossible not to allow that the law of its position proclaims that it should be attached to the United States. Abounding in those productions to which the soil and climate, both of Mexico and Colombia are best adapted, neither of them can want it: whilst, in that view of the subject, if the United States were to lend themselves to the suggestions of interest, it would, to them, be particularly desirable. If the population of Cuba were capable of maintaining, and should make an unprompted declaration of, its independence, perhaps it would be the real interest of all parties that it should possess an independent self Government. And then it would be worthy of serious consideration whether the powers of the American Continent would not do well to guarantee that independence against all European attacks upon its existence. What the President, however, directs you to do is to keep a vigilant attention upon every movement towards Cuba, to ascertain the designs of Mexico in regard to it, and to put him, early, in full possession of every purpose of the Mexican Government relative to it. And you are authorized, if, in the progress of events it should become necessary, to disclose frankly the feelings and the interests as here developed, which the people of the United States cherish in respect to that Island.

The Federal Constitution which the United Mexican States have adopted for themselves has evidently been formed after the model of that of the U. States.[15] You will impress their President with a due sense of the compliment which is felt to be thus paid to the illustrious founders of our own; and you will shew, on all occasions, an unobtrusive readiness to explain the practical operation, and the very great advantages which appertain to our system.

By an Act passed at the late Session of Congress,[16] of which a copy accompanies this letter, the President is authorised to appoint Commissioners to mark out a road from the western frontier of the State of Missouri, to the boundary line of the United States in the direction to Sante Fe, of New Mexico; and he is further empowered to cause the marking of the road to be continued from the boundary line of the United States to the frontier of New Mexico, under such regulations as may be agreed upon for that purpose, between him and the Mexican Government

You will accompany the communication of that Act to the Mexican Government by assurances that it has originated in a friendly spirit to open a commerce and intercourse between the two countries in that direction, which it is believed, would be mutually beneficial. And you will receive any propositions which may be offered for regulating that intercourse. It does not occur to the President, at present, to suggest any. In regard to the continuation of the road to Santa Fe, as the United States have taken upon themselves the expense of making the road within their limits, it is presumed that Mexico would readily assume that of continuing it to Santa Fe.

Information has been received at this Department, of an outrage committed on the 4th. January last, on the American Schooner Scott,[17] by the Forts of La Vera Cruz, which you will represent to the Mexican Government in terms suited to the nature of the outrage, and demand satisfaction for the injury. According to that information, it appears that the Schooner Scott, bearing the American flag, hove in sight of the Castle, San Juan de Ulloa,[18] in the afternoon of the 4th. of January; that the wind, blowing fresh from the northward, she came to anchor near the Castle, but within reach of the guns of the City, which position the vessel was obliged to take, by the heavy weather that prevailed; that a short time only elapsed, before the forts of Vera Cruz opened a dreadful fire on the vessel, tore her to pieces, wounded the mate severely, and finally compelled the Captain, in order to save the lives of his crew, to run the vessel ashore at the mouth of the Southern ditch of the Castle, where she immediately filled; & that the violence did not then close, the forts continued their fire, during the whole night of the 4th., and part of the next day, until they made the Schooner a complete wreck, and prostrated in the water the American flag, which had been kept flying the whole time, with a cannon ball that carried away both masts. A Letter detailing the circumstances of this attack, accompanies these instructions.[19] The pretext for it will probably be, that she was attempting to violate a blockade of the castle; but if she were not warned off, or if there were no Mexican

force at sea, present, to render her approach hazardous, the attack
can find no justification in the law of blockade.

Information has been also received at this Department,[20] respecting which, however, it is believed, there must be some mistake,
that American fabrics, and especially that of Cotton, which is every
day becoming more important, are subjected, on their entry at
the Custom Houses of Mexico, to higher duties than those of
similar manufacture of Great Britain are made to pay; and that the
inequality is so great as to threaten a total discontinuance of the
trade. The injustice and unfriendliness of such a discrimination,
if it exist, are so manifest, that the President cannot doubt that a
remonstrance which, in that contingency, you are instructed to
make, will be promptly followed with the desired corrective.

Mess'rs Samuel G. Arnold and Co., Richard J. Arnold, and
Ratcliffe Hicks, owners of the Ship Louisa, of Providence in Rhode
Island,[21] have a claim upon the Mexican Government, of which
Capt. Hicks, now in Mexico, is endeavouring to effect a payment.
The Letter of Mr. Samuel G. Arnold, addressed to the President,
under date the 15th. March, 1825,[22] accompanying these instructions, and to which you are referred, will put you into more full
possession of the case. It appears that the justice of the claim is
not contested by the Mexican Government, which has even made
some payments on account of it. Nevertheless, the claimants are
subjected to a ruinous procrastination in obtaining their rights.
You will render to Captain Hicks every assistance in your power,
and urge the immediate payment of his claim.

I have the honour to be, Sir, with great respect, Your obedient
& very humble Servant.   H. CLAY.

Copy. DNA, RG59, Dip. Instr., vol. 10, pp. 225-38 (M77, R5). AL draft, in DLC-HC
(DNA, M212, R7), and LS, in DNA, RG84, Mexico—both dated March 25, 1825.
Transmitted with personal instructions, below, Clay to Poinsett, March 27, 1825.

1 Extracts of Adams' letter to Richard C. Anderson, Jr., are found in Manning
(arr.), Diplomatic Correspondence . . . Latin-American Nations, I, 192-208; American
State Papers, Foreign Relations, V, 888-97; Alfred Tischendorf and E. Taylor Parks
(eds.), The Diary and Journal of Richard Clough Anderson, Jr., 1814-1826 (Durham,
N. C., 1964), 109-19.

2 See above, III, 186n.

3 Brazil had recognized the independence of the United Provinces of Río de la
Plata in July, 1821, as an accompaniment to assertion of its own jurisdiction over the
Banda Oriental (cf. above, II, 446n, 702n).

4 See above, Nelson to Clay, March 8, 1825, note. The relevance of American action
to the disruption of the plans of the European Allies has been minimized by most
modern interpreters of these events. See Temperley, The Foreign Policy of Canning,
129-30; Dexter Perkins, The Monroe Doctrine, 1823-1826 (Cambridge, [Mass.], 1932),
112-43, 225-27, 231-35, 255-58; Samuel Flagg Bemis, John Quincy Adams and the
Foundations of American Foreign Policy (New York, 1949), 381, 406. On the other
hand, diplomatic agents of the United States found that the desire to win recognition
from Great Britain induced the new American Republics to accord her preferential
treatment. See below, Forbes to Clay, March 30, 1825; Watts to Clay, May 10, 1825;
Allen to Clay, September 16, 1825.

5 See above, Clay to Salazar, March 21, 1825, and note.

[6] See above, Lorich to Clay, March 16, 1825, note.

[7] See above, III, 383n.   [8] See above, II, 678n.

[9] See above, Lorich to Clay, March 16, 1825, note; cf. below, Clay to Forbes, April 14, 1825.

[10] Dated March 14. Copy, in DNA, RG59, Ceremonial Communications, vol. 2, pp. 3-4.

[11] The original statement of the Monroe Doctrine (above, III, 542n).

[12] ALS, in DNA, RG59, Notes from Foreign Legations, Mexico, vol. 1 (M54, R1). José Anastasio Torrens, named Secretary of Legation for Mexico in the United States in September, 1822, had been accredited as Chargé from December, 1823, until November, 1824, when he was transferred to similar duties in Colombia.

[13] That is, Pinckney's Treaty.

[14] See above, Raguet to Secretary of State, March 11, 1825, note; cf. above, Tudor to Secretary of State, March 21, 1825, note.

[15] See above, III, 475n.

[16] Approved March 3, 1825. 4 *U. S. Stat.*, 100-101.

[17] Sailing from New Orleans; owners not identified.

[18] The last Spanish post on the mainland of North America; by proclamation of the President of the Mexican States, dated December 14, 1824, declared to be "under a rigid blockade . . . by sea and by land." On the final surrender of the fortress, see below, Poinsett to Clay, November 23, 1825.

[19] Not found. "The late master of the Scott complains severely of the transaction." *Niles' Weekly Register*, XXVIII (March 19, 1825), 35-36. The report of the incident by William Taylor, consul of the United States at Veracruz, written on January 5, 7, 1825, and received at the State Department on March 7, had differed markedly from this version. Taylor had noted that an American schooner, which he did not identify, "bound to the Castle with supplies from Havana, being chased by a Mexican vessel of war anchored under the Guns of the Castle, next to Vera Cruz"; the "Guns of the Town were immediately opened upon the Schooner whereupon . . . the Castle opened a heavy fire against the City"; "The firing Continued about 24 hours"; and finally, "the Castle having secured the provisions from on board the Schooner, and secured that vessel from the fire of the batteries on Shore, Ceased firing upon the City—" ALS. DNA, RG59, Cons. Disp., Veracruz, vol. 1 (M183, R1).

[20] A memorial from David Lewis and others, of Philadelphia, dated March 21, 1825, and addressed to the President, had asked that the United States Minister to Mexico be instructed to try to get the duties there on American manufactures placed on a footing with those of the most favored nation. An endorsement by Clay on the wrapper (AEI) states: "The object of these Memorials has already been comprehended in the instructions given to our Minister; but let copies of them be made out for him. 28 Mar. 1825 H. C." DNA, RG59, Misc. Letters (M179, R62). On May 14, Daniel Brent, at the direction of Clay, notified James Yard and others, memorialists of Philadelphia, that the object of their memorial, dated March 21 and addressed to the President, had been encompassed in the instruction to Poinsett. Copy. DNA, RG59, Dom. Letters, vol. 21, pp. 58-59 (M140, R19). See also, above, Biddle to Clay, March 10, 16, 1825; Clay to Biddle, March 12, 1825.

[21] The Arnolds were wealthy and prominent merchants of that port.

[22] Not found.

To Elisha Whittlesey

Dear Sir   Washington 26h. March 1825

I received today your obliging letter of the 17h. inst.[1] and was pleased to find from it that you had reached your home in safety. I am gratified to learn that the good people of your district are generally satisfied with the result of the Presidential election. From all quarters I received information of the same agreeable character. I never doubted that such would be the sobjer [*sic*] judgment of our Country. I have prepared and now have in the press an address to my Constituents in defence of my late course in regard to public events here;[2] and to quiet all your friendly apprehensions about it, I tell you before hand that you will find it perfectly temperate. I will direct a Copy to be sent to you.

The opposition to my nomination in the Senate[3] was greater than I expected; but considering its discordant materials one ought not to be surprized or mortified. Mr. Macon[4] took occasion to say explicitly to some of my friends that his vote was not influenced by my vote on the P. question; that he approved of what I had done; and that he could *prove* that I could not have consistently acted otherwise; but that he was governed by my opinions on the Constitution, alluding as I suppose to that respecting Internal Improvements and perhaps others.

We have no news. I find my new office not a bed of roses, but one that requires me to work 12 or 14 hours per day.

With my best wishes for your prosperity I am faithfully Yrs
The Honble E. Whittlesey.   H. CLAY

ALS. OClWHi.   1 Not found.   2 See above, this date.
3 See above, Commission, March 7, 1825, note.   4 Nathaniel Macon.

INSTRUCTIONS AND DISPATCHES   March 26, 1825

From JOHN M. FORBES, Chargé d'Affaires at Buenos Aires, no. 16. Transmits minutes of conferences with the Minister of Foreign Relations at Buenos Aires (Manuel José Garcia) on "the treaty lately concluded here by the British [above, Raguet to Secretary of State, March 11, 1825]" and "the views of this [the Buenos Aires] Government as to their future diplomatic intercourse with foreign Governments." Forbes reports having "obtained from the Minister a formal, written assurance of the readiness of this Government to Conclude a Treaty with the United States on precisely the Same bases of that Concluded with England.—" ALS. DNA, RG59, Dip. Disp., Argentina, vol. 2 (M69, R3). Addressed to Secretary of State. Published in Felipe A. Espil (comp., trans., and ed.), *Once Años en Buenos Aires, 1820-1831; las Cronicas Diplomaticas de John Murray Forbes* (Buenos Aires, [1956]), 355-56.

Forbes had returned from Denmark in the autumn of 1818 and in January, 1819, had submitted his resignation as consul general in that country. In June, 1820, he had been appointed agent for commerce and seamen in the Province of Buenos Aires and had set sail the following month. He was named Secretary of Legation at Buenos Aires in January, 1823, served as acting Chargé d'Affaires there from 1824 to 1825, and on March 9, 1825, became the Chargé, in which position he continued until 1831.

The enclosed memorandum on the second of the conferences, held March 24, notes that Garcia cited the inability of his country to support diplomatic establishments of the higher grade and, on the other hand, the embarrassment they would feel at "the presence of a very elevated class of foreign diplomatists."

From RICHARD RUSH, London, no. 426. Reports that "Mr. [Charles R.] Vaughan" is about to embark as Minister to the United States and that Stratford Canning has recently discussed with the Russian Government the differences between Russia and the United States on navigation in the Pacific; warns that British claims to the Columbia River and coast "will be followed up in a tone that will be unyielding." Interprets the program of the president of the Board of

Trade (William Huskisson), presented to the House of Commons in speeches of March 21 and 25, as "raising up the British colonies in our hemisphere as rivals to the United States, making them more powerful by widening their range of free action, and conciliating them by boons, so as to render for the future their union with the mother country more cordial and more efficient." Particular emphasis is being placed upon the settlement of Canada, Rush notes, with advertisement of British command of navigation at the mouth of the St. Lawrence and plans for a governmental commission of engineers to examine "the whole line of frontier between the United States and that province, and to make report on the state of the posts and fortifications at every point." He believes the great powers of Europe are reconciling themselves, though reluctantly, to British recognition of the new American States. ALS. DNA, RG59, Dip. Disp., Great Britain, vol. 32 (M30, R28). Addressed to Secretary of State; received May 19.

Stratford Canning, cousin of George Canning, had been Minister to the United States from 1820 to 1824; he had been sent thence to St. Petersburg; and from there, in 1825, he was transferred to Constantinople, where he served as envoy much of the remainder of his life. He was a member of Parliament from 1835 to 1841. On the dispute between the United States and Russia, see above, Clay to Tuyll, March 25, 1825, note.

Huskisson's program for revising the British policy on colonial trade (outlined in his speech of March 21—that of March 25 being devoted to general commercial policy) had been designed to counter the American legislation of March 1, 1823 (see above, III, 729n). He recommended that American vessels be subjected to general alien duties upon entry into the British colonies and that under such duties the colonies be opened to trade with all friendly states. Trade between Britain and her colonies, whether direct or circuitous, and all intercolonial commerce were, however, to be regarded as "coasting trade" and reserved entirely to British vessels. Importation of foreign goods into the colonies was to be permitted generally, under a scale of duties ranging from 7 ½ to 30 per cent ad valorem for all products formerly excluded; and only firearms, ammunition, and, in specific colonies, sugar, rum, and a few other articles locally produced were to be barred. All port fees were to be abolished, the customs officials to be placed on salaries paid out of customs receipts, which income was otherwise to be subject to appropriation by the colonial legislatures. A system of bonding and warehousing was to be established in the West Indies, designed especially to facilitate mercantile relations with the former Spanish-American colonies. These recommendations, together with a provision that goods imported into the British colonies through the United Kingdom should receive a remission of one tenth of the duties, were enacted on June 27 and incorporated into a general summary of British trade regulations adopted on July 5, 1825. "Exposition of the Colonial Policy of the Country, March 21," in William Huskisson, *The Speeches. . . , with a Biographical Memoir Supplied to the Editor from Authentic Sources* (3 vols.; London, 1831), II, 304-27; 6 *Geo. IV,* c. 114; *American State Papers, Foreign Relations,* VI, 301-21; *Annual Register, 1825,* "History," 101-106; Benns, *The American Struggle for the British West India Carrying Trade,* 107-108. For features of the legislation which American policy makers did not understand and which led to closing of American trade with the British West Indies, cf. below, Clay to Gallatin, June 19, 1826; Gallatin to Clay, August 19, September 13, 14, November 8, 1826. See also George Dangerfield, *The Era of Good Feelings* (First Harbinger Books edn.; New York, 1963), 372-75.

Looking forward to the time when "joint occupation" of Oregon would end (see above, III, 60n), the United States favored dividing the area west of the

Rocky Mountains along the parallel of 49 degrees, north latitude, to the
Pacific Ocean, while Britain agreed to a boundary at this line only so far as the
Columbia River, thence down that stream to the coast. British negotiators in
1818 had, in fact, proposed, in their only formal denomination of a boundary,
that the joint occupancy apply to the territory as far south as the forty-fifth
parallel. Miller (ed.), *Treaties. . .* , V, 18-19.

From CHARLES SAVAGE. Transmits residue of the Government *Gazette,* completing the file from March, 1824, to March, 1825, and one copy, each, of the
Constitution of this republic and of a discourse of the President. ALS. DNA,
RG59, Cons. Disp., Guatemala, vol. 1 (M-T337, R1). Addressed to Secretary
of State; received July 25. See above, Savage to Clay, March 18, 1825.

From JOHN WARNER. Reports rumors that Mexico has offered its protection
in case the Captain General of Cuba (Francisco Dionisio Vives) should
declare the island independent of Spain and has promised preservation
of slavery as it now exists. Seven American seamen, held as accomplices in a
murder aboard the brig *Noble* in 1823, have been brought to trial. LS. DNA,
RG59, Cons. Disp., Havana, Cuba, vol. 3 (M-T20, R3). On the case of the
seven seamen, see above, Perry to Clay, March 25, 1825; below, Bruce to Clay,
August 26, 1825; Warner to Clay, October 8, 1825; Clay to Rodney, October
29, 1825; Clay to Vives, November 14, 1825; Rodney to Clay, December 19,
1825; January 7, 1826; February 4, 1826.

MISCELLANEOUS LETTERS   March 26, 1825

To PETER A. BROWNE. Requests substantiation of charges against officials of
the Patent Office. Copy. DNA, RG59, Dom. Letters, vol. 21, p. 18 (M40, R19).
See above, Browne to Clay, March 7, 1825.

To Henry Unwin Addington

Henry U. Addington Esqe.
Chargé d'Affaires from Great Britain.   Department of State,
Sir,   Washington City, 27. March 1825.
   I have the honour to transmit to you herewith a Report made
by a Committee of the Senate of the state of Maine on the 18th.
day of January last, and extracts from certain Letters marked from
Ns. 1. to 5 inclusive, relating to encroachments by British subjects
upon the territory of the United States.[1] These documents shew
that an extensive system of depredation has been adopted and
persevered in, under which large quantities of timber have been
cut and removed from lands within the limits of the State of Maine,
belonging to that State and to the State of Massachusetts; that the
trespassers pretend to derive authority for their intrusions from
licences and permits which are said to have been granted by the
Government of the Province of New Brunswick; that the timber
is transported down to St. Johns and subsequently exported to the
dominions of His Britannic Majesty; and that schemes have been

probably formed by the Colonial authorities, if they are not now in a progress of execution for granting the lands within the State of Maine to British Subjects for the purpose of occupation and Settlement. It is entirely unnecessary to make any observation upon the character or impropriety of these proceedings, which must be altogether unauthorized by the Government of Great Britain. I am instructed by the President to demand that immediate and efficacious measures be adopted to put a stop to them all; and to communicate to you his just expectation that a full indemnity and reparation be made to the States of Massachusetts and Maine for the value of the timber which has been cut and removed from their lands.

I pray you, Sir, to accept the assurance of my distinguished Consideration.   H. CLAY.

Copy. DNA, RG59, Notes to Foreign Ministers and Consuls, vol. 3, pp. 205-206 (M38, R3). AL draft, in CSmH; published with the accompanying documents in *House Docs.*, 20 Cong, 2 Sess., no. 90, pp. 3-8. Addington, who had been in the British foreign service since 1807, retired in 1826, but was repeatedly recalled to active duty and was Under Secretary of State for Foreign Affairs from 1842 to 1854.

1 The commission established under Article V of the Treaty of Ghent, to fix the northeastern boundary of the United States (see above, I, 1006), had failed to reach agreement during conferences which had terminated in April, 1822. Controversy, stemming from the treaty ending the Revolutionary War, had continued between the United States and Great Britain and had grown more serious as settlers and timber cutters moved into the disputed area along the St. John's, Madawaska, and Aroostook rivers.

To Joel R. Poinsett

Instructions—Personal

No. 2   Joel R. Poinsett, appointed Envoy Extraordinary and Minister Plenipotentiary, U. S. to Mexico.

Sir,   Department of State   Washington 27. March 1825.

With this Letter you will receive the following papers, documents, and books, which will be found necessary or useful to you, in the discharge of the duties of the Mission to which you have been appointed.

1. A Commission as Envoy Extraordinary and Minister Plenipotentiary to Mexico.[1]
2. A Letter of credence to the United Mexican States.[2]
3. A Full Power for negociating concerning matters of Commerce & Navigation and Boundaries[3]

    Your General Instructions contain all the observations that I have to make with regard to the use of this Power.

4. A cypher to be used as occasion may require, in your correspondence with this Department, or with any other of the Ministers of the United States abroad.

5. An engraved design of the Uniform worn by the Ministers of the United States at Foreign Courts, on occasions when full dress is required

   In the Monarchial Governments of Europe, a Minister of the United States is compelled to conform to the established usages of appearing in the presence of the Sovereign, in a Court dress. He cannot, indeed, deliver his credential Letter without it, and this uniform was adopted for the convenience of using the same dress upon all necessary occasions, and at every Court. In the Republican Government of Mexico, it may be presumed that no such dress will be required or expected; and if not, you will have no occasion for using it. The use of it is, in no case, prescribed by this Government, and every Minister of the United States abroad, may wear, at his discretion, any dress conformable to the customs of the place where he may reside.

6. A Letter of credit upon the Bankers of the United States at London, authorizing them to pay your drafts upon them for your salary and the contingent expenses of the Legation. You will be careful, in availing yourself of this, not to exceed in the amount drawn, the sum to which you may be entitled in account, with the United States, at the time of the draft.

7. A set of the Laws of the United States in six volumes, and pamphlet copies of the Laws of the subsequent sessions of Congress.

8. A volume containing the Commercial regulations of the Foreign Countries with which the United States have commercial intercourse, collected, digested, and published by order of Congress, now furnished you, will serve as a guide to your enquiries into the Commercial regulations of the Government of Mexico, the result of which you will communicate, as soon as you may find convenient, to this Department.

9. A Set of Niles' Register, complete, 26 volumes, and one of Index.

10. A sett [sic] of Waites [sic] State Papers, 12 volumes.

    All the printed Books are for the use of the Legation, and at the termination of your Mission are to remain with the Chargé d' Affaires in case one should be left, or pass to your successor.

11. A Passport for yourself and your suite.

12. A Letter of General Instructions

13. A sample of Despatch-paper, and a set of lines adapted to its size.

Your allowance, as limited by Law, is nine thousand dollars a year, for all personal and other expenses, with an outfit equal to one years salary, and a quarters salary for your return. By a general rule, the salary commences from the time of the Minister's leaving home to proceed upon his Mission, and ceases on his receiving notice or permission to return; after which the additional allowance takes place. In your case your salary will commence on the day of the date of the confirmation by the Senate, of your nomination, and of your Commission, the 8th. of this Month.

The cost of Gazettes and Pamphlets transmitted to this Office; of Postage, Stationary [*sic*], *necessary* and *customary* presents to the menial attendants of the Public Functionaries at your presentation, and on other established occasions, (usually the Christmas or New Years days) are not considered as included under the denomination of personal and other expenses, and will form, as *contingencies* of the Legation, a separate charge in your accounts. It is hoped however, that there will be no such practice of making official presents in the Mexican Republic, and no contingent expenses are to be incurred without necessity, unless in compliance with the established usages, and no charge of any other description will be admitted not warranted by express directions from this Department. Exact vouchers, in all cases of expenditures, will be necessary for the settlement of your accounts; and, as some of these incidental charges are of a nature scarcely admitting of any other sort of voucher for every item, a separate account of them should be kept, and certified by the Secretary of the Legation.

These particulars are stated thus minutely that you may be relieved from all doubts on the subject of your accounts, which, you will keep in remembrance, are to be regularly transmitted, by duplicates, for adjustment, at the Treasury, at the close of every quarter, ending with March, June, September and December. These directions, and particularly that of forbearing to draw for any public money in advance, and that of the regular quarterly transmission of your accounts for settlement, are rendered the more indispensable for the due observance of the recent Act of Congress "concerning the disbursement of public money." (31. January 1823. See Acts of the 2nd. Session, 17th. Congress p.7)[4]

Among the most important general duties of a Minister of the United States in foreign Countries is that of transmitting to his Government, accurate information of the policy and views of the Government to which he is accredited, and of the character and vicissitudes of its important relations with other powers. To acquire this information, and particularly to discriminate between that which is authentic and that which is spurious requires steady and impartial observation, a free, though cautious correspondence with the other Ministers of the United States abroad, and friendly, social relations with the members of the Diplomatic Body at the same place.

You will find, it is presumed, at Mexico, no accredited Minister from any European Government, but there may be several from the other South American States.

In your correspondence with this Department, besides the current general and particular Politics of the Country where you are to reside, you will be mindful, as you may find it convenient, to collect and transmit information of every kind relating to the Government, Finances, Commerce, Arts, Science and condition of the Nation, not already known, and which may be made useful to our own Country. Books of Travels, containing statistical or other information of political importance; historical works not before in circulation, authentic maps, published by authority of the State, or distinguished by extraordinary reputation, and publications of new and useful discoveries, will always be acceptable acquisitions to this Department. The expense of procuring and transmitting all such Books or Pamphlets will form in your account a separate charge to the Department. But none of any considerable amount is to be incurred in any one account, without a previous express direction for it, from this Department.

It is the practice of the European Governments in the drawing up of their Treaties with each other, to vary the order of naming the parties, and that of the signatures of the Plenipotentiaries, in the Counterparts of the same Treaty; so that each party is first named, and its Plenipotentiary signs first in the copy possessed and published by itself. And in Treaties drawn up between parties using different languages and executed in both, each party is first named, and its Plenipotentiary signs first, in the copy executed in its own language. This practice having, on several occasions, been accidentally, or inadvertently omitted, to be observed, by the United States, the omission was followed by indications of a disposition in the Negociators of certain Royal European Governments to question its application to the Treaties between them and the United States. It became, therefore, proper to insist upon it, as was accordingly done with effect.[5] As it is understood to involve a principle, you will consider it as a standing instruction to adhere to this alternative, if, in any event, you should have occasion, as a Minister of the United States, to sign any Treaty, Convention or other Document, with the Plenipotentiary of any other Power.

The Consuls appointed to reside in the Republic of Mexico are James Smith Wilcox, at the City of Mexico, William Taylor, Vera Cruz, and Alvarado, George R. Robertson, Tampico, Thomas

Reilly, Aguatulco, Harvey Gregg, Acapulco, and John [*sic*] Mc-Goffin at Saltillo.[6]

In the practice of our Government, there is no immediate connection or dependence between the persons holding Diplomatic & Consular appointments in the same Country; but, by the usage of all the commercial Nations of Europe, such a subordination is considered as of course. In the transaction of their official duties, the Consuls are often in necessary correspondence with their Ministers, through whom alone, they can regularly address the Supreme Government of the Country wherein they reside; and they are always supposed to be under their directions. You will, accordingly, maintain such correspondence with the Consuls of the United States in Mexico as you shall think conducive to the public interest, and in case of any vacancy in their offices, which may require a temporary appointment of a person to perform the duties of the Consulate, you are authorised, with the consent of the Government to which you are accredited, to make it, giving immediate notice to this Department.

Among the ordinary functions of an American Minister abroad, is that of giving Passports to citizens of the United States, who apply for them. They sometimes receive applications for such Passports from the subjects of other countries; but these are not regularly valid, and should be granted only under special circumstances, as may sometimes occur in the case of foreigners coming to the United States. In times of war and internal commotions, such Passports are often solicited, and sometimes sought, by fraudulent means, to be obtained, to favour the escape of individuals having no right to such protection, and being in peril of their persons. It is not improbable that attempts of this kind may be made to procure Passports from you. Your vigilance will be exercised in guarding against such impositions, and your firmness in resisting such solicitations. Respect for the Passport of an American Minister abroad, is indispensable for the safety of his fellow citizens travelling with it, and nothing would be so fatal to that respect, as the experience that his Passport had been abusively obtained by persons not entitled to it. All Passports should be gratuitously given and a record or list kept of all those which you may deliver, containing the name and voucher of American Citizenship of the persons to whom they are given. They may be refused even to Citizens of the United States who have so far expatriated themselves as to have become bound in allegiance to other Nations, or who, in any other manner, have forfeited the protection of their own. Protections to seamen are not included under the denomination of Passports, nor are they ever granted by public Ministers. Seamen may, nevertheless, like other Citizens, occasionally want the Passport of the Minister, and be equally entitled to it.

A custom prevails among the European Sovereigns upon the conclusion of Treaties, of bestowing presents of Jewelry or other articles of pecuniary value, upon the Minister of the Power with which they were negociated. The same usage is repeated upon the Ministers taking leave, at the termination of his Mission. The acceptance of such presents by Ministers of the United States is expressly prohibited by the Constitution; and even if it were not, it can scarcely be consistent with the delicacy of intercourse with foreign Powers, for the Ministers of the United States to receive from foreign Princes such favours, as the Ministers of those Princes to the United States never can receive from this Government in return. The usage, exceptionable in itself, could be tolerated only by its being reciprocal.

It is expected by the President that every offer of such present which may in future be made to any public Minister or other officer of this Government abroad, will be respectfully, but decisively declined. This has been already a standing instruction to all the Ministers of the United States abroad, for several years, and is therefore repeated to you. It is probable that no such practice will be observed by the new Governments of South America, so that no offer of such present will be made; but should there be reason to expect it, at the termination of your mission, to avoid the apparent harshness of declining an intended favour, informal notice that it cannot be accepted, given in the proper quarter, may anticipate the necessity of a refusal.

You are requested to provide yourself with a sufficient supply of despatch paper, in size and quality corresponding with the sample herewith furnished, to be exclusively used in your correspondence with this Department. It has been found highly convenient and useful to have the original despatches from our Ministers abroad, bound up in Volumes. For this purpose, with a view to uniformity, the Despatches should be regularly numbered and, with the copies made at the Legation of all papers transmitted with them, should be written on paper of the same dimensions, 13¼ inches long, 8¼ broad, with the edges uncut, and a margin of at least, 1¼ inch round all its borders for stitching and cutting off the edges without injury to the text. The lines herewith furnished are adapted to the size of the paper, and mark the margin within which the manuscript should be confined, of which these Instructions also exhibit an example. Two Reams of the Despatch paper to be used in your correspondence with this Department, are herewith furnished.

Minute as these particulars appear, they are found to be very essential to the good order and convenience of business in the Department. I have the honour to be, with great respect, Sir Your very humble and obedient Servant.   H. CLAY.

Copy. DNA, RG59, Dip. Instr., vol. 10, pp. 238-45 (M77, R5). L draft, in DLC-HC (DNA, M212, R7). This document, except for the transmittal of the "Full Power for negociating concerning matters of Commerce & Navigation and Boundaries," is representative of the "personal instructions" which were sent to all diplomatic agents of the United States as an accompaniment of the "general instructions," the latter covering the specific problems of their missions. Hereafter routine "personal instructions" will be omitted.

1 Dated March 8. Copy, in DNA, RG59, Ceremonial Communications, vol. 2, p. 2.
2 Dated March 14. Copy, in *ibid.*, pp. 2-3.
3 See above, Clay to Poinsett, March 26, 1825.
4 3 *U. S. Stat.*, 723-24.
5 In the Treaty of Ghent Great Britain had been named first and the British negotiators had signed first. John Quincy Adams subsequently wrote that he had demurred at this arrangement privately to Albert Gallatin but that he "had then forborne to make a point of it only because we had no instruction to warrant us in so doing, and because I thought all the precedents of our treaties were the other way." Adams, *Memoirs*, III, 242. That the earlier American treaties, notably the Treaty of Paris of 1783, with Great Britain, had not given priority to the opposing party was tartly brought to Adams' attention in his instructions as Minister to Great Britain by Secretary of State James Monroe, on March 13, 1815, wherein the latter criticized the oversight in the preparation of the Treaty of Ghent, noted that in "the exchange of ratifications it was thought proper to advert to these circumstances," and called upon Adams at "a suitable opportunity" to "explain to the British government, the sentiments of The President on it." Miller, *Treaties. . .*, II, 583-84. This was the background of Adams' stand in controversy with Clay and Gallatin over the subsequent arrangement of the London commercial convention. See above, II, 54n. At the latter date Clay was reported to have "said he thought it a matter of no consequence; that Mr. Monroe's argument in the dispatch was a bad one. It was no good reason why we should make a point of such a formality because the European Powers thought it so important; for the most insignificant powers, such as Spain for instance, were those that insisted most upon these punctilios." Adams, *Memoirs*, III, 241-42.
6 Wilcocks, of Pennsylvania, and Taylor, of Virginia, had been appointed to these posts in January, 1823, and remained there until 1834 and 1831, respectively. Reilly, also of Pennsylvania, appointed in March, 1823, continued at Aguatulco until 1837. Robertson, of New York, Gregg, of Indiana, and James Wiley Magoffin, of Kentucky, had been appointed in the closing days of President Monroe's administration. Robertson remained until 1836, but the others held appointment for relatively short periods. Gregg, a former Kentuckian, residing in 1825 at Shelbyville, Indiana, had been named a State prosecuting attorney in August, 1824; he returned to resume that position in 1831 and thereafter lived at Indianapolis until his death in 1833. Magoffin, born in Harrodsburg, Kentucky, an elder brother of a later Kentucky Governor, Beriah Magoffin, embarked upon the Santa Fé trade around 1828 and continued in it most of his life. In 1835 he was appointed to, and briefly held, the post of register of the land office at St. Stephen's, Alabama. He settled at Independence, Missouri, in 1844 and, after the Mexican War, at the Mexican town of El Paso del Norte. Across the Rio Grande River from the latter community he founded a settlement later included in the present city of El Paso, Texas.

To Thomas Todd

My dear Sir   Washn. 27h. Mar. 1825

I cannot express to you how much solicitude I have felt about your health, nor how much I was delighted to learn from Charles, in a letter which I received from him of the 3d. inst.,[1] that you were better. I most sincerely hope that your health may be restored, and your life, in which so many of us feel a deep interest, may be preserved. The Chief Justice, Johnson and Story[2] expressed to me the greatest anxiety for your recovery.

I will not trouble you about politics, of which I have had a surfeit   I will triumph over all the villaney [sic] by which I have been cruelly assailed.

Tell Charles that I recd. his letter. The Bank,[3] I believe, does not intend to continue to employ a Counsel, in consequence of the diminution & settlement of so much of its Law business. If it did, I should take particular pleasure in recommending and urging the appointment of our friend Crittenden.[4]

With my best respects to Mrs Todd, I am faithfully Your friend

H. CLAY

ALS. KyU. Addressed: "The Honble Thomas Todd   Frankfort (K)."
[1] The letter, from Charles S. Todd, not found.
[2] John Marshall; William Johnson; Joseph Story.
[3] Bank of the United States.   [4] John J. Crittenden.

From John Tyler

Dr. Sir: Chs. City county Va. March 27t. 1825—

In the midst of the numerous accusations which have of late been urg'd against you from different quarters, and from none with more acrimony than from the seat of government of this State, I have deem'd it proper and in some measure call'd for, to make known to you that one of the million at least, still regarded you as I am satisfied you deserve to be regarded,— Instead of seeing in your course on the late presidential question ought [sic] morally or politically wrong, I am on the contrary fully impress'd with the belief that the U. States owes you a deep debt of gratitude for that course, resulting as it did in the speedy settlement of that distracting subject— Believing Mr. Crawford's chance of success to have been utterly desperate, you have not only met my wishes (which would be to you of little concern) but I do believe, the wishes and feelings of a large majority of the people of this your native State— I do not believe that the sober and reflecting people of Virginia would have been so far dazzled by military renown as to have confer'd their suffrages upon a *mere soldier*—one acknowledg'd on all hands to be of little value as a civilian— I will not withhold from you also the expression of my approval of your acceptance of your present honorable and exalted station— To have refus'd it would have been to have furnish'd your enemies with fresh ground of objection— Against an insidious and malitious attack you quoted [sic] an investigation not only before the Representatives of the people, but by accepting the office, before the Senate, and gave fresh evidence of your purity by your readiness to encounter your accusers supported as they were by the virulence and intemperance of party feeling on the part of some of your very judges.

For a time the tide may run against you, but when the ferment excited by the feelings of the day shall have subsided, and men shall regard things with unprejudic'd eyes, your motives and your acts will be justly appreciated and the plaudits of your country will await you— This is not the language of flattery to one lifted high in authority— As an American citizen I claim to be your equal— It is the voluntary offering of truth at the shrine of patriotism, and is call'd for by the circumstance of our having been in times past fellow laborers in the same vineyard of our common country, altho' I was at the time an unprofitable servant— When one, however, is assail'd by unjust reproaches the expression of confidence from a quarter even the most humble and the most retired, cannot but be acceptable— It is under the influence of this feeling and of this belief that I have thus ventur'd to address you   I pray you to accept assurances of my sincere regard and unshaken confidence—   JOHN TYLER
The Hon: Henry Clay—

ALS. DLC-HC (DNA, M212, R1).

INSTRUCTIONS AND DISPATCHES   March 27, 1825

From CHARLES SAVAGE. Refers to letters sent earlier, on March 18 and 26; transmits further issues of the Government *Gazette,* "which renders that file complete from March 1824 to this time." ALS. DNA, RG59, Cons. Disp., Guatemala, vol. 1 (M-T337, R1). Addressed to Secretary of State; received July 25.

MISCELLANEOUS LETTERS   March 27, 1825

From ACHILLE MURAT, Charleston, South Carolina. Requests the interference of the American Minister at Madrid in behalf of Murat's brother. Explains that the writer is a resident of the United States, in the process of becoming a citizen, and has no other government to which he can appeal. ALS. DNA, RG59, Misc. Letters (M179, R62). No addressee named; endorsed: "Care of Mess. Pitray [*sic*] and Viel   Charleston."

Charles Louis Napoléon Achille Murat, born in France, the elder son of Joachim Murat, King of Naples from 1808 until the fall of Napoleon, had emigrated to the United States in 1823 and applied for American naturalization. He shortly thereafter bought and began development of a plantation near Tallahassee, Florida, where he held various minor political offices and, in 1828, was admitted to the bar. Following the July Revolution of 1830 in France, Murat became an exponent of republican doctrines on the Continent. Denied permission to travel beyond Belgium, he published several widely circulated works descriptive of American governmental ideas: *Lettres sur les Etats Unis . . . à Un de Ses Amis d'Europe* (Paris, 1830) ; *Esquisse Morale et Politique des*

Etats-Unis de l'Amérique du Nord (Paris, 1832) ; and *Exposition des Principes du Gouvernement Républicain, tel qu'Il A Été Perfectionné en Amérique* (Paris, 1833). Returning to the United States, he later served in the Seminole War and was commissioned a colonel. He died in 1847.

His brother, Napoléon Lucien Charles Joseph François Murat, born in Milan, Italy, had also taken passage for the United States, in 1824, after persecution by the Austrian authorities during the political unrest of the early 1820s. Shipwrecked near Gibraltar, he had been seized and imprisoned in Spain for several months. His brother's pleas for American intercession in his behalf, addressed previously to President Monroe, had already proved effective; and the younger Murat arrived at Boston in April. He, too, applied for American citizenship, traveled extensively over the country, and lived for a time in Florida. In 1827 he settled in Baltimore and resided there during most of the period from then until his return to France after the fall of Louis Philippe, in 1848. Murat thereupon became a deputy in the French Constituent Assembly, 1848 and 1849, was appointed Minister to Turin in 1849, and in 1852 was made a Senator and given the title of Prince. He remained prominent in the imperial government until its fall in 1870, when he returned to the United States. At his death in 1878, he was again in Paris.

Lewis A. Petray and Just Viel were Charleston merchants.

APPLICATIONS, RECOMMENDATIONS   March 27, 1825

F. C. CLOPPER, Woodland Mills, Maryland, recommends for a clerkship in the State Department "a friend & former neighbour. . . , C H. W. Wharton Esq, at present residing in Washington." ALS. DNA, RG59, A. and R. (MR1). Clopper not further identified. Charles H. W. Wharton had been appointed a justice of the peace for the county of Washington, District of Columbia, in 1821 and was reappointed to that office for successive five-year terms in 1826, 1831, and 1836.

From John H. Eaton

WASHINGTON CITY, 28 MARCH, 1825.

SIR, In the National Journal of this morning, over your signature, I find my name introduced with the following remarks:

"A few days after the publication of my Card, another Card under Mr. Kremer's name was published in the Intelligencer. The night before, as I was voluntarily informed, Mr. Eaton, a Senator from Tennessee, and the biographer of General Jackson was closeted for some time with him. I pretend not to know the object of Mr. Eaton's visit to him. I state the fact as it was communicated to me, and leave you to judge. Mr. Kremer's Card is composed with some care, and no little art; and he is made to avow in it, tho' somewhat equivocally, that he is the author of the letter to the Editor of the Columbian Observer. To Mr. Crowninshield, a member from Massachusetts, formerly Secretary of the Navy, he declared he was not the author of that letter."[1]

The imputation which your phraseology would seem to convey

is this: that the letter which appeared in the Columbian Observer, and acknowledged by Mr. Kremer, was not written by him, but was, in fact, written by me; and that by *me* he was *made* to avow himself, "though somewhat equivocally," the author. Your language and meaning are somewhat equivocal too; but as, by fair interpretation, they appear to warrant this construction, I present myself before you to require you distinctly to state, whether or not any such meaning was, by you, designed to be conveyed. If this be the idea intended to be communicated, I will not persuade myself but that at least you are possessed of facts and circumstances to fix against me the opprobrious charge of writing a letter, which, as the inference must be, I was not merely afraid to acknowledge, but which, through finesse, arrangement, and closet management, I had caused to be avowed by one who was innocent of *producing it*.

I have the honor to be, Respectfully, Your most obedient,

Hon. HENRY CLAY, Sec'y of State.   JNO. H. EATON.

Washington Gazette, April 5, 1825. Published also in Washington *Daily National Intelligencer,* April 6, 1825; *Niles' Weekly Register,* XXVIII (April 9, 1825), 87; Lexington *Kentucky Reporter,* April 25, 1825.
1 See above, Address, March 26, 1825.

MISCELLANEOUS LETTERS   March 28, 1825

From GEORGE WARREN CROSS, Charleston (South Carolina). Solicits aid for his brother-in-law, (Thomas Lloyd) Halsey, in prosecuting a claim against the Government of Buenos Aires. ALS. DNA, RG76, Misc. Claims, Buenos Aires. Cross was a Charleston lawyer, former militia officer, and, briefly, member of the general assembly. After the death of his first wife, in 1808, he had married Frances Maria, sister of Thomas L. Halsey, of Providence, Rhode Island. Halsey, former United States consul in Buenos Aires, had furnished arms, ammunition, and money to the United Provinces of the Rio de la Plata before losing favor with Pueyrredón. His claim for payment was not settled until after his death, in 1855.

From JOHN C[OFFIN] JONES, Boston, Massachusetts. Complains against the Spanish consul at Boston (Ramundo Chacon) for failure to issue certificates for shipments to Spain without extra fee, application for such certification having been made by Jones' agent and son-in-law, Ebenezer Chadwick. ALS. DNA, RG59, Misc. Letters (M179, R62). Jones and Chadwick were both prominent Boston merchants, the former having also been active in local politics as a Federalist through the turn of the century, a career capped in 1802 by election to the speakership of the House of Representatives of the Massachusetts General Court.

On April 18, Daniel Brent, "by direction of the Secretary," informed Jones "that he had made a representation to the Spanish Chargé d'Affaires at Philadelphia [see below, Clay to Salmon, April 16, 1825], upon the conduct of M. Chacon . . . and that Instructions will be given to Mr. Everett . . . [see below, Clay to Everett, April 27, 1825] to bring it before the Government" of Spain for measures of counteraction. Copy in DNA, RG59, Dom. Letters, vol. 21, p. 33 (M40, R19).

To [John Quincy Adams]

Tuesday morning [March 29, 1825]

Mr. Clay's respectful compliments to the President and he sends for his perusal, at his leisure, two letters[1] which Mr. C. has received.

AN. MHi-Adams Papers, Letters Received (MR468). Endorsed at top of page, in unidentified hand: "29 March {1825}."
[1] Not found.

To James Brown

James Brown Esqr., Paris.— Washington 29 March 1825.
Dear. [sic]

Enclosed I transmit you a Letter for M: Scheffer,[1] which I must ask the favor of you to deliver to him.— It contains my acknowledgment, on the part of the House of Representatives, during the late session of Congress, of the receipt from him of a super-excellent Portrait of our good friend, General la fayette.[2] In delivering it, you will be so good as to intimate to M. Scheffer, in such a manner as, in no degree, to commit the House, that I was restrained myself from making any movement towards a more suitable return for this valued and acceptable present, by the advice of General la fayette and his son.— I am &c &c. HENRY CLAY.—

Copy. DNA, RG59, Unofficial Letter-Book of H. Clay, p. 1.
[1] Ary Scheffer; the letter not found.
[2] See above, Barry to Clay, January 10, 1825, note. The portrait hangs in the House Chamber.

To James Strong

My dear Sir Washn. 29h. Mar. 1825

I duly recd. your friendly letter dated at N. York on the 16h. instant.[1] In regard to the publication of the laws, according to usage, I have defered [sic] designating the papers until the commencement of the next session of Congress, when I shall be able to have the benefit of your advice and that of other friends.

Since you left us, Mr. Clinton declining to accept the English Mission, it has been offered to Mr. R. King.[2] I make this communication to you however in confidence, as he has not yet positively decided to accept. You will readily, I hope, see in Mr. Ks. weight of character, the estimate in which he is held both here and in England, his residence, and the place of his nativity, so deeply concerned in fixing our N. E. boundary, sufficient considerations for his appointment.

I have published an address to my Constituents,[3] of which I have directed a Copy to be sent you—Tell me frankly and freely what you and others think of it.

With great regard I am faithy Your friend   H CLAY
The honble JAMES STRONG.

ALS. ViU.   1 Not found.
2 Cf. above, Stuart to Clay, March 15, 1825, note. Rufus King had been offered the appointment by Adams' letter of March 17 and accepted on March 22. Issued a temporary commission during the recess of the Senate, he was formally nominated for the post on December 13, 1825, and the appointment was confirmed on December 20.   3 Above, March 26, 1825.

From Wade Mosby

My Dear Sir,   Powhatan C Vy. Mar. 29. 1825
It has been a long time Since I had the pleasure of seeing you, but time has not effaced my remembrance or friendship for you, I see you often, in print, as may be expected of every one who, as they become more conspicuous, will have their Enemies as well as friends, among the latter I have no doubt you place me, & my family   I was much disappointed that you should have lost the Vote of Louisa. & therby [sic] was thrown out from Congress, which I with much anxiety anticipated, & in which event, I thot your success almost sure, but we must take things as they go, if we cant will [sic] the first heat we must try to get the second, I see a great deal of fuss made by the disappointed, but it will soon settle down to insignificance in publick mind, I shall be glad when you have a leisure moment, to hear from you, & while I am on that subject shall be obliged to to [sic] drop me a line & inform me whether the place in Florida which Richard[1] was a candidate for has been filled or what State the business is in, I am Very anxious that he shoud [sic] be doing somthing [sic], & not be wasting the prime of his life in Idleness   please let me hear from you & diret [sic] to Cartersville, Cumberland County,[2] with respects of the highest order I am Yr. Friend & mo Ob.   WADE MOSBY

ALS. DNA, RG59, A. and R. (MR5). Addressed to Clay at Washington.
1 Richard H. Mosby. See above, Clay and others to Adams, February 3, 1825.
2 Where Wade Mosby lived for about two years.

DIPLOMATIC NOTES   March 29, 1825

To HENRY U. ADDINGTON. Transmits copy of a letter from "Mr. Tattnall," who wishes to obtain from the British archives copies of documents on the early history of Georgia. Copy. DNA, RG59, Notes to Foreign Ministers and Consuls, vol. 3, p. 206 (M38, R3). Also L draft, in CSmH. Edward F. Tattnall, of Savannah, Georgia, who had been State solicitor general, 1816-1817, and member of the State legislature, 1818 and 1819, was at this time a member of Congress,

1821-1827. Appointed appraiser of goods for the port of Savannah in 1832, he died later that year. On the subject of the Georgia documents, see above, Rush to [Clay], March 16, 1825.

INSTRUCTIONS AND DISPATCHES March 29, 1825

To JAMES BROWN, no. 6. Acknowledges receipt of his dispatch no. 24 and replies that with respect to his attendance at the coronation, "Whilst, on the one hand, the President does not wish the Foreign Representatives of the United States unnecessarily to assist in a mere pageant, he would not, on the other, have them omit shewing the usual respectful attentions. . . ." If Brown desides to attend, his "reasonable expenses will be allowed." Copy. DNA, RG59, Dip. Instr. vol. 10, p. 252 (M77, R5). AL draft in DLC-HC (DNA, M212, R7). Brown's dispatch no. 24 was dated February 12 and received in the Department of State on March 18. For a repetition of his inquiry relating to the coronation, see above, Brown to Clay, March 21, 1825.

From JAMES OMBROSI, Florence. Reports the arrival at Leghorn, in February, of an American vessel carrying a cannon and "various warlike ammunition" for the Greeks. Notes that the Government (of Tuscany), despite its neutrality, permitted these articles to be unloaded and reshipped, but Ombrosi warns that there is danger of seizure of future shipments of this kind. Cites the circumstances attending the arrest and pardon of an American sea captain as an indication of the need for a diplomatic or consular representative of the United States in Florence. ALS. DNA, RG59, Cons. Disp., Florence, vol. 1 (M-T204, R1). Addressed to Secretary of State; received August 18. Though Ombrosi, born in Florence, had been appointed as United States consul at that city in March, 1823, he had not yet been accredited by the Tuscan Government. Ombrosi to Secretary of State, January 1, 1825, in *ibid.* He retained the appointment until 1835 and served as acting consul from 1845 to 1847 and in 1851.

From [WILLIAM TUDOR], Lima, no. 25, extract. Reports the death of Judge (John B.) Prevost; urges appointment of a Minister to Peru; encloses correspondence with (Simón) Bolívar on Prevost's death. AL. DNA, RG59, Cons. Disp., Lima, vol. 1 (M154, R1). Addressed to Secretary of State; received September 4.

MISCELLANEOUS LETTERS March 29, 1825

From P[ETER] A. BROWNE, Philadelphia. Protests against the insult to the Franklin Institute by employees of the Patent Office in refusing to supply copies of patent papers; questions how one can know, without information on specifications, whether he infringes a patent; and charges Patent Office personnel with ignorance of the law and of their official duty, gross partiality, inconsistency, and extortion. LS. DNA, RG59, Misc. Letters (M179, R62).

From DANIEL WEBSTER, Boston. Introduces John C[offin] Jones and E[benezer] Chadwick. ALS. *Ibid.* See above, Jones to Clay, March 28, 1825.

From DANIEL WYNNE, New York. Acknowledges receipt of letter of March 25 (not found), extending the date of his departure for Santiago de Chile to September 1. ALS. DNA, RG59, Cons. Disp., Santiago de Cuba, vol. 1 (M-T55, R1). Cf. above, Wynne to Clay, March 21, 1825.

James Maury, United States consul at Liverpool, recommends Thomas Wilson, of Dublin, son of Joseph Wilson, former consul at the latter city, to succeed Thomas English in that post. ALS. DNA, RG59, A. and R. (MR4). Cf. above, Clay to Drayton, March 22, 1825; below, Drayton to Clay, March 30, 1825. The post remained vacant until Wilson's nomination, submitted to the Senate on February 17, 1826, was confirmed on March 17. He thereafter remained consul until 1847.

To John H. Eaton

Washington, 30th March, 1825.

Sir. Your letter, under date the 28th inst., was handed to me yesterday. After referring to an address of mine to my late constituents, published in the National Journal of Monday, and from which you quote certain passages, you observe, "the imputation which your phraseology would seem to convey is, that the letter which appeared in the Columbian Observer, and acknowledged by Mr. Kremer, was not written by him; but was, in fact, written by me; and, that by me, he was made to avow himself, though somewhat equivocally, the author. Your language and meaning are somewhat equivocal too; but, as by fair interpretation, they appear to warrant this conclusion, I present myself before you, to require you distinctly to state, whether or not, any such meaning was by you designed to be conveyed."

In the part of my address to which you refer, having stated a particular fact respecting you, I observe, "I state the fact as it was communicated to me, and leave you to judge." I cannot, therefore, admit your right to call on me for my inferences from a fact, which I have submitted to my constituents, leaving *them* to draw their *own* conclusions. But, in the spirit of frankness which has ever guided me, I have no hesitation in stating that, in regard to the letter in the Columbian Observer, I have not formed, and therefore did not intend to intimate, any opinion of the person who was its real author. I was satisfied to take Mr. Kremer's declaration that *he* was not the author of the letter, as made to the late Secretary of the Navy.

In the same spirit of frankness, however, it is proper for me to add that I did believe, from your nocturnal interview with Mr. K. referred to in my address, that you prepared or advised the publication of his Card, in the guarded terms in which it is expressed. I should be happy, by a disavowal on your part of the fact of that interview, or of its supposed object, to be able to declare, as, in the event of such disavowal, I would take pleasure in declaring, that

I have been mistaken in supposing that you had any agency in the composition or publication of that Card.

I have the honor to be, Your obedient servant,

The Hon. JOHN H. EATON.   H. CLAY.

Washington Gazette, April 5, 1825. Published also in Washington *Daily National Intelligencer*, April 6, 1825; *Niles' Weekly Register*, XXVIII (April 9, 1825), 87; Lexington *Kentucky Reporter*, April 25, 1825.

DIPLOMATIC NOTES   March 30, 1825

From H[ENRY] U. ADDINGTON, Washington. Acknowledges receipt of Clay's note of March 27, and enclosures; states that copies will be sent to the Governor of New Brunswick and the British Secretary of State. ALS. DNA, RG59, Notes from British Legation, vol. 13 (M50, R14). Published in *House Docs.*, 20 Cong., 2 Sess., no. 90, p. 8.

INSTRUCTIONS AND DISPATCHES   March 30, 1825

From JOHN M. FORBES, Buenos Aires, no. 17. Transmits copies of correspondence with the Government of Buenos Aires, requesting "that every political, religious or commercial right or privilege conceded to the subjects of his Britannic Majesty" under the recent treaty with England be extended to citizens of the United States under "similar reciprocal engagements." Mentions recent events in Peru and Chile; refers to the spirit of pecuniary speculation and the political difficulties in the Provinces of Rio de La Plata, to the influence exerted by England, and to the indifference toward the United States. States that he has, at the request of merchants engaged in the trade, made official representation, without success, against "the oppressive operation of a transit duty on flour," first imposed three years earlier. Transmits copies of his correspondence with Manuel José Garcia, the Foreign Minister, on this last topic, as well as a minute of his conference with the same official in which "the system of diplomatic intercourse which this Government proposes to adopt with other nations, is pretty clearly stated" (see above, Forbes to Clay, March 26, 1825, note). ALS, "Duplicate." DNA, RG59, Dip. Disp., Argentina, vol. 2 (M69, R3). Addressed to Secretary of State. Conclusion of the dispatch dated April 1. Published in Espil (comp.), *Once Años en Buenos Aires*, 351-53.

MISCELLANEOUS LETTERS   March 30, 1825

To JOSEPH E. CARO, Pensacola, Florida. Encloses his commission as keeper of the archives in West Florida. Copy. DNA, RG59, Dom. Letters, vol. 21, p. 19 (M40, R19). In a note addressed to Clay on April 30, 1825, Caro acknowledged receipt of this commission. ALS. DNA, RG59, Acceptances and Orders for Commissions (M-T645, R2). A native of Pensacola, he had been appointed to this office on March 7; he retained it until his death, around 1860. He was also appointed a justice of the peace for Escambia County in 1827.

From WILLIAM DRAYTON, Charleston (South Carolina). States his decision not to accept the Dublin consulate and expresses thanks for Clay's promptness and kindness in transmitting the President's offer. ALS. DNA, RG59, Misc. Letters (M179, R62).

APPLICATIONS, RECOMMENDATIONS   March 30, 1825

Jos[EPH] DUNCAN, New York, inquires about the success of his application for appointment as receiver of public moneys at Edwardsville, Illinois. ALS. DNA, RG59, Misc. Letters (M179, R62). See above, Letcher to Clay, March 5, 1825.

ELIAS K. KANE, New York, under belief "that the office of postmaster for this city will in the progress of a few months become vacant," in consequence of the present paralysis and probable death of the incumbent, solicits the appointment of his father, Elias Kane, "for many years one of the most . . . successful merchants of this city" but now, since his bankruptcy in 1815, a resident of Albany. ALS. DNA, RG59, A. and R. (M531, R4). Unaddressed. The younger Kane, born in New York and graduated from Yale, had begun legal practice in Nashville, Tennessee, before removing to Kaskaskia, Illinois, in 1814. A former secretary of state of Illinois (1820-1824) and member of the State legislature (1824), he had recently entered upon a term as United States Senator (1825-1835). Theodorus Bailey, a former member of Congress (1793-1797, 1799-1803) and United States Senator (1803-1804), had held office as postmaster of New York since 1804 and continued in that position until his death in 1828.

MOSES SHAW, Wiscasset, Maine, editor of the *Lincoln Intelligencer,* solicits appointment to publish the laws. ALS. DNA, RG59, P. and D. of L. Endorsed (AES) by Francis Cook, collector of customs at Wiscasset, who recommends the appointment.

JOHN TOD, Bedford, Pennsylvania, asks that Clay give favorable consideration to documents submitted to John Quincy Adams "about a year ago," including an application for a clerkship in the State Department "on behalf of Josiah M. Espy Esqr. of this place" and a "strong recommendation signed by all . . . of the most conspicuous men of the democratic side in this part of the Country, and backed by at least, twenty . . . of the members of Congress from this state." ALS. DNA, RG59, A. and R. (MR2). Espy received no appointment.

From John H. Eaton

WASHINGTON, 31 March, 1825.

SIR, Your letter, in answer to mine, was received at 4 o'clock yesterday:[1] from the delay I was disposed to think you had concluded not to reply.

On reading your communication to your late constituents,[2] I understood you as intending to convey the idea, not "by inference from a fact," but almost by actual averment, that the letter published in the Columbian Observer was written by me, and that, to escape or avoid responsibility, by me Mr. Kremer was made to acknowledge himself its author. Your reply to my letter disavows this, and states

that "you have not formed, and therefore did not intend to intimate, any opinion of the person who was its real author, being
satisfied to take Mr. Kremer's declaration that he was not the author
of the letter, as made to the late Secretary of the Navy."

Having nothing to do with this controversy further than as I
considered the introduction of my name intended personally and
directly to affect myself, I might omit any notice of the concluding
part of your remark derived from Mr. Crowninshield, lately Secretary of the Navy. In justice, however, to an absent individual,
with whom my name has been associated, I shall not forbear the
opinion, that Mr. Kremer never did use the language imputed to
him. It is a mistake—any thing but fact; and without intending to
ascribe the error to you, I claim the right of saying, that reason
revolts at the idea, that he should have made Mr. Crowninshield
his confessor, and to him uttered a language at war with his public
and repeated private declarations made to his friends.

The concluding paragraph of your letter expresses a belief that
I "proposed or advised the publication of his (Mr. K.'s) card in the
guarded terms in which it is expressed"; and you declare yourself
ready to acknowledge the mistake, if I will offer any disavowal.

If you had properly reflected as to what belonged to courtesy,
you would have sought from me information about this, before my
name was introduced before the public, and your belief formed.
You knew me sufficiently well to believe that I would not decline,
candidly, to answer any enquiries, necessary and proper to be
made: This was not done; but, on the information you had received,
you yielded it your confidence, and proceeded to a defence before
the public. Without intending to be understood as either admitting
or denying any thing respecting my imputed visit to Mr. Kremer,
on the evening preceding the publication of his card, suppose the
fact to be that I did visit him; and, suppose too, that it was, as you
have termed it, a "nocturnal visit," was there any thing existing
that should have denied me this privilege? or does it, therefore,
necessarily result, that I should have been engaged in any plan
against your rights, or conspiracy against you? There is no one
more interested than yourself, in denying the force of conclusion
as derived for [sic] circumstance; and, it is a little strange, that
while in your own case, you should object to it, as a rule of proper
application, you should, at the same time, claim it as rightfully
entitled to operate in the cases of others.

You will excuse me from making an attempt to remove any
belief which you may entertain upon this subject: it is a matter
which gives me no sort of concern. In the communication made to
you, my object was to ascertain distinctly your meaning as to the

letter published in the Columbian Observer, and to that you have frankly replied. Had you referred to me five days ago on this subject, I should with pleasure have answered you; but having exhibited your belief and opinions to the public, I am precluded from any explanation: you have no right to ask it, nor I in justice to yourself [*sic*] any right to give it.

Respectfully, Your most ob't. servant,

Hon. H. CLAY.   JNO. H. EATON.

Washington Gazette, April 5, 1825. Published also in Washington *Daily National Intelligencer,* April 6, 1825; *Niles' Weekly Register,* XXVIII (April 9, 1825), 87-88; Lexington *Kentucky Reporter,* April 25, 1825.

1 Above, March 30, 1825.   2 Above, March 26, 1825.

INSTRUCTIONS AND DISPATCHES   March 31, 1825

From JOHN M. FORBES, Buenos Aires, *"Private."* Complains of British influence over the Government of Buenos Aires. Referring to the comment on "the humble Class of diplomatic representatives which this Government has it in Contemplation to establish near the different Governments with which they are in relation," as indicated in the "official dispatch which accompanies this [dated March 30]," questions the appointment of a Minister Plenipotentiary from the United States and recommends that the rank of the post be changed by adding "Consul General" to his title. ALS. DNA, RG59, Dip. Disp., Argentina, vol. 2 (M69, R3). Addressed to Secretary of State. Published in Espil (comp.), *Once Años en Buenos Aires,* 355-56.

MISCELLANEOUS LETTERS   March 31, 1825

To WILLIAM P. DUVAL. Announces his reappointment as Governor of Florida and sends his commission. Copy. DNA, RG59, Dom. Letters, vol. 2, p. 21 (M40, R19). On April 25 Duval acknowledged, from Bardstown (Kentucky), receipt of the commission; cited the necessity for settling his "private concerns," after an absence from "this state" and from his family for more than two years; and requested Clay to assure the President that he would remain away from his post no longer than necessary. ALS. DNA, RG59, Acceptances and Orders for Comms. (M-T645, R2). Published in Carter (ed.), *Territorial Papers,* XXIII, 242-43.

To CHARLES JOHN SHERMAN [*i.e.,* STEEDMAN]. States that his application to publish the laws of Congress will be considered at the beginning of the next Session, when such appointments are made. Copy. DNA, RG59, Dom. Letters, vol. 21, p. 21 (M40, R19). See above, Steedman to Clay, March 24, 1825.

To GEORGE WALTON, Pensacola, Acting Governor of Florida. Transmits to him the commission of the legislative council of the Territory and requests that he make it known to the members individually. Copy. DNA, RG59, Dom. Letters, vol. 21, pp. 24-25 (M40, R19). On Governor Duval's absence from his post, see above, Clay to Duval, this date, note. Walton had been secretary for the Territory of Florida since April, 1822, and was reappointed for another four years, to run from April, 1826. On May 30, 1825, he acknowledged to Clay receipt of the commission. LS. DNA, RG59, Acceptances and Orders for Comms. (M-T645, R2).

From LANGDON CHEVES, Office of the Board of Commissioners under the Convention of St. Petersburg. Transmits copies of the answer of the British Commissioner (George Jackson), dated March 16, to Cheves' paper of February 25 (see above, Cheves to Clay, March 14, 1825) and of the full statement of Cheves' argument, an amplification of the journal extract filed earlier. Observes that the case made out in respect to the Couper claim was unusually conclusive, yet the British Commissioner deemed it defective; concludes "that if the same measure of proof shall be required in other Cases, the Convention will prove to be almost entirely nugatory." Notes the British Commissioner's reference "to the question of Slavery . . . and an attempt to draw into discussion the circumstances under which these Slaves were brought within their power"; explains that, in reply (dated March 23), Cheves relied on "a judgment of Sir William Scott showing how Such property is considered under the law of Nations" and "expressly declined entering into a discussion of the circumstances under which these Slaves joined the British forces." Expresses regret that the British Commissioner's most recent rejoinder, "read Yesterday at the Board," appeared "still more exceptionable" and promises that a copy of it will be forwarded soon. ALS. DNA, RG76, G.B.9-Folder 8. Received March 31. Copies of enclosures, with another copy of this letter, may be found in DNA, RG76, Indemnity for Slaves.

APPLICATIONS, RECOMMENDATIONS   March 31, 1825

ISAAC ENGLISH, Dublin, refers to an earlier letter by which he announced the death of his brother, Thomas, United States consul at that port, and solicited appointment to this office. ALS. DNA, RG59, Cons. Disp., Dublin, vol. 1 (M-T199, R-T1). Addressed to Secretary of State; received on May 18. Cf. above, Maury to Clay, March 29, 1825, note.

To John H. Eaton

WASHINGTON, 1st APRIL, 1825.

SIR, I received yesterday your note of the 31st. ult. With respect to mine in answer to yours' [sic] of the 28th, (in your reception of which you seem to think there was some delay) allow me to remark, that it was my intention to have transmited [sic] it through a friend, who when I sent for him happened to be out of the City, in consequence of which I despatched it through another channel; that amidst my official engagements I cannot mark the hours with the same precision as a gentleman can of your presumed leisure; that I received your own note the day after it bore date; and that by your own admission, you received my note at 4 o'clock, of the day, succeding [sic] that on which yours was delivered.

Whilst you disclaim having any thing to do with the controversy into which I have been most reluctantly drawn by others, under Mr. Kremer's name, you have chosen to observe, entirely in justice to that gentleman, that he never used the language to which Mr. Crowninshield testifies; "that it is a mistake; any thing but fact," and to claim the right of saying "that reason revolts at the idea that he should have made Mr. Crowninshield his confessor." Why this solicitude to defend Mr. Kremer? Why question the credibility of Mr. Crowninshield? He has not claimed to be the *confessor* of Mr. K.—a term the religious associations with which might have suggested to you the propriety of abstaining from its use, whatever occasion he may have for the office. The American public is the best judge whether a gentleman of Mr. Crowninshield's well known character, for honor, probity, and veracity, has falsely testified, or Mr. Kremer has been prevailed upon to avow himself the author of a letter which he never wrote.

In regard to your polite intimation that I had not properly reflected upon what belonged to courtesy, I have two observations to make, the first of which is that I am yet to be made sensible of any particular claim that you have upon me for an extraordinary observation of its rules; and the second is, that when I may think I shall have occasion to learn them, I shall not be tempted, even by a gratuitous offer, to renounce my indisputable right to choose my own preceptor.

I made no demand upon you for an explanation of the object of your interview with Mr. Kremer the night preceding the publication of his Card. The *privilege* of any one to derive from his society whatever enjoyments it can afford, literary, scientific or political, was never contested, as it never will be envied, by me. My intention was to afford you an opportunity of making an explanation of the object of your visit to him, if you chose to do so. In declining it, I acquiesce entirely in your determination.

                    I have the honor to be Your obedient servant
The Hon. JNO. H. EATON.   H. CLAY.

Washington Gazette, April 5, 1825. Published also in Washington *Daily National Intelligencer*, April 6, 1825; *Niles' Weekly Register*, XXVIII (April 9, 1825), 88; Lexington *Kentucky Reporter*, April 25, 1825.

To Wade Mosby

                                        Washington, 1. April 1825.
Wade Moseby Esqr.   Cartersville, Virginia.
Dear Sir,

I have just received your Letter of the 24th. Instant,[1] and have a very grateful sense of the kind sentiments which it exposes towards me.

A Mr. Claggett, of the State of Maryland, is appointed to the Place in Florida, which I understand was solicited in behalf of your

Son— Mr. Claggett was nominated to the Senate for that office by the late President, but the nomination was not acted upon: and the actual President included the same name for the same Office, I am told in one of his first nominations, and it resulted in a confirmation of the appointment.[2]

I am, Sir, truly and Respectfully, Your obedient Servant.

H. CLAY.

Copy. DNA, RG59, Dom. Letters, vol. 21, pp. 22-23 (M40, R19).
[1] See above, Mosby to Clay, March 29, 1825.
[2] Albert J. Clagett had been nominated as district attorney of West Florida by President Monroe on February 26, 1825; the nomination had been tabled in the Senate on March 3; but after a re-nomination by President Adams on March 8, the Senate had given its approval, March 9.

From J[ames] B[rown]

My dear Sir   Paris April 1st. 1825

At the date of the last letter which I had the pleasure to receive from you[1] your determination seemed to have settled down in favor of Mr. Adams as President and I have since heard he was elected. I congratulate you on the success of his election, for although you will be abused and censured by some of the friends of the other Candidates yet defeat would have rendered that censure and abuse more frequent whilst you now can receive the support of the majority of Congress if not of the nation. I am wholly at a loss to conjecture who will compose the cabinet of Mr Adams. It is believed here that Mr Webster[2] will be Secretary of State in case the appointment should not be offered to you. I rather doubt whether Mr Webster's opposition to the last War is forgotten sufficiently to make him popular in that important office. I hope soon to receive letters from Washington, which will remove all doubt as to the manner of filling these important places. Indeed we have waited for some days in anxious expectation of the arrival of the Packet of the 1st. of March which has been delayed by the prevalence of eastwardly winds. The election of Mr Adams, after the fact was known that the choice would be between him and Genl Jackson appeared to give great satisfaction in Europe. The character of Genl Jackson was considerably mistaken and still more the power he would have as a President of our Republic. It was beleived [sic] this [sic] his education had been entirely military and that he would if elected declare war on the slightest pretext or provocation— His conduct at Pensacola and at St Augustine had made him obnoxious to the Spaniards and their Continental friends whilst the British have neither forgotten the battles at New Orleans, nor forgiven the executions of Arbuthnot and Ambrister.[3]

I have received an invitation in common with the other Members of the diplomatic corps to attend the coronation at Rheims which will take place about the middle of June. Although this journey will be fatiguing and expensive yet the invitation was given in such terms and accepted by the whole diplomatic body that I could not without offense refuse to attend. I have written to the Secretary to know whether this extraordinary expense would be paid by the Government of the United States as it will be by all the Governments of Europe.[4] The death of the late King subjected me to a very considerable expenditure being obliged to put my carriage and servants in mourning, but I have not placed it in my account with the Government. The coronation will cost me in all probably near two thousand Dollars, a sum too considerable to be borne by a minister enjoying the smallest salary of any Minister at this Court—

Our claims against this Government appear to have taken a stand at the point at which Mr Gallatin left them and I do not know how or when we shall be able to drive the Ministry from their resort to the 8 Art of the Louisiana. [sic][5] I was surprized that the Committee of foreign relations, when informed that the real difficulty arose out of that Article, had not taken some pains to notice and explain their views of it in their report.[6] I hope if the subject is again brought before Congress instead of a loose report merely affirming the justice of our claims, the Treaty of Cession of Louisiana will be carefully examined and an argumentative report on the construction of it given to satisfy the Claimants that the interpretation contended for by France is not warranted by the Treaty. In the present state of the business I find France by no means to recede and indeed my two letters of the 23 of Octr. and the 18 Ulto. in which I have urged a separate discussion of the questions remain without any answer.[7]

The recognition of the Independence of the South American Governments[8] has produced much feeling on the Continent, but will not be immediately followed by war. The want of revenue, fleets, and the conflicting interests arising out of the affairs of Greece and Turkey will for the present prevent a resort to force. It is obvious however that England is viewed in no very friendly light by the Members of the Holy Alliance. Prince de Metternich has been in Paris for some time and frequent conferences are held by the Representatives of the great powers over all of which the veil of great secrecy is thrown. It is believed however that they relate principally to the affairs of Greece and Turkey. Austria it is said entertains serious apprehensions that the war with Greece, if continued much longer may so sensibly enfeeble Turkey that Constantinople will fall into the hands of the Emperor of Russia and increase his already overgrown Empire.

The Course pursued by the English Cabinet is well calculated to restore the influence of that nation on the Continent by exciting the admiration of all those who are in favor of liberal systems of Government. Although Europe is apparently tranquil yet symptoms of disatisfaction [sic] and discontent are to found [sic] in every part of it, and particularly in the small States over which the Holy Alliance is said to exercise a pretty rigid superintendance. The new King of Naples and Sicily[9] is anxious to escape from the Austrian yoke and it is said is very urgent with the Emperor to withdraw the army of occupation.[10] The King of Sardinia[11] is said to be in favor of a more liberal system of Government and the temper and disposition of the small powers of Germany has been soured by the intermeddling of the Allies in their systems of Government and the aversion shewn to the liberty of the press. France is prosperous and tranquil, and if we might draw our inferences from the measures now depending in the two chambers, expects the state of peace to remain uninterrupted for some time. A law has passed the Chamber of Deputies which allows indemnity of one Milliard of francs to the Emigrés, and adds thirty millions to the annual interest of the National debt[12]— The State of Spain is a miserable [sic] as you well imagine and that of Portugal but little better. How Spain can long exist without army fleet organization or revenue is beyond my comprehension.

The price of every thing necessary for living such as house rent, servants, provisions rises rapidly and I believe London is now as cheap as Paris. I have paid for my house for the present year 22,500 francs and now find I shall be forced to leave it in August as Prince Esterhazy[13] Ambassador of Austria has rented it for nine years. I do not believe I can procure one sufficient for my accommodation for less than 28,000 francs. You perceive no money is to be made by a foreign Mission— A house, servants, carriage, lights and fuel will exhaust my nine thousand Dollars leaving the other expences unprovided for. I shall however so long as I stay, endeavor to keep up an establishment nearly as respectable as that of the Ministers of my rank and I believe my country men who have reached Paris are generally satisfied with the reception I have given them—

A Mr Rhineholt of Philadelphia had commenced a suit for some lands on Johnstons fork which interfered with Mosby s claim.[14] I feel interested in the event and I hope you will be so kind as to have an eye to my interest in that quarter.

I hope John Humphreys[15] will not fail to remit to Mrs. Price the amount which I requested should be paid for her and her mother.[16] He has funds of mine for that purpose at his disposal.

I fear your vote for Mr Adams will affect your popularity in Kentucky, but as you have been already elected for the two next Sessions you will have time to remove any unfavorable impressions before your Constituents are again called upon to make a choice. It gave me great pleasure to hear that you were again nearly independent in your pecuniary affairs, and I hope your lands and real property will soon assume a higher value and completely extricate you—

We have now very few Americans at Paris but those who are here are generally of a very respectable order and conduct themselves with great propriety. Mr Lynch of new York[17] Lady Hervey and her sisters Mrs. Patterson and Miss Caton[18] are among the number. Washington Irving is also here and is much esteemed as is William West of Lexington by his fine and highly cultivated talent for painting— His picture of Lord Byron has attracted great notice and he has had full employment in making portraits since his arrival— He proposes to establish himself in London where I have no doubt he will meet with great encouragement.[19]

I shall enclose this letter to the Department of State to be sent to Lexington in case you should have left Washington. Remember me most affectionately to Mrs. C. and all our friends in Kentucky and receive assurances of the unabated friendship of Dear Sir Yours

J. B—

ALI. DLC-HC (DNA, M212, R1).
[1] Above, January 23, 1825.   [2] Daniel Webster.
[3] See above, II, 612n.   [4] Above, March 21, 1825.
[5] See above, III, 154n, 313n, 382, 383n.
[6] The "Report of the Committee on Foreign Relations, on the Petition of Archibald Gracie and Others," presented on May 24, 1824, had noted "with surprise" that the French Government had "not yet thought proper to enter upon the discussion" of the spoliation claims. "No other answers have yet been given to various official communications of the minister of the United States, than those required by the mere obligations of international courtesy." The committee, with the "hope and expectation, that attention will be given to this interesting subject by France, prior to the next session of Congress," had asked that they not be discharged. *House Reports*, 18 Cong., 1 Sess., no. 127.
[7] See above, Brown to Clay, March 23, 1825.
[8] By Great Britain. See above, Nelson to Clay, March 8, 1825, note.
[9] Francis I had ascended the throne on the death of his father, Ferdinand I, January 4, 1825.
[10] See above, III, 80-81, 82n. Austrian dominance, nevertheless, continued until 1849.
[11] Charles Felix.
[12] In January, 1825, Jean Baptiste (Guillaume Marie Anne Séraphin), Comte de Villèle, since 1821 Minister of Finance and, from 1822 to 1828, President of the Council of Ministers, had proposed, and the Chamber had adopted, legislation providing this indemnification for property seizures from the émigrés during the Revolution. The indemnity, which in actuality cost the French considerably less (around 630 million francs), was to be financed by refunding the public stock, currently outstanding on call at five percent interest, to provide for interest of three percent on stock purchased "at the price of 75" or $4\frac{1}{2}$ percent "at par, with a guarantee in both cases against being paid off till the 22nd of September, 1835."
[13] Prince Paul Anthony Esterházy.
[14] Suit not found. It probably related to the property of Wade Mosby, identified above, III, 119.
[15] John B. Humphreys, Brown's nephew, managed Brown's sugar plantation in Louisiana and was a partner in that enterprise.
[16] Susannah Price; Susannah Hart.

17 Dominick Lynch, wine merchant, singer, and introducer of Italian opera in the United States.

18 Louisa Catherine, wife of Sir Felton Bathurst Hervey; Mary Ann (Marianne), widow of Robert Patterson of Baltimore (son of William Patterson); and Elizabeth, yet unmarried, were daughters of Richard Caton.

19 William Edward West, born in Lexington, Kentucky, a son of Edward West, had gone to Europe in 1822 and remained abroad, as a painter, most notably of portraits, until about 1840. He exhibited regularly at the Royal Academy in London from 1826 through 1833.

MISCELLANEOUS LETTERS   April 1, 1825

To W[ILLIAM] STURGIS, of the firm of Bryant and Sturgis. Asks whether he would settle for $10,000 his claim against the Russian Government in the case of the *Pearl.* Copy. DNA, RG59, Dom. Letters, vol. 21, p. 22 (M40, R19). See Clay to Tuyll, above, March 25, 1825; below, April 19, 1825.

APPLICATIONS, RECOMMENDATIONS   April 1, 1825

HORATIO TURPIN, "Beech Park Gallatan [*sic*] Ct Kentucky," wishing "an appointment in the Military Academy at West Point" for his son, Philip O. Turpin, 16 years old, solicits Clay's "friendly Aid in obtaining it." ALS. DNA, RG94, Military Academy, Cadet Applications, 1825-207 (M688, R39). Horatio Turpin, born in Virginia and a veteran of the Revolution, had moved to Kentucky from Powhatan County shortly after the war and had been a resident of Lexington as early as 1787. He was an extensive property holder in Gallatin County at the time of his death in 1827. Cf. below, Crittenden to Clay, April 9, 1825. Philip O. Turpin, not further identified, was rejected for admission to the Military Academy.

From John H. Eaton

WASHINGTON, 2d, April, 1825.

SIR, Your letter of yesterday is received: as there is nothing now of enquiry or argument between us, I might forbear—offering a reply; but from a desire to correct some perversions given both to the meaning and expression of my last communication to you, I shall notice but one of them.

I do not assert that Mr. Kremer never used the language imputed to him, by you, as derived from Mr. Crowninshield: it is given as matter of belief only. "I cannot forbear the opinion" is the expression used, accompanied by a full and sufficient reason, why that opinion could not be incorrect; and that your informant must be mistaken. It was unnecessary for you to talk of Mr. Crowninshield's honor or veracity to me; I entertain as high an opinion of them as you can; but that he is mistaken, I have no more doubt, than I have, that Mr. Kremer is also a correct man. His differing with you, can assuredly not render him a better, or worse member of society.

I admit most cheerfully, that I have no "claims" on your courtesy, and to "any extraordinary observance of its rules." I have claims in this respect on no one: Society, not me, creates the claim; and has long since established amongst her subjects, that her's [sic] are rules every where in fashion, and always to be regarded. I am a little surprised that you should claim to enter any protest against them, while you evince such warmth of regard for the Catholic principle of confession. Permit me to assure you, that with such avowals before me, I have not the least desire, to question "your indisputable right, to choose your own preceptor."

For the privilege conceeded [sic] by you of visiting Mr. Kremer and of deriving "from his society, whatever enjoyments it can afford, literary, scientific or political" I ought to feel grateful, however I may omit to express my gratitude. Mr. Kremer is considered an honest man; he bears with him every where this reputation; and whilst he bears it, is fair company for any one, although he may not, like false coin, aim to assume any gloss, appearance, or to pass for any thing beyond a real value.

Respectfully, Your most obedient,   JNO. H. EATON.
Hon. H. CLAY, Secretary of State.

Washington Gazette, April 5, 1825. Published also in Washington *Daily National Intelligencer,* April 6, 1825; *Niles' Weekly Register,* XXVIII (April 9, 1825), 88-89; Lexington *Kentucky Reporter,* April 25, 1825.

From John Moody

New Canton Buckingham County. Virginia April 2d 1825—
Dear Sir

I wrote you Some five weeks past[1] and have not an answer   I Supose [sic] the Cause you so Engaged with Public Busness [sic] has prevented,,   The Purport of that Letter and this also was and is to State to you as a friend that I am Still Lying on my oars for want of Employment a Life I was not Brot up to and Time Lies heavuy [sic] on my hands   I have therefore to Request the kind favour of you to use your Influence with the President of the United States John Quincy Adams Esqr to Procure for Me Some Handsome Appointment under the fedral [sic] Goverment [sic]   There is Maney [sic] Places Vacant westward or was some time Past   I Conceve [sic] my self Qualified to fill any of them with Reputitation [sic] and Resposubility [sic] to the goverment,, Therefore I Pray you to Do Something for me in that way   If I had a Capital to goe [sic] into the Mercantile Busness I would Prefer that to any other,, But that not Being the Case I Cannot Run a Risque,   I am in good Health and able to Travell [sic] to any Point   I persue [sic] Steady Habits and Temprance [sic] as any Man in the union To which I

pledge my most Sacred Honour and I authorise you as a friend to averr [sic] this,, If my Character Should be Calld. in Quston [sic]— I Sent on to Mr. Stvenson[2] most ample Certificates placing my Character in a fair, point of Veiw [sic]. Beyond the Reach of Calumny and Cernsure [sic]   Relying on you [sic] goodness of Heart and Mind I Bid you farwell [sic] for the present in hopes of Hearing Something favourable[3]   I Subscribe myself with great Considerations [sic] your Most obt St   JOHN MOODY
P S I Expect Mr Stvenson filed my Certificate in Some of thee [sic] offces [sic] of Goverment,,   if So,, I Refer you to them for Satisfaction on all points in Queston [sic]   JOHN MOODY
I am Satisfied there is appointments wanting to the westward about the Indian Lands   There was Some ago a Mision [sic] Vaccant [sic] to portugal[4]   I am willing to goe to any Port and am of Oppinion [sic] I am fully Qualified   I am Yours   J. M

ALS. DNA, RG59, A. and R. (MR3). Addressed to Henry Clay, Secretary of State. Moody was a veteran of the Revolution.
  [1] Letter dated February 28, before Clay had assumed office, not found.
  [2] Andrew Stevenson.   [3] No reply found; Moody received no appointment.
  [4] Upon the recall of Henry Dearborn, who had held the post from May, 1822, until June, 1824, Thomas L. L. Brent, of Virginia, the Secretary of Legation, had served as Chargé ad interim. His commission as Chargé d'Affaires and letter of credence, from Clay to the Portuguese Minister of Foreign Affairs, had been dated March 9, 1825 (each, copy. DNA, RG59, Ceremonial Communications, II, 8-9, 20).

INSTRUCTIONS AND DISPATCHES   April 2, 1825

From ROBERT MONTGOMERY, Alicante. Comments on the "dearth of morality even in the higher classes of society [in Spain]" and on the bitterness of party hatreds. Notes rumors, which he has attempted to contradict, that the King (Ferdinand VII) "had refused to ratify the cession of the Floridas." Reports that the projected expedition to South America "is totally exploded"; suggests that the "onerous impositions" placed on American and British trade may have been occasioned by the King's hostility to these nations as "the fomenters of the revolution in his late colonies." Mentions the fall of the King's favorite, Ugarte, and the belief that there will be a new ministry. Cites the effects of severe drought and compares the calamities of Europe with the prospect of "our own favored land." ALS. DNA, RG59, Cons. Disp., Alicante, vol. 1 (M-T357, R1). Addressed to John Quincy Adams, Secretary of State; received May 22. Montgomery, a resident of Alicante since 1788, had been appointed United States consul there in April, 1824. Antonio Ugarte y Larrizábal had been dismissed in March as secretary to the Council of State; on the duration of the Ministry of Francisco de Zea Bermudez, see above, Brown to Clay, March 22, 1825, note.

From JOHN MULLOWNY, Tangier, no. 35. Reports that Captain (James) Allen (III) and his crew are in Tangier en route to Gibraltar and that their treatment furnishes proof of the Emperor's "friendly disposition toward Americans" and "the benevolence of the Musselmen of Morocco." ALS. DNA, RG59, Cons. Disp., Tangier, vol. 4 (M-T61, R4). Addressed to John Quincy Adams, Secretary of

State; received June 30. See above, Mullowny to Adams, Secretary of State, March 25, 1825. Abd-er-Rahman, II, was ruler of Morocco from 1822 to 1859.

MISCELLANEOUS LETTERS   April 2, 1825

From WILLIAM THORNTON, Department of State. Answers charges brought against him in the letter from Peter A. Browne to Clay, of March 29, 1825. ALS. DNA, RG59, Misc. Letters (M179, R62).

To George Ticknor

My dear Sir   Washn. 3d. April 1825

I pray you to excuse the delay which has arisen in my acknowledgment of the receipt of your obliging letter of the 23d. Feb.[1] with the two pamphlets, on your Free schools,[2] and the article on La Fayette,[3] which you did me the favor to transmit. Public affairs and public turmoils have left me but little leisure, of late, for my private correspondence. The return of tranquillity has enabled me to resume it. The school pamphlets afford me the information which I desired, and I attach much value to the sketch of Lafayettes life. Accept my thanks for all of them. I took the liberty of sending you a Copy of my Address to my late Constituents[4] which I trust you received, 'though I dare not hope, from its appalling but unavoidable length, that you could read it.

My lot having cast me in this City I propose to bring My family here in June. It will give me great pleasure, if you and Mrs. Tichnor [*sic*] should again come this way,[5] as I hope you may, to make you acquainted with Mrs. Clay and to receive you at my house. Should circumstances carry me to Boston I shall derive great satisfaction from accepting your kind invitation. I pray you to present me respectfully to Mrs Tichnor and believe me

Faithfully & cordially Yrs   H. CLAY

Geo. Tichnor Esq.

ALS. NhD. Ticknor, of Boston, was professor of French and Spanish and of belles lettres at Harvard from 1819 until his resignation in 1835. Most notable among his writings is the *History of Spanish Literature* (3 vols., New York, 1849).

1 Not found.

2 Probably James G[ordon] Carter, *Letters to the Hon. William Prescott, LL.D., on the Free Schools of New England, with Remarks upon the Principles of Instruction* (Boston, 1824) and an unsigned review article on this pamphlet in *North American Review*, XIX (New Series, X; October, 1824), 448-57. The review is attributed to Ticknor in *Life, Letters, and Journals of George Ticknor* (9th edn., 2 vols.; Boston, 1878), II, 507 (Appendix B).

3 Another unsigned review article, on two recently published memoirs of the life of Lafayette, had appeared in the *North American Review*, XX (New Series, XI; January, 1825), 147-80. Republished in Boston (1825) under the title, *Outlines of the Principal Events in the Life of General Lafayette, from the North American Review*, and, subsequently, in London and in Europe under slightly different titles, this review is also attributed to Ticknor by the Library of Congress.

4 See above, March 26, 1825.

5 Ticknor and his wife, the former Anna Eliot, of Boston, had visited Washington for three or four weeks during December, 1824, and January, 1825.

To Charles Hammond

My dear Sir   Washn. 4 Apl 1825

I cannot withhold from you the expression of my thanks for the able and efficient support which you have kindly given to my late political course.[1] I have been able to recognize you in the several articles of your composition. That in which you have so masterly [*sic*] treated Jackson's Swartwout letter will be republished here,[2] as all of them deserved to have been. I have sent you a Copy of my address to My Constituents.[3] You will perceive in it that I have taken the liberty to use your name in reference to a letter which I addressed to you prior to my departure from Lexn. of the receipt of which I have not been informed. If you have the letter (since I do not precisely recollect its contents) I submit it to your discretion whether it ought to be published or not.

The effect of my address is greater, on this side of the Mountains, than I even anticipated. Does it meet your approbation? Tell me without reserve; you know I can hear any thing from a friend.

I could not refuse the Dept. of State. The Conspirators would have abused me much more if I had declined it. Then how could I have refused the first office under a President whom I had contributed to elect? I know my *forte* is the H. of R. But I will endeavor to do my duty in this new office, and if God grant me life and health I will disappoint and triumph over my enemies.

You must recollect that we are still Charles Hammond & Henry Clay and write me accordingly.

Yr. faithful friend   H CLAY

ALS. InU.
1 In the *Liberty Hall and Cincinnati Gazette*.
2 On the Swartwout letter, see above, Clay to Brooke, January 28, 1825, note. Hammond's reply, published over the initial "L.," was reprinted from the *Liberty Hall and Cincinnati Gazette,* March 22, 1825, in the Washington *Daily National Journal,* April 5, 1825, and in the Lexington *Kentucky Reporter,* April 4, 1825. On the identification of Hammond as the author, see *City of Washington Gazette,* April 7, 1825, reprinting an item from the Cincinnati *National Republican,* March 25, 1825.
3 See above, Address, March 26, 1825.

From John Marshall

Dear Sir   Richmond April 4th. 1825

I have received your address to your former constituents;[1] and, as it was franked by you, I presume I am indebted to you for it. I have read it with great pleasure as well as attention, and am gratified at the full and complete view you have given of some matters which the busy world has been employing itself upon. I required no evidence respecting the charge made by Mr. Kremer, nor should I have required any had I been unacquainted with you or with the transaction, because I have long since ceased to credit charges destitute of proof, & to consider them as mere aspersions. The minuteness of detail however will enable your friends to encounter any insinuations on that subject which may be thrown out in their hearing. More of this may be looked for than any hostility to you would produce. There is unquestionably a party determined to oppose Mr. Adams at the next election, and this party will attack him through you. It is an old and has been a successful Stratagem. No part of your letter was more necessary than that which respects your former relatio[n] with that gentleman.

I am dear Sir with respect & esteem Your Obedt Servt

J MARSHALL

ALS. DLC-HC (DNA, M212, R1). Addressed to Clay.
1 See above, March 26, 1825.

DIPLOMATIC NOTES   April 4, 1825

From P[ETER] PEDERSEN, Philadelphia. Acknowledges receipt of Clay's note of March 25, 1825; urges that negotiation for a commercial convention be commenced "as early . . . as may be practicable," because of the "precarious nature of the communications with Copenhagen during the winter months"; states that he will communicate a "project" of the intended convention as soon as Clay intimates a wish to see him in Washington; encloses a copy of his full powers. ALS. DNA, RG59, Notes from Danish Legation, vol. 1 (M52, R1) .

INSTRUCTIONS AND DISPATCHES   April 4, 1825

From RICHARD RUSH, London, no. 427. Reports his interview with George Canning on April 2, in which Rush was apprized of the reaction of the European powers to British recognition of the new American States; transmits copies of memoranda of statements made by Russian, Austrian, and Prussian diplomats on this topic; and summarizes Spain's formal remonstrance. "In the end he [Canning] did not hesitate to say unequivocally, that he considered all danger to the peace of Europe as wholly gone by; he meant all immediate danger arising out of the measure in question, and he intimated that France was perhaps less disposed than any of the powers to make it a cause of breach." No reference was made to American recognition of the independence of the former Spanish colonies or to past conferences between Canning and Rush on that subject. Britain's recent negotiations with Russia on their differences respecting the northwest coast of America were mentioned; the convention, not yet displayed, is understood to have set the boundary of Russia's claims at 56 degrees north latitude and within ten leagues of the coast. The Under Secretary of State for the Colonial Department has reported that a total of 568 emigrants were sent from Ireland to Canada at the expense of the British Government in 1823. ALS. DNA, RG59, Dip. Disp., Great Britain, vol. 32 (M30, R28) . Extract published in Manning (arr.), *Diplomatic Correspondence . . . Latin*

American Nations, III, 1548-50. Addressed to Secretary of State; received May 21. On British recognition of the Latin American Republics, see above, Nelson to Clay, March 8, 1825, note. On the dispute relating to Russia's claims regarding the northwest coast of America, see above, Clay to Tuyll, March 25, 1825; Rush to Clay, March 26, 1825.

The boundary provision of the convention between Great Britain and Russia, signed February 28, 1825, had fixed the line between territories of the contracting parties in North America at the parallel 54 degrees 40 minutes north latitude, thence northward up the "Portland Channel" to 56 degrees north latitude, along the summit of the mountains lying parallel to the coast as far as 141 degrees west longitude, and along this meridian to "the Frozen Ocean." Should the summit of the mountains as specified prove to be more than ten marine leagues from the ocean, the boundary was to follow "a line parallel to the windings of the coast," not more than ten marine leagues inland. *Annual Register, 1825,* "Public Documents," 65.

The United States and Russia had already, on April 17, 1824, concluded a convention fixing the line of demarcation between their territorial claims at 54 degrees 40 minutes. Miller (ed.), *Treaties . . . ,* III, 153-54.

MISCELLANEOUS LETTERS   April 4, 1825

To ARCHIBALD GRACIE. States, in reply to his letter of March 25, that (Richard C.) Anderson (Jr.) will soon arrive in the United States, when his information will be made available. Copy. DNA, RG59, Dom. Letters, vol. 21, p. 23 (M40, R19). See below, Anderson to Clay, May 17, 1825.

To JOSEPH W[ILSON] PATTERSON, Baltimore (Maryland). Encloses his commission as a director of the Bank of the United States and requests acknowledgment of its receipt. Copy. DNA, RG59, Dom. Letters, vol. 21, p. 24 (M40, R19). Patterson had been appointed March 3, 1825, in the place of his father, William Patterson. The son was later head of a Baltimore firm of iron merchants and president of the Baltimore and Ohio Railroad. On April 5, 1825, he acknowledged receipt of the commission. ALS, in DNA, RG59, Acceptances and Orders for Comms. (M-T645, R2).

APPLICATIONS, RECOMMENDATIONS   April 4, 1825

A[LEXANDER] McNAIR, St. Louis, seeks appointment as a commissioner to Santa Fé, to obtain the cooperation of the Mexican Government in laying out a road between that city and St. Louis, and as an agent to bring the Indians under control along the route. Cites his qualifications as a former Governor of Missouri Territory (1821-1824) and now Indian Agent to the Osage. ALS. DNA, RG59, Misc. Letters (M179, R62). See above, Clay to Poinsett, March 26, 1825. McNair did not receive the appointments here requested.

From Francis T. Brooke

My Dear Sir.   St. Julien April 5. 1825

Your address to your former constituents[1] ought to put.to Silence the most obstinate of your enemies,   not so Mr Ritchie[2]   I am out of all patience with him,   the public must See that he is enlisted

body and Soul in the opposition—nothing can Satisfy him,   he is
evidently infinitely chagrined that the address is so lucid and un-
answerable,   it will have, I have no doubt a powerful effect,   as
I know it will be gratifying to you to See an example of its effect
I enclose you a letter from P N Nicholas[3]   the first part of it, alludes to an obituary notice of the death of that charming woman
Mrs Randolph[4] which you will See in the last Enquirer[5]— I received
before I left Richmd. a letter from Mr. Forsyth[6] of rather an extraordinary character and I have pondered the matter for Some time
before I have come to the conclusion that you ought to know its
contents,   though you were on the Spot and he might have applied to you to correct what he thought was wrong in your letter
to me in which you Spoke of his approbation of your acceptance
of the office you hold,[7] he thought proper to question me as to the
purport of that Letter,   my answer he has not replied to, nor do
I presume he will   your letter, as requested by you was Seen by
Mr Ritchie, and I believe its contents were made known to Mr
Forsyth by his partner[8] in a letter to Mr Stephenson,[9] I Shewed Mr
Forsyth's letter to Some of your friends who have Seen yours, and
to Gouch [sic] himself, none of whom perceived the Smallest difference between your account of the matter and his own— if however you wish to See Mr Forsyths letter I feel myself at perfect
liberty to inclose it to you,   I have but a Slight acquaintance with
that gentleman but have a very Sincere esteem for him,   his
father[10] was high in my estimation and while on the one hand I
think it due to you perfectly to understand him, I Should regret
it if his letter was to operate unfavorably to him,   like Mr Ritchie
he Seems to be under an indescribable infatuation in regard to
Mr Crawford,[11]   by the bye I have Seen no one, who Saw Mr C,
at Fredg who does not admit that he labours under mental and
bodily imbecility—   Yours very truly   FRANCIS BROOKE

ALS. DLC-HC (DNA, M212, R1). Addressed to Clay at Washington.
1 Above, March 26, 1825.   2 Thomas Ritchie.   3 Enclosure not found.
4 Mrs. Peyton Randolph (née Maria Ward), whose death had been reported in the
Washington *Daily National Intelligencer,* April 1, 1825. Mrs. Randolph had died in
Richmond on March 19.
5 Richmond *Enquirer.*   6 John Forsyth.   7 Above, February 18, 1825.
8 Ritchie's partner, Claiborne W. Gooch.   9 Probably Andrew Stevenson.
10 Robert Forsyth, Revolutionary War officer from Virginia, first Federal marshal
of Georgia.   11 William H. Crawford.

From Noah Zane

D Sir   Wheeling 5th. April 1824 [*i.e.,* 1825]
   The Barr [sic] of this County has recommended to the Government the appointment of Alexander caldwell as district Judge in the

place of John G. Jackson deceased[1]— I have been urged to sustain this recommendation by letters to you and Mr. Barbour[2] the Secretary of War   I have supported your Election as I did Mr. Barbours Election to the senate of the U.S. on national grounds and without the least notion that it could in any way personally be useful to either myself or others and I will now say to you that you will find by my future conduct that in no way will I ever claim any thing on this account— Personally I have no objection to Mr. Caldwells appointment but considerations of a higher Charecter [*sic*] induce me to state; that his appointment will not aid you or the administration in the Great Measures they have in View— Mr. Caldwell since your appointment has been Very Busy in producing the impression that your conduct in the late election has been *corrupt,* since the death of the Judge he has been silent but I submit to you whether under all circumstances he ought to receive the appointment; he is of Very moderate talents and of doubtful Politicks and an enemy of you Personally— I can with Truth say many things to the prejudice of Mr Caldwell but I forbear, he is your enemy and the enemy of Mr. Adams—as such I hope his apointment [*sic*] will not take place— you can in the Valley of Winchester select some one that may strengthen your [*sic*] in the administration rely upon it that this appointment cannot have that effect.

I wish this letter to be shewn to Mr. Barbour and the president, you may rely on on [*sic*] its Verity[3]—   your sincere friend
Hon H. Clay—   NOAH ZANE

ALS. DNA, RG59, A. and R. (MR1). A merchant, one of the developers of the Wheeling townsite, and proprietor of a bridge company, Zane was also a horse-racing enthusiast and had been a leader in introducing the Lancasterian system of education in the community (cf. above, II, 663n).

1 Jackson, who had been appointed judge for the Western District of Virginia in 1819, had died March 28, 1825. Caldwell, a lawyer of Wheeling, was not Adams' first choice as a replacement (cf. below, Clay to Pendleton, May 9, 1825; Smith to Clay, October 21, 1825) but was later appointed (see below, Clay to Caldwell, October 28, 1825). He retained the judgeship until his death in 1839.

2 James Barbour.

3 In an undated and unaddressed letter, sent to the State Department by the next mail, Zane wrote: "upon reflection I may have used stronger language than the actual conduct of Mr. Caldwell warrented [*sic*] I am incapable of injuring any one and have to request the withdrawal of my letter to you & to add my suffrage to that of his and your friends here family considerations have upon mature reflection induced me to take this course, if you should have shewn my letter to any one I will take it as a favor if you will remove any unfavorable impressions that may have been made

"I wish you to destroy my letter or inclose it to me— I will explain this matter satisfactorily to you when I see you   no one knows here that I have written it." ALS. DNA, RG59, A. and R. (M531, R2).

DIPLOMATIC NOTES   April 5, 1825

From the BARON DE TUYLL, *"Confidential."* States his intention "of writing to Count Nesselrode on the affair relating to *Tonnage";* reminds Clay "of a

certain *inofficial* paper it was his intention to send to Baron Tuyll" for use "in
preparing a Despatch concerning the same object, which he intends to communicate in a confidential way to the Secretary of State, before its transmission,
wishing that it may also be submitted to the previous consideration of the
President of the United States." AN. DNA, RG59, Notes from Russian Legation, vol. 1 (M39, R1). See below, Clay to Tuyll, this date.

To the BARON DE TUYLL. Encloses "Informal memorandum" (see above,
Tuyll to Clay, this date). Copy. DNA, RG59, Notes to Foreign Ministers and
Consuls, vol. 3, p. 214. The memorandum refers to Tuyll's note of February
16, 1825, in which the inequality in tonnage duties imposed on American and
Russian vessels entering Russian ports was said "to be nominal"; states that,
since no complaints have been received from Americans regarding this treat-
ment, the President is disposed "not to disturb the continued operation of the
Act of Congress of the 7 January 1824 until the pleasure of His Imperial
Majesty is known"; but adds that the United States expects equality "both
in form and in fact" without unnecessary delay. Copy. DNA, RG59, Notes to
Foreign Ministers and Consuls, vol. 3, p. 214. Both documents, AN draft, also
located in CSmH. On the act of January 7, 1824, see above, Lorich to Clay,
March 16, 1825, note.

INSTRUCTIONS AND DISPATCHES   April 5, 1825

To LEONARD CORNING, "Consul U. S. at the Island of Maranham [Brazil]."
Encloses commission, printed circular of instructions, and a blank consular
bond to be executed and returned. Copy. DNA, RG59, Cons. Instr., vol. 2, p. 349
(M78, R2). On August 1, 1825, Corning acknowledged this communication and
indicated his acceptance of the appointment. ALS. DNA, RG59, Cons. Disp.,
Maranham, vol. 1 (M-T398, R1). He remained at the post until 1830.

MISCELLANEOUS LETTERS   April 5, 1825

To GEORGE WARREN CROSS, Charleston, South Carolina. Acknowledges receipt of Cross's letter of March 28, which will receive consideration. Copy. DNA,
RG59, Dom. Letters, vol. 21, p. 25 (M40, R19). The copyist wrote Cross's name
as "Crox."

APPLICATIONS, RECOMMENDATIONS   April 5, 1825

J[OHN] GOTTFRIED BOKER, United States consul for the Prussian Provinces of
the Rhine, explains the importance of commercial relations between the United
States and Germany; solicits appointment as consul general for Prussia and
Saxony. ALS. DNA, RG59, A. and R. (MR1). Boker, of New York, remained
consul at Remscheid from 1821 until 1830, when he was appointed consul
general to Switzerland.

VINCENT GRAY, Havana (Cuba), solicits appointment as commercial agent at
Havana if John Warner, the incumbent, who has returned to the United States
because of illness, does not return; states that he will forward by the next vessel
letters from his and Clay's "mutual friend T. B. Robertson Esqr. late Governor
of Louisiana," and from Clay's "Brother in Law Jas. Brown Esqr.," and that
he has for years been on "terms of intimacy as a Correspondt." with Clay's
"Brother John," though not personally acquainted with him. ALS. *Ibid.* See

below, Robertson to Clay, April 20, 1825. Recommendation from Brown not found. Warner died at Baltimore on May 13. Washington *Daily National Intelligencer,* May 17, 1825. Gray did not receive the appointment but regularly served as vice consular commercial agent for the port during the summer and fall months, while the appointee, Thomas McKean Rodney, returned to the United States. Rodney, son of Caesar A., later became collector for the port of Wilmington and a prominent Republican leader.

THOMAS WILSON, Dublin (Ireland), seeks appointment as consul at Dublin; encloses letter from James Maury. ALS. DNA, RG59, A. and R. (MR4). See above, Maury to Clay, March 29, 1825.

To H[enry] U. Addington

H. U. Addington Esquire,
Chargé d'Affaires from Great Britain.   Department of State,
Sir,   Washington, 6th April, 1825.
   I have the honour to inform you that the delay, in the transmission of a definitive answer to your Note of the 6th. of November last, has proceeded from an anxious desire on the part of the late President of the United States, to ascertain the practicability of reconciling, if possible, the views of the Government of the United States with those which are entertained by that of His Britannic Majesty, in respect to the Convention for more effectually suppressing the Slave trade. With that object, the correspondence with your Government and the Convention in which it terminated, together with what has since passed between the two Governments, both here and at London, were submitted to Congress during its late Session.[1] Of that reference you were apprized by the Note of my Predecessor of the 4th. December last.[2] It has so happened that neither the Senate nor the House of Representatives has expressed directly any opinion on the subject. But on another Convention, having the same object, concluded with The Republic of Colombia, on the 10th. day of December 1824, which was formed after the model of that which is pending between the Governments of the United States and Great Britain, the Senate has expressed a very decided opinion. In the Colombian Convention, the coasts of America were excepted from its operation, and yet notwithstanding this conciliating feature, the Senate after full deliberation, in the exercise of its proper constitutional powers, has by a large majority, deemed it inexpedient to consent to and advise the ratification of this Convention.[3]
   The Government of His Britannic Majesty is well acquainted with the provision of the Constitution of the United States by which the Senate is a component part of the Treaty-making power; and that the consent and advice of that branch of Congress are indispensable in the formation of all Treaties. According to the

practice of this Government, the Senate is not ordinarily consulted in the initiatory state of a negotiation, but its consent and advice are only invoked after a Treaty is concluded, under the direction of the President, and submitted to its consideration. Each of the two branches of the Treaty-making authority is independent of the other, whilst both are responsible to the States and to the people, the common sources of their respective powers. It results, from this organization, that, in the progress of the Government, instances may sometimes occur of a difference of opinion between the Senate and the Executive, as to the expediency of a projected Treaty, of which the rejection of the Colombian Convention affords an example. The people of the United-States have justly considered that, if there be any inconveniences in this arrangement of their Executive power, those inconveniences are more than counterbalanced by the greater security of their interests, which is effected by the mutual checks which are thus interposed. But it is not believed that there are any inconveniences to Foreign Powers, of which they can with propriety complain. To give validity to any Treaty the consent of the contracting parties is necessary. As to the mode by which that consent shall be expressed, it must necessarily depend with each upon its own peculiar Constitutional arrangement. All that can rightly be demanded, in treating, is to know the contingencies on the happening of which that consent is to be regarded as sufficiently testified. This information the Government of the United States has always communicated to the Foreign Powers with which it treats, and to none more fully than to the United Kingdom of Great Britain and Ireland. Nor can it be admitted that any just cause of complaint can arise out of the rejection by one party of a Treaty which the other has previously ratified. When such a case occurs, it only proves that the consent of both, according to the Constitutional precautions which have been provided for manifesting that consent, is wanting to make the Treaty valid. One must necessarily precede the other in the act of ratification; and if after a Treaty is ratified by one party, a ratification of it be withheld by the other, it merely shews that one is, and the other is not willing, to come under the obligations of the proposed Treaty.

I am instructed by the President to accompany these frank and friendly explanations by the expression of his sincere regret that, from the views which are entertained by the Senate of the United States, it would seem to be unnecessary and inexpedient any longer to continue the negotiation respecting the Slave convention, with any hope that it can be made to assume a form satisfactory to both parties. The Government of His Britannic Majesty insists, as an indispensable condition, that the regulated right of search, proposed in the Convention, should be extended to the American Coasts, as well as to those of Africa and the West Indies. The Senate, even with the omission of America, thinks it unadviseable [*sic*] to ratify the Colombian Convention. And it is therefore clearly to be inferred that a Convention with His Britannic Majesty, with a similar omission, would not receive the approbation of the Senate. The decision of the Senate shews that it has made up its deliberate judgment, without any regard to the relative state of the Military or Commercial Marine; for all the considerations belonging to a view of that subject would have urged the Senate to an acceptance of the Colombian Convention. It is hoped, therefore, that His Britannic Majesty cannot fail to perceive that the Senate has been guided by no unfriendly feeling towards Great Britain.

Before closing this note, I must express my regret that I am unable to concur with you in the view which you have been pleased to present of the Act of the British Parliament, by which it has denounced, as piratical, the Slave trade; when exercised by British subjects. It is acknowledged that the Government of the United States considered such a denunciation as expedient preliminary to the conclusion of the projected Convention.[4] But the British Parliament, doubtless, upon its own sense of the enormity of the offence, deemed it proper to affix to it the character and the penalties of piracy. However much it may be supposed to have been actuated by an accomodating [*sic*] spirit towards the United-States, it can hardly be imagined that it would have given that denomination to the fact of trading in Slaves from motives of concession merely, contrary to its own estimate of the moral character of that act.[5] The Executive of the United-States believed that it might conduce to the Success of the negotiation, if the British Parliament would previously declare, as the United-States have done, the Slave-trade to be piratical. But it did not follow from the passage of that act that any Treaty, in which the negotiation might terminate, was to be taken out of the ordinary rule by which all Treaties are finally submitted to the scrutiny and sanction of the respective Governments. No peculiar advantage has accrued to the United-States from the enactment of that British Law. It's [*sic*] continued existence, moreover, now depends upon the pleasure of the British Parliament.

But there is no disposition to dwell longer on this subject. The true character of the whole negotiation cannot be misconceived. Great Britain and the United-States have had in view a common end of great humanity, entitled to their highest and best exertions. With respect to the desire of attaining that end, there is no difference of opinion between the Government of His Britannic Majesty and that of the United-States in any of its branches. But the

Senate has thought that the proposed Convention was an instrument not adapted to the accomplishment of that end, or that it was otherwise objectionable. And, without the concurrence of the Senate, the Convention cannot receive the Constitutional sanctions of the United-States. Without indulging therefore unavailing regrets, it is the anxious hope of the President that the Government of His Britannic Majesty should see in all that has occurred nothing towards it unfriendly on the part of the United-States, and nothing that ought to slacken their separate or united exertions in the employment of all other practical modes to effectuate the great object, so dear to both, of an entire extirpation of a traffic which is condemned by reason, religion and humanity.

I pray you, Sir, to accept the assurance of my distinguished Consideration.   H. CLAY.

Copy. DNA, RG59, Notes to Foreign Ministers and Consuls, vol. 3, pp. 207-11 (M38, R3). AL draft, in CSmH.

1 As an accompaniment to President Monroe's annual message to Congress, December 7, 1824. *American State Papers, Foreign Relations*, V, 359-68. The proposed convention for suppression of the slave trade, negotiated by Richard Rush and George Canning, had been submitted to the Senate by President Monroe on April 30, 1824. On May 22, this body had approved ratification, but only with amendments providing for termination of the agreement upon six months' notice and elimination of the words "of America" from line four of the first article, thus rejecting authorization of visit and search by British naval officers on vessels off the coasts of America. In his note of November 6 Addington had reported his Government's willingness, and his own accreditation, to renew negotiations accepting the proposed changes other than the omission of the right of search off the American coasts.

2 *American State Papers, Foreign Relations*, V, 367-68.

3 See above, Clay to Salazar, March 21, 1825.

4 In a note to Stratford Canning on March 31, 1823, John Quincy Adams, as Secretary of State, had cited the enactment of a law, approved May 15, 1820 (3 *U. S. Stat.*, 600-601), under which if citizens of the United States, "being of the crew or ship's company of any foreign ship or vessel engaged in the slave trade, or any person whatever, being of the crew or ship's company of any ship or vessel, owned in the whole or part, or navigated for, or in behalf of, any citizen or citizens of the United States," should seize, detain, "offer or attempt to sell, as a slave, any negro or mulatto not held to service" by the laws of the states or territories of the United States, they were to be subject to the penalties of piracy. Adams, at the direction of President Monroe, had proposed to Great Britain the adoption of "a mutual stipulation to annex the penalties of *piracy* to the offence of participating in the slave trade by the citizens or subjects of the respective parties. This proposal," he had stated, "is made as a substitute for that of conceding a mutual right of search, and of a trial by mixed commissions which would be rendered useless by it." *American State Papers, Foreign Relations*, V, 328.

The British Parliament having passed such an act on March 31, 1824 (5 *Geo. IV*, c.17), Addington, in his letter of November 6, had pointed to the measure as fulfillment of a "condition required of Great Britain prior to the signature of the treaty by the American plenipotentiary." He had then commented: "On the justice of accepting the value already paid for a stipulated act, and withholding the performance of that act, I leave it with confidence to your own sense of honor and equity to determine." *American State Papers, Foreign Relations*, V, 367.

5 Cf. below, Clay to Raguet, April 14, 1825.

To Francis T. Brooke

My dear Sir   Washn. 6 Apl. 1825.

From your letter of the 5h. inst. which I this day received I perceive you are at home and not at Richmond, to which I had transmitted for you one of my addresses to my Constituents. The favorable opinion entertained of it by such early and valuable friends as yourself and Nicholas is highly gratifying. Among other similar testimonies from Richmond, I have received from the Chief Justice a very satisfactory letter.[1] Prior to the publication of my address Mr. Tyler wrote me a letter, approving my course (since he believed Mr. Crawford to have been out of the question) and declaring, in strong terms, his unabated confidence in me.[2] From all quarters, in short, information is constantly pouring in on me, in every form, evincing general & hearty approbation of my late public course. My triumph will, as it ought to be, complete [sic] and entire over the base confederacy against me. As to Forsythe [sic], he certainly advised me in unqualified terms to accept the Department of State. I attached myself no particular importance to his opinion, 'though I supposed others might. He was with me on the 30h. or the 29h. of last month, had a long conversation, in the course of which he praised my address, and (entre nous) gave in his adhesion. I have no curiosity to see his letter. I understand him thoroughly. He did not mention one word about my letter to you or his correspondence with you. What could he say to me?

I share with you in your grief for the death of Mrs. Randolph. I have known her from my earliest youth. She deserved all that you have so well said in behalf of her memory.

I find my office no bed of roses. With spirits never more buoyant, 12 hours work per day are almost too much for my physical powers. An entire harmony as to public measures exists between Mr. Adams and me.

I return you Nicholas s letter. With great regard I am truly Your friend   H. CLAY
P.S. Was ever any thing so silly as for Eaton to publish his correspondence with me?[3] I am greatly deceived if he has not come out worse than he stood before   H C.

ALS. KyU. Addressed to Brooke at "St. Julien, Fredericksburg, Va."
[1] Above, Marshall to Clay, April 4, 1825.   [2] Above, March 27, 1825.
[3] Above, March 28, 30, 31, April 1, 2, 1825.

From R[obert] R. Henry

Sir   [6 April][1] 1825
You probably may have heard that the Committee on Commerce, did *not* report on Collector Clarks case, it being the wish of the late President[2] that they should *not*, owing no doubt to his

sympathy for Secy. Crawfords health &ca, and the consequences that would result to him, the Collector & others, from a report on the documents referred to in my letter to the Committee dated 11th March 1825.

By advices from St Mary's I find, that Mr Clark expects (*and that justly*) to be removed from office, by President Adams, and that he wishes either Robt L. Halcombe or Thomas H. Miller to be his successor[3]— Both those men are most deplorably and habitually intemperate, and have proved themselves in *Private* trusts unworthy of confidence

It is most important to the government that a man of high standing and character should be appointed to that station, as the recent law, relative to *Wrecked Property* (from the Florida Coast)[4] &ca. requires a Person of intigrity [*sic*] to be Collector, otherwise the Public will suffer, as they did with the *Intentional ship Wrecked goods* brought from Key Vacas to that Port[5]

I am happy to hear that Doctr Whipple Aldrich (formerly of Providence Rhode Island)[6] a gentleman of Property & talent, and in point of Character inferior to none in the Union, has been prevailed on to offer for the Collectorship, and I understand that the President has been Written to on the subject.[7]— Will you Permit me to recommend the Doctr to your good offices— You cannot bestow your Patronage on a more Worthy character & who I personally wish to see in the place of a man of the *very reverse* character as the documents on file at Washington conclusively shew— Excuse the liberty I take on this occasion, and I am respectfully Sir Your most obed Servt   R R HENRY
The Honble Henry Clay Secy of State [Washington] Cit[y]

ALS. DNA, RG59, A. and R. (MR1). Postmarked: "NEW YORK   APR 8"; endorsed on cover: "6 April 1825." See above, III, 571n.
    [1] MS. torn.   [2] James Monroe.
    [3] Halcombe, not identified; Miller, probably of St. Mary's, Georgia.
    [4] The law, regulating the handling and sale of goods salvaged from wrecked ships off the coast of Florida, had been enacted by "the governor and legislative council of the territory of Florida" in 1823. It was disapproved, and nullified, by act of Congress in 1826 (4 *U. S. Stat.*, 138).
    [5] Reference not found.   [6] At this time a resident of St. Mary's.
    [7] Aldrich to Adams, March 12, 1825. ALS. MHi-Adams Papers, Letters Received (MR468).

DIPLOMATIC NOTES   April 6, 1825

From JOSE SILVESTRE REBELLO. Requests an answer to his letter of January 28, which proposed a convention and an alliance between the United States and Brazil, directed against interference by any government in the conflict between Brazil and Portugal or the occupation by Portugal of any military position in Brazil. Observes that, if rumors of Portuguese recognition of Brazilian independence are correct, the proposed convention should "go no further than, to promote the Independence of the other new American Nations, this being one of the objects of the convention," because the reasons that induced Brazil to seek alliance with the United States will cease upon recognition by Portugal of the independence of the Empire of Brazil.

But, since the United States and Brazil ought to be united in ties of friendship, peace, and commerce, a treaty between them may now have a denomination more in keeping with the philanthropic principles that regulate the general interests of nations. While Brazil opposes principles not generally accepted as international law, she "will embrace them with pleasure provided they may become theorems in Public right by universal concurrence." LS, orig. and trans. DNA, RG59, Notes from Brazilian Legation, vol. 1 (M49, R1). Published in Manning (arr.), *Diplomatic Correspondence . . . Latin-American Nations,* II, 813-14.

From the BARON DE TUYLL, *"Confidential."* Acknowledges receipt of the confidential communication transmitted to him yesterday; encloses the minute of his projected dispatch; and, "Should any expressions made use of in that paper give rise to some difficulties," states his willingness "to call upon Mr. Clay and adjust the same in a manner which may suit the Secretary of State." AN. DNA, RG59, Notes from Russian Legation, vol. 1 (M39, R1). See below, Clay to Tuyll, April 8, 1825.

INSTRUCTIONS AND DISPATCHES   April 6, 1825

From NATHAN LEVY, Baltimore. Reiterates concern regarding the vice-consulate at St. Thomas; refers to ex-President (James) Monroe's promise to instruct (Christopher) Hughes on the subject, when his mission to Copenhagen was first contemplated; and cites a letter from Levy to the Department of State, dated June 4, 1821, together with the Danish vice-consulate instructions and the acts of Congress of March 27, 1804, and March 3, 1817, for fuller elucidation of the subject. LS. DNA, RG59, Cons. Disp., St. Thomas, vol. 2 (M-T350, R2). Levy, son of a prominent Baltimore merchant and Indian trader, was officially recognized at this time only as commercial agent.

The Danish instructions to which Levy referred had been issued September 12, 1802, and further recommended on July 13, 1809, by Peter Pedersen, consul general of Denmark in the United States, for the regulation of the vice consulates under his administration; they required, among other provisions, the deposit by Danish ship masters of their "passport and Ship Rolls, with all other public papers," with the consular offices within 24 hours after entering port. Quoted in Levy to Clay, February 11, 1829 (*ibid.*).

Levy appears to have erred in citing the act of March 27, 1804 (2 *U. S. Stat.,* 296), which he elsewhere (Levy to Clay, February 11, 1829) describes as the basis from which grew the act of March 3, 1817; his reference should have been to the act of February 28, 1803 (*ibid.,* 203), which provided, in section two, that masters of vessels belonging to United States citizens must, on arrival at a foreign port, deposit their "register, sea letter, and Mediterranean passport" with the American consular office, if there be one, at the port. The act of March 3, 1817, required that ships registers, together with clearance and other papers issued by customs officers to foreign vessels in United States ports, should be deposited with consular authorities of the nations to which the vessels belonged, within 48 hours after their entry into port, with the proviso that this measure should not extend to the vessels of nations who did not reciprocate this regulation, by providing for the deposit of such papers for American vessels with the United States consular offices, according to the provisions of the second section of the Congressional act of February 28, 1803. 3 *U. S. Stat.*, 362.

As "directed by the Secretary," Daniel Brent informed Levy, on April 8, that Christopher Hughes had been instructed (above, March 24, 1825, no. 2) in relation to the matter here discussed. Copy, in DNA, RG59, Cons. Instr., vol. 2, p. 350 (M78, R2).

From HUGH NELSON, Madrid, no. 54. Encloses documents showing that Spain still exacts a duty of 20 reals per ton on American vessels coming into port (see below, Clay to Everett, April 27, 1825, n. 8) ; reports "some sensation among the Ministers of the foreign powers here" resulting from accounts in English newspapers of the authorization by Congress for the use of "our cruisers" against pirates in the West Indies; summarizes an interview with the Spanish Secretary of State (Francisco de Zea Bermudez), who complained of the conduct of Commodore (David) Porter; states that the Spanish Government has renewed complaints against (John) Mullowny, United States consul at Tangiers, for protecting Spanish refugees; and transmits a copy of a note from Nelson to Bermudez, protesting the treatment of the American schooner *General Jackson,* which, though refused a landing permit in a Spanish port, was compelled to pay the tonnage duty. LS. DNA, RG59, Dip. Disp., Spain, vol. 24 (M31, R26).

In answer to two Senate resolutions requesting information concerning piratical depredations upon United States citizens and the measures adopted for their suppression, President Monroe on January 13, 1825, had suggested three possible courses of action: pursuit of offenders into settled, as well as unsettled, areas of the islands whence they emanated, reprisal on the property of inhabitants of the islands, and blockade of the ports of the islands. Such action, he had stated, could only be taken, with amity toward Spain, under a belief that neither the Spanish Government nor the governments of her Caribbean islands could suppress piracy, "and that the United States interpose their aid for the accomplishment of an object which is of equal importance to them as well as to us." Acting on this assumption, the President had requested "power, commensurate with either resource [*sic*] . . . to be exercised according to his discretion, and as circumstances may imperiously require." "Message from the President of the United States, Transmitting Information Relative to Piratical Depredations . . . January 13, 1825," *Sen. Docs.,* 18 Cong., 2 Sess., no. 15, p. 3. A Senate bill drafted to supply this authorization was so drastically amended by House action as to provide only for augmenting the United States naval forces with ten additional sloops of war. The House Committee on Foreign Relations had opposed further action by this government until Spain had been given additional opportunity to effect amelioration. 4 *U. S. Stat.,* 131 (March 3, 1825); *Register of Debates,* 18 Cong., 2 Sess., 714-17 (March 1, 1825); *Niles' Weekly Register,* XXVII (February 19, 1825), 391-93. See also, above, III, 338n.

Sensitivity on the issue of Spanish sovereignty over her West Indian islands was heightened at this time both by the independence movements emanating from Colombia and Mexico (see above, III, 596n; Clay to Poinsett, March 26, 1825; below, Robertson to Clay, April 20, 1825; Clay to Everett, April 27, 1825; Thomas to Clay, April 30, 1825; Clay to Middleton, May 10, 1825; Poinsett to Clay, June 15, 1825) and by the punitive action taken by Captain David Porter in the Fajardo (Faxjardo, Foxardo) incident. As reported by Porter to Samuel L. Southard, Secretary of the Navy, November 15, 1824, the commander of the West Indian Squadron had let a party of two hundred seamen and marines ashore at the port of Fajardo, a Puerto Rican town some two miles inland from the eastern coast of the island, had spiked the guns of the military installations, and had required the local alcalde and captain of the port to render public apology for imprisoning and insulting Lieutenant Commandant Charles T. Platt, of the United States schooner *Beagle,* who had visited the community in an effort to trace a quantity of dry goods supposed to have been stored there by pirates. The incident had been the subject of congressional inquiry under a House resolution of December 27, 1824; and Porter had been relieved of his command, with orders to return home for inquiry.

For earlier reference to the Mullowny case, see above, Salmon to Clay, March 16, 1825.

From JOHN SHILLABER, Batavia. Acknowledges receipt of his commission; reports that the Governor General refuses to acknowledge him "as Consul, having no instructions from His [*sic*] Sovereign so to do"; gives an optimistic view of the possibilities of American trade with "Java and the ports around"; refers to the trade rivalry in that area between the Dutch and the British; discusses the economy, people, and political situation of Java; and suggests "that it would probably be of benefit to American Commerce were some of her public armed vessels to visit these seas from time to time. . . ." ALS. DNA, RG59, Cons. Disp., Batavia, vol. 1 (M-T95, R1). Addressed to Secretary of State. Cf. below, Clay to Clark, April 16, 1825, note.

MISCELLANEOUS LETTERS   April 6, 1825

To WILLIAM HENRY ALLEN, St. Augustine. Transmits his commission as "Commissioner for ascertaining claims and titles to Land in Florida." Copy. DNA, RG59, Dom. Letters, vol. 21, p. 25 (M40, R19). In reply, on April 26, Allen commented: "Altho a stranger permit me sir to say (in accordance with a long-formed and often expressed opinion) that in my estimation you deserve the eternal gratitude of your country as having warded off one of the greatest possible calamities by preventing the setting so terrible a precedent as the elevation of a man to her highest office *merely* in consideration of military services. I have no doubt the great body of the American people will shortly think so too. Permit me to say too that I am rejoiced to see the absurdity of the allegations lately made against you so triumphantly exposed." ALS. DNA, RG59, Acceptances and Orders for Commissions (M-T645, R2). Allen, a native of Maryland, had been nominated for the post as commissioner on December 28, 1824; the appointment had been confirmed on March 3. On May 22, 1826, he was named receiver of public moneys for the District of East Florida and held that position for the next decade.

From ISAAC H. TIFFANY, Esperance, New York. Transmits a letter on Patent Office business from Horatio Gates Spafford to Clay. ALS. DNA, RG59, Misc. Letters (M179, R62). See below, April 7, 1825. Tiffany not further identified.

APPLICATIONS, RECOMMENDATIONS   April 6, 1825

H[ARVEY] GREGG, Shelbyville, Indiana, recommends Thomas Douglas for appointment to office in the Territory of Florida. ALS. DNA, RG59, A. and R. (MR2). Douglas, born in Wallingford, Connecticut, had attempted, unsuccessfully, to raise silk in St. Augustine, Florida, before removing to Madison, Indiana, where he was at this time a merchant, manufacturer, bank director, lawyer, and associate justice of the circuit court. He was appointed United States attorney for the District of East Florida in 1826 and reappointed for successive terms until

1845, when he resigned to become judge of the Eastern Circuit of Florida. In 1853 he became the first chief justice of the newly organized State supreme court.

MAGNUS M. MURRAY, Pittsburgh (Pennsylvania), requests appointment as a commissioner or surveyor on the road to be marked out from the western frontier of Missouri to New Mexico or on that from Little Rock to Cantonment Gibson, in Arkansas. ALS. *Ibid.* (MR3). On the proposed road to New Mexico, see above, McNair to Clay, April 4, 1825. Provision for commissioners to lay out a road from Little Rock to Cantonment Gibson had likewise been authorized in legislation approved March 3, 1825 (4 *U. S. Stat.*, 135). Murray did not receive an appointment.

To Jesse Bledsoe and Others

Gent   Washington 7h. April 1825

I ought earlier to have transmitted to you the inclosed letter from Genl. La Fayette,[1] but as it will reach you in time to be informed when he may be expected at Lexington, no injury will result from the delay. He left Augusta[2] on the 23d of March, and so far had been able to perform his journey according to the plan which he had arranged prior to its commencement. He expects to be in N. Orleans on the 3d. of May and in Lexington on the 11h. of that month;[3] but circumstances may retard or accelerate his arrival. If he give up his trip to St. Louis, he will be with you earlier.

It is my wish to meet him at Lexington, but I am not sure that my public duties will admit of the gratification of it.

I am Your obt. Servant   H. CLAY
The Honble J. Bledsoe
    Mr. Holley.
    Dr. Caldwell[4]   &c   &c   &c
    Mr. Bradford
    Dr. Richardson[5]

ALS. KyLxT. Addressed on attached sheet: "John Bradford Esqr, or The Revd. H. Holley   Lexington (K)." Published in Lexington *Kentucky Reporter,* April 25, 1825.
[1] See above, Lafayette to Clay, February 4, 1825.   [2] Georgia.
[3] Lafayette arrived in New Orleans on April 10; in Lexington, on May 16.
[4] Charles Caldwell.   [5] William H. Richardson.

To John Sloane

Dear Sir   Washn. 7h. Apl. 1825

I have this moment received your obliging letter of the 28h. Ulto.[1] and thank you for the agreeable information which it contains. Intelligence from all quarters flows in on me in a channel broad and deep, of the most perfectly satisfactory kind. Our triumph, my friend, over the wickendness [*sic*] which has assailed us will be thorough and complete. We have put down the

Military mania, and the Country will thank us for it. I have sent you my address to my constituents.[2] I do not say it in any boasting spirit, but its effect has been wonderful. It has swept clean from Boston to Charleston. You will also see a *little* correspondence which I have had with Eaton.[3] Was ever any thing so silly as for *him* to publish it? I have used in it a strain of irony and sarcasm which my friends need have no apprehension of my employing in my public correspondence.

Things are going on well here. There is entire coincidence between Mr. Adams and me on public affairs. By the bye, he paid you a high compliment (which I think was deserved, 'tho' you know we did not agree in the vote[4]) for your LaFayette letter.[5]
Your faithful friend   H. CLAY
The Honble J. Sloane.

ALS. IEN.   1 Not found.   2 See above, March 26, 1825.
3 See above, Eaton to Clay, March 28, 31, April 2, 1825; Clay to Eaton, March 30, April 1, 1825.
4 During House consideration of the bill honoring Lafayette (see above, III, 899n, 900), Sloane had first urged postponement of action and appointment of a committee to report the facts and accounts on which it was founded. Upon the defeat of this proposal, he had voted against the bill. *Register of Debates,* 18 Cong., 2 Sess., pp. 55-56.
5 Robert Walsh, Jr., editor of the Philadelphia *National Gazette,* had sharply criticized those who opposed the grant to Lafayette. James W. Gazlay, on December 31, in a letter addressed to the editors of the Washington *National Intelligencer,* had written a bitter reply, defending the minority opposition to a measure enacted without the customary procedure of report by legislative committee and denouncing the action of the majority as idolatrous and unrepublican. No letter identified with Sloane has been found; but an anonymous piece, signed "One of the Twenty-Six" and written from the House of Representatives on January 10, repudiated Gazlay's exposition as representative of the views of others who had opposed the bill. Washington *Daily National Intelligencer,* January 5, 11, 1825.

To [Josephus B. Stuart]

Dear Sir   Washington 7h. Apl. 1825
I am obliged by your letter of the 4h. instant[1]— I am glad to learn that my friend Worth[2] is so comfortable. I had some wishes about him which I will not entirely repress 'though I shall rejoice if *he* shall have no interest in their realization. You advised Mr. Leake[3] (with whom I am not personally acquainted, but of whom I have had favorable & friendly accounts) well. This is not the time, if there ever be one, to establish, in this Country, a merely political paper—

In regard to the local parties and politics of N. York— I mean to take no part, whatever interest it is impossible, on account of the important position of that great state, they should not create. The administration here will hope to merit the support of all of your parties, under every denomination. Yr's respectfy
                                    H CLAY

ALS. NcD.   ¹ Not found.   ² Gorham A. Worth.
³ Isaac Q. Leake, who, in the summer of 1824, had been induced to surrender his connection with the *Albany Argus* because of political differences with the Albany Regency. Marcy to Van Buren, February 15, 1824, and Van Buren to Worth, February 22, 1824, in Elizabeth Howard West (comp.), *Calendar of the Papers of Martin Van Buren, Prepared from the Original Manuscripts in the Library of Congress* . . . (Washington, 1910), 65, 66; Alvin Kass, *Politics in New York State, 1800–1830* (Syracuse, 1965), 35.

From Hugh Mercer

Fredericksbg April 7th. 1825—

I have received, my dear Sir, with very high & sincere gratification, your address to the people of your late district in Kentucky,¹ which you have done me the kindness to inclose to me— I consider it as a fresh & lively token of your friendship & esteem, which I value very highly—

I had read in my Intelligencer,² this able paper, with deep interest & pleasure, & altho' it is immediately addressed to your late constituents, yet it is an appeal to the whole American people, & will excite as it ought, much feeling & interest thro' out our country—a very large portion of which will sustain you in the patriotic, just & proper stand you decided upon (in my opinion) in the great presidential question— Many of the friends of the disappointed Candidates, particularly of Genl J— will probably continue sullen & dissatisfied—but this is what was looked for & expected, & you were prepared for the slanders which have been heaped upon you, especially by "Messrs. Geo. Kremer & co"— The abuse of such a Man as Mr K— I look upon as "extorted praise"— Genl J— in my humble Judgment, never will again be so near the first office in the Gift of the People, as he has been— I value him & feel grateful for his military Services, & so does our whole country— she has requited him for them, by her Gratitude, &c—; but it is impossible that he can be qualified for the great, responsible & diversified duties of the President of the U. States—besides, as a president, it would be seriously dangerous to the prosperity & liberties of this country to see any Man appointed to that high station, because of military Services only—

I have some hope, that I may have the pleasure to see you in all [*sic*] this month, as I have some business at Washington, which may call me thither— I am desirous too to pay my respects to Mr Adams, to whom I am not known— I doubt not but that his administration will be such, as to promote & secure the best interests of our Country, & of course such as will meet with the approbation & support of a large & decided Majority of his fellow Citizens—

I am, Dear Sir, very truly yr friend & ob St,   HUGH MERCER—

I have written of necessity in much haste, which you will excuse—
P.S. I have concluded that our Case in the Supreme Court, was not reached, & that it lies over for the next term, when we must trust it will be decided[3]— On this subject, we will converse when I have the pleasure to see you— You will not leave Washington, I have supposed, until some time in the Summer—   H.M.

ALS. DLC-HC (DNA, M212, R1). Addressed: "Honble. H. Clay   Secretary of State   Washington City."   [1] See above, March 26, 1825.
[2] Washington *National Intelligencer*.   [3] See above, III, 393, 396n.

From Nathaniel Silsbee

Dear Sir,   Salem April 7th. 1825
Your letter of the 1st. instant[1] was received by yesterdays mail. The intelligence of the appointment of Mr. Jeremy Robinson to the Consulate of Rio Janeiro[2] was, evidently, very unexpected to those who knew him here and called forth such remarks from some of our mercantile gentlemen as were indicative of great regret that it had been made. Soon after this intelligence reached here I was requested by two or three gentlemen to write to the Government on the subject, which I agreed to do if they would furnish me with a statement of facts, which, although promised, have not been handed me.

I do not *know* much of Mr. Robinson's character except from common & general report, and as your letter is a confidential one I do not feel at liberty to make it the foundation of a call on those who have had an opportunity of knowing it, for such facts as they might be able to communicate, but, unpleasant as it is to me to speak unfavorably of any one, I feel constrained to say that I have heard several gentlemen of respectability who have heretofore employed Mr. R. as an agent, in different foreign voyages, express a total want of confidence in his integrity— and I am sorry to add that the conversation which his appointment has been productive of amongst the merchants of this town seems to justify the belief that there is scarcely an individual of them who would willingly confide to him the consignment of a single shipment.

Mr. R. is a native of Boxford, an interior town of this County, he came here when a young man & resided with a Brother[3] who was, and who now is engaged in foreign commerce; it is now several years since he (Mr. J. R.) left this town, in which time he may have greatly improved the reputation he carried with him, nothing, however, seems to be publickly known here either of him or of his proccedings [*sic*] since his departure except that subsequent to that period his pecuniary drafts on his brother are said to have outlasted the brothers willingness to honor them.

My services to you on this or any other occation [*sic*], either of a public or private character, will, I assure you, always be readily & willingly rendered. You will please to consider this communication as a confidential one.

Mrs. Silsbee joins me in respectful acknowledgements of your friendly recollection and I beg of you to accept the assurance of my high regard & esteem   NATH SILSBEE
Hon. Henry Clay.

ALS. DNA, RG59, Misc. Letters (M179, R62).   1 Not found.
2 See above, Clay and others to Adams, March 1, 1825, note.
3 Probably Nathan Robinson.

From Daniel Webster

My Dear Sir   Boston April 7. 1825.

I am obliged to you for a copy of your Address to your Constituents.[1] It has been widely circulated here, is universally read, & highly commended. I have heard but one opinion, as to its general merits. Some think that part which relates to Mr. Kremer's letter, & the incidents connected with it, was an unneccesary [*sic*] laber [*sic*], at least so far as regards the state of public opinion this way. That transaction seems to have made no impression here. The part of your Address which sets forth your reasons for preferring another Candidate to Genl. Jackson is composed, in my opinion, with great skill & ability, & I have no doubt it will produce a very strong effect. It is a very good case, very ably managed.

We are very quiet, in this quarter. There is very little dissatisfaction, & no disposition that I discover, to opposition. With almost all, there prevails a very good spirit; and the exceptions are not important, from weight of character or influence.

I have heard nothing since I left Washington respecting the English Mission. If any thing has occurred,[2] not improper for me to know, I should be glad to learn it from you, at your leisure; as I shall be gratified also to hear from you, on other Subjects & occasions—   With entire regard, Yr Ob. Sert.   DANL. WEBSTER

ALS. DLC-HC (DNA, M212, R1). Addressed: "To the honble Henry Clay   Secretary of State   Washington."   1 See above, March 26, 1825.
2 See above, Clay to Strong, March 29, 1825. Webster had wanted the appointment for himself, and Adams had thought that "his ambition . . . might be gratified hereafter, but not immediately." Adams, *Memoirs,* VI, 469.

INSTRUCTIONS AND DISPATCHES   April 7, 1825

From ROBERT MONROE HARRISON, Antigua. Requests that attention be given to his earlier reports on the predicament of two Americans imprisoned on the Island of St. Christopher under a charge of murder aboard the brig

Stranger, of Middletown, Connecticut, and to an enclosed letter from a Mr. Tapshire, vice consul at that place, who complains of the disrespect shown him by American shipmasters, notably those from Connecticut. Recommends that the authority of consular officials be reinforced by issuance of either a circular or a letter suitable for publication in newspapers of the islands. ALS. DNA, RG59, Cons. Disp., Antigua, vol. 1 (M-T327, R1). Addressed to Secretary of State; received May 4. Enclosure not found. The vice consul at St. Christopher was George M. Tapshire, not further identified.

From CHRISTOPHER HUGHES, Stockholm. Summarizes the reply by the King of Sweden to a communication from the Russian Minister which enclosed copies of the protests by the Russian and Austrian Governments to George Canning, on British recognition of the new American Republics. Reports that Count Wetterstedt proposes that the Stralsund claims (see above, Hughes to Clay, March 19, 1825) be settled either by recommending "their liquidation to the next Diet" or by offering "a round sum" to John Connell (agent for the claimants), who has just returned from Copenhagen. The Count has proposed, incidentally, that the United States buy the Island of St. Bartholomew and take the amount of the claims from the purchase money. ALS. DNA, RG59, Dip. Disp. Sweden and Norway, vol. 4 (M45, R5). Addressed to Secretary of State; received May 27. Jean Bernadotte had ascended the throne of Sweden and Norway as Charles XIV in 1818. He had named Gustave, Count de Wetterstedt, formerly head of the Colonial Department, to become Minister of State and Foreign Affairs in June, 1824, upon the retirement of Lars, Count d'Engeström. General, and Count, Jan Pieter Suchtelen had served as Russian Minister in Sweden for more than a decade.

From CONDY RAGUET, Rio de Janeiro. Reports a decree ordering the execution of all persons, including James Hude Rodgers (Rogers), implicated in the rebellion at Pernambuco and gives details of Rodgers' case; mentions reports of continued unrest at this port. Transmits copies of correspondence with the Minister of Foreign Affairs (Luiz Joze de Carvalho e Mello) concerning seizure of the *Spermo* and the *Exchange;* states that the refusal of the Brazilian Government to interfere evinces "an unkind spirit towards the United States"; and argues that, in order to avert future annoyances, the United States must present a firm demand for justice. Notes the arrival, and departure for France, of Spanish officials from Peru, the Vice Roy "during his visit here [having] received no civilities of any sort from the Government." Refers briefly to the apathy concerning the approaching assembly of the Brazilian Legislature, to the introduction of a requirement that English be taught to the army, to announcement of pay increases for both the army and the navy, to advocacy by the Government newspaper of abolition of the slave trade, to the reception of a consul from Mecklenburg, to the activities of Lord Cochrane, and to Brazil's difficulties with Buenos Aires. Describes at some length the public excitement attending the innovation of capital punishment "for a publick offence" in Rio de Janeiro. LS. DNA, RG59, Cons. Disp., Rio de Janeiro, vol. 2 (M-T172, R3). Addressed to Secretary of State. On the events involving James Hude Rodgers, the *Spermo,* the *Exchange,* and Lord Thomas Cochrane, see above, Raguet to Clay, March 11, 1825. Carvalho e Mello, an eloquent orator, had been one of the leaders during the debates in the Brazilian *Cortes* of 1823 on the formation of the imperial constitution and, as Minister of Foreign Affairs, conducted the negotiations which culminated in Portuguese recognition of Brazilian independence (above, Raguet to Clay, March 11, 1825, note). The last viceroy of Spain in Peru (1821-1824) was José de la Serna.

APPLICATIONS, RECOMMENDATIONS   April 7, 1825

SAMUEL GREEN, publisher of the *New London Gazette* (Connecticut), urges
that he, rather than Joshua B. Clapp, be appointed publisher of the laws. The
Gazette, "the oldest paper in the state . . . has firmly advocated the present chief
magistrate, and your character; while Mr. Clapp's paper [the New London
Republican Advocate] has been distinguished for its virulent abuse of Mr Adams,
and of all who did not Support Mr Crawford." ALS. DNA, RG59, P. and D.
of L. Clapp, one of the founders of the New London *Republican Advocate,*
in 1818, retained the patronage of the State Department throughout the Adams
administration.

ROBERT MONROE HARRISON, Antigua, solicits the collectorship at Bath, Maine.
ALS. DNA, RG59, A. and R. (MR2). Cf. above, Harrison to Clay, March 10,
1825, note.

HORATIO GATES SPAFFORD, Troy, New York, acknowledges receipt of Clay's
letter of March 26, 1825 (not found), states Spafford's desire to recover a
reassignment of the copyright of his *Gazetteer,* and solicits an appointment "in
the offices" under Clay's control. ALS. DNA, RG59, A. and R. (MR3). Spafford had published *A Gazetteer of the State of New York . . .* (Albany, 1813)
and other works. He did not receive an appointment.

JOSEPH G. SWIFT, New York, recommends J. Gottfried Boker as consul general for the United States in Prussia and Saxony. ALS. DNA, RG59, A. and R.
(MR1). Swift, one of the first graduates of the United States Military Academy
and Chief Engineer of the Army from 1816 to 1818, was later engineer for several railroads and, from 1829 to 1845, for the United States Government, assigned to harbor improvement on the Great Lakes.

To Peter Force

Dr Sir   Friday evening [April 8, 1825]
    If you have space and time will you be pleased to have the inclosed
extract published in the Journal of tomorrow?

                                        Yrs   H CLAY
[Enclosure][1]
    Extract of a letter from a distinguished gentleman in Boston to
his friend in Washington—under date 4 apl—
    "We had a great Caucus last night— A Caucus for an union of
both political parties[2]— From 4 to 5 thousand persons were present—
Mr. Pickman, Mr. Jno. Everitt [*sic*], Mr. Davis[3] and two or three
other persons spoke— . . . . . . At last Mr. Webster[4] rose, and there
was a shouting and cheering that lasted a quarter of an hour. Never
was a man more plainly proclaimed to be the man of the people than
he was at that moment. When silence was at last obtained he made
a speech of about half an hour in length, interrupted constantly by
the most tumultuous applause, but with intervals of a dead silence
which was even a more honorable tribute to his power over the
vast multitude. His argument was, that this whole people are now

called by the Circumstances of the Country and of the world to such high objects that all party differences are become unworthy of us. In the course of his remarks he spoke of Mr. Clay and said, that he was perfectly satisfied that, in relation to the Presidential election, his whole course had been frank, honorable & high minded And that he owes the office he now holds *solely* to his merits and to the consideration in which he is held by the great Western states amidst which he lives and by the whole Country. This testimony to the purity of Mr. Clay's character was received with very great applause by the multitude— Indeed it is many years since we have had in Boston a caucus like the one last evening"

ALS. DLC-HC (DNA, M212, R2). Addressed: "Mr. P. Force   Present."
1 Not in Clay's hand; published in Washington *Daily National Journal*, Saturday, April 9, 1825.   2 Federalist and Republican.
3 Benjamin Pickman, Jr., several times a member of the State legislature in Massachusetts, Congressman (1809-1811), active in religious and educational matters; John Everett; and either Judge John Davis or John Davis, Worcester lawyer, member of Congress (1825-1834), Governor of Massachusetts (1834, 1835, 1841-1843), United States Senator (1835-1841, 1845-1853).   4 Daniel Webster.

From Manuel de Sarratea

Sen   Buenos Ayres 8 de Abril en 1825
    Aprobecho la Ocasion de pasar a esa mi Antiguo Amigo el Capitan Meani,[1] pa. pagar el tributo devido a su eficaz cooperacion en la favorable direccion politica de Nuestra Causa, ofreciendole mi mas cordial gratitud y reconocimiento por la parte que mi toca.
    En estos dias he tenido el gusto de leer sus sentimientos expresados, con aquel calor y gusto que Caracteriza sus producciones Justamte. Admiradas, en el brindis que Consagró a la memoria de sus hermanos Continentales, a la Republica de Colombia, y al General Bolivar. No hé podida resistir al deseo de mandar al mismo General el Articulo Original de la Gacta. satisfho [sic] que la Naturaleza del recuerdo unida a las Circunstancias de su Autor le Seran Altamente Satisfactorio
    El Capitan Meani ha querido encargarse de presentar a [. . .] al homaiage [sic] de mi profundo respt. y Consideracion con la que
    Tengo el honor de Ser Su mas Attto. ServOr.   Q. S. M. B.
Sen Dn Enrrique [sic] Clay   MANL. DE SARRATEA

ALS. DNA, RG59, Misc. Letters (M179, R62). Margin of MS. obscured in binding. Sarratea, born in Buenos Aires and educated in Spain, had been active in the Argentine revolution of 1810, had served as one of the triumvirs in the early revolutionary government, had led their forces against the Spanish in Montevideo in 1812, had acted as diplomatic agent in England and France in 1814, and, very briefly, had held the post of Governor of the Province of Buenos Aires during the anarchy of 1820. He returned to London as the Minister of the United Provinces of Río de la Plata from the fall of 1825 to the fall of 1826. He served as envoy extraordinary to Brazil, in 1838, and to France, from 1841 until his death in 1849.   1 Not identified.

From Joseph Story

Dear Sir   Salem April 8. 1825—

I am much obliged to you for the Copy of your Address to your late Constituents,[1] which you have been pleased to send me— I read it with great interest & satisfaction— As a vindication of your character & conduct it was to me wholly unnecessary, for I have never entertained the slightest doubt of the perfect correctness of the motives of your vote in the recent Presidential Election— I have considered it as a new proof of your integrity, independence, & firmness— Pardon me if I add, that if your vote had been other than it was, I should have found it somewhat difficult to have reconciled it with your known public opinions, on subjects intimately connected with Executive Duties—

I have no doubt, that the Address will meet with general approbation, I do not say, among warm partizans of other candidates, but among reflecting, considerate men of all parties— In this part of the Union it has received unqualified praise, & has given a new lustre to your public fame.

I hope you may long live to enjoy the confidence of the nation, & to remain a blessing to the Country— And I beg you will do me the favour of numbering me among those, who cheris[h] with the sincerest pleasure every expression of publ[ic] regard towards you—

I have the honour to remain with the highest respect Your obliged friend & servant   JOSEPH STORY

The Honorable Henry Clay Secretary of State &c &c—

ALS. DLC-HC (DNA, M212, R1).   1 Above, March 26, 1825.

DIPLOMATIC NOTES   April 8, 1825

To the BARON DE TUYLL. Returns his dispatch of April 6, with the comment that it conforms to their recent conversation regarding the act of Congress of January 7, 1824. Copy. DNA, RG59, Notes to Foreign Ministers and Consuls, vol. 3, p. 211 (M38, R3). AN draft, in CSmH. Cf. above, Clay to Tuyll, April 5, 1825.

INSTRUCTIONS AND DISPATCHES   April 8, 1825

From ANDREW ARMSTRONG, consular commercial agent of the United States at Port au Prince, Haiti. Reports passage of an act "placing British manufactures, imported in British ships, on the same footing as the produce of all other nations" and expresses a hope that this change will effect the objectives of his special mission. Extends congratulations on Clay's appointment to office. ALS. DNA, RG59, Cons. Disp., Cap Haitien, vol. 1 (M9, R-T5). Armstrong, a resident of Pennsylvania, had been appointed agent for commerce and seamen for the

United States at Port au Prince in March, 1820, and his status raised to that of consular commercial agent in January, 1824. He was later, in 1828, appointed United States naval agent for the port of Lima, Peru. He had been instructed to assist in collection of American claims incurred against the government of (Henri) Christophe and to report upon "the prostitution of our flag to cloak the trade of other nations." [John Quincy Adams] to Armstrong, January 31, 1821, in DNA, RG59, Cons. Instr., vol. 2, p. 225 (M78, R2).

From WILLIAM TAYLOR, Alvarado. Reports the arrival, at Veracruz on March 12, of the British Commissioner, (Henry George) Ward, who proceeded to Mexico City, "where he is now actively engaged in making a commercial Treaty with this Governt." Notes the laying of an embargo upon all vessels in Alvarado from March 15 to 28, at which latter date an expedition sailed from there for Campeche. ALS. DNA, RG59, Cons. Disp., Veracruz, vol. 1 (M183, R1). Extract published in Manning (arr.), *Diplomatic Correspondence . . . Latin-American Nations*, III, 1621. Addressed to Secretary of State; received May 2. Ward, who had been sent to Mexico in 1823, had just returned from a visit in England. He retired from the diplomatic service in 1827, was a member of the House of Commons from 1832 to 1849, and held administrative posts in the colonial service from 1849 until his death in 1860. On the treaty under negotiation, see below, Wilcocks to Secretary of State, April 9, 1825; Poinsett to Clay, May 5, 1825.

From BEAUFORT T. WATTS, Bogotá. Transmits letter from Pedro Gual, Secretary of Foreign Affairs of Colombia, to Richard C. Anderson, Jr., who has left for the United States. ALS. DNA, RG59, Dip. Disp., Colombia, vol. 3 (M-T33, R3). Addressed to Secretary of State; received May 22. Watts, born in South Carolina, was Secretary of the United States Legation at Bogotá, 1824 to 1826; Chargé d'Affaires there, 1826 to 1828; Secretary of Legation at St. Petersburg, Russia, 1828 to 1829; and secretary in the Governor's Office of South Carolina, 1834 to 1861. Gual's letter, dated March 25, 1825, expresses the satisfaction of the Colombian President with Anderson's conduct as Minister.

MISCELLANEOUS LETTERS   April 8, 1825

To RENSSELAER BENTLEY. States that the books recommended in his letter of March 18, 1825 (not found), had already been placed in the State Department before Clay became Secretary. Copy. DNA, RG59, Dom. Letters, vol. 21, pp. 26-27 (M40, R19). Bentley was the author of a spelling book and grammar, published in 1824, and, later, of a dictionary and a reader.

APPLICATIONS, RECOMMENDATIONS   April 8, 1825

J. C. WRIGHT, J. H. HALLOCK, and JOHN M. GOODENOW, Steubenville (Ohio), recommend Alexander Caldwell, of Wheeling, for appointment as judge for the Western District of Virginia, in the place of (John G.) Jackson, deceased. ALS by Wright, signed also by Hallock and Goodenow. MHi-Adams Papers, Letters Received (M469). Goodenow, born in New Hampshire, was a lawyer and former member of the Ohio Legislature (1823). He was elected to Congress as a Jacksonian Democrat in 1828 but served for only a year, when he resigned to accept appointment as a judge of the Supreme Court of Ohio, a post from which, for reasons of health, he also shortly resigned. In 1832 he removed to Cincinnati and the following year became judge of the court of common pleas.

DIPLOMATIC NOTES   April 9, 1825

From H[ENRY] U. ADDINGTON, Washington. Acknowledges receipt of Clay's letter of April 6. Despite the disappointment of the British Government at the termination of negotiations for a slave convention, it "will consider the unfortunate issue of this business as in no wise affecting the friendly feelings, which exist between the two Governments, and will accept with pleasure the expression of the Presidents desire that every exertion should still be used for effecting the entire extirpation of that odious traffic, which the Convention was designed to suppress." Explains that his comments in his letter of November 6, 1824, relative to passage of the act of Parliament denouncing the slave trade as piracy, were not intended as a demand but rather as an appeal to the United States; that the statute would not have been passed had the United States Government not expressly desired its enactment; that it conferred no power for suppression of the trade not already held by the British Government; and that a repeal of the law "is now, by the interposition of subsequent events, rendered tantamount to morally impracticable." ALS. DNA, RG59, Notes from British Legation, vol. 13 (M50, R14). Published in *Register of Debates,* 19 Cong., 1 Sess., Appendix, p. 39; *American State Papers, Foreign Relations,* V, 784.

INSTRUCTIONS AND DISPATCHES   April 9, 1825

From SANTIAGO [*i.e.,* JAMES] SMITH WILCOCKS, Mexico (City). Reports the signing of a treaty by Great Britain and Mexico, "founded on the basis of mutual reciprocity as respects the contracting parties, and of equality as relates to all other nations—" Urges the sending of a Minister from the United States, who will have the authority to apply the pressure requisite to win attention to the claims of American citizens, whose rights "have been shamefully neglected and I may say trampled upon, ever since the present Minister of the Hacienda came into office." Congratulates the President (Adams) "on the proof he has received, in his election, of the homage of the American people." ALS. DNA, RG59, Cons. Disp., Mexico City, vol. 1 (M296, R1). Addressed to Secretary of State; received May 27. On the treaty between Great Britain and Mexico, see also below, Poinsett to Clay, May 5, 1825. On José Ignacio Esteva, Minister of the Hacienda, see below, Wilkinson to Clay, August 20, 1825.

APPLICATIONS, RECOMMENDATIONS   April 9, 1825

JAMES BRECKINRIDGE, Fincastle (Virginia), recommends his neighbor, Allen Taylor, to fill the vacancy caused by the death of John G. Jackson (above, Zane to Clay, April 5, 1825, note) and adds: "I have read your address to your constituents with infinite satisfaction, not so much because it has produced any change in my mind as that it has in so masterly a manner exposed & demolished the villainies & villains [*sic*] with which you were so furiously beset." ALS. DNA, RG59, A. and R. (MR4). Taylor, a resident of Liberty, Fauquier County, Virginia, did not receive a Federal appointment but the following year was named judge of the Chancery Court for the Staunton, Wythe, and Greenbrier districts of Virginia.

J[OHN] J. CRITTENDEN, Frankfort, transmits a letter (above, April 1, 1825) from his "old uncle, Mr. Horatio Turpin"; states that "The son which he wishes disposed of in this manner is . . . a youth of fine appearance, & much promise";

and assures Clay that his help in this matter "will be remembered as additional evidence of" his "kindness." ALS. DNA, RG94, Military Academy, Cadet Applications, 1825-207 (M688, R39). Endorsed on cover by Clay: ". . . Refered [*sic*] to Mr. Secy [James] Barbour with Mr. Clays respects." Horatio Turpin was a great-uncle of Crittenden, an uncle of Judith Harris Crittenden.

SPENCER E. GIBSON, Jonesborough, Tennessee, encloses a letter from his Congressman (John Blair, also of Jonesborough), which shows Gibson to have been a friend of John Q. Adams; asks Clay's attention to recommendations, "probably now in the department of state," favoring Gibson for a government appointment. ALS. DNA, RG59, A. and R. (MR2).

JOSEPH TOWLER, Lexington, Kentucky, solicits a clerkship in either the State or Treasury Department. ALS. *Ibid.* (MR4). Towler had been employed as bookkeeper of a Lexington mercantile firm and as clerk of the Lexington Branch, Bank of the United States. He later became cashier of that office.

DIPLOMATIC NOTES   April 10, 1825

From HILARIO DE RIVAS Y SALMON, Philadelphia, "*Confidential.*" Encloses duplicate of a note addressed to President Adams on March 11, before learning that Clay "had entered upon the discharge of the duties of" his office, and requests an answer to the request there expressed for a loan, "this Legation having, at the present moment, no other resources to depend upon, but those the President may be willing to grant. . . ." ALS. DNA, RG59, Notes from Spanish Legation, vol. 8 (M59, R11). Salmon was here applying for a second loan, of five or six thousand dollars; a former one had not yet been collected from his Government (see below, Clay to Nelson, April 14, 1825; Everett to Clay, September 10, 1825).

INSTRUCTIONS AND DISPATCHES   April 10, 1825

From ROBERT MONROE HARRISON, Antigua, "*Private.*" Encloses a letter from his "confidential Agent at S. Barts" and vigorously supports its warning against the proposed appointment of one "Baily," recommended by Commodore (David) Porter, for the consulate or commercial agency at the Swedish port. States that the nominee is "an ignorant Englishman . . . a Creole of S. Christophers to which he dare never return—and possesses all the prejudices of Englishmen, as regards the U. S, without one of their good qualities." Attributes Porter's recommendation to influence exerted by the Governor, who is described as a drunken tyrant, the protector of piracy and the slave trade. ALS. DNA, RG59, Cons. Disp., Antigua, vol. 1 (M-T327, R1). Addressed to Secretary of State; received May 4. The enclosure, a letter from William Johnson, of St. Bartholomew, to Harrison, dated March 19, 1825 (ALS), deplores the reported appointment of "Bailey," a former "elected Counsellor . . . disapproved of by the King [Charles XIV] as an improper person to hold a seat in Council." Baily (or Bailey) not further identified.

MISCELLANEOUS LETTERS   April 10, 1825

From LEWIS CASS, Detroit, Michigan Territory. Acknowledges receipt of Clay's letter of March 23, 1825, and its enclosure; declares that all prisoners taken by the Indians at the Battle of the River Raisin, "who have not long since made their appearance, are far beyond the sympathies of their friends, or the aid of their Country." Cass encloses a letter to Hugh Goodwin, Jr., which he asks Clay to read and forward. LS. DNA, RG59, Misc. Letters (M179, R62).

APPLICATIONS, RECOMMENDATIONS   April 10, 1825

J[OSHUA] GIST, Frederick County, Maryland, applies through Clay to James Barbour for an appointment as a cadet at West Point for Mordecai Milton Gist, whose father is a resident of Ohio. ALS. DNA, RG59, A. and R. (MR2). Cf. above, III, 736.

Bill to Thomas Curry

Thos. Curry to H. Clay Dr.	[ca. April 11, 1825]
For Rent of Lower Rooms & Kitchen from 26 Mar 1824 til [sic] 28 Feby 1825 }	$121„10
Ditto from last date until this day 11 April 1 Mo. 11 ds. @ 130$ pr. yr. }	14„81.
Ditto of Upper Room from 23 Apl. 1823 to 11 April 1825 is 1 Yr. 11 Ms. 19ds. }	78.78
	$214„69
Warrants of Distress	„50
	215„19
By J M Pikes Accepte @ 30 d/s.	200„—
Balance	15„19
Sheriffs Commn	9„75
	24.94
8 Lights Glass broken @ 25	2 —
	26„94
Cr.	
By News paper Acct.	$3„13.
„ R Scotts do	87.

D, in Robert Scott's hand. DLC-TJC (DNA, M212, R16). Cf. above, Scott to Clay, February 2, 1825.

INSTRUCTIONS AND DISPATCHES   April 11, 1825

To RICHARD RUSH, no. 2. Directs that the papers of the Legation be committed to the care of John A(dams) Smith pending the arrival of Rufus King. Copy. DNA, RG59, Dip. Instr., vol. 10, pp. 252-53 (M77, R5). Also a copy in DLC-HC (DNA, M212, R7). Smith, brother of William Steuben Smith and nephew of John Quincy Adams, had been appointed Secretary of Legation for the United States in London in January, 1816.

To JOHN A[DAMS] SMITH. Informs him of his appointment as Secretary of

Legation in Madrid but directs him to remain in London until the arrival of
Rufus King, to whom he is to deliver the archives of the legation there. Copy.
DNA, RG59, Dip. Instr., vol. 10, p. 253 (M77, R5). Also a copy in DLC-HC
(DNA, M212, R7). Smith had been nominated for the change of assignment
by President Monroe, on February 11, 1825; the nomination had been con-
firmed on February 16. A copy of his commission, dated April 8, is located in
DNA, RG59, Ceremonial Communications, vol. 2, p. 12. On King's appoint-
ment to the British mission, see above, Clay to Strong, March 29, 1825, note.

From RICHARD RUSH, London, no. 429. Acknowledges receipt of the Secretary
of State's dispatch dated February 24, "relative to the Georgia historical documents," and a letter from Daniel Brent, dated February 16, regarding "the
papers in the case of the ship Calliope"; encloses copies of correspondence indicating that he has requested British assistance in supplying the documents
sought under the first inquiry; and explains that he has been unable to locate
the papers of the *Calliope*. ALS. DNA, RG59, Dip. Disp., Great Britain, vol.
32 (M30, R28). Addressed to Secretary of State; received May 19. Published
in *House Reports,* 19 Cong., 2 Sess., no. 91 (February 24, 1827), pp. 4-5.

On the Georgia documents, see above, Rush to Secretary of State, March 16,
1825, and note. The papers of the *Calliope,* which had been sent to John Quincy
Adams, as the United States Minister at London, in 1816 indicated that the
American vessel had been seized in the St. Mary's River during the War of 1812;
they were now needed to support a claim pending before the Joint Commission under the St. Petersburg Convention (see above, III, 736n).

MISCELLANEOUS LETTERS   April 11, 1825

From P[ETER] A. BROWNE, Philadelphia. Announces the quarterly meeting of
the Franklin Institute and asks again for Clay's determination in the dispute
with William Thornton regarding the granting of specifications of patents.
LS. DNA, RG59, Misc. Letters (M179, R62). See above, Browne to Clay, March
7, 15, 29, 1825.

From CHARLES F. MAYER, Baltimore. Notes that he wrote the Department of
State in January, 1825, "in behalf of the Trustees of Mr. John Hollins," relative to "the grievance which Mr. Hollins, for twenty five years, has been
suffering from the Judicial Tribunals of Havaña, in a suit which is now about
to be carried before the Council of the Indies at Madrid." Suggests that the
Minister (Alexander H. Everett) who is "soon [to] leave the United States
for Madrid . . . be charged to promote the fair investigation of . . . [the]
case"; solicits Clay's attention to the January letter; and requests a reply to
an "inquiry in that letter whether the United States will disburse upon our
credit the necessary monies for having the case brought to the Notice of the
Council at Madrid." LS. DNA, RG76, Misc. Claims, Spain. Mayer signs "for
himself, & the other Trustees. . . ."

On April 14, Daniel Brent, at Clay's direction, acknowledged receipt of this
letter and promised to transmit instructions to Everett "to employ his good
offices . . . towards the prosecution . . . of the appeal which has been entered . . . to the Council of the Indies at Madrid." Brent noted, however, that
the Government declined to disburse public funds "for the prosecution of
Judicial causes of private individuals. . . ." Copy, in DNA, RG59, Dom. Letters,
vol. 21, pp. 31-32 (M40, R19).

On May 4, Brent transmitted to Everett "copies of two Letters from Charles
F. Mayer, of Baltimore, to this Department, dated the 12th. of January and

11th. of April, in the present year," reported the contents of the above-noted reply to Mayer, and stated "the wish . . . of the Secretary, that . . . official aid should be given consistently with this engagement, for that purpose, in such way as it may be employed with propriety and advantage." Copy, in DNA, RG59, Dip. Instr., vol. 10, pp. 311-12. ALI draft, in Brent's hand, endorsed as Secretary of State to Everett, in DLC-HC (DNA, M212, R7). Hollins' case grew out of claims amounting to $250,000 for ship seizures under Napoleonic decrees prior to 1800. The claims were ultimately rejected by commissioners acting under a convention of 1834. *Sen. Doc.*, 35 Cong., 2 Sess., no. 18, p. 25.

From WILLIAM STURGIS, Boston. States, in reply to Clay's letter of April 1, that the owners of the *Pearl* have "looked only to an *indemnity* for the loss actually sustained"; estimates the loss to exceed $15,000 but indicates a disposition to be satisfied with whatever amount may be received; and expresses a preference for receiving the money at St. Petersburg. ALS. DNA, RG76, Misc. Claims, Russia.

APPLICATIONS, RECOMMENDATIONS   April 11, 1825

CHARLES HAMMOND, Cincinnati, recommends Alexander Caldwell to succeed (John G.) Jackson as judge of the Western District of Virginia. Comments: "It has been thought by his friends that my good opinion might be worth something with the President— I have no reason myself to suppose that it will: but I have nevertheless given it with great cheerfulness and sincerity." ALS. DNA, RG59, A. and R. (MR1). See above, Zane to Clay, April 5, 1825, note.

INSTRUCTIONS AND DISPATCHES   April 12, 1825

To JOSHUA PILCHER, "Consul U.S. for Chihuahua, New Mexico." Encloses commission, printed circular of instructions, and a blank bond to be executed and returned. Copy. DNA, RG59, Cons. Instr., vol. 2, p. 350 (M78, R2). The appointment of Pilcher, a St. Louis banker and merchant, had been approved March 7, 1825. Cf. below, Clay to Storrs, this date, note.

To AUGUSTUS STORRS, "Consul U. S.   Santa Fé." Similar in content to the preceding document. Copy. DNA, RG59, Cons. Instr., vol. 2, p. 351 (M78, R2). Storrs, born in Connecticut and removed to Howard County, Missouri, in 1816, had accompanied the expedition of traders to Santa Fé in 1824. His observations, published as "Answers of Augustus Storrs, of Missouri, to Certain Queries upon the Origin, Present State, and Future Prospect, of Trade and Intercourse, between Missouri and the Internal Provinces of Mexico, Propounded by the Hon. Mr. [Thomas Hart] Benton, January 3, 1825" (*Sen. Docs.*, 18 Cong., 2 Sess., no. 7), had formed the basis for recommendation that consular agents be appointed for the United States in Chihuahua and Santa Fé. Storrs' appointment had been approved on March 8.

From JAMES BROWN, Paris, "Private." Notes publication in Paris of the "official account of the capture of the army of the Viceroy of Peru, and a copy of the articles of capitulation"; comments that the declaration of Great Britain on December 31 and the successes of Bolívar "would now seem to have removed all cause of apprehension of any danger to the independence of the new republics." Reports frequent conferences of Metternich with the Minister of Foreign Affairs (the Baron de Damas) and the ambassadors of the great powers and speculation concerning the subject of these meetings. One rumor is that Metternich and Lord Granville have discussed the affairs of Brazil and "that the Austrian Government is favorable to the independence of that empire." Sir Charles Stuart is now at Lisbon and will shortly sail for Rio de Janeiro. Another rumor concerns the desire of the allied sovereigns to terminate the war in Greece, the proposal that all unite in obtaining an armistice, but the fear that the Porte will reject one. Transmits copies of documents obtained under an injunction against their publication by the United States Government, the answer by the Count de Lieven to (George) Canning after the British declaration of December 31 and the instructions to General Count Pozzo di Borgo before and after the British action had been communicated to the Court at St. Petersburg. LS. MHi-Adams Papers, Letters Received (M469). Addressed to Secretary of State; received May 16.

On the Spanish defeat in Peru, see above, Raguet to Secretary of State, March 11, 1825, note; on the British declaration of December 31, see above, Nelson to Secretary of State, March 8, 1825, note; on Metternich's Paris visit, see above, Brown to Secretary of State, March 22, 1825; on Stuart's mission, see above, Raguet to Secretary of State, March 11, 1825, note. Leveson-Gower, Lord Granville (in 1833 created the first Earl Granville and Baron Leveson of Stone), a former member of the House of Commons (1795-1815) and, since 1815, a member of the House of Lords, had been named British Ambassador to Paris as the replacement for Sir Charles Stuart, in the autumn of 1824.

On the proposal of an armistice in the war between Greece and Turkey, see below, Middleton to Secretary of State, April 21, 1825, note; on the Count de Lieven's communication to Canning, see above, Hughes to Secretary of State, March 25, 1825. The first of the dispatches to General Pozzo di Borgo, in December, 1824, here summarized, contained advice for reform of the interior administration of Spain and stressed the importance of establishing a stable and moderate regime as a basis to support her efforts against the colonies and as a measure to forestall Britain's political recognition of the new states, a resolution which, it was known, had been in contemplation for a year. The second dispatch to the Russian Ambassador outlined the course advocated for Spain, denounced the British action, and urged that the "comité de Paris" unite in representations to the Netherlands Government, which alone among the courts on the Continent appeared likely to follow the British example.

Charles André, Count Pozzo di Borgo, was a native of Corsica, identified with Russian diplomacy since the Napoleonic era, but long a supporter of monarchical forces in France, where he served as Russian Ambassador for some twenty years after the Restoration. He was the presiding officer of the "comité de Paris," otherwise known as the Ambassadors' Conference of Paris, a body consisting of the ministers of Russia, Prussia, and Austria in France and including, at this time, the French Foreign Minister (the British Ambassador having withdrawn from the sessions in 1823), which assembled at irregular intervals to evolve and maintain unified policy for the government of Europe. While the conferences were a generic outgrowth of the consultations entailed in administering the Treaty of Vienna, the emphasis at this period stemmed from the action taken at the Congress of Verona (above, III, 313, note 4). Throughout 1824 the ministers had urged that Ferdinand VII pursue a course of moderation at home while upholding his claims over the Spanish colonies. The influence of the Conference is supposed to have prevented the Netherlands in 1825 and Prussia in 1826, and perhaps also Sweden and Hamburg, from recognizing the Spanish-American states. Harold Temperley, "Canning and the Conferences of the Four Allied Governments at Paris, 1823-1826," *American Historical Review,* XXX (October, 1924), 16-43.

From ALEXANDER BURTON, Cádiz. Transmits a copy of a royal order, "by which it appears that license is given for the introduction of Wheat, *only,* and limited in its duration to the 31st. of the next month"; notes receipt of a letter from Hugh Nelson reporting failure to obtain modification of certain regulations on foreign vessels in Spanish ports; states that the French continue building up the defences of the "Isla," though work has been suspended on one or two batteries. ALS. DNA, RG59, Cons. Disp., Cádiz, vol. 4 (M-T186, R4). Addressed to Secretary of State; received May 25.

From RICHARD RUSH, London, no. 430. Reports information given by "A person high in diplomatic station here" that, some six or nine months ago, the British had offered to Spain "to guaranty to her the possession of Cuba, and to send British troops there for that purpose, should it become necessary; but that the offer was declined by Spain." Notes rumor that the ambassadors of the great continental powers, excluding Britain, are to meet shortly at Milan; comments on the deterioration of relations between these states and Britain in consequence of the latter's recognition of the new American Republics; and cites the recent refusal of Count (Karl Robert) Nesselrode to discuss the affairs of Greece with Stratford Canning. ALS. DNA, RG59, Dip. Disp., Great Britain, vol. 32 (M30, R28). Extract published in Manning (arr.), *Diplomatic Correspondence . . . Latin-American Nations,* III, 1550-51. Addressed to Secretary of State; received May 19.

The British proposal relating to Cuba had been extended in a note of April 2, 1824, and rejected by Spain on May 3. George Canning had emphasized, however, that the proffered defence "by maritime power" did not encompass landing of troops. Temperley, *Foreign Policy of Canning,* 139-40n.

The British Minister to Vienna, Sir Henry Wellesley, a brother of the Duke of Wellington, was present in Milan during May and June, 1825, together with the Emperor Francis I of Austria, Metternich, Christian (Count von Bernstorff, the Danish-born Foreign Minister of Prussia), and various Italian heads of state. On the political goals of this meeting, see below, Campbell to Clay, June 11, 1825.

From WILLIAM SHALER, Algiers, no. 83. Announces his intention of going to Europe until the next December for reasons of health. ALS. DNA, RG59, Cons. Disp., Algiers, French Africa, vol. 11 (M23, R13).

From W[ILLIAM] TUDOR, Lima, no. 26. Reports that General Bolívar has departed for a visit to "the Upper Provinces of Peru"; that (José María de) Pando, now acting as Minister of Finance, will "leave here next month to meet the Plenipotentiary of Colombia at Panama, to prepare the proceedings for a future congress of all the States of South America"; and that heavier batteries are shelling Callao, which is expected to hold out at least another month (cf. below, Tudor to Clay, February 23, 1826). Lists names of officials administering the government during Bolívar's absence. ALS. DNA, RG59, Cons. Disp., Lima, vol. 1 (M154, R1). Addressed to Secretary of State; received September 4.

Pando, born in Lima and educated in Madrid, had been prominent as a writer and diplomat in the service of Spain under the constitutional government (above, II, 789n). Returning to Peru in 1824, he became an active supporter of Simón Bolívar, who appointed him, first, Minister de Hacienda, then Minister to the Congress at Panama, and, for a few months, from 1826 to 1827, Minister of Exterior and Interior Relations. Pando was again prominent as an administrator in the Peruvian Government from 1833 until 1835, when he retired and returned to Spain. He was also noted as a literary writer and editor.

On April 23 President Adams noted that the Mexican Minister, (Pablo) Obregón, had suggested to Clay that the United States should send ministers to a proposed American Congress at Panama; that "Mr. Clay strongly inclines to it, and proposed a cabinet consultation concerning it." Four days later Adams reported that Clay had had conversations with both Obregón and (José Maria) Salazar on this subject, and that a Cabinet meeting would be held "to consult upon the expediency of it." Adams, *Memoirs,* VI, 531, 536-37.

MISCELLANEOUS LETTERS April 12, 1825

To J[OHN] J[AMES] APPLETON, Cambridge, Massachusetts, no. 1. Offers appointment as commercial agent at Naples, instead of as Secretary of Legation in London. His object will be "to sound the Government of Naples as to the practicability of getting indemnity for our Citizens for their numerous and large claims upon that Government." Copy. DNA, RG59, Dip. Instr., vol. 10, p. 254 (M77, R5). AL draft, in Clay's hand, in DLC-HC (DNA, M212, R7). Appleton had been nominated, and the nomination confirmed, for the post of Secretary of Legation at London in February of this year. His letter of acceptance is dated April 22. ALS. DNA, RG59, Dip. Disp., Sweden and Norway, vol. 5 (M45, R6). On the American claims against the Government of Naples, see above, II, 505, n.20.

APPLICATIONS, RECOMMENDATIONS April 12, 1825

E[DWARD] B[RAKE] JACKSON, Clarksburg, (West) Virginia, transmits recommendation of his "late Brother's friends, in favour of the claims of Colo. Pindall to be selected to supply the vacancy," and requests that their letter be laid before the President. ALS. MHi-Adams Papers, Letters Received (M469). The enclosure, dated April 5 and signed by eighteen members of the court and bar of Lewis County, recommends James Pindall to replace John G. Jackson as judge of the Western District of Virginia. Edward Brake Jackson had been a member of the Virginia House of Delegates (1815-1818), clerk of the United States Court for the Western District of Virginia (1819), and a member of Congress, succeeding Pindall and completing his unexpired term (1820-1823). Pindall did not receive the judicial appointment; he died in November, 1825.

To José Silvestre Rebello

Mr. José Silvestre Rebello,
Chargé d'Affaires from Brazil, Washington.   Department of State,
Sir,   Washington, 13th. April 1825.

I have the honour to acknowledge the receipt, at this Department, of your two Notes, the one under date the 28th. January,[1] and the other the 6th. day of April 1825. The delay, in transmitting an answer to the former, has arisen from arrangements incident to the formation of a new Administration, and not from any insensibility to the important propositions which it announces, or disrespect to the Government of Brazil or its Respectable Representative here. To those propositions, the President has given the most attentive

Consideration. They are 1st. that the United-States shall enter into a Convention with your Government to maintain its independence, in the event of Portugal being assisted by any foreign power to reestablish its former sway; and secondly, that a treaty of alliance and defence be formed between the United-States and the Government of Brazil to expel the arms of Portugal from any portion of the Brazilian Territory of which they might happen, in the progress of the war, to take possession.

The President of the United States adheres to the principles of his Predecessor, as set forth in his message of the 2d. December 1823 to the American Congress.[2] But with respect to your first proposition, as there does not appear, at present, any likelihood of Portugal being able to draw to her aid other powers to assist her in resubjugating the Brazils, there would not seem to be any occasion for a Convention founded upon that improbable contingency. The President on the contrary, sees with satisfaction that there is a reasonable probability of a speedy peace between Portugal and the Government of Brazil, founded upon that Independence of which the United-States were the first to acknowledge. In declining, therefore, to enter into the proposed Convention, you will be pleased to assure your Government, that the determination of the President does not proceed from any abatement of the interest which the United States have constantly felt in the establishment of the Independence of Brazil, but is dictated solely by the want of those circumstances which would appear to be necessary to justify the formation of such a Convention. If in the progress of events there should be a renewal of demonstrations on the part of the European Allies to attack the Independence of the American States, the President will give to that new state of things, should it arise, every consideration, which its importance would undoubtedly demand.

With respect to your second proposition of a Treaty of alliance offensive and defensive to repel any invasion of the Brazilian Territories by the forces of Portugal, if the expected Peace should take place, that also would be unnecessary. But such a treaty would be inconsistent with the policy which the United-States have heretofore prescribed to themselves, that policy is, that whilst the war is confined to the parent Country and its former Colony, the United States remain neutral, extending their friendship and doing equal justice to both parties. From that policy they did not deviate during the whole of the long contest between Spain, and the several Independent Governments which have been erected on her former American Territories. If an exception to it were now for the first time made, the justice of your Sovereign will admit that the other new Governments might have some cause to complain of the United-States.

Whilst I regret that these considerations of policy which the United States feel themselves bound to respect, will not allow them to enter at this time into either of the two compacts suggested by you, I have much satisfaction in concurring with you in the expediency of permanently uniting our two Nations in the ties of Friendship, Peace and Commerce— With that view I am instructed to say to you, that the United-States are disposed to conclude a Treaty of Peace, Amity, Navigation and Commerce with the Government of Brazil, and that they are willing to adopt, as the basis of the mutual regulations of the Commerce and Navigation of the two Countries, a principle of equity and perfect reciprocity. If you should be empowered to negotiate such a Treaty, I shall take great pleasure in entering upon the discussion and consideration of its terms at such time as may be mutually convenient.

I pray you, Sir, to accept the assurance of my distinguished Consideration.   H. CLAY.

Copy. DNA, RG59, Notes to Foreign Ministers and Consuls, vol. 3, pp. 212-14 (M38, R3). AL draft, dated April 11, in CSmH. Published in Manning (arr.), *Diplomatic Correspondence . . . Latin-American Nations*, I, 233-34.
1 To John Quincy Adams.   2 The Monroe Doctrine (see above, III, 542n).

INSTRUCTIONS AND DISPATCHES   April 13, 1825

From HENRY MIDDLETON, St. Petersburg, no. 45, "Private & confidential." Reports contents of communications between diplomats of Russia, on the one hand, and of Spain, the Low Countries, and Sweden on the other, indicative of the reaction of their respective governments to the announcement of British recognition of the independence of the former Spanish-American colonies. ALS. DNA, RG59, Dip. Disp., Russia, vol. 10 (M35, R10). Published in Manning (arr.), *Diplomatic Correspondence . . . Latin-American Nations*, III, 1870-72. Addressed to Secretary of State; registered September 21, 1825. See above, Nelson to Clay, March 8, 1825; Hughes to Clay, April 7, 1825.

MISCELLANEOUS LETTERS   April 13, 1825

From THOMAS GRIFFIN, Yorktown, Virginia. Transmits "authenticated copies of Depositions relating to Slaves deported by the enemy, in the late war," and requests that these documents be submitted to the commissioners assembled to consider compensation for such property (under the St. Petersburg Convention). ALS. DNA, RG76, G.B.5-Folder 3.

From JOHN A. LEAMY, Philadelphia. Cites his letter of March 18, 1825; wishes to know whether "the Government" has relinquished "the intention of urging the settlement of" claims against Colombia. ALS. DNA, RG76, Misc. Claims, Colombia.

On April 20 Daniel Brent, at the direction of the Secretary of State, replied

that the Department "is at no time remiss unless it be from accidental circumstances in its attention and efforts, where it can with propriety take any
steps in reference to all claims upon foreign Governments, brought to its notice
by Citizens of the U. S." Copy. DNA, RG59, Dom. Letters, vol. 21, pp. 34-35
(M40, R19). One day later Brent transmitted to Leamy an excerpt from a letter
of Richard C. Anderson, Jr. (above, March 18, 1825), "communicating the
result of his application to the Government of Colombia for indemnity. . . ,
in the case of the Schooner Liberty and Cargo. . . ." Copy. *Ibid.*, p. 39.

To John M. Forbes

No. 1. John M. Forbes, appointed Chargé d'Affaires, U. S. to
Buenos Ayres.

Sir,   Department of State   Washington 14. April 1825

I transmit you, herewith, your Commission as Chargé d'Affairs
[sic] to the Government near which you are now residing, with the
proper Letter of credence.[1] The President, with the concurrence
of the Senate, was happy to be able to render this honourable
testimony to your long, faithful, and zealous services, and of his
personal regard for you. Being already in the actual discharge of
the duties of the appointment thus conferred on you, and understanding well the relations between Buenos Ayres and the United
States, it is not necessary that I should enlarge much upon the
objects to which your attention should be directed.

With regard to the Slave trade, you will take a proper occasion
to signify to the Government of Buenos Ayres the high satisfaction
which the President derived from its prompt attention to the
wishes of the United States that the character and the penalties of
piracy should be affixed to that odious traffic.[2] But is is [sic] not
deemed necessary that you should continue the negociation for
forming any convention upon that subject. You have been made
acquainted with that which was in treaty between Great Britain
and the United States.[3] One after the model of it, which was
concluded and signed with the Republic of Colombia, in December
last, with the exception of the coasts of America from the regulated
right of search, was submitted by the President to the Senate, at
its late Session. After full deliberation, the Senate did not think
proper to advise and consent to the ratification of it;[4] and hence
it is to be inferred that, if you were to conclude a similar Convention,
it would not meet the approbation of the Senate. In declining,
therefore, further to treat on that subject, you will explain to the
Government of Buenos Ayres that this determination does not
proceed from any diminished sensibility to the evils of the Slave
trade, but from a disinclination to employ the qualified right of
search, as an instrument to accomplish the end in view.

No one knows better than yourself what a deep interest has been taken by the people and Government of the United States in the success of the Patriot cause of Spanish America throughout all its fortunes and struggles. The recognition of the Independence of the new Governments was made as early as it was possible, consistently with all those considerations of policy and duty which this Government felt itself bound to entertain towards both parties. In point of fact, with the exception of the Act of the Portuguese Brazilian Government, to which it was prompted by self interest, and which preceded that of the United States only a few months, this Government was the first to assume the responsibility, and to risque the consequences of acknowledging the new Governments formed out of Spanish America. The United States have never claimed, and do not now desire, any particular favour or concession to their Commerce or navigation, as the consideration of the liberal policy which they have observed towards those Governments. But the President does confidently expect that the priority of movement on our part, which disconcerted schemes meditated by the European Allies against the Independent Governments, and has tended to accelerate similar Acts of recognition by the European Powers, and especially by Great Britain, will form a powerful motive with the Government of Buenos Ayres, for denying to the Commerce and Navigation of any of those European States any favours or privileges which shall not be equally extended to us. If the assurances of the British Government are to be implicitly relied on,[5] that Government does not desire, and will not seek to obtain, from the new Governments, any privileges for their Commerce and Navigation which shall not be extended to other foreign Powers.

The President is desirous of placing the Commerce and Navigation between the United States and all the new Governments upon the liberal basis which is provided for in the Acts of Congress of 3rd. March 1815,[6] and 7th. January, 1824.[7] The equitable principles of those Acts have been already extended, by reciprocal measures, to the Kingdom of the Netherlands, Prussia, the Imperial Hanseatic Cities of Hamburgh, Lubec and Bremen, the Dukedom of Oldenburgh, the Kingdom of Norway, the Kingdom of Sardinia, and the Empire of Russia. They will shortly be applied to France, if the Convention between the two Countries should not be terminated.[8] Other European Powers have manifested a disposition to be availed of them. And Mr. Poinsett, our Minister to the United Mexican States, has been empowered to conclude a Convention embracing them.

Two modes exist of accomplishing the object of the Act of the 7th. January; the one by mutual regulations adopting its principle, and the other by a Convention. If it be effected by reciprocal measures, both parties retain the power, respectively, to put an end to the continuance of it, whenever either of them may think proper. By a Convention, that power is parted with, during the existence of the compact, and provision can be made for other subjects of a Commercial nature, which it may be desirable to arrange, and which are not comprehended in the Act of 7th. January. I am directed by the President to instruct you that, without waiting to ascertain the practicability of the two Countries being able to conclude a Commercial Convention, you immediately urge upon the Government of Buenos Ayres the expediency of accepting the proposal which is contained in that Act, and the adoption of the necessary regulations, accordingly. If, however, it be preferred to effect the object by Convention, the President has no objection to that course. In that event, he would consider it most advisable that the negociation of the Convention should be conducted at Washington; but should the Government of Buenos Ayres desire that the negociation should be carried on at Buenos Ayres, the President will yield to its wishes, and upon their being made known to him, the necessary powers will be transmitted to you.

A General Convention of Peace, Amity, Navigation & Commerce, was concluded between the United States, and Colombia, and signed at Bogota on the 3rd. of October, 1824. It has been ratified by the United States, and we are daily expecting the Colombian ratification.[9] The basis assumed by that Convention, for the regulation of the Commerce and Navigation of the two Countries, is that of the rule of the most favoured Nation. To that rule there are some objections, and the President would prefer the more liberal principle incorporated in the Act of 7th. January.[10]

[. . . .]

As connected with Commerce of the two Countries I am directed to express the surprise and regret which have been excited by the passage of the Law of the Provincial Junta of Buenos Ayres, prohibiting the importation of Flour.[11] Although your zealous exertions to prevent its passage were unsuccessful, the President indulges the hope that, upon a reconsideration of it, either by that Junta or the General Congress, its unfriendly tendency towards the United States will be perceived, and the law repealed. From any view which we have been able to take of it here, it does not appear to have been called for by the state of the agriculture of that Country, whilst it is manifestly injurious to the United States, and must react upon Buenos Ayres by diminishing the exportation of one of its important staples, itself a produce of a kindred pursuit to Agriculture.[12] You will, therefore, in conciliating, but firm and decided language, remonstrate against that impolitic law.

The President sees with much satisfaction, the increased demand for American Manufactures, and particularly for the important fabric of Cotton in the States of La Plata, and that this Article has been able to sustain itself against all the jealous rivalry of the British trade.[13] You will take every opportunity to urge upon the Government of Buenos Ayres the adoption of liberal regulations, so as to secure for our manufacturing interest, a fair and equal competition.[14]

[. . . .]

The series of your despatches from No. 6. to No. 12, inclusive, has been received. The President has been gratified with the funeral honours awarded by the Government of Buenos Ayres, to the late Minister of the United States, Mr. Rodney,[15] and the respectful attention subsequently shown to his memory. You will communicate to that Government the grateful sensibility which is entertained to their delicate and friendly testimonies on that melancholly [sic] occasion.

The Government of the United States is sincerely desirous to cultivate and maintain the most friendly relations with all the new States formed out of what was Spanish America. It is expected that every Representative of this Government near those States will constantly bear in mind, and seize every fit occasion to give effect to, this friendly policy. If amicable explanations are sought, of the nature of our institutions, and their social operation, they should be cheerfully and frankly rendered; whilst all improper interference in their public Councils, all expressions of contempt for their habits, civil or religious, all intimations of incompetency on the part of their population, for self Government, should be sedulously avoided. Entertaining these views, the President saw with approbation, the discountenance you gave to the proposed meeting of Supercargoes and Captains to remonstrate against the passage of the Law prohibiting the importation of flour, exceptionable as that Law is deemed.[16] Such a meeting of foreigners would not have been tolerated in our own Country, and we could not expect that what we should be the first to condemn in respect to ourselves, would be agreeable to others. If our citizens have complaints to make, they must not take justice into their own hands, but prefer all such complaints through the regular and accredited organs.

You will communicate to the Government of Buenos Ayres the pleasure which the President derives from beholding the prospect of a speedy conclusion of the war between Spain and her late Colonies. The recent decisive events in Peru have terminated it on the Continent in fact;[17] and there wants now only a Treaty which the interests of Spain would seem to recommend, that she should not longer delay negociating, to put an end to it in form. If you should find that you can impart any strength to the dispositions for so happy an event in the Government of La Plata, you will not fail to impress upon it, how very agreeable it will be to the United States to see the People of La Plata in the full enjoyment of all the blessings of Peace, Independence, and Free Government.

This Despatch will be conveyed to you by Mr. John Hambden [*sic*] Pleasants, the son of Governor Pleasants of Virginia,[18] a young gentleman who is particularly recommended to your kind offices. He will bear any communications to the Government which you may have a wish to make in return. Unless they should be very urgent, there is no wish to hurry him home until he shall have refitted and recovered from the fatigues of his voyage. Wishing you great success in your mission, I am your obedient Servant

H. CLAY.

P. S. The claim of Colonel Halsey[19] has already been under your care. Should your exertions in his behalf have been unattended with success, you will continue to employ them in your new official character as far as it may appear to be expedient and proper.

H. C.

Copy. DNA, RG59, Dip. Instr., vol. 10, pp. 258-66 (M77, R5). ALS draft, in DLC-HC (DNA, M212, R7). Extracts published in Manning (arr.), *Diplomatic Correspondence . . . Latin-American Nations*, I, 235-37. Cf. above, Clay to Poinsett, March 26, 1825.

1 The commission, dated March 9, and the letter of credence, dated April 14, both copies, are located in DNA, RG59, Ceremonial Communications, vol. 2, pp. 9, 13.

2 In letters to Foreign Minister Manuel José Garcia, dated September 17 and November 8, 1824, Forbes had urged passage of such legislation, which had been enacted on November 15, 1824, by the legislative Junta of the Province of Buenos Aires. Garcia to Forbes, November 22, 1824 (translation in DNA, RG59, Dip. Disp., Argentina, vol. 3 [M69, R37]). The original proposal had been urged as a preparatory step leading to conclusion of a convention or treaty authorizing "mutual search and examination of all such vessels as may be found in proximity to the scenes" of slave trade—both measures having been presented in accordance with instructions from Adams, as Secretary of State, to Caesar A. Rodney, then the American Minister to Buenos Aires, May 17, 1823. *American State Papers, Foreign Relations*, V, 332.

3 See above, Clay to Addington, April 6, 1825.

4 See above, Clay to Salazar, March 21, 1825.

5 See Rush to Adams, December 30, 1824, in Manning (arr.), *Diplomatic Correspondence . . . Latin-American Nations*, III, 1528.

6 Which had repealed, conditionally, legislation imposing discriminatory duties on imports and foreign vessels in American ports, the repeal to be effective in favor of any foreign nation that should satisfy the President of the United States "that the discriminating or countervailing duties of such foreign nation, so far as they operate to the disadvantage of the United States, have been abolished." 3 *U. S. Stat.*, 224.

7 See above, Lorich to Clay, March 16, 1825, note.

8 See above, III, 53n. The convention is still in force. Among its articles was a provision for gradual abolition of discriminating duties when the convention had been in effect two years without a declaration of discontinuance by either party. Miller (ed.), *Treaties. . .* , III, 82.

9 See above, Clay to Salazar, March 21, 1825, and note.

10 The portion of this document which repeats content beginning at this phrase on p. 169, above, and ending at the same phrase on p. 170, copied in accordance with Clay's instructions in his draft version, "substituting Buenos Ayres for Mexico," is here omitted by the editors.

11 The measure, enacted in November, 1824, had been reported in a dispatch from Forbes to John Quincy Adams, dated November 25, 1824, and received at the Department of State on February 17, 1825. ALS. DNA, RG59, Dip. Disp., Argentina, vol. 3 (M69, R3).

12 One argument in favor of the legislation had been the claim that the trade with the United States drained Buenos Aires of specie. Forbes had countered the assertion, in discussions with Garcia, by pointing to the fact that the trade was largely in exchange for "Jerk beef," carried to Havana. *Ibid.*

13 "Of our commerce the only articles which, in any manner, rival those of English manufacture, are some china silks, East India cottons and some of our humble domestic manufactures, particularly our unbleached cotton cloths." *Ibid.* The dispatch recounts particularly the failure of the British to produce a satisfactory imitation of the last item.

14 The two paragraphs which repeat content beginning at the second paragraph on p. 170, above, copied in accordance with Clay's instructions in his draft version, "substituting the Government of B. A. to that of Mexico," are here omitted by the editors.

15 Caesar Augustus Rodney had died June 10, 1824, in Buenos Aires.

16 Reported in Forbes to Adams, November 25, 1824.

17 See above, Clay to Poinsett, March 26, 1825, and note.

18 John Hampden Pleasants; James Pleasants.

19 See above, Cross to Clay, March 28, 1825.

Check to Benjamin W. Leigh

Washn. 14h Apl 1825.

Pay to B. W. Leigh Esqr. or order the sum of one hundred and twelve dollars and 44 Cents.[1] Cashr. of the Off. of Dt. & Dt. Washington City.[2] H. CLAY

ADS. DLC-TJC (DNA, M212, R16). Endorsements indicate that the draft was cleared to the credit of Charles Page.

1 Cf. above, III, 801, 897. 2 Richard Smith.

To Condy Raguet

No. 1. Condy Raguet, appointed Chargé d'Affaires, U. S. to Brazil. Instructions—General

Sir, Department of State Washington 14. April 1825.

The President having, by and with the advice and consent of the Senate, at its late session, appointed you Chargé d'Affaires of the United States to the Brazilian Government, I transmit, herewith, your Commission, and also a Letter of credence to be presented to the Minister of Foreign Affairs,[1] when you communicate to him your appointment. In the discharge of the duties of the honourable station to which you have been promoted, it is requested that you will continue to manifest the same zealous attention to the interests of the United States, that you have heretofore displayed in that of their Consul at Rio Janeiro. The Commerce of the United States, already considerable with the Brazilian territories, is susceptible of great augmentation, and you will, therefore, lose no opportunity to advance its interests, and increase its facilities. Both France and

Great Britain will probably strive to obtain for themselves peculiar privileges in the trade with Brazil. Great Britain will, no doubt, seek to secure with the new Government, the same extraordinary advantages as those which her Commerce has so long enjoyed with Portugal—advantages which have placed Portugal almost in the condition of a Colony or dependence of of [sic] Great Britain.[2] You will resist, firmly, and constantly, any concessions to the Commerce or Navigation of either of those two powers, which are not equally extended to the Commerce and Navigation of the United States. They neither claim nor desire, for themselves, any peculiar commercial privileges. But they are entitled confidently to expect, if not to demand, from all the circumstances by which they stand connected with the Government of Brazil, that no such peculiar commercial privileges be granted to others. The United States were the first to acknowledge that Government, disregarding all the risks incident to the fact, and to the nature of its recent establishment, and overlooking the anomaly of its political form in the great family of American Powers.[3] The United States do not claim, from this prompt and friendly measure, favour; but they insist upon equal justice to their commerce and Navigation. And the President is altogether unprepared to see any European State, which has come tardily and warily to the acknowledgment of Brazil, running off with commercial advantages which shall be denied to an earlier and more uncalculating friend

Mr. Rabello [sic], the Brazilian Minister here, addressed a note to this Department on the 28th. day of January last, and another on the 6th. instant, proposing, in substance, a Treaty of offensive and defensive alliance between the two Countries, against the European alliance; and also a similar Treaty against Portugal, if she should invade the Brazilian territories. He was answered on the 11th. Instant,[4] and copies of his notes, and of the answer accompany. this Despatch. You will observe that the President declines entering into either of the proposed Treaties, but the answer contains a proposition to conclude a commercial Convention, regulating the Commerce and Navigation of the two Countries. No reply to this proposal has been yet received;[5] but should one reach the Department before this Despatch leaves it, a copy will be sent to you. The decision upon Mr. Rabello's overtures has been made in conformity with that neutral policy which the United States have prescribed for themselves. It has not proceeded from any diversity of views between the late, and present, Administration, as to the principles announced in the Presidents Message to Congress of 2nd. December, 1823.[6] To those principles the President adheres; and you will embrace every proper opportunity to impress upon the Brazilian Government, the advantage which accrued to America from their promulgation at that epoch. There can be but little doubt that the ground then taken contributed to dissuade the European Allies from embarking in the cause of Spain, and, consequently, from uniting with Portugal, against their respective Colonies. You will also inculcate the utility of the Brazilian Government maintaining, in its correspondence and intercourse with the European Powers, the same principle which has been proclaimed here against the establishment, on this Continent, of new European Colonies.

If the two Governments shall unite in the expediency of concluding a Commercial Convention between them, it is preferred that the negociations shall be conducted here. But if a strong wish be manifested to have them carried on at Rio Janeiro, the President will yield to it; and, in that contingency, you will be furnished with the requisite powers and instructions. In the mean time, without waiting for the issue of any such negociation, if there should now exist, by the Laws or regulations of Brazil, any discriminating import or tonnage duty between the vessels of the two countries, and their cargoes, unfavourable to those of the United States, you will urge the adoption of the equitable principle of the Act of 7th. January, 1824.[7] By the 4th. Section of that Act, it is enacted "That, upon satisfactory evidence being given to the President of the United States, by the Government of any foreign Nation, that no discriminating duties of tonnage or impost are imposed or levied within the Ports of the said Nation, upon vessels wholly belonging to citizens of the United States, or upon merchandize, the produce or manufacture thereof, imported in the same, the President is hereby authorised to issue his proclamation declaring that the foreign discriminating duties of tonnage and impost, within the United States, are, and shall be, suspended, and discontinued, so far as respects the vessels of the said Nation, and the merchandize, of its produce or manufacture, imported into the United States in the same: the said suspension to take effect from the time of such notification being given to the President of the United States, and to continue so long as the reciprocal exemption of vessels belonging to citizens of the United States, and merchandize as aforesaid, thereon laden, shall be continued, and no longer." The President, being satisfied that Brazil has done away any such discriminating duty, operating against the Navigation or Commerce of the United States, would immediately issue the Proclamation provided for in that Section.

The Slave trade is still tolerated by Brazil. The United States were the first to put an end to that odious traffic, so far as their own Citizens were concerned in it.[8] They would gladly see all other Nations imitating so good an example. Its abolition in Brazil will encounter many obstacles in the obduracy of long indulged habits, the vast, fertile regions which are yet unsettled, the climate, and the illusions of individual interest. It is to be hoped that the prevalence of truer views of social duty and happiness, and the obligations of religion and humanity will, at no distant day, lead the Government of Brazil to the prohibition of that trade. In the mean time, it is wished that, in a manner perfectly conciliatory, and unoffending, you should contribute, as far as you can, to the hastening of this desirable event. That Government has undoubtedly the power to continue the trade, if it think proper to do so, and, however painful that may be, the interests of the United States, or the cause of humanity, are not likely to be promoted by our offensively encountering the prejudices of another people, or becoming importunate on a subject over which their jurisdiction is incontestible. It may not be amiss, too, to leave the new born zeal of Great Britain, in relation to the Slave trade,[9] to fret itself on the Brazilian Government, as it is most likely that it will be exerted, in a manner not very acceptable. Such an interposition may have the effect of checking any undue or improper influence which Great Britain might otherwise acquire in Brazil.

Your Letters of the 12th. 22nd. and 24th. April, 1824, 14th. June, 2nd. and 21st. August, 12th. September, 5th. October, 8th. and 27th. November, 9th. and 18th. December, and 17th. January 1825, have been severally received at this Department.

This despatch is carried by Mr. John H. Pleasants, the son of Governor Pleasants[10] of Virginia, and who is recommended to your friendly offices. I am, with great respect, Sir, Your obedient & humble Servant.   H. CLAY.

Copy. DNA, RG59, Dip. Instr., vol. 10, pp. 266-70 (M77, R5). ALI draft, in DLC-HC (DNA, M212, R7). In his diary entry for April 18, John Quincy Adams reports that he has returned Clay's draft of instructions to Raguet, "proposing omission of a paragraph respecting the slave-trade." Adams, *Memoirs,* VI, 530; MHi-Adams Papers, Diary (R36). The paragraph is the same in both the official letterbook and draft versions of the document, which appears to have been dispatched several days previous to Adams' entry.

1 The commission, dated March 9, and the letter of credence, April 14, both copies, are located in DNA, RG59, Ceremonial Communications, vol. 2, pp. 10, 12-13.

2 Under the Anglo-Portuguese Treaty of 1654 English merchants had been given extensive privileges in Portugal, including provision that, without their consent, they would never be required to pay customs duties of more than 23 percent. Portuguese efforts to counter the effects of foreign competition on their developing industries in the latter half of the seventeenth century, by banning importation of various manufactures, had been met by the commercial treaty negotiated by John Methuen, as envoy extraordinary from Britain at Lisbon, in December, 1703, which provided for the entry of English cloths as before the prohibitive legislation, in return for admission of Portuguese wines into Britain at a third less than the duty levied on the French. H. V. Livermore, *A History of Portugal* (Cambridge, [Eng.], 1947), 295-97, 326-28.

3 The reception of Rebello by President Monroe on May 8, 1824, had been celebrated in Brazil and at least implicitly acknowledged by Monroe, in his annual message of December 7, 1824, as the act of recognition; but delay in transmission of Raguet's accreditation as Chargé, instead of consul (see below, Clay to Pleasants, April 16, 1825; Pleasants to Clay, July 7, 1825; Raguet to Clay, November 12, 1825) cast some doubt upon the precedence of the United States in completing the formalities.

4 Dated April 13 in official file.

5 See below, Rebello to Clay, April 16, 1825.

6 See above, III, 542n; Clay to Poinsett, March 26, 1825.

7 See above, Lorich to Clay, March 16, 1825, note.

8 An act to prohibit the importation of slaves into the United States from and after January 1, 1808 (the earliest date possible under Article I, Section 9, of the Constitution) had been approved March 2, 1807 (2 *U. S. Stat.*, 426-30). See also, above, Clay to Addington, April 6, 1825, note.

9 The British Parliament had, in fact, resolved in June, 1806, that "they would, with all practicable Expedition, take effectual Measures for the Abolition of the African Slave Trade"; a series of acts of that year had regulated it in an attempt to eliminate the worst abuses; and by legislation of March 25, 1807 (47 *Geo. III*, c. 36), the trade had been "forthwith abolished and prohibited." In Britain, moreover, the religious and humanitarian movements which had generated this action, displayed a missionary fervor that not only pressed for abolition of slavery as an institution in the British colonies (enacted August 28, 1833, 3 and 4 *Wm. IV*, c. 73) but also promoted these reforms as goals of foreign policy throughout the period. The particular publicity which George Canning, as opposed to earlier ministers, focused upon his efforts in this campaign is discussed in Temperley, *Foreign Policy of Canning*, 313-14.

10 James Pleasants.

To William C. Somerville

No. 1. William C. Somerville appointed Chargé d'Affaires U. S. to Sweden.

Sir,   Department of State   Washington 14. April 1825.

As you have been already informed, the President has appointed you, with the advice and consent of the Senate, Chargé d'Affaires of the United States in Sweden, in the place of Mr. Christopher Hughes whom he has appointed Chargé d'Affaires in the Netherlands, and it is his wish that you set out with all convenient dispatch upon this mission. A Letter of introduction addressed to the Minister of Foreign Affairs of the Government of Sweden, and a copy of it for your own information, together with your Commission, are now transmitted to you.[1] You will receive the Archives and papers appertaining to the Mission, from Mr. Erskine[2] our Consul at Stockholm, with whom it is expected Mr. Hughes will have left them.

The principal object of your appointment being to cultivate and strengthen the good understanding which so happily exists between the United States and Sweden, it is the Presidents wish that you take advantage of all fit occasions, consistently with the interest of the United States, to promote that object.

Many citizens of the United States have well founded claims, to a considerable amount, upon the Government of Sweden, for property illegally sequestered, confiscated and sold with the permission, and by the orders, of the Swedish Government, within the

Dominions of Sweden, during the existence of the late European wars;[3] and you will not fail to urge the satisfactory adjustment and payment of them, by all the means in your power. With the nature and extent of these claims, you will be made more particularly acquainted upon your arrival at Stockholm, by Mr. Erskine, with whom, it is presumed, Mr. Hughes will have left the evidences and papers connected with the subject. Mr. John Connell of Philadelphia, was lately sent to Stockholm, by the claimants, charged with the special Agency of prosecuting their rightful demands; and Mr. Hughes employed his good offices, in aid of Mr. Connell's efforts, unfortunately to little or no effect.

If any wish should be suggested to you, or overtures made, on the part of the Swedish Government, that the Commercial relations between the United States and Sweden should be further regulated or modified by Conventional stipulations, you will refer all such overtures to this Department; and, in the mean time, you are authorised and directed to apprise that Government that it is the Presidents desire that the Commercial intercourse between the United States and all foreign Countries including Sweden, should be permanently established upon a footing of fair and perfect reciprocity.

Great inconvenience is often experienced by our Citizens in the Colonial possessions of this Hemisphere, from the policy of the European States to which they belong, in not allowing to the Consuls and Consular Agents of the United States residing in those Dependencies, the privilege of a full exercise of their functions. It is the Presidents wish that you should endeavour to procure a relaxation of the Rule in regard to the Island of St. Bartholomew;[4] that the interests of the Citizens of the United States, constantly resorting thither for mercantile and commercial purposes, may be under the care and protection, when necessary, of responsible agents of their own Government.

I am, with great respect, Sir, Your obedient and very humble Servant   H. CLAY.

Copy. DNA, RG59, Dip. Instr., vol. 10, pp. 255-56 (M77, R5). L draft, in Daniel Brent's hand with interlineations by Clay, in DLC-HC (DNA, M212, R7).

1 Copies of the commission, dated March 9, and the letter of credence, dated April 27, are located in DNA, RG59, Ceremonial Communications, vol. 2, pp. 10-11, 17-18.

2 David Erskine, a resident of Stockholm at the time of his appointment as consul, in December 1818.

3 See above, Hughes to Secretary of State, March 19, 1825, note.

4 The United States, having applied for permission to send a consul to St. Bartholomew's Island, had been informed by the Swedish Minister of Foreign Affairs, in 1822, that such an official could not be admitted because the island was a colony. Adams had not yet won acceptance of his view, then stated, that "European Governments excluded foreign Consuls from colonies because foreign commerce with them was interdicted . . . but where commerce was allowed, the Consul followed of course." Adams, *Memoirs*, VI, 32.

From Lewis Cass

Dear Sir,   Detroit April 14. 1825

I have just finished the perusal of your masterly address to your late constituents,[1] and I cannot refrain from expressing to you the high satisfaction it has afforded me. It is a triumphant refutation of the vile slanders, which have been propagated respecting the motives of your conduct in the peculiar circumstances, in which you were recently placed. You may safely commit your character to the judgement of your countrymen and of posterity. They will not fail to award you full justice.

I must ask your indulgence for this almost involuntary tribute to your claims and Services. So strong is the impression, which your appeal has made upon me, that I could not restrain this expression of my feelings. With warm regard, I am, Dear Sir, Sincerely yours   LEW CASS.
Hon. H. Clay.

ALS. DLC-HC (DNA, M212, R1). Endorsed on verso by Clay: "Govr. Cass Answd." Answer not found.   [1] Above, March 26, 1825.

INSTRUCTIONS AND DISPATCHES   April 14, 1825

To HUGH NELSON, no. 12. Transmits letter of recredence and instructions on his leaving the post as Minister to Spain, to be succeeded by Alexander H. Everett; commends Nelson on his services. Encloses a letter from Achille Murat (above, March 27, 1825) concerning the arrest of his brother in Spain and instructs Nelson to use his good offices, so far as proper, in this connection. Requests him to settle the case involving a bill of "Mr. Salmon" (Hilario de Rivas y Salmon), drawn on his Government and used as a remittance to United States bankers at London. Copy. DNA, RG59, Dip. Instr., vol. 10, pp. 255-56 (M77, R5). Draft, in Daniel Brent's hand with interlineations by Clay, in DLC-HC (DNA, M212, R7). A copy of the letter of recredence, dated April 8, is located in DNA, RG59, Ceremonial Communications, vol. 2, p. 11.

The case involving Salmon's bill concerned a draft for $6,000, drawn by the Spanish Chargé upon his Government for legation expenses. The United States Government, which had honored the draft with advance payment, had been unable to collect the sum, when, upon remittance of the draft, through Baring Brothers and Company to Wiseman, Gower, and Company, a Madrid commercial house, the property of the latter firm had been attached under bankruptcy proceedings.

From CHRISTOPHER HUGHES, Stockholm, "Private." Reports the sale of a Swedish warship to a commercial house in Stockholm, allegedly for the East Indian trade but known to be for the use of Mexico. ALS. DNA, RG59, Dip. Disp., Sweden and Norway, vol 4 (M45, R5). Addressed to Secretary of State; received June 7. See below, Hughes to Clay, July 8, 1825, note.

From RICHARD RUSH, London, no. 431. Acknowledges receipt "yesterday" of Clay's dispatch of March 10; states Rush's acceptance of the appointment as

Secretary of the Treasury and his intention to embark early in June, "sooner, should my successor in this mission arrive here sooner." ALS. DNA, RG59, Dip. Disp., Great Britain, vol. 32 (M30, R28). Received May 19.

MISCELLANEOUS LETTERS   April 14, 1825

To [John Douglass and Douglass Maguire,] the editor(s) of the Indianapolis *Indiana Journal*. Daniel Brent, at the direction of the Secretary of State, requests that this newspaper be sent regularly to the Department. Copy. DNA, RG59, Dom. Letters, vol. 21, p. 30 (M40, R19). Douglass, formerly a publisher and State printer at Vevay, Indiana, had moved to Indianapolis when the governmental offices were transferred there in 1824. Maguire, a former Kentuckian, long active as a Clay political supporter in Indiana, had been one of the publishers of the *Western Censor and Emigrant's Guide,* established in 1823. Acquiring full control of this journal, in January, 1825, Douglass and Maguire renamed it the *Indiana Journal*. Douglass continued as proprietor, part of the time as sole proprietor, for some fifteen years. The newspaper had been designated to publish the laws of the Second Session of the Eighteenth Congress and retained the patronage throughout the Adams administration.

On the same date, Brent wrote similar letters to [John P. Erwin,] the editor of the *Nashville Whig*, Tennessee, to [Charles Miner,] the editor of the West Chester, Pennsylvania, *Village Record,* and to [William Tanner,] the editor of the Louisville, Kentucky, *Morning Post and Commercial Advertiser.* All copies, in DNA, RG59, Dom. Letters, vol. 21 (M40, R19).

Miner, born in Connecticut, had moved first to Wilkes Barre, Pennsylvania, where he had founded and edited another newspaper from 1802 to 1809. In 1817 he had acquired the West Chester *Chester and Delaware Federalist* and the following year changed the name to *Village Record.* He remained publisher of the journal until 1832. A member of the Pennsylvania Legislature in 1807 and 1808, Miner had now become a Representative in Congress and served from 1825 to 1829.

Tanner, not further identified, in 1824 had acquired the Louisville *Morning Post and Commercial Advertiser.* He sold it in October, 1825, and left Louisville.

To Achille Murat. States that his letter requesting relief for his brother has been sent to Hugh Nelson, United States Minister to Spain, with a request for his good offices. Copy. DNA, RG59, Dom. Letters, vol. 21, p. 31 (M40, R19). See above, Murat to Clay, March 27, 1825; Clay to Nelson, April 14, 1825.

From Nathaniel Silsbee, Salem, Massachusetts, "Private." Transmits, in consequence of Clay's inquiry of April 1 (not found), letters concerning Jeremy Robinson. ALS. DNA, RG59, Misc. Letters (M179, R62). The only enclosure remaining in the file, written by Willard Peele, Salem merchant, and addressed to Silsbee, is highly uncomplimentary to Robinson and opposes his appointment to government service.

MISCELLANEOUS LETTERS   April 15, 1825

To [William Wirt]. Asks the opinion of the Attorney General on two questions arising from the controversy between (William) Thornton, of the Patent Office, and the secretary (Peter A. Browne) of the Franklin Institute in Philadelphia: (1) does the patent law "authorize any person, other than the Patentee, to demand the copy of any Paper respecting a Patent, that has been

granted, *prior* to the expiration of the term for which it was granted?" and
(2) "Is it lawful to allow copies of any Such papers" to be issued from the
Patent Office at a lower rate than "twenty cents for every copy sheet of One
hundred words?" N, in Daniel Brent's hand. DNA, RG60, Letters Received
from State Dept.

APPLICATIONS, RECOMMENDATIONS   April 15, 1825

THOMAS CORWIN, Lebanon (Ohio), recommends "Col. William A Camron,"
his "long time personal acquaintance & for several years . . . Neighbor in this
town," for a lieutenancy in the Marine Corps. ALS. DLC-Gideon Welles Papers
(DNA, M212, R22). Corwin, an Ohio lawyer and legislator, was a member of
Congress (1831-1840, 1859-1861), Governor (1840-1842), United States Senator (1845-1850), Secretary of the Treasury of the United States (1850-1853),
and Minister to Mexico (1861-1864). Camron not further identified.

To James Brown

Dear Sir   Washn. 16 Apl. 1825
The bearer hereof Mr. Lemoine[1] has been introduced to me as a
promising young gentleman, the son of a respectable Citizen of our
native State. He is about to visit Europe on business and personal
gratification. I pray you to extend to him any civilities in your power.
                          Yr's faithfy   H. CLAY
The Honble James Brown—

ALS. NcD.   1 Not further identified.

Rental Agreement with Mrs. Henrietta Warren
and Mrs. K. H. Blanton

                                         [April 16, 1825]
It is agreed between Henry Clay of the one part and Mrs. Henrietta Warren and Mrs. K. H. Blanton of the other, as follows—
The said Clay hereby leases to the said Warren and Blanton the
five rooms which they at present occupy in the house of said Clay
at the corner of short and Market Streets in Lexington and the
Kitchen and Yard thereto appertaining, for three months begining [*sic*] with the 17th. day of the present month, April 1825—
In consideration whereof the said Warren and Blanton agree to
pay the said Clay the sum of forty one dollars and 25c. in Ky.[1] on
or before the 16th. day of July next and to surrender the said
premises to said Clay on said 16th day of July next in as good repair
as they now are—natural decay and inevitable accidents excepted.
The right of distress for any of the rent in arrear is reserved to
the said Clay—and also the right of the other occupants of the 2nd.

Story in said building to use the passage and stairs and yard is reserved to them as well as the use of the yard to the occupants of the two lower rooms fronting market Street—

Witness the hands and seals of the parties this 16th. day of April 1825—   H. CLAY by ROBT SCOTT {Seal}
                              H WARREN {Seal}
                           K H BLANTON {Seal}

[Endorsements][2]
17 April to 1st Oct. is 5 Ms. 13 ds @ 41$25 pr. 3 Ms. is— $74,,71
Old balance $6,,12\frac{1}{2}$[3]
        due.—— $\overline{\$80.83\frac{1}{2}}$
                                                42.   [*sic*]

Memo. of Deficiencies—
3 Lights Glass out of lower passage Windows ⎫   3 Keys
12 — Do ————— upper Do —— Do ⎬   2 Keys in Doors.
1 Sash Missing in Garrett & 2 panes Glass broken out
By former agreement they were to Glaze all the windows
in the front rooms up Stairs & of course to leave them so—
All the Keys for these rooms are missing—
6 Lights & 1 Sash & Lights missing in the Kitchen below—
7. Do up Stairs in the Kitchen Missing—
No Keys to the Doors of the upper rooms—
No Key to Smoke House—
                                 R. SCOTT
1825 Nov. 3—By Coms.[4] Note $10—
        Deduct $6,,12\frac{1}{2}$ due on former lease $6,,12\frac{1}{2}$
                         Paid on this lease $\overline{\$\ 3,,87\frac{1}{2}}$
       ,,   U States[5] Notes 15$. —equal — $22,,50$
                                        $\overline{\$26,,37\frac{1}{2}}$
1826 Jany. 3rd. By Specie 11$—equal $16,,50$
            74 ,, 71 $\overline{42.87\frac{1}{2}}$
            $42 ,, 87\frac{1}{2}$
            $\overline{31.\ 83\frac{1}{2}}$

ADS by Scott, signed also by Mrs. Warren and Mrs. Blanton. DLC-TJC (DNA, M212, R16).
   1 Kentucky currency.
   2 The first, AE; the second, AES; the third (on verso), AE—all in Scott's hand.
   3 Cf. above, Scott to Clay, February 2, 1825.
   4 Bank of the Commonwealth.   5 Bank of the United States.

DIPLOMATIC NOTES   April 16, 1825

TO HILARIO DE RIVAS Y SALMON. Acknowledges receipt of his note of April 10, enclosing a copy of one dated March 12 (*i.e.*, March 11, addressed to Daniel Brent). "Both notes have been submitted to the President," who states "that he has no power to make the loan desired." Advances have sometimes been made "to foreign ministers . . . upon the credit of their orders upon their own Governments"; but, since this practice has led to "some inconvenience" and since "there is even danger in the instance of a former advance to you of the United States sustaining an ultimate loss of its amount, the President thinks it proper to discontinue this species of transaction." Copy. DNA, RG59, Notes to Foreign Ministers and Consuls, vol. 3, pp. 214-15 (M38, R3). AL draft, in CSmH. President Adams had been "inclined to accede" to Salmon's request; but Clay was reluctant, and Adams "authorized him to decline the advance." Adams, *Memoirs*, VI, 528. See above, Clay to Nelson, April 14, 1825, note.

To HILARIO DE RIVAS Y SALMON. Transmits a copy of the letter of John C. Jones (above, March 28, 1825). Copy. DNA, RG59, Notes to Foreign Ministers and Consuls, vol. 3, p. 215 (M38, R3). N draft, in CSmH.

To the BARON DE TUYLL, "Private and inofficial." Transmits a letter (not found) from (Isaac) McKim "on the subject of the indemnity which it might be proper to allow to the owners of the Pearl"; proposes, "With the view to the final settlement of that affair," a meeting of the Baron with Clay on the following Monday. Copy. DNA, RG59, Unofficial Letter-Book of Henry Clay, 1825-1829, p. 1.

From JOSE SILVESTRE REBELLO, Washington, Argues, on the basis of (James) Monroe's message of December (2), 1823 (above, III, 542n), that the United States should abandon its policy of neutrality between mother country and colonies once the United States has recognized their independence, if the mother country should attempt by force to retake possession of her former colonies; urges, more specifically, that the United States should "declare itself in alliance . . . with Brazil" if peace should not be established between the South American country and Portugal. LS, orig. and trans. DNA, RG59, Notes from Brazilian Legation, vol. 1 (M49, R1). Translation published in Manning (arr.), *Diplomatic Correspondence . . . Latin-American Nations*, II, 814-15. See above, Rebello to Clay, April 6, 1825.

INSTRUCTIONS AND DISPATCHES   April 16, 1825

To JOSEPH HILL CLARK, "Consul U. S. Lubec." Encloses commission, printed instructions, and blank bond. Copy. DNA, RG59, Cons. Instr., vol. 2, p. 353 (M78, R2). The appointment of Clark, a resident of Massachusetts, had been approved February 11; he remained at this post until 1831, when the consulate was discontinued.

On the same date Clay sent similar documents to HARVEY GREGG, "Consul U. S. for Acapulco Indianapolis, Indiana"; ABRAHAM B. NONES, "Consul U. S. Maracaybo"; GEORGE R. ROBERTSON, "Consul U. S. Tampico"; JOHN SHILLABER, "Consul U. S. Batavia, Java"; JOHN R. THOMSON, "Consul U. S. Canton"; WILLIAM WHEELWRIGHT, "Consul U. S. Guayaquil, Col[ombia]"; and DANIEL WYNNE, "Consul U. S. St. Iago de Chile." All copies. *Ibid.*, pp. 353-56. Nones, Shillaber, Thomson, and Wheelwright had all been given recess appointments, which had been confirmed early in January. Nones, a Virginian, held the position until 1832, when, it being noted that he no longer resided at Maracaibo, a successor was named. Shillaber and Wheelwright, both of Massachusetts, served until 1833. Thomson, a Pennsylvanian, resigned in 1826.

To JOHN H[AMPDEN] PLEASANTS, Richmond, Virginia. Orders him "to embark by the earliest opportunity" for the purpose of delivering dispatches to Condy Raguet, at Rio de Janeiro, and to John M. Forbes, at Buenos Aires; states that his allowance, of which the sum of $1950 is furnished in advance, will include

$900, actual travel expenses, and six dollars a day; and grants permission for him to remain "some days" at each destination for the purpose of rest "and the gratification of your curiosity." Copy. DNA, RG59, Dip. Instr., vol. 10, p. 278 (M77, R5). L draft, in DLC-HC (DNA, M212, R7).

To JOEL R. POINSETT, no. 3. States that, according to information received from (Pablo) Obregón, (William) Taylor, United States consul at Alvarado, has asserted that he cannot recognize the Mexican blockade of San Juan d'Ulloa until "officially notified of its execution by his own Government"; orders Poinsett to instruct American consuls in Mexican ports that "a Blockade being otherwise legal and maintained by the competent force, it is not necessary that its existence Should be communicated by a neutral to its public Agents, to entitle it to the respect which belongs to it." Copy. DNA, RG59, Dip. Instr., vol. 10, pp. 270-71 (M77, R5). AL draft, in DLC-HC (DNA, M212, R7).

To CONDY RAGUET, no. 4. Transmits evidence of claims of citizens of the United States against Brazil for the seizure and detention at Pernambuco of the sloop *Morning Star* and the ship *Spermo,* of New York; encloses, also, letters of William P. [sic] Sproat, of Philadelphia, and Thomas Buckley and Son, of New York, to the State Department, asking aid in obtaining indemnity for the seizures. Copy. DNA, RG59, Dip. Instr., vol. 10, p. 277 (M77, R5). L draft, in DLC-HC (DNA, M212, R7). Endorsed: "*Mem.* The original papers were sent with this Letter to Mr. Raguet." Cf. above, Peter W. Sproat to Clay, March 15, 1825.

From CONDY RAGUET, Rio de Janeiro. Relays information concerning the siege of Callao. LS. DNA, RG59, Cons. Disp., Rio de Janeiro, vol. 2 (M-T172, R3). Addressed to Secretary of State; received June 1.

MISCELLANEOUS LETTERS   April 16, 1825

From WILLIAM WIRT, "Office of the Attorney General of the U. S." Gives his opinion in response to the two questions submitted by Clay (above, April 15, 1825), relating to the eleventh section of the patent law: (1) the proviso to this section does not give to all citizens of the United States "the right to demand copies of papers respecting patents granted to others"; it "might well receive the strict construction which the Superintendent of the Patent Office has been disposed to place upon it," although it has been construed to extend the right to demand copies "to persons who have been sued for a violation of a patent right"; (2) it is not lawful to allow copies of any such papers, official or unofficial, to be issued from the Office for any purpose at a less rate than "twenty cents, for every copy sheet of one hundred words—" ADS. DNA, RG59, Misc. Letters (M179, R62). Document not dated; date supplied on the basis of related correspondence.

From N[icholas] C. Horsley

Sir,   Henderson, April 17th. 182[5]

A voucher of fourteen hundred dollars, being paid to you by Genl. Hopkin's [sic] Agents in 1818, is now before me, and only a day or two ago put in my possession; which was overlooked in the collection of vouchers for a settlement with you last fall at Lexington;[1]— and I find likewise omited [*sic*] in your account Current.[2]—. The following is the language of Mess Bartlett [*sic*] & Cox's letter:

"Genl Saml Hopkins   "New Orleans 29 March 1818."[3]

Dr Sir, The principal object of the present is to advise you we have this day remitted to Henry Clay Esqr. fourteen hundred dollars on your account in J. F. Gray & Jno. Taylors draft on John Bohlen of Phila. @ 60 days sight.   BARTLET & COX."

Mr. Lyne[4] and myself had to advance the money paid to you at the Sale in Lexington, which has not yet been refunded to us by the other heirs of Genl. Hopkins's Estate; and therefore, we feel a *peculiar* interest in having this matter adjusted with you.— Be so good Sir, as to let me hear from you as soon as convenient on this business.   Very Resply Sir, Yr Mo Ob St

Honble H. Clay.   N. C. HORSLEY

ALS. DLC-TJC (DNA, M212, R12).   1 No settlement found.
2 Cf. above, II, 917; III, 330.   3 See below, Ingersoll to Clay, May 7, 1825.
    4 George Lyne, of Henderson, had married in 1819 Martha, daughter of Samuel Hopkins.

To Antonio José Cañaz

Don Antonio José Cañaz,
Envoy Extraordinary and Minister Plenipotentiary from the United Provinces of the Centre of America. New York.

Sir,   Department of State, Washington, 18 April, 1825.

Your letter under date at Washington on the 8th. of February last was duly received at this Department.[1] The delay in answering it has proceeded from the termination of one, and the formation of another administration. I rely upon your goodness to perceive, in the pressure of indispensable business, incident to that change, a sufficient apology for this delay.

Your letter has been submitted to the President and attentively considered by him. And I am instructed to make known to you the very great sensibility with which he receives the expression of sentiments of consideration and friendship towards the United States which are entertained by the Government of the Republic of the Centre of America; and, at the same time, to assure you that they are most cordially reciprocated. The confidence of your Government in that of the United States is strongly manifested by the highly important proposition which your note communicates. That proposition is that the United States shall co-operate with the Republic of the Centre in promoting the opening of a Canal, through the Province of Nicaragua, to unite the Atlantic Ocean to that of the Pacific, and that by means of a treaty the advantages of that Canal may be perpetually secured to the two nations—

The idea has been long conceived of uniting those two seas by a Canal navigation. The execution of it will form a great epoch in the commercial affairs of the whole world. The practicability of it can be scarcely doubted. Various lines for the proposed Canal have been suggested and have divided public opinion. The evidence tending to shew the superiority of the advantages of that which would traverse the Province of Nicaragua seems to have nearly settled the question in favor of that route. Still on a project of such vast magnitude it is necessary to proceed with the greatest caution. A false step, taken in the first movement, might lead to the most mischevious [sic] consequences. The President has, therefore, determined to instruct the Chargé des Affaires of the United States, whom he has just appointed,[2] and who will shortly proceed upon his mission to the Republic of the Centre, to investigate, with the greatest care, the facilities which the route through the Province of Nicaragua offers, and to remit the information which he may acquire to the United States. Should it confirm the preference which it is believed that route possesses, it will then be necessary to consult Congress as to the nature and extent of the co-operation which shall be given towards the completion of the great work. The Chargé des Affaires of the United States will be specially directed to assure your Government of the deep interest which is taken by that of the United States in the execution of an undertaking which is so highly calculated to diffuse an extensive influence on the affairs of mankind; and to express to it also the acknowledgements which are justly due to the friendly overture of which you have been the organ.

I pray you to receive assurances of my highest and most respectful consideration.   H. CLAY.

Copy. DNA, RG59, Notes to Foreign Ministers and Consuls, vol. 3, pp. 215-16 (M38, R3). AL draft, in CSmH.

1 ALS. DNA, RG59, Notes from the Central American Legation, vol. 1 (M-T34, R1).

2 William Miller. See above, Clay to Miller, March 24, 1825, note; and below, Clay to Miller, April 22, 1825.

From Horace Holley

Dear Sir.   Transylvania University, April 18th, 1825.

I am much obliged to you for a copy of your address to your late constituents.[1] It appears to me to be able, frank, and satisfactory. Your immediate friends did not need such a communication to keep them from yielding to the calumnies, which were heaped upon you for the independent and magnanimous course that you pursued

in regard to the election of the President. The publication however will, I am convinced, do great good, or rather has done it already.
There is but one sentiment upon the subject in this vicinity, so
far as comments have reached my ears. All are satisfied with the
facts and the reasonings. I have no doubt that there are some among
us, who would be better pleased, if you had not defended yourself,
or if you had made your statement with less calmness, judgment,
and ability. This number cannot be great.

I have just read the correspondence between yourself and Mr
Eaton.[2] I am blinded, or it was weakness in him to publish it.
He has left the community to believe that he was concerned in
Kremer's conspiracy, even to a greater extent than might otherwise
have been supposed. He appears to begin with a demand for explanation, which is given only in reference to the first letter, and
ends the correspondence without obtaining any satisfaction upon
some of the most material points, and with new evidence fastened
upon him of connivance, and indeed of active exertions in the base
affair. I at first regretted to see Mr Eaton's name in your address,
but he has now shown himself worthy of reprobation from the
community.

We are at this moment somewhat excited by the course of an
Irishman in Lexington, William Bayley, a lawyer, who has purchased
the Monitor, and calls it the True American.[3] It is devoted zealously to Jackson, and probably will be hostile to the University,[4]
and defend the relief party.[5] Bayley is injudicious and rash. He has
had a quarrel with Edmiston;[6] another with John A Coyle;[7] and on
Saturday, at 7 o'clock in the afternoon, was assailed by Thomas
J Stevenson at Leavy's corner,[8] and stabbed him through the body
with a sword cane. Stevenson died on Sunday morning about 3
o'clock. Two magistrates were sitting all day yesterday upon the
case, and adjourned till to day. Bayley is in custody. It appears, by the
decision of the jury of inquest, that he killed Stevenson in self defence. We do not yet know the course, which the law will take.[9]
The Jacksonites sympathize with Bayley; and for the single act
of defending himself against Stevenson, we do not blame him much,
whatever may be our political feelings; but we have good reason
to keep him in coventry for his general misconduct. He is sprightly,
and will annoy us through our young men, though his first editorial
article shows no talent, and is not even English.

I am threatened with a political attack from the relief-party,
although I have always avoided all interference with the political
opinions of our students, and have taken no active part in our local
politics.[10] But I have expounded the Federalist, Vattel, and Say,[11]
as text books in our course of studies, and our leading men of the

dominant party have declared themselves dissatisfied with the principles taught to the young men. Mr Rowan has spoken against the University, and so has Mr Bibb.[12] Mr Barry[13] has not yet made any clear manifestations of histility [sic], but expresses regret that my friends have not been more faithful in warning me against any agency in politics. I shall wait calmly for the result in the next legislature, but shall maintain the course I have pursued, without either defying or fearing public opinion. I have aimed to be discreet on the subject of politics, while I claim the privileges of [. . .][14] man in common with my fellow citize[ns.]

Judge Bledsoe has resigned his prof[essorship] of law,[15] and talks considerably against the Trustees, and a little against myself. He is seeking a seat on the bench of the Court of Appeals,[16] and adapts his course to this end, possibly without knowing how far the end may influence his representations.

Your family are well, as are your friends in this place.

Very respectfully yours,   HORACE HOLLEY.

Hon: Henry Clay.

It is just reported, that Bayley is discharged, neither acquitted, nor committed for a future trial. The magistrates, two, J Bradford and E West,[17] divided in opinion.

ALS. DLC-HC (DNA, M212, R1).   1 Above, March 26, 1825.
2 See above, March 28, 30, 31, April 1, 2, 1825.
3 Bayley, who had very recently come from Philadelphia, changed the name of the Lexington *Western Monitor* to the *True American and Western Monitor*.
4 Transylvania University.   5 See above, III, 146n.
6 Probably Joseph W. Edmiston.   7 Not identified.
8 For about forty years William Leavy's store was located at the southwest corner of Main and Mill Streets, Lexington.
9 Stevenson had been employed by Bayley as printer; the encounter resulted "from circumstances which occurred in their relation of employer and employed." Lexington *Kentucky Gazette*, April 21, 1825.
10 For a fuller account of the criticism of Holley as president of Transylvania University, see Sonne, *Liberal Kentucky*, 250-54.
11 The major work of the French economist Jean Baptiste Say, *Traité d'Économie Politique* . . . , had appeared in 1803. A translation from the fourth edition had been published in Boston, in 1821, under the title, *A Treatise on Political Economy; or the Production, Distribution, and Consumption of Wealth* (2 vols.).
12 John Rowan; George M. Bibb—both prominently identified with the "relief" movement, Rowan having received the senatorial appointment in December, 1825.
13 William T. Barry.   14 MS. torn; one or two words missing.
15 Jesse Bledsoe had held this position since 1822.
16 He was not appointed to the position.
17 John Bradford; William (not Edward) West. Lexington *Kentucky Gazette*, April 21, 1825.

INSTRUCTIONS AND DISPATCHES   April 18, 1825

To JOSHUA BOND, "Consul U. S.   Montivideo [sic]." Encloses commission, printed instructions, and blank bond. Copy. DNA, RG59, Cons. Instr., vol. 2, p. 352 (M78, R2). The appointment of Bond, a resident of Maryland, had been approved February 16.

To DANIEL W. SMITH, "Consul U. S. Refugio [Mexico]." Similar in content to the preceding document. Copy. *Ibid.,* pp. 351-52. The appointment of Smith, a resident of Connecticut, had been approved February 11. He remained at this post until 1832, when he was transferred to Matamoras.

From JAMES MAURY, Liverpool. Notes a startling rise in the demand for cotton but an expectation that Egyptian cotton, the production of which is rapidly increasing, will soon become a formidable competitor to that of the United States in this market. LS. DNA, RG59, Cons. Disp., Liverpool, vol. 3 (M141, R-T3). Cultivation of long staple cotton, famous for its strength, elasticity, and twist, had been begun on Egyptian delta lands around 1822. The introduction of steam pumps, which permitted irrigation of the basin areas of Upper Egypt, also contributed to the agricultural development of the country in this period.

MISCELLANEOUS LETTERS   April 18, 1825

From ROBERT MCCLINTOCK, New York. Asks whether the Government would have any objection to the establishment at New York of a branch of the Alliance Insurance Office of London. ALS. DNA, RG59, Misc. Letters (M179, R62). See below, Ogden to Clay, this date.

From DAVID B. OGDEN, New York. Introduces Robert McClintock, a "merchant of great respectability in this city." ALS. DNA, RG59, Misc. Letters (M179, R62). Ogden had been graduated from the University of Pennsylvania in 1792, had studied law, and had begun practice in Newark, New Jersey. In 1803 he moved to New York City, where he became a highly successful lawyer, noted for his participation in numerous cases before the United States Supreme Court. Prominent in local politics as a Federalist and, later, a Whig, he held no higher office than membership in the State assembly in 1814 and 1838 and surrogate of New York County, 1840-1844.

APPLICATIONS, RECOMMENDATIONS   April 18, 1825

DAVID DAGGETT, New Haven, solicits appointment as Federal district judge in Connecticut. "Confidential." ALS. DNA, RG59, A. and R. (MR2). Cf. above, III, 437n.

JOHN EVERETT, Boston, solicits appointment as Secretary of Legation at Madrid, where his brother, Alexander H. Everett, is United States Minister. ALS. DNA, RG59, A. and R. (MR2). Cf. above, Clay to Smith, April 11, 1825; see below, Clay to Alexander H. Everett, April 26, 1825.

To Board of Navy Commissioners

19h. April 1825

Mr. Clay's Compliments to the Gentlemen of the Navy Board and he will be obliged to them to direct the payment to be made to him for the Ton of Hemp, made from the article in its unretted state, which he delivered to the use of the Navy last Autumn.[1]

AN. DNA, RG45, Navy Commissioners' Misc. Letters Received. Endorsed: "Recd 19. april."   [1] See above, III, 830, 844.

To J. Morrie and Others

Gent.   Washn. 19h. Apl. 1825.

Prior to the receipt of your letter of the 26 March[1] I had suggested to the President and to the Secy of War[2] most of the views contained in the memorial, of which a copy accompanied your letter. In extending the road from Wheeling,[3] it is proposed to let it out in sections of two miles so as to invite the greatest degree of competition, prevent speculation, and accommodate the poorer classes. It is intended to execute the road after the method of McAdams.[4] The appropriation of the last Session[5] will probably complete about thirty miles. I had wished the road to begin simultaneously at the point opposite to Wheeling and at Zanesville, but some difficulty would exist in the superintendance [sic] at points so distant. If, as I trust, an appropriation, at the next Session, shall be made to continue the work,[6] as there will then remain only about 50 miles to carry it to Zanesville the objection to going on with it, at the same time, from the opposite points, will be diminished, and I hope your wishes, in that respect may be gratified.after the next Session.

You are perfectly right in supposing that I take the most lively interest in this truly National Undertaking.

MESS. J MORRIE	JNO HAMM
SAML HERRICK	JAMES HAMPSON &
W SILLIMAN	APPLETON DONNER[7]

AL (signature removed). OClWHi. Name of addressee not clear with respect to the initial and final letter. Cf. below, Brent (Clay) to Dunlevy and Morris, August 25, 1825, note.   [1] Not found; date not clear.
[2] John Quincy Adams; James Barbour.   [3] The Cumberland Road.
[4] John Loudon McAdam, of Scotland, developer of macadamized roads.
[5] See above, Speech, January 17, 1825, notes.
[6] The act for completing the road to Zanesville, appropriating $175,000 for the purpose, was not passed until May 19, 1828. 4 *U. S. Stat.*, 275.
[7] All, except Morrie, identified as residents of Muskingum County, Ohio. Hamm, who had been a surgeon of infantry during the War of 1812, had held office as marshal for the District of Ohio from 1813 to 1822 and later (1830-1833) served as United States Chargé d'Affaires in Chile.

To [Joseph Vance]

Dear General.   Washn. 19h. Apl. 1825

I thank you for your friendly letter of the 7h. inst.[1] The information which it communicates is very gratifying, and accords with what I receive from all quarters. Our Country will do justice to the purity of our intentions to serve her in the late Presidential question.

Your friend Baldwin[2] has been provided for as you wished—at least the Secy of War[3] so promised me, and I presume his appointment has been notified to him.

I do not find my new office a bed of roses. I work from 12 to 14 hours per day, which I should not care for, if my health would bear it. The Western air which I hope shortly to breathe, and the Mountains' jostle which will intervene will put me to rights in that respect.

We go on perfectly well here, harmoniously, and all sincerely anxious to merit the public approbation.

Yr faithful friend   H. CLAY

ALS. ViU.   1 Not found.
2 Jonah Baldwin. See above, Vance to Clay, March 9, 1825.
3 James Barbour.

From William Bainbridge

Sir   Navy Commissioners Office 19th April 1825

The Commissioners of the Navy have had the honor of receiving your note of this morning.—until they received it, they had presumed that the Navy Agent at Baltimore had paid for the hemp, agreeably to the instructions sent to him, copy of which is enclosed[1]— payment will be made to your order in Baltimore; or if more agreeable to you, the Commissioners will direct the Navy Agent at Baltimore to send the account on to this place, and the payment can be made here.   I have the honor to be &c &c

Honorable H. Clay   WM. BAINBRIDGE

Copy. DNA, RG45, Navy Commissioners' Misc. Letters Sent, vol. 3, p. 396.
1 Instructions to James Beatty not found.

DIPLOMATIC NOTES   April 19, 1825

From the BARON DE TUYLL, Washington, "Confidential." Suggests that Clay consult the owners of the *Pearl* before transmitting an "official note" regarding the "arrangement verbally agreed upon in the conference of yesterday." N. DNA, RG59, Notes from Russian Legation, vol. 1 (M39, R1).

To the BARON DE TUYLL. States, in answer to Tuyll's note of this day, "that he (Mr. Clay) considers himself fully authorized by the owners of the Pearl to make the arrangement which was yesterday verbally agreed upon," that he sees no need to consult them again "before the proposed exchange of official notes," that he "has prepared an official note, which he now transmits to the Baron, for his examination and . . . suggestions . . . , prior to its formal delivery." Should the Baron still "think it desirable to consult the owners of the Pearl, previous to the exchange of the official notes, Mr. Clay will yield with pleasure to his wishes in that respect." Copy. DNA, RG59, Notes to Foreign Ministers and Consuls, vol. 3, p. 216 (M38, R3). AN draft, in CSmH. Cf. above, Sturgis to Clay, April 11, 1825.

To the BARON DE TUYLL. States Clay's understanding, as developed from conferences with Tuyll "on the affair of the claim of the Brig Pearl, . . . that His Imperial Majesty . . . has determined to order compensation to be made for the loss referred to." The loss suffered from the voyage, after the brig had been turned back from the northwest coast and, with its cargo, sold in the Sandwich Islands, amounted to $16,994.69. The alternative "standards of compensation" are summarized: (1) payment of a sum equal to the profits that might have been made from an uninterrupted voyage, double the loss sustained, "viz, $33,989.38 with interest"; (2) replacement of the sum lost, $16,994.69, with interest from January, 1822; or (3) "restoration of the capital without interest or other charges by the payment simply of a sum equal to $16,994.69." Though the owners probably prefer the first alternative and "The second corresponds better with what would seem to be proper," the Government of the United States will consider Russia's acceptance of the third "as terminating the present transaction in a manner entirely satisfactory." Copy. DNA, RG59, Notes to Foreign Ministers and Consuls, vol. 3, pp. 217-18 (M38, R3). AL draft, in CSmH; published in Miller (ed.), *Treaties . . .*, III, 201-202. See above, Clay to Tuyll, March 25, 1825.

INSTRUCTIONS AND DISPATCHES   April 19, 1825

From RICHARD RUSH, London, no. 432. Transmits copy of (George) Canning's answer to Rush's "notes respecting the historical documents of Georgia"; reports the British Government's willingness to permit "any respectable person whom the minister of the United states at this court may name, to inspect the proper archives of the British government and to make such transcripts from them as may be required for the purpose in view"; but explains that, since Rush is not authorized to incur the expense of hiring such a copyist, he can take no further action at this time. ALS. DNA, RG59, Dip. Disp., Great Britain, vol. 32 (M30, R28). Received June 25. Published in *House Reports*, 19 Cong., 2 Sess., no. 91, p. 6. See above, Rush to Secretary of State, March 16, April 11, 1825.

MISCELLANEOUS LETTERS   April 19, 1825

From WILLIAM KELLY, "Brown's Hotel." States that suit has been brought by John Smith, of Missouri Territory, in the United States District Court at Huntsville (Alabama) "against Lewis Dillahunty & others, Tenants in possession to try his title to the lands they claim under the U. S.—[and that] Smith claims under Zachariah Cox one of the Grantees., [*sic*] of the Tennessee company, under the state of Georgia—" As attorney for Smith, Kelly gives notice that trial is set for "the next July Term," with the intention of bringing the matter before the Supreme Court for final decision. He takes this action in the light of a letter from the defendants to Clay's predecessor, written "sometime last winter, notifying him that they were sued, & requesting, to be defended, by the United States. . . ." Requests acknowledgment of this notification. ALS. DNA, RG59, Misc. Letters (M179, R62). See below, Clay to Wirt, June 21, 1826; Wirt to Clay, June 24, 1826.

As a Federal case, the suit has not been found; it continued in the State courts of Mississippi for another twenty years. See Smith *vs.* Dillahunty, 8 *Miss. Reports* (7 Howard) 673 (1843). The dispute grew out of the claims of the Tennessee Company, of which Cox was one of the partners, relating to lands in northern Alabama, purchased from the State of Georgia under legislation of February 7, 1795, authorizing sale of the Yazoo holdings. The Legislature of Georgia having repealed this act the following year, the territory had been subsequently conveyed to the Federal Government and claimants under the Georgia law, after much litigation, had been compensated in non-interest-bearing stock certificates, redeemable from the proceeds of public land sale in Mississippi Territory, claimants under the Tennessee Company having been assigned $600,000 for their interest. 2 *U. S. Stat.*, 229-30 (March 3, 1803); 3 *U. S. Stat.*, 116-20 (March 31, 1814), 192-93 (January 23, 1815), 235-37 (March 3, 1815), 294-95 (April 20, 1816).

From STEPHEN PLEASONTON, Treasury Department, by Thomas Mustin. Encloses an agreement between William R. Higinbotham, United States commercial agent at Bermuda, and a Bermudan ship captain, "by which the latter engages to transport to the said States eleven destitute American seamen" at a charge of $25 per man; calls attention to the act of 1803 (2 *U. S. Stat.*, 204, approved February 28, 1803), fixing the sum of $10 as compensation for this service, and to instructions issued by the Secretary of State shortly afterward, authorizing payment, under certain circumstances, of larger sums; and submits the question whether the sum in this instance "be a reasonable charge or not." ALS by Mustin. DNA, RG59, Misc. Letters (M179, R62). Mustin, of Virginia, was chief clerk to the 5th Auditor.

In a letter addressed to Mustin on April 21, Daniel Brent, at the direction of the Secretary of State, approved the larger payment. Copy. DNA, RG59, Dom. Letters, vol. 21, p. 40 (M40, R19).

From William Bainbridge

Sir   20th April 1825

The Commissioners of the Navy have directed Commre. Tingey[1] to prepare an account of the hemp belonging to you, and delivered at the Yard under his command, for payment—allowing $170. per ton— the Government paying the freight from Baltimore to Washington.   I have the honor to be &c

Honorable Henry Clay.   WM. BAINBRIDGE

Copy. DNA, RG45, Navy Commissioners' Misc. Letters Sent, vol. 3, p. 397. See above, Clay to Board of Navy Commissioners, April 19, 1825; Bainbridge to Clay, April 19, 1825.

[1] Thomas Tingey, a native of England, had served in the navy and merchant service of both Britain and the United States. He had laid out the Washington Navy Yard, which he commanded, except for one brief interval, from its founding in 1800 until his death in 1829.

From Thomas B. Robertson

Dear Sir   Havana 20 April 1825

Mr Vincent Gray of this place has requested me to say that he would be well pleased to fill the office now held by Mr Warner[1] in the event of its becoming vacant. Mr Gray is doubtless known to the Govt   he acted as consul here some years ago and his pretensions can be properly appreciated without any remarks of mine but I should do violence to my feelings and injustice to him were I to withhold my good opinion of his zeal & patriotism as an American and his kindness and attention to his fellow Citizens visiting this Island either for recreation or business

I left New Orleans about six weeks ago on account of bad health and have since that time been in Matanzas and the neighbouring country— But situated as you are now I will not detain you with a discription [sic] of Cuba its soil climate productions &ca, but content myself with saying that in these respects it excels any country on Earth—probably you may be better satisfied with my views of its political situation—and these, crude and indigested [sic] as they certainly are, you shall have, concisely.

The situation of the Island then, is considered as Extremely critical— this is the remark of every one who speaks on the subject— Americans, Europeans & creoles all say that, the present state of things cannot last long. that their commercial & agricultural prosperity is not only destroyed, but their personal safety Endangered. Now that Bolivar is successful and released from further exertions in favor of Peru,[2] they look forward, some with joy, & others with fear, to an invasion of the Island. The foreigners who hold the offices, and constitute the Army, Navy & diciplined [sic] Militia, as well as a great portion of the talent & wealth which exist here, are opposed, not only to a connexion with south America, but to Independence itself. They say that the hostility which is manifested in Columbia [sic] and Mexico against Europeans, renders a union with them impossible; and that the same sentiment, felt to as great an extent by the creoles here, equally forbids an acquiescence on their part in an Independent Government—that an attempt to establish either, will be attended with dreadful consequences, and that there [sic] mutual hatred is such, there is reason to apprehend the unsuccessful party might call in the aid of the free people of colour— indeed of the slaves themselves— — they see then their escape from Civil commotion, in the continuation of Spanish protection—in the usurpation of the sovereign power by their present Governor—or in the protection of the U States or England—all these views have their partisans— among the foreigners, the first is the most popular, and the only difficulty it encounters arises out of the war Existing between Spain & south America; to do away this, under much alarm and terror of the consequences, they have sent to their king a memorial, setting forth the grievances of the Island—the danger of its being lost to him Entirely—and urging the recognition of the Independence of his former provinces that peace may be established & their commerce set free from its trammels. The interference of the U States or of England would be wished for only under the most desperate circumstances— But a despotism, with their present Governor at its head, if possessed of a respectable force, would be well supported by the foreigners & the priests. The Creoles wish for freedom and independence, and would join with alacrity, any standard under which, they might hope to establish and Enjoy these blessings. They count upon the aid of their bretheren [sic] of the continent, to assist in putting an end to European sway in this her last important strong hold in America. In no part of the world has she ever exercised a more poisinous [sic] influence—no where on Earth is reformation more necessary— a good & simple people are ruled by lazy, ignorant, & cunning priests—who keep them in a wholesome state of stupidity crush the first approaches of intellectual improvement, and instil [sic] into their minds, struggling to be free, prejudices against other nations & other institutions—endeavouring to make them view like the Romans of old, a stranger as an enemy— Schools except for a few *soi disant* in the Cities are no where to be found, and bridges & roads, where they exist at all, are whoely [sic] neglected. But I hear your old cry, *Order, the Gentleman will confine himself to the Question*

The Slave trade is in the full tide of successful operation. 5000 Africans have been introduced into the Island since the 1 January, and 20000 more are expected in all the year. The vessels are sent out from this port, and our own countrymen have a full share of interest in them—indeed I have heard that an agent of the govt. has been engaged in the business.

The political, as well as commercial interests of the U States here, are of no common importance; they ought to be confided to men of talents & character. The people ought to be taught to look upon us with respect, but this cannot be the case, whilst, we are represented by drunkards, Bankrupts, and violators of our own laws & principles

You have no doubt heard of the late Capture of pirates by Capt Mc Keever[3]— they have arrived here, and here in all probability, nothing will be done with them. Every body regrets that they were not sent, not to the U States, where they would be acquitted or if found guilty, pardoned, but to Jamaica. Mr Munroe[4] is much censured for his false & fatal humanity, and surely nothing can be considered as more unfortunate than the course, which in this respect, he has thought proper to persue [sic]. Country people, coming into Matanzas from the neighbourhood of the late Capture, State that 14 human skeletons, tied by their fleshless arms to trees, have been found in the adjacent forest. It is estimated here that the blood of a thousand of our fellow Citizens has been shed by these monsters— protected by the cold sophistry of a Tazewell,[5] and encouraged by the forbearance of the ex-president.

At this time but few piratical vessels venture out to sea. they have been deterred by our cruisers,[6] and those of Columbia & England—

but they yet infest the bays & shores in great numbers—sallying forth, & seizing on unarmed ships which may, unfortunately, pass too near their haunts— Should they be overhalled [*sic*] and examined, they produce a licence, and are let off as drogers engaged in the coasting trade of the Island. now the U States, should put a stop to the dangers growing out of this trade, by coercing the local authorities to take sufficient security of the Drogers that the trade shall not be abused—by insisting that it shall in future be carried on only in large vessels, say 200 tons & upwards. and should these experiments fail of producing the desired effect—let it be strictly & entirely inhibitted [*sic*]. It is the coasting trade, which furnishes all the facilities for that description of piracy, which may be considered if not the most dangerous, the most difficult to destroy.

I forgot to state in its proper place, that it would seem the French Monarch[7] has a recognised Consul in this City—at least so I infer from the *Guia de Forastoros* published *con permisso. Habana: oficiaro del Gobierno y Capitano general y de la R. S. P por S.M.*— where he is thus noticed. "Consul de S M Cristianisima residente en Esta Siempre fidelisima Ciudad. El Señor don Sant Iago Maria Angeluce, cabellero de la legion de Honor, consul de S M Cristianisima"[8]

The English too have an agent, whose talents manners & style of living, give him much influence & consideration— He is here ostensibly under an agreement concerning the Slave trade—but really, to take advantage of circumstances and to keep the govt well apprised of passing events

Of home politics I know but little, having been in the country where I saw no papers. Since my return I have seen the presidents message,[9] and a list of the heads of department— I congratulate you on your appointment, and so far as I understand it, am well pleased with the course you have pursued— My health is, I think reestablished and I take passage on saturday next for New Orleans

I am Dr Sir with much respect & friendship Yr ob St
Honorable Mr Clay   TH B ROBERTSON

ALS. DNA, RG59, A. and R. (MR1). Endorsed on cover: "forwarded by Yr mo. Ob Servt—V, Gray."   1 John Warner.
2 See above, Clay to Poinsett, March 26, 1825.
3 A force under Lieutenant Isaac McKeever, of Pennsylvania, commander of the United States sea galliot *Sea Gull*, with aid from the British frigate *Dartmouth*, had captured a pirate schooner off Matanzas on March 25. Five pirates were reported killed and nineteen taken prisoner. The officers of the *Sea Gull* reported finding the bodies of the victims as noted below in this paragraph. *Niles' Weekly Register*, XXVIII (April 28, 1825), 118.
4 James Monroe, whose use of his power of pardon to release condemned pirates, notably, as one of his last acts, in the case of seven convicted at Savannah, was much criticized. *Ibid.*
5 Littleton W. Tazewell, who had led opposition in the Senate to the proposed bill to combat piracy. See above, Nelson to Clay, April 6, 1825, note.

6 See above, III, 338n; Nelson to Clay, April 6, 1825.
7 Charles X.   8 Not further identified.
9 The inaugural address of John Quincy Adams.

INSTRUCTIONS AND DISPATCHES   April 20, 1825

From CHARLES MACNEAL, acting consul, "Carthagena de Colombia." Reports the
arrival in January of Henry H. Williams, a citizen of the United States, who
requested MacNeal's help in recovering a vessel that had been brought into
port by a Colombian privateer; MacNeal's subsequent withdrawal from this
agency when he discovered that the vessel was "fitted out for the slave trade";
his request, under instructions issued to consuls in 1803, that the Intendant
"prevent the departure of [John] Goldwaith her commander" and Williams;
his later request for release of Williams, for want of evidence; and the escape
of Goldwaith, when mistakenly released. MacNeal seeks reimbursement for the
commission lost by his withdrawal from the agency. ALS. DNA, RG59, Cons.
Disp., Cartagena, vol. 1 (M-T192, R1). Addressed to Secretary of State; received May 20. MacNeal, Williams, and Goldwaith not further identified.

MISCELLANEOUS LETTERS   April 20, 1825

To PETER A. BROWNE. States that the Attorney General has upheld the stand
of Dr. [William] Thornton in the controversy between the Patent Office and
the Franklin Institute and adds: "In considering the subject of those communications I trust that you will do me the justice to believe that I have been
actuated by a sincere desire to afford to the patriotic objects of the Franklin
Institute every aid and facility in my power—" Copy. DNA, RG59, Dom.
Letters, vol. 21, pp. 37-38 (M40, R19). See above, Wirt to Clay, *ca.* April 16, 1825.

To WILLIAM STURGIS. States terms of settlement, as arranged between Clay
and the Baron Tuyll, in the case of the *Pearl.* Copy. DNA, RG59, Dom. Letters,
vol. 21, pp. 36-37 (M40, R19). See above, Clay to Tuyll, April 19, 1825; below,
Tuyll to Clay, April 22, 1825. On April 25, Daniel Brent, "by direction of the
Secretary," transmitted a "copy of a communication . . . just made to Mr.
Middleton [below, April 25, 1825], . . . concerning the provisional arrangement
which he has concluded with Baron de Tuyll. . . ." Copy. DNA, RG59, Dom.
Letters, vol. 21, p. 44 (M40, R19).

From A[LEXANDER] H. EVERETT, Boston. Requests that (John A.) Smith not
be appointed Secretary of Legation in Spain—"Mr. Smith is more advanced in
age than I am & we have been in habits of private intercourse upon the footing
of an equality of station in the diplomatic services." Suggests that, in view of
(Richard) Rush's departure from London, Smith might remain there and that
(John J.) Appleton, instead of appointment as Secretary of Legation in London,
deserves promotion to a higher rank. Recommends Everett's brother, John, as
Secretary of Legation in Madrid. ALS. DNA, RG59, Dip. Disp., Spain, vol.
25 (M31, R27). Received April 25.

From S[AMUEL] L. S[OUTHARD], Navy Department. Encloses a copy of a letter
from Captain Lewis Warrington, commander of the United States naval
squadron in the West Indies, transmitting correspondence about two American
seamen. LS. DNA, RG59, Misc. Letters (M179, R62). The enclosed correspondence
relates to the case of two deserters from an American merchant vessel in Havana

Harbor, who had taken refuge on board the British frigate *Hussar*. Captain John Gallagher, of the United States schooner *Shark*, had demanded that the men be released to him; and, after brief delay, Captain George Harris of the *Hussar* had complied with the request.

APPLICATIONS, RECOMMENDATIONS   April 20, 1825

P[HILEMON] BEECHER, Lancaster (Ohio), recommends James Pindall for appointment as "District Judge for the Western District in Virginia—" ALS. DNA, RG59, A. and R. (MR1). See above, Jackson to Clay, April 12, 1825, note.

To Nathaniel Silsbee

Mr. Nathanl. Silsbee   Salem, MS.   Washington 21 April 1825.
My Dear Sir,

I have received your Letter of the 7th., and also that of the 14th. instant, with its Enclosures, respecting Mr. Jeremy Robinson, and I am greatly obliged by your prompt and friendly attention to my request.— The President nominated Mr. Robinson, as consul of Rio Janeiro, under a belief that he was a Native of Virginia, with no knowledge of the fact of his being born in Massachusetts, nor of his character being such as it appears to be. I will thank you to make this explanation to Messrs. Peel, Andrew [*sic*] and Nichols and Peirce,[1] as being due to the President. In this state of things what shall be now done with Mr. Robinson's appointment is under consideration.[2] Would those Gentlemen have any objection to a disclosure of their names, and of the transactions to which they refer, if circumstances should seem to render it proper? I am, respectfully your friend & humble Servant,   H. CLAY.—

Copy. DNA, RG59, Unofficial Letter-Book of Henry Clay, 1-2.
[1] Willard Peele; probably John Andrews, George Nichols, and either Jerathmiel Peirce or his son, Benjamin, all Salem merchants.
[2] A commission, "ready to be delivered to" Robinson, "was withheld in consequence of remonstrances . . . charging him with misconduct in trusts committed to him. . . ." Though informed that he would be given no office "until those transactions should be satisfactorily explained," he gave no "satisfactory explanation." Adams, *Memoirs*, VII, 524.

DIPLOMATIC NOTES   April 21, 1825

From the BARON DE TUYLL, Washington. Transmits "the minute of his intended answer to Mr. Clay's official note of the 19th. inst: requesting the Hon. Secretary of State to examine this paper at his leisure." The Baron is "particularly desirous" that the document "fully correspond with Mr. Clay's views of the subject to which it relates." N. DNA, RG59, Notes from Russian Legation, vol. 1 (M39, R1). Endorsed by clerk on wrapper: " (Confidential) . . . . Case of the Pearl."

To the BARON DE TUYLL. Acknowledges receipt of his note of this date; comments that no change in the enclosed "minute" appears necessary. Copy. DNA,

RG59, Notes to Foreign Ministers and Consuls, vol. 3, p. 218 (M38, R3). AN draft, in CSmH.

INSTRUCTIONS AND DISPATCHES   April 21, 1825

From CHRISTOPHER HUGHES, Stockholm, no. 11. Transmits copy of the Count de Wetterstedt's dispatch to the Swedish Minister at St. Petersburg concerning British recognition of the South American States and remarks: "I am disposed to believe, that you will approve of the Tone & Spirit, in which Count Wetterstedts despatch is conceived." ALS. DNA, RG59, Dip. Disp., Sweden and Norway, vol. 4 (M45, R5). See above, Hughes to Clay, April 7, 1825; Middleton to Clay, April 13, 1825.

From HENRY MIDDLETON, St. Petersburg, no. 46. Mentions a secret conference of the four Continental Powers which is supposed to have concerned "the affairs of Turkey & Greece," especially "a joint effort . . . to introduce the monarchical principle into the revolutionized Countries of Greece"; forwards a copy of the treaty concluded last year between Sardinia and Turkey; and reports the calling together of a Diet at Warsaw, from May 13 to June 13, under a new article, restricting publicity of debate, under the Constitutional Charter of Poland. ALS. DNA, RG59, Dip. Disp., Russia, vol. 10 (M35, R10). Addressed to Secretary of State; registered September 21.

A conference, called in January, 1824, by Emperor Alexander I, of Russia, to which George Canning had declined British representation, had brought together ministers of Austria, Prussia, Russia, and France in negotiations at St. Petersburg extending from February to May, 1825, to effect settlement of the conflict between Turkey and the Greek revolutionists (see above, III, 87n). On March 13, they had resolved to present a joint note to Turkey, offering mediation. Emperor Alexander had hoped that the conference would endorse the division of Greece into three separate principalities under Russian hegemony. Metternich had countered this proposal by suggesting that the pressure for Turkish concessions be supported by a threat to recognize Greek independence. On April 7, Turkey rejected the proposed mediation. The friction among the Continental Powers, manifest during the ensuing summer in their failure to reach agreement upon a course of action, led to the disruption of the alliance.

The treaty of commerce between Sardinia and Turkey, signed at Constantinople, October 25, 1823, was designed "for giving a public guarantee to the Maritime Commerce of both, and for throwing open the navigation of the Black Sea to the Royal [Sardinian] Flag. . . ." For the terms, see [Great Britain] Foreign Office (comp.), *British and Foreign State Papers, 1824-1825* (London, 1826), pp. 961-24. Ratifications had been exchanged on April 27, 1824.

The Polish Constitution, signed by Alexander I on November 27, 1815, had been notable for its liberality; but the Emperor's experience with two previous Diets, in 1818 and 1822, had induced him to accompany his proclamation convoking the third assemblage with a separate edict, dated February 13, 1825, which had provided that only the opening and closing sessions and those in which royal sanction was declared for projected laws should be public.

MISCELLANEOUS LETTERS   April 21, 1825

From S[AMUEL] L. S[OUTHARD], Navy Department. Transmits extract of a letter from Captain Thomas Macdonough, regarding "the reception given to Mr.

Coxe, Consul of the United States, at Tunis." ALS. DNA, RG59, Misc. Letters
(M179, R62). The enclosure, dated January 8, 1825, states that Coxe had been
well received despite reports that he would not be accepted because of "the prejudice of the Bey against his character." Macdonough now commanded the frigate
Constitution in the Mediterranean. Charles D. Coxe, originally of Pennsylvania
but at this time identified as a resident of New Jersey, had served previously
as commercial agent at Dunkirk and, in January, 1824, had been appointed
consul at Tunis. He was transferred as consul to Tripoli, by interim appointment (see below, Clay to Coxe, November 9, 1825), which was confirmed
December 19, 1825, and remained in this last position until his death in 1830.

To William Miller

No. 1. William Miller, appointed Chargé d'Affaires of the United
States to the United Provinces of the Centre of America
Sir,   Department of State   Washington 22. April 1825
The President having, by and with the advice and consent of the
Senate, appointed you Chargé d'Affaires to the Government of the
Federal States of the Centre of America, I have the honour to
transmit, herewith, your Commission, and also a Letter of credence[1]
which you will present to the Minister of Foreign Affairs, at your
first interview with him.

The Republic of Guatimala [*sic*] is of more recent formation
than those, the Independence of which was recognized by the
Government of the United States, in March 1822. But there are
circumstances in its origin and subsequent conduct, which give it
a claim to the interest and regard of the United States, perhaps
even superior to that which they have ever felt in any of the other
Southern Republics.

The Province of St. Salvador, one of the Constituent States of
the Republic of Guatimala, by a solemn Decree of its Congress,
freely chosen by the people, did, on the 5th. day of December,
1822, propose its annexation to our own Union, as one of these
United States.[2] This measure was adopted as an expedient for
escaping from the oppression with which they were menaced, of
being annexed, by force, to the Mexican Empire, while under the
Government of Yturbide. For the purpose of carrying it into
effect, three Commissioners were despached [*sic*], with full powers,
who came to the United States, and, in the beginning of September,
1823, repaired to the City of Washington. In the interval between
the time of their appointment and that of their arrival, here, a
Revolution in Mexico had overthrown the Government of Yturbide,[3]
and the Republican Rulers who succeeded to his power, acknowledged the right of the people of Guatimala to institute a Government
for themselves, and withdrew all claim of supremacy over them.
This course of events superseded the determination which the

Congress of St. Salvador had formed, of offering to unite their
fortunes with our Confederation, but in announcing this new
direction given to their affairs, the Commissioners Mess'rs Manuel
J. Arce, and Juan M. Rodriguez declared that the people, their
constituents, were animated with the sincerest sentiments of attachment to the Government of the United States; that there was a
great similitude of principles between them and the people of this
Union, and that, in every emergency, which might befal [sic] them,
they would place great reliance upon our friendship to support
them against the oppression of Tyranny.[4]

Whatever obstacle there might have been in physical relations,
or in the Constitutional arrangements of our own Government, to
the proposed Union, the proposal itself, and the spirit in which
it was made, were eminently adapted to inspire the warmest
sentiments of regard and attachment towards a foreign People,
speaking a different language, who thus confided in our honour
and justice, and thus gave, in the face of all mankind, the most
glorious of testimonials to the wisdom of our Institutions, and to
their sense of their tendency to promote the happiness of those
who live under them.

On the 8th. of February last, Mr. Cañaz, the Minister of the
Republic of the Centre, addressed a Note to this Department,
which affords a new, and highly interesting proof of the friendly
sentiments entertained by his Government towards the United
States. In that Note, after calling the attention of this Government
to the important object of uniting the Atlantic and Pacific Oceans
by a Canal Navigation, through the province of Nicarauguay [sic],
by the direction of his Government, he offers to that of the United
States to share in that great enterprize, and, by means of a Treaty,
perpetually to secure the advantages of it to the two Nations. To
that Note, an answer was transmitted on the   day of this month,[5]
and copies of them, both, accompany these instructions. From the
perusal of the answer, without declining the friendly proposal,
you will perceive that a decision upon it is postponed to the acquisition of further information; and you are desired to direct your
attention particularly to that object. It will, at once, occur to you
to ascertain if surveys have been made of the proposed rout [sic] of
the Canal, and if entire confidence may be placed in their accuracy;—
what is its length; what the nature of the Country, and of the
ground through which it is to pass;—can the supply of water for
feeders be drawn from the Lake Nicarauguay or other adequate
sources;—in short, what facilities do the Country and the state of
its population afford, for making the Canal, and what are the
estimates of its cost? It is not intended that you should inspire the
Government of the Republic of Guatimala with any confident

expectation that the United States will contribute, by pecuniary or other means, to the execution of the work, because it is not yet known what view Congress might take of it. What the President desires is to be put in possession of such full information as will serve to guide the judgement of the Constituted Authorities of the United States in determining in regard to it, what belongs to their interests and duties.

The Republic of the Centre of America being situated precisely at the Isthmus which forms the connexion between the two American Continents, and at the seat of Commerce carried on by the Bay of Honduras and the Musquito Shore, between the Gulph of Mexico, and the Southern Ocean, here drawn in their closest proximity to each other, the relations both political and commercial, between that Country and the United States, must acquire, from year to year, magnitude and importance. But of all the Countries of the Southern Continent, it is that with which we have hitherto had the fewest relations, and concerning which we have the least information. To obtain that information is one of the objects of your Mission, as well as to give proof to the worthy Republicans of those regions that the Government of the United States has felt, with great sensibility, the signal marks of confidence and friendship already received from them.

It will be a leading and constant object of your attention, then, to obtain, and to communicate to this Department, by every opportunity of conveyance, that may occur, information, as well respecting the physical condition of the Country, as the moral and political character of the inhabitants. The Geographical boundaries of the Republic, its standing with the neighbouring Countries of Mexico, Colombia and Peru; the present state of its Government; its prospect of forming a permanent Republican Constitution; and the State of its relations with European Powers will all form important subjects of enquiry. You will, especially, observe the Country, with reference to its future capabilities of a Commerce, mutually advantageous, with the United States, and communicate the result of your observations. You will avail yourself of every occasion to impress the Government of the Republic of Guatimala with the friendly dispositions towards it, of that of the United States. You will answer, in the most frank and full manner, all enquiries from that Government, having for their object information as to the practical operation of our own, or any of our Institutions. And whatever is peculiar in their own habits, religious or civil, should be treated with great indulgence.

It is not anticipated that any foreign Powers will endeavour to obtain for their Commerce and Navigation, peculiar concessions;

or if they should, that they will meet with success from the Republic of Guatimala. If, however, there should be any such attempt, you will firmly resist it. The Government of the United States has never sought for their Commerce and Navigation any advantage from the Governments of South America, which they were not willing should be extended to all other Powers. All that we have desired is fair competition, and that, at least, we have every right confidently to expect.

In order to strengthen the connexions between the two Countries, it might be well to conclude a Treaty of Amity, Commerce and Navigation between them, upon the basis of equity and perfect reciprocity; and you are, accordingly, authorised to propose such a Treaty. The President would, however, prefer that the Negociations respecting it, and the conclusion of it, should take place at Washington; but if a strong desire be manifested to have them in Guatimala, he will yield to it; and in that case, upon receiving information from you, the necessary Power and Instructions will be transmitted to you.

In the mean time, and without waiting the result of any such negociation, you will call the attention of the Government of the Republic of the Centre, to the Act of Congress of the 7th. January 1824.[6] By the last section of that Act, it is provided "that, upon satisfactory evidence being given to the President of the United States, by the Government of any foreign Nation, that no discriminating duties of tonnage or impost are imposed or levied within the Ports of the said Nation, upon vessels wholly belonging to citizens of the United States, or upon merchandize the produce or manufacture thereof, imported in the same, the President is hereby authorised to issue his proclamation, declaring that the foreign discriminating duties of tonnage and impost within the United States, are, and shall be, suspended and discontinued, so far as respects the vessels of the said Nation, and the merchandize of its produce or manufacture imported into the United States in the same; the said suspension to take effect from the time of such notification being given to the President of the United States, and to continue so long as the reciprocal exemption of vessels belonging to citizens of the United States, and merchandize aforesaid thereon laden, shall be continued, and no longer." It is very likely that there does not exist, at present, any discriminating duties of tonnage or impost, against the vessels of the United States or their Cargoes, in the Ports of Guatimala. If that be the case, and its Government will furnish you with authentic and satisfactory evidence of it, the President will, upon the reception of it, issue the Proclamation which he is empowered, by that Act, to put forth. Should there exist, on the contrary, such a discrimination, in duties of tonnage and impost, unfavourable to the Navigation and Commerce of the United States, you will urge the abolition of it, and assure the Government of Guatimala that a corresponding measure will be promptly adopted by this Government, placing the vessels of the United States and Guatimala, and their cargoes, (being of the produce of the respective Countries,) upon the liberal footing of fair and equal competition   I am, with great respect, Sir, your very humble and obedient Servant.   H. CLAY.

Copy. DNA, RG59, Dip. Instr., vol. 10, pp. 285-89 (M77, R5). Extract published in Manning (arr.), *Diplomatic Correspondence . . . Latin-American Nations*, I, 239-41. Redated and, with two major changes, sent also to John Williams, February 10, 1826.

1 Cf. above, Clay to Miller, March 24, 1825. A copy of the letter of credence, dated April 27, is located in DNA, RG59, Ceremonial Communications, vol. 2, p. 17.

2 The acts of the General Congress of San Salvador, dated November 22 and December 2, 1822, and the proclamation of the President, José Matéas Delgado, dated December 5, 1822, which provided for this proposal of annexation, are published in Manning, *op. cit.*, II, 873-79. Delgado of St. Vincente, was the first President of this state and a prominent leader in its assertion of independence from Mexico. He was also active in promoting the establishment of a separate bishopric of San Salvador, of which he became the first incumbent.   3 See above, III, 575n.

4 Cf. Vicente Rocafuerte, the third of these agents, to John Quincy Adams, October 16, 1823, in Manning, *op. cit.*, II, 880. Rodriguez had been delegate from Cojutepeqc and Arce (Arza), St. Salvador, in the General Congress of 1822. Rocafuerte, a native of Guayaquil, educated in France, and intimately associated with the revolutionary leaders of Latin America, had served as their European agent on various occasions and was at this time known in the United States as a publicist who had opposed the pretensions of Itúrbide. Later this year he became Minister Plenipotentiary for Mexico to the Government of Hanover and in 1826 served as negotiator of a treaty of friendship, commerce, and navigation for Mexico with Great Britain. He was subsequently imprisoned for activity in opposing Bustamente. Returning to Guayaquil in 1833, he became the second President of the Republic of Ecuador (1835-1839). His last years were spent as diplomatic agent for that State in Peru, Bolivia, and Chile.

5 See above, Clay to Cañaz, April 18, 1825.

6 See above, Lorich to Clay, March 16, 1825, note.

To [John] Sloane

My dear Sir   Washn. 22d. April 1825
I have received the enclosed strange letter[1] from a lad entirely unknown to me. Wild as it is, it indicates genius. Altho' New Lisbon[2] is some distance East of you I have thought that you may possibly have some opportunity of enquiring into the situation of the youth, whom we may find worthy of being appointed a Midshipman, or a Cadet at W. point. If it should prove entirely convenient, I would thank you to make some enquiries about him.

I see Mr. Ingham, it is announced, is about to answer my address.[3] If he does not come off better than his associate Genl. Eaton,[4] he may as well remain quiet.

Can you refer me to any member who knew of the fact of his getting hold of the written apology which Kremer designed to make me, and putting it in his pocket, as stated in my address? I heard it from several, 'though I do not now recollect who they were.

If you have not written, had you now better not defer it until you see what Mr. Ingham has to say? Your faithful friend
The Honble. Mr. Sloane   H. CLAY

ALS. MH.   1 Not found.   2 Ohio; now Lisbon.
3 For Clay's Address, see above, March 26, 1825; on Ingham's reply, cf. below, Clay to Brooke, April 29, 1825, and note.
4 Cf. above, Clay to Brooke, April 6, 1825; Clay to Sloane, April 7, 1825.

From Robert A. Ewing

Dr Sir   City of Jefferson April 22nd 182[5]
Report says that one or two of the Commissioners appointed to view and mark a road[1] from the Westeren [sic] boundary of this State to the confines of Mexico, and for other purposes, have refused to except [sic]; if this be the fact and you can believe me capable of this charge, I should like to receive the appointment, and would therefore beg leave, to solicit your friendship in procuring me the same

Being aware that your pr[esent] Honourable situation places it very much in your power to have favours of this kind bestowed, I hope you will pardon this privilege I take in soliciting your friendly aid in procuring any appointment the duties of which may be to be performed in the western Country, which may become vacant, and which I capable [sic] of performing for none other would I except; That you may be somewhat capable of judging of my integrity, & capability, I will just state that you formerly were somewhat acquainted with my Father[2] & connections in Kentucky; and will [ref]er you to Robert P. Henry Esq, Francis [John]son Esqr. J. J. Critenden [sic], Esqr. Henry P. Brodmax [sic] Esqr. and Presley Edwards Esqr.;[3] My business is the practice of the Law which I have persued [sic] with a tolerable degree of success for several years both in Kentucky and this State; I have a young family and am quite poor wherefore I would ask the public patronage in any [th]ing, I am capable of, and at [t]hese times it is very plain that those who procure, by the well performance of any duties assigned them, a draw at the paps of the public treasury fares [sic] the best

Excuse my freedom & trespass on your time & pacience [sic], and belie[ve me] the warm advocate of your public [. . . .][4]   Your &C.
                                        ROBT. A. E[WING]

ALS. DNA, RG59, A. and R. (MR1). MS. torn. Writer's name endorsed on cover. Ewing, a native of Logan County, Kentucky, had studied law under John J. Crittenden and had moved to Missouri to practice his profession.

1 See above, Clay to Poinsett, March 26, 1825.
2 Robert, brother of Urbin and Young Ewing, had been born in Virginia and had settled in Logan County, Kentucky, sat in the Kentucky General Assembly, and served as an officer in the War of 1812.
3 Russellville, Kentucky, lawyer; later, a member of the State Senate; brother of Ninian Edwards.   4 One word missing.

DIPLOMATIC NOTES   April 22, 1825

From the BARON DE TUYLL, Washington. Acknowledges receipt of Clay's note of April 19; states that "considérant la proposition que vient de lui adresser Monsieur le Secrétaire d'Etat, comme conforme aux principes d'équité et de modération que les deux Gouvernemens ont en vue, [Tuyll] a l'honneur d'accepter cette proposition" and will promptly communicate the arrangement "dont on vient de convenir" to the Ministry of the Emperor, in the hope that it will receive the full approbation requisite to definitive conclusion of the affair. LS. DNA, RG59, Notes from Russian Legation, vol. 1 (M39, R1). Endorsed: "Recd 21 [sic]. April." Published in Miller (ed.), Treaties. . . , III, 202-204.

INSTRUCTIONS AND DISPATCHES   April 22, 1825

From JOHN M. FORBES, Buenos Aires, no. 18. Reports excitement resulting from "the personal approach of Bolivar to these Provinces," the "deadly hatred and jealousy towards Bolivar entertained by the leading men now in power here," and the re-election of Bustos as Governor of Cordoba. Comments that the territorial dispute with Brazil can be settled only "by the daily expected arrival and important negociation of Sir Charles Stuart."

Final paragraph, dated April 23, notes that a meeting of the Provincial Junta, held "last evening" to declare on the recent election, in which regular troops and English sailors "were marched to the polls and voted," was "of a very violent character" and failed to reach a decision. LS. DNA, RG59, Dip. Disp., Argentina, vol. 2 (M69, R3). Published in Espil (comp.), Once Años en Buenos Aires, 356-57. Addressed to Secretary of State; received July 13. Juan Bautista Bustos had served as Governor and Captain General of the Province of Cordoba from 1820. On Stuart's mission to Brazil, see above, Raguet to Secretary of State, March 11, 1825, note. His attempt to mediate also the territorial dispute between Brazil and LaPlata (above, Poinsett to Clay, March 26, 1825, note 3; below, Forbes to Secretary of State, May 2, 1825) was unsuccessful.

From W[ILLIAM] TUDOR, Lima, no. 27. Transmits a copy of a decree, dated April 17, concerning which Tudor has "represented" to (José María de) Pando that "much uneasiness & remonstrance" would arise, especially since it allows insufficient time in which to warn merchants of the United States not to engage in the commerce, hitherto permitted; sends, also, copies of correspondence "in the case of the most brutal & savage ill treatment of Captain [Samuel] Lombard of the Ship Minerva of New Bedford," whose vessel in September, 1824, had been pressed into the service of Colombia to transport troops to Peru and who, himself, had been violently assaulted by a Captain Buchard, "a frenchman by nation." Although Bolívar had expressed to Tudor a wish that "all the canaille of foreigners who only entered their serv[ice] to disgrace it were shot &c.," as soon as the Liberator had departed, a court martial had assembled and acquitted Buchard. The case and the decree mentioned above are cited as showing the need for a minister to defend the interests of the United States.

Notes that the blockade presses severely on Callao.

Having read that a motion has been made "to furnish the correspondence of agents of the U. S. in this country to Congress," Tudor asks that his own letters not be published. ALS. DNA, RG59, Cons. Disp., Lima, vol. 1 (M154, R1). Addressed to Secretary of State; received August 24. Marginal note states that letter was completed on April 23. For a summary of the Peruvian decree, to become effective four months after its publication, see below, Clay to Hull, December 20, 1825. Lombard and Buchard not further identified. On the siege of Callao, see above, Tudor to Clay, March 21, 1825.

APPLICATIONS, RECOMMENDATIONS   April 22, 1825

THOMAS HART BENTON, St. Louis, recommends David Delaunay, "one of the French population of this place," for appointment to "a situation," preferably "in the custom House at New Orleans, or even in Florida," ALS. DNA, RG59, A. and R. (MR2). Delaunay, a civil and militia officer at St. Louis during the early territorial period and an insolvent debtor in 1823, did not receive an appointment.

PETER LITTLE, Freedom (Maryland), at the urging of "a Brother [Edward Brake Jackson] of the late Judge John G. Jackson," recommends Col. James Pindall for "the appointment vacated by the death of the Judge." Comments that he has known Pindall only in Congress: "you are better acquainted with his signal qullifications [sic] than I can be"; but expresses belief that they are "such as highly to recommend him for the Office beside . . . his appointment would be gratifying to the People of that Section of Virginia." ALS. *Ibid.* (MR1). Addressed to Clay as Secretary of State, Washington. See above, Jackson to Clay, April 12, 1825, note.

SAMUEL L. SOUTHARD, Washington, recommends Claudius F. LeGrand, who served in "the late War" as a captain in the 32d Regiment, as United States consul at Sola la Marina, Mexico. LS. DNA, RG59, A. and R. (MR3). LeGrand did not receive an appointment.

To Charles Hammond

My dear Sir   Washington 23d. Apl. 1825

I have this moment received your obliging letter of the 11h. inst. and reserving other parts of it for a reply a few days hence, in great haste, I wished to say a word or two to you about your accompanying letter for the printers.[1] I think the publication of it will be attended with good effect; 'though there are certain parts of my letter[2] which I should prefer to be omitted only because they would be liable to misrepresentation. I should erase them, and hand your letter to the editors (which I believe you intended to authorize) but I did not like to do it without your *express* consent. The parts which I would rather not have published are 1st. the last member [sic] in the third objection to Mr. Craw ord [sic] including these words "from his position & Southern support." 2d. The last paragraph which you have copied beginning "To each of the other gentlemen &c. And thirdly the paragraphs commencing with the words "What course my friends may take" &c and ending with the words "There are strong objections to each of the three gentlemen from whom we may have to make a selection."

After these parts are left out, what will remain will be sufficient for the general purpose of the publication which is to confirm the statement in my Address,[3] respecting Mr. Crawford, in which I took the liberty to refer to your name. I also, for a particular reason, should prefer your letter to be first published in the Nat. Journal.

There will not be time for me to receive an answer to this letter before I set out for home. I shall therefore leave your letter in the hands of a friend Dr. T. Watkins auditor &c with the erasures indicated; and if you consent to its publication in that form be pleased to address a letter to *him* conveying your permission, and also your willingness to change the address from the Intr.[4] to the Journal.

Your powerful commentary on Swartwout's letter[5] has had a most extensively wide circulation, and has produced great effect. The President was very much impressed with its ability.

I remain faithfully Your friend   H CLAY
C. Hammond Esq.

ALS. InU.
[1] Neither of these letters has been found. Cf. above, another letter from Clay to Hammond, April 11, 1825; below, Clay to Hammond, May 23, 1825; Hammond to Clay, August 31, 1825.
[2] To Hammond, October 25, 1824 (above, III, 870-72).   [3] Above, March 26, 1825.
[4] Washington *National Intelligencer*.   [5] See above, Clay to Hammond, April 4, 1825.

To Peter B. Porter

My dear Sir   Washington 23d. April 1825
I thank you for your very friendly letter of the 14h. instant,[1] from which I am glad to perceive that you approve of the Administration which has been formed. We might have had in it more talent with less harmony. I entertain no fears but that the latter object has been secured. Without knowing your wishes, it was my anxious desire to have had you a member of it. The President had towards you the best feelings; but the considerations which led him to the selection of the particular gentlemen who compose it had great weight; and these, when I shall have the pleasure to meet you, I will fully explain, as well as the motives which induced the offer to Mr. Clinton of the mission to England.[2] As to the dispositions of this gentleman towards the administration I believe you are right, as we have other concurring informations

[sic]. But, with such friends as yourself and others, and with the good intentions which prevail here, I have no serious apprehensions from his enmity.

I shall go to Kentucky in two or three weeks to bring my family. It will make such a large draft upon my time that I fear I shall hardly be able to visit you and my excellent friend Mrs. Porter this summer. But if I live I will have that gratification at no very distant day.

In the event of the P. Office vacancy[3] your friend Genl. Lynch[4] shall have his pretensions considered with the greatest kindness. With my best respects to Mrs. Porter I remain Faithfully & cordially Your friend   H CLAY
Genl. P. B. Porter

[Marginal note]

P S   I am greatly obliged by the honorable notice intended to be taken of me in the name of the new Steam boat[5] I shall be gratified to take a passage in her at some future day   H.C.

ALS. NBuHi.
[1] Not found. President Adams noted that Clay had read him part of the letter, "asserting that DeWitt Clinton is inveterately hostile to the present Administration . . . ." *Memoirs*, VI, 531.   [2] See above, Stuart to Clay, March 15, 1825.
[3] Cf. above, Kane to Clay, March 30, 1825.
[4] Probably James Lynch.
[5] The *Henry Clay,* 301 tons, built by the Lake Erie Steamboat Company at Black Rock, New York, was launched June 9, 1825.

INSTRUCTIONS AND DISPATCHES   April 23, 1825

From A[LEXANDER] H. EVERETT, Boston. Presents for consideration a statement regarding "the situation of the American Consuls in the ports of Holland and Belgium": following repeated complaints by these officers that they are discriminated against, he has "made several representations upon the subject to the Belgian Government" and has been informed that it is willing "to allow to the American Consuls within their jurisdiction precisely the same franchises as are allowed the Consuls of the Netherlands in the United States." His requests for instructions in this connection having brought no response, he urges that information and instructions be sent to (Christopher) Hughes. Suggests also that a decision be made in regard to a proposed method of settling the accounts of consuls and that these officials be sent, regularly, copies of the laws of the United States. ALS. DNA, RG59, Dip. Disp., Netherlands, vol. 7 (M42, R-T11A).

MISCELLANEOUS LETTERS   April 23, 1825

From JAMES H. CAUSTEN, Baltimore. Inquires when a report relative to French spoliations, called for by Senate resolution of March 5, 1824, may be expected. LS. DNA, RG76, Records re French Spoliations. See below, Causten to Clay, August 29, 1825; Clay to Adams, May 20, 1826. Causten, who in 1837 described himself as a notary public, residing in Washington, served as attorney and legal

representative for one of the spoliation claimants. The Senate resolution of
March 5, 1824, had requested that the President supply copies of the correspondence concerning such spoliations prior to 1800.

APPLICATIONS, RECOMMENDATIONS   April 23, 1825

EDWARD COLSTON recommends Philip C. Pendleton, of Martinsburg, (West)
Virginia, to fill the vacancy caused by the death of (John G.) Jackson. Comments: "You know Mr. Pendleton personally, and altho' not intimately, yet I
trust sufficiently to judge of the correctness of what I have stated." Emphasizes
the importance of the view that "this administration" should not confer judicial
appointment on any man sharing "the opinions of most of our politicians on
the subject of the strict construction of the powers of the federal government."
Pendleton's sentiments on this subject are well known to the writer, and he
believes they "agree with those of the present administration." ALS. MHi-
Adams Papers, Letters Received (M469). Postmarked at Martinsburg. Pendleton, uncle of John Pendleton Kennedy, was appointed and accepted the post
but apparently never served in it. Cf. above, Zane to Clay, April 5, 1825, note.

JOHN DAVIES, Harrisburg (Pennsylvania), solicits employment, either at Washington or "as a Surveyor in any situation the Government might please to
place" him. ALS. DNA, RG59, A. and R. (MR2).

INSTRUCTIONS AND DISPATCHES   April 25, 1825

To HENRY MIDDLETON, no. 22. Informs him of the arrangements agreed upon
in connection with the claim of Bryant and Sturgis in the case of the *Pearl.*
Copy. DNA, RG59, Dip. Instr., vol. 10, p. 295 (M77, R5). L draft, in DLC-HC
(DNA, M212, R7). See above, Clay to Tuyll, April 19 (2), 1825; Tuyll to Clay,
April 22, 1825.

From CHARLES L. BARTLETT, "Island of Trinidad." Reports that the Governor
of the island (Sir Ralph Woodford) has no authority to receive an American
agent until the appointment is "recognised by His Majesty's Government" and
that a copy of Bartlett's commission as consular agent "has been transmitted
to the Secretary of State for the Colonies." ALS. DNA, RG59, Cons. Disp., Trinidad, vol. 1 (M-T148, R1). Received June 6. Bartlett, of Haverhill, Massachusetts, had been appointed American "Consular Commercial Agent" at Trinidad
in November, 1824. He was listed as "Consul" there in the *Biennial Register*
of office-holders on September 30, 1825; but his appointment had never been
presented to Congress, and he was not accredited by the British Government.
He retained the post, which he identified as his "Consulship," as late as 1831
but was not listed in the *Biennial Register* of 1835. On the distinction between
a consul and a commercial agent, see below, Clay to Tattnall, June 12, 1826.
    Woodford, who had inherited property on the Island of Tobago, had been
named Governor of neighboring Trinidad in 1812. He held the position
until 1829.

To [John J. Crittenden]

My dear Sir   Washington 26 April 1825
    I recd. your letter of the 9h. inst. transmitting one from my worthy

old friend your uncle requesting his son to be appointed a Cadet at West Point.[1] It would have given me great satisfaction to have been able to have promoted his wishes; but there is unfortunately no vacancy at present and none is likely to occur during this year. Appointments are usually made about the 4h. of March, and they are regulated very much according to the recommendations of the several states among whom they are distributed. It would be calculated to advance your uncles desire, if he should persevere in it, to interest, in his son's behalf, some of our delegation at the next period of appointment. Be pleased to make this communication to him.

I hope to be able to leave here for K. about the 8h. or 10h. of next month. You must spare me as much as possible in the Federal Court until I reach Frankfort and make some final disposition of my business.

I have found the labors of my office very severe. But they have been increased by my desire to dispatch as many of them as were most urgent, prior to my departure.

Give my respects to Blair, Harvie and Judge Todd.[2]

Your's Sincerely   H CLAY

ALS. NcD.
[1] See above, Turpin to Clay, April 1, 1825.
[2] Francis Preston Blair; John Harvie; Thomas Todd.

To Alexander H. Everett

A. H. Everett Esquire, Boston,
Sir   Department of State Washington 26 Ap. 1825

I have received the Letter which you addressed to me, under date the 20th. instant, and submitted it to the President. After a deliberate consideration of its contents, and with every possible disposition to promote your ease and accommodation, I am directed by him to express his regret that he cannot comply with your request to make some other provision for Mr. Smith, in lieu of the place of Secretary to the Legation at Madrid, which he now holds. His appointment to that place was made by the late President,[1] who was somewhat influenced by the circumstance of the relation between Mr. Smith and the President. That same relation opposes an insuperable obstacle to the disturbance of that arrangement, if there were no other difficulties in the way. Towards your brother, Colo. John Everett, both the President and I entertain warm feelings of personal regard; and it would have been a satisfaction to both of us, if it had been practicable to have conferred the appointment of Secretary on him.

Your Instructions and other papers connected with your Mission, are nearly prepared.[2] I can have them at New York by this day week. Do you wish them sent to meet you there, or shall they be forwarded to Boston?

With high respect I am Your obedient Servant   H. CLAY.

Copy. DNA, RG59, Dip. Instr., vol. 10, p. 296 (M77, R5). ALS draft, in DLC-HC (DNA, M212, R7).
[1] See above, Clay to Smith, April 11, 1825.
[2] See below, Clay to Everett, April 27, 28, 1825.

INSTRUCTIONS AND DISPATCHES   April 26, 1825

From D[AVID] ERSKINE, Stockholm. Notes that, for reasons of health, he has been advised to travel during the summer and has appointed his brother-in-law, Gustaf Englehart, as vice-consul, to perform the duties of the consulate. (Christopher) Hughes has approved the appointment. ALS. DNA, RG59, Cons. Disp., Stockholm (M-T230, R-T1). Addressed to Secretary of State; received July 5. Englehart not further identified.

From HUGH NELSON, Madrid, [no. 55]. Reports the receipt of assurances that (José de) Heredia will be sent to the United States as soon as possible, to begin negotiations for the adjustment of claims (see above, Nelson to Secretary of State, March 8, 1825; below, Clay to Everett, April 27, 1825); encloses copies of correspondence with the Foreign Secretary (Francisco de Zea Bermudez), relative to payment of tonnage duties by American vessels entering Spanish ports in distress, and the proclamation of the King (Ferdinand VII) on April 19, stating his determination to exercise absolute rule. LS. DNA, RG59, Dip. Disp., Spain, vol. 24 (M31, R26). Addressed to Secretary of State; received June 22. The enclosed correspondence, culminating from Nelson's protest in the case of the *Dick* (above, Nelson to Secretary of State, March 8, 1825), conveys mutual agreement by the agents of the governments of Spain and the United States to a reciprocal admission of vessels under distress without payment of tonnage duties.

On the collapse of constitutional government in Spain, see above, III, 313n, 498n, 606-607. Released from confinement by the Spanish Cortes at Cádiz, to avert the horrors of protracted siege by the French, Ferdinand VII had promptly repudiated his pledge of amnesty and, supported by a French army of occupation, had instituted a reign of terror. The appointment of Zea Bermudez (above, Brown to Clay, March 22, 1825), having been interpreted as a step toward mitigation of this despotism, Ferdinand had issued a decree on April 19, 1825, contradicting the "alarming reports" that he had been obliged "to make reforms and innovations in the regime" and demanding, instead, the arrest of all who criticized the measures or agents of his government. *Annual Register, 1825,* "History of Europe," 168-69.

MISCELLANEOUS LETTERS   April 26, 1825

From B[ENJAMIN] BUISSON, editor of the *Natchitoches Courier,* Louisiana. Gives notification of the sale of the newspaper, "One of the number designated for publishing the Laws of the United States," to H. F. Deblieux, who will publish it in partnership with Milton Slocum, "under the firm of Milton Slocum & Co." ALS. DNA, RG59, P. and D. of L. Buisson, who had left France because he opposed the Bourbons, remained a French citizen throughout a long life spent mostly in New Orleans, as architect, surveyor, engineer, and editor. In 1824 he had assumed editorship of the *New Orleans Argus* (see below, Derbigny to Clay, May 28, 1825, note). The *Natchitoches Courier* retained the contract to publish the laws throughout the Adams administration. Milton Slocum and Company continued as publishers through 1827. Deblieux and Slocum have not been further identified.

From LANGDON CHEVES, Office of the Board of Commissioners under the Convention of St. Petersburg. Comments that perusal of the paper of the British Commissioner (George Jackson), dated March 30 (see above, Cheves to Clay, March 31, 1825), confirmed the apprehensions evoked upon first hearing it but that subsequent explanations have removed the principal objection. Reports conclusion and transmission of papers not previously filed in connection with the case of John Couper, which raised three points: the kind of evidence to be required from claimants; the question of interest or damages; and the refusal of the British Commissioner to execute the fifth article of the convention in connection with the disagreement on the question of interest. Notes the reluctance of the British Commissioner to make the documents available as required by the third article of the convention and his refusal to permit their inspection by the claimants, "under any circumstances," or to allow copying of them for the use of the State Department.

States that the case of Jumonville de Villiers raised a new question, one relevant to most of the Louisiana claims, in that the slaves at the conclusion of the war were on Dauphin Island, which the British Commissioner asserts was part of West Florida then claimed by Spain. Cheves has refused to argue the point, on the ground that the island was in the possession of the United States until seized by the British forces and surrendered to Spain, that the possession and not the title "is the fact with which these claims are coupled."

Reports the status of action on four other cases brought before the commissioners, these claims all being held in abeyance for varying reasons, the conclusion that nothing further can be done until the disagreement on the point of interest is resolved, and the decision to adjourn sittings of the Board until December 8. Relevant documents and arguments are enclosed. ALS. DNA, RG76, G.B.9-Folder 8. Copies of enclosed documents may be found, with another copy of this letter, in DNA, RG76, Indemnity for Slaves. On the issues raised in this document, see below, Clay to King, May 10, 1825. Jumonville de Villiers, of Louisiana, was claimant for twenty slaves carried away by the British after the conclusion of the War of 1812.

From LANGDON CHEVES, Washington—"Memoranda for the Secretary of State furnished at his request." Describes the rigidity of the approach of the British Commissioner (George Jackson) to claims (presented under the St. Petersburg Convention) and the consequent discouragement of claimants. Notes that this official has on several occasions refused to act to give effect to Article 5 (of the convention), specifically on disagreements relating to admission of cases to consideration when they had been omitted by clerical error from the "definitive list," to the question of interest on damages, and to the issue "whether Dauphine Island is a territory or place within the Treaty" (cf. above, Cheves to Clay, this date); that he has forbidden the secretary of the commission to supply Cheves with copies of documents obtained under article 3 of the convention, even for the use of the United States Government; and that he has refused claimants the right to see these documents prior to putting their cases to trial. Questions whether, in view of the disagreements prospective at each stage of the negotiation, "a tolerable compromise can be effected in the shape of an aggregate sum payable by the Government of Great Britain to this Government, distributed by the functionaries of the latter. . . ." Estimates that valid claims for compensation for slaves may amount to 500 from Virginia and Maryland, at $280, equalling $140,000; 250 from Louisiana, at $580, equalling $145,000; 900 from Georgia, at $390, equalling $351,000, totaling $636,000, which with interest at six per cent per annum, comes to $1,010,000, to which sum must be added $15,000 in principle and $90,000 in interest for general property damage—a total sum of about $1,250,000. Notes the probability of much contention in Maryland and Virginia because of widespread misunderstanding regarding the fact that compensation is authorized for slaves and property carried away only after the signing of the treaty of peace. Inasmuch as the commissioners have agreed that all official proceedings shall be in writing, Cheves has directed that a copy of the protocol certified by the secretary of the Board be sent to the Department of State. Copy. DNA, RG76, Indemnity for Slaves. Cf. below, Clay to King, May 10, 1825.

From JOHN W. SMITH, Columbus, Ohio. Asks when a commissioner is to be named for locating the National (Cumberland) Road west of Zanesville. ALS. DNA, RG59, Misc. Letters (M179, R62).

From SAMUEL L. SOUTHARD, Navy Department. Inquires whether information is available concerning the French brig *Calypso,* which, having been "stranded and abandoned, was saved by certain American and British Officers, carried to Thompsons Island [Key West] and . . . condemned to be sold for the benefit of the Owners, and Sailors"; also asks to borrow a copy of the laws of Florida "on the subject of wrecks, Salvage, &ca." ALS. *Ibid.* See below, Mareuil to Clay, May 6, 1825.

From WILLIAM STURGIS, Boston. Acknowledges receipt of Clay's letter of April 20; expresses thanks to Clay "for the very prompt & efficient attention" he gave "to the business"; and asks that (Henry) Middleton be directed "to pay over the money to the order of Bryant and Sturgis." ALS. DNA, RG76, Misc. Claims, Russia.

To A[lexander] H. Everett

No. 1. A. H. Everett appointed Envoy Extraordinary and Minister Plenipotentiary, U. S. to Spain.

Sir,   Department of State Washington, 27 Ap. 1825.

The President of the United States, by and with the advice and consent of their Senate, having appointed you Envoy Extraordinary and Minister Plenipotentiary to Spain, I now transmit you, herewith, your Commission in that character, together with a Letter of Credence to the King of Spain, to be delivered on your presentation.[1] It is the wish of the President that you proceed, without unnecessary delay, on your mission. Upon arriving in Spain, you will receive from Mr. Nelson,[2] if he shall not have returned to the United States, or, if he has, from the person in whose charge he shall have left them, the Archives and papers of the Legation. Accompanying herewith, you will also find such parts of those Documents as have been printed by the order of either branch of Congress. From a perusal of all these papers, you will obtain a full knowledge of the present posture of our relations with Spain. The Instructions of my Predecessor to Mr. Nelson, under date the 28th. April 1823,[3] exhibit the state of our affairs, and the view which the Executive had of them at that period. You will consider those Instructions as forming a guide for you so far as their objects have not been attained, and so far as they shall not be modified by these supplemental Instructions. It will be the principal purpose of these to direct your attention to intervening events and transactions, and to point out your duty in relation to them.

Those Instructions embraced three principal objects
1st. The Piracies.
2nd. Indemnity for spoliations on our commerce.
3rd. The state of our commerce in the Ports of Spain.

1. The failure of Spain to suppress the piracies committed by robbers issuing from the harbours of Cuba and Porto Rico may be ascribed partly to her weakness, and partly to the countenance and connivance which they experienced from some of the inhabitants, and some of the local Authorities in those Islands. So far as it has resulted from her weakness, whatever may be the strength of the obligation under which she lies to repress them, it would be both useles [sic] and impolitic, unnecessarily to press her. Recent events and intelligence demonstrate that a better spirit prevails among the local Authorities, and most of them have, accordingly, evinced a disposition to co-operate, as far as their means extend, with the forces of the United States,[4] in putting an end to those enormities. The Captain General of Cuba,[5] especially, has manifested, throughout the whole of his residence in that Island, unaffected zeal, and the best intentions on this subject. In making known the satisfaction which the Government of the United States derives from this display of better feeling, you will urge upon that of Spain, the propriety of an unremitted action upon the local authorities, to keep them in the line of their duty, and to afford all the aid in their power to the cruisers of the United States.

2— The spoliations for which indemnity is claimed by the United States, were the consequence of captures made by Spanish Privateers, fitted out principally from Porto Cabello and Porto Rico, under pretext of the blockade declared by General Morales.[6] Of the character of that illegal blockade, and the consequent duty of Spain to make ample reparation for the wrongs which have been inflicted under colour of it, nothing need be now added to what is contained in the instructions of the 28th. April, 1823. It appears from a note of Mr Zea Bermudez, addressed to Mr. Nelson, on the 19th. day of November 1824, communicating the appointment of Don Jose de Herida [sic], Envoy Extraordinary and Minister Plenipotentiary to the United States, that the Minister was to be charged with a negociation here, on the subject of those claims for indemnity, as well as alleged interests and claims of Spanish subjects against the Government and citizens of the United States.[7] It was stated in the Same note, that Mr. Herida would proceed on his mission as soon as possible; and yet more than five months have elapsed without his arriving in the United States, and without any certain information as to the time when he may be expected to arrive. In the neglect which was so long shewn to Mr. Nelson's repeated and earnest representations to the Spanish Government, upon the subject of those claims; in the intimation of a wish, the expression of which was so long delayed, to transfer the negociation from Madrid to Washington; and in the subsequent tardy movements of Mr. Herida, it is impossible not to recognize a spirit to procrastinate, incompatible with the just rights of the injured citizens of the United States. And what is to be gained by entering upon the discussions here? What is there indeed to discuss? It will not be attempted on the part of Spain to maintain that the Blockade of Genl. Morales, condemned as it unquestionably was by the public Law, condemned by Spain herself in the revocation of it,[8] condemned by Great Britain, in the threat of reprisals, in consequence of the capture of the vessels of her subjects, and condemned by Spain again in the arrangement which she made to redress those British injuries,[9]—was entitled to be respected by the Citizens of the United States. We should as soon believe it to be necessary to discuss any one of the best settled principles of the Law of Nations, as to engage in a discussion of such a Blockade as that of Genl. Morales. But if such a discussion were not perfectly idle and unnecessary, what advantages does Washington offer for conducting it, which are not equally held out at Madrid? There is no peculiar fact or local information possessed here, in relation to the subject, which is not equally possessed at Madrid. There is really nothing to do but for Spain to make provision for the indemnity due to our citizens, for the unlawful aggressions committed upon their property, under colour of that Blockade. If the negociation were to be opened here, we should soon find Mr. Herida without instructions, and proposing references to Madrid; and this would necessarily add to the delay, which has been already great. The President thinks that the negociation had better, at once, begin at the point where it would probably terminate if it were commenced here, and thus avoid that useless consumption of time. You are therefore authorised, at once, to propose, and conclude, at Madrid, a Convention for the settlement and payment of the claims to which reference has been made; and a Power for that purpose accompanies these instructions.[10]

With respect to the interests and claims of Spanish subjects, to which Mr. Bermudez alludes, as existing against the Government and citizens of the United States, his notice of them is not very precise, nor is it distinctly understood to what he refers. In regard to any such claims or interests on the part of Spanish subjects against the citizens of the United States, our tribunals are alike open to Spanish subjects and to American citizens to obtain redress for any injuries which they may have respectively suffered, in their persons, property or reputation. And any such case hardly can be immagined [sic] in which the Government of the United States ought to be held responsible. But with respect to any just claims which Spanish subjects may have upon this Government, it is always as ready to render justice to them, as it is prompt in the demand of it in behalf of the citizens of the United States, from Foreign Governments. And if any such just claims upon this Government shall be substantiated to your satisfaction, you are authorised to comprehend a provision for them in the proposed Convention

3rd. The commerce of the United States with Spain is subjected to many burthensome restrictions injurious to both parties, and forming a just subject of complaint on the part of this Government, since some of those restrictions apply exclusively to the United States. Most of them are enumerated in a memoir presented on the 1st. of December last[11] by your Predecessor to the Spanish Government with a request that it should be laid before the Junta of Aranceles which was engaged in preparing a system of Commercial regulations for Spain. If you shall find that those restrictions continue to operate, you will urge their immediate abolition. The most grievous of them are those by which all American vessels, without regard to the places or the periods of their departure from the United States, are required to perform a quarantine as unnecessary as it is vexatious; and by which, when they are, at last, admitted to an entry, they are subjected to a rate of tonnage duty twenty times greater than that which is levied upon all other Foreign vessels. If both the spirit of existing Treaties, and the disposition to cultivate friendly relations should not lead to a revocation of these unequal and unwise regulations, it might be supposed that an adequate motive would be found for their discontinuance, in the interest of Spain. For, undoubtedly, the direct commerce between the two countries is more advantageous to her, than it is to the United States.

You are authorised to repeat the proposition made by Mr. Nelson, to place the commerce of the two Countries upon the liberal footing which is provided for by the Act of Congress of the 7th. of January, 1824.[12] There are two modes of accomplishing the object of that Act; one by Treaty, and the other by mutual regulations of the two Countries. The latter is liable to the objection that, after the adoption of these reciprocal regulations, they may be abolished by either party, at its pleasure, and without previous notice to the other. And this objection applied to Spain, has great weight, from her actual condition, and the consequent frequent changes in her ministry and fluctuations in her councils. The President, therefore, deems it best that you should endeavour to effect the object by a Convention of Amity, Commerce and Navigation, of which that made with England on the 3rd. July 1815, will furnish a model.[13] A Power to conclude such a Convention, accompanies these Instructions.[14] In connection with this subject, you will call the attention of the Spanish Government to the desire of the United States, so often expressed, to have Consuls admitted in such of the Colonial Ports as are open to the Commerce of the United States. This privilege ought to have been yielded upon the ground of friendly accommodation alone; but, in regard to the Havanna [sic] the United States have now a strict right to demand the admission of a Consul. By the 19th. Article of the Treaty of 1795[15] it is stipulated that "Consuls shall be reciprocally established, with the privileges and powers which those of the most favoured Nation enjoy, in the Ports where their Consuls reside or are permitted to be."

It appears from a work published at the Havanna, entitled "Strangers Guide of the Island of Cuba, and General Calendar,"[16] which is believed to be official, that a Consul of France is established at that Port: and consequently, the United States, by the express terms of that Article, have the same right. On their part, they have ever faithfully executed the provisions of that Article, by freely admitting Spanish Consuls in all the Ports of the United States in which it was wished they should reside.

In regard to the Palmyra, mentioned in the Instructions to Mr. Nelson of the 28th. April, 1823, as a case pending before the Supreme Court, on the trial before that Court, it was remanded to the Court below; and if any disposition has been there since made of the cause, information of it has not reached this Department.[17] Lieut. Wilkinson whose arrest is noticed in the same instructions, was, upon full investigation, acquitted by the Court.[18]

Besides the preceding objects to which your attention will be directed, others of great interest will also claim it. Of these, that of the highest importance is the present war between Spain and her former Colonies, on this Continent. The President wishes you to bring this subject, in the most conciliatory manner possible, before the Spanish Government. It would be as unnecessary, as unprofitable to look to the past, except for the purpose of guiding future conduct. True wisdom dictates that Spain, without indulging in unavailing regrets on account of what she has irretrievably lost, should employ the means of retaining what she may yet preserve from the wreck of her former possessions. The war upon the Continent, is, in fact, at an end. Not a solitary foot of land from the western limit of the United States to Cape Horn owns her sway; not a bayonet in all that vast extent, remains to sustain her cause. And the Peninsula is utterly incompetent to replace those armies which have been vanquished and annihilated by the victorious forces of the new Republics. What possible object, then, can remain to Spain to protract a war which she can no longer maintain, and to the conclusion of which, in form, there is only wanting the recognition of the new Governments by Treaties of peace. If there were left the most distant prospect of her reconquering her Continental Provinces, which have achieved their independence, there might be a motive for her perseverance. But every expectation of such reconquest, it is manifest, must be perfectly chimerical. If she can entertain no rational hope to recover what has been forced from her grasp, is there not great danger of her losing what she yet but feebly holds? It should be borne in mind that the armies of the new States, flushed with victory, have no longer employment on the Continent: and yet whilst the war continues, if it be only in name, they cannot be disbanded, without a disregard of all the maxims of just precaution. To what object, then, will the new Republics direct their powerful and victorious armies? They have a common interest, and a common enemy; and let it be supposed that that enemy, weak and exhausted as he is, refuses to make peace; will they not strike wherever they can reach? And from the proximity and great value of Cuba and Porto Rico, is it not to be anticipated that they will aim, and aim a successful blow too, at those Spanish Islands? Whilst they would operate from without, means would, doubtless, be at the same time, employed to stimulate the population within to a revolt. And that the disposition exists among the inhabitants to a considerable extent, to throw off the Spanish authority, is well known. It is due to the United States to declare that they have constantly declined to give any countenance to that disposition.[19]

It is not, then, for the new Republics that the President wishes you to urge upon Spain the expediency of concluding the war. Their interest is probably on the side of its continuance, if any

nation can ever have an interest in a state of war. But it is for
Spain herself, for the cause of humanity, for the general repose of
the world, that you are required, with all the delicacy which belongs to the subject, to use every topic of persuasion to impress
upon the Councils of Spain, the propriety, by a formal pacification,
of terminating the war. And, as the views and policy of the United
States, in regard to those Islands may possibly have some influence,
you are authorized, frankly and fully to disclose them. The United
States are satisfied with the present condition of those Islands, in
the hands of Spain, and with their Ports open to our commerce, as
they are now open. This Government desires no political change
of that condition. The population itself, of the Islands is incompetent, at present, from its composition and its amount, to maintain self government. The maritime force of the neighbouring
Republics of Mexico and Colombia is not now, nor is it likely
shortly to be, adequate to the protection of those Islands, if the
conquest of them were effected. The United States would entertain
constant apprehensions of their passing from their possession to
that of some less friendly sovereignty. And of all the European
Powers, this Country prefers that Cuba and Porto Rico should
remain dependent on Spain. If the war should continue between
Spain and the new Republics, and those Islands should become the
object and the theatre of it, their fortunes have such a connexion
with the prosperity of the United States that they could not be indifferent spectators; and the possible contingencies of such a protracted war might bring upon the Government of the United States
duties and obligations, the performance of which, however painful
it should be, they might not be at liberty to decline. A subsidiary
consideration in favour of peace, deserving some weight, is, that
as the war has been the parent cause of the shocking piracies in
the west Indies, its termination would be probably followed by
their cessation. And thus the Government of Spain, by one act,
would fulfil [sic] the double obligation under which it lies, to foreign Governments, of repressing enormities, the perpetrators of
which find refuge, if not succour, in Spanish territory,[20] and that to
the Spanish Nation itself, of promoting its real interests.

With respect to the unauthorised incursion made in November
last, into the Island of Porto Rico, by Commodore Porter, and a
part of the forces under his command, and his threatened attack
upon Foxardo, you will impress his Catholic Majesty with the very
high respect for his territorial rights which the Government of the
United States promptly manifested by the recall, in consequence
of those acts, of that officer, and the order of a Court of enquiry
to investigate his conduct.[21] That Court will shortly convene, and

the Representative of Spain here will be invited to lay before it any evidence pertinent to the case, which he may think proper to adduce, if, after what has happened, Spain can, any longer feel an interest in an affair which has occasioned her no real injury.[22]

The accompanying papers in relation to the conduct of the Spanish Consul at Boston, demonstrate a disregard of his official duty which would have well justified an immediate revocation of his Exequatur.[23] If this Government has forborne to take that disagreeable step, it has been from a spirit of moderation which Spain ought duly to appreciate, and from a hope that the proper corrective will be applied without the necessity of a resort to it by the President.

Tendering you my best wishes for an agreeable voyage and a successful mission,

I am, with great respect, Your obedient Servant   H. Clay.

Copy. DNA, RG59, Dip. Instr., vol. 10, pp. 297-305 (M77, R5). ALS draft, in DLC-HC (DNA, M212, R7).

[1] The commission, dated March 9, and the letter of credence, dated April 27, both copies, are located in DNA, RG59, Ceremonial Communications, vol. 2, pp. 14-15.

[2] Hugh Nelson.

[3] *American State Papers, Foreign Relations*, V, 408-19.

[4] See above, III, 338n; Nelson to Clay, April 6, 1825.

[5] Francisco Dionisio Vives, who had assumed the post of Captain General and Governor of Cuba in May, 1823.

[6] In the spring of 1822, following directly upon the action by the United States Government to accord recognition to the Republic of Colombia (above, III, 186n), General Francisco Tomás Morales, recently appointed commander in chief of the Spanish forces, had re-established the blockade of the coast of the Main as formerly imposed, and subsequently lifted, by General Pablo Morillo (above, II, 560n). From May through July, journals in the United States reported shocking atrocities committed by the crews of two large brigs and two schooners fitted out in, and sailing from, Puerto Rico under papers authorizing them to serve as privateers for enforcement of the blockade. *Niles' Weekly Register*, XXII (April 27, May 18, July 13, 1822), 134, 181, 309; Washington *Daily National Intelligencer*, July 3, 1822.

[7] Copy, in DNA, RG59, Dip. Disp., Spain, vol. 24 (M31, R26). On the Spanish claims, see above, Nelson to Clay, March 8, 1825.

[8] In obedience to a royal decree of December, 1822, which opened the commerce of Spain's colonies on the Main to world trade, General Morales had issued a proclamation on March 8, 1823, lifting the blockade; but at the same time he had warned that foreigners bringing arms in aid of the Colombians would be treated as enemies of war. *Niles' Weekly Register*, XXIV (May 3, 1823), 141; Hugh Nelson to Luis Maria de Salazar, September 7, 1824 (DNA, RG59, Dip. Disp., Spain, vol. 24 [M31, R26]; *American State Papers, Foreign Relations*, V, 424).

[9] The British warship *Falmouth* had been reported under orders to call at Puerto Cabello in May, 1822, to notify the local commandant that the British Navy would treat as pirates any privateers attacking vessels of that nation. *Niles' Weekly Register*, XXII (June 1, 1822), 223. When the British Government had subsequently protested against the blockade, the royal decree cited above, note 8, had been issued and the Spanish Cortes had appropriated 40,000,000 reals as reparation for damages to British subjects. Adams to Nelson, April 28, 1823, in *American State Papers, Foreign Relations*, V, 411.

[10] Dated April 27. Copy, in DNA, RG59, Ceremonial Communications, vol. 2, pp. 18-19.

[11] A copy of the memorandum is located in DNA, RG59, Dip. Disp., Spain, vol. 24 (M31, R26). It protests against the Spanish imposition of "vexatious & oppressive" quarantine regulations; the refusal to permit amendment of cargo manifests once they have been filed with Spanish customs officers; the levy of excessively heavy tonnage duties (20 reals on vessels from the United States, as contrasted with one real on those

of all other commercial nations), whether the ships enter in ballast, merely to visit, or to trade; the system of fixing duties upon staves, which is computed on quantity rather than value—all of which restrictions are said to be specifically directed against American commerce. Of more general impact, but cited as also injurious to United States trade, are the requirement that masters of foreign vessels entering Spanish ports in transit to other foreign markets must post bond for certification, by the Spanish consuls at the ports of destination, that the goods have arrived as specified and the prohibition against introduction of gold and silver into Spain unless accompanied by a Spanish consular certificate. Nelson concludes by recommending adjustment "to place the vessels and cargoes of the respective nations on a perfect equality in regard to tonnage and other duties in the ports of each other."

12 See above, Lorich to Clay, March 16, 1825, note.

13 See above, II, 57-59.

14 Dated April 27. A copy is located in DNA, RG59, Ceremonial Communications, vol. 2, p. 16.

15 Pinckney's Treaty, with Spain.

16 See above, Robertson to Clay, April 20, 1825.

17 The *Palmyra* (otherwise known as *Panchita*), the most notorious Spanish privateer from Puerto Rico, had been captured in 1822 by the United States schooner *Grampus*, under Lieutenant Francis H. Gregory, of Connecticut, on charges of robbery of the American schooner *Coquette*, of Georgetown, District of Columbia, and firing upon the *Grampus*. A decree of the United States Circuit Court for the District of Charleston, awarding damages of over $10,000 against Lieutenant Gregory, had been appealed to the Supreme Court, which under an opinion by Justice Story, issued January 15, 1827, upheld the lower court's release of the vessel from condemnation but denied the damages. The Supreme Court ruled: "The whole circumstances present such well-founded grounds for suspicion of the piratical character and conduct of the privateer, as required Lieutenant Gregory, in the just exercise of his instructions . . . to subdue and send her in for adjudication." 25 *U. S.* (12 Wheaton) 1-18.

18 In February, 1823, Lieutenant Jesse Wilkinson, of the United States brig *Spark*, had seized the Spanish schooner *Ninfa Catalana* (*Catalan Nymph*, known also as the *Santissima Trinidad*) off Havana as a pirate, on grounds that her crew had plundered an American schooner near Honduras the preceding October. Placing her sailors in irons and a prize crew aboard, he had sent the vessel into Norfolk, where the prisoners had been discharged for want of sufficient evidence. Lieutenant Wilkinson had been called before a naval court of inquiry. *American State Papers, Foreign Relations*, V, 387-88, 413; Washington *Daily National Intelligencer*, April 7, 1823.

19 Cf. above, Clay to Poinsett, March 26, 1825; Robertson to Clay, April 20, 1825.

20 Cf. above, Nelson to Clay, April 6, 1825, note; Robertson to Clay, April 20, 1825.

21 See above, Nelson to Clay, April 6, 1825.

22 See below, Clay to Salmon, April 29, 1825.

23 See above, Jones to Clay, March 28, 1825.

From John Eaton

Honourable Sirs　　　　　　　　　　Morristown Ohio April 27th 1825

May I have the assureance [sic] of addressing a few lines to you on the Subject of the Road[1] James Barnes Who Lives South of the Road now Located by the Commissioners who I Presume you have full Confidence in their Judgment and Integrity as to their Report is about to trouble you with a lengthy Petition to have a Review on his Rout [sic] I hope you will not delay the making the Present Road although Mr. Barnes wears a Strait Coat there is full as much Confidence to be Put in other men that do not Make So much Pretentions [sic] as to Honesty he has been troubleing [sic] the Post Master General for ten years Back and Could not Succeed in Getting the mail Rout through his Place in Consequence of it being off the Direct Rout and the old Established Road, if you feel at a Loss I will Refer you to Mr. Ruggles Mr. Patterson and Mr. Caldwell[2] of St. Clairsville for Information but I hope there is no need   yours most Respectfully   JOHN EATON

ALS. DNA, RG77, Letters Referred, 1819-1825, no. 838. Addressed to Clay or "Mr. Barber [sic] Secretary of War." Eaton, postmaster at Morristown, had been a Clay supporter in the campaign of 1824. Cf. below, Caldwell to Clay, April 28, 1825.
    1 The National Road.
    2 Benjamin Ruggles; John Patterson; and James Caldwell, merchant, banker, and former member of Congress (1813-1817).

MISCELLANEOUS LETTERS   April 27, 1825

From WILL[IAM] DUNCAN, London (England). Requests that the United States Minister in London (Rufus King) be instructed to lay before "Mr. Secretary [George] Canning" a memorial and claim against Edward Tyrrel Smith and the British Government. ALS. DNA, RG59, Misc. Letters (M179, R62). Received July 17. Edward Tyrrel Smith, Knight of the Bath, had been named Admiral of the Blue in 1812. On the claim at issue, see below, Taliaferro to Clay, July 12, 1825.

From WILLIAM C. SOMERVILLE, Washington. States that, since he may delay his departure for a few months, in the event of his death before embarkation, his heirs "will return the outfit, {of four thousand five hundred dollars} which was advanced." ALS. DNA, RG59, Dip. Disp., Sweden and Norway, vol. 4 (M45, R5). See below, Ingersoll to Clay, May 7, 1825, and note.

APPLICATIONS, RECOMMENDATIONS   April 27, 1825

JOHN SCOTT, St. Louis, recommends David Delaunay for appointment to office. ALS. DNA, RG59, A. and R. (MR2).

To F[ielding] L. Turner

Dear Sir   Washn 28h. Apl. 1825
    You may well imagine that it gave me much gratification to receive your letter of the 26h. March,[1] coming as it does from one who has known me so long and so well, and between whom and me there has ever existed a reciprocal friendship. The events in Louisiana by which I was accidentally kept out of the House have passed by,[2] and I have long since ceased to regard them even with any regret. The House could not have done better; and I am rejoiced to learn that the State of Louisiana will generally approve the decision. We shall continue to see some spasms in the Military fever, but they will not last; the Constitution and the Civil principle have triumphed. Reason and Mind have prevailed over phrenz [sic] and idolatry.
    I send you one of my Addresses to my Constituents.[3] Its good effect has surpassed my most sanguine expectations; and testimonies,

public and private, from all quarters have reached me of cordial
and general approbation.

We have every reason to believe that we shall have a prosperous
Administration. We shall undoubtedly have it, if zeal, industry
and good intentions can secure it.

With great respect I am faithfy & Cordially Yrs
The Honble F. L. Turner.   H. CLAY

ALS. KyLoF (photostatic copy of MS. owned by Charles F. Mansfield). Addressed
to New Orleans.   1 Not found.
  2 See above, III, 900, 904-905.   3 Above, March 26, 1825.

From James Brown

My dear Sir,   Paris April 28. 1825
I wrote you by the last Packet which sailed from Havre, but as
I had presumed that before it could reach Washington you would
have commenced your journey westward, I directed it to you in
Lexington.[1] The Newspapers received since the date of that letter
inform me of your having entered upon the duties of the Department of State, and I pray you to accept my congratulations on that
agreeable event. You will no doubt find the Office laborious or
at least more confining than the place you formerly filled, but I
hope you will find your Compensation in having a permanent
residence instead of those long and fatiguing journies, which had
an unfavorable influence on your health and spirits—

You will see by my several letters to Mr Adams that all my efforts
to extract from the present Minister of foreign Affairs a definitive
answer to the proposal made for a separate discussion of the question of Claims and that arising under the Louisiana Treaty have
been unavailing.[2] The Baron Damas who now fills the Office of
foreign Affairs is said to rely much upon the President of the
Council Mr De Villele for the direction which he gives to all diplomatic discussions, and as that Minister is now overwhelmed with
business in his own department (the finances) it is probable he
will not have time to give his assistance in examining the question
of our claims until after the adjournment of the two Chambers
which will not take place before the month of July, or the middle of
June. The present Ministry having carried the elections as they
wished, and passed a law to keep the Deputies in place for seven
years have large majorities on all questions and will carry all the
laws which have been proposed. The Bill for punishing sacrilege
with death after the *Amende honorable,* and that for giving a
Milliard of francs as an indemnity to the Emigrés for their estates
which had been confiscated and sold under the revolutionary

Government, have already passed.[3] Both of these laws are very unpopular, particularly the latter which seems to displease all parties. The Emigres wished either a restoration of their Estates or their value as an indemnity, instead of which they obtain only the amount for which they were sold without interest. Other classes of individuals who were ruined by revolutionary measures complain of the hardship of granting an indemnity to Emigrants only and refusing it to those who adhered to the Country under all its changes, whilst the Mass who also suffered during the long struggle consider it a peculiar hardship to be taxed for the benefit of Emigrants— The parade and expenditure at the Coronation[4] may for a while allay these discontents, but it is evident that they are deeply felt and will in all probability be more strongly expressed, after the adjournment of the Chambers.

There is much conjecture afloat respecting a meeting of the Allied Sovereigns at Milan.[5] Prince Metternich spent some weeks in Paris and had almost daily conferences with the Ministers of this Government and with the Ambassador of Russia. Although every means was tried to discover the objects of these conferences, I have seen no one who could give any satisfactory information on the subject.[6] It is said the Ambassador of England was not present at any of them.

My health is considerably improved, but is very far indeed from being confirmed. My situation compels me to expose myself to night air and I hardly ever do so without suffering from it.

I hope after a careful examination of the correspondence with France I shall have the pleasure of hearing from you on the subject of our Claims. I am exceedingly mortified that I have been unable to obtain a satisfactory answer or even to know when one might be expected   I am Dear Sir with great regard Yours sincerely

JAMES BROWN

PS. You will readily perceive that this is any thing but an official letter   J B.

ALS. DLC-HC (DNA, M212, R1).   1 See above, April 1, 1825.

2 See above, Brown to Secretary of State, March 23, 1825; Brown to Clay, April 1, 1825.

3 On the second measure, see above, Brown to Clay, April 1, 1825. The law punishing sacrilege had been passed on April 15 and provided the death penalty for public profanation of the communion utensils, if they contained the consecrated elements, the execution to "be preceded by the *amende honorable* of the condemned person before the principal church of the place where the crime shall have been committed, or of the place where the Court of Assize sits." *Annual Register, 1825*, pp. 139-40. Unworkable because of its imprecise definition of the crime, the law was never enforced; but it connoted the pietism of the ruling party and precipitated vigorous opposition. J[ean] Lucas-Dubreton, *The Restoration and the July Monarchy* (Tr. by E. F. Buckley; New York, 1929), 109-10.

4 Of Charles X.

5 See above, Rush to Secretary of State, April 12, 1825.

6 See above, Brown to Secretary of State, March 22, 1825.

From James Caldwell

Dear Sir   St. Clairsville 28th April 1825

The Interest which you have ever taken in the Location and Construction of the Cumberland road, has induced me to address you on that subject—The Superintendant [sic] is now ingaged [sic] in grading on the location between Canton and this Town, and it is the anxious desire of at least 9 tenths of the Citizens of this County, and of those to the west, that the road should be made on the rout [sic] recommended by the Commissioners Col McCrey[1] &c, and that the Superintendant may be permitted to proceed, without interuption [sic],   on this subject no doubt would be entertained, were it not for a James Barnes of the Town of Barnesville (in this County) who passed through this place on yesterday on his way to the City with a Petition to the President, requesting a review of the rout from Canton to Zanesville,   his object is to have the location so varied as to pass through Barnesville, where he has large possessions thence passing south of the location & the old road from 4 to 10 miles untill [sic] it would intersect near Zanesville,   passing through a very rough country and very thinly inhabited, this rout would be much inferior to the located rout, to say nothing of the increased distance, as well as leaving out all the Towns from this place to Zanesville, & that too for the sole purpose of accommodating Barnesville

Mr Barnes is capable of telling a plausable [sic] tale and I fear that his straight coat will give to his representations a credit that they are not entitled to, and would not have, even in his own society (the Friends) where he is well known.—

The President will not probably do anything on this subject, without consulting You,   should a review be in contemplation I hope that you will exert your influence to prevent it[2]—   I have no interest where the road may go, after it passes this place, other than the publick good—I have made this communication at the earnest request of the citizens of this Town, who are sensible that the publick would sustain a very great injury, were the rout so altered as to pass through Barnesville,   in deed it is my opinion that should it pass through that Town, it ought not to pass through this—should Barnes succeed in obtaining a review it will consume so much time, that no part of the road will probably be made this year—Yours very respectfully   JAMES CALDWELL

P S a Remonstrance against Barnes Petition will be forwarded to the President within a few days—singned [sic] by a few Indivduals [sic] in this Town and the citizens of Morris Tow [sic] Fairview Washington & Cambridge   all the citizens of this Town would

have signed the remonstrance had it been deemed necessary to
present it to them— JC
Hon H. Clay.

ALS. DNA, RG77, Letters Referred, 1819-1825, no. 839. Cf. above, Eaton to Clay,
April 27, 1825.
1 William McRee, of North Carolina, who with Abner Lacock and David Shriver,
Jr. (one of the founders of "Union Mills," Carroll County, Maryland—at this time
a resident of Cumberland, Maryland—and a civil engineer, who had been superintendent of location and construction of the Reistertown turnpike and of the Cumberland Road, east of Wheeling), had filed their report on January 2, 1822, as commissioners for laying out the road between Wheeling and Zanesville. *American State
Papers, Miscellaneous,* II, 797-98. In January, 1825, McRee had been appointed
surveyor of the public lands for Illinois, Missouri, and Arkansas, which position he
held until 1832, when, as a resident of Missouri, he was appointed commissioner to
mark out the boundary between the United States and Mexico.
2 On May 5, before receiving this letter, Clay had already presented Barnes to the
President, on which occasion the petitioner had "argued his cause with earnestness."
But at a Cabinet meeting on May 7, Clay was "strongly averse to any change" in
the proposed route for the Cumberland Road. Adams noted that "Several letters
and remonstrances [had been] received against Barnes's application." Adams, *Memoirs,*
VI, 540, 542

From Amos Kendall

Dear Sir,   Mount Pleasant Franklin County April 28th 1825—
    You are no doubt apprized of the events which have occurred in
Lexington within a few days; how the Monitor has been converted
into a Jackson paper and how the Editor has whipped one man
and killed another.[1] I do think your friends there, have, for some
time, been pursuing a rash and imprudent course. There was in
this state a very general feeling of dissatisfaction at the result of
the Presidential election, which, in my opinion, should have been
left to subside instead of being irritated by discussion. Yet a formal
and warm discussion was commenced in the Reporter.[2] This was
calculated to bring out the representation who voted for Jackson,
and I am inclined to think, will actually produce that effect. When
this new editor went to Lexington, he should have been wholly
neglected. There is no surer way to give a man importance than
to attempt fighting him down. The general impression is, that this
has been attempted in the case of this Editor, and it has already
raised a strong sensation in his favor. The natural consequence is
a wider circulation and more influence to his paper. As things now
stand, a discussion seems inevitable, and I acknowledge I have some
apprehensions as to its result. Besides being engrossed with local
politics, we are so situated in Frankfort that we cannot, at present,
be of much service in such a controversy to any side.
    Your favor of the 5th. inst. came to hand two days ago.[3] On the
subject of the situation you mention, I am inclined to be explicit
at once. If it would be expected, that I should write steadily and

systematically in support of the administration, or be under any obligation to write for newspapers at all, I should certainly decline it. If I were offered a situation not too laborious, with a liberal compensation attached to it, and left entirely free to sport my pen as I pleased, I should accept it. I am too much disgusted with the life of a party Editor to abandon the situation I am in for another like it in name or in reality. Yet I take pleasure in writing, and should hardly desist were I in Washington. Employed in the administration, I should certainly not write against it, and I should take some pride in vindicating you from the aspersions with which your enemies would overwhelm you. I do not say this, because I suppose that you thought of employing me merely as a writer, but because the little talent I have that way may have entered into your mind, and because I would accept of no place under you without first apprizing you what I would not do as well as what I might do. If, under these circumstances, you should offer me a place not too laborious (for I cannot stand the labor of 12 or 14 hours in 24) and supported by sufficient pay, I should certainly accept it[.]

I have some anxiety to know your inte[*ntions*] as soon as possible; for they will much inf[*luence my*] private affairs. If I enter on such a situat[*ion, the*] loan I mentioned will not be wanted, or a[*t any*] rate, but a small sum, as I should dispose of my property here except this little farm and mills.[4] If nothing of the kind takes place, then I shall seek to prosecute that object. You will therefore see the importance to me of shortly knowing the result of this affair.— — The current of public opinion here is setting almost furiously against the old Judges.[5] Depend on it, the majority against them will be increased in the next Legislature. Your friend

AMOS KENDALL.

ALS. DLC-HC (DNA, M212, R1). Addressed to Clay at Washington. MS. faded and torn.
  [1] See above, Holley to Clay, April 18, 1825.
  [2] See, e.g., Lexington *Kentucky Reporter,* March 21, 1825, and succeeding issues.
  [3] Not found.
  [4] Cf. above, Kendall to Clay, February 19, March 23, 1825.
  [5] See above, III, 902 and note; cf. above, Kendall to Clay, February 19, March 23, 1825.

DIPLOMATIC NOTES   April 28, 1825

From SEVERIN LORICH, Philadelphia. Requests acknowledgment of his note of March 16. ALS. DNA, RG59, Notes from Swedish Legation, vol. 3 (M60, R2).

INSTRUCTIONS AND DISPATCHES   April 28, 1825

From CHARLES D. COXE, Tunis. Gives details of his quarrel with Dr. S. D. Heap, acting consul prior to Coxe's arrival, based in part upon a letter in which a local official had asked Heap to inform his Government that Coxe was not acceptable to the Bey (Hassein, who had ascended the throne late in 1824 and who ruled until 1835). Coxe has learned that the Bey had understood that the American consul there in 1815 (Mordecai M. Noah) was to have been re-appointed and that the objection was against the latter rather than himself. Documents pertaining to the quarrel are enclosed. LS. DNA, RG59, Cons. Disp., Tunis, vol. 5 (M-T303, R5). Addressed to Secretary of State. Cf. above, Southard to Clay, April 21, 1825. Samuel D. Heap, born in Pennsylvania, had held a commission as a Navy surgeon since 1804. Stationed in the Mediterranean in 1825, he succeeded Coxe as consul at Tunis in December of that year and remained in the position until 1842.

From RICHARD RUSH, London, no. 433. Reports that he performed the official ceremony of taking leave from his post, at the King's levee of the preceding day; that nothing occurred "requiring special recapitulation"; and that he will continue "to attend to the publick business of the Legation" until his successor arrives, unless this event should be delayed beyond June 5, in which case the Secretary of Legation will be given *ad interim* charge of its affairs. Encloses copies of the correspondence involved in arranging for his audience of leave from this Court. ALS. DNA, RG59, Dip. Disp., Great Britain, vol. 32. Received June 25.

MISCELLANEOUS LETTERS   April 28, 1825

From H[ENRY] and D[AVID] COTHEAL and ABRAHAM S. HALLETT, New York. Review their efforts, successful only in small part, to obtain restitution for loss of vessel and cargo in the case of the *Mosquito,* captured in 1823 by a privateer from Puerto Rico; conclude that they "have no resource [*sic*] for redress except from" their "own government or that" their "just claim may be made to the King of Spain" (Ferdinand VII); transmit various documents relating to the claim. LS. DNA, RG76, Misc. Claims, Spain. The Cotheal brothers were proprietors of a counting house and shipping firm in New York, trading particularly along the coasts of Latin America. Hallett not further identified. The claim for indemnity in the case of the *Mosquito* was finally resolved among the awards under a convention of 1834. *Sen. Docs.,* 35 Cong., 2 Sess., no. 18, p. 121.
    On May 18, Daniel Brent, by Clay's direction prior to his departure, sent Alexander H. Everett copies of the letter from the Cotheals and Hallett with its enclosures and stated "the Secretary's wish" that Everett should aid in obtaining "a just indemnity." Copy, in DNA, RG59, Dip. Instr., vol. 10, pp. 361-62 (M77, R5).

From A[LEXANDER] II. EVERETT, Boston. Requests copies of "all the papers re-lating to our foreign affairs which have been published by order of Congress" and of all papers in the State Department that throw light on the questions of suppression of piracy in the West Indies and claims against Spain for "spoliations committed upon our citizens in the same quarter"; also asks for a list of vessels "captured either by pirates or privateers." Suggests that a notice be inserted in the newspapers, requesting all who have suffered by such captures to send detailed information to the Department. ALS. DNA, RG59, Dip. Disp., Spain, vol. 25 (M31, R27).

To Francis T. Brooke

My dear Sir   Washington 29 Apl. 1825

I have just received your favor of the 27h.[1] I did not know that the extract published by Mr. Pleasants[2] was from a letter written by you. The same thing has been told to me by several, and amongst others by Mr. Wilson Allen of the Bowling Green[3] and Col. H. Mercer. I think you ought to take no notice of the contradiction of Mr. Ritchie.[4] Your name is not before the public as the writer of the letter. If it were you might be considered as pledged to sustain the assertion. Mr. Allen told me that Mr. Crawford's[5] warmest friends in Fredericksburg, after seeing him, admitted his incompetency for the office. I think I would let it stand where it does. We ought to make great allowances for chagrin and disappointment. I wish Mr. Crawford could have been seen at Richmond. Mr. Van Buren[6] told me that they had committed a great error in not withdrawing him in May last, on account of his want of health.

From all quarters the testimony which I get, public and private, of the public approbation of my late conduct, is full complete and triumphant. They are preparing in Kentucky to give me an enthusiastic reception. But you see they will not let me alone. Ingham has just made his appearance, and I wish he would write by the league, instead of the yard.[7] The next shot will be from McDuffie, or from Nashville or from both.[8]

Ever Faithfully Yr friend   H. CLAY
The Honble F. Brooke.

ALS. KyU.   1 Not found.
2 John Hampden Pleasants. The "extract" has not been identified.
3 A racing and social center, the county seat of Caroline County, Virginia.
4 Thomas Ritchie.   5 William H. Crawford.
6 Martin Van Buren.

7 On April 22, the Washington *Daily National Intelligencer* had noted an announcement that an address by Samuel D. Ingham to his constituents would appear in the next issue of the *Doylestown Farmer* (not found). The document, "Address to the People of the Counties of Bucks, Northampton, Wayne, and Pike, Pennsylvania," was published in the *Intelligencer* on April 30; also in *Niles' Weekly Register*, XXVIII (April 30, 1825), 134-38.

8 George McDuffie; Andrew Jackson.

To Langdon Cheves

My dear Sir   Washington 29h. April 1825

I received the papers from your Board[1] which you intended for me, with the exception of the protocol, which I dare say I shall get in due time. I thank you most heartily for the memo.[2] which will save me much trouble. I do not distinctly understand whether it is of that or of the protocol that you desire a copy. If you will have the goodness to inform me it shall be sent you.

And now about the House that I told you I would avail myself of your friendly disposition to make some enquiries concerning. I should be glad if you would ascertain from Mr. Caldwell[3] (who I understand is a gentleman of the profession) what is the lowest rent he would be willing to receive for the House, if taken for a term of three or four years; and whether he would now have it put in a state of reparation, if it want it?

I am faithfully & cordially Your friend   H. CLAY
Langdon Cheves Esqr.

ALS. ScHi. Addressed to Philadelphia.
[1] See above, Cheves to Clay, March 14, 31, April 26 (1), 1825.
[2] See above, Cheves to Clay, April 26 (2), 1825.
[3] Probably Timothy Caldwell, of Philadelphia, who had advertised for rent the house and premises formerly occupied by Stratford Canning, in Washington. Washington *Daily National Intelligencer,* November 27, 1823. The Washington *Daily National Journal,* May 16, 1825, reported that this property was "undergoing a complete repair, for the reception of Mr. [Charles R.] Vaughan, the new Minister from Great Britain, whose arrival may be shortly expected."

To E[dmund] P[endleton] Gaines

General E. P. Gaines   Washington 29 April 1825
Sir.

Having met with Genl. Brown[1] to day, and fearing that I might not have the pleasure to see you, I requested him to make a communication to you respecting an incident which occurred in the President's House a few days ago. Upon calling at your Lodgings this morning, I was unfortunate in not finding you at them. The incident to which I allude, is this— Upon leaving the President with whom I had been engaged in official consultation, I unexpectedly met on coming out of his receiving room at the door of it, in the adjoining room, Genl. Brown, yourself, and a young Gentleman, Mr. Butler,[2] to whom as your aid, I was introduced by Genl. Brown. Both the meeting and the in[tro]duction were entirely unexpected by me. Upon being presented to Mr. Butler, I walked up to him and offered my hand—in my usual manner, which he declined receiving. I remarked nothing offensive in his countenance, but he distinctly evinced an unwillingness to reciprocate that mode of salutation. Attaching no particular virtue to the touch of his hand, I turned off and left the room. Upon reflexion on the occurrence, it appeared to me that if the young gentleman designed an affront to a total stranger, he could not have possibly selected an apartment of the President's house, at the very door of his receiving room, and within the hearing, if not in the view of the Chief Magistrate, to give the affront. I had a right therefore to conclude that he had some cutaneous disease with which he was unwilling to infect me, or that, as he kept his hand enclosed in his coat or waistcoat, that some newly established etiquette forbade the ancient & unfashionable mode of salutation. But on my return from the office to my lodgings yesterday afternoon, I perceived your visiting card, unaccompanied by that of any other person; from which I have supposed that I may have misconceived the intentions of Mr. Butler and that he really meditated offering me an insu[lt.] Upon that supposition this Note is addressed to you, with the sole object, that you may impress upon the member of your family to whom I refer, the utility of the observance of urbanity, as a necessary part of that discipline, for which the American Army, generally, is so eminently distinguished. I have the honor to be with great respect Your obedient servant   H. CLAY

LS (the formal closing in Clay's hand). DLC-HC (DNA, M212, R1). Endorsed by Clay: "This letter was sent to Genl. Gaines at his lodgings in the City of Washn. on the date of its date; but he had left it and the letter was never transmitted to him. HC." MS. torn.
1 Jacob J. Brown. See Adams, *Memoirs*, VII, 8.
2 Edward George Washington Butler, godson and former ward of Andrew Jackson.

From Chauncey Whittelsey

My Dear Sir   New Orleans April 29th. 1825
My friend Nathl. Chamberlain formerly of the house of Peabody & Chamberlain of this City, has made application for the place of Consul at Mexico, which it is said is soon to become vacant.[1]

Mr Chamberlain is an able Merchant, & is well qualified in my opinion for the Office. He has requested me to express my opinion to you, & I do it cheerfully.

I have been somewhat disappointed in not hearing from you; tho' I am aware that your labours this past winter must have been great. In my last[2] I mentioned that I had bro't Suit against Cox & Trudeau[3] in the State Court, & gave you my reasons for it. The Cause can be brot to Trial at any time, when you choose—after we receive Cox's original letter to you. Judge Robinson[4] is at Havanna, & will probably never hold another Court—tho' he may live a year or two it is not probable he will ever have health, to enable him to perform the Duties of his Office. I have been very unwell this winter, but am now able to attend Court, tho not perfectly restored. I remain D Sir with much respect Your friend & Obedt Servt.   CHAUNCEY WHITTELSEY
Honble Henry Clay.

ALS. DNA, RG59, Misc. Letters (M179, R62).

1 On Chamberlain, see below, John Clay to Henry Clay, May 23, 1825. He did not receive the appointment.   2 Not found.
3 Nathaniel Cox and Charles L. Trudeau. See below, Account, *ca.* May 27, 1826.
4 Thomas B. Robertson. See above, III, 249n.

DIPLOMATIC NOTES   April 29, 1825

To HILARIO DE RIVAS Y SALMON, Philadelphia. Invites him to present any evidence he may wish to the court of enquiry which will convene at the Washington Navy Yard, May 2, to examine into the conduct of Captain David Porter at Fajardo. Copy. DNA, RG59, Notes to Foreign Ministers and Consuls, vol. 3, p. 219 (M38, R3). ALS draft in CSmH. Published in Washington *Daily National Intelligencer,* August 22, 1825; *Niles' Weekly Register,* XXIX (September 3, 1825), 12. See above, Nelson to Clay, April 6, 1825, note.

INSTRUCTIONS AND DISPATCHES   April 29, 1825

From C[ORTLAND] L. PARKER, Curaçao. Reports the wreck of the schooner *Magdalena,* of Philadelphia, and the rescue of the crew from Indians on the coast of Colombia by sailors of an English merchant sloop, whose captain asks payment of $300. Parker thinks this sum excessive but wants a statement of policy concerning reward for such rescues. LS. DNA, RG59, Cons. Disp., Curaçao, vol. 1 (M-T197, R1). Received May 19. No answer found.

MISCELLANEOUS LETTERS   April 29, 1825

From ARCHI[BALD] GRACIE, New York. Encloses a "Copy of a memorial presented in 1823," explaining his claim against France, and requests Clay to present the case to the French Minister (Baron Durand de Mareuil). ALS. DNA, RG76, Misc. Claims, France.
   On May 23, 1825, Daniel Brent, "by direction of the Secretary," informed Gracie that his "claim will not fail to receive all the attention to which it may be entitled . . . in common with others of the same nature. . . ." Copy, in DNA, RG59, Dom. Letters, vol. 21, pp. 47-48 (M40, R19).

From DUDLEY L. PICKMAN, Salem (Massachusetts). Requests Clay's intervention in behalf of William Gomez, a nineteen-year-old American merchant seaman, of Portuguese descent, who was imprisoned at Santiago de Cuba on July 4 of the preceding year on a charge of stealing bacon. ALS. DNA, RG59, Misc. Letters (M179, R62). Gomez was a resident of Salem.

From SAMUEL L. SOUTHARD, Navy Department. States that a court of enquiry has been ordered to convene at the Washington Navy Yard on May 2, to examine into the conduct of Captain David Porter at Fajardo the preceding November. LS. *Ibid.* A copy is located in DNA, RG45, Executive Letterbooks, 1821-1831, p. 107. Published in Washington *Daily National Intelligencer,* August 22, 1825. See above, Nelson to Clay, April 6, 1825, note.

From JOHN WEBSTER, clerk of the District Court, Clarksburg, (West) Virginia. Points to the urgency of filling "the vacancy in the office of Judge of the District Court at this place." ALS. DNA, RG59, Misc. Letters (M179, R62). See above, Zane to Clay, April 5, 1825; Breckinridge to Clay, April 9, 1825; Hammond to

Clay, April 11, 1825; Little to Clay, April 22, 1825. Webster had been active
as a Jeffersonian politician since before the turn of the century.

From Henry B. Bascom

Mr. Clay.   Pittsburgh P. 30. Apl. *1825*.
my Dear Sir,
    I am requested to recommend to your notice Mr Wm. Connelly
of Franklin P. who is an applicant for a clerkship in Washington[1]—
He is a man of *intelligence* & *integrity,* and is one of the best
Clerks in the U. States.
    If you can find a vacancy for him I shd. be glad as he has been
unfortunate—
    You have many friends here—the *"Effigy"* business,[2] an eternal
disgrace to Pittsburg [*sic*], did you no harm— You are unquestionably gaining ground in this section of P. Wishing you perpetual
happiness, I am my Dear Sir your constant friend, H. B. BASCOM.
Hon. H. Clay.

ALS. DNA, RG59, A. and R. (MR1). Bascom, a Methodist minister, had held
pastorates in Ohio and Kentucky and, in 1823, through Clay's influence, had been
elected Chaplain to Congress. He was now residing at Pittsburgh, where he had
moved early in March of this year, following appointment to that city. In 1826 he
was assigned to Uniontown, Pennsylvania, where he helped found Madison College,
of which he was the first president (1827-1829). He was later an agent for the American
Colonization Society (1829-1831), a professor at Augusta College, Kentucky (1832-
1842), president of Transylvania University (1842-1849), and bishop of the Methodist
Episcopal Church, South (for a few months until his death in 1850). He was active
in bringing about the sectional division of his denomination, was for a time editor
of the *Southern Methodist Quarterly Review,* and was the author of *Methodism and
Slavery* (1847) and two volumes of *Sermons* (1849).
    1 Connelly, not further identified, did not receive an appointment.
    2 See above, Address, March 26, 1825, note 8.

From Samuel J. Donaldson

Dear Sir   Balto April 30th 1825
    I Send a Copy of the Chancellors Order on Your Petition & that
of the Crs of S & R Purviance, by which he appoints me trustee
for the settlement of the Unfinished Business of the Estate.[1] The
Bond required will be filed during the Ensui[ng . . .][2] then be
Competent to receive Conveyances for the [. . .][3] and the Mortgage
agreed on in February last to Secu[re] the payme[nt] of the Notes
drawn by You on the 16th of that Month,[4] & which you said would
be Executed at Lexington on Your return to Kentucky[.] Oblige
me by Stating when Convenient, at what time You Expect [to be]
in Lexington.
    I recd. your favour Enclosing a Letter from Your frien[d][5]
relative to the depredations Committed on the Lands in Hen-

d[erson's] Grant,[6] for which I thank you. Mr Prentiss[7] has been written to, on the Subject & requested to take immediately Such Steps as may be Necessary in regard to them.

    I am Sir respectfully Yours   SAML J. DONALDSON
Mr Clay

ALS. DLC-TJC (DNA, M212, R16). MS. stained and torn. Endorsed by Clay: "Answd." Answer not found.

1 A copy of the order, signed by Theodorick Bland, chancellor, dated April 23, 1825, is enclosed. "The Petition of Henry Clay filed on the 20th Instant praying to be discharged from the Office of Trustee for the benefit of the Creditors of Samuel and Robert Purviance to which he was appointed by an Order of this Court made on the 27th February 1811" has not been found. See above, I, 547; Donaldson to Clay, February 26, 1825.   2 Three or four words missing.
3 Three or four words missing.   4 See above, Agreement, February 16, 1825.
5 Neither letter has been found.   6 See above, I, 494n.
7 Probably William H. Prentiss.

From Philemon Thomas

    Baton Rouge State of Louisiana   Apriel [*sic*] 30th 1825 Old frend [*sic*], I Receaved your friendly Leter[1] [*sic*] And am hapy [*sic*] to hear of your helth [*sic*], but Should be hapy to Receave a line from you.more frequent, for I sinsearly wish your prosperity, and altho we have lost you for President am hapy that you have agread to fill that of Secretary of theas united States and Still hope to se [*sic*] the day that you will fill the other,   I beleave that this State [is ve]ry well Satisfied with Mr Adams as they failed in geting [*sic*] you,   Jactions [*sic*] frends hear make a grait [*sic*] nois [*sic*], while your frends are of the more moderate, and had not jactions frends maid a Compromise with Mr Adamses frends, you wood have got the votes of this State, but your frends wished a fair Election and wood not Enter into any improper Compromise,   In the Second Balet had no Compromis [*sic*] taken plas as above Mr Adams frends wood have voted for you   But tis now over and Cant Be Changed therefore we may now let it go,   I will only ad [*sic*] that I think our delegation or the Majority of them in Congress did Rite in there voting for Mr Adams, and before the four years expueres [*sic*] I think all the Citazens will be of my way of Thinking, for tis very Rair to find a grait Military man and a Statesman blended in The same purson,   our grait Washington was one of those Exceptions, but Sho [*sic*] me another, in the united States, that has prove [*sic*] him Self so,   I Recolect [*sic*] none, it apears [*sic*] from information we shall have Boliver [*sic*], very near us fiting [*sic*] to free his Felow [*sic*] Cuntry [*sic*] men in Cuba,[2]   if he Should be Sucksesfull I shall be hapy for I want to se all Nations free,   There is and will be wanting I prosume [*sic*] Many Consels [*sic*], Sent to the difrent Seports in the Republicks,   I therefore

Beg leave to Recomend [*sic*] to your and the Presidents Consideration Mr Diego Pintado,[3] who is a Spanyard by Burth and a Man
who I have been aquainted [*sic*] with for twenty years, and who
is a firm Republican, to be apointed [*sic*] to sum of those Republicks
or ports as a Consul,   he is a man Of Sound understanding speak
[*sic*] thi [*sic*], Inglish french & Spanish, and do beleave that he
wood be firm and independant in what Eaver plase [*sic*] that he mite
be apointed to fill,   Mr Gurley[4] is well aquainted with him and
may Say Sumthing on that Subject,   I have nothing more that is
worth your hearing   I am your Real frend and Hle Svt
The Honorable Henry Clay   PHILN THOMAS

ALS. DNA, RG59, A. and R. (MR3). A native of Virginia and veteran of the
Revolution, Thomas had settled in Mason County, Kentucky, which he had represented
in both Houses of the State legislature (1796-1803). Removing to Louisiana in 1806,
he had also served in the legislature of that State, had led an uprising against Spanish
rule in West Florida, and had been major general of Louisiana militia during the
War of 1812. He later represented Louisiana as a Jacksonian Democrat in the
United States Congress (1831-1835).   1 Not found.
2 Cf. above, Clay to Poinsett, March 26, 1825; Robertson to Clay, April 20, 1825;
Clay to Everett, April 27, 1825.
3 Not further identified. He received no appointment.   4 Henry H. Gurley.

From Elisha Whittlesey

Sir   Canfield Trumbull County Ohio April 30th 1825
   The bearer Mr Hall Smith will visit Washington for the purpose
of communicating to the President what information he possesses
of this section of the Country and its adaptation for canals. Mr
Smith has long been a resident of this country and is well acquainted
with that part of it, contiguous to the South Shore of Lake Erie,
its waters &c. He feels a deep interest in having the Chesapeake
and Ohio canal[1] located on the Chenango[2] rout, and that its
termination should be at the mouth of the Ashtabula Creek, near
which he resides. He is a gentleman who sustains a good character,
is enterprising and industrious in business. An introduction to
the President and any other civilities extended to him will be thankfully received by him, and gratefully acknowledged by Sir Yours
Most Respectfully   E WHITTLESEY—
Hon H Clay—Secretary of State—

ALS. DNA, RG59, Letters of Introduction. Endorsed: "Recd 10th June."
1 See above, III, 593n.
2 The Shenango River, in western Pennsylvania.

MISCELLANEOUS LETTERS   April 30, 1825

From NATHANIEL SILSBEE, Salem (Massachusetts). Solicits aid for the objective
expressed in the enclosed letter from Dudley L. Pickman. ALS. DNA, RG59,
Misc. Letters (M179, R62). See above, Pickman to Clay, April 29, 1825. On

May 6, Daniel Brent, "by the Secretary's direction," acknowledged Silsbee's letter and transmitted to him a copy of "a letter from this Department to Mr. James J. Wright, the Commercial Agent of the United States at St. Iago de Cuba, instructing him in an especial manner to employ his good offices in such way as might prove effectual, towards procuring the enlargement of William Gomez from imprisonment. . . ." Copy, in DNA, RG59, Dom. Letters, vol. 21, p. 51 (M40, R19).

Wright, born in New York, resigned from his position as commercial agent in 1826 (see below, Wright to Clay, August 10, 1826) and subsequently settled in Ohio. In 1844 he was re-appointed to Santiago, now as consul, where he died the following year. A copy of the letter from Brent to Wright, also dated May 6, 1825, is found in DNA, RG59, Cons. Instr., vol. 2, p. 356 (M78, R2).

APPLICATIONS, RECOMMENDATIONS   April 30, 1825

CALEB KIRK, "Stark County Ohio (Near Attwater Post office Portage County.)," solicits employment; states: "I wrote thee a year or two ago concerning the Land Offices in Ohio; and thee verry kindly replied that it would give thee pleasure to aid me. . . ; But that I must first settle myself in the State. This I have since done, and wrote thee from here, in february last. . . ." ALS. DNA, RG59, A. and R. (MR2). Undated; postmarked April 30. The letters mentioned have not been found. On Kirk's former residence, see above, III, 397n.

On June 14, 1825, Daniel Brent, in Clay's absence, acknowledged receipt of a letter dated May 25 (not found), in which Kirk had reiterated his request. Brent informed him that the letter had been referred to the Secretary of the Treasury (Samuel L. Southard), who was vested with the power of appointment to land offices. Copy. DNA, RG59, Dom. Letters, vol. 21, p. 96 (M40, R19). Kirk received no appointment.

INSTRUCTIONS AND DISPATCHES   May 1, 1825

From CHARLES D. COXE, Tunis. Presents the case of Ambrose Allegro, formerly secretary to the consulate at Tunis, who has received no pay since 1810, and recommends that he "receive some relief, in his declining years. . . ." ALS. DNA, RG59, Cons. Disp., Tunis, vol. 5 (M-T303, R5). Addressed to Secretary of State. Allegro not further identified. See below, Clay to Heap, April 20, 1826.

MISCELLANEOUS LETTERS   May 1, 1825

From AMBROSE ALLEGRO, Tunis. States that he has served the American consulate at Tunis since 1801, "in the triple capacity of Chancellor, Secretary and Interpreter," but that he has received no salary since 1810; petitions for "some salary or remuneration for the future; by which he may be enabled to support himself and soften the infirmities of age." ALS. DNA, RG59, Cons. Disp., Tunis, vol. 5 (M-T303, R5). Addressed to Secretary of State.

APPLICATIONS, RECOMMENDATIONS   May 1, 1825

H[ENRY] M. BRACKENRIDGE, Pensacola, recommends Robert Mitchell, "of this place," for appointment as naval storekeeper. ALS. DNA, RG59, A. and R.

(MR5). Brackenridge was at this time United States judge in West Florida, a position to which he had been appointed in 1822. Mitchell, who did not receive appointment as storekeeper, was named collector of customs at Pensacola in April, 1826, and continued in that post for some twenty years.

Edmund H. Hopkins, Henderson, Kentucky, solicits appointment as Secretary of Legation at London. ALS. *Ibid.* (MR2). A graduate of Transylvania University, with A.B. and M.A. degrees in 1820, Hopkins became an outstanding lawyer, notably in chancery and land litigation. On the appointment here desired, cf. below, King to Clay, May 6, 1825, note.

Robert Mitchell, Pensacola, expresses a hope that the "annexed letter [above, Brackenridge to Clay, this date] will claim . . . consideration"; states that other communications on the same subject are being forwarded to the President; and, to explain the necessity of this activity, adds: "our late Delegate Genl. [Richard K.] Call, has, since his return, used his endeavours to prevent my success, & advocate others, in consequence of his considering (in true *military* style) an honorable political opponent, a personal enemy; occasioned by his exception to some Essays of mine, in which I reprobated the course pursued in relation to the events, preceding and subsequent to the Presidential election, and which also tended to prostrate his political career in this Territory." ALS. DNA, RG59, A. and R. (MR5). Mitchell's "Essays" not found.

To Charles Hammond

My dear Sir   Washington 2d. May 1825

Your young friend Mr. Ruffin[1] cannot be received in the Academy at West point this year. Mr. Calhoun[2] not only filled all the vacancies pror [*sic*] to his leaving the Department of War, but has provided for many that will arise, by anticipation. But I have prevailed on the Secy of the Navy[3] to promise to appoint him a Midshipman on the first of the ensuing October. Remind me of it at that time (with Mr. Ruffin's christian name) and the Warrant shall be forwarded.

You would do wrong to quit politics. You occasionally write better than almost any body I know. There are but two things for you to guard against, one is the loss of temper (of which I saw some evidence in an article in reply to very rude attacks upon you)[4] and the other I will not now mention. You see altho' often wanting it myself, I nevertheless can give good advice. I wrote you about my letter, extracts from which you were kind enough to transmit to me, accompanied by some pertinent observations of your own; for the press. As you only professed to publish *extracts,* I wished some parts of what you had copied not to be published. And I wrote to you for your permission to omit them.[5] The publication, if made at all, will be delayed until you are heard from.

I have received your favor of the 18h.[6] Your good opinion of my Address[7] gives me more confidence in it. I have letters from all parts of the Union, and from some of the most eminent men in it, speaking

of it in the most satisfactory manner— These letters would fill a
volume. As a composition I have no doubt it has many faults. I
have not much confidence in my capacity to write; but I did not
aim at elegance. I endeavored only to narrate, in clear language,
the naked truth. Its effect has been overwhelming to my opponents. Of that I have the most abundant evidence, public and
private.

There is really no contradiction between my letter to you, and
my conversations with Dr. Drake.[8] You must attend to dates and
circumstances. My letter to you bears date the 25h. October[9]   In
my letter to you I say, "What course my friends may take, what it
may be proper for me to pursue, in the event of my not being returned to the H. of R. I have not yet determined. I have indeed
purposely postponed the consideration of that question." &c Now
my conversations with Dr. Drake were I think from the first to the
fifteenth of Novr. The last was probably on the 14h. In them I say
as between Adams & Jackson I shall decide for the former.[10]
Recollect that important events were then rapidly passing. The
election for electors had just taken place in Ohio, and on the 14h.
Novr. I did not know the result of it. I heard the final issue of it
for the first time on the Kanawha, in my route to this City.[11] In
my letter to you I was speaking of the whole subject. It was evident
that, although I strongly inclined against Mr. Crawford, I had not
absolutely decided against him. I found the state of his health worse
than I had even anticipated it to be; and this, on my arrival here,
confirmed me agt. him. In my conversations with Dr. Drake I was
speaking of a part of the subject. But even if I had postponed the
decision of the question, on the 25h. of Octr., I might even some
days after, from the influence of passing events, have decided it,
without inconsistency.

While on this subject of apparent contradictions, I will notice
one, which is merely superficial, that has been carped at between
my address and Dr. Drakes letter.[12] In my address I say that the
opinion of the Ohio delegation formed a *collateral* consideration
&c. Now it is said that if, as I told Dr. Drake, I had decided in K.
to prefer Adams to J. the opinion of your delegation could not have
contributed to the formation of my own. But I do not use it as creating but only as *confirming* my opinion. I say, in the the first part
of my address, after it was known who were returned to the House,
I deliberately examined &c. and "weighed all the facts before me,
upon which my judgment was to be formed or *reviewed*." Now this
implied that I had previously formed an opinion. I then proceed
to state the *direct* considerations which led to my determination,
and bring in as *subsidiary* that of the Ohio delegation. Altho' I

would have made great sacrifices to go along with it, I certainly never meant to give up my *deliberate* judgment to it or to any other men.

Ingham has appeared,[13] and he makes a figure as silly as Eaton.[14] I shall not write about him. He wants to be Governor of Pennsa. and is afraid Kremer[15] will run away with all the honor. Neither ought to be Govr. of Pennsa., but if I had to decide between them I would give it to Kremer, fool as he is, rather than Ingham who is both knave and fool. The former, in honest hands, might be made some thing of; but out of the latter, in no hands, could good spring. The next fire will be from McDuffie or Nashville.[16] I hope they will all write—God send them "pen ink and paper," it is all I want to prove the Conspiracy.

I send you a poem just published here with keys to the dramatis personae.[17] I know nothing of the author. It is calculated (though devoid of any elegance) to strike the mass of plain readers. Perhaps it might not be amiss to republish it at Cincinnati.

Mr. Kane[18] is mistaken about Mr. Adams' friends in N. York— The majority of them (and it is impossible to please every body) are well satisfied. Both parties (that of Clinton and that of V. Buren[19]) are vieing [*sic*] with each other to be considered as the warmest supporters of the Admon. Tho' I have no doubt that Clinton will ultimately go into the opposition, if he think he can make any thing of it.

I shall leave here next week for home, where I hope to get about the 20h. of May. I should be very glad to see you when in the West, having a thousand things to say, which I have not time to commit to paper. The labors of my office have been excessive. I have toiled 12 or 14 hours per day. I wish to God I had your assistance, in some way or other. You are right in saying that I have sacrificed much. But I think I shall convince you, when I have the pleasure to see you, that you were wrong as to my accepting it. If my health can be preserved, I *will* perform its duties, arduous as they are, and I *think* (at least I hope) I shall not disappoint you and my other friends.

I have but little leisure for the luxury of private correspondence. My respect for you cannot be better testified than by the fact that this is the longest private letter which I have written since I have been in this office. With my best regards to Dr. Drake, you may shew it to him if you please—   Sincerely Your friend
Charles Hammond Esqr.   H. CLAY

ALS. InU.
1 Charles K. Ruffin, born in Ohio and appointed a midshipman from that State on October 24, 1825.   2 John C. Calhoun.
3 Samuel L. Southard.   4 Specific item not identified.

5 See above, Clay to Hammond, April 23, 1825.
6 Not found.   7 Above, March 26, 1825.
8 Daniel Drake.   9 Above, III, 870-72.
10 See above, Address, March 26, 1825.
11 Cf. above, III, 884, 887.
12 Dated at Lexington, Kentucky, March 21, 1825, published in Washington *Daily National Intelligencer,* April 4, 1825, and widely reprinted in contemporary journals. In this document Drake wrote that, in several conversations "last fall," Clay had "expressed himself as having, long before, decided in favor of Mr. Adams, in case the contest should be between that gentleman and General Jackson."
13 See above, Clay to Brooke, April 29, 1825, note.
14 John H. Eaton.   15 George Kremer.
16 George McDuffie; Andrew Jackson.
17 A copy of the effusion, a broadside entitled "THE CONCLAVE—A POEM, *Descriptive of a scene at Washington previous to a late important election, in which the dramatis personae are characteristically delineated, and the object and the means of their united councils clearly unfolded,"* is located in MHi-Adams Papers, Letters Received (M479, R469).
18 Probably Elias Kent Kane.   19 DeWitt Clinton; Martin Van Buren.

To Rufus King

My dear Sir   (Private)   Washington 2d. May 1825.

Your instructions are nearly completed, and I shall be able to put them in your possession in the early part of next week.[1] They will not extend to the objects of the negotiation begun and suspended last year,[2] for the present. I have been obliged to defer the preparation of instructions on those objects, in consequence of the great pressure of official business, but they will follow you to England in due time. If you should like to have your outfit, your wishes being indicated on that matter will be promptly attended to.

You are well acquainted with the point of difference between G.B. and the U.S. in respect to the Colonial trade, that is, whether the produce of the U.S. shall be introduced into one British Colony on the same terms as if it were carried from another British Colony. Can we maintain that ground? Can we distinguish it from the claim, if it were asserted by G.B., to have the sugar of the W. Indies admitted into the Atlantic ports of the U.S. on the same terms as that of Louisiana? At present the alien duties levied upon British vessels, coming from the Colonies, and their Cargoes, in the ports of the U.S. are countervailed by equivalent alien duties levied on American vessels and their Cargoes entering those Colonial ports. As much the greater part of the tonnage employed in the trade is American, do we not suffer most by the continuance, and should we not gain the most, by a reciprocal abolition of those alien duties? Would not, in other words, the abolition have a favorable effect on our tonnage? Can we not maintain a successful competition with the produce of the Northern B. Colonies, even with the British protecting duties against us if all alien duties were abolished by both Countries, from our proximity and superior natural advantages?[3]

What will be the effect of Mr. Huskisson's late motions in Parliament upon the trade, American and European, with the British West India Colonies?[4]

I trouble you with these enquiries, because I know that your familiarity with the subject is much greater than mine. You will oblige me by an answer to them.

I was extremely gratified that you consented to serve our Country in your contemplated mission. And I sincerely hope that you may be the means of cementing, more and more, the two Countries together. G. B. appears to be resuming her natural position, that is the head of liberal principles, commercial and political, in Europe.

With great regard & esteem I am faithfully Your ob. servant

The Honble R. King   H. CLAY

ALS. NHi. Endorsed by King: ". . . ansd *copy infra* 6 May—"
[1] See below, May 10, 1825.
[2] On trade between the United States and the British colonies in America. See above, III, 729, note 21.
[3] On May 2 President Adams noted that Clay, preparing King's instructions "upon the Colonial Trade question; thinks there is more than plausibility in the British claims, and that we ought to concede something on this point." *Memoirs*, VI, 540.
[4] See above, Rush to Clay, March 26, 1825. Huskisson's speech of March 21 had been published in the Washington *Daily National Journal*, April 28, 1825.

DIPLOMATIC NOTES   May 2, 1825

From HILARIO DE RIVAS Y SALMON, Philadelphia. Acknowledges receipt of Clay's recent letter (above, April 29, 1825) ; presents an extract of the journal of the Captain General of Puerto Rico for November 23 and a Government *Gazette* treating the (Fajardo) occurrence; and explains the detention of the American landing party, upon which Captain Porter based his complaint, as a natural reaction to the appearance of "a few foreigners . . . justly liable to suspicion, from their having neither passports nor papers, nor any uniform to distinguish them from enemies," and this "at a time of war with some neighboring governments, and when the island was exposed to an invasion." Expresses appreciation for the promptitude with which the President has ordered the return of Captain Porter and the investigation of his conduct. LS (in Spanish). DNA, RG59, Notes from Spanish Legation, vol. 8 (M59, R11). Translation (quoted) published in Washington *Daily National Intelligencer*, August 22, 1825. Miguel de la Torre, Count of Torrepando, was Captain General of Puerto Rico, 1823-1837.

From the BARON DE TUYLL, Washington, "Private." Thanks Clay for notification, by "private communication" of April 30 (not found), that the owners of the *Pearl* "are satisfied with the arrangement lately concluded." N. DNA, RG59, Notes from Russian Legation, vol. 1 (M39, R1).

INSTRUCTIONS AND DISPATCHES   May 2, 1825

From JOHN M. FORBES, Buenos Aires, no. 19. Reports rumors of the beginning of operations against Brazilian outposts in the Banda Oriental and of Brazilian reinforcement of the garrison at Montevideo; notes the "more particular solicitude of this government" in the victory of the Patriot cause in Upper Peru and its "extreme uncertainty as to the ultimate views of Bolivar in relation to the Provinces of Upper Peru, now fallen under his power. . . ." Concluding paragraphs, dated May 8 and 11, report triumphs of the forces attacking the Brazilians in Banda Oriental and at Montevideo. Comments finally: "The Government has not yet publickly participated in these measures, but I am assured that the Executive has this morning proposed to Congress to sanction military movements towards Uruguay and even to extend them generally to aid the war against the Brazilians in Monte Video." ALS. DNA, RG59, Dip. Disp., Argentina, vol. 2 (M69, R3). Addressed to Secretary of State; received July 13. Published in Espil (comp.), *Once Años en Buenos Aires*, 357-60. On the dispute with Brazil, see above, Clay to Poinsett, March 26, 1825, note 3.

From RICHARD RUSH, London, no. 434. Encloses copies of the notes between the Spanish and British governments relating to the latter's recognition of the new American States. ALS. DNA, RG59, Dip. Disp., Great Britain, vol. 32 (M30, R28). Received June 25. Cf. above, Rush to Secretary of State, April 4, 1825.

APPLICATIONS, RECOMMENDATIONS   May 2, 1825

NATHAN BRIDGE, Boston, Massachusetts, recommends Thomas Wilson for appointment as consul at Dublin; states that the writer is known to President Adams. ALS. DNA, R59, A. and R. (MR4). See above, Maury to Clay, March 29, 1825. Bridge was, perhaps, the well-known schoolmaster of Salem Street.

To Peter B. Porter

My dear Sir   Washington 3d. May 1825

I recd. your favor recommending Mr. Grant for the office of Collector of Oswego, and inclosing a letter from Mr. Bronson in his behalf.[1] I immediately directed an enquiry to be made at the Treasury, and learned that the office was not vacant, and that Mr. Grant had as yet prefered [*sic*] no application for it. Should he make one, every consideration will be given to it.

I pray you to be assured that, in recommending any of your friends, so far as I may have any agency in the appointments which they may happen to desire, I will give always to your recommendations the most full & friendly consideration, whether I may write you on the occasion or not. With respect to appointments, the administration will act upon one general rule, which is not to commit itself by *previous* pledges or promises, which I am sure you will approve.

I shall take my departure for K. next week— With my best regards always to Mrs. Porter, I remain Faithfy & Cordially Your friend
Genl. P. B. Porter   H. CLAY

ALS. NBuHi.
[1] Neither letter has been found. The latter was probably written by Alvin Bronson and addressed to the Acting Secretary of the Treasury (Samuel L. Southard), rather than to Clay. If a letter by Porter was addressed to Clay, it apparently covered one

addressed to the Acting Secretary of the Treasury, recommending John Grant, Jr., a local judge of Oswego, New York, for the office of collector of customs at that port (AN, draft, undated, in NBuHi). Grant was nominated for the position a year later, on April 25, 1826, and the appointment was promptly approved.

DIPLOMATIC NOTES   May 3, 1825

To SEVERIN LORICH. Promises to send "in a few days an answer to his notes of the 16th. March last, the 2d. September and the 25th. July 1824"; refers to the difficulty of transacting business with "Foreign ministers" who do not reside in the City of Washington but concedes that in the case of Lorich, "merely charged ad interim with the affairs of Sweden it might be highly inconvenient to him to remove to Washington." Copy. DNA, RG59, Notes to Foreign Ministers and Consuls, vol. 3, p. 219 (M38, R3). See above, Lorich to Clay, April 28, 1825.

From HENRY U. ADDINGTON, Washington. Returns "the interesting paper" loaned him yesterday and comments: "I should almost despair of success from any further representation to the Court of Spain, did I not recollect several instances in which the word *'never'* used diplomatically has been found in practise to be synonimous [sic] with *'immediately.'* May it be so in this case!" ALS. DNA, RG59, Notes from British Legation, vol. 13 (M50, R14). The "paper" probably encompassed the segment of Everett's instructions (above, April 27, 1825) relating to the effort to persuade Spain to recognize the independence of the new Latin American States. See also below, Clay to Middleton, May 10, 1825; Clay to King, May 11, 1825; Clay to Brown, May 13, 1825.

MISCELLANEOUS LETTERS   May 3, 1825

To the SECRETARY OF THE TREASURY [SAMUEL L. SOUTHARD]. Requests information on two points: (1) under what conditions was remission of forfeiture, for illegal importation of ten cases of gin, granted last August in the case of the Swedish vessel *Carl John (Johan)*; and (2) under what terms are vessels of Sweden, Norway, and the Island of St. Bartholomew admitted in ports of the United States. Copy. DNA, RG59, Dom. Letters, vol. 21, p. 47 (M40, R19).

From A[UGUSTE] P[IERRE] CHOUTEAU and JULES DE MUN, St. Louis, Missouri. Present, through Clay to the President, complaint of an injury received from the Government of New Mexico in 1817, when, on a trading expedition, the writers were seized on American soil, conveyed to Santa Fé and imprisoned for six weeks before being released, without their property, and allowed to get home as best they could. Claim that their goods were worth $30,000 and that interest and damages bring the amount due them to $50,000; ask that the United States Minister to Mexico (Joel R. Poinsett) be instructed to plead their cause; and state that they had hoped to recover in the Florida claims indemnity (see above, II, 678n) but that their case was ruled non-applicable. LS, "Duplicate," both signatures by Chouteau. DNA, RG59, Misc. Letters (M179, R62).

Chouteau, born in St. Louis and graduated from the United States Military Academy, had served in the Army briefly on the southwestern frontier and again throughout the War of 1812. He had led a trading party into the Mandan country in 1807 and, as one of ten partners of the Missouri Fur Company, of St. Louis, had conducted an expedition to the mouth of the Knife River during 1809 and 1810. In 1815 he and De Mun had headed a similar venture under license from the Governor of Missouri Territory to trade in the region of the upper Arkansas. Rebuffed by Spanish authorities in an effort to open trade with Santa Fé, the Americans had headed northward, when, as they maintained, severe weather forced them to remain in the area north of the Arkansas and east of the first chain of mountains. There they had been seized by a Spanish military force. Chouteau had subsequently traded among the Osages in western Missouri and in 1823 purchased a trading post at the junction of the Verdigris and Arkansas rivers (present day Oklahoma), where he lived as a "frontier baron" the remainder of his life.

De Mun, born in Santo Domingo and educated in France, had escaped to England during the revolutionary purges of the seventeen nineties. From 1803 to 1808 he had operated a coffee plantation in Cuba and thence had come to the United States, settling at St. Louis and entering upon the fur trade. Following the losses incurred at Santa Fé, he had returned to Cuba, in 1820, and remained there during the next decade. In 1830 he moved back to St. Louis and, shortly thereafter, was appointed secretary and translator to the Federal board of commissioners adjusting claims to French and Spanish land grants. He became register of the United States Land Office at St. Louis in 1837 and recorder of deeds for St. Louis County in 1842.

On June 21, 1825, Daniel Brent, in the absence of Clay, assured Chouteau and De Mun that he had transmitted a copy of their letter of May 3 to Poinsett in Mexico and recommended "to his attention in an especial manner, the claim to which it refers. . . ." Copy, in DNA, RG59, Dom. Letters, vol. 21, pp. 101-102.

The matter was not settled, however, until 1849, when under the terms of legislation in fulfillment of the terms of the Treaty of Guadelupe Hidalgo, by which the United States Government assumed the obligation of paying unliquidated claims of citizens against Mexico, an administrator *de bonis non* for Chouteau and De Mun was paid $30,380, as principal, and $51,392, as interest. John Bassett Moore, *History and Digest of the International Arbitrations to Which the United States Has Been a Party, Together with Appendices Containing the Treaties Relating to Such Arbitrations, and Historical and Legal Notes. . .* (*House Misc. Docs.,* 53 Cong., 2 Sess., no. 212; 6 vols., Washington, 1898), II, 1286.

From A[LEXANDER] H. EVERETT, Exeter, New Hampshire. Acknowledges receipt of Clay's letter of April 26; provides schedule for departure, planned for June 1. ALS. DNA, RG59, Dip. Disp., Spain, vol. 25 (M31, R27).

To Samuel Smith

Dear Sir   Washington 4h. May 1825.

I return you the letter of Mr. Canning and that of Mr. Hughes with the perusal of which you have favored me. I also shewed them to the President. They afforded to both of us much gratification.[1] I should fall in love with Mr. Canning, if I were to read many more of such letters from him. He has seen and is fearlessly treading the true path of glory for England and for him. His predecessor[2] was the great rallying point of unmitigated Legitimacy. Under his ministry, England was rapidly ceasing to be England and becoming subservient to the politics and the views of the Continental allies.

Mr. Canning is placing England in her natural attitude that of being the head of European liberal principles, political and commercial. With such an enlightened minister, and such views, I can have no fears of the U. States maintaining, with G. Britain, relations of the most perfect frankness & friendship.

I do not think at present that any change can be made in the grade of our representative at the Hague. You ought to reflect that something has been done for Hughes by his transfer from Stockholm. He goes to a better climate, as cheap a Country & gets an outfit. He must be patient. I took great pleasure in promoting his late appointment. And he knows the friendship of both the President and myself for him.

I do not understand your objection to late appointments. Do you mean that of Mr. King?[3] I have no doubt that it was a highly proper and will be generally a very popular appointment.

I am faithfy Yr's   H. CLAY

Genl. S. Smith.

ALS. DLC-Samuel Smith Papers (DNA, M212, R22). Endorsed: "Ansd. 5h." Answer not found; cf. below, Clay to Smith, May 7, 1825.

[1] John Q. Adams noted, on April 30: "Clay, H., brought letters from C. Hughes and S. Smith, of Baltimore. Hughes's enclosed copy of an answer received by him from G. Canning, which has put him out of his wits with exultation—his letter is a dissertation to prove that the whole science of diplomacy consists in giving dinners; and Smith thinks that our diplomatic appointments have not strengthened the Administration." Adams, Memoirs, VI, 539. Smith's letter to Clay has not been found.

[2] Viscount Castlereagh.   [3] Rufus King.

INSTRUCTIONS AND DISPATCHES   May 4, 1825

From HEMAN ALLEN, Valparaiso, no. 14. States that "The arrival of the treaty between England and Buenos Ayres [cf. above, Raguet to Secretary of State, March 11, 1825] has induced . . . [him] to renew in writing . . . representations to this government" relative to the claim of the United States "for reciprocal rights"; transmits a copy of his note "to the new Minister, [Francisco R. de] Vicuña, upon that subject, and of his satisfactory reply"; points out that, in view of his restricted instructions with regard to a treaty, he has thus done everything he can to resist "in Chile, the acquisition of those commercial advantages on the part of England, that she is looking to in all parts of the world, and to no part . . . with more present anxiety, than to the South American States"; comments on English methods of acquiring trade and influence in Chile; predicts that "When England shall have recognized the independence of Chile, as it is understood here, that she has that of Mexico, Colombia and Buenos Ayres [see above, Nelson to Secretary of State, March 8, 1825, note; cf. below, King to Clay, September 4, 1825], she will no doubt, proceed immediately to the execution of a treaty with the former, if she thinks the government sufficiently permanent for that purpose"; cites the "vacillating state of affairs" and the monopoly on "tobacco and other articles" as "great barriers" to a treaty between the United States and Chile; but adds that the monopoly may "soon be done away." Expresses satisfaction with "the qualifications of . . . Vicuña." Notes that "The Sovereign Congress still continues in session," although "It is pretty generally expected that the Provinces will soon separate, and form Provincial Legislatures, subject, however, to some general government, to be continued at Santiago."

Reports on the financial stringency encountered by the Chilean Government, which lacks "the means of sending a Minister to the United States." Cites information received from Commodore (Isaac) Hull that (William) Tudor, in Peru, "had declined advocating the claims of American citizens"; explains that "Our trade with Chile is now of trifling amount, and all our vessels that come round the Horn, necessarily pass on to the ports of Peru, where captures, confiscations and other injuries have been very frequent"; and urges "the appointment of a publick agent to that place, to whom our citizens can resort with safety for assistance in redress of their repeated [sic] violated rights." LS, "Duplicate." DNA, RG59, Dip. Disp., Chile, vol. 1 (M-T2, R1). Addressed to Secretary of State, received September 17.

The British Government did not formally recognize the independence of Chile until 1831.

MISCELLANEOUS LETTERS   May 4, 1825

From THOMAS HART BENTON, St. Louis. States, with regard to the claim of Auguste Chouteau and "Julius" de Mun against Mexico: "After almost losing hope, their spirits are suddenly revived by your accession to the department of State." "The French look to you as a friend, and from New Orleans to St. Louis the feeling is universal among them that, in you they will find a patron ready to listen to their complaints, and anxious to redress their wrongs." Argues that "The Federal government . . . has no right to overlook the injury done by a foreign power to the persons and property of American citizens." Identifies Chouteau as "the nephew of Col. Auguste Choteau [sic] the founder of this town and the head of the French population" and DeMun as "the brother of the Count Louis de Mun . . . French Secretary of Legation in the suite of the Baron de Neuville."

Refers to the dissatisfaction of the "French inhabitants of this country" with their treatment by the Federal Government, particularly in regard to confirmation of land titles, which led "several [to] reveal their grief to Lafayette in his late visit to this place" and others (including Jules de Mun, now in Cuba) to "quit the country in disgust and go off to France, Mexico and the West Indies." Comments: ". . . your accession to the department of State has opened new prospects before them. They expect justice from *you*, and this affair of Choteau & Demun is the first instance in which they look to you for aid. Through your agency they expect these gentlemen to be paid, and, in fact, I think you will find no difficulty in satisfying their just expectations. The question of indemnifying them seems to me to address itself exclusively to the Executive branch of the government, I had almost said, *to yourself alone,* for in a question of indemnity to *western* citizens, depending upon the agency of the State department, I should suppose that the President would be decidedly influenced by your advice."

Urges that, in the negotiations about to begin with Mexico, the United States assume the amount of this claim "in return for equivalent advantages." ALS. DNA, RG59, Misc. Letters (M179, R62). For the negotiations with Mexico, see above, Clay to Poinsett, March 26, 1825; on the claim of Chouteau and DeMun, see above, their letter to Clay, May 3, 1825.

APPLICATIONS, RECOMMENDATIONS   May 4, 1825

J[OHN] McLEAN, Shawneetown (Illinois), recommends John C. Rives, now in Washington, for appointment to a clerkship. ALS. DNA, RG59, A. and R.

(MR3). McLean, a lawyer, had been born in North Carolina, had grown up in Logan County, Kentucky, had been elected as the first member of the United States House of Representatives from Illinois (1818-1819), and had served briefly in the United States Senate (November 23, 1824-March 3, 1825). He was again Senator from Illinois from 1829 until his death in the next year. Rives, a native of Virginia, had also lived in Kentucky before moving to Illinois, where, at Edwardsville, he had been a bank clerk and, at Shawneetown, cashier of another bank. Failing to obtain the appointment for which he was here recommended, he was employed for a time by a Washington newspaper; was appointed to a clerkship by President Andrew Jackson; and became an employee and, in 1833, a partner of Francis P. Blair in publishing the Washington *Daily Globe* and the *Congressional Globe*.

ALBERT O. NEWTON, Matanzas, Cuba, reports the death of his brother-in-law, Francis Adams, commercial agent at Matanzas, and solicits his own appointment to the vacancy. ALS. DNA, RG59, A. and R. (MR3). Both Newton and Adams were from Alexandria, District of Columbia. Adams, one of the partners of Latting, Adams, and Stewarts, had been United States consul at Trieste before his appointment, in 1823, to the post at Matanzas. He had died May 1, at Mount Vernon Plantation, Cuba. Newton, also a merchant, did not receive the desired agency.

DIPLOMATIC NOTES   May 5, 1825

From JOSE MARIA SALAZAR, Washington, no. 3. Submits observations for the purpose "of concurring in some manner with the good offices which the Government of the United States may interpose . . ., and with the philanthropic powers of their Secretary of State," for mediation of a peace between Spain and the independent states of South America; stresses the economic benefit that would follow reduction in size of armies; asserts that Spain should learn the bitter truths that the American cause is based on public opinion supported by the first families, that reconquest is impossible, and that war will accelerate the ruin of Spain; and argues that peace would end piracy in the Spanish islands of Cuba and Puerto Rico, where it compromises Spanish honor, would cause the return of Spanish families driven from South America, and would heal deep wounds of humanity. LS (and copy in translation). DNA, RG59, Notes from Colombian Legation, vol. 1, pt. 2 (M51, R2). Translation published in Manning (arr.), *Diplomatic Correspondence . . . Latin-American Nations*, II, 1283-86. Cf. above, Clay to Everett, April 27, 1825.

INSTRUCTIONS AND DISPATCHES   May 5, 1825

From JOEL R. POINSETT, Veracruz, no. 1. Announces his safe arrival at this port and his welcome with military honors "and with every distinction the public authorities could pay to the representative of a friendly and favored nation." Reports the quelling of a mutiny on the Island of Sacrificios, shortly before his arrival there, en route, and the peaceful removal of Santa Anna from command at Campeche in Yucatán. Notes that the arrival of the commissioner of the British Government has preceded his own by two months, that a treaty between Mexico and Great Britain has already been negotiated, and that it has been ratified by the lower house of the legislature, after heated debate, which centered on provisions for freedom of worship and for most favored nation treatment. Poinsett will leave for the capital in the morning. LS. DNA, RG59, Dip. Disp., Mexico, vol. 1 (M97, R2). Received August 10.

Antonio López de Santa Anna, Mexican military and political leader, had been appointed Military Governor of Yucatán in April, 1824, and, shortly afterward, had been made Civil Governor as well. Complicity in a scheme to invade Cuba had caused his removal from both offices in April, 1825. Later, he was several times President of Mexico (once, during the war with the United States).

On the arrival of the British commissioner, see above, Taylor to Secretary of State, April 8, 1825. The proposed treaty of amity and commerce between Mexico and Great Britain (see above, Wilcocks to Secretary of State, April 9, 1825) was approved by the Mexican Congress in spite of an unfavorable committee report; but when the British Cabinet subsequently proposed alterations which required that the document be again submitted to the Mexican Congress, which had in the meantime adjourned, the ratification was deferred indefinitely. *Annual Register, 1825,* "History," 205.

MISCELLANEOUS LETTERS   May 5, 1825

To SAMUEL L. SOUTHARD. Notes that Clay has received letters from (Hilario de Rivas y) Salmon relating to the case of Commodore (David) Porter and that they will be transmitted when translated. Copy. DNA, RG59, Dom. Letters, vol. 21, p. 49 (M40, R19). See above, Salmon to Clay, May 2, 1825.

From JAMES CORNELL, Port Gibson, Mississippi. States that the *Port Gibson Correspondent* has been sold to George B. Crutcher and Benjamin F. Stockton, who are to be paid for publishing the laws. ALS. DNA, RG59, P. and D. of L. Cornell had become associated with the paper (founded in 1818) in 1821. Stockton had been one of his employees. For a few months in 1820, Crutcher had been part owner of the Russellville, Kentucky, *Weekly Messenger* (cf. below, Justice to Clay, August 1, 1825, note).

From SAMUEL L. SOUTHARD. Transmits extract from a letter by "Commodore Isaac Hull, commander of the United States Naval Force in the Pacific Ocean." ALS. DNA, RG59, Misc. Letters (M179, R62). The enclosure notes the uncertainty attending the case of the *China,* held by the Royalist forces at Callao, which are now under blockade by Chilean and Colombian vessels (see above, Tudor to Clay, March 21, 1825). Trial of the vessel by the Royalists has been postponed "in the expectation of the Spanish Fleet returning to Callao." Hull is standing by.

The *China,* owned by N(athaniel) L. and G(eorge) Griswold, New York merchants active in trade with China and the West Indies, had been seized by the Spanish authorities at Callao, in November, 1824, on a charge of smuggling.

On May 25, Daniel Brent transmitted to Alexander H. Everett, by Clay's direction, documents "received . . . from the Navy Department . . . relative to outrages on the persons and property of citizens of the United States, committed during the last year by the Spanish Authorities in Peru." The documents related to the cases of the *China,* the *General Carrington* (see below, Southard to Clay, December 12, 1825), and the *Nancy* (captured in August, 1824). Everett was instructed to claim indemnity for "the extraordinary treatment of the Masters and crews of these vessels, and the insults offered the United States Naval officers in the Port of Callao. . . ." Copy, in DNA, RG59, Dip. Instr., vol. 10, pp. 364-65 (M77, R5).

From Rufus King

Dr Sir,   Private   Jamaica 6 May 1825

By the last mail I received your obliging letter of the 2d. instant, and have been gratified by the satisfaction which you express that I have accepted the mission to England, though I have not confidence that we shall soon be able to adjust all our questions with England, some of which are of long standing, and the settlement of wh [sic] I heretofore was unable to effect[1]— I cannot suppose that my own Powers have increased, thoh I have confidence that those of the Country have, & that its influence has become more considerable, so that our just demands must in the End prevail. in the late commercial measures, so wisely pursued by the Parliament,[2] the force of our arguments in relation to the commercial Intercourse with the Eng. Colonies will suffer an alteration. On this matter I will as you request communicate to you my views.[3] I ask you to be good enough to furnish me with instructions, particularly in Relation to the costume of the Minister, and to other things referring to him personally, such as the mode & periods in which his Appointments are made.[4] when I was heretofore in England, the appointsments [sic] were paid quarterly by the Banker, and to avoid the more, or the less, than the true allowance, by the variation of the Exchange, the Salary was rated at Par, estimating the Dollar at 4/6 sterling.

In Regard to the Outfit, as I shall want it in England, where the Expenses will occur, I shall therefore be obliged to you to send me a Draft on our Banker for the amount thereof.[5] Mr. J.A.K. expects the appointment of secretary of Legation to England, & has already made his arrangements accordingly, and having taken our Passage for the 1. of June, the owners of the Packet expect that we confirm or give up the Passage as soon as your Opinion is known[6]

with great Regard & Esteem I am respecfully [sic] yr. ob. serv.

honble H Clay   Department of State   RUFUS KING

ALS. NHi.   [1] See above, I, 767-68, 774n.
[2] See above, Rush to Clay, March 26, 1825.   [3] Not found.
[4] See below, Clay to King, May 11, 1825.   [5] See below, Clay to King, May 9, 1825.
[6] A copy of John A. King's letter of appointment, signed by John Quincy Adams and Clay and dated May 5, 1825, is located in DNA, RG59, Ceremonial Communications, II, 20-21.

From D. A. Thornetine

Sir,   May 6, 1825

Being a citizen of South-Carolina, and having made some enquiries relative to the Improvements on Roads—And observing, as one of the Members of Congress, Mr. McDuffie,[1] was passing thro' Cheraw, a wish was expressed, by the Inhabitants of the Town, that the Lower Mail Road should be made to pass thro' said Place;— He objected "because there was no *Stone* to enable them to form the road"— I would beg, thro' you, to call the attention of the Commissioners, or Engineers (who are to make the Lower National Turnpike)[2] to a few suggestions:—

The *Sandy-soils,* in the South (and probably every where else) are Flat and Level. In the absorption of long and heavy Rains, *Quick-sands* are formed; and thro' these the superabundence [sic] of water escapes, forming Springs in the bowels of the Earth. These quick-sands abound, and will render Roads composed of *heavy materials,* constantly out of repair. I made an effort to fill one of these outlets with broken bricks, its visible Diameter about 3 feet— In 5 or 6 years it swallowed up 20 cart loads, and to appearance, was the same, as when commenced.

The *Inhabitants* of the Middle and Eastern States are surrounded with *Stone,* together with a Stiff-Clay soil; to which may be added (in the consideration of the construction of Roads) *severe & deep Frosts,—these* find the hard and *heavy* material, Stone, best, in Improving Roads— And *we,* in the South, with our loose, light and Sandy Soil, find the Articles which Nature furnishes, in abundance, producing equal, if not superior Roads than those of the North—for our Roads are *Level,* and somewhat *Elastic.*

Our method is this,— First, to "Pole the Road," that is, to cross it with small Saplings—then cover these with a sufficiency of Marsh-mud—then saturate the mud with Sand—and lastly, strew it over with the fallen Pine leaves. This Road, kept well ditched, *on both sides,* and these ditches being kept clean with a free outlet to carry off any surplusage of water, will last considerably longer than any Stone Turn-pike, I have seen, and will seldom require repair. This Road can only be injured by suffering the Water to *lay upon it*— Hence their durability depends upon the keeping the ditches clean, and they being sufficiently large to contain and carry off all the Water— Altho we know this to be the best and most substantial mode of Road-making, *few* obtain in the State! However, specimens are to be found between the Little & Great Pedee [sic] rivers, not on, but to the left of the Lower Great Mail Line. Should a Mr. McLean,[3] who resided, 4 years since, at the Stage house, on the Banks of the Little Pedee, (on the great Southern road) be still there, he will readily point out the Roads above noted, and give much useful information on their construction.

The Country being intersected with Swamps, these, where ever practicable, ought to be avoided, as, in constructing Causeways thro' them, great difficulty is found to render them durable. The Swamps on the margin of Rivers are still more difficult to manage in constructing the Causeways, and more so, in keeping them in Repair.— It is stated, a foreigner, a Frenchman constructed one of the most difficult and best, near Beaufort, S.C.

What are termed Bridges in South Carolina, in Causeways, are contemptable [sic],— But it is maintained, by Judicious men with us that the Plan & Materials of our old-bridges over Creeks & rivers, ought to be preferred to those recently constructed by Workmen from the North— They state, that *durability* & *economy* give the old a decided preference. On this head I would simply remark,— The Atmosphere is deemed Dry, in the North & East,— Whereas the South is unquestionably, humid & Wet.

Should these remarks prove useful, it will afford me the only satisfaction I wish. Very respectfully, your hble Servt

                                                   D A THORNETINE.

ALS. DNA, RG77, Letters Referred, 1819-1825, no. 842. Endorsed: "Philadelphia May 6, 1825. D A Thornetine to Hon H Clay. . . . refd by H Clay to Scy of War & by S W to Enginr Dept." Thornetine not further identified.

    1 George McDuffie.

    2 From March to August, 1825, a board of investigation composed of Brigadier General Simon Bernard and David Shriver (Jr.), assisted by Captain William Tell Poussin, of the Topographical Engineers, Lieutenant George Dutton, of the Corps of Engineers, and "Lieutenant T. [sic] Trimble, of the Artillery," United States Army, traveled over two regions proposed as routes for a post road from Washington to New Orleans—the first, by way of Richmond, Raleigh, Columbia, and Milledgeville; the second, or intermediate zone, covering various suggested paths west of the first, but east of the mountains. A third district, west of the other two, running through the valleys beyond the Blue Ridge—by way of Fairfax, Rockfish Gap, Lexington, Abingdon, Knoxville, New Philadelphia, Ashville, Centerville, and Demopolis— was investigated by Poussin and Trimble later in the year. The report of these preliminary surveys was filed April 8, 1826. "Letter from the Secretary of War, Transmitting the Report of the Board of Internal Improvement upon the Subject of a National Road from the City of Washington to New Orleans, April 12, 1826," *House Docs.*, 19 Cong., 1 Sess., no. 156. Poussin, born in France, served as a topographical engineer in the United States Army from 1817 to 1832, when he resigned with the rank of major. Dutton, born in Connecticut and graduated from the United States Military Academy, served in the Army from 1822 until his death, as a major, in 1857. Trimble, probably Isaac R., born in Virginia but appointed to the United States Military Academy from Kentucky, after graduation from that institution in 1822, served in the Artillery until his resignation from the Army in 1832.

    3 Not further identified.

DIPLOMATIC NOTES   May 6, 1825

From the BARON [DURAND] DE MAREUIL. States that the French ship *Calypso,* from Havre, after leaving Santo Domingo had been taken by pirates on November 1, 1824, but abandoned by them some days later upon the approach of the English ship *Lion,* the United States schooner *Terrier,* and two American cargo vessels; that the *Calypso* was taken into Key West, where the indemnity for her rescue was set at 80 per cent of the value of the ship and cargo saved; and that, to discharge this indemnity, the ship and cargo were sold. The Baron quotes the American law on salvage and requests an investigation of the "exorbitant" charges. LS (accompanied by a translation). DNA, RG59, Notes from French Legation, vol. 9 (M53, R7). The Baron de Mareuil had arrived in Washington as Envoy Extraordinary and Minister Plenipotentiary from France in August, 1824.

MISCELLANEOUS LETTERS   May 6, 1825

To SAMUEL L. SOUTHARD. Transmits Salmon's letter and two documents on the affair of Commodore Porter at Fajardo last November. Copy. DNA, RG59, Dom. Letters, vol. 21, p. 50 (M40, R19). See above, Salmon to Clay, May 2, 1825; Clay to Southard, May 5, 1825.

From HENRY ADAMS, Huntsville, Alabama. States that he has transferred the *Alabama Republican* to H. Orlando Alden and that it has been united with the *Alabamian* to form the *Southern Advocate and Huntsville Advertiser.* ALS. DNA, RG59, P. and D. of L.

APPLICATIONS, RECOMMENDATIONS   May 6, 1825

H. ORLANDO ALDEN, A. WOODWARD, and D. FARISS, solicit a continuance of patronage for themselves, "Proprietors & Publishers of the Southern Advocate & Huntsville Advertiser." LS, in Henry Adams' hand. DNA, RG59, P. and D. of L., an endorsement on Adams to Clay, this date. Postscript identifies the new firm as Dandridge, Fariss and Company. Woodward, a lawyer, had been, earlier in this year, editor of the *Alabama Republican,* of which Adams was publisher. Woodward and Alden were now editors of the newly established journal. Fariss has not been further identified. On the renewal of the printing contract, see below, Campbell, Woodward, and Fariss to Clay, November 26, 1825, note.

WILLARD HALL, Wilmington, recommends Thomas W. Robeson, "the bearer," for consul at Havana. ALS. MHi-Adams Papers, Letters Received (M469). Hall, born in Massachusetts and graduated from Harvard University, had begun the practice of law in Dover, Delaware, in 1803, and had served as secretary of state of Delaware (1811-1814, 1821), member of Congress (1817-1821), member of the Delaware Senate (1823), and Federal district judge for Delaware (1823-1871). He compiled the *Revised Code of Delaware* in 1829. Robeson, of Delaware, did not receive the appointment.

To Samuel Smith

Dear Sir   Washn. 7h. May 1825

In reply to your letter of the 5h.[1] I would observe that Mr. Adams does think well of Hughes,[2] 'though he perhaps believes that he attaches more political effect to a good dinner than belongs to it, whatever other good effects may belong to it. Mr. Hughes has acquitted himself very well in Sweden, and has furnished from time to time valuable information.

In regard to the recent appointments abroad to which you refer I do not know that they will impart any particular strength to the Admon, except that of Mr. King[3] which I believe will. It is probable it may be disapproved in some parts of the South, but it will be generally deemed judicious. He is old, and that in my opinion is the only objection to him; but his mind is believed to be yet in full vigor, and if we can extract any good out of it, we should not, on account of his age, neglect to do it.

I should like, at your perfect leisure, to have your views on the Colonial question between G.B. & the U.S.[4] Do we not contend for too much in insisting upon the introduction into the W. Indies of our produce on the same terms with that of Canada? In the mean time are we not now suffering more than the British from the existing alien duties of the two Countries? Yr's faithfy
Genl. S. Smith.   H CLAY

ALS. DLC-Samuel Smith Papers (DNA, M212, R22). Endorsed on verso: "Ansd. 9h. but dated 10h. by mistake." Answer not found.
   1 Not found.   2 John Quincy Adams; Christopher Hughes.   3 Rufus King.
   4 See above, III, 729n; Rush to Secretary of State, March 26, 1825, note; Clay to King, May 2, 1825.

To [Samuel L. Southard]

Sir   Washn. 7h. May 1825
   I beg leave to recommend to you for a Midshipman's appointment Geo. Nicholas Hawkins, a son of the late Joseph H. Hawkins, of Kentucky. This young gentleman is connected with the Nicholas family of Va. with the Mess. Smith's of Balto.[1] and his father, my personal friend and my successor in the H. of R. when I was sent to Europe, was a gentleman of great worth. I am Yr. ob. Servant
                                                                         H. CLAY

ALS. DLC-John Nicolay Papers (DNA, M212, R22).
   1 Young Hawkins' mother was George Anne, a daughter of Mary and George Nicholas. Mrs. Nicholas had been a sister of Robert and Samuel Smith. The young man was appointed a midshipman in the Navy on March 1, 1826, and remained in the service for about ten years.

From Edward Ingersoll

Dear Sir.   Philada. May 7. 1825
   Mr Bohlen is in full life, and I have seen him on the subject of the inquiry you desire.

   He will write to you, he says, in a day or two; and he volunteer'd the information to me that such a draft as that you mention was accepted and paid in 1813.,[1] which year he supposes you to mean, as in 1818 no such transaction could have occurred.

Mr. Ingham has, like Gen. Eaton,[2] succeeded in establishing the facts stated by you respecting him. The putting Mr. Kremer's apologetic paper into his pocket and the busy part taken by him in the scene, which you attributed to him,[3] he has admitted, & to a greater degree even, his self love and egotism have induced him to admit it, than was charged.[4]   I furnished the Democratic Press[5] with a few paragraphs on the subject, intended to indicate particularly the effect of his admissions on his friend *Governor* Kremer, and also the logic with which he ascribes to you a menace, as he calls it, against the whole Pennsylvania delegation—, and the ingenious dilemma that he chuckles so much about. Mr. Binns[6] has printed my paragraphs with a full share of typographical blunderings, making nonsense of some sentences—. Perhaps it is as well to let the thing alone, to work its own condemnation, but there is a pleasure in exposing absurdity, and particularly when the absurdity is very malignant.

Mr. Ingham had just been here, after a visit to Harrisburgh, so that I infer his address had the benefit of a "multitude of counsellors"— He was soliciting meetings, and conferences, little caucuses, at which he inveighed against the Administration, and against you especially, and urged, much, the necessity of an early organization preparatory to the next Presidential election—*and* of a vigorous opposition in the interim. The Franklin Gazette[7]—in which I believe he has a pecuniary interest,—he pledged to be ready to carry on the attack—. I became acquainted with these caballings partly through Bernd McCredy,[8] who was one of our Committee in the autumn, and continues to be a very firm friend of yours. Ingham mistook him for a Jackson-man, and opened his plans to him, at Geo. Dallas's where there was a small collection of chosen men, to the assemby [sic] of whom McCredy had been invited without any intimation of the object—. McCredy is a pretty plain speaking man, and, he says, when he gave them his mind upon the subject, they scattered as if a hand-grenade had been thrown in among them. Ingham was a stranger and might be excused for not knowing his men, but how our friend George should make such a mistake I can't imagine;—he is not often so unwary as to *catch a Tartar.*

I understood subsequently from Majr. Barker,[9] an ardent Jackson man but not an admirer of Mr. Ingham, that the conference resulted in an opinion that it was not wise to do *much* at present—. But that the Franklin Gazette is to improve it's [sic] circulation quietly, and be ready to come out distinctly, as soon as it shall find an opportunity.

I have no patience nor toleration for that Franklin Gazette and wish all governmental patronage were withdrawn from it.

I am very glad Somerville has a chance of reconciling his two interfering blessings[10]—. His situation between the mission and the miss was somewhat like the lover who sings (in the Beggar's opera I believe), how happy could I be with *either*, were t'other dear charmer away[11]—. I advised him to tell his whole story frankly and freely to you and the President, and told him I was sure you would contrive some method of relieving him from a quandary so perplexing—. I have some misgivings as to the sincerity of the lady—and can't but suspect there is some coquetry in the case—if so however the sooner he puts it to the test the better.

This is a very *light* letter to send to a Secretary of State—but I address you unofficially and prate without premeditation. Very devotedly & respectfully Yours   EDWARD INGERSOLL Hon. H. Clay.

ALS. DLC-HC (DNA, M212, R1). Endorsed by Clay on verso: ". . . [Samuel] Hopkins's business—bill on Bohlen." Cf. above, Horsley to Clay, April 17, 1825.
1 See above, II, 917.   2 Samuel D. Ingham; John H. Eaton.
3 See above, Address, March 26, 1825.
4 See above, Clay to Brooke, April 29, 1825; Clay to Hammond, May 2, 1825.
5 Philadelphia.   6 John Binns.
7 The Philadelphia *Aurora* and the *Franklin Gazette* had been merged in November, 1824, to form the *Aurora and Franklin Gazette*.
8 Bernard McCready.
9 James Nelson Barker, of Philadelphia, playwright, poet, and political writer; officer in the War of 1812, with the rank of major as Deputy Adjutant General of the United States Army in 1815; and an employee of the Treasury Department from 1829 until his death in 1858, during which time he held posts as collector of the port of Philadelphia (1829-1838) and First Comptroller of the Treasury (1838-1841).
10 President Adams and Clay had agreed, on April 25, that William C. Somerville "should be allowed to postpone his departure for Sweden till July or August, to accomplish his matrimonial project with Miss Cora Livingston, at New Orleans, his salary not to commence till he shall depart upon his mission." Adams, *Memoirs*, VI, 533. The young lady, born in 1806, was the daughter of Edward Livingston. She did not marry Somerville, who died a bachelor, in France, en route to his mission, January 5, 1826.
11 John Gay, *The Beggars' Opera*, Act II, Scene XIII, Air XXV.

MISCELLANEOUS LETTERS   May 7, 1825

To [SAMUEL BARNES,] editor of the Frederick, Maryland, *Political Examiner*. Daniel Brent, at the direction of the Secretary of State, requests that this journal be sent to the Department. Copy. DNA, RG59, Dom. Letters, vol. 21, p. 53 (M40, R19). Barnes, who had earlier published a newspaper in Baltimore, had founded the *Political Examiner* in 1813.

From SAMUEL HOLLINGSWORTH, Baltimore. Requests Clay to instruct (James) Brown to aid in the prosecution of a claim against the French Government in the case of the schooner *Two Brothers*, owned "by the late House of Thos. & Saml Hollingsworth" and lost by action of French forces in the West Indies in 1805. ALS. DNA, RG76, Misc. Claims, France. The Hollingsworths, born in Maryland, had been mill owners and merchants in Baltimore from the close of the Revolutionary War. Thomas had been prominent in the organization of the Bank of Maryland in 1790 and had become one of the first councilmen upon the organization of the city government. Samuel, a veteran of the Revolution, remained active in business until shortly before his death, in 1830. On French spoliation claims generally, see above, I, 527n; III, 134-55n, 313n; Brown to Clay, April 1, 1825.

On May 14, 1825, Daniel Brent, at the direction of the Secretary of State, informed Hollingsworth that his claim would receive attention "in any arrangement for . . . indemnity to Citizens of the United States. . . ." Copy. DNA, RG59, Dom. Letters, vol. 21, p. 60 (M40, R19) .

MISCELLANEOUS LETTERS   May 8, 1825

From JOHN SCOTT, St. Louis, Missouri. Presents plea for consideration of the French population in this State, with specific reference to the claims of (Auguste) Chouteau and (Jules) DeMun. Stresses the hopes aroused by the accession of the new administration: ". . . they [the French inhabitants] expect to see justice done to Chouteau and Demun, because Mr Adams when Secretary of State advocated their claims with warmth and Sincerity: and you being a Western [man] and connected to the french in lower Louisiana they expect more exertions from you than from any other person." ALS. DNA, RG59, Misc. Letters (M179, R62). See above, Chouteau and DeMun to Clay, May 3, 1825; Benton to Clay, May 4, 1825.

To James Brown

Dear Sir   Washn 9h. May 1825

Count de Menou, who carries this letter[1] at the same time affords me an opportunity of writing to you, and an apology for not writing much—a sort of excuse which the labors of my present office make me eagerly embrace. He is so much of an American that he will tell you all the news. These the papers will have put you in possession of. From them you will learn the event and the incidents of the Presidential election, including my part, as principal, and accessory in it. In this latter character I have indeed been made very important. Because, under all the actual circumstances, I prefered Mr. Adams I have been assailed in the grossest manner. I send you my address to my Constituents,[2] though I dare say it will have reached you through other channels. My triumph over my assailants has been every where complete and signal. In the West the approbation of my conduct is general, sincere and ardent.

I shall leave this City on the 14h. for Kentucky. I have been, since the adjournment of Congress, laboriously engaged in the arduous duties of my new office, which I find any thing but a bed of down. You may estimate their extent and fatigue when I tell you that, besides the current business of the office, I have prepared instructions to six new and old missions,[3] some of them reaching to twenty pages, and all requiring much reading of previous correspondence and documents relating to each. I have no fears however of being able to subdue the business of the station, and keeping it under my control. This very day I have had interviews with four different foreign ministers on matters of great public importance, and each of considerable duration.

I shall bring Mrs. Clay and my family on my return which will not be until early in July. We shall board in the first instance, and I have even conceived the folly of building a house, in which event we may not go to House keeping until the fall twelvemonth. I shall be the subject of some conversation if I take that course, but I am getting quite used to all that. The leisure of a Boarding house will afford us ample opportunity to look around us in making preparations for house keeping and we shall be able both to commence it with greater advantages, and in the mean time to œconomize, which is still necessary to us. Can we get any thing in France better, or on better terms, than in the U. S. to make up our establishment? My present inclination is to bring but very little of our furniture from Kentucky.

All our friends I believe are well in K. Dr. Brown has resigned his professorship in Transyl:[4] and Mason Brown is married to Miss Bledsoe.[5]

To revert to the public affairs. I have not been yet able to look much into those of your mission. I have had two or three long interviews with Baron de Mareuil on the Comml. convention,[6] in the course of which he has manifested the restleness [sic] of France with its operation. I have given him kind words, and solemn shrugs, and told him that we can make no change in it more favorable to France. He says he will advise France to put an end to it, which I told him she had a most undoubted right to do; but that it was worth enquiry whether, if his Govt. resorted to separate legislation, we ought to throw all the trade into English hands.

I shall send you a despatch in a few days of some consequence relating to the War of the Spanish Colonies & Spain.[7] I am very desirous for peace between them.

We shall have no serious opposition. The powder of the malcontents is already beginning to fail, and their guns are heard weaker and weaker. Calhoun will try to carry on a business under the firm of the Hero,[8] but it will only be in the small way.

Tell Mrs. Brown that she must not forget to supply her sister[9] with the new fashions &c. She has been so much out of society that I am afraid it will be difficult to renew her taste for it. I understand however that she is cheerfully and I hope happily making arrangements to accompany me here. I expect to find at Ashland Mrs Duralde with her two sons,[10] and Mrs. Erwin[11] without either son or daughter, altho' she tells me that she has a disposition to follow the good example of her elder sister. I am afraid there is something in names.[12]

My health was not good during the three last months. It is now better, and I anticipate much of improvement in it from my approaching journey. With my kindest and best respects to Mrs Brown I am Faithfy Your friend   H CLAY.
James Brown Esq.

ALS. DLC-HC (DNA, M212, R1).
1 Count Charles Julius de Menou, whose position as French Chargé d'Affaires in the United States had been supplanted with the arrival of the Baron de Mareuil as Minister (above, Mareuil to Clay, May 6, 1825), remained in Washington until May 11, 1825, when he left for New York to take passage for Havre.
2 Above, March 26, 1825.
3 Above, to Hughes, March 24, 1825; to Poinsett, March 26, 1825; to Forbes, April 14, 1825; to Raguet, April 14, 1825; to Miller, April 22, 1825; to Everett, April 27, 1825.
4 See above, Drake to Clay, February 20, 1825.
5 Mason, son of John Brown, and Judith Ann, daughter of Jesse Bledsoe, had married on March 10, 1825. Young Brown, a graduate of Yale, received the LL.B. degree from Transylvania University later this spring and ultimately attained prominence as a lawyer, commonwealth's attorney, circuit judge (1838-1849), secretary of state of Kentucky (1855-1859), and, for several years before his death in 1867, United States district attorney.
6 See above, III, 53n, 382, 383n.   7 See below, Clay to Brown, May 13, 1825.
8 John C. Calhoun; Andrew Jackson.   9 Mrs. Clay.
10 Mrs. Martin Duralde (Jr.); Martin Duralde III; Henry Clay Duralde.
11 Mrs. James Erwin.
12 Mrs. James Brown, for whom Mrs. Erwin had been named, had no children.

To Rufus King

Dear Sir   Washington 9h. May 1825
I have just received your favor of the 6h. instant. I shall send a messenger this week with your instructions, and a Commission for your son Mr. John A. King as secretary of the Legation, who will reach New York about the 16h. instant. Your personal instructions will afford you all the information you desire upon the affair of Costume, Salary &c. As to your outfit I apprehend that we shall have to make payment of that here, according to the general practice. I will look into what has been usual with every disposition to accommodate you, in this particular, if possible.
I am with great regard Faithfully Your ob. Servt.   H CLAY
The Honble R. King
P.S. I will forward your *personal* instructions by mail tomorrow or the next day.   H.C.

LS, postscript also in Clay's hand. NHi.   L draft, in DLC-HC (DNA, M212, R7); copy, in DNA, RG59, Dip. Instr., vol. 10 (M77, R5).

To [Samuel Smith]

Dear Sir,   (Confidential)   Washington 9th. May 1825
Will you allow me, at your perfect leisure, to trouble you for your opinion and the result of your observations as to the question

now pending between Great Britain and the United States, in
respect to the Colonial trade. You are aware that, on our part, it
is contended that the produce of the United States ought to be
admitted in a British Colony on the same terms, and paying no
higher duties than similar produce is received when coming from
another British Colony. In other words, that Great Britain ought
not to give, in her own Colonies, to the produce of Canada, for
example, any preference over that of the United States. On the
other hand, Great Britain contends that to renounce the right of
giving such preference is, in effect to give up her Sovereignty, is
to do what no Nation ever has done, and what the United States
themselves do not, under analogous circumstances, in reference
to the Sugar of Louisiana. We now subject British Vessels and their
Cargoes coming from the British West Indies, to alien duties which
are countervailed by similar duties levied on the British side.[1] In
as much as we employ much the greatest amount of tonnage in
that trade, do we not suffer most by the continuation of those alien
duties? And would not the competition of our tonnage with that
of Great Britain be improved by the mutual abolition of those
duties? Would it be advisable to consent to such abolition, leaving
Great Britain free to give the preference for which she contends
to the produce of her own Colonies? Can we maintain the ground
which we have heretofore taken? How is the British doctrine to
be distinguished from that relative to the Coasting trade? Or from
their corresponding pretension to have the sugar and molasses
of the British West Indies admitted in the Ports of the United
States on the same terms with those of Louisiana and Florida?

I shall leave this City in a few days for Kentucky, and if you
should favor me with an answer to this letter, it will arrive in
time, if I get it by the last of June. With great respect, I am your
obedient Servt.   H. CLAY

LS, the word "(Confidential)" also in Clay's hand. DLC-Samuel Smith Papers (DNA,
M212, R22). A copy of this letter, addressee unknown, is located in PPL-R. Replies
from John Holmes (below, June 8, 1825), James Lloyd (below, June 27, 1825), and
Daniel Webster (below, September 28, 1825) indicate that additional copies (not
found) were sent out. Cf. above, Clay to Smith, May 7, 1825.
[1] See above, III, 729, note 21; Rush to Clay, March 26, 1825, note.

DIPLOMATIC NOTES   May 9, 1825

To HILARIO DE RIVAS Y SALMON. Replies to notes of January 15 and March
16, stating that no information has been received by the State Department
concerning the conduct of John Mullowny other than that communicated by
Salmon and by the Spanish Government through Hugh Nelson, that a communication from Mullowny is expected soon, and that, when all facts in the
case are known, "if there has been any impropriety of conduct on his part
injurious to Spain, the President will hasten to cause the proper corrective to

be applied." Comments: "If Mr. Mullowney [*sic*] has exceeded the rights of hospitality and what is due to the unfortunate, and has allowed his house to be used for the purpose of forming plans of rebellion and disorder against Spain as suggested by you, his conduct in that respect will receive no countenance from this Government, which is desirous, upon all occasions and every where to maintain with yours relations of the most perfect frankness and friendship." Copy. DNA, RG59, Notes to Foreign Ministers and Consuls, vol. 3, pp. 219-20 (M38, R3). AL draft, in CSmH. See above, Nelson to Clay, April 6, 1825.

INSTRUCTIONS AND DISPATCHES   May 9, 1825

From WILLIAM TAYLOR, Alvarado (Mexico). Notes the arrival at Veracruz on May 5 of (Joel R.) Poinsett and his suite, who proceeded immediately to Mexico City, "where he has been long anxiously expected." Reports the conclusion of a treaty of commerce between Mexico and Great Britain, after considerable opposition, "so much so, that at one point the [British] Commissioners demanded their Pass ports, with the intention of leaving the Country." ALS. DNA, RG59, Cons. Disp., Veracruz, vol. 1. Received June 4. On the difficulties attending completion of the British-Mexican treaty, see above, Poinsett to Clay, May 5, 1825, note.

MISCELLANEOUS LETTERS   May 9, 1825

To PHILIP C. PENDLETON, "Judge of the United States for the Western District of Virginia, Martinsburg." Forwards commission for this office. Copy. DNA, RG59, Dom. Letters, vol. 21, p. 54 (M40, R19). Pendleton replied, May 12, stating his acceptance of the office. ALS. DNA, RG59, Acceptances and Orders for Commissions (M-T645, R2).

From ROBERT McCLINTOCK, New York. Encloses duplicate of his letter of April 18 and requests a reply. ALS. DNA, RG59, Misc. Letters (M179, R62).

From WILLIAM B. QUARRIER, Norfolk. Calls attention "for the third time" to the enquiry, addressed to John Quincy Adams, August 21, 1824, by Robert Hatton, former captain of the American brig *Undaunted,* concerning the legality of charges for the distressed seamen's fund, levied by the American commercial agent at Anguilla, where the vessel had been condemned as unfit for sea; expresses surprise "that not the slightest information" has been obtained "altho' so frequently asked"; and requests a reply. ALS. *Ibid.* On Quarrier, see below, Quarrier to Clay, February 3, 1827. On the distressed seamen's fund, see below, Clay to Quarrier, May 12, 1825.

From WILLIAM REYNOLDS, St. Augustine. Encloses copies of his correspondence, as newly appointed keeper of the public archives (of East Florida), with William H. Simmons and E (dward) R. Gibson, who refuse to give up the records without directions from the President or Secretary of State; requests that the necessary directions be given. LS. DNA, RG59, Misc. Letters (M179, R62). Published in Carter (ed.) *Territorial Papers,* XXIII, 247-48. Reynolds' appointment had been confirmed March 7, 1825. Simmons and Gibson were members of the Legislative Council of Florida, of which Reynolds had also been a member.

From [SAMUEL L. SOUTHARD,] Secretary of Treasury. In answer to Clay's inquiry of May 3, transmits all the information available in the Treasury Department on the matter in question. AL. DNA, RG59, Misc. Letters (M179, R62). The enclosures are two letters, both addressed to Southard and dated May 4, 1825: the first, from S(amuel) M. McKean, states that in the case of the *Carl Johan,* seized at New Orleans in June, 1824, for bringing in ten cases of liquors not the produce of Sweden, the Secretary of the Treasury, in response to a petition, had remitted the forfeitures upon re-exportation of the liquors and payment of the duties; the second letter (a copy), from Joseph Anderson, Comptroller, cites the treaty of September 4, 1816, between the United States and Sweden, various acts of Congress, and the Presidential proclamation of August 20, 1821, in explaining the terms on which vessels of Sweden, Norway, and the Island of St. Bartholomew are admitted to American ports. Cf. above, Lorich to Clay, March 16, 1825, note.

McKean, a native of Pennsylvania, probably a grandson of Thomas McKean, was a clerk in the office of the Secretary of the Treasury.

To John Bohlen

Sir   Washington 10h. May 1825

I thank you for the information contained in your letter of the 7h. instant,[1] which I have just received.

I shall take pleasure in giving my best attention to the official letter which you intimate it to be the purpose of your House to address to me.   With high respect I am Your ob. Servt.

Mr. John Bohlen.   H. CLAY

ALS. Owned by Thomas D. Clark, Lexington, Kentucky.
[1] Not found; cf. above, Ingersoll to Clay, May 7, 1825.

To Rufus King

No. 1. Instructions—General
Rufus King, appointed Envoy Extraordinary
and Minister Plenipotentiary, U. S. to G. Britain

Sir,   Department of State, Washington 10. May 1825

The President having appointed you Envoy Extraordinary and Minister Plenipotentiary to the United Kingdom of Great Britain and Ireland, I transmit you, herewith, your Commission, in that character, together with the usual Letter of Credence, to be delivered, on your presentation, to the King.[1] And it is the desire of the President that you should proceed on your mission without any unnecessary delay. In the discharge of the duties of the honourable and highly interesting trust which is thus confided to you, great reliance is placed on your experience, ability, zeal and fidelity. And I will add, that much satisfaction is felt with your consenting to allow the public to be availed of your services, from the employment of which it has a right to anticipate the most beneficial results.

If Mr. Rush[2] shall not have taken his departure from England upon your arrival there, you will receive from him the Archives of the Legation. If you do not find him there, you will receive them from Mr. J. Adams Smith, in whose charge he will have left them. They will put you in full possession of the present state of the relations between the two countries. In the mean time, I now transmit you the message of the President of the United States to the Senate, of the 19th. of January last, with the accompanying documents, all of which have, by its order, been confidentially printed.[3] From those Archives and documents you will learn that a negociation was opened early in the last year, between Mr. Rush and Messrs. Huskisson[4] and Stratford Canning on many important points of difference between the two Governments, and that it terminated on the 28th. of July without the parties being able to come to an agreement on any one of them, except that which related to the suppression of the slave trade. The whole correspondence at Washington, and at London, in relation to the Convention which was concluded and signed on this latter Subject, embracing the modifications of it which were desired by the Senate, and assented, or objected, to by the British Government, was laid before Congress by the President, with his message, at the commencement of the last session.[5] The object of submitting it to Congress, was, to afford to that body, or to either branch of it, an opportunity of expressing its opinion upon that instrument. It has so happened that Congress has not, collectively, or either branch of it, separately, expressed any direct opinion on that Convention. But the United States having, on the 10th. day of December, 1824, concluded a Convention with the Republic of Colombia, for the same object of more effectually suppressing the slave trade, which was free from the objection of extending the qualified right of search to the American coasts, this latter Convention was submitted, during the last session, to the consideration of the Senate. And that Body, in the exercise of its Constitutional participation of the Treaty making power, has deemed it inexpedient to advise and consent to the ratification of the Colombian Convention.[6] From this decision the inference was irresistible, that, even if the British and American Governments could come to an agreement to exclude from the operation of the proposed Convention between them, the American coasts, it would be, still, unacceptable to the Senate. Under these circumstances, the further continuation of the negociation seems entirely useless; and I, accordingly, addressed a note to Mr. Addington, on the 6th. day of April 1825, (of which a copy, together with a copy of his answer to it,[7] accompanies these Instructions) informing him that the President declined treating any longer upon that subject. You will communicate this determination of the President to Mr. Canning,[8] in the most friendly and conciliatory terms, and assure him, that it has not proceeded from any abatement of interest on the part of the American Government, or any portion of it, in the great object of an entire suppression of the slave trade. But that, on the contrary, it will continue to afford its hearty co-operation by all practicable means of which its judgement shall approve in the attainment of that most desirable end.

With respect to the other objects of the negociation which was suspended on the 28th. of July last, their great importance, and the new lights which are thrown upon them by subsequent events, and especially the effect on the Colonial trade which is likely to be produced by the measures recently proposed in the British Parliament by Mr. Huskisson,[9] the matured form of which has not yet reached us, require the most cautious and deliberate consideration. My recent entry upon the duties of the Department of State, and the great pressure of the mass of other business which called for immediate attention, have not allowed me yet to bestow on those objects the time which is indispensably necessary to the formation of a satisfactory judgement. I am not, therefore, now ready to communicate to you the instructions of the President which they require. To detain you for them, might have the effect of occasioning some injury to the current affairs of the Legation, and to other interests demanding your presence at London. I have, therefore, the approbation of the President in requesting that, without waiting for them, you proceed on your voyage. As soon as I return from Kentucky, for which I expect in a few days to depart, I will commence the work of preparing them, and hope to be able to place them in your possession early in September. This delay is the less regretted, because, from the engagement of Mr. Huskisson in Parliament, who will probably be again associated in the negociation, and from other obvious causes, it is not likely that it can be renewed before the approaching autumn, and no great intermediate mischief will probably accrue to any of the interests to which it relates. In the interval your time may be usefully dedicated to the object of a full and clear comprehension of the present state of the relations between the two countries, to the transaction, after your arrival in England, of occasional official business, as it arises, and to an affair of much immediate practical consequence, to which I shall now proceed to direct your attention.

You are aware that a Convention between the United States and His Brittanic [sic] Majesty was concluded and signed at St Petersburg, under the mediation of the Emperor of all the Russias on the 30/12 day of May/June 1822 (see appendix to the Acts of the session of 1823) for the purpose of carrying into effect the award of His Imperial Majesty, as Arbitrator of the difficulties which had arisen between Great Britain and the United States out of the Treaty of Ghent, in regard to Slaves and other property, carried away by the British forces in contravention to this Treaty.[10] By that Convention a mixed Commission was to be constituted, to settle the just indemnification which His Imperial Majesty awarded to be due to the Citizens of the United States, for the slaves and property so deported. On the part of this Government, Mr. Langdon Cheves was appointed, and on that of Great Britain, Mr George Jackson. The Commissioners met at Washington, on the 25th. day of August, 1823, and after various adjournments, their session continued until the 27th. of April, 1825, when they adjourned to meet on the 8th. of December following. The proceedings of the Board have been arrested by a most extraordinary refusal of Mr. Jackson to execute the 5th. Article of the Convention; and it cannot be again made to move on to the accomplishment of the objects of its institution, without the interposition of the British Government.[11] Before I call your attention particularly to the exceptionable course which that Commissioner appears to have considered himself bound to adopt, I will make some observations upon the nature of the constitution of the Board. By the 5th. Article it is provided that, "in the event of the two Commissioners not agreeing in *any particular case,* under examination, or of their disagreement upon *any question* which may result from the stipulations of this Convention, then, and in that case, they shall draw, by lot, the name of one of the two Arbitrators, who, after having given due consideration to the matter contested, shall consult with the Commissioners; and a final decision shall be given conformably to the opinion of the majority of the two Commissioners and of the Arbitrator so drawn by lot." The whole practical inconvenience of such a general provision for submitting every question that might arise in every cause, to arbitration, in the event of the non-concurrence of the Commissioners, was probably not foreseen at the Conclusion of the Convention. Experience has fully developed it. All interlocutory points; every preliminary question about the forms of trial; the authentication of evidence; its effects, and the rules of proceeding (and what a multitude of such points and questions may not occur?) are thus to be referred in the contingency but too often happening of a disagreement between the Commissioners. If the settlement of one question settled the whole class to which it belonged, in all analagous [*sic*] cases, the evil which then would be still great, might be borne. But, unfortunately, the very same question (the sufficiency, for example, of the authentications of a deposition, or any other) may arise in different, cases, and be determined according as the lot for the Arbitrator may be cast. And thus it may, and most probably will, happen, that the proof or [*sic*] the claim of one individual will be rejected under precisely the same circumstances of those of another, which will be received and allowed.

The malformation of the Tribunal could have only been remedied by a spirit of mutual concession and accommodation between its component members. Such a spirit has, unfortunately, not been evinced, in the course of its proceedings, by Mr. Jackson. The Protocol of the Commissioners, and so much of the correspondence between them, as is necessary to put you in possession of what has been and of what has not been, done, accompany these Instructions.[12] From a perusal of those Documents, you will not fail to observe that he has manifested throughout, the most impracticable [*sic*] disposition. I shall only advert to some of the instances of his course of conduct, to sustain that remark

1. It became important, by some general rule, in the commencement of the proceedings of the Board, to notify claimants of the species of authentication of their Depositions which would be required. The usual form of authenticating such acts is by the signature of the Justice who takes them, accompanied by the certificate and seal of the Governor of a State, Judge of a Superior Court, or Notary. This did not satisfy Mr. Jackson, who must also have the certifying officer to state that he *knew* the hand writing of the officiating Justice. Now this extraordinary requisition (for, by what Tribunal, British, or American, was it ever before made?) it is, in many cases, almost impossible to comply with. It may be asked, why did the American Commissioner concur in the adoption of such a rule? Because it was better to have some known rule, even a bad one, than none; and because it did not bind him to exclude testimony which should be authenticated in the usual and established forms.

2nd. In the case of Cowper,[13] a question arose which is applicable to all the cases, and that is, whether interest should be allowed upon the ascertained value of the property carried away in violation of the Treaty of Ghent, as a part of that just indemnification which His Imperial Majesty awarded. Mr. Cheves thought interest was equally due with the principal. Mr. Jackson rejected it as wholly inadmissible. The discussions on this point have been extended to a great length. You will find them in the voluminous correspondence between the Commissioners themselves, and in the papers of Mr. Tazewell and Mr. Livingston,[14] in behalf of the claimants. If I could add any thing to what has been so ably urged in support of the demand, it would be unnecessary. Mr. Jackson endeavors to sustain his argument by a literal criticism on the text of the Convention, rejecting as unworthy of material consideration the contemporaneous Imperial acts. Mr. Cheves maintains his side of the question from the text also, of the Convention, from the terms and the spirit of the Imperial decision, from analagous cases, and from the reason of the thing. And surely there can be no adequate conception of a just indemnification for injuries, the redress of which has been so long delayed, which does not comprehend interest. What is, briefly, the case? Great Britain, by the most solemn of compacts, stipulates not to transport from the American territories, the most productive description of property. Her faith is promptly and perseveringly invoked to fulfil her obligations and do justice to the injured American proprietors. She withholds it, upon the plea that she was not bound to the surrender of the property. The two Governments appeal to the Emperor of Russia to decide this point of difference, and His Imperial Majesty determines that Great Britain was bound by the Treaty of Ghent to surrender the property, and awards a just indemnification. The Convention which was subsequently concluded is merely the means of giving effect to the Imperial award. And the question is, whether the parties who, more than ten years ago, ought to have had their property, with all its intervening use and profits, will have been justly indemnified without interest, for the very great, and, as the Imperial decision proves, unjust, delay, which Mr. Jackson is increasing by the very course which he has felt himself authorised to adopt. But I have said that it is not necessary, nor do I mean to discuss the point of interest. Whether it be just or not is not material in considering the exceptionable resolution to which he has brought himself. That resolution is, not even to refer the claim of interest to the arbitrament expressly provided for in the fifth Article of the Convention. That article declares that, in the event of the two Commissioners not agreeing *in any particular case under examination* &c, it shall be referred to a tribunal composed of them and an arbitrator to be designated by lot. A particular case is under examination,— the Commissioners disagree in it. The *casus fœderis* occurs, and Mr. Jackson refuses to execute the fifth Article. And on what pretext is this extraordinary refusal attempted to be supported? Upon the allegation that interest is, in his judgement, clearly excluded from the Convention. He, no doubt, thinks so— Mr. Cheves, with equal honesty of intention, thinks otherwise. And this difference between them is precisely one of those cases of non-concurrence which were foreseen, and all of which, without exception, when, unfortunately, they shall arise; are to be submitted to the arbitrator. If Mr. Jackson is justified in the refusal, in this particular, to constitute the triple tribunal, what is to prevent his declining the reference, in every other case? Undoubtedly if an unjust claim be preferred, either as it regards the right, or the sufficiency of the evidence by which it is attempted to be substantiated, it is not within the Convention; and Mr. Jackson may therefore refuse the reference in all cases in which he shall decide against the claimant. If, as he supposes, the claim of interest is not comprehended in the Convention, that will be a sufficient ground for the determination of the Arbitrator against it. The refusal to bring it to the test of the Convention, implies some distrust of the correctness of his own judgement, or an unreasonable want of confidence in the rectitude of the Umpire. It is evident that if the Commissioner, representing one party, has the right to predicate his refusal to refer a subject to the Arbitrator, upon his separate notion that it is not embraced in the Convention, the great object of that instrument, is defeated. For that object undoubtedly was, that neither party should absolutely decide, but that a mixed tribunal, in which both were to be represented, should pronounce on all controverted questions, in which both are interested. And neither in the spirit, nor in the terms of the Convention is any countenance to be found for the idea that one class of controverted cases, more than any other, is excepted from its operation. If it be urged on the one hand, that the effect of this broad ground of reference might be to draw within the jurisdiction of the mixed Tribunal, claims upon Great Britain which were never designed to be included in the Convention, the argument will be answered on the other, by stating that the opposite ground might put without their jurisdiction, claims to which it was evidently intended to extend. The true answer is the same to both; and that is, that they are extreme cases, against which the only security is to be found in the integrity, intelligence and obligations of the Board.

3— In the case of Jumonville de Villiers, a Citizen of Louisiana, the claim of indemnity for twenty slaves, carried away from Dauphin Island, in the Bay of Mobile, does not appear to have been questioned by Mr. Jackson upon the ground, either of the sufficiency of the proof by which it was established, or the time of the transportation of the slaves. But to the allowance of the claim he objected, upon the pretence that Dauphin Island was no part of the Territory of the United States, but belonged to West Florida. Mr. Cheves, declining to discuss our incontestible right to that Island, derived from the cession of Louisiana, of which it constituted a part, offered to refer the difference between him and his associate, agreeably to the provisions of the fifth Article of the Convention. But Mr. Jackson, having erected himself into a Judge of what belonged to us, and what to Spain, decided that Dauphin Island was not an appendage of Louisiana but of West Florida, and therefore belonged to Spain, at the period of the exchange of the ratifications of the Treaty of Ghent, and refused to consent to the proposed reference. Dauphin Island was, during the late war, reduced and occupied by the British arms, as a part of the territory of the United States. Had it not been a part of their territory, the military occupation of it by Great Britain, would have been an unprovoked act of war on her part against Spain, with whom she was then in peace. It was, on the return of peace, surrendered to the United States, as a "Territory, place or possession" (to use the language of the Treaty of Ghent) taken from them during the war. Thus, in order to screen the British Government from the indemnity due to American citizens for one or two hundred Negro Slaves, Mr. Jackson would represent his Nation as having committed an act of deliberate and wanton war upon the territories of a friendly and unoffending Sovereign; And, as having, after perpetrating that act of enormity, transferred the Territory, violently wrested from that Sovereign, to the United States, who had no right to it! The mere statement of the case, which truth compels me to make, must wound the sensibility of His Brittanic Majestys Government. If it were creditable to discuss the question of the right of the United States to Dauphin Island, it would be easy to show that the Province of Louisiana which was ceded to them on the 30th. of April, 1803, extended as far east as the Perdido,[15] and, of course included the Bay of Mobile; that, prior to the late war with Great Britain, the United States had actually taken possession of the whole Province up to that limit; that they had incorporated the Bay of Mobile, including Dauphin Island, in one of their Territories, and governed it by their Laws; and that the Treaty with Spain of the 22nd. day of February 1819,[16] did not operate as an original cession, but only as a confirmation of their previous title acquired under that with France, to the country lying between the Perdido and the Island of New Orleans. It would have been a more compendious mode of disposing of this claim on the part of Mr. Jackson, to have drawn in question our title to any part of Louisiana, as was done during the conferences at Ghent.[17] He would then have gotten rid of the territory, the claimant and his slaves. But the conclusive answer to his plea is to be found in the terms of the first article of the Treaty of Ghent. They stipulate that "all territory, places and possessions whatsoever, taken by either party from the other, during the war, or which may be taken after the signing of this Treaty, excepting only the Islands herein after mentioned shall be restored without delay, and without causing any destruction, or carrying away any of the artillery or other public property, originally captured in the said forts or places, and which shall remain therein upon the exchange of the ratification of this Treaty, or any slaves or other private property."[18] Dauphin Island was not one of those which were excepted from surrender. That article binds the high contracting parties to a mutual restoration of territory, places and possessions, without regard to the consideration of title. The mere fact of possession prior to the war, determined the duty of restoration on the return of peace. It was so intended, and well understood by both parties. Under that Stipulation, as being one of the possessions taken from us during the war, the mouth of the Columbia has been restored,[19] although our title to it was subsequently contested by Great Britain.[20] And from none of the places or possessions thus to be restored, was Great Britain to carry away any slave or other property. If this impeachment of our title to, or possession of, Dauphin Island (for which, at an earlier period, Mr. Jackson might have been entitled to the grateful acknowledgments of Spain, but which, at this late day, will hardly be made) had been even colourable, the claim of D'Villiers might have presented a fit subject of reference to the Arbitrator of the Convention. Incontestible as both title and possession were, Mr. Cheves, in consideration of what belonged to the character and dignity of his Government, would not have been without justification, if he had declined an arbitration of the question had it been offered by the other Commissioner. In tendering it himself, you cannot fail to perceive manifested by him, the greatest moderation, and the strongest disposition faithfully to execute the fifth Article of the Convention. Nor can you avoid contrasting the conduct of the two Commissioners in this respect. Whilst Mr. Jackson refuses to refer, to say the least of it, the debateable [sic] question of interest, Mr. Cheves is willing to refer a case in which our *clear* and *indisputable* right to Dauphin Island was the only point to be collaterally adjudicated.

4. By the third Article of the Convention His Brittanic Majesty engaged "to cause to be produced, before the Commission, as material towards ascertaining facts, all the evidence of which His Majesty's Government may be in possession, by returns from His Majesty's officers or otherwise, of the number of Slaves carried away."[21] On the 25th. of October last, Mr. Rush requested of Mr. Canning the fulfilment of that undertaking. Mr. Canning, in a note to Mr. Rush, under date the 16th. of February last, informed him that he lost "no time in directing the necessary returns to be prepared. This has been done in as far as the records in the possession of His Majesty's Government could supply the information re-

quired, and the returns have been forwarded to Mr. Jackson at Washington, for the use of the mixed British and American Commission." From the well known fairness and straightforwardness of Mr. Canning, there can be no doubt that Mr. Jackson was made the medium merely of communicating, unconditionally, the information thus collected, to the Board. Instead of promptly performing that duty, keeping the Documents in his own possession, he opened a negociation with Mr. Cheves, as to the uses which should be made of them, after they came into the joint possession of the Board. He insisted, as one of the conditions upon which they should be delivered over to the Commission, that all access to them should be denied to the claimants, until the testimony was closed in their respective cases, and they were put down for final trial; and then, that each claimant might be cautiously allowed to inspect so much of the returns as related to his particular case, and no more. The object of the stipulation undoubtedly was, to supply all the testimony which might happen to be in the custody of the British Government, respecting facts very difficult to prove. Its operation was in the nature of a discovery of evidence, which the ordinary tribunals of the two countries, in cases of individual litigation, would have enforced, but which, in national concerns, could only be provided for by Treaty. The evidence thus discovered and produced might supply the defects of other proof, or might, itself, require the explanations which other testimony could render. But how were these explanations to be made if the returns were to be locked up from the view of the parties whose interests were to be affected? Mr. Jackson seems to have supposed that testimony which was to be furnished for the benefit of both parties, ought to be employed exclusively for that of one of them, as a check upon what might be produced by the other. The party was, according to him, to be indulged, at the last moment, as a gracious favour, with a view of that evidence which was possibly to defeat his just expectations although a timely examination of it would have enabled him to have adduced the most conclusive explanatory proof. And where does Mr. Jackson find any precedent for the extraordinary condition which he would have imposed? Surely not in the enlightened judicial codes of either of the two countries, unless he goes as far back as to the proceedings of the Star chamber. The case which he puts, (and which is believed to be one of rare occurrence) where, during the examination of one witness in Court, other witnesses are kept out to prevent their hearing him, will not bear him out. For in that case, the party to be affected by the testimony is allowed to hear it, and may during the progress of the trial, by cross examination, or adducing other witnesses in his behalf, counteract its effect. The condition which Mr. Jackson would have imposed, was, doubtless, founded upon the apprehension of an improper use being made by the claimants, of the returns, so as to subject the British Government beyond its just responsibility. But it ought to be borne in mind that the definitive list of property for which indemnity was to be made, required by the Convention, was given in to the Commissioners, and that the claimants, consequently, could make no addition of other property to it. The Convention having stipulated the production of the returns, without any conditions, it is hardly necessary to add that Mr. Cheves rejected those which Mr. Jackson had no authority from that instrument, and it is believed, none from his Government, to propose. The returns were then produced and filed. The proceedings of the Board will shew that Mr. Jackson persevered in rejecting every general and special application which was made in behalf of the claimants, for a sight of them. Mr. Cheves then proposed that the Secretary of the Board should be directed to prepare a transcript of the returns, to be transmitted to his Government, to facilitate the discharge of his duty, and to afford to it an opportunity of seeing how far a compliance had been made with the stipulation of the third Article. To this Mr. Jackson also objected, without some pledge or guaranty should be given to him, that this Government would make no other use of the returns than such as he deemed proper. I put it to the candour of Mr. Canning to suppose a change of positions, and to ask himself what would have been his estimate of a demand of such a pledge or guaranty, if it had been required at London by an American Commissioner? Mr. Cheves, it is useless to say, refused to be the organ of making such an affrontive proposal to his Government.

It is painful to me to have been obliged to dwell so long upon the conduct of the British Commissioner. I might have greatly extended a list of the examples of his unaccommodating spirit, but those which I have selected must be sufficient to bring a conviction of it home to the British Government. It would have been much more agreeable to have seen in his official course here, manifestations of that liberality, frankness and mutual good feeling, which happily characterise the subsisting relations, generally, of the two countries, and which it will be my constant purpose and pleasure to labour to increase.

You cannot avoid remarking, in the scheme of the Composition of this Board, the great difference in the relative situation of the parties, and the disadvantageous attitude in which the claimants are placed. The British Government is the party from which indemnity is exacted for a large amount of property. The Government of the

United States, in its corporate character, has no interest in the affair. It is to pay nothing.—to receive nothing. It is the guardian only of the rights of its citizens, who are in the pursuit of that indemnity. If, when the two Commissioners are divided in opinion, the British Commissioner refuses the reference for which provision is made in the fifth Article that refusal is tantamount to a decision in favour of Great Britain. And if the refusal were extended to every case of division (and it really does not appear likely that there will be many of concurrence) the result would be, that the object of the Convention would be almost entirely defeated. Should the British Government sanction this course of proceeding of its commissioner, which is not, however, to be supposed, it would turn out that one party absolutely made that decision which was to flow from the common consultations and joint judgment of both. We might, indeed, again invoke the friendly interposition of His Imperial Majesty, and he might again lend his friendly offices, and pronounce a new award. Out of this new award fresh questions might spring, dividing the judgements of the Commissioners, rendering further appeals to his umpirage necessary, and presenting a never ending circle.

From a Commission so constituted and so executed, no practical benefit is likely to flow. It should be the mutual desire of both parties to be delivered from it. We have had reason to believe, from some former intimations, that the British Government is anxious to dispense with it by an agreement fixing upon some gross amount for all the indemnities which the Convention promises. This is the only hypothesis upon which the course of Mr. Jackson is explicable. Believing that it is the interest of the claimants to make a reasonable compromise, you are requested to sound the British Government upon the subject; and if such an arrangement be attainable, you are authorised to make it. A power for that purpose accompanies these instructions.

The difficulty is in fixing on a proper sum. We can only make an approximation, but even that will probably be nearer the justice of the case, than any aggregate amount which may be expected to be awarded by the present, or any other, commission which would be created under the Convention. The total number of slaves on the definitive list, to which the Board is now restricted, is 3601, the details of which may be seen in the accompanying paper designated A.[22] The aggregate sum of their values, estimated by the average price which has been agreed upon by the Board is $1.183.200. Ten years interest upon that sum, at six per cent per annum, amounts to $709.920, giving as the total of principal and interest, $1.893.120. The entire value of all personal property, other than slaves for which, as having been carried away, or destroyed, in contravention to the Treaty of Ghent, claims have been laid before the Board, according to the best estimate which can be made is $500.000. Ten years interest upon that sum would be $300.000, making an aggregate, in principal and interest, of $800.000. The entire amount of the value of all property, including slaves, for which indemnity is claimed, and including interest, may be stated at $2.693.120. If, therefore, you could obtain that sum, every claimant might be fully compensated. But that can hardly be expected; and I will, therefore, endeavour to exhibit views of the deductions from that sum which would, probably, be made if the Commission proceeds to fulfil its duties.

1st.— As to the slaves. Of these, upwards of two thousand four hundred were carried away from the States of Virginia and Maryland, and, of this number, not more than five hundred will probably be brought by the proof, within the terms of the Treaty of Ghent. Of the residue of the 3601, after deducting the 2400, the principal part of them were taken from the States of Georgia and Louisiana, and all these are supposed to be comprehended in the provision of that Treaty. The average values fixed by the Board were, for the slaves carried from Virginia and Maryland $280. each; for Louisiana $580. each, and for the other southern States $390. each. The slave account, then, it may be conjectured, would probably stand thus;—

    500 from Virginia and Maryland, at $280 $140.000.
    250 from Louisiana   „ $580   145.000.
    900 from Georgia &c   „ $390   351.000.
                                                     ─────────
    producing together a total sum without interest of $636.000.

2ndly. As to the personal property, other than slaves. The estimated value of all that is claimed, is about $500.000. But many of these claims are clearly not within the terms of the Treaty of Ghent. For example, a large item in the list, (a copy of which designated B accompanies this Letter) is for tobacco *destroyed* in 1814. However just it may have been to compensate the owners of that property for their loss, it is not provided for. It is believed that $250.000, principal, may be assumed, as as large an amount as would be obtained for all the property, other than slaves, under the most liberal exercise of the powers of the Board. The aggregate amount, then, of the indemnity for every description of property which would probably be awarded by the Commission, may be safely assumed, it is believed, at $886.000. exclusive of interest. If to that sum be added ten years interest, amounting to $531.600, the total of both principal and interest would be $1.417.600. A compromise, therefore, by which the British Government would agree to pay the sum of \$1.417.600 would be deemed advisable. With respect to the question of interest, if the British Commissioner, in the event of the Board being again put in motion, should consent to refer it to the Arbitrator, the reference could take place in every individual case; and the lot for the Arbitrator would be cast in each case. Upon the only supposition on which we can reason, that of an equality between the parties in the result of that appeal to chance, it would turn out that the British choice of the Arbitrator would prevail as often as the American. And we may safely conclude that, as often as the British Arbitrator had to decide upon the claim to interest, it would be rejected. In conjecturing the amount of interest which may possibly be obtained, on the contingency of the progress of the Board, we must deduct one half from the preceding estimate, that is \$265.800, which being taken from the aggregate of \$1.417.600, would leave \$1.151.800, as the highest sum which it may be fairly presumed would be awarded by the Commission, if it be not abolished. This sum, therefore, of \$1.151.800, you will consider, in treating, as the minimum to which you can fall. I observed in the estimates laid before Parliament for the British service of the present year one of £250.000 sterling to cover the awards of the Commission.[23] This sum being very near the same as that to which you are limited, it is probable that they may have adopted some such process to arrive at it, as I have employed, and it is, therefore, anticipated that you will have no difficulty in coming to the agreement with the British Government which you are now authorised to conclude.

In the event of your being able to effect this arrangement it would be proper to insert in the Convention which you may conclude, that the gross amount shall be distributed among the persons entitled to indemnity under the Treaty of Ghent, and the award of His Imperial Majesty, and the Convention signed at St. Petersburg, in pursuance of it, in such manner, by an American Commission, as the Congress of the United States may, by law, direct. It would be well, also, to insert a clause declaring that, in the distribution thus to be made, the average value of the slaves which has been fixed by the Commissioners, should govern; and that the Commission should be restricted to the definitive list of slaves and other property which has been given in to the mixed Commission, with such additions to it as ought to be equitably made, in consequence of omissions in the Department of State. This would simplify the duty to be performed, avoid the necessity of establishing the value of each particular slave, and prevent the uncertainty which would attend a new search after a just average. It would likewise be proper to provide in the Convention that, if the aggregate sum, stipulated to be paid by Great Britain, should fall short of the amount of claims to be ascertained by the American Commission, under the Act of Congress, there should be a rateable deduction from the sum adjudged to each claimant. If, on the contrary, there should be an excess, that excess should be distributed by the same Commission, among such other owners of slaves and personal property, carried away or destroyed by the British forces, as Congress may direct.

If you should be unable to come to any agreement to put an end to the present Commission, by substituting, in lieu of it, a gross sum, to be apportioned among the claimants, you will then urge the British Government to infuse a better spirit into their Commissioner; and, especially, that they instruct him to execute the fifth Article of the Convention according to its true intent and meaning, by referring to the Arbitrator all the questions on which he and Mr. Cheves have disagreed. And to prevent the delay which would arise from resorting again to the British Government, he ought to be charged with a similar reference of all other questions, on which, from time to time, the Commissioners, during the future progress of the Board, may, unfortunately, happen to disagree.

I am, with great respect, Sir, Your very humble and obedient servant.   H. CLAY.

Copy. DNA, RG59, Dip. Instr., vol. 10, pp. 314-30 (M77, R5). AL draft and LI draft (with interlineations by Clay), in DLC-HC (DNA, M212, R7).

1 Both dated May 5, 1825. Copies, in DNA, RG59, Ceremonial Communications, II, 21, 23.   2 Richard Rush.

3 President Monroe's message, Secretary Adams' report, and a list of the documents transmitted are found in *American State Papers, Foreign Relations,* V, 510-11.

4 William Huskisson.

5 *American State Papers, Foreign Relations,* V, 353-68. On the convention, see above, Clay to Addington, April 6, 1825.

6 See above, Clay to Salazar, March 21, 1825.

7 Addington to Clay, April 9, 1825.   8 George Canning.

9 See above, Rush to Secretary of State, March 26, 1825.

10 See above, III, 318n, 736n; Rush to Secretary of State, March 8, 1825.

11 See above, Cheves to Clay, April 26 (1 and 2), 1825.

12 Cf. above, Cheves to Clay, March 14, 31, April 26 (1 and 2), 1825.

13 John Cowper (Couper). See above, Cheves to Clay, March 14, 31, April 26 (1), 1825.

14 Littleton W. Tazewell; Edward Livingston. Briefs not found.

15 See above, I, 516n.   16 See above, II, 673, 674n, 678n.

17 See above, I, 983.   18 See above, I, 1006.

19 In 1811 the Pacific Fur Company, founded and controlled by John Jacob Astor, had established Astoria, a trading post on the south bank, near the mouth, of the Columbia River. The partners on the scene had sold out to a rival British firm in November, 1813, one month before the arrival of a British sloop-of-war, which took possession of the post and renamed it Fort George. Under Article I of the Treaty of Ghent, Astoria, as territory, though not as a trading operation, had been restored to the United States in 1818.

20 See above, Rush to Secretary of State, March 26, 1825, note.

21 See above, Rush to Secretary of State, March 8, 1825.

22 Enclosures "A" and "B" not found. On the following estimates for slave and property claims, respectively, cf. above, Cheves to Clay, April 26 (2), 1825.

23 Frederick John Robinson, as Chancellor of the Exchequer, had included this sum

as a "Miscellaneous" entry in the estimates contained in his speech reviewing the financial situation of the country, delivered before the House of Commons on February 28. *Annual Register, 1825,* "History," 118.

To Henry Middleton

No. 1: Henry Middleton, Envoy Extraordinary and
Minister Plenipotentiary, U S. to St. Petersburg.

Sir,   Department of State Washington 10 May, 1825.

I am directed by the President to instruct you to endeavour to engage the Russian Government to contribute its best exertions towards terminating the existing contest between Spain and her Colonies. Among the interests which, at this period, should most command the serious attention of the Nations of the old and new world, no one is believed to have a claim so paramount as that of the present war. It has existed, in greater or less extent, seventeen years. Its earlier stages were marked by the most shocking excesses, and throughout it has been attended by an almost incalculable waste of blood and treasure. During its continuance, whole generations have passed away without living to see its close, whilst others have succeeded them, growing up from infancy to Majority, without ever tasting the blessings of peace. The conclusion of that war, whatever, and whenever, it may be, must have a great effect upon Europe and America. Russia is so situated as that, whilst she will be less directly affected than other parts of christendom, her weight and her councils must have a controlling influence on its useless protraction or its happy termination. If this peculiar attitude secures her impartiality, it draws to it great responsibility in the decision which she may feel it proper to make. The predominance of the power of the Emperor[1] is every where felt. Europe, America and Asia all own it. It is with a perfect knowledge of its vast extent, and the profoundest respect for the wisdom and the justice of the august Personage who wields it, that his enlightened and humane councils are now invoked.

In considering that war, as in considering all others we should look back upon the past, deliberately survey its present condition, and endeavour, if possible, to catch a view of what is to come. With respect to the first branch of the subject, it is, perhaps, of the least practical importance. No statesman can have contemplated the Colonial relations of Europe and Continental America, without foreseeing that the time must come, when they would cease. That time might have been retarded or accelerated; but come it must, in the great march of human events. An attempt of the British Parliament to tax, without their consent, the former British Colonies, now these United States, produced the war of our Revolution, and

led to the establishment of that Independence and freedom which
we now so justly prize. Moderation and forbearance on the part of
Great Britain might have postponed, but could not have prevented,
our ultimate separation. The attempt of Bonaparte to subvert the
ancient Dynasty of Spain, and to place on its throne a member of
his own family,[2] no doubt hastened the Independence of the Spanish Colonies. If he had not been urged, by his ambition, to the conquest of the Peninsula, those Colonies, for a long time to come,
might have continued quietly to submit to the parental sway.
But they must have, inevitably, thrown it off, sooner or later. We
may imagine that a vast continent, uninhabited or thinly peopled
by a savage and untutored race, may be governed by a remote
Country, blessed with the lights, and possessed of the power, of
civilization. But it is absurd to suppose that this same Continent,
in extent more than twenty times greater than that of the parent
Country, and doubling it in a population equally civilized, should
not be able, when it chooses to make the effort, to cast off the distant
authority. When the epoch of separation between a parent State
and its Colony, from whatever cause, arrives, the struggle for self
government on the one hand, and for the preservation of power on
the other, produces mutual exasperation, and leads to a most embittered and ferocious war. It is then that it becomes the duty
of third Powers to interpose their humane offices, and calm the passions, and enlighten the councils of the parties. And the necessity
of their efforts is greatest with the parent Country, whose pride,
and whose wealth and power, swelled by the Colonial contributions,
create the most repugnance to an acquiescence in a severance which
has been ordained by Providence.

In the war which has so long been raging between Spain and
her Colonies, the United States have taken no part, either to produce, or to sustain it. They have been inactive and neutral spectators of the passing scenes. Their frankness forbids, however, that
they should say that they have beheld those scenes with feelings
of indifference. They have, on the contrary, anxiously desired that
other parts of this Continent should acquire, and enjoy, that independence with which, by the valour and the patriotism of the
founders of their liberty, they have been, under the smiles of Heaven,
so greatly blessed. But in the indulgence of this sympathetic feeling,
they have not, for one moment, been unmindful of the duties of
that neutrality which they had deliberately announced.[3] And the
best proof of the fidelity with which they have strictly fulfilled its
obligations, is furnished in the fact that, during the progress of the
war, they have been unjustly accused by both parties, of violating
their declared neutrality. But it is now of little consequence to

retrace the causes, remote, or proximate, of the revolt of the Spanish
Colonies. The great, and much more important consideration which
will, no doubt, attract the attention of His Imperial Majesty, is the
present state of the contest. The principles which produced the war,
and those which may be incorporated in the Institutions of the new
States may divide the opinions of men. Principles, unhappily, are
too often the subject of controversy. But, notorious facts are incontestible. They speak a language which silences all speculation
and should determine the judgement and the conduct of States,
whatever may be the school in which their rulers are brought up or
practiced, and whatever the social forms which they would desire
to see established. And it is to the voice of such facts that Europe
and America are now called upon patiently to listen.

And in contemplating the present state of the war, what are the
circumstances which must forcibly strike every reflecting observer.
Throughout both Continents, from the western limits of the United
States to Cape Horn, the Spanish power is subdued. The recent decisive victory of Ayachuco [*sic*] has annihilated the last remains of
the Spanish force.[4] Not a foot of territory in all that vast extent,
owns the dominion, not a bayonet sustains the cause, of Spain.
The war, in truth, has ended. It has been a war between a contracted corner of Europe, and an entire Continent; between ten millions of people, amidst their own extraordinary convulsions, fighting at a distance across an ocean of three thousand miles in extent,
against twenty millions, contending at home, for their lives, their
liberty, and their property. Henceforward it will present only the
image of a war between an exhausted dwarf, struggling for power,
and empire, against a refreshed giant combating for freedom and
existence. Too much confidence is reposed in the enlightened
judgement of His Imperial Majesty to allow of the belief that he
will permit any abatement of his desire to see such a war formally
terminated, and the blessings of peace restored, from sympathies
which he may feel, however strong, for the unhappy condition of
Spain. These very sympathies will naturally lead His Imperial
Majesty to give her the best, and most friendly advice in her actual posture. And in what does that consist? His Imperial Majesty
must be the exclusive, as he is the most competent judge. But it
will not be deemed inconsistent with respect to enquire, if it be
possible to believe that Spain can bring the new States again under
her dominion? Where does the remotest prospect of her success
break out? In Colombia, Mexico, or Peru? The re-conquest of the
United States by Great Britain would not be a more mad and
hopeless enterprize than that of the restoration of the Spanish power
on those Continents. Some of the most considerable of the new

States have established Governments which are in full and successful operation, regularly collecting large revenues, levying and maintaining numerous and well appointed armies, and already laying the foundation of respectable marines. Whilst they are consolidating their institutions at home, they are strengthening themselves abroad by Treaties of alliance among themselves, and of amity and commerce with Foreign States. Is the vain hope indulged that intestine divisions within the new States will arise, which may lead to the recal [sic] of the Spanish Power, as the Stuarts were recalled in England,[5] and the Bourbons in France,[6] at the close of their respective revolutions? We should not deceive ourselves. Amidst all the political changes of which the new States are destined to be the theatre, whatever party or power may be upermost [sic], one spirit will animate them all, and that is, an invincible aversion from all political connexion with Spain, and an unconquerable desire of independence. It could not be otherwise. They have already tasted the fruits of Independence. And the contrast between what their condition now is, in the possession of free commerce, liberal Institutions, and all the faculties of their Country and its population, allowed full physical and moral development, and what it was under Spain, cramped, debased and degraded, must be fatal to the chimerical hope of that monarchy, if it be cherished, by any means whatever to re-establish her power. The cord which binds a Colony to its parent Country, being once broken, is never repaired. A recollection of what was inflicted, and what was borne, during the existence of that relation; the pride of the former governing power, and the sacrifices of the interests of the Colony to those of the parent, widen and render the breach between them, whenever it occurs, perpetual. And if, as we may justly suppose, the embittered feelings, excited by an experience of that unequal connexion, are in proportion to the severity of the parental rule, they must operate with irresistible force on the rupture which has taken place between Spain and her Colonies, since, in no other instance has it been exerted with such unmitigated rigour.

Viewing the war as practically terminated, so far at least as relates to Spanish exertion on the Continent, in considering the third branch of the enquiry which I proposed, let us endeavour to anticipate what may be expected to happen if Spain obstinately perseveres in the refusal to conclude a peace. If the war has only a nominal continuance, the new Republics cannot disband their victorious armies without culpable neglect of all the maxims of prudence and precaution. And the first observation that occurs is, that this protracted war must totally change its character and its objects. Instead of being a war of offensive operations, in which

Spain has been carrying on hostilities in the bosom of the new States, it will become one to her of a defensive nature, in which all her future exertions must be directed to the protection and defence of her remaining insular possessions. And thus the Peninsula, instead of deriving the revenue and the aid so necessary to the revival of its prosperity, from Cuba and Puerto Rico, must be further drained to succour those Islands. For it cannot be doubted that the new States will direct their combined and unemployed forces to the reduction of those valuable Islands.[7] They will naturally strike their enemy wherever they can reach him. And they will be stimulated to the attack by the double motive, arising from the richness of the prize, and from the fact that those Islands constitute the rendezvous of Spain, where are concentrated, and from which issue, all the means of annoying them, which remain to her. The success of the enterprize is, by no means, improbable. Their proximity to the Islands, and their armies being perfectly acclimated, will give to the united efforts of the Republics great advantages. And if, with these, be taken into the estimate, the important and well known fact, that a large portion of the inhabitants of the Islands is predisposed to a separation from Spain, and would therefore form a powerful auxiliary to the Republican arms, their success becomes almost certain. But even if they should prove incompetent to the reduction of the Islands, there can be but little doubt that the shattered remains of Spanish commerce would be swept from the ocean. The advantages of the positions of Colombia and Mexico for annoying that commerce in the Gulph of Mexico, and the Caribbean Sea, must be evident from the slightest observation. In fact, Cuba is in the mouth of a sack, which is held by Colombia and the United Mexican States. And if, unhappily for the repose of the world, the war should be continued, the coasts of the peninsula itself may be expected soon to swarm with the privateers of the Republics.

If, on the contrary, Spain should consent to put an end to the war, she might yet preserve what remains of her former American possessions. And surely the retention of such islands as Cuba and Porto Rico is eminently worthy of serious consideration, and should satisfy a reasonable ambition. The possessions of Spain in the West Indies would be, still, more valuable than those of any other Power. The war ended, her commerce would revive, and there is every reason to anticipate, from the habits, prejudices and tastes of the new Republics, that she would find in the consumption of their population, a constantly augmenting demand for the produce of her industry, now excluded from its best markets. And her experience, like that of Great Britain with the United States, would demonstrate that the value of the commercial intercourse would more than indemnify the loss, whilst it is unburthened with the expense incident to political connexion. A subordinate consideration, which should not be overlooked, is, that large estates are owned by Spanish subjects, resident in Spain, which may possibly be confiscated if the war be wantonly continued. If that measure of rigour shall not be adopted, their incomes must be greatly diminished, during a state of war. These incomes, upon the restoration of peace, or the proceeds of the sales of the estates themselves, might be drawn to Spain, and would greatly contribute towards raising her from her present condition of embarrassment and languishment. If peace should be longer deferred, and the war should take the probable direction which has been supposed, during its further progress, other powers, not now parties, may be collaterally drawn into it. From much less considerable causes, the peace of the world has been often disturbed. From the vicinity of Cuba to the United States, its valuable commerce, and the nature of its population, their Government cannot be indifferent to any political change to which that Island may be destined. Great Britain and France, also, have deep interests in its fortunes which must keep them wide awake to all those changes. In short what European State has not much at stake, direct or indirect, in the destiny, be it what it may, of that most valuable of all the West India Islands? The reflections and the experience of the Emperor, on the vicissitudes of war, must have impressed him with the solemn duty of all Governments to guard against even the distant approach of that most terrible of all scourges, by every precaution with which human prudence and foresight can surround the repose and safety of States.

Such is the view of the war between Spain and the new Republics which the President desires you, most earnestly, but respectfully, to present to His Imperial Majesty. From this view it is evident that it is not so much for the new States, themselves, as for Spain, that peace has become absolutely necessary. Their independence of her, whatever intestine divisions may, if intestine divisions shall, yet, unhappily await them, is fixed and irrevocable. She may, indeed, by a blind and fatal protraction of the war, yet lose more: gain for her is impossible. In becoming the advocate for peace, one is the true advocate of Spain. If the Emperor shall, by his wisdom, enlighten the Councils of Spain, and bring home to them a conviction of her real interests, there can be no fears of the success of his powerful interposition. You are authorized, in that spirit of the most perfect frankness and friendship which have ever characterized all the relations between Russia and the United

States, to disclose without reserve, the feelings and the wishes of the United States, in respect to Cuba and Porto Rico. They are satisfied with the present condition of those Islands now open to the commerce and enterprize of their citizens. They desire, for themselves, no political change in them. If Cuba were to declare itself independent, the amount and the character of its population render it improbable that it could maintain its independence. Such a premature declaration might bring about a renewal of those shocking scenes, of which a neighboring Island was the afflicting theatre.[8] There could be no effectual preventive of those scenes but in the guaranty, and in a large resident force, of Foreign Powers. The terms of such a guaranty, and the quotas which each should contribute of such a force, would create perplexing questions of very difficult adjustment, to say nothing of the continual jealousies which would be in operation. In the state of possession which Spain has, there would be a ready acquiescence of those very Foreign Powers, all of whom would be put into angry activity upon the smallest prospect of a transfer of those Islands. The United States could not, with indifference,[9] see such a transfer to any European Power. And if the new Republics or either of them, were to conquer them, their maritime force, as it now is, or for a long time to come, is likely to be, would keep up constant apprehensions of their safety. Nor is it believed that the new States desire, or will attempt, the acquisition, unless they shall be compelled, in their own defence, to make it, by the unnecessary prolongation of the war. Acting on the policy which is here unfolded, the Government of the United States, although they would have been justified to have seized Cuba and Porto Rico, in the just protection of the lives and the commerce of their citizens, which have been a prey to infamous Pirates, finding succour and refuge in Spanish Territory,[10] have signally displayed their patience and moderation by a scrupulous respect of the sovereignty of Spain, who was herself bound, but has utterly failed, to repress those enormities.

Finally, the President cherishes the hope, that the Emperor's devotion to peace, no less than his friendship for Spain, will induce him to lend the high authority of his name to the conclusion of a war, the further prosecution of which must have the certain effect of an useless waste of human life. No power has displayed more solicitude for the repose of the world than Russia, who has recently given the strongest evidence of her unwillingness to disturb it in the east by unexampled moderation and forbearance.[11] By extending to America the blessings of that peace which, under the auspices of His Imperial Majesty, Europe now enjoys, all parts of this continent will have grateful occasion for regarding him, as the United States ever have, as their most potent and faithful friend

This Despatch is confided to your discretion, to be communicated in extenso, or its contents disclosed in such other manner, to the Government of Russia, as shall appear to you most likely to accomplish its object.

I have the honour to be, Sir, with great respect, Your obedient and very humble Servant.   H. CLAY.

Copy. DNA, RG59, Dip. Instr., vol. 10, pp. 331-38 (M77, R5). AL draft and L draft, with interlineations by Clay, in DLC-HC (DNA, M212, R7). The major change in these various versions lies in the re-writing, in Clay's hand, of the next to the last paragraph, designed to express the same views more felicitously rather than to change the meaning.   1 Alexander I.
2 See above, II, 516; 539, note 6.   3 See above, II, 292n.
4 See above, Raguet to Secretary of State, March 11, 1825, note; cf. above, Tudor to Secretary of State, March 21, 1825, note.
5 On the restoration of Charles II, see above, I, 897, 899n.
6 See above, I, 873, 885.
7 Cf. above, Clay to Poinsett, March 26, 1825; Clay to Everett, April 27, 1825.
8 Haiti. See above, II, 504, note 3.
9 The last two words interlined, replacing the phrase "without serious inquietude," crossed out, in the original draft.
10 See above, Nelson to Clay, April 6, 1825; Clay to Everett, April 27, 1825.
11 See above, Clay to Middleton, April 21, 1825, note.

From James Brown

Dear Sir,   Paris May 10. 1825
I received your letter of the 29 March enclosing one directed to Mr Scheffer acknowledging on the part of the House of Representatives the receipt of his excellent portrait of our good friend General Lafayette presented to that body. This letter I delivered to Mr Scheffer on the 5th Inst and at the same time intimated to him in such terms as could in no way compromit the House, that you had been restrained only by the advice of General Lafayette and his son[1] from making a movement towards a more suitable return for that valuable present. Mr Scheffer expressed his entire approbation of the course which had been recommended by his friends, and assured me that the acknowledgement had been made in the manner, most agreeable to his feelings and wishes   I am Dear Sir very sincerely Your faithful Servt   JAMES BROWN
Honle Henry Clay

ALS. DLC-TJC (DNA, M212, R13).
1 George Washington Lafayette.

From George McClure

Dear Sir   Bath Steuben County 10h. May 1825
I have taken the liberty of addressing you freely on the subject

of my concerns, and solicit your aid in procuring for me some profitable employment under the Government of the U. States, in this or any other State in the Union, Having invested my all (about $30,000) in a Woollen factory, at a time when I flattered myself that such establishments would not be suffered to languish for want of Govermental [sic] protection, besides in order to complete my works I borrowed of the State $10,000 and mortgaged the whole of my property to secure the payment of the same, from the whole of this investment I cannot say that I have rcieved [sic] one dollar profit. I did not expect to be called upon by the State for the am,t loaned, until I should find it convenient to pay, provided the interest was anually [sic] paid, nor was it ever intimated to me by the Comptroler [sic] that the principal would be called for, until the last day of our November session, when in the presence of a number of Gentlemen, he demanded payment & threatened a foreclosure of the mortgage unless I should immediately comply—and before I reached home he advertised my property for sale,

This scene of persecution by our State Officers (for they were all combined against me) grew out of my opposition to their will in relation to the late struggle for the Presidency, had I united with them in the support of Mr, Crawford every possible favour & indulgence would have been afforded me, consequently I was obliged to apply to the Legislature for relief, which was granted by extending the time of payment.—

The late additional tariff of 5 pr. cent on Woollen cloths is not felt, it is overballanced [sic] by a duty of 10 pr. cent on the raw material imported,[1] At present it is not an object worthy of my attention, and I have concluded to transfer the management of the factory into the hands of my sons,[2] provided I can obtain some other profitable employment. I have had an impression that in the land office department in Michigan, or some of the Western States will afford employment for a number of Officers, such as Registers & receivers &c— Should there be any vacancies in that, or any other quarter of the Union of any Office of which you may deem me quallified [sic] to fill, I would esteem it a verry [sic] great favour, if through your influence I can obtain an appointment[3]—

As it respects my quallifications [sic], I can only say that I have been actively & extensively engaged in Mercantil [sic] business for nearly thirty Years, until the time I embarqued in manufacturing— If a recommendation however is necessary I can readily procure such a one as I presume will be sattisfactory [sic]—

I shall be pleased to hear from you, and in the mean time accept assurances of the esteem & regard of your friend & Servt.

Hone. H. Clay—   GEO. MC.CLURE

P, S, I recd. Your late address to your constituents as well as Your corraspondance [sic] with Eaten[4] & it gives me great pleasure to find that Your friends are perfectly sattisfied, and as it respects your Enemies their mouths (generally speaking) are shut, some few Jacksonites, *alias Clintonians* occasionally shew their teeth, but they cannot bite, I would advise you to write no more, I think you have paid Old *hickery* [sic] with compound interest—

ALS. DNA, RG59, A. and R. (MR3).
[1] Cf. above, III, 756n. Prior to the act of May 22, 1824, the rate of duty on raw wool had been 15 per cent, ad valorem, and that on manufactured woollens, 25 per cent. "Comparative Statement of Duties. . . ," *House Docs.,* 18 Cong., 1 Sess., no. 38, p. 3.   [2] Not identified.
[3] He received no appointment.
[4] See above, Address, March 26, 1825; Eaton to Clay, March 28, 31, April 2, 1825; Clay to Eaton, March 30, April 1, 1825.

DIPLOMATIC NOTES   May 10, 1825

To SEVERIN LORICH. Replies to notes of July 25 and September 2, 1824, and March 16, 1825; explains remission of forfeiture in the case of the *Carl John (Johan)* ; asserts that, immediately after ratification of the convention between the United States and Sweden, its provisions were applied to Swedish and Norwegian vessels in American ports and Clay knows of no violations; states, concerning suggested reciprocation of privileges granted in Sweden, allowing importation in American vessels of goods not manufactured in the United States, that the President is favorably disposed but that the decision rests with Congress. Copy. DNA, RG59, Notes to Foreign Ministers and Consuls, vol. 3, pp. 220-21 (M38, R3). AL draft, in CSmH. On the case of the *Carl Johan,* see above, Southard to Clay, May 9, 1825; on the commercial convention of the United States with Sweden, see above, Lorich to Clay, March 16, 1825, note.

INSTRUCTIONS AND DISPATCHES   May 10, 1825

To THOMAS L. L. BRENT, no. 1. Transmits his commission as Chargé d'Affaires to Portugal and an introductory letter to the Minister of Foreign Affairs in Lisbon; acknowledges receipt "at this office" of dispatches numbered 1 through 5 and "private" letters of September 19, 1824, and January 13, 1825; and promises an inquiry into complaints of the Portuguese Government against an American ship captain for robbery "at one of the Cape de Verd Islands" and "against Samuel Hodges, our Consul there, for promoting a contraband and illicit trade, and the escape of some Portuguese subjects in banishment at the same Islands. . . ." Copy. DNA, RG59, Dip. Instr., vol. 10, p. 339 (M77, R5). AL draft, in CSmH; L draft, in hand of Daniel Brent, in DLC-HC (DNA, M212, R7). Samuel Hodges, Jr., born in Massachusetts and appointed in 1818 as consul at the Cape Verde Islands, was retained in this position until his death in 1828. For fuller details of the incidents about which the Portuguese complained, see below, Hodges to Clay, July 28, 1825.

From BEAUFORT T. WATTS, Bogotá. Reports discussion with Dr. (Pedro) Gual concerning special privileges accorded to Great Britain by Colombia in the recent commercial treaty: the concessions were deemed necessary to gain British recognition of Colombian independence; Colombia stands ready to extend the same privileges to the United States. ALS. DNA, RG59, Dip. Disp., Colombia, vol. 3 (M-T33, R3). Received July 22.

The Treaty of Amity, Commerce, and Navigation between Colombia and Great Britain, signed April 18, 1825, had provided for reciprocal freedom of commerce between Colombia and all British territory in Europe, with most-favored-nation treatment for Colombia in British dominions outside Europe; reciprocity of tonnage duties and equality of rates on goods, whether they be carried in British or Colombian bottoms; security of conscience and freedom of worship for each other's nationals, provided it be done in private houses with due decorum; and Colombian agreement to cooperate in abolition of the slave trade. *Annual Register, 1825,* "Public Documents," 80-84.

MISCELLANEOUS LETTERS   May 10, 1825

From E[DWARD] BATES, United States district attorney, St. Louis (Missouri). Requests copies of the laws of the United States, with which neither the judge nor any other officer of the district court has been supplied and which cannot be bought in the State. ALS. DNA, RG59, Misc. Letters (M179, R62). Endorsed in strange hand: "Sent August 25th. 1825." Bates, a native of Virginia, had moved in 1814 to St. Louis, where he engaged in the practice of law. He was district attorney from 1821 to 1826, a member of Congress, 1827 to 1829, and United States Attorney General, 1861 to 1864.

From JOHN FITZGERALD and JOHN W. TOWNSEND, Mobile. Announce transfer of the *Mobile Mercantile Advertiser* from Fitzgerald to Townsend and a change of name to *Mobile Commercial Register.* ALS by Fitzgerald. DNA, RG59, P. and D. of L. Addressed to Secretary of State. The *Mobile Commercial Register* was not newly formed; it had been founded in 1821, with John W. Townsend as one of the proprietors.

In the spring of 1824 Fitzgerald had become printer of the *Mobile Mercantile Advertiser for the Country.* He had earlier (in March, 1819) edited another Mobile newspaper, which appeared for only a few issues. He is, perhaps, the same John Fitzgerald who from May, 1819, until January, 1820, published a journal at Clarksville, Tennessee, and in 1826, as one of the State printers, published a Nashville journal for a brief period.

APPLICATIONS, RECOMMENDATIONS   May 10, 1825

DAVID DELAUNAY, St. Louis, expresses disappointment at the necessity of abandoning plans to visit Kentucky and of renouncing "the Gratification of being acquainted with one who is so Justly Esteemed here and particularly by my Countrymen"; encloses papers explaining his claim for an appointment. ALS. DNA, RG59, A. and R. (MR2). The enclosures were probably a statement by Delaunay, dated March 28, 1825, a certification by William Clark, dated March 29, 1825, and a deposition by A(lexander) McNair, dated April 3, 1825—all unaddressed documents referring to Delaunay's early military service in Louisiana and Missouri. DNA, RG59, A. and R. (M531, R2). See above, Benton to Clay, April 22, 1825.

ROBERT WRIGHT, "Blakeford," solicits a consulship "in South America or elsewhere" for his son, William Henry De Coursey Wright, who has been "bred in a Counting House, been Several Trips a Super Cargo from Baltimore, [and] has had a good Education. . . ." Speaks of himself as "your old friend." ALS. MHi-Adams Papers, Letters Received (M469). On Robert Wright, see below, Barney to Clay, May 14, 1825 (no. 2). On his son's appointment as consul to Rio de Janeiro, see below, Clay to Wright, September 14, 1825.

To Nicholas Biddle

Dear Sir   Washington 11h. May 1825
   I received your obliging letter of the 9h. inst.[1] informing me of a small addition made by the Board to the compensation allowed to Mr. Mentelle at the Lexn. office.[2] I entertain a grateful sense of the kind consideration which the Board has been pleased to give to the expression of my wishes;[3] and I have no doubt that the comforts of a most worthy family will be increased by the recent generous act of the Board.
           With great respect I am faithfully Your ob. servant
N. Biddle Esq &c. &c. &c   H. CLAY

   ALS. DLC-HC (DNA, M212, R1).   [1] Not found.
   [2] Augustus Waldemarde Mentelle had been employed as porter by the Lexington Branch of the Bank of the United States since 1817.
   [3] No letter found.

To Rufus King

No. 3. Rufus King, appointed Envoy Extraordinary and
Minister Plenipotentiary, U. S. to Great Britain.
Sir,   Department of State Washington 11. May 1825.
   The coincidence in the policy of the United States and Great Britain, and the friendly communications which the British Government has made to this, in regard to the war between Spain and the new States on this Continent,[1] require that there should be observed the utmost frankness in the intercourse between the two Countries. It is in this spirit that you are requested to make known to the Government of Great Britain, the desire which animates the President, to see that War honourably terminated. Its further prosecution can be attended with no beneficial affect to Spain herself, and if she is made sensible of her true interests, and the dangers to which her insular possessions are now exposed, it is believed that she would consent to put an end to it. Instructions have been given to Mr. Poinsett,[2] and will be given to others of our Ministers, near the new States, to strengthen in them, if necessary, a disposition to peace. Mr. Everett is charged with similar instructions to operate at Madrid.[3] The same object will be confided to our Ministers at Paris and St. Petersburg.[4] I transmit you herewith, a copy of my

official note, addressed to Mr. Middleton, as best explaining the
views which are entertained by the President. You are authorized
to make such use of it with the British Government as your judgment
shall approve. It is understood that the local Government of Cuba
has petitioned the King of Spain[5] to make peace, by acknowledging
the Independence of the new States. If Great Britain, and the other
principal European Powers, would heartily unite with the United
States in these pacific endeavours, the President entertains the confident hope that a stop would be put to the further, and unnecessary effusion of human blood.

I am, with great respect, Sir, Your very obedient and humble
Servant.   H. CLAY.—

Copy. DNA, RG59, Dip. Instr., vol. 10, pp. 345-46 (M77, R5). AL draft, in DLC-HC
(DNA, M212, R7).
[1] See above, Rush to Clay, April 4, May 2, 1825; Addington to Clay, May 3, 1825.
[2] Above, March 26, 1825.   [3] Above, April 27, 1825.
[4] James Brown (below, May 13, 1825); Henry Middleton (above, May 10, 1825).
[5] Ferdinand VII. Cf. above, Robertson to Clay, April 20, 1825.

MISCELLANEOUS LETTERS   May 11, 1825

From PETER A. BROWNE, Philadelphia. Encloses opinion, relating to his dispute
with the Patent Office, signed by Horace Binney and John Sergeant, at variance
with that of William Wirt; inquires whether Clay has come to any conclusion
on other charges in his letters concerning the Patent Office. LS. DNA, RG59,
Misc. Letters (M179, R62). Dated "May 1825." The enclosure is dated May
10. Endorsed on cover: "Recd 13th." See above, Wirt to Clay, *ca.* April 16, 1825.

To John J. Appleton

John James Appleton, appointed special agent of the U. S. at Naples.
Sir,   Department of State Washington 12 May 1825
Some citizens of the United States have large claims upon the
Government of Naples, founded upon the seizure and condemnation of their vessels and cargoes, during the reign of Murat, in 1809.
Mr. Pinckney[1] was sent in 1816, on a temporary Mission to Naples,
as Envoy Extraordinary and Minister Plenipotentiary of the United
States, for the purpose of requiring indemnity and satisfaction
for those claims. His Mission was not attended with the success
which the evident justice of the object of it, authorized us to anticipate. There have been received at this Departure some communications from Mr. Hammett, the American Consul at Naples,[2]
importing that he had reason to believe a better disposition to
render justice to the claimants, prevailed in the Government of
Naples. Whatever that may happen to be, it is the determination
of this Government not to abandon those claims, but to continue

to assert them until satisfaction is made for them. Their great amount, the long delay which has intervened since the wrongs were perpetrated, and the information derived from Mr. Hammett, justify the renewal of endeavours to obtain the indemnity which is justly due. But the President does not think it proper, at present, to send a Representative of this Government, cloathed with a formal commission. He has considered it better adapted to the circumstances of the case, to appoint you a commercial Agent. I transmit, however, an informal Letter of introduction to the Minister of Foreign Affairs of Naples,[3] which you are authorised to present. The object of your Agency will be to ascertain, by such means as may appear to you best calculated to elicit, the present temper and disposition of that Government in respect to those claims. You will enquire of Mr. Hammett, on what ground he has formed the opinion that a better prospect existed for obtaining justice from Naples, and avail yourself of whatever information and assistance you can derive from him. You will let it be known to the Government of Naples that the United States still hold it responsible for the injuries inflicted upon their citizens, at the period, and in the manner, before mentioned; that this responsibility, far from weakening, acquires, in the view of the President, augmented strength, by the lapse of time, and that it never will be considered as cancelled, until full indemnity is made.

If you should conclude, from all the circumstances which you may be able, on the spot, to observe and weigh, that there is a reasonable hope of obtaining an acknowledgement of the obligation of Naples to pay the claims, and a provision for their payment, at even a distant day, a Commission will be sent you as chargé d'Affaires, to agree upon a Convention for that object. If, on the contrary, no favourable prospect exist, you will return to the United States. The duration of your abode at Naples, is necessarily left to your discretion, to be regulated by all the facts that may present themselves. I herewith transmit you a copy of the instructions formerly given to Mr. Pinckney, and the correspondence which passed between him and the Government of Naples; all of which are to be found in the 11th. volume of Wait's State Papers, from page 486 to the end of the volume. I also place under your care, to be used if necessary, the papers and documents in support of the respective claims.

Your compensation will be at the rate of $4500. per annum, computing from the day of your acceptance of this Agency, to that of your return to the United States. Your reasonable expenses in going and returning, will also be allowed you, exclusive of those which may be incurred during your residence in Naples.

I am, Sir, with great respect, your very humble and obedient
Servant   H. Clay.

Copy. DNA, RG59, Dip. Instr., vol. 10, pp. 352-54 (M77, R5). AL draft, in DLC-
HC (DNA, M212, R7).
1 William Pinkney. See above, II, 501, 505n.
2 Alexander Hammett, of Maryland, held this post from 1809 to 1860. In a letter
written to John Quincy Adams, as Secretary of State, June 12, 1824 (received September 2), Hammett had spoken of "our Confiscated property" as "Shamefully abandoned" and referred to both the American and Neapolitan authorities as "seemingly
alike indifferent thereto." Previously, in a letter of February 1, 1823, also addressed
to Adams, he had stated that the Neapolitan Minister of Finance, (Luigi) di Medici,
had predicted that the United States would return to its claims and would compel
payment. Hammett believed that William Pinkney's earlier departure without pressing a "Categorical" demand, "with the menace of reprisals," represented pusillanimity
and "tended only to place us on a worse footing than before." A more recent communication, dated June 16, 1824, without mentioning the subject of the claims, had
reported a royal decree calling for liberalized trade restrictions, designed to develop
commerce with the United States and, through this connection, with Latin America.
Cf. below, Hammett to Clay, June 1, July 1, 1825.
  Luigi di Medici, Duc di Sarto, had long served as financial adviser to Ferdinand
I. In 1822 he had become President of the Council of Ministers and subsequently
assumed the additional posts of Minister of Foreign Affairs and of Police.
3 Dated May 12, 1825. Copy, in DNA, RG59, Ceremonial Communications, vol.
2, p. 24.

To Robert McClintock

R. M. Clintock [sic] Esqr.   New York.
Sir,   Department of State, Washington, 12th May 1825.
    I duly received your Letter of the 9th. inst. as I had that of the
12th.[1] of April to which it refers. The delay in answering the letter
has proceeded entirely from the pressure of public business and also
from the belief that any answer which could be given would really
possess very little value.
    You state that the Alliance Insurance Company of London, gov-
erned by gentlemen some of whom are here well known and highly
esteemed, is desirous of establishing an Agency of that institution
in the United States for Insurance purposes only; and you desire
to be informed of the views of the Executive in reference to such
an Agency. It is a subject respecting which the President can hardly
be supposed to entertain any particular views, which ought to have
influence on the resolutions of the Company. And I therefore am instructed to inform you, that he cannot say any thing either to invite
or to prevent the contemplated establishment. It must be left like
all other enterprizes to the enlightened judgment of the concerned
exercised on the knowledge which they possess of the state of our
Laws and the liberality of our institutions.
    I have the honour to be, with high respect, your obedt. Servt.
                                                          H. Clay.

Copy. DNA, RG59, Dom. Letters, vol. 21, pp. 56-57 (M40, R19).
1 That is, 18th.

To Joseph B. Nones

Sir   Washington 12h. May 1825
  Immediately on the receipt of your letter of the 7h. Ulto.[1] I directed the Superintendant [sic] of the patent office to attend to the subject of your application for a patent.[2]

The specimen of Nankeen which you forwarded is very beautiful. As far as I am competent to judge, your success in the preparation of the color has been complete. And I most ardently hope that you may realize all the advantages which cannot fail I think to flow from so important a discovery.

I am highly obliged by the kind consideration of me which has lead [sic] you to think of confering [sic] my name on your Infant establishment.[3] As you have been pleased to ask my consent, I can only say that I feel highly honored by your intention.

                    Wishing you great prosperity I am Your ob. Servant
J B. Nones Esqr.   H. CLAY

ALS. Owned by S. Stanwood Menken, New York, New York. Nones, brother of Abraham B. Nones, had served in the United States Navy from 1812 to 1822 and had subsequently become a merchant in Philadelphia.
  1 Not found.
  2 On April 28, Nones had been granted a patent for an improvement in "making yellow nankeen or buff colors." *House Docs.*, 19 Cong., 1 Sess., no. 22, p. 10.
  3 Not identified.

INSTRUCTIONS AND DISPATCHES   May 12, 1825

From THOMAS ASPINWALL, United States consul at London. Reports that William Tisdale, master of the ship *Hantania,* of Portsmouth (New Hampshire), has abandoned crewmen in England; comments that the frequency of such irregular discharges necessitates rigid infliction of legal penalties. LS. DNA, RG59, Cons. Disp., London, vol. 11 (M-T168, R-T11). Aspinwall, of Massachusetts, had been appointed to this post in 1816 and remained there until 1853. On the law relative to distressed seamen, see below, Clay to Quarrier, this date, note.

Daniel Brent responded to Aspinwall's note by a letter, dated June 21, addressed to Daniel Humphreys, United States attorney for the District of New Hampshire, enclosing papers on the subject so that he might "institute such judicial proceedings against Captain Tisdale upon his return to Portsmouth, as shall appear to be required by the circumstances which they disclose." Copy. DNA, RG59, Dom. Letters, vol. 21, p. 102 (M40, R19).

From CONDY RAGUET, Rio de Janeiro. Reports the probability of war in the Banda Oriental and Brazilian preparations for this eventuality. Attributes (Thomas) Cochrane's continued presence at Maranham (Maranhão) to a quest for money, explaining that Cochrane seized a gold reserve in the public treasury at Maranham, which he claimed as payment for bills that the Brazilian Government has declined to honor; cites reports that Cochrane "has been several times recalled" and surmises "that he will never trust himself at Rio de

Janeiro, where he is literally detested by all parties." Notes friction in the provinces between "Portugues [sic] Europeans and the native Brasileans [sic]"; encloses copies of correspondence with the Minister of Foreign Affairs (Luiz Joze de Carvalho e Mello) relative to the execution of James Hude Rodgers (Rogers) and to "acts of violence" against four Americans. States that Raguet has appointed William Whitaker, British vice consul for Santos, American consular agent for "all . . . ports of the Province of St Paul." Refers briefly to the celebration of the birthday of the Queen of Portugal (Carlota Joaquina, sister of Ferdinand VII of Spain), to privileges granted to English mining companies, and to the slave trade; discusses events connected with the politics and internal affairs of Brazil; and mentions the expectation of Sir Charles Stuart's arrival. Expresses pleasure at the election of Adams and "the nomination of a Chargé de Affairs [sic] for Rio de Janeiro." LS. DNA, RG59, Cons. Disp., Rio de Janeiro, vol. 2 (M-T172, R3). Addressed to Secretary of State; received July 16. Extracts published in Manning (arr.), *Diplomatic Correspondence . . . Latin-American Nations,* II, 816-17. On the case of James Hude Rodgers and the mission of Sir Charles Stuart, see above, Raguet to Secretary of State, March 11, 1825, notes.

From RICHARD RUSH, London, no. 435. Acknowledges receipt of Clay's letter of April 11; lists the unfinished business of Rush's correspondence with the British Foreign Office, relating to the case of John McDonell, the establishment of lights on the Island of Abaco, and "certain royal proclamations touching forfeited lands in the Floridas"; explains the reasons why the British have appeared reluctant to act in these matters; and encloses the papers in the case of the *Calliope.* ALS. DNA, RG59, Dip. Disp., Great Britain, vol. 32 (M30, R28). Received June 19.

McDonell, a resident of Detroit and a naturalized citizen of the United States, had been arrested by the authorities of Sandwich, in Upper Canada, on charges of high treason for the part he had played as a militiaman against Great Britain during the War of 1812. Having escaped from confinement, he had been declared an outlaw and his property holdings in Canada had been confiscated. After intercession by the American Minister in London, the outlawry was removed, with entry of a *nolle prosequi* on his case in 1826; his property, however, was not recovered. "Memorial of John McDonell," *House Docs.,* 23 Cong., 2 Sess., no. 16.

By resolution of December 23, 1823, the House of Representatives had requested that the President negotiate with Great Britain for cession of land on the Island of Abaco, in the Bahamas, and at such other places on the Bahama Banks as were necessary for the erection and maintenance of beacons and buoys for the security of navigation in that passage (U.S. H. of Reps., *Journal,* 18 Cong., 1 Sess., pp. 83, 87). The British had refused to give possession of the territory but had offered to provide the lights if the United States would designate the appropriate sites and pay for their maintenance. Questioning how the fees requisite for support of such a service might be collected under this arrangement, Rush had dropped the matter. Rush to Adams, September 16, 1824, in *American State Papers, Foreign Relations,* V, 484-85.

MISCELLANEOUS LETTERS   May 12, 1825

To WILLIAM B. QUARRIER. Answering his letter of May 9, states: "the delay of which you complain has proceeded from the pressure of public business, and from no disrespect to yourself or Mr. Hatton." While Quarrier's inquiry "involves a question of Law, the solution of which does not strictly belong to this Department," Clay explains that under section three of the act of Congress of February 28, 1803 (2 *U. S. Stat.*, 203-204), "it has been usual and is considered as the intention of the Law, upon the discharge from whatever cause of a Seaman or Mariner in a Foreign Country, for the Master or Commander of the vessel to advance three months pay for every Seaman or Mariner so discharged," without distinction whether they be bond or free. Copy. DNA, RG59, Dom. Letters, vol. 21, p. 57 (M40, R19).

APPLICATIONS, RECOMMENDATIONS   May 12, 1825

RICHARD PETERS, JR., Philadelphia, requests State Department patronage, both within the United States and by distribution abroad, for a mercantile journal published under the title *Grotjan's Philadelphia Public Sale Report*. ALS. DNA, RG59, Misc. Letters (M179, R62). The journal had been established by Peter A. Grotjan in 1812.

To James Brown

No 1.   James Brown, Envoy Extraordinary and
Minister Plenipotentiary, U. S. to France.
Sir,   Department of State   Washington 13. May 1825.
The President entertains a strong desire to see the war between Spain and her former Colonies terminated. Besides the considerations of humanity which, alone, would be quite sufficient to create such a desire, the danger to the peace of other States, and of the United States especially, gives much additional strength to the sentiment. With the view to promote that interesting object, Mr. Poinsett has been, and others of our Ministers to the new States will be, instructed to use their best exertions.[1] But it is in Europe more than in America that our efforts must be directed. And the strong ground to take is that peace is more necessary to Spain than to the new Republics. Accordingly, Mr. Everett has been instructed to endeavour to make Spain sensible of the advantages to her of putting an end to the war, and the dangers which hang over her by its further useless prosecution.[2] I have also, by the directions of the President, addressed a note to Mr. Middleton, to enlist the Government of Russia in the cause of peace.[3] Mr. King has received similar instructions, in reference to Great Britain.[4] And you are requested to open the matter to the French Government, in the hope that they may co-operate in the great object. To enable you to lay before that Government our views, I transmit you, herewith, a copy of the despatch to Mr. Middleton, the use of which is committed to your discretion. A like copy has been put into the possession of Mr. King. Information has reached us, that the local Authorities of Cuba have petitioned the

King of Spain to acknowledge the new Republics, and close the war.[5] By a concerted system of action, direct and collateral, on Spain, it is hoped that she may be made to see the necessity of peace. And great confidence would be placed in this hope, if Russia and France, the Powers most likely to influence the Councils of Spain, would lend their hearty co-operation.

I am, with great respect, Sir, Your obedient & very humble Servant.

H. CLAY.—

Copy. DNA, RG59, Dip. Instr., vol. 10, p. 356. (M77, R5). AL draft, in DLC-HC (DNA, M212, R7).
1 See above, Clay to Poinsett, March 26, 1825.
2 See above, Clay to Everett, April 27, 1825.
3 See above, Clay to Middleton, May 10, 1825.
4 See above, Clay to King, May 11, 1825.
5 See above, Robertson to Clay, April 20, 1825.

DIPLOMATIC NOTES   May 13, 1825

To the BARON [DURAND] DE MAREUIL. Acknowledges receipt of note of May 6 and promises further communication on the subject after "the requisite information" has been obtained. Copy. DNA, RG59, Notes to Foreign Ministers and Consuls, vol. 3, p. 221 (M38, R3). AN draft, in CSmH.

On May 14, Daniel Brent, at Clay's direction, wrote to Samuel L. Southard, enclosing a translation of Mareuil's note and requesting Southard's "good offices toward procuring . . . from the Officers of the Terrier, or otherwise a full statement of all those circumstances." Copy. DNA, RG59, Dom. Letters, vol. 21, p. 59 (M40, R19).

INSTRUCTIONS AND DISPATCHES   May 13, 1825

To ALEXANDER HAMMETT, "Consul U. S.   Naples." Requests Hammett's "good offices" in aid of John James Appleton, appointed "Special Agent of the United States at Naples in relation to the Claims of sundry citizens of the United States upon the Government of the King of the two Sicilies, for the seizure and confiscation of their property many years ago. . . ." Copy. DNA, RG59, Cons. Instr., vol. 2, p. 358 (M78, R2). See above, Clay to Appleton, May 12, 1825.

MISCELLANEOUS LETTERS   May 13, 1825

To PETER A. BROWNE. Comments on Browne's letter (above, May 11, 1825), conveying the views of (Horace) Binney and (John) Sergeant: "The high respect which I entertain for the judgments of those Gentlemen will induce me on my return from Kentucky, for which I am on the eve of my departure, to look again into the subject. . . ." Regarding Browne's charges having "for their object the removal from office of the persons having charge of the Patent Office," Clay asserts: "It has not yet appeared to me that my interposition is justly called for to effect that purpose." Copy. DNA, RG59, Dom. Letters, vol. 21, p. 58 (M40, R19).

Check to John Davis

14 May 1825

Pay to John Davis or order Three hundred and thirty five dollars and 50 Cents.   H. CLAY

Cashr. of the Off. of Dt. & Dt. Washington[1]

ADS. DLC-TJC (DNA, M212, R16). Endorsed on verso (AES): "John Davis." Cf. above, III, 531n.   [1] Richard Smith.

Check to Jo[seph] Wood

14 May 1825

Pay to Mr. Jo. Wood or order fifty dollars.

Cashr. of the Off. of Dt. & Dt. Washington   H. CLAY

ADS. DLC-TJC (DNA, M212, R16). Endorsed on verso (AES): "Jo: Wood," probably the painter of two studies of Clay, one a seated figure, full length, in 1825, and the other, half-length, in 1829. Born in New York, Wood had begun his career as an artist in 1803. In 1813 he had moved to Philadelphia and in 1816 to Washington.

DIPLOMATIC NOTES   May 14, 1825

From HILARIO DE RIVAS Y SALMON, Philadelphia. Reports that he has transmitted to the Spanish Government Clay's note of May 9. LS. DNA, RG59, Notes from Spanish Legation, vol. 8 (M59, R11).

INSTRUCTIONS AND DISPATCHES   May 14, 1825

From HUGH NELSON, Madrid, no. 56. Reports conversation with the (Spanish) Secretary of State (Francisco de Zea Bermudez) in which Nelson urged "the prompt dispatch of Mr Heredia" to Washington "with full powers to adjust our differences"; the Secretary's subsequent inquiry regarding Nelson's means of passage to return home, his proposal that Heredia be carried with Nelson by United States frigate, and his request that Nelson present this suggestion to his Government; and the latter's note, on his own responsibility, to Commodore (John) Rodgers in the Mediterranean, asking for such accommodation as a measure to promote "the early departure of Mr. Heredia." Nelson speculates that the effectiveness of the operations of Colombian cruisers against Spanish shipping, "in view from their ports even, and with impunity," has occasioned this scheme. Notes that Zea Bermudez also commented upon the success of cooperative efforts by Spanish authorities and the American (Caribbean) squadron in capturing and bringing to justice the pirates in the vicinity of the islands (Puerto Rico and Cuba). LS. DNA, RG59, Dip. Disp., Spain, vol. 24 (M31, R26). Received July 17. See above, Nelson to Secretary of State, March 8, April 6, 1825; Clay to Nelson, April 14, 1825.

MISCELLANEOUS LETTERS   May 14, 1825

From JAMES H. CAUSTEN, Baltimore. Requests a reply to his letter of April 23. ALS. DNA, RG76, Records re French Spoliations (MNP-8, R2).

From ROBERT RALSTON, president of the Philadelphia Chamber of Commerce. Calls attention to the excessive duty levied in Mexico on articles of American manufacture, particularly on cotton goods; expresses apprehension that such goods may be prohibited; encloses extract of a letter from Taylor, Sicard and Company to the Philadelphia Chamber of Commerce, dated March 5, 1825, and an official statement from the latter body to the United States Secretary of State (undated; ALS by Ralston) in this connection. LS. DNA, RG59, Misc. Letters (M179, R62). Cf. above, Biddle to Clay, March 10, 16, 1825; Clay to Poinsett, March 26, 1825. Ralston not further identified. The statement from the chamber of commerce notes that Taylor is the American consul at Alvarado (William Taylor); other members of the Alvarado firm have not been identified.

APPLICATIONS, RECOMMENDATIONS   May 14, 1825

JOHN BARNEY, Baltimore [no. 1], recommends appointment of a commercial agent at Havana and suggests J. W. Symington, of Baltimore, as possessing the requisite mercantile experience. Notes that the widow and children of (John) Warner "are left in reduced circumstances, requiring the aid of their friends, among whom Mr. Simonton [sic] stands prominent, and should he be successful in his application a portion of the emoluments of the office will be appropriated to assisting Mrs Warner to educate & provide for her children. . . ." ALS. MHi-Adams Papers, Letters Received (M469). On Symington (Simonton), who did not receive the appointment, see below, Smith to Clay, this date.

JOHN BARNEY, Baltimore [no. 2], recommends, as commercial agent at Havana, W. H. De C. Wright, "Son of one the [sic] oldest politicians in our State [Robert Wright] who has successively filled the important station of Delegate to the General Assembly, Member of the House of Representatives   Senator of the U. S.   Governor of Maryland, and is now [1823-1826] a Judge in his former Congressional District. . . ." ALS. MHi-Adams Papers, Letters Received (M469).

G[ABRIEL] DUVALL, Baltimore, introduces William (H. De C.) Wright, the bearer, son of Governor (Robert) Wright, whom Clay knows; recommends the son as successor to (John) Warner, "as Consul U. S. at Havanna in the Island of Cuba." LS. MHi-Adams Papers, Letters Received (M469). See above, Wright to Clay, May 10, 1825, note.

A[LEXANDER] H. EVERETT, Boston, recommends William Willink, Jr., as banker for the United States at Amsterdam, noting that the two senior partners "in the late House of William & John Willink . . . had retired in a great measure . . . a good while before their connexion with the House was formally dissolved; and of the two junior ones the present applicant was understood to be the leading man." ALS. DNA, RG59, Dip. Disp., Spain, vol. 25 (M31, R27). Received May 18. Nicholas and Joseph Van Staphorst are still listed at this time as partners in the firm of Willinks and Van Staphorst (above, I, 876), together with R. Van Staphorst and the younger Willink. They continued bankers for the United States under joint signature, as "William Willink, Jr., and N. & R. & J. Van Staphorst."

ISAAC MCKIM, Baltimore, recommends the bearer, William H. D. C. Wright to fill the vacancy caused by the death of (John) Warner. ALS. MHi-Adams Papers, Letters Received (M469). See above, Wright to Clay, May 10, 1825, note.

S[AMUEL] SMITH, Baltimore, introduces "J. W. Simonton [Symington]," a resident of this city, who was born in (New) Jersey; recommends him to fill the vacancy occasioned by the death of (John) Warner, whose impoverished family will be aided if Symington is appointed. While not known to Smith personally, the nominee has been favorably reported by a reliable friend. ALS. MHi-Adams Papers, Letters Received (M469). See above, Barney to Clay, this date (no. 1).

Receipted Bill from Thomas Cookendorfer

[May 15, 1825]

Honbe. Henry Clay To Tho Cookendorfer Dr.
1825 May 15. Passage to Fredericktown[1] $4.00
                    Recd payment   THO COOKENDORFER

ADS. DLC-TJC (DNA, M212, R16). Cookendorfer not identified.
[1] Maryland.

MISCELLANEOUS LETTERS   May 15, 1825

From JAMES RAY and others, Philadelphia. Request that the documents in the case of the *James Lawrence,* a brig which, with cargo, was condemned by a "Marine Court at Havana in September 1824," be sent "under the authority of Government, to the American Consul General in Spain, with directions to present and prosecute the appeal [already pending] at Madrid before the Spanish King to its final issue." LS. DNA, RG76, Misc. Claims, Spain. Dated: "May 1825"; endorsed on cover: ". . . Recd 18th." Signed by Ray and four other persons. The vessel, owned by Ray, of Wilmington, Delaware, had been captured by a Spanish privateer and brought to trial, originally, in Admiralty Court at St. John's, Puerto Rico, in 1823. Everett to Salmon, February 13, 1828, in *House Docs.,* 20 Cong., 2 Sess., no. 56, pp. 20-22.

APPLICATIONS, RECOMMENDATIONS   May 15, 1825

VICTOR DU PONT, Brandywine (Delaware), recommends his friend, John Mountain, as commercial agent at Havana, he "having acted there since the appointment of the late John Warner as his deputy." Comments that since the State congressional delegation will recommend Mountain strongly, further testimony "would be superfluous; But as it affords me an opportunity to renew the expression of my most sincere Respect & regard, I embrace it with pleasure and hope you will excuse the liberty now taken to introduce and recommend a friend to you." ALS. DNA, RG59, A. and R. (MR3). Mountain, a resident of Delaware, did not receive the appointment.

JOHN HOLLINS, Baltimore, recommends Vincent Gray for appointment as commercial agent at Havana. ALS. *Ibid.* (MR1). See above, Gray to Clay, April 5, 1825.

JOHN MOODY, New Canton, Buckingham County, Virginia, renews his application for employment. ALS. DNA, RG59, A. and R. (MR3). See above, Moody to Clay, April 2, 1825.

S[AMUEL] SMITH, Baltimore, notes that he "yesterday" gave a letter of introduction to (J. W.) Simonton (Symington), who is seeking appointment as commercial agent at Havana; hereby recommends William Wright, "Son of your Old acquaintance Governor [Robert] Wright," for the post. Concludes: "It will afford to me and to many of your friends, among others to Govr. Loyd [Edward Lloyd] great pleasure if Mr Wright shall be the successful Candidate." ALS. MHi-Adams Papers, Letters Received (M469). See above, Wright to Clay, May 10, 1825, note.

SAMUEL SMITH, Baltimore, recommends Samuel Purviance "for the vacant Commercial Agency" at Havana. The nominee is a brother of John Purviance, the Baltimore lawyer, "son of the late Collector [Robert Purviance]", and nephew of Samuel Purviance, who "was an important Character in Maryland during the War of the Revolution." ALS. DNA, RG59, A. and R. (MR3). Young Purviance received no appointment.

INSTRUCTIONS AND DISPATCHES   May 16, 1825

From JOHN MULLOWNY, Tangier, no. 36. Offers "some remarks relative to the long established custom of giving presents to the King [of Morocco], and his officers"; cites the kindness shown Captain (James) Allen as "a strong and *singular* mark of benevolence toward Americans"; but maintains that he (Mullowny) presents his gifts as "favours, and neither a debt, or tribute." States that he has not heard from the Department of State since May, 1824. ALS. DNA, RG59, Cons. Disp., Tangier (M-T61, R4). Received August 31.

APPLICATIONS, RECOMMENDATIONS   May 16, 1825

ISAAC MCKIM, Baltimore, recommends appointment of Samuel Purviance (the younger) as "Consul" at Havana. ALS. DNA, RG59, A. and R. (MR3). See above, Smith to Clay, May 15, 1825 (no. 2).

L[OUIS] MCLANE, Wilmington, Delaware, recommends appointment of John Mountain as commercial agent at Havana. ALS. DNA, RG59, A. and R. (MR3). See above, DuPont to Clay, May 15, 1825, note.

THOMAS RANDALL, Washington, recommends John Mountain, of Delaware, to fill the vacancy "in the office of Consul of the United States for the Port of Havana." ALS. MHi-Adams Papers, Letters Received (M469). Addressed to Secretary of State. See above, Du Pont to Clay, May 15, 1825, note. For the past two years Randall had been "Agent of the United States for Commerce and Seamen, for the Islands of Puerto Rico & Cuba, and for the Ports on the Spanish Main" and "commissary under the 2nd Art. of the Florida Treaty." He had recently resumed the practice of law in Washington.

FRANCIS SHOEMAKER, of the firm of L. and F. Shoemaker, merchants of Philadelphia, trading in Cuba, recommends his brother, Lewis, for the past four years a resident of Matanzas, Cuba, for appointment to the vacancy as commercial agent at Havana; comments that he addresses Clay upon the recommendation of John Binns. ALS. DNA, RG59, A. and R. (MR1). Addressed to Clay at Lexington; a copy (ALS) is addressed to him as Secretary of State at Washington. *Ibid.*

On May 23, Daniel Brent, "in the absence of the Secretary," transmitted to Lewis Shoemaker a commission as "Consular Commercial Agent of the

United States at Matanzas" and "a copy of the printed Circular Instructions to Consuls." Copy, in DNA, RG59, Cons. Instr., vol. 2, p. 359 (M78, R2). Shoemaker was raised to the rank of consul at Matanzas in 1831 and held that post until 1839.

N[ICHOLAS] VAN DYKE, New Castle (Delaware), recommends appointment of John Mountain as commercial agent at Havana. ALS. DNA, RG59, A. and R. (MR3). Van Dyke, United States Senator from Delaware from 1817 until his death in 1826, had practiced law, had served in both houses of the State legislature, and had been a member of the United States House of Representatives, from 1807 to 1811. On Mountain, see above, Du Pont to Clay, May 15, 1825, note.

From Richard C. Anderson, Jr.

Dear Sir   New York May 17. 1825.

I arrived here last evening with my unfortunate children[1] from Carthagena. On tomorrow or the next day, I shall proceed to Washington, and hope to be able to see you by this day week at farthest. My own health is tolerably good; my children have been very sick and are not yet well.

My letter of the 19th. of Jany. addressed to the Department, and received probably before you took charge of the Office, will have informed you of the reason which I considered as compelling my return at this time without delay or leave[2]—

In Colombia there is nothing important. Every thing is tranquil. Callao had not surrendered at the last advices from Peru[3]—

Negotiations for a Commercial Convention were opened at Bogota between the British & Columbian [sic] Commissioners on the 4th. of April[4]— With respect I am truly yours—

R. C. ANDERSON JR

ALS. DNA, RG59, Dip. Disp., Colombia, vol. 3 (M-T33, R3). Received May 19.
[1] Anderson's wife, the former Elizabeth Gwathmey, of Louisville, Kentucky, sister of John Gwathmey, had died January 9, 1825, from the complications of "something like the dysentery" and premature childbirth. The son then born died within a few days of his mother, leaving three surviving children, Elizabeth C., Arthur, and Ann (Annita Nancy). Tischendorf and Parks (eds.), *Diary and Journal of Richard Clough Anderson, Jr.*, 182-83, 288.
[2] Written shortly after the death of his wife and son and while another child was yet ill, the letter stressed Anderson's anxiety to return to Kentucky briefly so that he might place his remaining children "in safety with their Grand-parents." ALS. DNA, RG59, Dip. Disp., Colombia, vol. 3.
[3] See above, Tudor to Clay, March 21, 1825, note.
[4] See above, Watts to Clay, May 10, 1825.

From Stephen W. Foreman

Sir,   Advocate office, St. Louis, 17th May, 1825.

During the Presidential contest, the public journals of this State, by Some means had been Secured against you; and from a wish to advance your political views, I was induced to take charge of the Editorial department of a paper, published in St. Charles, the Seat of Government.[1] After the Election had passed from the hands of the people, the paper of which I had the control, was, during the last winter, enlarged, and published under the title it now bears, by myself and Mr. Keemle,[2] who was also your political friend. The result of the presidential election, produced no change in our conduct towards you, and after we established the press in this City,[3] we forwarded a few numbers of the paper to yourself and Mr. Adams, that you might collect the public Sentiment. Under these circumstances, you can perhaps better imagine, than I can describe, the mortification of feeling produced by the reception of a letter from your department, of the 9th of April,[4] breathing a temper, better Suited to the Editor of the *Columbian Observer*,[5] than to those who attempted to shield you from the assault of your enemies. The fact of your requesting the discontinuance of the *Missouri Advocate,* gave not the least uneasiness; it was your privilege to do so—but the style of your letter is inexcusable. Surely, Sir, if there is nothing due to disinterested friendship, you should have had some regard for the rules of common civility, and been satisfied with intimating in language becoming a gentleman, that you were unwilling to be troubled with the *Advocate.* The Editors of the *rejected* "Advocate," give you the Strongest assurance, they were not actuated, in forwarding their paper, by any hope of reward from you or Mr. Adams;—that they feel as indignant at any act unbecoming a gentleman, as either of you; and are strangers to any part of their character, which could have induced you to suppose them capable of charging for a paper, which they gratuitously Sent you. "By birth, Virginians; by choice, Missourians, they scorn an act, which would disgrace a *Yankee,* and pledge their honor's *never to present you again, with the Missouri Advocate.*

I have the honor to be, With great respect, Your Obedient Servant,

STEPHEN W. FOREMAN

Hon. Henry Clay.—   One of the Editors of the Advocate[6]

ALS. DNA, RG59, Misc. Letters (M179, R62). Foreman not further identified.

[1] The *Missouri Advocate* had been established at St. Charles (capital of the State from 1820 to 1826) in December, 1824.

[2] Charles Keemle, born in Philadelphia, had been associated with newspapers in Virginia, Indiana, and Missouri and from 1820 to 1824 had been employed by a fur company.

[3] In February, 1825. Late the following summer the editors acquired Duff Green's *St. Louis Enquirer* and published the journal under joint title as *Missouri Advocate and St. Louis Enquirer.* Green, born and educated in Kentucky and married to Lucretia Maria Edwards, a sister of Ninian Edwards, had moved in 1816 to St. Louis, where he was active as land speculator, merchant, lawyer, and member of the State legislature. In 1823 he had purchased the *Enquirer* as an organ for support of the Presidential candidacy of Andrew Jackson. In 1826 he removed to Washington, where he was to become one of the leading Jacksonian journalists and politicians.

[4] The letter, sent on April 13, from Daniel Brent to the editor of the *St. Louis*

Enquirer, was a duplicate of a circular written on April 9 to editors of seventeen journals, with sixteen others added to the list on the later date and sixteen more on April 23, 1825, giving notice that an order, originally issued by President Monroe, in May, 1821, was hereby renewed, discontinuing all newspapers addressed to the Executive Department, "with notice that payment would be made for all papers, furnished by his orders, and for none others." The circular had been occasioned, it was stated, by receipt at the State Department of an account "charging for a daily newspaper" for which there was "neither authority, nor fund, existing at this place, from which payment of it can be made; and as several newspapers are still received by the President, some addressed to him, and others to the Executive Department, for which no orders have been given. . . ." Copy, in DNA, RG59, Dom. Letters, vol. 21, pp. 28-30, 41-43 (M40, R19).

5 Stephen Simpson.

6 On June 9, 1825, Daniel Brent, in Clay's absence, acknowledged receipt of this letter and explained that the circular of April 9, sent out by the State Department, "was written at the instance exclusively, and by direction of the President of the United States," and addressed to 54 newspapers, "which he had discovered were habitually sent to him as President or the Executive Department of the United States," to warn them that no funds were provided for such accounts. Brent further explained that the circular had been intended "as the renewal of" Monroe's order, that Adams had not been, nor would he be, informed of Foreman's protest, and that "it would be a subject of much concern to him . . . to learn" that exception had been taken to the circular. Copy, in DNA, RG59, Dom. Letters, vol. 21, pp. 92-93 (M40, R19).

INSTRUCTIONS AND DISPATCHES   May 17, 1825

From W[ILLIAM] TUDOR, Lima, no. 28, "Confidential." Expands on remarks addressed to the Department (of State) in April, 1824, in which he had proposed a plan to increase the amount of specie, "the only export from this country," going from Peru to the United States. He advocates a scheme for using American warships to transport the specie and urges that they be barred from "receiving on board . . . any article of the precious metals prohibited by the laws" of Peru from export. Regulations by the United States to discourage smuggling, however, "would necessarily require the same on the part of the English government." ALS. DNA, RG59, Cons. Disp., Lima, vol. 1 (M154, R1). Addressed to Secretary of State; received September 5.

MISCELLANEOUS LETTERS   May 17, 1825

From SAMUEL L. SOUTHARD, Treasury Department. Asks that the State Department procure a copy of the Spanish "Royal *instruction*" of October 15, 1754, for use in determining the land titles in East Florida. LS. DNA, RG59, Misc. Letters (M179, R62). Published in Carter (ed.), *Territorial Papers,* XXIII, 249-50.

APPLICATIONS, RECOMMENDATIONS   May 17, 1825

OGDEN EDWARDS, New York, recommends Andrew S. Garr, "of this City, Counseller at law," with a knowledge of the Spanish and French languages, for appointment as commercial agent at Havana. ALS. DNA, RG59, A. and R. (MR2). Garr did not receive the appointment.

JAMES G. FORBES, Washington, solicits appointment as commercial agent at Havana. ALS. MHi-Adams Papers (M469). Forbes, of St. Augustine, Florida, a brother of John M. Forbes, had published *Sketches, Historical and Topographical, of the Floridas; More Especially of East Florida* (New York, 1821). He had previously held a recess appointment, not confirmed upon subsequent nomination, as United States marshal for East and West Florida (1821). He did not receive the appointment here sought.

From Alexander Reed and Others

[May 18, 1825]
[Expresses the esteem of the citizens of Washington, Pennsylvania, for Clay's public character, their confidence in his political integrity, and gratitude for his services.]

Their motive, however, for wishing to give a marked expression of their approbation at this time, is not limited by the sentiments of respect, esteem and gratitude which they cherish: they are influenced by views of a more general nature, at a time when it is obvious that a spirit of detraction and calumny is abroad; which, regardless of the candor and courtesies that renders [sic] society amiable, seems determined to sacrifice truth, honor and justice at the shrine of disappointed party zeal; they consider it as their duty to oppose and resist, or, at least, to express, in the most unequivocal manner, their abhorrence of such a course. They regret that you, sir, have been exposed to the shafts of malevolence and falsehood; and, although they have no doubt that the darts aimed at you will recoil upon your assailants themselves, yet, your friends here are anxious to be permitted to declare to this nation and to the world, that they will never consent to abandon to unmerited aspersion and unjust calumny, a man who has done so much for the country, and who, in their opinion, has always been actuated by pure principles and a disinterested public spirit. They believe you, sir, incapable of any act unworthy of a gentleman, and they *know* that no proof has been offered to sustain any charge which would lessen their confidence and esteem. With these views and sentiments, an invitation is now tendered you, on behalf of our citizens, to partake of a dinner at Mr. Morris's[1] tavern, on to-morrow, at 2 o'clock P. M.

With much respect and esteem, we are, respectfully, your obedient servants, ALEXANDER REED, WILLIAM SAMPLE, THOMAS McGIFFEN, T. M. T. McKENNAN, RICHARD BARD, committee of arrangements.[2]

Niles' Weekly Register, XXVIII (June 18, 1825), 243. Reed, one of the original lot holders of Washington, Pennsylvania, was prominent in community affairs—a burgess (1810, 1811, 1816), borough treasurer (1813-1815), member of the town council (1817), and later director and president of the principal bank (1836-1842).
[1] The proprietor was probably David Morris, another of the original lot-holders of Washington, member of the town council (1814), and burgess (1817). Morris's tavern had been operating as early as 1804 and was then known as the "Sign of the Indian Queen." Bayrd Still, "To the West on Business in 1804," *Pennsylvania Magazine of History and Biography*, LXIV (January, 1940), 11.

382 SECRETARY OF STATE

2 Sample, formerly borough auditor (1817-1818) and clerk of the court of quarter sessions (1818-1821), was now prothonotary (1819-1821, 1823-1830). McGiffin was a lawyer, bank director, member of the town council (1813-1815, 1826), and, briefly, a member of the State legislature (1836). Thomas McKean Thompson McKennan was a lawyer, member of Congress (1831-1839, 1842-1843), Secretary of the Interior for a brief time in 1850, president of the Franklin Bank of Washington from 1843 and of the Hempfield Railroad Company from 1850 until his death in 1852. Bard not further identified.

To [Alexander Reed and Others]

[May 18, 1825]

Gentlemen: I accept, with much pleasure, the invitation contained in your note of this day. The value of the distinguished compliment intended me, is greatly enhanced by a consideration of the time, the place, and the kind expressions with which it is connected. You have done me no more than justice in the estimate which you have made of the motives of my public action, although your partiality has led you greatly to exaggerate its importance to the community. With respect to the recent attack upon my conduct and character, I never doubted that the nation would put down the conspiracy and the conspirators. The manifestation, which my fellow citizens here have been pleased to make of their continued confidence in me, is but one of a multitude of testimonies to the justice and magnanimity of my country, spontaneously called forth by the late occasion. I exercised only the rights of an independent freeman. I wish never to exercise the right of any other.

I pray you, gentlemen, to accept my thanks for the very obliging manner in which you have communicated the invitation with which I am honored.

Niles' Weekly Register, XXVIII (June 18, 1825), 243.

DIPLOMATIC NOTES   May 18, 1825

From HILARIO DE RIVAS Y SALMON, Philadelphia. Encloses copies of instructions which he issued to the Spanish consul in Boston (Ramundo Chacon) following the complaint by J(ohn) C. Jones, as expressed in Clay's note of April 16, and of the consul's reply; notes that the matter has been reported to the Spanish Government. LS. DNA, RG59, Notes from Spanish Legation, vol. 8 (M59, R11).

INSTRUCTIONS AND DISPATCHES   May 18, 1825

From RICHARD RUSH, no. 436. Transmits copies of his correspondence with the British Government preparatory to his departure, requesting replies to unanswered diplomatic notes, explaining that the business of the legation was being placed in the hands of (John Adams) Smith, and asking for Rush's passport and for issuance of the orders necessary to permit loading of his baggage without hindrance. ALS. DNA, RG59, Dip. Disp., Great Britain, vol. 32 (M30, R28). Cf. below, Watkins to Clay, June 24, 1825.

APPLICATIONS, RECOMMENDATIONS   May 18, 1825

STEVENSON ARCHER, Baltimore, recommends William Wright, "the son of our very worthy friend Governor [Robert] Wright," for appointment as commercial agent at Havana. ALS. MHi-Adams Papers, Letters Received (M469). Cf. above, Wright to Clay, May 10, 1825.

H[ENRY] C. DE RHAM, Swiss consul for the northern part of the United States, New York, suggests the advantage of appointing an American consul in Switzerland and favorably mentions for the office the name of I[saac] Iselin, now residing at Basle, "a native of Switzerland, but a naturalized citizen of the United States, where he passed many years of his life," and a former partner in the New York mercantile firm, LeRoy, Bayard, and Company. ALS. DNA, RG59, Misc. Letters (M179, R62). De Rham, who had come to New York from Switzerland, was senior partner of the firm De Rham, Iselin, and Moore, the largest importers of "French Goods" into the United States. Iselin, who in 1801 had also emigrated from Switzerland, had been a partner in the firm since 1809. He had first worked in the counting house and in 1808 as a supercargo for the firm headed by Herman LeRoy and William Bayard, one of the largest American mercantile houses of the period, prior to its failure in 1827.

ANDREW S. GARR, New York, apologizes for misdirecting the original version of the enclosed letter, "to the President, instead of the Secretary of State," and requests that Clay lay the application before the President, "in the ordinary way." ALS. DNA, RG59, A. and R. (MR2). The enclosure is a copy of an application by Garr for appointment as commercial agent at Havana. See above, Edwards to Clay, May 17, 1825, note.

Toasts at Washington, Pennsylvania, Banquet

[May 19, 1825]

Henry Clay, our guest—the patriot—the orator—the statesman. In every situation he has been found just in his principles, honorable in his purposes, and independent in his actions—our confidence in his political integrity is unshaken. We admire him for his talents, we esteem him for his private worth, and we thank him for his public services.

{After a short speech, in reply to this compliment, which is said to have been a "happy specimen of that commanding eloquence which is equally the pride and delight of every American who has witnessed his efforts," Mr. Clay gave—

"The governor of Pennsylvania."[1]}

Niles' Weekly Register, XXVIII (June 18, 1825), 243. At the dinner "the room was crowded to overflowing. Thomas H. Baird presided, and Hugh Workman acted as vice president. One of the invited guests was Henry Baldwin, of Pittsburgh, who

was casually at Washington." *Ibid.* Baird, a lawyer, formerly a member of the town council (1817) and president of the Bank of Washington (1818), was presiding judge of the district court (1818-1838). Workman had been a member of the town council much of the time from 1810 to 1823 and in 1826 became a burgess.
1 John A. Shulze.

From Nicholas Biddle

Dear Sir,   Bank of the U. States May 19. 1825
I had the honor on the 25th of Jany last to ask your attention to some improper practices which the Agent at Cincinnati[1] imputed to the District Attorney[2] of that place in conjunction with Mr Jesse Hunt & his family and to a proposition made by the Agent for a transfer to the Bank of the claim of the U.S against Jesse Hunt, with a view to the more successful prosecution of their respective rights against him. Your impression, as conveyed in your answer of the 31st of January, was that the transfer was scarcely practicable, and of doubtful utility—but that it might be well to bring the conduct of the Attorney to the view of the Executive. I have since received from the Agent a letter of which the inclosed is a copy[3] & which I was about to send to you at Washington, when the papers announced your having left that city for Kentucky. I now forward it to you because as the deportment of the District Attorney falls naturally under your official supervision, your visit to the West may furnish a fit occasion to make the necessary enquiries with regard to him.
I have the honor to be with great consideration Yrs
N BIDDLE Prest.
Honble Henry Clay   Secretary of State   Lexington Ky.

ALS. DLC-HC (DNA, M212, R1).   1 George W. Jones.
2 Joseph S. Benham.   3 Not found.

From John Binns

Dear Sir,   Phila. May 19. 1825.
This letter will be delivered you by Mr H. Shoemaker[1] in behalf of whose brother Lewis Shoemaker, as an applicant for the office of Commercial Agent at Matanzas. Since that time the U. S. Comm'al Agent [*sic*] at Matanzus [*sic*] and at Havanna [*sic*], have both[2] died. Under these circumstances Mr. Shoemaker asks the appointment of Comm'al Agent at Havanna. His brother will do himself the honor to submit to your consideration the commercial and other recommendations he carries with him in favor of the appointment.
I would urge the appointment of Mr. Shoemaker not only on commercial but political considerations. In this city the family of Mr. Shoemaker is numerous and influential and all rank with the

Democratic party; as I have before repeatedly done myself the pleasure to submit to you my veiws [*sic*] as to the political state of Penna. and the probability if the appointments of the Genl. Govt. be judicious of bringing Pennsa. into the support of Mr. Adams' Administration, I will not now trouble you further than to remark that in this point of light the appointment of Mr. Shoemaker will be most judicious. From these considerations and personal respect for some members of his Family I respectfully yet earnestly press upon you the appointment of Mr. Lewis Shoemaker.

  With Respect & Esteem. I have the honor to be Yr. Ob Sert
Hon. Henry Clay   U. S. Sey of State.   JOHN BINNS.

LS. DNA, RG59, A. and R. (MR1). Addressed to Clay at Washington. See above, Shoemaker to Clay, May 16, 1825, note.
  1 Not further identified.   2 Francis Adams; John Warner.

From Philander Chase

Dear Sir;   Worthington May 19. 1825
  I fear I shall tax you too heavily for your very kind promise of assisting me in my English correspondence. The reflection, however, that whatever is done in this way is intended for public benefit, in cherishing a mutual respect and friendship between the two nations especially in respect of our infant Church in the west— will create I am confident in a mind like yours a sufficient apology.—
  Our June Convention[1] approaches after which if I conjecture rightly I shall shall [*sic*] call on you to do the promised kindness of *Umpire Ship*.[2]
  In the mean time tho' immersed in care I am your faithful & attached Friend   PHILR. CHASE
The Hone. H. Clay
P. S. Please send the letters for Europe which accompany this by channels as shall seem most advisable, for expedition, to yourself: and have the goodness to *frank* one to my dear wife's mother,[3] Kingston, Ulster Cy. N York.   P. C.—

ALS. DNA, RG59, Misc. Letters (M179, R62).
  1 Of the Protestant Episcopal Diocese of Ohio.
  2 See above, III, 865.
  3 In 1819 Chase had married Sophia May Ingraham, daughter of Duncan and Susanna Ingraham, of Poughkeepsie, New York.

INSTRUCTIONS AND DISPATCHES   May 19, 1825

From THOMAS L. L. BRENT, Lisbon. Sends translation of an article in the *Portuguese Gazette* of this date, reporting attendance of the Portuguese King (John VI) and the Infantas (Isabel Maria and Francisca) at a ball on His Britannic Majesty's ship *Wellesley* in celebration of the conclusion of negotiations by Sir

Charles Stuart looking to settlement of the conflict between Portugal and her rebellious colony, Brazil. ALS. DNA, RG59, Dip. Disp., Portugal, vol. 6 (M43, R5). Received July 17. On Stuart's mission, see above, Raguet to Secretary of State, March 11, 1825, note.

MISCELLANEOUS LETTERS May 19, 1825

From A[LEXANDER] H. EVERETT, Boston. Repeats statement of his plan to depart for New York on May 25 and to take passage on the packet leaving June 1; also reiterates his expectation that his instructions will be ready for him "to embark early in June." ALS. DNA, RG59, Dip. Disp., Spain, vol. 25 (M31, R27). See above, Everett to Clay, May 3, 1825.

APPLICATIONS, RECOMMENDATIONS May 19, 1825

JOHN CROWELL, Princeton, Creek Nation, recommends William Triplett as United States marshal for Georgia, in the event of resignation of the incumbent. ALS. DNA, RG59, A. and R. (MR1). Crowell, born in North Carolina and resident in Alabama, had been Territorial delegate and member to Congress from Alabama, 1818 to 1821. He had been appointed agent for the Creek Indians in the latter year and held that position until 1831. William M. Triplett, of Georgia, who had been an infantry officer in the United States Army during the War of 1812, did not receive appointment. Cf. below, Morel to Clay, January 29, 1826.

INSTRUCTIONS AND DISPATCHES May 20, 1825

From CONDY RAGUET, Rio de Janeiro. Reports receipt of intelligence of the outbreak of rebellion in the Banda Oriental, the retreat of (Brazilian) Government forces into the city of Montevideo, and the preparations for a military expedition to that area. Raguet expects the involvement of Buenos Aires, a blockade of the Plate River, and illegal seizures of American vessels. He advocates placing "one or two Publick Ships on this station" and authorization for himself to adopt a strong tone concerning violations of American rights. LS. DNA, RG59, Cons. Disp., Rio de Janeiro, vol. 2 (M-T172, R3). Addressed to Secretary of State; received July 6. Published in Manning (arr.), *Diplomatic Correspondence . . . Latin-American Nations*, II, 817-18.

Toasts and Remarks at Wheeling Banquet

[May 21, 1825]

Our distinguished guest, HENRY CLAY—Fearless as he is honest, and patriotic as he is enlightened—"what is a public man worth, if he will not expose himself, upon fit occasions, for the good of his country."*

. . . .

VOLUNTEERS.

By Mr Clay. James Pleasants—More honouring by his bland character, than honoured by the high dignity of the Chief Magistracy of Virginia.

. . . .

* This toast was received with loud reiterated cheering. As soon as silence was restored Mr Clay rose, and in an eloquent and feeling manner, expressed to the company his grateful acknowledgements for the generous sentiment they had expressed in his behalf. He adverted to the motives which had governed his conduct in the presidential election, and acknowledged the satisfaction he felt at finding his conduct approved by the citizens of Wheeling. He concluded by wishing to them continued health, prosperity and happiness.

Lexington *Kentucky Reporter*, June 13, 1825, from *Wheeling Gazette*. On May 20, Clay, accompanied by "a respectable cavalcade of gentlemen," had ridden from Washington, Pennsylvania, westward to the State line, "where he was received by a number of gentlemen from Wheeling and its vicinity. . . ." At the public dinner on the next day "Noah Zane, Esq. presided, assisted by Col. A. Woods."

Archibald Woods, a native of Albemarle County, Virginia, and a veteran of the American Revolution, had been one of the delegates at the Virginia convention upon ratification of the Federal Constitution, one of the original trustees of the town of Wheeling, and president of the Northwestern Bank of Virginia since its founding in 1817.

APPLICATIONS, RECOMMENDATIONS   May 21, 1825

HUMPHREY PEAKE, Alexandria (District of Columbia, now Virginia), recommends appointment of A(lbert) O. Newton as commercial agent at Matanzas. ALS. DNA, RG59, A. and R. (MR3). Peake not further identified. On the appointment, see above, Newton to Clay, May 4, 1825.

To [Charles Hammond]

My Dear Sir   Ohio river 23d. May 1825.

My detention at Washn. having exceeded my expectations, your letter to Dr. Watkins[1] reached the City prior to my departure. The publication of the extracts from my letter of Oct.[2] with your remarks would appear in the N. Intellr. a day or two after I left the City.[3] There was no part of that letter, viewed in a candid and liberal spirit, to which just exception could be taken; but there were some passages which would have supplied aliment to malignity and I was glad therefore that you consented to their omission. I recd. your letter addressed to me at Wheeling.[4]

My reception West of the Mountains so far has exceeded my expectations. I was invited to a public dinner at Union town, which I was obliged to decline, in consequence of previous engagements at Washn. & Wheeling.[5] In all the villages through which I passed crowds of decent orderly citizens visited me and with much kindness & cordiality welcomed me. Public dinners, well attended and accompanied with warm and enthusiastic sentiments, were given me at Washn. & Wheeling. I was eschorted by 15 or 20 gentlemen from the former place & from Claysville to the Virginia line, where I was met by as many more from Wheeling who advanced to greet me. I was not allowed to pay any expence in the villages from Union to Wheeling inclusive. Even the owner of the Ferry at the former place refused to receive my ferriage. I do not mention these things, my dear Sir, in a spirit of pride or vain boasting. In my opinion they do as much, if not more, credit to the hearts of my Countrymen than to the object of them. I knew that you would take an interest in hearing them.

I shall land to day at about six OClock p.m. at Maysville, where I understand other friendly demonstrations await me.[6] I expect to remain in K. the greater part of June. My return home has been thrown so far forward into the summer, that I apprehend I shall hardly be able in going back with my family to the City to avail myself of the facility of the Steamboat. In that case I shall return through Ohio, and on my route should like to perform the act of umpirage refered to me by the English donors to the Episcopal church.[7]

The agitation of the Steamboat,[8] which renders what I have written scarcely legible, obliges me to conclude, which I do with a renewal of assurances of my being faithfly.

Your friend   H. CLAY

ALS. InU.   1 Tobias Watkins.
2 Above, III, 870-72.
3 They were not published. See below, Clay to Hammond, September 23, 1825.
4 Not found.
5 Cf. above, Toasts, May 19, 21, 1825.
6 See below, Langhorne and others to Clay, this date.
7 See above, Chase to Clay, May 19, 1825.
8 The *Pennsylvania*, 107 tons, built at Pittsburgh in 1823, "worn out" and abandoned in 1827.

From Maurice Langhorne and Others

MAYSVILLE, May 23, 1825.

Dear Sir: The citizens of Maysville and its vicinity have appointed the undersigned a committee to congratulate you on your return to Kentucky, and request that you will honor them with your company to a dinner at Capt. Maurice Langhorne's, on to-morrow afternoon at 3 o'clock. They have likewise requested us to assure you of the undiminished reliance they place in your patriotism, and their unabated confidence in your spotless integrity. At any other time, such assurances would have been omitted as superfluous. The approbation you have received from Kentucky, has never been ambiguous, and her public testimonials of applause have ever accompanied you, during your long political life. But at the present moment calumny is not idle; your independent and manly course,—during the late Presidential election, has unmasked many secret enemies, who not content with expressing their own disappointment, have ventured to assert, that your constituents disapprobate your conduct. We, sir, are not your *immediate* constituents: nor do you, *as a representative*, look to us for approbation. Yet we have ever regarded you as one to whom the interests of the whole western states are dear, and are happy in the present opportunity of meeting you on the verge of our state, and assuring you that your consistent manly, and independent course, meets with the entire approbation of the citizens of Maysville and its vicinity.

Accept for yourself, considerations of our high personal regard.

M. LANGHORNE,	WM. B. PHILIPS,[2]
WILSON COBURN,[1]	WM. MURPHY,
MASON BROWN,	FR. TAYLOR,
	L. L. HAWES.[3]

Lexington *Kentucky Gazette*, June 2, 1825, reprinted from Maysville *Eagle*.
[1] A physician.
[2] Member of the State House of Representatives from Mason County, 1820.
[3] Lowman L. Hawes, Maysville lawyer.

To Maurice Langhorne and Others

MAYSVILLE, 23d May, 1825.

Gentlemen: After an absence from home of more than six months, the affectionate reception and congratulations of my fellow citizens of this town and vicinity, on my here first touching Kentucky ground, afford me the highest satisfaction. And I take particular pleasure in accepting their obliging invitation, conveyed in your note of this day. The cause of this generous manifestation of attachment and confidence gives to it, in my estimation, much additional interest. I ought to be thankful to those who have recently sought to impair my public character. Their wanton and groundless attack has been the occasion of demonstrations of regard and kindness towards me, on the part of my countrymen and my friends, which more than compensate for all the pain which it inflicted. Grateful as I am, and ever shall be, for these demonstrations, they are not more honorable to the object of them, than they are creditable to the justice and generosity of an enlightened people.

I beg, you, gentlemen, to accept my respectful thanks for the very friendly manner in which you have communicated the sentiments and wishes of the citizens of this town and neighborhood.

I have the honor to be, Faithfully, your obt. servt.   H. CLAY.
Messrs. M. Langhorne, Wilson Coburn, Mason Brown, Wm. B.
Philips, Wm. Murphy, Fr: Taylor, and L. L. Hawes.

Lexington *Kentucky Gazette*, June 2, 1825, reprinted from Maysville *Eagle*.
1 While at Maysville, Clay also received an invitation (no letter found) to visit
Cincinnati (cf. below, Toasts and Speech, July 13, 1825). Lexington *Kentucky Reporter*,
May 30, 1825.

DIPLOMATIC NOTES   May 23, 1825

From HENRY U. ADDINGTON. Replies to Clay's letter of March 27, 1825, copies
of which have been sent by Addington to the Governor of New Brunswick and
to the British Government. Summarizes the response received from the Governor, Sir Howard Douglas, who states that the charge of encroachments by
British subjects on "the *acknowledged* territory" of Maine and Massachusetts
is groundless as far as his Government is concerned; that he will "use his best
endeavours to put a stop to such practices"; that British sovereignty has long
been exercised over the "Ristook and Madawaska settlements," which were
"well understood to belong to New Brunswick" but were subsequently claimed
by the American boundary commissioners—a claim to which "no disposition
was ever shewn by Great Britain to accede"; that "documents in the possession
of the British Colonial Department" indicate "that the settlement of Madawaska in the Province of New Brunswick was made under a grant from the
Crown upwards of thirty years ago"; that the territory along the "Ristook"
is claimed by both parties; and that under the circumstances he feels "it im-
perative on him to apply immediately for still more precise instructions for the
guidance of his conduct in a matter of so much delicacy." Addington concludes
by stating that his lengthy communication is not intended "to provoke discussion here" but to show "that whatever measures, it may be found expedient
to take on the subject of your representation, cannot originate with the Authorities of New Brunswick, but must be derived directly from His Majesty's
Government. . . ." ALS. DNA, RG59, Notes from British Legation, vol. 13
(M50, R14). Published in *House Docs.*, 20 Cong., 2 Sess., no. 90, pp. 8-9; William R. Manning (arr.), *Diplomatic Correspondence of the United States, Canadian Relations, 1784-1860* (Publications of the Carnegie Endowment for International Peace, Division of International Law; 4 vols., Washington, 1940-1945),
II, 490-91.

Sir Howard Douglas, third baronet of Carr, Perthshire, after previous military
service in Canada and Spain and as commandant of the military college at High
Wycombe, had become Governor of New Brunswick in 1823. He remained in this
position until 1831, after which he served as High Commissioner of the Ionian
Islands (1835-1840) and member of Parliament (1842-1847).

INSTRUCTIONS AND DISPATCHES   May 23, 1825

From JOHN M. FORBES, Buenos Aires, no. 20. States that he has "received the
pleasing news of the termination of the long pending election of President and
the formation of the new Cabinet"; acknowledges notification of appointment as
Chargé d'Affaires at Buenos Aires and comments that he looks "to the justice
of Government to allow . . . the accustomed outfit . . . granted to others of
same rank." Reports on the progress of the conflict in South America and en-

closes local newspapers and a translation of the President's (John Quincy Adams') inaugural address, which he has published at Buenos Aires and forwarded to Chile. ALS. DNA, RG59, Dip. Disp., Argentina, vol. 2 (M69, R3). Published in Espil (comp.), *Once Años en Buenos Aires*, 361-64. Part of the letter was written on May 25, and it was completed on May 26. Received July 25.

APPLICATIONS, RECOMMENDATIONS   May 23, 1825

JOHN CLAY, New Orleans, recommends Nathaniel Chamberlain for appointment to some office. "Mr C is originally from Boston & is a relative of the Honble D. Webster." ALS. DNA, RG59, A. and R. (MR1). Chamberlain was probably related to Webster's mother-in-law, Rebecca Chamberlain (Mrs. Elijah) Fletcher, of Hopkinton, Massachusetts. On the appointment, see above, Whittlesey to Clay, April 29, 1825, note.

From John Chambers and Others

To the Honorable Henry Clay
Sir   Washington[1] 25th. [*i.e.,* 24] May 1825
The distinguished confidence which the people of Kentucky have uniformly reposed in your integrity and devotion to the interests of the Union from the moment of your first entrance into public life would on an ordinary occasion have rendered it unnecessary for us as the organ of the Citizens of Washington and its vicinity to have tendered to you any evidence of their undiminished esteem and regard and of their unlimited confidence in your integrity talents and devotion to the best interests of the Country. But the extraordinary and unparralleled [*sic*] manner in which you have been assailed because in the exercise of the Constitutional duty which devolved upon you as one of the representatives of Kentucky, you dared independently to be governed by your own judgment in selecting from the Candidates returned to the House of Representatives the most suitable person to fill the high and dignified office of President of the United States, demands in the opinion of the inhabitants of this town and its vicinity the expression of the high sense they entertain of your public services and their undiminished confidence in your integrity and patriotism. By their direction therefore we avail ourselves of the opportunity which the first moment of your arrival in Kentucky affords to greet you on their behalf with that warmth of affection and cordiality of esteem which as Kentuckians they have ever felt for her favorite son, and to assure you that they consider you as they ever have, the able and eloquent defender of their rights and the rights of the whole American people, the bold and intrepid advocate of freedom and the rights of man throughout the world. With pride and pleasure they have ever found you the faithful representative of Kentucky the

open candid liberal statesman unfettered by local prejudices or sectional feeling. And so far from their confidence having been diminished by the attempts which have been made to impeach your integrity they consider your conduct in the late presidential election as affording a new and distinguished proof that the confidence Kentucky has always reposed in your firmness talents and integrity has not been misplaced.

Permit us individually to assure you of our hearty concurence [*sic*] in the sentiments we have expressed on behalf of our fellow citizens and to join with them in tendering you our best wishes for your health and happiness.

JOHN CHAMBERS	DAVID V. RANNELLS
WALKER REID	A. BEATTY.
PETER LEE	JNO, GREEN
DAVID DAVIS	B. DUKE[2]
JAS. ELLIS	

LS. DLC-HC (DNA, M212, R1). Published (and dated May 24) in Lexington *Kentucky Reporter,* June 6, 1825; *Niles' Weekly Register,* XXVIII (June 25, 1825), 268.
1 Kentucky.
2 Reid, a lawyer, had been a member of the Kentucky House of Representatives and was later a circuit judge; Lee, Davis, and Green had been pioneer settlers of Mason County, Davis having been named one of the trustees of the town of Washington at its founding, in 1793; Ellis had been an officer of Kentucky militia in the War of 1812; and Rannells had established at Washington a female academy in 1813 and a newspaper, the *Union,* which he had published from 1814 to 1824.

To John Chambers and Others

GENTLEMEN.   Washington, 24th May, 1825.

I receive, with very great satisfaction, the kind congratulations of my Fellow-Citizens of this town and neighbourhood, communicated in your friendly address.[1]

If the recent attack upon me was without precedent and without principle, I have derived the greatest consolation from the generous support which I have received from all quarters. That of which you have been the organ, is the more acceptable, because it is rendered by citizens of my own state, many of whom have known me well and for a long series of years. You have stated the cause correctly gentlemen; it was because I "dared independently to be governed by my own judgment," that some, who happened to think differently from me, have chosen to assail me with the most persevering malignity. They have furnished, however, an occasion for an exhibition of magnanimous sympathy and prompt justice, as creditable to the American people, as it is honorable and cheering to the grateful object of those noble sentiments.

I pray you Gentlemen, respectively, to accept assurances of the high esteem and strong personal regard of

Your faithful and obedient servant.   H. CLAY.

Messrs. John Chambers, A. Beatty, B. Duke, David Davis, Walker Reid, John Green, David V. Rannells, James Ellis, Peter Lee.

Lexington *Kentucky Reporter,* June 6, 1825.   1 Above, this date.

Toasts and Remarks at Maysville Banquet

[May 24, 1825]

Our distinguished guest, HENRY CLAY—In his recent vote for President, as a representative of the people, *"conscience"* was his *monitor*—he *obeyed,* and the great majority of the people of Kentucky *approve* its dictates.

{Mr CLAY arose, and in a short, but very feeling and eloquent address, expressed his sincere acknowledgments for the kind attention of the citizens of Maysville and its vicinity, which was rendered peculiar [*sic*] dear to him, on account of the recent attempt to destroy his political character.}

Mr CLAY gave—*The State of Kentucky*—In all our local divisions, may we ever recollect that they are among friends, brothers and countrymen.

Lexington *Kentucky Reporter,* May 30, 1825, reprinted from Maysville *Eagle.* The toast to Clay was given after the diners had drunk "to the memory of Washington and the heroes of the Revolution, and to the health of Jefferson, Madison, Monroe and the President of the United States."

INSTRUCTIONS AND DISPATCHES   May 24, 1825

From WILLIAM TAYLOR, Alvarado. Transmits communication dated May 14, from (Lucas) Alamán, Secretary of State of the Mexican Government, giving notice that after sixty days the ports of Mexico will be closed to all vessels arriving from Thompson's Island (Key West) ; explains that, since his residence at this port, there has been but one American ship entered from Thompson's Island and it merely transferred a cargo from a Philadelphia schooner shipwrecked at the Island en route to Alvarado; comments that "so far as relates to the Ports within this Consulate the Mexican Government has acted upon very erronious [*sic*] information." Notes that the treaty between Mexico and Great Britain has not yet been signed. ALS. DNA, RG59, Cons. Disp., Veracruz, vol. 1 (M183, R1). Received June 29. The enclosed document (copy, certified by Taylor) transmits a copy of the above-mentioned order, dated May 11, which, it is asserted, has been issued in consequence of the Mexican Government's belief that Key West has served as a base for transshipment of Spanish goods from Havana, in contravention to Mexican commercial restrictions. On the proposed treaty between Mexico and Great Britain, see above, Wilcocks to Clay, April 9, 1825; Poinsett to Clay, May 5, 1825.

MISCELLANEOUS LETTERS   May 24, 1825

From John A. Leamy, Philadelphia. Notes that a memorial presented in 1817
in the case of the schooner *Liberty* listed John Coulter as owner of the vessel,
although she had been purchased from him abroad earlier in that year; submits documentary evidence of that purchase (by Leamy as agent of Ledlie and
Leamy). ALS. DNA, RG76, Misc. Claims, Colombia. Coulter, a director of the
United States Bank, was a merchant active in the East India trade. The firm,
Ledlie and Leamy (James F. Ledlie and John A. Leamy), appears to have
operated from Martinique, as the West Indian exchange for Philadelphia
merchants.

From William Lytle

Hon H. Clay   Acting Exr of James Morrison Esqr.
Sir,   Cincinnati 25 May 1825.
    I have transferred all my claims as locator for one third of Survey
No. 4251 & 4451—in the name of Jas. Morrison & James O.Hara
& N Bowsman each for 500 acres of land[1] to Henry Avery[2] of this
City—to Whom I request you to convey the Land or Settle with
him therefor— Your compliance will much Oblige your friend and
humble Servt.   Wm. Lytle

    ALS. DLC-TJC (DNA, M212, R13).
    [1] Cf. above, III, 878. The tract was probably a location listed by Morrison as about
1400 acres on the Miami in Ohio, of which Morrison claimed 934 acres, with the
balance to be transferred to Lytle in compensation as locator. Fayette County, Will
Book F, 73.   [2] Not further identified.

INSTRUCTIONS AND DISPATCHES   May 25, 1825

From Heman Allen, Valparaiso, no. 15. Reports his belief that the provinces
of Chile will separate and attempt a federal system. Requests, for the sake
of his family, permission to continue to live at Valparaiso, since the Secretary
of Legation resides at Santiago. ALS. DNA, RG59, Dip. Disp., Chile (M-T2,
R1). Addressed to Secretary of State; received September 17. Cf. above, Allen
to Secretary of State, March 19, 1825.
    Samuel Larned, of Rhode Island, had been appointed Secretary of Legation
in Chile in 1823. Left in charge of the mission in 1827, he was officially appointed Chargé d'Affaires to Chile in February, 1828, and to Peru, from December, 1828, to March, 1837.

From James H. Bennett, Pernambuco (Brazil). Reports that "The Military
Government was revoked by order of his Imperial Majesty [Pedro I], and a
President installed on the 23d. Inst. under the Same Laws— The City is gar-
risoned by German Soldiers. . . ." Brazilian troops will probably land at
Montevideo, which is besieged by a Spanish force. A letter from the United States
consul at Rio de Janeiro (Condy Raguet) brings information of an embargo
"on all vessels bound for the River Plate." ALS. DNA, RG59, Cons. Disp.,
Pernambuco, vol. 1 (M-T344, R1). Addressed to Secretary of State; received
July 28, 1825. Bennett, of Virginia, had been appointed consul at Pernambuco

in February, 1821. On the siege of Montevideo, see above, Forbes to Clay, May 2, 1825.

MISCELLANEOUS LETTERS   May 25, 1825

From JAMES H. McCULLOCH, Collector's Office, Customs House, Baltimore. Reports the impressment, by "the Portuguese Brazilian navy" at Rio de Janeiro about August 1, 1824, of Toby Maddon, colored, age 32, a resident of Baltimore, and a seaman on board the ship *Meridian*. Captain John Myers, of this vessel, has applied, without success, to Admiral (Thomas) Cochrane for discharge of the seaman, whose wife has asked for help in obtaining her husband's release. ALS. DNA, RG59, Misc. Letters (M179, R62). McCulloch, a veteran of the Revolution and the War of 1812, had been a delegate to the Maryland Assembly (1800) and a State Senator (1806-1808); he was collector of customs at Baltimore from 1808 until his death, in 1836.

From WILLIAM SHALER, Marseilles (France). Requests permission to insert, in an appendix to a historical sketch of Algiers which he is preparing for publication, two letters "written by the President to the Dey of Algiers in the years 1815 and 1816." ALS. *Ibid.* (M179, R63). See below, Sparks to Clay, December 25, 1825, note. Shaler's volume, *Sketches of Algiers, Political, Historical, and Civil . . . ,* was published at Boston in 1826.

APPLICATIONS, RECOMMENDATIONS   May 25, 1825

G. G. AND S. HOWLAND, New York, recommend for appointment as commercial agent at Matanzas their brother, Joseph, whom Clay knew at Ghent and who "has determined to remove his Establishment from Charleston S. C." to Matanzas. LS. DNA, RG59, A. and R. (MR2). Gardiner Greene Howland, a commission merchant in the West India trade, had in 1816 taken his brother, Samuel Shaw, as a partner. Joseph Howland, not further identified, did not receive the appointment.

From John M. Forbes

(*Private*)   Buenos Ayres 26th May 1825.
Honble. Henry Clay   Secretary of State Washington
My Dear Sir,

It has only been within the last three days that I have received the welcome intelligence of Mr Adams' election to The Presidency of the U.S. and the formation of his Cabinet.

I Can say, Sir, without fear of any Charge of insincerity, that I am delighted to see you at the head of the Department of State, because I have been honoured with enough of personal intercourse with you, to be penetrated with a due sense of the warmth of your heart and the elevation of your Sentiments on all Subjects, especially in regard to every thing Connected with the Welfare of our Common Country.—

At the same moment that these events have reached me, I received also the unofficial, but certain information of my nomination as *Chargé d'Affaires* here,[1] and this new proof of the approbation of my Government, having entirely filled the Cup of my ambition, I trust that the present homage of personal feelings towards you, will be received without the smallest suspicion as to the purity of its motive.— It is, in a degree, a general practice (and has always been mine) to communicate in the freedom of personal Correspondence, to the Secretary of State, such facts as are not of a nature to be Consecrated to the diplomatic Archives, and I hope that you will indulge me in the Continuance of this practice.

Presuming to refer you to my official Communications and the Gazettes forwarded by this opportunity to the Department, for the passing events of the moment in this vicinity, I pray you to accept my most Cordial wishes for the Continuance of your health and of every personal blessing and the increase (if possible) of your Fame.—

I am, very faithfully Your devoted friend & Humble Servant

J M Forbes

ALS. DNA, RG59, Dip. Disp., Argentina, vol. 2 (M69, R3).
1 See above, Forbes to Clay, March 26, 1825, and note.

INSTRUCTIONS AND DISPATCHES   May 26, 1825

From James Brown, Paris, "Private." Reports that the ministers to France from various countries, in meetings which Brown has been unable to attend, have "resolved to decline the *banquet royal*," at the coronation at Rheims, "unless permitted to dine in the same hall with the Ambassadors" and have drawn up a resumé of reasons (copy enclosed) for their decision. LS. DNA, RG59, Dip. Disp., France, vol. 22 (M34, R25). On the coronation, see above, Brown to Secretary of State, March 21, 1825, and note.

From W[illiam] Tudor, Lima, no. 29, "Confidential." Transmits copies of his correspondence with the Peruvian Government concerning the case of Captain (Samuel) Lombard, a decree prohibiting importation of Spanish goods, and a demand "on resident American citizens to perform militia duty." The Americans and English have resisted the demand upon foreigners to perform military duty and in retaliation have been subjected to a discriminatory impost. Comments that Bolívar's arrival at Quilca (Peru) coincided with the capture there of General Espartero, who was returning to South America after a year's absence, and that the siege of Callao continues. News of Adams' election has been received. ALS. DNA, RG59, Cons. Disp., Lima, vol. 1 (M154, R1). Extract published in Manning (arr.), *Diplomatic Correspondence . . . Latin-American Nations,* III, 1781-82. Addressed to Secretary of State; received September 5. On the case of Samuel Lombard, see above, Tudor to Clay, April 22, 1825.

Baldomero Espartero had first come to America in 1815, as a young officer attached to the staff of General Pablo Morillo. After participating in numerous engagements and being seriously wounded, he had returned to Spain in 1823. He later led the forces of Queen Isabella II against the Carlists, in the conflict for succession to the throne of Ferdinand VII. Following her victory, he became prime minister from 1840 to 1843, acting as regent the last two years, and again served as chief minister from 1854 to 1856.

MISCELLANEOUS LETTERS   May 26, 1825

From WILLIAM BULLITT, New Orleans. Solicits Clay's "aid and friendship" in obtaining an appointment as "naval Officer of this port," the application for which is being sent to Washington by way of New York. Bullitt adds: "I was partly raised in Kentucky, in this state I have been one of your warm supporters." ALS. DNA, RG59, A. and R. (MR1). Addressed to Lexington. William was probably the nephew of Thomas and the son of Cuthbert Bullitt, partners in a Louisville mercantile firm. The young man did not receive an appointment. For his application, see below, Bullitt to Clay, May 29, 1825.

From PLATT H. CROSBY, Lima. Protests against consideration of a copy of his statement on the cruise of the *Franklin* as his own production after the document had been amended and forwarded to the State Department by the late (John B.) Prevost (see above, III, 483-84n). Discusses revolution and politics in Peru and the proposed "Congress of Plenipotentiaries for the purpose of establishing a *general Federation,* or alliances offensive and defensive against Spain not only, but the *Holy Alliance,* and even, should occasion require, prospectively against Don Pedro of the Brazils." Reports 54 American vessels on the Peruvian coast, most of which brought cargoes of flour, which "is a mere drug" on the market; recalls Clay's warning in his speech on the tariff, that the demand for flour in South America was temporary (above, III, 690); and concludes that "It would have been well" if the merchants had believed him. ALS. DNA, RG59, Misc. Letters (M179, R62). On the proposed Pan-American Congress, see above, April 12, 1825.

From Bartholomew Shaumburgh

Sir   New Orleans May 27th. 1825.

Captain James Sterret[1] who held the office of Naval Officer in the Custom House at this Port took his departure for an other world this morning— His loss need not to be regreted [*sic*] because He was an Enemy to you & Mr. Adams—

Mr. Durald[2] has promiss'd to join me in prayers to you, that should you think my Claim just, to be so good and use your influence with the President of the U. States to bestow that Office on me—

I make the application with a Conviction that old & long service will *Now* be rewarded—

I must Confess Sir, that present necessity does not Compell me to make the application, I make it because I am gitting Old, and in order to prevent that necessaty which may follow—The Salary annex'd and the ease of the office, together with my other little income, would dragg me through this rugged world tolerable smooth, and enable me to make my sons what they should be, "defenders of their country & useful & respectable members of Society"—

pardon Sir the liberty I have taken, and please to accept the assurance of my high Esteem and respect— I have the honor to be—

Sir Your very humble Servant   BARTHOLOMEW SHAUMBURGH

Honorable Henry Clay   Secretary of State United States—

[Endorsement on cover][3]

Col. Shaumburgh (the writer of the within) was formerly an officer in the army of the U. S. and is a gentleman of worth, integrity and capacity.   H CLAY

17. June 1825

ALS. DNA, RG59, A. and R. (MR3). Shaumburgh, born in Germany, had entered the United States Army from Pennsylvania and served as an officer from 1791 to 1802. In 1804 he had been licensed to establish trading houses at Natchitoches and Ouachita, Louisiana, where he had held rank as a colonel of militia during most of the next decade. In 1812 he had been commissioned a deputy quartermaster general of the United States Army, and at the Battle of New Orleans he had acted as aide to Governor W. C. C. Claiborne. He did not receive the appointment here requested.

1 Born in Pennsylvania, commissioned an officer of the United States Army from 1794 to 1805, and assigned to Natchitoches at the time of his discharge, Sterret had been appointed to the New Orleans customhouse sometime after 1816. Clay had urged Adams, on May 13, to remove him from the position. Adams, *Memoirs*, VI, 545-47. On his death, see below, R. D. Richardson to Clay, May 28, 1825.

2 Martin Duralde (Jr.).   3 AES.

INSTRUCTIONS AND DISPATCHES   May 27, 1825

From JAMES BROWN, Paris, no. 28. Acknowledges receipt of Instructions no. 6 (above, March 29, 1825); states that "a severe recurrence of rheumatism" has disrupted his plans to attend the coronation. LS. DNA, RG59, Dip. Disp., France, vol. 22 (M34, R25). See above, Brown to Secretary of State, March 21, 1825.

APPLICATIONS, RECOMMENDATIONS   May 27, 1825

NATHANIEL MACON, "Buck Spring," Virginia, transmits a letter from William Smyth (addressed to Macon and dated February 9, 1825) requesting employment as a consul or commercial agent; notes that he is not personally acquainted with Smyth, who as a lieutenant in a rifle corps, was wounded "during the last war," that Smyth is now on the pension list and is apparently residing at St. Thomas in the West Indies. ALS. DNA, RG59, A. and R. (M531, R7). Smyth, not further identified, did not receive an appointment.

From Francis P. Blair and Others

THE HON'BLE H. CLAY.   *Frankfort, May* 28, 1825.

Sir.—A number of the people of Franklin County and many other persons now brought together at the seat of government from distant parts of the state, participating in the general gratification felt at your return to Kentucky, welcome you to the bosom of your family and the society of your friends.

To the approbation which they have so often manifested for the arduous and successful exertion of your talents and virtues in behalf of the state as its representative, they would now add an expression of the sense they entertain, of the unblemished political integrity and the signal public services by which you have deserved, and of their confidence in your ability to fill, the high department of the national Government which you are called to administer. For the purpose of giving a public demonstration of their sentiments and of mingling their personal congratulations with a tribute of respect, a meeting of your fellow-citizens has directed a public dinner to be given at Capt. Weisiger's[1] tavern, to which we are deputed to invite you. You will therefore be pleased to inform us whether it will be convenient to accept this invitation; and if so, when it will be most agreeable to you to afford the pleasure of your company.

F. P. Blair	J. Swigert,[2]
J. Harvie,	J. Dudley,
P. H. Darby,	J. J. Crittenden

Lexington *Kentucky Reporter,* June 13, 1825.   [1] Daniel Weisiger.
[2] Jacob Swigert, Frankfort lawyer, who had been born in Washington, District of Columbia, had been brought up in Fayette County, Kentucky, and became clerk of the Kentucky Court of Appeals from 1825 to 1858.

From Robert D. Richardson

Dear Sir,   New Orleans, May 28th. 1825.

In November last, I was in a measure compelled to make sale of the office and establishment of the Louisiana Gazette, and the purchaser was James McKaraher,[1] who has for some months conducted and disgraced its columns. This wretched imitation of an Editor never paid me a cent of the purchase money, but after embarrassing the establishment permitted the office to be advertised for sale for rent— I heard of it just in time to reach this place and by becoming purchaser of my own office at public sale, have saved that much from being totally lost, as it was evidently the intention of this man to have it bought in by a friend of his (who bid for it at the sale) and take the benefit of the insolvent law and swindle me out of the whole concern. My family are at Baton Rouge. I shall endeavor to revive the character and standing of the paper—and make up for the pain which I have experienced in seeing a paper which was once mine and published in my name, so disgracefully conducted. After I shall have accomplished this

object, I will dispose of the newspaper to a man of correct principles—in hopes of finding some other employment.[2]

Col. James Sterret, the naval officer at this station—departed this
life yesterday.— I have no doubt but that there will be many
applicants for the situation which has now become vacant.— I
should, in a change of situation, prefer Washington city, where
there would be a better prospect of educating my two interesting
daughters—and my two promising Boys—but should there be no
vacancy which I could fill in the city, I should be pleased to obtain
the appointment of Naval Officer in the custom House of this city.

I beg to be allowed my Dear sir, to speak to you with freedom
and frankness with regard yourself. I consider you this day, and I
am far from being alone in the Opinion, as the most popular man
in the U. States— If not so at this moment, your political march
thro'. life, and particularly your recent movements will render
you so in a short time. I consider you as on the successful road of
establishing that popularity upon a basis as *durable as brass*. You
have already written enough— I would notice nothing more— You
are beyond the reach of any thing which may be said—and your
friends do wish [*sic*] to see *you* take one step in condescension to
any man—or of what any man or set of men can say in print. Your
address to your constituents[3] is beyond the reach of candid criticism.

Your Brother[4] is in good health—we spent some hours together
last evening. Excuse this scraul [*sic*], as I write in great haste—but
believe me as ever, most truly and sincerely Your friend & Obt.
Sert.   R. D. RICHARDSON
H. Clay, Esq.   Lexington Ky

[Endorsement on verso][5]

Mr. Richardson (the writer of the within) was a Captain (I believe)
formerly in the Army of the U S.[6] Mr Gurley[7] of Louisiana displayed a particular interest in his behalf, when he was at the City.
This letter is forwarded that the President may be apprized of
the wish of Mr Richardson (who is poor) to obtain the office
vacated by Capt Sterrets death.[8]   H. Clay   11 June 25

ALS. DNA, RG59, A. and R. (MR3).
1 Who had been owner and publisher of *L'Ami des Lois* (New Orleans) from
February, 1819, to April, 1820.
2 After engaging in several bitter editorial controversies during the summer and
fall of 1825, Richardson again sold his interest in the journal to McKaraher. Albert
[E.] Fossier, *New Orleans, the Glamour Period, 1800-1840* . . . (New Orleans, [c.
1957]), 187.   3 Above, March 26, 1825.
4 John Clay.   5 AES.
6 Richardson had been appointed captain, deputy commissary of Ordnance, in 1813,
had transferred to Infantry in 1821, and had resigned from the Army in 1822.
7 Henry H. Gurley.
8 Cf. below, Richardson to Clay, May 31, 1825.

From William H. Richardson and Others

DEAR SIR.   LEXINGTON, MAY 28th, 1825.

The undersigned, a committee on the part of the citizens of Lexington and Fayette county, are authorised to invite you to a Public Dinner, on Wednesday next at Fowler's[1] Garden.

It affords us peculiar pleasure at this time to offer you this public expression of our entire confidence in the able and impartial manner you have discharged your various public duties.

You became our Representative at an important and critical juncture of our country; during the whole time, you have been the inflexible advocate of rational liberty and the steady supporter of public justice. There has occurred no session of Congress, out of the many you have been a member, that your political acts were more completely in accordance with our wishes and views of national prosperity and repose, than the one which terminated the arduous and responsible relationship that subsisted between us.

You have been called from us to discharge the duties of an elevated and distinguished station in another department of the government; rest assured Sir, you carry with you our highest confidence in your superior talents, experience, and unshaken integrity.

We avail ourselves of this opportunity to renew to you assurance of our great personal regard and esteem. With sentiments of the most distinguished consideration, we are your obd't servants.

<table>
<tr><td>WM. H. RICHARDSON,</td><td>E. YEISER,</td></tr>
<tr><td>M. FLOURNOY,[2]</td><td>A. DUDLEY,[3]</td></tr>
<tr><td>JNO. TILFORD,</td><td>JAMES SHELBY.</td></tr>
<tr><td>THOS. BODLEY,</td><td></td></tr>
</table>

Lexington *Kentucky Reporter,* June 6, 1825.

[1] John Fowler.

[2] Matthews Flournoy, at this time a resident of Fayette County, which he had represented in the State Senate from 1821 to the session of 1824-1825 and continued to serve in the State House of Representatives during the succeeding session.

[3] Ambrose Dudley, veteran of the War of 1812; brother of Benjamin W., Jephthah, and Peter, nephew of William Dudley; later a resident of Cincinnati.

INSTRUCTIONS AND DISPATCHES   May 28, 1825

From HUGH NELSON, Madrid, no. 57. Transmits copies of a note from the Secretary of State (Francisco de Zea Bermudez) announcing a new decree "relative to the article of Salt to be exported" from Spain; of Nelson's reply, urging repeal of the tonnage duty on vessels entering Spanish ports in ballast for salt cargoes to be carried to the United States; and of a note by Nelson protesting the requirement of a second tonnage duty, at Cádiz, charged against the master of the American brig *Cobossee Contee,* which had earlier paid duty at Teneriffe and had not since visited any foreign port. Reports recent agreement by Spain to accredit consuls of France in the West Indian Islands and

Nelson's intention of renewing his request for such accreditation of agents of the United States.

Addendum, dated May 31: Despite rumor that the accreditation of French consuls in the West Indies is granted in return for a promise that France will not "recognise the Independence of the South American states," Nelson has requested an interview with the (Spanish) Secretary (of State) and argued for extension of such recognition to the American agents as a means of better suppressing piracy in the area. The Secretary has promised his answer on the next Saturday. Speaking with pride of Spain's efforts to combat piracy, he (Bermudez) also announced the revocation of all privateering commissions by his Government.

Nelson further notes that the Spanish Government, following the refusal of the King (Ferdinand VII) to recognize debts contracted by the Cortes (under the Republic), has failed in its attempt to obtain a loan in Holland. LS. DNA, RG59, Dip. Disp., Spain, vol. 24 (M31, R26). Received July 23. On actions of the Spanish colonial officials to suppress piracy, see below, Smith to Clay, July 14, 1825, note.

From JOEL R. POINSETT, Mexico (City), no. 2. Announces his arrival at the capital on May 25 and his friendly welcome along the way. Encloses a copy of the British treaty. LS. DNA, RG59, Dip. Disp., Mexico, vol. 1 (M97, R2). Received July 5. On the British treaty with Mexico, see above, Wilcocks to Secretary of State, April 9, 1825; Poinsett to Clay, May 5, 1825.

From RICHARD RUSH, no. 438. Transmits copy of letter, dated May 25, to (John Adams) Smith and states that Rush will embark "in a few days." ALS. DNA, RG59, Dip. Disp., Great Britain, vol. 32 (M30, R28). Received July 17. The enclosure is a copy of Rush's letter formally investing Smith with the duties of the mission.

APPLICATIONS, RECOMMENDATIONS   May 28, 1825

P[IERRE AUGUSTE CHARLES] DERBIGNY, New Orleans, recommends Manuel Cruzat, "a creole of New-Orleans, who wishes to be appointed naval officer of this port in lieu of James Sterret deceased." ALS. MHi-Adams Papers, Letters Received (M469). Cruzat was owner of the *New Orleans Argus,* renamed from *L'Ami des Lois,* which he had purchased in the spring of 1824. He was given an interim appointment as naval officer in August, 1825; his formal nomination to the post was confirmed on January 9, 1826. He was elected to the city council, as an alderman, the following year.

CHARLES W. DUHY, former editor of the *Louisiana Gazette,* now senior editor of the *Mercantile Daily Advertiser,* New Orleans, cites "an acquaintance of some years' standing" with Clay and requests recommendation to the President for appointment as naval officer of this port. Mentions his understanding of the French, Spanish, and English languages, his financial stability, his eighteen years of residence in Louisiana, and his service in its defense, as qualifications for the office; and presents an account of his service in behalf of the administration:

"I became principal editor of the *Mercantile Advertiser,* about six months ago. This paper, from its commencement, has advocated the election of Mr. John Q. Adams, and until a few weeks back, it was the only paper in the city that dared to publish a line in favor of either Mr. Adams or Mr. Clay. The moment I began my editorial career anew, I left nothing undone by writing myself, or publishing the pieces of others, which could establish the claims of

Mr. Adams to the presidency, or support his administration after it began. This frankness on my part, did not fail to procure many enemies for myself and paper; some withdrew their subscription; others threatened to mob me. In fact, when on the 5th of April, I made some commentaries upon Jackson's letter to Swartwout, three papers of this city assailed me with all sorts of abuse. I was personally insulted, challenged and fought, and prosecuted for a libel. Altogether, I had to spend three or four hundred dollars of my own money, and witness a combination which cost me many subscribers."

ALS. MHi-Adams Papers, Letters Received (M469). Addressee not named. Charles William Duhy had printed a paper in Rhode Island for a brief time in 1807. In 1817 he had been admitted to partnership in the New Orleans *Louisiana Gazette* and, after his partner's death in 1820, had conducted the paper alone until he sold it three years later. On Andrew Jackson's letter to Samuel Swartwout, see above, Clay to Brooke, January 28, 1825, note.

[JOHN H.] PLEASANTS and [ALEXANDER W.] JONES, Richmond, Virginia, offer to publish the laws on the usual terms. ALS. DNA, RG59, P. and D. of L. Jones, later (1830-1834) a member of the Virginia House of Delegates, had become co-editor of the Richmond *Constitutional Whig* in April, 1825, and remained with that journal until the following February.

MISCELLANEOUS LETTERS   May 29, 1825

From A[LEXANDER] H. EVERETT, New York. Reports his arrival "at this place yesterday from Boston," his receipt of "the trunk containing . . . instructions and the documents and books accompanying them," also his receipt of letters from (Daniel) Brent "under the date of the 18th. 19th. (three in number) and 25th. with their respective enclosures," and completion of arrangements for departure. ALS. DNA, RG59, Dip. Disp., Spain, vol. 25 (M31, R27).

APPLICATIONS, RECOMMENDATIONS   May 29, 1825

WILLIAM BULLITT, New Orleans, solicits appointment as naval officer at this port. ALS. DNA, RG59, A. and R. (MR1). See above, Bullitt to Clay, May 26, 1825; Derbigny to Clay, May 28, 1825, note.

GABRIEL MOORE, "Near Huntsville, Ala.," recommends, for "some respectable appointment in this state," William L. S. Dearing, "who has recently removed from the State of Tennessee to Ala." Clay "will doubtless recollect an acquaintance with . . . Dearing." ALS. DNA, RG59, A. and R. (MR2). Dearing not further identified.

To John Harvie and Others

ASHLAND, MAY 30, 1825.

Gentlemen—I have the honor to acknowledge the receipt of your obliging note of the 28th instant,[1] communicating the kind congratulations of a number of my fellow citizens of Franklin County, and others assembled at the seat of government from different parts of our State, on the occasion of my return home, and also an invitation to a public dinner at Frankfort.— The friendly and cordial testimonies of their highly esteemed approbation afford me the greatest gratification. They are worthy of public services much more eminent and arduous than any which I have ever been able to render. I accept with much pleasure, the invitation, and will have the honor of dining with my fellow citizens, of whom you have been the obliging organ, on Saturday next, or on such other day as they may be pleased to designate, if any other shall better suit their convenience.

I pray you gentlemen to be assured of the very high respect which is entertained for you personally by Your obedient servant,

H. CLAY.

Messrs. *J. Harvie, J. J. Crittenden, J. Swigert, J. Dudly* [*sic*], *P. H. Darby & F. P. Blair.*

Lexington *Kentucky Reporter,* June 13, 1825.
1 From Blair and others.

To William H. Richardson and Others

GENTLEMEN.   ASHLAND. 30TH MAY, 1825.

I received, with very great satisfaction, the note which you did me the honour to address to me on the 28th instant; and I accept, with much pleasure, the invitation which it conveys.

No man more highly estimates the public approbation than I do. I have sought however to deserve it (I hope I may venture to assert without arrogance as it is said with perfect truth) by zeal, fidelity, and integrity, and by the exertion of the utmost of my humble powers. I have never sought it by any mean compromises or unworthy arts. But I have desired the good opinion of no portion of the public more anxiously, than that of my immediate constituents. Judge then, gentlemen, what inexpressible gratification I derive from your assurances of the entire confidence which is reposed in me by my fellow citizens of Lexington and Fayette, who comprise, at the same time, my nearest and most intimate friends and neighbours, and a highly respectable and considerable part of my late constituents. Their kind extension of the same unshaken confidence to the new station, to which I have been summoned, adds to the numberless obligations under which they have placed me. Among the objections which I had to the acceptance of that office, none had more weight than that arising out of my repugnance to close a connection which has so long subsisted between the people of this district and me. As their representative I have experienced, without interruption, their liberality, affection and confidence. I can offer only, in return, unbounded gratitude and ardent devotion.

I tender to you, gentlemen, the homage of my sincere respect and high personal regard. Your obedient servant, H. CLAY.
Messrs W. H. Richardson, M. Flournoy, Jno. Tilford, Thomas Bodley, E. Yeiser, A. Dudley, & James Shelby.

Lexington *Kentucky Reporter,* June 6, 1825.

From Samuel H. Woodson and Others

HON. H. CLAY. MAY 30th, 1825.

Sir.—The citizens of Jessamine County having heretofore enjoyed the honor of composing a portion of your congressional district, have witnessed with admiration and delight the commencement and progress of your most useful and brilliant career, not only in the councils of the state, but as their immediate Representative in those of the nation; they feel gratitude for your past services, your constant and zealous devotion to the true principles of our own free government, your noble and eloquent exertions to promote their highest interests and glory, and advance the cause of liberty wherever her standard has been erected, and the happy union, and powerful display of virtue, talent, unbending integrity and characteristic firmness as a man and politician, demand of those who best know, and therefore most appreciate your private and public worth, to embrace the opportunity afforded by your return, and temporary residence among them, (especially at this peculiar period, when envy and disappointed ambition have vainly attempted to sully the lustre of your character, and thereby shade the escutcheon of America) of rallying around their most faithful and distinguished public servant, and offering him a sincere but humble testimony of their highest approbation and esteem. With this view we have been requested, earnestly to solicit the honor of your company at a public dinner in Nicholasville on the 15th June next. In the discharge of this duty, the greatest pleasure is derived by Your sincere friends and most ob't serv'ts.

S. H. WOODSON,	JO. H. CHRISMAN,[3]
WM. H. RAINY,[1]	REUBEN B. BERRY,[4]
C. R. LEWIS,[2]	WM. CALDWELL,
GEO. I. BROWN,	A. LOGAN.

Lexington *Kentucky Reporter,* June 20, 1825.

[1] Born in Pennsylvania, Rainy had been prominent as a lay leader of the Presbyterian Church in the Blue Grass area of Kentucky since early in the century. He was at this time an elder of the Nicholasville church; by 1829, he had moved to Lexington, where he then became ruling elder of the Second Presbyterian Church. For over a decade he operated a dry-goods business in Lexington, after the failure of which he removed to Harrison County.

[2] Courtney R. Lewis, born in Jessamine County, which he represented in the Kentucky Legislature of 1830. He later settled in Lafayette, Louisiana.

[3] Possibly Joseph Chrisman, Jessamine County farmer.

4 A physician and farmer, who resided on the Nicholasville Road in Fayette County, four and a half miles from Lexington.

DIPLOMATIC NOTES   May 30, 1825

From HILARIO DE RIVAS Y SALMON, Philadelphia. Encloses copies of letters which support his contention that the Colombian privateer *Polly Hampton* is using Key West as a base of operation against Spain. LS. DNA, RG59, Notes from Spanish Legation, vol. 8 (M59, R11). The enclosures assert that the *Polly Hampton* has again arrived at Key West with a prize and is in the habit of cruising off Cuba, running Spanish vessels aground, where a wrecker is then employed to bring the vessel and cargo into Key West for sale "to discharge the pretended claim of salvage which in fact goes into the pockets of the Captors."

INSTRUCTIONS AND DISPATCHES   May 30, 1825

From THOMAS L. L. BRENT, Lisbon, no. 7. Reports the arrival, on March 25, of Sir Charles Stuart, "charged to offer to this Country the mediation of Great Britain between it and Brazil"; the acceptance of his services; and his departure for Rio de Janeiro on May 24. Noting the great secrecy surrounding these negotiations, Brent hazards the opinion that "although the prejudices in Portugal are infinitely less strong than in Spain with regard to the former Colonies, yet . . . it is doubtful whether these people are yet ripe for an unqualified acknowledgment of the independence of Brazil, rendering it wholly unconnected with Portugal. . . ." ALS. DNA, RG59, Dip. Disp., Portugal, vol. 6 (M43, R5). Received August 28. See above, Raguet to Secretary of State, March 11, 1825, note.

From Robert Breckinridge and Others

LOUISVILLE, Ky. May 31, 1825.

The Hon. Henry Clay.—Dear Sir, Your friends in Louisville and its vicinity are solicitous to have an opportunity of paying to you in person, that respect which is due to eminent talents, sound integrity, and important public services. They are the more anxious at this time, to shew their high regard for you as a man, a patriot, and a statesman, in consequence of the base attempt made last winter by some of your enemies to rob you of the good opinion of the American people.

The undersigned, a committee appointed for that purpose, do earnestly solicit the honour of your company at a public dinner in Louisville to be given at such time as will best suit your convenience and for the purposes stated in the enclosed resolutions. With sentiments of the highest esteem and respect we are, your obedient humble servants,

ROB'T. BRECKINRIDGE,	COLEMAN ROGERS,
JAMES HUGHES,[1]	N. BERTHOUD,
THOMAS M'CLANAHAN,	N. B. BEALL.

Lexington *Kentucky Reporter,* August 1, 1825, from the Louisville *Morning Post.* This invitation resulted from action taken at a meeting in Louisville, on May 30, at which Dr. Coleman Rogers had served as chairman and H (orace) B. Hill, secretary. Resolutions, of which a copy was enclosed with this document, had been adopted, appointing committees to formulate the invitation, present it, and arrange the dinner. Robert Breckinridge and Norborne B. Beall were named to "wait upon" Clay and present the letter. The banquet committee comprised Isaac Thom, Ruggles Whiting, John Peay, Benjamin Lawrence, Jacob Miller, Richard Hall, George W. Chambers, Dr. (William C.) Galt, and Dr. (Richard) Ferguson.

Rogers, Louisville physician and surgeon, born in Virginia, had been trained under Samuel Brown in Lexington and at the University of Pennsylvania, where he had received his M.D. degree in 1817. He had been a partner of Ephraim McDowell at Danville in 1810, had served briefly as adjunct professor of anatomy at Transylvania University in 1817, had then been associated with Daniel Drake in practice and as professor at the Ohio Medical College until 1823, when he had removed to Louisville. He later (in 1833) became one of the incorporators of the Louisville Medical Institute, where he was appointed to the chair of anatomy.

Dr. Galt, another of the incorporators of the Louisville Medical Institute and its first president, was a prominent civic leader, manager of the Louisville Library Company at its founding in 1816 and an active Mason. Dr. Ferguson, also a prominent Mason, had been born in Ireland, had emigrated to Virginia in 1792, and had removed to Louisville in 1803, where he practiced medicine for fifty years. Miller, in 1831, Hall, from 1828 to 1832, and Chambers, a lawyer, in 1836, served as members of the Louisville Board of Councilmen. Hill, Peay, and Lawrence have not been further identified.

[1] President of the Louisville branch of the Bank of the United States, elected in 1823.

INSTRUCTIONS AND DISPATCHES   May 31, 1825

From JAMES H. BENNETT, "Consulate of the United States   Pernambuco [Brazil]." Acknowledges receipt of letter of February 17, agreeably to which he has ceased to perform the functions of his office and submits herewith documents explaining his "justification in the case of the representations made in behalf of John Bayard Kirkpatrick." Asserts that evidence contained in these documents will absolve Bennett "of the charge of having taken advantage of . . . official character in order to procure the arrest of the complainant." ALS. DNA, RG59, Cons. Disp., Pernambuco, vol. 1 (M-T344, R1). Addressed to Adams as Secretary of State; dated "May 1825." Enclosures dated in early June indicate that the letter was mailed somewhat later. Received July 28. The enclosed documents give details of a purported assault upon Bennett by Kirkpatrick, a native of New Jersey.

From GEORGE MOORE, Trieste. Reports the arrest of "General ['Don Juan'] Devereux a Citizen of the United States," on May 16, "by Order of the Austrian Government," and his confinement in Venice. Moore has been unable to learn "the real cause of detention." Devereux, who has been released, informed him of a hint "that it might be a 'mauvais tour' of the Spanish Ambassador at Rome." Notes reports of successful opening of the Greek campaign "both by Land & Sea, especially . . . against the Egyptian Forces." ALS. DNA, RG59, Cons. Disp., Trieste, vol. 1 (M-T242, R1). Received July 30. Moore, a native of Great Britain, had been appointed consul for the United States at Trieste in February, 1821; he served until 1845. On Devereux's arrest, see below, Brown to Clay, June 27, 1825.

Moore's information on the progress of the war in Greece was erroneous. The Greeks had enjoyed brief satisfaction from a successful foray against the Egyptian fleet at Modon on May 12; but Ibrahim Pasha, commander of the Egyptian forces sent the previous winter to aid the Turks, had not permitted this action to divert his operations. The Greeks, who had abandoned their own siege of Patras (Patrai) to reinforce their defenses in Messenia, had been forced to surrender the island of Sfakteria and the fortresses of Pylos and Navarino by May 21. Ibrahim then overran almost the whole of the Morea, while the Greeks fell back for a defense of Missolonghi (Mesolongion), which had been under attack by Turkish forces from the north since late in April.

Ibrahim subsequently campaigned in Syria and served as governor there from 1833 to 1839. He became regent of Egypt in 1848 but died later that year.

APPLICATIONS, RECOMMENDATIONS   May 31, 1825

H[ENRY] JOHNSON, New Orleans, recommends appointment of Paul Lanusse, of New Orleans, as consul at Mexico (City). ALS. DNA, RG59, A. and R. (MR3). Lanusse, a merchant and banker, had been a major in the Territorial militia, justice of the peace (1805), president of the chamber of commerce (1806), and member of the town council (1813). He did not receive the proposed appointment.

ROBERT D. RICHARDSON, New Orleans, withdraws his application for appointment as naval officer at New Orleans and recommends, instead, Ebenezer Fiske, "long . . . an able Merchant of this city." ALS. *Ibid.* (MR2). Addressed to Clay at Lexington. Cf. above, Derbigny to Clay, May 28, 1825, note.

Toasts and Response at Lexington Banquet

[June 1, 1825]

Our respected Guest, beloved fellow citizen and late able representative, Henry Clay—We rejoice in the occasion of expressing to the world, and *emphatically to his enemies,* our undiminished confidence in his incorruptible integrity, and our unqualified approbation of his conduct from his *first* to his *last* most important act, as our representative.

{Mr. CLAY rose and after thanking his constituents for this and many other expressions of kindness and affection towards him, addressed the company at considerable length on the recent election of the Chief Magistrate and the new administration. When he adverted to the base attacks upon his reputation, and the attempts to *bully* him, by the Kremer conspirators,[1] a feeling of indignation against his enemies seemed to pervade the whole company. With respect to his acceptance of Secretary of State, he remarked, that *all* his friends, particularly his Western friends, were of opinion that he ought not to decline it.— Their pressing solicitude on the subject had great weight with him; it could not indeed, under the circumstances in which he was placed, be disregarded. In accepting the appointment therefore he had yielded to a sense of duty, and the strong desire of the West to have a representative in the cabinet. He adverted to the harmony which prevailed between the President and all the members of the administration, their desire to promote alike the interests of every section of the Union, and to administer the government on fair and liberal republican principles.

Volunteer by Mr. CLAY. Lexington and the University[2]—Fayette and its Agriculture.

Formal toast and response, Lexington *Kentucky Reporter*, June 6, 1825; volunteer, Washington *Daily National Intelligencer*, June 20, 1825. Charles Wilkins presided over the affair, assisted by John Bradford, William Morton, Benjamin Merrell, and James Trotter, vice presidents. Merrell, a veteran of the Revolution, had long been a resident of the northern district of Fayette County.

[1] See above, Address, March 26, 1825.   [2] Transylvania.

INSTRUCTIONS AND DISPATCHES   June 1, 1825

From ALEXANDER HAMMETT, Naples. Reports the appointment of "the Count Lucchesi" as "Consul General in the U. States, to reside at Washington." The Count plans to reach Washington at about the time Congress meets, and Hammett thinks "his views are more to penetrate the intentions of the American Government relative to our just claims, than commercial. . . ." ALS. DNA, RG59, Cons. Disp., Naples, vol. 1 (M-T224, R-T1). Addressed to "J. [*sic*] Clay Esqre. Secy. of State"; received September 10 (a copy was received September 9). Count Ferdinando Lucchesi-Palli di Campofranco, after a prominent military career, had been appointed to the American post on April 6. On the claims of the United States against Naples, see above, II, 505n; Clay to Appleton, May 12, 1825.

From SAMUEL LARNED, Santiago de Chile. Transmits pamphlets on the revolution and the present state of the country. ALS. DNA, RG59, Dip. Disp., Chile, vol. 1 (M-T2, R1). Received October 5.

From CONDY RAGUET, Rio de Janeiro. Congratulates Clay on his appointment as Secretary of State and acknowledges having learned unofficially of his own appointment as Chargé des Affaires in Brazil. Explains that his dispatches have been, and will continue to be, designed "to shew the progress of the revolution and the actual condition of affairs" in this country.

Remarks that "Although the Revolution in favour of *Independence* in Brasil, may be considered to have reached its consumation [*sic*], yet the revolution in favour of *Liberty* is yet to be accomplished." Mentions briefly the celebration of the birthday of the King of Portugal (John VI) jointly with the anniversary of the conferring of title upon Dom Pedro as "Perpetual Defender of Brasil"; the subscription to the authorized level of stock for the Bank of Brazil, payment in 1824 of a dividend of 19 per cent, and the probability that it will amount to 10 or 12 per cent this year; the sending of "A Political Agent" to Mecklenburg; the probable arrival of additional troops from Germany, their general unreliability, and the fact that none have yet been sent to the Banda Oriental; news of (Thomas) Cochrane's operations in constituting himself a court of admiralty for condemnation of Portuguese vessels entering Maranham and the "hatred and party spirit between the Europeans and Brazilians" at that place; and the probable effect of news that disaffection exists in both the north and the south of the country. Summarizes information reaching Rio de Janeiro from Montevideo and Buenos Aires concerning the rebellion in the Banda Oriental and describes the military expedition which has been dispatched there. Discusses at length the frustration of efforts of the Emperor and his followers to arouse sentiment for absolute rule; comments that Dom Pedro stands in a "delicate" position, the "moral force" of his government having been weakened both by recent political events and by his elevation of "his favourite mistress" to "*first lady*" of the Court"; but reports, also, mounting support for monarchy, generated partly by "the clamours, respecting the late Presidential election, by some of our editors, who have done infinite mischief to the great cause of liberty and free government, throughout the world, by their intemperate and indiscreet language, which has not only shaken the faith of the Liberals in the stability of our Republick & in the superiority of our form of government, but has furnished materials to the Monarchists, by which they can stregthen [*sic*] their arguments against popular and frequent elections." Relays news received from Upper Peru and Lima on the activities of Bolívar. Expresses a belief that arrival of his (Raguet's) credentials as Chargé is awaited with interest by the Government and notes the appointment of a "Political Agent of this Empire near the Government of Bueynos Ayres." States that American merchants have suffered severe losses in shipments of flour to South America during the past year. LS. DNA, RG59, Cons. Disp., Rio de Janeiro, vol. 2 (M-T172, R3). Received July 27. Extracts published in Manning (arr)., *Diplomatic Correspondence . . . Latin-American Nations*, II, 818-22. On the conflict in the Banda Oriental, see Forbes to Clay, April 22, May 2, 1825; Raguet to Clay, May 12, 20, 1825.

Pedro's "favourite mistress" was the wife of an overseer, named Castro, on one of the Emperor's estates in São Paulo. She was titled the Viscountess of Santos by imperial decree of October 12, 1825.

MISCELLANEOUS LETTERS   June 1, 1825

From C[HARLES] F. MERCER, Leesburg, Loudoun County, Virginia. Transmits a letter, addressed to himself, and a protest, both from James H. Bennett, relative to Bennett's encounter with John B. Kirkpatrick. ALS. DNA, RG59, Cons. Disp., Pernambuco, vol. 1 (M-T344, R1). Addressed to Secretary of State; received June 2, 1825. See above, Bennett to Adams, as Secretary of State, May [31], 1825.

To Robert Breckinridge and Others

FRANKFORT, 2d JUNE, 1825.

Gent.—Messrs. Beall and Breckinridge did me the honour to deliver to me personally the Resolutions adopted by a meeting of my friends at Louisville, on the 30th ult. and your note of the next day, written in conformity to them, inviting me to a public dinner in that place. I will thank you to communicate to the gentlemen, who propose me this distinguished compliment, that I have received, with the most lively sensibility, the testimonies of their kind consideration of me; to assure them that I derive high gratification from the public manifestation of their respect and confidence; and that I shall ever cherish a grateful recollection of the generosity of the motive which has dictated, at this time, the expression of their feelings and opinions. It would give me great pleasure to meet them at Louisville, prior to my return to my official duties; and I indulge the hope I shall be able to have that satisfaction, towards the close of the present month. But at present, such is the nature and variety of my engagements, that I cannot designate a day. Should I not be prevented by circumstances from visiting Louisville, I will in due time apprise you of the day on which it will be in my power to meet my friends.

I offer you gentlemen my respectful acknowledgments, for the very polite and obliging manner in which you have communicated with me on this occasion; and also assurances of the high and cordial esteem which is entertained for you by,

Your obedient servant,   H. CLAY.

Messrs. Robert Breckinridge, Coleman Rogers, James Hughes, N. Berthoud, Tho. M'clanahan [*sic*], Norborne B. Beall.

Lexington *Kentucky Reporter,* August 1, 1825. AL draft, in DLC-HC (DNA, M212, R1), differs slightly in the arrangement but not in the content of the text.

To Samuel H. Woodson and Others

Gentlemen: ASHLAND, 2d June, 1825.

I have received, and accept with much pleasure, the invitation of my fellow citizens of Jessamine county to a public dinner, communicated in your friendly note of the 30th ult. Next to the approbation of those whom I had the honor lately to represent, there is no portion of my countrymen, of the value of whose good opinion I am more sensible, than I am of that of the people of Jessamine. I once had the honor to represent them, and they sustained me, in a critical period of my public life, with a degree of zeal and unanimity, of which I shall ever retain a grateful recollection.[1] The immediate cause of the honorable testimony, which they are now pleased to render, is in entire consonance with their high sense of justice, and the magnanimity of their character. It affords a new incentive to continued and increased exertion on my part, to preserve their esteem.

I thank you, gentlemen, for the flattering and obliging manner in which you have addressed me; and offer my cordial wishes for your individual prosperity.

I am truly, your ob't servant,   H. CLAY.

Messrs.—*S. H. Woodson, W. H. Rainey, C. R. Lewis, Geo. I. Brown, Jo. Chrisman, Reuben Berry, Wm. Caldwell, and A. Logan.*

Lexington *Kentucky Reporter,* June 20, 1825.
[1] See above, I, 484, 716; II, 98-99, 225, 592. In the congressional election of 1816 (see above, II, 182n), Jessamine County had given Clay a majority of 210 votes, while Woodford County had provided a 49-vote majority for Pope. The results in neither of these counties had been decisive, however.

MISCELLANEOUS LETTERS   June 2, 1825

From CHARLES MCALESTER and JOHN LEAMY, Philadelphia. Acknowledge receipt of "a Letter from the Department of 30th Ulto." (see above, Anderson to Secretary of State, March 18, 1825, note), with reference to bills of exchange in the amount of $21,750 to be paid to the claimants in the case of the *Josephine;* state that they had understood that (Richard C.) Anderson (Jr.) had recovered their "claims in full" ($42,000) ; and inquire "how so great a difference has occurred." LS. DNA, RG76, Misc. Claims, Colombia. McAlester signs as president of "the Insurance Co of the State of Penna." On the discrepancy between claim and payment, see below, Clay to Anderson, September 16, 1825.

APPLICATIONS, RECOMMENDATIONS   June 2, 1825

H[ENRY] JOHNSON, New Orleans, recommends Nathaniel Chamberlain for appointment as consul to Mexico (City). ALS. DNA, RG59, A. and R. (MR1). See above, Whittelsey to Clay, April 29, 1825, note.

From Micah Taul and Others

Hon'ble H. Clay,   WINCHESTER, June 3, 1825.
SIR—At a large and highly respectable collection of the citizens of Clarke county, at the court house on the 23d ult., being county court day, the undersigned were appointed a committee, to prepare and deliver to you, a suitable Address approbatory of your conduct, as the representative of this district in the Congress of the U.S. particularly in relation to the election of President; and to invite you to partake of a public dinner, &c.

In the discharge of the duty devolved upon us by our fellow-citizens, we are proud to say, "That in the office, which you have just left, you have not abused our confidence or betrayed our interests." On the contrary, we are free to declare, that in the exercise of your duty under the constitution, as well in relation to the ordinary business of legislation, as in voting for a Chief Magistrate for these U. States, we see that you have been actuated by the same views, which throughout a long course of public service, had marked your conduct—the promotion of the interest, honor and happiness of the Nation.

In the election of President, your situation was peculiar and no doubt embarrassing; it is a source of great satisfaction to us, that all the means, which were used, to awe and influence you, were borne by *you,* as *our* representative ought to have borne them.

Your conduct upon that occasion has been like your whole life, honorable and without reproach. We delight to tell you so.

When we saw the charge first made against you of betraying the interests of your country, in the vote which you would be thereafter called upon to give, we viewed it in no other light than that of ineffable contempt. We saw in it, nothing but the puny effort of blind and misguided zeal or something worse, to overawe a man of whose firmness and character, the authors of that ridiculous charge seem to have been totally ignorant. And we should feel ourselves unworthy of being your constituents, if we did not say to you, in the most decided terms, that we felt and still feel indignant at seeing the name of HENRY CLAY, coupled with the charge of treachery to his Constituents or his Country. No, Sir, you had no occasion to betray your trust, or resort to the mean arts of little politicians, to promote your own views, personal or political.

In yielding to (we have no doubt) the voluntary and unsolicited request of the President to accept the office of Secretary of State, you have manifested your continued devotion to your country.

In the office which you now fill, you have and will continue to have the "cheering countenance" and support of your late constituents, and we hope of a great majority of the people of the Nation, until some better evidence is produced of your having betrayed our interests, than that which is furnished by the Washington conspirators, of "assertions without proof, of inferences without premises."[1]

We should be pained at the separation which has taken place between us, and the consequent loss of your valuable services in the Congress of the United States, if we did not see that you were placed in a situation, where your usefulness to the country, and the great cause of liberty and human happiness, particularly in this Western Hemisphere, can be continued.

We congratulate you, on your safe return, after a long absence to the bosom of your family, at your favorite retreat at Ashland, and by the directions of the citizens of Clarke, invite you to dine *with them*, at Col. Colby H. Taylor's,[2] on Saturday the 11th instant.

In conclusion, we beg leave to say to you, that it affords us great pleasure to have been made the organs of this communication; and to assure you, that the sentiments therein contained, are those which are cherished individually, by Sir, respectfully, Your ob't servants,

M. Taul,	*James Clark,*
James Simpson,[3]	*Hubbard Taylor,*
Samuel Hanson,	*Isaac Cunningham,*
Richard Hawes, Jr.	*Ben. H. Buckner,*[9]
Chilton Allan,[4]	*Samuel M. Taylor,*[10]
Thomas R Moore,[5]	*R. T Dillard,*[11]
John Mills,[6]	*James Anderson,*[12]
James Brasfield,[7]	*Thomas Hart,*[13]
James P. Bullock,[8]	*Thomas Wornall.*
Colby H. Taylor	

Lexington *Kentucky Reporter*, June 20, 1825. Taul, after serving in the War of 1812 and for one term in Congress (1815-1817), had in 1817 removed from Wayne County

to Winchester, Clark County, Kentucky, where he practiced law. Early in 1826 he
moved again, to Winchester, Tennessee.

1 Both the phrases quoted in this paragraph are taken from the Address, above,
March 26, 1825.

2 Colbyville Tavern, located five miles from Winchester on the road to Lexington.

3 Probably the Winchester lawyer, later a judge of the circuit court of Clark County
(1835-1847), judge (part of the time chief justice) of the State court of appeals (1847-
1860), and member of the Kentucky Senate (1861).

4 Winchester lawyer, born in Virginia, member of the State House of Representatives (1811, 1815, 1822, 1830) and Senate (1823-1827). He later became a Representative in Congress (1831-1837) and president of the State Board of Internal Improvements (1837-1839).

5 Clark County stock farmer.   6 Not further identified.

7 Later settled in Platte County, Missouri, where he died in 1839.

8 Veteran of the War of 1812; succeeded his father, David, as clerk of Clark County
court from 1814 until 1850.

9 Winchester merchant and banker, later a resident of Jackson County, Missouri.

10 Of Winchester, for many years clerk of the circuit court of Clark County and,
from 1844 to 1848, State Senator for Montgomery and Clark Counties. He was a son
of Jonathan Taylor, nephew of Edmund, and cousin of George G. Taylor.

11 Ryland T. Dillard, a native of Virginia, who, as a young man, had come to
Winchester, Kentucky, studied law, and (in 1821) commenced practice. In 1825 he
left the law and became a Baptist minister. He became State superintendent of public
instruction from 1843 to 1847 and later owned a large farm in Fayette County.

12 Winchester merchant.   13 Not further identified.

APPLICATIONS, RECOMMENDATIONS   June 3, 1825

ALBERT O. NEWTON, Matanzas (Cuba), although already an applicant for
appointment to the consular office at Matanzas (above, Newton to Clay, May 4,
1825), solicits appointment to the post at Havana. ALS. DNA, RG59, Misc.
Letters (M179, R62).

ASHER ROBBINS, Newport, Rhode Island, recommends George C. Mason, of
Newport, a brother of Mrs. Oliver Hazard Perry, as a purser in the Navy. ALS.
DNA, RG59, A. and R. (MR3). Before marriage Mrs. Perry had been Elizabeth
Champlin Mason.

Toasts and Remarks at Frankfort Banquet

[June 4, 1825]

HENRY CLAY—In giving him to the nation, Kentucky rejoices
that she does not resign her claims on one who has so long, so faithfully, so satisfactorily, served her, and who, in devoting to the advancement of liberal principles, his splendid genius, has shed a
lustre on her name.

When the applause which followed this toast had subsided, *Mr
Clay* rose and thanked the company for the respect shown him,
as well by the occasion as by the sentiment expressed; alluded to
the late circumstances of the presidential election; declared he had
been governed by the good of his country, viewed with the best
lights of his understanding, and that he would excuse the enemies
who had assailed him on that score, because their attacks had brought
forth both public and private testimonials of respect, the pleasure

of which was heightened by their vain efforts to injure and destroy him. He concluded by saying, there were many questions which he thought ought to be settled by long acquiescence and lapse of time. Of this nature was the question relative to the seat of government. Twenty years ago he had been in favor of removing it from Frankfort;[1] but so many interests of our fellow citizens had now been connected with it; so many would be seriously injured without any material public benefit, that he thought it ought not now to be removed. He therefore gave the following toast.

The Capitol—May it be rebuilt on its former site, by the only means compatible with the justice, with the honor and the dignity of the state.[2]

Lexington *Kentucky Reporter,* June 20, 1825. Cf. above, Blair and others to Clay, May 28, 1825; Clay to Harvie and others, May 30, 1825.
[1] See above, I, 314n.   [2] See above, III, 879n, 881n.

INSTRUCTIONS AND DISPATCHES   June 4, 1825

From JOEL R. POINSETT, no. 3, Mexico (City). Reports his reception by the President of the United Mexican States on June 1; comments on the magnitude of the crowd which attended this ceremony in contradistinction to that which, on the preceding day, had witnessed the similar audience accorded to the British Chargé d'Affaires, (Henry George) Ward; and notes that he availed himself "of the opportunity to set the conduct of the United States towards these countries in its true light." Reports, in a coded paragraph, that the British "have made good use of their time and opportunities," that they have won the President and the secretaries of state, treasury, and ecclesiastical affairs to their interest, but that "We have a very respectable party in both houses of Congress and a vast majority of the people in favor of the strictest union with the United States." Encloses copies of his discourse to the President, the latter's reply to it, and the latter's speech on reception of the British Chargé. LS. DNA, RG59, Dip. Disp., Mexico, vol. 1 (M97, R2). Received July 15. Code translation interlined by Daniel Brent. Published in Manning (arr.), *Diplomatic Correspondence . . . Latin-American Nations,* III, 1626. Guadalupe Victoria, whose real name was Manuel Félix Fernández, born in Durango and attached to the revolutionary movement since 1810, had supported the uprising against Itúrbide in 1823 and served as first President of the Republic from 1824 to 1829.

From WILLIAM SHALER, Marseilles, no. [84]. Notes that, at the time of his departure from Algiers, May 11, United States relations with that country rested "upon the most safe and amicable footing and without the slightest appearance of any danger of interruption"; also that he intends to return to his post in November. Reports information which he has learned in Marseilles that an American vessel, under the United States flag, sailed as a transport in the Egyptian flotilla to the Morea "in the grand expedition which sailed . . . last year . . . under the command of Ibrahim Pashaw," and that, after the reverses suffered by that fleet, the ship "returned to Alexandria and Sailed again for the Morea in Company with about thirty Sail of other transports and vessels of war." Comments that "it obviously tends to tarnish the purity of our Flags and to injure the national character in this part of the world." ALS. DNA, RG59,

Cons. Disp., Algiers (M23, R-T13). On Egyptian participation in the Turkish war in Greece, see above, Moore to Clay, May 31, 1825; on the response to Shaler's information, see below, Clay to Somerville, September 6, 1825.

From J[OHN] ADAMS SMITH, London, no. 1. Transmits copies of three treaties, with brief comment on each, concluded in February between Great Britain and, respectively, Buenos Aires, Russia, and Sweden. (Charles R.) Vaughan will embark in a few days for the United States. ALS. DNA, RG59, Dip. Disp., Great Britain (M30, R28). Addressed to Secretary of State; received July 22. On the new British treaties, see above, Raguet, to Secretary of State, March 11, 1825; Rush to Secretary of State, April 4, 1825; and Hughes to Clay, July 10, 1825.

From W[ILLIAM] TUDOR, Lima, no. 30. States that Callao still holds out; cites trouble caused by parties of banditti composed of former Spanish soldiers; refers to an independence movement in Upper Peru; expresses an opinion that Bolívar's presence "is necessary to the quiet of Peru, there are two [sic] many symptoms to shew that it will be torn by factions the moment he leaves it." Cites the recent dismissal of a court of justice "on account of an unjust decree against some English property" and suggests that this "may be the means of saving the ship General Brown & brig Elizabeth Ann, which have been for upwards of four months in a state of detention. . . ." ALS. DNA, RG59, Cons. Disp., Lima, vol. 1 (M154, R1). Addressed to Secretary of State; received November 1. Extracts published in Manning (arr.), *Diplomatic Correspondence . . . Latin-American Nations*, III, 1782-83. On the vessels *General Brown* and *Elizabeth Ann*, see below, Tudor to Clay, June 8, 1825.

MISCELLANEOUS LETTERS June 4, 1825

From JOSEPH PEABODY and GIDEON TUCKER, Salem. Acknowledge receipt of a bill of exchange, "drawn by the Colombian Government," as payment of their claim in the case of the *Tiger*. LS. DNA, RG76, Misc. Claims, Colombia. Cf. above, Anderson to Secretary of State, March 18, 1825.

APPLICATIONS, RECOMMENDATIONS June 5, 1825

WILLIAM L. S. DEARING, "Near.Huntsville," acknowledges receipt of Clay's letter of April 21 (not found), expresses gratitude "for the Courtesy . . . extended" in it, explains that (Gabriel) Moore erroneously inferred (above, Moore to Clay, May 29, 1825) a "probable acquaintence" of Clay with one of Dearing's relatives, and asks that Clay "will have the goodness to absolve him [Moore] of error from that cause in regard to the appointment which was a part of the subject of a former [com]munication [not found]." Renews application for the position to be filled "when the present incumbent receives the appointment under this state of which" Dearing had written. ALS. DNA, RG59, A. and R. (MR2). Cf. below, Crawford to Clay and Tait to Clay, both September 25, 1825.

To Mathew Carey

Dr Sir   Ashland 6h. June 1825
   I received your letter of the 18h. May[1] with the Copies of your

papers containing an examination of the later British doctrines as they have been unfolded by Mr. Huskisson, in their new policy.[2] I was glad to see you so usefully employed in exposing the mischieveous tendency of that policy, as applied to the condition of the U. States, although its propriety may be admitted in regard to England. It is based upon the selfish principle, which has ever guided British Statesmen.

I have put your valuable papers in a course of distribution.

I remain faithfy Yr. ob. Servant   H CLAY

ALS. ViU. Addressed on attached sheet: "Mathew Carey Esqr. Philadelphia."
[1] Not found.
[2] The papers, issued as "Hamilton—Eighth Series," I-VIII, were first printed in the Washington *Daily National Intelligencer*, April 15, 27, May 6, 14, 17, 27, June 9, 20, 1825. The work was subsequently republished, again under the pseudonym, "Hamilton," as *Cursory Views of the Liberal and Restrictive Systems of Political Economy; and of Their Effects in Great Britain, France, Russia, Prussia, Holland, and the United States, With an Examination of Mr. Huskisson's System of Duties on Imports,* By a Citizen of Philadelphia (2d. ed., enl. and improved, Philadelphia, 1826).
On William Huskisson's program regarding British colonial policy, see above, Rush to Secretary of State, March 26, 1825, note. Huskisson's speech of March 25, 1825, had covered broader ground, proposing a revision of tariff policy toward a general and drastic reduction of import duties, together with the encouragement of shipping and navigation by repeal or marked reduction of quarantine and stamp duties and of fees upon ships trading in the colonies or registering with British consular officials abroad. Huskisson, *Speeches . . .* , II, 327-62.

Power of Attorney to Felix Grundy

[June 6, 1825]

I Henry Clay sole acting Exor of James Morrison deceased, do hereby authorize Felix Grundy Esq. of the State of Tennessee to recieve [*sic*] from Robt. Purdy[1] of said state Seventy Dollars in the notes of the Nashville bank in full satisfaction of a claim on sd. Purdy by sd. Morrisons Exor, and to execute a full reciept for sd. claim upon the payment of sd. $70—And whereas the sd. Purdy apprehends that a note may have been given for said claim to sd. Morrison or some other person, the sd. Grundy is hereby further authorized for me as acting Exor of sd. Morrison to execute a writing of indemnity to sd. Purdy, covenanting to save him harmliss [*sic*] from sd. supposed note or other writing, if it should hereafter be enforced against him—Witness my hand & seal this 6th. day of June 1825—

H. CLAY sole acting Exor
of J. Morrison deceased {LS}

Witness present
Robt. Scott

DS, in Scott's hand. NcU.
[1] Purdy, who had entered the army as an ensign, from Pennsylvania, in 1792, had been discharged as a colonel in 1815, had been appointed Federal marshal for the District of Western Tennessee in 1820, and was reappointed to this position quadrennially thereafter until his death in 1831.

To Micah Taul and Others

Gentlemen: ASHLAND, 7th June, 1825.

I have received and perused, with strong emotions of gratitude, the address which you did me the honor, on the third instant, to transmit to me, in conformity to the previous resolutions of my fellow citizens of Clarke County; and also the resolutions themselves, and the proceedings of the public meeting at which they were adopted. I shall ever regard and cherish these as among the most honourable and gratifying testimonials with which I have ever been favoured. They emanate from a people, whose sense of justice, intelligence and patriotism I have long known. To learn in a manner so unequivocal, that my humble endeavors to serve my country, and especially those which I exerted on a late memorable occasion, in the H. of Representatives of the U. States, have received the approbation of such a people, affords me inexpressible satisfaction. I never doubted that my constituents would display their accustomed magnanimity in sustaining their representative against a wicked, malignant and presumptuous conspiracy, who vainly hoped to deprive him of their affection and confidence. But their cordiality, unanimity and enthusiasm greatly exceeded my fondest expectations. These friendly demonstrations increase much the regret which I felt in the dissolution of the connexion which has so long subsisted between us. The circumstances, however in which I was placed left me no option. My friends in Congress, I believe with one voice, advised me to accept the office which the President did me the honor to tender me. They thought that, if I declined it one of the principal objects of the conspirators would be accomplished. Other members of Congress, whom I had not the good fortune to rank my political friends, concurred in the opinion, that I ought not to refuse the Department of State. If I had have declined it, the very persons who most wished that determination, would have immediately charged me with a want of confidence in the Chief Magistrate, to whose election I had felt it my duty to contribute. I am rejoiced to find that my constituents approve of the decision which I made.

I pray you gentlemen to accompany my grateful acknowledgments to my late constituents of Clarke with a communication of the sentiments and views here exposed; to assure them, that it will ever be an object with me of anxious solicitude to continue to merit their good opinion; and to allow me to seize this opportunity of expressing to you individually the high personal regard and esteem of
         Your faithful and obedient servant,   H. CLAY.
Messrs. M. Taul, James Simpson, Sam. Hanson, Richard Hawes Jun,

Chilton Allan, Thomas R. Moore, John Mills, James Brassfield, James Bullock, Colby H. Taylor, James Clarke, Hubbard Taylor, Isaac Cunningham, Benj. H. Buckner, Sam. M. Taylor, R. T. Dillard, Jas. Anderson, Thomas Hart and Tho. Wornall. *Com'tee* &c. &c. &c.

Lexington *Kentucky Reporter,* June 20, 1825.

Property Deed, Executors of Thomas Hart, Jr., to Trustees of Louisa Hart Taylor

[June 7, 1825]

[Eleanor Hart, executrix, and Henry Clay and John W. Hunt, surviving executors of Thomas Hart, Jr., transfer to Eleanor Hart, John J. Crittenden and George W. Anderson, as trustees for Hart's youngest daughter, Louisa A. B. Hart, who has married Edmund H. Taylor, property to secure Hart's legacy "to her and her heirs," he having devised that, when any one of his daughters marries, her portion of his estate "shall be assigned to her and one half of such portion shall be vested in trustees to secure the same to her and her heirs." The executors transfer to the trustees seven slaves, "with their increase," and "such an interest in one undivided fourth part of the property" in Lexington bought by Hart from (Samuel) Smith and (Wilson Cary) Nicholas and Thomas D. Owings, and occupied now by Robert Wickliffe, Bruce and Gratz, and John McCracken, "as will when sold produce the sum of three thousand dollars." The transaction is agreed to by Taylor. Deed signed by Eleanor Hart, Clay, Hunt, and Anderson; recorded June 7, 1825, in the office of the Fayette County clerk.]

Fayette County Court, Deed Book Z, 252-54. Louisa Hart had married Taylor, of Frankfort, on October 26, 1824. Probably a grandson of Edmund and nephew of George G. Taylor, he was at this time a clerk in the Bank of the Commonwealth and later became a successful banker. The property to which reference is made in this deed was that assigned to Thomas P. Hart, above, II, 313-14. Cf. also, *ibid.,* 616. McCracken was a farmer on the Winchester Road at the edge of Lexington.

Property Deed, Executors of Thomas Hart, Jr., to Alexander Black

[June 7, 1825]

[Eleanor Hart, executrix, and Henry Clay and John W. Hunt, executors of Thomas Hart, Jr., deceased, and Edmund H. Taylor, convey to Alexander Black 39 acres, 107 poles in Fayette County "on the waters of Elkhorn." The property has been sold by Taylor (husband of Hart's daughter, Louisa), with the assent of the court, to Black for $20.18 an acre. Signed by Eleanor Hart, Clay, Hunt, and Taylor; recorded in the office of the Fayette County clerk, June 7, 1825.]

Fayette County Court, Deed Book Z, 249-50.

Property Deed, Executors of Thomas Hart, Jr., to John and James Wardlaw

[June 7, 1825]

[Eleanor Hart, executrix, and Henry Clay and John W. Hunt, surviving executors of Thomas Hart, Jr., deceased, and Edmund H. Taylor and Louisa his wife, convey to John and James Wardlaw of Fayette County, 74 acres, 13 poles of land on the "waters of South Elkhorn." The property has been sold by Taylor (husband of Hart's daughter, Louisa), with the assent of the court, to the Wardlaws for $20.18 an acre. Signed by Eleanor Hart, Clay, Hunt, and Taylor; recorded in the office of the Fayette County clerk, June 7, 1825.]

Fayette County Court, Deed Book Z, 248-49. The Wardlaw brothers lived on the Versailles Road, five miles from Lexington. James was probably the doctor who had practiced in Shelbyville, Kentucky, at the turn of the century, had been postmaster there from 1801 to 1802, and had represented Shelby County in the State House of Representatives during the session of 1803-1804.

From Andrew Erwin

Mr. H. Clay   Shelbyville Ten. June 7th. 1825.

Sir— This will be handed to you by Mr. Thomas G. Bradford,[1] a citizen for many years of Tennessee, and late Editor of the Nashville Clarion a paper you may have seen— his reputation as a man of business and of correct deportment, warrant [sic] me in Seconding a desire he has, to obtain a clerkship in one of the departments at Washington.[2] Several of your friends, as well as myself would be gratified if you could give him a situation in your office or assist him in procuring one in some other department.

I am respectfully your Obt. Svt.   ANDREW ERWIN

[Endorsement on cover][3]

To be sent to Mr. Rush the Secy of the Treasury   H C.

ALS. DNA, RG59, A. and R. (MR1).
[1] Bradford, son of Fielding Bradford, had helped establish a succession of newspapers (with each of which he maintained only a brief connection): the Georgetown (District of Columbia) Columbian Repository (1803), Chillicothe Ohio Herald (1805), and Huntsville (Alabama) Madison Gazette (1812). In 1808 he had purchased from his cousin, Benjamin J. Bradford, the Nashville Clarion (title varies), which he had published until he sold it in September, 1820.
[2] He did not receive an appointment.   [3] AEI by Clay.

MISCELLANEOUS LETTERS   June 7, 1825

From ARCHIBALD GRACIE, New York. Acknowledges receipt of Clay's letter of April 4, 1825, concerning the cargo of the schooner *Mechanic;* encloses copies of documents showing that the Hope Insurance Company (of New York) has also paid a claim in this case and wishes this claim presented with that of the Atlantic Insurance Company. ALS. DNA, RG59, Misc. Letters (M179, R62).

Toast at Barbecue in Woodford County, Kentucky

[June 8, 1825]

Our Guest and late Representative, HENRY CLAY, the eloquent and enlightened Statesman—His distinguished services in the cause of freedom, his indefatigable exertions in promoting Internal Improvements and Domestic Manufactures; and his recent vote in the Presidential Election, entitle him to our warmest approbation.[1]

Lexington *Kentucky Reporter,* June 13, 1825. "On Wednesday last a Barbecue was given to Mr Clay . . . by the citizens of Woodford county. The company was large and respectable, there being present 500 gentlemen or more. . . . The table was spread under an arbour in a beautiful grove adjoining the town of Versailles. . . ."
[1] Clay responded by addressing "the company in his usual strains of eloquence, and with complete success as to those points of difference which were supposed to exist between himself and some, at least, of his late constituents." *Ibid.*

From John Holmes

Dear Sir   Alfred[1] 8 June 1825.

I have as far as my time would permit Attended to the subjects of enquiry in your letter of the 9th ult.[2] I was in the house of representatives when the navigation act of the 15th of May 1820 was passed[3] and voted against it. That act however, passed with great unanimity, there being but sixteen in the house and one in the senate against it.[4] The principal provisions were to exclude British vessels from the ports of the United States, coming from ports closed to American vessels, and to prohibit our own vessels from importing from the British American colonies any articles which were not the product of those colonies. This Act was retaliatory and its prohibitions continued in force until the act of parliament of[5] opened our trade with certain specific ports in the West Indies, and the North American colonies, whereupon the President by his proclamation[6] opened the ports of the United States to British vessels coming from the places specified in the act of parliament. The act of the first March 1823[7] sanctions a direct trade with the colonies in British vessels to and from the specified ports in the products of the colonies and authorized the President on satisfactory proof that we are admitted in those ports on the same footing as British subjects to accord to them the same privileges. The British government however, never having done this, we continue to exact the alien duty.

You inquire "inasmuch as we employ much the greatest amount of tonnage in that trade do we not suffer most by the continuation of those alien duties"? It is impossible to determine what would have been the effect had Great Britain relaxed her colonial system to the extent anticipated by the act of the first of March 1823. A perfect reciprocity is what we have ever been willing to accede to. What provisions would make this trade perfectly reciprocal is a point not easily settled. Our claim to trade with her colonies on the same footing as her own subjects, without an equivalent, would be unreasonable. To consider these colonies as a part of her dominions and, as we permit her to trade in all the ports of the United States, consequently, we should have the corresponding right to a trade with her colonies, is losing sight of the local situation of these colonies. Had *we* colonies in her immediate vicinity, our cases would be similar. That Great Britain, therefore, should open to us a free trade with *all* the ports of *all* her American colonies is more than we should exact, and more than we have ever expected. Their vicinity and even contiguity to the United States, their comparatively limited means in tonnage, mechanics seamen &c. and her distance from them, and above all our *enterprise,* would give us advantages to which Great Britain would never accede. Consequently, we, in our act of the first March of 1823 established as a rule of reciprocity, that her colonists should be admitted into *all* the ports of the United States, on the same terms as our own citizens, on her according to us the same privileges in those only which were specified in that act. And if I recollect rightly the act of parliament not only limited the *ports* but the *Articles of Commerce.* In answer to this part of your enquiry then, there can be no doubt, that a free and unlimited trade with the British American colonies would be very advantageous to the United States. How far the advantages of our situation, our means, and our enterprise, would justify a yielding to her colonists an unlimited trade with us upon a concession of a limited trade with them and to what limitations as to places and articles we ought to accede, I must leave to the negotiator who will endeavor to obtain as good terms as he can. By recurring to the statements of the commerce and navigation of the United States made by the Secretary of the Treasury on the 16th February last[8] according to the provisions of the act of 10th January 1820,[9] we find that during the year ending 30th September 1824 our imports from the British West Indies were

	2.758.067.
And from her American colonies	705.931.
making	3.463.998.

Of this 3.060.097 was in American and 403.676 in foreign vessels.

Our exports to these colonies were during the same period 3.546.732 of which 3.361.572 were in American, and 185.160. in foreign vessels. So that of the exports and imports more than 7/8 was in American vessels.

By an average of arrivals and departures during the same period we find that the tonnage employed was, American 144.123 foreign 13.640, a little more than 9/10 American. It further appears that of the exports to the British West Indies and their other American colonies being 3.546.732, 3.523.810 is of domestic growth and manufacture.

With these facts before us, the question is presented "would not the competition of our tonnage with that of Great Britain be improved by the mutual abolition of these alien duties?" Considering the discrimination of each nation as exactly countervailing that of the other, there can be no doubt that a mutual abolition would give us the decided advantage. The *commerce* relieved from the alien duty would be more valuable to the seller and less expensive to the buyer, as both would probably in the course of trade share in the benefit of this abolition. Should this removal of these restrictions be general, embracing all Colonial ports and all articles the growth of the colonies and the United States respectively, we should be by far the gainers. Should this reciprocity be limited to comport with the Act of the first of March 1823, it would benefit our existing commerce, and I do not see, how it would injuriously affect our tonnage.

In this, what benefit Great Britain would gain in our ports, we should experience in hers. We having the tonnage now actually engaged, and the advantage of proximity and enterprise, could engage in the Competition with facilities which would countervail all the limitations with which it would be encumbered. Notwithstanding our convention with Great Britain places the parties on a perfect equality so far as regards the United States and the British European dominions[10] the American tonnage in the trade bears a proportion to that of Great Britain as 140.000 to 42.000. In any commercial regulation established on the basis of equality we can successfully compete with any nation on earth.

I have as little doubt as to your other question "whether it would be adviseable to consent to such abolition, leaving Great Britain free to give the preference, for which she contends to the produce of her own Colonies?" I think it would not. Commercial restrictions for purposes of coercion should never be hastily *adopted* nor *abandoned*. I was among the last to come into this measure, and I would be the last to *retract*. Besides it has been long in operation, your commerce has conformed to it, and your tonnage is engaged.

Open your ports to the colonists, with the same privilege as your own citizens while they have the preference *at home,* and your shipping interest would engage in a vain and fruitless competition, with no prospects of success. The influx of British tonnage would reduce the freights and consequently give a *temporary* improvement to the value of the article in the hand of the grower or manufacturer. This however would be *but temporary.* The American shipping would be driven from the trade, the carriers would be exclusively British, and having no others to compete with, freights would assume their former prices, and the articles of export and import settle to their ordinary standard.

You ask "how is the British doctrine to be distinguished from that relative to the coasting trade, or from their corresponding pretension to have the sugar and molasses of the British West Indies admitted into the United States on the same terms with those of Louisiana and Florida?" I confess I can see no analogy in the cases. We do not claim of Great Britain to carry on her coasting trade. We propose to trade with that part of her dominions in our immediate vicinity on terms of reciprocity. We will permit all her subjects to trade with us from that portion of her dominions on precisely the same terms that she will permit us to trade with them. She is apprehensive that we can supply them and obtain their produce cheaper than she can. The prospect of her North American colonies supplying her West Indies, it is believed, she has about abandoned. That she has the right to exclude us from this trade, or any other trade, not conceded by treaty, no one doubts. And we have the corresponding right to countervail every regulation which is to build up the trade of the Colonies at our expense. That the colonies suffer more than we do, without a corresponding advantage to the Mother country admits I think of no doubt. It appears to me that the law of 1st. March 1823, goes as far as we ought, & this I think should be our *ultimatum.* As to the admission of British sugars on the same terms as those of Louisiana, it would be an arrogant pretension. *We* have *no* colonies, and Louisiana being one of the United States is included within the Commercial Convention and its commerce with Great Britain is like that of every other state in the Union. If there were any thing in this pretence the West India sugars must be admitted free of duty, and the same reasoning would apply to other articles transported from one state to another. It is no concern of ours on what terms Great Britain regulates the intercourse between different portions of her own dominions, and as little of hers how the sugars of Louisiana are admitted at Boston. (To us her colonists are foreigners. As foreigners and a part of her dominions we expect to trade with them on terms of reciprocity giving them in the ports of both the parties an equal chance with ourselves. Permit me however to enquire whether *at this time,* negotiations on this subject ought to be pressed? The complaints of the Colonists have been heard in Parliament with feelings which indicate a willingness to relieve them. Should *we* be in haste to remove the pressure, the Mother country might with safety refuse to relax and the colonists would obtain at our expense, what by a little delay they might obtain from parliament. Should an act of parliament be passed in the spirit of ours, the President has power by proclamation to place this trade on equitable ground. You may perhaps entertain the opinion that this last suggestion is gratuitous and obtrusive. But as your enquiries are broad and appear to be made with that frankness for which you are so much distinguished, the answers are given in the same spirit. It is to be sure a superficial view of the subject, but as it is, it is submitted to your candour, by yours very affectionately.   J HOLMES

LS. DNA, RG59, Misc. Letters (M179, R62).   1 Maine.
2 See above, Clay to Smith, May 9, 1825, note.   3 See above, III, 729, note 21.
4 The final House vote was not reported. Cf. U.S. H. of R., *Journal*, 16 Cong., 1 Sess., 526-27. For the Senate vote, as stated, see U.S. Senate, *Journal*, 16 Cong., 1 Sess., 302.   5 Date omitted; see above, III, 729, note 21.
6 Dated August 24, 1822. James D. Richardson (comp.), *A Compilation of the Messages and Papers of the Presidents, 1789-1897* (10 vols., [Washington], 1901), II, 184-85.   7 See above, III, 729, note 21.
8 "Letter from the Secretary of the Treasury, Transmitting Statements of the Commerce and Navigation of the United States, during the Year Ending on the 30th September, 1824," *Sen. Docs.*, 18 Cong., 2 Sess., no. 33.
9 Incorrectly cited. The act had been passed February 10, 1820. 3 *U.S. Stat.*, 541-43.
10 See above, II, 57-59.

INSTRUCTIONS AND DISPATCHES   June 8, 1825

From W[ILLIAM] TUDOR, Lima, no. 31, "Confidential." Reports that "the most important event that has occurred here, is the retirement of Mr Hères from the Ministry."

States that the ship *General Brown,* of New York, "which arrived here some months since from Gibraltar with some Spanish passengers & partly laden on Spanish account, was this week cleared, . . . so far as the property was neutral, which was the case of the Ship a part of her cargo on account of the owners, and a part shipped for account of English merchants." The case has been appealed, "and another long delay will probably occur before a final decision." The case of the *Elizabeth Ann,* of Philadelphia, "which arrived soon after, from Gibraltar with goods on neutral account, except a part consigned to a merchant here now an emigrant to Callao, is still under trial."

Encloses copies of correspondence in which it was agreed that American merchants should pay five dollars a month, "towards the expenses of the police in the City," in lieu of the discriminating duty levied for failure to comply with the requirement of military service. Refers to difficulties encountered in execution of consular duties; cites the need for reformation of the conduct of American seamen as well as for amelioration of their treatment; and complains of never having received acknowledgment of his letters. ALS.

DNA, RG59, Cons. Disp., Lima, vol. 1 (M154, R1). Addressed to Secretary of State; received November 1.

Tomás de Hères, born in Angostura, Venezuela, had at first supported the Spanish forces against the revolutionaries but in 1820 had transferred his efforts to the latter. Rising rapidly through a succession of governmental posts under Bolívar, Hères in 1825 had been named a general and appointed Minister of State of Peru, from which post he shortly retired because of ill health. He later served as a deputy and senator in the legislature and for brief periods as a provincial governor.

The case of the *General Brown* was not finally resolved until 1847, when, in accordance with awards provided for under a claims convention signed with Peru in 1841, the owners of the vessel and cargo, Henry Eckford, "Porter" (probably Peter) Harmony, and G(ardiner) G(reene) and S(amuel) S(haw) Howland, were allotted a sum of $201,768.18. Moore, *History and Digest of . . . International Arbitrations. . . ,* V, 4591-93, 4598, 4605.

Eckford, a native of Scotland, who had attained prominence as a shipbuilder in New York during the War of 1812 and at the Brooklyn Navy Yard from 1817 to 1820, had broadened his interests to include a directorship of the New York office of the Bank of the United States from 1823 through 1825 and active support of William H. Crawford's presidential candidacy in 1824. On Harmony, cf. below, Burton to Clay, November 23, 1825.

Under awards growing out of the same claims convention as that covering the *General Brown,* owners of the *Elizabeth Ann* and its cargo received $3,950.50 as compensation for damage to the vessel, liability to a charterer, detention, injury, and partial loss of their property.

MISCELLANEOUS LETTERS   June 8, 1825

From RICHARD W. HABERSHAM, Savannah. Transmits copies of an affidavit by Francis Flournoy and of the presentment of the grand jury of the United States Circuit Court for the District of Georgia (concerning the murder of three Creek Indian chiefs by a band of Indians, accompanied by one white man, in protest against the cession of Indian lands). ALS. DNA, RG59, Misc. Letters (M179, R62). Habersham, United States attorney for the District of Georgia, resigned early in 1827 in a dispute over the conflicting authority of the Federal Government and the State of Georgia, involving the Creek land cession (cf. below, Clay to Southard, July 3, 1825, note). He was a member of Congress from 1839 until his death in 1842.

On June 17, 1825, Daniel Brent, in Clay's absence, acknowledged receipt of Habersham's letter and reported that it had been referred to the President. Copy. DNA, RG59, Dom. Letters, vol. 21, p. 97 (M40, R19).

From ROBERT CRITTENDEN, Louisville. Presents a claim for horses lost "During the Seminole campaign" (see above, II, 612, note) by the company of Kentucky troops which he commanded and which "was attached by a *general order* to Genl Jacksons person as a Life Guard"; notes that he is "Relying confidently on the justice and even Kindness of the President. . . ." ALS. DNA, RG107, Letters Received (Unentered), H-Misc. 1824. Endorsed by clerk: "Respectfully referred to the Secy of War."

APPLICATIONS, RECOMMENDATIONS   June 8, 1825

SAMUEL SMITH, Baltimore, recommends William Wright, son of Governor

(Robert) Wright, for appointment as consul at Rio de Janeiro. ALS. DNA, RG59, Misc. Letters (M179, R62). See below, Clay to Wright, September 14, 1825.

From John Mosely and Others

Jessamine County, June 9, 1825.

Dear Sir—The undersigned a committee on behalf of the citizens of Nicholasville and Jessamine county, are authorised to invite you to a Public Dinner at Capt. Coger's,[1] as a further testimonial of their high respect and entire approbation of your political course as their former representative; and more particularly as it respects your decisive, patriotic, and magnanimous firmness in the late Presidential election.

It is with peculiar pleasure, sir, that we are enabled to seize upon the present opportunity to express our unreserved gratitude for your highly distinguished past services, and to give a grateful token of our approbation of your conduct in the last session of Congress. We would have deemed such an expression of sentiment as altogether unnecessary at any other time than the present, (knowing that Kentucky has heretofore entertained the highest sentiments of regard and respect for you,) were it not attempted to attach impurity of motive, and to disseminate calumny against you;[2] and that upon grounds which we deem false, and most ungenerous. We are further instructed to say, sir, that you have our entire confidence, both as it regards your integrity and the purity of your motives; and that it is our sincere hope, that your present elevation may only prove a prelude to a higher and more honorable one, so long as you continue to be the able defender of virtuous liberty and equal rights, and that in your temporary separation from us, you may carry this along with you as a testimony of our warmest affection, and most earnest wishes for your present welfare, and future prosperity. With sentiments of the highest respect and esteem, we are your most obedient servants,

John Mosely,	*Geo: W. Broun* [*sic*],
John Barkley,	*Joseph Crockett,*
Thos S. Smith,	*Hugh Chrisman,*
Jeremiah Frazier,	*Thompson Howard,*
Nathaniel Dunn,	*John Whip* [*sic*],
Thos: T Coger,	*John Cunningham,*
Samuel Barkley,	*Archd: Young,*
Benjn: Bradshaw,	*David Steele,*
Julius C. Howard,	*William Clarke,*
Daniel B. Price,	*James Williams.*[3]

The Hon: H. Clay.

P.S.—You will please to select a day which may be most convenient

to yourself, after the day on which you will dine in Nicholasville.[4]
Yours &c.   *Committee.*

Lexington *Kentucky Reporter,* June 20, 1825. Mosely, born in Buckingham County, Virginia, and a veteran of the Revolutionary War, had settled in Jessamine County around 1793.

[1] Thomas T. Cogar conducted a large trade and shipping business at Cogar's landing (Brooklyn) on the Kentucky River. Much later (1867-1871) he represented Jessamine County in the State legislature.

[2] See above, Clay to Gales and Seaton, January 30, 1825, note.

[3] George Washington Brown, who later this year became the son-in-law of Hugh Chrisman, served as representative of Jessamine County in the Kentucky legislative sessions of 1829 and 1832. Cunningham, a colonel of militia, was a State representative in 1828. Clarke became a State senator from 1838 to 1842. Young was postmaster of Nicholasville. The Barkleys and Howards, Smith, Frazier, Dunn, Bradshaw, Chrisman, Whips, Steele, and Williams have not been further identified.

[4] See above, Woodson and others to Clay, May 30, 1825.

APPLICATIONS, RECOMMENDATIONS   June 9, 1825

LEWIS CASS, Detroit, recommends that publication of the laws be given to Edward D. Ellis and the Monroe *Michigan Sentinel;* cites the need for such publication in the territories. LS. DNA, RG59, P. and D. of L. On July 5, 1825, in the absence of the Secretary of State, Daniel Brent replied to Cass, announcing a decision to appoint Ellis as publisher of the laws and requesting that he be given this information. Copy. DNA, RG59, Dom. Letters, vol. 21, p. 109 (M40, R19).

Ellis, born in New York, began publication of the *Michigan Sentinel,* the first journal south of Detroit in Michigan Territory, on June 24, 1825. He sold the establishment in 1836. Ellis, as a Whig, was a member of the Territorial Senate in 1835; but running as a Democratic candidate for the governorship in 1837, he was defeated. A member of the State constitutional convention of 1835, he led the movements for provision of common schools and township libraries.

SAMUEL SMITH, Baltimore, presents William Wright, "Son of our good friend Govr [Robert] Wright," and recommends him for appointment as consul to Rio de Janeiro; adds, as a postscript: "Maryland has very few of the Consuls." ALS. DNA, RG59, A. and R. (MR4). See below, Clay to Wright, September 14, 1825.

From Philip S. Markley

Dear Sir   Norristown June 10th. 1825.

Your friendly letter of the 7th. of April in reply to mine[1] I received some time the latter end of Apl., after my return home from attending the Courts, and should have answered it immediately, but was apprehensive a letter would fail reaching you previous to your departure from Washington for your residence in Kentuckey— No one is more sensible than my self of the sincerity of the friendly feelings, expressed in your last letter towards Pennsylvania, and I hope providence may preserve to our Country your life, to witness the auspicious period, when the honest yeomanry of Pennsylvania, will have an opportunity afforded of evincing their gratitude, for your able and indefatigable exertions in support of those great measures of national policy identified with her interest and prosperity.

Your address to your constituents[2] has made a very favourable impression on the minds of the people of Penna,   all the Editors of the numerous papers printed in the City of Phila., with the exception of the Columbian Observer and Franklin Gazette,[3] have given it an insertion in their papers, and it has found a place generally in all the papers printed through out the interior of the State— Many of the Editors who had previously to the appearance of your address expressed an unfavourable opinion respecting the course you pursued in regard to the Presidential question have since retracted their hasty opinions, and become your faithful friends, and zealous champions— there is no section of the State your address has made a greater impression than in the German settlements,   it has been published in nearly all the German papers,   a highly respectable German residing in an adjacent County informed me a few days ago that they were about getting it published in the German language in his County in pamphlet form   the Germans of Penna are your friends and they are a people when their confidence and friendship is fixed, it is almost immoveable, and not easily to be shaken: they constitute the great bane of the democracy of the "Key stone of the federal arch"— Governor Shulze[4] still continues to be your friend and the well wisher of the Administration of the General Government— *Our old friend* Kremer[5] is talked of by the violent partizens [*sic*] of Jackson as the Candidate to oppose Shulze at the expiration of his present Term which does not take place until next October a year— this opposition is thus early started with Kremer as their humble instrument, with a view of keeping up the embers of military enthusiasm in Pennsylvania, to bear on the next Presidential election—but you may confidently rely on it, that all their schemes and plans will prove abortive, and whilst the administration of the General Government pursues the track commenced, it cannot fail to inspire confidence and will not receive the support of Penna but will be sustained by the whole nation—

I presume you have perused Mr Inghams Address[6]— it has obtained him verry [*sic*] little credit in the State; Since its appearance he has fallen much in public estimation,   it contains neither pith nor marrow, but a degree of bitterness and malignancy truly characteristick of the *man*— in the Congressional District which he represents I have ascertained from a recent excursion through parts of it, that he has received a political defection from which he will not soon recover— so much so, that he & his friends have become alarmed respecting their future hopes of political aggrandisement—

I am satisfied my self from information received from the best sources throughout the State that Mr Ingham's political standing is considerably lower than ever it was in Pennsylvania— in my District where there are five public journals printed his address has been published in none of them, but all have contained editorial remarks of reproof & disapprobation of his course & conduct   The general impression throughout the State respecting his address is, that it is wanting in skill, temperation, good feeling & discretion & instead of refuting completely justifies what you said of him— it has not been generally published in the republican papers throughout the State—

The appointment of Mr King[7] to England has been better received in Pennsylvania than I had anticipated— his conduct during the war and his election to the United States Senate by the republican Legislature of the State of New York, recconciled [sic] the Democratic feeling of Penna very much in favour of the appointment

I some time ago gave a letter of introduction to Mr Paterson[8] to you— he is a promising young man,   any thing you can do for him in the Western Country I would esteem [. . .][9] particular favour—

[. . .][10] friends in Penna have expressed a hope that on yo[ur return] to Washington City this summer you will pass through this State and take Harrisburg, Reading, Norristown, and Phila in your way   I assure you nothing would be a higher gratification to your friends than the realization of such a hope, which would afford to them the opportunity of testing [sic] the sincerity of their friendship and their unlimited confidence in your political integrity— should [sic] be happy to hear from you as soon as convenient   I am extremely anxious to learn the political feelings of the West in relation to Mr Adams & more particularly as it respects yourself— I am very truly your friend   PHP. S. MARKLEY
Honbe Henry Clay

ALS. DLC-HC (DNA, M212, R1). Addressed to Lexington, Kentucky. MS. partially obliterated.   1 Neither letter has been found.
2 Above, March 26, 1825.
3 Cf. above, Ingersoll to Clay, May 7, 1825, note.
4 John A. Shulze.   5 George Kremer.
6 See above, Clay to Brooke, April 29, 1825, note.
7 See above, Clay to Strong, March 29, 1825, note.
8 Not identified; the letter not found.
9 Three or four words.   10 Two or three words.

APPLICATIONS, RECOMMENDATIONS   June 10, 1825

J[OHN] P. ERWIN, Nashville, introduces Thomas G. Bradford, "formerly a citizen of this place, but at this time a resident in Virga.—Mr Bradford has heretofore been recommended to the Treasury Department, for a clerkship, in some of its Offices— He now expresses a wish to obtain a similar Situation" in the State Department. "He was for some years Editor & proprietor of a respectable paper in this place, has filled several public stations, and possesses the good will of a large number of his fellow citizens of this State, in addition to a highly respectable Connexion." ALS. DNA, RG59, A. and R. (MR1). Endorsed (AEI) by Clay: "To be sent to Mr. Rush." See above, Erwin to Clay, June 7, 1825, note.

WILLIAM WILSON, Freeport, Harrison County, Ohio, solicits appointment "as a Recorder or Clerk in the Department of State." ALS. DNA, RG59, A. and R. (MR4). Wilson, not further identified, received no appointment.

Toasts at Clark County Banquet

[June 11, 1825]

The Hon. Henry Clay, Secretary of State of the United States— He owes his present elevation to his distinguished talents, eminent public services, and the high estimation in which he is held by the nation; his conduct in the Presidential election has our unqualified approbation, and we rejoice in the opportunity of giving him our feeble aid in shielding him from the malicious darts of his enemies and of proclaiming our undiminished confidence in his purity and integrity.[1]

. . . .

VOLUNTEERS.

By *Mr Clay*—The Fair of Clarke County—The single married and happiness to all.[2]

Lexington *Kentucky Reporter,* June 20, 1825. The dinner was held at "Col. [Colby H.] Taylor's Inn in Clarke county"; "between two and three hundred gentlemen and 60 or 80 ladies" were present. *Ibid.,* June 13, 1825. Hubbard Taylor and "H[ay]. Battle [Battaile]" served as presidents; (Richard) Hickman and (John Thornton) Woodford, as vice presidents. Battaile, born in Caroline County, Virginia, a member of the Virginia Legislature from 1815 to 1820, had recently come to Clark County. Hickman, also a Virginian, a veteran of the Revolution, and one of the early settlers of Clark County, had been a delegate to the Kentucky constitutional convention of 1799, had served in the Kentucky House of Representatives from 1793 to 1798, in the State Senate from 1800 to 1812 and from 1819 to 1823, and as Lieutenant Governor and Acting Governor in 1812 and 1813. Woodford, also of Caroline County, Virginia, had moved to Kentucky about 1820; he was a cousin of Mark Catesby Woodford.
1 Following this toast Clay "addressed the company." His remarks were not recorded.
2 Micah Taul remembered the toast as: "The Ladies of Clarke County: good husbands for the single ones and happiness for all." "Memoirs of Micah Taul," Kentucky State Historical Society, *Register,* XXVII (1929), 627.

From William Jennings and Others

LANCASTER, KY. June 11th, 1825.

DEAR SIR—The citizens of Garrard unconnected with you by any other ties, than the sympathies of common interest, and common fame, and country, have been vigilant and impartial observers of

the manner in which you have discharged the various duties which
have devolved on you, in your long and eventful career of public
service: and it is with great pleasure, that in presenting to you the
enclosed resolutions of a respectable portion of them, we are able
to assure you of their increased confidence in your undeviating
firmness, purity and patriotism. They cherish a lively and grateful
recollection of the many eminent services which you have rendered
to the West, and are duly sensible of their obligations to you for
the large contributions which your talents and well directed phi-
lanthropy, have made to the prosperity and fame of our own
country, and the happiness of others. The memorials of most of
these will survive the age in which we live, and would derive no
aid from any transient testimonial of your fellow citizens; but your
conduct in the recent Presidential election by the House of Representatives of the Union,[1] (in our opinion) deserves and demands
a specific and emphatic expression of public approbation—not to
panegyrize you, but to do you justice.

Placed unavoidably in a situation of peculiar delicacy and
responsibility, and beset with difficulties, which to many would have
been appalling, and to any embarassing [sic], you have, by following
alone (as we believe you have ever done) the dictates of your own
conscience, and the suggestion of your own impartial judgment, subjected yourself (as was to have been expected) to the imputation of
unworthy motives, and to unjust and acrimonious animadversions
by many, whose hopes your firmness aided in disappointing, and
some whose ambition you succeeded in prostrating.

No act of your political life has been more gratifying to us and
to those whom we represent, than your vote in that momentous
contest. In your whole conduct on that subject we have seen nothing
to censure, everything to approve and much to applaud. Any other
course than that which you persued [sic], would (we think) have
been inconsistent with the principles which have characterised
your past, and unfriendly to the usefulness of your future, life—
and repugnant (we assure you) to the wishes of almost all your
fellow-citizens in this quarter, and as we confidently believe, to a
large majority of those of our whole state, and of the United States.
And, sir, allow me to say that we are sure, that your conduct was
uninfluenced by any assurance or expectation of your own preferment. And some of us have satisfactory reasons for believing, that
you did not desire the station which you now occupy, and accepted
it with hesitation in obedience to a sense of duty, and of respect
for the opinion and wishes of many of your friends.

Approving as they do, your conduct in this affair, as wise and
magnanimous, and having seen attempts made to impair your usefulness, and embarrass the administration with which you and they

are now identified, by misrepresenting your motives and acts, the citizens of our county are desirous to tender you some testimonial of the continuation of their confidence, and the increase of your claims on their gratitude.

We have therefore been instructed to invite you to a public dinner, which they propose to give you in Lancaster at such time as you may select. Anxious to offer you personally the humble tribute of their respect, they have forborne to designate any particular day, lest by its possible interference with some pre-engagement, you might be unable to attend; but if you are allowed sufficient leisure, they hope that you will select some day most suitable to yourself, and it will therefore be most agreeable to them.

Allow us, sir, in conclusion, to assure you of our entire confidence in the new administration, of which you are a member, and pray you to accept for yourself and the other members of that administration, our united wishes for *your* and *their* prosperity, and triumph over all factious opposition to your acts, as long as they shall, as we hope they will be, wise, national and benificent [*sic*]. Very respectfully, Your obdt, humble serv'ts.

W. JENNINGS,	MOSES O. BLEDSOE,	
BENJ: LETCHER,	JNO: YANTIS,	} *Managers.*[2]
J. HOPPER,	SAML: M'KEE,	

Lexington *Kentucky Reporter*, June 27, 1825. At a meeting of citizens of Garrard County, held at the courthouse June 9, 1825, "in pursuance of public notice," resolutions had been adopted inviting Clay to a public dinner at Lancaster, "as an evidence of the undiminished confidence of the people of Garrard county, in his integrity and patriotism," inviting also Robert P. Letcher, John Boyle, and William Owsley (the judges of the old court of appeals), and appointing a committee on arrangements. The latter body was composed of the signers of this letter and, in addition, Francis P. Horde, John Faulkner, and John Rout. Jennings had served as chairman of the gathering and James Hughes Letcher as secretary.

Jennings, who had held office as a justice of the peace and sheriff in Garrard County prior to the War of 1812, had attained rank as a general of militia during that conflict. Faulkner, a major of militia, had come to Garrard County from Virginia around 1780 and served in the Kentucky Legislature much of the time from 1810 through 1834. Rout has not been further identified. James Hughes Letcher, probably a cousin of Benjamin and Robert P. Letcher, was clerk of Clark County from 1825 to 1836.

1 See above, Clay to Adams, January 9, 1825, note; Clay to Brooke, February 10, 1825, note, *et passim*.

2 Benjamin Letcher, prominent in Garrard County since before the turn of the century and a general of militia in the War of 1812, had served as clerk of county court from 1797 to 1825; he was a brother of Robert P. Letcher. Yantis, a veteran of the Revolution and captain of militia in the War of 1812, had also settled in Garrard County at an early date, had served in the State legislature much of the period from 1809 to 1821, returned to that body from 1825 to 1828 and again in 1830, and finally moved to Lafayette County, Missouri, in 1832. Hopper and Bledsoe have not been further identified.

INSTRUCTIONS AND DISPATCHES   June 11, 1825

From ROBERT CAMPBELL, Genoa. Summarizes his last communication to the State Department (addressed to John Quincy Adams, January 31, 1824 [*i.e.,*

1825]), noting, among other subjects, that a treaty had been concluded between Sardinia and Turkey (see above, Middleton to Clay, April 21, 1825, note); states that the "Court of Sardinia has been here for upwards of a month and last Week the King [Charles Felix] received a Visit from the Emperor of Austria [Francis I] the King of Naples [Francis I], Prince of Lucca, Duchess of Parma (late Empress of France [Marie Louise]) Prince Metternich and various other Ministers"; cites a rumor that the Emperor attempted, without success, to establish a confederation with himself as head; and concludes that some alterations in territory are to occur among the smaller states, without, however, affecting American trade. ALS. DNA, RG59, Cons. Disp., Genoa, vol. 1 (M-T64, R1). Received August 17. Campbell, a British merchant residing in Genoa, had been appointed the United States consul in 1823. Charles Louis, Prince of Lucca, later reigned as Charles II, Archduke of Parma.

APPLICATIONS, RECOMMENDATIONS   June 11, 1825

WILLIAM CARROLL, Nashville, introduces Thomas G. Bradford, "who is desirous to procure the appointment of clerk in some of the departments at Washington." Notes that "Mr. Bradford has numerous relations and friends in Tennessee who would be highly gratified with his success. He is an honorable prudent man, in whom great confidence can be placed; and . . . has been, and now is your friend." LS. DNA, RG59, A. and R. (MR1). Addressed to Lexington. Endorsed (AEI) by Clay: "To be sent to Mr. Rush on his arrival." Postscript (AE) by Carroll on verso: "The belief that Colo. Erwin will be elected has gained strength since I last wrote you, though a combination of the interests of other candidates may yet defeat him." On the defeat of Andrew Erwin, in the current congressional campaign, see below, Carroll to Clay, October 4, 1825.

To John Moseley and Others

ASHLAND, 12th JUNE, 1825.

Gentlemen—I know not how I shall make suitable acknowledgments for the very great obligations under which I am placed by the citizens of Nicholasville and Jessamine. The additional proof of their esteem and confidence, contained in your obliging note of the 9th instant, coming as it does from those with whose suffrages I was once honored, gives me the highest gratification. Many of them and several of you, have known me well throughout the greater part of my life. Whilst, in the instance of my public conduct, to which you have been pleased kindly to refer, I have sought an investigation before every competent tribunal,[1] I have been particularly anxious in respect to the judgement of my friends and fellow citizens in Kentucky. The spontaneous and honorable decision of all whom I have had, at any time, the honor to represent in the House of Representatives of the U. States, ought to satisfy even those who have been impelled by vindictive and malignant feeling, to assail me.

I regret extremely that I am not able to accept the polite invitation to the public dinner at Capt. Coger's. I should be very happy to meet there again my friends of Nicholasville and Jessamine. But I have to lament that the necessity of arranging my private affairs, prior to my return to Washington City, and the urgency of my official duties will not permit me to partake of their generous hospitality.

I pray you to tender to them my warmest and affectionate regards, and to allow me to present to each of you my best wishes for your prosperity and happiness.

I am respectfully, your ob'dt. servant, H. CLAY.

Messrs John Mosely, John Barkley, James Williams, Thomas S. Smith, Jeremiah Frazier, Nathl. Dunn, &c &c &c.

Lexington *Kentucky Reporter*, June 20, 1825.
[1] See above, Appeal, February 3, 1825.

INSTRUCTIONS AND DISPATCHES June 12, 1825

From W[ILLIAM] TUDOR, Lima, no. 32. Describes the injurious effect, on American commerce with Peru, of a ten per cent duty on cotton cloth, from which inferior goods of British manufacture are exempt. ALS. DNA, RG59, Cons. Disp., Lima, vol. 1 (M154, R1). Addressed to Secretary of State; received November 1.

Advertisement of Auction

Ashland, June 13, 1825.

CASH SALE.

The subscriber will sell, at his residence
near Lexington,

On Friday the 24th and Saturday the 25th inst.

A GREAT VARIETY OF

HOUSE & KITCHEN FURNITURE,

CONSISTING OF

BEDS, and Bedsteads, Sofas, Chairs, (hair bottomed, mahogany, flag, &c.) Tables, Carpets, Chandeliers, Mirrors, Lamps, Pendules, Clocks, and Busts, a Piano Forte, and other Articles:

AND ALSO A LARGE QUANTITY OF

STOCK,

Including Horses, Mares and Colts, Mules, English Cattle, both of his own importation[1] and other improved breeds, and about 120 Sheep of the Merino breed chiefly.[2] Also, four tons of Hemp, and several Stacks of *Timothy Hay*. The Sale will commence at 12 o'clock on Friday the 24th inst. if the morning of that day should not be unfavourable, in which case it will begin on Saturday the 25th instant, and it will be for chash [*sic*] in hand. The objects first put up will be the Stock. H. CLAY.

Executor's Note Account with Morrison Estate

[June 13, 1825]

As only acting executor of the estate of James Morrison, Clay files an account of the settlement in notes of the Bank of the Commonwealth covering the period from June 8, 1824, through June 13, 1825. A commission of five per cent on receipts of $5,488.90 is allowed the executor. Examined and certified, June 13, 1825, by commissioners appointed by the court; approved by the Fayette County court at the June Term, 1825, and ordered to record. Fayette County, Will Book G, 167-68.

Executor's Specie Account with Morrison Estate

[June 13, 1825]

As only acting executor of the estate of James Morrison, Clay files an account of "specie funds received and paid," from June 8, 1824, through June 13, 1825. A commission of five per cent on receipts of $29,762.93 is allowed the executor. Examined and certified, June 13, 1825, by commissioners appointed by the court; approved by the Fayette County court at the June Term, 1825, and ordered to record. Fayette County, Will Book G, 173-77.

From Daniel Breck and Others

DEAR SIR: RICHMOND, June 13th, 1825.

We have been chosen a committee by the citizens of Madison County to invite you to partake of a public dinner at David C. Irvine's[1] Spring in the vicinity of Richmond on any day that may suit your other engagements, and which you will have the goodness to designate, should you find it convenient to accept this invitation.

We could not on any occasion have been delegated to perform a more enviable service than to tender to an individual alike pre-eminent as an orator, a statesman, and philanthropist, the friendship and hospitality of the citizens of Madison; and our pleasures are very much enhanced by the circumstances under which we have been called to the discharge of this duty. We have been charged by the citizens of Madison county to express to you their elevated sense of your public services and their undiminished confidence in the firmness and integrity of your character, and in your patriotic devotion to the best interests of the American people. Although they have not been your immediate constituents, they have felt a deep interest in your public career and ultimate destinies. They have witnessed with mingled emotions of contempt and indignation the foul attempt which has been lately made to sully a reputation identified with the prosperity and glory of our country.[2]

They have seen you in the morning of professional life, the eloquent advocate of liberal principles, equal rights and rational liberty; and in the vigor and maturity of meridian developement they have marked your path in the second struggle for our freedom and independence. They have gone with you across the Atlantic and mingled in the deep toned feeling which pervaded the negotiations at Ghent, and justly appreciated your invaluable services in restoring our beloved country to an honourable peace. In a moment of great public excitement, when the union of these states, the strongest safeguard of our independence, was threatened with immediate dissolution, your opulent mind, rich in expedients, presented to the national legislature a plan by which the most opposite views were harmonized and another star[3] added to the American constellation.—They have with conscious pride and inexpressible pleasure seen you embracing within the enlarged sphere of your philanthropic affections the people of two hemispheres—raising your voice in defence of republican liberty and the rights of men, as well in the classic land of Homer and Epaminondas as in the two Americas.[4]— They too have beheld the bold, manly and independent stand you took in support of Domestic Manufactures and an American system of internal improvement, and the wisdom of your enlightened policy, confirmed by the unexampled prosperity and happiness of the nation.

In the part which you have lately acted in the election of a chief Magistrate,[5] we have another instance of your disinterested devotion to the public good. These considerations have sunk deep into the hearts of the citizens of Madison county, and whatever views others may express or entertain, they believe when party strife shall cease, and the tongue of slander be silent, your name and character will float down the tide of time associated with those of Washington, Jefferson and the good La Fayette. While they deeply regret parting with you as a citizen of Kentucky, they most cordially approve your appointment to and acceptance of an office in another department of the government. Be assured, Sir, you carry with you their warmest affections and their unbounded confidence in your pre-eminent qualifications for the discharge of the high duties to which you are called. Suffer us individually to embrace this occasion of tendering you the homage of our sincere respect and great regard.

DANIEL BRECK,	T. C. HOWARD,	
SQUIRE TURNER,	THOMPSON BURNAM,	COMMITTEE.
W. H. CAPERTON,	A. WOODS, JUNR.	
T. A. CLARKE,	A. W. ROLLINS,[6]	

THE HON. H. CLAY, *Secretary of State.*

Lexington *Kentucky Reporter,* June 27, July 11, 1825. Reprinted from Richmond (Kentucky) *Farmer's Chronicle,* June 17, 1825. Breck, brother of Samuel Breck, had been born in Massachusetts and in 1812 graduated from Dartmouth College. Two years later he had been admitted to the bar and had begun practice of law in Richmond, Kentucky. He served in the State legislature from the session of 1823-1824 to 1828 and again in the session of 1834-1835; he was a judge of the State court of appeals from 1843 to 1849 and a member of the United States Congress from 1849 to 1851. Prior to his election to the State court and following his service in Congress, he was president of a Richmond bank.

1 David C. Irvine, a representative in the Kentucky legislative session of 1816-1817 and a nephew of William Irvine, had died in 1820. His property here mentioned was probably a tract of three acres near town on the Lexington Road, adjoining land owned by Thomas A. Clarke.

2 See above, Clay to Gales and Seaton, January 30, 1825.

3 Missouri. See above, III, 26-50 *passim.*

4 See above, II, 402-405, 508-62, 667-68, 853-60; III, 597-99.

5 See above, Clay to Adams, January 9, 1825, note; Clay to Brooke, February 10, 1825, note.

6 Turner, born and trained as a lawyer in Kentucky, had been admitted to the bar in 1815, after service in the War of 1812. He was a member of the Kentucky Legislature from 1823 to 1827, during the sessions of 1830-1831 and 1831, and again during the session of 1839-1840; he later became a member of the State constitutional convention of 1849. By 1823 Thomas A. Clarke had moved from Jessamine to Madison County, where he at that time also became deputy sheriff. Burnam, born near Raleigh, North Carolina, had been brought to Madison County as a child, around 1792; he later became prominent as a merchant and farmer and served part of one term in the State legislature (1844). Archibald Woods, Jr., who was not a son of Archibald Woods of Wheeling, had represented Madison County in the Kentucky Legislature from 1816 to 1820 and in the session of 1824-1825; he served as a State senator from 1826 to 1829. Dr. Anthony W. Rollins, born in Westmoreland County, Pennsylvania, had attended Jefferson College in Pennsylvania (founded in 1794), studied medicine at Transylvania Medical College, and practiced successfully until 1830, when, his health failing, he removed to Boone County and engaged in agriculture. He was a leader in livestock importation and agricultural improvement.

INSTRUCTIONS AND DISPATCHES   June 13, 1825.

From J[OHN] ADAMS SMITH, London, no. 2. Reports the departure of (Richard) Rush and family "on board the Packet Ship York" on June 1, with prospects of "a prolonged passage." Smith has been left in charge of "the business of the Mission at this Court." ALS. DNA, RG59, Dip. Disp., Great Britain, vol. 32 (M30, R28). Addressed to Secretary of State; received August 11.

To Daniel Breck and Others

ASHLAND, 14th June, 1825.

GENTLEMEN—I have received the note which, as a Committee of my fellow citizens of Madison County, you did me the honor to address to me on the 13th instant, inviting me to a public dinner in their county. I thank them, most cordially, for this obliging proof of their friendly consideration of me. And it would have afforded me particular satisfaction to have been able, at this period, to partake of their generous hospitality; but I regret extremely, that indispensable engagements, now existing and extending to the residue of the time which I shall remain in Kentucky, will not allow me that honor. In reluctantly yielding to the necessity under which

I am placed of declining their kind invitation, they will I hope, permit me to seize the occasion to make my respectful acknowledgements as well for the compliment intended me, as for the favourable and flattering opinions and sentiments which they are pleased to entertain towards me. Madison county is endeared to me by many early recollections. I have had the happiness during a period of nearly thirty years, to know intimately many of its inhabitants. Their respectability is exceeded by that of no community of equal size in any part of our country. To know that I possess the confidence and affection of such a people; to learn that, in my public career, I have obtained their approbation, and to be assured that I have their respected sanction for the part I acted, in a memorable instance, during the last session of Congress, affords me a gratification as lasting as it is inexpressible. Those who have recently assailed me, in consequence of that part, have done me an essential service. They would have sacrificed me to their malignant and ambitious passions. The nation has seen and condemned their machinations. They would have deprived me of the attachment and confidence of my constituents. My constituents have overwhelmed me by general and emphatic manifestations of their regard and esteem. They would have infused distrusts into the minds of the people of my state of the integrity of my public action. Kentucky never displayed more entire satisfaction with me, than at the present, to me, happy moment. Their signal defeat is a new demonstration of the wisdom of our social structure and of the competancy [sic] of the people to discriminate between the suggestions of calumny and the accusations of truth. And they have impressed upon me, more strongly my obligations of gratitude to my country, of ardent devotion of the utmost of my humble abilities to its service, and of unceasing prayers for its welfare and prosperity. In the new office to which I have been called, and my acceptance of which you are pleased to have seen with satisfaction, I hope to be able, by zeal and industry, to evince that I am not insensible to the distinguished evidence of honor, affection and confidence, of which I have been so long and so often the favoured object.

I will thank you gentlemen to expose these feelings and sentiments to my fellow citizens of Madison, and to accept for yourselves individually assurances of the high regard and esteem of Your ob't. humble serv't.   H. CLAY.

Messrs, *Daniel Breck,*   *T. C. Howard,*
       Squire Turner,   *Thompson Burnam,*
       W. H. Caperton,   *A. Woods,* Junr.
       T. A. Clarke,   *A. W. Rollins.*

Lexington *Kentucky Reporter,* June 27, 1825. Reprinted from Richmond (Kentucky) *Farmer's Chronicle,* June 17, 1825.

From Alexander H. Everett

Dear Sir: New York. June. 14. 1825.

I take the liberty of addressing you a few lines—on the eve of my embarkation—for the purpose of bidding you farewell and of offering you individualy [sic] my best wishes for your success in the high station you occupy in the councils of the country. I have noticed with sincere satisfaction the symptoms of unabated respect & attachment on the part of your constituents in the West which have been called out by your presence among them. They afford at once the most gratifying reward for the real service you rendered the country at the late session of Congress and the most promising omen of the future progress of events. I may venture I think to assure you that the East will cordialy [sic] harmonise with the West in all the great points of national policy: and I very much doubt whether the middling interest (to use a Boston phrase) although bridgd[1] by its canals or the Southern—headed as it is by a military chieftain[2]—will be able to prevail against such a coalition.

My brother Edward and myself—with a view of providing the administration with a more efficient instrument of the Kind than they now possess at the Eastward—have determined in unison with my brother John to found a new paper[3] at Boston of which he will be the immediate Editor   He will be aided by contributions from us as well as from several vry [sic] respectable gentlemen of our part of the country including Messrs. Blake and Webster and Judge Story.[4] We venture to hope that such an establishment will meet with your approbation and patronage. The proposals will be issued very shortly and the first number about the 4th. of July. Both will of course be transmitted to you as soon as they are published.

I have already acknowledged in an official form the receipt of your instructions which I found at this place on my arrival.[5] Permit me to avail myself of this occasion to express to you most particularly the deep sense I feel of the confidence with which I have been honourd [sic] by the President & yourself and my determination to do every thing in my power to justify it. With a government so wretchedly constituted and administered as that of Spain now is—the best directed efforts might however fail of success. I can promise nothing but zeal & industy [sic]—and it would not be surprising if they should be found unavailing. I venture to hope that you will look with indulgence upon the errors into which I may probably fal [sic] In the management of the important concerns which will devolve upon me and that you will judge of my exertions—not wholly by their results—but in part by the evidence I may give of sincere and active devotion to the public service.

I propose to embark tomorrow on the ship Edward Quesnel for

Havre. I shall of course take the liberty of addressing you immediately after my arrival in Europe and remain, in the mean time with sincere respect & esteem, dear Sir, your friend & servt.

Mr. Clay   A. H. EVERETT.

ALS. DNA, RG59, Dip. Disp., Spain, vol. 25 (M31, R27).
[1] Word not clear.   [2] Andrew Jackson.
[3] Possibly the Boston *Traveller,* which began publication on July 5, 1825, and still continues.
[4] George Blake, prominent Boston Republican, a lawyer, formerly a member of the State Senate, United States district attorney from 1820 to 1829, and for a time editor of a Worcester newspaper; Daniel Webster; Joseph Story.
[5] See above, Clay to Everett, April 27, 28, 1825; Everett to Clay, May 29, 1825.

INSTRUCTIONS AND DISPATCHES   June 14, 1825

From ANDREW ARMSTRONG, Port au Prince. Encloses copies of new revenue laws placing "our commercial rival" (Great Britain) on the same footing as the United States. Refers to a problem arising from the protection offered by Haitians, in violation of shipping articles, to colored seamen deserting from American vessels and suggests in this connection that the commercial agent of the United States residing here might be recommended in a semi-official manner to the Government—a maneuver that has benefitted Britain. Cites the "contracted and jealous policy" of the Haitian Government, which has limited enterprise here, though there has been considerable educational progress. Reports on the military status of the island, its population and revenue, and its imports and exports, the former being predominantly from the United States until the first of this year, since which date they have declined fifty per cent. States that the Government denies American claims for spoliations committed under (Henri) Christophe but would pay them to prevent ill feeling. Armstrong requests leave for a few months. ALS. DNA, RG59, Cons. Disp., Cap Haitien (M9, R-T5).

As "instructed by the Secretary of State," Daniel Brent informed Armstrong, on November 11, that the President had granted his request for leave. Copy, in DNA, RG59, Cons. Instr., vol. 2, p. 372 (M78, R2).

APPLICATIONS, RECOMMENDATIONS   June 14, 1825

NICHOLAS RIDGELY, Dover (Delaware), recommends appointment of Maskline Clark, formerly of Dover, as consul at Arica, Peru. ALS. DNA, RG59, A. and R. (MR1). Ridgely, a distant cousin of Nicholas Greenberry Ridgely, had been born in Dover and had become one of the leading lawyers of Delaware. Long active in political affairs of that State, he had served for ten years (1791-1801) as State attorney general and for five terms (1792, 1796, 1797, 1799-1801) as a member of the State House of Representatives prior to his appointment in 1802 as chancellor, which last position he retained until his death in 1830. Clark, a native of Kent County, Delaware, had held positions as recorder of deeds and register in chancery of this county until he was commissioned a second lieutenant in the War of 1812; thereafter he had been employed for a time in the customhouse at Philadelphia and for the last three or four years had been engaged "in commercial pursuits," primarily in South America. He did not receive consular appointment.

Toasts at Nicholasville Banquet

[June 15, 1825]

Our distinguished guest and fellow citizen *Henry Clay,* the pride of the West—Each successive act of his brilliant public life, particularly his late participation in the election of John Quincy Adams as President of the U. States, adds a brighter link to that chain of confidence and affection by which we are bound to him. His known integrity, talents and virtue must form a shield empervious [*sic*] to calumny and unhallowed ambition.

{Mr. CLAY expressed his acknowledgments to the company for the full and unequivocal expression of their approbation conveyed in this toast.}

. . . .

Our highly respected Guest and distinguished Statesman, H CLAY— We rejoice in the occasion of expressing to the world, and particularly to Messrs Kremer[1] & Company, our unshaken confidence in his incorruptible integrity.

Lexington *Kentucky Reporter,* June 20, 1825. The dinner, given Clay by the citizens of Jessamine County, Kentucky, was prepared by Benjamin Netherland, founder and proprietor, from 1793 to 1838, of "Mingo Tavern." Joseph Crockett presided, and Archibald Logan served as vice president. The first toast was given as part of the formal program; the second was volunteered.
1 George Kremer.

INSTRUCTIONS AND DISPATCHES   June 15, 1825

From HUGH NELSON, Madrid, no. 58. Reports his confidential introductory conversation with the Secretary of State (Francisco de Zea Bermudez) on the subject of accreditation of consular agents of the United States in Cuba and Puerto Rico, in which the Secretary protested against American recognition of the Spanish American Republics and pointed out the injury to Spain if she "admitted our Consuls to day, [and] tomorrow a state of things might occur in which we might be called upon to recognize the Independence of those islands, and policy or necessity might operate on our Govt. to adopt the same course which we had heretofore adopted." States that Nelson assured Zea that the policy of the United States had been "produced by a necessity, to which the Govt. had found itself compelled to yield, growing out of the uninterrupted course of events in these new countries, and by an irresistible pressure of public sentiment, expanding thro' the whole of the North American Continent. That it could not be unknown to the Govt. of HM. that the Executive of the United States, had repeatedly set itself in opposition to the measure, altho' sustained by the most distinguished talents in the other departments of the Govt. and had only adopted it when it was seen to be sustained by the universal opinion of the undivided country." Notes that this interview provided Nelson's first opportunity to follow his instruction "to announce to Spain the sincere desire of the United States Govt. that these islands should remain to Spain as parts of her dominion, and should not pass into the hands of any other power."

Encloses copies of a memorial received from Americans protesting their imprisonment and seizure of their vessel in the Canary Islands, of Nelson's note to the Spanish Secretary of State in this connection, and of the latter's reply to Nelson's previous inquiry about the "Tarifa light money." Gratefully acknowledges receipt of Clay's letter of April 12 (*i.e.*, 14), "conveying my letter of recredence."

Expresses fear that the United States will lose much of the money in "the transaction of the Six thousand dollars" (see above, Clay to Nelson, April 14, 1825). Explains that "The case of young Murat [see above, Murat to Clay, March 27, 1825] had been terminated" before receipt of Clay's "suggestions on the subject."

Reports that Commodore Rodgers was unable to release a frigate to transport "Mr. Heredia" to the United States (see above, Nelson to Clay, May 14, 1825) but that he offered the *Cyane,* which returns by way of the Coast of Africa and the West Indies; that the Secretary of State (Bermudez) declined this arrangement because of the hazard to the health of Heredia's family at this season on this route; that Heredia has himself informed Nelson that illness renders him unable to embark upon his assignment to the United States. LS. DNA, RG59, Dip. Disp., Spain, vol. 24 (M31, R26). Received August 21.

Nelson's instructions to inform the Spanish Government of the views of the United States relating to the continuance of Spain's possession of Cuba and Puerto Rico had been issued by John Quincy Adams on April 28, 1823. Adams, *Writings,* VII, 379-81.

Under a decree of 1818 the special fees required of American vessels entering Mediterranean ports, for support of the lighthouse at Tarifa, were supposed to have been included in the twenty reals charged as a tonnage duty upon American shipping. A letter from Nelson to Secretary of State Adams, March 3, 1825, had reported the demand by port authorities at Barcelona for the "Tarifa light money" as an additional charge.

The *Cyane* was a United States naval corvette, captured from the British during the War of 1812.

From JOEL R. POINSETT, Mexico (City), no. 4. Reports receipt of information of the surrender at Acapulco of the Spanish warship *Asia* and a smaller "vessel of war" (the brig *Constant*), which had "sailed from *Callao* immediately after the Capitulation of Ayacucho" (see above, Raguet to Secretary of State, March 11, 1825), supposedly headed for Manila; also of the dispersion of the Royalist forces in Upper Peru, which latter event has led Bolívar to urge an earlier sitting, no "later than July next," of the (Pan) American Congress proposed for October. "The object of hastening the meeting of this American Congress," Poinsett writes, "is doubtless, to concert measures for attacking Cuba." Notes that proposals to the Mexican States, presented by the Minister from Colombia, urging a joint attack on Cuba, have been rejected by the Congress in secret session, partly from fear of British opposition, but (in a coded section) that the Mexican States "have ambitious views" on Cuba "and would prefer undertaking the expedition without the aid of Colombia." Asserts that the Mexican delegates will not be ready to attend a July meeting of the American Congress; adds (in a coded section) that the Government is not disposed to hasten their departure and that it also "entertains some views with regard to Guatemala." LS, coded passages deciphered in State Department file. DNA, RG59, Dip. Disp., Mexico, vol. 1 (M97, R2). Received August 7. Extract published in Manning (arr.) *Diplomatic correspondence . . . Latin-American Nations,* III, 1626-27. On the Spanish vessels, cf. below, Poinsett to Clay, June 18, 1825; on the Pan American Congress, see above, Tudor to Clay, April 12, 1825, note.

The Colombian Minister to Mexico was Miguel Santa María, Mexican by birth but a supporter of Bolívar and a member of the Colombian General Congress at the time of his appointment, in October, 1821.

From J[OHN] ADAMS SMITH, London, no. 3. Transmits copies of letters "relative to the case of John McDonnell." ALS. DNA, RG59, Dip. Disp., Great Britain, vol. 32 (M30, R28). Addressed to Secretary of State; received August 10. In one of these documents addressed to Richard Rush, June 9, 1825, George Canning states that "In fulfillment of my promise, not to the Minister from the United States, but to Mr Rush . . . authority has been given to the Lt. Governor of Upper Canada to direct the entry of a *noli* [sic] *prosequi* on the Indictment against your friend (or your friend's friend) Mr Macdonnell who may therefore return to his Province when he pleases." See above, Rush to Clay, May 12, 1825.

From WILLIAM TAYLOR, Alvarado (Mexico). Reports the outbreak of yellow fever at this port; comments on the annoyance of Mexican authorities at the recent arrival of a number of Spaniards, hostile to Mexican independence, who travel under passports as United States citizens; notes that the castle of San Juan de Ulloa remains faithful to Spain; and transmits several gazettes from Mexico City, including that for June 3, which published (Joel R.) Poinsett's speech upon his presentation to the President of Mexico (Guadalupe Victoria). ALS. DNA, RG59, Cons. Disp., Veracruz, vol. 1. Received July 15. On the fall of San Juan de Ulloa, see above, Clay to Poinsett, March 26, 1825, note.

MISCELLANEOUS LETTERS June 15, 1825

From WILLIAM MILLER, Washington. Reports going to New York in May for the purpose of obtaining passage to Guatemala; encloses a copy of a letter from J. A. Alvarado, a native of that country. ALS. DNA, RG59, Dip. Disp., Central America, vol. 1 (M219, R2). Cover missing; no addressee given in letter. Alvarado (not further identified), who also wishes passage to Guatemala, suggests the possibility of their being conveyed together on a public vessel.

From WILLIAM MILLER, Washington. Inquires about the propriety of drawing on his salary and of accepting the use of a furnished house offered by a resident of Guatemala. ALS. *Ibid.* Cover missing; addressee not given.

APPLICATIONS, RECOMMENDATIONS June 15, 1825

T[HOMAS] CLAYTON, Dover (Delaware), recommends appointment of Maskline Clark as consul at Arica, Peru. ALS. DNA, RG59, A. and R. (MR1). Cf. above, Ridgely to Clay, June 14, 1825, note. Clayton, born in Maryland, was United States Senator from Delaware (1824-1827, 1837-1847). Admitted to the bar in 1799, he had begun practice at Newcastle, Delaware, served in both houses of the legislature and as attorney general of his adopted State, and sat in the United States House of Representatives from 1815 to 1817. He was later chief justice of the court of common pleas of Delaware (1828) and of the State superior court (1832).

H[ENRY] M. RIDGELY, Dover, recommends appointment of Maskline Clark as consul at Arica, Peru. ALS. DNA, RG59, A. and R. (MR1).

Thomas B. Robertson and Joshua Lewis, New Orleans, recommend appointment of Nathaniel Chamberlain as consul at Mexico (City). ALS by Lewis. *Ibid.* Cf. above, Whittelsey to Clay, April 29, 1825.

To William Jennings and Others

ASHLAND, 16th June, 1825.

GENTLEMEN—I have had the honor to receive your letter of the 11th inst. transmitting the resolutions of the citizens of Garrard, in which they have had the goodness to invite me to a public dinner. I have derived peculiar satisfaction from this honorable testimonial of their approbation, and from the friendly sentiments with which you have been pleased to accompany the communication of it. Although I never enjoyed the honor of directly representing the people of Garrard, their well known independence, intelligence and patriotism, give a high value to their expression of confidence and esteem. I am happy to learn that they approve of my well meant endeavors to serve my country, although I am sensible that their kindness and partiality have induced them to estimate them too highly. It gives me very great pleasure to know, that after weighing all the difficulties in which I was placed, on a late memorable occasion, they are entirely satisfied with the choice I made. And I concur with you in the opinion, that if I had taken a different course, I must have acted inconsistently with the whole tenor of my previous life and, I will add, with all the reflections and observations which I have ever made. In respect to the office which I now hold, it was tendered to me voluntarily, and without solicitation, by the President. I never sought from him or from either of his predecessors, any office whatever. My determination to vote for him was made, without the slightest reference to any composition of his cabinet. If I had previously known and disapproved of the gentlemen whom he intended to introduce into it, I should still have voted for him. My acceptance of my present situation was not without much hesitation; but neither my friends nor my enemies left me at liberty to decline it. I thank you gentlemen, in behalf of the President and my colleagues, as well as for myself, for the assurance of your confidence in the new administration. If good intentions, ardent zeal, concord in the adoption, and hearty co-operation in the execution of public measures can command success, we shall not disappoint your friendly wishes. The administration may encounter opposition, but if it should, it must be one founded upon a sincere and an honest difference of opinion. Such an opposition is neither to be dreaded nor deprecated. No other can find countenance or support from the American people.

It would have afforded me much pleasure to have met my fellow-citizens of Garrard, my late colleague, their worthy represen-tative,[1] and the other highly esteemed gentlemen, whom they have directed by one of their resolutions to be invited to the proposed dinner; but the pressure of my engagements and the necessity of my speedy return to Washington, will not allow me that gratifica-tion. I pray you to communicate the regret I feel in yielding to the urgent duties, which constrain me to decline their invitation—and to assure them of the deep sensibility with which I have re-ceived and shall ever cherish their distinguished and affectionate testimonies. And allow me, gentlemen, to offer to you my acknowl-edgments for the flattering and obliging manner in which you have had the kindness to address me.

I am with high respect and esteem, Your obedient serv't,

H. CLAY.

Messrs W. Jennings Benj Letcher, J. Hopper, Moses O. Bledsoe, Jno. Yantis, and Saml M'Kee.

Lexington *Kentucky Reporter,* June 27, 1825.   [1] Robert P. Letcher.

INSTRUCTIONS AND DISPATCHES   June 16, 1825

From JOHN CUTHBERT, "Consulate of the United States of America   Hamburg." Reports on grain shipments "from this Port for British America for the purpose of introducing it into England as Canada wheat" and on shipments "of Flour, Bread and Salt Provision . . . to Nova Scotia for consumption." States that "the Bread and Salt Provision is prefered [*sic*] to the American, the Flour not." ALS. DNA, RG59, Cons. Disp., Hamburg, vol. 3 (M-T211, R3). Received Au-gust 22. Cuthbert, of Pennsylvania, was at this time acting as consul for Edward Wyer, who held the appointment from 1817 until his resignation in March, 1826. Cuthbert was then named to the post and continued in it until 1848.

MISCELLANEOUS LETTERS   June 16, 1825

From THOMAS BUCKLEY AND SON, New York. Encloses a copy of an earlier letter to John Quincy Adams, then Secretary of State (concerning the seizure of the ship *Spermo*), to which no reply has been received; solicits "the attention of Government to the subject. . . ." ALS. DNA, RG76, Misc. Claims, Brazil. Cf. above, Clay to Raguet, April 16, 1825.

APPLICATIONS, RECOMMENDATIONS   June 16, 1825

MARGARET HARRISON, Portsmouth (New Hampshire), solicits appointment of her husband, Robert M. Harrison, to some lucrative situation in his own coun-try, "such as a collectorship at Bath, or any other Port in America. . . ." Noting that "Ten years residence in a Tropical Climate has considerably impaired his health," she comments: "His present circumstances are most distressing; he finds himself at an advanced age with a competency scarcely adequate to the support of himself and family; and in order to maintain the respectability of his situation, he has been under the necessity of submitting to a painfull separation; sending his wife and children to the United States." Also states that two of their sons are in the United States Navy, the elder on the *Spark,* the younger on the *Grampus,* and asks that Clay have the latter "appointed a full Midshipman." Refers also to their "large family of younger children, whom . . . [they] wish if possible to educate in America." ALS. DNA, RG59, A. and R. (MR2). Mrs. Harrison has not been further identified. The elder son, born in the West Indies, was Charles P. C. Harrison, commissioned a midshipman in 1823. The younger boy, Robert Monroe Harrison (II), born in Sweden, received his commission as midshipman on November 9, 1825.

To Samuel L. Southard

My dear Sir   Ashland 17 June 1825
The only contingency on which you exacted a promise that I should write you has not happened. I have not been burnt either in p. p.[1] or in effigy since my return, and yet I will not refuse myself the pleasure of writing you a few lines.

My reception in K. has greatly exceeded in cordiality and enthusiasm any which I ever before obtained. I have been the object of as many public manifestations of regard nearly as La Fayette was. Public dinners, Barbacues [*sic*] and Balls have left me but little leisure to restore my health or transact my private business. I have been obliged to decline four or five, and do not mean to come under any new acceptances, for the want of funds and time. The good feelings towards me are extended to the administration, and, if we avoid error, I have no doubt of its stability and popularity in this quarter. Do not imagine that the exhibition of popular feeling, to which I have refered [*sic*], has any intoxicating effect with me. On the contrary I regard it with perfect coolness, considering it as flowing from a just indignation against the conspiracy of last winter.

I hope to leave home for Washn. in about a fortnight. I shall have a hot and tedious journey, for the state of the Ohio river will not I apprehend admit of the navigation of Steam boats. Be pleased to present my respectful compliments to the President and our Colleagues.   I am respectfy & Faithfy Yr ob. servant
Mr. Southard   H. CLAY

ALS. NjP-Samuel L. Southard Papers. Endorsed: "H. Clay   recd. 1 July—no ans—he is travelling."   1 Propria persona.

INSTRUCTIONS AND DISPATCHES   June 18, 1825

From JOEL R. POINSETT, no. 5. Corrects his earlier report (June 15, 1825) by noting that the *Asia* and the *Constant* (Spanish war vessels) were surrendered at Monterey only after the crew had mutinied and put the officers ashore in the Marianas. Transmits memoranda from a copy of "Mr. [George] Canning's answer to the remonstrance of the Spanish Minister Zea" (Bermudez; see above, Brown to Clay, March 22, 1825), which Poinsett has seen through the courtesy of the British Minister (Henry G. Ward). Reports that the (Mexican) Secretary of State (Lucas Alamán) has objected to making any arrangement relating to "the road from the Western limit of Missouri to Santa Fé . . . until the Boundary line shall be settled"; transmits copy of a note on this subject which Poinsett has written to the Mexican official. LS. DNA, RG59, Dip. Disp., Mexico, vol. 1 (M97, R2). Registered September 21. Poinsett's note, dated June 17, on the proposed road to Santa Fé, outlined the project (see above, Clay to Poinsett, March 26, 1825) and sought Mexican cooperation and sharing of the expense in continuing the road from the border to Santa Fé.

Bill to Kentucky Penitentiary

[*ca.* June 20, 1825]

The Penitentiary of Kentucky To Henry Clay Dr.

For rent of a Store Room from 16th. March to 20th. June 1825— is 3 Ms. & 5 days @ 200$. per Anm. $52.75

D, by Robert Scott. DLC-TJC (DNA, M212, R16). See above, III, 777-78.

MISCELLANEOUS LETTERS   June 20, 1825

From AUGUST NEALE, Richmond County, Virginia. States that the British Commissioner (George Jackson) under the St. Petersburg Convention has agreed to accept, as evidence of claims, copies of depositions, relating to "the desertion of slaves to the enemy," taken in the county courts of Virginia, provided these documents are properly authenticated; requests that the depositions, perhaps 2,000 in number, be returned to Virginia for authentication in time to have them ready by December 8, the date for the next meeting of the Board of Commissioners under the convention. Neale writes as attorney "for numerous claimants under the Ghent treaty." ALS. DNA, RG59, Misc. Letters (M179, R62). On November 19, Daniel Brent at the request of the Secretary acknowledged receipt of a letter of November 10 (not found), enclosing a copy of the above request, and explained that Clay's absence from Washington during the summer "and the accidental omission afterwards to bring it under his notice, have produced the delay. . . ." He noted that Clay had the subject of Neale's "application for the authentication of the evidence concerning Slaves carried off by the British forces . . . under consideration" and that Neale would be informed of the decision. Copy. DNA, RG59, Dom. Letters, vol. 21, pp. 193-94 (M40, R19).

APPLICATIONS, RECOMMENDATIONS   June 20, 1825

N. ROBINSON, Huntsville, Alabama, recommends appointment of James B. Craighead, nephew of Samuel and Preston Brown, as receiver of public moneys in Alabama. ALS. DNA, RG59, A. and R. (MR1). Robinson not further identified. Preston, brother of John, James, and Dr. Samuel Brown, had been born in Virginia and was also a physician, with a large practice at Frankfort,

Kentucky, and in the vicinity of his residence in Woodford County. Craighead, a son of the Browns' elder sister, Elizabeth, later practiced law in Mobile and operated a plantation in Marengo County, Alabama. He did not receive a Federal appointment.

Rental Agreement with John D. Dillon

[June 21, 1825]

An agreement entered into this 21st. day of June 1825 Between H. Clay and John D. Dillon.

The said Clay hereby leases to the said Dillon for the term of four years commencing this day the house situated on Short street, fronting the public square, lying between Tibbatts's and the corner house occupied by Bruce and Gratz,[1] with the lot attached thereto,[2] which said house and lot are at present in the possession of the said Dillon.

In consideration whereof the said Dillon hereby agrees and binds himself to pay to the said Clay for each & every year of the term aforesaid the sum of sixty dollars in specie, to be paid in quarterly payments of fifteen dollars specie each.

And as the said House is very old and in a decaying condition it is stipulated by the parties that the said Clay is to be at no expence or trouble about any repairs whatever.

The right to destrain [sic] for the rent, as it becomes due, and also the right to reenter and take possession of the premises, for non payment of the rent, are both hereby reserved to the said Clay.

Witness the hands and seals of the parties the day and year aforesaid   H CLAY {Ls}

JOHN D DILLON {Ls}

Sealed & Delivered ⎫
In presence of   ⎬ Theo: W. Clay
                              ⎭

[Endorsement][3]

Rent due quarterly from 21 June 1825—$32¼ pd. by Moses P. Ellis Conste.[4] 25 Septr. 1829 In full of the balce. due on this lease

[Endorsement on verso][5]

15 Oct. 1825 recd. fifteen dollars, the first quarters rent due
21st. day of last month   R SCOTT
13 Jany 1826 recd. a qrs rent say 15$ due 21st. Decr. 1825

16 May— „ —	Ditto—	do 15$ —	21. March 1826
10 July— „ —	Ditto —	do 15$ —	21 June 1826
5 Feb 1827—	Ditto 2—	do 30$. —	21—Decr. 1826.
20 Mar 1828	Ditto 4—	do 60 —	21 Decr. 1827—

ADS, signed also by Dillon. DLC-TJC (DNA, M212, R16).
[1] I.e., Gratz and Bruce.   [2] See above, III, 880.
[3] AE by Robert Scott.   [4] Constable.   [5] AE by Scott.

From Christopher Hughes

Private   Stockholm, 21: June; 1825.
My dear Mr Clay

[Explains that he has delayed several weeks before acknowledging receipt of Clay's communications in the hope of being able to report the results of (John) Connell's efforts to settle the Stralsund claims. A round sum in cash has been offered; Connell wants $10,000 more; a decision, "in one way or another," will be reached "in a very few days." For his success, Connell owes much to the Count de Wetterstedt, "a most kind-hearted, honourable and able man," who prevailed over the cupidity of the King (Charles XIV) and his Council. Hughes claims some credit for himself in the connection, for having "sustained Mr Connell to the utmost of my power; but as to the princip[al] and the amount of liquidation & *compromise,* I have carefully abstained from mixing myself up with that matter." Beyond "formal presentation of Mr. Connell's Memorial, I have had *no official* connection whatever with the Minister, on this subject, so far as any projects or principles of *compromise* were suggested, or acted on!"]

I am sure, my dear Sir, that you will excuse my continuing to write to you, frankly & without reserve and allow me to cherish the valued conviction, that you continue to think of me, with friendship, and I may say affection. True, our letters have been *"few & far between,"* but I have ever hugged to my heart, as one of my dearest persuasions, that you feel towards me, not as to a common Friend; & though you have now become my immediate chief, yet you will never show to me the repelling [. . .] of office; but still allow me to commune with you as I have *ever* been wont to do, when I communed with you *at all;*— id est. as I do with my own heart! I shall go on & eat this fruit, until you tell me 'tis *forbidden.*

I am exceedingly grateful to Mr. Adams, for having thought of me; & to you, for having supported my transfer to Brussels;[1] I know the kind way, in which you *both,* did me the honour to speak of me to General Smith;[2] & I shall endeavour to retain my place in the esteem of you both! I am exceedingly gratified at my dislocation [*sic*]; for I have had enough of the bold & cold & ossian scenery of Sweden! But I should have been overjoyed, if the interests of the Country, & the benevolence of both your Excellencies, had united in giving me a promotion.

Yet I got, what I asked; and (to use Mrs. Goulburns,[3] idiom) when *one* gets what *one* asks, *one* ought to be satisfied: and so I am; au moins, pour le coup!

Breaking up my establishment here, has been no easy or trifling

affair! it was *rather* extensive; and, though I have not committed
any *major* breaches of the wise and friendly counsel, with which
you kindly followed me to Europe (with your letter in 1816:)[4] as
to hospitality & scale of living: (which letter, I found & read
'tother day;) still, I have not exactly been as *thrifty*, as I might have
been; &, in strictness, *ought* to have been, with a view to the future!
However, we grow grave & gray and economical, with time; & I have
got a valuable stock of *notions* & resolutions, for the time to come!
Besides, General Smith's misfortunes,[5] & the depression in the value
of real property, all *came over me*, in destruction of all my hopes &
calculations; & idle as they almost always are, who is *so sage* as not
to indulge in them!!!

[States that he has followed the advice of Sir Charles Bagot, now
Ambassador at Brussels "(who asks all about you, & with great professed anxiety & friendship, especially in reference to your new
place)" to ship household furniture to his new station rather than
sell it. Some articles are being sent to Baltimore, where part of them
will be wanted, "as we mean to pass the winter, agreeably to Leave
of absence, my private affairs, & the affairs of the Estate of my
Father, & of all my family, require that I should do so!" A "little
english hunting carriage and a sledge" will be shipped to New
York, freight free, through the courtesy of Swedish friends.]

I have written already a *mortal* letter; but *you may* remember,
that I am long-of-wind, & given to circumlocution & penphrase—
certainly, *I do* remember one fierce lesson you gave me, & with
a pruning & unsparing hand, at Ghent!! You cut down, in a trice,
a letter of mine from *lines* to *words!* But it is not *every* one who
has the spartan style! I remember how my *comb* was cut; & if I
could have been allowed, by lapse of recollection, ever again to
raise my *feathers*, our Humane & tenacious Friend, Mr. Russell,[6]
would not have permitted it; for, with a *charity*, not confined to
home, he took occasion, in 1819, *here* to put-me-in-mind-of the
Busby[7] dressing and the merciless amputation, I suffered, at your
hands! It was kind & civil in Gentle Brother Jonathan! I have
not forgotten either the origin, or the humanity, of this exemplary
exercise of memory, on his part!

Mrs. Hughes, (whose health is far from being good:) and my
son & daughter[8] (all, God has spared to us:) leave this, in 5 or 6
days; they go about 1/3 of the way to Copenhagen, & wait me, at
a friend of ours, Baroness Rebausen's Chateau! I leave Stockholm
about the 15th. July, & we then go on to Denmark. The Rebausens
are our most intimate friends. She is a Sister of Mrs. Genl.
Humphreys;[9] & we pass our few last days, in Sweden, under their
Roof!—

Mr. Connell's business *may* delay me a few days longer; but I hope not, it, & winding up my affairs, after 8½ years residence, have rendered it impossible for me to move sooner! But it was not important, that I should! The King of Denmark [Frederick VI, who reigned from 1808 until his death in 1839] will not return from Schleswig, until the end of [August] & when he is absent, nothing is *done;* he leaves no *Alter[nate]* at *Copenhagen!!!* Mr. Somerville wrote me, that he did not expect to be in Europe until August! So all chimes in [. . . .]

                                           25 June

Lord Bloomfield,[10] the English Minister, sends a special courier, and that enables me to *inflict* a still longer letter upon you! [Hughes describes the flattering attention shown him on the preceding day by the King and then continues:] about an hour after, The King called me to him; took me into an alcove of the Pavilion; requested me to sit down beside him; & we had a most edifying conversation of some 20 minutes, about our Country—about South-America—he wished to know my opinions of the new Republics—if I thought them to be solidly established—he spoke of Sweden, of his own administration. The gradual disappearance of ancient prejudices & amelioration of the commercial system— his hope ere long, to get rid entirely of the antiquated Product-Placat (Navigation Law,[11] founded on the most rooted prohibitive principles) said— "We shall soon renew our Treaty with your Country, you may rest assured, Monsieur Hughes, that whatever extension may be possibly given to its basis— indeed— Whatever your Government may ask, shall be granted—where we get, we will willingly give:— we will even be the first to *give:*— in the hope of *getting*— we will do by Treaty (& have already done a great deal:) that, which I should find great difficulty to do *at once* & by enactment;— we will destroy ancient & contracted prejudices, & root up the prohibitive system! *You* shall be satisfied with *us;* I hope you have had reason to be satisfied with our treatment of your country's ships & merchants; & I flatter myself, knowing your observing faculty, that you have perceived a slow, but certain & solid amelioration in this Country, since you came here; I have done a good deal; I leave to my Soon [*sic*] to carry on & complete the work: &c. & &c." He then spoke again of my going away, in the kindest terms. [Nearly a page on this subject here omitted by editors.]

I have very little hope of doing any good at Copenhagen;[12] the present Minister of Foreign Affairs, Ct. Schimmelman,[13] is a superannuated Statesman, & the Foreign estate of Denmark was put out *to nurse,* when placed in his hands; however, I will clap John Doe & Richard Roe upon his Danish Majesty's back; & make my stay as short as circumstances may seem to make advisable.

I hope to be arriving at Brussels at the end of August, or beginning of September, & my project is to be nearing my dear native Land in November.

Our old Ghent Friends have written me Lots of kind Letters, on reading the newspaper statement that I was to go to their Court; they say, that they look on it as if Mr. Adams meant to do "un acte de Galanterie à leurs bonne Ville de Gand"! and really, nothing can *exceed* the affectionate & flattering terms, in which those good people have written to me! The d'Hanes, VanConeghems[14] &c. &c. The new Dutch Minister, just arrived here, is a [. . .] Baron Von Crombrugghe;[15] you may remember the name; they were intimate with the d'Hanes! & among *our* friends, however, the Baron says, "They are *all* our friends; for they brag & talk about us to this day"; & they glory and boast because one of the Congress has been chosen President! He has been several years at Copenhagen, & is a favourite of his King: He says, the Danes will never pay a sou; nor will Old Schimmelman do any business effectually; that I should have had a better chance with the late Minister Rozencrantz![16] Now *we* know, & so did Mr. *Erving*,[17] what *that* chance was worth. However, nous verrons!—

Mr. Brown[18] is a Martyr to the Govt. & I hear that Mr. Sheldon's[19] health is very, almost hopelessly bad,— I regret all this from my heart! Mr. & Mrs. Brown are amazingly Popular.—

And now, my dear Sir, I think I may afford to spare you any more reading of my dull phrases! May I pray you to mention me most respectfully, to the President, & to recal [*sic*] me, in the kindest terms, to the memory of Mrs. Clay! In conclusion, let me commend myself to a continuation of your friendly feelings, for your's ever & devotedly   CHRISTOPHER HUGHES

ALS. DNA, RG59, Dip. Disp., Sweden and Norway (M45, R5). Received September 4. Ellipses indicate illegible words.

1 See above, Clay to Smith, March 1, 1825.

2 See above, Clay to Smith, May 7, 1825.

3 Jane Montagu Goulburn (Mrs. Henry Goulburn).

4 See above, II, 259.   5 See above, II, 698n.

6 Jonathan Russell.

7 The name of Richard Busby, headmaster of Westminster School, London, from 1638 to 1660, had become proverbial for severity as a pedagogue.

8 Charles John and Margaret S. Hughes. Cf. below, Hughes to Clay, October 28, 1825.

9 Neither the Rebausens nor the Humphreys have been identified.

10 Benjamin, first Baron Bloomfield, had risen to the rank of major general of horse artillery (1814) and served as member of Parliament (1812-1818) and private secretary and confidant of George IV (1817-1822) prior to his appointment to Stockholm. He had been raised to the Irish peerage earlier in 1825.

11 Issued in 1724 and 1726.

12 See above, Clay to Hughes, March 24, 1825.

13 Count Ernst Heinrich Schimmelmann, who, after serving as Finance Minister from 1784 to 1814, had assumed the post of Foreign Minister upon the death of Niels Rosenkrantz in 1824. Schimmelmann continued in the latter office until his own death, in 1831.

14 Neither family has been identified.

15 P. von Crombrugghe, not further identified.

16 Niels Rosenkrantz.
17 George W. Erving. See above, I, 571n; Clay to Hughes, March 24, 1825.
18 James Brown.
19 Daniel Sheldon, who in 1816 had been appointed Secretary of Legation for the United States in France.

INSTRUCTIONS AND DISPATCHES   June 21, 1825

From JOSEPH PULIS, Malta. Reports the boarding and plundering of an American vessel by a Greek privateer. ALS. DNA, RG59, Cons. Disp., Malta, vol. 1 (M-T218, R1). Addressed to John Quincy Adams, Secretary of State; received September 1. Pulis, a resident of Malta, held the position of United States consul at that port from 1801 until 1828.

MISCELLANEOUS LETTERS   June 21, 1825

From JOSEPH E. READ, Troy, Massachusetts. Acknowledges information from the State Department relative to the case of the *Minerva* (see above, Anderson to Clay, March 18, 1825, note); inquires "what sort of discharge will be Necessary for the owners to give on receiving their money. . . ." LS. DNA, RG76, Misc. Claims, Colombia. Read signs as "Acting owner of the Schooner Minerva."

To Nicholas Biddle

Dr Sir   Lexington 22d June 1825
   Col. Charles S. Todd and his father the honble Thomas Todd (though the latter is still in bad health and very feeble) came up from Frankfort yesterday and have seen me to day, to execute on their part the arrangement made with the B.U.S.[1] and I believe have their papers prepared or very nearly so to complete it. Upon adverting however to the resolution of January, adopted by the Board, I observed that the extension of time for the accomplishment of this business expired in April; and as I had not heard directly from you, and as my professional relation with the Bank had ceased,[2] I felt some apprehensions that I might not consult [*sic*] the wishes of the Board if I entered on the business. I have stated this feeling to the gentlemen and advised Col. Todd to apply to the Bank for its authority to Mr Wickliffe[3] or any other gentleman that it may choose to designate, to conclude the matter. I have ventured to say, from my knowledge of the liberality and equitable dispositions of the Board, that I did not doubt that the requisite authority would be accordingly promptly given. There is no diminution, as far as I know or believe, of the motives which I presume led the Bank to agree to the proposed arrangement. In justice to Col Todd I ought to add that immediately upon my coming out to Kentucky he applied to me, expressed his readiness to complete the arrangement, and his present visit to Lexington has been made

in pursuance of my request to enable me to examine into the condition of the affair. Indeed he has throughout manifested an honorable solicitude to comply fully with the arrangement.

I am with great respect Your ob. servant   H. Clay
Nicholas Biddle Esqr &c &c &c

P.S. With respect to the effect of a release from the Bank to Col Todd, undoubtedly it would be to release the other parties who are bound with him, though except Mr. Sneed,[4] all of them are, I am fully persuaded, insolvent. To guard against that operation of the release, I have suggested to Col. Todd that the Bank could adopt a resolution not to prosecute him, with which he says he would be content, and which would not have the above effect   This course has been occasionally pursued by the Bank of K.[5]   H C.

ALS. DLC-HC (DNA, M212, R1).
[1] On the younger Todd's debt to the Bank of the United States, see above, III, 414, 415n, 811, 881.
[2] See above, Clay to Biddle, March 8, 1825.
[3] Robert Wickliffe.   [4] Achilles Sneed.   [5] Kentucky.

Mortgage Deed to Louis Marshall

[June 22, 1825]

[James B. January, James Logue, Robert S. Todd, and Henry Clay, on behalf of the Grand Lodge of the Free and Accepted Order of Masons of Kentucky, convey title to the property of the Lodge on West Main Street in Lexington, contingent upon their failure to pay by January 1, 1835, the sum of $10,630.66 due to Dr. Louis Marshall as winner of the $20,000 prize in the Grand Masonic Lottery.]

Fayette County Court, Deed Book 1, pp. 16-19.
Logue, a native of Ireland who had come to Lexington in 1813 and opened a school, was for twenty-five years, at varying periods, librarian of the Lexington Public Library. In 1846 he was elected mayor of Lexington. Later he removed to Ohio.
The Grand Masonic Lottery, authorized by the Kentucky General Assembly (*Acts, 1814-1815*, pp. 290-92) to raise funds for construction of the Hall here mortgaged, was held as a series of drawings ranging from 1818 to 1841. The $20,000 ticket had been drawn March 18, 1820. When the Lodge was unable to pay the sum due as here stipulated in 1835, the building, which had been estimated to cost $21,000, was sold to Marshall at auction for $6,000. The Lodge paid the remainder of the debt to Marshall on November 26, 1839. Coleman, *Masonry in the Bluegrass,* 97, 101-103.

Property Deed from Andrew McCalla and Others

[June 22, 1825]

[Andrew McCalla, Alexander Wake, Richard Sharp, deputy of Leonard Young, "late Sheriff of Fayette County," and George I. Brown and Thomas E. West, commissioners of the Farmers Bank of

Jessamine, join in a deed to Henry Clay clarifying title to property on Short Street in Lexington, purchased by Clay from the commissioners. The property, conveyed by McCalla to Wake under deed of trust, dated April 13, 1820, to secure payment of a debt due the Farmers Bank of Jessamine, was bought by the commissioners of the bank on May 22, 1821, at a Fayette County sheriff's sale, under foreclosure proceedings brought against McCalla. Whereas the commissioners have not received title from either the sheriff or his deputy and "all the parties aforesaid of the first part are desirous to vest in . . . Clay a good and valid title . . . ," the present indenture is executed. Signed by McCalla, Sharp, Brown, and West only; recorded in the office of the Fayette County clerk, June 22, 1825.]

Fayette County Court, Deed Book Z, 268-69. See above, III, 880. Wake, born in Fauquier County, Virginia, in 1797, had been brought to Woodford County, Kentucky, around the turn of the century, had studied law, and had been admitted to the bar in 1820. The above-mentioned deed of trust from McCalla to Wake (recorded in Fayette County Court, Deed Book T, 337-39) had authorized the latter to conduct sale of the property, as subsequently transacted by the sheriff, in the event that McCalla's debts to the bank commissioners and others were not paid within three months. Wake later became an extensive property owner in Nicholasville, Jessamine County, and county judge from 1850 to 1858.

Leonard Young, who had also served for many years from 1797 as a Fayette County justice of the peace, had died in October, 1821, while holding office as sheriff.

INSTRUCTIONS AND DISPATCHES   June 22, 1825

From HENRY MIDDLETON, St. Petersburg, no. 47. Acknowledges receipt of Clay's letter of April 25 and encloses copies of gazettes reporting all that has been announced concerning the proceedings of the Diet in Poland. ALS. DNA, RG59, Dip. Disp., Russia, vol. 10 (M35, R10). Addressed to Secretary of State. See above, Middleton to Secretary of State, April 21, 1825.

APPLICATIONS, RECOMMENDATIONS   June 22, 1825

WILLIAM R. KING, Cahaba, Alabama, recommends "Doctr. Charles Douglass [sic] of Franklin County Alabama" for appointment as Secretary of Legation or consul in South America. ALS. DNA, RG59, A. and R. (MR2). In March, 1827, Douglas was appointed consul at Barcelona; late the following year he was transferred to Guazacualco (Coatzacoalcos), Mexico, where he remained until 1830. Cf. below, Douglas to Clay, June 30, 1825; May 26, 1827.

APPLICATIONS, RECOMMENDATIONS   June 23, 1825

WILLIAM RICHARDSON, Lexington (Kentucky), transmits, with his own recommendation, a letter by which "Mr [Eben.] Fiske" solicits an appointment. ALS. DNA, RG59, A. and R. (MR3). Addressed to Clay at Ashland. Endorsed, probably in a clerk's hand: "The Enclosure referred to not recd with this Letter." Richardson, born in Massachusetts, had lived in New Orleans briefly before settling in Lexington in 1819. Trained as a merchant, he became a successful manufacturer of woolens. In 1837 he removed to Louisville, where he served as cashier, later president, of the Northern Bank of Kentucky. He was an active member of the Masonic Order, a life member of the Kentucky Colonization Society, for thirty years a ruling elder of the Presbyterian Church, and, politically, a strong Clay partisan. On the recommended appointment, cf. above, Richardson to Clay, May 31, 1825, note.

Statement of Auction Sale

Sales at auction for Acct. of H. Clay at Ashland			24 June 1825
	Articles.	Amt	To whom
paid	1. Cow & Calf (yellow & white Back	$pd. 6 25	A Atcheson[1]
paid H. C.	1. Brindle Cow (Harrison)[2]	5 —	Jno. Hart[3]
paid H. C.	1. Young red Cow & Calf (white face)	13 50	Mr. Smeade[4]
pd. H C.	1 Red Cow & Calf (Harrison)	25 —	J. Shelby[5]
pd. H C.	1 Pided[6] Cow & Calf (red head & neck)	8 50	do
paid	1 Red Cow, white face, & Calf	30 —	Jno. Brand.
pd. H. C.	1 Ditto little do—	14 —	J Shelby
pd. H. C.	1 Red hieffer [sic] White Jaws & Calf star & white on rump	14 —	do
pd H. C.	1 Red Cow—White on shoulder	8 50	do
paid H C.	1 Large Red Cow. (Big Bag)	23 50	do
pd. H C.	1 Red Cow, hieffer, some white in face	17 —	do
pd. H. C.	1 Large Pennsa. Cow & Calf	25 50	do
pd	1 Black long horn. Pennsa. Cow & Calf	pd. 24 50	Mr. Speirs[7]
pd. H C.	1 dark red Cow, a little white in face & back	13 —	J Shelby
pd. H. C.	1 Red Cow, spotted Belly & white face	15 —	do
pd. H. C.	1 Do— Stoop down horns	12 —	do
pd. H. C.	1 Do—White belly & legs & White face	17 —	do
paid H. C.	1 fat red Cow— (imported)	30 —	G. Coons[8]

pd. H. C.	1 Red Hieffer, spotted Jaws, never calved	14 —	J Shelby
pd. H C.	1— Do— White face & back	17 50—	do
paid H. C.	1— do— Do— & belly (spayed)	16 —	G. Coons.
pd. H. C.	8 Steers— @ 16$—	128 —	E. Cartmill[9]
pd. H. C.	1 Yellow hieffer & Bull Calf	21 —	J Shelby
pd. H. C.	1 Sorrel Buzzard[10] Mare (old)	25 —	do
pd. H. C.	1 Bay Mare (old)	36 —	do
	1 Bay diomed[11] Horse 4 yr old	33 —	Thee. Clay
paid H. C.	3-2 Yr. Old Mules @ 55/50	166 50	Harbin[12]
	Forwarded	$759 25	
	Sales continued	759 25	
paid H. C.	3 One yr. old Mules @ 35$25	105 75	Jno. Clark[13]
paid H C.	1 Brown Mare & spotted Colt	63—	Wm. Offut L P C Bufford[14]
paid	1 Iron Grey Colt—	35 50	S Cooper[15]
paid H C.	1 Black Colt Horse—	40 —	L P. C Bufford
pd. H C—	1 Bay 3 yr. old filly—	45 —	Mr. Smead—
paid H C.	1 Sorrel 3- Do—do	60 —	L P. C. Bufford
pd.	1 Bay Colt 1 yr. old (not deld.)	16 pd.	B Berry[16]
pd. H C.	1 Brown Mare & Colt (old mare)	50 —	Mr Smead
pd.	1 Sorrel Horse 3 yrs. old pd.	61 —	TH. Pindell
	1 Sorrel Colt 2 yr. old—	35 —	F G Hawkins
paid	20 Sheep 1st. choice (excepg. 4) @ 5$.	100 —	W E Dudley[17]
paid	1 Brown Mare & Blaze Colt 40$ & $5 more if she shold [sic] have a Mule Colt	40 —	S. Cooper 25 June 1825.[18]
Furniture	(Household & Kitchen.) 4 Large parlour & dining room mirrors	$300.	Geo. C. Thompson
	2 Demijohns @ 1.50c. pd.	3 —	Shelby
paid	1 do	1 50	R Higgins[19]
	2 do pd	3 — pd.	H Lewis[20]
paid	1 Fender (small)	2 25	T Nelson[21]
	1 Small pr. Kitchen Andirons	„ 62½	Jno. Carr[22]

	1 Large do do pd.	75	J Shelby
H C pd	1 Smallest do do	37	D Castleman[23]
pd. H. C.	1 Lot Castings 8 ps	3 50	Mr. Smead—
pd	1 do 7	4 —	do
	1 do 10	3 25	Mr. Wickliffe[24]
	1 do 10 pd.	3 75	J Shelby
	1 Copper Coffee Pot & Bell } pd. Metal Kettle	3 50	J Shelby
	1 Lot Tin Ware pd.	1 75	Dunlap[25]
	1 Bathing Tubb [sic] pd.	8 50	J Shelby
	1 pr Brass Andirons, largest pd	12 50	D. Bryan[26]
	Shovel Tongs & poker pd.	6 —	do
paid	1 pr. Brass Andirons 2nd. size	4 —	C Williams[27]
paid	Shovel & Tongs	1 —	T Nelson
	1 pr. Brass Andirons 3rd pd	1 —	R. Gray[28]
	1 do do (Eagle) pd.	6 —	J Shelby
	1 do do. Smallest One bent) pd.	3 25	do
H. C.	1 Biscuit Table & one small do	1 —	Mr. Smead
	1 Stand Candle Moulds pd.	3 25	Shelby
H C	1 Wash stand Cherry	2 25	Smead
	1 Do—Pitcher & Ewyer [sic]	4 50	Do
H C	1 Wash stand	1 25	Castleman
	1 Portable Desk pd.	87	R Gray
	Sales contd.		
	1 High post Bed Stead & bottom pd.	4 —	Wm. Long[29]
pd	1 Low post Do pd.	3 25	Wm Boman[30]
paid	1 Woms. Saddle	5 —	S. Cooper
	1 Childs. Bedstead & bottom	1 75 }	Jno Carr
	1 Cradle	1	
paid	12 Rush bottom fancy Chairs 225c.	27 —	Mr. Holly[31]
paid	6 & the balance „	13 50	do
paid	1 Iron bd. Millers Bbl	2 50	do
pd	4 Waiters & 2 Bread Baskets pd.	2 50	Mr. Hart
pd	1 Cherry Table	87	Mr Smead

pd	2 Toilet Tables	50	D Castleman
paid	2 ps. new Carpeting @ 87c.	27 40½	Brand
			Majr Robb[32]
paid	2 Do (sewed) 85		
paid	1 Carpet	7 25	S Cooper
paid	2 Ladies work Tables 212½c	4 25	R Higgins
	1 do do not pd. pd.	„ 75	T. Smith
pd	1 Easy Chair	6 50	D Castleman
pd	1 Side Board Table	2 50	Smead
	1 Circular front Bureau	5 —	Theo. Clay
paid	1 Column do	10 62	Majr. Robb
paid	1 Knife Case	2 25	E Warner[33]
pd	1 Back Gamn. Table pd.	1 25	J Shelby
paid	1 Square Bureau	2 25	H Holly
paid	2 Settees 275c	5 50	T Smith
	1 Dressing Glass	55 —	Mr Wickliffe
paid	1 Doz Mahogy. Chairs @ 5$	60 —	R Higgins
pd	1 Sopha	51	E Warner
	1 Piano Fortie [sic]	150 —	J. T. Johnson
	12 Chairs @ 225c.	27 —	(T Smith)
	Sales contind.		
	1 Chandelier	50 —	Mr. Wickliff [sic]
paid	1 Carpet (dining room)	27 50	C Williams
H. C	2 doz. Bottles assd 9½c	2 28	Mr Smead
H. C	1 ditto 8½	1 02	do
	1 ditto 8¼	1 — pd.	Wallace[34]
paid	Remainder 7		Higgins
paid H C.	1 Mirabeau	11 —	Dishman[35]
paid H C.	1 Franklin	6 50	do
paid.	1 Side Board	13 50	E W. Craig
	1 Plateau pd.	27 50	L Caldwell[36]
pd	8 Glass Jarrs @ 35c	2 80	D Castleman
pd 212	4 Plate Heaters 106	4 24	pd 212 (Mr. Lewis) do
pd	1 Caster	6 50	E Warner
pd	1 pr. Cut Glass Lamps	11 50	D Castleman
	1 pr. Snuffers & Tray @ 262½	2 62	E Warner
paid	1 pr. Branch Lamps	25 —	H Holly
pd Broken[37]	1 Alabaster Candlestick	1 12½	E Warner
	1 Comr. Perry[38] pd	62½	Bryan
paid	1 La belle Polenies[39]	1 12	Craig
paid	1 Ninon Do	1 25	R Higgins
paid	1 Innocence	1 37	do
	1 Thos. Jefferson	25	do

	2 Pictures	pd	1 —	D Bryan
	1 Adam	pd.	1 50	D Long[40]
	1 Cains[41] departure	pd.	1 25	Do
	1 Josephs Dream		2 62	
	1 Redeemer	pd	6 75	E Warner
	1 Gardner [sic]	pd	1 12½	do
	Sales continued			
pd	1 View of Paris No 8		1 62	E Warner
pd.	1 Joseph Sold		4 —	do
paid	1 Passage Lamp		14 50	Brand
paid	1 Lot Glassware &			
	Stand		14 —	do
	1 Lot Queensware		50	Jno Carr
	1 Alabaster Time piece			
	& Ornams. pd.		45 —	Jos. I. Lemon[42]
paid	⌈Demostenes [sic] &			
	3⟨ Niobe @ 20$		40 —	R. Chinn[43]
paid	⌊Cicero		20 —	do
pd	1 Bellows pd.		„ 81¼	Mr. Thompson
	1 pr. Card Tables		10 — pd.	Mr Wallace
	Dining Tables			
	(3) @ 250c		7 50	Mr Smead
	Carpet Rods 21c.			E Warner
	1 Lot Cut Glass			
	(not sold)			
	1 Hair Matrass [sic]		15 75	E Warner
paid	1 Clock		38 —	C McAlear[44]
paid	3 Stacks Hay			
	(choice—8$50		25 50	S Cooper
paid	1 Do		9 —	T Smith
paid	1 Pendule			
	(Washington)		75 :	H Holley—[45]

5000

AD by Robert Scott, except as noted. DLC-TJC (DNA, M212, R16). The word "paid" and its abbreviation are in Clay's hand, as are his initials with a few exceptions. See above, Advertisement, June 13, 1825.

1 Alexander Atchison.

2 Probably from the stock of Daniel Harrison. Cf. above, II, 703n.

3 John Hart (Sr.).   4 Abraham K. Smedes.

5 James Shelby.   6 Pied.

7 Probably Greenberry Spiers.

8 George Coons, an inhabitant of Kentucky since the turn of the century, at first a brewer in Lexington, now owned a small farm on the outskirts of town.

9 Elijah Cartmell, a resident of the South Elkhorn district of Fayette County.

10 Cf. above, I, 322-24.

11 Cf. above, I, 234n. Diomed, imported into Virginia in 1798, was one of the most famous sires of race horses ever brought into the United States. Since he had died in 1807 or 1808, the reference indicates lineage.

12 John Harbin, Lexington livery stable keep· r.

13 Of Tate's Creek Road.

14 Probably William C. Offutt, of Fayette County; Bufford not identified.

15 Spencer Cooper.

16 Benjamin Berry, born in Virginia, now resided in Woodford County, Kentucky.

17 William Eylett Dudley, of Winchester Pike, Fayette County, a brother of Ambrose, Benjamin Winslow, Jephthah, and Peter Dudley; nephew of William Dudley. On this transaction cf. below, Clay to Beatty, September 24, 1825.

18 This line and the next one are in Clay's hand.

19 Richard Higgins.

20 Possibly Hudson Lewis, of Clark County, Kentucky.

21 Thomas Nelson, Lexington merchant.   22 Probably John H. Kerr.

23 David Castleman.   24 Robert Wickliffe.

25 Probably William Dunlap, who owned land on Hickman Creek in Fayette County.

26 Daniel Bryan.   27 Caleb Williams, Lexington shoemaker.

28 Probably Richard Gray, who held a considerable acreage on South Elkhorn Creek in Fayette County.

29 Who owned property on South Elkhorn Creek and Hickman Road in Fayette County.

30 Bowman, proprietor of a livery stable in Lexington.

31 Horace Holley.

32 Joseph Robb, a farmer of the southern district of Fayette County.

33 Probably Elijah Warner, Lexington cabinet maker.

34 Possibly Thomas Wallace.

35 John Dishman. His purchases were, presumably, busts.

36 Probably Leaming, son of Dr. Charles Caldwell.

37 A line, crossed out, recorded the sale of "1 Small Looking Glass" to T. Smith for $2.75.   38 Oliver H. Perry (portrait).

39 Probably Polonaise. This and the succeeding eleven entries were apparently pictures.

40 Probably Daniel Long, of the Silver Creek area, Madison County.

41 Word not clear.   42 Lexington merchant.

43 Richard H. Chinn.

44 Probably Charles McLear, married in Fayette County in 1822.

45 This line in Clay's hand.

To W[illiam] J[ordan] Morton [Jr.] and Others

Gent.   Ashland 24 June 1825

I have duly received the letter which you did me the honor to address to me on the 17h. instant.[1] I thank you, and the Citizens of Russellville and its vicinity, most cordially, for the friendly expressions of confidence and approbation which it contains. If I have been assailed with unparallelled [sic] malignity, because I would not, on a late occasion, sacrifice my own deliberate convictions to gratify others, not even Citizens of Kentucky, I have, on the other hand, enjoyed the highest gratification, in the general and enthusiastic demonstrations of affection with which I have been surrounded since my return to Kentucky. Those which your magnanimity have prompted you to make are as honorable and acceptable, as the recollection of them will be grateful and lasting.

It would have given me inexpressible satisfaction to have been able to partake of the generous hospitality to which you have kindly invited me. Having seen your interesting part of our State twenty six years ago,[2] and but once since,[3] a visit to it now would have afforded me the agreeable opportunity of observing its progress and again seeing many valuable friends and acquaintances. But I regret that the urgency of my duties, public and private, will not admit of my indulging in that happiness. Whilst I submit, therefore, to the necessity of declining acceptance of the honor intended me,

I beg my fellow Citizens of Logan to be assured that it will be my earnest and constant endeavor to continue to deserve their highly esteemed confidence and attachment.

To you, gentlemen, among whom I recognize several of my earliest and undeviating friends, I offer the respectful acknowledgments of
Your faithful friend & obedient Servant   H. CLAY

Mess. W. J. Morton   Chas. S. Morehead
      Edward Jones   Thomas Foster
      Robt. Ewing   Edwn. R. Wallace
      Richard Bibb   A R. Macey &
      E. W [sic]. Ewing   Richard Bibb Junr[4]
                            &c. &c. &c.

ALS. ICU. Morton, born in Louisa County, Virginia, had settled in Logan County, Kentucky, in 1810. A lawyer, he had served one term in the State legislature (1818-1819) and was now postmaster of Russellville (1824-1827). He later became county attorney and, in 1855, county judge.   1 Not found.

2 During his trip to Nashville in 1799. See above, I, 24 and note.

3 On his return from New Orleans in 1819. Cf. above, II, 696-98.

4 Jones was a lawyer. Foster had probably resided near Great Crossings, Scott County, Kentucky, at the turn of the century. They, with Wallace and Macey, have not been further identified.

Richard Bibb, father of George M. as well as of Richard, Jr., was a Virginian and a veteran of the Revolution, who had come to Kentucky in 1789 and for a brief period had lived in Lexington. He had then purchased a salt works in Bullitt County and, in 1803, had represented that district in the Kentucky Legislature. Subsequently he had removed to Logan County, where he was a Methodist minister and a prominent businessman, president of the Russellville branch of the Bank of Kentucky. Richard Bibb, Jr., was a Russellville merchant.

Ephraim McLean Ewing, son of Robert, had studied law at Transylvania University and successfully practiced that profession in Russellville. He became a member of the Kentucky Legislature from 1830 to 1832, an associate justice of the court of appeals in 1835, and chief justice of the latter body from 1843 to 1847.

Charles Slaughter Morehead, graduated with a degree in law from Transylvania University in 1820, practiced that profession in Christian County, which he represented in the Kentucky Legislature from 1828 to 1830. He thereupon removed to Frankfort, where he served as State attorney general from 1830 to 1835 and representative in the State assembly from 1838 to 1843 and again in 1844-1845, serving as speaker the last three sessions. He was a member of Congress from 1847 to 1851, a member of the Kentucky Legislature again in 1853-1854, and Governor of the Commonwealth from 1855 to 1859.

INSTRUCTIONS AND DISPATCHES   June 24, 1825

From HEMAN ALLEN, Valparaiso, no. 16. Now that the Chilean Congress has adjourned, Allen has filed the claim of the owners of the ship *Macedonian* but anticipates that a proposal for organizing a federative government will further delay action. An assembly to begin formation of that government has attacked the junta in power; Vicuña has resigned, and (Juan de Dios) Vial del Rio has replaced him. Postscript notes that the Spanish squadron in the area is disintegrating—crews are mutinying and surrendering to local officials. ALS. DNA, RG59, Dip. Disp., Chile, vol. 1 (M-T2, R1). Addressed to Secretary of State; "Recd 5 October." In 1818 the *Macedonian*, of Boston, owned by John S. Ellery and commanded by Eliphalet Smith, had made a trading voyage to the Spanish-Peruvian port of Callao. During Captain Smith's journey home, the profits of the expedition, amounting to over $145,000, had been seized by

Chilean officials. A memorial requesting intervention by the United States Government, in behalf of the owners of the cargo, had been lodged with the Department of State in 1820.

From AB[RAHAM] B. NONES, Maracaibo (Colombia). Acknowledges receipt of Clay's letter of April 16. Reports his inability to procure the arrest of a deserter from the crew of an American vessel because of instructions received by local officials "not to render any assistance to the Consul of the U.S. in arresting deserters in consequence of Colombia not enjoying equal rights in the United States." Nones has forwarded a statement of the case, and copies of the correspondence, to the American Chargé in Bogotá (Beaufort T. Watts, acting Chargé). LS. DNA, RG59, Cons. Disp., Maracaibo, vol. 1 (M-T62, R1). Received August 5.

MISCELLANEOUS RECEIVED   June 24, 1825

From ORAN FOLLETT, Batavia (New York). Announces transfer of the (Batavia *Spirit of the*) *Times* to his brother, Frederick Follett, "who has in fact managed the business of the concern for a number of years past." Oran Follett is "soon to come into a controlling influence over the" *Rochester Telegraph* and wishes that the present proprietor not be given the appointment to publish the laws. ALS. DNA, RG59, P. and D. of L. The proprietor of the *Rochester Telegraph* was at this time Everard Peck, who had founded the journal in 1818. He sold it later in the summer of 1825 to Thurlow Weed. See below, Hayden to Clay, August 27, 1825.

From GEO[RGE S.] WATKINS, Baltimore. Explains that illness caused his delay in delivering dispatches from (Richard) Rush and his transmittal of them "through the public mail." ALS. DNA, RG59, Letters from Bearers of Dispatches. The delayed dispatches appear to have been those, above, Rush to Clay, May 18, 1825.

Account with [John] Sheley

[*ca.* June 25, 1825]

Computed at twenty dollars an acre for 92 acres, that is, $1840, of which $200 had been paid in August, 1822, $1274 on September 20, 1822, and $226 on October 15, 1824, the account shows interest and principal charges of $191.20 due on June 15 (1825), upon which Sheley paid $69.20 on June 25, leaving a balance of $122 yet unpaid. D, the line reporting Sheley's payment of June 25 in Clay's hand. DLC-TJC (DNA, M212, R16). Cf. above, III, 272.

Property Deed to John Sheley

[June 25, 1825]

[For the sum of $1840, in notes of the Bank of the Commonwealth, Henry Clay and (Isham) Talbott sell to "John Sheely [*sic*]" a tract of 92 acres in Scott County, bounded with reference to points in the lines of (Charles) Whitaker, Greenup,[1] and John Waters.[2] Title guaranteed against "all and every person whatever." Acknowledged by Clay before J. C. Rodes, clerk of Fayette County court, July 2, 1825; recorded by Ben B. Ford,[3] deputy for Elijah Hawkins, clerk of Scott County court, January 20, 1826.]

Scott County Court, Deed Book G, 204-205. Recorded copy partially destroyed. See above, Account, this date.

1 Possibly Samuel Greenup, not further identified.

2 Probably the early settler of Mason County who had died in 1800.

3 Born in Virginia, Ford had moved in 1811 to Georgetown, Kentucky, where he had taught school in 1812 and had begun the practice of law in 1816. He became clerk of the Scott County court in 1827 and held that office for many years.

From James Brown

My dear Sir,   Paris June 25. 1825

I had the pleasure of receiving your very acceptable letter by the Count de Menou,[1] and was happy to learn that your health was not so bad as I had been induced to apprehend, and that you bear up with your usual fortitude against the attacks of your political enemies and the scurrility of the newspapers paragraphs directed against you since the result of the Presidential election has been announced. The administration of Mr Adams will no doubt be assailed by a combined attack of the friends of the dissappointed [sic] Candidates, but before the next election a division must necessarily take place, and the present Incumbent will find his chances of success increased by a division of the forces opposed to him under their several Chiefs. In the mean time I sincerely hope you will preserve your health, your firmness, and what is not the least difficult nor the least important of all a perfect command of your temper however envenomed the assaults which may be made upon your feelings. Party bitterness when sustained by no essential political principle, may be softened down and ultimately dis olved by forbearance, condescension, and bland manners, and I am sure you are as capable as any one with whom I am acquainted of bringing these into operation when a proper occasion for their employment occurs. The solid understanding, long experience, and extensive acquirements of Mr. Adams must have their weight, and although some may complain of the coldness of a first reception, a further acquaintance with him cannot fail to remove prejudice and to increase the number of his friends. Mrs. Adams is eminently qualified by her talents, knowledge of the usages of good society, and disposition to please, to fill the place assigned her, and to become the rival of Mrs. Mrs. [sic] Madison in popularity. Her social and truly pleasing qualities will now be exerted on a wider sphere, and I have no doubt with increased effect. Time however can alone decide how all will operate and we must patiently wait for the result.

In my late dispatches you have been informed of the wretched state of my health, which although somewhat improved is yet very far from being so good as I could desire. My Physician has advised me to pass two or three weeks at the hot mineral waters of Aix in Savoy as the only certain means of eradicating the rheumatism from my system and I believe I should have ventured to take a furlough of that length had the health of Mr. Sheldon[2] been such as to have left him in charge of the Legation until my return. He has suffered for some weeks with a bad cough and fevers and with the hope that a change of air would be serviceable to him has fixed himself near Montmorency at about 12 miles distance from Paris. I hope his indisposition will be of short duration and that he will be perfectly recovered in a few days. He is an excellent man, attentive to business and exceedingly well qualified for the place he has so long occupied. We were both deprived of the pleasure of witnessing the coronation although I had made my preparations for the purpose.[3] My expence will not exceed fifteen hundred francs and I presume will be considered moderate by the Government. I have reason to believe that those of the other Ministers have in no instance been under ten thousand and even those of the Chargé d'Affaires of Switzerland amounted to two thousand. This subject however will be mentioned to you officially when I send on my next account— My accounts and Vouchers having been transmitted with great regularity, I should be glad to be informed that they had been passed and closed.

You mention your intention of building in Washington and enquire whether your furniture could not be better procured here than in the U States. Perhaps Time pieces, Candelabras, porce laine, mirrors and a few other articles might be advantageously procured here, but the greatest part of what you want can be had on better terms at home or in England. If you determine on buying any thing here I shall be happy if you command my services. Your plated ware will be best if bought in England & the gilt is better in France. All articles in Mahogony [sic] are better and cheaper in the U States than in any other Country— The Damasks of India are perhaps equally beautiful with silk of France for curtains and chairs and cost less— The fringe can only be had here— Carpets of the finest kind can be had here but they are very expensive— Inferior kinds are better and much cheaper in England—

Although this is any thing but a public letter yet I cannot help expressing my wish that you would lose no time in looking into the question of our claims and giving me your opinion as to the Course I ought to pursue— You will perceive that four or five of my letters on that subject remain without any answer[4]— Indeed I found the Baron de Damas so entirely unacquainted with the subject, and so unwilling to take the trouble of examining it, that I had but little expectation that an answer would be had until the Chambers had adjourned and the bustle of the Coronation had gone by when Mr Villele would be at leisure to bestow his attention on the question— You may refer to his letter to Mr Gallatin[5] for his opinion which I have reason to believe has underwent no change— I have no ground for a hope that he will agree to discuss the Claims, unless in connexion with the 8 Article of the Louisiana Treaty, and in case we consent to that order of negociating he will make our admission that the treaty has been broken a preliminary to the adjustment of the claims. The French come in for so small a portion of the navigation between the two countries, that it is not impossible that the hint you have received from the Baron de Mareuil that the Convention will be terminated,[6] may be acted on— and that we may have that troublesome question again to adjust— I have heard nothing said on the subject here, and I believe the Merchants are generally satisfied with the present state of things.

I have had a letter of a late date from Mr Nelson[7] who is waiting with great impatience for the arrival of Mr Everett[8] in order to return to the U States— He has passed a very unpleasant time in Spain, and has had no society from which he could derive advantage or pleasure— Mr Hughes[9] has not yet arrived at the Hague but is hourly expected—

The Arabian Manuscript[10] was placed in the hands of a Professor of Oriental languages for translation— He did not consider it as worthy of a translation, as it contained nothing of an interesting nature. He has made out in French the substance of what it contains from which you will perceive, that a translation of it could not answer any valuable purpose—

Mrs. Brown is well and joins me in love to Mrs. Clay. I am Dear Sir Yours Sincerely   JAMES BROWN
Honle. Henry Clay—

ALS. DLC-HC (DNA, M212, R1).
1 Above, May 9, 1825.   2 Daniel Sheldon.
3 See above, Brown to Clay, May 27, 1825.
4 See above, Brown to Clay, March 23, April 1, 28, 1825.
5 Albert Gallatin.   6 See above, Clay to Brown, May 9, 1825.
7 Hugh Nelson.   8 Alexander H. Everett
9 Christopher Hughes.
10 Not found. On August 12, 1825, Daniel Brent, in Clay's absence, transmitted to J (ohn) L (ouis) Taylor, of Raleigh, North Carolina, the papers relating to the Arabian manuscript enclosed in Brown's letter, with the explanation that the document had presumably been sent to Brown for translation in compliance with Taylor's request. Copy. DNA, RG59, Dom. Letters, vol. 21, p. 126 (M40, R19). Taylor, born in London, England, and educated at William and Mary College, had been a prominent North Carolina legislator and jurist since 1792. He had been the first chief justice of the State supreme court, the compiler of several series of case reports, later incorporated in the *North Carolina Reports*, and author or collaborator in revisions of North Carolina's statute laws, published in 1821 and 1825.

Promissory Note from James Graves, Jr., and James Graves, Sr.

[June 25, 1825]

On or before the 18th. day of December 1825 we promise to pay to Henry Clay or order the sum of One hundred dollars with interest thereon from the 18th. day of December last, for value received. Witness our hands this 25th. day of June 1825.

JAMES GRAVES JR
JAMES GRAVES SENR

[Endorsement][1]
Interest from 18 Decr. 1824 til
24th. Augt. 1827 is 2 Ys. 8 Ms. 6 ds. $16.10.

DS, in Clay's hand, signed by both Graveses. Fayette Circuit Court, File 660. Copy, in DLC-TJC (DNA, M212, R16). The younger Graves was a Lexington merchant; the elder has not been further identified.

A second promissory note (DS, in Robert Scott's hand), from the same source (copy in DLC-TJC [DNA, M212, R16]), bearing the same date, is similar to this except for the date of maturity: "the 18th. day of December 1826."

On August 30, 1827, Clay filed two suits against the Graveses to collect the notes, plus interest. Judgment, by default, was given in his favor, September 20, 1827. Fayette Circuit Court, Civil Order Book 6, p. 274.

[1] AE by Scott.

From Samuel Smith

Sir   Baltimore 25' June 1825

It has taken some time to collect the information necessary, to enable me to answer your letter[1] to my own satisfaction; Nor have I been able to obtain all I wished. For a correct understanding of the causes which have intervened to check a free commerce between the United States and the British Colonies in America, and their West India Islands, it may not be irrelavant [sic], to revert to certain occurences [sic], and make some introductory observations.

Commerce and Navigation are by many considered as one great whole, but you know, that they are *separate* and *distinct* interests, however nearly allied; Commerce can exist without the Nation being its own carriers, but certainly not with the same advantages, activity or enterprize.

The Eastern States own nearly one half of all the Shipping of the United States, they have little of their own produce *comparatively,* and therefore are compelled to seek employment in the Southern States and elsewhere for their Ships. Their Merchants in consequence look attentively to every thing that relates to navigation. The Southern States having the great and valuable articles of export, are more attentive to Commerce. It is not of such vital importance to them, whether their produce be carried by the vessels of the one or the other nation.— From these views, it may be, that the middle and southern States might be perfectly content with the trade on the terms offered by the Act of Parliament of June 1822.[2] When it may not be quite as agreeable to the Eastern States. I ought however to observe, that the Commerce of Norfolk and North Carolina with the British West India Islands, is much the same as that from the Eastern States.

[Smith reviews, in the next four pages, the proposed legislation, the acts of Congress and of Parliament, the Convention of 1815, and the proclamations since "1802 or 3" involved in relations between the United States and Great Britain concerning trade with the West Indies.]

Permit me to take a view of the Act of Parliament,[3] to see whether its operation is such as to insure to British Ships, an *undue* proportion of the carrying trade between the U. S. and the Colonies alluded to in the Act.

That Act opens to the vessels of the U. S. certain ports, in which certain specified duties are charged on articles of the U. S., whether the same be imported *direct* from the United States in British or American vessels or *circuitously* in British from the European possessions of Great Britain; but no duty whatever is imposed on similar articles the produce &c &c of G Britain or Ireland or of the North American Colonies. Thus the flour of Canada, Great Britain, & Ireland, and the lumber of the Colonies, may be imported free of duty. The duty on a barrel of flour in Jamaica is $1.05, which is equal to the freight and Insurance from any port in the United States; it is probable however that the freight for Montreal and Quebec may cost more; in addition to this difference our vessels pay the Alien tonnage duty of 94 cents, a charge of about 10 cents pr Bbl, which with the 10 p Ct additional duty makes a charge of 15½ cents pr bbl. on flour when imported in An American vessel, more than would be payable if imported in a British vessel from the United States; if we had not charged the Alien duties, they would not have imposed their retaliation, and the only thing we could have complained of (as to that article), would have been, that the flour of Great Britain and of Canada was admitted duty free whilst ours paid $1.05 pr bbl. Great Britain (it is known) exports little of her *own* flour to the West Indies, but actually supplies them with *our* flour, which is imported into Liverpool and Warehoused for exportation. The Canadas can only export during six months in the year; they actually export none to Jamaica. The Islands are generally supplied from the United States either *direct*, or with our flour from Nova Scotia or Great Britain, *all paying the same duty*. If then we were relieved from the Alien duties of Import and tonnage, there can be little doubt that our flour would go *direct,* and that ⅔ds at least perhaps ¾ths thereof would be carried in American vessels. Even under all these disadvantages, it is certain that more than ten Bbls flour are exported to the Colonies in American vessels for one in British, on that point you may obtain better information from Mr Nourse.[4] If I am correct, then, the retaliation of Great Britain is a serious tax on the trade, for which we get a trifling addition to the Revenue; I must think that the spirit of the act of 1815[5] would have fully justified the Government for imposing the Alien duties on the vessels of *any* Nation, *where no Alien duties existed* (none existed in the West Indies). The administration thought differently, and therefore the act of the 7 Jany 1824[6] was passed, and probably the Treasury Circular[7] issued from the same cause.

Lumber is charged with duties when from the United States, and pays no duty when imported into the British West Indies from her American Colonies, this gives an advantage to the Colonial vessels over those of .the U. S. in particular kinds of lumber. But it is a mistake to suppose that the disadvantage falls "on the Eastern States *only* and *particularly* on Maine," for the fact is, that lumber is exported in great quantities from all the Southern States to the British West Indies, but particularly from North Carolina and Norfolk, white pine boards and plank, it is true, are exported and in great quantities from the Eastern States, but pitch pine in plank & boards, shingles & staves are exported chiefly from North Carolina and Norfolk, large quantities of staves were formerly exported from Maryland and other States, and many are still exported.— The duty (Mr Adams says)[8] is 10 pr Cent on the cost, I cannot think, that so small a duty would operate very powerfully, we could not be worse off, for we have now, not only to pay that duty, but 10 pr Ct thereon, and what is more onerous the 94 cents of tonnage duty, which I should think must together amount nearly to an exclusion of the export of our white pine boards and plank in our vessels to the British West Indies.

Flour and lumber are (I believe) the articles on which we bottom our complaint; indian corn may be another, it is free of duty from Nova Scotia, none however has ever been imported from thence into Jamaica, indeed, I am informed that the corn of the United States is imported into that Colony for its own consumption. Our corn pays the heavy duty of 12½ cts pr bushel, being 25 pr Cent on its average cost, and may have been imposed to induce the planters to continue its cultivation.

There are several valuable articles necessary to the West Indies which can *only* be drawn from the U. S. the retaliating duties on which fall heavily on the Merchant and Cultivator. I am surprised that they are not carried by British Ships alone, if however they are carried (as I am told they are) principally in our vessels, they are subjected to the heavy charge of Alien duties which might have been avoided, the articles are, Rice, Corn meal (kiln dried) Tar, Pitch, Turpentine, Tobacco, Peas, Ship bread, Pilot bread, Crackers, Indian corn Livestock, and pitch pine boards, plank & timber, those articles with few exceptions are from the South & middle States.

Mr Adams (in his letter to Mr Rush[9] of 23 June 1823) mentions an export duty in the West Indies payable on articles permitted to be exported to the United States of 4 to 5 pr Cent, not imposed on the same, when exported to the *North American Colonies,* he justly considered it as an additional injury to a fair intercourse; but is such duty really charged? It certainly is not on the exports from Jamaica— I have before me an Invoice of coffee dated 28 November 1823 for account of Mr McKim, and one of Sugar, coffee and other articles for Mr Patterson[10] of December 1823, in which no such charge has been made, nor is any such duty In Jamaica known to any of our Merchants, I have conversed with two Agents from Commercial Houses in Jamaica, and they say they know of no export duty, except on Cocoa & Ginger (which is paid by all parties) from that Island. One of them supposes that the idea of such a duty may have arisen from the following fact.— In the year[11]   Parliament passed an act imposing a tax on the planters of 4 pr Cent on all the exports from their Estates, that tax was resisted by the Islands as being in violation of their Charters, after much controversy, Jamaica offered in lieu thereof, that the Colony would pay the white troops employed for its defence— their offer was accepted. The other Islands being unable to adopt the compromise have paid the 4 pr Cent; if Collected on export it must have been paid by the North American Colonies and Great Britain, he thinks but he is in Error that it is paid by and is simply a tax on the planters, who cannot make it a part of the price of his [*sic*] produce, for its price will be regulated by that at which similar articles can be procured elsewhere.

The same Agent (who married and resides in this City) informs me that in 1807 or 1808, there were 347 entries of American vessels in Jamaica, that he beleives [*sic*] 200 vessels entered from the U. S. the last year, of which, he appears confident, that not more than ten were British, he says that he never knew of any Canadian flour arriving in Jamaica, that he has known British flour imported into that Island, the quantity small and of little importance.

An inequality certainly exists in the trade as it has been authorized under the act of Parliament, to wit, That many articles permitted to be carried from the American Colonies and from Great Britain and Ireland, are prohibited from the U. S. such as, Fish, Beef, Pork, Lard, Butter, and all and every manufactured article, other than those specifically named.

It certainly would be a great advantage & convenience if we could be permitted to introduce these articles, but ought we to insist on it? when we know, that they are considered *all important* by Great Britain, to their American Colonies and Ireland, their prohibition is not of vital importance to the U. S.

We could with equal propriety complain that we are prohibited from selling these and other articles for consumption when imported from the U. S. in the ports of Great Britain and Ireland— There is however one article which has been admitted into the Islands, but may by fair construction of the Act of Parliament be prohibited, it is that of Shooks; for your information, they are Molasses and Rum Hhds, completely put together, the staves and heading of each numbered, then shook and put up in separate bundles, on arrival in the West Indies, they are again set up, and hooped with hoops carried out for the purpose, this mode is economical, the purchase of Hhds made in the West Indies would be too great an expense especially on the article of Molasses, they have been considered heretofore as staves, but as a doubt has arisen in one of the Islands, it ought to be made certain, it may appear a trifle but is nevertheless of importance.

When our Alien duty was retaliated by an order in Council, the money was directed to go to the King, unless the Assembly of the several Colonies should pass a law to the same effect. In that case it was to accrue to the benefit of the Colony. Jamaica passed the necessary Act and the Alien duties form a part of her revenue. So that I fear there will be the greater difficulty in undoing what has been done, if you can succeed you will deserve some credit.

The public papers have announced, and letters from Jamaica confirm, that the excessive port charges imposed in the Islands are to be repealed. If they should be, it will be a great relief to the Commerce between them and the United States, the same liberal spirit may facilitate a repeal of the Alien duties, which I flatter myself will be met with equal liberality on our part.

Look at our Act of March 1823, it appears to me, that if that Act had passed before the British Government had imposed the Alien duties that we could not have enforced our Alien duties on their Ships.— This is an Error the word Elsewhere interposed & protected the Government.[12]

The port charges & pilotage of vessels from the United States are the same in Jamaica whether they be British or American (except only the retaliatory duties).— British vessels from the N American Provinces pay precisely the same port charges and pilotage as those from the United States.

The only export duty in Jamaica is on Cocoa $1.75 per 100 lbs and on Ginger 15¾ cents per 100 lbs these have of late been collected under a very old Colonial law, without reference to the Country exported to, or whether the vessel be british or foreign. Cocoa is now principally imported into the United States from South America, none from Jamaica, and almost all the ginger wanted comes from Calcutta, so that these duties are of no sort of consequence to the United States. Our Alien duties fall very heavy on Sugar Coffee & rum imported in British Ships, and may be the cause why so few of them are now employed in the trade between the United States and the West Indies, the extra duty on rum from Jamaica amounts to 5 cents pr gallon and from the other Islands to 4 & 4 ½ cents according to the proof. On sugar 33 ⅓ cents per 112 lbs. On Coffee ½ a Cent pr lb So that if the Alien duties on both sides be repealed we may expect to see a greater number of British vessels entering our ports. It is proper that you should be apprized of that probable consequence, lest it might escape your observation.

It is idle for us to complain that British ships *only* are permitted to carry from one Colony to another, that is to all intents the same as our coasting trade. Great Britain & her Colonies do not form one great whole, where the duties and charges are the same in every port, as is the case in the United States. I therefore doubt whether the case of Louisiana Sugar will exactly apply, the principle might be made to operate powerfully against us.— for instance if a *high* export duty on the produce of the Islands were charged on articles to the United States and none charged, where the British ship *cleared* for the North American Colonies, and no bonds taken compelling a discharge in those Colonies, such Ships might and *most certainly would* proceed direct to the U. S. and thus avoid the export duty, manifestly to the great injury of our carrying trade, but they have not as yet done so, and if they should, then we could by law refuse the entry of every vessel from the Colonies whose clearance did not specify that the same was cleared actually to the United States, and in addition the British Government might be prevailed on to compel bonds to be given "that the Cargoes cleared for the N American Colony should actually be landed therein," this would be so reasonable, that I should suppose there could be no objection to it—but until such export duty shall be imposed, we ought to be silent on the subject, lest we should admit, that which we might hereafter regret. Again. If Canada, Great Britain & Ireland were able to supply the West Indies with their own flour, on which *no duty* would be payable whilst ours paid a duty, then our trade with the Islands would be less useful but we would have no just cause of complaint, the same principle exists now, for the grain & flour of Canada is admitted into Great Britain when the average price in the market is less, than *that* when the same may be imported from the United States; still we should have the supplying of the Islands with many articles which *cannot* be supplied from Great Britain or any of her possessions.— I cannot perceive any cause we have to fear a competition in the article of flour, or in *any other article* which we are permitted to import into the Colonies, on the terms proposed by the Act of Parliament. Let the Alien duties be repealed on both sides, and our *enterprize,* our *proximity* and *our articles* essential to the Islands will do the rest, the profit to the Merchant in the West India trade is trifling, in general it scarcely pays a moderate freight, but the trade gives employ to our vessels and seamen, and demands *much* of our produce. Jamaica alone consumes more than Sixty thousand bbls of flour annually, and about as much is consumed in all the other British Islands. Canada (if ever able to supply) can only do it as I have already said for six months in the year and there is little danger of Great Britain and Ireland furnishing the quantity necessary for the other six months with *their own flour.* vessels from Canada cannot make more than one voyage in the year to Jamaica, when ours can make four or five.

Since writing the above, I have obtained some further information relative to the export duty. I have seen Invoices from Barbadoes and Antigua, of sugar &c &c *just arrived,* on both of which an export duty, of something less than 4 per Ct. on the *actual cost* is charged; a Captain just arrived from Turks Island paid $100, export duty on salt— yet, on an Invoice from Trinidad there is no export duty charged. I have received the following answer to an inquiry made of a Merchant lately arrived from Barbadoes "The export duty on Colonial produce is 4 per Ct paid by the Shippers, whether shipped to Great Britain or elsewhere, the duty I think is confined to Barbadoes and Antigua only, in some of the other Islands there is an export duty but not so heavy."— He emphatically says *"whether shipped to Great Britain or elsewhere,"* and how can it be otherwise? the act of Parliament passed when foreign intercourse *was prohibited;* of course the duty could fall, *at that time,* on none but Great Britain and her Colonies; and if so, it is imposed on them as well as on the United States, and can do no injury that I can perceive, the price of the article must be so much less; for (as I have already observed) the price must, and will be regulated by its relative value in other Islands. The Collector of Eastport[13] can easily ascertain whether the Merchants of New Brunswick are charged with the export duty or not; you could inform yourself fully and completely by writing to the United States Consul at Antigua, His name is Robert M. Harrison a very respectable gentleman, or if you prefer it, I will write to him on the subject.

The papers say, that Great Britain has lately admitted on a very low duty the wheat of Canada. Quere? If it be true and she should permit that wheat to be ground, for exportation & allow a drawback of the duty when exported. Whether such flour *being free of duty* in the West Indies Islands might not seriously interfere with the export of the flour of the United States? therefore the necessity of an early understanding with Great Britain on the subject on liberal terms. Our vicinity, and possessing articles for consumption *which they have not,* would enable us to compete with them, notwithstanding that we should have to pay a duty from which they would be free, if we were only clear of the alien duties in the Islands.— The freight of five bushels of wheat from Montreal (required to make a barrel of flour) is more than equal to the duty of $1.05 which we would have to pay.— That freight would of course place us on equal terms with them, and why need we fear competition   Yours truly & sincerely
Honble Henry Clay Secretary of State   S. SMITH

LS. DNA, RG59, Misc. Letters (M179, R62). With the letter was enclosed a schedule of prices at Kingston, Jamaica.
[1] Above, May 9, 1825.   [2] See above, III, 729, n. 21.
[3] The act of June 24, 1822 (3 *Geo. IV*, c. 45), upon which the British action of the following month was based.   [4] Joseph Nourse.
[5] See above, II, 37, n. 7.
[6] See above, Lorich to Clay, March 16, 1825, note.
[7] "A Digest of the Recent Commercial Regulations of Foreign Countries, with Which the United States Have Intercourse . . . Prepared Conformably to a Resolution of the House of Representatives of the 21st January, 1823," in "Message from the President of the United States Transmitting. . . ," *House Docs.,* 18 Cong., 1 Sess., no. 130, p. 243. A discriminatory duty of ten per cent was charged against British vessels entering ports of the United States from those of British American or West Indian possessions.
[8] Dated August 25, 1824, it required payment of alien duties on British vessels entering from the Colonies.
[9] Richard Rush.   [10] Probably Isaac McKim; William Patterson.
[11] Date obliterated by writer; statute not found. Cf. Robert Harry Inglis Palgrave (ed.), *Dictionary of Political Economy* (3 vols.; London, 1925), I, 795-96, which discusses the continued application of the duty of four and a half per cent ad valorem, introduced in 1663.   [12] This sentence added in Smith's hand.   [13] Maine.

From CHRISTOPHER HUGHES, Stockholm. States that his household and private effects have been sent to Baltimore, to be delivered to his brother-in-law, (Samuel) Moore, and that other articles will be transported to New York, free of freight, in a Swedish ship; requests that the Secretary of the Treasury be informed so that instructions may be sent to collectors at these two ports to permit Hughes' friends to take possession of the goods. ALS. DNA, RG59, Dip. Disp., Sweden and Norway (M45, R5).

From WILLIAM MILLER, New York, New York. Requests copies of correspondence between the American Government and (Antonio José) Cañaz, mentioned in Miller's instructions (above, April 22, 1825). ALS. *Ibid.,* Central America, vol. 1 (M219, R2). Cover missing; addressee not named.

From DANIEL WYNNE, New York. Determined to proceed to Chile the next month, requests that his commission and consular bond be sent to him. ALS. DNA, RG59, A. and R. (MR4). On June 29 Daniel Brent, in the absence of the Secretary of State, replied to Wynne that his commission had been sent on April 16, 1825, probably addressed to the collector of customs at New York. A duplicate was promised if the original were not found. Copy. DNA, RG59, Cons. Instr., vol. 2, p. 361 (M78, R2). Cf. below, Hogan to Clay, November 16, 1825.

APPLICATIONS, RECOMMENDATIONS   June 25, 1825

DAVID E. EVANS, WILLIAM U. TISDALE, HENRY BROWN, C. CARPENTER, DAVID TISDALE, JOHN T. ROSS, and RICHARD SMITH, Batavia, New York, recommend continuation of the Batavia *Spirit of the Times,* now published by Frederick Follett, an an organ for printing of the laws. DS. DNA, RG59, P. and D. of L. Enclosed in Follett to Clay, July 9, 1825. Evans, a former member of the New York Senate (1819-1822) and Council of Appointment (1820, 1821), was elected to Congress in 1826 but resigned before that body met. Other signatories not further identified. The printing contract was shifted out of Batavia before the next Session of Congress.

To Peter Hagner

Dear Sir   Ashland 27 June 1825
   In the case of Henry Webster, which you mentioned to me, I enclose an exact copy below of his receipt.[1]   I have no doubt that in the other (the name I do not recollect) payment has been made.
   I find the business of arranging my private affairs will not admit of my return to the City quite as early as I wished and expected. It will be towards the last of next month before I can rejoin you.
                         Yr's Respectfy   H. CLAY

ALS. DNA, RG217, Fugitive Items. Addressed to Hagner at Washington.
[1] The enclosure, omitted by the editors, is a copy of the document of April 19, 1817 (above, II, 342).

From James Lloyd

Dear Sir.–   Boston June 27h. 1825.

As it would at all times afford me a sensible gratification to meet your wishes, in reference to an exposition of any views, or information I might possess, connected with the public interest, I shall with readiness, and in compliance with your request, reply to your favor under the 9th. of May[1] within the time you have mentioned, but from the occupations which a long absence from home have unavoidably multiplied, and my engagements during the visit of the distinguished Guest of the Nation,[2] and the Jubilee which the semi-centenial [sic] celebration of the Bunker hill battle[3] has occasioned, I shall be compelled to treat the subject less elaborately, and perhaps usefully than I might otherwise endeavor to do; this however will be the less important, as the topic to which the communication will principally refer, has been so much a subject of attention and the diplomatic discussions with regard to it, have been so ample and long continued, that I am not conscious of the ability to throw any new lights on it, which would be worthy of much consideration.–

The leading, fair, and honorable principle of our commercial intercourse with foreign nations undoubtedly is, and should be, that of *reciprocity*;–it is a principle from the various views, with which, it is connected, alike of National self-respect, and interest, to which I should at all times be disposed to adhere, with great steadiness, even at the expense of some present accomodation [sic] and advantage; from the hope, that by so doing, and steadfastly setting it up, as the great land mark of our commercial policy, it might induce its adoption by others towards us, and thereby produce a corresponding and greater benefit hereafter, more than equivalent to the endurance of a present inconvenience.–

[Lloyd explains in three manuscript pages that he had assented to the Convention of 1822 with France,[4] notwithstanding its failure to provide reciprocity, in the belief that it was the best arrangement that could be negotiated at that time.]

–I adduce these suggestions, merely for the purpose of making known to you, how *strong* my attachment is, to the single, untrammelled principle of *reciprocity*.– so far as it can be maintained in our intercourse with foreign powers, not only in fact, but in terms; still however I am fully aware, that to every contract, National & Individual, there must be two wills and two interests to be consulted, and that he who comes to an agreement under them, certainly does well, if he secures the greatest good, that is attainable, improves his present situation, and materially compromits no future

interest in the doing it.—   And probably, after all, it is to this
ground we must consent to come at last, in our commercial arrangements with other powers; as with the greater trading Nations of
Europe, we can scarcely expect to establish the broad unreserved
principle of reciprocity, for a long course of years to come, if at any
time hereafter; for even their limited prohibition of importations,
so long as it continues, and of its total removal there can be little
expectation, is of necessity at variance with our System, which
from choice imposes no interdictions; which will always make a
distinct, and in some degree contradictory feature of commercial
policy between us and them; and so far as it goes, must qualify
the principle of reciprocity some what in their favor, if we are to
have any commercial intercourse with them.—

—The depending question in our discussions on this head with
Great Britain, then is, whether, without inpinging any of the leading principles of her policy, or injuriously affecting any of the great
branches of her domestic industry, she is willing to admit the
United States to an intercourse with her colonies in the West
Indies, or on the Continent, on terms which would be fair, and
equable in their operation, and which would produce the benefits
to both parties, which it is the avowed disposition of each to accord?—or in other words, would the benefit of opening to us, the
British West India ports under existing laws & usage Colonial as
well as National, be reciprocal, or nearly so, or would it be partial
and unequal. [sic]

And so far as I understand this question as at present existing,
I should contend the latter would be the fact; for it is this very want
of actual reciprocity, which has, as I presume restricted, and crippled
our commercial intercourse with the British Colonies in the West
Indies, since the opening of their ports, by the act of Parliament
of June 1822,[5] which has also very properly induced the Government
of the United States, to continue the discriminating duties on importations from thence in British vessels, and which has become,
a subject both of comment and complaint, on the part of the British
Government.—

The trade between the United States, and the British West
Indies, if it could be prosecuted on equal terms, would be one,
of very considerable interest, and of profit to us; inasmuch, as it
would take off a quantity, of some importance of our most bulky
articles of domestic and agricultural product, —such as lumber,
live stock, vegetable productions, provisions, fish &ca.—, thereby
not only opening another market for the fruits of our industry.—
but requiring the occupation and employment of proportionately a
large tonnage, and number of seamen, thereby affording a mart

for our smaller traders and navigation, and giving an increased degree of activity to the lesser sea-ports, along almost the whole Atlantic border of the Country.—

—It was therefore with gratification, that I witnessed, even the limited and qualified opening of the British Ports in the West Indies, in consequence of the Act of Parliament before referred to, the Presidents proclamation, & the law of Congress of March 1823.—

—But not finding, that the beneficial effect had resulted, from the apparent removal of the restrictions between the United States, and the British West Indies, which I had hoped, I was induced at the close of the year for my own satisfaction, to endeavor to obtain some precise information from the Collectors of the Customs, as to the extent to which this trade had been prosecuted; this I did from Passamaquoddy to Philadelphia, not having extended my inquiries farther south, and regretted to find it still more inconsiderable, than from casual observation I had anticipated, and which was the more unexpected, as it was reasonable to conclude, from the West India markets having been for some years closed to us, and that for articles we could better supply than others, and which they had formerly been in the habit of receiving from the United States, either in their own vessels, or ours, that those markets would have been in a comparative state of exhaustion, and in consequence on the re-opening of the flood gates would have required, even a greater than usual amount of such articles as we were permitted to supply them with, from this Country.—

The failure of this to be the case, induced me, to attempt to develope the causes which led to the disappointment of expectations that seemed so well founded; these I was soon convinced, notwithstanding the limited list of permitted articles, and the injurious exclusion from them, of our salted fish & provisions, arose in a material degree from circumstances which were easily discernible, And unfortunately, more than sufficiently conclusive; —from sources, which have I believe, the most, if not all of them, been made the subject of diplomatic discussion.—

—They were principally, the embarrassments, expences and vexations, to which American vessels and property entering the British West India ports were subjected on the one Side, and on the other, the discriminating duties which were still kept up, and with good reason, on British vessels coming from thence to the United States.

[In the next seven manuscript pages Lloyd states that the embarrassments to American trade in the British West Indies arise from "the inequality of duties on the same articles, when imported from the United States and from the British Colonies;—from the unfriendly & vexatious regulation, said to have been practised in some, if not many of the Ports, obliging an American vessel to unlade at the first port she entered, whether the markets were good or bad"; "The exaction of a cash payment for duties," which impels the small shipper to make a forced sale of at least a part of his cargo or to make a "disadvantageous consignment of it to a resident merchant or Broker"; the imposition, by "many . . . British settlements in the West Indies," of an export duty, which "we cannot constitutionally countervail," on return cargoes; the requirement in the West Indies of bonds guaranteeing that an American vessel "shall return only to the specified port or ports in the United States"; and the imposition of heavy "port charges and expences" on American vessels.] Some of the previous regulations it is admitted, have been retaliated, but this forms no palliation for their original imposition; for where they have been adopted by the United States, they still do not operate equally on the British, as on ourselves, and have been forced on us, not as a subject of election, but as a matter of form, of self-respect, or of supposed necessity—; Still independently of these, there remains, more than a sufficiently marked diversity in the regulations between the two Countries, in reference to this trade, manifestly to shew the different temper and dispositions with which the parties go into it, and the dissimilar operation upon them;—for.—

—neither the Cash payment for duties, nor the sacrifices incident to it, do we require.—

—An export duty we do not, and cannot impose,

We interdict none of the products of the West Indies from an entrance to our Ports,—and altho' we do by the provisions of the Act, to regulate the intercourse between the United States and certain British Colonial Ports of March 1823. require bond to be given, corresponding with the stipulations of the British Act of Parliament, for the delivery of the cargoes taken from the United States at the places specified; yet from the peculiar circumstances of the trade, it is a restriction in the one case, vexatious and onerous, and in the other of no importance, consisting more in words than in fact, in form than in substance.

—This will be demonstrable, from the different modes and objects of the trade, and the different description of vessels in which it is prosecuted by the respective parties.—

—The British vessel coming to the United States is generally a large European freighting ship sent out for the receipt of a cargo from a particular port in the West Indies, generally to be delivered at London, Liverpool, or Bristol;— from the failure or disappointment of receiving such cargo, at the regular season, a casual temporary employment is sought for the vessel by sending her to the United States, commonly only, for a return cargo of lumber & live stock, to be paid for most frequently, not by merchandize or produce brought out, but by bills of exchange on England, and to return therewith to the same port in the West Indies, to which the ship was originally destined, when coming out, and where it is expected, a cargo will by the time of her arrival be ready for her, to take back to Europe.—

—This transaction on the face of it, requires an established correspondence and agency, and such vessels are in consequence, almost invariably consigned to some regular mercantile house in the United States, which purchases the return Cargo, endorses and makes sale of the bills, and is willing to give bonds for the return of the vessel to the Port in the West Indies from which she came, as she could in fact go no where else; This therefore is done without difficulty or reluctance, as the parties are Capitalists feeling a mutual confidence in each other, probably arising from a long continued, and acceptable intercourse between Individuals of sufficient standing to ensure an absence of all risk, from negligence, ignorance, or deviation, for the latter of which, it is apparent no adequate motive could exist.—

—This regulation therefore, as it regards the British trade is nugatory and harmless;—   not so however, is the operation of it on the American, or United States trade, which is carried on by vessels of a lower class, most frequently in small sloops, and schooners, the ownership of the cargoes of which, is distributed, among a number of adventurers, each of whom in the lesser ports makes his individual shipment; while the vessels are navigated by skippers, or masters, of little property or standing in the Community, whose object after getting into Port, used formerly to be, and still is, to barter the various articles they carry out for the returns of the West Indies; and to transact their own business free of expense; —and who can therefore, neither pay prompt cash duties, nor heavy commissions, nor procure sureties to enter into engagements, to the value of half the amount of the exports, that they shall not on their return unlade their cargoes at Philadelphia instead of Wilmington; at Norwich instead of New London;— or at Providence instead of New Port; provided the doing it should be to their advantage, and provided also, they should have omitted, or not been astute enough to have inserted half a dozen ulterior contingent ports in their clearances, before leaving the West Indies.

These are I believe, the principal practically injurious effects of the regulations of our intercourse with the British West Indies under the act of Parliament of 1822 upon the vessels of the United

States, and so long as this system of regulations continues, the wonder is, not that the trade is comparatively crippled, & unimportant, but that it should have any existence at all, as I confess I do not perceive how they could be otherwise than fatal to it;—

—The discriminating duty in the United States, undoubtedly also puts a ban upon the British trade to our Ports from the West Indies; and which from all these causes, until a more equitable policy in regard to it, is adopted on the part of that Government, can only have the sickly existence it at present possesses.—

—The question, as to the right to claim, or extort, an unreserved intercourse with the colonies of a nation on the same terms as the mother country enjoys it, opens another, and a different field of argument, and possibly one in which we could not very successfully or strenuously contend as of right, for an equal participation.—

—Colonies planted and sustained by a parent Country at great cost, undoubtedly become affiliated with it, as a part of the Domestic establishment of that Country; and so long as the parties themselves are willing to assent to it, the Colonists must be considered, as in a state of tutelage, or guardianship under the parent Country, and in which State while the Parent, and the offspring alike abstain from wrong to others, and are satisfied with their own relative condition, third parties can certainly have, no very well grounded pretence forcibly to interfere with it; nor can they very well, unless the principle of reciprocity is not only set up, but applies, very well sustain themselves, in advocating the enjoyment of advantages which they did not create,—in which they have no common right, and to the cost of maintaining which they do not contribute;—and it will probably be admitted, that it would not be an easy task to select very strong ground, for claiming, as of right, an intercourse with the Colonies of a Nation, any more than with the members of a family within their own immediate peculium, or Castle, without the consent, or permission of the head of it.—

Such an intercourse can only originate, and be based in feelings of good will, and a sense of mutual present or future interest, of which, as with regard to the conditions of any other contract, or bargain, the Parties will probably assume to be the best Judges for themselves; hence the want of Colonial possessions on the part of the United States, is not necessary to support the narrow policy of their opponents, in witholding such intercourse, if they choose to do it.

In a consideration of this principle of reciprocity, it is not however, the merely granting letter for letter, or opening port for port, that should be adverted to; it ought undoubtedly to be governed, if it is admitted to be the condition of the intercourse, by the general scope and effect, and by the respective regulations, and comparative benefit, to which it gives rise between two Countries; —and if the one, as in the case of the United States, admits most unreservedly, every British production into her ports for two thousand miles extent of sea-coast, precisely, if it so please Great Britain, in British vessels, on the same terms, as if imported in their own, while Great Britain in return, excludes a host of articles of American produce and manufacture, and gives on like terms, admission for a limited number of articles only, and comparatively to a few Ports, it is palpable, that the United States, do, without the possession of any colonies, afford to this principle of reciprocity, an equivalent many times over, more than equal to the limited permission, alike as to Ports and merchandize, Great Britain is willing, under any circumstances to allow; and this would be felt by her to be true, if we adopted, what would border a little, upon the so often designated Chinese policy.— and excluded from our ports, and consumption, her productions of a similar description to those which she interdicts the importation of when going from the United States, and to avoid our doing which, if indispensable, she would probably be willing to pay, ten times over the price of an intercourse with her settlements in the West Indies.—

But such a policy comports, neither with our system, nor with our interest, and is adduced only to shew the fallacy of the reasoning of Great Britain on our want of Colonial possessions, which is however, certainly as well supported, as a claim, for a participation in the coasting trade, or an equally free admission of the sugar & molasses of her Colonies into our markets as those of Louisiana & Florida —& about which she will be better enabled to hold an argument, when she permits on the same terms, the City of London to be supplied with fuel from New Castle by American vessels, and allows the importation into the English markets, the cloths, and cottons, and wheat and sugar of the United States, at the same rates, as the woolens and calicoes from Leeds & Manchester—the corn from the interior, or the Sugar & molasses from the West Indies; and when she does this, it will be sufficiently in season to ascertain, what under such a state of things might convert a sophism into an analogy, and furnish some reasonable ground for discussion.—

—The inquiry then comes up, how is this state of things to be remedied, and what are the means for its improvement?— to which I can only reply, the answer has been already given;— it is to be hoped for, from the present popularity, and extension of correct views and liberal principles of commerce on the part of Great Britain, (in her measures with regard to which however, if I mistake not, there is something more of both method and safe calculation, than at the First blush meets the eye,) and from the mutual interest as I conceive of the two Countries; as well also, as from the earnest desire of the Inhabitants of the West Indies among whom memorials & petitions are now getting up, and forwarding to Great Britain.—

—It is also to be looked for from the professed good dispositions between the two Countries, a state of relation undoubtedly highly desirable and useful to each and which an equable and fair intercourse with the British West India Colonies, would tend to strengthen & increase;—but this desirable result, must be attained if at all, by some other process, than that of fallacies and embarrassments, and the strife to obtain petty advantages, and until this may be the case, if one of the Parties chooses to play the Dog in the manger at its own cost, I know not, that it would be expedient for the other, under existing circumstances, to make the doing it a subject of serious contention, in preference to suffering a continued inconvenience to work out in its own time, its own cure.—

—Our progress is happily, so splendid, rapid, and forward, as to enable us to rest confidently, on the unrivalled, and constantly developing advantages we enjoy, and to wait with some degree of patience, on the operations of good sense & the constantly recurring privations, of those with whom we are negotiating, for the attainment of objects, which are not exclusively at our command, and in the securing of which, others have an interest, even paramount to our own.—

—I have thus hastily run through this subject, so far as it appeared to me, useful to do it, unavoidably repeating and amplifying in some degree, remarks which must in many instances, have been before familiar to you, with a view of giving to them such a practical illustration, as might not be without its uses;—in doing it, having intentionally avoided entering into fiscal calculations and details, as you have them much more correctly at your command from the Treasury Department than I could give them, did the time admit of my attempting it.—

I am much pleased to learn, that you have thus early, and zealously engaged, in a consideration of the important questions, yet depending with Great Britain.   —the present amicable dispositions of the two Countries towards each other, forbids [sic] the apprehension of any particularly unpleasant results respecting them; still the interests incorporated with all of them, are of so imposing a character, as to make it greatly desirable, they should be brought to a favorable issue, as speedily as may be practicable.—

—The vexatious interruption of our fishermen,[6] the unwarrantable claim, for a considerable part of the territory of the State of Maine, coupled with the felling & carrying off the timber, by special permission, from the British local authorities, as I believe; the denial of Mr. Addington notwithstanding, from lands long admitted, at least sub silentio, to have been within the jurisdiction of Massachusetts & Maine,[7] and even partially sold by the former Government to Individuals, are circumstances not unlikely in themselves, to lead to serious difficulties, and perhaps even hostile collisions which heretofore have probably, been prevented by the comparative sparseness of the population, in the immediate vicinity of these aggressions, as well as the entire reliance of our citizens, on the General Government, for the protection of their property, and an early adjustment & settlement of the disputed boundary.—

—And to these objects are to be added, the free navigation of the St. Lawrence,[8] and the recognition of our Territorial title on the Pacific,[9] all of them presenting topics of great magnitude, which will undoubtedly receive the constant and vigilant attention of the Government, until they may be finally disposed of; while the two first mentioned appear however to require a more prompt arrangement, from the desire, and expediency of avoiding, the immediate inconveniences and difficulties, which the present state of them, might possibly give rise to, at no very distant period—

—With a perfect conviction, that all our claims on the subjects before stated, are founded, on the fair principles of reciprocity, and of mutual interest, so far as respects the Commercial part of them; and on rights too well established to be ultimately resisted as it regards the others, I can only further express to you, the persuasion I feel that they will be, alike ably and efficiently supported; accompanying this assurance with my best wishes, for the unreserved success of your efforts acceptably to adjust them,

Having the honor to be With great respect Your Obedt st

JAMES LLOYD

The honorable Henry Clay, Secy of State of the U: S: &c &c &c.

ALS. DNA, RG59, Misc. Letters (M179, R62).

[1] See above, Clay to Smith, May 9, 1825, note.

[2] Lafayette.   [3] The battle had been fought June 17, 1775.

[4] See above, III, 53n.

[5] See above, Smith to Clay, June 25, 1825, note.

[6] During the summer of 1824 a more rigid enforcement of the restrictions under the Anglo-American Convention of 1818 (above, II, 611n), barring American fishermen from entry within the three-mile limits of the British-American dominions, except for delimited territories and under specified conditions, had resulted in seizure of seven vessels. One notable instance, involving the *Ruby* and the *Reindeer*, sailing from Lubec, Maine, had occasioned counteraction by a group of armed Americans from Eastport, who had overtaken and recaptured the vessels. The United States, on the basis of testimony that the Americans had entered the British waters under the emergency provisions of the treaty, had requested reparations. The British had rejected the complaint. "Message from the President . . . Transmitting Copies of Correspondence, &c. upon the Subject of the Capture and Detention, by British Armed Vessels, of American Fishermen, during the Last Season, February 18, 1825," *House Docs.*, 18 Cong., 2 Sess., no. 93; "Message from the President . . . Transmitting

a Further Report from the Secretary of State, on the Subject of the Capture and Detention of American Fishermen . . . in the Bay of Fundy, February 26, 1825," *ibid.,* no. 101.

7 See above, Clay to Addington, March 27, 1825; Addington to Clay, May 23, 1825.

8 See below, Clay to Gallatin, June 19, 1826.

9 See above, Rush to Secretary of State, March 26, April 4, 1825; Clay to King, May 10, 1825, note 19.

From Ralph Lockwood

The Honble. H. Clay.   New York June 27. 1825.
D Sir,

As I have not had the honor of hearing from you in reply to what I took the liberty to suggest to you, some time since in relation to the appointment of a *Chargé d'affaires* to *Prussia,*[1] I take the liberty to recal [*sic*] your attention once more to the subject.— I have thought it not improbable that the President might be averse to extending that class of diplomatic agents beyond the number appointed in Europe by his Predecessors.— If this should be so, I suppose the objection might in some degree be removed if not entirely if the person selected, should waive all claim to the *salary* affixed to the office, in case the Senate should decline to confirm the appointt. For myself, I should most cheerfully accept it on that condition—fully persuaded that that body would at once recognise the propriety reciprocating [*sic*] the diplomatic courtesy which the Prussian Government has so long maintained toward us without an interchange on our part. With this condition, I should conceive that all objection to make an appointment of *some person* would be obviated. And I can see nothing inadmissible in the stipulation.—

If, from this or any other consideration, the President's objections should be removed, if such objections indeed exist, I rely upon your past indulgence and goodness to favor my application, as well as to excuse the trouble I have taken the liberty to give you.

I have the honor to be with the highest respect Your most obedient Servt   RALPH LOCKWOOD

ALS. DNA, RG59, A. and R. (MR3).

1 No letter found. The United States had no Minister in Prussia from 1801 to 1835.

From Richard H. Mosby

Sir,   Petersburgh Va: June 27th 1825—

When in Washington last winter I had a conversation with you in relation to an application I then had before the Executive for the appointment of District Atty: for West Florida; You will recollect Sir (at my request) you were pleased to say that you would join my friends from Va: in representing me favourably to the Presi. which I have since learnt from Mr Stevinson[1] you did[2] and for which Sir permit me now to tender you my most sincere acknowledgments—

Since my departure from Washington I have not heard one word in relation to the subject whither [sic] the appointment was made or not;[3] if it is not made will you be so good as to inform me, as I am still anxious to go to that country, and if I should, this appointment would every way be desirable to me; if further recommendations should be necessary (which by the by [sic] I cannot believe) I could readily obtain them   If any other appointments should be vacant in either of the Florida's I should like to know, my anxiety to go to country [sic] is very great, I would accept of any thing which would inable me to sustain myself even but for a short time, as my object in going there would be the practise of my profession—

By answering this communication[4] you will confer a singular favour upon your Obt: St: R: H. MOSBY
To the Hble Henry Clay   Secretary of State

ALS. DNA, RG59, A. and R. (MR5).
[1] Andrew Stevenson.   [2] Above, February 3, 1825.
[3] Cf. above, Wade Mosby to Clay, March 29, 1825, and Clay's reply, April 1, 1825.
[4] No answer found; Mosby received no appointment.

DIPLOMATIC NOTES   June 27, 1825

From JOSE SILVESTRE REBELLO. Complains of Condy Raguet's abusive language and his accusations against the Brazilian Government in relation to the impressment aboard a Brazilian vessel, of John Williams, an American seaman. Rebello explains that Brazilian officials thought Williams, who had been picked up from a shipwreck and lacked papers, was a British seaman deserted from the Brazilian navy. ALS; accompanied by translation, AL. DNA, RG59, Notes from Brazilian Legation, vol. 1 (M49, R1).

INSTRUCTIONS AND DISPATCHES   June 27, 1825

From JAMES BROWN, Paris, no. 30. Gives information concerning the imprisonment of General ("Don Juan") Devereux, as follows: In February the general, bearing a passport signed by (Richard) Rush, with visas of the United States and Austrian Legations in Paris, had gone to Italy for his health. Early in June word had been received from Devereux's traveling companion, Charles Oliver, of the general's imprisonment by Austrian officials in Venice, "accused as Mr Oliver understood, of entertaining dangerous political opinions and of having aided Bolivar in the cause of Columbian [sic] Independence." Upon Brown's remonstrance to the Austrian Ambassador, Baron Vincent, concerning this report, he had been assured that there must be a mistake about the cause of imprisonment. Soon afterward Devereux had appeared in Paris, stating that he had been released after ten days' confinement and that he was unable to obtain "official information as to the cause of his arrest." Brown expects to receive "some explanations from the Austrian Ambassador," which he will forward as soon as possible. LS. DNA, RG59, Dip. Disp., France, vol. 22 (M34, R25).

Charles Oliver, of Baltimore and Paris, was the son of Robert Oliver. Baron Karl Freiherr von Vincent held the position of Austrian Ambassador in Paris from 1806 until his retirement later in the summer of 1825.

Devereux had been arrested at Rovigo on May 13 and imprisoned in the ducal palace at Venice. His papers and some property were reported to have been seized and sent to Milan for examination in the presence of the Emperor (Francis I). Washington *Daily National Intelligencer,* July 25, 1825, reprinting dispatches from New York *Evening Post.*

From JOHN M. FORBES, Buenos Aires, no. 21. Reports the probability of armed conflict between the provinces of La Plata and the Andes, on the one hand, and Brazil on the other; comments that an invasion of Upper Peru by Brazilian troops appears imminent and that it will be opposed by the Patriot army under Bolívar and Sucre; observes that Brazilian vessels are already reconnoitering off Buenos Aires in preparation for a blockade. Forbes recommends sending a sloop of war and a vessel of light draft to protect American commerce. He gives details of growing British economic influence in the area and predicts "that this Province, at least, will Shortly become a British Colony, not chargeable with an expensive and responsible government, but subject to equivalent political and moral influences." ALS. DNA, RG59, Dip. Disp., Argentina, vol. 2 (M69, R3). Published in Espil (comp.), *Once Años en Buenos Aires,* 365-69. Antonio José de Sucre y de Alcalá, born in Cumaná, Venezuela, had served as one of Bolívar's principal officers in the struggle for South American independence. Hero of the battles which gave liberty to Ecuador and Peru, most notably of the victory at Ayacucho (above, Raguet to Secretary of State, March 11, 1825), Sucre in 1826 became the first President of Bolivia.

MISCELLANEOUS LETTERS   June 27, 1825

From NOAH NOBLE, Brookville (Indiana). Notes that "Some weeks since" he wrote requesting copies "of all the recommendations given the members in Congress" from Indiana in favor of (John) Vawter or himself for appointment as marshal. States that Noble had suspected that a nomination "had been made without consuting [*sic*] the wishes of four fifths of the members from the State," but that he now has some doubts. Reiterates his request. ALS. DNA, RG59, A. and R. (MR3). The earlier communication not found. In January, 1826, Noble, brother of James Noble, was appointed receiver of public moneys at Indianapolis. He was Governor of Indiana from 1831 to 1837. On Vawter's reappointment, see above, Clay to Parke, March 16, 1825.

To John Quincy Adams

Dear Sir   Ashland 28h. June 1825
I have defered [*sic*] the honor of writing to you until I could speak, with some degree of certainty, as to the time of my departure from Kentucky. That I am now enabled to do. I shall leave my

residence on the 6h. or 7h. of July and, passing by Louisville, I shall join my family at Cincinnati and proceed thence to the City, by Land or the river, as circumstances may require. I apprehend that it will be the last of July before we shall reach Washington. I hope that I shall not have abused, in the duration of my absence from my post, the privilege which you kindly gave me of an indefinite furlough. I do not believe that I have wasted any time. A removal more than 500 miles of a tolerably large family, from a residence of more than 25 years, cannot be instantly effected. The regulation of my private and professional business, the sale of stock and furniture[1] not retained &c. have required more time than I anticipated. I should, nevertheless, have been abler to have abridged the period of my sojourn here, if it had not have been for the public festivals which have been offered to me since my return home. From the time I left the Allegheny mountains until I reached this place, in every village through which I passed, some testimonial of respect has been tendered to me. In Kentucky, and especially in my own district and the surrounding Counties, the strongest evidences of public confidence and attachment have been exhibited, in public dinners, barbacues [*sic*], balls, public eschorts &c.   La Fayette's transit through the Country has hardly occasioned more excitement than my return. I have been obliged to decline many invitations to public dinners. Otherwise I believe I might have gone the tour of the whole State. I have been invited to public dinners to *three* of the four districts whose representatives voted for Genl. Jackson;[2] and from the fourth, which happens to be the remotest from me in the State, I have the most abundant evidence of the satisfaction of the people. All my expectations, as to the cordiality of my reception, have been more than realized. There is not a murmur existing against me. Those who, in the first moments after the election, felt a disposition to disapprove my vote, have from policy or conversion united in the general demonstrations. I pray you to believe Sir that I do not advert to these things in any vain spirit of exultation. I thought a communication of them to you due to the friendly interest which you have been pleased to take in what relates to me.

My health has not been improved in as great a degree as I had hoped. I attribute this to the want of more tranquillity and abstraction from the bustle and the crowd. I count much upon my return journey.

With my respectful Compliments to Mrs. Adams, I remain Faithfully and cordially Your ob. servant   H. CLAY
Mr. Adams.

ALS. MHi-Adams Papers, Letters Received (M479).
1 See above, Statement, June 24, 1825.

2 That is, at Nicholasville (above, Woodson and others to Clay, May 30, 1825), which was part of the district represented by Thomas P. Moore; at Louisville (above, Breckinridge and others to Clay, May 31, 1825), which was included in the district of Charles A. Wickliffe; and at Georgetown (below, Toasts, July 2, 1825), the residence of John T. Johnson. See above, Kendall to Clay, February 19, 1825, note.

Receipted Account with Beach and Hedenberg

Henry Clay Esq.—Dr.   [*ca.* June 28, 1825]
To Beach & Hedenberg Lexington June 1. 1824

July	18 1823	To Spring Saddle	$42..00
		To Housand & Sturips	11..00
		to Martingail —	4..50
August	18 —	to Mending Martingail	37½
Sepr–	21 —	to 1 pair of Bridle rains	87½
Oct	8 —	to Wagon Harnis	40„50
	31 —	to Wagon Wip [*sic*]—	2..50
Nor.	25 —	to Pading [*sic*] Cart Saddle—	2..50
		to Straps—	50
D[ec]r.	6 —	to „ Atop Curtans[1] [*sic*]	6.00
April	2 1824	to Filling Stud bridle	4
		to a Halter—	2
			$116–75
June 30		to mending Bridle for Son	0„25
August	19	To Bair Skin on holsters	2„ —
		To Sirsingle for Son	1„25
27		To repairing Whip	—„12½
		To one Spring Saddle	40„ —
		To one pair of Stirup [*sic*] irons	5„ —
		To Saddle Cloath	6„ —
Sepr,,	18	To Bridle and Martingale	9„ —
		To two pair of rains in Bridle	1„50
Decmr	22	one pair of Buffilow Socks	3„0
			$184„87½

[Endorsement on verso][2]
Recd. 28 June 1825 of H Clay the amount of the within a/c
                                                JAMES BEACH

AD, by James Beach. DLC-TJC (M212, R16). The firm, Beach and Hedenberg, Lexington saddlers and harness makers, was composed of James Beach and Peter Hedenberg.   1 MS. torn; line not clear.   2 ES, in Clay's hand.

APPLICATIONS, RECOMMENDATIONS   June 28, 1825

A[TKINSON] H[ILL] ROWAN, Louisville, recommends, for appointment as naval officer at New Orleans, Dr. B (enjamin) F (ranklin) Harney, brother of Rowan's deceased brother-in-law. Dr. Harney, "one of the eldest Surgeons in the U S Army. from which he is about to retire . . . . has the reccomendation [*sic*] of Govr. [Henry] Johnson & many others. . . ." ALS. DNA, RG59, A. and R. (MR2).

Rowan was a son of John Rowan, whose daughter, Eliza Cooper, had married Dr. John Milton Harney. Eliza had died in 1815; her husband, in January, 1825. Dr. Benjamin Franklin Harney, born in Delaware, had entered the Army as a resident of Mississippi, serving in the War of 1812. He did not receive the appointment here requested.

Tax Receipt from Elijah C. Berry

STATE OF ILLINOIS, AUDITOR'S OFFICE,
Dolls. 27 18/100   Vandalia, June 29. 1825
Received into this office of Henry Clay the Treasurer's receipt for Twenty Seven Dollars and Eighteen Cents, being the amount of his Land Tax_____for the year 1825 on Sec. 7. W $\frac{1}{2}$ 18, SW 8. & SE 6. 14 N. 10 W & SE 12 14 N. 11W—
(Duplicate)   E. C. Berry, Aud.

DS, partially printed. DLC-TJC (DNA, M212, R16). Cf. above, III, 134-35, 291.

From Robert Sterrett

Dear Sir   Military Academy West Point June 29th. 1825
The Kentuckians have been peculiarly unfortunate this year at West Point,   on standing an examination I was found difficient [sic] in orthography, which will be seen by examineing [sic] the reports. I appeal to you Sir to appeal to the Secretary of War,[1] and endeavour to obtain for me a new examination by Sept next.   my appointment was procured by F Johnson[2]
             your most humble servant   Robert Sterrett.

ALS. DNA, RG59, Misc. Papers, Military Academy, File F, Serial no. 106. Addressed to Clay at Washington. Sterrett has not been further identified; he was not graduated from the Military Academy.
[1] James Barbour.   [2] Francis Johnson.

To Adam Beatty

Dear Sir   Ashland 30 June 1825
Inclosed is a note of Genl. Bodley and Genl. Pogue[1] the amount of which ($265 with interest) I will thank you to collect for me. It is payable in Specie; but to prevent controversy I am willing it should be settled at the depretiation [sic] of 20h. Oct. 1820, its date, if there were any depreciation at that time. Be pleased to inform me by letter, if the note comes safely to your hands.
             With great regard I am Yr's faithfy   H Clay
Adam Beatty Esq.

ALS. Owned by Earl M. Ratzer, Highland Park, Illinois.
[1] Thomas Bodley; Robert Poague. The note has not been found.

Power of Attorney to Richard Hawes, Jr.

[June 30, 1825]

Know all men by these presents that I Henry Clay sole acting
Executor of James Morrison decd. who was surviving Executor
of George Nicholas decd. have Constituted and appointed, and by
these presents do make Constitute & appoint, Richard Hawes Junr.
my attorney in fact, for me & in my name to attend to all the land
claims of the said George Nicholas in the Counties of Montgomery
Bath Morgan or Estill,[1] and to sue for & recover the same by any
suits in law or Equity that the said Hawes may deem expedient—

I do further Authorize the said Hawes as my Attorney in fact to
enter upon any of the lands owned by the sd. Nicholas in his life
time in any of the above named Counties & the same to lease for
one or more years, and to adjust settle & compromise any land disputes which may be on said lands, and to adjust settle & compromise
all such claims but especially the Claims belonging to or claimed
by the representatives of sd. Nicholas in the name of William
Davis[2] for 10,000 acres & of Littleberry Mosby heir at large of John
Mosby for 3000 acres— I do further Authorize the sd. Hawes to
Sell and Convey any part of any of sd. Davis' or Mosbys claims or
any other of the lands of sd. Nicholas in sd. Counties, in any manner
he may deem proper, and the Same to convey by deed to any person
or persons who may purchase or compromise, but the Said Hawes
is only to convey by deed with Special warranty such claim or title
as I may have in the character of Executor as aforesaid—

As witness my hand & seal this 30th. day of June 1825 as Executor
aforesaid   H CLAY {seal}

Copy. DLC-TJC (DNA, M212, R16).   [1] All in Kentucky.
[2] Davis, a Virginian who had died in 1798, had held some 75,000 acres of land in
Kentucky, under entries made during the decade of the seventeen eighties.

Receipted Bill from Hugh Foster

Mr. Henry Clay   Dr to H Foster   June 30th 1825
1823[1]

Sept 11	To one pare super blue overalls (son Thos)	$24
	making and trim black vest	3-50
	one pare suspenders	1-50
Oct 1st	one super blue coat	52 00
		$ 81-00

Recd payment in full   H FOSTER

ADS. DLC-TJC (DNA, M212, R15).
[1] The figure "3" superimposed on "4".

INSTRUCTIONS AND DISPATCHES   June 30, 1825

From ALEXANDER BURTON, Cádiz (Spain). Reports that on June 1 the French forces "in possession of this Island of Leon" began enforcing quarantine regulations and that no vessel from the United States is allowed to enter the port. Comments that this discrimination is "contrary to the Decree of the Supreme Board of Health at Madrid, whose list of prohibited Ports [of origin] includes only those south of Rhode Island. . . ." Explains that the general reduction in trade between the United States and Spain, now confined largely "to a commerce between Spain and Cuba, under Special Licenses . . . purchased from the Chief of this miserable country," results from restrictions on importation of foreign produce and manufactures. Grain and flour are still barred, "and the Duties on Codfish, amount, nearly, to seven dollars per quintal." The new tariff will soon be published, but "No reliance can be placed . . . on the fair execution of any law adopted here." A duty of one dollar per ton is exacted from American vessels in Spanish ports, compared to five cents per ton charged vessels of other nations. Burton cites a case, about which he wrote in February, of the charge having been levied on an American vessel entering the port of Cádiz in distress. He has learned from (Hugh) Nelson that in this instance the duty is to be refunded and that in future cases of this nature the vessels will be exempt from tonnage duties as long as Spanish vessels receive the same treatment in American ports.

Burton reports that, under an agreement between France and Spain "to receive the Consuls of each other, in their respective Colonies," French consuls have been sent to Cuba and Puerto Rico.

Preparations for a military expedition to Cuba proceed slowly for lack of money and credit. A large quantity of ordnance is being sent, "It is said, . . . with a view to afford aid to the discontented in Mexico." French forces remain in Cádiz, although "the project . . . for putting the Isla de Leon in a complete state of defence . . . appears for the present laid aside." Spanish vessels of war here "keep in Squadron, for mutual protection, against the numerous Colombian Privateers on this coast, some of which appear almost daily in sight of this Port." ALS. DNA, RG59, Cons. Disp., Cádiz (M-T176, R4). Addressed to Secretary of State; received August 31. The American vessel about which Burton had written on February 15 was the brig *Dick*.

From BEAUFORT T. WATTS, Bogotá, Colombia. States that he has been asked about the attitude of the United States toward the Congress at Panama and has replied that he could venture only "a conjectural opinion, that so important a convention of National Representatives, having in View the grand object of a continental Congress, for the security of constitutional principles, a safeguard to Republics, and the promotion of a perpetual alliance, would not be regarded with indifference by the United States." Reports that (Pedro) Gual, who will be one of the Colombian delegates and is ready to set out, expressed an "ardent wish" that the United States "would not only be represented but that her Government take a prominent part in promoting the views of the Congress."

Comments that Miralla, who says he had "the honor of your acquaintance some years ago in Washington," left Bogotá some weeks since to report on operations in Cuba and Puerto Rico, "as the conquests of those Islands is a favorite enterprize of Bolivar & this Government." ALS. DNA, RG59, Dip. Disp., Colombia (M-T33, R3). Received September 4. Endorsed on wrapper by Clay: "☞To be sent to the President."

On the Panama Congress, see above, Tudor to Secretary of State, April 12,

1825, note. José Antonio Miralla was an Argentine scholar and poet, a skilled linguist, who died later this year in Puebla, Mexico.

APPLICATIONS, RECOMMENDATIONS   June 30, 1825

CHARLES DOUGLAS, Tuscumbia, Alabama, expresses thanks for a letter of introduction (not found), once obtained from Clay by request of Felix Grundy, "to Col John D. Bradburn of Mexico," and now solicits aid in procuring an appointment as Secretary of Legation or consul in one of the Latin American Republics. Douglas has lived in Mexico and would like to return there. Refers Clay to an accompanying letter of recommendation from William R. King (above, June 22, 1825) and to an earlier communication (not found). States that Henry Chambers has written to (John Quincy) Adams in behalf of Douglas, whose brother, Richard, of Chillicothe, Ohio, has promised to address Clay "on the same subject." ALS. DNA, RG59, A. and R. (MR2). Addressed to Clay at Lexington. Richard Douglas, born in New London, Connecticut, had moved to Chillicothe in 1808, had been admitted to the bar shortly thereafter, and practiced until his death in 1852. He had represented Pickaway County in the Ohio Legislature in 1812 and remained actively interested in politics, delivering a nominating speech for William Henry Harrison at the Whig Convention of 1836.

JAMES OMBROSI, Florence (Italy), reports the failure of Campbell, Levers, and Company of Genoa, "an event which by the law of the United States deprives R. Campbell of the Consulship . . . in that City," and applies for appointment to fill the vacancy. ALS. DNA, RG59, Cons. Disp., Florence (M-T204, R1). Duplicate, also ALS, in DNA, RG59, A. and R. (MR3). Addressed to Secretary of State; received September 12. Other members of Campbell's firm have not been identified. He retained his appointment until 1834. On Ombrosi's position, see above, Ombrosi to Secretary of State, March 29, 1825, note.

Promissory Notes to Richard Smith

43. 75/100   City of Washington, July 1st. 1825
    On the first day of January eighteen hundred and twenty-Seven I promise to pay to the order of Richard Smith.Agent forty three Dollars and Seventy five Cents, for value received. on Pew No.
in St Johns Church   H. CLAY

DS, partially printed. DLC-TJC (DNA, M212, R16). Endorsed on verso: "Rd. Smith Agent for St. Johns church   1143 H Clay   43.75 1/4 Jany 1827." Two additional notes, bearing the same date and located in the same source, are virtually identical, except for the dates of maturity, respectively April 1 and July 1, 1827, and for the numbers on the endorsements, 1144 and 1145. St. John's Episcopal Church, located across Lafayette Square from the White House, had been erected in 1816.

Receipt from Moses Dawson

[July 1, 1825]
Recd. 1st. July 1825 from the Hon: H. Clay Seven dollars and 50

Cents for two and a half years of his subscription for the Cincinnati Advertiser—by the hands of Mr. Scott Harrison   Moses Dawson

ADS. DLC-TJC (DNA, M212, R16). Dawson, an Irish revolutionary, had come to the United States in 1817 and in the same year had accepted an invitation to conduct a school in Cincinnati. In 1821 he had begun writing for the *Cincinnati Advertiser,* and in January, 1823, he had become its editor and proprietor. Under his leadership until 1840, the journal developed as a leading organ in support of Andrew Jackson's political views.

John Scott Harrison, commonly identified by his middle name, was the third son of William Henry Harrison. Graduated from Cincinnati College in 1824, young Harrison had married and begun farming on a tract in Ohio bordering the Indiana line. He later became a local magistrate and served as partner in management of his father's farm.

From John M. Forbes
(*Private*)   Buenos Ayres 1st July 1825.
Honble. Henry Clay Secretary of State, Washington.
Dear Sir,

Referring to my despatch No. *21*.[1] by this Vessel for general news, I am about to trespass on your pressing occupations by a few words Concerning my affairs in Connection with the public service here.— [Requests payment of salary to "a Copyist and general assistant" whom he has found it necessary to employ; asks that additional volumes, beyond the first five of "Bioren's Corrected edition" of the laws of the United States[2] be sent to continue his own set and a set he has given to the public library in Buenos Aires; and expresses a wish also to receive the acts of Congress, after each Session, and "Force's 'National Register'[3] annually."] Any Packages or Communications for me, if forwarded *franked* to Messrs. De Forest & Son of New York, will be more Promptly and Carefully sent on, than in the usual mode of Sending them to the Collector; because many Vessels Sail with fictitious Clearances, destined for this place[4] and Such destinations are best known to Merchants in active business.—

On another Subject I touch with embarrassment inasmuch as it is Connected with your name.— It has ever been an object of earnest desire and Constant effort on my part to impress this ungrateful People with a due sense of the friendship of the U.S. towards them and as a Part of my Plan, I have never Ceased to Speak of your efforts in their Cause and have Published here, in the language of the Country, several of your Speeches.— but the one most directly Connected with the Subject (that on the motion made in Congress by you and which is alluded to in the engraving Published of your Portrait[5]) is wanting.— Having Presented one of those Engravings to the Public Library here and intending to Present another to the General Congress now sitting, I will thank you to Send me, if in your power, a translation into Spanish (which I understand was sometime since published) of that Splendid Speech which I had the greatest pleasure in hearing.[6]— I wish to accompany the Engraving by a Copy of that Speech.— These People are so servilely English that they wish to forget or deny any obligation to us.— I am quite ashamed of myself, My Dear Sir, for having so long importuned you, in your unceasing public occupations, and Have the honour to be, With the greatest respect, Your devoted & very Obedient Servant

J M FORBES

ALS. DNA, RG59, Dip. Disp., Argentina, vol. 2 (M69, R3). Published under date of June 29 in Espil (comp.), *Once Años en Buenos Aires*, 369-70.

1 Above, June 27, 1825.   2 See above, II, 560n.

3 Probably Force's *National Government Journal, and Register of Official Papers, from December, 1823, to December, 1824* (Washington, 1823-1824). This volume, only, is listed in Joseph Sabin, *Bibliotheca Americana, a Dictionary of Books Relating to America, from Its Discovery to the Present Time* (Begun by Joseph Sabin and continued by Wilberforce Eames for the Bibliographical Society of America [29 vols.; New York, 1868-1936]), VI, 64. Cf. below, Davis and Force to Clay, September 21, 1825.

4 Cf. above, Raguet to Secretary of State, May 20, 1825.

5 See above, III, 242n, 413. The picture had been engraved by Peter Maverick, of New York, from a portrait (now hanging in the Corcoran Art Gallery, Washington) by Charles King. The latter, born in Rhode Island and educated in London, had established himself in Washington in 1816, where he remained for the next forty years as a painter of eminent men. The engraving bears the inscription, "To Congress United States of North America   February 10th. 1821," followed by the resolution as published above, III, 29.

6 On Forbes' foreign assignments, see above, Forbes to Clay, March 26, 1825, note. He could not have heard Clay's remarks in connection with the resolution of February 10, 1821, or the more famous speeches of March 24, 28, 1818 (above, II, 512-62). He probably refers to that of May 10, 1820 (above, II, 853-60). No translation has been found.

Property Deed from Richard and Sally Higgins to Executor of James Morrison

[July 1, 1825]

[Richard Higgins and wife, Sally, of Fayette County, convey to Henry Clay, sole acting executor of James Morrison, 43 acres on "the Woodford Road" at Merino Street, part of a tract purchased by Higgins and Lewis Sanders from Robert Patterson. The transfer is made "for and in consideration of the Compromise of a certain action of ejectment . . . against . . . Richard Higgins instituted for the recovery of one half of a tract of land purchased by" Higgins and Sanders from Patterson, "part within and part without the *town* boundary of Lexington by which Compromise the sd parties to said Suit have agreed to *divide* the sd. one half Sued for . . . and for the further consideration of One dollar in hand paid. . . ." Signed by Richard and Sally Higgins; recorded in the office of the Fayette County clerk, July 1, 1825.]

Fayette County Court, Deed Book Z, 280-81.

Property Deed, Executor of James Morrison to
Richard Higgins

[July 1, 1825]

In "consideration of the Compromise of a Suit in ejectment pending in the Fayette Ct. Ct. in the name of . . . James Morrison against . . . Richard Higgins . . . instituted for the recovery of one half of a tract of land purchased by said Higgins and Lewis Sanders of Robert Patterson by which the parties have agreed to divide the one half . . . and in further Consideration of one dollar this day paid," Henry Clay, as executor of James Morrison, transfers to Richard Higgins "the whole of sd. tract purchased by . . . Sanders and Higgins of Robert Patterson remaining unsold by them . . . except the forty three acres supposed to be one fourth of the part of said tract which is unsold and which is this day conveyed to . . . Clay by . . . Higgins. . . ." Signed by Clay; recorded in the office of the Fayette County clerk, July 1, 1825.]

Fayette County Court, Deed Book Z, 281-82.

INSTRUCTIONS AND DISPATCHES   July 1, 1825

From ALEXANDER HAMMETT, Naples. Reports that the Count Lucchesi awaits the return of "the Minister, Mr. De Medici, now absent with the King," before setting out for the United States. The Count has informed Hammett that he has proposed to De Medici certain modifications in restrictions on American trade, in response to which the Minister has asked what would be given in return. Hammett has explained to the Count the footing on which other nations trade in the United States, observing that, in the case of Naples, a "serious difficulty" exists under the act of Congress of March 3, 1815, because their trade in tobacco, a principal article of American production, is a government monopoly, which has been farmed out for six years. Notes that the Count seems uneasy about his reception in the United States and attributes this anxiety to "the reflexion of the wrongs we had Suffered in this Country, & the view in which the American Government might Still consider them," a subject which neither party has mentioned but on which Hammett believes the Count has secret instructions, "to watch the intentions of our Cabinet. . . ." ALS. DNA, RG59, Cons. Disp., Naples, vol. 1 (M-T224, R-T1). Addressed to "J. Clay"; received September 10. On the act of March 3, 1815, see above, Clay to Forbes, April 14, 1825, note.

From CHARLES MACNEAL, "Carthagena [*sic*] Colombia." Owing to ill health, and under authority left with him by John M. MacPherson, United States consul for Cartagena, MacNeal has this day appointed "William Berrien Esq. a Citizen of the United States resident in this City" to act in his place. ALS. DNA, RG59, Cons. Disp., Cartagena, vol. 1 (M-T192, R1). Received September 5. MacPherson, of Pennsylvania, remained titular consul for the United States in Cartagena from 1823 until 1837. William Berrien, his nephew, formerly of Philadelphia, died in July, 1826.

Toasts and Remarks at Georgetown Banquet

[July 2, 1825]

HENRY CLAY, *Secretary of State*—The soul of Kentucky: the tried Republican. Domestic Manufactures Interna[l] Improvement, Universal Liberty, and Liberal Principles, find in him an advocate indeed. His unshaken integrity and splendid genius have shed a lustre on his country.

After the applause which succeeded this toast had subsided, Mr *Clay* rose, and in a very feeling and elegant address, thanked the company for the respect they had shewn him, as well by the occasion as by the sentiment they had expressed. He adverted to the circumstances attending the late Presidential election; declared that he had been governed alone by a wish to promote the welfare of his country; and that according to the best lights he had received on the subject, he could not, without doing violence to his conscience, have acted otherwise; but disclaimed a wish to be understood as casting the slightest censure on any man for acting differently from himself, believing that they had been governed by the purest and best of motives. He concluded by offering the following toast.

The revival of the prosperity of Geo. Town, and the happiness of the people of Scott.

Lexington *Kentucky Reporter*, July 4, 1825, reprinted from Georgetown, Kentucky, *Sentinel*. The dinner, given Clay by citizens of Georgetown and Scott County, was attended by "Col. R. M. JOHNSON, one of our Senators in Congress, Maj: J. T. JOHNSON, our late, and Col. JAMES JOHNSON, our present Representative in Congress. . . . Owing to the shortness of the notice given, it was not generally known through the County, that a Dinner was to be given on that day; the company was, however, large and highly respectable. At about 3 o'clock, the company sat down to an elegant Dinner, prepared by Mr B. H. EVANS. No incident occurred during the day to disturb the harmony and good feelings that pervaded the whole company." The toasts followed the meal.

Bennett H. Evans had taken out a tavern license in February of this year; he renewed it the following year but thereafter dropped from the record.

Mortgage Deed to Samuel J. Donaldson

[July 2, 1825]

[Indenture by which Henry Clay and Lucretia, his wife, convey to Samuel J. Donaldson of Baltimore, Maryland, trustee for the creditors of Samuel and Robert Purviance, the Kentucky Hotel property on Short Street, Lexington, Kentucky, and property at Short and Market Streets in Lexington, as security for the payment of notes. The debt consists of three notes, each for $5,175.96, dated February 16, 1825, and payable in one, two and three years. The Kentucky Hotel property is subject to an existing mortgage by Clay to the Bank of the United States.[1] Signed by Henry and Lucretia Clay; recorded July 2, 1825, in the office of the Fayette County clerk.]

Fayette County Court, Deed Book Z, 284-87. Cf. above, Agreement, February 16, 1825.
[1] See above, II, 876-77.

Deed of Emancipation, as Executor of James Morrison

[July 2, 1825]

[Deed of emancipation, executed by Clay, sole acting executor of James Morrison, for a "mulatto man Slave John commonly called John Taylor," Morrison in his will having empowered his executors to free John two years after Morrison's death, "if during that time his conduct should in their discretion be such as to merit it." Signed by Clay and witnessed by Theodore W. Clay and J. W. Edmiston; recorded in the office of the Fayette County clerk, July court, 1825.]

Fayette County Court, Deed Book Z, 342-43.

Receipt from James Harper

[July 2, 1825]

Recd. 2. July 1815 [sic] of H. Clay as a collateral Security of the debt which he owes the Bank of the U States at its Office of Discount & Deposit in Lexington and for which the Said officer holds his Note[1]— the following bonds & notes—

George C Thompson— payable 1st March next—	$300[2] —
Jas Graves Jr & Jas Graves Sr paye. 18 Decr next—	100 —
Same—& Same paye. 18 Decr 1826	100[3] —
W W Worsley s accpts.—due 11. Octr 1826—	1000[4]
Danl Bryan & W Romans Note due 8 Decr 1824 for—	6621.[5]

The above (Note of Bryan & Roman) is entitled to the following credits—to wit $1000. on the 11. Octr 1825
                      1000—   11 Octr 1826.
                      1150. pd. 28 Octr 1824[6] to be
                      credited when the Note become [sic] due

Alexr Parker & W Warfield due 22 Decr 1828—	2400.
W Warfield & A Parker due 8 Decr 1828 ——	1320

These two carry interest from date— Int pd up to last Decr[7]

E Payne D Mc Payne & David Howard Replevy bond due 19 Decr 1826	1430[8]
S Trotter, J Trotter & C Wilkins due 25 Decr 1826	1911.88[9]

The Notes & Securities above mentioned are assigned by H Clay & agreed to be taken by the Bank on the condition that no claim or plea shall be made by him for the want of due diligence on the part of the Bank in proceeding upon them or any of them—Executed

in duplicate & interchanged between H Clay & J Harper Cashr for
the Bank of the United States——   J HARPER Cashr.

ADS. KyLxT.
1 See above, II, 876-77; cf. above, III, 532-33.
2 See above, Auction Sale, June 24, 1825.
3 See above, Promissory Note, June 25, 1825.
4 Not found. Cf. above, II, 249.
5 See above, III, 296, 298n, 892n.   6 See above, III, 872.
7 See above, III, 519, 525, 549, 550n; Scott to Clay, January 3, 1825.
    8 Cf. above, III, 519, 525-27, 550n. The replevy bond, not found. Howard was
probably a kinsman of the Paynes, whose mother, Elizabeth (Mrs. Edward) Payne,
was a sister of Benjamin Howard (who died without issue), of Mary Howard (Mrs.
Alexander) Parker, and of Margaret Howard (Mrs. Robert) Wickliffe. Orlando Brown,
Memoranda of the Preston Family (Frankfort, Ky., 1842), 10.
    9 Cf. above, III, 519, 550n. This also appears to have been a replevy bond, co-
signed by Charles Wilkins.

From Charles Humphreys

2 July. 1825.

H. Clay has given his receipt[1] for a note of W. C. Cowan for $1000
dated the 8 March 1821 due 12 months after date, with interest
from the date,[2] on account of a debt due from McConothy Tibbatts[3]
and myself to John Postlethwait Trustee &c, for which Judgment
has been recovered in the Fayette Circuit Court.[4] The note of
said Cowan was payable in the Currency and has, with my assent,
been this day settled (principal & interest) at $777 16/100 for which
sum of $777 16/100 the debt aforesaid is to be credited as of this day.

CH HUMPHREYS

    DS, in Clay's hand DLC-TJC (DNA, M212, R16). Endorsed on wrapper by Clay:
". . . Certificate on a/c of Cowan's note recd. on a/c of debt of said Humphreys, Mc-
Conothy and Tibbatts in their debt due in the name of Postlethwaite [*sic*]." Cowan
was a brother-in-law of Humphreys.
1 Not found.   2 Cf. above, III, 293-94.
3 Probably Jacob McConathy, Thomas Tibbatts.
4 Case not found.

INSTRUCTIONS AND DISPATCHES   July 2, 1825

From J[OHN] ADAMS SMITH, London, no 5. Reports that a copy of the British
treaty with Colombia has arrived but has not been laid before Parliament. The
"Representative from Buenos Ayres," "the Envoy from Colombia Mr [Manuel
José] Hurtado," and "General Michelena the Minister from Mexico who
arrived . . . last year" have not been officially received. Lord Cochrane has landed
at Portsmouth. ALS. DNA, RG59, Dip. Disp., Great Britain, vol. 32 (M30, R28).
Addressed to Secretary of State; received August 21. On the British-Colombian
commercial treaty, see above, Watts to Clay, May 10, 1825. On the disagreement
between Lord Thomas Cochrane and the Government of Brazil, see above,
Raguet to Secretary of State, March 11, 1825, note; May 12, 1825.
    Bernardino Rivadavia, a native of Buenos Aires, distinguished for military
leadership during the British attacks upon that city early in the century, and

an active proponent of Argentine independence from 1810, had been placed in charge of negotiation to win European support for the republican movement during the period from 1814 to 1820. Returning to Argentina in the latter year, he had served for three years as Chief Minister. Upon a change of government in 1824, Rivadavia had been named envoy to England. Returning to Argentina in February, 1826, he was elected President of the United Provinces of River Plate and served until forced out of office in June, 1827, by the mounting dissension between the interior provinces and the city of Buenos Aires.

José Mariano Michelena, after early imprisonment for revolutionary activities in Mexico, had been named as one of the alternates for the triumvirs who constituted the provisional government of that country from 1823 to 1824. Sent to England in the latter year as a representative of Mexico, he was recalled later in 1825 to become a delegate to the Panama Congress. He later, in 1837, served briefly as Minister of War and Navy.

To Samuel Southard

Dear Sir   Ashland 3. July 1825
    I send you by this Mail the communication which I received from the Pacific respecting the cruise of the Franklin and of which I spoke to you.[1]
    You appear at Washington to have your hands full of business with Commodore Porter,[2] Govr Troup and the Creek Indians.[3] I shall not be able before the end of the month to reach my post to share the labors and the responsibility with you on the two latter affairs. As to the first, I think you ought to move on steadily in the course determined on. Your's with great respect   H. CLAY
The Honble Mr. Southard &c &c &c

ALS. NjP.
[1] Probably Alsop to Clay, September 1, 1823 (above, III, 481-84).
[2] See above, Nelson to Clay, April 6, 1825; Southard to Clay, April 29, 1825; Salmon to Clay, May 2, 1825; Clay to Southard, May 6, 1825.
[3] Under the Treaty of the Indian Springs of February 12, 1825 (7 *U.S. Stat.*, 239-40), a group of Creek chiefs had committed their people to cession of all their lands in Georgia; the State was to come into possession by September 1, 1826. Meanwhile, Governor Troup had opened negotiations with the same group of Indian leaders to permit survey of the lands prior to the cession date, so that they might be opened to settlement promptly. On April 29, three of the Creek leaders who had agreed to the treaty and survey had been murdered (cf. above, Habersham to Clay, June 8, 1825). Troup charged that the Federal Indian Agent, John Crowell, had incited the violence. When other Federal officers, Timothy Patrick Andrews (an Army paymaster, later distinguished for service during the Mexican War; and, from 1862 to 1864, paymaster general) and General Edmund Pendleton Gaines, sent to investigate the manner in which the Treaty of the Indian Springs had been negotiated, adopted the view that the cession had been arranged with minority leaders who could not win tribal endorsement, the Secretary of War, James Barbour, on July 21, 1825, informed Governor Troup that President Adams would not authorize the survey. The Georgia Legislature subsequently maintained belief in the fairness of the treaty and insisted upon the State's right to the lands at the specified date. President Adams instituted negotiations with other tribal leaders for a new treaty, signed at Washington, January 24, 1826, with a supplementary clause of March 31, 1826 (7 *U. S. Stat.*, 286-90), which provided for cession of the Creek lands east of the Chattahoochee in Georgia but deferred entry into the ceded zone until January 1, 1827. Tension between

Federal and State authorities brought threat of armed conflict when in September, 1826, the Secretary of War forbade entry into the area before the end of the year. In December, 1826, the Georgia Legislature declared the abrogation of the original treaty unconstitutional, and Troup ordered a survey of all the Creek lands in Georgia. The impasse was finally resolved by further agreements of November 15, 1827, and January 3, 1828 (7 *U. S. Stat.*, 307-308), under which the Creeks surrendered title to their remaining holdings in the State. Ulrich Bonnell Phillips, *Georgia and State Rights, a Study of the Political History of Georgia from the Revolution to the Civil War* . . . (American Historical Association, *Annual Report . . . for 1901*, II; Washington, 1902), 56-65.

Banquet Toast at Connett's Inn

[July 4, 1825]

HENRY CLAY, *Secretary of State:*
"The man resolved and steady to his trust,
Inflexible to ill, and obstinately just."[1]
On the eve of his departure we renew to him the assurance of unabated confidence in his integrity, and tender to him our "heart-felt warm adieu."[2]

Lexington *Kentucky Reporter,* July 11, 1825. The dinner, at which "Mr CLAY, Major Gen. SCOTT and Capt GALT of his Staff, were guests," was held at "Mr CONNETT'S," where "the party of ladies and gentlemen was very large. . . ." The toasts followed the meal.

General Winfield Scott was serving a tour of duty, from 1824 to 1825, as commander of the Western Department of the United States Army, with headquarters at Louisville, Kentucky. Patrick Henry Galt, of Virginia, who had served in the War of 1812 and later was distinguished for service in the Mexican War, was not formally commissioned a captain until May 15, 1829. W. C. Connett's Inn was located on the Georgetown Road, about four miles from Lexington.

1 Source not found.   2 No reply has been found.

Property Deed from James Minter

[July 4, 1825]

[Indenture by which, for and in consideration of one dollar, James Minter conveys to Clay a tract of land in Fayette County, containing 221 acres and 30 poles, with appurtenances, formerly the property of Thomas Wallace, now in possession of Nathaniel Petit, bounded as follows: "Beginning on the Winchester road the North East side at a stake corner to Robert Wickliffe and Richard Downton, thence North 44 degrees East 304 poles to a large sugar tree, thence South 32 degrees 20 minuets [*sic*] East 151 poles and two tenths to a broken top hickory corner of John Price,[1] thence South 45 degrees West 186 poles and 4 tenths of a pole to a large elm on the South West side of the aforesaid Winchester road, thence North 76 degrees West along the said road to the beginning 162 poles and eight tenths of a pole. . . ." Minter covenants to defend the title "except against two mortgages one given to the B. of the U. States, and the other to the Commonwealths Bank, which by an agreement, bearing even date herewith the said Clay has agreed to extinguish." Witnessed by Theodore W. Clay and Henry Clay, Jr., proved on their testimony, and recorded by J. C. Rodes, clerk of Fayette County, July 5, 1825.]

DS, in Clay's hand. DLC-TJC (DNA, M212, R16). Cf. above, III, 806-807.
1 Probably John R. Price. Cf. deeds, Levi Todd to John Price, August 17, 1805; John Price to Bird Price, January 8, 1806—both in Fayette Circuit Court, Deed Book B, 150-51, 264-66.

Agreement with James Minter

[July 4, 1825]

An agreement entered into this 4h. day of July 1825 Between H. Clay and James Minter.

Where as the said Minter has not removed and is unable to remove the mortgages in the preceding agreement mentd[1] to the Bank of the U. States and the Commonwealths Bank, the former now amounting to two thousand dollars specie and the latter to seventeen hundred and sixty dollars in Commths bank paper, with a small amount of interest upon each: It is therefore agreed between the parties that the said Clay shall assume the payment of the said two mortgages for the amount due thereon as aforesaid: And in consideration there of the said Minter agrees to resell to the said Clay the Tammany Mills in the preceding agreement mentioned, in the condition in which they now are, possession of which he is to deliver to the said Clay on the first of January next, without removing any thing attached to the realty from or impairing the present condition of the said property. And it is further agreed between the parties afd. that Nathaniel Petit shall retain possession of the farm in the preceding agreement mentioned for three years from the first day of March 1826. And it is further agreed that, if the said Clay shall sell the said Tammany Mills property at any time within three years from the date here of, at a sum greater than twenty five hundred and fifty dollars specie with interest thereon from this date then that the said Minter shall receive such excess beyond the said sum; but if no sale there of is effected within the said period of three years then the said Minter is to have no claim upon the said Clay if after that period he shall sell it for more, nor is the said Clay to have any on the said Minter if he should sell it for less. This stipulation is not intended by the parties to operate as a mortgage, but flows from a disposition of the said Clay to accommodate the said Minter. It is further agreed between the parties that the said Clay is to be released from the payment of the sum of nine hundred and fifty eight dollars on the

first of Octr. 1825 (and his note is surrended [*sic*] accordingly) a part of the said sum having been placed against the rents of the farm during the three years occupancy of the said Petit as afd. and the residue thereof being applied to reduce the afd. mortgages to the sum of $2550 as afd. Witness the seals of the parties this 4 July 1825 and hands.   H. CLAY {LS}
Teste Theo. W. Clay   JAMES MINTER {LS}

[Endorsement][2]
Although H. Clay did not make Sale of the Tammany Mills within the time above limited, he has from motives of generosity this day paid me one hundred dollars, which I have recd. in a spirit of thankfulness; and I do hereby acknowledge that I have no claim whatever upon him.   9h. May 1835   JAMES MINTER.

ADS, signed also by Minter. DLC-TJC (DNA, M212, R16). Cf. above, Property Deed, this date.   [1] Above, III, 806-807.
[2] ES, in Clay's hand.

Agreement with Nathaniel Petit

[July 4, 1825]

An agreement between Nathl. Petit & H Clay. The said Clay agrees that the said Petit shall retain possession of the farm which he now occupies in Fayette County, adjoining the farm of R. Wickliffe, formerly the property of Thomas Wallace, for three years, from the first day of March 1826. And the said Clay expecting to get fifty acres adjoining from Mrs. Russell[1] he agrees (if he should obtain it) that he shall have that also for the aforesaid term of three years. In consideration whereof the said Petit agrees to relinquish all claim whatever that he has upon the said farm, growing out of any right or lien either from Thomas Wallace or James Minter. He also agrees to surrender the aforesaid land to the said Clay on the first day of March 1829, without removing in the Mean time any wood or timber therefrom. He further agrees (in consideration of the use of the fifty acres adjoining as aforesaid) to put the fences upon both the farm and the fifty acres in good tenantable order, and to leave in good order fifty acres of the land in red clover—

Witness the hands & seals of the parties this 4 July 1825.
Teste William C.C. Claiborne   NATHL. PETIT {LS}
                                            H. CLAY {LS}

ADS, signed also by Petit and Claiborne. KyLxT. Cf. above, Agreement with Minter, this date.
[1] Mary Owen Russell. See below, Memorandum, July 6, 1825.

From Benjamin Netherland

My dear Sir   Nicholasville July 4. 1825

I have discovered in the Clarkes office of this place, a Copy of all the lands [t]hat were Sould under the decree of the Federal Court at Frankford, where I was plaintiff & May and others deft.[1]—the land that were patternd [sic] to you & Mr. Walker were all Sould under that decree,[2] also them [sic] of 9491½ Acres 133 is now laying in the Office not pattern & assignd [sic] to you, I send your Sisters[3] letter, I have no doubt of you doing me Justice   I look up to you as a a [sic] Father, I beg you will look into that and if any think [sic] can be done for me I Know you can do it   I shall rest on what ever you say. I wish you would wright me by male what time you will go. as I wish to See you, respecting my Servises as and [sic] Officer in the Armny [sic] of the U S— I had three years pay due me I have never receiv d any Lands on my Compation[4] what ever, which in Consequence I am Intited [sic] to half pay[5]   when I see you I will State in wrighting the Circumstance, and do as you direct— May God Perserve [sic] you   B NETHERLAND

ALS. DLC-TJC (DNA, M212, R13). Addressed: "The Honbe [Henry] Clay   Lexington."   [1] See above, I, 803-805.
[2] See above, *ibid.*, 192, 486-88.
[3] Word not clear. The letter has not been found.
[4] Compensation.
[5] Under a resolution of the Continental Congress on September 16, 1776, officers who served for the duration of the Revolutionary conflict were to receive land grants in accordance with their rank; under a resolution of November 12, 1776, officers who enlisted for only three years were to receive a bounty and pay, but not land grants. By resolution of October 21, 1780, officers then in service who continued on duty to the end of the war or who became supernumerary while in service were to be retired at one-half pay for life. Finally on March 22, 1783, the Congress determined to commute the half pay for life to five years at full pay. The State of Virginia had enacted comparable legislation, except for the commutation provision. [Walter S. Franklin, comp.], *Resolutions, Laws, and Ordinances Relating to the Pay, Half Pay, Commutation of Half Pay, Bounty Lands, and Other Promises Made by Congress to the Officers and Soldiers of the Revolution* . . . (Washington, 1838), 9-10, 12, 14, 20; W. T. R. Saffell, *Records of the Revolutionary War: Containing the Military and Financial Correspondence of Distinguished Officers; Names of the Officers and Privates of Regiments, Companies, and Corps* (New York, 1858), 492-95, 507-508.

Netherland, however, does not appear on the military rolls at either governmental level. Following his heroism in rallying the defeated Kentuckians after the Battle of Blue Licks, in August, 1782, he had been nominated to the War Office of Virginia, for a major's commission; but the request had been denied. Gwathmey, *Historical Register of Virginians in the Revolution.* . . , 581.

Property Deed from William Pollock

[July 4, 1825]

[For the sum of $250, paid and acknowledged, William Pollock conveys to Henry Clay the tract for which Clay holds Pollock's bond,[1] this deed being in discharge of that bond—the land lying in Fayette County, part of the tract which Jesse Bledsoe purchased

from Dr. Charles Lewis of Virginia and which Bledsoe deeded
to John Pollock, amounting to 5¾ acres and 20 poles, beginning
at a stake corner to the tract formerly owned by Stephens, Fisher,
and Company[2] on which the Fayette Paper Manufacturing Company established their buildings, thence with their line N 18¾ E
23 poles to a stake, thence S 71½ E 40 poles to a stake, thence 18¾°
W 24 poles to a stake in Benjamin Minst's[3] line, and with it N 70°
W 40 poles to the beginning—the property now being in Clay's
possession and adjacent to the tract he purchased at the sale of
Lewis Sanders' property to satisfy the claim of the Bank of Kentucky.[4] General warranty of title. Recorded July 4, 1825.]

Fayette County Court, Deed Book Z, 279.
[1] Above, III, 130.
[2] Luther Stephens, Hallet M. Winslow, and Maddox Fisher. For their deeds trans-
ferring the property to the Fayette Manufacturing Company, see Fayette County Court,
Deed Book N, 185-87; Q, 121-22.
[3] Probably Benjamin Merrell.   [4] See above, III, 151-52.

INSTRUCTIONS AND DISPATCHES   July 4, 1825

From ANDREW ARMSTRONG, Port au Prince. Reports a French squadron in port
under a flag of truce and apparently on a friendly mission. Asks, if the independence of Haiti is to be recognized, would it not be well for the United States
to be among the first to negotiate a commercial treaty? ALS. DNA, RG59, Cons.
Disp., Cap Haitien, vol. 5 (M9, R-T5). On recognition of Haitian independence, see below, Holden to Clay, July 16, 1825.

From JOHN M. FORBES, Buenos Aires. Encloses a newspaper which gives "an
account of the organization of a temporary Patriot Government in the Banda
Oriental. . . ." ALS. DNA, RG59, Dip. Disp., Argentina, vol. 2 (M69, R3).
Published in Espil (comp.), *Once Años en Buenos Aires*, 370.

Promissory Note to Esther Morrison

[July 5, 1825]

Twelve months after date I promise to pay to Mrs. Esther
Morrison the sum of One thousand dollars, with interest thereon
from this date, the interest to be paid half yearly until this note
is finally discharged.

Witness my hand & seal this 5 July 1825
[Endorsements on verso][1]

Paid the interest up to 5 July 1826 by a check on the Office of
the Bank U.S. this 7 Aug. 1826 at Lexington.   H. CLAY

Do. Do. 13 July 1827 up to 5 July 1827.   H.C

Do. Do 5 Septr 1829 up to the 5th. July 1829 in a check on the
B. B. of the U.S. at Lexn.   H. C.

Int. paid 22d. Novr. 1830 in a check on the Off. B. U S.   H.C.

Int. paid in a check 17h. Nov. 1831   H.C

  do. do. 24 Nov. 1824. [*sic*]   H.C.

AD (originally ADS; signature crossed out). DLC-TJC (DNA, M212, R16). Cf.
above, III, 518. Mrs. Morrison's annuity, under the terms of her husband's will, was
$2,000, to be paid in semiannual installments. Fayette County, Will Book F, 62.
  1 The first, AES; the remainder, AEI.

Bill of Complaint against Robert Wickliffe

[*ca.* July 5, 1825]

To the Honble the Judge of the Circuit Court of Fayette County
in Chancery sitting.

Humbly complaining sheweth unto your honor your orator
Henry Clay,

That on the 18h day of June 1808 your orator entered into a written agreement with a certain William Lytle (of which a copy is hereto
annexed, the original being in his custody ready to be produced
when this Court may so direct)[1] by which they mutually engaged
to exchange certain real estate therein described: That the said
Lytle has constantly enjoyed and possessed that which your orator
agreed to give in exchange, to which, according to the said agreement, he has executed a conveyance: That, among the parcels of
property to which the said Lytle agreed, in the said written
contract, to convey to your orator, is one described therein as
"also the stable and lot hitherto used for the purpose of the said
tavern on Market Street, adjoining the lot at present occupied by
William T. Barry Esqr.": That as the said agreement imports the
value of the said stable and lot chiefly consisted in its being an
appurtenance to the Tavern in the said agreement mentioned, and
the value again of the stable and lot chiefly consisted in the stable,
which was a large brick building of much capacity for the accommodation of horses belonging to persons stopping at the said
tavern: That your orator took possession of the property agreed
to be given by the said Lytle in exchange as aforesaid and remained
therein: That, finding that he could dispense with the use of the
said stable & lot, by converting the tavern into a sort of boarding
house and tavern, on the 9h day of Novr. 1808 he agreed to sell
the said stable and lot to a certain John P. Wagnon, by a written
contract (of which a Copy is hereto annexed as part of this bill,
the original being in his custody ready to be produced when this
Court shall so direct:)[2] That the said Wagnon agreed to pay your
orator therefor $1800, of which he paid eight hundred dollars in
four Chandaliers, and for the balance of $1000 he gave your
orator his note[3] which he still holds, payable in three years, with
interest from the first day of November 1808: Your orator shews

that he received the said Chandaliers at a price greatly beyond
their intrinsic value, in consideration of the whole transaction,
and he has recently sold one of them to Robert Wickliffe Esq. at
the price of fifty dollars: That the said Wagnon afterwards transfered the said written contract with him to Genl. Geo. Mathews (he
to pay the balance due your orator) and he assigned it to W. T.
Barry Esqr. who assigned it to John T. Mason Junr. who again
assigned it to Robert Wickliffe Esqr. That your orator presumes
though he cannot so allege that each of the said assignees was to
stand, as it respects your orator, in the original condition of Wagnon:

And your orator further shews that the said Wagnon and his
said assignees or some of them took possession of the said stable
and lot and remained therein: That whilst they had the said
possession they sold and removed or caused or authorized to be
removed the materials of which the said stable was built from the
said lot, thereby reducing the said lot to the mere value of the
ground, without its principal improvement, which value your
orator charges is not above $500 and at no time exceeded that
amount: That after the removal of the said stable, the said
Wickliffe as the Counsel of   Phillips or of McDermid's heirs
brought a suit in Ejectment against the person in possession for
the said ground in the Circuit Court of Fayette,[4] and having
recovered a Judgment therein, on the   day of   181   took
possession thereof: That the said Lytle, being desirous to quiet
your orators title thereto derived from him, on the   day of
in the year 181   agreed to purchase of the said Wickliffe the title
in fee to the said lot and to give him therefor $ for which the
said Lytle executed his note, upon which the said Wickliffe has
prosecuted a suit and obtained a Judgment in the Circuit Cou[rt
of the] U. States for the district of Kentucky:[5] That whether the
said Wickliffe (who retains the possession of the said lot obtained
as aforesaid under the Judgt. of Fayette Circuit Court) has really
obtained from the said Philips or McDermids heirs the title to the
said lot & is now competent to convey the same, your orator knows
not and calls upon him to shew and prove: That by the agreement
as afd. between the said Wagnon and your orator, your orator has a
lien upon the said stable and lot for the balance of the consideration money due him, as by the said agreement will appear; and he
annexes hereto a Copy of the said Wagnon's note (the original being
in his possession ready to be produced when this Court shall so
order).

And your orator had well hoped that the said Wickliffe and
Lytle by adjusting the title to the said lot (for the stable is gone
as aforesaid) would settle between them and pay to your orator
what is really due to him, which in justice he ought to receive:

That he purchased the said Stable and lot without knowing or suspecting any defect whatever in the title: But now so it is &c   In tender Consideration whereof &c   To the end therefore that the said William Lytle John P. Wagnon, William T. Barry, John T. Mason and Robert Wickliffe (whom your orator prays may be made defendants hereto) may upon their Corporal oaths make as full answer to the allegations of this bill as if they were herein again repeated in the form of interrogatory: that the said Wickliffe may set forth and establish his title to the said lot, and also whether, by the terms of the assignment from Mason to him, he is bound to pay to your orator what is due to him upon the contract as afd. with Wagnon, or whether he is so bound by agreement either with the said Mason or either of the previous assignees; that the said Wickliffe may be decreed [. . .][6] the title to the said lot to the said Lytle and he to your orator; that the same may be decreed to be sold to pay what remains due to your orator; that if any thing be due to the said Wickliffe, in consequence of the purchase by the said Lytle from him, he may be decreed to pay it, and if he fails your orator is willing and hereby offers to do whatever, under all the circumstances of the case may be [. . .][7] proper and equitable; and that your orator may have such other and proper relief as may be deemed agreeable to Equity and good conscience   May it please your honor &c   H CLAY

ADS. KyLoF. MS. torn. On July 5, 1825, Thomas Bodley, clerk of the Fayette Circuit Court, ordered the sheriff to summon William Lytle, John P. Wagnon, William T. Barry, John T. Mason, Jr., and Robert Wickliffe to appear before the court on September 1, "to answer a bill in Chancery exhibited against them by Henry Clay...." *Ibid.*   [1] See above, I, 348-49.
    [2] See above, I, 383-84.   [3] See above, I, 382-83.
    [4] Cf. above, II, 383. The suit, brought by John Doe, on demise of Edmond Phillips and Milly, his wife, against Richard Roe, *i.e.*, Francis Walker, the tenant in possession, had been initiated at the September Term, 1817, of Fayette Circuit and, after various continuances, had been decided, by jury verdict, on April 7, 1819. Fayette Circuit Court, Civil Orders, R, 407-408; U, 34-35.
    [5] Suit not reported in Complete Record or Order Books, but a general index entry identifies the suit as no. 2392 and the judgment as "Abated" in June, 1823.
    [6] One or two words missing.   [7] Word illegible.

Receipted Account with John Bryan and Son

		H Clay Esqr. To John Bryan & Son	[July 5, 1825] Dr.	
1822				
Decr.	21st	To dressed buckskin		2 50
	26	To Repg. bridle & Saddle		‖ 25
	28	To 2 Circingles @ $1.25—To Kirb bridle @ $2		4 50
1823		To pr. Coat strops		‖ 25
July	1	To Elastic saddle $40—pr. Boneyed stirrups $7		47 ‖
		To best saddle Cloth $7 drawrein bridle $8		15 ‖

25   To pr. Martingales $3. .... 3 „
                                                                    $72 50
[Endorsement][1]
Recd. payment 5 July 1825   JOHN BRYAN & SON

D. DLC-TJC (DNA, M212, R15).   [1] ES, in Clay's hand.

Receipted Account with Lexington Post Office

                                                        [July 5, 1825]
The Honbl Henry Clay   To the Lexington P office   Dr.
1825
April 1 To Amt Postage to this day ....   29—01
July —1 To Postage to this date ....   3—40
          To letters for Mr Irwin[1]   —2 19
                                                           34 . 60

          By the post to you in the
              month of Novr enterd. over charged ....   20 . 26½
          Recvd Payment in full July 5th. 1825 $14 „ 33½
14 33/100   JOSEPH FICKLIN

ADS. DLC-TJC (DNA, M212, R10).
[1] James Erwin. Cf. above, Clay to Brown, May 9, 1825.

Receipted Account with Thomas Kane

                                                        [July 5, 1825]
The Honble Henry Clay.   To Thomas Kane   Dr.
1824
Septr 1st „ A Vest superf: Eng. black Clo: fash. dress. Coat, $32..00
         „ A pair superf. dress black cassimier pantaloons   12..00
  — 14th „ A Rich figured velvet vest   7..00
1825
June 4th „ A Vest superf: Eng: blue Cloth Coat &c &c   33..00
                    Amt of Thos. Clay Esqr acct $84..00
[Endorsement][1]
Recd. payment 5 July 1825, of H Clay   THOS. KANE

D. DLC-TJC (DNA, M212, R16).   [1] ES, in Clay's hand.

Check from James Harper

OFFICE OF DISCOUNT & DEPOSITE,
Bank of the United States.
No. 507   LEXINGTON, July 5th 1825
Cashier of the Bank of the United States,
    Pay this my Second Check, (First unpaid) to the Order of Hone
H. Clay, Three thousand dollars ....
——3.000 Dollars 00/100   J HARPER Cashr

[Endorsement][1]

Pay to the order of the Cashr of the Off of Dt. & Dt in the City of Washington.   H. CLAY

ADS, partially printed. PHi-Etting Collection.
[1] AES. Cf. below, Clay to Smith, July 6, 1825.

Receipt from John Wirt

[July 5, 1825]

Recd. Lexington July 5th. 1825. of Henry Clay Seventy Dollars & Sixty five cents his Town Tax for the present Year.

JOHN WIRT, Colr. T T.

ADS. DLC-TJC (DNA, M212, R16).

Receipt from John Wirt

[July 5, 1825]

[John Wirt acknowledges receipt of nine dollars, Lexington town tax for 1825, from Clay for the heirs of Thomas Hart, Sr.]

ADS. DLC-TJC (DNA, M212, R16).

INSTRUCTIONS AND DISPATCHES   July 5, 1825

From JOHN MULLOWNY, Tangier, no. 37. Encloses translation of a letter announcing the opening of the port of Mazagan, which, he thinks, will prove of no advantage to the United States. Recommends appointment of an American as agent at Mogador and states his intention of making such an appointment "should it so happen, that a native citizen of the U.S. sought a residence" there. Notes that he has been "without any communication from the Department of State, since May 1824." ALS. DNA, RG59, Cons. Disp., Tangier, vol. 4 (M-T61, R4). Dated: "Tangier 5"; the enclosure is dated June 19, 1825. Received: "Sep. 1825."

MISCELLANEOUS LETTERS   July 5, 1825

From JOHN P. SHELDON, Detroit. Reports dissolution of his partnership with Ebenezer Reed. ALS. DNA, RG59, P. and D. of L. Sheldon and Reed, who individually had both previously published journals in New York State, had established the *Detroit Gazette* in 1817 and had been publishers of the laws of the United States from the beginning. Sheldon was appointed inspector of the port of Detroit in 1830 and register of the public land office at Mineral Point, Michigan, in 1834. Reed continued as editor of the *Gazette*.

APPLICATIONS, RECOMMENDATIONS   July 5, 1825

JOSEPH M. WHITE, Saratoga (New York), recommends Samuel R. Overton and

Robert Mitchell for appointment as naval agent and naval storekeeper, respectively, at Pensacola. ALS. DNA, RG59, A. and R. (MR5).

White, a lawyer, born in Franklin County, Kentucky, and there admitted to the practice of law, had moved to Florida in 1821, had been appointed to the Territorial legislative council in 1822, and was now (1825-1837) Delegate to Congress. In 1823 he had been appointed one of three commissioners to ascertain claims and titles to land in West Florida under provisions of the act of Congress of May 8, 1822 (3 *U. S. Stat.*, 709-718). He published several accounts of land law, most notably *A New Collection of Laws, Charters, and Local Ordinances of the Governments of Great Britain, France and Spain, Relating to the Concessions of Land in Their Respective Colonies . . .* (Philadelphia, 1839).

Samuel R. Overton, a son of Waller and brother of Dr. James, John W., and Thomas J. Overton, had fought in the War of 1812 and thereafter had moved to Tennessee. In May, 1822, he had been appointed one of the Florida land commissioners and in February, 1825, register of the land office at Tallahassee. He had already been offered the appointment as naval agent at Pensacola, on May 26; he accepted the position on July 17 and on December 28, 1825, this appointment was confirmed by the Senate, retroactively. Carter (ed.), *Territorial Papers,* XXIII, 254.

Memorandum to Robert Scott

Memo for Mr. Scott.   6 July 1825

I leave a power of attorney[1] to you to take possession and sell the slaves of Mr. Mason agreeably to what passed yesterday.[2] I also leave with you The bill of Sale.[3]

I have a number of boxes and trunks at Ashland to be sent to the City of Washington. They contain china, glass, books, furniture &c. and require very careful handling. I wish you to engage a faithful waggoner or waggoners to carry them to Mess: January & Sutherland (Maysville),[4] and inform them of the necessity of careful attention to the articels [sic] in forwarding them to Wheeling. There is also some wine & whiskey in barrels. Be pleased to forward me to Washington a descriptive list of the boxes &c.

Don't forget to procure from Mr. R. Todd[5] the large barrel containing (120 gallons) and having [sic] it filled with old whiskey at the farm and sent to Genl. James Shelbys for me

Give Mr. Kerr[6] (my overseer) about the 15 or 20 August when he calls on you for it $50 in Commths notes to purchase bacon for the Negroes on the farm.

I leave the following notes for collection.

Geo. W. Morton   (payable in Commths paper) pd.[7] $150
Dr. John Todd   do.   do   50—[8]
B. Bosworth   (in Specie) pd.[9]   84[10]

    C. Williams   in specie (due a year hence)—   30[11]
    E. B Pearson $30:96/100 in whatever you can get[12]
Mrs. Russells agent (Mr Downing)[13] has agreed to let me have
Fifty acres of land on the Winchester road, near Mr. Wickliffes[14]
farm to adjoin a tract of 221 Acres owned by me, formerly the
property of Tho Wallace, now occupied by N. Petit.[15] The land
is to be laid off on the Nort [sic] East of my tract adjoining the
whole length of my line. I wish you to apply to Mrs. Russell or
Mr. Downing, get it surveyed and take a deed from her to me
for it.[16]   H. C.
[Endorsements on verso][17]
Memo. for Mr. Scott. Furnish Mr. Kerr with Salt for the farm
                                                        HC.

Receive from Mr M. Richardson[18] the money in their [sic] hands as
Deputy Sheriffs [sic] for me   H. C.

ADI. DLC-TJC (DNA, M212, R16).
1 Not found.
2 John T. Mason. The event to which reference is made has not been identified.
3 Not found.
4 Andrew M. January and William Sutherland, successors to the earlier partnership
of Winans and January.
5 Probably Robert S. Todd.   6 John H. Kerr.
7 This word in Scott's hand. Morton's note has not been found.
8 See above, III, 428-29.   9 This word in Scott's hand.
10 Cf. above, III, 97n. The note has not been found.
11 Cf. above, Statement, June 24, 1825. Williams' note has not been found.
12 Note not found.   13 Mary Owen Russell; Francis Downing.
14 Robert Wickliffe.
15 Cf. above, Agreement with Petit, July 4, 1825.
16 See below, Property Deed, November 2, 1825.
17 Each AEI.
18 Marquis D. Richardson. At this point the words "& Tho Wallace" have been
crossed out.

To [Richard] Smith

Dear Sir   Ashland 6 July 1825
    I transmitted to you, under date yesterday, two Checks one for
$3000 and the other for $500,[1] which I wished to be applied to the
payment of my note[2] under discount at your Office. I now inclose
two other Checks[3] both drawn by the office at N. Orleans   one
for $500, on the office at New York, and the other for $250 on
the parent institution, the amount of which I wish applied to
the same object. I am Yr. ob. servant   H. CLAY
Mr. Smith &c &c &c

ALS. NN-A. W. Anthony Collection.
1 See above, Check from Harper, July 5, 1825. The second check has not been found.
2 Cf. above, III, 886.
3 Not found.

Receipted Account with Elijah and Richard Henry

[July 6, 1825]

Henry Clay Esqr. To E. & R. Henry   Dr.

1824

July 1 To Shoeing 2 horses one year from this date	@	$16 ,, 00
,, 1 To 4 Shoes & 4 remove [*sic*]	@	2 ,, 25
,, 17 To 1 Shoe & 4 removes	@	1 ,, 50
,, 22 To 1 Shoe on Sorrel horse	@	,, ,, 50
August 2 To 1 Shoe & 3 removes	@	1 ,, 25
,, ,, To 3 Shoes & 1 remove	@	1 ,, 75—
Septr. 1 To 4 Steel Toed Shoes by Clark[1]	@	2 ,, 75—
,, 6 To mending pump handle New Axle &C.	@	1 ,, 50
,, 6 To new hook on pump rod		,, ,, 75
Oct. 9 To 1 Shoe	@	,, ,, 50
Novr. 9 To 6 Shoes & 2 removes	@	3 ,, 50—
Decr. 24 To 2 Shoes	@	1 ,, 00
		$33 25

[Endorsement on verso][2]
Recd. payment 6 July 1825   R HENRY for E & R Henry

D. DLC-TJC (DNA, M212, R16). Elijah and Richard Henry, probably brothers, were Lexington blacksmiths.

1 Not identified.   2 ES, in Clay's hand.

INSTRUCTIONS AND DISPATCHES   July 6, 1825

From JOHN M. FORBES, Buenos Aires, no. 22. States that "the affair between the Brazilians and these Provinces" approaches a crisis. Brazilian warships have appeared "off our Roads," and their admiral has warned that, unless the local government renounces claim to the Banda Oriental, "he . . . has orders to establish a vigorous blockade and to Commence hostilities." Forbes hopes "that the presence of a Small naval force on our part, will Soon keep in check" abuses on American commerce. ALS. DNA, RG59, Dip. Disp., Argentina, vol. 2 (M69, R3). Received September 1. Published in Espil (comp.), *Once Años en Buenos Aires*, 370-71. On the conflict between Brazil and the United Provinces of Río de la Plata over control of the Banda Oriental, see above, Clay to Poinsett, March 26, 1825, note; Forbes to Secretary of State, May 2, 1825. Rodrigo José Ferreira Lobo, Vice Admiral of the Brazilian Navy, was in charge of the operations off Montevideo.

APPLICATIONS, RECOMMENDATIONS   July 6, 1825

JOEL POINSETT, Mexico (City), transmits a letter urging a consular appointment for "Mr. Delaporte." Notes that those recommending him "are respectable men." DNA, RG59, A. and R. (MR2). The enclosure, undated and addressed to Poinsett by Hodgson Penny and Brother, recommends Lewis Delaporte, of Guadalaxara, a citizen of the United States, as "Vice Consul of the United States for the Port of San Blas." Delaporte did not receive an appointment. The firm recommending him has not been further identified.

Toasts and Remarks at Shelbyville Banquet

[July 7, 1825]

Our distinguished guest, Henry Clay. The arrows of malevolence which have been pointed at him, have been inoperative   as it is with him so may it ever be, let inflexible integrity triumph.

.   .   .   .

When the 3rd toast was drank [*sic*], MR. CLAY rose and addressed the company in his usual eloquent style, and in a peculiarly impressive manner, to the inexpressible gratification of all present. He then proposed as a toast, The memory of Col. *John Allen*[1]. . . .

Lexington *Kentucky Reporter,* July 18, 1825, reprinted from *Shelbyville Compiler.* The gathering was described as "large." D(avid) White, Jr., was among the invited guests. Judge (probably Samuel) Venable presided and M(ark) Hardin served as vice president.   [1] See above, I, 817n.

From John H. Pleasants

My dear Sir,   Liverpool July 7th. 1825.

If you are surprised at the date of my letter, I am scarcely less surprised at the circumstance myself— To be in England at all, is what I never expected—to be here, when I expected to have been in Buenos Ayres, seems rather the affect [*sic*] of enchantment, than of ordinary causation. It remains Sir, for me to account for this apparent dereliction of duty, and I Cannot but hope, that a plain Statement of the circumstances which changed my destination, will exculpate me from any blame in your eyes; Solicitous as I am, to preserve that good opinion, which procured for me the charge conferred by the Department of State—

After many ineffectual attempts to secure an earlier passage, in which I was baffled by the diminished intercourse between the U States, and the Provinces of S. A. which lie beyond the Spanish Main, I succeeded at last in procuring a passage in the Brig Wm. Tell, which sailed from New York on the 28h. May, for the River Plate. This vessel was not Such An one, as I should have selected had I had any ch[oice]— Being simply a merchant ship, it was destitute [of co]mfortable accommodation. Nevertheless becoming impatient for action, and foreseeing that if I neglected that opportunity, I might meet with no other, I availed my self of it, and sailed as stated, on the 28h. May— I speedily had cause to regret my precipitation in choosing such a ship— The cabin not 15 feet square, was destined to accommodate, in a voyage which would occupy from 60 to 90 days, 25 passengers— The quantity of these individuals was in no respect[1]   by their respective

qualities. They were for the most part, mechanics emigrating to that country, and the filth of their persons, and obstreperous[2]
of their deportment, was by no means corresponding to the Republican respectability of their professions— When the horrors of sea sickness, were superadded to the other painful circumstances attending my situation, my sufferings became greater than I can describe— Deprived of every comfort—with not 10 feet square for exercise—a pestilential air and most offensive smell, pervading every part of the Ship, and even without the most common medicines, I assure you Sir, that death would have been no unwelcome visitor. I was seized with a high fever, and in 10 days reduced in my own opinion, and in that of those around me, to the brink of the grave. At this time, we spoke an American Ship from N. Y. bound to Antwerp. The Captain, [who] was likewise ill, was bearing for Fayal in the Az[ores a]nd by great persuasion was induced to take me on board in a miserable Condition. Two day [sic] after this removal, my new Captain recovered his indisposition, and resumed his Course for Antwerp. Having no inclination to visit Holland, I determined to avail myself of the next Ship that we might speak, and return to the U. S. or go to England. From the time that I boarded the vessel in which I then was, I had begun slowly to recover from the superior Comforts of its accommodations. On the 20h. June, we Spoke the Brig Olive, from N. Y. to this Port, and the Captain consenting to receive me, I arrived in Liverpool on the 1st. ins. having been at sea, 33 days— The despatches which were entrusted to my care, I forwarded to Mr Forbes,[3] in charge of Capt. Hinman,[4] of the Wm Tell, to whom he was consigned— stating the reasons of my not bearing them in person, and requesting him to forward those for Mr Raguet[5] at Rio— If the Wm Tell goes safely, the despatches will safely reach their destination.

These sir, are the circumstances which have brought me to England—and I hope that they are such as to excuse my abandonment of my charge. As I am here, I have determined to devote a few weeks to the purpose of seeing the Country, after which I shall have the pleasure of giving you in person, a more detailed account of my voyage. With high Respect, Yr. Obt. Sert,

JNO. H PLEASANTS

P. S. The vessel that carries this is on the eve of Sailing—may I ask the favor of you to forward this letter to my father.

ALS. DNA, RG59, Letters from Bearers of Dispatches. Addressed to Clay.
1 Space for one word follows in MS.
2 Space for one or two words follows in MS.
3 John M. Forbes.   4 Not further identified.
5 Condy Raguet.

From JOHN W. PARKER, Amsterdam. Repeats an earlier "request to be put in possession of the Acts of Congress as they are passed"; encloses copies of his correspondence with the Minister of Foreign Affairs relative to the imprisonment at Dordt "some months since," of the mate from the American ship *Superb,* of Philadelphia. ALS. DNA, RG59, Cons. Disp., Amsterdam, vol. 2 (M-T182, R-T2). Received November 11. Parker, born in Virginia, had been appointed consul at Amsterdam in April, 1820, and remained in that post until 1837. His enclosures reveal that George Lee, second mate of the *Superb,* had been taken from his ship and imprisoned for wounding a member of his crew, a native of the Kingdom of the Netherlands. The Foreign Minister of the Netherlands in 1825 and 1826 was Patrice-Charles-Gislain, le Chevalier de Conincke, a native of Bruges and a legal scholar, who had headed the Interior Department from 1817 to 1825.

From Christopher Hughes

Private. *To Mr. Clay.*   Stockholm; 8th. July: 1825.
My dear Sir,

I wrote you a mortal letter,[1] by last Post: it is not my intention to inflict such another, at present, upon your time and patience! Nothing decisive has taken place, yet, in Mr. Connell's business; but, I think, we shall come to a conclusion, before the 12th., when, (as I have officially notified the Government, & demanded my audience de Congé;) it is my intention to weigh anchor; prospects are encouraging; but Mr. Connell *decides,* and *acts,* for *himself;* neither the Government, or myself, it's humble agent, shall be compromised; or *"compromitted,"* as say our orators of the Capitol.

Lord Bloomfield[2] went off on a Russian tour on the 28th., he wrote a despatch to Mr. Canning,[3] the day before his departure, communicating the *important* approaching event of my leaving this Court; he kindly sent me an Extract; I cannot now lay my hands on it, in the Chaos of papers on my table! Suffice it, that he made out, to *my* entire satisfaction, that your old Secretary is a prodigious clever fellow, & an upright, honest man; he said, the King had told *him* so; & that the King had spoken of me in the highest terms of respect & esteem & had lamented my going away; so, (assures Lord Bloomfield,) do all my Colleagues & all society &a. &a.; & that the Royalty even mixed up a sort of *affection,*[4] in their regrets; indeed, everybody has expressed similar feelings; even persons whom I *don't* know, personally, (perhaps, that explains it!) have sent me their most affectionate adieus & good wishes; ex. gr. Baron Erenheim [*sic*] Minr. of Foreign affairs to Gust: Adolph IV: & who has retired from public life, since the expatriation of the Vasas,[5] & devoted himself to study & the sciences, & very much distinguished himself by his late works; & who is (& this is much more:) looked on as one of the most dignified, virtuous men in Europe; as he is one of the most celebrated here in the North—: Bn. Erenheim, the Scandinavian Cato, sent me a card, as follows— "Le Bn. d'Erenheim a l'honneur de souhaiter le bon voyage á Mr. Hughes, qui laisse, il le scait des regrets bien profonds &— bien sincères, á toutes ses connaissances. [*sic*] Now this gave me great pleasure, for it is only by general report, that this virtuous &— venerable man can know anything of me; I never was but once in his company, & that is 7 years ago. In a word, they, the Swedes, could not more lament the Aurora Borialis [*sic*], if it were to emigrate; *& my name*, in Swedish, means Light! Lumiere!—Ljus! The English Chargé d'affaires, St George, sent me the within despatch,[6] it is a precious production! I think it very important, for *you* & Mr. *Adams* to know, all these proofs of my *uncommon* & *unexpected* worth & success; & as no one will mention them, unless I do, why I cheerfully go through the labour! What is the use of honours & orders, unless one shows them? This was the creed &— practice of Lord Nelson;[7] & they *shot* him, for making himself so conspicuous! I expect the reverse consequences from my candid exposé of my own dazzling merits. The old Russian General Suchtelen & Daughter,[8] have just been to see me, in my Bachelors-Rooms; & in a word, I really am, & I enjoin you to give faith, quite a miraculous sort of a personage! Now, I implore you to be persuaded!!! The old Genl. S. came, in person, to ask me to a dinner d'adieux, for Sunday: but the Minister of Foreign affairs Ct. Wetterstedt, had already named that day, for a similar important purpose![9] I suppose, I shall have mes audiences de Congé, about the 11th. or 12h. & in a day, or two after, I shall leave, join my family, & go on to Denmark.

We have nothing new, excepting that Alvardo [*sic*], the Spanish Chargé d'affaires,[10] has written a Mercuriale to this Government, on the subject of the late sale of 2. ships of the line, & 3 Frigates to Goldsmiths, London, for the ostensible purpose of a commercial enterprize to the Indies; but *undoubtedly* for the Government of Colombia.[11] In my former letter, & of the sale of the first 2 Ships, I mentioned Rothschild[12] & Mexico; I was misinformed; no matter; so as one of our liberated and brave neighbours gets the vessels, it is no matter which; I openly rejoice at it; & the King likes the cash terms. I hope to send you, by next mail, a Copy of Alvarado's Note; 'tis said to be spirited & well written, with here & there some *Castilianisms,* & some absurdities[;] however, he is the most insupportable brute, in the world him self, & an arrant ass! Some one wrote *for him!* Bodisco, the Counsellor of the Russian Legation,[13] has been here just now bombarding me on the subject; it is plain, that the Spaniard is backed by the Russians, or Bodisco would not have spoken so Furiously; I gave him my opinions, as I always do, openly; & said, "I thought that the King of Sweden had as good a right to sell his ships to Bolivar, as the C. of R. had to sell his to Ferdinand:[14] that, besides, the Swedish were in excellent state & the Russians were Rotten &c." He said, "Genl. Bubona[15] was quite right to arrest Genl. DeVreux;[16] & so would *he* have done, & *'peeped into his papers.'* I replied, "of course I dont speak of *you, Bodisco;* but I think Genl. Bubona, has behaved like the tool of a Tyrant; & Peepers in to Papers always deserve the Carcan, the Pillory; at least we Americans think so." He laughed, & so did yr. friend   C. HUGHES

ALS. DNA, RG59, Dip. Disp., Sweden and Norway, vol. 4 (M45, R5). Received September 8.   1 Above, June 21, 1825.
2 Benjamin, first Baron Bloomfield.   3 George Canning.
4 At this point Hughes adds a footnote: "not affec*tation*???"
5 Former ruling family of Sweden, of whom Charles XIII was the last. Frederick Wilhelm von Ehrenheim, Swedish Minister of Foreign Affairs, 1797, and President of the Chancellery, 1801 to 1809, had since then lived in retirement as a natural philosopher and writer. He died in 1828.
6 The dispatch, from Charles M. St. George to Canning, concerns the refusal of the Holy Alliance to permit the return of Joseph Bonaparte, the Count de Survilliers, to Europe to visit his wife, now in ill health. Bonaparte, residing in the United States, has a "matrimonial connection" with the Royal Family of Sweden. (Bonaparte, who called himself the Count de Survilliers after coming to America as a refugee in 1815, and Charles XIV had married, respectively, Julie and Desirée Clary, sisters, of Marseilles.)
St. George adds that he obtained this information from Hughes, "who had several very interesting Conversations with the Qn. of Sweden on the Subject, who may,— from his being a personal Friend and correspondent of Joseph Bonaparte,— &— from his intimate Footing with the Royal Family here be deemed good Authority, on this point,— as far as Sweden is concerned.—
"Nearly Eight Years intimate acquaintance with Mr. Hughes, will, I trust, be my Excuse for touching on his departure [. . .] so soon after Lord Bloomfield's latest Despatch on the Subject:— He is as much regretted as he was liked and esteemed by all,— nor is this feeling confined to his diplomatic Colleagues, it being universal in Society here.—"
At the end of the copy of St. George's letter Hughes wrote (AES):
"Mr. Clay will oblige me by showing this Despatch as well as my letter to the President; with the tender of my most perfect respect.   C Hughes."
7 Horatio, Viscount Nelson, Vice-Admiral of the British Navy, hero of the battles of the Nile and Trafalgar, against the French, during the former of which he had been wounded and during the latter, killed.
8 Count Jan Pieter Suchtelen; his daughter, not identified.
9 Cf. above, Hughes to Clay, June 21, 1825.
10 Felix Ramond Alvarado, not further identified.
11 See above, Hughes to Secretary of State, April 14, 1825. Great confusion of rumor emerged from the sale and projected sale of these vessels by the Government of Sweden during the summer and autumn of 1825. Two of them, the *Tapperheten,* a ship of the line, and *Af Chapman,* a frigate, were purchased by B. A. Goldsmidt and Company, a London banking house, which in 1824 and 1825 had underwritten large Mexican loans. These ships, however, were designed for delivery to Colombia, reportedly at a cost of about $700,000 to that Government, while negotiation continued for three others to be sent to Mexico. The latter arrangement was suspended before the ships left European waters (cf. below, Hughes to Clay, December 1, 1825). The Goldsmidt's firm failed later in the year and their representatives in America were unable to meet a demand by the Swedish Government that the officers and crew of the vessels sent to Colombia should be paid return passage before the delivery. The vessels rapidly

deteriorated and, diverted to New York for repairs, were finally sold there under order of the Federal District Court, in August, 1826, after suit by the Swedish officers and crew for the amount of their wages, supplies, and return passage. *Niles' Weekly Register,* XXXI (September 9, 16, 30, 1826), 32, 37, 68.

12 Probably Nathan Meyer Rothschild, founder in 1805 of the London branch of a banking business established by his father, Meyer Amschel Rothschild, at Frankfurt, which dealt very largely in governmental financial transactions.

13 Alexandre de Bodisco, who from 1838 to 1854 served as Russian Minister to the United States.

14 Ferdinand VII of Spain.   15 Not identified.

16 Probably "Don Juan" Devereux. See above, Brown to Clay, June 27, 1825.

MISCELLANEOUS LETTERS   July 8, 1825

From SAMUEL SOUTHARD, Navy Department. Announces that a court martial has begun the trial of David Porter upon charges, among others, resulting from the Fajardo incident. Suggests that "the representative of the Spanish Government" be informed that the documents transmitted by him "were rejected by the Court, as incompetent evidence, and not properly authenticated." ALS. DNA, RG59, Misc. Letters (M179, R62). Cf. above, Clay to Southard, May 6, 1825.

Toasts and Speech at Louisville Banquet

[July 9, 1825]

Our distinguished guest Henry Clay.—A bright occidental star in the horizon of American worth, may prejudice not dim its lustre, nor faction impede its progress, until it culminates in the zenith.—

Mr. C. rose with the most lively and grateful sensibility to make his respectful acknowledgments for the flattering sentiment just drank [*sic*]. Such a sentiment (however unmerited he felt it to be) expressed on such an occasion, any where, would have afforded him high gratification. But I own that uttered here with so much cordiality, at the present period, by so numerous an assembly, comprehending so much worth intelligence and respectability, it gives me inexpressible satisfaction. It is not necessary that I should affect ignorance of the generous allusion, in one of the topics of the toast. I have no self reproaches on account of my agency on the occasion which has excited the prejudice to which you kindly refer.[1] The question submitted to my judgment was one the decision of which did not depend upon the possession of military attainments, however great and splendid they might be, but on that of qualifications for Civil Administration.[2] Of the two gentlemen, between whom the competition chiefly existed, I never could have doubted, and do not now doubt, as to the choice which it became me to make. If we had been called upon, in a season of War, to designate a General to conduct our armies to victory and glory, and had selected the distinguished Citizen of Tennessee in preference to his late rival, would it not have been most unreasonable, in any of the partizans of the latter, to have assailed us with reproach and abuse? Whilst I claimed and exercised the right to bestow my vote, for my Constituents and for my Country, according to the best lights with which I was favored, I equally recognized a similar right in every other member of the House of R. I have accused no man, I have called in question the motives of no man for differing in opinion with me. But I yield to none in purity of purpose, or in honesty of pursuit after the public good. In a Country and under institutions like ours where the elective franchise is happily so greatly extended, and consequently is so often exerted, there ought to be mutual toleration, liberality and forbearance. The prevalence of a contrary spirit—of a spirit of crimination, denunciation and abuse, in consequence of a difference of opinion as to the fitness and competency of Candidates for public stations, would produce the most mischievous effects. It would perpetually disturb our social harmony at home, and impair our public character abroad. Why should I have been selected, because I prefered [*sic*] one eminent Citizen to another, as an object of condemnation and abuse? On a subsequent occasion the unsuccessful Candidate, in the exercise of his incontestable privilege to form his own judgment and express his own opinion, thought proper to interpose his negative upon the nomination with which the President, as the Chief Executive organ of the Union, honored me.[3] Doubtless his vote was the result of a full conviction that the President was mistaken, in supposing me capable of rendering him the requisite assistance in his Administration, and the illustrious Senator and I do not disagree at all on that subject; for he would not have made a more humble estimate of my abilities than that which I have formed myself. And I never have, do not now, and never will complain of the advice which he gave to the President in that instance.

But I will turn from this egotism, which I pray you gentlemen to pardon, in consideration of the injustice of my assailants. In making up my judgment in the H. of R. I could not forget the exalted Condition of my Country. I could not conceal from myself that she is the great Steward of the Human family, invested with the most interesting trust that ever was confided to the discretion of a Nation. The principal, if not the exclusive, depository of regulated and established liberty, the eyes and the hopes of the friends of free and liberal institutions, from all quarters of the Universe, are anxiously cast upon her. It is not the short lived race who now fill the busy scenes around us—it is not the present generation that is alone concerned as to the manner in which we shall fulfill the high duties of that most important trust. No! Our posterity,

in the countless numbers who are destined to succeed us, the new
States just springing into existence in South & North America
and copying our institutions all Europe, all Christendom are
deeply interested and may be materially affected by the wisdom
or indiscretion which shall mark the fulfillment of that Steward-
ship. The H. of R. was called upon, it appeared to me, to weigh
well the responsibility of its lofty position, to look before and behind
us and to elevate itself to the contemplation of the important
relations in which we stand to every part of the world— And it
was required, by the highest of all human obligations, to abstain
from the exhibition of hazardous and inconsiderate examples to
those who are disposed to honor us by following in our footsteps.
With these views (I repeat that I quarrel with no one for entertaining others) I could not and did not believe that it was my
duty to bestow my suffrage on a gentleman who came recommended to my choice by military qualifications chiefly, if not
exclusively. For that exercise of my best judgment an accusation
has been prefered by citizens of other States against me of violating
my obligations to the district which I lately had the honor to
represent. There I have been longest & best known, and whether
I have or have not disregarded the wishes of those whom I represented they must best know. If there be any who remain under
such a delusion let them go to those enlightened, liberal & just
constituents, by whose confidence & attachment I have been so
highly distinguished. They will there learn that, by an unexampled
unanimity, with a general acclamation, the ratification of my vote
has been pronounced in a voice the most decisive. And that the
imputations of the Conspiracy against me have been rejected with
contempt and indignation.

I am about gentlemen to leave you to resume the duties of that
arduous station to which I have been appointed. This is the last
occasion which I may have for some time, if not forever, of addressing a Kentucky audience. In spite of all the consolation that I
endeavor to draw from the reflection that I shall probably again
and again have the gratification of seeing you, and of finally depositing my earthly remains among you, there is an indescribable feeling
of melancholy excited in my mind by the separation. The utmost
exertion of reason and of hope is not sufficient to assure me that
there is not some resemblance between my present situation &
that lasting and awful separation to which we are all doomed.
Whether my removal be temporary or not, however I may be
separated by time or distance from you, whatever may be my
fortunes, I shall never cease to cherish the most grateful emotions
for the many instances of affectionate confidence, and especially
for the recent Signal proofs of regard & esteem, which I have

experienced in Kentucky. Although I have been greatly afflicted by the unhappy divisions which prevail here on a local subject, and although my opinion on the question which agitates us is well known,[4] I have found no difference between the two great parties in the zeal, cordiality & enthusiasm with which I have been every where received and entertained. I pray you gentlemen to be the last repository of my grateful & hearty thanks for all these demonstrations of kindness and attachment; and to be assured that whatever party or power among us obtains the ascendancy my constant and fervent prayers will be for the happiness, the honor and the character of our Commonwealth. And in conclusion allow me to offer a sentiment connected with a most interesting part of it for whose welfare I shall ever feel great solicitude

The completion of the Canal at Louisville[5] and [the][6] consequent growth & prosperity of this commercial metropolis of K.

The first toast, Lexington *Kentucky Reporter,* August 1, 1825, reprinted from Louisville *Morning Post.* The speech and closing toast, AD draft, in DLC-HC (DNA, M212, R2); published in Washington *Daily National Intelligencer,* August 4, 1825; Lexington *Kentucky Reporter,* August 22, 1825. Cf. above, Breckinridge and others to Clay, May 31, 1825.
1 See above, Clay to Adams, January 9, 1825, note, *et passim.*
2 See above, III, 906; Clay to Featherstonhaugh, January 21, 1825; Clay to Brooke, January 28, 1825.
3 See above, Commission, March 7, 1825, note.
4 Cf. above, Kendall to Clay, March 23, 1825.
5 See above, Speech, January 17, 1825, note 19.
6 MS. torn.

INSTRUCTIONS AND DISPATCHES   July 9, 1825

From CONDY RAGUET, Rio de Janeiro. States that since his last communication, of June 1, "nothing particularly important has transpired"; gives a lengthy discussion of news and rumor from various provinces of the country, including a report that Admiral (Thomas) Cochrane has escaped from Maranham, where new disturbances have broken out; discusses events and politics within the capital; notes the status of the cases of the *Exchange* and *Spermo,* the conjecture concerning terms being brought by Sir Charles Stuart, and the arrival of Felizberto Caldeira Brant (Pontes), "one of the Brazilean Agents at London." LS. DNA, RG59, Cons. Disp., Rio de Janeiro, vol. 2 (M-T172, R3). Extracts published in Manning (arr.), *Diplomatic Correspondence . . . Latin-American Nations,* II, 822-23. General Brant Pontes, as one of two commissioners, had been sent to Europe a year earlier to seek aid from England and Austria in obtaining settlement of the Brazilian controversy with Portugal.

APPLICATIONS, RECOMMENDATIONS   July 9, 1825

FREDERICK FOLLETT, Batavia (New York), applies for continuation of the appointment to publish the laws in the *Spirit of the Times.* "The paper will be a strong supporter of the present administration, as long as it is conducted with the wisdom and energy that has thus far characterized it; and will be a supporter of the *probable* successor of Mr. Adams. Your good offices in this case are earnestly solicited." ALS. DNA, RG59, P. and D. of L. Cf. above, Oran Follett to Clay, June 24, 1825; below, Hayden to Clay, August 27, 1825, note.

INSTRUCTIONS AND DISPATCHES   July 10, 1825

From ANDREW ARMSTRONG, Port au Prince. Reports French recognition of the independence of Haiti, whose President has pressed for a commercial treaty with France. Armstrong fears that the French force, concentrated at Port au Prince, is in reality bound for Cuba. ALS. DNA, RG59, Cons Disp., Cap Haitien, vol. 5 (M9, R-T5). On recognition of Haitian independence, see below, Holden to Clay, July 16, 1825. The President of the Republic of Haiti was Jean Pierre Boyer, who had succeeded to power over a small area in the southern part of the island in 1818 and over practically the whole of it in 1822. He ruled until 1843, when he was forced to resign.

From THOMAS L. L. BRENT, Lisbon, no. 8. Acknowledges receipt of his personal instructions and commission on June 23 and notes that presentation of his credentials to the Portuguese Government served as the occasion for notification to him that (Frederico) Torlade (de Azambuja) had been appointed as Portuguese Chargé d'Affaires at Washington. The implication of this transaction was that Torlade's departure had been held up by the delay in Brent's accreditation, but the latter has been privately informed that the real reason lay in the reception by the United States of a Chargé from the Empire of Brazil while her dispute with Portugal remained unsettled. Reports the terms for such a settlement as carried by Sir Charles Stuart. Mentions the complaint of Portuguese authorities over the "imputed robbery" of a vessel at the Cape Verde Islands and actions of the United States consul, Samuel Hodges. ALS. DNA, RG59, Dip. Disp., Portugal, vol. 6 (M43, R5). Received September 15.

   Torlade did not arrive at Philadelphia until August, 1828, and was not accredited until October, 1829. He terminated his duties in July, 1834. On Stuart's mission, see above, Raguet to Secretary of State, March 11, 1825, note. On the difficulties of the United States consul with the Portuguese officials at the Cape Verde Islands, cf. above, Clay to Brent, May 10, 1825; below, Hodges to Clay, July 28, 1825.

From JAMES BROWN, Paris, "Private." Reports that the departure of the Haitian commissioners without having achieved recognition of their Republic has caused complaints in France, where "A Strong current of public opinion" favors such recognition. Brown has been told in confidence that a French vessel has sailed for St. Domingo carrying "a Royal *ordonnance* declaring the Emancipation . . . of the Republic" on condition that its government pay "Indemnity to the ancient Colonists" and grant certain commercial advantages to France. He does not know whether the consent of Spain, necessary because that country claims a part of the island as a former colony, has been obtained. LS. DNA, RG59, Dip. Disp., France, vol. 22 (M34, R25). Published in Manning (arr.), *Diplomatic Correspondence . . . Latin-American Nations,* II, 1411-12. See above, Armstrong to Clay, this date. Negotiations between the Haitian commissioners and the French had been broken off because the latter, while willing to recognize the independence of the Republic, had demanded an acknowledgment of French "suzeraineté." *Annual Register, 1824,* p. [213].

From CHRISTOPHER HUGHES, Stockholm. Transmits a copy of the treaty between Sweden and Great Britain for the suppression of the slave trade. ALS. DNA,

RG59, Dip. Disp., Sweden and Norway, vol. 4 (M45, R5). For the treaty, signed at Stockholm November 6, 1824, and presented to Parliament May 16, 1825, see *British and Foreign State Papers, 1824-1825* (London, 1826), 3-28.

From CHRISTOPHER HUGHES, Stockholm, "Private." Transmits copies of (Felix Ramond) Alvarado's remonstrance to the Government of Sweden for the sale of vessels to "M. Goldschmidt" of London; notes that the Mexicans rather than the Colombians are getting these vessels; and comments on the King's (Charles XIV's) "love of Gold." New paragraph, dated July 12, states that a copy of Count (Gustav de) Wetterstedt's reply to Alvarado's note is enclosed and that Hughes has just heard that the King of France (Charles X) has sent a vessel to Haiti bearing a royal order declaring the independence of that Republic. ALS. *Ibid.* Received September [. . .] (date obliterated). On the sale of the Swedish vessels, see above, Hughes to Clay, July 8, 1825, note.

From HUGH NELSON, Madrid, no. 59. Encloses a copy of his last note to the Spanish Secretary of State (Francisco de Zea Bermudez), regarding an application for admission of United States consuls into Cuba and Puerto Rico, "the aversion of the American Govt. to see the island of Cuba pass into the hands of any other European power, and our Disclaimer of all views on our part in ·ference to the same subject." Not having yet received permission concerning the consuls, Nelson has concluded to leave the matter to his successor.

In regard to the bill of (Hilario de Rivas y) Salmon for $6,000, though the Spanish Government is cooperative and a portion of the sum has been obtained, Nelson fears that "fraud and chicanery" will prevent recovery of the whole. Power to collect is left in the hands of (Obadiah) Rich, who has acted as Secretary of Legation since (John J.) Appleton's departure and whom Nelson recommends "to the Department."

Ill health has forced (José de) Heredia's resignation as Minister to the United States. Another appointment will soon be made, at a lower rank ("Minister resident instead of Plenipotentiary") owing to the necessity of reducing salaries. The Spanish Secretary of State wishes to transfer negotiations on subjects under discussion from Washington to Madrid.

Nelson has presented his letter of recredence, has taken leave of the King, and intends departing on July 12. The archives of the Legation are being left with Rich until the arrival of (Alexander H.) Everett. LS. DNA, RG59, Dip. Disp., Spain, vol. 24 (M31, R26).

On Nelson's efforts to procure accreditation of United States consuls in Cuba and Puerto Rico and his assurances to the Spanish Government concerning American views about Cuba, see above, Nelson to Clay, June 15, 1825; on the matter of Salmon's bill for $6000, see above, Clay to Nelson, April 14, 1825, note. Rich, born in Massachusetts, had been appointed consul at Valencia in 1816. He was named United States consul at Port Mahon, for Minorca and the Balearic Islands, in 1834 and remained at that post until 1845.

From J[OHN] ADAMS SMITH, London, no. 7. Reports that, in response to a question raised in the House of Commons on July 1, (George) Canning explained to that body on July 5 that the envoy from Buenos Aires had not been presented at the last levee because "he had no regular credentials." Notes an expectation that Lord (Thomas) Cochrane, recently arrived in London, will "withdraw from the naval service of the Brazils" and speculation that his rank in the British Navy may be restored. ALS. DNA, RG59, Dip. Disp., Great Britain, vol. 32 (M30, R28). Addressed to Secretary of State; received August

22. Extract published in Manning (arr.), *Diplomatic Correspondence . . . Latin-American Nations,* III, 1552.

INSTRUCTIONS AND DISPATCHES   July 11, 1825

From THOMAS L. L. BRENT, Lisbon, no. 9. Transmits correspondence relating to complaints on seizure of the cargo of the American brig *Osprey* at Bahia in March, 1824, as supply for a Portuguese squadron; on the imprisonment of the master and crew of the brig *Ironsides* at the Cape Verde Islands, which the American consul, Samuel Hodges, has protested as "an insult offered to himself as well as to the flag of the United States"; on the arrest, also at the same place, of William G. Merrill, appointed consular agent during Hodges' absence, "together with his own male servants"; and on the treatment accorded Captain Charles Preble of the American ship *Champion* at Porto Praya, "when in ignorance of, and contrary to the regulations, he attempted to enter that port after sun set." Brent has referred all these matters to Clay for instructions. ALS. DNA, RG59, Dip. Disp., Portugal, vol. 6 ((M43, R5). Received September 15. Enclosed documents show that Portuguese officials claimed the cargo, salted meat, of the *Osprey* from Salem, was seized after the captain and consignee of the vessel had sought to evade a contract for sale of the provisions; payment, it is conceded, will be provided, but only under the general measures yet to be adopted for settlement of the debts incurred by the expedition to Bahia. Affidavits also enclosed by Brent assert that the *Champion,* of Boston, putting into Porto Praya, on November 3, 1824, for emergency supplies of canvas, bread, and water, had been delayed by light winds until after sunset, when the vessel had been fired upon. Documents on the complaints involving the *Ironsides* and William G. Merrill are not here included; regarding those incidents, see below, Hodges to Clay, July 28, 1825, no. 1. Merrill succeeded Hodges as consul for the United States in the Cape Verde Islands and served from 1828 to 1837.

MISCELLANEOUS LETTERS   July 11, 1825

From RICHARD RUSH, "Packet ship York, The Narrows." Reports Rush's arrival after a voyage "of forty one days from London." He will visit New York and Philadelphia on his way to Washington. ALS. DNA, RG59, Dip. Disp., Great Britain, vol. 32 (M30, R28).

From Susan Watkins and Others

To the Hon. Henry Clay.   July the 12th 1825—
Sir.

We have the honor to inclose you a copy of the proceedings of a meeting of the ladies of Lawrenceburgh[1] expressing their high regard for your private character, and the exalted opinion so unanimously entertained for your public and political one: And permit us Sir: with pride to acknowledge our profound respect & gratitude for your distinguished Services in advocating the interest of the west, The independence of South America & of clasic [*sic*]

Greece, The principle of Internal improvement, Domestic Manufacture and Agriculture, And for your eloquent and Successful exertions in every thing that could add to the happiness and Glory of our country. And permit us Sir: through you to tender our high esteem & regard, for Mrs Clay as the wife of the most distinguished polition [sic] and orator of our country, and as an example of every femenine [sic] virtue.

We sincerely regret that it was not convenient for you to accept the invitation[2] given you by the gentlemen of this place, that we might have had the pleasure of paying our respects personaly [sic] to your lady.

With ardent feelings of gratitude we will ever remember you and hope you and your family may enjoy health at your new residence, and that the present administration may tend to the Glory and happiness of the Union, and of those by whom it is conducted.

Susan Watkins	Mary S Randolph
Almeria Buell—	Lucy B Dennis
Mary Lane	Sarah Wardell[3]

LS. DLC-HC (DNA, M212, R1). Addressed to Clay at Cincinnati, "Politeness of Mr. Lane." Amos Lane, Lawrenceburg, Indiana, lawyer, who had lived in Boone County, Kentucky, from 1808 to 1814, had been a member of the Indiana House of Representatives (1816-1817). He became an ardent supporter of Andrew Jackson and, from 1833 to 1837, served as a Representative in Congress.

[1] Indiana. The enclosure has not been found.

[2] Not found.

[3] Mrs. Mary Foote Hawes, of Connecticut, had married Amos Lane in 1804 and had operated a school during their residence in Boone County, Kentucky. Mary Skipwith Randolph was the widow of Thomas Jefferson's cousin, Thomas Randolph, for six years (1800-1806) a member of the Virginia Legislature from Amelia County, attorney general of Indiana Territory in 1811, killed at the Battle of Tippecanoe in 1812. Lucy B. Dennis later (in 1828) married Milton Gregg (see below, Holman to Clay, October 24, 1825, note). Sarah Wardell was probably the wife of Thomas Wardell, a Lawrenceburg lawyer; she may have been the Mrs. Wardell who in 1851 taught school in that town. Almeria Buell not identified.

INSTRUCTIONS AND DISPATCHES   July 12, 1825

From George Moore, Trieste. Gives details in "A Case of extraordinary Insubordination" involving members of "the Crew of the Ship Canton, Robt. Lewis Master, of New York, which was followed up with a degree of obstinacy without precedent in this Port," and encloses documents pertaining to the matter; comments that, judging from unofficial reports, "affairs have taken a much more favorable Turn" for the Greeks. ALS. DNA, RG59, Cons. Disp., Trieste, vol. 1, (M-T242, R-T1). Received September 4.

MISCELLANEOUS LETTERS   July 12, 1825

From John Taliaferro, "Hagley" (his residence, near Fredericksburg, Virginia). Transmits letters concerning the claim of William Duncan, "a very respectable man—a native of Virginia—and not long since extensively engaged in the West India trade from Baltimore." ALS. DNA, RG59, Misc. Letters (M179, R62).

Received July 17. The enclosures are Duncan's letter to Clay, above, April 27, 1825, and a letter (which transmitted the Duncan communication for forwarding to Clay) from D (avid) Henderson, Jr., New York, to Taliaferro, June 28, 1825. In the latter document Henderson explains that the claim originated in the seizure of Duncan's vessel by "Admiral [Edward Tyrrel] Smith of the British Navy" for use in transporting British troops in the West Indies; that "Admiral Smith admits the justice" of the claim; and that Duncan expects a favorable settlement, if it can be presented to (George) Canning "in a formal shape." Duncan desires Henderson to solicit Taliferro's "friendly aid" in getting Clay to act, "as the case may require, to obtain an early decision." Duncan and Henderson, probably both born in Augusta County, Virginia, have not been further identified.

On July 29, 1825, Daniel Brent, in Clay's absence, acknowledged receipt of Duncan's letter and assured him that Rufus King had been informed of the claim. Copy. DNA, RG59, Dom. Letters, vol. 21, p. 123 (M40, R19). Brent's letter to King, also dated July 29, transmitted Duncan's correspondence and reported that he had been assured that he could count upon King's "good offices." Copy. DNA, RG59, Dip. Instr., vol. 10, p. 375 (M77, R5).

Toasts and Speech at Cincinnati Banquet

[July 13, 1825]

Our distinguished guest Henry Clay—An illustrious Statesman and incorruptible Patriot: frank, fearless, and devoted to his country.

After the applause with which it was received had subsided, Mr Clay addressed the company.

In rising (he said) to present, as I beg permission to do, my respectful thanks for the sentiment just expressed, I feel in a situation at once gratifying and embarrassing. The number and respectability, the worth and intelligence of the gentlemen here assembled, the place, the occasion, and the presence of the distinguished gentlemen who honor us with their attendance, would serve to explain, as they had produced, the mingled sensations which I now feel. Whilst I am sensible of not meriting the high compliment which has been offered, I can but be extremely gratified with the friendly sentiments which are here entertained towards me, and which have been impressively evinced by the enthusiastic reception of the toast. If indeed I have any claim on account of my public services, to your favorable considerations of me, it rests mainly upon some of those great national measures, in which I had the happiness to concur with my fellow citizens of Ohio. With respect to one of those measures, the cause of internal improvement, in which all parts of the union are so deeply concerned, and in which the west has ever taken so lively an interest, I am glad to be able to offer you my hearty congratulations, on its success in the national councils. The power of the general government, long, ardently and perseveringly contested, has been finally maintained by repeated majorities in Congress, and has at last obtained the support of the President. The argument honestly and sincerely pressed on both sides, has been completely exhausted, and henceforward, we have nothing to do but stand by our arms!—those arms, the spade and pickaxe, which were so gloriously exercised by two of your guests, (Govs. Clinton and Morrow) on a recent auspicious occasion.[1] Hereafter we may confidently hope that the beneficent power, thus successfully upheld, and the application of which has already commenced in the east and in the west, by the extension of the Cumberland road into the state of Ohio,[2] will advance with no other restraints than the character, the object and the convenience of the public treasury, until every geographical tendency to disunion shall be subdued, and made to bend to the power, the durability, and the prosperity of our confederacy. {*Loud and long continued applause*} The satisfaction which we must now feel in the vindication of this truly national interest, is much increased by the presence among us of one of its most enlightened and efficient supporters. {Pointing to Governor Clinton.}

The success which attends another national concern, not less important than that to which he had just adverted, and intimately allied with it, was in a high degree cheering and animating. The progress of the arts, under the wise policy of the general government, is such as already to leave no doubt of their attainment at no distant day in America, of all the perfection at which they had arrived in any other country. If all the opponents of the American system could have witnessed that gratifying collection of specimens of American skill and ingenuity, hastily made and exhibited during the late session of Congress,[3] their number would be greatly diminished. I hope that we shall not be diverted from the steady pursuit of that policy by the recent alleged departure from the restrictive system, by a nation which exerts a most powerful influence over the moral and physical interests of the world.[4] The object of the prohibition, to which Great Britain has longer and more rigorously adhered than any other nation, was by an exclusion of all foreign fabrics from British consumption, to secure the uncontested home market to British industry; and her ultimate aim was the perfection of the arts by the operation of that great stimulus. Her policy has accomplished its purposes, and British skill and industry have conducted them to a state of improvement which is equalled by that of no other nation. Now, when she can any and every where enter into successful competition in foreign countries, with foreigners, she proposes, under certain modifications of her tariff, to allow them a competition with her at home, which she knows they cannot sustain. She has cautiously retained restriction, where the superiority was on the side of the foreigner, and removed them [sic] only where it was incontestibly with her. British ability to put down all competition is frankly avowed, and proclaimed in parliament.[5]—Her policy in both instances—in the adoption and in the partial removal of restrictions, has been precisely the same; that is, to secure and enlarge the sphere of the consumption of British produce. If she can by her example prevail upon foreign nations to abolish their restrictions and thus open new markets to her, she knows perfectly well, that she will throw a much greater amount of her produce into their consumption, than they can of theirs into her consumption. Great Britain ought not to be condemned for thus endeavoring to advance her own interests. But those nations would justly excite surprise, who, seduced by her nominal liberality, should abandon the care and protection of their own industry.

In passing from those objects on which I had the satisfaction to coincide with most of you, I approach one respecting which it was not my fortune to concur with a majority of the citizens of Cincinnati.[6] But I should have no pretension to some of the characteristics which you have done me the honor to assign me, if I did not here, and on all other proper occasions, freely avow and vindicate my opinion. The alternative prescribed to my choice, during the last session of the house of representatives, was that of a soldier, covered it is true with never fading laurels, won on the glorious field of Orleans, but still a soldier: and a distinguished citizen, eminently endowed, experienced in the public affairs of the country at home and abroad, a practised statesman.[7] The qualifications required were those adapted to civil administration. Whilst I respected the motives, and shared in the grateful emotions of those with whom I differed, my deliberate judgment pointed too clearly to my duty, to allow me to act on the convictions of others, I claimed only for myself the independence and the integrity which I never disputed in them. I had a right to the uncontroled exercise of my suffrage, the enjoyment of which I never censured in them.

Yes, gentlemen, I felt on the memorable occasion to which I am alluding, strongly impressed with a sentiment which you have just drank [sic]; I did believe that the eyes of all nations are upon us, closely observing our examples. The great trustee of human liberty, one portion of mankind is ever ready to chuckle at the indiscretions of our country: whilst another is encouraged and rejoiced at instances of her prudence and wisdom.—With the friends of liberty and liberal principles throughout the world anxiously gazing at us;

with the new republics of the south turning to us with filial affection, and gathering seeds from our institutions to plant in their own free and fertile land; with all our responsibility to present and after generations, I did not think it became me to assist in setting an example which, if unattended with present, I believed productive of future danger. I was aware that, like every other public functionary, I was under the moral cognizance of the whole American people, but I recognize an official responsibility only to my immediate constituents. Those to whom I was almost a stranger, have allowed themselves, in the transports of their zeal, and in the charities of their nature, to arraign me at the bar of the Republic. If there be any who yet doubt as to this alien accusation, I would refer them to the high-minded people of that state which I have just left, and of which I am proud to be an humble citizen. I would entreat them to go among those affectionate, generous and enlightened constituents, who have known me from my earliest youth. They will there witness the general concurrence that prevails in the sanction and ratification of my vote, and hear the unanimous verdict, pronounced in a tone as enthusiastic as authoritative. {*General burst of applause.*}

I am sensible, gentlemen, that I have been too prominent a figure, and have engrossed too much of your time, in the address which your politeness alone has tolerated. Allow me to call your attention to a subject more congenial with my feelings, and which must be more acceptible [*sic*] to yours: I beg leave to offer as a toast,

The States of New York and Ohio—One has executed, and the other projected,[8] a public work worthy of a nation's enterprize and energies.

Lexington *Kentucky Reporter,* July 25, August 15, 1825, reprinted from the *Cincinnati Gazette.* The "largest dinner party ever before given in Cincinnati" had begun at about four o'clock with "Governor [DeWitt] Clinton, Gov. Morrow," Clay and other guests present. "Ethan Stone, Esq. officiated as President—Col. Borden and Wm. Corry, esq. as Vice-Presidents." The meal was "creditable to Col. Mack and the occasion." See above, Clay to Langhorne and others, May 23, 1825, note; below, Clay to Crittenden, July 25, 1825.

Samuel Borden, a grocer, and Corry (or Cory), an attorney, had been active supporters of Clay in Cincinnati during the campaign of 1824. Corry had been a member of the Ohio Legislative Assembly in 1819-1820. Andrew Mack, at first a Clinton and finally a Jackson proponent in the 1824 campaign, a representative in the State legislature from 1817 to 1819, and State senator from 1827 to 1829, was manager of the Cincinnati Hotel. Born in Connecticut, Mack had been a sea captain and had engaged in merino sheep and mercantile ventures; he was probably the debtor to the Bank of the United States prosecuted by Clay in 1823 and 1824 (above, III, 539-40n, 805).

[1] On July 4 Clinton and Morrow had begun the excavations for the Ohio and Erie Canal in a ceremony at Licking Summit near Newark, Ohio. Later in the month, on July 21, Clinton participated in a similar ceremony at the beginning of the Miami and Erie Canal at Middletown.

[2] See above, Speech, January 17, 1825, notes.

[3] An exhibition of American manufactured goods, featuring such productions as broadcloths, furniture, and machines, had been held in the rotunda of the Capitol during the week beginning February 22.

4 See above, Clay to Carey, June 6, 1825, note.

5 For example, see speech of William Huskisson on March 25, 1825, in his *Speeches. . . ,* II, 330.

6 Jackson had amassed his largest Ohio pluralities in Butler and Hamilton counties.

7 See above, Clay to Adams, January 9, 1825, note.

8 The Erie Canal, completed by New York (above, II, 311n), and the Ohio to Lake Erie canals undertaken by Ohio (above, Stuart to Clay, March 15, 1825, note). Ceremonies marking "the wedding of the waters" at the completion of the Erie Canal were celebrated in October of this year.

INSTRUCTIONS AND DISPATCHES   July 13, 1825

From HUGH NELSON, Madrid, no. 60. Reports that he has delayed his departure for two days in order to obtain an answer to his request for accreditation of American consuls in the Spanish islands; now encloses copies of two letters just received. LS. DNA, RG59, Dip. Disp., Spain, vol. 24 (M31, R26). Both enclosures are dated July 12 and addressed to Nelson from (Francisco de) Zea Bermudez. The first states that the King (Ferdinand VII) "has at no time thought of ceding to any Power the Islands of Cuba and Porto Rico" and that, when the United States puts an end to the use of its ports and coast by rebellious subjects of the King of Spain to harass Spanish commerce and attack these islands, or promote revolution in them, "His Majesty will hasten to take into consideration" the proposal concerning consuls. The second communication announces the acceptance of Heredia's resignation and the appointment of Francisco Tacon, now in London, as Minister Resident in the United States. Cf. above, Rush to Clay, April 12, 1825; Nelson to Clay, June 15, 1825.

From WILLIAM TAYLOR, "Consulate U. S. America Alvarado" (Mexico). Transmits copy of his letter of January 12, to Lucas Alamán, which, he has learned from (Joel R.) Poinsett, "seems to have given rise to the communication made to you by Mr Obregon in April. . . ." ALS. DNA, RG59, Cons. Disp., Veracruz, vol. 1 (M183, R1). Received August 19. See above, Clay to Poinsett, April 16, 1825. No letter from Pablo Obregón to Clay in April was registered in the State Department.

From ———— Quesnel, Sr.

Hon'ble Henry Clay   Havre 14 July 1825
    Washington

Sir

I hand you herein Bill of Lading[1] for One small Case sundries shipped on board the D. Quixote Captain Clark[2] for New York and to your address by order of our mutual friends Messrs. R B Rhodes & Co.[3] of Paris.

On the other side you will find note[4] of my shipping charges thereon amounting to frs. 8 » » to the debit of said friends in Account. Very respectfully Sir your most obedt. St.

                                   [. . .] QUESNEL L'AINÉ
                                    [. . . .][5]

ALS. DLC-TJC (DNA, M212, R13). Endorsed on cover, AE by Clay: "Mr. Edw. Quesnel of Havre {forwarded the bill of lading 22d. Aug. to the Collector of N. York—" See below, Brown to Clay, July 15, 1825. Quesnel, initials illegible, was probably associated with an old Petersburg, Virginia, importing firm, Quesnel and Company.   1 Not found.
2 Not further identified.
3 The firm not further identified. Ralph Brown Rhodes, a citizen of the United States, died in Paris, in 1835, at the age of 36.
4 Omitted by editors.   5 Name, or expression, not clear.

From Samuel Smith

Sir/   Baltimore 14' July 1825

On recurring to Mr. Rush's letter of 12 Augt last.[1] I find that the Export duty is confined to the Islands of Antigua, St Kitts, Montserrat, Barbadoes, Nevis and the Virgin Islands, that it is paid on exports to G. B. but he did not know whether it was paid when the exports were to a N. American Colony from those Islands,— The Collector of Eastport Can easily ascertain that fact—

The proposition of Mr. Rush in the 1st protocol marked A was met by a refusal as must have been expected—

There appears a great Spirit of liberality in permitting our Vessels to sell part their [sic] Cargoes at one Island and to proceed to others (without any new Charge) for the sale of the residue— That fact is not generally known to the merchants. It would be well to Cause it to be published—

The British paper marked L. is rational. That marked W. not easily answered, or controverted. That of L. might be assented to especially if a proviso Could be obtained to wit. If the export duty is not paid on B. Vessels bound to a N. A. Colony. "That Bonds should be given to land the Cargo in such Colony— Or that no British Vessel with Colonial produce shall be admitted into the U. S. unless Cleared from the Island for some port therein. Specified in her Clearance.

I still must believe that the export duty is paid by all— — Such a proviso might be tried or an Act of Congress might provide the remedy.

Being on the move to the Country I put my letter to you in the P. Office yesterday. I shall for sometime be within two miles of the City where I receive my letters daily. I come seldom to town during the summer.

I understand that the Foxardo business[2] is generally approved by the people. They think that it was Spirited and had a proper influence on the Governor of Porto Rico. and induced him to execute the Pirates[3]   yours truly   S. SMITH

ALS. DNA, RG59, Misc. Letters (M179, R62). Addressed to Clay, "Secy. of State Washington"; received August 4. Cf. above, Smith to Clay, June 25, 1825.

1 A lengthy extract, including the supplementary papers cited below, is published in *American State Papers, Foreign Relations*, VI, 235-44.

2 See above, Nelson to Clay, April 6, 1825, note.

3 In March, 1825, the crew of the schooner *Grampus*, of the United States Navy, had captured seventeen pirates off the east coast of Puerto Rico, where they had been turned over to local officials and hanged. *Niles' Weekly Register*, XXVIII (April 16, 23, 30, June 4, 1825), 112, 118, 129, 212.

INSTRUCTIONS AND DISPATCHES   July 14, 1825

From JOHN T. MANSFIELD, Pernambuco (Brazil). Reports his arrival at that port on June 28 and his reception by the provincial authorities. James H. Bennett has stated "that he had no Papers or Documents appertaining to the Consulate, and that he could not consent to deliver up the Seal as it was his own private property." Bennett has since loaned the seal to Mansfield. ALS. DNA, RG59, Cons. Disp., Pernambuco, vol. 1 (M-T344, R1). Received September 2.

From JOEL R. POINSETT, Mexico (City). Forwards complaints, "by a respectable merchant of Charleston S. C.," against the United States consul at Cartagena, for detention of a vessel. ALS. DNA, RG59, Dip. Disp., Mexico, vol. 1 (M97, R2). The complaint, by "[John B.] Lemaitre Junr," a commission merchant, is directed against Charles MacNeal.

MISCELLANEOUS LETTERS   July 14, 1825

From DAVID BLACKWELL, Belleville (Illinois). Announces transfer, in "January last," of the (Vandalia) *Illinois Intelligencer* to Robert Blackwell and Company. ALS. DNA, RG59, P. and D. of L.

From 1816 to 1820 Robert Blackwell, with various partners, had published the journal, first as the Kaskaskia *Western Intelligencer,* in 1818 renamed as the Kaskaskia *Illinois Intelligencer,* and in 1820, under the latter name, removed to Vandalia. In December, 1820, he had disposed of his interest to William H. Brown; but when controversy over the slavery issue had developed in the State in 1823, Brown's interest had been regained by Blackwell, who espoused the pro-slavery cause. Under financial difficulties in the spring of 1824, the journal had then been transferred to Robert Blackwell's brother, David, of Belleville, a lawyer, a Methodist minister, and Secretary of State under Governor Edward Coles, who provided the money for it to be issued as an anti-slavery organ. Following the resolution of the slavery controversy in the Illinois election campaign of 1824, the journal had been transferred to Robert Blackwell and Company (the partners not identified) and on June 24, 1825, to Robert Blackwell, alone. David Blackwell had been elected to the State legislature in 1824; Robert later served in the assembly from 1832 to 1836 and in the senate from 1840 to 1842.

From James Brown

Dear Sir,   Paris July 15. 1825

In my former letters you have been informed of the bad state of my health. I was attacked by a severe renewal of rheumatism of a more painful and inflamatory [*sic*] character than any I had hitherto felt, and for several weeks I was unable to leave my chamber. I am now nearly free from pain, but have been left so weak and reduced that my physician has enjoined it upon me to resort to the hot sulphur mineral waters in Savoy at a short distance from Lyons. I had nearly finished my preparation for the journey when I received your dispatch on the subject of the war between Spain and her Colonies.[1] Believing it to be important that the views of the President should be communicated to the Government of France with the least possible delay I postponed my journey and endeavored to comply with your instructions by submitting the subject to the consideration of the Minister of foreign Affairs.[2] You will receive by the ship which sails on the 25 a dispatch[3] which whilst it will prove that the Government here has been put in possession of the leading arguments in favor of the policy recommended by the President, will throw but little light on the course which France may be disposed to pursue. The public opinion in France is in favor of that policy, and certain circumstances of a financial nature, are calculated to recommend it to the Ministry. The popularity of Mr de Villele in a great measure depends on the State of the rentes, and the success of a law passed at the last Session for the conversion of the five per cents into four per cents.[4] The report of the acknowledgement by this Government, of the independence of St Domingo[5] has produced a favorable change in the price of stocks, and there can be no doubt but that they would advance considerably upon an acknowledgement by France of the Independence of the New Republics. I am inclined however to think that the difficulty in taking this step is opposed by the Governments to the north and east,[6] and that if they Could be induced to yield, Spain would be compelled to abandon the further prosecution of the war— I have not the least doubt of the disposition of England to urge the policy recommended by the President, but England is not viewed in the most favorable light by the Continental sovereigns, and perhaps the idea that we are too friendly with that power may in some degree lessen our influence— Perhaps instead of saying that this circumstance lessens our influence, I might be more correct in the remark that it increases our weight, but impairs the friendly feelings which some of the powers entertained for us.

Mr Sheldon[7] has been for some time in such bad health as to have thought proper, by the advice of his physician to pass a fortnight in the Country. He has returned to Paris and will remain during the four or five weeks of my absence. I am sorry that I am compelled to take this journey but as my absence will be so short, I am sure the public interest will not suffer by it— You will oblige me by mentioning the subject to the President and solliciting [*sic*] him to excuse the liberty I have taken of being absent without leave— I have suffered so much, and suffered so patiently, that I think myself entitled to a short absence when by it I may avoid decrepitude, and render myself more useful on my return— a son of Mr. Barnet our Consul[8] has been employed to assist Mr Sheldon until his health is restored—

Mrs. Brown sent to Mrs. Clay a small box which was given to the Agent of the Packet Ship Don Quixote [*sic*] which sails this day from Havre to New York.[9] You may find it by addressing a letter to the Agent of the line of Packets at New York or perhaps he will inform you of its arrival. Mrs. Brown enjoys excellent health and joins me in affectionate remembrances to Mrs. Clay

I am Dear Sir very sincerely Your faithful Servt   JAMES BROWN
[Postscript]

The inclosed letter is from Mrs. Brown's housekeeper (a very good and trusty woman) to her husband[10] on board Capt Hulls vessel[11] If Mr Southard[12] will let it go when he sends out his dispatches I would be much obliged to him

Honle Henry Clay

ALS. DLC-HC (DNA, M212, R1).   1 Above, May 13, 1825.
2 Ange-Hyacinthe-Maxence, Baron de Damas.
3 See below, Instructions and Dispatches, Brown to Clay, this date.
4 Cf. above, Brown to Clay, April 1, 1825, note.
5 See above, Armstrong to Clay, Brown to Clay, both July 10, 1825.
6 France; Russia; Austria.   7 Daniel Sheldon.
8 Isaac Cox Barnet, born in New Jersey, had been consul for the United States at Brest (1797-1801) and commercial agent at Bordeaux (1801-1803), Antwerp (1803), and Havre de Grace (1803-1816) before his appointment as consul at Paris, where he served from 1816 until his death in 1833. The son mentioned by Brown was probably William A. G. Barnet. See below, Barnet to Clay, March 13, 1826.
9 See above, Quesnel to Clay, July 14, 1825.
10 Not identified.
11 The *United States*, Commodore Isaac Hull.
12 Samuel L. Southard.

INSTRUCTIONS AND DISPATCHES   July 15, 1825

From JOHN J. APPLETON, Havre (France), no. 1. Reports his arrival and intention to proceed to Naples by way of Paris and Geneva. "Before leaving the United States, . . . [he] had, in compliance with the wishes of the Department, an interview with Mr. [Robert] Oliver of Baltimore," who put under Appleton's "care, for his agent in Naples a sealed package, containing . . . Papers in support of his claims. He appeared much pleased with the early attention shewn to these claims by the new administration." ALS. DNA, RG59, Dip. Disp., Sweden and Norway, vol. 5 (M45, R6). Received August 20. Cf. above, Clay to Appleton, April 12, May 12, 1825.

From JAMES BROWN, Paris, no. 31. Acknowledges receipt of instructions no. 1 (above, May 13, 1825) and gives details of an interview, held in accordance with them, with the Baron de Damas, Minister of Foreign Affairs, on the subject of the war between Spain and her colonies. To Brown's presentation of the position of the United States in this connection, Damas replied that he believed the "statement of facts to be substantially correct." He observed, in regard to Spain, that acknowledgment of the independence of her colonies "would be humiliating to her pride and derogatory to her character," that Governments friendly to Spain should respect her feelings, that "the harmony prevailing on the continent must be preserved, by the good understanding prevailing among the sovereigns on questions of general interest," and "that Spain would, he hoped, be able to find the means" to protect Cuba. LS. DNA, RG59, Dip. Disp., France, vol. 22 (M34, R25). Received September 4. Published in Manning (arr.), *Diplomatic Correspondence . . . Latin-American Nations,* II, 1412-16.

From JOHN M. FORBES, Buenos Aires, no. 23. Reports that negotiations between "this Government" and Brazil are being transferred to Rio de Janeiro and that Admiral (Rodrigo José Ferreira) Lobo, in command of the Brazilian naval force in the "Outer Roads" (off Buenos Aires), disclaims hostile intentions and professes to wish only "to prevent Supplies going to the insurgents in Banda Oriental and the Sailing of *pirates,*—one of which was a fine Baltimore brig, . . . now fitting out under Command of one Robert Beasley, a renegade citizen of the United States," who is "more known than respected in the District of Columbia." Comments also on a quarrel between members of the Congress of the United Provinces of Río de la Plata which led to an attack on the Government. "It is said that Mr. [Manuel José] Garcia will give up the Foreign Department" and be replaced by Manuel Sarratea, in which case "the British influence will, *if possible,* be augmented." Adds news and rumors concerning "the war against Brazil." ALS. DNA, RG59, Dip. Disp., Argentina, vol. 2 (M69, R3). Parts of the letter were written on July 16 and 18. Received September 21. Published in Espil (comp.), *Once Años en Buenos Aires,* 371-73.

From JOHN M. FORBES, Buenos Aires, *"Private."* Transmits copy of a letter addressed by Forbes to (George W.) Slacum, consul of the United States at Buenos Aires, distinguishing between the functions of a legation and a consulate; discusses the jurisdictional dispute that evoked that communication. ALS. DNA, RG59, Dip. Disp., Argentina, vol. 2 (M69, R3). Received September 21. Published in Espil (comp.), *Once Años en Buenos Aires,* 374-75. Slacum, of Alexandria, Virginia, for a decade or more a justice of the peace of Fairfax County during the early 1800's, had been appointed consul at Buenos Aires in 1824 and remained in that position until 1834. He later performed the same duties at Rio de Janeiro from 1837 to 1843.

From CHRISTOPHER HUGHES, Stockholm, "Private." Forwards additional copies of Alvarado's note and Wetterstedt's reply, sent on July 12 (see above, Hughes to Clay, July 10), for fear of accident to the earlier dispatch "over the continent" owing to "much *prying* into Letters at Hamburg"; dilates on the friendship shown Hughes by the royal family, especially by the King (Charles XIV), whose manifestations of "personal respect and consideration" have been exhibited before the "Corps diplomatique" to show "the esteem & kindness with which he honours the Americanska *Ministern"*; and, in a paragraph dated July 16, reports that "Connell's business" was settled yesterday by a decision of the Council to make a cash payment of $60,000, "about one half of the Sum the Swedish Government acknowledge to have received for the goods sold at Stralsund in 1810-1811!" Hughes considers it "a miracle that he got so much."

ALS. DNA, RG59, Dip. Disp., Sweden and Norway, vol. 4 (M45, R5). Received September 8. On John Connell's agency, see above, Clay to Hughes, March 24, 1825, note.

From J[OHN] ADAMS SMITH, London, no. 8. Transmits correspondence with (Rufus) King, who is expected soon to have recovered sufficiently from his voyage to proceed to London; notes that "Mr. [George] Canning is confined to his residence . . . by a renewed attack of gout. . . ." ALS. DNA, RG59, Dip. Disp., Great Britain, vol. 32 (M30, R28).

From FREDERICK JACOB WICKELHAUSEN, "Consulate of the United States of America at Bremen." Congratulates Clay upon his appointment to the Secretary-ship of State; states that the election of Adams to the Presidency "has given general satisfaction in this City, and . . . in all Germany," and that the "Senate of Bremen" requested Wickelhausen "to convey its sentiments of high respect and esteem to this great and enlightened Statesman." Remarks briefly on the tranquility characterizing "the present political State of the german Empire." ALS. DNA, RG59, Cons. Disp., Bremen, vol. 1 (M-T184, R-T1). Received October 26. Wickelhausen, a resident of Bremen, was consul for the United States at that port from 1796 to 1833.

MISCELLANEOUS LETTERS   July 15, 1825

From JOSEPH M. WHITE, Black Rock (New York). States that lands west of the Apalachicola River, in West Florida, "should not be ordered into market by the President, before the latter part of next winter, or spring" and that certain persons "desire sale before the crops of the planters can be sold" and before application can be made to Congress for a preemption law similar to that in force in other Territories. ALS. DNA, RG59, Misc. Letters (M179, R62). A number of special acts after 1801 had permitted acquisition of public land by preemption. Probably the legislation of most general importance and relevance to White's concern had been encompassed in acts of March 3, 1807, and January 19, 1808. The first of these provided that occupants currently residing on lands ceded to the United States by treaty with a foreign nation or cession from any State might apply for permission to continue on such tracts, up to 320 acres in size, as tenants at will of the United States. The subsequent act, passed as a supplement to legislation for disposal of lands south of the State of Tennessee, had granted preference in becoming purchasers at public land sale to those who, on March 3, 1807, actually inhabited and cultivated such tracts and who had obtained permission to remain on them under the terms of the earlier act. 2 *U. S. Stat.*, 445-46, 455.

APPLICATIONS, RECOMMENDATIONS   July 15, 1825

MARK HARRIS, Portland (Maine), refers to his "short . . . acquaintance" with Clay and, "anticipating . . . a removal of the Collector at Bath should that be the event of the present inquiry," recommends the appointment of John B. Swanton. ALS. DNA, RG59, A. and R. (MR3). Harris, a Portland merchant, had been a member of Congress from December 2, 1822, to March 3, 1823. He later held local and state offices before moving to New York City in 1842. In November, 1825, Swanton, a native of Maine, was named interim collector of customs and inspector of the revenue at the port of Bath and his nomination for a regular appointment was confirmed in January, 1826.

The incumbent collector, Mark L. Hill, had been appointed to the position in May, 1824, after the Senate had rejected the nomination for reappointment of Joseph Ferdinand Wingate, who had held the position since 1820. Both Hill and Wingate were engaged in private mercantile business and both were active in politics, Wingate having served in the Maine Legislature in 1818 and 1819 and later (1827 to 1831) becoming a member of Congress. As early as January and February, 1825, Wingate had been urging investigation of charges against Hill and proposing a replacement. Adams, *Memoirs,* VI, 467, 501, 512, 515.

JAMES WEIR, Lexington (Kentucky), recommends, for an appointment, Andrew Stainton, with whom he has "been intimately acquainted . . . for the last twelve years," first as an employee of (Lewis) Sanders and, later, of Weir, himself. ALS. DNA, RG59, A. and R. (MR3). Enclosed in Stainton to Clay, July 25, 1825. Stainton had been a bookkeeper and accountant for Sanders and, in 1816, had operated a grist mill and commission business. He did not receive a Federal appointment.

INSTRUCTIONS AND DISPATCHES   July 16, 1825

From ALEXANDER H. EVERETT, Havre de Grace (France), [no. 1]. Reports his arrival "after a short and agreeable voyage of about thirty days." ALS. DNA, RG59, Dip. Disp., Spain, vol. 25 (M31, R27). Received August 21.

From JAMES A. HOLDEN, Aux Cayes. Reports that the French fleet brought to Port au Prince, on July 3, the Baron de Mackau as negotiator for the independence of the island (Haiti). Terms of agreement have not been announced, but it is rumored that the island is to pay $30,000,000 in five years, that French vessels are to pay only half the export and import duties required of "most favored" nations, and that exports of the island in French vessels are to be admitted to France upon payment only of colonial duties. Holden fears, if this be true, injury to the trade of the United States. ALS. DNA, RG59, Cons. Disp., Aux Cayes, vol. 1 (M-T330, R1). Holden, of New York, had been appointed consular commercial agent for the United States at Aux Cayes, Haiti, the previous January. Ange-René-Armand, the Baron de Mackau, was a career officer of the French Navy, at this time holding the rank of rear admiral, later (in 1847) raised to admiral. He served in the French Chamber of Deputies (1830) and Senate (1852); became chief of the French sea and land forces in the Antilles and Governor of Martinique (1836), French Minister to the Provinces of Río de la Plata (1840), and French Minister of Marine (1843-1847). The terms reported as a basis for French recognition of Haitian independence, including the monetary compensation covering indemnity to French citizens forced to emigrate from Santo Domingo during the insurrection, proved to be correct. Cf. below, Brown to Clay, May 10, 1826, note.

APPLICATIONS, RECOMMENDATIONS   July 16, 1825

THOMAS CORWIN and others, "Lebanon Warren Co. Ohio," recommend William Miner for appointment to a clerkship in the State Department and states that his "conduct as Clerk of the Supreme court for this County" shows him qualified for the position. ALS by Corwin, signed also by Benj(amin) Collett, Jacob Dixon Miller, George J. Smith, A. H. Dunlevy (Dunlavy), Phineas Ross, Thomas R. Ross, Francis Dunlavy, John Woods, Matthias Corwin, and Jos[eph] S. Benham. DNA, RG59, A. and R. (MR3). Miner, not further identified, did not receive an appointment. Miller was elected to the State Senate in 1826; Smith was a member of the State House of Representatives (1825-1827) and later of the State Senate (1836-1839); and Anthony Howard Dunlevy (Dunlavy), brother-in-law of Thomas Corwin, subsequently became a member of the State House of Representatives (1837-1838). Francis Dunlavy, father of Anthony Howard, had been born in Virginia and settled in Ohio, after previous residence in Pennsylvania and Kentucky; he was a veteran of the Revolution, had served as a senator in the first legislative assembly of Ohio (1803) and for fourteen years (1803-1817) as president judge of the western circuit of the State court of common pleas, and was still practicing law. Matthias Corwin was either the father or the brother of Thomas: the father, elected an associate judge of the State court of common pleas in 1817, had also been a member of the State House of Representatives from 1804 to 1812, 1813 to 1816, and 1824 to 1825; the brother was clerk of Warren County court. Benjamin Collett and Phineas Ross have not been identified.

FELIX GRUNDY, Nashville, recommends, for a consular appointment, Dr. Charles Douglass, "formerly of this State, now of Alabama," who has lived in Mexico and knows the Spanish language. ALS. DNA, RG59, A. and R. (MR2). See above, King to Clay, June 22, 1825, note.

From Ninian Edwards

Dear Sir   (*Confidential*)   Belleville Illinois July 18. 1825
     Convinced of the justice of my claim upon the Government for compensation for my services as Superintendent of the U. S. Wabash Saline,[1] and reposing the most implicit confidence in your magnanimity, I take the liberty of inclosing to you my statement[2] upon the subject, trusting that, you will give to my application that support which you may conceive it justly merits.
     Postponed for a long time in consequence of the relations which subsisted between Mr Crawford & myself[3] this claim was submitted to the late President at the last session of congress, when, a decision upon it was evaded, as I verily believe, from a fear of the consequences, in Virginia, of doing me justice. This impression causes me infinite regret, that it had not been presented at an earlier period. It is unpleasant enough to have to encounter the injustice of avowed enemies, but a tame acquiescence in the neglect & ill treatment of professed friends, proceeding from motives of policy, would betray a mean & abject spirit equally worthy of contempt & abhorrence. My disposition is such (and I do not regret it) that I would put every thing to hazard, rather than permit either foe or friend, to with hold from me, especially on political considerations,

that justice which had been extended to others, and is equally
due to myself— I could, easily, have shewn from a great many precedents of the last administration that, the President could not, consistently, have refused to allow my claim, & had I been at Washington, last winter, as I intended, I would, whatever advice I might
have received to the contrary (for in such cases I yield to the advice
of no one) have had him called upon to exhibit to congress every
case in which compensation for extra services, or under his incidental
powers, had been allowed; and to have stated in what my case was
distinguishable, in principle, from them; and why some compensation had not been allowed me— With such a text book I could in
my leisure moments, and I would, in the most temperate and dispassionate manner, have demonstrated to the satisfaction of every
rational mind either that, enough had not been done for me; or
that too much had been done for others. I never was, nor will
I ever be, mean enough to place myself under such obligations to
any man as to forbid my doing myself justice—and I should have
been the less disposed to brook such treatment from a suspicion
that it might have proceeded, in part, from a belief [*sic*] that I
had been completely prostrated—

If such an idea has been entertained, I can assure you, nothing
can be more erroneous— My sphere of influence has always been
an humble one— It has been, principally, limited to my own state—
Within which, it never was greater than at present— It is, at least,
such that, all the politicians of the state combined, whatever may
be their party or politics, could not prevent my being elected the
next Governor— And I shall be obliged to be a candidate in my own
defence, for, I find that, to be even reasonably respected abroad,
it is necessary to be pretty strong at home— I regret this necessity,
very much, on account of the effects it may have on Mr Cook's
election[4]— It doubtless will injure us both, in some degree, that, the
father in law, & son in law should be candidates, at the same election,
for the two highest stations in the gift of the people. I however,
believe we *can* both be elected—but whether, or not, the situation
in which I am placed will not permit me to forego the opportunity
of availing myself of the most unequivocal testimony of the unim-
paired confidence which my fellow citizens repose in me— There
may be much talk, and some parade about entering the lists with
me, but, I shall be disappointed, if I even have a competitor at the
polls. Mr Cook will have serious opposition, in consequence of his
vote for President, but, if I were not a candidate, it would be fruitless. As it is however, it is impossible, at this time, to judge with
any kind of certainty, how it will eventuate— I am however, digress-
ing from the intended subject of this letter— I return to my claim.

It does appear to me that $500 per annum is the least compensation that ought to be allowed me, but I am willing to submit that matter wholly to the President. He has, as yet, established no precedents, nor can I tell how far he may conceive himself bound by those of his predecessors, but, if he should be disposed to allow me any thing upon precedent, or on principle (which last fully justifies it) I wish to have a credit allowed me upon the account against me for the outfit that was advanced to me as Minister to Mexico.

You are probably apprized that my resignation was produced by Noble's testimony against me[5]— Improbable & false as it was, I could not think of serving my country with so foul an imputation resting upon me. Time has proved that I was right, for, I am now fully prepared to demonstrate— Yes, not only to demonstrate, but to force irresistable [sic] conviction on the minds of both friends & foes, that his statements were false, & that he is utterly unworthy of belief. In fact, I have no idea that, when he made his statements, he was expected to be called upon to swear to them. I shall completely demolish him— As to Mr Crawford, though my indisposition, and the want of time, during the session of the committee, did not enable me to do complete justice to the case, it has been seen that, notwithstanding the committee were invited & challenged by me to do so, they were not able to detect a single inaccuracy in any one of my statements against him— All defects however, are now amply supplied, and much additional matter of corroboration & illustration drawn from his last copious report (which I then had not sufficient time to examine) in a reveiw [sic] which I have since written.[6] I have no fear of permanent injury to my character from that contest— But I am extremely anxious to settle up for my outfit, which, as soon as I made up my mind to resign, I determined to return, not as a matter of right, but of choice— This however, I have, as yet, been only able to effect in part— It has not been without considerable sacrifices, and some pecuniary embarrassment, (to which I had hitherto been a stranger) that I have been able to accomplish as much as I have done in that way— My looses [sic] in consequence of this business must be very considerable— The far greater part of the articles purchased for my outfit are still on hand, & cannot be disposed of, for any thing like the first cost—some of them are yet more than a thousand miles apart, and others I fear will be totally lost. The President, I understand told Mr Cook that, if I would make out an accurate statement of my losses, they should be allowed me— Had I known this in time I might have availed myself of it— It is now too late— Considering however, that I resigned a highly honorable & important station; that I incurred great expenses preparatory to my departure; that I both left, and returned to the city under the positive orders of the President &c, I do think it right that I should retain the amount of my salary for the time I held the office, and by virtue thereof was subject to the President's orders— With this, I should still be a looser [*sic*] by that affair, but I would be perfectly content, if a settlement on these terms would be satisfactory to the administration— If you see no objection thereto, I should be highly gratified with your private opinion, given confidentially, if you please, on this subject. I may not be a good judge in such a case. And my wish is to give entire satisfaction to the administration in regard to this matter— But though, my property is considerable, it is unproductive, and such is the present pressure of the times, in this state, that it is impossible to raise money without enormous sacrifices— Great, however, as they may be, I will make them, if it is thought right, or even wished, that I should do so—

I submit the inclosed statement to whatever disposition you may think proper to make of it—

I have the honor to be with the highest respect Sir Yr Mo Ob. St. Hon. H. Clay.   NINIAN EDWARDS

PS. As this letter is more of a medley than I intended it, I will risque the rendering it a little more objectionable in that respect by one or two suggestions that have no connection with the original design of it.

A favorite object, and indeed a political hobby, that supercedes [*sic*] all other, in this state & Missouri is a canal to connect Lake Michigan & the Illinois river.[7] Nothing could sustain the administration or its friends in these two states, so effectually as its countenancing this measure— Connecting the waters of Lake Erie & the Wabash is also a desirable object in a part of this state and Indiana.[8] Ohio is executing a similar project.[9] Now, do I venture too far, in suggesting that it might be very judicious in the President without descending to any particular case, to introduce into his message to congress some sentiment favorable to the connection of our great Lakes with the Atlantic & Western waters?[10] This might probably satisfy the friends of all these different projects. I know it would contribute greatly to the support of the friends of the Administration. I could say much more, and am half inclined to do it, but there are considerations which admonish me to forbear.

As however, I have alluded to my being a candidate for Govr. I will inclose for your inspection, one, among the multitude of letters I am constantly receiving from different parts of the state, on that subject. This is from Judge Young[11] who is decidedly one of our most popular characters. I will only observe that the people of the District he refers to, actually consider me a friend of Mr. Adams— You will please to return the letter—

Dr John Todd of Edwardsville is, and long has been a very warm friend to you. He was a candidate in your favor in this District. He is a very popular, and very worthy & intelligent man. I should be very happy if you should find it in your power to serve him.[12] Vancancies [sic] in office are frequently occurring, which would, I am sure, be very acceptable to him, though I never have spoken a word to him on the subject—   Yrs   N. EDWARDS

ALS. ICHi.

[1] See above, II, 166n. Edwards' claim, "for attending to leasing the Wabash Saline, &ca &ca.," had been rejected by the United States Treasury Department as early as 1814. Edward Tiffin to Edwards, July 9, 1814, in Carter (ed.), *Territorial Papers . . .* , XVI, 443.   [2] Not found.   [3] See above, III, 744-45n.

[4] Edwards, in 1826, was elected Governor of Illinois by a narrow plurality of 6,280 votes to 5,833 for his major opponent; Daniel P. Cook was defeated by about 900 votes.

[5] James Noble had been one of the witnesses before the House committee investigating the charges against Crawford in 1824. His assertion that Edwards assured him that he was not the author of the "A. B." letters proved decisive in shifting the criticism of the committee from the alleged maladministration of Crawford to the prevarication of Edwards.

[6] Cf. below, Edwards to Clay, December 15, 1825.

[7] An engineering report on the possibilities of such an improvement had been made by the Federal Government in 1819, and the Illinois General Assembly at that time had passed a resolution requesting the State's congressional delegation to seek Federal aid. Daniel P. Cook and the Edwards faction had been leaders in this agitation. By act of March 30, 1822 (3 *U. S. Stat.*, 659-60), provision had been made for a right-of-way of ninety feet on each side of the proposed canal through the public lands; but the State legislature found such support inadequate. Congressional bills for an increased Federal grant, proposed in the sessions of 1825 and 1826, culminated in passage of the act of March 2, 1827 (4 *U. S. Stat.*, 234), which allotted to the State alternate sections of public land to a depth of five miles on each side of the proposed canal, which was to be commenced within five years and completed within twenty and to be free from toll for use by the United States Government. Financial, political, and engineering difficulties subsequently delayed the beginning of construction until 1837, and legislation extending the earlier time limits by five years was enacted on March 2, 1833 (*ibid.*, 662). The Illinois and Michigan Canal, joining Chicago to the Illinois River at La Salle, was not completed until 1848. Theodore Calvin Pease, *The Frontier State, 1818-1848* (*The Centennial History of Illinois*, II; Springfield, 1918), 194-215.

[8] By act of Congress of May 26, 1824 (4 *U. S. Stat.*, 47-48), the State of Indiana had also been authorized to build a canal through the public lands, from the Maumee to the Wabash, under terms similar to those first extended to Illinois (above, n. 7). The legislature of Indiana, similarly condemning the grant as niggardly, had rejected it and pressed for more generous support. In May, 1826, the Government ordered an engineering survey of practicable routes, and by act of March 2, 1827 (4 *U. S. Stat.*, 236), Congress provided for a grant at a rate and under conditions as described for those ultimately accorded for construction of the Illinois and Michigan Canal. Though the State accepted this grant, negotiations for the termination of the route through Ohio delayed the beginning of construction until 1832. The canal was completed between the Maumee and the Wabash by 1835; the route from Toledo, Ohio, to Lafayette, Indiana, was in use by 1840; but Evansville was not reached until 1851. Jacob Piatt Dunn, *Indiana and Indianans, a History of Aboriginal and Territorial Indiana and the Century of Statehood* (4 vols.; Chicago and New York, 1919), I, 387-91.

[9] See above, Stuart to Clay, March 15, 1825.

[10] Adams' annual message of December 6, 1825, spoke of the "enlightened enterprise" of one State (New York) by which "the waters of our Western lakes mingle with those of the ocean," but he spoke only generally of the value of roads "and canals" as "among the most important means of improvement." Richardson, *A Compilation of the Messages and Papers of the Presidents*, II, 311, 316.

[11] Richard M. Young, born in Fayette County, Kentucky, had begun the practice of law in Nicholasville before moving to Jonesboro, Illinois, in 1817. He had been a member of the Illinois Legislature (1820-1822), was a circuit judge (1825-1827), and became a United States Senator (1837-1843), associate justice of the State Supreme Court (1843-1847), Commissioner of the General Land Office (1847-1849), and Clerk of the United States House of Representatives (1850-1851).

¹² Dr. Todd was appointed register of the public land office at Springfield, Illinois, in January, 1827, but was removed from the position under the Jackson administration, in 1829. He remained a resident of Springfield, where he became a prominent physician, long a member of the local board of health, and one of the founders of the Illinois State Medical Society.

INSTRUCTIONS AND DISPATCHES   July 18, 1825

From JOEL R. POINSETT, Mexico (City), no. 6. Acknowledges receipt of Clay's communication no. 3 (above, April 16, 1825); reports that steps have been taken "to inform the Consuls of the United States, of the laws and usages in relation to blockades"; encloses a copy of his recent "representation . . . to this government, respecting the high duties levied upon a cargo of American cotton shirtings"; and states that one of the subjects to be considered by the next extraordinary session of the (Mexican) Congress is a new tariff. LS. DNA, RG59, Dip. Disp., Mexico, vol. 1 (M97, R2). Received September 20. The enclosure relates to shirtings consigned to Taylor, Sicard and Company.

From JOEL R. POINSETT, Mexico (City), no. 7. Reports agreement with the (Mexican) Secretary of State (Lucas Alamán) on separation of "the negociations for the Treaties of Commerce and of Limits between the two nations" and on the desirability of an early conclusion to negotiations for the former. The Secretary was gratified at Poinsett's suggestion that, though the United States "held itself bound to carry into effect the Treaty of Limits concluded with the King of Spain, 22nd of February, 1819 [above, II, 678 and 816, n. 19]," an effort should be made to establish a "more easily defined" boundary and, in turn, proposed the appointment of "Commissioners to make a reconnaissance of the country bordering on the line formerly settled with Spain. . . ." Poinsett objected to the proposal, and it was agreed that the Secretary should send him a note stating his Government's views in this connection. LS. DNA, RG59, Dip. Disp., Mexico, vol. 1 (M97, R2). Received September 20. See above, Clay to Poinsett, March 26, 1825.

INSTRUCTIONS AND DISPATCHES   July 19, 1825

From O[BADIAH] RICH, Madrid. States that (Hugh) Nelson has left with him the papers of the legation and authorized him "to prosecute the recovery of the 6000 Dollars proceeding from Mr Salmons bill on his Govt."; relays information "that the new Minister from Spain Mr [Francisco] Tacon is a relation of the late Marquis of Casa Yrujo that he has been Chargé d'affaires at Constantinople, but that he is 'little versed in diplomatic affairs.'" ALS. DNA, RG59, Dip. Disp., Spain, vol. 24 (M31, R26). Received September 9. On Salmon's bill, see above, Clay to Nelson, April 14, 1825; Nelson to Clay, July 10, 1825.

APPLICATIONS, RECOMMENDATIONS   July 19, 1825

From O[BADIAH] RICH, Madrid, "Private." Calls attention to his services to "this Legation for several years past," when he kept himself "from starving" by purchasing "rare books and MSS, which have been sold in London at exorbitant prices: a traffic in no wise discreditable . . . , since some of the most respectable foreign Ministers are engaged in the same"; solicits appointment as Secretary of Legation, a position promised by Adams' "worthy Predecessor [James Monroe]," or as "Consul and Agent for claims and for seamen" for Madrid; states that, under his commission as "Consul for Valencia and all parts nearer thereto than to any other Consul," he has constituted himself consul for Madrid. ALS. DNA, RG59, Dip. Disp., Spain, vol. 24 (M31, R26). Received September 9.

APPLICATIONS, RECOMMENDATIONS   July 20, 1825

T[HOMAS] C[HURCH] BROWNELL, Hartford, Connecticut, requests an appointment, as bearer of dispatches, for a professor of Washington College going to Europe to purchase philosophical apparatus. ALS. DNA, RG59, Misc. Letters (M179, R62). Brownell, born in Massachusetts, had been appointed bishop of the Episcopal Diocese of Connecticut in 1819 and the first president of Washington (now Trinity) College, at Hartford, in 1823. In 1831 he resigned from active service in the college and devoted his time solely to administration of the episcopate and to religious writing.

On August 4, 1825, Brent, in Clay's absence, acknowledged receipt of Brownell's letter and informed him that the State Department had no need for a bearer of dispatches to Europe. "In this time of general Peace the Packet Ships and post Offices are found by experience to be perfectly safe, expeditious and convenient mediums of conveyance, and this Department makes use of them, almost exclusively, for its Despatches." Copy. DNA, RG59, Dom. Letters, vol. 21, p. 124 (M40, R19).

WILLIAM SMYTH, St. Thomas (Virgin Islands), encloses a letter (not found) promising him an appointment and asks Clay "to remind Mr. Adams of his promise and to beg him for God [sic] sake, give" him employment. ALS. DNA, RG59, A. and R. (M531, R7).

"In the absence of the Secretary," Brent replied, August 18, that the purported letter "from the late Secretary of State . . . , dated 10th. of January, 1824 . . . is altogether a counterfeit. . . ." Copy, in DNA, RG59, Cons. Instr., vol. 2, p. 363 (M78, R2). See above, Macon to Clay, May 27, 1825, note.

To John Q. Adams

Dear Sir   Lebannon [sic] (Ohio) 21st. July 1825

I have been detained with my family at this place a week by the illness of one of my children, a daughter of about twelve years of age.[1] Upon the arrival of my family at Cincinnati on the 12h. she had fever, which we hoped was merely the effect of the journey from Lexington and its incidental excitements. But on reaching this place, about 30 miles East of that City, we found it necessary to call in a physician, who pronounced her fever remittent, and her condition to be unfit for the prosecution of our journey. It has not yet yielded to the remedies which have been applied, but, on the contrary, a symptom has appeared this morning which excites some apprehension. I cannot say when her situation will admit of my continuing the journey, but I shall resume it, without any unnecessary delay. I regret extremely the occurrence, as it protracts an absence from my post which had been previously extended beyond my expectations.

My reception at Cincinnati was in a high degree cordial and distinguished. On no former similar occasion was a public dinner so numerously and respectably attended. Between your political friends and mine entire concord & co-operation prevail. The disaffected would have been glad that some public manifestation should have been given of an unfriendly character, during my sojourn in that City. The best proof of their weakness and decline is that they were awed from the execution of such a purpose. In every other part of this State there is not a mere acquiescence but a high degree of satisfaction in the events of the last Session. Of this I am assured by Governor Morrow[2] and others as it is demonstrated by many public testimonies. The vast multitude which was assembled promiscuously from all parts of the State, and therefore may be considered as having fairly embodied public feeling and sentiment, displayed at the commencement of their Great Canal more sensibility when a toast was drank [sic], relating to those events,[3] than was exhibited in reference to any other.

Govr. Morrow has just told me that Mr. Clinton[4] allowed himself, in a large circle at Louisville, to speak very disparagingly of the capacity of Mr. King.[5] He stated that his physical and intellectual powers were both impaired, and that he always had enjoyed a much higher character for talents than he merited. With this opinion of Mr. King is it not extraordinary that Govr. Clinton should have made a recommendation of him to the Legislature of N. York as a Senator of the U. S.?[6] A recommendation which, if justifiable at all, could only be defended upon the ground of Mr. King's possessing uncommon attainments. Govr. Morrow remarked that he felt hurt, and he thought many others in the circle were also hurt, that Mr. Clinton should have indulged in such observations.

> With high respect I am Your ob. servant   H. Clay

Mr. Adams.

ALS. MHi-Adams Papers (MR471).   1 Eliza.   2 Jeremiah Morrow.
3 See above, Toasts and Speech, July 13, 1825.
4 DeWitt Clinton.   5 Rufus King.
6 Probably a reference to the support of King by Clinton forces in the New York Legislative session of 1820, when, however, the vote was unanimous. On the ramifications of this election, see Hammond, *The History of Political Parties in the State of New York* . . . , I, 482-85, 514-17; Van Buren, *The Autobiography* . . . , 100-101; Fox, *The Decline of Aristocracy in the Politics of New York*, 220-21. No reference to a revival of Clinton's support, as pressure for continuation of King in office after expiration of his term in 1825, has been found.

INSTRUCTIONS AND DISPATCHES   July 21, 1825

From Andrew Armstrong, Port au Prince. Encloses account of ceremonies of recognition of (Haitian) independence; summarizes ordonnance of the King of France, covering the terms of agreement; concludes that the United States will have little chance to participate in the export trade but will still be unrivalled in the import trade and, consequently, that a good understanding with these people is worth-while. If a treaty is not wished, it can be avoided by offering reciprocity, which they cannot accept because of their commitment to France. Negotiations might, however, settle problems concerning seamen and the Christophe spoliation claims, and Armstrong wishes to be appointed diplomatic agent to conduct them. ALS. DNA, RG59, Cons. Disp., Cap Haitien, vol. 5 (M9, R-T5). On French recognition of Haitian independence, see above, Holden to Clay, July 16, 1825; on the problems here mentioned by Armstrong, see above, Armstrong to Clay, June 14, 1825.

From W[ILLIAM] R. HIGINBOTHAM, Bermuda. Encloses a copy of a letter by Higinbotham to the collector of customs at New Haven, "from which you will observe how much difficulty, I experience. in the execution. of the duties of my Office, a remedy for which I beg leave respectfully to request." LS. DNA, RG59, Cons. Disp., Bermuda, vol. 1 (M-T263, R1). Received August 8.

The enclosed letter, dated July 21, complains that Captain William Tyler of the American schooner *Industry,* bound to New Haven, failed to comply with the United States law "in reporting his vessel . . . on arrival, and refused when notice had been given him. . . ." Also enclosed is a copy of the vessel's register, "taken from the Custom House at St Georges Bermuda where it was deposited, and never shewn at this Office." Tyler is identified as a resident of Bradford County, Connecticut, and part owner, as well as master, of the *Industry.*

From JOHN RAINALS, Copenhagen. Refers to his letter of May 22 (not found); reports a change in "the Bonding or Transit duty on goods landed for Exportation" and that, as a result of "the late Treaty with Great Britain," the difference in measurement of Danish and foreign vessels for the calculation of port charges has been eliminated; and notes the sale of two Swedish vessels to Colombia. ALS. DNA, RG59, Cons. Disp., Copenhagen, vol. 3 (M-T195, R3). Received December 16 (the "Duplicate" was received December 8). Rainals, a Copenhagen merchant, born in Great Britain, had been appointed consul for the United States at that port in 1820 and held the position until 1834. On the sale of the Swedish vessels, see above, Hughes to Clay, July 8, 1825, note.

MISCELLANEOUS LETTERS   July 21, 1825

From JONATHAN THOMPSON, New York. Transmits copies of documents from the United States consul at Pernambuco (James H. Bennett), charging Captain Thomas Carter, "of the Brig Ambuscade," with discharging his crew at that port without paying them according to law; notes that Carter's bond is "in this office" and Carter himself is in New York; and asks for directions relative to putting the bond in suit. Adds that Carter claims that his agent at Pernambuco paid the seamen fully after receipt of the consul's letter. ALS. DNA, RG59, Misc. Letters (M179, R62). Thompson, born on Long Island and for many years engaged in the shipping and importing business in Brooklyn, had served as collector of the direct tax from 1813 to 1819 and thereafter (until 1833) as collector of the port of New York. From 1840 until his death, six years later, he was president of a New York banking house. He was long active in political affairs, having been chairman of the Democratic-Republican executive committee for ten years. No reply to this letter has been found.

INSTRUCTIONS AND DISPATCHES   July 22, 1825

From JOSHUA DODGE, "Consulate of the United States," Marseilles. Transmits copies of two letters, "received from the Board of Health of this place," concerning an outbreak of the plague on "two French Vessels arrived from Alexandria in Egypt"; encloses also "a Statement received from Egypt" relative to "the growing commerce of that country." ALS. DNA, RG59, Cons. Disp., Marseilles, vol. 2 (M-T220, R-T2). Received September 9. Dodge, born in Massachusetts, was consul at Marseilles from 1820 to 1830 and at Bremen from 1834 to 1840. On the developing commerce of Egypt, cf. above, Maury to Clay, April 18, 1825.

From JOEL R. POINSETT, Mexico (City), no. 8. Transmits (translation of) "a note from the Secretary of State [Lucas Alamán], on the subject of the road from the frontier of the State of Missouri . . . to Santa Fè [*sic*] of New Mexico, and respecting the proposed treaties of commerce and limits"; states "that this Government regards all our movements towards Texas and New Mexico with jealous apprehension"; and expresses a fear that "they are resolved to postpone marking out the road in question through their territory, until Commissioners are appointed to make a regular reconnoissance of that portion of the country with a view to" a boundary settlement. LS. DNA, RG59, Dip. Disp., Mexico, vol. 1 (M97, R2). Dated, erroneously, June 22. The enclosure, dated June (*i.e.* July) 20, 1825, proposes negotiations on a treaty of commerce and the appointment of commissioners by the two governments to obtain exact information upon which the boundary might be established. To this document is appended a communication from Poinsett to Clay (ALS), also misdated June 22, 1825, stating that Alamán's note had been returned in order that a part of it, based on erroneous reading of an American document, might be expunged. Having previously translated the note, Poinsett sends the translation.

On the proposed treaty of commerce, road to Santa Fé, and boundary settlement, see above, Clay to Poinsett, March 26, 1825; Poinsett to Clay, July 18, 1825.

APPLICATIONS, RECOMMENDATIONS   July 22, 1825

EBENEZER HERRICK, Bowdoinham (Maine), refers to an expectation of "a vacancy in the office of Collector of the Customs for the Port of Bath in this State" and to the probability that "a strong effort will . . . be made to keep the office in the hands of some one, belonging to the same party, to which the person incumbent [Mark L. Hill] is considered attached, a party avowedly hostile to the present administration." Endorses the recommendation of John B. Swanton for appointment and adds the hope that Clay "will find an opportunity of suggesting to the President the importance of not aiding his enemies in a triumph over his friends." ALS. DNA, RG59, A. and R. (MR2). Herrick, a lawyer and former member of the Legislatures of Massachusetts and Maine, was, from 1821 to 1827, a United States Congressman. See above, Harris to Clay, July 15, 1825.

Mortgage Deed from John Trimble

[July 23, 1825]
[Indenture by which John Trimble of Fayette County conveys to Henry Clay, executor of James Morrison, "a certain negro man

Steve," as security for payment of a note for $178.45, due May 23, 1826. Signed by Trimble; recorded in office of the Fayette County clerk, July 23, 1825.]

Fayette County Court, Deed Book Z, 333.

INSTRUCTIONS AND DISPATCHES   July 23, 1825

From ROBERT CAMPBELL, Genoa. Reports that "the House in Trade" with which he is connected has been forced to suspend payment but that arrangements with its creditors are such as to require no change in his place of abode; solicits, therefore, a continuation of his appointment. ALS. DNA, RG59, Cons. Disp., Genoa, vol. 1 (M-T64, R1). Received October 12. Cf. above, Ombrosi to Secretary of State, June 30, 1825.

From J[OHN] ADAMS SMITH, London, no. 9. Transmits copies of correspondence with (Rufus) King, whose indisposition from seasickness has obliged him to remain at Cheltenham; states the probability that King and (George) Canning may have an interview there. ALS. DNA, RG59, Dip. Disp., Great Britain, vol. 32 (M30, R28). Received September 8.

To John Q. Adams

Dear Sir   Lebannon [*sic*] (Ohio) 25 July 1825
I am still detained here by the illness of my daughter,[1] of the termination of whose case we can neither anticipate the time nor the manner. I am greatly mortified and distressed by the occurrence. Mr Erwin,[2] my son in law, who will have the honor of delivering you this letter, will explain her situation more fully. His business obliges him to leave us. I shall lose no time that is not unavoidable in reaching the City.   I am with great respect Your ob. servant
Mr. Adams   H. CLAY

ALS. MHi-Adams Papers, Letters Received (MR471).
[1] Eliza.   [2] James Erwin.

To John J. Crittenden

Dear Sir   Lebannon (Ohio) 25 July 1825
I omitted, in passing through Frankfort, to request the favor of you to appear in a cause in the Court of Appeals between Genl. Richard Hickman of Clarke and his family. The case is one involving a division of the Estate of his father, and it went up from Fayette.[1] I was of Counsel for Genl Hickman in the Court below, where the great point involved was the validity of the Will of the father. That point was settled, and I believe is not carried up. I do not think my engagement for Genl. Hickman requires me to appear in the Ct. of Appeals but as he may take a different view of the matter,

and as he is an old friend for whom I entertain high esteem, you will oblige me if you will represent me and appear on his Side, unless you should be retained by his antagonist.

I am detained here by the illness of one of my children, a daughter of 12 years of age.[2] She has fever which has confined her here 10 or 11 days, and we are not yet able to see when or how it will terminate.

My reception at Cincinnati and here has been extremely cordial and gratifying.[3] I met there and here with Mr. Clinton,[4] who is nominally on a tour of observation of Internal improvements, but in fact in pursuit of political advant[age.] My friends tell me (and I incline to think with them) that h[e] does not make a favorable impression. He is reserved, al[oof] and has rather a haughty air. They flatter me by drawing favorable conclusions from the comparisons made between us. At the public dinner given me in Cincinnati (which was attend[ed] by from 180 to 200 persons), I spoke when toasted, and he when also toasted was silent. He does not appear to be gifted in that way, whatever other attainments he may have.   With great regard I am Yr's truly   H. CLAY
John J. Crittenden Esq

ALS. NcD. Margin of MS. ragged.
1 Two cases involving the heirs of James Hickman were carried to the Kentucky Court of Appeals, in December, 1827, and April, 1828, where Crittenden served as one of the attorneys for Stephen Holliday and others in opposition to General Richard Hickman and others. In both contests the appellate court upheld the Fayette Circuit Court decisions, supporting the validity of the will and providing for the division of the property. Fayette Circuit Court, Order Book X, 296-301, 318-19, 450-58; Order Book 1, pp. 299-304; 22 *Ky. Reports* (6 T. B. Monroe) 376-80, 582-92. James Hickman, Sr., an uncle of Paschal Hickman, had been born in Hanover County, Virginia, and had died in Clark County, Kentucky, in 1816. Stephen Holliday, a farmer of Clark County, was the husband of Richard Hickman's sister, Ann. Both Ann and her husband had been born in Culpeper County, Virginia.
2 Eliza.   3 See above, Toasts and Speech, July 13, 1825.   4 DeWitt Clinton.

From Andrew Stainton

Hble H Clay   Lexington July 25. 1825—
Dr. Sir

My friend Mr. R Scott informs me that you are very much disposed to meet my wishes but that any application for an appointment must be accompany'd with such recom dations as shall remove all doubts of its propriety— I have procured the inclosed from Mr. James Wier[1] whose reserve on such occasions is so well known to you that if unmerited it could not been [sic] extracted from him— Mr. S and myself advised Mr. Gratz,[2] who is now in Philadelphia that a recom endation from that place would be of service to me and if his friendship has not very much abated he will address you on my behalf— I could procure similar introductions from every influential character in this State but well knowing it depends only on your own pleasure and that these will remove all *your* doubts of my ability or integrity I have no wish to increase your annoyance which must be very great and shall rest the success of my application thereon without I am inform'd by you that more are necessary— I am personally acquainted with the Secretary of War.[3] but unfortunately his knowledge of me was unprofitable for in a trade I made with him when I was rich as I thought in Ky. lands & by a purchase of his. I was compell'd to become a Clerk to our Frd. Mr. L Sanders— I was 26 times thro yr. wilderness before I moved to Ky. and spent an independant fortune in defending my claims and travelling after my land— Mr. Barbour is a magnanimous man and without his feelings of good will towards me have worn off by time he would not oppose my Interest— I should be glad to serve ye U S in any business either stationary or if it took me from my family ½ my time it would make no difference   I am fond of travelling indeed the desire of seeing the world brought me from England and the want of means only has prevented me from gratifying my curiosity more extensively— I can only observe that if you are pleased to place me in any situation that will enable me to make my escape from my present disagreeable office of Superintending a mad House[4] where my sympathies are eternally on the rack, I will to the best of my abilities manifest my gratitude by taking care not to disappoint any expectations you may form of me— With sentiments of esteem I Remain   Dr Sir Your most obed Serv   ANDW. STAINTON

ALS. DNA, RG59, R. and R. (MR3). Endorsed by Clay: "Andw. Stainton's application for an appointment— To be filed—"
[1] Above, Weir to Clay, July 15, 1825.
[2] Benjamin Gratz.   [3] James Barbour.
[4] Incorporated in 1816 as the Fayette Hospital, privately financed, for the care of the insane, the institution had been taken over by the State following passage of legislation in 1822 to establish a "Lunatic Asylum." It had begun accepting inmates on May 1, 1824, and by November, 1825, accommodated fifty-four. Ky. Gen. Assy, *Acts, 1822-1823,* pp. 174-76; Ky. Senate, *Journal, 1824-1825,* pp. 173-75; *1825,* p. 76.

INSTRUCTIONS AND DISPATCHES   July 25, 1825

From J[OHN] ADAMS SMITH, London, no. 10. Transmits a copy of a letter from the American consul at Antigua (Robert M. Harrison) to (Richard) Rush, with an enclosure, seeking clarification of the British regulations concerning the importation of shooks into that island. Smith is permitting the matter to rest pending the arrival of (Rufus) King. ALS. DNA, RG59, Dip. Disp., vol. 32 (M30, R28). Received September 8.

APPLICATIONS, RECOMMENDATIONS   July 26, 1825

ROBERT R. STEWART, Trinidad de Cuba, solicits appointment as "Commercial Agent for this place," to fill the vacancy caused by the death of James Baker.

ALS. DNA, RG59, A. and R. (MR3). Endorsed: "Appointed." Baker had been residing in Trinidad at the time of his appointment in November, 1824. Stewart, who also resided in Trinidad, was probably a partner in the mercantile firm based at Matanzas. Cf. above, III, 454.

Receipt from Henry Allen

[July 27, 1825]

Henry Allen, collector, in a document similar to the Receipt, above, III, 489, acknowledges payment "from Henry Clay by the hand of Col. T. H. Blake six dollars and four cents" for taxes for the year 1825 on two tracts of second rate land in Vigo County, Indiana. The State tax is now $1.28 on each tract; the county tax, $1.10; and the road tax, $.64. ADS. DLC-TJC (DNA, M212, R16). Endorsed by Clay on verso: "Sent a Check [not found] for $22:56/100 drawn by the branch bank [of the United States] at Washn. on Philada.—the 7. Jan: 1826. H. C." Cf. above, III, 877; below, Blake to Clay, July 30, 1825.

From James Wilkinson

Dear Sir   City of Mexico July 27th. 1825

It has been my intention to write you a long Letter of congratulation, on the issue of the Presidential Election, & your own elevation to the office of State; but my purpose is arrested by a Topic on which I consider it a duty to give you the earliest advice, yet I cannot forbear to offer you, on the present occasion, the hearty thanks of a veteran patriot & Soldier, of 1775, for your conduct & motives in the selection of Mr. Adams to occupy the highest office of our Country, (altho I could have preferred another) nor will I suppress the avowal of my surprize [sic] & my pity, for the unaccountable delusions of some men of experience, & virtue & Intelligence— The Idea of the Goth Jackson for President of the United States, always reminds me of of [sic] my old Friend Mr. G. Morris & Lucius Horatio Stockton[1]—Lord! Lord! Lord!—The sympathies of His whore & another of the same class, in New Orleans, first suggested the Idea of running this Man Monster for the Presidency;[2] vain & presumptuous as he may, [sic] he did not dream how far a Body of active interested partizans, could impose Him on a credulous People, to whom he was as much a stranger, as are the merits of his blind operations before N. Orleans; but he was willing to lend His name to distract your Interests, because you had dared to question the constitutionality of His Conduct pending the Simenole [sic] War,[3] for which you merited the "Corona civica" instead of the censures of the ignorant, of the malignant & envious—for when the motives, the conduct & conclusion of that War, shall be calmly examined by the impartial Historian, neither Mr. Monroe nor His administration, nor General Jackson can escape the reprobation of our Country & of mankind— What ever may be the result of these things, or of the Spade & Trowel conflict which seems to be impending, your inimitable appeal to your Country has secured the approbation of all unprejudiced Persons, & what must be of more worth to you, the "mens conscia cibi recti"

However I may reprobate secret information, in the general, I cannot witness conspiracies, cabals & Intrigues, for the exaltation of the vicious or the depression of the virtuous, without an impulse of detestation, & much less will my Sense of Patriot duty permit me, by silence, to connive at a meditated imposition on the national executive— The Facts I am about to state, with a single exception, are as obvious as the meridian Sun, & that exception may be sustained by my oath

John F. Gould formerly, as He has informed me, a Carpenter in Boston, but as others say a Brick-Layer, arrived in this City in the year 1822, as the Agent of Robert McQueen Machinist in New York,[4] who had contracted with our Consul Saint Iago S. Wilcocks[5] for a Steam Engine, to be delivered & put in operation by the said McQueen, for certain unknown mine-owners in this Country— In course of the transactions which ensued, much bickering, chicanery & strife arose between the said Gould & the said Wilcocks, about their respective rights, prevoliges [sic] & advantages; Mr. Gould resided some part of the time under the same Roof with me, during which period he took great pains to convince me that Saint Iago was the greatest Villain in existence, who at the same time treated the said Gould as a Sot, a Brute & Blockhead unworthy of his consideration or Society.—

Mr. McQueen in the year 1823, having heard of some improprieties in the Conduct of Mr. Gould, who at that time drank freely & had become a Gambler, sent out a very decent young Man by the name of Black,[6] to scrutinize Goulds Conduct & if he found it culpable to remove Him otherwise not— Mr. Black soon discovered that Gould was gambling & speculating on Mr. McQueen, He therefore took the business into his own Hands as his duty enjoined, with which Saint Iago appeared to me to be well-pleased, but soon after this J. F. Gould did actually consult me, whether he should abandon the Interest of his former employer McQueen, & attach Himself to Mr. Wilcocks, for redress of certain grievances real or supposed, my advice was of course that he should preserve his Integrity, and subsequent to that period, a close & intimate connection has ensued between the Said Wilcocks & Gould, accompanied by circumstances of such a Character as to excite the disgust & distrust of every observer—

Well, now, this Gould left this City on the 21st. Ultmo. for the U. S. it said [sic] with dispatches from our Legation & also from this Republick, under circumstances as is reported which will protect Him against process in the U. S., and this silly extravagance is credited here, because it originates with high authority—

There are mysteries hanging about this transaction which I do not comprehend, but I verily believe this Gould goes to the U. S. as the envoy of St Iago, and therefore I have felt it my duty to give you this advice for your government, and am in haste & with unfeigned respect & regard   Your Friend & Servt.   JA WILKINSON
The Honble H. Clay.

[Endorsement on verso][7]

Commodore Porter has been proposed as the Commander of the Mexican Navy, & yesterday I was told he was Elected[8]—& tis said the young man OBryan[9] recommended Him—but who introduced Him to OBryan— Anon.—

ALS. DLC-HC (DNA, M212, R1).

[1] The incident (not found) probably involved Gouverneur Morris, born in New York, admitted to the bar (1771), active in the Continental Congress (1777 and 1788) and in the framing of the Articles of Confederation (1775) and of the Constitution of the United States (1787), Commissioner to England (1789), Minister to France (1792-1794), and United States Senator (1800-1803). Lucius Horatio Stockton, of Trenton, New Jersey, appointed United States attorney for that State in 1789, had been nominated in 1801 as Secretary of War. Two days after his nomination had been presented to the Senate, action upon it had been postponed; four days subsequently Stockton had declined appointment for the stated reason that the illness of his mother, Anice Boudinot (Mrs. Richard) Stockton, barred his acceptance of the office. Stockton to Adams, January 20, 1801, in MHi-Adams Papers, Letters Received (MR400).

[2] The discovery, in December, 1793, that Rachel Donelson Robards had been still the wife of Lewis Robards at the time of her marriage to Jackson, approximately two years earlier, had led to a second wedding ceremony in January, 1794, and to persistent gossip, which eventually became injected into politics. Marquis James, *The Life of Andrew Jackson* (complete in 1 vol.; Indianapolis, [c. 1938]), pp. 71-74, 462-68. In February, 1815, Mrs. Jackson had joined her husband in New Orleans, where they had been lavishly entertained in the home of Edward Livingston, who had subsequently become one of the first to consider Jackson as a candidate for the Presidency. Mrs. Louise Moreau Livingston, to whom Wilkinson also apparently refers, had been at the time of her marriage to Edward Livingston, in 1805, "a refugee from the black uprising in French Santo Domingo, . . . the young widow of a Jamaica planter." James Parton, *Life of Andrew Jackson* (3 vols.; New York, 1860), II, 350; III, 17-18, 30.   [3] See above, II, 636-62.

[4] Gould and McQueen not further identified.   [5] James S. Wilcocks.

[6] John Black, of New York, resided in Mexico City some forty years and served as United States consul there from 1843 to 1860.

[7] AE by Wilkinson.

[8] On July 4 the Executive Department of the Mexican Government had recommended David Porter for the appointment, but the Council did not give final approval to the proposal until July 30. Washington *Daily National Intelligencer*, September 24, 1825. Porter went to Mexico the following May and by early July had accepted the appointment. This information, together with the fact that he had resigned his commission in the United States Navy, was announced in the Washington *Daily National Intelligencer*, on August 9, 1826; but the resignation was not officially effective until August 18. See also *Niles' Weekly Register*, XXX (June 24, 1826), 304; C. Harvey Gardiner (ed.), *Mexico, 1825-1828, The Journal and Correspondence of Edward Thornton Tayloe* (Chapel Hill, [c. 1959]), 127; *Senate Docs.*, 19 Cong., 1 Sess., no. 1, pt. 4, p. 106.

[9] Possibly Donat Henchy O'Brien, born in Ireland, a captain in the British Navy on duty off the coast of South America from 1818 to 1821. He had thereupon returned to Britain, attaining the rank of rear admiral, but saw no further sea duty.

INSTRUCTIONS AND DISPATCHES　　　　　　　July 27, 1825

From ALEXANDER H. EVERETT, Paris, no. 2. Reports his arrival in Paris and encloses copy of his request to the Spanish Foreign Minister (Francisco de Zea Bermudez) for such orders to border authorities as will facilitate entrance into Spain. Notes the apparent unsettled state of Spain and the formation of two French military camps near Bayonne and Perpignan. Transmits a pamphlet by Chateaubriand on "the affairs of the Greeks," whose "prospects seem . . . less favorable than they were last year." ALS. DNA, RG59, Dip. Disp., Spain, vol. 25 (M31, R27). Received October 3.

François Auguste René, Vicomte de Chateaubriand, of the French nobility, had visited the United States in 1791 and lived as an emigré in England during the French Revolution, had returned to his homeland to become the leading literary figure of the Napoleonic period, and, upon the restoration of the Bourbons, had come into political prominence as Minister of the Interior (1814-1816), French Ambassador to Berlin (1821), London (1822), and Rome (1827), and Minister of Foreign Affairs (1823-1824). His pamphlet *Note sur la Grèce* had recently (1825) been published in Paris.

From HENRY MIDDLETON, St. Petersburg, no. 48. Acknowledges receipt of instructions no. 1 (May 10, 1825) and reports discussion of the proposal with Nesselrode. Though receiving "at first no great encouragement," Middleton prepared a copy of the instructions, with an introductory note (copy here enclosed), to be laid before the Emperor. Middleton believes "that the proposition is in consideration between *the Allies;* it being a fundamental maxim with them not to take any determination in matters affecting the general policy, without the mutual consent of the parties to the Alliance." ALS. DNA, RG59, Dip. Disp., Russia, vol. 10 (M35, R10). Addressed to Secretary of State; received January 6, 1826. Published in *American State Papers, Foreign Relations,* V, 849.

From JOEL R. POINSETT, Mexico, [no. 9]. Transmits copies of the note from the Mexican Secretary of State (Lucas Alamán), mentioned in Poinsett's last dispatch, with his reply thereto, and reports "great apprehension in . . . this country that the Government of the United States contemplate renewing their claim to the territory North of the Rio Bravo del Norte [Rio Grande] . . . ." In a concluding paragraph (in cipher, decoded by State Department clerk) Poinsett cites the importance of gaining time if the United States wishes to extend its territory beyond the line specified in the treaty of 1819 (the Adams-Onís Treaty). Poinsett comments, further: "Most of the good land from the Colorado to the Sabine has been granted by the State of Texas, and is rapidly peopling with either grantees or squatters from the United States, a population they will find difficult to govern, and perhaps after a short period they may not be so averse to part with that portion of their Territory as they are at present." LS. DNA, RG59, Dip. Disp., Mexico, vol. 1 (M97, R2). Received September 17.

APPLICATIONS, RECOMMENDATIONS　　　　　July 27, 1825

ROBERT WRIGHT, "Blakeford" (Queen Anne's County, Maryland), introduces his son, William H. D. C. Wright, applicant for a consulship. Comments: "My long and intimate Connexion with You, in the public Councils of the Nation in trying times, inspires me with the Sure Hope, that you will feel peculiar pleasure in promoting my honest wishes for the public Good— Your attentions to my Son will be a sure proof of the Sincerity of our mutual Respect—" ALS. DNA, RG59, A. and R. (MR4). See below, Clay to Wright, September 14, 1825.

From Frances Wright

Baltimore July 28th 25.—

May I request your perusal my dear Sir of the enclosed paper.[1] It relates to a subject wch I feel assured has often engaged yr attention & interested yr feelings as a Man a patriot & a statesman.

The undertaking I am about to engage in wd indeed be presumptuous were I not sustained by the countenance & assistance of many distinguished citizens in the South & North. It is among the former that I am most anxious to find support & counsel. Cd I add your name to those friendly to the undertaking I shd embark in it with additional energy & pleasure. I am about to set out for Tennessee by the way of Pittsburgh Ohio & Kentucky; & after collecting the valuable assistants who generously devote their time to the work, I trust the location will be made & establishment opened by the month of Janry.[2]   Shd the subject appear worthy your intention [sic] I mt perhaps request of yr kindness to furnish me with the names of any citizens in your state or the South west generally who you consider likely to view the plan favorably. & to furnish it assistance—

Excuse my dear Sir this intrusion on your valuable time & permit me to subjoin the assurance of my very highest respect

FRANCES WRIGHT.

Until the 15th August my address will be to the care of Mr. Rapp[3] Economy below Pittsburgh Penna.   afterwards Nashville Post office Tennessee—

ALS. DLC-HC (DNA, M212, R1). Addressed to Clay, Secretary of State, Washington.
[1] Not found; it was probably a draft of her pamphlet, *A Plan for the Gradual Abolition of Slavery in the United States without Danger of Loss to the Citizens of the South*, published at Baltimore in September of this year. Her proposal sought donation of public lands in various sections of the South for establishment of farms on which Negroes might work to repay the cost of their emancipation while being educated for freedom. The plan included colonization outside the United States for freed Negroes.
[2] "Nashoba," Miss Wright's experimental model community, on Wolf River, about thirteen miles northeast of Memphis. The project terminated in 1828, when the slaves then enlisted were resettled in Haiti.
[3] George Rapp, born in Württemberg, Germany, and there occupied as a farmer and vintner, had come to the United Stats in 1803 as leader of a colony of religious separatists. They founded communal settlements first at Harmony, in Butler County, Pennsylvania, from 1814 to 1824 at New Harmony, in Posey County, Indiana, and then at Economy, eighteen miles below Pittsburgh, on the Ohio River, in Pennsylvania.

DIPLOMATIC NOTES   July 28, 1825

From C. D. E. J. BANGEMAN HUYGENS, New York. Announces his arrival as
Envoy Extraordinary and Minister Plenipotentiary from the Netherlands to
the United States and his expectation of reaching Washington toward the
middle of the next month; requests a friendly reception in American ports
for a corvette used in training naval students. ALS (in French). DNA, RG59,
Notes from Netherlands Legation, vol. 1 (M56, R1). The Chevalier Huygens
served as the Netherlands Minister from 1825 to 1832.

INSTRUCTIONS AND DISPATCHES   July 28, 1825

From GEORGE G. BARRELL, Malaga. Requests a copy of the treaty between the
United States and Colombia, about which he has had inquiries; discusses the
case of five sailors, claiming to be United States citizens, who, after serving on
a Colombian privateer, are in Spanish custody. ALS, "Duplicate." DNA,
RG59, Cons. Disp., Malaga, vol. 2 (M-T217, R-T2). Barrell, a native of
Massachusetts, served as consul for the United States at Malaga from 1817
to 1839. On the treaty between the United States and Colombia, see above,
Clay to Salazar, March 21, 1825.

From SAMUEL HODGES, JR., "Consulate U. States Cape de Verd Islands   Villa
da Praya   St. Iago." Transmits copies of documents relative to "the wanton
Seizure" of "the Brig Ironsides Long Boat" and to the imprisonment, and
subsequent release, of the captain and crewmen from the same vessel, already
reported by Hodges to the State Department, in a dispatch of September 28,
1824; also encloses documents relating to the treatment of (William G.)
Merrill. LS. DNA, RG59, Cons. Disp., Santiago, vol. 1 (M-T434, R1). Received
September 17.
   The enclosed documents assert that the *Ironsides,* of Boston, had been sent
to the Isle of Mayo, on Hodges' orders, to transport salt which he owned at
that port; that he had been requested, and had refused, to purchase additional
salt from the local commandant; that this officer had harassed the masters not
only of the *Ironsides* but of two other vessels sent to load salt already owned
by Hodges. Hodges charges, in his dispatch of September 28, 1824, that his
difficulties with the Portuguese officials arose from his unwillingness to cooperate
in the graft conducted by the local commandant. The specific incident involving
the arrest of the captain and four of the crew of the *Ironsides,* however, grew
out of efforts of the crewmen, purportedly without the captain's knowledge,
to sell two kegs of tobacco to residents of the Island in contravention of customs
regulations. Hodges' specific grounds of complaint at their treatment stemmed
from the requirement by the local officials that the seamen sign statements
written in Portuguese, which they did not understand, and without prior
consultation with him, as United States consul. The incident provided basis
for the charges preferred by Portuguese authorities against Hodges, as cited
above, Clay to Brent, May 10, 1825; Brent to Clay, July 10, 1825.

From SAMUEL HODGES, JR. Transmits copies of a letter received from (Thomas
L. L.) Brent, at Lisbon, and of documents sent by Brent "relative to the
disposition of the Government here towards citizens of the U. States," including
a report injurious to Hodges' character. Hodges considers the imprisonment
of (William G.) Merrill to have been "a flagrant violation of all privileges
granted to consuls." He asks permission to return to the United States the

next spring, stating that he had intended resigning but cannot do so in the face of the accusations against him. ALS. DNA, RG59, Cons. Disp., Santiago, vol. 1 (M-T434, R1). Received September 19. See above, Clay to Brent, May 10, 1825; Brent to Clay, July 10, 1825; Hodges to Clay, this date, no. 1.

From SAMUEL HODGES, JR., "Private." Refers to unfavorable reports against himself, doubtless received by the State Department, through (Thomas L. L.) Brent, from the Portuguese Government; discusses the "despotic and cruel conduct" of "the Governor of this place," whom he believes the originator of the complaints; and states that an article from the *Boston Patriot,* referring to treatment received by the ship *Champion* "here last Novr.," is enclosed. ALS. DNA, RG59, Cons. Disp., Santiago, vol. 1 (M-T434, R1). Received September 19. Having failed to enclose the document referred to here, Hodges transmitted a copy of it on the following day. ALS. *Ibid.* Received September 17. On the *Champion,* see above, Brent to Clay, July 11, 1825. See also above, Clay to Brent, May 10, 1825; Brent to Clay, July 10, 1825.

From SAMUEL HODGES, JR. Encloses an affidavit concerning a British vessel, consigned to Hodges, which in 1820 had been "cut out of this port by Convicts and Soldiers of the Garrison," and expresses fear that the complaint of Portuguese officials against him may relate to this incident, "as the Govr. at that time insinuated to some persons, that I had fitted her out as a Piratical cruiser, to screen himself from the blame of not protecting her." ALS. DNA, RG59, Cons. Disp., Santiago, vol. 1 (M-T434, R1). Received September 17.

From SAMUEL LARNED, Santiago (Chile). Transmits, in addition to various publications, "an unfinished posthumous work of the late Monteagudo, on the subject of a general Congress of the American States, which seems at this moment to engage much of the attention of their respective governments, and is understood to be a favourite project with the Liberator Bolivar." ALS. DNA, RG59, Dip. Disp., Chile, vol. 1 (M-T2, R1). Bernardo Monteagudo, born in Tucumán and educated in law at Córdoba, had been one of the first leaders of the independence movement in Spanish America, active in Argentina, Venezuela, and Peru. In 1821 he had been named Secretary of War in Peru and the following year, for a few months, Minister of State and Foreign Relations of that country. Earlier in 1825 he had been assassinated. An editor of several publications supporting the independence movement, his volume here mentioned was entitled: *Ensayo sobre la Necessidad de una Federacion Jenereal entre los Estados Hispano-Americanos, y Plan de su Organizacion* (Lima, 1825).

Remarks at Lebanon Banquet

[July 29, 1825]

Invited to a public dinner to be held in his honor at Lebanon, Clay had declined because of the illness of his daughter, Eliza. He did, however, attend a dinner given in honor of DeWitt Clinton; and after a toast to Clay's health had been drunk, "he returned thanks in a most pathetic and eloquent address, as well for the affectionate regard manifested for his person by the citizens of Lebanon, as for their kindness and attention to his family during his stay among them." Lexington *Kentucky Reporter,* August 15, 1825, reprinted from Chillicothe *Supporter.* On Clinton's visit to Ohio, see above, Toasts and Speech, July 13, 1825.

INSTRUCTIONS AND DISPATCHES   July 29, 1825

From JOEL R. POINSETT, Mexico (City), no. 10. Reports the status of the claim of Jethro Mitchell, an American citizen, on the Mexican Government; notes that, upon the basis of his own inquiry, the Mexican agents hold themselves responsible to Samuel Gelston, of New York, rather than to Mitchell. LS. DNA, RG59, Dip. Disp., Mexico, vol. 1 (M97, R2). Received September 23.

In separate letters, dated September 24, 1825, addressed to Mitchell and Gelston, both of New York (not further identified), Daniel Brent, at Clay's direction, transmitted copies of Poinsett's dispatch. Copies, in DNA, RG59, Dom. Letters, vol. 21, p. 115 (M40, R19).

The claim, for "seizure of specie in 1822 . . . for the use of the Mexican Government," was conceded by that Government in 1842. *House Docs., 27 Cong., 2 Sess., no. 291, p. 52.* Payment of the claim was not, however, fully liquidated until after the War with Mexico.

MISCELLANEOUS LETTERS   July 29, 1825

From PHILIP C. PENDLETON, "Bath, Berkeley Springs" (Virginia). Requests Clay "to lay before the President" an enclosed letter (not found) "of resignation of the office of Judge of the United States for the Western District of Virginia"; explains that ill health prompted this action; expresses "earnest wishes for the success of the Administration. . . ." ALS. DNA, RG59, Letters of Resig. and Declin.

From Thomas H. Blake

Dear Sir,   Terre Haute July 30th. 1825

On my return from a visit to the lower Wabash Country I received yours of the 3rd instant,[1] and I felt not a little ashamed that I had kept you so long in suspense concerning your lands in Vigo. I have however a short apology to trouble you with. When I last wrote you, in the fall,[2] I expected shortly to see you in Washington and consequently declined writing again, and when the result of the then pending election was finally made known, you had become engaged in your arduous duties at Washington, and that period of deep interest had arrived when almost every thing had to yield to the consideration of the Presidential question. To have addressed you at such a time I should have deemed an intrusion, and since that crisis, your new employments, and more especially the compliments and felicitations of your friends from every quarter, must I think have kept you very much engaged. Add to this, I indulged the belief that you would have every confidence in my attention to your business.

You will find enclosed the receipts of the Collector of this County for your land tax, for 1823, 24 & 25,[3] and you will find in the first a small charge for advertising, as that was the first advice I received of your lands being in this County, and taxable, when I took the liberty without knowing your pleasure to have them charged to me. The tax is very high and indeed so are the taxes of every kind in the State, owing to its poverty at the commencement of the Government and some peculiar pecuniary embarrassments shortly afterwards,[4] but the financial matters of the State have changed very much for the better, taxes are diminishing, and in a few years this obligation will be very little more than nominal. Your lands lie in the north western corner of this County, and are second rate, and are not so valuable on that side of the river as they would be on this, although, if Vermillion County which lies immediately north, should be extended further down the river, which is contemplated by many, and the village of Clinton made the County seat, your lands must be included and their value enhanced. There are some very fine farms at present in the neighborhood, and the Country around is generally improving. No lands in this Country however, except some choice spots, or where they are well improved, will command a good price, and I am satisfied that you could not now get for your lands what you gave for them at first; which is owing principally to so much fine Country having been brought into the market north and north east of us, and which has been very much sought after. When the national road is marked out through this Country[5] there will probably be a rise in landed property,—but independent of every other consideration, it is a fact, that this Country is nearly out of its pecuniary embarrassments and is beginning to be more prosperous than it ever has been.—

I avail myself of this occasion Sir, to assure you that your conduct in relation to the election of President, is warmly approved of in this State by all who have heretofore been your friends, and that your popularity has very much improved. It has had the effect of making many persons (myself among them) friendly to Mr Adams, who never expected to be so, and on the other hand of making the friends of Mr. Adams, who were very hostile to you, devotedly your friends. The friends of Adams and Clay are now harmonizing in the most perfect accord, and seem to participate equally in the triumph of late events, while occasionally is to be heard the muttering of some Jacksonite,—but the cause of the General is certainly down, such a turbulent spirit can not be revived among us.— Poor Call[6] it seems, became engaged last Winter to be married to a Miss Van Horne of the District, being engaged at the same time to a Miss Aigen of Vincennes.[7] He returned, the Wedding day was appointed, but he fled from the fair one to Kentucky, where it is said he is mentally deranged, and of which I have no doubt. I outran him at the last election, but the returns were not brought in in time to render me any service,—at the next election unless something extraordinary should happen I shall

certainly be elected.[8] Whatever may happen to me Sir, I sh [*sic*]
ever be warmly alive to your elevation, prosperity and happiness
    I have the honor to subscribe myself Your Friend & Obt. St.
The Hon. H. Clay.   THO. H. BLAKE
P. S. The tax paid for you, you will please remit by Mail
                                                        T.H.B.—

ALS. DLC-TJC (DNA, M212, R10).
[1] Not found.   [2] Not found.
[3] See above, III, 489, 877; Allen to Clay, July 27, 1825.
[4] Probably a reference to the depression of the period 1818 to 1821, which had
been particularly severe in Indiana. Sickness associated with settlement of the swamp
lands also had depopulated a number of communities in the years 1820 and 1822.
Murray N. Rothbard, *The Panic of 1819, Reactions and Policies* (*Columbia Studies in
the Social Sciences*, no. 605; New York and London, 1962), 41, 78-80; Logan Esarey, *A
History of Indiana from Its Exploration to 1850* (Indianapolis, 1915), 234-36, 247.
[5] See above, Speech, January 17, 1825, note.
[6] Jacob Call, born in Kentucky, had been admitted to the bar and had practiced
law in Vincennes and Princeton, Indiana. He had been a judge of Knox County
circuit court (1817, 1818, 1822-1824) and a member of Congress (to complete an
unexpired term from December 23, 1824, to March 3, 1825). He died by suicide in
April, 1826.   [7] Neither young lady has been identified.
[8] To Congress. See above, Clarke to Clay, September 15, 1823, note.

INSTRUCTIONS AND DISPATCHES   July 30, 1825

From JOHN CUTHBERT, Hamburg. Reports on shipments of grain, "salted Provisions, Bread and Flour" from this port directly to British America. ALS.
DNA, RG59, Cons. Disp., Hamburg, vol. 3 (M-T211, R3).

From JAMES MAURY, Liverpool. States that the "wonderful advance" in cotton
prices is now succeeded by "a depression equally wonderful." LS. *Ibid.*,
Liverpool, vol. 3 (M141, R-T3). Addressed to Secretary of State.

From CONDY RAGUET, Rio de Janeiro. Reports the arrival, July 17, of Sir Charles
Stuart, whose negotiations are the subject of much speculation; states that his
own credentials as Chargé have not arrived; refers to court action on the cases
of the *Exchange* and the *Spermo,* to the discharge of an American seaman who
had been impressed on board a Brazilian vessel, and to an American merchant
at Pernambuco, (Joseph) Ray, who is seeking reversal of an order from the
Imperial Government to leave Brazil, under charges that he "intermeddled in
the political affairs of that Province during the rebellion. . ." (cf. below,
Watson to Clay, December 9, 1826); notes receipt of information that Lord
(Thomas) Cochrane has resigned from the service of Brazil and refuses to
return to Rio de Janeiro; and discusses news from Montevideo which indicates
a weakening of the rebellion in the Banda Oriental and a strengthening of
Brazilian land and naval forces there. LS, "Duplicate." DNA, RG59, Cons.
Disp., Rio de Janeiro, vol. 2 (M-T172, R3). Extract published in Manning
(arr.), *Diplomatic Correspondence . . . Latin-American Nations,* II, 824-28. Ray,
of Pennsylvania, had been appointed in 1816 as consul for the United States
at Pernambuco; but upon demand of the Brazilian Government, which had
suspended delivery of his exequatur, his commission had been revoked in
December, 1818. He was later, in 1836, renamed to the office and served there
until 1842. On the recent rebellion in Pernambuco, see above, Raguet to
Secretary of State, March 11, 1825, note.

MISCELLANEOUS LETTERS   July 30, 1825.

From Isaac Auld, Edisto Island, near Charleston, South Carolina. Requests that a letter be forwarded to Joel R. Poinsett, asking him to send exotic or valuable seeds to the St. Johns, Colleton (County), Agricultural Society. ALS. DNA, RG59, Misc. Letters (M179, R62). Auld was a Charleston physician and one of the founders of the Supreme Council, Mother Council of the World, Ancient and Accepted Scottish Rite of Freemasonry.

INSTRUCTIONS AND DISPATCHES   July 31, 1825

From James J. Wright, Santiago de Cuba. States that the principal competition for trade in this port is between France and the United States; that the tonnage duty of $2.50 per ton, imposed in February on foreign vessels, injures trade "with the Eastern States"; that French consulates have been established at Havana and this port and accredited by the Spanish Government; and that the United States should demand most favored nation treatment. If rumors of impending attack on this colony by Colombia be true, United States naval vessels should be ordered to protect American citizens and property. ALS. DNA, RG59, Cons. Disp., Santiago de Cuba, vol. 1 (M-T55, R1).

MISCELLANEOUS LETTERS   July 31, 1825

From Simon Cameron (Harrisburg, Pennsylvania). Requests payment for publishing the laws. Comments: "Pennsylvania is regenerating. Time will cure her disease." ALS. DNA, RG59, P. and D. of L. Place and date of writing supplied by postmark. Cameron, later United States Senator (1845-1849, 1857-1861, 1867-1877), Secretary of War (1861-1862), and Minister to Russia (1862), was one of the editors of the Harrisburg *Pennsylvania Intelligencer*.

INSTRUCTIONS AND DISPATCHES   August 1, 1825

From Alexander Hammett, Naples. States that Count Lucchesi will set out in fifteen days for his post as Sicilian consul general in the United States. ALS. DNA, RG59, Cons. Disp., Naples, vol. 1 (M-T224, R-T1). Addressed: "J. Clay, Esqre. Secy. of State Washington"; received November 10.

From Christopher Hughes, Copenhagen. Reports his arrival, reception by the Minister of Foreign Affairs, Count (Ernst) Schimmelmann, and expectation that his mission will not be successful. ALS. DNA, RG59, Dip. Disp., Sweden and Norway, vol. 4 (M45, R5). Received September 15. See above, Clay to Hughes, March 24, 1825.

From Robert Montgomery, Alicante (Spain). Reports leprosy in the Province of Catalonia and apprehensions of an outbreak of plague in Marseilles; states that there is no direct trade between Spain and the United States; and notes rumors of a reduction in the "extra duty" on salted fish, to 65 cents per hundredweight, from the first of September. ALS. DNA, RG59, Cons. Disp., Alicante, vol. 1 (M-T357, R1). Addressed to Secretary of State; received October 14.

DAVIS FLOYD, St. Augustine (Florida), recommends "Samuel Blair Esqr. a practising attorney of this place," for appointment to membership in "the Legislative Council of this Territory." Reminds Clay that Blair was educated in Lexington (Kentucky). ALS. DNA, RG59, A. and R. (MR5). Floyd, born in Virginia, had been presiding justice of an Indiana circuit court prior to his removal to Florida in 1823 to serve as one of the United States commissioners to settle land claims. He later became treasurer of Florida Territory. For the appointment of Blair, probably a son of Samuel and brother of William W., see below, Clay to Blair, August 22, 1825.

From William Lytle

Hon. H. Clay   Cincinnati 3rd. August 1825.
Sir

Your favor of 28th. was duly recd. and contents considered, finding myself at a loss for a clear understanding of this business, I have copied your letters of 24th.[2] and 28th. July, and enclosed the same to Judge Rowan[3] with a request of his attention to the same.

I find Judge Barry[4] was my agent in purchasing of Mr. Wickliffe[5] and the letters I have from him leads [sic] to expect he has a Deed from the McDermid heirs for the Lot,[6] in his possession. I have therefore wrote Judge Barry for the Deed if he has it, if he has not to let me know what my rights actually are agreeable to the contract he made.

If on receiving his answer it shall appear there is no Deed in his hands, and that by his contract I am not at present entitled to a Deed, and it shall be out of my power to satisfy Mr. Wickliffes Bond of $1250. & interest. I request you to state if you please what terms I can make within my ability to perform, whereby I can accomidate the business so as to satisfy yourself, Mr Wickliffe & Judge Rowan and close the same, as I apprehend if $1500 or $1800 in cash is requisite, it will not be in my power at present to raise such a sum. Since I wrote you Mr. Kirby[7] has returned from Kentucky without effecting the arangements [sic] I alluded to in my letter of the 25th. July.[8]

I enclose you a Statement of my Acct. with the estate of Colo. Morrison relative to a payment I made for Colo Morrison to Robert Fielding for a Coach, with Mr. Robert Scotts endorsement on the same, of his being satisfied of the correctness of the claim,— likewise my receipt for a Deed for 100 Acres of land, & for a transfer of 125 Acre [sic] of Land.— these lands I have long since sold & am paid for, and I wish you to make the titles so as to quiet the owners.— I shall be much obliged if you send me the

Deed & transfer as Mr. Scotts [*sic*] states you have them with you. If you will not do so, please return the receipt.

My further Claim upon Colo. Morrison as locater [*sic*] for the O Hara & Bowsman & Jas Morrisons Survey[10] which you have conveyed chiefly to Mr. Holmes,[11] I had assigned to Mr. Mr. [*sic*] Avery in may last[12] on a valuable Consideration received by me as far back as 1820, Mr. Scott acknowledged notice of the transfer, but now declines doing anything either to pay my assignee for his claim, or to convey him the land, as this is a fair and Just claim, I hope you will be so good as to settle it, either by payming [*sic*] for the land, or making the conveyance.

I will be prompt in attending to the matter of the Lot as you have requested me, and will endevour [*sic*] to compromise it in some shape if it can be done, without further delay—

I am Sir respectfully Your Ob. Servt.   WM. LYTLE

I did not discover this sheet of paper was torn until I turned over and the mail starting prevents my copying it—

In haste yours &c.   W.L.

ALS. DLC-TJC (DNA, M212, R13). Addressed to Clay at Lebanon, Ohio.
1 Not found.   2 Not found.
3 John Rowan.   4 William T. Barry.
5 Robert Wickliffe.   6 See above, Complaint, *ca.* July 5, 1825.
7 Probably Timothy Kirby.   8 Not found.
9 Cf. above, III, 878.   10 See above, *ibid.*
11 Probably James Holmes, nephew of James Morrison, who under the terms of the latter's will was to be given $4,000 worth of unspecified land, to be selected from an accompanying listing and evaluation of Morrison's holdings. Fayette County, Will Book F, 65, 71, 73.
12 See above, Lytle to Clay, May 25, 1825.

INSTRUCTIONS AND DISPATCHES   August 3, 1825

From JOEL R. POINSETT, Mexico (City), no. 11. Refers to a dispute between Mexico and Guatemala over the Province of Chiapa. On the advice of Poinsett the Minister from Guatemala has addressed "a note to the Secretary of State [Lucas Alamán] setting forth the evils which would inevitably result to both parties from any act of violence on the part of Mexico; and proposing to refer the settlement of this dispute to the Congress which is shortly to be assembled at Panama." Poinsett hopes this "will produce a good effect." Transmits copies of correspondence with Alamán concerning "a foolish publication" on the treatment of foreigners. LS. DNA, RG59, Dip. Disp., Mexico, vol. 1 (M97, R2). Received September 16. Juan de Dios Mayorga was at this time Guatemalan Minister in Mexico.

APPLICATIONS, RECOMMENDATIONS   August 3, 1825

GEORGE BLAKE, Boston, testifies to the respectability and veracity of (Zebedee) Cook (Jr.), the writer of an accompanying letter. ALS. DNA, RG59, A. and R. (MR1). See below, Cook to Clay, this date.

ZEB[EDEE] COOK, JR., Boston, recommends, in view of newspaper statements that the King of Spain (Ferdinand VII) refuses to accredit (Robert) Montgomery as United States consul for Alicante, the appointment to this position of George Bright Adams, a native of Boston, for "several years" a commission merchant at Alicante. ALS. DNA, RG59, A. and R. (MR1). Cook, also born in Massachusetts, was president of the Eagle Insurance Company, of Boston, which he had established in 1822, after an earlier venture in the mercantile commission business. He was one of the founders of the Massachusetts Horticultural Society, in 1829, and an active politician, serving as a Whig member of the Massachusetts House of Representatives from 1835 to 1838. Adams, as a resident of Pennsylvania, was appointed United States consul at Alicante in 1827 and held the post until 1834.

INSTRUCTIONS AND DISPATCHES   August 4, 1825

From JOSHUA DODGE, Marseilles. Transmits a copy of another letter from the Board of Health, Marseilles, on the subject of the plague on two French vessels from Alexandria. ALS. DNA, RG59, Cons. Disp., Marseilles, vol. 2 (M-T220, R1). Received October 5.

From F[RANCIS] B[ENJAMIN] FAURES, "Point Peter Guadelupe." Transmits an ordinance, issued by the Governor of the Island, concerning reopening of the ports following a recent hurricane, and describes the damage resulting from the storm. Requests instructions in regard to a dispute with local authorities over the punishment of an American sailor for resisting arrest. ALS. Ibid., Guadeloupe, vol. 1 (M-T208, R-T1). Faures, a Pennsylvanian, was United States commercial agent at Pointe-à-Pitre until 1831.

From HARRIS E. FUDGER, Santa Marta (Colombia). Reports that his efforts to take charge of the property of Charles Hildebrand have been frustrated by action of (Charles) MacNeal, acting consul at Cartagena, who claims jurisdiction. Requests the Secretary's opinion on the subject. LS. Ibid., Santa Marta, vol. 1 (M-T427, R1). Addressed to Secretary of State; received September 25. Fudger, of Boston, had been appointed consul for the United States at Santa Marta in July, 1823. He died there in 1826. Hildebrand, a naturalized United States citizen of German birth, had drowned near Santa Marta in April, 1825. Fudger, who on April 25 had reported Hildebrand's death to the State Department, on October 12, 1825 (routine documents omitted by editors), filed an inventory of the estate. Ibid.

MISCELLANEOUS LETTERS   August 4, 1825

From WILLIAM SMYTH, Island of St. Thomas. Asserts that the United States should acquire an island in the West Indies; suggests that the American claims against Denmark (see above, Clay to Hughes, March 24, 1825, no. 1) be settled, in part, by the cession of one of her West Indian possessions; and discusses in considerable detail the advantages that would accrue from ownership of the Island of St. Johns. Smyth asks that this information, and his name, be kept secret, that he be informed in advance if action should be taken in this connection, and that he be appointed to some office. ALS. DNA, RG59, Misc. Letters (M179, R63).

INSTRUCTIONS AND DISPATCHES   August 5, 1825

From JOEL R. POINSETT (Mexico City), no. 12. Describes the opening of the extraordinary session of the Mexican Congress; encloses a statement of the finances of the country; stresses the bias of the Government in favor of Great Britain and the indifference with which the United States is regarded; discusses (in code) certain Mexican officials and the probability that, without a change of administration "or unless this government is controlled by the congress of Panama," the country "will not form a part of the great American system"; refers to the constitutions adopted by the Mexican States and to religious matters; expresses (in code) anxiety about the boundary line and a conviction that the United States should extend its territory "toward the river del norte [Rio Grande]"; and states (in code) that "the invasion of Cuba is one of the subjects to be treated of in secret session." LS, coded passages deciphered in State Department file. DNA, RG59, Dip. Disp., Mexico, vol. 1 (M97, R2). Received October 3.

Check to William Ferguson

Lebanon[1] 6 August 1825

Pay to William Ferguson or order one hundred and seventy five dollars.   H. CLAY

Cashr. of the Off. of Dt. & Dt of the B. U. States   Washington City[2]

ADS. DLC-TJC (DNA, M212, R16). Endorsed by Ferguson to Allen and Grant; presented for payment, after additional endorsements, by "W. A. Bradley Cas by Jno. H. Reily Teller—" The Clays stayed at the Ferguson house while in Lebanon. William A. Bradley, later mayor of Washington, was cashier of the Bank of Washington. Reily not further identified.

[1] Ohio.   [2] Richard Smith.

From Finis Ewing

Dear Sir,   Boonville August 6. 1825

Your favour of the 16. June[1] was not recd 'till two days since. I am aware, from its nature, that your "new office is any thing but a bed of Roses" therfore [sic] I do not expect to enjoy, on my part, the luxury of *your* private correspondence as *often* as would otherwise be desirable—

I have seen your address to your constituents,[2] & can assure you it was a great feast to myself & others of your old & stable friends— Said one, of no common intelligence, "it is a *complete* refutation of all the charges &c"— I think there has not been much change of publick oppinion [sic], here, since I wrote you last   there is still a noise kept up by Duff Green & his Minions   I regret that his paper[3] has so extensive a circulation in this State— Some of his Subscribers, however will discontinue their patronage.— There is, & will be a mighty effort to oust Col. Scott[4]— The hobby is that "he violated the known will of his Constituents"—this, however, is

not quite so certain, yet,   I am impressed that, at the time Col.
Scott voted, a majority of his Constituents were in favour of Genl.
Jackson i e in preference to Mr. Adams— But, I have never heard
of any thing like formal instructions being sent to him, or given
him except to Vote for yourself. It is, at this time quite unceartain
[sic] wheather [sic] he can be re elected— it will depend, in a great
measure, on the course of the president, with regard to the western
Country between this & next August— If Scott should not be
re elected, the Vote of Missouri will probably be given to Genl,
Jackson, in case the election should again go to the House.—

I do most cordially approve your sentiments with regard to
previous promises &c. in the appointment of offices by the Genl,
Government they accord with your whole political course— I am
gratified that you express a good oppinion [sic] of our mutual freind
[sic] Col. Reeves.[5] He is "honest faithful & capable"—

It gives me great pleasure to hear you say with such emphasis
that the president &c. "are animated with the best intentions &
warmest zeal to promote the publick good." You are aware Sir,
that the *Western* people have long looked on Mr. Adams as one
who felt inimical to their growth prosperity &c— If he ever felt
such sentiments I hope he does not now   if he do, I am sure he
was unwise in selecting H. Clay. for his *first* adviser— While I
feel & express my wish for the promotion of the interests of the
West, I would not be understood as disregarding the interests of the
East the *North,* the *South.*—

There is one particular subject which the people of the West,
particularly the States of Missouri, Illinoise]sic[, Indiania [sic] &c,
&c. feel a deep, very deep interest in—. That is the graduation of
the price of publick lands— I am persuaded that nine-tenths,
perhaps more, of the people are exceedingly anxious that such a
law should pass and I am persuaded Sir, if the president could
make personal observations on the situation &c, of the several
States & Teritories [sic] in which the Gov ment hold lands, he
would think that such a measure would be *wise, humane, & Just.*
I cannot give you, in the limits of a letter, the reasons why such a
law should pass— I will only now say, that it is the unshaken
beleif [sic] of many well informed Gentlemen, that the interests
of the General Government would be promoted, & benefit extended
to thousands of worthy citizens— There are multiplied Millions
of Acres of land that will not sell, perhaps in a century to come
at the present prices,[6] a great deal of which would sell in a few
years if the prices were graduated according to their vallue [sic]—
and why not? Does not every individual who sells land sell it on
that principle?— If the president would take time to contemplate

this subject, & it should meet with his approbation, & he recommend it, if in but a few words, to the next Congress,[7] I have no doubt, but it would fasten him in the affections of tens of thousands of the citizens of the West— & who of the East or else where could reasonably object?— I may be mistaken, but I think that you Sir will approve of the measure, if so, permit me to say, you would do your Country a great benefit to urge the measure on the attention of the president, and by doing so you would bring the western people under additional obligations to one who has always been their most prominent centinal [sic] in the councils of this Nation

I speak, you will perceive with great plainness & freedom, but beleive me, that it is with the adage fully in view that, "flatery [sic] is falshood [sic]"— Feeling as I do, great solicitude on this subject for many substantial reasons, I will take the liberty to request, if consistant [sic] with your views of propriety, that when you shall have obtained the presidents views on this subject, that you will have the goodness to communicate them, with your own, to me as soon as it may suit your conveniance [sic]— I repeat that I don't expect you to answer *all* my scribles [sic] (for I may frequently drop you a line on various subjects) but I do wish an answer, when convenient to this[8]— May Heaven give you health & peace in time & eternity.   FINIS EWING

ALS. DLC-HC (DNA, M212, R1). Addressed to Clay at Washington. Ewing, a native of Virginia, brother of Robert, Young, and Urbin Ewing, had lived for a brief time in Tennessee before settling in Logan County, Kentucky, in 1794. He had been ordained a Presbyterian minister in 1800 and, in 1810, had helped found the Cumberland Presbyterian Church, of which he became a leader. He had moved to Missouri in 1820. The Cumberland Presbyterian Church had broken from the Presbyterian Synod of Kentucky in 1810, in protest against the latter's educational requirements for the ministry, its adherence to the doctrine of pre-destination, and its assertion of hierarchical authority.

1 Not found.   2 Above, March 26, 1825.
3 The *St. Louis Enquirer*.   4 John Scott.

5 Benjamin H. Reeves had moved from Virginia to Christian County, Kentucky, about 1800, as a boy, and in 1818 had removed to Howard County, Missouri, where he had become a delegate to the State constitutional convention (1820), State senator (1822-1824), and Lieutenant Governor (1824-1825). After again serving as a Missouri State senator in 1832 and 1834, he returned to Kentucky and represented Todd County in that State legislature from 1838 to 1841.

6Under the act of April 24, 1820, public land prices were now set at a minimum of $1.25 an acre, with the land to be first offered at public auction to the highest bidder. 3 *U. S. Stat.*, 566-67.

7 In his annual message, December 6, 1825, President Adams made no recommenda-tion for alteration in the price of public lands, though he did urge relief for public land claimants by extension of the time limits under previous legislation, most recently the act of May 18, 1824, which had expired on April 18, 1825 (4 *U. S. Stat.*, 24-25), for payment of old credit contracts through relinquishment of fractional holdings. Richardson (comp.), *A Compilation of the Messages and Papers of the Presidents. . . ,* II, 305.   8 No answer has been found.

INSTRUCTIONS AND DISPATCHES   August 6, 1825

From CHRISTOPHER HUGHES, Copenhagen, no. 1. Reports his reception by the

King (Frederick VI). ALS. DNA, RG59, Dip. Disp., Sweden and Norway, vol. 4 (M45, R5). Received October 25.

MISCELLANEOUS LETTERS   August 6, 1825

From RICHARD RUSH, Treasury Department. Encloses a letter concerning illegal tonnage duties charged American vessels at St. John's, New Brunswick, and requests that the British Government be asked to order "their proper officers in North America and the West Indies" to abstain from such charges and to refund sums already paid. LS. DNA, RG59, Misc. Letters (M179, R63).

INSTRUCTIONS AND DISPATCHES   August 7, 1825

From ALEXANDER BURTON, Cádiz. Transmits "a copy of a Royal Order, obtained through our Legation at Madrid, directing the repayment" to Burton of the duty exacted from the American Brig *Dick,* "and, further, exempting American Vessels hereafter entering the Ports of Spain, in distress, from the like tax"; also transmits copies of a decision of the Spanish Government, refusing to place foreign vessels in the colonial trade under Spanish licenses on the same footing as its own, and a decree relative to a dispute between Spanish and French officials over a search for contraband; reports that French ships continue to enforce the quarantine of the port against vessels from the West Indies and the United States, even against an American ship from Antwerp carrying furniture for (Alexander H.) Everett; and notes movement of Spanish vessels preparatory to an expedition to Cuba. ALS. DNA, RG59, Cons. Disp., Cádiz, vol. 4 (M-T186, R4). Received October 3.

From CHRISTOPHER HUGHES, Copenhagen, no. 3. Describes his audience with the King (Charles XIV) upon taking leave of the Court of Sweden. ALS. DNA, RG59, Dip. Disp., Sweden and Norway, vol. 4 (M45, R5). Received September 30.

From Susan Clay Duralde

My dear mother and father   Near N. Orleans 8th. August 1825
I hope this letter will find you safely arrived at Washington. I have heard that you regret leaving Ashland very much, but for my part I am very glad of it for I think you worked too much, stay'd at home too much and you were too much plagued there, at Washington you will be forced to go more into the world and although you will perhaps not like it much at first, you will soon get accustomed to it. I am glad of your removal to Washington on another account, it will be more convenient for us to visit you there because we can leave here in June and return as soon in the fall as we please there being at all times sufficient water in the sea. Mr Duralde[1] promises me that we shall go next summer, he has even told all of his friends that we intend to do so, however I will not be so certain as I was last spring for fear of being again disappointed.

My eldest son[2] enjoys very good health but his poor little brother[3] has been sick for a long time, he has always been delicate and now he is cutting his teeth, he has also had the fever caused by a large abcess which was forming in his side, since we have had it lanced he has been a good deal relieved but he still suffers so much from his teeth that we are sometimes fearful we will not be able to raise him. Mr Duralde and myself are both well. I have had the fever two or three times occasioned by my having eaten too much fruit. New Orleans continues to be quite healthy and as the season is advancing we are in hopes we will pass it off without any yellow fever.

I wish you would let me know what you intend to do with Eliza,[4] whether you inten[d] to send her to Philadelphia or to keep her with you. You have quite a small family now. I suppose Mr & Mrs Erwin will stay with you until she is confined.[5] I advised her to do so, because it is much better to be with one's relations at such a time than to be amongst strangers as I suppose she would be if she left you. I am in hopes they will visit N.O. again this winter. Ann never writes to me, I do not know whether to attribute it to her indifference for me or to her laziness, I hope it is the latter. Mr Duralde wrote a few days ago to Papa.[6] Give my love to him, to Ann & her husband and kiss Eliza and the little boys[7] for Your affectionnate [sic] daughter   S. DURALDE.

ALS. Elsie Jackson Kelly Collection, Henry Clay Memorial Foundation, Lexington, Kentucky. Addressed to Clay at Washington.
[1] Martin Duralde (Jr).   [2] Martin Duralde III.
[3] Henry Clay Duralde.
[4] See above, Clay to Crittenden, July 25, 1825; below, Clay to Crittenden, August 22, 1825, note.
[5] Julia D. Erwin, first child of Anne Brown Clay Erwin and James Erwin, was born December 24, 1825.   [6] No letter found.
[7] James Brown Clay and John Minor Clay.

INSTRUCTIONS AND DISPATCHES   August 8, 1825

From CHRISTOPHER HUGHES, Copenhagen, no. 4. Encloses documents relative to the conclusion of negotiations between (John) Connell and officials of the Government of Sweden. ALS. DNA, RG59, Dip. Disp., Sweden and Norway, vol. 4 (M45, R5). Received September 30. Cf. above, Hughes to Clay, July 15, 1825.

INSTRUCTIONS AND DISPATCHES   August 9, 1825

From RUFUS KING, Cheltenham (England), no. 1. Explains his continued presence at Cheltenham; incorporates into this communication copies of his correspondence with (George) Canning. States that he expressed, in an interview with Canning, the desire of the United States "to engage Russia, France and Great Britain to influence Spain to make peace with the New States [of South America] by acknowledging their Independence," to which

"Canning *soon* replied that such a hope was desperate, that Russia was unchangeable on this point." Reports Canning's views concerning French activity in the Caribbean, his statement that England felt herself "so greatly reinforced and sustained by the Views of the United States" that she had directed her "efforts to prevail on Spain to conclude an Armistice with the New States," and his suggestion that a note drawn up by England, the United States, and France might lead Spain to "consent to such armistice, especially if . . . it be provided that Cuba and Porto Rico shall remain under the Dominion of Spain." Canning promised to put his views in writing, but King has not yet heard further from him. LS. DNA, RG59, Dip. Disp., Great Britain, vol. 32 (M30, R28). Received September 22. Published in *American State Papers, Foreign Relations,* VI, 246.

APPLICATIONS, RECOMMENDATIONS   August 9, 1825

SAMUEL BLAIR, St. Augustine, solicits appointment as a member of the Legislative Council of the Territory of Florida. ALS. DNA, RG59, A. and R. (MR5). See below, Clay to Blair, August 22, 1825.

JOSEPH M. HERNANDEZ, St. Augustine, declines appointment as a member of the Legislative Council of the Territory of Florida and recommends Peter Mitchell, formerly a member of that body, in his place. ALS. DNA, RG59, A. and R. (MR5). Hernandez, born in St. Augustine, owned a large sugar plantation and other land at the head of the Matanzas River. He had become an American citizen upon the transfer of Florida to the United States, had served as Territorial delegate to Congress during the session of 1822-1823, and was now a member of the Territorial legislature. He became a brigadier general of militia during the Indian conflicts of the late 1830's in this area. Mitchell, born in Scotland, was a resident of St. Augustine and had represented St. Johns County on the legislative council for the last two years.

From William DuVal

Dear Sir,   Buckingham County Virga Augt 10th. 1825.
    I was much pleased to observe that your Constituents & the Kentuckians in General & your Western Friends approved of your Vote in Congress in favor of electing Mr Adams as President of the United States in preference to the other Candidates   Many in this state think now, that you made the best Selection, & that you exercised a Sound discretion
    I received a Letter from my Son John P. DuVal of Fauquir [sic] County last Week requesting me to write to you to endeavor to obtain for him an Appointment of a district Judge when ever a vacancy happens. or the Appointmen [sic] of Navy Agent at Pensacola or any other that is worth about $1000 per Year[1]
    John P. DuVal before he was 21 Years Old entered the Service. & before the close of the War he was promoted to a Captaincy
    It is probable that Mr Francis T Brooke, Governor Pleasants,

& Judge Dade[2] of Virginia may write to you on this Subject. I gave John a Liberal Education, his Talents are above mediocrity, he is said to be a good Lawyer temperate and moral & a sincere Friend to his Country. he has an amiable Wife and Three Children

I will candidly inform you that such an appointment would be convenient to him— I gave him a debt of $1200. another of $5000 the Lawyer Recd the money & died Insolvent— The large Debt was against Colo Richard M Johnson & his Brother James Johnson as Heirs to their Father[3] It said [*sic*] Little can be obtained from them. Having emancipated my Slaves & given John good Land on Green River I supposed the above would have settled him with every Conveniency, He can't in Consequence of the above losses, do so. John, is not extravagant—

Altho he is my Son, I would not have said a word in his favor, if I did not believe, that he would discharge any appointment of minor Consequence with Honor to him self & Credit to his Country. I am with great Esteem, Yr obedient Servant.

WILLIAM DUVAL

ALS. DNA, RG59, A. and R. (MR2). Addressed to Clay.

[1] John Pope DuVal, brother of Samuel Pope DuVal and of William Pope DuVal, had been born and educated in Virginia, had been admitted to the bar in 1811, and since then, except for a period of service in the War of 1812, had practiced his profession in Richmond. In 1827 he moved to Tallahassee, Florida, though he did not receive a governmental appointment, as here requested. From 1832 to 1836 he lived at Bardstown, Kentucky, where he recruited volunteers for the Texan war of independence. Thereafter he returned to Florida, served as secretary of the Territory from 1837 to 1839, and in 1840 published a *Compilation of the Public Acts of the Legislative Council of the Territory of Florida, Passed prior to 1840.*

[2] James Pleasants; William A. G. Dade, judge of Fauquier Circuit Court for single terms in 1824 and 1828.   [3] Robert Johnson.

INSTRUCTIONS AND DISPATCHES   August 10, 1825

From JOEL R. POINSETT, Mexico (City), no. 13. States (in code) that the Secretary of State (Lucas Alamán) is wholly devoted to England and that he has commented, in secret session of the Senate, that Mexico should regard the United States as an enemy, that she "had Ever-y-thing to fear from our am-bit-ion and noth-ing to hope from our fri-end-ship." Poinsett doubts that the Ministry will be able to maintain itself "against the str-ong party of the opposition." LS, coded passages deciphered in State Department file. DNA, RG59, Dip. Disp., Mexico, vol. 1 (M97, R2). Received October 3.

INSTRUCTIONS AND DISPATCHES   August 11, 1825

From SAMUEL HODGES, JR., "Villa da Praya   St. Iago." Transmits copies of documents announcing a prohibition of importation "of Gun Powder, Cotton, Tobacco, Wine and Spirits" and of exportation of specie and "Portuguese Copper Coin." LS. DNA, RG59, Cons. Disp., Santiago, Cape Verde, vol. 1 (M-T434, R1). Received September 23.

From RUFUS KING, Cheltenham [no. 2]. Transmits a copy of "Mr. Canning's promised Communication" (see above, King to Clay, August 9, 1825), which constitutes an effort to sustain the British proposal in preference to that of the United States. King adds that, in the absence of (James) Brown from Paris (see above, Brown to Clay, July 15, 1825), he has "no means of counter-vailing" a statement by Canning that France has "returned a negative answer" to Brown's presentation of the American project. LS. DNA, RG59, Dip. Disp., Great Britain, vol. 32 (M30, R28). Received September 15. Extract published in Manning (arr.), *Diplomatic Correspondence . . . Latin-American Nations*, III, 1557-60. Canning's note, dated August 7 and marked "Confidential," states that information received from Lord Granville leaves "no doubt that the French Government have returned a negative answer to Mr. Brown. . . ." Of the great powers, Canning notes, France has most to gain from an adjustment of Spain's differences with Latin America, but her "awe . . . of the Continental Alliance prevents her" acting. Russia, he continues, is "the moving Soul" of that entente, "and the United States are grievously mistaken if they imagine that the Emperor of Russia is . . . open to the blandishments of flattery, so far as to be led to use the influence he possesses, and is proud to be thought to possess in Europe, in a Direction quite different from that which his principles, his prejudices, and *perhaps* his interests prescribes." Since the intervention of the Continental Allies for effecting peace between Spain and her former colonies "is hopeless," Canning proposes that Britain and the United States "consider what we can do, to preserve Cuba to Spain. . . ." He therefore suggests a tripartite agreement by Britain, France, and the United States, "disclaiming each for for [sic] ourselves, any intention to occupy Cuba and protesting each against such occupation by either of the others." The "mutual and reciprocal respect for each other is a security for . . . mutual abstinence" on the part of the United States and Britain; but "France," Canning argues, "is swayed so much by the humor of the day, and proceeds in a course of policy so devious and vacillating, that she is really capable of *blundering* into a maritime War, without having seen its danger much less calculated its consequences." As an instance he points to the danger posed by the recent service of the French fleet as convoy for a Spanish troop movement from the Philippines to Havana, with no awareness of the possibility of consequent involvement in the Spanish war with the Latin American States. The French Government, having confessed its ignorance of the fleet action, had then protested that Count Dongelot, the Governor of Martinique and captain general of French forces in the West Indies, carried "clear instructions for the only case in which there was any probability of his being called upon to interfere in Spanish Colonial concerns. . . . Nothing less than to send French Troops to the Havanna if the Governor of that place should ask his assistance to put down Internal Disturbance!"

DIPLOMATIC NOTES   August 12, 1825

From SEVERIN LORICH, Philadelphia. Acknowledges receipt of Clay's note of May 10, 1825; argues at length, citing navigation laws of both Sweden and the United States and treaties between the two countries, that the seizure of the *Carl John* (*Johan*) should not have occurred. ALS. DNA, RG59, Notes from Swedish Legation, vol. 3 (M60, R2). Cf. below, Clay to Lorich, September 20, 1825.

INSTRUCTIONS AND DISPATCHES   August 12, 1825

From JAMES E. BRICE, Cap Haitien. Notes the threat of an uprising, after French recognition of the independence of Haiti (above, Holden to Clay, July 16, 1825), and the restoration of order. ALS. DNA, RG59, Cons. Disp., Cap Haitien, vol. 5 (M9, R-T5). Brice, a native of Maryland, was commercial agent for the United States at Cap Haitien.

From ALEXANDER H. EVERETT, Paris, no. 3. States his intention to leave for Madrid on August 15; expresses regret that (James) Brown's absence (see above, Brown to Clay, July 15, 1825, no. 1) has made it impossible "to obtain a copy of the instruction to Mr. Middleton on the subject of the intervention of the Allied Powers in the affairs of Spain and South America" (above, Clay to Middleton, May 10, 1825); and declares his intention of replying to a note, received by (Hugh) Nelson after the latter had taken leave of the King of Spain (see above, Nelson to Clay, July 13, 1825), by presenting "a detailed review of the present state of" relations between the United States and Spain, in an effort to show the advantages of cultivating American good will. Comments that French influence on the Spanish Government will be used in favor of acknowledgment of the independence of the South American Republics and that, because of the opening of French ports and of Gibraltar to South American privateers, the latter are now "swarming round the coasts of the mother country." Discusses French recognition of the independence of Haiti, the failure of an attempt "to convert the French five per cent stocks into threes" (above, Brown to Clay, April 1, 1825, note), and reports from Greece announcing the capture of Ibrahim Pasha (cf. above, Moore to Clay, May 31, 1825, note). Observes that (Daniel) Sheldon, whose ill health has caused him to leave Paris, will probably not live longer than three or four months. ALS. DNA, RG59, Dip. Disp., Spain, vol. 25 (M31, R27). Received September 25. Extracts published in Manning (arr.), *Diplomatic Correspondence . . . Latin-American Nations,* III, 2056-58.

From SAMUEL HODGES, JR. "Villa da Praya   St. Iago." Reports "a flagrant outrage" committed last month on the American flag by the British "ship Redwing D. C. Clavering Esqr. Commander," which fired on "the Brig Ruby of Bucksport, Maine Benjamin Shute, Master," and then sent a boarding party to search her, in the harbor of St. Nicholas. LS. DNA, RG59, Cons. Disp., Santiago, Cape Verde, vol. 1 (M34, R1). Received September 23. Neither Clavering nor Shute has been further identified.

From THOMAS M. RODNEY, Wilmington. Two letters enclose extracts of correspondence from Havana. LS. *Ibid.,* Havana, vol. 3 (M-T20, R3). One enclosure states that a small American naval squadron is in the harbor and that the city is sickly. A second enclosure reports that the French fleet is in the harbor and that France has reportedly acknowledged the independence of the Island of St. Domingo.

INSTRUCTIONS AND DISPATCHES   August 13, 1825

From CHRISTOPHER HUGHES, Copenhagen, "Private." Discusses the reaction in Europe to the sale of ships by the King of Sweden "to the Goldsmith's of London, for the account of Mexico" (see above, Hughes to Clay, July 8,

1825, note); expresses a conviction that his own mission (see above, Clay to Hughes, March 24, 1825) will not be successful; reports great interest among Danish officials concerning the proposed commercial treaty with the United States (see above, Pedersen to Clay, April 4, 1825). ALS. DNA, RG59, Dip. Disp., Sweden and Norway, vol. 4 (M45, R5). Received September 30.

From J[OHN] ADAMS SMITH, London, no. 11. Notes the departure of (Hugh) Nelson from London, the reception in England of that country's treaty with Mexico, which will be returned for alterations (see above, Poinsett to Clay, May 5, 1825, note), and a report that Buenos Aires will not within the next year send a Minister to England but will soon send one to the United States; encloses recent acts of Parliment concerning trade; and states that (Rufus) King will probably be presented at Court around the first of October. LS. *Ibid.*, Great Britain, vol. 32 (M30, R28). Addressed to Secretary of State; received September 22. Extract published in Manning (arr.), *Diplomatic Correspondence . . . Latin-American Nations,* III, 1561.

From Young Ewing

State of Missouri   Lillard County   Lexington August 15th 1825.
Dear Sir.

there being a vacancy in the office of receiver of public monies of the Land office in this place by the resignation of Genl W. D. Mc.Ray.[1]

I have thought proper to be an applicant to fill said vacancy.

[States that he is not personally known to Clay; that he "was a Kentuckian"; that he supported Clay in the presidential election; that Clay probably knows his uncles, Robert, Young, Urbin, and Finis Ewing, and his cousin, E. M. Ewing,[2] of Russellville (Kentucky); and that he is "not the man who applied for the appointment of receiver when this office was first established."[3] He has no personal acquaintanceship with the Missouri congressional delegation, although he may be remembered by (Thomas H.) Benton; he is known by John J. Crittenden and Francis Johnson.]

I will only say to you with the exception of a party about St Louis aided by Genl. Duff. Green as Editor we are will [*sic*] satisfied that you did not vote for the "Military Cheiftain [*sic*]" as President of the United States,. Your speech on the subject of internal improvement[4] has with the better informed honest part of this western population added much to your. political character   Your exertions for our ad[missi]on as a State into the union[5] ar[e] not altogether forgotten,   Your. freind [*sic*] the Honbl. David Todd whom we elected as. an Elector from the western district is your frend [*sic*] in deed any attention you may think proper to bestow in promotion of my. views will be greatfully [*sic*] acknowledged by. Your. sincere freind [*sic*]   YOUNG EWING
Honbl H. Clay

ALS. DNA, RG59, A. and R. (MR2). Endorsements indicate that this letter was "Referred to the Commr of the Land Office" and, by the Commissioner, George Graham, to the Secretary of the Treasury (Richard Rush). Ewing, a nephew of John Ewing and a cousin of Robert A. and William Y. C. Ewing, as well as kinsman of those herein mentioned, had formerly served as sheriff of Logan County, Kentucky. He now resided in Lafayette (earlier known as Lillard) County, Missouri, where he had been clerk of both county and circuit courts. After receiving a temporary appointment in November, 1825, as receiver of public moneys, he was formally named to this position in May, 1826.

1 William D. McRay, a resident of Missouri, had been appointed to the office in January, 1824.   2 Ephraim McLean Ewing.
3 William Y. C. Ewing, son of Urbin Ewing.
4 Above, January 17, 1825.   5 See above, III, 15-50 *passim*.

INSTRUCTIONS AND DISPATCHES   August 15, 1825

From CHARLES SAVAGE, Providence, Rhode Island. Reports his return to this country from his consulate, which he left on May 6; explains his inability to come to Washington, because of fatigue and weakness from illness. Transmits the congratulations of President "Arza" (Manuel José Arce), of Centre-America (Federation of Central America), to John Quincy Adams upon his elevation to the Presidency, "that pleasure . . . [being] augmented from the circumstances of his [Arce's] having a personal acquaintance with" Adams. Expresses gratitude for the helpfulness encountered in his relations with the Government of Centre-America. ALS. DNA, RG59, Cons. Disp., Guatemala, vol. 1 (M-T337, R1). Received August 20.

MISCELLANEOUS LETTERS   August 15, 1825

From JAMES PH. PUGLIA, "professor of for. Langs., Mount Airy's College, Germantown, Philada. Co., Pennsylvania." Claims that a patent, granted to an Englishman, Nathaniel Sylvester, for an "Invention of *preventing fraud on bank-notes, Checks* &c.," conflicts with his own *"original* Invention of preventing and detecting Forgeries on all kind [*sic*] of documents," for which a patent was granted August 13, 1822. ALS. DNA, RG59, Misc. Letters (M179, R63). Puglia has not been further identified. Sylvester was listed as a resident of New York when his patent was issued, on July 12, 1825.

From RICHARD RUSH, Washington. Transmits a copy of a note from (George) Canning, written after Rush's departure from England, which seems to settle "the case of Mr Macdonnel." LS. DNA, RG59, Dip. Disp., Great Britain, vol. 32 (M30, R28). See above, Smith to Secretary of State, June 15, 1825.

DIPLOMATIC NOTES   August 16, 1825

From CHARLES R. VAUGHAN (Washington). Announces his arrival as Envoy Extraordinary and Minister Plenipotentiary to the United States to succeed Stratford Canning. LS. DNA, RG59, Notes from British Legation, vol. 14 (M50, R15).

MISCELLANEOUS LETTERS   August 16, 1825

From WILLIAM C. SOMERVILLE, Washington. Reports that he left his "residence in Virginia yesterday the 15 of Augt." to proceed on his mission to Sweden. His departure has been delayed by a severe illness, from which he has "not yet entirely recovered." ALS. DNA, RG59, Dip. Disp., Sweden and Norway, vol. 4 (M45, R5).

APPLICATIONS, RECOMMENDATIONS   August 16, 1825

EDWARD HALL, deputy collector of the port of Mobile, recommends Henry Hitchcock for appointment as United States district attorney for the District of Mobile. ALS. DNA, RG59, A. and R. (MR2). Hall has not been further identified. Hitchcock, born and educated in Vermont, had moved in 1815 to Alabama, where he had served as secretary of the Territory in 1818 and thereafter as State attorney general. He now received an interim appointment as Federal attorney for the Southern District of Alabama, to which office he was formally appointed in December, 1825, and held this position for the next decade. In 1836 he was named an associate justice in the State judiciary and the following year became chief justice of the State.

JAMES LANMAN, Norwich, Connecticut, solicits appointment as United States district judge for Connecticut, mentions his aversion to returning to the practice of law "after a considerable absence and having practised at the Bar of the Supreme Court for twenty years." ALS. DNA, RG59, A. and R. (MR1). Lanman, who had been defeated as a candidate for reappointment to the Senate in 1825, did not receive the position here requested, but he became a judge on the State superior and supreme courts (1826-1829), mayor of Norwich (1831-1834), and a member of the State legislature (1833).

INSTRUCTIONS AND DISPATCHES   August 17, 1825

From JOEL R. POINSETT, Mexico (City), no. 14. Transmits "the final answer" of the Mexican Government in regard to the road from Missouri to Santa Fé. Poinsett has not made further proposals in writing because he "ascertained they would not have been acceded to." LS. DNA, RG59, Dip. Disp., Mexico, vol. 2 (M97, R3). In the enclosure, dated August 16 (a translation), Lucas Alamán informs Poinsett that a decision on the road must await a regular session of the Mexican Congress but that, if informed of the demarcation of the road by the United States "to the presumed frontier," a Mexican custom house "might be situated in a convenient position, and the necessary measures might be taken for the safety of travellors [sic]." Alamán is pleased that the two negotiations, for commerce and boundaries, have been separated and expresses willingness to begin conversations, although "the limits cannot be definitely settled until the reconnoissance of the country has been made. . . ." Received September 19. See above, Clay to Poinsett, March 26, 1825; Poinsett to Clay, July 18, 22, 1825.

From JOEL R. POINSETT, Mexico (City), no. 15. Transmits a translation of a note, dated August 16, from the Mexican Secretary of State, and Poinsett's reply. Reports that the receipt of information of a large French force at Martinique and of a squadron of French warships moving toward Havana "has produced a great sensation here—& a strong disposition exists . . . to take very decisive measures against the French residents & against the commerce of that nation—a disposition which . . . [Poinsett will] use every exertion to soften and restrain within due bounds." This dispatch is being forwarded by a courier sent by the British Chargé, "by way of New-York," to carry "intelligence of these events" to his Government. LS. DNA, RG59, Dip. Disp., Mexico, vol. 2 (M97, R3). Received September 19. Published in *American State Papers, Foreign Relations*, VI, 364.

In the first enclosure, Lucas Alamán views the presence of the French force as "an act positively hostile to the Independent States of America, or at least so suspicious as justly to attract the attention of this government"; states that the Government of the United States "has declared in the most solemn manner, that it never will consent that any third power should interpose in the question pending between Spain and the Independent States of America, which formerly formed a part of her dominions"; asserts that "The conduct of France . . . is certainly an interposition"; expresses the hope that the United States will demand of France "such explanations as the occasion requires." Poinsett, in reply, states that he does not doubt that the President of the United States will ask explanations of France and that the principles of "the declaration made by the late President of the United States to Congress," December 2, 1823, are cherished by "the present President." He observes, however, that the movement of French forces does "not necessarily imply hostile intentions" and that Mexico should take no measures which would give "just cause of complaint" to France if it should develop that the presence of French forces was unconnected with designs against the Americas.

From JOEL R. POINSETT, Mexico (City), no. 16. Notes that items relating to the French expedition were "yesterday published" in a local paper, with an expression of editorial opinion that "this movement can have no other object than to cover the Island of Cuba from the designs of the United States and from those attributed to Colombia and Mexico." Believing Alamán to have been the author of the statement, Poinsett has expressed to him his "surprise at the tenor of it" and addressed "a private note to him on the subject." Copies of Poinsett's note and Alamán's reply are enclosed. LS. DNA, RG59, Dip. Disp., Mexico, vol. 2 (M97, R3). Received September 19.

In the communication to Alamán, Poinsett asks application of his influence upon the editors of the paper "to correct an expression . . . in some degree injurious to the character of the United States" and declares that "The Government of the United States never did entertain designs against the Island of Cuba, and have on every occasion disavowed all such intentions." In response, Alamán engages to have a correction inserted in the newspaper.

MISCELLANEOUS LETTERS   August 17, 1825

From P[ETER] A. BROWNE, Philadelphia. Congratulates Clay on his return to Washington and solicits his "promised attention to the application of the Franklin Institute for copies of the specifications of patents. . . ." Enclosing resolutions adopted by the Board of Managers of the Institute, Browne expresses the "hope that upon a reconsideration of the case our request will be complied with." ALS. DNA, RG59, Misc. Letters (M179, R63). See above, Clay to Browne, May 13, 1825.

MISCELLANEOUS LETTERS   August 18, 1825

From ISAAC RUSSELL, Greencastle, Pennsylvania. Wishes to know "how to compel the payment of" an annuity, left to his wife in Cork, Ireland. The estate agent has refused to honor the most recent bill, drawn for a payment due, on the ground that he supposed Mrs. Russell dead. Thanks Clay for answer to a former letter (not found) and asks reply to this one. ALS. DNA, RG59, Misc. Letters (M179, R63). The Russells have not been further identified.

From Henry Daingerfield

Hone. Henry Clay,   Alexandria 19 August 25
Sir

Supposing that you will be in want of a house on your return to Washington I take the liberty of offering you the one known as the residence of the late Robert Sewall near Col Wm. Brents[1] It is probably one of the most pleasant houses in the City—has four rooms on a floor two of which are large handsome, a very wide and cool passage, extensive back buildings for servants, a first rate stable and Carriage house and a small office with a good garden attached to the premises   If you are in want of such an establishment it will be put in good order at a very short notice such as repairing the inclosure to the garden and some papering in the house   The rent will be moderate say from four to four hundred & fifty Dollars per annum according to Circumstances   If you will drop me a line by mail I will Call on you at any time and shew you the house   with great Respect Yr Obedt St

HENRY DAINGERFIELD

ALS. DLC-HC (DNA, M212, R1). Daingerfield not further identified. Cf. below, Rental Agreement, October 11, 1825.
[1] William Brent, a brother of Daniel, had been, for a brief period, secretary to President Thomas Jefferson and, for many years, clerk of the circuit court of the District of Columbia. Sewall has not been further identified; the house has not been located.

INSTRUCTIONS AND DISPATCHES   August 19, 1825

From CHRISTOPHER HUGHES, Copenhagen. Announces his intention to resume immediately his journey to the Netherlands; transmits copies of correspondence with Count (Ernst Heinrich) Schimmelmann on matters referred to in Clay's instructions (of March 24, 1825, no. 1); comments on the friendly disposition of the King (Frederick VI) and "Prince Christian Frederick Presumptive Heir to the Throne" toward the United States and on "the universal anxiety felt here, for a favourable termination of Mr. Pederson's [Peter Pedersen] negotiation"; and observes that there exists in Copenhagen a disposition, based on the desire for trade with the United States, "to go into an examination" of the American claims but warns that the claimants must be ready to compromise, "for, as to admitting, or paying, the whole Sum claimed, there does not exist here, either the will, or the ability." ALS. DNA, RG59, Dip. Disp., Sweden and Norway, vol. 4 (M45, R5). Included among the enclosures is a letter, dated August 18, 1825, from Count Schimmelmann, announcing that the King had authorized him to state that a consul of the United States at St. Thomas would be recognized and permitted to exercise the functions of his office.

Prince Christian, whose adherence to the forms of constitutional authority had incurred the hostility of the continental powers in 1814, lived in relative retirement at Copenhagen until he ascended the throne as Christian VIII in 1839.

From James Wilkinson

Dear Sir   City of Mexico August 20th. 25

The Evangelical prescription "do unto all Men as you would they should do unto you" I have endeavoured to make the Rule of my Life, tho it is very probable an ardent temperament, may too often have beguiled my understanding & perverted my Judgement—I shall however never fail to atone for my Errors when it may be in my Power.—

It is therefore I now seek to correct some observations respecting the hardened Sinner Gould & his patron Santiago, which I exhibited in my Letter of the 27th. Ultmo., as I have been since informed, it is doubtful whether Goulds mission to the united States, is for the promotion of Santiago's consular views, or to favour some swindling mining speculations, in which Hundreds of English men & Americans are at present engaged in this Country

It is neither my right nor my inclination to interfere with the sordid deceptive speculations of any Person, however I may detest them, and surely at my time of Life I should avoid controversies, which are not forced upon me by conscience or love of Country, having myself been the victim of persecution & Injustice, throughout the greater part of my Life— I am therefore desirous to leave Gould & His Patron to pursue their private fortunes without opposition, by all the nefarious means in their Power—

You have under cover a Memo.[1] respecting the mining Companies of London, all of which have been got up since my arrival in this Country, and there are many minor swindlers from the Queen of Isles, busily engaged with our own *conscientious* Countrymen, in bating [*sic*] Hooks with the same species of lure, to catch Gudgeons where ever they may be found; and it is therefore my desire to warn our fellow Citizens against the facination [*sic*]; for verily this mining mania, even to those who have grown with the soil, proves ruinous nine times out of Ten. what then must be the Fortunes of distant & ignorant adventurers, in the Hands of agents who whilst *drawing* like oxen, to increase their commissions & keep up delusions, dash about in their Coaches, keep Mistress's, give sumptuous Dinners & suppers & Balls, and with gross presumption emulate the Rank & distinction of European Princes.—

To this very day I do not beleive [sic] a single Dollar has been *cleared* either by an English or American adventurer in the Mines, tho' *I know* of Hundreds & Hundreds of thousands which have been spent (dissipated) in vain pursuits— It is true that a few, a very few Mines, have been got into partial & feeble operation, and that inconsiderable quantities of the precious metals have been raised, but such is the extravagant expense of the Works under the conduct of ignorant Managers, intent only on making their own fortunes, that I am assured the mines of of [sic] Guanajuato which are the most productive, do not yield a Dollar to the proprietors for less than twelve Bitts [sic], i.e. 50 pr Ct. advance— It is currently reported here, that the weekly expense of the Anglo Mexican Mines, which include that of Valenciana, of which the Baron Humboldt has given us such marvellous [sic] details,[2] amounts to $60.000 per week, at a loss of 50 pr Ct.—inveracity, among all class's & complexions, is unfortunately but too current in this Country, & therefore I may be deceived in some of these Statements, but my own Senses cannot deceive me & of consequence I know them in the main to be correct—

In fine were I, with all the information I have acquired, called on to give an opinion respecting the Mines of this Country, I should say that those which have been most wrought are least valuable, because of their exhaustion & the profound Abyss's you are obliged to explore in search of mineral, and that those which have not been tested, are utterly precarious in their products & will disappoint the Undertaker four times in five— In conversation some time since with a Gentleman, of immense fortune in Mines & extensive Tracts of improved Territory, His grand Father having netted in one year five Millions of Dollars from a single mine in this vicinity, the Real del Monte,[3] on which a British Company has been labouring more than a year, in quest of that which they have not yet discovered, under the superintendance [sic] of of [sic] a Capt. Vetch[4] I understand; I was surprized to hear this Gentleman speak in terms of reprobation of the occupation, which He compared to gambling or Privateering, and expressed his deep regret that their [sic] should be a Mine in the Country; "were not this the case said He, we should be enabled to cultivate the Earth & the poor Mexican might live in comfort—but the Mines in operation draw off & destroy our working Hands; by their modes of Labour & Habits of Life, whilst our Luxuriant Fields lie waste & unproductive, and the Bread of Life is held at an exorbitant Price" These are sound reflections & I would they were common to Men in official trust here, but this is not the case, as you may presently perceive by their commercial regulations, which if I am rightly advised, (I have no communication on this

subject with Mr. P . . . . . . t⁵) will disfigure the impending tariff &
disgrace its projector, a Mr. Estiva,⁶ from Vera Cruz, where he was
not not [*sic*] long since a pedestrian pedling [*sic*] contrabandist,
now Secretary of the Treasury & a favourite of the President
Victoria— I understand that He considers the simple simple [*sic*]
Rule of three the standard for regulating the impending tariff—
i.e. if a yard of cloth taxed one Dollar, should be taxed two Dollars,
it will increase the publick Revenue 100 pr Ct, without reflecting
that the augmented Tax will operate as a bounty to contraband,*
& will probably reduce the receipts of the Treasury at least 66⅔
pr Ct.— in the mean time it may not be unseasonable for you to
know, that Mr. Estiva quotes your own arguments, in favour of
restrictions, to favour our manufactories, in order to justify His
own propositions

This is intended for your information & advisement, and my
detention here will depend on the caprice of this Government, in
respect to their publick debt, (a subject which unfortunately has
occupied me more than three & an half years)   the Event is precarious, altho' my present prospects lead me to Hope for a satisfactory adjustment in a couple of Months; in the mean time your
bare acknowledgement of my Letters will be highly satisfactory,
and through the Hands of your Brother in New Orleans,⁷ will
reach me in this place or that City

The right to a mine is Established either by discovery or denunciation—and The last being the most prompt & facile mode it
is the general resort of our Country Men particularly— The process
is simply this   a Yankee, for example, determines to turn minor
[*sic*], as he does not prosper at Monte or the Roulet,   He accordingly becomes a naturalized Citizen, or should he prefer it, as has
frequently happened, he seeks a sprinkling from the Holy Font
& becomes an Idolator in exterior—   thus prepared He sallies forth
in quest of abandoned Mines, of which their are thousands in the
Country, lays claim to such as he may fancy, and at a small expense,
say $60 or $100, He procures a forfeiture of the former occupant
& the investiture of the title in Himself according to Law;— a
History & a *Picture* of the mine, its former fame & products, are
then easily procured, under the Sanction of Seals, Signatures &
Cyphers of whatever Character you may desire, with Certificates
at once so plausible & solemn, as to silence the exceptions of the
most incredulous; the mine being thus identified & located, it is
partitioned into shares at a Given price, on which a small Sum is
advanced, and then it is fitted for speculation & is accordingly sent
into the market to catch Gulls, among whom I implore Heaven
our fellow-Citizens may not be included.—

You will doubtless hear of great exceptions to the veracity, the

moral rectitude, stability & consistency of this People; but with
the Evidences of commercial cupidity, avarice, apostacy, gambling,
ostentation & venal speculation, which a needy, greedy hosts [*sic*]
of adventurers from all Countries, daily exhibits to them, we should
be sparing of our censures & tender in our criminations.— make
Such use of this Letter as discretion may suggest, without my
Name.— I wish you fame & happiness and Am truly thine
The Hon ble Henry Clay—   JA: WILKINSON
   * which is in itself a species of commerce in this Country, as I
will show you in my next—

ALS (dateline in a different hand). DLC-HC (DNA, M212, R1). Postmarked at
New Orleans, Louisiana, October 28; endorsed on verso: "Forwarded by J[ohn] Clay";
endorsed on verso by Clay: ". . . {Answered 24 Novr. 1825}." Answer not found.
   1 Not found.
   2 The mines of Guanajuato (Guanaxuato), including that of Valenciana, were
described by Alexander de Humboldt in his *Political Essay on the Kingdom of New
Spain*, III, 171-204, one of the additional volumes of the London publication (4 vols.,
1811), not the New York edition as cited above, II, 539n.
   3 One of the oldest and most productive of the Mexican silver mines.
   4 James Vetch, a captain of the Royal Engineers, had retired from the army in
March, 1824, to assume management of the Real del Monte and of several other
mines. He remained in Mexico until 1829 and returned there from 1832 until 1835,
during which time he was active in road construction and mapping. He was
later honored for his engineering services in England in the fields of harbor development,
sanitation, and drainage. In 1843, a decade before the French began to give serious
consideration to the project which evolved as the Suez Canal, Vetch published a
proposal for such a link between the Mediterranean and the Red Sea.
   5 Joel R. Poinsett.
   6 José Ignacio Esteva, who had come into office with the administration of Guadalupe
Victoria.   7 John Clay.

INSTRUCTIONS AND DISPATCHES   August 21, 1825

From JOEL R. POINSETT, Mexico (no. 17). Explains the circumstances attending
the correspondence, concerning the presence of the French fleet in the West
Indies, enclosed in his "last letter" (*i.e.* his dispatch no. 15, August 17). The
lengthy account states that the Mexican Secretary of State (Lucas Alamán)
had consulted the British Chargé, Henry George Ward, who had then sought
Poinsett's cooperation in acting upon the report. Poinsett had agreed, with
the condition that the Mexican Government in its communications with
them should place both their governments "on precisely the same footing."
When Ward had later found that Alamán ignored this stipulation, he had
carried a protest to the President (Guadalupe Victoria), who thereupon had
expressed dissatisfaction with the conduct of his minister. Poinsett, in the
course of the discussions, assured Alamán that the United States "would not
view with indifference the occupation of the Island of Cuba by France" but,
at the same time, suggested that the imprudent conduct of some Mexican
commanders, for example, Santa Anna, "might have induced Spain to cede
that Island to the French. . . ."
   Adds that Mexican invasion of Cuba has been discussed in secret sessions
of the House of Representatives, without a decision "but their wish to anticipate
Colombia in this affair is manifest" (see above, Poinsett to Clay, June 15,
1825); that the House has decided that the Province of Soconusco should be

taken, and, if the Senate agrees, the Guatemalans will be driven out of it, "if they do not retire peaceably"; that he has seen a letter from Bolívar, urging "the necessity of the Congress at Panama" and characterizing "the Emperor of Brazil [Peter I] as a powerful agent of the European league and a dangerous enemy to the republics of America"; and that he gathered from this letter that Bolívar "had resolved to drive the Brazilians out of" the Province of Chiquitos in Upper Peru. Reports that, in response to an appeal from the Guatemalan Minister (Juan de Dios Mayorga), requesting the good offices of Poinsett and the British Chargé in the dispute with Mexico, he has advised that the matter, if not settled earlier, be referred to the "congress of Panama." LS. DNA, RG59, Dip. Disp., Mexico, vol. 1 (M97, R2). Received November 26. Extracts published in *American State Papers, Foreign Relations,* V, 909-10.

MISCELLANEOUS LETTERS   August 21, 1825

To John A. Leamy, Philadelphia (Pennsylvania). Inquires whether "the firm of Ledlie & Leamy" still exists, and, if it does not, to whom payment should be made "of the sum shortly to be received from the Colombian Government for the Cargo of the Schooner Liberty." Copy. DNA, RG59, Dom. Letters, vol. 21, p. 129 (M40, R19). See above, Anderson to Secretary of State, March 18, 1825.

To John J. Crittenden

My dear Sir   Washington 22d. Aug. 1825
   Upon my arrival here yesterday I found your agreeable favor of the 7h. inst.[1] Altho.' it is a moment of severe affliction with me,[2] I cannot refuse myself the satisfaction of addressing a line to you. I rejoice most heartily in the event of our elections.[3] I rejoice in your election,[4] to which I attach the greatest importance. I rejoice that the vile and disgusting means employed to defeat you have failed, as they ought to have failed. Your presence in the H. will be highly necessary. The pruning knife should be applied with a considerate and steady hand. The majority should dismiss from their minds all vindictive feelings, and act for the good and the honor of K. and for the preservation of her Constitution. You will have some trouble in preserving the proper temper in them, but you should do it. Nothing should be done from passion, nor in passion. Undoubtedly, restore the Constitutional judges.[5] Repeal bad laws, but preserve good ones, even if they have been passed by the late dominant party. Where you have the power of appointment, put in good & faithful men. But make no stretches of authority even to get rid of bad ones. Such would be some of my rules, if I were a member of the G. Assembly.
   I hope we shall preserve the public peace with Georgia, notwithstanding the bad humor of her Governor.[6] Nor do we intend that the Treaty with the Creeks shall be executed before the time

fixed by its own stipulations for its execution, which happily will again bring that instrument in review before Congress.

Give my respects and my congratulations to Harvie.[7] Your faithful friend   H. CLAY

John J. Crittenden Esqr.

ALS. DLC-John J. Crittenden Papers (DNA, M212, R20).
[1] Not found.
[2] Clay's daughter, Eliza, had died August 11. Cf. below, Clay to Lucretia Hart Clay, August 24, 1825.
[3] The Kentucky election of August 1-3, 1825, which followed a bitter campaign between the Old Court and New Court Parties. See above, III, 902n; below, Bodley to Clay, August 23, 1925.
[4] To the House of Representatives.
[5] See below, letters to Clay by Bodley, August 23, 1825; Hammond, August 31, 1825; Beatty, September 13, 1825; Theodore W. Clay, November 10, 1825; Kendall, December 25, 1825; Crittenden, December 26, 1825.
[6] See above, Clay to Southard, July 3, 1825, note.
[7] John Harvie.

DIPLOMATIC NOTES   August 22, 1825

FROM SEVERIN LORICH, Philadelphia. Acknowledges receipt of Clay's note of May 10, 1825; argues at length, citing navigation laws of both Sweden and the United States and treaties between the two countries, that the seizure of the *Carl John* (*Johan*) should not have occurred. ALS. DNA, RG59, Notes from Swedish Legation, vol. 3 (M60, R2). Cf. below, Clay to Lorich, September 20, 1825.

INSTRUCTIONS AND DISPATCHES   August 22, 1825

From SAMUEL HODGES, JR., "Villa da Praya   St. Iago." Reports his efforts to ascertain whether goods from an American vessel were on board a pirate ship captured by Portuguese authorities and cites the high-handed action of Captain (D. C.) Clavering, commander of the British ship *Redwing*, "who respects the neutrality of no Port, nor the Flag of any nation," in plundering the vessel after the Portuguese had taken it. Suggests, for the protection of American commerce, "that a National Vessel occasionally cruise here and on the Coast of Africa, to protect the Commerce of the United States against Pirates and certain British Cruisers, whose Commanders respect no flag." LS. DNA, RG59, Cons. Disp., Santiago, Cape Verde, vol. 1 (M-T434, R1). An official copy, in NHi. Received December 16.

From O[BADIAH] RICH, Madrid. Encloses copies of a letter addressed by (Hugh) Nelson to the Spanish Secretary of State (Francisco de Zea Bermudez), "containing a request made by Come. [John] Rogers [Rodgers] to be allowed to deposit at Mahon" stores brought from the United States for the use of the American naval squadron in the Mediterranean, and of the reply, granting the request under certain conditions. ALS. DNA, RG59, Dip. Disp., Spain, vol. 24 (M31, R26). Received October 26.

MISCELLANEOUS LETTERS   August 22, 1825

To SAMUEL BLAIR, St. Augustine. Forwards commission for membership in

Legislative Council of the Territory of Florida. Copy. DNA, RG59, Dom. Letters, vol. 21, p. 129 (M40, R19). Blair's commission was dated August 20. He was reappointed in 1828 and later served as United States marshal for the Eastern District of Florida, from 1831 until his death in 1837.

From LITTLETON DENNIS TEACKLE, Washington. Defends his character against a charge that he is "a Common or Professional Gambler." Encloses "testimonials." ALS. DNA, RG59, A. and R. (M531, R8). The enclosures were written, without address, by William Thornton and P. D. Stelle, respectively, on August 6; by Richard Hall, on August 9; and by S. Handy, Jr., on August 15. Cf. below, Teackle to Clay, August 23, 1825.

Stelle had been proprietor of a Washington hotel for many years, until its destruction during the British invasion of Washington in 1814. Handy was probably proprietor of "S. Handy's Boarding House," on Pennsylvania Avenue, between 12th and 13th Streets, in Washington. Hall not identified.

APPLICATIONS, RECOMMENDATIONS   August 22, 1825

T[HOMAS] H. HUBBARD, Utica, recommends Nathan Williams, of Utica, now a State circuit judge, for appointment as judge of the Northern District of New York. Should, however, Samuel Beardsley, the district attorney, be preferred over Williams as district judge, Hubbard recommends Greene C. Bronson to fill the vacancy as district attorney. ALS. DNA, RG59, A. and R. (MR4). Hubbard, clerk of the New York Supreme Court, 1825-1835, had been born in New Haven, Connecticut, had been graduated from Yale College (1799), and in 1804 had begun the practice of law in Hamilton, New York. He had served as surrogate and as district attorney in Madison County and as a member of Congress, 1817-1819 and 1821-1823, before moving to Utica in 1823.

Williams, a native of Williamstown, Massachusetts, had begun the practice of law in 1785 at Utica, where he held various local offices. He had been a Representative in Congress, 1805-1807, an officer during the War of 1812, a member of the State Assembly, 1816-1819, and was circuit judge from 1823 to 1833. Appointed clerk of the State Supreme Court in 1834, he died in the following year.

Beardsley had been appointed United States attorney for the Northern District of New York in 1823 and remained in that position for seven years. He had been an officer in the War of 1812 and a member of the State Senate, 1823. He was twice a member of Congress, 1831-1836 and 1843-1844, resigning each time to accept a judicial appointment. He was a circuit judge, 1836, attorney general of the State of New York, 1836-1838, an associate judge of the New York Supreme Court, 1844-1847, and chief justice of that body in 1847.

Bronson, born in Oneida County, New York, practiced law for many years at Utica. He had been elected surrogate of that county (1819) and a member of the State Assembly (1822). He later served as State attorney general (1829-1836), a judge of the supreme court (1836-1847), and chief justice of that body in 1845. Subsequently removing to New York, he practiced law and for one year (1853-1854) held the position of collector of customs. He received no other Federal appointment.

WAY AND GIDEON, Washington, solicit "a share of the Printing & Bookbinding of" the State Department. ALS. DNA, RG59, Misc. Letters (M179, R3). The cover is marked "Private." Andrew Way, Jr., and, probably, Jacob Gideon were editors of the Washington *Republican*.

From Thomas Bodley

Dear Sir   Lexington August 23d 1825

I take the liberty of enclosing to you the Schedule & Certificate of Littleton Jeeter an old Revolutionary Soldier, who I beleive [*sic*] merits, & stands in need of, the aid of Government,[1]

I do not enclose it to you, with a view of your personal attention to it; knowing your arduous engagements in buisiness [*sic*]; but do it at the request of the old Soldier, & solicit the favour of you to put it into the hands, of some Gentleman, who will attend to it & procure & forward an a[nswer] as soon as practicable— Your friends [here] are all well— The Elections have terminated in favour of the Old Court, in the H. R about 64 to 36   In the Senate about 17 for the old Court & 21 for the new.[2]

Judge Todd[3] left my house this morng. with his Family, intending to go to the Olympian Springs, where he will spend a week or two, if it agrees with him, & if he gains sufficient strengh [*sic*], will proceed on to Virginia, if not, return— He is extremely feeble & much reduced, has had some severe spells, lately; and I have but little hopes of his recovery. Sincerely your friend & hube Servt

THOS: BODLEY.

ALS. DLC-HC (DNA, M212, R1). MS. torn. Addressed to Clay.
1 Jeter, who had served as a private in the Virginia Line, now resided in Fayette County, Kentucky. He was placed on the pension roll in December, 1828.
2 See above, Clay to Crittenden, August 22, 1825. Subsequent developments proved membership in the senate evenly divided between partisans of the two courts. See below, Kendall to Clay, December 25, 1825, note.   3 Thomas Todd.

MISCELLANEOUS LETTERS   August 23, 1825

To S[AMUEL] SMITH, Baltimore. Explains that absence from the city has prevented Clay's earlier acknowledgment of Smith's letter of June 26 (*i.e.*, 25) "with the interesting communication, respecting the British Colonial trade, which accompanies it"; extends thanks "for both papers." AL (signature removed). DLC-Samuel Smith Papers (DNA, M212, R22).

From LITTLETON DENNIS TEACKLE, Washington, "Private." States that he had first intended relying on his "public character" and on testimonials written in his behalf; "but, understanding that the President would require some more especial notice of the matter [the charge of gambling]," he asks that the enclosure (probably his letter, above, August 22), "with the accompanying documents, may be laid before the President." ALS. DNA, RG59, A. and R. (MR4). Cf. below, Teackle to Clay, September 6, 1825. No reference to an application for a State Department appointment has been found prior to that of September 6.

APPLICATIONS, RECOMMENDATIONS   August 23, 1825

A[NDREW] G. WHITNEY, Detroit, solicits appointment to a clerkship in the

Department of State. ALS. DNA, RG59, A. and R. (MR1). A lawyer, Whitney
had resided in Michigan Territory since its organization and had held appointments as judge advocate of the militia and, since 1824, as Federal district
attorney. He died in the autumn of 1826.

To John Quincy Adams

Wednesday morning [August 24, 1825]
Mr. Clay's respectful compliments to the President and he sends
three letters for his perusal.

AN. MHi-Adams Papers. Endorsed: ". . . 24 Aug 1825. . . ." Enclosures not
identified.

To Lucretia Hart Clay

Washington 24th. August 1825
I wish, my dear wife, I could offer you some consolation for the
severe affliction which Providence has seen fit to send us. I did
not hear of the sad event until Sunday morning last when, taking up
an Intellr.[1] at breakfast about 20 miles from this place, I first
acquired the information. I am yet without a knowledge of the
changes which took place in my poor Eliza's situation between the
period of my leaving her and the day when God was pleased to take
her from us. I cannot describe to you my own distressed feelings,
which have been greatly aggravated by a knowledge of what your's
must have been, in the midst of strangers, and all your friends far
away. We must bow, with religious resignation, to decrees which
we have no power to revoke.

I have received a letter from Mr. Erwin,[2] in which he writes
that you expect to reach Hagers town on friday evening. There is
scarcely time for me to reach there, if I could set off tomorrow;
but I have some business in my office that would make it very
inconvenient for me to go before saturday. I will leave here on
saturday morning and get to Mrs. Scholls[3] that night. If you should
get to Hagers town on friday night you will be able, by making an
early start, to reach Mrs. Scholls also on saturday night. If you
should not get there, I will either remain there until you come
or proceed on towards Frederick to meet you.

Mr. Erwin does not tell me how my dear Anne bore our common
loss. Her situation is such as to make me entertain serious apprehensions for her.[4] I have received several letters[5] from home
since I left you. Your Mama[6] had been unwell but had got better.
I have a letter from Thomas,[7] who tells me that he is doing well.
You will see Eliza Ross and her daughter[8] at Hagers town.

I am living at the house[9] where I expected we should board and rooms will be prepared to receive you.

I inclose some letters for Mr. Erwin which I have received for him, and also one for you from Mrs. Brown,[10] and one for Anne.

I also send you a letter,[11] with some inclosures (I have not opened it) which I wrote you on the road, and which has returned from Lebanon.

Give my love to Anne and Mr. Erwin, and kiss my James and John.[12] Ever Your affte. husband   H. CLAY
Mrs Clay

ALS. NHi.
1 Washington *Daily National Intelligencer,* August 20, 1825.
2 James Erwin. The letter has not been found.
3 Probably Mary Catherine Brengle (Mrs. John) Scholl, Frederick County, Maryland. Scholls' Tavern, which had been in operation more than a decade, was located on a high ridge near the Montgomery County line.
4 See above, Susan Clay Duralde to Clay, August 8, 1825.
5 None has been found.   6 Susan Hart.   7 Thomas Hart Clay.
8 Eliza's husband, George G. Ross, had died in 1818. They had two daughters, Margaretta and Ellen, both at this time unmarried.
9 Mrs. Eliza Clark's boarding house.
10 Mrs. James Brown.   11 Not found.   12 Clay's sons.

To Nathaniel F. Williams

Dear Sir   Washn. 24h. August 1825
I received your obliging letter of yesterday,[1] and thank you for the friendly sympathy which it expresses. The surviving members of my family, I thank you, enjoyed good health when I left them and when I last heard from them. My own health is neither very good nor very bad. It would have been better if I had been subjected to less excitement & less anxiety during my late visit to the West. I think it will be quite [g]ood in a few weeks.

I did not see Mr. F. Johnson[2] during my abode in K. His residence is a considerable distance from mine, but I heard from & of him. He was doing well in all respects.

With great respect I am faithfully Your ob Servant   H. CLAY
Nath. F. Williams
I return the letter inclosed, thanks for its perusal.

ALS. KyLoF. Williams, a veteran of the War of 1812 and an active Republican politician, had recently become one of the editors of the *Baltimore Patriot,* established in 1812 and conducted as an Adams organ during the campaign of 1824.
1 Not found.   2 Probably Francis Johnson.

INSTRUCTIONS AND DISPATCHES   August 24, 1825

From RUFUS KING, London, no. 3. Transmits "a further confidential communication from Mr. [George] Canning" and his own reply. LS. DNA, RG59,

Dip. Disp., Great Britain, vol. 32 (M30, R28). Extract published in Manning (arr.), *Diplomatic Correspondence . . . Latin-American Nations,* III, 1564. Having ascertained French willingness to sign a tripartite agreement of the nature proposed by him (above, King to Clay, August 9, 1825), Canning sends to King a draft of such an agreement. King replies that he is referring the matter to his Government for instructions.

MISCELLANEOUS LETTERS   August 24, 1825

From CHARLES H. BAKER and JOHN RIANHARD, Philadelphia. Transmit copies of documents substantiating their claim to the sum recovered in the case of the *America* (see above, Anderson to Secretary of State, March 18, 1825); request Clay to direct payment of the bill of exchange to them. ALS by Baker, signed also by Rianhard. DNA, RG76, Misc. Claims, Colombia.

From WATERS SMITH, Marshal for East Florida, "St. Augustine, Florida." Transmits copy of a letter from Archibald Clark, collector of St. Marys, and admits that he has refused to follow Clark's instructions to release certain property "taken on Executions in favour of the United States, issued from the District Court, for the District of Georgia." Solicits an inquiry into his conduct. ALS. DNA, RG59, Misc. Letters (M179, R63). Published in Carter (ed.), *Territorial Papers,* XXIII, 312-13. In the enclosure, Clark states that he will make representations, "before the proper department at Washington City," concerning Smith's "highly censurable" conduct. Endorsed on cover by Clay (AEI): "Inform Mr. Smith that his letter has been recd. but that no charges have been exhibited at this office agt. him. HC." On September 23, 1825, Daniel Brent answered Smith's letter in accordance with these instructions. Copy, in DNA, RG59, Dom. Letters, vol. 21, p. 154 (M40, R19). Smith, who had been appointed to his position in 1823, remained in office at least until the mid-thirties.

APPLICATIONS, RECOMMENDATIONS   August 24, 1825

PLATT H. CROSBY, Lima, discusses at length conditions in Peru and Chile; states that his family now resides at Buenos Aires and that he can be reached there; and applies for appointment as Secretary of Legation to Peru or to an equivalent position anywhere in South America. ALS. DNA, RG59, Misc. Letters (M179, R63).

To Isaac Russell

Mr. Isaac Russell   Washington 25 August 1825
Green castle Penna.
Sir,

I should be very happy to afford you any information in my power respecting the drawing of your wife's annuity, as requested in your Letter of the 18th. instant, but the case (which, by the bye, is altogether a private affair, which one versed in the Irish laws would be most competent to solve) is too imperfectly stated by you to allow me to offer any satisfactory suggestions. If the agent of Westroppe requires proof of the continued existence of Mrs. Russell (which, as I understand you, is the fact) I suppose you had better furnish it.— Considering the distance of her residence from Ireland, it would not be deemed a very unreasonable requisition. What proof, and what mode of authenticating it will satisfy him, I cannot undertake to say.— But I should suppose that an affidavit of some person who knows her, taken before a Notary Public, or before a Justice of the peace, would be deemed sufficient. In the latter case the official character of the Justice should be properly certified.— I am your obedt. Servt.   H. CLAY.

Copy. DNA, RG59, Unofficial Letter-Book of Henry Clay, 1825-29, p. 2.

MISCELLANEOUS LETTERS   August 25, 1825

To A[NTHONY] H[OWARD] DUNLEVY and I. MORRIS, editors of the Lebanon, Ohio, *Spirit of Freedom*. Daniel Brent, at the direction of the Secretary, requests that the Department of State be considered a subscriber for this journal. Copy. DNA, RG59, Dom. Letters, vol. 21, p. 131 (M40, R19). Morris (the initial could be "J.") may have been Isaiah, who had settled in Lebanon in 1803 but in 1811 had opened a road to Wilmington and there established the first store and became the first postmaster. He had represented Clinton County in the State legislature in 1812 and 1814. *The Spirit of Freedom* has not been found.

From VINCENT GRAY, Havana. States that he would not have sought appointment as consul for Havana had he known that (Thomas M.) Rodney was an applicant for the post. Adds that since the French consul general in Havana has been recognized, they are "bound to acknowledge the American Consul." Comments that the British have obtained trade advantages in Buenos Aires and Mexico, which, he presumes, the United States will counteract "by insisting on being placed upon the same footing as Great Britain. . . ." ALS. DNA, RG59, Misc. Letters (M179, R63). On the commercial treaties of Great Britain with the United Provinces of Río de la Plata and Mexico, see above, Raguet to Secretary of State, March 11, 1825, note; Poinsett to Clay, May 5, 1825, note.

From WILLIAM REDWOOD, Philadelphia. Notes that the cashier of the Bank of the United States (Thomas Wilson) is unwilling to divide the proceeds of the bill from the Colombian Government in the case of the *Josephine* between "the Insurance Co of the State of Pennsylvania & the Marine Insurance Co of Philadelphia"; solicits "the views of the Department [of State]—As to the proportions in which" the division is to be made and what further proofs are needed. LS. DNA, RG76, Misc. Claims, Colombia. Redwood signs as "Prest pro. t." of "the Insurance Co of the State of Pennsa."

APPLICATIONS, RECOMMENDATIONS   August 25, 1825

HECTOR KENNEDY, New York, renews recommendation, first made in 1823, of John Young, "a native of Baltimore but for many years a resident of Trinidad in the Island of Cuba," for appointment as commercial agent at Trinidad.

ALS. DNA, RG59, A. and R. (MR1). Neither Kennedy nor Young has been further identified; the latter did not receive the appointment recommended.

From James Brown

Dear Sir,   (Private)   Paris, August 26. 1825

My former letters will have made you acquainted with the State of my health which has been much worse generally since my arrival in Europe than it had ever been in Washington. I was confined to my house for nearly three months, and my Physician, after applying to my obstinate disease all the resources of his skill, gave me distinctly to understand that unless I could be relieved by the use of the Mineral Waters, I had but too much cause to apprehend that I should be reduced to a state of incurable decrepitude— With such an alternative I could not hesitate to decide on visiting the Waters, and I had made every preparation for my journey when I received your letter[1] containing a Copy of the Instructions sent to Mr Middleton relative to the war between Spain and her Colonies. I felt some difficulty in deciding whether I would not wait until Mr Middleton should have laid the subject before the Emperor[2] and then mention it to the Minister of foreign affairs in this place. But as your instructions were silent as to the place and time of bringing forward the measure, and as I thought it possible that if the policy recommended by the President should be favorably received by the French Government, it might prevent Spain from sending additional troops against her Colonies, I concluded to have a conference immediately with the Baron de Damas, the result and nature of which you have been made acquainted with by my Dispatch[3] of which a duplicate is sent with this letter. Since my return, I have visited many of the Ministers of the Continental Governments, and think that their opinions have undergone some change on the Subject of Spain and her Colonies. Some of those who once thought that the Mother Country possessed the power to reduce them to obedience, now acknowledge their mistake and admit their Capacity to maintain their independence— So soon as this fact is generally admitted, it will follow, that a general wish will prevail to extricate Spain from a war which so long as it continues will exhaust her few remaining resources, and protract the period of her return to peace and prosperity. As a perfect union yet prevails among the great powers any Communication made to one of them is immediately known to all, and I have no doubt but that the conversation which I had with the Baron de Damas on Spanish affairs was immediately made known to each of the Ministers of Austria Russia and Prussia in all its details. Events which are constantly occurring in Spain, and which are calculated to prove the weak distracted and declining State of that Monarchy, will at this moment powerfully recommend the course of policy advised by the President, and induce the Sovereigns to advise its adoption.

Accounts from Madrid to the 20 have arrived which represent the condition of that Kingdom as being more wretched than it has ever been since the last revolution. A plot has been discovered to dethrone the King and place the crown on the head of his brother.[4] Many of the most distinguished persons in the State and Church are said to be implicated. The Swiss troops have been ordered from Madrid to St. Ildephonso for the greater security of the Court, and the King has issued a proclamation denouncing [sic] severe punishments against all who are concerned in the Conspiracy. Bessiere,[5] whose Monarchial principles, and loyalty, have been the subject of so much praise, as well in Spain as in this Country has left Madrid and placed himself at the head of a small corps of the malcontents with the professed purpose of rescuing the King from the power of his Ministry but with the real design of forcing him to abdicate in favor of Don Carlos. With the aid of the French troops these insurrectionary movements will no doubt be repressed, but the arrests, imprisonments, proscriptions and banishments which will follow, will add fresh fuel to the flame of discontent, and produce new plots against the Governments. All attempts to raise money, either by wars or taxes have been abortive, and the soldiery from whom pay has long been witheld [sic] are becoming mutinous and will soon be ready for revolt. Under circumstances so very distressing to Spain and at a moment when her affairs are nearly as desperate as they can be, I cannot but hope that the course of policy advised by the President will be approved by the great Continental powers and acquiesced in by the Spanish Monarch. At all events the proposal will do credit to our Government, and afford convincing proof of the wisdom by which her Councils are directed— Having now nearly reestablished my health, I shall be able to mingle in society, and have frequent occasions to see and converse with those whose opinions and advice have great weight on this subject, and I shall not fail to use my most strenuous efforts to give to the policy of Spain a judicious direction—

The recognition of St. Domingo by France,[6] however it may operate in other respects, will have a favorable effect in relation to the New Republics. It is a first step on the part of France towards recognizing their Independence. Having afforded the example in emancipating her own Colony, France may now advise Spain to follow it, and to this course the Government will be strongly urged by the public feeling which is decidedly in favor of it. Addresses have poured in from all the Commercial cities urging the adoption of that policy and Complaining that England, in consequence of the unwillingness of France to acknowledge the new Republics would enjoy the exclusive advantage of their trade. To this suggestion the answer of the Ministerial papers has always been, that French trade to those countries could be carried on as advantageously without as with a recognition of their sovereignty, and that England and the United States had derived no advantages from their treaties with those former Colonies. An intimation which has lately appeared in the English papers, that the trade of such nations as should continue to decline acknowledging the existence of the new Governments would be subjected to additional duties has excited some alarm and will encrease the anxiety of the French that their Government should no longer delay the recognition—

The policy of Great Britain corresponding as I believe it will with that of our Government, her efforts to terminate the War in South America will have a powerful influence when combined with those which may be exerted by the United States. The moral influence which Great Britain has acquired in Europe under the liberal administration of Mr. Canning[7] will give that power more weight than it had when a Member of the Holy Alliance or connected with it for certain objects—

We have received no very late intelligence from Greece of an authentic character. The general impression however is that the war has taken an unfavorable turn for the Greeks[8] and that unless aided by some other power, they must soon be reduced to their ancient state of Slavery.

Mr. Sheldon[9] who has for four or five months suffered by a complaint in his breast, left Paris a few days before my return for Dieppe with the hope of improving his health by a change of air and exercise. When I last heard from him he was at Havre and had experienced but little improvement in his health from the journey—

I shall write you again in a few days and am Dear Sir with great regard Your most faithful servt   JAMES BROWN
Honb Henry Clay

ALS. DLC-HC (DNA, M212, R1).
[1] Above, May 13, 1825.   [2] Alexander I, of Russia.
[3] Above, July 15, 1825, no. 31.
[4] Don Carlos María Isidro de Borbón, known for his extreme piety and firm commitment to the principle of the divine right of kings. Supported by clerical reactionaries who long opposed Ferdinand VII, Carlos refused to act against the reign of his brother but, following the latter's death in 1833, led an unsuccessful six-year conflict to assert his own claim to the succession.
[5] Jorge Bessières, a French adventurer who had supported first the Spanish republican government (above, II, 789n) and then the royalist regime of Ferdinand VII, attaining the rank of field marshal in the Spanish Army, had now espoused the cause of

extreme absolutism. On August 25 he had been arrested, while leading revolutionary forces in Aragon. He and seven companions were shot on the date of Brown's letter.
6 See above, Holden to Clay, July 16, 1825.   7 George Canning.
8 See above, Moore to Clay, May 31, 1825, note.   9 Daniel Sheldon.

INSTRUCTIONS AND DISPATCHES   August 26, 1825

From ALEXANDER BURTON, Cádiz. Transmits a copy of a decree by which Spain has "abolished the Monopoly of dried Cod and Stock Fish, together with the Duty heretofore paid thereon," and notes the duty remaining to be paid on these products by vessels under the American flag. ALS. DNA, RG59, Cons. Disp., Cádiz, vol. 4 (M-T186, R4). Received October 27. Published in Washington *Daily National Intelligencer,* October 27, 1825.

MISCELLANEOUS LETTERS   August 26, 1825

To CHARLES H. BAKER and JOHN RIANHARD, Philadelphia. Acknowledges receipt of their letter of August 24; asks that they secure authorization from owners of the cargo of the brig *America* to receive the amount obtained from the Colombian Government, "as soon as it is collected." Copy. DNA, RG59, Dom. Letters, vol. 21, pp. 133-34 (M40, R19).

To WILLIAM REDWOOD. Acknowledges receipt of his letter of the preceding day; urges agreement between the Insurance Company of Pennsylvania and the Marine Insurance Company relative to division "of the amount which will be shortly payable for the Brig Josephine and Cargo." Copy. *Ibid.,* pp. 132-33.

From GEORGE BRUCE, Wilmington, Ohio. Reminds Clay of a promise, made at Lebanon, to institute inquiry about Bruce's brother, Benjamin Franklin Bruce, a native of Frederick County, Virginia, imprisoned in Havana for over two years. ALS. DNA, RG59, Misc. Letters (M179, R63). Neither of the Bruces has been further identified.

On September 8, 1825, Daniel Brent, at Clay's direction, transmitted to George Bruce a copy of the letter from Warner to Clay, above, March 26, 1825, and commented: "We have had no later intelligence in relation to the Prisoners particularly referred to in that Letter, including your Brother; but I have no doubt that they have all been released." Copy. DNA, RG59, Dom. Letters, vol. 21, p. 145 (M40, R19). Cf. below, Diamond to Clay, October 8, 1825; Clay to Rodney, October 29, 1825; Clay to Vives, November 14, 1825; Rodney to Clay, December 19, 1825; January 7, 1826; February 4, 1826.

APPLICATIONS, RECOMMENDATIONS   August 26, 1825

MATHEW CAREY, Philadelphia, recommends George B. Adams for appointment to the consulship at Alicante. ALS. DNA, RG59, Misc. Letters (M179, R63). See above, Cook to Clay, August 3, 1825, note.

To John Adams

Sir   Washington 27 August 1825
   Mr. Rabello[1] being about to visit Boston and your residence,

and being very desirous of the honor of your acquaintance, I take particular satisfaction in introducing him to you as the Chargé des Affaires of the Emperor of the Brazils and as a gentleman whose official and private intercourse with me has inspired me with high respect for him. I have the honor to be with great respect Your obedient Servant   H. CLAY
John Adams Esquire

ALS. MHi-Adams Papers (MR471).   1 José Silvestre Rebello.

INSTRUCTIONS AND DISPATCHES   August 27, 1825

From CONDY RAGUET, Rio de Janeiro, "Duplicate." States that his application in favor of (Joseph) Ray of Pernambuco was unsuccessful; that reports of the resignation of (Thomas) Cochrane, now in Europe, may have been premature; that troop transfers are being made within Brazil to discourage rebellion; that much speculation attends the presence of Sir Charles Stuart. Gives current information on the war in the Banda Oriental and on relations between Brazil and Buenos Aires, which he does not believe will lead to war. Notes that Brazil has disavowed the union of Chiquitos, in Upper Peru, to the Empire. LS. DNA, RG59, Cons. Disp., Rio de Janeiro, vol. 2 (M-T72, R3). Received October 29. Extract published in Manning (arr.), *Diplomatic Correspondence . . . Latin-American Nations,* II, 828-31. See above, Raguet to Clay, July 30, 1825.

MISCELLANEOUS LETTERS   August 27, 1825

To ALFRED CONKLING, "Judge of the United States, for the Northern Dist. of New York." Transmits commission for this office. Copy. DNA, RG59, Dom. Letters, vol. 21, p. 134 (M40, R19). This was an interim appointment (cf. below, Clay to Conkling, December 20, 1825). Conkling, a lawyer, formerly of Canajoharie, had been prosecuting attorney for Montgomery County from 1818 to 1821 and a member of Congress from 1821 to 1823, before moving to Albany. He served as Federal judge from 1825 to 1852. Briefly he held the position of United States Minister to Mexico (1852-1853) and then practiced law in Omaha, Nebraska, for eight years before returning to New York. He became the author of several widely used treatises on the organization of the Federal courts and the powers of the Executive.

APPLICATIONS, RECOMMENDATIONS   August 27, 1825

M[OSES] HAYDEN, "York Liv Co" (New York), recommends, as printer of the laws, Thurlow Weed, editor and proprietor of the *Rochester Telegraph*. ALS. DNA, RG59, P. and D. of L. Weed had begun his career as a publisher of small journals in support of DeWitt Clinton. Moving to Rochester, penniless, in 1822, he had procured work as printer and junior editor of the *Telegraph,* where he had endorsed the presidential candidacy of John Quincy Adams. He was himself elected to the State Assembly in 1824 and, on August 29, 1825, purchased the Rochester newspaper. Becoming active in the anti-Masonic movement generated the following year, he then relinquished the *Telegraph* to publish an anti-Masonic organ. This was the basis of the political support which returned him to the State legislature in 1829 and upon which he founded the *Albany Evening Journal* in March, 1830. He retained the editorship of the latter newspaper until 1863 and during the intervening period became one of the principal national spokesmen for the Whig Party. The contract for publication of the laws was shifted by the Adams administration from Batavia to Rochester but not to the journal edited by Weed. Cf. below, Marshall and others to Clay, December 17, 1825, note.

To James Erwin

Dear Sir   Washington Sunday 28h. Aug. 1825
I met Mrs. Clay yesterday evening at Mrs Scholls,[1] and we have reached the City this evening. You can imagine what the feelings of both of us must have been on our first interview after our late calamity.[2] There is no remedy for such a severe affliction but time.

I was mortified to learn from her that two packets which I addressed to her at Hagers town (care of Dr. Dorsey[3]) had not been received. I put them into the post office (or rather sent Charles[4] to do it) on thursday night last, within one hour after I received your letter[5] from Washington, or Beamers town, in Ohio. One of those packets contained two letters to you, and one or two letters to Anne[6] from yourself. They were expected by me to reach Hagers town the same night that you got there and would have done it, if they had been mailed. But I presume either from neglect, or from being put into the office too late, they were not sent, and that they were carried up in the mail that went this day. I have accordingly written to Hagers town and requested them to be returned to me here, and as soon as I receive them I will forward your letters to you at Lewisburg.[7] I presume that I shall get them again tomorrow evening, and I will lose no time in forwarding them to you. I write you now to apprize you of the fact. One of your letters was from Savannah; I did not observe where the other came from.

Although my presence at Lebanon could not have averted the melancholy event which occurred there, I regret extremely that I left it. I should not have done so but that Dr. Ross[8] was so confident of the convalescence of my poor Eliza. I had some forebodings which have been but too sadly fulfilled. I cannot think without extreme concern of the situation in which Mrs. Clay and Anne were, on such a mournful occasion, in the midst of strangers.

Give my love to Anne and believe me Affectionately Yrs
Mr. James Erwin   H. CLAY

ALS. THi.
1 See above, Clay to Mrs. Clay, August 24, 1825.
2 See above, Clay to Crittenden, August 22, 1825.
3 Frederick Dorsey, born in Anne Arundel County, Maryland, but a resident of

Washington County since 1795, pursued a distinguished medical career until his death in 1858. He had been made an honorary member of the Philadelphia Medical Society in 1804 and had been awarded an honorary M.D. degree by the University of Maryland in 1824.

4 Probably Charles Dupuy.   5 Not found.   6 Mrs. Erwin.
7 Probably at the White Sulphur Springs.   8 Possibly Phineas Ross.

MISCELLANEOUS LETTERS   August 29, 1825

From BORIE AND LAGUERENNE and others, Philadelphia. Certify the power of attorney held by Charles H. Baker, John Rianhard, and William L. Hodge (now in Europe), "Jointly and severally," to act in the case of the *America*. LS by Borie and Laguerenne and representatives of six other firms. DNA, RG76, Misc. Claims, Colombia. John Joseph Borie, a French Huguenot refugee from Santo Domingo, was a prosperous Philadelphia merchant; his partner not further identified. The firm was engaged in the Mexican and Chinese trade. Hodge was a Philadelphia merchant, trading with Latin America.

From JAMES H. CAUSTEN, Baltimore. Presses Clay for an answer, early in the next Session of Congress, to the Senate resolution of March 5, 1824, concerning the surrender, in the convention of September 30, 1800, of American spoliation claims against France; asks for a copy of the "Conjectural note," not published, attached to the convention of April 30, 1803, with France. ALS. DNA, RG59, Misc. Letters (M179, R63). Under the Franco-American Convention of September 30, 1800, as originally signed, article two had stated the inability of the parties to agree "upon the indemnities mutually due, or claimed. . . ." The United States Senate had agreed to ratify the document only after the elimination of this article. France had thereupon announced that, if the second article were expunged, "the two states renounce the respective pretensions which are the object of the said article." A Senate resolution, with two-thirds of the members concurring, had finally approved the convention under this stipulation. Miller (ed.), *Treaties. . .*, I, 459, 482, 484. The "Conjectural Note" attached to the convention of April 30, 1803, concerned the extent of the private claims to be indemnified as an offset to the United States payment under the Louisiana purchase agreement. On the dispute concerning the private document meant to be attached to the latter convention, see *ibid.*, I, 517, 524-28.

From JOHN A. LEAMY, Philadelphia. Acknowledges receipt of Clay's letter of August 26 [*i.e.*, 21]; states that the firm of Ledlie and Leamy no longer exists; that his father, John Leamy, of Philadelphia, has full power to act in the younger Leamy's absence; that no other person has any authority in this connection; and that "The power & all the papers relative to the transaction are deposited in the Dept of State." ALS. DNA, RG76, Misc. Claims, Colombia.

From DAVID B. MACOMB, Tallahassee. Complains of the absence of judges, and of Territorial officials who might appoint them, which renders it impossible to obtain a writ against "Forcible entry & detainer." He has been removed by (Ambrose) Crane, publisher of the *Florida Intelligencer,* in violation of contract, as editor of that paper, for publishing a criticism of officials of the local land office. ALS. DNA, RG59, Misc. Letters (M179, R63). Macomb, a brother of Alexander Macomb and son-in-law of Thomas Worthington, had been born in Canada and had been a resident of Chillicothe, Ohio, prior to his settlement in Tallahassee around 1824. He was admitted to the Florida bar in January, 1826, and subsequently served as a judge of Leon County court. In 1835 he removed to Texas, where he was active in the movement for independence. Crane, a native of Connecticut, had been one of the founders of the *Florida Intelligencer,* a Jacksonian organ, the first number of which had been issued in February, 1825. He was appointed the postmaster of Tallahassee, in 1825, surveyor and inspector for the port of St. Marks, from 1826 to 1837, and collector of customs, in 1837.

APPLICATIONS, RECOMMENDATIONS   August 29, 1825

RICH[ARD] T. BRYAN, New York, encloses memorial of "sundry Merchants" of New York recommending the appointment of William Bryan as consul for Pernambuco. ALS. DNA, RG59, A. and R. (MR1). Neither of the Bryans has been further identified; William did not receive the appointment recommended.

EDWARD LIVINGSTON, Red Hook, New York, recommends appointment of William A. Duer as United States judge for the Northern District of New York. LS. DNA, RG59, A. and R. (MR2). Duer had begun the practice of law in association with Livingston and had followed him to New Orleans. Duer had returned to New York, however, in 1806. He did not receive the appointment for which he was here recommended.

To Henry B. Bascom

My dear Sir   Washington 30h. Aug. 1825
    I thank you for your kind & condoling letter of the 24h. instant.[1] Our recent affliction is indeed most severe.[2] Our little daughter was the only unmarried one that we had, and her mother had anticipated much gratification from her society and from completing her education in this City. I know, my dear Sir, our duty is to bow, with submission, to unalterable decrees; and we must strive to perform our duty.
    I regret to hear that your health is bad. I am afraid that you tax your Constitution too much in the professional vocation which you have chosen. That you may soon find it re-established and in all other respects enjoy prosperity will ever be the anxious of [*sic*] Yr's faithfully & cordially   H. CLAY.
The Revd. H. B. Bascom.

ALS. KyU.   1 Not found.
2 See above, Clay to Crittenden, August 22, 1825.

To James Erwin

Dear Sir   Washington 30h. August 1825.
    According to my expectation the packets sent to Hagerstown[1] were returned last evening and received by me this morning, and

I now inclose you the letters for you which they contained, together with some others which I have received by the mail since.

We are yet at Mrs. Clarke's[2] boarding house, where we shall remain a month or two. I have not yet had it in my power to obtain a house, or even to look or enquire much about one. Mrs. Clay has received a letter from her sister, Mrs. Brown,[3] who has forwarded to her several dresses and other articles, of which in her present situation, under recent circumstances, she can make no use.

Your father, it appears, has been again disappointed in his election.[4] Your brother,[5] from whom I have received a letter, attributes his failure to sinister causes.

You see my opinions about the fall in the price of Cotton are in a progress of realization. You would have made a bad bargain with me to purchase Cotton at 15 Cents.

Give my love to Anne,[6] and do let us hear frequently both from her & yourself. Yr's faithfully   H. CLAY
James Erwin Esqr.

ALS. THi.
1 See above, Clay to Erwin, August 28, 1825.
2 Mrs. Eliza Clark.   3 Mrs. James Brown.
4 See below, Carroll to Clay, October 4, 1825.
5 Probably John P. Erwin. The letter has not been found.
6 Mrs. James Erwin.

To James Lloyd

The Hon. James Lloyd   Washington 30th. Augt. 1825.
Boston.
Dear Sir,

My absence from this city has delayed my receipt and acknowledgment of your obliging favor of the 27th. June, for which I feel much indebted to you. I derive great aid from it, in the consideration of the interesting subjects of which it treats, and particularly that of our trade with the British Colonies.— I apprehend that it will be very difficult, if not impracticable, to prevail upon the British Government to let us into the trade with those colonies upon the same terms and conditions as trade is carried on between one British Colony and another British Colony, or between a British Colony and the Mother country. I understand it to be willing to allow us to trade with the colonies in the same manner as any other foreign Nation. But the British argue that their Empire, including all of their possessions, however separated, or distant from each other, is to be regarded as one whole; that the trade carried on between these several parts is in the nature of a coasting trade; and that, without subjecting themselves to the imputation of illiberality, or giving any fair ground of complaint, they may, between the parts of their Empire, allow privileges, both as to the admission of produce and navigation, which are not extended to foreign Governments. And they say that, if they may not grant to the produce of Canada, for example, when imported into their West India islands, advantages not extended to similar produce of the United States, when introduced into the same islands, neither ought the United States to allow the produce of one of the States to be brought into any other upon more favorable terms (the exemption from duties, for example) than the same kind of produce is permitted to be imported from the British Colonies into the United States— If the position be granted that all parts of the British Empire make but one whole, the consequence which they claim would not be very unreasonable.—

If Great Britain cannot be induced to agree to the introduction of produce of the United States, upon the same terms that similar produce is brought from one British Colony into another or from the parent country, it appeared to me to be worthy of consideration, whether it would not be for our interest to agree to the mutual abolition of alien duties. Our alien duties, far from compelling the British Government to let us trade with their Colonies, upon the same favorable footing, as those Colonies trade with each other, and with the parent country, are met by countervailing alien duties on the British side, intended to be fully equal to ours— The reciprocal alien duties then neutralize each other, and Great Britain remains unmoved from her ground.— Now, as it happens in point of fact that, of the tonnage employed in the trade, about seven eighths is American, and about one eighth only British, we must pay in the same proportion, that is to say, seven eighths more of those alien duties than the British; and, consequently, by a reciprocal abolition of them, that we should gain seven to one. It would seem that we ought to advance to the imposition of higher discriminating duties, to secure the reciprocity which our system requires, or, by agreeing with the British Government to mutually do away all alien duties, avoid the disproportion to which I have adverted. In the first contingency, we should, doubtless, be promptly met by an augmentation of the British duties, and ultimately we should again arrive at a total non-intercourse with the British West India Colonies, unless one or the other party gave away— What surprizes me is that, with the evident advantage to their navigation on the British side, in the duties, in point of fact we engross almost the whole of the tonnage employed in the trade. In a state of things so propitious, it would, perhaps, be better not to introduce any disturbance if it required an effort— But the British Government is understood to be desirous of a reciprocal repeal of all alien duties, and I confess that I am inclined to think that such a measure would be an improvement for us of the existing relations between the United States, and the British W. India Colonies.— With great regard, I am faithfully your obedt. Servant,   H. CLAY.—

Copy. DNA, RG59, Unofficial Letter-Book of Henry Clay, 1825-29, pp. 2-4.

From Francis P. Blair

My dear Sir   Canewood: Aug: 30. 1825

You have had an account from those who were most pleased to give it, of the success of the antirelief party.[1] There never was I think a more extraordinary or more unexpected victory atcheived [sic] by any party. The House of Representatives is completely "reorganized:" And there will be exactly the same majority in that body against the new Judges this session, as was found against the Old Court upon the address last year.[2] In the Senate the strength of the respective parties is changed but by a Single vote. From this State of things it might be inferred that the strife must be protracted, but I hope for a different result. The friends of the new court cannot without a violation of all their principles take advantage of the little majority in the senate to defeat the public will so decidedly expressed. I have had however but little communication with my defeated friends since the elections— After putting the business of my Office[3] in a train, I have retreated with my family from the atmosphere of Frankfort, & am endeavoring to right my own feelings, aloof from public commotion I do not therefore know what are the intentions of those with whom I act, but I trust their conduct will be governed by the principles they have hitherto professed. Many of them attribute the late disaster to other causes, than a conviction of the unconstitutionality of the law establishing the new court. The want of confidence in some of the Judges—raising the salary—increasing the number of incumbents[4]—Misrepresentations industriously circulated both with regard to the acts of the last legislature & the conduct of the new court— All these are circumstances to which the change is somewhat attributable— The Governor too & his wretched son[5] have weighed upon our strength like the terrors of a guilty conscience, & have given confidence, enthusiasm & all the credit they have detracted from us to our opponents. The beleif [sic] that the elections have turned on upon [sic] these collateral causes, may probably induce some to wish that the principles involved in the question may be tested in another trial before the people, in the hope that adventitious weights may somehow be thrown off— Such individuals will be disposed to consider the late result as merely breaking the heats, & not as winning the race, & will therefore be unwilling to give up the stakes— For my part I am ready to surrender,— I consider it the duty as well as the policy of the new court to yeild [sic]— The friends however of the new tribunal will in both branches of the Legislature insist also on the resignation of the Old Court simultaneously.[6] If the majority in the lower House contend that their election is proof of the public inclination to get rid of the new establishment, the majority in the Senate will declare that they too were pledged at the poles [sic] to get rid of the old Court. It is probable then that no satisfactory adjustment can be made but by mutual concession—to begin with the resignation of all the Judges, & to conclude by the appointment by the governor of two on each side, to be recommended by the respective parties. An arrangement of this sort however it might fail to gratify the animosities of the leading men on either side, would I am sure give satisfaction to the Country generally & its confidence to the tribunal—A Circumstance which can never happen if the bench be filled from either side exclusively—especially if by those for whom the controversy has been waged—Such can hardly be, & will never be deemed, impartial.

As it regards my private interest involved in these public Concerns, I expect, & am prepared for the worst. I think my chance would be best in the long run—in another race— Sneed will never resign & take his chance in a mixed court.[7] And although he was very willing to turn traitor & "serve the new court only" he will now doubtless insist on serving the old Court only, & he will surely have reason to complain, if he can be saved on *no principle*. If all the Judges should resign, Sneeds pretensions will in all probability, form the only obstacle to an accomodation [sic]. His claims if made a subject of Legislation, will bring up the controversy in all its violence & he will doubtless be sustained by the triumphant party for the sake of principle only, for they will not consider it a great merit in him, that he denounced the "usurpers," because they would not allow him to serve them. This difficulty might be avoided possibly by leaving to the Court to decide as to the Clerk—

If all attempts at compromise fail, the defeated party if they are wise, will enter the lists on their old principles & prove their willingness to give full effect to public opinion as expressed at the last as well as at the previous elections which have turned on the Judicial contest— The moderation of giving up one half the tribunal to their adversaries will go far to support them & the new proposal which would thus be made will excite hopes & afford room for speculations in which each politician will indulge his own Eutopian [*sic*] views— The other side imagine that the public are tired of controversy—that repose is its natural state—but they should remember that when the people have become accustomed to agitations, the habit thus contracted will not be instantly repressed, but that as long as causes of excitement remain, they will be taken up by the body politic, with the eagerness that a habitual drinker will seek his stimulants— But believe me I do not judge in this instance from my own feelings— I am disposed for a permanent peace— I have never witnessed a political contest productive of so much ill feeling It not only makes men entertain the worst opinion of each other, but in a great degree makes them deserve the mutual abhorrence.

After having enlarged myself to the measure of my new office I know not how I can shrink to the dimensions of a Circuit Court Clerk— The prospect of independance [*sic*] which I have for a moment enjoyed, will render me restless in an employment, which is literally living from hand to mouth— Upon this eclipse of my expectations I must take up a subsidiary calling, & in default of it, I feel strongly inclined to go to some of our new countries where the size of the society is more in proportion to my means, & where my children may find the way to rise in the tide of emigration—

I go to Frankfort day after to morrow to vote for a president of the Comwealths Bank. I shall vote for Davy White, although it is painful to me to vote against Weisiger[8]— If White be elected I hope he will have the countenance of your particular friends to assist in supporting him in his reelection before the *House*.[9]

I took leave of Judge Todd[10] in Lexington a few days since on his way to Mudlicks,[11] & from thence to Virginia if his health permit. I fear I shall never see him again. His decline is gradual, but continuously progressive.

Be pleased to mention me to Mrs Clay, as one who feels a sincere concern in her happiness. Although her removal from Kentucky has been attended with circumstances of the deepest greif [*sic*], I hope she will yet find a consolation in the perfect restoration of your health & that her cheerfulness will return & mingl[e] with the joy that event will impart to all your friends. And to none let me assure you, more than to your affectionate friend

F. P. BLAIR

ALS. DLC-HC (DNA, M212, R1). Addressed to Clay at Washington. Endorsed on verso by Clay: ". . . Answered." Answer not found.
1 See above, Bodley to Clay, August 23, 1825.
2 See above, III, 902.

3 See above, Blair to Clay, February 11, 1825.

4 The act of December 24, 1824, establishing the new court of appeals, had provided for a chief justice and three associate justices, in lieu of the total of three justices under the old system. Supplementary legislation had provided for a salary of $2,000 annually, instead of $1,500, as formerly. Ky. Gen. Assy., *Acts . . . 1824-1825*, pp. 44, 107-108; Littell (comp.), *The Statute Law of Kentucky . . .* , II, 443; III, 358; V, 41-42; Frankfort *Argus of Western America*, August 24, 1825.

5 Joseph Desha; Isaac B. Desha.

6 See below, Crittenden to Clay, December 26, 1825.

7 Achilles Sneed died September 18 of this year.

8 Upon being elected to the legislature (see above, Clay to Crittenden, August 22, 1825), Crittenden had resigned as president of the Bank of the Commonwealth. As his successor, until the legislature should act in this connection, the board of directors, of which Blair was a member, on September 16 chose David White, Jr. Daniel Weisiger was also an aspirant for the position.

9 In December the legislature chose John J. Marshall as president of the bank and, among other changes, replaced Blair as a member of the board of directors.

10 Thomas Todd.   11 Olympian Springs.

MISCELLANEOUS LETTERS   August 30, 1825

To JOHN A. LEAMY (Philadelphia, Pennsylvania). Acknowledges receipt of his letter of August 29; encloses order for Ledlie and Leamy to collect from the cashier of the Bank of the United States the sum of $9,461.40, for the cargo of the *Liberty;* also encloses a direction to the cashier to pay over to the firm the proceeds of a bill for £1,848:8:5, on the Colombian agent in Landon. Copy. DNA, RG59, Dom. Letters, vol. 21, pp. 136-37. See below, Clay to Wilson, August 30, 1825. The second bill provided payment of $4,372.70 as interest on the principal sum.

To DANIEL SMITH, "Judge of the United States for the Western District of Virga., near Harrisonburg." Transmits commission for this office. Copy. DNA, RG59, Dom. Letters, vol. 21, p. 138 (M40, R19). Smith, born in Reading, Berks County, Pennsylvania, had been appointed in 1811 as a State judge for the district encompassing the counties of northwestern Virginia. He continued in the State service until 1830. Cf. below, Smith to Clay, October 21, 1825.

To THOMAS WILSON, cashier of the Bank of the United States, Philadelphia. Requests payment to Ledlie and Leamy of proceeds of two bills, when collected: one, for $9,461.40 on "Col. Palacio" (Leandro Palacios); the other, for £1,848:8:5, "on Mr. [Manuel José] Hurtado, Colombian Agent in London." Copy. DNA, RG59, Dom. Letters, vol. 21, p. 136 (M40, R19). See above, Clay to Leamy, August 21, 30, 1825.

From CHARLES H. BAKER and JOHN RIANHARD, Philadelphia. Transmit, in accordance with Clay's letter of August 26, "the Declaration of the concerned in the Goods per the Brig America . . ." (above, Borie and Laguerenne and others to Clay, August 29, 1825). ALS by Baker, signed also by Rianhard. DNA, RG76, Misc. Claims, Colombia.

From CHARLES MCALESTER, Philadelphia. States, in answer to Clay's letter of August 26 (to William Redwood), the willingness of "The Insurance Co. of the State of Pennsylvania . . . to Receive a joint order with The Marine Insurance Co of Philadelphia—on the Bank of the United States for the Amount of" the bill in the case of the *Josephine,* "Relying on the continued exertions of the Government to have the Error corrected, which unfortunately occurred in Copying the Documents Relative to the claim furnished to the Department of State." LS. *Ibid.*

ARCHIBALD ALLAN, Louisville, solicits aid in obtaining an appointment "to the Military Accadimy [*sic*] at West Point" for his son, James Chilton Allan, fifteen years old, "a youth of the Most Morral [*sic*] habits," who "never has made use of one Profane Word in his life, . . . has not amongst his associates or School mates an enemy; . . . [and] is very Studious. . . ." Notes that "those are the reasons which induced Genl. [Edmund Pendleton] Gains [*sic*]" to urge that application be made for the appointment. Comments: "I presume this [the appointment] cannot be done without the assistance of Some Friend, and believing you to be one have made thus free to request your Kind assistance. . . ." ALS. DNA, RG94, Military Academy, Cadet Applications, 1825-1855 (M688, R37). Endorsed by Clay on cover: ". . . Refered [*sic*] to the Secy of War [James Barbour] with the recommendation of H. C." The Allans have not been further identified; the young man received no appointment at the Military Academy. General Gaines had commanded the Western Department of the United States Army, with headquarters at Louisville, from 1822 to 1824.

CHARLES D. MCLEAN, Jackson, Tennessee, recommends publication of the laws in the *Jackson Gazette*. ALS. DNA, RG59, P. and D. of L. McLean, who had formerly published newspapers at Clarksville and Nashville, Tennessee, had established the *Jackson Gazette* in May, 1823. The journal was substituted for the *Sparta Review* as publisher of the laws of the next Congress.

To John Holmes

The Hon. John Holmes Saco   Washington 31st. August 1825.
Dear Sir,

My absence from this City has occasioned delay in my receiving and acknowledging your obliging favor of the 8th. June last, most sincerely, for your kind attention to my letter of the 9th. of May. Your views and observations will render me essential aid in considering the interesting subject of our trade with the British West India colonies.— You ask if negotiation on that subject ought, at this time, to be pressed? You will recollect that, at the last session of the Senate, the correspondence and other proceedings in a negotiation between Mr. Rush and the British Commissioners at London, embracing various matters, and that of our Colonial trade among them, were confidentially communicated to the Senate.[1] That negotiation had paused, with an understanding that it was to be resumed. And it was in reference to its resumption, that I was desirous to enlighten myself by appeals to the better informed judgments of others.— Considering the superiority of the tonnage, at present employed by us over that of Great Britain, in the trade with her west India Colonies, a more propitious state of things for us in that respect, could hardly be expected to exist— Still if, without any teazing efforts of Negotiation, she would consent to the mutual abolition of the Alien duties of the two Countries, it appeared to me to be worthy of enquiry, whether we had better not agree to it. Such an abolition, simply, unaccompanied by any other measure would increase the trade, without augmenting the proportion of the British tonnage employed in it.

With great regard &c &c   H. CLAY.

Copy. DNA, RG59, Unofficial Letter-Book of Henry Clay, 1825-29, p. 4.
1 See above, Clay to King, May 10, 1825.

From C[hristopher C.] Graham

Dear Sir,   Harrodsburg, August [31,] 1825—

Haveing [sic] a thirst for travelling and seeing distant parts, and not knowing but that I might do it with more facility in the Service of my country, I write for information on that subject. Should there be a mission of any kind that will pay expenses, it would, most probably, suit me, for higher offices of honor and gain will ever elicit much competition, anexiety [sic] and suspense from which I wish to be freed.— Honor or pecuniary gain is not, therefore, what I ask.

I have travelled much, both within and out of the United States, and have, thereby, received a stock of knowledge which I would be much pleased to increase. My situation in the army of the U. S. for two years of the last war, together with much experience in life, have, I think, prepared me for the execution of any ordinary mission. I am independent, and do not solicit a birth [sic] gain. I am fond of the sciences of Natural History and mineralogy, which travelling so much extends. My cabinet is already respectable, and I wish to enlarge it. I am not seeking office, but prefer living at home in privacy and independence; yet I find an occasional peregrination agreeable.

I lived in Lexington some years, part of the time in University, and part of it a Pupil with Doct. Dudley,[1] where I formed an acquaintance with you, and have since renewed it, by occasional interviews. The last time I saw you was at Harrodsburg springs, at which time we had a conversation on my Mexican visit.

My character is well known to Doct. Dudley, and the other Professors, as well as to most other persons in this section of country. I am, at present, Proprietor of the Harrodsburg springs, which I am improveing for much company. This is getting to be a place of great resort, and should you visit our country in the summer, it would be well to give us a call. Your political opponents are trying to make head against you, but I believe we shall be able to regulate them and bring all things right again. Capt. Moore,[2] my particular Friend, who I have often heard assert that Genl. Jackson; [*sic*] had not a claim to the Presidency, and that his ignorance was such that "he could not write three lines of english to save his life, but had got others to write those publications to which he had affixed his own name," now thinks the Genl. a most accomplished and diplomatic character, and the author of all that has ever appeared in his name!— All this you understand.

I should be pleased to know the probability of Mr. Rafinesque's success in his Banking schemes,[3] as he has flooded me with letters, appointing me *sole Agent* in all his operations. I know him to be so visionary, that I have given the subject but little attention.

Knowing your situation, Dear Sir, I shall not be a troublesome correspondent. Most respectfully Yrs.   C. GRAHAM, M. D.

ALS. DNA, RG59, A. and R. (MR2). Addressed to Clay at Washington; postmarked: "HARRG. K. SEP 9." Graham, born near Danville, Kentucky, had been a silversmith until the outbreak of the War of 1812, when he had raised a regiment of volunteers and fought in several engagements. Following the war, he had acquired a tract of land at Harrodsburg, where in 1820, he had opened a spa, known alternatively as Harrodsburg or Graham Springs. Enlarged in 1827 through his purchase of the nearby Greenville Springs, it was a popular vacation and health resort for over thirty years. In 1825, at the age of 38, Graham had just received a degree from the Medical Department of Transylvania University. During the Black Hawk War, he acquired a large lead interest at Galena, Illinois. Subsequently he served as a volunteer in the Texas war of independence and, in 1855, as surgeon to the military party surveying a southern route for a transcontinental railroad.
1 Benjamin W. Dudley.   2 Thomas P. Moore.
3 Constantine Samuel Rafinesque, born in Turkey, of French and German extraction, a resident of the United States since 1815, taught botany, natural history, and modern foreign languages at Transylvania University from 1818 to 1826 and then removed to Philadelphia. Widely travelled, his principal contributions lay in description, often vague and inaccurate but frequently original and perspicacious, covering the plants and fishes he observed. He provided statements of the modern theory of evolution and the modern system of botanical classification over a quarter century before their general acceptance. His voluminous writing covered a wide range of topics, including a project for "Divitial Institutions," which should issue divisible certificates for bank stocks and deposits to circulate like money, a concept which later found acceptance in the coupon as an instrument for payment of interest on bonds. He patented this scheme in August, 1825, and appointed Christopher Graham his agent in promoting banking institutions on his plan, the profits to the promoters to be realized from a commission of one to five per cent on the amount of "divitial operations." Rafinesque succeeded in having such an institution established at Frankfort later in the year and himself launched a savings bank on similar lines at Philadelphia in 1835. The latter appears to have been fairly successful, at least until 1838, but Rafinesque succumbed to stomach cancer two years later and died in great poverty. Harry B. Weiss, *Rafinesque's Kentucky Friends* (Highland Park, N. J., 1936), 14-15; Francis W. Pennell, "The Life and Work of Rafinesque," *Transylvania College Bulletin*, XV (September, 1942), 32-35, 53-54.

From Charles Hammond

My dear Sir—   Cincinnati. August. 31. 1825.

Writers, upon the laws of nations, Seem to confine the right to navigate a Straight to cases, where the navigation of the connected seas is common to *all*, or to *most* nations.— This was the actual situation of the Mediterranean Euxine & Baltic seas. to which the doctrine principally applied—It was broad enough for all the purposes of those who maintained it, and it was but prudent in them to limit the doctrine within the bounds assigned to it.— But when the entire Shores of an immense Sea are owned by two nations only, and one of them commands its communication with the ocean the principle certainly applies with as much force, as if ten different nations were located upon the interior Sea— The common right of two to navigate is impeded if the one that commands the Straight deny a passage. And where a common right is admitted to exist its appurtenant priviledges [sic] must be the Same, whether the right be common to *all* to *most* or to but *two*.

It Seems to be well settled that the power in possession of a Straight, in the proper case, cannot refuse passage to others, without injustice. And the passage duty which he may lawfully impose must be moderate, not more than enough to indemnify him for trouble and Expense,—all which is a proper Subject to be regulated by treaty— I find that so early as three hundred years before the Christian era, the Byzantines levied a toll upon all ships passing into the Pontic sea— The Rhodians, then the most commercial people in the world, resented the attempt to collect this toll, made it cause of War, and compelled the Byzantines to give it up— This is I presume the most antient precedent upon the subject— and is *a case in point* for us— The application of these doctrines to our Lakes and to their communication with the ocean by the channel of the St Lawrence may be well insisted upon[1]— Very possibly a suggestion of this nature will call forth no little discussion—and tho we may have no Such men as Selden and Grotius, Sarpi or Bynkershoek[2] to conduct the controversy, I doubt not that much will be written and well written on both Sides— We shall have no latin quartos, Mare clausum, a De domino Mari,[3] but we shall have Smart pamphlets and ponderous newspaper essays in abundance— I feel within me that I could contribute some thing myself—if a proper occasion offerred [sic]—

The conviction of Commodore Porter[4] does not Set well with our folks— They are resolved to consider him a persecuted man, and to curse the administration. I have been much surprised at the conduct of such men in respect to this affair— They are determined to misunderstand it. We received the intelligence on Sunday night. On Monday young Mr. Worthington[5] insisted that Lieutenant Plat[6] was Sent by Porter to look after a captured Vessel and was Seized by the Foxardians— The Same day Judge Burnet[7] asserted that Plat was Sent by Porter to inquire respectfully after Pirates, that he was detained and that Porter landed to rescue him— When respectable men, and men not devoted to faction, thus misconceive and mistate [*sic*] facts, there is reason to fear the consequence of such misconceptions and Error—

I have seen Rowan[8] since the Kentucky election[9]   The result he says is a mere ebullition of temporary Excitement. The people have been misled for a moment, But will return to their Senses—. Till then the Governor and Senate must perform their functions, and preserve the balance of Government— So I suppose the struggle is not at an End— H. Marshall is frantic in exultation— He is belabouring my *Strictures*[10]— Heaven save the mark! were I to review them myself the[y] would come much worse off—

I have addressed a line by the mail that carries this to Gales & Seaton requesting them to return my manuscript to Dr. Watkins,[11] and asking an Explanation of the course they have pursued— I kept no copy of that article, I wish when they return it, you would enclose it to me—

We shall be glad to hear that you are again located and surrounded by your family, in health, and recovered from the fatigues and distresses of their recent journey   God bless you, Yours &C

C. HAMMOND

ALS. OHi. Addressed to Clay.
1 Cf. below, Clay to Gallatin, June 19, 1826.
2 John Selden, English jurist (1584-1654); Hugo Grotius (Hugo de Groot), Dutch jurist, historian, and theologian (1583-1645); Paolo Sarpi, Venetian scholar and patriot (1552-1623); and Cornelius Van Bynkershoek, Dutch jurist (1673-1743). All had published voluminously.
3 In rejoinder to Grotius, *Mare Liberum* . . . (1609), Selden had published a treatise entitled *Mare Clausum seu de Dominio Maris* . . . (London, 1635).
4 On August 17, the decision of the Navy court-martial had been announced, convicting Commodore David Porter on all charges and sentencing him to suspension from duty for six months.
5 Probably Vachel Worthington, born at Crab Orchard, Kentucky, in 1802, and graduated from Transylvania University in 1822, who had begun the practice of law in Cincinnati in 1824 and married Mary Ann Burnet, daughter of Jacob Burnet, in May, 1825. Worthington continued in practice until 1877, taking little part in politics, except for one term in the Ohio Senate, 1874-1875.
6 Charles T. Platt.   7 Jacob Burnet.
8 John Rowan.
9 See above, Clay to Crittenden, August 22, 1825.
10 In March, 1825, Humphrey Marshall had begun publishing the *Harbinger* at Frankfort, chiefly as an organ in support of the old court of appeals. In September, following the Kentucky election, he disposed of his interest in the journal. Cf. above, III, 460n.
11 Tobias Watkins. See above, Clay to Hammond, April 23, May 23, 1825.

INSTRUCTIONS AND DISPATCHES   August 31, 1825

To RUFUS KING, no. 4. Requests his assistance to Richard Caton and John McFaden, of Baltimore, in the prosecution of a claim against the British Government "on account of the capture by a British cruiser, and the consequent loss, to them, of the Brig Ariel and Cargo." Copy. DNA, RG59, Dip. Instr., vol. 10, pp. 376-77 (M77, R5). McFaden (or McFaddon), who had long been associated with Caton in mercantile operations, was at this time also a partner in an insurance agency. Further reference to the case of the *Ariel* has not been found.

From ABRAHAM B. NONES, Maracaibo. Reports that Americans trading at Maracaibo are still forced "to pay the old rates of Dutch Tonnage &c," owing to the absence of orders from Bogotá to carry the treaty between the United States and Colombia into effect; expresses doubt that any change will occur "until Colombia may form a treaty with some other foreign power"; and adds that the treaty between Colombia and England, if ratified, cannot be put into effect for six months, during which American commerce will pay the old rates while Colombia enjoys most favored nation treatment in American ports. Nones has asked the American Chargé d'Affaires at Bogotá (Beaufort T. Watts, acting Chargé) for information that might enable him to reclaim the amount of overcharges on American commerce and now requests "any information or explanation" Clay may wish to communicate. LS. DNA, RG59, Cons. Disp., Maracaibo, vol. 1 (M-T62, R1). On Colombia's treaty with the United States, see above, Clay to Salazar, March 21, 1825; on her treaty with Great Britain, see above, Watts to Clay, May 10, 1825.

From JOHN RODGERS, "U. S. Ship N. Carolina, Smyrna," "Secret." Reports his having left Gibraltar on August 10 "on a cruise of observation among the Greek Islands" to protect American commerce and to interview "the Captain Pashaw of the Turkish fleet." Having found the Turkish fleet besieging Missolonghi, he has postponed the interview. States that the "Greek Cause really appears to be in a hopeless condition," that European intervention in behalf of the Greeks appears unlikely "unless the British Government should take them under its protection. . . ," that agents of France and Austria are secretly aiding the Turks and Egyptians, and that "Many persons" think a war between England and the continental powers "not unlikely." ALS. DNA, RG59, Dip. Disp., Turkey (M46, R2). The Captain Pasha of the Turkish fleet since 1823 had been Khosref Mehemet, called "Topal," or "the lame pasha." On Rodgers' reasons for seeking the interview, see below, Clay to Rodgers, September 6, 1825.

MISCELLANEOUS LETTERS   August 31, 1825

To C[HARLES] H. BAKER and JOHN RIANHARD (Philadelphia). Acknowledges receipt of their letter of the preceding day, enclosing their authorization, which Clay accepts, to receive payment of a bill obtained by (Richard C.) Anderson (Jr.) by arrangement with Colombia, in compensation for "the cargo of the Brig America, seized at St. Martha in 1821." Copy. DNA, RG59, Dom. Letters, vol. 21, pp. 139-40 (M40, R19).

To WILLIAM GASTON, "at Newbern, N. C." States, in reply to a letter of inquiry (below, this date), that the treaty of October 8, 1782, between the United States and the Netherlands is in full force. Copy. *Ibid.,* 139.

To THOMAS WILSON, "Cashr of the Bank of the U. S. Philadelphia." Directs payment, to C(harles) H. Baker and John Rianhard of a bill "on Colonel Palácio" (Leandro Palacios). LS. NN.

From WILLIAM GASTON, "Brent-Wood." Inquires, in connection with a controversy over a tract of land in North Carolina, whether the treaty of October 8, 1782, between the United States and the Netherlands is still in force. ALS. DNA,

RG59, Misc. Letters (M179, R63). "Brentwood," near Washington, had been the home of Robert Brent, until his death in 1819, and remained the property of this family. The treaty to which reference is made concerned amity and commerce and included an article (6) which provided that "Heirs, subjects of one of the Parties, and residing in the Country of the other, or elsewhere, shall receive such successions. . . , even although they shall not have obtained Letters of Naturalization. . . ." Miller (ed.), *Treaties*. . . , II, 65. For Clay's reply to the inquiry, see above, this date.

From JOHN H. PLEASANTS, London. Hopes that the explanation offered in his letter of "the 8th [*i.e.*, 7th] July" will provide "a satisfactory justification of the apparent abandonment of a mission, which had been as kindly bestowed. . . , as it was zealously sought and gratefully accepted. . . ." Remarks that he "could not do less after getting here, than take time sufficient to look at what was most worthy of being seen in England." Notes that he "of course can have no claims upon the Treasury" but that he has drawn on Clay "for the means of returning" to the United States. Promises to "replace the amount" as soon as he reaches Richmond. Refers to (Rufus) King's ill health and to recent events in Europe. ALS. DNA, RG59, Letters from Bearers of Dispatches.

APPLICATIONS, RECOMMENDATIONS   August 31, 1825

JOHN MOODY, New Canton, Buckingham County, Virginia, states that he wrote in February in quest of public employment, that he is a veteran of the Revolutionary War, and that he intends petitioning Congress for support. ALS. DNA, RG59, A. and R. (MR1). Addressed to Clay, or, in his absence, to James Barbour. Cf. above, Moody to Clay, April 2, May 15, 1825.

To David Daggett

Dear Sir   Washington 1 September 1825
    I recd. your letter of the 27h. Ulto.[1] Anxious to obtain any information I could, on the subject of it, I addressed a note to the French Minister[2] requesting any which he could communicate, and I now transmit his reply. We have not the particulars of the late arrangement between France and Hayti, in any official form, but I should presume that your French teacher was one of the very class of persons for whose benefit the one hundred & fifty millions of franks were intended.[3] I beg leave to reciprocate, most cordially, the friendly sentiments expressed in your letter and to assure you that I shall ever recollect our acquaintance, formed in the Nat. Councils, with high satisfaction.
        I am faithfully & respectfly Yr. ob servant   H CLAY
D. Daggett Esqr.

ALS. CtY.   1 Not found.
2 Baron Durand de Mareuil. The note and the reply have not been found.
3 Cf. above, Holden to Clay, July 16, 1825, note; below, Clay to Brown, October 25, 1825; Brown to Clay, January 9, 1826.

INSTRUCTIONS AND DISPATCHES   September 1, 1825

From HEMAN ALLEN, Valparaiso, no. 17, "Duplicate." States that he learned, from an American newspaper only a few days earlier, "the name of the distinguished individual" whom he addresses "as the Head of our Foreign relations" and declares his "satisfaction on this occasion" as he "beheld at once in that station, the accomplished statesman, the able and constant defender of his country's rights, and the great champion of South American freedom." Cites his earlier dispatches as revealing his "rather gloomy apprehensions" concerning Chile but comments that he does not think "the friends of freedom should despair." Asserts that "A most wicked and abandoned clergy, still directs the destiny of the State, which nothing but the hand of time, and the progress of knowledge can ever remove," and that it is necessary to look to the next generation "for the downfal [*sic*] of that bigotry and superstition, that has so long blighted the prospects of this fair region and still holds her sons in bondage." Nevertheless, he rejoices that "the sun of colonial oppression has forever set, and . . . the dominion of Spain no longer exists."

In regard to the relationship between the United States and Chile, Allen writes: "The fact is, the theory and practice of these people towards us, is very opposite; they profess much gratitude, but exercise very little; perhaps, they are so constituted at present, as to be incapable of that noble sentiment. At any rate, from the kindness and friendship we have shown them, they think to avail themselves of our forbearance, and regardless of the obligations, of either justice or gratitude, to sport with impunity with our rights. Deeply therefore, as I should lament the necessity, of any coercion on our part, yet I firmly believe, that a little chastisement would do much good, and perhaps a bare indication of it, might spare the disagreeable resort."

Notes that he has "endeavoured, by original and duplicate despatches," to keep the Government informed but has received no instructions in return. Repeats that he has not been successful in pressing the claims of American citizens.

Because of the unsettled state of the country, he has not proposed a commercial treaty. He thinks little more can be done "at this time"; and, if it be thought that his services there are no longer required, he will return home. ALS. DNA, RG59, Dip. Disp., Chile, vol. 1 (M-T2, R1). Received January 13, 1826. Extract published in Manning (arr.), *Diplomatic Correspondence . . . Latin-American Nations*, II, 1103-1104.

MISCELLANEOUS LETTERS   September 1, 1825

To JOHN LEAMY and CHARLES MCALESTER. Acknowledges receipt of McAlester's letter of August 30 and encloses the joint order. Copy. DNA, RG59, Dom. Letters, vol. 1, p. 141 (M40, R19). See above, Clay to Redwood, August 26, 1825, note.

To M[ORDECAI] M. NOAH, New York. Daniel Brent, at the direction of the Secretary of State, requests that the Department be considered a subscriber for the *New York National Advocate*, "of which it is understood you are the Editor...." Copy. DNA, RG59, Dom. Letters, vol. 21, p. 142 (M40, R19). Cf. above, Stuart to Clay, March 15, 1825, note.

To THOMAS WILSON, Cashier of the Bank of the United States, Philadelphia.

Authorizes payment of the bill for $21,750, with interest from January 27, 1819, drawn on (José Leandro) Palacio(s), transmitted by (Daniel) Brent to Wilson on May 30, to John Leamy, for the Marine Insurance Company of Philadelphia, and to Charles McAlester, for the Insurance Company of the State of Pennsylvania. Copy. DNA, RG59, Dom. Letters, vol. 21, pp. 141-42.

From JOHN LEAMY, "Office of The Marine Ins: Co. Philadelphia." Requests that, on the payment of the bill for $21,750, with interest, from the Colombian Government in the case of the *Josephine,* his company be allotted $12,000. LS. DNA, RG76, Misc. Claims, Colombia.

To Francis T. Brooke

My dear Sir   Washington 2d. September 1825
   I received your kind letter of the 29h. Ulto.[1] and thank you for the friendly expression of sympathy which it contains. Our late affliction was rendered still more severe by the circumstances under which it occurred. I did not yield to the urgent calls of duty here, until I had the strongest assurances from the attending physician that there was no danger. And, after leaving Lebanon, the first information which I received of the sad event which occurred there reached me, when I was within about 20 miles of this place, through the Intellr.[2]
   I received, perused and now return Judge Duval's[3] letter. His wishes in behalf of his son will be considered; but the fact that he has one son a Governor[4] under the General Government and another holding a Captains Commission (this latter now applying for another appointment)[5] will operate somewhat against his success.
   You must feel gratified that our old friend Troup has finally concluded to abstain from surveying the Creek lands, and of course that all danger is dissipated of disturbing the public peace.[6]
                          I am faithfly Your friend   H CLAY
The Honble F. Brooke &c. &c. &c.

ALS. KyU.   1 Not found.
2 See above, Clay to Mrs. Clay, August 24, 1825.
3 William Duval.   4 William P. Duval.
5 Probably John P. Duval, who had been promoted to captain of infantry in 1814 but honorably discharged from the army in the following year. On his recent application, see above, Duval to Clay, August 10, 1825.
6 Cf. above, Clay to Southard, July 3, 1825, note.

DIPLOMATIC NOTES   September 2, 1825

From C. D. E. J. BANGEMAN HUYGENS, Washington. Requests Clay to take action for the detention of the ship *Celia,* her cargo, and her master, Captain Lloyd, should they enter a port of the United States. Captain Lloyd, an American, engaged in February, 1823, to transport a cargo of salt and spice under the flag of the Netherlands to Borneo, has not reached his destination. He was last seen in December, 1823, in Rio de Janeiro. His conduct is considered piracy. NS, in French, translated in State Department file. DNA, RG59, Notes from Netherlands Legation, vol. 1 (M56, R1). Lloyd has not been further identified.

To D[aniel] Parker

Dear Sir   Washn. 3 Septr. 1825.

I am desirous to obtain and am now looking out for a house to accommodate my family. It has been mentd. to me that you might be possibly disposed to part with yours, I therefore take the liberty of enquiring,

1 Whether you would rent it, without the furniture, and on what terms?

2 If you wd. rent it with the furniture (making of course such exceptions as you might think proper) and on what terms? and.

3 If you wd. nether [*sic*] rent it with or without the furniture, on what terms you would sell?

The house is not exactly adapted to my family, but if you would have the goodness to answer the above enquiries, it might possibly enlarge the field of selection.   Yr's with great respect   H CLAY

ALS. PHi. Addressed: "Genl. D. Parker Care of Genl. C[allender] Irvine Philadelphia." Parker, born in Massachusetts and educated as a lawyer, had been chief clerk in the United States War Department in 1810, adjutant and inspector general in 1814, and paymaster general from 1821 to 1822. He returned to the Department as chief clerk from 1841 until his death in 1846.

INSTRUCTIONS AND DISPATCHES   September 3, 1825

From ROBERT MONTGOMERY, Alicante. States that the outbreak of leprosy, reported in his dispatch of August 1, has not developed further; discusses the duty on salt fish, which prevents the American product from competing with the English; reports that political tranquillity is not yet restored in Spain and that "Commerce continues in a most deplorable state. . . ." ALS. DNA, RG59, Cons. Disp., Alicante, vol. 1 (M-T357, R1). Addressed to Secretary of State; received November 1. On the high Spanish duties, see also above, Burton to Clay, June 30, 1825.

From JOHN RAINALS, Copenhagen. Reports that, at the suggestion of Christopher Hughes, who left for Holland about fourteen days ago, he has appointed "Mr. John Alexander Balfour of Elsenure [*sic*] . . . to be Vice-Consul of the United States at that port . . . ," and expresses hope that Clay will approve; offers his own services in the collection of claims against Denmark but notes that (John) Connell is still there; and comments upon the controversy concerning the Swedish men of war "purchased for South American account," which, "It is now said . . . may proceed, but no Sweedish [*sic*] Officers will be allowed to accompany them." ALS. DNA, RG59, Cons. Disp., Copenhagen, vol. 3 (M-T195, R3). Received September 8. See above, Hughes to Clay, July 8, 1825, note.

From JOHN LEAMY, "Office of the Marine Ins: Comp. Philadelphia." Acknowledges receipt of Clay's letter of September 1 (above, to Leamy and McAlester) and of "a *joint order*" for the sum paid by Colombia in the case of the *Josephine;* refers to his company's request (above, Leamy to Clay) of September 1; and returns the *"joint* order, as this Company did not authorise such an arrangement." LS. DNA, RG76, Misc. Claims, Colombia.

From JOHN A. LEAMY, Philadelphia. Expresses thanks for Clay's letter of August 30; states that (Thomas) Wilson had earlier requested "the Barings" to hold the proceeds in the case of the *Liberty* "subject to the orders of the Dept of State"; requests a duplicate order "to those gentlemen" to pay the bill of exchange. ALS. *Ibid.* Endorsed on verso by Clay: ". . . Give the order in duplicate requested on the Mess Barings." Cf. above, Clay to Wilson, August 30, 1825.

From THOMAS WILSON, "Bank United States." Transmits "a receipt from Messrs Ledlie & Leamy for $13834.10 and from Chs H Baker & John Rianhard for $26663.12 . . . agreeably to the instructions contained in" Clay's "letters of the 30th & 31st Ulto." States that the bill on (Manuel José) Hurtado "for £1848, 8.5 Stg" received earlier from (Daniel) Brent has been "transmitted to Messrs Baring Bro & Co. London, for the credit of the Secretary of State. . . ." Adds that "Saml Keith Esq Presdt Delaware Ins. Co. has called on" him "for payment of their claim in the case of the Minerva." ALS. DNA, RG76, Misc. Claims, Colombia.

To James Brown

My dear Sir   Washington 4h. September 1825

Upon my return to the City about a fortnight ago, I found here your letter of the 25h. June, from which I was sorry to learn that your health was not yet re-established. I must refer you to my letter accompanying this to Mrs. Brown[1] for an account of a most heavy domestic affliction which we have recently experienced and for other private affairs.

My reception in the Western States, on my recent trip, was marked by the greatest enthusiasm. From the Alleghany [*sic*] to Lexington going and returning through Ohio, I scarcely passed a village in which I was not pressed to accept of some public manifestation of regard. The demonstrations which were made of public esteem and consideration, in the case of Genl. La Fayette, hardly exceeded those of which I was the object. If the public effect of this species of testimony is favorable, its operation upon my health was not so propitious. I have returned without having laid in as good a stock of it, as I should have done if I had been more abstracted and less compelled to mingle in crowds. The extraordinary heat of the past summer has not been favorable to disorders such as mine, and I look forward with strong hope of a good effect from the more bracing weather of the autumn & winter.

The Administration gets along very well. The number of unfriendly prints and persons is I think considerably diminished, and the tone of those which remain is somewhat softened. We have been threatened with a civil war with Georgia, about the Creek Indian lands, by the intemperance of Govr. Troop [*sic*];[2] but the moderation dignity and decision of the Executive have commanded out of Georgia, the undivided voices of the American people, and the Govr. has, by conforming to the wishes of the general Government, saved us, for the present at least, from Civil commotion.

Commodore Porters trial[3] has also commanded much of the public attention; but altho' the factious have been endeavoring to make something out of his case,[4] I have no doubt that the great body of the intelligent people of America will cordially approve what has been done. It was time to neutralize the effect of the bad precedent furnished in Genl. Jacksons case.[5] If Porter had been acquitted, or had not been brought to trial, hereafter the peace of the Country would have been in the hands of every military and naval commander of an expedition.

I must refer you to Genl. La Fayette for more particular accounts of public matters. He has seen all parts of our Country and seen and conversed with all persons in it. The popular feeling has been kept up to the last in regard to him. I feel much concern in relation to his future life. It ought to be passed in dignity and tranquillity, abstaining from public affairs, and most cautiously guarding against giving the least ground for the imputation of his being concerned in any Conspiracy. I think this is his determination, and I pray that he may adhere to it.[6]

You express a wish that instructions should be sent you in respect to our claims on France. The business of my office has increased so much, by the establishment of the new states to the South as well as from the natural growth of the Country, and I have been obliged to be so much absent from it since I entered it, that I am compelled to attend to the more pressing matters first. I have however not neglected to think of our French concerns, and I hope in the course of the fall to be able to take up that subject and to suggest some practicable plan for putting the business in motion again.

In my letter to Mrs. Brown, I have requested her to have purchased for us some articles which I have enumerated. I do not know what they will amount to, or I would send a bill to pay for them. I presume however that there is very little difference between drawing from Paris upon the U.S. or drawing from here on France. I must request that you will get the person, whom Mrs. Brown may engage to make the purchases, to draw on me for the amount, or get a bill in some other way disposed of on me, and I shall not fail to discharge it on presentation. I am glad to be able to tell you that I have continued to feel the most sensible benefit from the system of œconomy and exertion which I adopted to get out of my pecuniary difficulties; and that I have so far succeeded as to no longer entertain any fears for my family, if I were suddenly taken off. Still we mean to persevere in the practice of œconomy, and I do not intend, in my disbursements here, to exceed my salary. To that limit, I think it my duty as well as my interest, to restrict myself.

A most thorough and signal change has at last taken place in Kentucky. The dominant (that is the relief party) at the lat [*sic*] Session of the legislature put out the Judges of the Court of Appeals, by an act of ordinary legislation. The effect of that and other measures of the party has been such that, at the elections in the last month, the Anti relief party has succeeded by a majority of about two thirds.[7] I am highly gratified with this result. The character of our State will I hope be recovered, and we shall again command respect. It was contemplated by some of the leaders of the fallen party to attack me, if (which I think they could not have done) they could have carried their party along. The change therefore is no less favorable to myself than to the State at large.

I am truly & faithfy Yr's   H Clay

James Brown Esq.

ALS. DLC-HC (DNA, M212, R1).
1 Letter not found; see above, Clay to Crittenden, August 22, 1825.
2 See above, Clay to Southard, July 3, 1825.
3 See above, Nelson to Clay, April 6, 1825, note; Southard to Clay, July 8, 1825; Hammond to Clay, August 31, 1825, note.
4 Cf. above, Hammond to Clay, August 31, 1825.
5 See above, II, 612n, 636-62, 667.
6 On Lafayette's departure from the United States, see below, Clay to Somerville, September 6, 1825, note. Upon his return to France, he resumed his career in the Chamber of Deputies, serving from 1825 until his death in 1834, and also, as head of the national guard during the revolution of 1830, was active in establishing the constitutional monarchy under Louis Philippe.
7 See above, Cowan to Clay, January 1, 1825; Bodley to Clay, August 23, 1825.

INSTRUCTIONS AND DISPATCHES   September 4, 1825

From Rufus King, London, no. 4. States that, when (George) Canning returns from "the North of England," King "will call his attention to the Commission at Washington concerning slaves" (cf. above, Clay to King, May 10, 1825); notes that he has asked (James) Brown to let him know "what has passed between him and the French Government on the subject of Mr. [Henry] Middleton's instructions" (Clay to Middleton, May 10, 1825) and that he has "in like manner written to Mr. Middleton"; reports that he has met the representatives of Chile (Mariano Egaña), Colombia (Manuel José Hurtado), and Mexico (José Mariano Michelena), that the representative of Buenos Aires

(Bernardino Rivadavia) and the Minister from Mexico have returned home, and that "None of these persons have . . . been received as Ministers. . . ." The treaty with Buenos Aires (see above, Raguet to Secretary of State, March 11, 1825, note) has been ratified, and it is said that a representative of that Government will be received upon offering a letter of credence. Chile has no treaty with England. A treaty with Colombia (see above, Watts to Clay, May 10, 1825, note) awaits ratification. The Mexican treaty (see above, Poinsett to Clay, May 5, 1825, note) has "gone back" for alteration of a provision "which as it stands, would sanction the rule that Free ships make Free goods." When the correction has been made it is expected that a Mexican Minister will be received. King points out that "England insists—First—upon the conclusion of a treaty, and Next, that the New Ministers severally comply with all the formalities of the old states in the form of their Credentials." LS. DNA, RG59, Dip. Disp., Great Britain, vol. 32 (M30, R28). Received October 25. Extract published in Manning (arr.), *Diplomatic Correspondence . . . Latin-American Nations,* III, 1564. Mariano Egaña, educated as a lawyer and driven into exile under the royalist regime, had held a series of governmental positions, as public prosecutor and departmental secretary, from his return in 1817 until he became Minister of State and Foreign Relations in 1823. In 1824 he had been sent as Minister Plenipotentiary to various European courts, where he remained until 1829. Shortly after his return, he became a member of the Chilean Parliament and was elected president of that body. From 1836 until 1841 he served as Minister of Justice.

From JOHN R. THOMSON, Philadelphia. Reports his arrival from Canton, which he left in March on account of ill health. The duties of his office as consul will be performed, during his absence, by Rodney Fisher, whom he has appointed consular agent. ALS. DNA, RG59, Cons. Disp., Canton, vol. 1 (M101, R1). Fisher was also a native of Philadelphia.

MISCELLANEOUS LETTERS   September 4, 1825

From JOHN A. LEAMY, Philadelphia. Refers to his letter of the previous day; informs Clay that on that same day (Thomas) Wilson paid him "the amount of the Bill of Col [José Leandro] Palacios"; requests a negotiable draft rather than the order (for the payment of the claim in the case of the *Liberty*). ALS. DNA, RG76, Misc. Claims, Colombia.

APPLICATIONS, RECOMMENDATIONS   September 4, 1825

JOHN D. GODMAN, Philadelphia, recommends George B. Adams for appointment as consul at Alicante. ALS. DNA, RG59, A. and R. (MR1). See above, Cook to Clay, August 3, 1825, note.

To John A. Leamy

John A. Leamy Esqr.   Department of State, 5th. September 1825.
Sir,
          Your Letters of the 3d. and 4th. instant are received. Agreeably

to the request contained in the former an order is enclosed[1] on Mess. Baring Brothers & Co. of London to pay over the proceeds to you of the bill for £1848.8.5. Sterling remitted to them, from this Office, through the Bank of the U. S. I cannot comply with the request communicated in your Letter of the 4th. to furnish you with negociable drafts instead of the order. If there has been some incidental official delays [sic] in the transmission of that bill, occasioning you the loss of a small amount of interest, you should reflect upon the multifarious duties belonging to the Office, which prevent an exclusive attention to any one matter, however important to the individual particularly interested that matter may be. Besides, the arrangement with the Colombian Government is marked by a high degree of liberality towards you. I should imagine that you can have no difficulty in drawing upon England, upon the Credit of the Bill, I am, Your Obt Servant   H. CLAY.

Copy. DNA, RG59, Dom. Letters, vol. 21, p. 143 (M40, R19).
[1] Below, this date.

INSTRUCTIONS AND DISPATCHES   September 5, 1825

From JOHN MULLOWNY, Tangier, no. 38. Reports the sale of a "Sardinian Schooner . . . to the Officers of the Emperor" (Abd-er-Rahman II); describes it as no match for "the smallest vessels of the Navy of the U. S."; and states a belief that "no injury or offence will be offered to any Christian power." ALS. DNA, RG59, Cons. Disp., Tangier, vol. 4 (M-T61, R4). Received November 8.

MISCELLANEOUS LETTERS   September 5, 1825

To BARING BROTHERS AND COMPANY, London. Requests payment, to John A. Leamy for Ledlie and Leamy, of a bill of exchange for £1848.8.5, drawn by authority of the Colombian Government on (Manuel José) Hurtado. Copy. DNA, RG59, Cons. Instr., vol. 2 (M78, R2). Cf. above, Clay to Leamy, August 30, 1825; Clay to Wilson, August 30, 1825; Wilson to Clay, September 3, 1825.

To JOHN LEAMY, President of the Marine Insurance Company, Philadelphia. Acknowledges receipt of Leamy's letter of September 3, refuses to settle the question of division of the sum recovered, returns the order "heretofore given," and leaves the two insurance companies to settle the matter between themselves. Copy. DNA, RG59, Dom. Letters, vol. 21, pp. 144-45 (M40, R19).

From J[AMES] L. E[DWARDS], "War Dept. Pension Office." Replying to Clay's note of September 3 (not found), states that the claim of Littleton Jeter "was rejected several years ago, on account of his property, which, although inconsiderable, was considered sufficient, with his own exertions, and the labor of his family to keep him above the necessity of public or private charity." Concludes, from "the schedule last exhibited," that his property has not diminished and that, while it "would appear to be a hard case . . . the decision was in strict conformity with the rules observed in such cases." Copy. DNA, RG15, Letter Books, General, vol. 17, p. 25. Cf. above, Bodley to Clay, August 23, 1825, note.

From W[ILLIAM] L. PRALL (Trenton, New Jersey). States that "James J. Wilson Esq. the original proprietor, of the Trenton True American, died on the 29 „ July 1824"; that his son, Allen N. Wilson, became publisher of the paper, while Prall served as editor; and that *"the whole* of the establishment" has passed into Prall's hands. AES. Endorsement on Wilson to Clay, this date. Prall and Allan N. Wilson have not been further identified. James J. Wilson, born in Essex County, New Jersey, had joined in publishing the *True American* a few months after its establishment in 1801 and continued the journal alone after 1808. A militia officer with the rank of brigadier general at his death, he had also served in the United States Senate from 1815 to 1821 and as postmaster of Trenton from 1821 to 1824.

From JAMES PH. PUGLIA, "Mount-Airy's College, Germantown" (Pennsylvania). States that he has been informed that his letter of August 15 was held by (William) Thornton on account of Clay's absence but hopes that it has now been delivered; complains again of Thornton's issuance of a patent to Nathaniel Sylvester; argues that he should not be subjected to the expense of litigation to protect his own right; announces abandonment of his patent, for which he expects the Government to provide "equitable compensation"; threatens, if his plea is unheeded, to bring the matter before Congress, though dreading that the nature of his case "may afford matter of detraction to ill disposed Editors & Scribblers, who eagerly seize every opportunity for scandalously inveighing against the most liberal of earthly Governments." ALS. DNA, RG59, Misc. Letters (M179, R63).

From ALLAN N. WILSON, Trenton (New Jersey). Certifies that he has transferred the Trenton *True American* to William L. Prall. ALS. DNA, RG59, P. and D. of L.

To Platt H. Crosby

Sir,　　　　　　　　　　　　Department of State, 6th. September 1825.

Your Letter of the 26th. May 1825, is received at this Department, just at the moment of the acquittal of Captain Stewart[1] of the charges preferred against him, arising out of the cruize of the Franklin in the Pacific. Your Letter, therefore transmitted through Mr. Prevost must have had whatever effect belonged to such a letter, upon the supposition of its entire genuiness [*sic*], and its having been transmitted with the knowledge and assent of its author. Your protest against it will be regarded in future.

With suitable acknowledgements for the information communicated in your Letter of the 26th. May respecting the politics, Military affairs and commerce of South America, I am, with great respect, Your Obedt. Servt.　　　　　　　　　H. CLAY.

Platt. H. Crosby Esqr. Lima.

Copy. DNA, RG59, Dom. Letters, vol. 21, p. 184 (M40, R19). Copy also in DNA, RG59, Cons. Instr., vol. 2 (M78, R2), p. 451.
1 Charles Stewart. See above III, 483n.

To John Rodgers

(Secret)   Department of State, Washington 6 Septr. 1825.
John Rodgers Esqr. Commanding U. S. Squadron in the
Mediterranean, U. S. Ship North Carolina.
Sir,

I have the honour to transmitt [*sic*] to you, enclosed a copy of a
Treaty between Turkey and France, or rather, in the language of
Turkish Diplomacy, of Capitulations, conceded by the Porte, to
France. Being in French, it is accompanied by a Translation, which
has been hastily made. From a perusal of this Document you will
see what has been granted to France.[1] The President wishes to
obtain similar advantages for the Commerce of this Country, and
you were instructed by a letter from this Office, under date the
7th. day of February 1825, to ascertain, through the Captain Pacha
of the Turkish fleet,[2] the probability that existed of this Government being able to procure them. It was expected that you were
to sound him, not treat with him, for which neither he nor you
would have Powers. But the interview may possibly lead to your
both being hereafter invested with powers to accomplish the object,
as being a mode preferable to sending a Minister to Constantinople.
Our wish is 1st. to trade with all the ports of Turkey, in whatever
quarter of the Globe situated, on the footing of the most favoured
Nations: 2ly. to obtain a free ingress and regress, through the
Dardanelles, to and from the Black sea, and 3ly. to be allowed to
appoint Consuls to reside at such Ports as the interests of our
Commerce may require.

Possibly the Captain Pacha, who was believed to entertain
friendly sentiments towards this Country, may not now be in
command, and may be succeeded by another, not cherishing a
similar disposition. In the event of such a change it will be left to
your discretion to decide whether it will be expedient, or not,
to open the business to such successor.[3]

I have the honour to be your obedt. Servt.   H CLAY.

Copy. DNA, RG59, Dip. Instr., Special Missions, vol. 1, pp. 30-31 (M77, R152).
Copy also in MHi-Adams Papers, Letters Received (MR472).
1 Probably a copy of the French-Turkish agreement of 1816, which in itself was not
favorable to the French but which had been put into effect in 1820 with applicaton
to France, under most-favored-nation precedents, of "all newer and lower specific
duties" found in schedules negotiated with Austria (1818) and Great Britain (1820).
Vernon John Puryear, *France and the Levant from the Bourbon Restoration to the
Peace of Kutiah* (University of California, *Publications in History*, XXVII; Berkeley,
1941), pp. 6-7.

2 Khosref Mehemet. In the spring of 1824 it had been reported to Secretary of State Adams that the Captain Pasha of the Turkish squadron in the Mediterranean, who "had been for several years the avowed and acknowledged patron of the American nation at the Porte," had proposed a meeting with the commander of the American squadron, at which the latter should make "such proposals for a treaty as the American Government might desire." The Turkish officer "would then communicate them directly to the Sultan," thus circumventing interference by European powers to forestall such an arrangement. Adams, *Memoirs*, VI, 320. After prolonged delay Adams had instructed Rodgers on February 7, 1825, "to ascertain in what manner a Treaty of Commerce, founded upon principles of reciprocity, and by which, access to the navigation of the Black-Sea, should be secured to the commercial shipping of the United States," might be obtained. DNA, RG59, Dip. Instr., Special Missions, vol. 1, p. 28 (M77, R152).

3 Negotiations were not successfully entered into until 1830. See Miller (ed.), *Treaties. . .* , II, 541-98.

To William C. Somerville

William C. Somerville &c. &c. &c.　　(Secret)

Sir,　　　　　　　　Department of State, Washington, 6 Septr. 1825.

The very deep interest which the People of the United States naturally feel in the existing contest between Greece and Turkey has induced the President to appoint you an Agent for the Government of the United States to proceed to Greece. You will accordingly embark on board the United States frigate, Brandywine, which is to carry General La Fayette to France,[1] and, upon your arrival there, you will thence continue in that vessel or proceed, without delay, in such other manner as may appear to you most eligible, to the point of your destination. Upon reaching Greece, you will repair to the actual seat of Government and communicate to the existing authorities your arrival and your appointment. You will let them know that the people of the United States and their Government, throughout the whole of the present struggle of Greece, have constantly felt an anxious desire that it might terminate in the re establishment of the liberty and independence of that Country, and that they have consequently observed the events of the war, with the most lively interest, sympathizing with Greece when they have been unfortunately adverse, and rejoicing when they have been propitious to her cause— Nor ought any indifference, as to its issue, on the part of the United-States, to be inferred, from the neutrality which they have hitherto prescribed, and probably will continue to prescribe, to themselves. That neutrality is according to the policy which has characterized this Government from its origin, which was observed during all the Revolutionary wars of France, and which has been also extended to the contest between Spain and her American Colonies. It is better for both the United States and Greece that it should not be departed from in the present instance.

It is a principal object of your Agency to collect, and transmit, from time to time, to this Department information of the present state and future progress of the war, by land and at sea; the capacity of Greece to maintain the Contest; the number and condition of her Armies; the state of her Marine; of the public Revenue; the amount, dispositions and degree of education of her population; the character and views of the Chiefs,—and, in short, whatever will tend to enable the Government of the United-States to form a correct judgment, in regard to the ability of Greece to prosecute the war, and to sustain an independent Government.

Without any officious interference in their affairs, or obtruding your advice upon them, you will, whenever applied to, communicate all the information which may be desired, as to this Country and its institutions; and you will, on suitable occasions, lend your friendly office to heal any difficulties or soothe any angry passions, in the way to that harmonious concert between the Grecian functionaries and Commanders, without which their cause cannot prosper.

You will also render any aid that you can to our commerce and seamen in the ports and harbours of Greece. Information, which, it is hoped, is not correct, has reached this Department, of one or two American Merchantmen having engaged in the Turkish service, to transport military men or means.[2] If any such instances should fall within your observation, you will acquaint the parties concerned with the high displeasure of the President at conduct so unworthy of American Citizens, and so contrary to their duty, as well as their honour; and that if they should bring themselves, in consequence of such misconduct, into any difficulties, they will have no right to expect the interposition of their Government in their behalf.

The compensation which the President has determined to allow you is at the rate of four thousand five hundred dollars per annum. Your Commission, as Chargé d'Affaires to Sweden, will be considered as terminating on your arrival in Europe, and as the Salary which it carried along will then cease with it, the above compensation will begin on that day.

I have the honour to be your obedt. Servt.   H. CLAY—

Copy. DNA, RG59, Dip. Instr., Special Missions, vol. 1, pp. 31-33 (M77, R152).
1 Lafayette set sail from Washington on September 7. The *Brandywine* had been newly commissioned and assigned to the Mediterranean Squadron.
2 See above, Shaler to Clay, June 4, 1825.

DIPLOMATIC NOTES   September 6, 1825

From HILARIO DE RIVAS Y SALMON, "Legacion de España," Philadelphia. Transmits copies of two letters, received from the Spanish consul at Baltimore

(Juan Bautista Bernabeu), relative to claims "in the cause pending of the Porto Rico Privateer *'Palmyra'* " (see above, Clay to Everett, April 27, 1825, note). LS, in Spanish, with translation appended in State Department file. DNA, RG59, Notes from Spanish Legation, vol. 8 (M59, R11).

INSTRUCTIONS AND DISPATCHES   September 6, 1825

From ALEXANDER HAMMETT, Naples. Reports information from Count Lucchesi that the Sicilian King (Francis I) and Minister of Foreign Affairs (Luigi di Medici) seem disposed to remove discriminating duties against the United States and "fix a reasonable quarantine" for American vessels and, though "afraid of England to do so," have taken steps toward these ends. Lucchesi has also told him that a Minister Extraordinary from the United States to the Court of Naples is on his way and that Lucchesi, himself, has been instructed to be prepared to embark in time to reach Washington when Congress meets. Hammett adds that a local merchant admitted to him the use of false weights in the sale of American cargoes by the customhouse (cf. above, II, 505n; Clay to Appleton, May 12, 1825, note) and that "it is well known there are many of these Neapolitans who owe their wealth to American plunder and we are so far the dupes as to leave them in the quiet possession of it." ALS. DNA, RG59, Cons. Disp., Naples, vol. 1 (M-T224, R-T1). Addressed to "J. Clay Esqr. Secy. of State"; received November 23.

From ROBERT MONROE HARRISON, Antigua. Encloses triplicate of his letter (to John Q. Adams) of June, 1824; states that he has had an attack of apoplexy; reports that "no one is satisfied with" (William) Huskisson's "famous colonial intercourse bill" (see above, Rush to Secretary of State, March 26, 1825, note), which goes into effect in January, 1826, because of the tax on "articles of the first *necessity*," heretofore free; expresses a hope "that our Government will insist on having Consuls formally acknowledged where we have occasion for them"; and notes that British colonial law requires "Masters of vessels to enter into bonds to take away all persons they bring with them. . . ." ALS. DNA, RG59, Cons. Disp., Antigua, vol. 1 (M-T327, R1). Received October 8.

APPLICATIONS, RECOMMENDATIONS   September 6, 1825

LITTLETON DENNIS TEACKLE, Washington, encloses copies of correspondence from (George E.) Mitchell (relating to an application by Teackle for a position in the Treasury Department) ; states that he has requested recommendation by Secretary (Richard) Rush for appointment to a consulate "in the absence of any services at home. . . ." ALS. DNA, RG59, A. and R. (M531, R8). The enclosures include Mitchell to Rush, August 1, 1825, and Mitchell to Teackle, August 12, 1825. Cf. above, Teackle to Clay, August 22, 23, 1825. In an undated note addressed to Clay, L(ittleton) D. T(eackle) again referred to his reluctance to defend his character but added: ". . . it must be obvious that a rejection, from that cause, may prove a source of incalculable injury to me." ANI. DNA, RG59, A. and R. (M531, R8). Teackle received no appointment.

Mitchell, a graduate of the Medical Department of the University of Pennsylvania, had served as a member of the Maryland Legislature (1808), as president of the Maryland Executive Council (1809-1812), and as an officer in the War of 1812. He was a representative in Congress from 1823 to 1827 and from 1829 until his death in 1832.

To James Brown

Dear Sir   Washington 7h. Sept. 1825
  I have only time on this day of bustle, being that of Genl. La Fayette's departure, that [*sic*] since I wrote by Capt. Morris[1] your letter of the 15h. July has come to hand. I regret very much to hear of the renewal of your rheumatism. The President does not disapprove of your visit to the waters of Savoy, but sees in your state of health ample justification for your resort to them and wishes that they may produce the desired effect.
  I was aware that in the work of pacification between Spain and the Colonies, Russia was the important power to put in motion. I hope that our efforts may have some favorable effect on her; and if the Emperor[2] could be induced to interest himself on the side of Peace, Spain could not well resist the concerted movements in Europe and America to bring the War to a conclusion.
  We have no news. Yr's faithfully   H. CLAY
James Brown Esq.

  ALS. KyLxT-Haupt Collection.
  [1] Charles Morris, in whose care Clay apparently gave his letter, above, to Brown, of September 4, had commanded the *Brandywine* during its voyage to return Lafayette to France. For this duty he was on leave from the Board of Naval Commissioners, where he was assigned from 1823 to 1827 and from 1832 to 1841. He commanded the Boston Navy Yard from 1827 to 1832 and the United States naval squadrons off Brazil and in the Mediterranean from 1841 to 1844.
  [2] Alexander I.

DIPLOMATIC NOTES   September 7, 1825

From ANTONIO JOSE CANAZ, New York. States that his own ill health and the absence of Clay from Washington have prevented him from proceeding to the negotiation of the treaties, which are the object of his mission; asks to be informed whether the "Supremo Gobierno" is willing to negotiate with "la Republica del centro." LS. DNA, RG59, Notes from Central American Legations, vol. 1 (M-T34, R1).

INSTRUCTIONS AND DISPATCHES   September 7, 1825

From JOSHUA DODGE, Marseilles. Requests leave of absence from his consulate, which would be left in the charge of Thomas Oxnard, an American citizen. ALS. DNA, RG59, Cons. Disp., Marseilles, vol. 2 (M-T220, R1). Received October 30. Oxnard was from Portland, Maine. On November 11, 1825, Daniel Brent, "by direction of the Secretary," acknowledged receipt of Dodge's letter and informed him that the President acceded to his request. Copy. DNA, RG59, Cons. Instr., vol. 2, p. 373 (M78, R2).

From CHRISTOPHER HUGHES, Brussels. Reports his arrival, on September 5, and the delivery of his credentials to De Conincke, Minister of Foreign Affairs, to whom he explained the circumstances necessitating his impending leave of ab-

sence. ALS. DNA, RG59, Dip. Disp., Sweden and Norway, vol. 4 (M45, R5).
Received October 22.

From JOHN MULLOWNY, Tangier, no. 39. Gives eight reasons why the United
States should own a house in Tangier for the residence of the American consul
and offers to sell, for $6,000, the house in which he resides and which he built
over a period of years from 1821 to 1824; states that he has had no letter from
the Department of State since May, 1824; and reports that he has informed
the King (Abd-er-Rahman II), who wishes to purchase American vessels of war,
that he cannot "act in such affairs without the consent of the President of the
United States," which he does not expect to obtain. LS. DNA, RG59, Cons.
Disp., Tangiers, vol. 4 (M-T61, R4). Received February 26, 1826.

MISCELLANEOUS LETTERS   September 7, 1825

From P[ETER] A. BROWNE, Philadelphia. Again calls Clay's attention to "the
application of the Franklin Institute for the specifications of patents"; states
that "The Commee of examination of the Franklin Institute . . . experience
considerable inconvenience in being deprived of a perusal of these documents."
ALS. DNA, RG59, Misc. Letters (M179, R63). A printed circular notice, signed
by Browne, of the appointment of a committee of the Institute to examine and
report on all new inventions and the printed report of that committee on the
invention of "Messrs. [Nathaniel] Sylvester and Evans, of this city, to prevent
alterations in checks, Bills of Exchange, and other instruments of writing,"
had been sent to Clay on September 6. Evans has not been further identified;
the patent had been issued to Sylvester alone. See above, Puglia to Clay,
August 15, 1825, note.

From ALEXANDER SCOTT, Georgetown. Refers (without date) to an earlier letter
to Clay, requesting a revision of Scott's account as agent to Venezuela; submits
additional documentary material in this connection; and cites instances of other
accounts having been reopened, after being settled, and additional compensation
having been made. ALS. DNA, RG59, Misc. Letters (M179, R63). Scott, a
native of Maryland, who had been collector for the port of Pensacola from
1821 to 1824, had earlier, in 1812 and 1813, served as political agent of the
United States in Venezuela, charged, in addition to his diplomatic duties, with
distribution of provisions donated by the United States for inhabitants of
Caracas suffering as the result of an earthquake. Scott had been paid a salary
at the rate of $2,000 a year, without allowance for expenses incurred while
abroad. In response, probably, to the earlier letter, Clay had informed Scott
(communication not found) "that 'he did not think it proper to disturb an
account so long settled.'" *House Reports,* 20 Cong., 1 Sess., no. 182, p. 4. Scott
thereafter submitted successive memorials to Congress and additional letters
(omitted by editors) to Clay urging favorable action on his claim. Finally, by
act of May 29, 1830 (6 *U. S. Stat.,* 436), Congress authorized payment to
him of $1,471.97 as reimbursement for his expenses abroad.

APPLICATIONS, RECOMMENDATIONS   September 7, 1825

C[ORNELIUS] P. VAN NESS, Burlington (Vermont), recommends William L.
Reaney, of Boston, for the consulship at Puerto Rico. ALS. DNA, RG59, A. and
R. (MR3). Reaney, not further identified, received no appointment.

To John J. Crittenden

Dear Sir   Washington 8h. September 1825
   Genl. La Fayette introduced to me in a very particular manner
the bearer Mr. Frederick List,[1] formerly a member of the Assembly
of Wurtemberg [sic], and professor of public law and political
œconomy in the University of Tübingen. Being on a visit to the
West, I could not refuse to myself the opportunity of making known
[sic] to you in the hope that the interest with which he has inspired
me may be also felt by you. Your's faithfully   H CLAY
J. J. Crittenden Esqr.

ALS. KyU.
[1] George Friedrich List, who had begun his teaching career in 1817, had resigned
shortly thereafter because of governmental opposition to his activities in promoting
German customs unity. He had been elected to the Diet of Württemberg in 1819, but
again his liberal ideas and advocacy of economic reform, particularly in aid of industry,
had brought him into governmental disfavor. Following an indictment and prison
sentence for sedition, he had escaped into exile for four years. When he had thereafter returned to his homeland in 1824, he had been re-arrested and was released only
upon condition that he leave the country. He had arrived in the United States in June,
1825, and traveled in the party with Lafayette much of the time until the latter's return
to France (see above, Clay to Somerville, September 6, 1825). The following year
List became editor of a Jacksonite German newspaper at Reading, Pennsylvania,
and during the latter part of the decade he was actively engaged in the coal and
railway development of that area. A naturalized American citizen, he returned to
Europe as United States consul at Hamburg (1830-1831), at Mannheim (1832-1834),
at Leipzig (1834-1838), and at Stuttgart (1843-1845).

DIPLOMATIC NOTES   September 8, 1825

To C. D. E. J. BANGEMAN HUYGENS. States in reply to Huygens' note of
September 2, that the United States will cooperate in the arrest of Captain
Lloyd. Copy. DNA, RG59, Notes to Foreign Legations, vol. 3, p. 229 (M38,
R3). ALI draft, in CSmH.

INSTRUCTIONS AND DISPATCHES   September 8, 1825

From A[LEXANDER] H. EVERETT, Madrid, no. 4. Reports his arrival in Madrid,
August 28; describes his journey from Paris, interview with Zea Bermudez, and
reception by the King (Ferdinand VII); and notes that Zea, "observing that
they were occupied in making a new arrangement of the Tariff," advises postponement of negotiation for a commercial treaty but is ready to discuss
indemnities "and requested . . . a written statement of the claims of the United
States, and of the principles upon which we desire that they may be adjusted."
In regard to the subject of "acknowledgment of the South American States,"
Zea "did not think it safe (in his own interest) . . . even to allow it to be
supposed that he had the most distant inclination to" suggest it to the King.
Everett adds that, as (Obadiah) Rich has already reported (above, August 22,
1825), Spain "has restored the privilege of depositing naval stores at Port
Mahon" and that "the affair of the Six thousand dollars [see above, Nelson to
Clay, July 10, 1825] is still in suspense." Copies of various documents relating
to formalities of Everett's arrival, including his "short address . . . to the

King" (see below, Poinsett to Clay, January 14, 1826), are enclosed. LS, partly in cipher, decoded in State Department file. DNA, RG59, Dip. Disp., Spain, vol. 25 (M31, R27). Received November 7. Extracts published in Manning (arr.), *Diplomatic Correspondence . . . Latin-American Nations*, III, 2058-59.

From HENRY MIDDLETON, St. Petersburg, no. 49. Transmits a copy of Nesselrode's reply to Middleton's note communicating to the Russian Government his instructions from Clay (above, July 27, 1825); considers "this answer to be *in substance*, (when divested of its diplomatic garb,) in every respect as favorable to the views" expressed by Clay "as could possibly be expected to be given by this Government standing in the predicament it now does." Infers from the document "that the proposal that the Emperor [Alexander I] shall lend his aid towards the conclusion of the war between Spain & her Colonies by interposing his good offices in the form of pacific counsel to the Mother Country, has been communicated to the allied Cabinets. . . ." Adds: "For obvious reasons we must not expect to learn *officially* that such advice as that alluded to above has been given, unless it should be attended to." ALS. DNA, RG59, Dip., Disp., Russia, vol. 10 (M35, R10). Dated: "27 Augst./8 Septr 1825"; addressed: "To the Secretary of State. . . ." Received December 8. Published in *American State Papers, Foreign Relations*, V, 849-50.

In the enclosure, dated August 20, 1825, Nesselrode wrote: "His Imperial Majesty has ever thought, that Justice, the law of Nations, and the general interest in having the indisputable titles of Sovereignty respected, could not allow the determinations of the Mother Country in this important case, to be prejudged or anticipated. On the other side, whenever Spain has wished to discuss the future condition of South America, she has addressed overtures to all the Allied Powers of Europe. It will not be possible therefore for His Imperial Majesty to change principles in this negociation, nor to institute it separately (*insolément*); and until positive information has been received of the ulterior views of Spain in regard to her American possessions, of her decision upon the proposition of the United States, and of the opinions of her Allies in relation to the same subject, Russia cannot give a definitive answer.

"She is however, in the mean while, pleased to hope, that the United States becoming every day more convinced of the evils & dangers that would result to Cuba and Puerto Rico from a change of government, being satisfied, as Mr Clay has said in his dispatch, with the present commercial legislation of these two islands, and deriving an additional motive of security from the honorable resolution of Spain not to grant to them, any longer, letters of marque, will use their influence, in defeating as far as may be in their power, every enterprise against these islands, in securing to the rights of His Catholic Majesty constant and proper respect, in maintaining the only state of things that can preserve a just balance of power in the sea of the Antilles, prevent shocking examples, and as the Cabinet of Washington has remarked, secure to the general peace, salutary guaranties."

From HENRY MIDDLETON, St. Petersburg, "Private." Congratulates Clay on the prospect of "obtaining the Russian mediation between Spain & the new American States." States that Clay's "paper [above, May 10, 1825] having been admirably translated into french, so as to preserve all its original force, was forwarded to the different Allied Courts, where it has been much admired." Declares that he knows "positively that Prince Metternich approves of" the proposal, and, "as France no doubt wishes something of the kind . . . and as Prussia assents to every thing which is agreeable to the majority of the allies," he (Middleton) considers "the question as settled." Asserts that *"The advice *will be given,* provided Pozzo di Borgo does not get up some Hobgoblin Spectre to prevent it," and expresses a belief "that *it will be accepted."* Adds that "a good deal has been gained" by Russia's delay in answering, "as at first the proposal seemed to be not a little *staggering."* ALS. DNA, RG59, Dip. Disp., Russia, vol. 10 (M35, R10). Dated "27 Augst./8 Septr 1825"; received December 8. Published in Manning (arr.), *Diplomatic Correspondence . . . Latin-American Nations,* III, 1877-78.

MISCELLANEOUS LETTERS   September 8, 1825

To GEORGE MURRAY, St. Augustine. Encloses copy of a letter addressed to him "by the Agent of this Department in June last," relative to money overpaid to him, and requests that he "will not hesitate in correcting" the error. Copy. DNA, RG59, Dom. Letters, vol. 21, p. 146 (M40, R19). In the letter to which reference is made (*ibid.,* 100-101) W(illiam) Browne states that Murray received overpayment of $100 for services as prosecuting attorney (in St. John's County court) in 1822-1823 and district attorney for East Florida in May, 1823. Murray, born in Virginia, had been an officer in the War of 1812, had held appointment as a member of the Florida Legislative Council (1823-1824), and in May, 1824, had been named land commissioner for the East Florida District.

From SAMUEL KEITH, Philadelphia. Notes that (Thomas) Wilson, of the Bank of the United States, has not received instructions from the State Department respecting payment of the insurance company's proportion of the sum obtained from Colombia, in the case of the *Minerva,* and requests Clay's attention to the matter. LS. DNA, RG76, Misc. Claims, Colombia. Cf. above, Keith to Clay, March 11, 1825; Wilson to Clay, September 3, 1825.

APPLICATIONS, RECOMMENDATIONS   September 8, 1825

C[HARLES] TAIT, Claiborne, Alabama, recommends, for appointment as United States attorney for the Southern District of Alabama, Henry Hitchcock, grandson of Ethan Allen, the Revolutionary War hero. ALS. DNA, RG59, A. and R. (MR2).

To John M. Forbes

J. M. Forbes Esqr.   Bs Ayres.
Dear Sir   (private)   Washington 9th. Septr. 1825
    I duly received your very friendly letter of the 26th. May last, and thank you for your kind congratulations on my appointment to the Department of State. It is not one of the least agreeable incidents of that situation that I shall be brought . . . . . . [*sic*] into official contact with you, though, I fear, I cannot often indulge in the luxury of private correspondence.—
    Your letter of the 1st. July has also been received— Your accounts will be looked into with a liberal eye, and with an anxiety to find their passage reconcileable [*sic*] to law and to duty. The transmission of the laws of Congress, and of the Journal, which

you desire, shall not be neglected, nor the Speech, if a copy of it can be procured.—

Your despatches have been very regularly received, and display additional proofs of zeal and ability, in the service of our Country.— I have not yet heard of your reception of your Commission, as Charge des Affaires, which I took pleasure in transmitting by Mr. Pleasants, with your instructions.[1]—

The Administration moves on very well— The Georgia business[2] is well disposed of, until the Meeting of Congress; and the trial of Naval Officers[3] is concluded— Genl. La Fayette left us the day before yesterday.[4]— I am, my Dr. Sir, faithfully Yr. obedt. Servant,

HENRY CLAY.—

Copy. DNA, RG59, Unofficial Letter-Book of H. Clay, 1825-29, p. 5.
[1] Above, April 14, 1825. Cf. below, Forbes to Clay, September 18, 1825.
[2] See above, Clay to Southard, July 3, 1825.
[3] David Porter; Charles Stewart.
[4] See above, Clay to Somerville, September 6, 1825, note.

INSTRUCTIONS AND DISPATCHES   September 9, 1825

From HEMAN ALLEN, Valparaiso, no. 18. Reports that the Province of Santiago has elected delegates to a general Congress, supposed to convene September 5 under a mandate issued by (Ramón de) Freire, that other provinces "disobeyed the summons," and that the members from Santiago, "by some wonderful magick, peculiar to these countries, have been transformed into a provincial Assembly, and as such, are now in session"; states a belief "that these proceedings will tend very greatly to the revival of the federative system," which, however, is opposed by the aristocracy in the Province of Santiago. Repeats his opinion that little can be done toward settlement of claims and negotiation of a commercial treaty; urges continued presence there of "a competent public agent" to aid American commerce and to take advantage of a favorable moment for negotiation; and recommends (Samuel) Larned, Secretary of Legation, for the duty, although Allen, himself, is willing to continue his services. ALS. DNA, RG59, Dip. Disp., Chile, vol. 1 (M-T2, R1). Received January 13, 1826. Freire, born in Santiago, Chile, had pursued an active military career in the forces of both Chile and Argentina, in opposition to Spanish rule. In 1823 he had been named Supreme Executive of his native land and ruled until 1830, when he was overthrown and forced into exile. He returned to Chile in 1842 but spent the last decade of his life in retirement.

From T[HOMAS] M. RODNEY, Havana. Presents specific inquiries concerning official policy toward American vessels sailing under Spanish coasting license, American vessels transferred to foreign ownership, and American vessels sold to other United States citizens. LS. DNA, RG59, Cons. Disp., Havana, vol. 3, (M-T20, R3).

MISCELLANEOUS LETTERS   September 9, 1825

From JAMES FERGUSON, Baltimore. Inquires when (William) Huskisson's bill (see above, Rush to Clay, March 26, 1825, note) goes into effect and whether, under it, imports of butter, lard, candles, and soap from the United States are admissible in the Barbados. ALS. DNA, RG59, Misc. Letters (M179, R63). Ferguson not further identified; cf. above, I, 545.

On September 12, 1825, Daniel Brent, at Clay's direction, replied to Ferguson that the Department of State had no copy of the bill as it had passed Parliament. Copy. DNA, RG59, Dom. Letters, vol. 21, pp. 148-49 (M40, R19).

From WILLIAM THORNTON, Patent Office. Acknowledges receipt of the letter from James Ph. Puglia to Clay, September 5; explains that, in regard to the patent granted to (Nathaniel) Sylvester, he did not think there was interference with that previously granted to Puglia, but that in any case he has no discretionary power to deny an application; and asserts that, while he warns applicants when he thinks interference exists, only the courts can decide between contending parties. ALS. DNA, RG59, Misc. Letters (M179, R63).

From Walter Dun

Dear Sir   Chillicothe September 10. 1825

Agreeably to promise I now take the liberty of inclosing to you your two receipts, dated July 15. 1823;–one to myself as Exr. of John Graham, deceased,[1] and the other to James Herons Executor,[2] with the Clerks tickets which you sent from Kentucky to Mr Creighton,[3] for comparison; and to enable you more readily to do so I have subjoined a statement of the amounts formerly paid, on the different accounts, with the sums charged by the Marshall and Clerk, agreeably to the inclosed tickets, which shews a balance against me of $10.21/100, and principally on account of Mr. Call.[4] I beg of you to give this matter your earliest attention, and return your two receipts to me; and whatever be the amount of the balance against me be pleased to direct in what manner I shall pay it. With the greatest regard I am   Dear Sir, Your Mo Ob Servant   WALTER DUN

July 15. 1823–Amount paid by W D to Clerk $6.36 to
     Marshal $2.50 ....$8.86
now charged by Clerk Pr. inclosed Tickets $3.19 & by
     Marshal $4.50 ....7.69
                  Balance in favour of W D $1.17

July 15. 1823–Amount paid by Herons Exr. to Clerk $26.91–
         & to Marshal $18.90 ....$45.81
now charged by Clerk Pr. inclosed Tickets $29.27 & by
    Marshal $18.90 ....48.17
                  Bale. in favour Mr Clay ....$ 2.36
           Off balance in favour W Dun 1.17
                                      $1.19
Amount now charged by Clerk & Marshal to D Call 9.02
          Final Balance in favour of Mr: Clay $10.21

P.S. I have had the plat and Certificate of survey No: 12521 of 300 acres in the General Land Office since March last; and although I wanted a Patent for it as soon as it could have issued, and removed two difficulties, the last in June, I have not yet got the Patent. I had got thus far when it occured [*sic*] to me that your interference in my behalf might make matters worse with Mr: Graham,[5] and I concluded to write to himself again upon the subject. I will rather put up with neglect and delay than trouble you with that which is always, in its very nature, unpleasant and disagreeable. I know your willingness to oblige me, but your kind endeavours might make matters worse.—   W D

ALS. DLC-TJC (M212, R13). Addressed to Clay at Washington. See above, III, 199, 449-50.
1 Graham had died August 6, 1820.   2 James Taylor, Jr.
3 William Creighton. See below, Clay to Dun, September 22, 1825, note.
4 Daniel Call.   5 George Graham.

INSTRUCTIONS AND DISPATCHES   September 10, 1825

To BEAUFORT T. WATTS, "Chargé d'Affaires, U. S. at Bogota." Informs him "that a Bill of one thousand Dollars," drawn by him on the State Department, April 8, 1825, "was, this day, presented, unaccompanied by any Letter of advice or explanation," and that the state of his accounts caused Clay "reluctantly . . . to decline it." Copy. DNA, RG59, Dip. Instr., vol. 10, pp. 379-80 (M77, R5) .

From JAMES BROWN, Paris, no. 33. Encloses copies of a letter, dated July 26, from the Prince de Castelcicala, Sicilian Ambassador (to France) , informing Brown of "the appointment of Count Ferdinand Lucchesi Palli de Campo-franco as Consul General of His Sicilian Majesty in the United States of America to reside in Washington . . . ," and of Brown's reply. LS. DNA, RG59, Dip. Disp., France, vol. 22 (M34, R25) . Received October 31. Fabrici Ruffo, Prince de Castelcicala, born in Naples, had served as diplomatic agent of his Government at London, prior to the turn of the century, and at Paris, since 1815.

From A[LEXANDER] H. EVERETT, Madrid, no. 5. States that his predecessor (Hugh Nelson) has probably informed Clay "of the proceedings that have taken place in regard to the sum of six thousand dollars due to the United States" (see above, Clay to Nelson, April 14, 1825; Nelson to Clay, July 10, 1825) ; reports failure of the assignee (Wiseman, Gower, and Company) to pay more; discusses written invitations of a local judge for an American agent to attend a meeting of creditors of the assignee and their rejection, by the American consul, (Obadiah) Rich, on the advice of Everett; expresses an opinion that it would be inconsistent "either with the dignity or interest of the Country to expend a great deal more time and paper upon a claim . . . of trifling consequence"; and encloses copies of correspondence on this matter. LS. DNA, RG59, Dip. Disp., Spain, vol. 25 (M31, R27) . Received November 7. In one of the copied letters Everett has stated to Zea Bermudez that, despite the King's decree, the sum of $6,000 due the United States from the property of Wiseman, Gower, and Company has not been paid in full; that it is the duty of the King's officials to enforce his decree; that the Spanish Chargé d'Affaires in the United States (Hilario de Rivas y Salmon) has applied to the American Government for a second loan of $6,000; and that the President would "readily comply with this request" but that his "ability . . . to accommodate in this way his Majesty's servants must of course depend altogether upon the punctuality and promptitude with which the reimbursements are made at home." See above, Salmon to Clay, April 10, 1825; Clay to Salmon, April 16, 1825.

MISCELLANEOUS LETTERS   September 10, 1825

To SAMUEL KEITH, President, Delaware Insurance Company, Philadelphia. Transmits, in response to Keith's letter of September 8, an order on the Bank of the United States for payment, from "proceeds of the Bill upon Col. Palacio [José Leandro Palacios] for $20,000. on account of the Minerva, $13,500. with interest. . . ." Copy. DNA, RG59, Dom. Letters, vol. 21, pp. 146-47 (M40, R19).

To THOMAS WILSON, Cashier of the Bank of the United States, Philadelphia. Requests payment, from proceeds of the bill on Palacios, "to the President of the Delaware Insurance Company or his agent the sum of $13,500. with interest. . . ." Copy. *Ibid.,* 147.

From SAT[ERLEE] CLARK, New York, "Confidential." States that, "With a view to expose the abuses which exist in the War Department . . . , introduced by the late Secretary [John C. Calhoun]," he has begun publishing a series of articles, two of which have appeared in the New York *National Advocate,* over the signature, "Hancock"; declares that he has found it necessary, in order to achieve publication, to pose as an opponent of (John Quincy) Adams, for whom he has "the highest respect," and that he will eventually show that the abuses of which he complains are attributable to the preceding administration; attacks Calhoun for having him dismissed from military service unfairly and without a trial; and requests Clay to communicate as much as he thinks proper of this letter to the President. ALS. MHi-Adams Papers, Letters Received (MR472). Clark, of Vermont, had attended the United States Military Academy, held a commission as first lieutenant during the War of 1812 and served as a district paymaster from 1810 to 1816 and as district and battalion paymaster with the rank of major from 1816 until his dismissal from the service on August 5, 1824. He was publicly identified as a "defaulter" and charged with failure to settle his accounts within the prescribed period; suit to recover over $13,000 had been instituted against him by the Treasury Department in the Federal court for the Southern District of New York. When an arbiter found Clark entitled to counterclaims leaving a balance in his favor of nearly $28,000, the Government withdrew the case and carried it to jury trial. Prodded by judicial instructions suggesting that the usual commission rates might be reduced in view of the size of the funds involved, a jury in 1827 reduced the balance owed Clark to $15,632, which sum the Government still refused to pay. A congressional committee some months after Clark's death, in March, 1848, finally recommended payment of the jury award, and a law making such provision was enacted on March 3, 1849 (9 *U. S. Stat.,* 784). The issue rested upon Clark's claim for a commission and travel expenses incurred in paying militia, as distinct from regular army personnel. *House Reports,* 19 Cong., 2 Sess., no. 79, p. 153; 24 Cong., 2 Sess., no. 164; 30 Cong., 1 Sess., no. 727.

APPLICATIONS, RECOMMENDATIONS   September 10, 1825

JOHN P. PHILIPS, Fredericksburg, Virginia, applies for a clerkship in the Department of State. ALS. DNA, RG59, A. and R. (MR3). Endorsed by Clay on cover: "Inform him that his application will be duly considered when vacancies occur, of which there are none at present." On September 12, 1825, Daniel Brent answered the letter in accordance with Clay's instructions. Copy. DNA, RG59, Dom. Letters, vol. 21, p. 148 (M40, R19). Philips not further identified.

INSTRUCTIONS AND DISPATCHES   September 12, 1825

To JOEL R. POINSETT, no. 4. Encloses copy of a letter from Charles J. Ingersoll (not found), "soliciting the interposition of this Government to obtain the restitution of part of the Cargo of the Brig Express, of Philadelphia," seized at Mocambo, Mexico, "on the charge of its being the produce of Spain, when it is stated to have been, in fact, the produce of France." Requests Poinsett to take such action as he thinks proper and necessary. Copy. DNA, RG59, Dip. Instr., vol. 10, p. 378 (M77, R5).

On the same day, Daniel Brent wrote to Ingersoll, enclosing Clay's letter to Poinsett, "under a flying seal," with the comment: "It is the wish of the Secretary that you should make use of the enclosure, and your own further representations, to engage the good offices of Mr. Poinsett in the case, in such manner as you may think advisable and proper." Copy. DNA, RG59, Dom. Letters, vol. 21, pp. 147-48 (M40, R19). The case of the *Express*, not further identified; for further reference to the matter, cf. below, Poinsett to Clay, November 19, 1825. Ingersoll was now (1815-1829) United States district attorney for Pennsylvania.

From JAMES BROWN, Paris, no. 34. Encloses copies of correspondence "relating to the appointment of Mr. [Christian] Mayer of Baltimore" as consul general in the United States for Württemberg. LS. DNA, RG59, Dip. Disp., France, vol. 22 (M34, R25). Received October 31.

MISCELLANEOUS LETTERS   September 12, 1825

To P[ETER] A. BROWNE. States that, upon examination of "the Law in regard to the right claimed by you, in behalf of the Franklin Institute, to obtain copies from this Office of the specifications accompanying unexpired patents," Clay believes he is "authorized to direct the copies required to be furnished on application." Copy. DNA, RG59, Dom. Letters, vol. 21, p. 149 (M40, R19). See above, Browne to Clay, March 7, 15, 29, April 11, May 1, August 17, September 7, 1825; cf. above, Clay to Browne, April 20, May 13, 1825.

From JOSIAH JONES and WILLIAM SIMONS, Providence (Rhode Island). Report that the *Providence Patriot*, "formerly published by Jones & Wheeler, is now printed by Jones & Simons," the new partner being William Simons, recently of the Newport *Rhode-Island Republican*. ALS by Simons, signed also by Jones. DNA, RG59, P. and D. of L. Jones and Bennett H. Wheeler had become co-proprietors of the journal, under its original title, *Providence Phoenix,* in 1807. The name of the organ had been changed somewhat over the years; and in January, 1819, it had been designated the *Providence Patriot.* Wheeler, who had previously worked on other journals in Providence, Boston, and Portland, had terminated his connection with the *Patriot* in 1823 and shortly thereafter had become postmaster of Providence. Simons had been publisher of the *Rhode Island Republican* since 1809.

From SAMUEL KEITH, Philadelphia. Advises "that in conformity" to Clay's letter of September 10, the claim of the insurance company in the case of the *Minerva* has been paid; expresses thanks to the State Department and "to the able Negociator Richard C. Anderson junr. . . ." LS. DNA, RG76, Misc. Claims, Colombia.

APPLICATIONS, RECOMMENDATIONS   September 12, 1825

WILLIAM C. KEEN, Vevay, Indiana, noting that the *Evansville Gazette* has been discontinued, renews his application for appointment to publish the laws in the Vevay *Indiana Register*. ALS. DNA, RG59, P. and D. of L. The *Evansville Gazette,* established in 1821, had been discontinued after the issue of August 27, 1825. See also below, Harrison to Clay, September 16, 1825, note.

WILLIAM SIMONS, Providence, states that he has disposed of the Newport *Rhode Island Republican* to James Atkinson and William Read, whom he recommends to "the consideration of government." ALS. DNA, RG59, P. and D. of L. Neither Atkinson nor Read has been further identified.

Check to Eliza Clark

13. September 1825.

Pay to Mrs. Eliza Clarke or order Fifty dollars.   H. CLAY
Cashr. of the Off. of Dt. & Dt. Washington City.[1]

ADS. DLC-TJC (DNA, M212, R16). Cf. above, Clay to Mrs. Clay, August 24, 1825; Clay to Erwin, August 30, 1825.   [1] Richard Smith.

From Adam Beatty

Dear Sir   Washington 13th. September 1825.

I availed myself of the first opportunity, after the reception of the note you enclosed me on Genls. Bodley & Pogue,[1] to see the latter, on the subject of its payment. He assured me it should be settled, without suit, but begged of me to give him time to consult with Genl. Bodley, respecting some credits, which he understood he was entitled to. Genl. Bodley has since met with me, at the Fleming circuit court and states, that he has fee bills against you individually and in cases in which you are bound as security, amounting to $213.46 cents, which he has held up, for two years back, to meet the payment of the note in question. At my request he made off the enclosed list, which I forward for the purpose of having your advice on the subject.[2] He had the original fee bills with him, and has left them with Genl. Pogue, for my examination, not having had time to do so at the Fleming court. Will you be so good as to advise me as early as will suit your convenience, whether I shall allow a credit for these fee bills, or any part of them, and take them up.

I understand you are desirous of disposing of your flock of merino sheep.[3] I have been engaged in raising this species of sheep, for a number of years past, and have had some thought of extending my flock, now amounting to about 240. If you are inclined to sell yours, I would thank you to mention, in your answer to this letter, upon what terms you would dispose of the whole or a part of them? How many do you own? What are their grades? Where have you usually sold your wool, and at what price, washed and unwashed, taking the average of the whole flock? At what time you will require payment? &c. &c.

From present appearances it is probable the party, now in power, in this State, will not yield to that construction of the constitution, in relation to the judiciary department, which has been so decisively maintained by the people, at the late Annual election. The Senate Stands 17 to 21 and relying upon the majority in their favor, in this body, they will, I have now no doubt, be disposed to try the result of another election.[4] Mr. Denny, of Louisville, it is understood, will redeem his pledge, by resigning.[5] His place will doubtless be filled by a constitutionalist; when the Senate will stand 18-20. Still, however the act of the last Session[6] cannot be repealed, unless some one or two of the Senators shall feel themselves bound to conform to the sentiments of their constituents, as evidenced by [th]eir vote at the late election. I think this hardly probable, as much pains are taking to render the phalanx firm, and to preserve it unbroken. I have no fear of the result, in the event of another trial of strength. There will certainly be a change in two Senatorial districts, and very probably three, unless the people can be deceived, by some new system of misrepresentation. The Senate will then stand 20 or 21 (supposing Denys [sic] district changed in the mean time) for the constitution, and 17 or 18 for Legislative supremacy.

Yours cordially & sincerely   A. Beatty

P.S. Mr. Adams' decisive course, in relation to the pertinacious disposition of the Governor of Georgia, to survey the Creek lands,[7] meets with general, I might say unusual, approbation. At least I have heard none yet speak on the subject, who does not speak of it in strong terms of approbation.   A.B.

ALS. DLC-HC (DNA, M212, R1). Addressed to Clay at Washington. Postmarked at Washington, Kentucky.

1 Cf. above, Clay to Beatty, June 30, 1825.

2 Addressed by Bodley to Beatty, September 8, 1825, the itemized statement covers fees due to Bodley as clerk of Fayette Circuit Court, including an entry of $103.98 for fees against Clay "in his own name &c.," seven entries for "old fees in cases where Mr Clay is bound to pay," and a fee of $11.11 relating to a suit of "James Brown vs. Owings &c." that brings the total to $203.46. From this sum an unexplained deduction of $30.78 is made, leaving a balance of $172.68 against Clay. The sums included under the second category stemmed from litigation involving "Maddon & Mounts

heirs" (case not found), Mary and John P. Usher (see above, I, 410n), Farish Coleman and wife, Michael Leib (cf. above, II, 106, 112n), Davidson and Goddard, Susanna(h) Jackson (see above, I, 406n), and Edmund W. Rootes.

Clay had conducted Kentucky suits for Farish Coleman and Catherine, his wife, of Caroline County, Virginia, against John Rogers, Mrs. Coleman's brother, regarding settlement of an estate. The High Court of Chancery in Virginia had found in 1802 that Rogers, who was not present to offer defense, was liable to the Colemans. When the latter had undertaken to institute action upon this decree in Fayette Circuit Court, Rogers had attempted to introduce evidence in his defense, which, in deference to the Virginia action, the Kentucky court had refused to consider. In 1808 the Kentucky Court of Appeals had reversed the latter ruling upon the ground that Rogers had not had adequate opportunity for defense; but upon retrial in Fayette Circuit Court in 1810, Rogers failing to appear, the Colemans had been awarded a default judgment, covering principle and interest on their claim since 1803. Fayette Circuit Court, File 184; Civil Orders, E, 251-58; G, 24; 3 *Ky. Reports* (1 Hardin) 422-29.

Clay had represented the firm of Charles Davidson and John Goddard, merchants of Baltimore, in their suit to collect for goods furnished Elijah Craig and his son, Joel, in 1800. Suit had been instituted in Scott Circuit Court, which had awarded judgment to Davidson and Goddard in 1802. Clay, having been assigned the debt for collection, had become personally involved in the litigation when disagreement subsequently arose over the valuation of cordage exchanged as payment. In 1808 Clay had arranged transfer of the action to Fayette Circuit Court, where the case had been continued until 1810 before it was dropped from record. Fayette Circuit Court, File 206.

Clay had represented Edmund W. Rootes in a successful action to collect a debt against Lewis Sanders and Robert C. Nicholas in 1809. Fayette Circuit Court, Civil Orders, E, p. 518.

The Brown *vs.* Owings suit, here cited, was probably that filed in 1811, when Brown had sought to collect on a note for $1200 signed by Thomas Deye Owings. Brown had won a judgment in Fayette Circuit Court in 1814. Fayette Circuit Court, File 296. Cf. above, III, 119n.

[3] Cf. above, Advertisement, June 13, 1825; Statement of Auction Sale, June 24, 1825.

[4] Cf. above, Bodley to Clay, August 23, 1825; Blair to Clay, August 30, 1825; Hammond to Clay, August 31, 1825; below, Kendall to Clay, December 25, 1825; Crittenden to Clay, December 26, 1825.

[5] James W. Denny returned to the senate but voted in opposition to that body's proposed amendment which rejected the house bill repealing the new court legislation. He was reported to have declared that he so acted, not from his own belief that the law was unconstitutional, but from a desire to redeem a pledge to his constituents. His discomfort in the whole action was evidenced by his failure to vote upon final adoption of the senate amendment. Frankfort *Argus of Western America,* November 30, 1825; Ky. Sen., *Journal, 1825,* pp. 126, 129.

[6] See above, III, 902; Cowan to Clay, January 1, 1825.

[7] See above, Clay to Southard, July 3, 1825, note.

DIPLOMATIC NOTES   September 13, 1825

To ANTONIO JOSE CANAZ. Acknowledges receipt of Cañaz' note of September 7; expresses friendly concern relative to his health; states that Clay will be glad to see him at any time on the business of his mission. Copy. DNA, RG59, Notes to Foreign Ministers and Consuls, vol. 3, pp. 229-30 (M38, R3). ALI draft, in CSmH.

INSTRUCTIONS AND DISPATCHES   September 13, 1825

From JAMES BROWN, Paris, "Private." Discusses "The affairs of the Peninsula [Spain], which for the last twenty months have been daily going on from bad to worse, whilst they compel the European sovereigns to discuss questions of the most embarrassing nature," but which "operate favorably to the views and wishes of the President in relation to the New Republics of America." Reports, from conversations he has heard, that "All now admit that the contest on the part of Spain,": against her former colonies, "is utterly hopeless," although "It is even at this time hoped by many that the New Republics might be persuaded like the Haitians to purchase an acknowledgment of their independence—" Notes that two alternatives are proposed for ending the "embarrassing if not alarming" situation of France, resulting from her intervention in Spain (see above, III, 313n; Nelson to Clay, April 26, 1825, note): either France should withdraw and leave the contending factions to determine their own form of government or she should send additional troops, sufficient to render Spain "tranquil at least if not prosperous." Cites evidence for expecting that, whatever choice may be made, "an attempt will shortly be made to persuade Spain to make a peace with the American Republics."

States his fear that the situation of the Greeks is "very critical and alarming," but adds: "It is rumored that Lord [Thomas] Cochrane is preparing to sail, and that two or three armed vessels bought and manned in Sweden [cf. above, Hughes to Clay, July 8, 1825, note] are now in Ireland waiting to go under his orders."

Comments that (Daniel) Sheldon's health is improving and that he may soon return to Paris. ALS. DLC-HC (DNA, M212, R1). Published in Padgett (ed.), "Letters from James Brown to Henry Clay," *Louisiana Historical Quarterly,* XXIV (October, 1941), 952-56. Cochrane did not arrive in Greece until March, 1827, and then brought only a small yacht. The steamers and frigates to have been built for the Greeks were not yet ready.

From RUFUS KING, London, no. 5. Encloses copies of an exchange of letters with George Canning, notes Canning's "anxiety respecting the friendly and confidential nature of his letters" to King, and states that King will "with confidence assure him of the discretion" of the Government of the United States. LS. DNA, RG59, Dip. Disp., Great Britain, vol. 32 (M30, R28). Published in Manning (arr.), *Diplomatic Correspondence . . . Latin-American Nations,* III, 1567-68. In the enclosures, Canning, by note dated September 8, expresses disappointment that King did not find himself "at Liberty to concur in so simple a measure, as the reciprocal disavowal by our two governments of designs which most assuredly neither of them entertains, without any previous reference to Washington," especially since France has declined to concur in such a declaration; he further argues the British point of view. King's reply, dated September 13, asserts that the British plan "can gratify nobody but Spain," while that of the United States "is Calculated to pacify the New States, by leading them to wait for the influence of the interference of their friends. . . ." Cf. above, King to Clay, August 9, 1825.

From SAMUEL LARNED, Santiago de Chile. Encloses "sundry pamphlets . . . having relation to the affairs of these countries and which may serve to throw some light upon their recent military and political history." ALS. DNA, RG59, Dip. Disp., Chile, vol. 1 (M-T2, R1). Received January 13, 1826.

From JOEL R. POINSETT, Mexico, no. 18. Reports that at "a second conference with the Plenipotentiaries of the Government," he presented a projet of a treaty containing "the principle of perfect reciprocity in the commerce and navigation of the two Countries," to which a counter proposal was made "to introduce the fourth article of their Treaty with Great Britain," permitting the granting by Mexico of special privileges to "the American nations which were formerly Spanish possessions." Poinsett "strenuously opposed" this exception. He warns, however, that Mexican officials are "obstinately bent on carrying this point" and asks instructions on this matter. States that a junta composed of army and navy officers, members of the Congress, and "a few Emigrants from Havanna [*sic*]," formed "to promote the Emancipation of Cuba," has memorialized Congress in favor of "an Expedition to assist the Patriots of that Island to shake off the yoke of Spain"; that the project will have executive support; and that some action will be decided on, although a Cuban invasion would "certainly be a very rash step in the present state of the finances of this Country." LS, partly in cipher, decoded in State Department file. DNA, RG59, Dip. Disp., Mexico, vol. 1 (M97, R2). Extract published in *American State Papers, Foreign Relations*, V, 852.

MISCELLANEOUS LETTERS   September 13, 1825

From JOHN A. LEAMY, Philadelphia. Acknowledges receipt of Clay's letter of September 5 with its enclosures. Explains why he preferred negotiable drafts (cf. above, Leamy to Clay, September 4, 1825) but expresses "perfect satisfaction with the other arrangement." ALS. DNA, RG76, Misc. Claims, Colombia.

From W[ILLIAM] WILLINK, JR., and N[ICHOLAS] and R. and J[OSEPH] VAN STAPHORST, Amsterdam. Advise sale of the American Hotel at the Hague, formerly the residence of the American Ministers, now uninhabited and in a bad state of repair. LS. DNA, RG59, Misc. Letters (M179, R63).

From THOMAS WILSON, "Bank United States." Transmits "a receipt from S. Keith Esq. President of the Delaware Insurance Company" for $17,322.75, in conformity with Clay's instructions of September 10. ALS. DNA, RG76, Misc. Claims, Colombia.

APPLICATIONS, RECOMMENDATIONS   September 13, 1825

C[OPELAND] P. L. ARION and THOMAS BERRYMAN, Madison, Indiana, solicit appointment to print the laws in the Madison *Indiana Republican,* of which they are publishers. ALS. DNA, RG59, P. and D. of L. The *Indiana Republican* had been established in January, 1817, and two years later Arion had become one of the publishers. Berryman has not been further identified. They did not receive the requested appointment during the Adams administration.

WILLIAM HENDRICKS, Madison (Indiana), recommends the editors of the Madison *Indiana Republican* for appointment as public printers. ALS. *Ibid.*

J[OHN] MCKINLEY, Huntsville (Alabama), recommends the appointment of Henry Hitchcock as district attorney for the Southern District of Alabama. ALS. DNA, RG59, A. and R. (MR2). See above, Hall to Clay, August 16, 1825, note.

JOHN WRIGHT, Philadelphia, solicits appointment as "Consul to the Port of Tampico de los Tamolipas [*sic*]," if one is to be appointed there, the location being separated by a lake from "the port of Pueblo Viejo de Tampico," where (George R.) Robertson is United States consul. States that he has lived in "that Country" (Mexico) eighteen months and contemplates "returning there, to reside." ALS. DNA, RG59, A. and R. (MR4). Wright, not further identified, received no appointment. On September 22, 1825, Daniel Brent, at Clay's direction, replied that there was no intention to separate the consular administration of the Port of Tampico de los Tamaulipas. Copy. DNA, RG59, Dom. Letters, vol. 21, p. 153 (M40, R19).

Rental Agreement with Nelson Nicholas

[September 14, 1825]

[Clay leases to Nicholas "the front and adjoining rooms and two Cellars in the corner of his Brick House on short and market Streets, for one year commencing with this day—" Nicholas agrees to pay, in quarterly instalments, $125, "in gold or silver coin of the United States," and to surrender the premises in good condition. ". . . Clay reserves the right of distress for any of the rent which may remain in arrear—and each party reserves the right of discontinuing this lease upon giving one months notice. . . ."]

ADS by Robert Scott, for Clay; signed also by Nicholas. Endorsements on verso by Scott: the first (AES) reveals that the first quarter's rent was paid January 10, 1826; a second (AE) comments: "Dead and insolvent." Nicholas died July 10, 1826.

INSTRUCTIONS AND DISPATCHES   September 14, 1825

To WILLIAM H. D. C. WRIGHT. Encloses his commission as United States consul for Rio de Janeiro, printed circular instructions, and a blank consular bond; requests him to inform the Department of State of the time he intends to embark. Copy. DNA, RG59, Cons. Instr., vol. 2, p. 364 (M78, R2). Wright remained at this post until 1831.

From A[LEXANDER] H. EVERETT, Madrid, no. 6. Encloses copies of an exchange of letters with (Francisco de) Zea Bermudez, who gives "notice that the King has consented to grant an exemption from the tonnage duty of 20 reals in favour of foreign vessels entering" Spanish ports to take on "salt and barilla, provided the value of the cargo exceeds the amount of the duty." LS. DNA, RG59, Dip. Disp., Spain, vol. 25 (M31, R27). The enclosures reveal that the concession resulted from a proposal made by Everett's predecessor, (Hugh) Nelson. See above, Clay to Everett, April 27, 1825, note.

INSTRUCTIONS AND DISPATCHES   September 15, 1825

From CONDY RAGUET, Rio de Janeiro. Asserts that the commission of Leonard Corning, as consul at Maranham, which Raguet has transmitted to the Minister of Foreign Affairs (Luiz Joze de Carvalho e Mello) is "no doubt" the first document to be presented from the head of a foreign state to "The Emperor of Brasil." Encloses copy of the treaty concluded between Brazil and Portugal (see above, Raguet to Secretary of State, March 11, 1825, note); comments on his own non-appearance at Court, on the occasion of the announcement of the treaty; and expresses his assumption that the failure of his credentials to arrive by that time was by design of his government (cf. above, Pleasants to Clay, July

7, 1825). Notes dissatisfaction with the treaty, among the Portuguese, who wished reunion with the mother country, and the Brazilians, who expected complete separation.

Reports that Felizberto Caldeira Brant Pontes has been appointed Ambassador to Portugal, but that "the time of his departure is uncertain." Informs Clay of reports that negotiations for a treaty with Great Britain have begun (see below, Raguet to Clay, October 26, 1825, note). States that "Bolivar is said to be" too weak in troops to aid Buenos Aires and that war between that Government and Brazil is not likely. LS. DNA, RG59, Cons. Disp., Rio de Janeiro, vol. 2 (M-T172, R3). Received November 3. Extract published in Manning (arr.), *Diplomatic Correspondence . . . Latin-American Nations,* II, 832-35.

MISCELLANEOUS LETTERS   September 15, 1825

From SAMUEL L. SOUTHARD, Navy Department. Requests that "the circumstances" of the enclosed "Copy of a communication from Commodore Lewis Warrington, Commanding U. S. Naval force in the West Indies, with Copy of the Affidavit of Ferdinand S. [*sic*] Madden, . . . be represented to the Colombian Government." LS. DNA, RG59, Misc. Letters (M179, R63). Copy in DNA, RG45, Executive Letter book, vol. 1821-1831, p. 131. The enclosures relate to the robbery of a small vessel carrying goods belonging to Ferdinand I. (or J.) Madden, by a Colombian privateer flying the American colors. Warrington, who states that Madden is a native of the United States but now a Spanish subject, not only refers to the illegal conduct of the privateer but adds that Cuban pirates "believe or affect to believe" that such acts "are really committed by American vessels; and are thus stimulated to exertion by the double motives of revenge and avarice." Madden has not been further identified.

To Richard C. Anderson, Jr.

No. 1. Richard C. Anderson, Minister Plenipotentiary U. S. Bogotá.

Sir,   Department of State Washington, 16. Sept. 1825

By the Treaty recently concluded between Great Britain and Columbia [*sic*],[1] it is understood that the vessels of the two Countries, and their cargoes are admitted into their respective ports, upon the payment, without discrimination, of the same duties of Impost and Tonnage, whenever the cargo consists of the produce of the Country to which the vessel belongs. Colombia having adopted the system of protecting her own Tonnage, by subjecting native vessels and their cargoes to a less rate of duty than that which is demanded on foreign vessels and their cargoes, these discriminating duties are paid by all foreign nations with which she has not agreed to equalize them. But the Treaty between the United States and Colombia,[2] has not stipulated for the equalization of those duties, and, consequently, the vessel and its cargo, of each country, now remains subject, in the ports of the other, to alien duties. The United States would have had just cause to complain of the advantage conceded to Great Britain, if, by the second Article of our Treaty with

Colombia, we had not a right to demand the same concession, and if Mr Gual had not, in a friendly spirit, in the course of the Month of June, last, informed Mr. Watts "that the United States, whenever its Government desired, would be invested with all the privileges and powers which had been surrendered to England."[3]

The President wishes, and you are authorized to propose, a mutual abolition of those discriminating duties. No difficulty on the part of the Government of Colombia, in acceding to this proposal, is anticipated; and it is only necessary to inquire into the best way of accomplishing the object. This may be done in either of the two following modes.

I—By the 4th. section of the Act of Congress of the 7th. January, 1824, it is enacted, "That upon satisfactory evidence being given to the President of the United States, by the Government of any foreign Nation, that no discriminating duties of Tonnage or Impost are imposed or levied within the ports of the said Nation, upon vessels wholly belonging to Citizens of the United States, or upon merchandise, the produce or manufacture thereof, imported in the same, the President is hereby authorized to issue his proclamation, declaring that the foreign discriminating duties of Tonnage and Impost, within the United States, are, and shall be, suspended and discontinued, so far as respects the vessels of the said Nation, and the merchandise, *of its produce or manufacture*, imported into the United States in the same; the said suspension to take effect from the time of such notification being given to the President of the United States, and to continue so long as the reciprocal exemption of vessels belonging to citizens of the United States, and merchandize [*sic*] as aforesaid, therein laden, shall be continued, and no longer."[4] This Act, conceived in a genuine spirit of liberality, makes a general proposition to all Nations. The same offer had been made by a previous Act of Congress, and it has been embraced by the King of the Netherlands, Prussia, the Imperial Hanseatic Cities of Hamburg, Lubeck and Bremen, the Dukedom of Oldenburg, Norway, Sardinia, and Russia.[5] A Convention between the United States and Great Britain, and a treaty with Sweden, adopt the same principle,[6] and Mr. Poinsett has been instructed to propose it to Mexico.[7] The President is desirous that all Nations would see, and appreciate, the fairness of the principle of reciprocity and competition upon which the Act of Congress is based. To enable the President to give effect as it respects any particular foreign Nation, to the act, by issuing the proclamation for which it provides, all that is requisite is, that *satisfactory evidence* should be given to him ["]that no discriminating duties of Tonnage or Impost, are imposed, or levied, within the Ports of the said Nation, upon vessels wholly belonging to citizens of the United States, or upon merchandise, the produce or manufacture thereof, imported in the same." In regard to Colombia, an Act of its Congress, abolishing all such discriminating duties, or a Diplomatic Note from its Minister of Foreign Affairs, declaring that no such discriminating duties exist against the United States, would be deemed by the President, evidence sufficiently satisfactory to authorise the issuing of his proclamation; and it would, accordingly, upon the production of such evidence, be by him issued.

II. A Convention might be concluded between the two Powers, effecting the purposed mutual abolition of alien duties; and, in that case, the second Article of that which, on the 3rd. of July 1815, was formed between the United States and Great Britain, (6th. Volume of the Laws of the United States, page 603)[8] will supply a model that may be safely followed. It is not very important which of these two modes be adopted; but the President rather prefers the latter, because the proposed equalization of duties would not, when depending upon compact, be so liable to a sudden termination as if it rested on separate Acts of the two parties, revocable at the pleasure of either. But if a strong inclination to the other mode should be manifested by the Government of Colombia, you are authorized to accede to it. A Commission empowering you to conclude and sign a Convention, if that should be the form selected, accompanies these Instructions.[9]

During the last spring the Ministers of Colombia and Mexico near this Government, made separate, but nearly simultaneous, communications to this Department, in relation to the contemplated Congress at Panama.[10] Each of them stated that he was instructed by his Government to say, that it would be very agreeable to it that the United States should be represented at that Congress; that it was not expected that they would take any part in its deliberations, or measures of concert, in respect to the existing war with Spain, but that other great interests affecting the Continent of America, and the friendly intercourse between the Independent Nations which are established on it, might be considered and regulated at the Congress; and that, not knowing what might be the views of the United States, a previous enquiry was directed to be made, whether they would, if invited by Colombia or Mexico, be represented at Panama; and if an affirmative answer were given, each of those Ministers stated that the United States would be accordingly invited by his Government to be represented there. The President instructed me to say, and I accordingly replied, that the communication was received with great sensibility to the friendly consideration of the United States, by which it had been dictated;

that, of course, they could not make themselves any party to the existing war with Spain, or to councils for deliberating on the means of its further prosecution; that he believed such a Congress as was proposed, might be highly useful in settling several important disputed questions of public Law, and in arranging other matters of deep interest to the American Continent, and to the friendly intercourse between the American Powers; that before such a Congress, however, assembled, it appeared to him to be necessary to arrange between the different Powers to be represented, several preliminary points, such as, the subjects to which the attention of the Congress was to be directed; the nature, and the form, of the Powers to be given to the Ministers, and the mode of organizing the Congress. If these preliminary points could be adjusted, in a manner satisfactory to the United States, the Ministers from Colombia and Mexico were informed that the United States would be represented at the Congress. Upon enquiry, if these preliminary points had yet engaged the attention of the Government either of Colombia or Mexico, they were unable to inform me that they had, whilst both appeared to admit the expediency of their being settled. Each of them undertook to communicate to his Government the answer which I had been instructed by the President to make; and nothing further has since passed. It has been deemed proper that you should be made acquainted with what has occurred here on this matter, in order that, if it should be touched upon by the Colombian Government, you may, if necessary, be able to communicate what happened. Should the President ultimately determine that the United States shall be represented at Panama you will be designated for that service, either alone, or associated with others, and you will hold yourself in readiness accordingly. We shall make no further movement until we hear from the Government of Colombia or Mexico.

You have already been informed, both by a Letter from Mr. Brent,[11] and verbally, of the mistake which occurred in this office, in June 1822, in the transcript of a paper relating to the case of the Brig Josephine, by which the amount of the claim of the Insurance Company of Pennsylvania, for the cargo of that vessel is reduced from $15000. to $1500. The mistake occurred by the accidental omission of a figure. As soon as the mistake was ascertained, a Letter, during my absence in the past summer, was, on the 18th. of June, addressed by Mr Brent to Mr. Watts[12] (of which a copy is now furnished) instructing him to bring the error to the notice of the Colombian Government, with a request that it would direct the payment of the further sum of $13,500, with fifty per cent damages, and interest, as were allowed in the other cases arranged by you,[13] so as to complete the measure of justice which it intended, to the claimants. As the justice of the claim was admitted without regard to its amount, it is not apprehended that any difficulty will arise in obtaining the desired correction, which is further recommended by the courtesy and consideration which are due to incidental official errors, from which no bureau is, at all times, wholly exempt. If Mr. Watts shall have failed in his endeavour to effect the object, you will renew the effort to accomplish it.

On the 10th. day of May last, I addressed an official note, by the direction of the President, to the Minister of the United States at St. Petersburg,[14] (of which a copy is herewith transmitted to you) having for its object to engage the friendly offices of Russia, to hasten a peace between Spain and the new American States. The same note, or the substance of it, has been communicated through the Ministers of the United States, to the Courts of Paris and London,[15] with the same purpose of peace. The hope has been indulged that, by a common exertion, and especially by the interposition of the Emperor of Russia, Spain may be made sensible of her true interests, and consent to terminate a war which she has no longer the ability to prosecute. No information has been yet obtained from Russia, of the manner in which the Emperor[16] has received this appeal to his humanity and his power. From the reception given to the application, by France,[17] we are confirmed in the previous impression of the importance of the movement of Russia, and new efforts, if they shall be considered likely to be useful, will be employed to urge her to the great work of pacification. In the mean time, it is deemed proper to put you in possession of what has been done, and of the copy of the note itself, which you are authorised to communicate to the Government of Colombia, or such parts of it as may appear to you to be expedient.

Complaints have been made to this Department through several channels, against Mr. Macniel, the American Vice Consul at Carthagena. Copies of the papers containing them, are now forwarded to you. If they are not fully and satisfactorily explained, they make out a case requiring his removal. Your early attention to the matter, is requested, and your exercise of the power of removal, if you shall find it necessary.[18]   I am your obedient Servant   H. CLAY.

Other copies of papers containing complaints against Macniel, the acting Consul at Carthagena, will be forwarded to you, tomorrow or the next day—

Copy. DNA, RG59, Dip. Instr., vol. 10, pp. 380-85 (M77, R5). ALS draft, in DLC-HC (DNA, M212, R7).
1 See above, Watts to Clay, May 10, 1825, note.
2 See above, Clay to Salazar, March 21, 1825.
3 See above, Watts to Clay, May 10, 1825.

4 4 *U. S. Stat.,* 3.

5 See above, Clay to Forbes, April 14, 1825.

6 See above, II, 57-58, 427n-28n; Lorich to Clay, March 16, 1825, note.

7 See above, Clay to Poinsett, March 26, 1825.

8 8 *U. S. Stat.,* 228-29. See above, II, 57-58.

9 Copy, in DNA, RG59, Ceremonial Communications, II, 25.

10 See above, Tudor to Clay, April 12, 1825, note.

11 Daniel Brent. The letter is dated June 23, 1825. Copy, in DNA, RG59, Dip. Instr., vol. 10, p. 371 (M77, R5).

12 Beaufort T. Watts. A copy of the letter is in *ibid.,* 370-71.

13 Relative to the *America,* the *Liberty,* and the *Minerva.* See above, Anderson to Secretary of State, March 18, 1825.

14 Henry Middleton.

15 See above, Clay to Brown, May 13, 1825; Clay to King, May 11, 1825.

16 Alexander I.

17 See above, Brown to Clay, July 15, 1825 (2): cf. above, Brown to Clay, September 13, 1825.

18 See above, Poinsett to Clay, July 14, 1825; Fudger to Secretary of State, August 4, 1825.

INSTRUCTIONS AND DISPATCHES   September 16, 1825

From HEMAN ALLEN, Valparaiso, no. 19. Encloses correspondence relative to his protest concerning import and export duties levied on public stores imported into Chile for the use of the United States naval squadron. Comments bitterly on the character of Chilean officials, their ingratitude and injustice toward the United States, "from whom they think, they have already obtained all their desires," and their preferential treatment of Britain and France, from whom they "desire to obtain the recognition of their independence." ALS. DNA, RG59, Dip. Disp., Chile, vol. 1 (M-T2, R1). Received January 13, 1826. Extract published in Manning (arr.), *Diplomatic Correspondence . . . Latin-American Nations,* II, 1104-1105. Among the enclosures is a copy of a letter, dated July 14, 1825, from Allen to Isaac Hull, commander of United States naval forces in the Pacific Ocean, concerning a Peruvian decree relating to neutral commerce (see above, Tudor to Secretary of State, April 22, 1825, note). To the first article, providing for confiscation of goods owned by Spanish subjects, "under whatever flag they may be found," Allen sees no objection if certain conditions are observed by the captors. The second article, providing that, after a stated period, vessels carrying Spanish property "shall be declared lawful prize," he considers contrary to international law. He advises Hull, therefore, to "put a stop to such unjust and arbitrary proceedings by refusing the execution even of the first article of the decree, and employ the armed force at your disposal to that object, should the occasion require."

MISCELLANEOUS LETTERS   September 16, 1825

From P[ETER] A. BROWNE, Philadelphia. Acknowledges receipt of Clay's letter of September 12, conveying an opinion "highly gratifying, but not unexpected." LS. DNA, RG59, Misc. Letters (M179, R63).

From E[LISHA] HARRISON, Evansville, Indiana. Requests withholding payment, for publishing the laws of the 18th Congress, 1st and 2d Sessions, from "William Monroe as Editor of the Evansville Gazette" and from "Thomas Evans, or any person for him," as editor of the same paper, "until an adjustment of matters can take place here." Explains that the appointment for printing the laws was given to Harrison and Monroe and that Harrison has not relinquished his interest in the publication of the laws and his ownership of the press, although a change in the editorship occurred for a brief time. ALS. DNA, RG59, P. and D. of L. Harrison, a second cousin of William Henry Harrison, had been a pioneer resident of Indiana, representing first Warwick and later Vandenburgh county in the State legislature. He had founded the Evansville *Gazette*. William Monroe had been listed as editor during most of 1824 and Thomas Evans, formerly of Clark County, Indiana, during the early part of 1825. Cf. below, Harrison to Clay, April 6, 1826.

APPLICATIONS, RECOMMENDATIONS   September 16, 1825

WILLIAM KELLY, Huntsville (Alabama), recommends David Rust, of Mobile, for appointment as district attorney. Adds that (Henry) Hitchcock, who will probably be an applicant for the appointment, is well qualified but not acceptable politically "to the people of the State generally—" ALS. DNA, RG59, A. and R. (MR3). Rust, probably until 1822 a militia officer in Dutchess County, New York, did not receive the appointment.

Draft from Charles March

$927,,76—   NEW YORK, 17 Septr—1825
Sixty days—*after* sight—*Pay to the Order of* Corns. Heyer Esqr.[1] Cashier—Nine Hundred and twenty seven 76/100——— *Dollars, for value received, and charged to the account of*   as advised by
                                                       CHARLES MARCH

To The Hon. Henry Clay   Washington
[Endorsement on verso (following successive endorsements from Heyer to John Hooff, Cashier, and from the latter to Richard Smith)][2] Accepted 20 September 1825   . H CLAY

DS, partially printed. DLC-TJC (DNA, M212, R16). March has not been identified.
[1] Not identified.   [2] AES. Hooff, not identified.

MISCELLANEOUS LETTERS   September 17, 1825

From PLATT H. CROSBY, Lima. States that, "As a supplement to" his last letter (above, August 24, 1825), he now addresses "a few observations . . . upon the Commerce of Peru, and more particularly, as in reference to that of our own Country." Comments (in three pages) on the present government of the country as a "Military Despotism" and (in the next twenty-two pages) describes the "ancient commerce of Spanish America," the changes brought about by independence, the present state of commerce, tariff regulations, the competitive position of goods imported from the United States, and Peruvian production. Declares that, in order to enjoy commerce with "this coast," Americans "must come here, in some measure, as the rivals of the English" and must encourage manufacturing at home. Notes rumors of continued "hostile demonstrations" by Brazilians "on the frontiers of *Alto Peru,*" where a boundary dispute has long existed, but asserts that, if war occurs, the true reason "no doubt, will be the secret concurrence of the Emperor Don Pedro, in the views of the Holy Alliance, of whom he seems to be a protegé." Reports that *"Alto Peru* has recently been erected into an independent Republic, and as is reported, takes the name of *Bolivar,*" and that "The Castles of Callao still hold out," although their surrender is expected imminently (cf. below, Tudor to Clay, February 23, 1826). ALS. DNA, RG59, Misc. Letters (M179, R63). The republic of Bolivia had been proclaimed August 10, 1825.

From A. W. JONES, "Richmond Whig Office" (Virginia). Inquires when John H. Pleasants, "special Messenger from the Government of the United States to one of the Southern Republics, is expected to return," and, "on behalf of the concern with which he is connected, declines being considered an applicant for the Public Printing. . . ." AN. DNA, RG59, P. and D. of L. See above, Clay to Pleasants, April 16, 1825.

From HORATIO GATES SPAFFORD, Lansingburgh, New York. States that he has invented "an engine" for removing obstructions to navigation of the Mississippi River and its branches; that he wishes to construct a model to exhibit in Washington and to sell the invention to the Government; that he is too poor to raise the money necessary for this purpose, unless he has assurance his invention would be purchased at a fair price; that he applies for advice to Clay, whose "patriotism & public spirit" are known; and that "In no event," will he trust his "invention to the protection of our present law of Patents." ALS. DNA, RG59, Misc. Letters (M179, R63).

From P. W. SPROAT, Philadelphia. Presents the case of Asa Pendleton, born in Maine, impressed in 1810 from an American vessel into service on a British warship, where he remained until, delivering himself up as a prisoner of war in 1812, he had been imprisoned from the latter date to 1815. Requests compensation to Pendleton, if any be allowed in such cases, or that the matter be brought before Congress. Notes that "as he was a seaman in the british [*sic*] navy and drew the same pay as british seamen his case is distinct from many others." ALS. *Ibid.* Pendleton has not been further identified.

From THOMAS WILSON, "Bank United States." Transmits "the joint receipt of Chs McAlester for Insce Co. of the State of Pennsylvania & John Leamy Presdt. Marine Insurance Compy of Philadelphia" for $29764.87. ALS. DNA, RG76, Misc. Claims, Colombia. Cf. above, Clay to Leamy, September 5, 1825.

APPLICATIONS, RECOMMENDATIONS   September 17, 1825

HENRY HITCHCOCK, Cahaba, Alabama, solicits appointment as United States attorney for the Southern District of Alabama. ALS. DNA, RG59, A. and R. (MR2). See above, Hall to Clay, August 16, 1825, note.

From Wilson Allen

Dr. Sir   (Confidentl.)   Bowl: Green Va. Sept: 18h. 1825.
     I have been expecting for sometime to visit Washington and intended when I did so to call and see you—but the peculiar state

of my family will probably prevent my leaving home now for sometime— am therefore induced to suggest to you as a friend that I apprehend you are much annoyd by the person acting as temporary assistant P. M. Genl. & know that Mr. Adams is extremely blamed for giving countenance to a man laboring under the charges alledged against the Major.[1] I however shou'd not now trouble you on this subject but that I rec'd a letter yesterday from a friend in Richmond in which he says "I met with Colo. Gooch one of the Editors of the Enqr.[2] yesterday (14h.) in an afternoons ride when the subject of Major Lee's appointmt. was accidentally mentd. The Colo. express'd astonishment that a man charged with the offences that the Major is & who is oblig'd to leave his native state to seek society shou'd be so far countenanc'd by a new administration & one brought about too under peculiar circumstances as to be placed in a high and responsible office under it's [sic] patronage—some thing he said must be wrong—there is some rotten in the core—or such characters wou'd not be call'd in to it's support however he said the public wou'd soon be satisfied about it for they have a number of communications on the subject which have been kept back for particular reasons—but which they wou'd now soon be oblig'd to publish."

On reading the letter I at first determined to communicate it's contents to Mr. McLean,[3] but I recollected that he had been told of the dissatisfaction given by the appointmt.—of all the charges against the Major & advised by one at least of his best friends to discharge him— therefore concluded that advice or information from me wou'd be unavailing & that the purity of my motive might be questiond—consequently declined writing him.

The Editors of the Enquirer[4] both view the appointment, as men, in a very unfavorable light, but as Editors enlisted in the opposition I have no doubt feel a secret gratification and have declined giving publicity to the communications on the subject. The truth is there is very little matter now afloat in this state upon which to feed their bloated opposition & independent of the means afforded by the peculiar situation of the Major who is at the fountain of information & who gives occasional hints, I know of nothing saveing [sic] his appointment that is now charged against the administration—the Creek controversy[5] excepted & that confined to Richmd.—. I but rarely interfere in political affairs & certainly shou'd not in this but that I feel anxious you & those acting with you shou'd at least have justice done you. Major Lee says he was placed in his present situation by Mr. Calhoun[6]—with what view I leave you to judge— at any rate he is in an office of as much patronge & influence as any under government and placed as near the head of it too as he can well be. The Washington City

Gazette I have good reason to know is often furnish'd with your name from that source & have good grounds to beleive [sic] that all the members of the administration come occasionally under animadversion from same quarter. However be that as it may— you have my best wishes for a successful & easy administration & when any thing occurs within my limitted [sic] circle of acquaintance that can benefit you—it shall be promptly & with pleasure communicated by your old acquaintance & frd.   WILSON ALLEN

ALS. DLC-HC (DNA, M212, R1). Addressed to Clay at Washington. Endorsed on verso by Clay: "Answd." Answer not found.
1 Henry Lee, of Virginia, a son of "Light Horse Harry" Lee, had been given a minor position in the Post Office Department, through the influence of John C. Calhoun. In November, 1826, Adams presented Lee with a bundle of anonymous letters which charged that the latter had been writing and using his office in opposition to the administration. Lee then informed Adams that he had resigned from the position and regretted the trouble he had occasioned. Adams, *Memoirs*, VII, 180. He shortly thereafter joined openly in support of Andrew Jackson and lived at the "Hermitage" during the campaign of 1828. Lee, who had married Anne McCarty of Westmoreland County, Virginia, in 1817, had fallen under social opprobrium because of his seduction in 1821 of his wife's sister, Elizabeth, who was his ward.
2 Claiborne W. Gooch; Richmond, Virginia, *Enquirer*.
3 John McLean, who continued as Postmaster General in the Adams administration.
4 Gooch and Thomas Ritchie.
5 See above, Clay to Southard, July 3, 1825, note.   6 John C. Calhoun.

INSTRUCTIONS AND DISPATCHES   September 18, 1825

From JOHN M. FORBES, Buenos Aires, no. 24. Acknowledges receipt of his commission as Chargé d'Affaires and his instructions; states that he has "received no continuance of the laws of the United States" and is "without any volumes of Niles' Register subsequent to 23d."; presumes that Clay knows of (John H.) Pleasants' "abandonment of his voyage and return to the United States" (see above, Pleasants to Clay, July 7, 1825, note); expresses regret that his credentials arrived later than those of (Woodbine) Parish, causing Forbes to lose "that precedence" due to his "Country, from the priority of her efforts in the cause of the independence of these people," and to himself, from his "much longer residence than that of any foreign Agent here." Reports that he has addressed to (Manuel José) Garcia a remonstrance against the prohibition of importation of flour and a note on the "general Subject of our commercial relations, transmitting exact and certified Copies of the Acts of Congress of 1815 & 1824" (see above, Clay to Forbes, April 14, 1825, note; Lorich to Clay, March 16, 1825, note); characterizes Garcia as "far more ready to promise than to perform on all occasions." Adds: "This arises, partly from levity and duplicity of character, and, partly from . . . insatiable love of power which induces him to retain . . . four important offices—Secretary of Government—of Foreign Affairs (national)—of Foreign Affairs (Provincial) and of Treasury." Presents a lengthy and gloomy view of "the present State of these Provinces." Continues, under date of September 23, by reporting the receipt of Garcia's "project of repeal of the prohibitory law of flour," which "is a miserable, evasive measure, and by an enormous duty of Six dollars per barrel, continues, in effect, the odious measure it affects to supercede [sic]." Reports, also, receipt of a reply to his note "on general Commercial intercourse," which he has not had time to digest and translate. Encloses copies of official correspondence and minutes of interviews. ALS. DNA, RG59, Dip. Disp., Argentina, vol. 2 (M69, R3). Received December 9. Published in Espil (comp.), *Once Años en Buenos Aires*, 375-85; extracts, in Manning (arr.), *Diplomatic Correspondence . . . Latin-American Nations*, I, 650-51. Woodbine Parish, having served in minor Foreign Office assignments since 1814, had been sent as British consul general to Buenos Aires in 1823. After concluding a treaty of amity and commerce between the two governments in February, 1825, he was appointed British Chargé d'Affaires in the South American Republic and remained in that position much of the time for the next decade. He was active in effecting a settlement of the dispute between Brazil and the Provinces of Río de la Plata, in 1828. Following his return to Britain, he published in 1839 a descriptive volume on Buenos Aires and the Provinces. He was knighted at the conclusion of his South American duty and later served as British negotiator of commercial agreements with Naples.

From RUFUS KING, London, no. 6. Encloses copy of "a Confidential Despatch from Mr. Canning." LS. DNA, RG59, Dip. Disp., Great Britain, vol. 32 (M30, R28). ALS copy, in NHi. Received October 29. Extract published in Manning (arr.), *Diplomatic Correspondence . . . Latin-American Nations*, III, 1569. In the enclosure, dated September 15, George Canning expresses surprise that his "letters have been actually transmitted to" King's government, for "They were not written with that intention," and deplores "The confounding of confidential with official letters." In regard to the proposals relative to Spain and her late colonies, he writes: "France has, as I presume you know, decided *against* your plan of joint interference; and the proposal of it has (if I am not misinformed) been received in Russia as cooly—as (to say the truth) it was natural to suppose it would be. . . ." He professes willingness to consider favorably any proposition conceived "in the Spirit of peace and good Will to Spain" and her late colonies and offering "a reasonable prospect of success." On Canning's earlier protest against King's reference to his government of the proposal for a tripartite statement regarding the independence of Cuba, see above, King to Clay, September 13, 1825, note. On the French and Russian reactions to the United States proposal requesting use of their good offices to promote Spanish recognition of the independence of her American colonies, see above, Brown to Clay, September 13, 1825; Middleton to Clay, September 8, 1825.

From JOHN SHILLABER, "Batavia (Java)." Acknowledges receipt of (Clay's) letter of April 16; refers to his own letter of April 6 (not found) to the Secretary of State, citing the refusal of local officials to acknowledge consuls of foreign countries "unless directed so to do by" the King of the Netherlands (William I); suggests, "As the American trade to Java is extensive and valuable," the desirability of applying to the King in this connection; notes that an insurrection is under way against Dutch rule in the vicinity of Djokjakarta; expresses a hope that one or more large war ships will be sent by the United States "into these seas . . . to make commercial arrangements with Native Governments for trade to their ports" and points out, specifically, that "an arrangement with . . . Siam would be beneficial." Continues, under date of September 30, reporting the seizure by the British of an American vessel allegedly attempting to enter the port of Singapore, the expectation of a battle between Dutch forces and rebels, and the opinion among Europeans that the insurrection will soon end. Encloses documents. ALS. DNA, RG59, Cons. Disp., Batavia, vol. 1 (M-T1, R1). Received April 9, 1826.

To A[lexander] W. Jones

Sir,   Washington 19th. September 1825.

In reply to your Note of the seventeenth instant, I have to say that the state of Mr. Pleasants' health, during his voyage to the River Plata, was such as to render it necessary, in his opinion, to abandon the voyage, and to proceed to Europe. Confiding the despatches, therefore, with which he was charged to other hands, he passed on board a vessel bound to Europe, and the last account I have of him represented him to be near a British port.

The subject of designating the printers of the Laws is not usually acted upon until the commencement of Congress. Your request to be considered as having declined the application to be one of them will be recollected.

I am, Respectfully, Your Obedient Servant,   H. CLAY.
A. W. Jones Esqr. Richmond.

Copy. DNA, RG59, Dom. Letters, vol. 21, p. 152 (M40, R19).

From Richard C. Anderson, Jr.

Hon: Henry Clay   New York   Sep: 19 1825.
Sir

There is no prospect of my getting a conveyance to Colombia, before the first of October, and very probably not before the tenth. On this day I shall go towards Boston, and return about the first of the month. Mr. Bayard[1] hopes to send a Vessel to Carthagena in the first days of October.

Any communication from you addressed to me at this place, within that time, will be received.

The situation of our navigation as affected by the late treaty between Colombia and England, was a subject, which you thought required a communication to that Government[2]—

It occurs to me that in making an application for the correction of the mistake in the Case of the Josephine, it would be best for me to have the Copy of the letter actually used at the settlement. I think that Doctor Gual would immediately recognize the paper; at any rate, it would enable me to state the cause of mistake with more explicitness.

If you should find it prop[er] (now or hereafter) to give any farther instructions, in relation to the Captures made by Captain Chase[3] during the last summer, you will see the points on which I should desire instructions, fully presented in the letter of the late Secretary to me, & in mine to the Colombian Minister of foreign Affairs—

If you have time to write to me (apart from any official communication) you know that I would most gladly hear from you—I am with respect &C Your obt. Servant.   R. C. ANDERSON JR.

ALS. DNA, RG59, Dip. Disp., Colombia, vol. 3 (M-T33, R3). Received September 21.
1 Probably William Bayard.
2 See above, Clay to Anderson, September 16, 1825.
3 John Chase. See above, Anderson to Clay, March 18, 1825, note.

From James Brown

Dear Sir,   Paris Septr. 19. 1825.

Since my return from Aix my health continues to improve and if the incessant fall of cold rains which we usually experience during the winter months, and the sudden changes of air to which I may be exposed by late visits *of duty* at parties where no apology but that of bad health is admitted, do not produce a renewal of my complaint, I may perhaps pass the busy season here with some share of comfort. Should I unfortunately be once more confined by the same complaint, a sense of the duty I owe to my Country will compel me respectfully to request the President to name my Successor, and to permit me to seek a climate where I may find, if not a cure, at least some alleviation of my sufferings—

It afforded me great pleasure to learn by the perusal of a file of Lexington papers, that every step of your journey West was a triumph over your enemies. I was no less pleased at discovering that the election of Mr Adams which gave such universal satisfaction in Europe is now generally approved even by those who once strenuously opposed it. If his administration shall be fairly tried by its measures, I have every reason to believe that it will daily become more and more popular. At home our affairs are prosperous to a degree which excites the envy or admiration of all Europe, and when considered on a broad scale our foreign relations are in a more favorable condition than we could, two years ago, have anticipated. All dangers of a war, by the combined Monarchs against the new Republics seems [*sic*] to have vanished. America is permitted peaceably to pursue its own interests and promote its own prosperity. The Holy Alliance finds full employment in tranquilizing Spain and in settling the affairs of Greece without attempting to crush the Spirit of liberty in the American Hemisphere.

[A request, by "a portion of the Greeks," for the protection of Great Britain has been transmitted to the British Government. "This measure is disapproved by the French who believe that it has been brought about by the intrigues of British agents.[1] Remonstrances of a strong character will probably be made to the British Government against this measure by more than one power." There is much speculation on the course Britain will follow, "frequent conferences are held on this subject which . . . is one on which there is much difficulty in reconciling the views of the principal powers." Many believe "that if Greece can sustain herself until the end of the present Campaign," the number of belligerents will increase.

["The arrests at Madrid . . . prove that the Conspiracy of Bessieres[2] has had more extensive support than was at first believed." Further arrests and a widening of "the breach between the Ministry and the Ultra royalist party" are expected. Some people believe that the defeat of the plot to overthrow the King (Ferdinand VII) "will tend to improve the condition of Spain . . . that the influence of the Clergy . . . will be diminished" and their estates taxed or sold for the benefit of the Treasury, that "the spirit of opposition will be crushed, and a party in favor of milder measures, and a more liberal administration of Government will be formed and predominate— that to bring about this state of things, all the influence of the Courts of Europe will be exerted," that Spain "will Consent to emancipate her Colonies—that for this recognition a large sum will be paid to her by the New Republics—That England and France will guarrantee [sic] to Spain Cuba and Porto Rico. . . ."

[The opposing point of view is "that tranquility can be restored in Spain only by permitting the King to pursue freely that course of policy with which he commenced when liberated from the restraints of the Constitution . . . that any attempt to impose upon the nation a more liberal system of government" will always meet formidable resistance, and that advocates of a free system of government must be crushed.

[Although it is difficult to predict the course that will be recommended to Spain by her allies, it appears that the support of Zea Bermudez will continue. One "universally expressed" wish in France is "that of opening commercial relations with the New Republics." The prevailing opinion is that the colonies are "irrevocably lost." It is "generally believed" that France and England will urge Ferdinand to acknowledge them and that, as "the exact state of affairs is known" in Spain, their recognition "will not be so strongly opposed."

[Although requested, by a letter of last August, to separate the question of American claims "from that arising under the 8th. Art [sic] of the Louisiana Treaty," the French Minister of Foreign Affairs (the Baron de Damas) has never replied.[3] "I have asked an interview for to morrow, the object of which is to press him to answer my letter. If he is opposed to our claims we will have little prospect of their being granted by the present Ministry." This "Ministry is said to be very unpopular" but to "possess the entire confidence of the King."[4] It appears doubtful "that the cause of liberal principles would gain much by a change of Ministry," although probably no change would result in stronger opposition to our claims.]

I have been very anxious for your return to Washington as it of [sic] great importance that I should as frequently as possible hear from the Government on every subject touching my duties. I should be glad to know whether in case I find a disposition to decide against our claims I had better press for a decision or wait for a more favorable moment which a change of Ministry or in the situation of affairs may one day present— I am convinced that a positive rejection of them although it cannot cancel them or impair the right to demand or the obligation to pay has a very injurious effect. It not only uselessly disturbs the relations between the two Countries, but in the answer already prepared, in the decision already given by one Ministry furnishes a mode of disposing of the question to which subsequent Ministers are always willing to resort—

I have just been informed that Mr Sheldon[5] whose health was much impaired, and who has been for some weeks on the sea shore with a view of recovering it, is greatly relieved and may soon be expected in Paris. You know him well and will readily conceive how much I should regret his loss. I did fear that he was rapidly declining with a pulmonary complaint, but it is now thought that his indisposition proceeded from debility produced by a sedentary life, and by residing too long in the same atmosphere.

I have had only a few lines from Mr King[6] since he landed in England. His health is said to have been very much impaired by the voyage. He however derived some benefit from the waters of Cheltenham and his friends think that he will soon enjoy perfect health—

It gave us great pain to find from the newspapers that your journey through Ohio had been arrested by the ill health of your daughter.[7] I sincerely hope she has recovered and that Mrs. Clay after the examplary [sic] life of retirement at Ashland, may have nothing to damp her enjoyments in once more entering on the gay theatre at Washington. You have always had warm and kind friends and with your dispositions you are now placed in a situation where you may add daily to their number. Mrs. Adams will make the Great House more gay than it has ever been since the days of Mrs. Madison, and strangers will return to Europe not to ridicule but to boast of the reception they have met with at the Presidential residence. I often wish we were with you. There is much to admire in the gay Circles of Paris, but there is a cordiality a warmhearted-ness in our own dear Country which I find in no other place.

The Ambassador of Austria[8] having a larger salary than the American Minister has taken a lease for ten years of the fine Hotel where I resided last year—the Danish Minster[9] having obtained a Congé for some months has permitted me to take his place. The Hotel is more splendid than that which I formerly occupied but the situation is more retired it being in the Faubourg St Germain. I obtain it however on more moderate rent it only being 16000 fr. whilst the former one cost 22,000 pr Ann.

Be so good as to present us most affy to Mrs. Clay and receive renewed assurances of the friendly of [sic] Dear Sir Your very faithful sevt.   JAMES BROWN
Hon. Henry Clay   Secretary of State

ALS. DLC-HC (DNA, M212, R1).
[1] Cf. below, Somerville to Clay, October 11, 1825, note.
[2] See above, Brown to Clay, August 26, 1825.
[3] Cf. above, Brown to Clay, June 25, 1825.
[4] Charles X, whose chief minister was still the Comte de Villèle.
[5] Daniel Sheldon.   [6] Rufus King.
[7] Eliza. See above, Clay to Crittenden, July 25, August 22, 1825.
[8] Baron Karl Freiherr von Vincent.
[9] Von Juel, first name not known, had served as Danish Minister Plenipotentiary in France in 1823, had been raised the following year to the rank of Envoy Extraordinary, and continued at Paris in the latter capacity for at least six more years.

From [Étienne] Mazureau

Most Respected Sir,   Nw. Orleans September 19th. 1825.
I am requested by the friends of Duralde[1] to make to you a very painful Communication, and when I consider the cruel blow the all mighty has recently inflicted upon your paternal Heart,[2] and the effect which the one he has recently received himself from the Same hand must have upon you and mistress Clay, I must beg leave to express my regret that the task has devolved on me, feeling as I do that it is not in my power nor perhaps in the power of any man to offer any of those Consolations which both of you will Stand in need of, after you have read this letter.

But a few days ago Duralde was yet looked upon by all those who knew him and his most accomplished lady[3] as one of the happiest men in the world—he Continued to find and enjoy in her Compagny [sic] all the blessings and happiness which can render life dear or amiable.— The unheard of healthiness of this place, and its neighbourhood during this Season, made them indulge the hope that those blessings and happiness could neither be destroyed or altered by any of those dreadful afflictions which divine providence, too often perhaps, Sends to the most virtuous. alas! in one instant that hope vanished. She who was most dear to his heart was to be taken from him.

On Tuesday last your beloved Daughter was attacked with a fever to which She paid So little attention as to refuse taking any of the remedies prescribed by her physician. on friday She thought herself So much better that She Sat at table and dined with her husband— In the evening, however, She felt a little more uneasy, but refused again every assistance, Saying it was unnecessary— on Saturday, early in the morning, her malady begun [sic] to assume a more Serious Character. Duralde Sent for a Second physician whom She herself named. This, in the absence of the first, came immediately to See her, appeared to find nothing alarming in her Situation, and Said that at five, in the afternoon, he would come again, in company with the other, and that they would Consult together as to the treatment most proper to adopt— at the hour appointed they both attended, but the disease had made Such rapid progress that both Seemed to be confounded— They resolved to call other Physicians. Three more were accordingly Sent for, and met Shortly after. after a most deliberate consultation they all declared that [the] disease was a malignant fever of the most dangerous kind, which left Scarcely any hope of recovery— They however agreed that Blisters Should instantly be resorted to, and, on their being informed that She had Constantly refused to take as yet any kind of physic, one of them, Doctor Gros,[4] the Physician of my own family, a man of long experience and great acknowledged abilities, prevailed upon her to take Some beverage which they all agreed Should be administered to her— alas! my Dear Sir, it was already too late. no medical aid could restore her to life— and yesterday at nine o'Clock in the evening, She was no more. "I regret to die without Seeing my Father & mother" were the last words She uttered, after having recommended her beloved children[5] to her most unfortunate husband, in the presence of Several friends who during her malady constantly bestowed upon her their kindest attentions.

This Morning at ten o'Clock, She has been Conveyed to her last abode— I need not tell you that her loss has been most Sensibly felt by all those who knew her, and by your numerous friends— a large Concourse of people amongst whom were Seen our most respectable Citizens attended her funerals—

Duralde's Situation cannot be described— I have Seen him half an hour ago— he was Surrounded by his two Systers[6] [sic] and Some intimate friends— If he Speaks, it is only to lament his irreparable loss & the cruel effect the first intelligence of it will produce upon you and your Lady: I do not believe that he will Soon be able to write to you; & to be Candid I will tell you that I am afraid he will himself be Sick.

I Shall not endeavour to tender you any Consolation. I feel

convinced that no tongue, no pen is adequate to the task. I am
myself the father of most dear children,[7] & I Can not believe that
it would be in the power of any human being to persuade me to
bear with any degree of fortitude the loss of any of them. But I
beg of you to rest assured that no man Sympathises more heartily
with you on this Sorrowful occasion than Sir Your humble Servant
& True friend   Mazureau
The Honble. Henry Clay   Secretary of State.

ALS. DLC-HC (DNA, M212, R1). Mazureau had been awarded an honorary
degree, LL.D., at Transylvania University on July 13 of this year.
    [1] Martin Duralde (Jr.).
    [2] By the death of Eliza Clay. See above, Clay to Crittenden, August 22, 1825.
    [3] Susan Clay Duralde.
    [4] Probably D. Gros, influential in local political affairs and a regent of the University
of Orleans in 1812.   [5] Martin and Henry Clay Duralde.
    [6] Julie Duralde Clay and Louise Duralde Soniat du Fossat.
    [7] One son, Adolphe, was at this time a student in the junior class at Transylvania
University. He later became a prominent New Orleans lawyer. Other children not
identified.

DIPLOMATIC NOTES   September 19, 1825

From Hilario de Rivas y Salmon, "Legacion de España," Philadelphia. Encloses a complaint of an assault upon himself, by Juan Gualberto de Ortega,
former acting consul of Spain at Charleston, and demands punishment of the
attacker and protection for himself. ALS, in Spanish, with accompanying
translation. DNA, RG59, Notes from Spanish Legation, vol. 8 (M59, R11).
In July, 1825, Ortega had become commercial agent for Colombia in Philadelphia.

INSTRUCTIONS AND DISPATCHES   September 19, 1825

To John Tucker Mansfield. Encloses commission as United States consul
for Pernambuco, Brazil, printed circular instructions, and a blank consular
bond. Copy. DNA, RG59, Cons. Instr., vol. 2, p. 365 (M78, R2). Cf. above,
Clay to Mansfield, March 18, 1825, note.

From Heman Allen, Valparaiso, no. 20. Transmits a copy of a letter sent
this day to Commodore (Isaac) Hull. ALS. DNA, RG59, Dip. Disp., Chile, vol.
1 (M-T2, R1). Received January 13, 1826. The enclosure elaborates views on
the Peruvian decree already discussed in Allen's letter to Hull, July 14, 1825
(see above, Allen to Clay, September 16, 1825, note). In the present note Allen
discountenances execution of the first article of the decree "within the waters
of Peru, and farther it cannot extend," thus calling for rejection of the decree
in its entirety.

From Alexander Burton, Cádiz. Encloses copy of an order, issued by the
Spanish Government, exempting from tonnage duty all vessels entering ports
of the Spanish Peninsula in ballast for the purpose of loading salt and barilla
(see above, Everett to Clay, September 14, 1825). Points out that the amount
of duty on American vessels "is nearly equal to one half of the cost of a Cargo
of Salt." States that he enclosed in his letter of August 7 a decree (not found)

authorizing the search of "dwellings of Foreigners for contraband goods, without the Consul of their nation being present," and that he now encloses a decree cancelling the earlier one. ALS. DNA, RG59, Cons. Disp., Cádiz, vol. 4 (M-T186, R4). Received November 7.

From J[OHN] ADAMS SMITH, London, no. 12. Encloses copies of correspondence with the Baron de Cetto, Bavarian Chargé d'Affaires in London. Reports that (Rufus) King, whose "health and strength is [*sic*] very precarious," has arrived in London. ALS. DNA, RG59, Dip. Disp., Great Britain, vol. 32 (M30, R28). Addressed to Secretary of State. The enclosures relate to efforts of the Bavarian Government to deliver "two judicial Summons" to Christian Augsburger, of Butler County, Ohio. A note, from Smith to De Cetto, dated September 17, concludes the exchange, stating that (Rufus) King believes "there is no probability whatever" of serving the papers, which are therefore returned.

From WILLIAM TAYLOR, Veracruz. Reports the arrival, at Mocambo, from England, of a Mexican vessel of war and the anticipated arrival of two more. The Mexicans will then be able to isolate the Castle of San Juan de Ulloa, which, it is believed, should fall within two months. ALS. DNA, RG59, Cons. Disp., Veracruz, vol. 1 (M183, R1). Received November 8. Cf. above, Hughes to Clay, July 8, 1825, note.

MISCELLANEOUS LETTERS   September 19, 1825

From C[HARLES] J. INGERSOLL, Philadelphia. Encloses copy of an affidavit of Hilario de Rivas y Salmon concerning the assault upon him by (Juan) Gualberto de Ortega, on the night of September 17; states that Ingersoll, in Salmon's behalf, caused a warrant to be issued for Ortega's arrest and now requests instructions relative to submitting the case to the United States Circuit Court; and adds that Ortega has been arrested and held to bail. ALS. DNA, RG59, Misc. Letters (M179, R63).

From S[AMUEL] L. S[OUTHARD], Navy Department. Acknowledges receipt of Clay's "note of the 17th. instant" (not found) and states that no appointment can be given immediately to (George N.) Hawkins. Copy. DNA, RG45, Executive Letterbook, vol. 1, p. 131. Cf. above, Clay to Southard, May 7, 1825, note.

APPLICATIONS, RECOMMENDATIONS   September 19, 1825

TIMOTHY FULLER, Boston, recommends William L. Reaney for appointment as consul in Puerto Rico. ALS. DNA, RG59, A. and R. (MR3). See above, Van Ness to Clay, September 7, 1825, note.

Check to John Forsyth

20 Septr. 1825

Pay to the Honble John Forsyth four hundred and forty five dollars.   H. CLAY

Cashr. of the Off. of Dt. & Dt. Washington City.[1]

ADS. DLC-TJC (DNA, M212, R16).   [1] Richard Smith.

To Severin Lorich

Department of State, 20th. September, 1825.
M. Severin Lorich, Chargé d'Affaires from Sweden
Sir,

I have, according to the request contained in the note which you did me the honor to address to me, on the 22d. ultimo, submitted it to the President, who has given to the contents of it the most attentive consideration, and by whose direction I now have the pleasure of transmitting this answer.

With respect to the case of the Swedish Ship Carl John, referring to my note of the 10th. of last May, and considering the unimportance of the only point in issue between us, that of the usual condition of the payment of costs on the remission of a forfeiture, incurred by a violation of the laws of the U. States, it is hardly necessary to protract the discussion.

The U. States have ever been scrupulous in the observance of good faith, in the execution of treaties which they have contracted with foreign powers. They are not sensible of the violation of any obligations which they have come under to Sweden, in the Treaties of 1783 and 1816.[1] The second article of the former, to which you refer, provides for a reciprocal grant by the two contracting parties of any particular favor, in relation to commerce and navigation, which may be extended to other nations, freely, if the concession were freely made, or on allowing the same compensation if the concession were conditional. If you will point out any particular favor granted, by the U. States, to the commerce and navigation of other nations, which Sweden does not enjoy, prompt measures will be taken to give to Sweden, in regard to such favor, all the effect which was intended by the second article of the treaty of 1783.

In regard to the 7th. 8th. and 9th. articles of the treaty of 1816. The seventh provides "that the citizens or subjects of one of the contracting parties, arriving with their vessels, on any coast belonging to the other, but not willing to enter into port, or being entered into port and not willing to unload or break bulk, shall have liberty to depart and to pursue their voyage without molestation" &c. They are nevertheless, whilst within the jurisdiction of either party to conform to the laws and regulations of that party concerning navigation.

The eighth article allows of a partial discharge of the Cargo, limits the payment of duties to that part, and allows the vessel to depart freely with the residue. The duties on the vessel itself are however to be paid where she first breaks bulk.

Of the benefit of both these articles of the Treaty Swedish vessels are believed to be in the full enjoyment. They do not confer a right so to introduce the produce of all countries indiscriminately. That depends upon the laws of the U. States and Sweden respectively; and whatever they allow to be imported may be brought in and either not discharged at all or partially discharged as stipulated in the seventh and eighth articles.

The ninth article merely provides "that the citizens or subjects of one of the contracting parties shall enjoy, in the ports of the other, as well for their vessels as their merchandise, all the rights and privileges of entrepot which are enjoyed by the most favored nations in the same ports." Before any violation of this article can justly be alleged, it must be shewn that some particular nation enjoys rights and privileges of entrepot in the ports of one of the contracting parties which are withheld from the other. If you will be pleased to particularize any foreign nation that enjoys such rights and privileges in the ports of the U. States, to the exclusion of Sweden, you will make out a case requiring the interposition of the Government, and it would immediately afford its interposition.

The act of the 7 January 1824[2] was intended, as to duties, to place the vessels of the powers enumerated in its first section, and their cargoes, being of the produce and manufactures, of those countries respectively, on the same footing, when entering the ports of the United States, as their own vessels and cargoes. It was not intended to allow the vessels of the enumerated powers to import the produce and manufactures of other foreign countries on the same terms with our own, with the exception only in the second section, which was designed to cover the peculiar condition of some German rivers which do not discharge themselves within the jurisdiction of the countries in which they take their rise.[3] All the vessels and their cargoes of the enumerated powers are now, in respect to duties, subject to the same rule; or if there be any exception to the disadvantage of Norway, it is unknown and would be instantly corrected when known.

The U. States are not prepared alone to adopt the policy of allowing the vessels of any foreign nation, indiscriminately to import the produce and manufactures of all foreign nations. Whenever the maritime powers shall be disposed so to enlarge the privileges of navigation, and to put down all restrictions founded on the place of origin of the articles composing the cargoes of vessels, the U. States, which have never been backward in enlightened and liberal systems of navigation and commerce, will be ready to second their expanded views.

You ask that the vessels of Norway and of the Island of St. Bartholomew may be permitted to import into the U. States other foreign produce and manufactures than those of Sweden upon the condition of the payment of no higher duties than would be chargeable upon the importation of like articles in vessels of the U. States. If that demand be placed on treaty stipulations it is believed not to be sustainable. Neither party has ever so interpreted the Treaty. Sweden does not now admit the vessels of the U. States to carry the productions of other nations indiscriminately into her ports. If her exclusion of them is not absolute; if she allows the vessel of the U. States to carry the produce of any of the West Indian Islands into her ports, this partial relaxation does not proceed from the obligations of the Treaty but from other considerations, to the friendly character of some of which this Government has heretofore expressed its sensibility.[4] If the demand rests upon the act of Congress of 7 January 1824, that act does not authorize it. It limits the principle of equalization, on which it is based, to the importation, in the vessels of the enumerated powers, of the produce of those powers respectively.

So far as respects the Island of St. Bartholomews, if the President possessed the power of opening, by proclamation, the ports of the U. S. to foreign vessels when laden with the produce of other countries than their own, he could not in justice to the U. States accede to a proposition which should be limited to that Island. The fourth section of the act of 7. January 1824, supposes *all* the ports of a foreign nation to be opened to the vessels of the U. States to warrant the issuing of the proclamation for which it provides. There would be no reciprocity in opening all our ports to a foreign nation which should occlude the greater part of hers: And when it is recollected that St. Bartholomew is a small island of scanty population and of inconsiderable trade, the inequality is more manifest.

The regret which is felt on account of the different views which are taken by the President and by you of the provisions of the treaty of 1816 is mitigated by the consideration that, as it expires in little more than a year from this time, the whole subject of our relations of commerce and navigation will be brought shortly under review. Whenever that is done, I trust that they will be so adjusted as to confirm and strengthen the amity and good understanding which have ever happily subsisted between the two countries.

I pray you to accept renewed assurances of the very distinguished consideration of Your obedient humble servant.   H. CLAY.

Copy. DNA, RG59, Notes to Foreign Legations, vol. 3, pp. 230-32 (M38, R3). ALI draft, in CSmH.
1 For the treaty dated April 3, 1783, see Miller (ed.), *Treaties* . . . , II, 123-50; on the treaty of 1816, see above, Clay to Lorich, May 10, 1825.
2 See above, Lorich to Clay, March 16, 1825, note.
3 The clause suspended discriminating duties against "such produce and manufactures as can only be, or more usually are, first shipped from a port or place in

the said territories in Europe [that is, the enumerated countries covered by the statute] of either of them, respectively, the same being imported in vessels truly and wholly belonging to the subjects or citizens of each of the said nations, respectively. . . ." 4 *U. S. Stat.*, 2.

4 In a note dated April 3, 1824, Count Lars d'Engeström had notified Christopher Hughes of Swedish concessions permitting American vessels to import colonial produce into Swedish dominions upon paying the same duties as Swedish ships bringing goods to Sweden from European ports, that is, indirectly. DNA, RG59, Dip. Disp., Sweden and Norway, vol. 4 (M45, R5).

The "satisfaction" of the United States at this pronouncement had been expressed on June 28, by Secretary of State Adams in a note addressed to Baron Berndt Robert Gustaf Stackelberg, who had transmitted a copy of the d'Engeström note. DNA, RG59, Notes to Foreign Ministers and Consuls, vol. 3, pp. 181-82 (M38, R3).

From George Eustis

New Orleans, Septr. 20th, 1825

Sir   I am charged to communicate to you intelligence of the most melancholy kind, and when I think of the wound about to be inflicted on affectionate parents to whom affliction has lately been so severely dealt, I shrink from the task I have undertaken.[1]

Your daughter was taken sick on the 13th. ins. The news of the death of her sister[2] weighed heavily on her; it depressed her spirits and perceptibly affected her health. The attack was not violent, but it was insidious; and her danger was not apprehended until the disease had so far advanced as to render all remedies unavailing. She expired on the 18th at nine o' clock in the evening.

I abstain from communicating to you the details of her sickness and treatment. Let it suffice to say, that the best physicians in the city were with her constantly and she was attended by the relations of Duralde—Mrs. Clay & Soniat,[3] and several of his friends—whose unremitting labours and watchings proved how much they loved your daughter. The sufferings of Duralde have been dreadful. His bodily health is not impaired, but grief has worn him down. The youngest child,[4] who is not yet weaned, will be taken by Mrs. Soniat and nursed by her daughter Me Boisblanc:[5] the other[6] goes to his Aunt's Mrs. J. Clay. They are both well.

The deceased died of a malignant fever, as it is called here. The organs of the stomach were vitally affected thirty six hours before dissolution: the brain was not affected and she preserved her senses until the last hour. She was perfectly aware of her situation and manifested throughout a most wonderful self-possession: she was more calm than the distressed friends who surrounded her death bed. She took an affectionate leave of her husband and her children and added these words "I hope you will always remember that these children are mine & yours." She dwelt with intense feeling on the sufferings her parents would experience: she appeared to feel more for you than for herself.

She was buried yesterday from my house, in the city—Duralde's residence being two miles distant—and a numerous concourse of the most respectable inhabitants followed her to the tomb.

Should any thing occur, which it may be necessary for you to know I shall take the liberty of advising you of it, as Duralde *cannot* write for the present. I take this opportunity—and a most melancholy one it is—to beg of you to be assured of my highest respect.   GEORGE EUSTIS.

Hon. H. Clay.

ALS. DLC-HC (DNA, M212, R1). Eustis, a nephew of William Eustis, had been born in Boston, educated at Harvard, and admitted to the bar in New Orleans (1822). He later served in the Louisiana Legislature, was State attorney general (1830-1832), secretary of state for Louisiana (1832-1834), a justice of the State supreme court (1838-1839), and chief justice of the revised State judiciary (1846-1852).

1 Cf. above, Mazureau to Clay, September 19, 1825.
2 Eliza Clay.
3 Julie Duralde Clay; Louise Duralde Soniat du Fossat.
4 Henry Clay Duralde.   5 Not further identified.
6 Martin Duralde III.

INSTRUCTIONS AND DISPATCHES   September 20, 1825

To JAMES H. BENNETT, Pernambuco. Refers to a letter from the State Department, February 17, 1825 (relative to accusations made against him by John Bayard Kirkpatrick), requiring him to offer explanation and justification for his conduct and suspending him from exercising consular functions until further notice; informs him that President Adams, having found in the evidence no ground for reinstating him, "has thought proper to appoint Mr. [John T.] Mansfield as Consul at Pernambuco" in his place. Copy. DNA, RG59, Cons. Instr., vol. 2, pp. 365-66 (M78, R2).

From JOEL R. POINSETT, Mexico, no. 19. Reports an interview with the Mexican Secretary of State (Lucas Alamán) "on the subject of the boundary line between the two Republics," during which the Secretary expressed a desire "to specify the ancient boundary [defined by the Pinckney Treaty of 1795], until the new line was agreed upon." Poinsett replied that the treaty of 1795 antedated the cession of Louisiana, after which the United States had "claimed to the Rio bravo del Norte, and Spain to the Mississippi"; that the (Adams-Onís) treaty of 1819, which resolved disputed claims, was binding on Mexico, having "been acknowledged by their accredited agent in the United States of America"; and that the United States had refrained from carrying the latter treaty into effect only from "motives of delicacy towards Mexico." The same motives, Poinsett further stated, had induced him to propose a new treaty, but he "did not intend to yield one square inch of land which was included within the limits of the United States according to the boundary" agreed upon in the Treaty of 1819. He thought "a more advantageous boundary might be drawn," but "such a line was not to be sought for east of the Sabine, or north of the Red River or the Arkansa [*sic*]; and . . . no article such as . . . proposed [by Alamán] could be inserted in the Treaty, without . . . renewing in it the claim of the United States to the Country north and east of the Rio bravo del Norte."

Notes the probability that Lucas Alamán will soon be succeeded by "one

Camacho" as Secretary of State; that a commissioner from the Netherlands has arrived in Mexico; that (José Mariano) Michelena, Mexican commissioner to England, has returned home; that the Mexican fleet is being augmented by purchases abroad; and that the memorial alluded to in his last dispatch (of September 13) has been presented to Congress. LS. DNA, RG59, Dip. Disp., Mexico, vol. 1 (M97, R2). Received November 4.

On the proposed boundary negotiation, see above, Clay to Poinsett, March 26, 1825; Poinsett to Clay, July 18, 22, 1825; on the augmentation of the Mexican fleet, cf. above, Taylor to Clay, September 19, 1825.

Sebastián Camacho, born in Veracruz, had been a member of the constitutional assembly and of the first legislative session following the recognition of Mexican independence. In the fall of 1825 he became Secretary of State and Foreign Relations and the following year was sent as Mexican Minister to England, France, and the Low Countries to complete commercial negotiations which marked the recognition of Mexican independence. He resumed the post as Minister of Foreign Relations later in the decade and, having withdrawn from public affairs after a change in political power during the early thirties, he returned to the same office in 1844. He was a member of the Mexican Senate in 1837 and Governor of the State of Veracruz in the late thirties and again in 1846.

MISCELLANEOUS LETTERS   September 20, 1825

From HUGH NELSON, "Belvoir" (Albemarle County, Virginia). Encloses a copy of his "address to the King of Spain on taking leave," as printed in a Spanish journal; states that he "thought it of so little consequence" that he did not send it until he saw "the bad translation of it" that appeared in the Washington *Daily National Journal*. ALS. DNA, RG59, Dip. Disp., Spain, vol. 24 (M31, R26).

From James E. Davis

Dear Sir.   Lexington September 21st. 1825.

I wish to rent your stone house on water street. In looking about, I find no house in the town of Lexington that will suit me better than it will— I applied to your Son, & to Mr. Scott; they directed me to Mr. Minter;[1] I saw Mr. Minter—He seems unwilling that I should make any attempt to get the house, says he is entitled to the rent of it, till Christmas, & intends to rent it afterwards to Carry on his business. I told him plainly that in his present embarressed [sic] condition (& there is in my opinion no possibility of his getting relieved from it) that it was folly to talk of commencing business there—*he cant do it*— I therefore wish you to write me,[2] what you will take for it the next three years, & also what you will sell it for to be paid, any time during the three years— I want to rent it with leave to buy it at the price you hold it at— In your proposition to rent or sell, I wish you to take into Consideration; that of all the houses in world [sic], it has been the most abused, & is the most out of order; there is not a window sash or glass in it— It will take besides sash, & doors, 500 panes of glass to make it tenantable— The board fence is torn down & burnt; & every outhouse is in the same condition— It is true that there is a very very good shed & inclined wheel put there by Minter— He claims the wheel, but from the wording of your Compromise,[3] I am of opinion you intended by *"fixtures"* to imbrace [*sic*] the wheel &c. It is my Candid opinion that it will be to your interest to rent me the house, upon the best of terms to me, Please instruct your agent here, to do it, upon such terms as will be fair & right[.] I trust I shall be able to buy in the course of the time mentioned, upon any liberal proposition you may make me, & which I wish you to make in reply to this— The house is only Calculated for manufacturing, & I don't honestly believe Mr. Minter will be able to Commence business in it; of Course it will make agt. your interest to have it unoccupied, & especially as it is going more & more to wreck I shall be much obliged to you, to get an answer as soon practicable. I shall want the house immediately, & shall have to make some very considerable sacrifice I am pretty certain to get out it out [*sic*] of the possession of Minter— I have no news of consequence— Boyle & Trimble this day (after being here several days) refused their appt. in the U— Burnett [*sic*] did the same some days ago[4]—

I have honor to be, &c.   JAMES E. DAVIS

H. Clay Esq

ALS. DLC-HC (DNA, M212, R1). Endorsed on verso by Clay: "Tammany Mills."
1 Probably Theodore W. Clay; Robert Scott; James Minter.
2 No answer found, but cf. below, Agreement, October 24, 1825.
3 See above, Agreement, July 4, 1825.
4 John Boyle, Robert Trimble, Jacob Burnet, declining appointment to the faculty of Transylvania University.

From Benedict Joseph Flaget

Dear & Hble. Sir   Bardstown,[1] 7ber. 21th. [*sic*] 1825.

In Sending my long report to the Hble. Lough Borough[2] J wrote as to the Presidt. of a committy [*sic*] charged to See into the amelioration of litterary [*sic*] institutions, & J contented my Self to anSwer as exactly & candidly as J could, all the questions he had been pleased to put to me. But in writting [*sic*] to you it Seems to me that J correspond with a Genuine Kentuckn a deep Statesman, & give me leave to add, with a friend to the old biShop at Bardstown.

By what J wrote to you once,[3] & by what you Will See in my letter to the Secretary P. T. you will be Convinced that though a Frenchman by birth, J am a Sincere American by choice & adoption— That J have Spent the most precious time of my life in the

United States, & that at all times & every where J endeavoured to make my Self useful to the people with whom J lived. The inhabitants of Vincennes in Indiana State, the Gentlemen of George town College near Fœderal City, thoSe of St. Mary's in Baltimore with whom Successively J have Spent the best part of my life, will never complain of me, & the Kind treatment J receive from them all, at this very time, is a proof of the Sincere affection they entertain for me—

Though J'am now about Sixty years of age, yet J feel the Same desire, the Same eagerness for public Good which J felt when thirty years of age. Dear Sir, there are great [sic] many good works J would do in Ky. were J Supported properly by our Govt. or by rich & Generous friends. Last year J intended to Go to Europe for Several good purposes.

Ily. To procure in Bordeaux two or three Sisters of Charity[4] who direct in that City a Manufacture Carried on by little Orphan Children— 15 years ago J visited my Self the Said manufacture, & J Saw Several of these children Seven or eight years old making more than their living by applying to trades Suitable to their age. 2ly. J intended also to procure, if possible, two or three Nuns of an order Called in French *Dames de la Sagesse*,[5] who understand how to instruct Deaf, & dumb,. J Know that there is in Danville an institution of the Kind[6]— But the School is a promiscuous one: & J have always ConSidered Such Schools as extremely pernicious to Sound morals.

3ly. J expected to procure in Paris, where J have numbers of excellent friends, a learned Chymist: & as J correspond regularly with people of the first rank in Rome, J expected to Collect there fine paintings & engage Some celebrated painters & Musicians to accompany me to Bardstown, && But want of means & Some domestik reasons prevented me— J have received Several invitations to visit Europe once more before J die, & J am almost determined to do it next Spring,[7] or at least to Send in my place a Clergyman of my utmost Confidence, in order to enrich as much as possible, My Dear Kentans. with learning & fine arts.

J freely & friendly unboSom my heart to your own, because J Know that your views for public good are entensive [sic], & that you are possessed with the noble ambition of making the United States independent of Europe. J feel animated with the Same Sentiments, & if you have it in your power to encourage them, do it, if you please, & you will never repent for it. As for me, J declare it with Confidence, J do not want foreign assistance. A man who lives with pleasure on Bacon & potatoes has no need of applying to our Generl. Govt. for Such provisions, he will find them in plenty

in Ky. it is not So when J have a Mind of erecting public institutions.   With unfeigned Sentiments of esteem & Sincere
friendShip J remain Dear & Hble. Sir, Your most obedt. & affectionate Servt.   BENEDICT JOSEPH FLAGET BiSHP. of Bardstown

ALS. DLC-TJC (DNA, M212, R10). Addressed to Clay at Washington. Flaget, born
in Contournat, France, had been educated for the priesthood at the Sulpician Seminary,
Clermont, France, and ordained in 1786. After teaching at various seminaries in
France, he had come to the United States as a refugee of the revolution, in 1792. He
had been assigned first as a parish priest to Vincennes, Northwest Territory, from
1795 to 1798 as vice-rector and teacher at Georgetown College (founded at Washington, District of Columbia, in 1789), from 1798 to 1801 as an emissary to aid in
founding a seminary in Havana, Cuba, from 1801 to 1809 as a teacher at St. Mary's
College, Baltimore, Maryland (founded in 1799), and since 1810 as bishop of the
see at Bardstown, Kentucky (removed to Louisville in 1841). Except for a brief
period in 1832, he held this charge until his death in 1850.
  1 Kentucky.
  2 Preston S. Loughborough, assistant secretary of state of Kentucky, had been acting
as secretary *pro tempore* during the interval before James C. Pickett assumed office.
See above, Clay to Wharton, February 5, 1825, note.
  The report, a statistical record of the religious and educational institutions under
Flaget's jurisdiction—their number, the size of the staff and student body, and the
capital investment—is summarized in M[artin] J[ohn] Spalding, *Sketches of the Life,
Times, and Character of the Rt. Rev. Benedict Joseph Flaget, First Bishop of Louisville* (Louisville, 1852), 302-303.
  3 Letter not found.
  4 Sisters of Charity of St. Vincent de Paul, founded at Paris in 1633, as "Servants
of the Poor," identified initially with the care of the sick but also, almost immediately,
with the care of foundlings.   5 Not identified.
  6 The Kentucky Asylum for the Tuition of the Deaf and Dumb, founded by
legislative act of December 7, 1822, was administered by a committee of twelve women,
appointed by the trustees of "Central [*sic*] College [Centre College, founded in 1819]
at Danville." Ky. Gen. Assy., *Acts . . . 1822*, pp. 179-81.
  7 Flaget had returned to Europe in 1809-1810, prior to accepting the assignment at
Bardstown. He was again abroad from 1835 to 1839, under a papal commission to
raise funds for missions in the American Mid-West. On the failure of his plans for
such a visit in 1825, see J. Herman Schauinger, *Cathedrals in the Wilderness* (Mil-
waukee, 1952), 290-91.

DIPLOMATIC NOTES   September 21, 1825.

From P[ETE]R PEDERSEN, Philadelphia, "Private." Inquires when he may come
to Washington to negotiate a commercial convention. ALS. DNA, RG59, Notes
from Foreign Legations, Denmark, vol. 1 (M52, R1) .

MISCELLANEOUS LETTERS   September 21, 1825

From JOSEPH ANDERSON, Comptroller's Office, Treasury Department. In answer
to Clay's inquiry at the Treasury Department "this morning," concerning duties
exacted from vessels of St. Bartholomew and Norway in American ports,
encloses copies of two letters addressed, in 1822, respectively to Severin Lorich
and (Henry A. S.) Dearborn, collector at Boston; expresses an opinion that,
under a broad interpretation of the act of Congress of January 7, 1824, Norwegian vessels carrying cargoes not the product of that country are entitled
to enter American ports upon paying tonnage duties at the domestic rate.
ALS. DNA, RG59, Misc. Letters (M179, R63). Dearborn, son of Henry Dearborn, was collector of customs at Boston from 1812 to 1829. He had served as

a brigadier general of volunteers in the War of 1812 and was later a member of the State legislature (1829, 1830) and of Congress (1831-1833).

From FREDERICK C. BAKER, Havana. Reports the death of William Miller, of yellow fever, at Key West. ALS. DNA, RG59, Dip. Disp., Central America, vol. 1 (M219, R2). Baker not identified.

APPLICATIONS, RECOMMENDATIONS   September 21, 1825

[JOHN B.] COLVIN solicits "some employment to enable him to subsist himself and his family for the present"; suggests that Clay might, "without subjecting any person to improper censure or remark," permit him to supervise the publication of "The Register of Public officers," which he would do for compensation of $100 or less, and which "might be done through the medium of the printer, Mr. [Peter] Force"; thanks "Clay for his good intentions in the case of Mrs. Colvin," although, "as there was no extra work in the Department, they were unavailing"; states that "He would call upon Mr. Clay in person but not having the advantage of a previous acquaintance, is induced to express himself through a friend." AN. DLC-HC (DNA, M212, R1).

Colvin's employment as a State Department clerk had been terminated by John Quincy Adams in 1822, his absences from office and neglect of duty "increasing with his habits of intemperance, till they could no longer be tolerated." Adams, Memoirs, VI, 94-95. Mrs. Colvin (A. S. Colvin) has not been further identified.

In a letter dated September 24, 1825, Daniel Brent, at Clay's direction, informed Colvin that provision had already been made for compiling the Biennial Register but that if he was "disposed to undertake the recording such of the laws of Congress as may be designated by this Department . . . from the Copy in the printed Pamphlets, leaving Blanks for the Presidents name and those of the presiding Officers of the two Houses, to be supplied when the Record is ultimately compared with the Roll, Mr. Bt. is authorised to propose that employment . . . ; it being understood that it is to be executed at Mr. Colvin's own Lodgings, and at the rate not exceeding fifteen cents the hundred words." Copy. DNA, RG59, Dom. Letters, vol. 21, pp. 155-56. On September 26, Brent, again at Clay's direction, wrote to Colvin, in reply to a note addressed to Brent on September 25, and informed him that Clay "would with great pleasure cause an advance to be made . . . of the sum of Seventy dollars, upon account, for recording the Laws of the United States, were he not restrained from doing so by the Law prohibiting such advances," but that if arrangements can be made with Mrs. Arguelles, proprietress of a Washington boarding house, to whom Colvin in indebted, "by which payments can be contingently secured," Clay "will with pleasure give effect to it . . . from time to time, as the work advances, for not less than twenty dollars each." Ibid., p. 156. On January 12, 1826, Brent, at Clay's direction, informed Colvin "that he declines for the present employing any extra aid to Record the Laws of the United States." Ibid., p. 244.

DAVIS AND FORCE, Washington, solicit "the contracts for printing the 'Register of Officers' Etc. and the Laws, under the same terms on which they have heretofore been done." ALS. DNA, RG59, Misc. Letters (M179, R63). From 1820 to 1828 Peter Force and William A. Davis, the latter a former newspaper publisher in New York, held the contract for printing the Biennial Register of Government office holders.

WILLIAM HENDRICKS, Madison (Indiana), recommends the appointment of the Richmond (Indiana) *Public Ledger,* edited by (Edward S.) Buxton, as publisher of the laws. ALS. DNA, RG59, P. and D. of L. The *Public Ledger* did not receive the patronage of public printing under the Adams administration. Buxton, not further identified, withdrew in the autumn of 1826 as publisher of the journal.

J[ACK] T[ERRILL] Ross, St. Stephens, Alabama, recommends Henry Hitchcock for appointment as district attorney for the Southern District of Alabama. ALS. DNA, RG59, A. and R. (MR2). Ross, born and educated in North Carolina, a lieutenant in the United States Army from 1813 to 1817, had entered business as a merchant at St. Stephens and engaged extensively in such operations after moving to Mobile in 1824. He also owned large plantations in Greene and Clarke Counties. He had served as Territorial, later State, treasurer and was now sheriff of Mobile County. He was elected to the State House of Representatives in 1826, 1827, and 1835 and to the State Senate in 1828.

To Walter Dun

Dear Sir   Washington 22d. Sept. 1825
    I received your favor of the 10h. with its inclosures now returned.[1]
    You are substantially right in your statement. I have nothing to receive from you but the fees in Mr. Calls case, and those in Chancery in Mountjoy's[2] Suit, which amount to about the sum stated by you of $10:21. which you will be pleased to pay to Mr. Creighton.[3]
    It would have given me pleasure to have served you in your business with Mr. Graham, if you had thought it advisable to have desired my aid. As it is I hope he will do what is proper.
    With great regard I am faithfy Yrs   H. CLAY
[Endorsement][4]
Otr. 1st 1825. Recd. of Walter Dun Esqr. Ten dollars and twenty one Cents. Clerks tickets in the case of Daniel Call Exr. of R Means vs Carneal in the Circuit Court U States Kenty for H Clay.
                                              W CREIGHTON JUN

ALS. Ross County Historical Society, Chillicothe, Ohio. Addressed to Dun at Chillicothe, Ohio.
    1 Enclosed with the letter are only two fee bills in the case of Daniel Call, executor of Means: the first, from the marshal, District of Kentucky, for $6.25, signed by Chapman Coleman; the second, from the clerk of the Circuit Court, Kentucky District, for $2.77, signed by John H. Hanna.
    2 Thomas Mountjoy, Jr.   3 William Creighton, Jr.
    4 AES by Creighton.

From John J. Crittenden

My Dear Sir,   Frankfort Septr: 22nd 1825
    Your valued letter of the 22d of August has been received, and

I thank you for your friendly congratulations on my election—
You are pleased to attach more consequence to it, than it deserves—
The general result of our late elections I regard as a real triumph,
& a just subject of congratulation among all the friends of constitutional government— It is my misfortune that so much is
expected of me at the ensuing session of the Legislature— I speak
it more in sorrow, than in vanity— The Anti-reliefs, & the Reliefs,
(to use names familiar here) both have their eyes fixed upon me—
The former expect me to do a great deal, the latter to forbear a
great deal— My situation will be delicate & responsible, & I may
well fear that I shall not be equal to it—

As to the course which the party (the majority) ought to take,
& the temper with which they ought to pursue it, I entirely concur
with you— They ought to do nothing "from passion, nor in
passion"— We ought in fact to do very little at the approaching
session— Nothing but what is indispensable, & necessary to be
done—leaving all other matters for future regulation & reform,
where such reform is proper— We must retrench & economise as
far as practicable— And finally we must have a very short session—
say one month— If the majority will take such a course they may
look to the future without fear; & certainly they can not be too
careful to avoid every act of indiscretion or impolicy that might
turn from them, or change, the public feeling & opinion—

It is not certain what course the new judges[1] will pursue—
They have not yet resigned—And some of their party talk of their
holding out to the last extremity. Supposing them to take such
a course, & supposing the Govnr.[2] & Senate to defeat the passage
of a bill for the repeal of the Act under which these new judges
were created[3]— Ought not the H: of Rep: to declare, by resolution, that act to be unconstitutional—and that Boyle Owsley &
Mills are the only constitutional judges?[4] and ought not those
judges, under these circumstances, to resume their functions, &
co-erce the redelivery of, or take by force, the records that were
wrested from their clerk by the new court?[5] Or would it be
better, leaving this new court in possession of the records & in
the exercise of its unconstitutional jurisdiction, to appeal again
to the people at the next election? What would be the most correct
& politic course for us to take under these circumstance [sic]? We
could certainly appeal to the people again with great effect, we
could point to these judges as sheltering themselves from the
constitution & the people & taking protection from both, under
a Govnr. & Senate &c &c   We could succeed again before the
people, & probably by an increased majority— But in the mean
time we should be leaving the new court, & their party [cur]rently
in power— And this might [be] attended with its disadvantages—

Upon the whole it is quite a perplexing subject to me, & I should like to hear your views of it, if you can venture to give them to me in confidence—

The Madman of Georgia,[6] I am glad to s[ee] has, agreed to defer his desperate resolution of surveying the Indian lands— It is well for him that he has some "method in his madness"— The conduct of the President in relation to this affair is, I beleive [sic], almost universally approved of with us—

Your Son Thomas supped with me last night & left here this morning for Judge Boyle's[7]— He is well— Our old acquaintance, A. Sneed died on sunday last   Yr Friend   J J CRITTENDEN
Hon: H. Clay, Secty &c

ALS. NcD.
1 William T. Barry; James Haggin; John Trimble; and Rezin H. Davidge.
2 Joseph Desha.   3 See above, III, 902n.
4 John Boyle; William Owsley; Benjamin Mills.
5 See above, Blair to Clay, March 7, 1825, note.
6 George M. Troup. See above, Clay to Southard, July 3, 1825, note.
7 Cf. above, Boyle to Clay, January 10, 1825.

From John T. Kirkland

Dear Sir: Harvard University. Cambridge Sept. 22nd. 1825.

I have the honor of informing you, that the Government of Harvard University did, at the last Commencement,[1] in expression of their sense of your professional and general attainments, & your distinguished character and standing, confer on you, the honorary Degree of Doctor of Laws.

The Diploma will be made out & sent to you. In the hope of your favourable consideration of this token of our respect, I have the honor to be with high esteem Your ob Servt.
Hon. Henry Clay   J. T. KIRKLAND President.

ALS. DLC-HC (DNA, M212, R1).   1 Held August 31.

DIPLOMATIC NOTES   September 22, 1825

From JOSE MARIA SALAZAR, New York. Extends condolences upon Clay's bereavement (the death of Eliza Clay). States that the health of Madame Salazar has caused him to remain in New York and to send to Washington the Secretary of Legation (Juan Maria) Gómez, who has recently returned from Europe, to confer upon public matters. Explains that he (Salazar), being uncertain of the duration of his commission to the United States, has decided not to renew his lease upon the house of (Richard) Forrest and to offer to Clay as much of the furniture as would prove useful. ALS, in Spanish. DNA, RG59, Notes from Colombian Legation, vol. 1, pt. 2 (M51, R2). Gómez was transferred in November, 1826, as Secretary of Legation to Brazil. In 1834 he conducted Colombian negotiations to resolve a dispute with France, and for six months in 1845 he served as Colombian Minister of Foreign Relations. On Clay's rental of the Forrest house, see below, Agreement, October 11, 1825.

From HILARIO DE RIVAS Y SALMON, "Legacion de España, Philadelphia." Cites specific instances of ships of war being built in New York and Baltimore and of armaments and munitions being sent from Philadelphia to South American States; asks that this information be laid before the President. ALS, in Spanish, with translation. DNA, RG59, Notes from Spanish Legation, vol. 8 (M59, R11). Received September 25.

INSTRUCTIONS AND DISPATCHES   September 22, 1825

From JOEL R. POINSETT, Mexico (City), no. 20. Transmits information, just received, of a report by a Mexican secret agent concerning a French scheme "to prevail upon the King of Spain [Ferdinand VII] to renounce his right to Mexico in favor of Francisco de Paula the youngest of the Spanish Bourbons," to land the Prince with a large force on the Mexican coast, and to announce to England a French disposition to recognize the independence of the former Spansh colonies as limited monarchies but not as republics; explains why he gives some credence to this report; states that Great Britain will oppose placing a Bourbon on the throne of Mexico; and notes that nothing has been said to him on the subject, although the Mexican President (Guadalupe Victoria) has conferred with the British Chargé d'Affaires (Henry G. Ward). LS, in code. DNA, RG59, Dip. Disp., Mexico, vol. 1 (M97, R2). A decoded copy, from which quotation is taken, is found in NHi. Decoded copy published in Manning (arr.), *Diplomatic Correspondence . . . Latin-American Nations*, III, 1632-33. Francisco de Paula Antonio de Borbón, born in 1794, was known primarily for his interest in the fine arts.

From GEORGE W. SLACUM, Buenos Aires. Transmits a copy of a report (not found) prepared "by a Committee of British Merchants long residents in this Country" for submission to the British Government; attributes to British influence the decree excluding American flour from "this Province" (see above, Clay to Forbes, April 14, 1825); comments on the jealousy of English merchants toward United States traders, who are able to compete successfully on equal terms; and congratulates Clay upon his appointment as Secretary of State. ALS. DNA, RG59, Cons. Disp., Buenos Aires, vol. 2 (M70, R3). Received December 9.

APPLICATIONS, RECOMMENDATIONS   September 22, 1825

JOHN T. KIRKLAND, "Harvard University Cambridge," recommends William L. Reaney "for the office he desires at Porto Rico." ALS. DNA, RG59, A. and R. (MR3). Cf. above, Van Ness to Clay, September 7, 1825, note.

WILLIAM L. REANEY, Boston, a 47-year-old widower, solicits appointment as consul in Puerto Rico or, if that vacancy be filled, "any other Office in your Gift either abroad or at home. . . ." ALS. DNA, RG59, A. and R. (MR3).

JOHN TALIAFERRO, "Hagley," introduces the bearer, W. R. Mason, and recommends him for a clerkship. ALS. *Ibid.* Wiley Roy Mason, of Fredericksburg, Virginia, shortly thereafter took up the study of law and was admitted to the bar in 1828.

To Charles Hammond

My dear Sir   Washington 23d. September 1825

I received your letter of the 31st. August, and thank you for the result of your researches on the Public Law of Straights, of which I shall be able to make a valuable use.

Dr. Watkins will have informed you of the cause which prevented the publication in the Intellr. of the extract from my letter to you, with your introductory remarks.[1] The President seems to have thought, upon the whole, that it was better not to make the publication, and I acquiesce in his opinion.

The view taken of Porter's case in the Liberty Hall[2] is very judicious. Public opinion is rapidly settling down in the approbation of the judgment of the Court, and I have no doubt that will ultimately be the almost unanimous opinion of the community. Porters recent indiscretion in a wanton attack upon Col. Monroe will increase the number who condemn his conduct.[3]

The Georgia affair would have gone off very well but for some ill-judged letters recently written by Gaines.[4] The Governor had abandoned the design of making the survey, and all was passing off well. These letters have provoked him to make a demand for the arrest and trial of Gaines, under the articles of War. The President has declined acceding to the demand, but he has caused his strong disapprobation to be signified to Gaines both for writing and publishing his late letters.[5] I should not be surprized if the effect of these letters should be the re-election of Troup.[6]

So Mr. Rowan has found that majorities are not always right. The resistance of the Senate, which he seems to desire, to the late decisive expression of public opinion, will only serve to throw his party into a still smaller minority. Their best course would be to chearfully [sic] acquiesce in the popular decision and to contribute all in their power to obliviate the Relief system.

I am faithfully & Cordially Yrs   H CLAY
C. Hammond Esqr.

ALS. InU. The word "Confidential" was written by Clay in the margin beside the fourth paragraph of this letter.

[1] See above, Clay to Hammond, April 23, May 23, 1825.

[2] Cincinnati *Liberty Hall and Cincinnati Gazette.*

[3] In a letter dated September 1, 1825, Commodore David Porter, declining attendance at a banquet proposed in his honor, had referred to his own apparent misunderstanding and erroneous interpretation of "orders and instructions, which the Court and the public, & I believe, also, the government, have only been able to comprehend, by the voluntary aid of him under whose superintendence they were framed, and who, in his own justification, undertook the difficult task, without having the orders under which I acted before him, or a distinct recollection of their contents, of giving a solution, corresponding with the *intention*, although at variance with the *letter*. . . , and having placed my entire confidence in one, who has proved both an accuser and a witness against me, and whose testimony alone has condemned me, it is no small solace to me that I have found favor and indulgence in the eyes of that public to

whom I so confidently appealed for justice. . . ." *Washington Gazette,* September 3, 1825.

4 In a series of letters, notably those dated July 10 and 28 and August 16 and 29, 1825, General Edmund Pendleton Gaines had engaged in dispute with Governor George M. Troup regarding the validity of the treaty of cession of the Indian lands in Georgia and the State's determination to survey the tract (see above, Clay to Southard, July 3, 1825, note), controversy which developed into highly personalized criticism. The fact that some of the correspondence was released to the press before delivery to the addressees enlarged the matter into a contest for public favor. General Gaines, as a military agent of the Government, was widely condemned for participating in such a debate. See Washington *Daily National Intelligencer,* September 10, 1825. The correspondence was published in that journal during August and September, *passim,* and in *House Reports,* 19 Cong., 2 Sess., no. 98.

5 Troup had presented his demand in a letter addressed to Adams, on August 31, 1825. On September 19, Secretary of War Barbour had replied to Troup, reporting the President's rejection of the request for Gaines' arrest, but had also informed Gaines of Adams' "regret that in the letters published . . . you have permitted yourself to indulge a tone, whose effect will be to destroy that harmony which the President is so much disposed to cherish; and the publication of which is calculated to inflame those differences which moderation and forebearance would not fail to allay." *House Reports,* 19 Cong., 2 Sess., no. 98, p. 559.

6 Troup was re-elected on October 3 for a second two-year term as Governor, defeating John Clark by only 688 votes out of over 40,000 cast. Gaines himself had noted that he was charged with meddling in State politics and, on September 12, had announced his decision to withhold further publication of his views until after the election. Washington *Daily National Intelligencer,* September 27, 1825.

MISCELLANEOUS LETTERS   September 23, 1825

From JOSEPH E. CARO, Public Archives Office, Pensacola. States that, in conformity with the act of Congress of March 3, 1825 (4 *U. S. Stat.,* 126), calling for translation of all Spanish records and documents having relation to land claims, he has translated all documents relating to land grants from the Spanish Government on record in his office; requests instructions regarding translation of private deeds and conveyances on file there. ALS. DNA, RG59, Misc. Letters (M179, R63). Published in Carter (ed.), *Territorial Papers. . . ,* XXIII, 325.

From JOSEPH DELAFIELD, New York. Reports that the surveyors employed by the American Commissioner (Peter B. Porter) have finished their survey and are preparing their maps, "under the 7th article of the Treaty [of Ghent]," for the next meeting of the Board, in December; notes that other surveyors, not yet returned, were sent out by the British Commissioner (Anthony Barclay) to find "a water communication" south of the established route between Lake Superior and the Lake of the Woods, which, with some uncertainty concerning the identification of Long Lake on Mitchell's map, would lay the basis for contention in support of the southern route. Believes that the British will find a southerly route, but states that he has obtained from the President's father (John Adams) testimony to identify the Long Lake of Mitchell's map with that of the Treaty of 1783, and asserts that he (Delafield) has explored a northerly route which he is prepared to claim in case of disagreement. Though doubting the sincerity of the British Commissioner, Delafield anticipates that a settlement of the boundary will be achieved at the next meeting of the Commission. ALS. DNA, RG59, Misc. Letters (M179, R63).

Delafield, born in New York, educated at Yale University, and admitted to the bar, had been an officer with the rank of major at the close of the War of 1812. From 1821 to 1828 he was in command of field parties as a United States agent for delineating the northern boundary, under articles six and seven of the Treaty of Ghent (above, I, 1006; II, 162n). He was later prominent for his interest in natural history and for his operation of a very successful lime kiln at Yonkers.

Anthony Barclay, of Nova Scotia, who had served in 1816 as secretary to the British boundary commissioner under the fourth article of the Treaty of Ghent, had been named as the British Commissioner for the negotiations dealing with articles six and seven. He later, from 1842 to 1856, served as British consul in New York.

John Mitchell, probably born in the British Isles though later a resident of Virginia, had been educated as a botanist and physician at the University of Edinburgh. His *Map of the British and French Dominions in North America with the Roads, Distances, Limits, and Extent of the Settlements,* published at London in 1755, became the standard used in treaty negotiation relative to the boundary between the United States and the British North American dominions.

From R[ICHARD] H[ENRY] TOLER, Lynchburg. Announces transfer, from Toler and Colin to Fletcher and Toler, of the Lynchburg *Virginian* and of all debts due that establishment. ALS. DNA, RG59, P. and D. of L. Toler had become editor of the *Virginian* in January, 1824, and continued with that journal until 1846. He then edited the Richmond *Whig* (originally the *Constitutional Whig*) until his death two years later. John B. Colin had been Toler's associate on the *Virginian* until January 13, 1825, when he had been replaced by Elijah Fletcher, who remained with that journal until 1841. Born and educated in Vermont, Colin had begun teaching in Alexandria, Virginia, in 1810. Between 1817 and 1819, he had removed to Lynchburg, where he had become active in civic affairs. He served several terms on the town council and in 1831 as mayor.

APPLICATIONS, RECOMMENDATIONS   September 23, 1825

NICHOLAS DAVIS, Limestone, Alabama, recommends Henry Hitchcock for appointment as district attorney for the Southern District of Alabama. LS. DNA, RG59, A. and R. (MR2). Born in Hanover County, Virginia, Davis had served there as a Federal marshal before moving to Kentucky in 1808. By 1817 he had resettled in Alabama, where two years later he had become a member of the first constitutional convention and of the first State legislature. He sat in the State Senate from 1820 to 1828, presiding over that body the last five sessions. As a Whig, he later ran for congressional and gubernatorial office, respectively, without success. On Hitchcock's appointment, see above, Hall to Clay, August 11, 1825, note.

To John Quincy Adams

Sir   Washington 24 September 1825
   I comply with the request of Majr. Clark[1] in laying this letter before you. It is the only letter I ever received from him, and my knowledge of him is not sufficient to enable me to affix an estimate upon his communication.
   The Secretary of War[2] will have informed you of the fact that Genl. Gaines, if not now in the City, will be here in a day or

two. This movement is unexpected and may render necessary a consideration of the contingencies of his return to Georgia.[3]

I shall transmit, for your inspection and direction, early in the next week, a letter of instructions for Mr. Poinsett which I have prepared and which are [*sic*] now copying.[4]

Hoping that this letter will find you at the safe termination of your journey,[5] I am, with great respect, Your obedient servant The President.   H CLAY

ALS. MHi-Adams Papers, Letters Received (MR472).
[1] Above, Clark to Clay, September 10, 1825.
[2] James Barbour.
[3] Cf. above, Clay to Hammond, September 23, 1825.
[4] See below, Clay to Poinsett, this date; Clay to Adams, September 26, 1825.
[5] Adams had left Washington on September 20, for a visit with his father in Quincy, Massachusetts. He returned to the capital on October 26.

To Adam Beatty

Dear Sir   Washington 24 September 1825

I received your letter of the 13h. instant, with Genl. Bodleys list of fees. I have other demands against him which will meet any fees he has against me, or for which I am responsible. But you may allow $172:68 of the note of Poague and himself to be suspended if the residue of it is paid, until I go out to K. and have a settlement with him, or until I otherwise direct. Of the list forwarded that sum is as much, if not more than I am chargeable with.

I have about 100 sheep. I cannot undertake to say what part of them are full blooded. All that I know is that I have been breeding from full blooded Merino rams ever since they were introduced into the State (about 12 or 13 years) and that I commenced with one or two full blooded ewes. I would take four dollars specie a piece for them including a ewe that I bought from Steubenville[1] and her produce which I believe is two ewes. Or I would sell the choice of fifty of them at five dollars a piece. That was the price at which I sold twenty at my Sale, and stopt the Sale.[2] I have directed a pair to be sent to my farm from Mr. Dickensons flock near Steubenville, but have not heard of their being sent.[3] Should they arrive they must be excepted. If you wish them this letter may be presented as your authority for receiving them, and I would be satisfied to receive paymt. next Spring or Summer as may be most convenient We generally worked up our wool in the family. I never exported any.

I think you will find that a sufficient number of the majority of the Senate will give way to insure a restoration of the old Constitutional order of things. They will hardly withstand the recent decisive expression of public opinion.

We have no news here. Your's faithfully   H. CLAY.
Adam Beatty Esq

ALS. Owned by Earl M. Ratzer, Highland Park, Illinois. Endorsed: "Answd. 22nd. febr. 1826." Answer not found.   1 Cf. above, III, 384.
2 See above, Statement, June 24, 1825.
3 Cf. below, Clay to Dickinson, November 1, 1825.

To Joel R. Poinsett

No. 5.   Joel R. Poinsett, Envoy Extraordinary and
Minister Plenipotentiary. U. S. Mexico
Sir   Department of State   24th. September 1825.
I have the pleasure now to acknowledge the receipt of your several Despatches, from No. 1. to No. 16, inclusive (with the exception of No. 9 and No. 13)[1] and I shall proceed, in this Despatch, to take such notice of them, as is deemed necessary.

The Convention with Colombia, referred to in your general Instructions, of the 25th. March last,[2] has, since their date, been ratified by the Government of Colombia, and the ratification [sic] of the two Governments have been exchanged at this place.[3] Subsequent to the date of that Convention, a Treaty was concluded between Great Britain and Colombia,[4] according to which, the Commerce between those two powers has been placed upon the footing of that of the most favoured Nation, and their navigation upon the principle of equality which is stipulated in the second Article of our Convention with Great Britain, under date the 3rd. July 1815,[5] (see 6th. Volume of the Laws of the United States, page 603)[6] and which is proposed in the Act of Congress of the 7th. January, 1824.[7] That second Article is almost literally copied into the Treaty between Colombia and Great Britain, where it will be found in its fourth, fifth, and sixth Articles. As, by our Convention with Colombia, no such provision was made for the regulation of the navigation of the two Countries, and as, by the Laws of that Republic, foreign vessels and their cargoes are subject to alien duties, advantages have been conceded to Great Britain which were not granted to the United States. These advantages would have formed a subject of just complaint, on our part, if the Government of Colombia, sensible of what is due to us, had not promptly informed Mr. Watts, charged with the affairs of the United States at Bogota, in the absence of Mr. Anderson, that it was ready to extend them to us.[8] Accordingly, instructions have been given to Mr. Anderson, who is just about returning to his post, to concur with that Government in the adoption of the necessary regulations for securing to our Commerce and Navigation, in all respects, the same advantages which have been yielded to Great Britain.[9] The result, undoubtedly will be, to place our commerce and Navigation with Colombia,—1st.— On the footing of the most favoured Nation, and 2ndly.— That the vessels of each party, laden with its own produce and manufactures, shall pay in the ports of the other, the same duties and charges as its own vessels importing similar produce and manufactures.

If you shall not have concluded the Treaty of Commerce, when this Letter arrives, you will be able to urge upon the Government of Mexico the example of Colombia and Great Britain, and what has been done, and is proposed to be completed, between the United States and Colombia, as motives for acceding to the principles which the President is desirous of introducing into the Treaty which you are authorized to negotiate.

I observe that, by the 6th. Article of the Treaty which has been concluded between Great Britain and Mexico (a copy of which is transmitted in your despatch, No. 2)[10] "the products or manufactures of each of the contracting parties, when imported in their own vessels, into the ports of each, respectively, shall not pay any higher duty than is now, or shall hereafter be, paid by the vessels of the most favoured nation; and the same on exportation of the products and manufactures of each, in the vessels of the other. When the Mexican mercantile marine shall have increased so as to be sufficient for its commerce, then there may be established by common consent, a perfect equality of duty &c. on the importation and exportation of the products and manufactures of the respective dominions and states, indifferently, in vessels of both Nations." This provision may possibly be urged by the Mexican Government as an objection against adopting, in the Treaty with the United States, that principle of perfect equality between the vessels of the two countries, which is desired. If the intrinsic merit of the principle itself, the example of Colombia and the irritating tendency of countervailing legislation, the inevitable effect of an attempt by one nation to secure advantages to its own navigation, denied to that of foreign Powers, shall not enable you to prevail on the mexican Government to agree to the perfect equality which is proposed, you will consider yourself authorised to accede to an article embracing the same principles as are contained in the Sixth Article of the British Treaty.

The President approves of your consenting to treat on the two subjects of Commerce and Limits separately.[11] Indeed it was never contemplated that one of them should be dependent on the other. As the ratification on the part of Great Britain, of the Treaty with Mexico, has been suspended with a view to effect some alterations in it,[12] the present is an auspicious period for pressing your negociation for the Commercial Treaty. Should the negociation be still pending, you will bear in mind the expediency of inserting a provision in the Treaty similar to that which is found in the first part of the second Article of the Convention of London of 1815, exempting the produce and manufactures of the United States from paying in the Ports of Mexico, higher duties than similar produce and manufactures of other Countries. The provision may be made reciprocal. Its necessity is suggested by the representation made to this Department, heretofore communicated to you, that our cotton fabrics were subjected to higher duties than like British fabrics.[13] If that representation were unfounded, such is the British jealousy of a competition with our rising manufactures, that an attempt may be made to depress them, by rendering them liable to more burthensome duties than are paid by the rival fabrics of Great Britain.

The President sees with regret, the reluctance, on the part of the Mexican Government, to agree to the opening of the road from Missouri towards Santa Fe.[14] The road was intended for purely commercial purposes, and doubtless the people of both countries would be benefitted by the exchanges which it would facilitate. No misconception could be greater than that of its having originated in views of Territorial acquisition. If either party could lose by it, it would probably be the United States, many of whose enterprising citizens might be tempted by the intercourse to which it would lead, in consequence of the greater cheapness, or other advantages, of the lands of the Internal Provinces to migrate thither. The connexion between the fixation of limits and the proposed road is not perceived. Wherever the limits may now, or hereafter shall, be established, the road will be useful. It proposes no disturbance in existing, or contemplated, limits. In fact, an imperfect trace or road, such as it is, is now used, and the sole question is, whether it shall be rendered more convenient to the persons whose interest or inclination shall induce them to travel it. To defer making the road more visible and comfortable, for an indefinite period; to deny to the parties mutually a certain benefit, in prospect of a future and contingent arrangement, to which it has no necessary relation, does not seem advisable.

Nor does the President perceive the utility of a joint appointment by the two Governments, of Commissioners "who, by examining, together, the Country within a given latitude from one sea to the other, might present exact information upon which the limits might be established, as is desired."[15] After agreeing upon the principles on which a line of demarcation between the Territories of two Nations should be run, it has been usual to appoint, conjointly, Commissioners to proceed to mark and abut the line. Their duty is then prescribed, and if any variance arises between them, observations and experiments with proper instruments generally enable them to reconcile it. But it has not been customary to send forth Commissioners either to agree upon a suitable boundary, or to collect data upon which the parties are subsequently to establish one. Such a course would be to reverse the order of proceeding which is recommended by the practice and experience of Nations. It would probably leave the state of information which should guide the two Powers, pretty much as it now is. There is but little likelihood that the Commissioners would agree, and each set would be influenced by the separate views of policy which it might happen to take of the particular country which it represented. If it were needful for both parties to acquire the knowledge which the Mexican Government supposes to be wanted, it would be better for each to send out its own exploring Commissioners, under its separate instructions. For ourselves, although much, undoubtedly, remains to be known of the Countries through which the line may be fixed, we believe that the stock of our information is sufficient to enable us, to agree upon a boundary that would be satisfactory to us. In declining, however, to accede to the measure of creating a joint Commission, the President would not be understood as objecting to a resort by the Mexican Government, for its own satisfaction, to the appointment of Commissioners for the purpose of collecting any information which it may desire. Should it persist in attaching importance to such a measure, the hope is indulged that no unnecessary time will be lost in sending out the Commission, so that the negociation in regard to the limits may be resumed with as little delay as possible.

The prevalence of British influence in Mexico, to which you refer,[16] is to be regretted. If it be the mere effect of British power, and British capital and enterprize, fairly exerted; if it be not manifested in the form of regulations favourable to British Commerce and Navigation, to our prejudice, nor in that of cherishing British subjects, whilst the citizens of the United States are treated unfriendly in their commerce and intercourse with Mexico, we can hardly make it the subject of a formal complaint. Against any partiality or preference shewn to any foreign Nation or its subjects to the disadvantage of the United States and their citizens, you will, if necessary, firmly remonstrate. And you will urge the uniform friendly tenor of the whole conduct of the United States towards the United Mexican States, from the earliest establishment of their Independence. As a further, and strong, proof of the friendly interest which is taken by the Government of the United States in the prosperity of Mexico, I transmit you, herewith, a copy of a

Note addressed on the 10th. day of May last, to Mr. Middleton, our Minister at St. Petersburg. The object of that note, you will observe is to bring about a peace, if possible, between Spain and the new States established in America. A copy of it has been transmitted to each of our Ministers at the Courts of London, Paris and Madrid[17] to be used in the endeavour to accomplish that desirable object. Russia is the Power whose movement will be most likely to operate on the Councils of Spain, and we wait, with solicitude, to hear from her. You are at liberty to communicate such parts of the contents of the note, to the Mexican Government, as you may think proper. Whatever may be the result of the effort, that Government cannot fail to appreciate the friendly motives in which it originated.

During the last Spring the Ministers of Mexico and Colombia, near this Government, made separate, but nearly simultaneous, communications to this Department, in relation to the contemplated Congress at Panama.[18] Each of them stated that he was instructed by his Government to say, that it would be very agreeable to it, that the United States should be represented at that Congress; that it was not expected that they would take any part in its deliberations or measures of concert in respect to the existing war with Spain, but that other great interests affecting the Continent of America, and the friendly intercourse between the Independent Nations established on it, might be considered and regulated at the Congress; and that, not knowing what might be the views of the United States, a previous enquiry was directed to be made whether they would, if invited by Mexico or Colombia, be represented at Panama; and if an affirmative answer were given, each of those Ministers stated that the United States would be, accordingly, invited to be represented there. The President directed me to say and I accordingly replied, that the communication was received with great sensibility to the friendly consideration of the United States by which it had been dictated; that, of course, they could not make themselves any party to the existing war with Spain, or to Councils for deliberating on the means of its further prosecution; that he believed such a Congress as was proposed might be highly useful in settling several important controverted questions of public Law, and in arranging other matters of deep interest to the American Continent, and to the friendly intercourse between the American Powers; that before such a Congress, however, assembled, it appeared to him to be necessary to arrange between the different powers to be represented, several preliminary points, such as, the subjects to which the attention of the Congress should be directed, the nature, and the form, of the Powers to be given to the Ministers, and the mode of organizing the Congress. If these preliminary points could be adjusted in a manner satisfactory to the United States, the Ministers from Mexico and Colombia were informed that the United States would be represented at the Congress. Upon enquiry if those preliminary points had yet engaged the attention of either the Government of Mexico or Colombia they were unable to inform me that they had, whilst both appeared to admit the expediency of their being settled. Each of them undertook to communicate to his Government, the answer which I delivered to their invitations; and nothing further has since transpired. It is deemed proper that you should be made acquainted with what has occurred here on this matter, in order that, if it should be touched upon by the Mexican Government, you may, if necessary, be able to communicate what passed. We shall make no further movement in it, until we hear from the Government of Mexico or Colombia.

You will, by this time, have learned that the operations of the French fleet during the past summer, in the West Indies, had no relation to the occupation of Cuba or Porto Rico, as was apprehended at Mexico. Your interposition to prevent hostile measures, founded upon that erroneous supposition, being adopted against France, was seasonable and proper.[19] If the Spanish Government is to be credited, there not only has been no cession to any Foreign Power, of either of those Islands, but Spain is resolved never to make any such cession, Mr. Bermudez, on the 12th. day of July last, having, in an official Note to Mr. Nelson, stated, that "His Majesty has at no time, thought of ceding to any Power, the Islands of Cuba and Porto Rico, and, so far from such a purpose, is firmly determined to keep them under the dominion and authority of his legitimate sovereignty."[20]

The translations which you propose to send, in future, of such official papers as you may transmit, will be acceptable. I am, with great respect, Your obedient Servant   H. CLAY.

Copy. DNA, RG59, Dip. Instr., vol. 10, pp. 385-91 (M77, R5). ALI draft, in DLC-HC (DNA, M212, R7).

1 Dated July 27, 1825; August 13, 1825.
2 See above, Clay to Poinsett, March 26, 1825.
3 See above, Clay to Salazar, March 21, 1825, note.
4 See above, Watts to Clay, May 10, 1825, note.   5 See above, II, 57-58.
6 8 U. S. Stat., 228-29. Clay cites the compilation published by John Bioren and William John Duane.
7 See above, Lorich to Clay, March 16, 1825, note.
8 See above, Watts to Clay, May 10, 1825.
9 See above, Clay to Anderson, September 16, 1825.
10 Above, May 28, 1825.
11 See above, Poinsett to Clay (no. 7), July 18, 1825.
12 See above, Smith to Clay, August 13, 1825.
13 See above, Clay to Poinsett, March 26, 1825, note 20.
14 See above, Poinsett to Clay, June 18, August 17, 1825.
15 See above, Poinsett to Clay, July 22, 1825.

16 See above, Poinsett to Clay, June 4, August 5, 10, 1825.

17 See above, Clay to King, May 11, 1825; Clay to Brown, May 13, 1825; but cf. Everett to Clay, August 12, 1825. Clay had expressed similar arguments to Everett, April 27, 1825.

18 See above, Tudor to Clay, April 12, 1825, note.

19 See above, Poinsett to Clay, August 17 (nos. 15 and 16), 1825.

20 See above, Nelson to Clay, July 13, 1825.

DIPLOMATIC NOTES   September 24, 1825

To PETER PEDERSEN, Philadelphia. Offers an apology for not having addressed him earlier on the subject of negotiations relative to commerce and navigation; requests further deferment of a meeting until the President's return, about October 20. Copy. DNA, RG59, Notes to Foreign Ministers and Consuls, vol. 3, pp. 232-33 (M38, R3). ALI draft, in CSmH.

To HILARIO DE RIVAS Y SALMON. Acknowledges receipt of his note of September 19; states that the United States attorney for the District of Pennsylvania has already "instituted judicial proceedings" against Ortega. Copy. DNA, RG59, Notes to Foreign Ministers and Consuls, vol. 3, p. 233 (M38, R3). ALI draft, in CSmH. See above, Ingersoll to Clay, September 19, 1825.

INSTRUCTIONS AND DISPATCHES   September 24, 1825

From JAMES BROWN, Paris, no. 35. Reports an interview, on September 20, with the French Minister of Foreign Affairs, Damas, during which Brown reminded him that discussion of American claims against France had been halted by French insistence that they be considered "only in connexion with the question arising out of the 8th. Article of the Louisiana Treaty of Cession" and expressed a hope that the matter of claims could be taken up "as a separate and distinct subject of negotiation." Damas argued that the United States had no "well founded Claim to indemnity," that the wrongs complained of "were the consequences of a war, during the progress of which, injuries and acts of injustice had been committed upon other nations by France, to an amount which rendered it utterly impossible for her to make adequate reparation," that France had limited her indemnities to the most flagrant cases, "that this principle had been observed in the Treaties made between her and the European powers," that other nations "had been excluded from indemnity," that the United States had no right to expect preferential treatment, and that the United States should have "urged payment . . . when France was entering into engagements to pay large sums to other powers. . . ." Brown summarizes his reply to these contentions, encloses a copy of a letter he sent Damas on September 21, and concludes that he gained from the interview no encouragement to hope that a settlement of claims could be obtained "from the present Ministry." LS. DNA, RG59, Dip. Disp., France, vol. 22 (M34, R25). Received November 10. Cf. above, III, 382, 383n; Brown to Clay, March 23, September 19, 1825.

In the enclosure, Brown reminds Damas that the question that had been the occasion for their interview had not been settled, that he had not expected a discussion of the claims themselves, and that he hoped a decision on the question of indemnity would be suspended "until the obstacle which has arrested the negociation shall have been removed" or until a full discussion of the claims could be had.

From JOEL R. POINSETT, Mexico, no. 21. Reports that the Secretary of State (Lucas Alamán) has communicated to him the information contained in his dispatch no. 20 (above, September 22) and has given the same information to the British Chargé d'Affaires, "not being aware that the President had previously shown to that Gentleman the Letter of their Agent in Paris." LS, in cipher, decoded in State Department file. DNA, RG59, Dip. Disp., Mexico, vol. 1 (M97, R2). Published in Manning (arr.), *Diplomatic Correspondence . . . Latin-American Nations,* III, 1633-34.

MISCELLANEOUS LETTERS   September 24, 1825

From [JAMES MADISON]. States that, since mentioning to Clay "the name of young Mr Waugh who wishes to be a bearer of public despatches," he has learned that the applicant is younger than he thought "and probly [*sic*] without that sort of knowledge of the world which would be useful at any age, and could alone supply the want of age"; refers Clay, in case Waugh's name arises, to "members of Congress connected with this part of the Country." AL draft. DLC-James Madison Papers (DNA, M212, R22). Waugh, not identified, received no appointment.

From STANHOPE PREVOST, Lima. Reports, in the temporary absence of (William) Tudor from the city, "the condemnation of the American Ship Genl. Brown and her Cargo" (see above, Tudor to Clay, June 8, 1825); states that he "protested against the Sentence immediately"; encloses his "letter and its answers"; comments on "the rebuff Com. [Isaac] Hull met with in attempting to interfere in the business"; and criticizes the conduct of American naval commanders who have served in that area, as well as the failure of the United States Government to heed the "official communications" of his father (John B. Prevost). Declares: "I shall not expose myself Sir, to have my Communications, because they may be disagreeable, treated with the neglect that has uniformly attended his, and believing moreover from the general result of the Court martials, which have been hitherto held on naval Chiefs in the U. S. [cf. above, Clay to Crosby, September 6, 1825], that Such would be the Case, I shall abstain from taking any Steps in the business"; but "again" observes "that the only effectual means of restoring and preserving the high Character, to which the liberal policy of our Government would Entitle us, is to put the incentive of private Emolument out of the way of duty, and abolish entirely the right of a Commander, to exact a deposit, or freight Commission, on bullion or moneys that may be placed on board his Ship." ALS. DNA, RG76, Misc. Claims #1-235, File 1887, Box 4. Addressed to the Secretary of State. Stanhope Prevost had been appointed by William Tudor, early in 1825, vice consul for Lima. He was nominated in 1843 to be consul and served in that office until 1850. On the transportation of bullion by Navy vessels, see above, III, 483n; Tudor to Clay, May 17, 1825.

From George W. Owen

Dr Sir   Claiborne Sepr. 25h 1825—
    A few days past I learned casually that our present District Judge would in *all* probability resign his place soon,[1]   if this should be the case will [you] pardon me for asking of you the favour to

advise me of the vacancy,   my reason for making this request is frankly this, Offices & some of them important, have been vacated & filled before it was known to the public that any vacancy existed, and this in my District,   I have no name to submit for the place but I wish my friends to have a fair start—

I am requested by two of my acquaintances & friends to submit their names to the executive Department, to fill the vacancy of District Atty for the South of Ala. caused by the election of Mr. Crawford[2] to the Senate of our State Legislature,   they are James Dellet[3] & David Rust,   for both I can say that they possess ample legal acquirements to discharge the duties of the office,   I am obliged to bear this Testimony without participating in my own feelings for the success of either application,   it is shere [sic] justice to the very highly respectible [sic] members of the bar whose names are mentioned,   as others will write you upon this subject—you may decide in favour of which may seem to you proper— I can say for both (not to give weight however) that both these individuals were & are still the friends of our present President— The former one on the Adams electoral ticket [became] his w[ar]m [a]dvocate—

These [writ]ings are to [sic] you upon the principle which was settled when I saw you last in candour & perfect regard—

"Alabama has not revolted" the people look to the acts of the administration they are not as much devoted to men—

Our cotton crops do not promise well   even the Tariff[4] I fear will not sustain the cotton grower,   Mathew Carey & Agricola make a bad contest[5]   we had much better argument and much more zealous controversies in the House of Representatives—

I hope that you have heard from my Brother,[6]   he is truly grateful to you for your hospitable kindness & friendship,   he is your zealous advocate *even* in Tennessee—   I am with sentiments of regard your obt. Svt.   G. W. OWEN
Hon Henry Clay

ALS. DNA, RG59, A. and R. (MR3). MS. torn.
1 For Charles Tait's resignation, see below, Tait to Clay, February 1, 1826.
2 William Crawford, born in Virginia, had moved to St. Stephens, Alabama, upon his appointment as Federal district attorney in 1817. He had been elected to the State Senate in 1825 but resigned his seat the following year to accept appointment as Federal district judge, which position he held until his death in 1849.
3 A Claiborne, Alabama, lawyer, born in New Jersey, graduated from the University of South Carolina, for several terms a member of the State legislature, and later (1839-1841, 1843-1845) a member of Congress. On the appointment to fill this vacancy, cf. above, Hall to Clay, August 16, 1825, note.
4 See above, III, 756n.
5 Two more series of letters by Mathew Carey under the pseudonym "Hamilton" (ten numbers in the first and two in the second) were published in 1825. The Washington *Daily National Intelligencer,* which carried these letters, was also publishing, during the summer and fall of that year, a series of answering communications by a correspondent (not identified) who signed as "Agricola." Carey

later commented that recognition of his efforts had been withheld in 1825 and 1826, "lest it might offend two gentlemen in high stations, who had violently opposed the Tariff, and whose doctrines I had refuted." *Mathew Carey Autobiography (Research Classics*, no. 1; [Brooklyn, New York], 1942), p. 132.

6 John Henry Owen, a younger brother of George W., had been graduated from Transylvania University in 1824.

INSTRUCTIONS AND DISPATCHES   September 25, 1825

From A[LEXANDER] H. EVERETT, Madrid, no. 7. Transmits a long account of conversations with (Francisco de) Zea Bermudez, a reply from him to Everett's note regarding the six thousand dollars (see above, Everett to Clay, September 10, 1825), and copies of various documents. Everett asserted to Zea Bermudez the right of the United States under the (Pinckney) treaty with Spain to the admission of a consul at Havana; Zea agreed, "if matters could be restored precisely to the situation in which they stood in 1795." To an inquiry whether "our recognition of the independence of the New States [is considered] as having annulled the treaty," Zea replied in the negative, "thereby yielding perhaps the only plausible ground he could have taken in support of his point"; and Zea "said that he must examine the subject." Notes the difficulties experienced by Spain in attempting to obtain a foreign loan and the report that a Spanish emissary "has gone on to Paris to negotiate with the Haytian deputies on the subject of the recognition of the independence of the Spanish part of the island." LS (except for a postscript, in Everett's hand). DNA, RG59, Dip. Disp., Spain, vol. 25 (M31, R27). Received November 28. Published in *American State Papers, Foreign Relations*, V, 867. Among the enclosures are a copy and a translation of a letter in which Zea Bermudez informs Everett that the King (Ferdinand VII) has ordered completion of payment of the $6,000 "due from the house of Wiseman Gower and Co. to the Government of the United States."

MISCELLANEOUS LETTERS   September 25, 1825

From DANIEL SMITH, Wheeling. Acknowledges receipt of Clay's letter of August 30; states that he will inform Clay in October of his decision on acceptance of the appointment. ALS. DNA, RG59, Misc. Letters (M179, R63). See below, Smith to Clay, October 21, 1825.

APPLICATIONS, RECOMMENDATIONS   September 25, 1825

WILLIAM CRAWFORD, St. Stephens (Alabama), submits his resignation as United States attorney for the Southern District of Alabama and recommends the appointment of Henry Hitchcock as his successor. ALS. DNA, RG59, A. and R. (MR2). On Hitchcock's appointment, see above, Hall to Clay, August 16, 1825, note.

To John Q. Adams

Sir   Washington 26h. September 1825
    I transmit you herewith instructions which have been prepared for Mr Poinsett,[1] founded upon the despatches which have been

received from him. If you should approve them, it will perhaps be best to cause them to be forwarded to the Collector of New York[2] that he may take advantage of the first opportunity to send them to their destination. It is desirable that he should get them with as little delay as possible.

The report of Genl. Gaines' near approach to this place[3] does not seem to have been well founded.

I regret to hear of Mrs. Adams' indisposition; and hope that she has so far recovered as to admit of the continuance of your journey.[4] I am, with high respect, Faithfy Yr. ob. Servant
The President.   H. CLAY

ALS. Adams Papers, Letters Received (MR472). A copy in DNA, RG59, Unofficial Letter-Book of Henry Clay, 1825-29, p. 5, indicates that the document is addressed to Adams at Boston.   [1] Above, September 24, 1825.
[2] Jonathan Thompson.
[3] See above, Clay to Adams, September 24, 1825.
[4] Because of Mrs. Adams' "indisposition," the President and his party had been detained at Philadelphia. On Monday, September 26, after a stop of four days, Adams continued the journey alone, "Mrs. Adams being by no means dangerously ill. . . ." Washington *Daily National Intelligencer*, September 27, 29, 1825.

Check to Eliza Clark

26 Septr. 1825
Pay to Eliza Clark or order Fifty dollars. Cashr. of the Off. of Dt. & Dt. Washington City[1]   H CLAY

ADS. DLC-TJC (DNA, M212, R16). Endorsement on verso: "Eliza Clark." Cf. above, Clay to Lucretia Hart Clay, August 24, 1825.
[1] Richard Smith.

To Joel R. Poinsett

No 6.   Joel R. Poinsett, Envoy Extraordinary and Minister Plenipotentiary, U. S. to Mexico.
Sir   Department of State   Washington 26. Sept. 1825
I have prepared Instructions[1] founded upon your various dispatches, received up to this time, which I this day forward to the President, now at Quincy, for his examination and approval; after which they will be transmitted to you, with as little delay as possible. If you should not have brought your Treaty on the subject of Commerce, to a close on the receipt of this letter, perhaps it will be well enough to protract the negociation until the receipt of those instructions.

I avail myself of the occasion to remind you of the claim upon the Mexican Government, of Messrs J. [*sic*] P. Chouteau and Julius De Mun,[2] adverted to by Mr. Brent, in his Letter of the

27th. May last,[3] written in my absence from the office. It is a claim, of the justice of which, upon Spain, or upon the Government of Mexico, there can be no doubt; and it is one for the liquidation and payment of which, great interest is felt in Missouri, by others, as well as by the claimants themselves.

I have the honour to be Your obedient Servant,   H. CLAY.

Copy. DNA, RG59, Dip. Instr., vol. 10, pp. 392-93 (M77, R5). ALS draft, in DLC-HC (DNA, M212, R1).   1 Above, September 24, 1825.
[2] See above, Chouteau and De Mun to Clay, May 3, 1825.
[3] Daniel Brent to Poinsett—copy in DNA, RG59, Dip. Instr., All Countries, vol. 10, pp. 365-66 (M77, R5).

INSTRUCTIONS AND DISPATCHES   September 26, 1825

From RUFUS KING, London, no. 7, "Duplicate." Encloses his reply to (George) Canning's letter, transmitted in dispatch no. 6 (above, September 18). Adds: "Mr. Canning has invited me to meet him at half past two oclock, which will constitute our first meeting in London." LS. DNA, RG59, Dip. Disp., Great Britain, vol. 32 (M30, R28). Received November 9. Extract published in Manning (arr.), Diplomatic Correspondence . . . Latin-American Nations, III, 1571.

In the enclosure King generally concurs with Canning's views, except in regard to Russia, of which he writes: ". . . my deference for the elaborate Instruction of my Government to my Colleague Mr. Middleton [above, May 10, 1825], and the uncertainty as I apprehend of any fixed policy in Russia, have created in my mind more hesitation. . . ." He explains why he forwarded Canning's "private friendly and confidential letters to Washington" and asserts that "you may rely upon our discretion." The United States, he notes, has informed Mexico and Colombia of its "interference with Russia and elsewhere" (see above, Clay to Anderson, September 16, 1825; Clay to Poinsett, September 24, 1825) and has told Spain "that we renounce all desire to occupy Cuba, preferring the status quo of the country" (see above, Clay to Everett, April 27, 1825). Of the policy of his government concerning Spain and her former colonies, beyond that of which Canning is informed, King has no knowledge but believes "that in any measures which may be suggested respecting this matter, we shall act in full and unreserved confidence with England."

From JAMES MAURY, Liverpool. Acknowledges receipt of Clay's letter of May 12 (not found), introducing (George S.) Watkins; states his inability to meet Clay's views owing to the small sum received by the consulate in fees; gives a statement of income and expense of the office during the preceding year. ALS. DNA, RG59, Cons. Disp., Liverpool, vol. 3 (M141, R-T3).

MISCELLANEOUS LETTERS   September 26, 1825

From PHILIP KEARNY, New York. Requests perusal of a memorial to Congress, forwarded earlier, concerning French spoliations on American commerce; notes that Clay "will perceive our claims on the Dutch are equally founded"; asks that either Holland or France be called on to pay them. ALS. DNA, RG59, Misc. Letters (M119, R63). Kearny, who had served as a New York militia officer during the War of 1812, had been prominent in founding the New York Stock Exchange in 1817. The claim related to spoliations, antedating 1800, perpetrated against the business of James Kearney, probably Philip's brother. The family long remained active as New York importers.

APPLICATIONS, RECOMMENDATIONS   September 26, 1825

ADDIN LEWIS, New Haven, Connecticut, recommends the appointment of Henry Hitchcock as United States attorney "for the Alabama District." ALS. DNA, RG59, A. and R. (MR2). Lewis, collector of the port of Mobile, Alabama, had been appointed to that office in 1811, while a resident of Fort Stoddert, Mississippi Territory.

To James Ph. Puglia

Sir,   Department of State, 27th. September 1825.

I regret extremely to learn, from your communications to this Department,[1] that you labor under the belief that injustice has been done you in the Patent Office, by the issuing of a patent to Mr. Nathaniel Sylvester on the 12th. July 1824, for preventing the forgery of Bank Notes. That patent you suppose interferes with yours, granted for the same object, on the 13th. August 1822; and you think the interference ought to have been avoided by a refusal to issue the patent to him. To have refused it, would have required an assumption of the power to judge of and determine upon your respective rights, if they really do conflict. And if that had been done in your case, it must also be done in all other instances of alleged interference. This, you will readily perceive, would be a very important and extensive power, thus exercised. If the Law required it of this Office, it ought to be done, however important extensive and responsible the perform-ance of the duty might be. But it has been the constant practice of the Office, adopted I believe after full consideration, to grant patents to all who apply for them, and who in other respects comply with the Law, without regard to the question of interference with prior inventions or patents. The patentees are then left to the action of the Judiciary, much more competent and endowed with ampler means, to investigate and decide upon nice and difficult questions of controversy than this Office. If a patent is obtained for what is not new, or what had been before patented, it is declared void by the Judiciary. Even if the Department were to assume and exercise a jurisdiction over the question of an alleged interference, the decision which it might happen to make would not be definitive. The losing party would still resort to the Judiciary, if he supposed injustice to be done him. So that between the existing practice, and that which you wish should prevail, the difference is only that of a litigation prior or subsequent to the emanation of the patent.

Perhaps it would be well that Congress should establish some tribunal to decide, in the first instance, upon all cases of interference, and that it should make the decision of such tribunal final and conclusive. But until that is done, and the consideration of its expediency belongs to Congress, we could not undertake to change a long established usage.

If the rule for which you contend had been pursued, perhaps in its practical application you might yourself have experienced inconvenience. For if your patent be prior to Mr. Sylvesters, other patents still prior to yours were obtained for the same object of preventing the forgery of Bank Notes. Whether any of those preceding patents present an interference with your's I have not enquired, but it may exist, and if in fact it do not the Office may have erroneously supposed it to exist and refused you a patent.

I am, Sir with great Respect, Your obedt. Servant. H. CLAY.
Mr. James Ph. Puglia.

Copy. DNA, RG59, Dom. Letters, vol. 21, pp. 156-58 (M40, R19). Cf. above, Thornton to Clay, September 9, 1825.
1 Above, August 15, September 5, 1825.

From James Brown

Dear Sir,   Paris Septr. 27. 1825

In my conference with the Baron de Damas, on the 20. Inst.,[1] he alluded to the Convention between France and the United States[2] which he seemed to consider as very advantageous to us and very unfavorable to the navigating interests of this country. I told him that I could not [perceive][3] what bearing that subject could have on the one to which our conversation related, that I thought it extraordinary that France should not be satisfied with being placed on the same footing in relation to her navigation with that of England Holland and other powers with whom we had commercial relations, and that as the basis of the conventton [sic] was one of reciprocity it promised to be as durable as it was just. He said that France was a sufferer by it and that her situation as it respected the Marine was in the a [sic] worse situation than when the intercourse between the two Countries was entirely suspended. I expressed my surprize at his remark, and he immediately gave to the conversation a different direction—

Although I had not heard any thing said for some time on the subject of the Convention yet from the manner in which it was introduced by the Baron, and from the strong terms in which he expressed his disapprob ion [*sic*] of it, I cannot doubt that it is under consideration, and that we have some ground to expect that they will terminate it—

I have reason to think that several circumstances which have taken place within the last few years have a little Changed the good feeling of this Government for the United States The recognition of South American Independence, the visit and reception of General Lafayette, and an impression generally felt that we are on terms of growing friendship with great Britain may be mentioned as among the causes of this change of feeling— In this opinion I may be mistaken having formed it rather from loose conversations of persons not connected with the Court, than from any thing intimated to me by those concerned in the administration—

You will find in my dispatch which goes with this letter[4] that the present Ministry is prepared to reject our claims, as they say they will those of Denmark— It is possible that I may receive that rejection notwithstanding the letter I wrote to Baron de Damas on the 21— Should he delay giving me an answer I wish you to advise me whether I ought to press for one or endeavor to postpone a decision in the hope of a change in the Ministry— A rejection of our claims, with the proceedings in our house of Representatives to which it will lead, may have an unpleasant effect on the relations of the two countries whilst it can be of no benefit to the Claimants— In taking such a step I should wish to have the advice of the Government as the state of things as well at home as abroad ought to be considered—

I send by the Vessel a dispatch from Mr Everett[5] which I have this moment received— I am Dear Sir with great regard Your faithful servant   JAMES BROWN
Honb. Henry Clay Secretary of State—

ALS. DLC-HC (DNA, M212, R1).
[1] See above, Brown to Clay, September 24, 1825.
[2] See above, III, 53n.   [3] Word illegible.
[4] Above, September 24.
[5] Probably the letter from Alexander H. Everett to Clay, September 14, 1825.

INSTRUCTIONS AND DISPATCHES   September 27, 1825

From HEMAN ALLEN, Valparaiso, no. 21. Transmits a handbill, just received from Arica, relative to the conversion of Upper Peru into a republic bearing Bolívar's name (see above, Crosby to Clay, September 17, 1825, note); reports a "general impression" that this step "will not be acceptable, either to Lower Peru, or to Buenos Ayres." States his understanding that the provincial assembly, mentioned in his dispatch no. 18 (above, September 9, 1825), "has declared itself a *section* of the general Congress intended to have been elected," has invited other provinces to send representatives to join it, and "is proceeding to the deliberation of the affairs of the nation." Notes reports from Lima that Callao has not yet surrendered. ALS. DNA, RG59, Dip. Disp., Chile, vol. 1 (M-T2, R1). Received January 13, 1826. Extracts published in Manning (arr.), *Diplomatic Correspondence . . . Latin-American Nations,* II, 1106.

From Daniel Webster

My Dear Sir,   September 28. 1825. Boston.

I have deferred to the present moment, any reply to yours of the 9th of May,[1] partly on account of my absence from home for Several weeks, and partly because I thought the measures in progress in the British Parliament, of the consummation of which we have not been, till recently, advised, were likely to have a bearing on Some of the questions in regard to which you are kind enough to ask my opinion.

As to the first topic, mentioned in your letter, I confess I do not See any firm ground on which to support our claim. It Seems to me England has a perfect right to receive the products of one of her Colonies, into another, with low duties, or without duties, as she may chuse, from considerations of her own interest; and that the mode in which She may see fit to exercise this right, raises no obligation, on her part, to regulate or modify, in the Same manner, the duties imposed by her laws on the importation of articles, the produce of a foreign State. The recent acts of Parliament,[2] although they do not, and cannot, *change* the rights of England, in this respect, have a tendency nevertheless, to Shew the existence of such rights Somewhat more clearly; inasmuch, as, these acts have been passed for the purpose of making the Colonies more truly and properly an integral *part of the Empire.* The new system seems to contemplate them in this light. This, certainly, does not alter the nature of our claim; but, I fear, it shews more clearly its want of a solid foundation. Why might we not as well contend that our corn should should [*sic*] be admitted into England on the Same terms as the corn of Canada, as that our produce Should be received in Jamaica subject to no higher duties than are levied on the produce of the North American Colonies? I should be glad to See Some ground to stand on; but, at present, I am afraid the principle is against us.

The Subject of the discriminating duties is more complex and embarrassed. It would seem, on first view that, as, in the intercourse between us and the British west India Islands, more United States Tonnage is employed than British, our interest would be promoted by a mutual abolution [*sic*] of all Such duties. But the question has various bearings; & many consequences, rather indirect than immediate, may follow which may well deserve consideration. I know not whether any thing but experience can decide, how far our interest may be benefitted by abolition of duties; and, therefore, if an arrangment [sic] Should be made, perhaps it may be well to consider it as an *experiment,* and to limit its duration to a fixed period. I think I can perceive Some advantages which, in the present state of British Law, the abolition of the discriminating duties might give to the navigation of *England, to our loss.* A British vessel, for instance, under this System, may bring a cargo from any part of Europe to Jamaica; there load with Sugar, coffee, rum, pimento, &c. or, going to the Bahamas, with Salt; proceed to the United States; in the United States load with cotton, Tobacco, rice, flour lumber, or other articles of foreign or domestic produce, and proceed, either back again to the West Indies, to Great Britain, or to any other part of the world. In other words, *a great part of the World is free to Such a vessel;* and she may go from port to port, earning successive freights, without feeling the influence of foreign prohibitions, and without loss of time.

But Suppose an American vessel to load in the United States for Jamaica, and there to Sell her cargo; if she there load with the produce of that Island, or any other produce, she must *return to the United States.* Or if an American vessel carry a cargo to Europe, she cannot bring an European cargo to the west Indies. Therefore the British west Indies are made a most useful *intermediate trading place* to the British vessel, but are not Such to the vessel of the United States..

Connected with this, in the policy of England, is the extension of the ware-house System to Kingston Halifax &c. These various regulations appear to have been made with great skill, and in the execution of a well considered and Systematic policy, the object of which is to extend the commerce of England, and especially her carrying trade. we have no right, perhaps, to complain of it, but then it is our duty to endeavor to *counter act,* as far as we can, any part of it that threatens to operate injuriously to ourselves. The abolition of discriminating duties, on both Sides, will complete this British System; and, although, we Shall derive *Some* advantages from such abolition, it may Still be a question, whether these advantages will not be more than counterbalanced by the new facilities which may, by this means, be given to the British competition against us. I consider the whole system as a master stroke of commercial policy on the part of England, and as one that should awaken all our vigilance, and exercise all our wisdom.

In one other point of view, perhaps, the probable future state of things may deserve consideration. The making of Halifax, St John, &c. *great Commercial Depots* may not a little endanger our revenue from the facility of Smuggling. On many articles, important to us in a financial respect, the duties imposed in the British Colonies are much lower than ours. Coffee, for example, pays, I beleive [*sic*] little more than a *cent* a pound while with us it pays *five*. This difference will be Sufficient encouragement, perhaps, to run the hazards of illicit trade.

But to return to the carrying trade: I very much fear that Should the discriminating duties be repealed, though there may be a *nominal,* there will hardly be a *real* equality; in as much as our commerce with the British West Indies must still be confined to the direct trade, whereas they may come to us from any place, and go to any place from us. It is obvious, that the British Government have not intended to benefit us much in the way of *a market.* Their exclusion of provisions, fish, oil, &c. must doubtless have been aimed principally at the trade of the United States. Lumber, live stock, and vegetable productions, Such as their necessities require, and as they cannot obtain from their own Colonies, are admitted now, and probably will continue to be so, on duties not very high. I do not See that the change of system, on the part of England, is likely to enable us to find a greatly increased market for our productions in her Colonies.

As far as the direct trade between the United States and the British west Indies is concerned, I think it probable we may by the proposed change rather gain than lose. we should then be able to bring an *assorted cargo* from her ports home; and it is probable enough, if she should succeed in making her ports of deposit large Entrepots, that a variety of articles for the composition of cargoes may be found in them. But then we lose *freights;* and, as far England [*sic*] Shall Succeed in bringing to our doors, whatsoever we want cheaper than we can bring it ourselves, so far we lose the business and the profit of *carrying.* Our object, therefore, Should be to continue ways and means of carrying as cheaply as she can. Now the advantage likely to accrue to England, from her present System, in my apprehension, is, that her ships will be able to make continuous voyages, and double voyages; whereas we shall be confined to the Single voyage out & home. And this advantage might be very decisive, in Some branches of trade, so close is the present actual competition.

Our whole trade to the British west Indies is not so important as might be at first imagined. Whether in present enjoyment; or in future prospect, it is trifling, compared with that to Cuba and Hispaniola. The mass of our productions is likely to be permanently excluded from the British Islands in all events. For the sake, therefore, of gaining a little greater facility to this branch of trade I Should not incline to adopt any measures of an injurious, or of a doubtful tendency, as to our general commerce, or our means of sustaining a general competition with England in the carrying trade. You are aware that her Colonial Tonnage is increasing astonishingly, and that our ship owners find a new and vigorous competition Springing up in Nova Scotia and New Brunswick. The recent measures of Parliament, doubtless, encourage and favor this interest in the Colonies. Shipwrights have recently gone, thither, from the New England States in considerable numbers. These considerations would induce me, I think, to pause, before I assented to an unconditional abolition of the discriminating duties. If England will allow us to proceed from her west Indies ports where we chuse, & to come to them from any place whatever, then there will be something like a *real* equality. Perhaps you may think it worth a little consideration whether this might not be suggested.

I am, Dr Sir, with constant regard, Your Obt. Servt

DANL. WEBSTER

LS. DNA, RG59, Misc. Letters (M179, R63). Cf. above, Holmes to Clay, June 8, 1825; Smith to Clay, June 25, 1825; Lloyd to Clay, June 27, 1825.

1 Cf. above, Clay to Smith, May 9, 1825.

2 See above, Rush to Clay, March 26, 1825, note.

From Daniel Webster

Dear Sir   Boston Sep. 28. 1825

Under another cover I send you what has occurred to me on the subject of our trade with England.[1] The object of this is, to express my sympathy for your domestic calamity[2] & to offer my congratulations on the welcome, so ardent & so universal, which seems to have greeted you among your fellow citizens of the West. The same kindness of feeling which has been expressed in that quarter, exists, I believe, in other places. I have been thro New York, in the course of the Summer, and I found, almost every where, a hearty approbation, and every where else, at least, an entire & not uneasy acquiescence, in regard to the events of last winter, & to your own agency in producing those events. In New England, with here & there a little expression of spleen from the disappointed, the great majority of the People have the best disposition towards the Government, in all its parts. Our *ability*, in Congress, is not so great as it might have been, & as it ought to have been. But that evil admits of no immediate cure.

You must allow me to admonish you to take care of your *health*.

Knowing the ardor, and the intensity, with which you may probably apply yourself to the duties of your place, I fear very much you may over-work yourself. Somebody, (was it not an Austrian Minister?) on being asked how he could get thro so much business, replied that he did it by repudiating two *false maxims,* which had obtained currency among men; that, for his part, he never did any thing *today,* which he could put off till *tomorrow;*—nor anything *himself,* which he could get *another* to do for him. Without following his example strictly & literally, I still think you ought to be a good deal governed by the same rules, especially the last.— I am, Dr. Sir, most truly Your Obt. Sert   Dᴀɴʟ. Wᴇʙsᴛᴇʀ

ALS. DLC-HC (DNA, M212, R1).
[1] Above, this date.   [2] See above, Clay to Crittenden, August 22, 1825.

INSTRUCTIONS AND DISPATCHES   September 28, 1825

From Aʟᴇxᴀɴᴅᴇʀ Bᴜʀᴛᴏɴ, Cádiz. Encloses a list of (12) "natives of the United States" formerly serving on Colombian privateers and now imprisoned at Cádiz; states that he has forwarded to (Alexander H.) Everett "such evidence as these persons could furnish of their American Character. . . ." ALS. DNA, RG59, Cons. Disp., Cádiz, vol. 4 (M-T86, R4).

From Jᴏᴇʟ R. Pᴏɪɴsᴇᴛᴛ, Mexico (City), no. 22. Notes that Lucas Alamán has resigned, that (Sebastián) Camacho has been appointed his successor, and that the Secretary of War, Gómez Pedraza, has been made Minister of Foreign Relations *ad interim,* empowered to continue the negotiations with Poinsett.

Reports, in detail, these negotiations of recent date, which have not reached a conclusion because of Mexican insistence on the exception, contained in the treaty concluded between Great Britain and Mexico, alluded to in Poinsett's dispatch no. 18 (above, September 13). The Mexican position is based on fraternal ties binding the American nations formerly Spanish possessions and on British acceptance of the point at issue. Poinsett has argued that no distinctions should be made among "members of the great American family"; that "the Republics of America were united by one and the same interest"; that it was to the interest of Europe to divide these Republics "into small confederations"; that the British may have considered it "important to lay the foundation" for such division; that the policy which the United States had followed "entitled us to be considered, at least, on equal footing with any of the American Republics"; that the exception was not included in the treaty between the United States and Colombia (see above, Clay to Salazar, March 21, 1825) nor in treaties possibly, by this time, concluded with Buenos Aires (the Provinces of Río de la Plata) and Chile; that this exception was not sanctioned by the American Republics other than Mexico; and that the treaty signed by the British plenipotentiaries would probably be rejected by England. In reply to an allusion, by the Mexicans, to the identity of interest of the infant Republics relative to Spain, Poinsett has asserted "that against the power of Spain they had given sufficient proof that they required no assistance, and the United States had pledged themselves not to permit any other power to interfere either with their Independence or form of Government; and that, as in the event of such an attempt being made by the powers of Europe, we would be

compelled to take the most active and efficient part and to bear the brunt of
contest, it was not just that we should be placed on a less favorable footing
than the other Republics of America. . . ."

States that it would be more to the interest of the United States to have
no treaty with Mexico than to conclude one "with this condition"; that he
will continue to oppose it; and that, "If the President take a different view,"
he wishes "to be informed as early as possible. . . ." LS. DNA, RG59, Dip.
Disp., Mexico, vol. 1 (M97, R2). Received December 9. Extracts published in
American State Papers, Foreign Relations, V, 852-54. Manuel Gómez Pedraza,
who had formerly served in the Royalist army and, after its defeat, as a partisan
of Itúrbide, had been named Secretary of War in 1824. He was later President,
in 1833 and again in 1850, but was overthrown in both instances after a few
months in office. During the intervening years he remained active in the
government, as Minister, deputy, and Senator at various periods.

To John E. Hall

Sir　　　　　　　　　　　　　　　　　　Washington 29h. Septr 1825

I have received your obliging letter of the 27h. instant,[1] stating
your purpose to continue the life of Lafayette, began [*sic*] by Mr.
Waln and left unfinished by his premature death; and enquiring
whether I would wish to make any alterations in the Address, as
it appears in the Intellr., which I delivered from the Chair of the
H. of R. to the Genl., and which you propose to insert in the
contemplated work.[2]

I am greatly indebted for your delicate and kind consideration
of me. I believe, I have no wish to make any changes in the
address, as it was published—material ones I should not feel
authorized to make. I am with great respect Your ob. Servant

Mr. J. E. Hall.　　　　　　　　　　　　　　　　　　H CLAY

ALS. ViU.　　　　　　　　　　　　　1 Not found.

2 Robert Waln, Jr., of Philadelphia, active in the family importing business and in
literary pursuits, had issued proposals in 1824 for subscriptions to such a publication.
The manuscript had been nearly completed before his death on July 4, 1825. The
first edition of Waln's *Life of the Marquis de La Fayette; Major General in the Service
of the United States of America, in the War of the Revolution,* published by J. P.
Ayres at Philadelphia, in 1825, lacks an account of Lafayette's American tour. Later
editions, including one in 1825, differing in pagination but without indication of
revision, and second and third editions in 1826, were also published by J. P. Ayres.
The last of these, at least, and probably all after the first, included a lengthy additional
chapter, reporting the honors accorded Lafayette on his American visit and quoting
Clay's address of December 10, 1824 (above, III, 893-94).

Check to Elijah H. Reed

　　　　　　　　　　　　　　　　　　29 Septr. 1825

Pay to Elijah H. Reed or order Fifty dollars. Cashr. of the Off.
of Dt. & Dt. Washington City[1]　　　　　　　　　　　　　　H CLAY

ADS. DLC-TJC (DNA, M212, R16). Endorsement on verso: "E. H. Reed." Reed,
not identified.　　　　　　　　　1 Richard Smith.

MISCELLANEOUS LETTERS   September 29, 1825

From E[DWIN] LEWIS, Mobile (Alabama). Requests that papers, sent earlier to Clay but which he has not laid before the House of Representatives, be submitted to the President; expresses a hope that the conduct of the court and the marshal involved in the matter will be taken up by the House at the next Session, in conformity with the resolution of (Charles Fenton) Mercer; and asserts that Judge (Charles) Tait is implicated in a "sham sale" of Africans under order of condemnation. Complains of "the manner of adjusting land sales in this quarter." Charges, in a postscript, that brick for a courthouse built under orders of Judge Tait was made by the Negroes, mentioned above, while in custody, that appointments to office in Alabama are based upon recommendations from Tennessee, and that bankrupts often are appointed to office. ALS. DNA, RG59, Misc. Letters (M179, R63).

Lewis, who formerly had engaged in business in Savannah, Georgia, and in 1819 had served as deputy marshal in Alabama, had become involved in acrimonious controversy with Judge Tait, when the latter objected to the procedure by which Lewis had attempted to qualify for legal practice before the Federal district court. After investigation in 1823, the Committee on the Judiciary of the House of Representatives had declined to entertain charges against Judge Tait. *House Repts.*, 17 Cong., 1 Sess., no. 69. The subject of current dispute concerned the action taken regarding seizure of three slave ships, the *Constitution, Louisa,* and *Marino,* captured off Pensacola while that port was held by Andrew Jackson in 1818 (above, II, 612n). The ships had been American owned; their cargo, purportedly the property of Spaniards, who had been transporting the slaves from Havana to Pensacola. Under a decision of the United States Supreme Court in February, 1824 (6 *U. S.* [9 Wheaton] 391-407), the General Court of Alabama had issued decrees of restitution, covering the claims of owners of the cargo, in accordance with terms of Article 9 of the Adams-Onís treaty of 1819, which pledged the United States to give satisfaction for injuries suffered by Spanish inhabitants from the late operations of the American Army in Florida. Miller (ed.), *Treaties. . . ,* III, 12; *House Docs.,* 19 Cong., 1 Sess., no. 163, *passim.* On February 15, 1825, Mercer had introduced a resolution, adopted by the United States House of Representatives the following day, calling upon the President "at the commencement of the next session of Congress," to report the proceedings of the Federal court and marshal for the District of Alabama with respect to the cargoes of the slave vessels "and to communicate especially the fact whether any of the African natives, comprising part of those cargoes, have been sold within the United States. . . ." U. S. H. of Reps., *Journal,* 18 Cong., 2 Sess., 236-37. Cf. below, Armstrong to Clay, March 6, 1826, note; Clay to Adams, March 7, 1826; Mercer to Clay, March 18, 1826; Clay to House of Representatives, March 8, 1826; April 6, 1826, note.

From SAMUEL R. SMITH, "Littles Town   Adams Cty   Penna." Offers his recently discovered cure for rheumatism, to Clay or any other member of the Cabinet if afflicted with this ailment, without charge except for a testimonial "should it effect a Cure." ALS. DNA, RG59, Misc. Letters (M179, R63). Smith not further identified.

APPLICATIONS, RECOMMENDATIONS   September 29, 1825

NEWTON CLAYPOOL, "Representative of Fayette County in the Legislature of Indiana," recommends "the [Richmond, Indiana] Public Ledger to the favorable notice of the Hon. Henry Clay, Secretary of State of the United States." ANS.

DNA, RG59, P. and D. of L. Claypool, born in Virginia and an early settler of Ohio, had removed to Indiana as a pioneer. Proprietor of a hotel in Connersville, he represented Fayette County in both branches of the general assembly for many years.

Check to Moses Poor

30 Septr. 1825.

Pay to M. Poor or bearer four hundred and thirty five dollars and twenty Cents. Cashier of the Off. of Dt. & Dt Washn. City.[1]

H. CLAY

ADS. DLC-TJC (DNA, M212, R16). Poor was a Washington auctioneer and commission merchant. On the date of this check he had conducted an auction of drawing room and other furniture, "all nearly new, and of the best quality," at the residence of José Maria Salazar, in Washington. *Washington Gazette,* September 29, 1825.   [1] Richard Smith.

INSTRUCTIONS AND DISPATCHES   September 30, 1825

From ROBERT MONROE HARRISON, Antigua. Encloses an act of Parliament for "regulating the Trade of His Majesty's possessions in America and the West Indies" (see above, Rush to Clay, March 26, 1825), in which, he points out, there is "nothing in the least favorable to the U States, or *their* own *Colonies* as articles which were before free are now taxed most uncommonly." Concludes that "the present British Ministry" has instituted a policy designed to make the colonies less dependent on the United States. LS. DNA, DG59, Cons. Disp., Antigua, vol. 1 (M-T327, R1). Received October 29.

From HENRY MIDDLETON, St. Petersburg, no. 50, "CONFIDENTIAL." Forwards copies of correspondence between the Spanish Chargé d'Affaires at Stockholm (Felix Ramond Alvarado) and the Swedish Government, which, though incomplete, indicates that the vessels "it had been agreed to deliver to the supposed agents of Mexico, will not be permitted to sail." Reports nothing to add to his last dispatch (above, September 8, 1825), concerning the proposition made to Russia under Clay's instructions of May 10, and that, until an answer is received from Spain, "the question cannot be again taken up in the Cabinet of the Emperor [Alexander I]." Describes the delays in transmission, through the postal system, of intelligence from Greece, where the Porte has failed in its "Campaign of this year" but where, in view of "the determined policy of the Allied Courts," the struggle for independence appears to be doomed. Austria perseveres in an adverse policy; Russia will do nothing; and the "fall of Greece must then hinge upon the determination of England and France, neither of whom seem [*sic*] disposed to take any decided step." ALS. DNA, RG59, Dip. Disp., Russia, vol. 10 (M35, R40). Dated 18/30 September. Received June 12, 1826. Extract published in Manning (arr.), *Diplomatic Correspondence . . . Latin-American Nations,* III, 1878-79. On the issue involving the transfer of Swedish ships to Mexico, see above, Hughes to Clay, July 8, 1825, note. On the progress of the war in Greece, see above, Moore to Clay, May 31, 1825, note.

APPLICATIONS, RECOMMENDATIONS   September 30, 1825

STEPHEN B. HOWE, Boston, encloses "a recommendation signed by the Agents of the Republick of Columbia [*sic*] for the New England States, and some of the first Merchants in this City for the appointment of a Consular Agent of this Government to reside in the Capital of the Province of Cumana in Colombia"; states that he is "about to establish" himself at that place; and solicits the appointment. ALS. DNA, RG59, A. and R. (MR2). Endorsed on cover by Clay: ". . . To be submitted to the President." Dated October 30, but cf. below, Howe to Clay, October 13, 1825. The enclosure, dated September 15, 1825, was signed by J. and L. H. Pickins and Sons and nine other firms. Howe, not further identified, received no appointment.

To [John Thornton] Kirkland

Dear Sir   Washington 1st. October 1825

I received this day your obliging letter of the 22d. Ulto., informing me that the Government of Harvard University, at the last Commencement, had confered [*sic*] on me the honorary degree of Doctor of Laws. I am extremely thankful for this kind and distinguished consideration of me; and I must pray you, My dear Sir, to make my respectful acknowledgments to the Government of Harvard for its unexpected, and I fear unmerited, notice of me. I shall preserve the Diploma,[1] which you promise to send me, as one of the most honorable & gratifying testimonies which I could receive. I have the honor to be, with great regard, Your obedient Servant   H. CLAY

President Kirkland. &c. &c. &c.

MH-University Archives.   [1] Not found.

Check to Jose Miguel Arroyo

1st. October 1825.

Pay to Mr. Arroyo or order Two hundred and thirty dollars and 25 Cents. Cashr. of the Office of Dt. & Dt. Washington[1] H. CLAY

ADS. DLC-TJC (DNA, M212, R16). Endorsement on verso: "J. Migl. Arroyo." Arroyo was at this time on the staff of the Mexican Legation in Washington. At various periods from 1852 to 1855 he was charged with the conduct of Mexican foreign relations.   [1] Richard Smith.

Rental Agreement with Mrs. Henrietta Warren and Mrs. K. H. Blanton

October 1, 1825

It is agreed between Henry Clay of the one part and Mrs Henrietta Warren and Mrs. K H. Blanton of the other as follows—

The said Clay leases to the said Warren and Blanton all the upper rooms, except that occupied by Mr. Wheeler[1] in his Brick House, corner of Short and Market Streets in Lexington, and the

Kitchen thereto appertaining, with the joint use of the yard with the tenants who occupy, or may occupy the Lower rooms of that part of the House highest up Market Street, for the term of one year commencing with this day—and ending on the 30th. day of September 1826—

In consideration whereof the said Warren & Blanton hereby oblige themselves to pay to said Clay the sum of One hundred dollars in gold or silver coin of the United States payable quarter yearly from this day—and to surrender to said Clay, on the said 30h. day of September 1826, the said premises, in as good repair as they now are, or in which they may be rendered at the expense of said Clay—natural decay and inevitable accidents only excepted

The right of distress for any of the rent in arrear is reserved to the said Clay—and also the right of the tenants, who occupy or may occupy the two lower rooms highest up Market Street in said house to the joint use of the yard &c—

Witness the hands and seals of the parties this first day of October 1825—   H. CLAY
                                               by ROBT. SCOTT }{Seal}
                                               K H BLANTON {Seal}
                                               HENRIETTA WARREN {Seal}

[Endorsement][2]

Memm.   There are but three Keys to the doors in the above—say two for the passage doors, and one for the room up stairs opposite the Kitchen—

Kitchen—6 Panes & One Sash and Glass out below

7 Lights broke [sic] on 2nd. Story—

No Key to the Smoke House—

All the Glass in the passage and the up stairs of the main house are complete and are to be left so at the expiration of the lease—
Teste   ROBT. SCOTT

ADS by Scott; signed also by Mrs. Blanton and Mrs. Warren. Cf. above, Rental Agreement, April 16, 1825.
[1] Leonard Wheeler, who had come to Lexington from Boston in 1816, after an earlier business failure in Richmond, Virginia, was a clerk in a dry-goods store. By 1838 he had established his own business as a dealer in hatters' furs and trimmings. Cf. above, II, 684, 685n, 708, 709.   [2] AES by Scott.

From John Boyle

Dear Sir   October 1st 1825.

Your letter of the 5th of July togather [sic] with a check for $100 on the U states Branch Bank at Lexington was handed to me on the day after its date[1]   I ought long since to have answered it—

Your delay in the state of Ohio[2] prevented me for a while from doing so; but for not writing to you at an earlier date since your departure from that state I have no apology to offer but that which my natural indolence & invincible repugnance to writing furnish

Your son Thomas I find is very impatient to commence the practice of the law. He thinks he is qualified & I am of opinion myself his qualifications are sufficient to justify his entering upon the practice if when he does so he would devote his leisure hours to improving his knowledge of the law   He says he will & he thinks he will do what he says but I have some apprehension he may not   He will no doubt read, but it will not be law, unless he is urged to it by motives which I fear he may not have when he shall first commence the practice   For light reading, Novels. poetry. plays, magazines & revieus [sic] he has an undissembled fondness & he reads every thing of that sort with an insatiable appetite; but for law he has not yet acquired much taste & he reads it as a task imposed upon him by a sense of duty   If he should therefore turn out to practice as it is probable he will this winter I would suggest the propriety of your frequently writing to him & advising him as to the course of his reading. I would not deprive him of the enjoyment to be derived from occasionally reading those lighter works but with the stock of legal knowledge he has he will find it necessary in order to be successful in the practice to devote a portion of his time to increase that stock. Three hours of each day or even less may be sufficent [sic] for that purpose. He ought also to give a part of his leisure to history, of which I apprehend he has but an imperfect knowledge

Shortly after he came to live with me he commenced Humes History of England[3] with great ardour & spirit, but quit it after he had read a volume or two & he has not I believe attempted any other important historical work since. Thomas has capacity & talents enough for any business of life if they can only be directed to their proper object, but to enable him to do this he will stand in need of the counsel & encouragement of his friends. What ever may be his fortunes or his misfortunes he will always have my most sincere wishes for his happiness & welfare   Honest, sincere. ardent, high minded liberal & affectionate it is impossible to know him without esteeming him & although he has some defects in his character, he is sensible of them himself & only requires the aid of a little encouragement from his friends to cure them.

When I sat down to write I thought before I concluded I would say something to you upon our state & national politics but I have really such bad pen ink & paper that I fear you will hardly be able to decypher what I have already written,   I will therefore

only remark that on Monday next the old court will meet at
Frankfort. Sneed is no more[4] & the first thing the court must do
will be the appointment of a clerk;[5] what course the court will
then take I am unable to say. Public sentiment seems to require
we should do some thing: Some are of opinion we should immediately take steps to regain the papers of which the office has
been robbed[6]   some think we should delay this measure till the
legislature meets & others that no step for that purpose ought to
be taken at any time. The new court it is understood will meet
on the same day & we shall thus again have the farce of two courts
of Appeals in session at the same time acted over again. What the
new court will do when it meets is as uncertain—as what will be
the course of the old court— I think however it is probable from
what I can learn that the new court judges will resign on the
meeting of the legislature.[7] The majority of the senate however
you know are new court-men, & it is believed that they will not give
way to the expression of public sentiment at the late election. If
they remain obstinate the new judges may not resign or if they
do others will be appointed by the governor to fill their places.
In this situation of things you may readily conjecture my situation
is an unpleasant one,   I am indeed truly weary of the part I am
compelled to act in these scenes so well calculated to render ourselves ridiculous & our state contemptable [sic],   I am not without
some hope that events will turn out more favourable than present
appearances would prognosticate

Things however will shortly come to a crisis, & you will then
learn better than I can now predict the result   Your fried [sic]
JOHN BOYLE

ALS. DLC-HC (DNA, M212, R1).
1 Neither the letter nor the check (probably in part payment of charges for instructing Thomas Hart Clay) has been found.
2 See above, Clay to Adams, July 21, 1825; Clay to Crittenden, August 22, 1825.
3 David Hume, Scotch philosopher and historian, had begun publication of his
History of England at Edinburgh in 1754. As completed, in 1762, his account, comprising six volumes, published by A. Millar of London, and covering the period from
Julius Caesar to the revolution of 1688, became the standard work in the field.
Subsequent editions, with additions by other writers, carried the history down to
current times.
4 See above, Crittenden to Clay, September 22, 1825.
5 See below, Kendall to Clay, October 4, 1825.
6 Cf. above, Blair to Clay, March 7, 1825, note.
7 Cf. below, Kendall to Clay, December 25, 1825.

From William Cox

Sir,   1st. October 1825
I have a large payment to make on Tuesday next, which I hope

will apoligise [*sic*] for presenting my account[1]   Very Respectfully
Sir Yr. Most Obt. Sevt.   WILLIAM COX
To The Honble, Henry Clay

ALS. DLC-TJC (DNA, M212, R16). Endorsed on verso by Clay: "Wm. Cox's a/c.
{Washn. City—paid 4 Oct 1825}." Cox's wine and tobacco shop was located across
from Williamson's Hotel, on Pennsylvania Avenue.
[1] See below, this date.

Account with William Cox

[October 1, 1825]

The Hon, Henry Clay   To William Cox D
1824

Decr. 17th	To 3 Galls Cognac Brandy		$ 6.00
"	"	" 4½ Galls Old Whiskey 125	" 5.62½
"	"	" ½ Dozen Champaigne	"12.00
"	"	" One quarter Box Segars	" 5.00
"	"	" 2 Demijohns	" 3.00
1825			
Jany 3	" One Quarter Box Segars		" 5.00
" 10	" One Do. Do. Do.		" 5.00
" "	" One Bundle Do.		" ".87½
March 21	" One Bundle Do.		" ".87½
" "	" 3 Galls Old Spirits		" 6.00
" 26	" 2 Bundles Segars		" 1.75
Apl 2	" 2 Bundles Do.		" 1.75
" 9	" 2 Bundles Do.		" 1.75
" 14	" 2 Bundles Do.		" 1.75
" 20	" 2 Bundles Do.		" 1.75
" 22	" 2 Bottles J.C.[1] Champaigne		" 4.50
" "	" 1 Bottle Old Port		" 1.50
" 28	" 2 Bundles Segars		" 1.75
May 5	" 2 Bundles Do.		" 1.75
May 11	" 1 Bundle Do.		" 0.87½
	" ½ Dozen Champaigne	February	
	19th 1824 Pr Mr	Thos. H Clay	12.00
			$80.50

[Endorsements on verso][2]
Recd. of H. Clay Seventy five dollars and 50 Cents on a/c of the within,
said Clay objecting to the paymt. of one box of Segars. 4 Oct. 1825.
                              WM COX By Wm Dawson[3]
Recd. five dollars the balance of the within   8h. Oct. 1825
Recd payt Octr. 8th.   pr.   T Mc.Keedin[4]

D. DLC-TJC (DNA, M212, R16). On the dating of this account, see above, Cox
to Clay, this date.
[1] Possibly a contraction for the brand name of J. C. Denet (Dinet), advertised by
Cox in Washington *Daily National Intelligencer*, February 17, 1826; January 3, 1827.
[2] The first, ES, in Clay's hand; the second, AE, by Clay; the third, AES.
[3] Not identified.   [4] Not identified; name not clear.

From Amos Lane

Dear sir.   Brookville 1d.[1] October 1825—

I am in great haste, having left home this morning to attend to some important business in this place, and being under the necissery [*sic*] of returning this evening, I have but a moment to Drop you a few hints, in relation to a subject to the citizens of this place as distressing, as to you & Mr Adams, it may be important —The sudden and unexpected, death of Mr Lazarus Noble the receiver of Public moneys at this place,[2]   He died on his way to the Seat of Govt. to which place the office had been directed to be moved, by the President— This is one of the most important offices in the State, and if Judiciously bestowed, will have a greater Tendency to add strength to the Present Administration than any other that may perhaps happen in the first four years of Mr Adams Admtn., which I can assure you is and will be my only solicitude. I have no other interest in the appointment, no particular friend, no connection who will be an applicant—: I have no time for explination [*sic*]. But will barely remark—That a Capt. Thomas Porter[3] of our place will be an applicant. Of him I will only say that of you and Mr Adams he has gone greater leangth [*sic*] to abuse than perhaps any other man in the Govt.   I have heard him State in public that you was the damnest corrupt Scoundrell in the nation, that you sold yourself to Mr Adams. yes he even threatned [*sic*] to insult you had you excepted our invitation to dine[4]— To transfer Capt. Vance[5] from fort Wayne to this office would be extremely unpopular   To Mr McCarty[6] who will apply the same or nearly the same objections as to Porter exist   both violent Jackson men. Of All I have heard named as applicants there is no question but Genl. Noah Noble the Brother of the deceased and of the U. S. Senator. Genl. J. Noble. he will be the most popular and politic appointment.[7] He is well qualified, a man of more or equal weight of popularity with any man in this State—In the last Election was your friend and voted the Clay Ticket, and has expressed on all occations [*sic*] his approbation of the result of that contest— Excuse this scrall. I will at Leisure explain at Large—   and [. . .][8] in haste your sincere and devoted friend.   AMOS LANE

Hon H Clay—

ALS. DNA, RG59, A. and R. (MR3).

1 Written from Brookville, Indiana; originally dated "2d."

2 See below, Noble to Clay, October 2, 1825. Lazarus Noble had been appointed to this position in 1820 and reappointed four years later.

3 An early resident of Indiana and a veteran of the War of 1812, at this time employed as a bank cashier, Porter did not receive a Federal appointment.

4 Cf. above, Susan Watkins and others to Clay, July 12, 1825.

⁵ Samuel C. Vance, father-in-law of Lazarus Noble, had been appointed register of the land office at Fort Wayne in 1823. He was reappointed to that office in 1827 but removed in 1829.

⁶ Abner McCarty was proprietor of a general store at Brookville and, during the 1830's, operated the stage line between that place and Cincinnati. He received no appointment under the Adams administration but under President Jackson, in 1834, was named receiver of public moneys at the Indianapolis land office and during the next four or five years received generous contracts for transporting mail.

⁷ Cf. above, Noble to Clay, June 27, 1825, note.

⁸ Word illegible.

DIPLOMATIC NOTES   October 1, 1825

From SEVERIN LORICH, Philadelphia. Acknowledges receipt of Clay's note of September 20; asserts that, since the differences between Sweden and the United States in regard to interpretation of the treaty of 1816 grow from "a posterior act of Congress" (of January 7, 1824), he sees "no benefit to be derived from" pointing out that vessels of other nations mentioned in the act receive more favorable treatment; states that, although he objects to the American construction of the treaty, he will not protract the discussion; declares that "The demand regarding equalisation of tonnage duty for St. Bartholomew vessels" was made under the act of January 7, 1824, and the treaty of 1783 and under the belief that, if conceded, it would confer only that which "is allowed to vessels belonging to the small Islands of the Netherlands." ALS. DNA, RG59, Notes from Swedish Legation, vol. 3 (M60, R2).

APPLICATIONS, RECOMMENDATIONS   October 1, 1825

JONATHAN JENNINGS, Charleston, Indiana, recommends Abner McCarty for appointment as "Receiver of Public Monies at Brookville." LS. DNA, RG59, A. and R. (MR3). Endorsed (AES): "I concur in the above and request a compliance therewith   John Test." Postmarked at Hamilton, Ohio, October 3. Jennings and Test, both natives of New Jersey, were congressmen from Indiana. Jennings had been Clerk of the Indiana Territorial Legislature, Delegate to Congress (1809-1816), and first Governor of the State of Indiana (1816-1822). He had been elected to Congress to fill the unexpired term of William Hendricks and served from 1822 to 1831. Test, a Brookville lawyer, had been a circuit judge in Indiana (1816-1819) and was a member of Congress (1823-1827, 1829-1831). He later removed to Mobile, Alabama, where he practiced law, but returned to Indiana sometime before his death, in 1849. On the recommended appointment, cf. above, Lane to Clay, this date, note.

JOSEPH KENT, "Rose Mount," recommends, for appointment as consul at some post in Europe, Edward Taylor, a native of Virginia, now a Maryland merchant. ALS. DNA, RG59, A. and R. (MR4). Enclosed in Taylor to Clay, February 27, 1826.

GEORGE PETER, "Montgomery Cty Md.," recommends Charles Bunting, "of this County," for appointment to "a Clerkship under the General Government." LS. DNA, RG59, A. and R. (MR1). Peter, a Montgomery County planter, cousin of John Peter, had been an army officer (1799-1809 and during the War of 1812), a congressman (1816-1819), and a member of the State legislature (1819-1823). He was again a member of Congress, from 1825 to 1827. Bunting, not further identified, received no appointment.

From James Noble

Sir,   Brookville[1] Oct. 2d. 1825

I write you in haste, and under afflicting circumstances. You can tell the loss of a relative, from *experience*,[2] which is all powerful.

My brother Lazarus Noble the Receiver of public monies at this place died on the morning of the 29th. Ultimo, about nine miles from this place, on his way to Indianopolis [sic], the place where his office was to be removed within the last month by the order of the President of the U. S. His personal property, the *books, papers,* and *furniture* of his *office* was sent on in waggons [sic], and the next day he set out with his wife and child in bad health, though we advised him to stay, he refused because he was anxious to obey the order of the President, and upon reaching Judge Mounts,[3] nine miles from this place, his sickness encreased, and on the 8th day after confinement he died. I refer you to a letter that I have written this day to Mr Rush[4] the Secretary of the Treasury, and among other things I have refered [sic] to certain recommendations on file in your office in favour of Noah Noble for the office of Marshal in this state made last winter.[5] Among others the almost Unanimous recommendation of the members of the Legislature, including our present Governor J. B. Ray.[6]

Will you do a distressed friend the favour to call on Mr Rush, and present to him this letter, if you chuse, and particularly the recommendations for Noah Noble for the office of Marshal, and likewise Mr Adams.

The circumstance of the Marshal you recollect, and so does Mr Adams.

My brother Noah Noble is recommended to be the Successor[7] of my decd. brother, and the letter of mine to Mr. Rush, gives minutely the standing of the office refered to. The most distressing occurrence that has happened me [sic] for years is the death of my brother, but added to it, that, unfeeling men was watching round to ascertain the last breath for pecuniary interest, and self aggrandizement, and in four hours after, (and while his relatives was preparing the corpse for the *grave,* and endeavouring to prepare for the last tribute of regard,) one Abner McCarty, and others mounted horses in every direction, and proceeded some to Hendricks[8] and Jennings[9] who reside 90. and 120 miles from this place, others to Cincinnati Ohio to Genl. Harrison,[10] to procure recommendations to succeed to the office. If one shake of my pen could have procured a successor, under the circumstances, I would have considered if I attempted it, myself degraded everlastingly. I will venture to say that Govr Hendricks and Genl. Harrison will both write to the

President recommending Noah Noble and so will the securities of my decd. brother, and even say to the President that they will consider themselves bound till the Successor is appd.   I must ask you to consult with the President, and if you can render him any aid, it will be appreciated. Mr Rush will shew you my letter, and I have asked him to lay it before Mr Adams.

I have the honour to be Respectfully Yr obd Svt   JAMES NOBLE
P.S. I send the letter of Mr Lane,[11] it was offered voluntary,   it is ardent, but it is truth I have no doubt, The excitement produced here, at the *few* and thank God but a *few* who watched for death to do its office upon my brother, gave rise to Lanes letter, and I am sorry any excitement occurred and more particularly the cause

J NOBLE

ALS. DNA, RG59, A. and R. (MR3). Addressed to Clay.
[1] Indiana.
[2] See above, Clay to Crittenden, August 22, 1825, note.
[3] David Mount, of Metamora, had been a member of the Indiana General Assembly (1816-1817) and, since 1822, an associate judge of the State Circuit Court. He remained on the bench for over a decade and from 1837 to 1843 served in the State Senate.   [4] Richard Rush.
[5] Cf. above, Noble to Clay, June 27, 1825.
[6] James Brown Ray, born in Jefferson County, Kentucky, and educated for the law in Cincinnati, Ohio, had begun practice at Brookville, Indiana. He had served as a State prosecuting attorney from 1819 to 1822, had been elected to the State Senate from Franklin County in 1822, and, elected president *pro tempore* of that body in 1824, had become Governor following the resignation of William Hendricks in February, 1825. Ray was elected and re-elected to the last position and served until 1831. He subsequently practiced law in Indianapolis.
[7] See above, Noble to Clay, June 27, 1825, note.
[8] William Hendricks. No letter of recommendation by him, relative to this position, has been found.
[9] Cf. above, Jennings to Clay, October 1, 1825.
[10] William Henry Harrison. See above, Jennings to Clay, October 1, 1825, note concerning postmark. No letter of recommendation from Harrison, relating to this position, has been found.   [11] Above, October 1, 1825.

To John Quincy Adams

Dear Sir   Washington 3d. October 1825
A Mr: Clarke[1] our Consul at Lubec, who has some mercantile connexions in Cuba, has lately returned from that place and was with me to day conversing on the affairs of the Island. He appears to be an intelligent man possessed of a good deal of information respecting Cuba. He thinks that matters are fast hastening to a crisis there, and that there must be shortly an explosion. The islanders dread the black troops of Colombia, and prefer a connexion with Mexico, but look anxiously and ultimately to the U. States. He thinks that, if the Mexicans can appear in force off the island, a movement within would be made which, by the co-operation, would speedily and certainly end in throwing off the

Spanish yoke. A considerable jealousy exists according to him (and in that his information is confirmed by Mr. Poinsett) between the Governments of Colombia and Mexico.[2]

It appears to me that the public interest would be promoted by establishing some channel through which we may obtain authentic information. Mr. Rodney's[3] official station, his youth and his want of experience are obstacles to the acquirement of it through him. Judge Robinson was there during the last winter, in pursuit of health, which he still wants, and I received from him then some valuable information, a part of which was an account of a deputation from the Local Government to the King of Spain to prevail upon him to conclude a peace with the new Republics.[4] I have not yet learnt the result of that effort at peace. Judge Robinson's long residence in Louisiana has made him acquainted with the Spanish character; and his liberal opinions and feelings would secure for him the confidence of the party in favor of Revolution. The condition of his health would cover the object of his visit.

I take the liberty therefore of suggesting, for your consideration, the propriety of sending him to Cuba, as a secret agent; to put us in possession of useful knowledge. I would propose that his commission should be one of enquiry simply, without holding out any encouragement or offering any stimulus to Insurrectionary Movements. I think it worthy to be thought of whether he had not better be instructed rather to repress any disposition to revolt.

I have had no direct communication with Mr. Robinson, but I have reason to believe that the service will be acceptable to him.

 I have the honor to be Faithfully Yr. ob. Servt. H. CLAY
The President.

ALS. Adams Papers, Letters Received (MR472).
[1] Joseph Hill Clark.
[2] See above, Poinsett to Clay, June 15, August 21, 1825.
[3] Thomas M. Rodney.
[4] Above, Thomas B. Robertson to Clay, April 20, 1825.

To David A. Sayre

Sir   Washington City 3d. October 1825.

I received your letter of the 20h. Ulto. with a bill for $150 drawn by Theodore on me,[1] inclosed in it. According to the request contained in your letter, I have this day transmitted a check[2] for that sum drawn on the B. U S. by its office here to Alexandrine Benson of Philada[3] {I could not make out very clearly the christian name, but I took it to be Alexan*drine*.}

   I am respectfully Your ob. servant H. CLAY

ALS. ICU. Addressed to Sayre at Lexington. Sayre, born in New Jersey, had moved to Kentucky in 1811 and engaged in silver plating. He had expanded his activities to include, in 1823, brokerage and, in 1829, banking. He amassed a large fortune, much of which he devoted to philanthropic projects in Lexington, notably the founding of Sayre Female Institute in 1854.
1 Theodore W. Clay. The letter and bill have not been found.
2 Not found.
3 Probably of Alexander Benson and Company, a banking firm.

From Porter Clay

Dr Sir   Frankfort 3rd. October 1825

Yours of the 6h ult[1] came to hand in due time and I thank you for the kind advice which it contains and which I have followed, we now have the curious specticle of two supream courts seting [*sic*] in our town at the same time,[2] and both performing buisness [*sic*] that the constitution has confided to one   you may easily imagin [*sic*] the state of perplexity we are in as well as the thousands of enquiries as to the ultimate result,   there are some fears whispered (but not openly) that Mr Pope[3] is about to act the Trator to the anties and take a seat upon the bench of the new court in place of Mr Barry[4], but off [*sic*] the trouth of this I know nothing only that Mr B and him have been much togeather here of late   first Mr B went to Lebanon[5] and sent for Mr P from whence B went with him to his house and remained some time   Mr P in return has been to Lexington and spent some time with Mr B. and it is possible that this is the grounds of the fears mentioned above, you know the gentlemen better than I do and also you can trace the effects of such a combination of circumstances as well as any one can for you. this much I can say I have mighty little confidence in the virtue or integrity of either of men [*sic*]

I have called on Mr Haggan with your note[6] and have received for answer that it is entirely out of his power to pay you untill the first of Jany next at which time he *seemes* [*sic*] to be confident he will pay,   I shall wait your further orders in relation to that, as well as the claim upon Mr Broadhead[7] who says he positively assured you he could not pay this faul,   he talks some thing about including the whole payment when a suit shall have been determined which is now depending in the U S Spuream [*sic*] court,[8] he also stated that you had not succeeded to the extent of your engagement.

I have nothing of interest save that we are all well and our country generally healthy   give my respects to Lucretia and family

                    yours &c   PORTER CLAY

ALS. DLC-TJC (DNA, M212, R10). Addressed to Clay.
1 Not found.   2 See above, Boyle to Clay, October 1, 1825.   3 John Pope.
4 William T. Barry, who remained on the court until it was dissolved.
5 Kentucky, a few miles from Springfield, where Pope resided.

6 Probably James Haggin, now a member of the new court of appeals. The note has not been found.

7 Lucas Brodhead, born in Ulster County, New York, and graduated from Union College, Schenectady, whence he had come to Kentucky in 1820 to look after land interests of his uncle, Lucas C. Elmendorf, practiced law and resided in Frankfort for the remainder of his life.

8 Clay had argued for the plaintiff on appeal from the Federal Circuit Court, for the District of Kentucky, in the United States Supreme Court, in March, 1822. The decision, which had been announced in March, 1825, had reversed that of the lower court, upheld the claim of Elmendorf, and remanded the case for appropriate action. 23 *U. S.* (10 Wheaton) 152-81.

From George Gibson

Sir,   October 3, 1825

Messrs. Thomas McGiffin & Wm Hawkins[1] of Washn Pa. are the lowest bidders for three important Contracts. They have by letter of 23d Sept. referred to you for information as to character and responsibility.

Any information which you may be pleased to communicate relative to those persons will be thankfully received.

Yr. mo. ob St.   GEO. GIBSON C. G. S.

The Hon. H. Clay, Secy of State.

Copy. DNA, RG192, Office of Commissary General of Subsistence, Letters Sent, vol. 4, p. 446. On September 29, 1825, Clay reportedly had written (presumably to Gibson; letter not found) that he had received many requests from Kentucky and Ohio for recommendations of applicants for contracts and that he would, on reference to him, supply all the information he possessed on persons who obtained them. *Ibid.,* Register of Letters Received.   1 A prosperous farmer.

INSTRUCTIONS AND DISPATCHES   October 3, 1825

From CONDY RAGUET, Rio de Janeiro. States that "general acquiescence" in the arrangement between Brazil and Portugal "is to be anticipated" but "that the Liberal party of the Brasileans" are resentful toward Great Britain and Sir Charles Stuart "for having . . . betrayed their country into the hands [of] The Holy Alliance" (see above, Raguet to Clay, March 11, 1825, note) ; expresses fear that the Brazilian settlement will now serve as a precedent for intervention by "The Holy Alliance in conjunction with Spain" in the former Spanish colonies. Notes propagation in the Government paper of the doctrine of legitimacy as the basis for the monarchical form of government; reports that an early meeting of the General Assembly is not expected. Negotiations for a treaty with Great Britain "are progressing." "It is said" that Luiz Joze de Carvalho e Mello has resigned as Minister for Foreign Affairs and will be succeeded by Felizberto Caldeira Brant Pontes. ALS. DNA, RG59, Dip. Disp., Brazil, vol. 4 (M121, R6). Extract published in Manning (arr.), *Diplomatic Correspondence . . . Latin-American Nations,* II, 835.

APPLICATIONS, RECOMMENDATIONS   October 3, 1825

WILLIAM SEBREE, Lawrenceburg, Indiana, recommends Thomas Porter, of Lawrenceburg, for appointment as receiver (of public moneys) at Indianapolis. ALS. DNA, RG59, A. and R. (MR3). Porter did not receive the appointment.

JAMES TAYLOR, Bellevue, Kentucky, recommends Dr. David Oliver for appointment as "Receiver of Public Monies at Brookville, Indiana"; states that he is informed that Oliver is "a Senator of Indiana." ALS. *Ibid.* Oliver, of Brookville, had been a member of the Indiana General Assembly from 1823 to 1825 and, in August of the latter year, had been elected to the State Senate. He did not receive the appointment here recommended.

Check to William Cox

Office of Discount & Deposit, Washington,   4 Octr.— 1825
PAY to William Cox or order—
Seventy five dollars .... *dollars,* 50/100
75 DOLLS. 50/100

H. CLAY

ADS, partially printed. DLC-TJC (DNA, M212, R16). Endorsed on verso: "William Cox." Cf. above, Account, October 1, 1825.

To Horatio Gates Spafford

Sir,   Washington 4th. Octr. 1825.
I received your Letter of the 17th. ultimo in regard to the navigation of the Mississippi and its great branches, and to an engine which you think you have invented adapted to the removal of the obstructions, commonly called "planters, Sawyers snags" &c.

You do not appear to be aware of the fact that two or three years ago, Congress appropriated seventy five thousand dollars for the removal of those very obstructions from Pittsburgh to the Balize;[1] that for less than that sum Mr. Bruce[2] of Kentucky contracted for their removal, in all that extent; and that work is now in progress. I have not very precise information (that will be acquired probably this winter) as to the degree of success which attends his labors, tho'. I have heard a rumor that the work is not well done, and that its difficulties are greater than he anticipated.[3] Mr. Bruce was the inventor of the Machine by which he intended principally to operate. I have not yet learnt how it has answered. I believe of many that were exhibited, at the period of making the Contract, his was deemed best by the Engineer Department.[4]

If Mr. Bruce is successful in his undertaking of course Government would not, I apprehend, be disposed to purchase your invention. If he should not succeed, I doubt whether you could obtain any thing to *assist* you in making the experiment. Congress has lent itself on one or two occasions to assist inventors with money to make experiments with their inventions. Thier [*sic*] experience in those instances has not been such as to induce them to engage often in that species of patronage. They have thought that, in the general, it is best to leave those matters to the care of individuals, especially as it is extremely difficult to discriminate. I state to you frankly what are my impressions as to the reception which Congress might give to your application for aid. If you had a model of your invention, I have no doubt that the Corps of Engineers would carefully examine it and ascertain its practical utility.

How would it do for you to address Mr. Bruce? If your's is a better invention than his I presume he would gladly compensate you for it.

The clearing out the navigation of the Mississippi and some of its principal branches is a National object for the accomplishment of which I am very anxious. With respect to the Mississippi, all that can be done, in the present state of the population and resources of this Country, is in my opinion to remove the planters, Sawyers and snags; and I entertain no doubt that it is practicable to effect that object, at a rate of expense far beneath its importance.

I am, Sir, Your Obedt. Servant.   H. CLAY.
Mr. H Gates Spafford. Troy, New York.

Copy. DNA, RG59, Dom. Letters, vol. 21 (M40, R19), pp. 162-63.
1 New Orleans. See above, III, 749n-50n.
2 John Bruce. Cf. above, III, 810.
3 The *Cincinnati Gazette*, reporting the progress of the work from Pittsburgh to Maysville, commented that the operation consisted merely of cutting off the largest trees at the low water mark, leaving the logs to float down the river where they "prove more injurious to navigation than when they first presented themselves." Reprinted in *Washington Gazette*, October 18, 1825.
4 His machine had been awarded a premium of $1,000. Lexington *Kentucky Reporter*, March 14, 1825.

From William Carroll

My dear Sir;   Murfreesboro. October 4 1825.

I have to acknowledge the receipt of your kind letter from Lexington,[1] to which it has not heretofore been entirely convenient to reply, particularly as I was desirous to communicate to you the result of our congressional elections. Six of the old members are returned and three new ones. Colo Mitchell, who represents Standifers district, is a grade superior in talents to Houston[2]—he is excessively vain and easily moulded to any honest purpose. Colo. Polk, by whom Colo. Erwin and others were defeated is a young man of sprightly talents, and will probably remain several years in congress; and may hereafter have a share of influence in the political concerns of the State.[3] Doctr. Marable, who succeeds Reynolds,[4] is alike destitute of capacity and moral character—

I have heretofore stated to you, that notwithstanding the great excitement among the friends of General Jackson, I did not believe that he would be run for the presidency at the end of Mr. Adams' first term.[5] This opinion is greatly strengthened by circumstances that are daily developing themselves, the most prominent of which is, that many of the Generals warmest friends have become loud in their praises of De Wit [sic] Clinton and some have gone so far as to say that an opposition by him would be successful against Mr. Adams. I never was the advocate of Mr. Adams, but I cannot consent that his administration shall be disturbed while it accords with the principles of our government by a man, against whom, as I conceive, objections exist which ought to have great weight in the western States. He was, if my memory serves me correctly, a violent apposer [sic] of the war, and on that account was brought out for the presidency in opposition to Mr. Madison by the Federal party.[6] This circumstance will distroy [sic] every effort in his behalf even in Tennessee.

Rumour says that General Jackson will leave the Senate after the present Session,[7] if it be discovered that his chance for the presidency is declining. I am unable to speak personally on the subject, though I think it intirely [sic] probable. Should that be the fact we shall have to elect two Senators within the next two years, and I have no doubt that your correspondent Major Eaton will be permitted to remain at home. I look upon it as almost certain that two gentlemen will be elected who are not unfriendly to you.[8] At the next election, I expect that a great change will take place in our representation in congress— A number of young men of talents will be candidates, some of whom will doubtless succeed— I have lately heard some conversation on the subject of printer of the laws of the United States in West Tennessee. Norvell & Erwin[9] were the publishers untill [sic] a year ago, when an appointment was forwarded by Mr. Adams to Mr. Murry[10] who is a good young man, completely under a certain influence, and has been bitter in his denunciations against Mr. Adams and yourself ever since the presidential election. I would not presume to offer advise [sic] in the case, but I may be permitted to say that do as you will, you cannot expect the forgiveness of your enemies.

Mr. James Erwin and lady passed through here a few days ago, on their way to his fathers:[11] They were both in good health, and intended proceeding immediately to the lower country.[12]

I have for several years been desirous to [visit] Washington, but have heretofore been unable to accomplish it. I think however that I shall certainly be able to do so this winter if health permits, particularly as I am under obligations to see, perhaps the last time, an aged mother[13] in the neighbourhood of Pittsburgh.

I shall be very happy to hear from you as often as your leisure permits you to write.

With a tender of my respectful compliments to Mrs Clay. I am, dear Sir, Most sincerely Yr. friend   WM. CARROLL

Hon: Henry Clay Secy. of State, Washington city.

ALS. DLC-HC (DNA, M212, R1). MS. faded. Endorsed on verso by Clay: "Answd. 21st." Answer not found.   1 Not found.

2 James C. Mitchell, a native of Virginia and a lawyer, served two terms in Congress (1825-1829), became a circuit judge in Tennessee from 1830 to 1836, after which he moved to Mississippi. James Standifer had been a member of Congress from 1823 to 1825, was again elected to that body in 1828, and served until his death, in 1837. Samuel Houston, among those re-elected, had been born in Virginia, had moved to Tennessee about 1806, and, after serving in the War of 1812, had begun the practice of law at Lebanon, Tennessee, in 1818. He had been State district attorney in 1819, State adjutant general in 1820, and member of Congress since 1823. He served as Governor of Tennessee from 1827 until 1829. After leading the Texas forces in revolt against Mexico, he became the first President of the Republic (serving from 1836 to 1838 and again from 1841 to 1844), Senator from the State of Texas upon its admission into the Union (1846-1859), and Governor of Texas (1859-1861).

3 James K. Polk, who had been a member of the Tennessee House of Representatives (1823-1825), was beginning the first of seven terms in Congress (1825-1839), during the last two of which he was Speaker of the House. Born in North Carolina, he had moved with his parents to Tennessee in 1806, had been graduated from the University of North Carolina, and practiced law in Columbia, Tennessee. He became Governor of Tennessee (1839-1841) and President of the United States (1845-1849). One of his opponents in 1824 had been Andrew Erwin.

4 John H. Marable; James B. Reynolds. Marable, born in Virginia, had studied medicine in Philadelphia and settled near Nashville, Tennessee, in 1806. He had been a member of the State Senate in 1817 and 1818, served two terms in Congress (1825-1829), and then returned to the practice of his profession.

5 The statement has not been found.

6 See above, III, 364-65, 366n.   7 He resigned October 14, 1825.

8 Hugh L. White was elected to the vacancy caused by Jackson's resignation and retained the seat until 1840, but John H. Eaton was re-elected in 1826.

9 Joseph Norvell and John P. Erwin, of the *Nashville Whig*. Norvell had been one of the founders of this journal, which then had changed hands several times. He had returned to the paper in 1819 and was conducting it alone when joined by Erwin, as editor, in 1824.

10 Abram P. Maury, a native of Tennessee, had edited newspapers as a very young man in St. Louis and Nashville and, now at the age of 24, was one of the publishers of the *Nashville Republican and Tennessee Gazette*, established the previous year. The appointment to publish the laws was returned to Norvell and Erwin for the Congress beginning in December, 1825; the *Nashville Republican* was sold to other owners in 1826; and Maury began the study of law. He served in the State House of Representatives in 1831, 1832, 1843, and 1844, as a Whig member of Congress from 1835 to 1839, and as a State Senator in 1845 and 1846.

11 Andrew Erwin.   12 See below, Erwin to Clay, November 7, 1825.

13 Mary Montgomery (Mrs. Thomas) Carroll, not further identified.

From Amos Kendall

Dear Sir,   Frankfort, Oct. 4th 1825.

Yesterday both sets of Judges met here,[1] and the new Judges will proceed to business. The old Judges appointed Jacob Swigert, Clerk, in the place of Sneed; but I am not apprized to their ultimate intention.

Yesterday in a playful conversation, Squire Turner of Richmond said to me 'we heard, up our way, that you was to have a place in the Department of State at Washington for the purpose of writing for Adams and Clay.' I enquired who told him so; but he gave it as a report. Before the election, I heard that George Robertson said in Mercer county, in so significant a manner as to cause it to be noticed, that they would not have me to contend with much longer. A suspicion thence arose among some of my political friends, that I was to be with drawn from the contest,[2] and almost of course, you was suspected of being the agent to accomplish this purpose. It is impossible that these men could have heard any thing on this subject from me or my political friends. After I saw you I mentioned it to nobody, and to bar against accident, burnt your letters.[3] Some person to whom you had mentioned the subject, must have told it, and it has been circulated in a manner injurious to you and myself. I therefore feel free to make such explanations to my friends as will vindicate your motives and mine.

The prospect now is, that our contest here will be renewed and continued with more bitterness than ever. I confess, the lies published on me and those with whom I act, have so stimulated my feelings that I shall meet it with alacrity, if it can be confined to our local question. But I apprehend a different course. The impression is general among the friends of the New Court, that you have interfered in this question and thrown your influence against us.[4] I believe no such thing; but in the irritable, suspicious state of men's minds, it is impossible to vindicate you satisfactorily. Hence I apprehend, the new Court Party here will, almost universally, take up Jackson for the next President to be run against Adams at the end of his first four years. For myself, I feel indifferent towards those two men, and, circumstances aside, would about as soon support the one as the other. But on account of the ultimate object, I cannot join my political friends in the support of Jackson. My situation will, therefore, be a difficult one. Your friends here will be my enemies, and mine will be yours. I see no course left me but perfect neutrality.

Not having heard from you, I presume you have made no arrangements to offer me such a place in your Department as would afford me a pecuniary inducement to abandon my present business. Perhaps it would injure both you and myself, were you to offer and I accept such a place under present circumstances. Sure I am, that I could not accept it without retaining the Argus[5] and writing for it long enough to shew friends and foes, that I was not purchased off from this controversy and that you were not a purchaser. I want nothing to induce me to quit political discussions but an opportunity to do so on honorable terms. Rather than quit it on any other, I will die an Editor.

You see I do now, as I have done heretofore unbosom myself to you most frankly. I have not requested you to consider what I write as confidential, because from its nature you must know it to be so. Not that I would care if the world saw every word of it, were the world *honest;* but malice perverts the best feelings and designs.

Give my respects to Mrs. Clay. I shall ever wish her the best of Heaven's blessings. Very respectfully Your friend

AMOS KENDALL

ALS. DLC-HC (DNA, M212, R1).
1 Cf. above, Boyle to Clay, October 1, 1825.
2 That is, from the old court-new court struggle.
3 None have been found for the period since Clay was in Kentucky.
4 Cf. above, Blair to Clay, March 7, 1825; Clay to Crittenden, August 22, 1825; Clay to Beatty, September 24, 1825.
5 Frankfort *Argus of Western America.*

DIPLOMATIC NOTES   October 4, 1825

From the BARON DE MAREUIL, Washington. Points out that his letter of October 3, last year, concerning difficulties encountered relative to execution of article 6 of the convention of 1822 and the return of "marine déserteurs," remains unanswered; cites the case of a deserter from a French warship, at Norfolk, and the refusal of local officials to aid in his apprehension on the pretext that the article in question applies only to sailors from merchant vessels; requests issuance of orders to prevent a similar refusal by local authorities to carry out the stipulation of the treaty. LS, in French, with translation. DNA, RG59, Notes from French Legation, vol. 9 (M53, R7). Translation published in *American State Papers, Foreign Relations,* V, 787. Cf. above, III, 53n. Article 6 of the convention had provided that consular officials might "cause to be arrested the sailors being part of the crews of their respective Nations, who shall have deserted from the said vessels, in order to send them back and transport them out of the Country." Those not returned within three months were to be liberated and "no more arrested for the same cause." Miller (ed.), *Treaties. . . ,* III, 80-81.

MISCELLANEOUS LETTERS   October 4, 1825

From DANIEL WYNNE, New York. Requests his commission. ALS. DNA, RG59, A. and R. (MR4). Endorsed by Clay on wrapper: "Send it to him"; endorsed in strange hand: "Sent 7h. Oct. 1825." The original commission (see above, Clay to Wynne, April 16, 1825) had not reached Wynne.

APPLICATIONS, RECOMMENDATIONS   October 4, 1825

DOUGLASS MAGUIRE, Indianapolis, recommends, for appointment as "Receiver of Public monies in the Land Office at this place," John Hawkins, of Indianapolis, a native of Kentucky, who "was educated at Transylvania University" and who "was a warm supporter of yours for the Presidency, and is now a supporter of the administration. . . ." ALS. DNA, RG59, A. and R. (MR2). Hawkins, not further identified, received no appointment.

JAMES NOBLE, Brookville, encloses papers relative to recommendation of his brother (Noah—see above, Noble to Clay, October 2, 1825); states that "the whole force of this Abner McCarty" will be exerted against the appointment; notes that the papers are being sent because he understands that "politics will be hinted at, God forbid such a course, . . . and . . . that Govr. [James B.] Ray is hostile . . . on that acct."; adds that he has given recommendations to all who asked, "even to Majr Gay, Govr. Rays father in law." ALS. *Ibid.* (MR3). John Gay, born in Rockbridge County, Virginia, and commissioned an ensign of Virginia militia in 1779, attaining the rank of major before his resignation in 1803, had also served for many years as a magistrate of Rockbridge County. An early settler of Wayne County, Indiana, he there acted as deputy county clerk; he did not receive a Federal appointment. His daughter was probably Mrs. Esther Booker, widow of Samuel P. Booker, a native of Virginia and, at his death in July, 1823, wealthy proprietor of a general store in Centerville, Indiana. Mrs. Booker and Ray had been married in September, 1825.

Memorandum of Commissioner's Sales

[*ca.* October 5, 1825]

1 Commrs Report of October 1823			
Nett [*sic*] amount	....		$ 1190
Deduct for purchases made			
by Majr. Dallam .... David the Abinoe [*sic*][1]	$ 90		
Mahogany Setee [*sic*] & 2 Demijohns	73	163	
		$ 1027	
First sale was on 28h July 1823[2]—			
at which H Clay purchased Jenny at $ 250			
Second Sale 15h. Sept. at which			
John Smith[3] purchased David at	345.		
James Vance Littlejohn[4]	460		

2 Commrs. Report of sales on the 5h. Octr. 1825.			
Gross amt. of Sales	....	....	$ 1305:80.
Expences of Sale to be deducted	....		35:
			1270:80

AD, by Clay. DLC-TJC (DNA, M212, R15). Endorsed on verso by Clay: "Memo of Commrs. Sales." Cf. above, III, 492n.

[1] The property disposed of at the commissioner's sale included several slaves, among whom were two albinos, David and Jenny. Lexington *Kentucky Reporter*, June 2, 1823.

[2] Originally advertised for June 24, the sale had been rescheduled for July 28. *Ibid.*, June 30, 1823.

[3] Lexington bagging manufacturer.   [4] Littlejohn, another slave.

From James B. Ray

Hon. Henry Clay

Dr. Sir.   Executive Department Indianapolis, Indiana Oct 5. 1825—

In behalf of One of Our most worthy citizens, and an acquaintance of yours, permit me to address you.

Lazarus Noble the late receiver of public monies for a land Office in this State is no more. It is expected that the President will make an appointment immediately, until the meeting of Congress, to fill the vacancy. Should he do so, let me humbly request that you would submit the name of Major John Gay of this State to the favourable consideration of the President. Major Gay says he is acquainted with you. I am acquainted with him,[1] and can safely say that he combines every qualification for a receiver of public monies. He is a surviving Officer of the Revolutionary war, and an honest man. He is the choice of the people; and his success would not fail to strengthen the present administration. I anxiously wish he may succeed.— I am well aware that I am a stranger to you; and it is altogether probable that you have never heard of me, as I am a Young man just emerging into notice, in the political world. You will, however, allow me to assure you, that I have made myself familiar with your character, and identified myself with your destiny. The people of Indiana will tell you that I was the first to come forth the warm and public advocate of Henry Clay for the Presidency. I hope that I may be the last to abandon him. Nothing will give me more real satisfaction, Sir, than to see you President of these United States at such a time, as you may think fit to present yourself. You may enroll me amongst your most devoted friends; and consider me a supporter of the present administration. Your vote in favour of Mr. Adams is approved of by a majority of the people.

One of the judges of the Supreme court of this state, and One of the Electors for Mr. Adams, was my Opponent for Governor in Augt. last, but I was elected by a large majority.[2] Pardon me, Sir, for giving you this intimation.

I am anxious that Major Gay may succeed in getting the place above alluded to. I know that you feel a delicacy in interfering with these matters, yet should you feel inclined, I know it would have weight, and the favour would be gratefully acknowledged—

Should you ever wish to communicate any fact to me, which I can make use of to your advantage, you can do so with safety; and it will afford me pleasure to further your views, and advance the public good. I have the Honor to be Sir Very respectfully Your most Obt. Servt.   JAMES B. RAY

ALS. DNA, RG59, A. and R. (MR3). Postmarked: "Brookville (Indiana) October the 4th [*sic*] 1825."

1 See above, Noble to Clay, October 4, 1825.

2 Ray's opponent had been Isaac Blackford, born and educated at law in New Jersey, where he had been graduated from Princeton College; a resident of Indiana since 1812; clerk of the Territorial legislature in 1814; judge of the first judicial circuit from 1814 to 1815; a representative of Knox County and Speaker in the State's first legislature; a judge of the Indiana Supreme Court from 1817 to 1853; and a judge of the United States Court of Claims from 1855 to 1859.

INSTRUCTIONS AND DISPATCHES   October 5, 1825

To RUFUS KING, London, no. 6. Encloses copy of the letter of Samuel Hodges relative to an outrage inflicted on the American vessel *Ruby* (above, August 12, 1825); requests King to inquire into the matter and, if necessary, to call upon the British Government for explanation or redress. Copy. DNA, RG59, Dip. Instr., vol. 10, p. 393 (M77, R5). L draft, in DLC-HC (DNA, M212, R7).

From ANDREW ARMSTRONG, Port au Prince. Encloses copy of the French "ordonnance" recognizing the independence of Haiti; points out that the only American export affected seriously is flour, on which the low duties for French vessels give them an advantage of two dollars a barrel, and that the real benefit to France is that all return cargoes will be in French bottoms; surmises that the local government probably regrets the gains by France; asserts that it would be well for the United States to enter into diplomatic negotiations as an offset. ALS. DNA, RG59, Cons. Disp., Cap Haitien, vol. 5 (M9, R-T5). See above, Holden to Clay, July 16, 1825. The "ordonnance" was published in *Niles' Weekly Register,* XXIX (September 24, 1825), 63.

MISCELLANEOUS LETTERS   October 5, 1825

To DEWITT CLINTON. Introduces (José Silvestre) Rebello, who is concerned with the case of a Brazilian subject imprisoned in New York; states that Clay, without "any very particular knowledge" of the matter, would be happy if Clinton should find it possible to exercise his pardoning power. ALS. NNC.

To DAVID B. MACOMB, Tallahassee. Acknowledges receipt of Macomb's letter of August 29, which will be submitted to the President upon his return to Washington; states that Macomb's controversy with Crane appears to be a private matter; adds that "The absence of the public functionaries from their Territorial posts, if it is without sufficient cause, is undoubtedly improper" and that the President "would not hesitate, on that supposition, to apply" the proper remedy. Copy. DNA, RG59, Dom. Letters, vol. 21, pp. 163-64 (M40, R19). Published in Carter (ed.), *Territorial Papers,* XXIII, 333.

APPLICATIONS, RECOMMENDATIONS   October 5, 1825

JOHN WATTS, Dearborn County, Indiana, recommends Thomas Porter, of Lawrenceburg, for appointment as receiver of public moneys in Indiana. ALS. DNA, RG59, A. and R. (MR3). Postmarked at Versailles, Indiana. See above, Sebrec to Clay, October 3, 1825, note. Watts, born in Culpeper County, Virginia, had resided near Lexington, Kentucky, from 1789 to 1796 and in Boone County, Kentucky, from the latter date until 1816, when he had removed to Dearborn County, Indiana. He had been a judge of circuit court in both Kentucky and Indiana, had been a member of both houses of the Indiana Legislature, and, since 1800, had engaged in the Baptist ministry.

From Robert Scott

Dr, Sir,   Lexington 6th. Octr. 1825
[On th]e 2nd. inst. I enclosed your private A/C with me and

3 Patent Certificates for Land in Missouri[1]— Herewith you will receive the A/C of Colo. Morrison's estate with you from 1st. August to 30th. Septr. Ulto.[2]—

Since my last have recd. your favor of 23rd. Ulto[3]— Mr. Waring[4] is in town and will see him on the subject of your letter and if he does not pay the amt of his bond will issue execution as you direct—

On the 3rd. inst. I paid 600$. the ½ years interest due on the Legacy to T. University[5]—

Several [local] citizens were at Frankfort in the beginning of the week a[ttending th]e meeting of the Court of Appeals— As you will have observed the former clerk A Sneed is no more, and the old Court have elected J Swigart [sic] their Clerk—and it is said the old court and the new are both doing [business][6]— Is not this an extraordinary state of things?

We are all well— very respectfully yr. obt. Servt. ROBT. SCOTT The Honble H. Clay.

P. S. J. C. Rodes has made [you an] official copy of your A/C with Co[lo Morrisons Es]tate[7]— Shall I send it to you—or [retain it unti]l your return   R S.

ALS. DLC-TJC. (DNA, M212, R13). MS. defaced.
[1] The letter and enclosures have not been found.
[2] Not found; cf. below, Private Accounts, August 12, 1826.
[3] Not found.
[4] John Upshaw Waring, a lawyer and property owner in both Woodford and Franklin Counties.   [5] See above, III, 496n.
[6] See above, Porter to Clay, October 3, 1825.
[7] Cf. below, Accounts, July 8, 1826.

INSTRUCTIONS AND DISPATCHES   October 6, 1825

To WILLIAM SHALER, Algiers. Acknowledges receipt of his dispatches numbered 75 to 83, except number 82, over a period of two years; expresses approval of his conduct; requests any information he may be able to communicate concerning American interests at Tripoli, including his opinion on the necessity of an agent of the government at that port, from which the United States consul has been absent more than two years. Copy. DNA, RG59, Cons. Instr., vol. 2, p. 368 (M78, R2). Thomas D. Anderson, of Pennsylvania, consul to Algiers from 1816 to 1819, had held the consular post in Tripoli from 1819 to 1825. For two years before his replacement he had left the affairs of his office in the hands of Joseph Nicholas Morillo (not further identified), while Anderson sought treatment in Europe for an eye disorder.

From JOEL R. POINSETT, Legation of the United States, Mexico, no. 23. Encloses copies of the treaty of alliance between Mexico and Colombia, of "The representation to Congress, made by the society for promoting the liberty of Cuba," and of certain pamphlets; notes that the proposed commercial treaty between Mexico and Colombia has not been ratified, for reasons given in his last dispatch (above, September 28, 1825); reports that the duties paid by Taylor, Sicard and Company, "on the exorbitant valuation" of goods referred to in his dispatch no. 6 (above, July 18, 1825), have been refunded; and states that he is "not disposed to prefer without instructions" a claim sent to him by John Sergeant, for "an Insurance office in Philadelphia," involving a cargo delayed by shipwreck, transferred at Havana to a second vessel, and seized at Alvarado for violating a law which had become effective after the original voyage had begun. LS. DNA, RG59, Dip. Disp., Mexico, vol. 1 (M97, R2). Received December 16. On September 20, 1825, announcement had been made in Mexico City of the ratification of a treaty of defensive alliance between Mexico and Colombia, including provision for formation of a congress, which "the other cidevant Spanish states of America" should be urged to enter, "to confirm and establish intimate relations between the whole and each one of the states; . . . serve as a council on great occasions; a point of union in common danger; a faithful interpreter of public treaties, in cases of misunderstanding; and as an arbitrator and conciliator of disputes and differences." Colombia agreed to provide facilities for meeting of the Congress at Panama; Mexico, to afford similar arrangements should occasion arise for a change of site. *Niles' Weekly Register,* XXIX (January 28, 1826), 356-57, translation reprinted from Washington *National Journal.* For earlier references to the seizure of the vessel at Alvarado, see above, Taylor to Clay, May 24, 1825.

APPLICATIONS, RECOMMENDATIONS   October 6, 1825

JOHN BARNEY, Baltimore, recommends the appointment of William Flemming Taylor as consul at the ports of Quilca and Arica. ALS. DNA, RG59, A. and R. (MR4). Taylor, born in New York but now a resident of Maryland, was appointed early in January, 1826, and remained at these Peruvian ports for over a decade.

WILLIAM DAILY, Connersville, Indiana, solicits appointment as receiver of public moneys at Indianapolis. ALS. *Ibid.* (MR2). Daily, not further identified, received no appointment.

JONATHAN JENNINGS, having "found that there will be considerable strife" attending the appointment of a "Receiver of Public monies for the Brookville Landed District," wishes "to recall" his request in this connection (above, October 1, 1825); gives as his reason: "it might affect you more than advantage me." ALS. *Ibid.* (MR3). Postmarked at Corydon, Indiana.

PHILIP C. PENDLETON, Martinsburg, Virginia, recommends appointment of the *Martinsburg Gazette,* edited by Washington Evans, to publish the laws. ALS. DNA, RG59, P. and D. of L. The *Martinsburg Gazette* received the appointment covering the next Session of Congress but not subsequently. Evans, not further identified, had become the editor in 1822.

Check to James Dee

7 Oct. 1825.

Pay to James Dee or order for Wood thirty five dollars and seventy five cents.

$35:75   H. CLAY

Cashr. of the Off. of Dt. & Dt. Washington City[1]

ADS. DLC-TJC (DNA, M212, R16). Endorsed on verso: "James Dee." Dee, not further identified.   [1] Richard Smith.

INSTRUCTIONS AND DISPATCHES　　　　October 7, 1825

From JAMES MAURY, Liverpool. Reports that three American vessels have been held for want of manifests for tobacco brought into this port; states that American vessels are occasionally denied entry for violating the British requirement that the master and three-fourths of the crew must be United States citizens; suggests that these requirements be circulated at home. LS. DNA, RG59, Cons. Disp., Liverpool, vol. 3 (M141, R-T3).

MISCELLANEOUS LETTERS　　　　　　　October 7, 1825

From JOHN DORR, Boston, "Agent for Owners ship Esther & Cargo." Replies to statements, relating to seizure of the ship *Esther* and cargo at Lima, addressed to the Secretary of State in 1823, as yet unanswered; requests information on the present state of the claim; requests, also, copies of all papers in the Department of State relative to the case, for use in preparing a "memorial, under the supervision of the Hon'ble Mr Webster, to Government. . . ." ALS. DNA, Dip. Disp., Special Agents, vol. 6 (M37, R6). Dorr, a resident of Dorchester, Massachusetts, and a prominent Boston merchant, was himself one of the principal owners of the *Esther*. The vessel had sailed from Boston in December, 1821, bound for Valparaiso, Chile, but had then continued, under separate charter arrangements, to several other ports, including entry and return to Callao. Upon the latter occasion the ship had been seized under the charge that she had been engaged in trade with Spanish supporters at Chiloe and had transported a spy from Chiloe as a passenger. Since Chiloe had not been included within the posted limits of blockade, the Peruvian contention was rejected under an arbitration award and settlement finally negotiated in 1841 and paid in 1847. Moore, *History and Digest of . . . International Arbitrations. . .* , V, 4595-98, 4603.

INSTRUCTIONS AND DISPATCHES　　　　October 8, 1825

To ROBERT M. HARRISON, Antigua. Acknowledges receipt of his letter of September 6; encloses a copy of a letter, on the same subject, from the Department to William B. Quarrier, May 12; states that it is impossible to answer every letter from consular agents. Copy. DNA, RG59, Cons. Instr., vol. 2, p. 369 (M78, R2).

From F. M. DIAMOND, Havana. Notes that four of seven American seamen imprisoned in Havana two years earlier, on suspicion of participation in the death of a Spanish soldier, have never been brought to trial and, unless the United States intervenes in their behalf, will die in this "most lothsome of prisons"; reports that he has protested the boarding of the Philadelphia ship *Thalia* by Spanish troops who took off the mate in response to the steward's complaint of chastisement on the high seas, ten days before entering port. LS. DNA, RG59, Cons. Disp., Havana, vol. 3 (M-T20, R3). Endorsement on cover, by John Quincy Adams, recommends that Clay write Francisco Dionisio Vives relative to these matters (see below, Clay to Vives, November 14, 1825). Diamond, vice consul at Havana, not further identified. On the plight of the seven seamen, see also below, Clay to Rodney, October 29, 1825; Rodney to Clay, December 19, 1825; January 7, 1826; February 4, 1826.

MISCELLANEOUS LETTERS   October 8, 1825

From C[HARLES] J. INGERSOLL, Philadelphia. States that he has directed that
Daniel Brent be summoned, in the trial of Juan Gualberto de Ortega for
striking (Hilario Rivas y) Salmon (see above, Salmon to Clay, September 19,
1825), to prove Salmon's accreditation as Chargé d'Affaires; adds that, if any
other person in the State Department can be spared more conveniently, he
may come instead of Brent and be served with a subpoena after his arrival.
ALS. DNA, RG59, Misc. Letters (M179, R63).

APPLICATIONS, RECOMMENDATIONS   October 8, 1825

WILLIAM CRAWFORD, Georgetown (District of Columbia), states that he was
born in Georgetown; that he was a classmate and friend of Clay's sons, Theodore
and Thomas, in the school of "Dr. James Carnahan, now President of Princeton
College"; and that he is now in his twenty-first year of age and studying law
in his "native town," with the intention of ultimately setting up practice in
Michigan Territory. Solicits appointment as bearer of dispatches to Europe,
so that he may acquire knowledge of the French language and people. ALS.
DNA, RG59, Misc. Letters (M179, R63). Crawford, who appears not to have
received the appointment, resided near Pontiac, Michigan, in the mid-1830's.
Carnahan, born in Pennsylvania and graduated from the College of New Jersey
(Princeton), conducted a classical academy at Georgetown from 1812 to 1823.
He was president of the College of New Jersey from the latter date until his
retirement in 1854.

ROPES, REED AND COMPANY, Boston, recommends retention of Robert Campbell
as consul at Genoa despite the failure of his firm. LS. DNA, RG59, A. and R.
(MR1). Cf. above, Ambrose to Clay, June 30, 1825. The partners in Ropes,
Reed, and Company, a mercantile firm, not further identified.

APPLICATIONS, RECOMMENDATIONS   October 9, 1825

L[AWRENCE] DE CRUISE, New Orleans, mentions that he wrote (to Clay) "some
months ago" and that Henry S. Thibodaux promised to deliver the letter (not
found; cf. below, Thibodaux to Clay, February 27, 1827). Refers to "the
friendly promises . . . made . . . several years ago, that . . . he [Clay] would be
of service . . . when ever an opportunity should offer." Solicits appointment as
Chargé d'Affaires "to some part of Europe," preferably Italy or Greece. States
that he was born in Ireland and reared in Germany, that he was named by
Commodore (John) Rodgers and Colonel (Tobias) Lear to serve as interpreter
in the negotiations leading to the treaty with Tunis in 1805, that he came to
the United States in 1806, was sent to New Orleans as an officer of the Marine
Corps (1807-1809), and has resided in that city since then, holding several
offices "of honour, and responsibility. . . ." ALS. DNA, RG59, A. and R.
(M531, R2). Unaddressed. De Cruise did not receive the desired appointment.
Thibodaux, born at Albany, New York, of French-Canadian parentage, had
settled in Louisiana in 1794, had become a member of the Territorial legislature
in 1805, a justice of the peace of Lafourche Parish in 1808, three times a
member of the State Senate, and Governor, to complete an unexpired term,
in 1824.

H[ARVEY] GREGG, Indianapolis, recommends appointment of John Hawkins as "Receiver to the land-Office in this place." ALS. DNA, RG59, A. and R. (MR2). See above, Maguire to Clay, October 4, 1825, note.

MISCELLANEOUS LETTERS   October 10, 1825

To CHARLES J. INGERSOLL. Acknowledges receipt of his letters of September 19 and October 8; approves his submission of the case in question to the circuit court; instructs him "to take the necessary steps" to lay it before the Supreme Court, if necessary; states that the subpoena for (Daniel) Brent has not arrived, that official certificates to establish the desired fact are herewith enclosed, and that Brent or another clerk "will be deputed to obey the summons." Copy. DNA, RG59, Dom. Letters, vol. 21, pp. 164-65 (M40, R19).

APPLICATIONS, RECOMMENDATIONS   October 10, 1825

JAMES ATKINSON and WILLIAM READ, Newport, Rhode Island, state that they have purchased, from William Simons, the (Newport) *Rhode Island Republican;* solicit continuation of that journal's appointment for publishing the laws. ALS by Atkinson, signed also by Read. DNA, RG59, P. and D. of L. The patronage of the journal was continued throughout the Adams administration.

JAMES DILL, Lawrenceburg (Indiana), requests Clay to recommend to (Richard) Rush, for appointment as "receiver of publick monies" at Indianapolis, Dill's son, Alexander Hamilton Dill. ALS. DNA, RG59, A. and R. (MR2). The young man did not receive a Federal appointment.

DANIEL WORTH, Winchester, Indiana, recommends appointment of the Richmond (Indiana) *Public Ledger,* edited by Edmund S. Buxton, to publish the laws. ALS. DNA, RG59, P. and D. of L. Worth signs as a member of the Indiana House of Representatives from Randolph and Allen Counties. He later became prominent as an antislavery leader in Indiana. On the patronage of the journal, see above, Hendricks to Clay, September 21, 1825, note.

Check to Eliza Clark

11 Oct. 1825

Pay to Mrs. Eliza Clark or order sixty five dollars and 62½ Cents. Cashr. of the Off. of Dist. & Dt. Washington City.[1]

H. CLAY

ADS. DLC-TJC (DNA, M212, R16). Endorsed on verso: "Eliza Clark." Cf. above, Clay to Erwin, August 30, 1825; below, Agreement with Forrest, this date.
[1] Richard Smith.

Rental Agreement With Richard Forrest

[October 11, 1825]

Articles of agreement made and entered into this Eleventh day

ber 1825, between Richard Forrest of the City of Washing-
, in the District of Columbia of the one part, and Henry Clay
of the aforesaid City and District of the other part:

The said Richard Forrest on his part, agrees to rent, and hereby
does rent for the term of three years from the date hereof unto
the said Henry Clay, a three Story brick dwelling, situated on F
Street in the City of Washington, between 14th and 15th Streets,
the property of the said Richard Forrest, for the Annual rent of
Five hundred dollars, payable quarter yearly to commence on the
Eleventh day of October instant.

The said Henry Clay covenants and agrees, and hereby binds
himself to pay to the said Richard Forrest, the said annual rent
of Five hundred dollars, as aforesaid, during the term aforesaid.

The said Richard Forrest and Henry Clay, do hereby mutually
agree, that either of the said contracting parties shall have the
power of rescinding and annulling the whole of this agreement,
by giving to the other party six months previous notice of his
intention so to do.

In witness whereof, the parties aforesaid have hereunto Set their
hands and Seals the day and year first herein before written.

Witness   RICHD. FORREST {Seal}
                                       H. CLAY   {Seal}

ADS by Forrest, signed also by Clay.

INSTRUCTIONS AND DISPATCHES   October 11, 1825

From WILLIAM C. SOMERVILLE, Paris, no. 1. Reports his arrival in France after
a rough voyage; encloses two newspapers, one giving an account of Lafayette's
reception in France and the other containing comments on a letter, relative
to Greece, written by a person named Washington, thought by some to be a
nephew of (George) Washington. Comments that the letter was "calculated
rather to increase than allay the discord which unhappily prevails in some
parts of Greece," that Washington "may have been induced to take this
imprudent step by Gen: Roche whom he accompanied, it appears, from Napoli
di Romania," and that the latter, ostensibly the agent of the Greek Committee
in France, "is believed by a part of the Committee" to be acting "in the interest
of the family of Orleans . . . labouring to create a party in favour of the
elevation of a member of that House to the throne of Greece." States that
Greece was in a perilous situation last summer but her prospects appear somewhat brighter; Ibrahim Pasha's forces were reported by mid-September
"straightened for provisions," while "Egyptian reinforcement will not be
prepared to sail before the middle of October. . . ." Notes that he has discussed
his mission *"in confidence"* with (James) Brown. ALS. DNA, RG59, Dip.
Disp., Sweden and Norway, vol. 4 (M45, R5). Received November 28.

William Thornton Washington, probably a great-great nephew of George
Washington, had attended the United States Military Academy from 1819 to
1823 but had not been graduated; had served as a second lieutenant of

artillery in the United States Army from August, 1823, until May 1, 1825, when he had been dropped from service; and had thereupon set sail for Greece, where he had arrived in mid-June. Claiming to act as an accredited representative of the United States, he had joined General Roche at the end of July in a published protest, opposing the petition of the Greeks which had placed their political existence under the protection of Great Britain. See above, Brown to Clay, September 19, 1825; below, Brown to Clay, October 13, 1825; *Niles' Weekly Register*, XXIX (November 5, 1825), 153; Douglas Dakin, *British and American Philhellenes* (Thessaloniki, 1955), 107-109. Washington was killed during an outbreak of civil strife among the Greeks, in July, 1827.

Antoine-Charles-Étienne-Paul La Roche-Aymon, attached to the French royal guards as a youth, named a peer and placed in command of various military departments under Louis XVIII, and promoted to lieutenant general during the French expedition into Spain in 1823 (above, III, 313n), had become the agent of an intrigue to place the Duc de Nemours on the throne of Greece. For discussion of the proposal, see Dakin, *op. cit.*, 98-99. Louis-Charles-Philippe-Raphaël d'Orleans, Duc de Nemours, was the second son of Louis-Philippe-Joseph, Duc d'Orleans, who from 1830 to 1848 occupied the throne of France. Nemours, at the age of twelve, in 1826, entered the French army, where he had a distinguished career and rose to the rank of lieutenant general in 1837. He refused the crown of Belgium in 1831 and, though heir apparent to the throne of France in 1848, found it unwise to press that claim.

MISCELLANEOUS LETTERS   October 11, 1825

To SAMUEL L. SOUTHARD. Inquires whether "the circumstances which led to the resignation of Edwin Welsh, as a Midshipman, were such as to render the restoration of his warrant to him liable to insuperable objections"; states that Welsh's uncle (John McKinley—cf. below, McKinley to Clay, January 9, 1826), who has written Clay (letter not found), wishes the young man reinstated. AN. DNA, RG45, Misc. Letters Received, vol. 6, 1825, p. 92. Young Welsh, born in Alabama, had received his warrant as midshipman in May, 1822. He had been assigned to the West India Squadron when his service was terminated in 1825. He was not reinstated.

APPLICATIONS, RECOMMENDATIONS   October 11, 1825

ANDREW STEWART, Uniontown (Pennsylvania), recommends T(homas) Porter for appointment as receiver of public moneys in Indiana. ALS. DNA, RG59, A. and R. (MR3). See above, Lane to Clay, October 1, 1825, note.

To Samuel Smith

Dear Sir   Washington 12h. Oct. 1825

I received your letter of yesterday,[1] with the paragraph inclosed. I have not seen the publication to which it refers, and which certainly was not authorized by this Department. I think it hardly worth while to say any thing in the prints about it, but if you

Mrs. Brown feels much pleasure in executing your order and has written to her sister[3] on that subject. The funds can be arranged without difficulty. With respect to Mirrors ours were left in the Keeping of our excellent friend Colo Bomford[4] who was so kind as to promise to permit them to remain in his house so long as they were safe, but to remove them to his own dwelling in case of their being exposed to injury where we left them. Mrs. Brown says we left no orders for selling them and if you think they will suit you, Colo. Bomford will oblige me by giving them to you until my return, when I can either bring you others or supply myself here as we may understand each other on that point.

[Discusses in some detail the situation of Greece, whose cause was believed, in France a few weeks earlier, to have been hopeless. Faced with destruction, the Greeks have appealed, without success, for aid from France and Britain. The repulse of assaults on Missolonghi and an outbreak of rebellion in Candia (on Crete), however, have led to the belief that Greece "will hold out until the end of this Campaign" unless reinforcements reach Ibrahim Pasha. The Greek cause has been injured by Austrian and French aid to Turkey, if rumor be true (cf. above, Rodgers to Clay, August 31, 1825; Clay to Rodgers, September 6, 1825), by disunion among the Greeks, by jealousies "amongst the great powers," and, probably, by suspicion and dislike of the republican form of government adopted by the Greeks.

[The Greek appeal to England has offended "The Agent[5] of the Greek Committee," who, "in conjunction with Mr Washington, has entered a protest against it,"[6] which has offended both friends and enemies of the Greek cause. English newspapers criticize Washington for indiscretion and using "the name of the U States without any authority derived from them to speak or act for them." Some English newspapers sneer at their government's proclamation of neutrality by saying that "Greece offered but four Millions of consumers of British *Manufactures,* whilst Turkey offered fifty millions and therefore Great Britain determined to leave the former to be *massacred* by the latter—"

[He has just seen an American who has received letters from Alexandria and Greece indicating "that the cause of the Greeks is less unpromising than it has been represented. . . ." Reinforcements for Ibrahim Pasha would not be ready to leave Alexandria for two months, and the Greek navy is trying to block the channel to prevent their departure. Meanwhile, "The army of Ibraham [*sic*] Pasha . . . could not hold out, unless relieved, for more than one month—"]

Genl. Lafayette has arrived in good health at La Grange, and I sincerely hope he will wisely avoid any interference in public affairs, and content with the honors he has received in the United States, will pass the remainder of his days in tranquillity [*sic*].

Mrs. Brown enjoys excellent health—my own is better than it has been for three years. We beg you to present us affectionately to Mrs. Clay and to receive assurances of the affectionate regard with which I am Dear Sir Your friend   JAMES BROWN
Honb Henry Clay Secretary of State

ALS. DLC-HC (DNA, M212, R2).   1 Above, September 4, 1825.
2 Mrs. Martin Duralde (cf. above, Mazureau to Clay, September 19, 1825); Mrs. James Erwin.   3 That is, Mrs. Clay.
4 George Bomford, born in New York, commissioned a second lieutenant of engineers in 1805, elevated to the rank of lieutenant colonel by 1815, and renowned as an expert on ordnance, was the owner of "Kalorama," famous Washington mansion, noted for its botanical garden and for its hospitality.
5 Antoine-Charles-Etienne-Paul La Roche-Aymon.
6 See above, Somerville to Clay, October 11, 1825, note.

DIPLOMATIC NOTES   October 13, 1825

From PETER PEDERSEN, Philadelphia, "Private." Acknowledges receipt of Clay's note of September 24; announces that he will call upon Clay by the time suggested "or very soon after." ALS. DNA, RG59, Notes from Danish Legation, vol. 1 (M52, R1).

MISCELLANEOUS LETTERS   October 13, 1825

To JOSEPH E. CARO, Pensacola. States, in reply to Caro's letter of September 23, that no exception should be made in the execution of the act. Copy. DNA, RG59, Dom. Letters, vol. 21, p. 168 (M40, R19).

APPLICATIONS, RECOMMENDATIONS   October 13, 1825

STEPHEN B. HOWE, Boston, states that he addressed Clay "on the 3d. [*sic*] Ulto. encloseing [*sic*] a recommendation" that Howe be appointed consul or commercial agent to Cumaná; notes that he is leaving "this day for that Place," and that he has "appointed Edward Sharp Esqr. of Boston to attend to any Communication" Clay may make in this connection. ALS. DNA, RG59, A. and R. (MR2). Postmarked: Boston OCT 14." Cf. above, Howe to Clay, September 30, 1825. Sharp not further identified.

INSTRUCTIONS AND DISPATCHES   October 14, 1825

From JOHN RODGERS, "U. S. Ship N Carolina Gibraltar Bay." Reports that he was unable to carry out his intention, announced in his letter of August 31 last, of having "an interview with the Captain Pashaw of the Ottoman Fleet" (Khosref Mehemet) and has written him instead; states that, although the Captain Pasha has been a favorite of the Sultan, "it is supposed" that he will be disgraced if he fails to capture Missolonghi, against which he is expected to make another effort; suggests that, in view of "the existing perturbed state" of relations between Turkey and the European powers, the United States should authorize some person to negotiate a commercial treaty with the Porte; declares that, judging from the American newspapers he has seen, the "real situation" of the Greeks is not known in the United States and that, in reality, their struggle for independence appears hopeless. ALS. DNA, RG59, Dip. Disp., Turkey, vol. 1 (M46, R2). Received November 28. The Sultan of Turkey, from 1808 to 1839, was Mahmud II.

MISCELLANEOUS LETTERS   October 14, 1825

From JAMES NEALE, Baltimore. Inquires whether a Mexican blockade of the Castle of San Juan de Ulloa has been declared. ALS. DNA, RG59, Misc. Letters (M179, R63). See above, Clay to Poinsett, March 26, 1825, note 18. Neale not further identified.

INSTRUCTIONS AND DISPATCHES   October 15, 1825

From JOHN M. FORBES, Buenos Aires, no. 25. Reports that "In our affairs here nothing decisive has taken place" and that "The affair of the new law about flour has . . . given way to a . . . discussion on the question of religious tolerance. . . ." States that "Upper Peru is most idolatrously prostrated before Bolivar," who is expected now "to assist in expelling the Brazilians from the Banda Oriental," and that the General Congress is holding secret sessions in attempting to decide whether or not to "receive the Deputies named by the Provincial Junta of the Banda Oriental." Encloses "a bulletin of a late very decisive victory obtained by the patriots over the Brazilians"; states that he was visited by a group of patriots celebrating this victory and that, "although unable to resist British influence with a venal Government," they have given him assurance of the very best feelings . . . of the patriot party" toward himself. Notes the return of "Bernardino Rivadavia, late Minister in England." Adds that he has just learned of an outrage, committed by Brazilian vessels in the outer roads, "on the American brig 'Henry,' Capt. Whittredge." Repeats a request that the United States send a small naval force to those waters. LS. DNA, RG59, Dip. Disp., Argentina, vol. 2 (M69, R3). Continued on October 20 and completed on October 21. Received February 9, 1826. Published in Espil (comp.), *Once Años en Buenos Aires*, 387-91. On the case involving the *Henry*, of Salem, see below, Slacum to Clay, November 5, 1825. Captain H. T. Whittredge, master of the *Henry*, not further identified.

MISCELLANEOUS LETTERS   October 15, 1825

To JOHN DORR, Boston. Acknowledges receipt of his letter of October 7; states that the communications mentioned by him are, with one exception, on file in the Department, "but no documents explanatory of the causes of seizure and condemnation of the ship Esther, and on which only, representations could have been made by the Secretary of State to our Agent in Peru, for the purpose of reparation," have ever been received; adds that "Measures for such redress as may be deemed proper, will . . . be adopted" when the necessary documents shall be furnished and after appointment, soon to be made, "of a Public Agent to the Government of Peru." Copy. DNA, RG59, Dom. Letters, vol. 21, pp. 169-70 (M40, R19).

From CHARLES HAY, Navy Department. Transmits copy of a letter from L (ewis) Warrington reporting the death of William Miller. ALS. DNA, RG59, Misc. Letters (M179, R63).

APPLICATIONS, RECOMMENDATIONS   October 15, 1825

JAMES TALLMADGE, Poughkeepsie, recommends L. H. Redfield, of Onondaga, for appointment to publish the laws. ALS. DNA, RG59, P. and D. of L. Lewis Hamilton Redfield, born in Connecticut, had founded the *Onondaga Register* in 1814. He did not receive the patronage here requested. In 1828 he moved the journal to Syracuse, where, as the *Onondaga Register and Syracuse Gazette,* it was published under his editorship until 1830. Redfield in 1834 became mayor of Syracuse and subsequently was long active in banking there.

INSTRUCTIONS AND DISPATCHES   October 16, 1825

From R[ICHARD] C. ANDERSON, JR., New York, no. 30. Acknowledges receipt of Clay's "Communication No. 1" (above, September 16, 1825), with its enclosures; states that he sails "this day" and expects to reach Bogotá in a few weeks. ALS. DNA, RG59, Dip. Disp., Colombia, vol. 3 (M-T33, R3).

From A[LEXANDER] H. EVERETT, Madrid, no. 9. Transmits a copy of his note to "the Minister" (Zea Bermudez) urging "the admission of our Consul at the Havana"; reports that "The purchase of Ships in our ports by the Agents of the South American States is the real point of difficulty"; transmits also a copy of a note informing "the Minister" of the outcome of the case of Commodore (David) Porter (see above, Hammond to Clay, August 31, 1825, note); states that "the result of the trial has made a favorable impression on" the Spanish Government and that "the Minister" will suggest payment by the United States for "damages to individuals occasioned by the Commodores inroad." LS. *Ibid.,* Spain, vol. 25 (M31, R27). Received December 12. Extract published in Manning (arr.), *Diplomatic Correspondence . . . Latin-American Nations,* III, 2065.

APPLICATIONS, RECOMMENDATIONS   October 16, 1825

E[LISHA] HARRISON, Evansville, Indiana, requests payment for publishing the laws in the *Evansville Gazette* but notes that the dispute with (Thomas) Evans is pending in the courts. States that the *Gazette* will resume publication, and solicits continuation of appointment as public printer. ALS. DNA, RG59, P. and D. of L. Cf. above, Harrison to Clay, September 16, 1825; Clark to Clay, October 12, 1825.

THOMAS CONTEE WORTHINGTON, "Frederick Town" (Maryland), recommends his brother, William G. D. Worthington, for appointment as Chargé d'Affaires in Guatemala. ALS. DNA, RG59, A. and R. (MR2). Thomas C. Worthington, a native of Maryland, veteran of the War of 1812 and brigadier general of militia, had begun the practice of law in Annapolis in 1817 but removed to Frederick the following year. He had served in the State House of Representatives in 1818 and had been elected to the Nineteenth Congress (1825-1827), after which service he returned to the practice of law. William G. D. Worthington, of Baltimore, had held the position of secretary of East Florida from

1812 to 1822, acting as Governor after Andrew Jackson's departure from Pensacola in October, 1821. In April, 1822, Worthington had been appointed marshal for East Florida; but, following rejection of his nomination as a land commissioner the following month, he had declined the previous appointment. In May, 1824, he had been approved as a land commissioner, but he did not receive a diplomatic post, as here and later requested. In 1846 he was named a judge of the Baltimore city court.

To Rufus King

No. 7 Rufus King, Envoy Extraordinary and
Minister Plenipotentiary, U. S. London
Sir,   Department of State Washington 17. Oct. 1825.

Your dispatch under date the 11th. August, at Cheltenham, with Mr. Canning's communication of the 7th. of the same month, has been duly received; as also that of the 21st.[1] of August, at London, transmitting his note, with the Tripartite instrument which he proposes to be signed by the Governments of the United States, Great Britain and France. These several papers have been laid before the President, and been deliberately considered.

He sees, with much satisfaction, the entire coincidence which exists between the Governments of the United States and Great Britain, as to the expediency of terminating the war between Spain and her former Colonies, and their concurrence also, in the fitness of the Island of Cuba continuing to abide in the possession of Spain. Agreeing, as the two Powers do, in those two important objects, the hope is indulged that they may ultimately be induced to think alike as to the means best adapted to their accomplishment.

The great object—that which is recommended alike by the interests of all parties, and of humanity—is the termination of the war. Whatever dangers threaten Cuba, within, or from without, are to be traced to the war. That ceasing, they will quickly disappear. And they will equally vanish, whether peace is concluded by recognizing the new States, or a simple suspension of hostilities takes place, without such recognition. With this view of the matter, the President, shortly after the commencement of the present administration, thought it advisable to direct the efforts of this Government towards bringing about a peace. Aware of the hopelessness of a direct appeal to Spain herself, it was thought best to invoke the interposition of the great Powers of Europe and especially of Russia, believed to have a preponderating influence in the councils of Spain. Accordingly a Note was transmitted to the American Minister at St. Petersburg, to be communicated to the Government of Russia, and a copy of it was also forwarded to you, and to Mr. Brown at Paris, to be used in communications with the respective Govern-

ments of Great Britain and France.[2] In that note, it was attempted
to be shewn that, if it were the true interest of both belligerents, it
was evidently still more that of Spain, to put an end to the war;
that, so far as respected the object of the recovery of her dominion
over the Colonies, the war was concluded; and that its further
prosecution could only be attended with an useless waste of human
blood, and the probable loss of Cuba and Porto Rico, with the danger
of involving in its calamities, other Powers, not now parties to it.
It was also distinctly stated in that Note, that the United States, for
themselves, desired no change in the political condition of Cuba;
that they were satisfied it should remain, open as it now is, to their
commerce, in the hands of Spain; and that they could not, with
indifference, see it passing from Spain to any European Power.

Absolute confidence in the success of these pacific exertions,
however it might have been warranted by the actual state of the war,
has never been cherished. They were justified by the purity of the
motives which dictated them, and whatever may be their result, no
regret can ever be felt on account of their having been made. Mr.
Canning is greatly mistaken in supposing us to have counted upon
the impression, to be made, by the employment of the blandishments of flattery with Russia; nor can it, for a moment, be admitted
that the Emperor[3] would be susceptible to their influence. They
are instruments foreign to our habits, to our principles, and to our
institutions, which we have practiced neither on that, or on any
previous occasion. If it were possible for us to employ such auxil-
iaries, we should have to resort to other climes and to other schools
to qualify ourselves for their rise[4] [sic]. Our relations with Russia
have been generally satisfactory, and characterized by mutual amity;
but we have every reason to believe that this happy result has proceeded from a sense of the justice of the two Powers to what was
due to the interests of each, and not to attainments, of the possession of which we are altogether unconscious. If, in the note to Mr.
Middleton, the power and preponderating influence of Russia are
dwelt upon, they are notorious facts, and we have the authority of
Mr. Canning himself for considering her as the "moving soul of
the Continental alliance."[5]

We have heard from France, and although the answer given by
Count de Damas to Mr. Brown is not so encouraging as could have
been wished, it has not yet divested us altogether of hope.[6] He thinks
the present period not favourable to peace; but he, at the same
time, admits the correctness of the views presented by this Government as to the state of the war, and in regard to the real interests of
Spain. The difficulties, he believes, which lie in the way of peace,
grow out of the personal character of the monarch, and the morti-

fied pride of Spain. Mr. Brown infered [sic], from what occurred
at his interview with the French Secretary, that which we, before,
well knew, that the first movement on Spain, must come from
Russia, and that France would follow, rather than lead. From Russia
we have not yet heard. Mr. Canning may be right in predicting a
failure of the attempt; but we would not willingly believe in such a
discouraging issue, for the reasons which he assigns. It is possible that
the principles and prejudices of the Emperor of Russia may be
opposed to the establishment, in Spanish America, of free Governments springing out of a revolution. But, if they be, in fact, established; if the power of Spain is altogether incompetent to their overthrow, and the recovery of her former dominion, it is difficult to
conceive that he should dissuade her from yielding to a necessity
absolutely incontrollable. We know that the Emperor of Russia
does maintain the most perfectly friendly relations with a State[7]
whose social forms are directly opposite to those of Russia. If the
Emperor of Russia advised Spain to refuse an acknowledgement of
the independence of the former Colonies, and to persevere in the
war, that advice must have been given when a gleam of hope remained. Now that it is forever obscured, to suppose that he would
persist in that advice after subsequent events, and especially after
the decisive battle of Ayachuco[8] [sic], would be to attribute a degree
of perverse obstinacy to the Emperor, utterly incompatible with
the fidelity of the friendship which he entertains for Spain, and which
should be very reluctantly credited. If he has lost the opportunity
of taking the lead in that line of policy which the United States
and Great Britain have wisely adopted, that remains to him, of
being the great pacificator between the Continent of America and
Spain. And, bearing in mind that principle of our nature which
impels us anxiously to hope for the possession of a desired object,
not yet within our grasp, and even to exaggerate its importance beyond that which we attach to acquisitions already made, there is
reason to believe that, by now becoming the successful agent of
peace, the Emperor may regain, in the view and affections of the new
States, and in the consideration of the world, even more than he
has yet lost by any tardiness in his acknowledgement of their Independence. Mr Canning supposes Spain to be ruined, and that the
Emperor has pushed her on in her blind folly. Her condition is
indeed bad enough, whether viewed at home or abroad. But the
nation remains, and yet presents elements which, if wisely combined, and directed, would make it a powerful and respectable State.
With a population not much short of 10 millions, at home, a fine
country, genial climate, and the ample Colonial possessions of
Cuba and Porto Rico, to say nothing of other insular domains, Spain

wants only wise Government, and peace. If, as is alleged, by pursuing the advice of the Emperor, she has lost, or has been unable to reconquer, her American Continental possessions; and if, by continuing in a state of hostilities, she puts in eminent[9] peril what remains to her in this hemisphere, we must be disposed to believe that he will inculcate upon her, other councils [*sic*], unless, (which cannot be believed) he has not the intelligence to comprehend, or the sincerity to recommend, that, which, in the present state of things, is the obvious interest of Spain. These are some of the views which lead us yet to cling to the hope that Russia may interpose her good offices to produce peace, notwithstanding the contrary predictions so confidently put forth by Mr. Secretary Canning. That object is, however, in itself so desirable, that all fair and practicable means of bringing it about should be considered with the utmost candour and deliberation. It is in this state of feeling that Mr Canning's proposal has been taken up, and attentively and respectfully examined.

That proposal is, the signature by the United States, Great Britain and France, either of three Ministerial notes—one between Great Britain and the United States,—one between the United States and France, and one between France and Great Britain;—or one Tripartite note, signed by all, disclaiming, each for himself, any intention to occupy Cuba, and protesting against such an occupation by either of the others. And the draft of such a paper as is contemplated by the latter alternative, accompanies Mr. Canning's note of the 7th. of August. He thinks that Spain apprehends danger to Cuba from the suspected ambition of the old Powers (Great Britain, France and the United States) whilst she thinks comparatively but little of that which impends over it from the new; and he cherishes the belief that, when we jointly go to Spain with this disclaimer of all designs upon Cuba, in our hands, she will be soothed, and disposed to listen to our united Councils, which, otherwise, would be heard with suspicion, and repelled with resentment.

Considered as a measure of peace, I am not satisfied that Mr. Canning's estimate of the value of his proposal, is not too high. Whatever follies the King of Spain[10] may have committed, we must still treat of him [*sic*] as a rational being, operated upon by similar motives to those which generally influence the conduct of Rulers. His fears now are, that, taking advantage of his weakness, and of vicissitudes in the existing war, one of the great maritime Powers of Europe or America may wrest Cuba from him; and his interests require security for that important Island. Whilst the danger continues, both his fears and his interests would seem to unite on peace, by which it may be effectually removed. But if he is quieted as to the greatest source of his apprehensions, and thus made secure in his possessions, a powerful motive of peace would be withdrawn. And he might then, with perfect composure, calculate the cost, and the comparatively little danger to Cuba from the new States, arising out of the protraction of the war. If, as is quite likely, Spain entertains the alleged suspicions of the old Powers, she ought to suppress them, the moment they advise the conclusion of peace, a state unpropitious to their realization, being founded altogether on the contingency of the continuance of the war. And I confess, I am not sure that Spain, tranquilized in all her apprehensions about further Colonial losses, would not find herself strengthened in her resolution to prolong the war, in the hope of re-establishing her antient power on some part of this Continent. After all that has happened, it would be too sanguine to believe that the United States and Great Britain can place themselves in any attitude that would induce Spain to take counsel from them, as from sincere, disinterested, and acceptable advocates of peace. And it may be doubted whether it would not be better, in aid of the cause of peace, to leave her to the operation of the full force of all her apprehensions about the possible contingencies which may assail her West India possessions in the further progress of the war, rather than give her the proposed security against those which she now most dreads.

We cannot, then, in the proposal of the British Government, discern the tendency towards peace which they believe it to possess. On the contrary, it is to be feared that, instead of its hastening the termination of the war, the sanction of the three Powers being known by Spain to be given to it, may retard the arrival of peace. If, instead of approaching Spain, with a diplomatic instrument, lulling her most serious apprehensions about Cuba, she were left to speculate upon all the possible dangers, from every quarter, which may assail her most important Colonial possession; and if, moreover, she were told by the three Powers, or by Great Britain and the United States, that, in the event of the people of Cuba declaring their independence, those Powers would guarantee it, she would be much more effectually awakened to a true sense of the perils to which perseverence in her present misguided policy might expose her. But if we are mistaken,—if the proposal of Mr. Canning would conduce to peace, by a suspension of hostilities, at least, as he supposes, there is no incompatibility between it and the previous attempt, on the part of this Government, to bring it about through the instrumentality of Russia, and the great maritime Powers of Europe, acting in concert with the United States. That attempt was founded on the belief that the existing inducements of Spain to terminate the war, are of themselves abundantly sufficient, if the naked truth should be exposed to her under such united, and distinguished auspices. Mr. Cannings proposal proceeds upon the idea of the utility of qualifying some of the parties in this common exertion, more effectually to espouse the cause of peace, by so manifesting their forbearance and disinterestedness as to lead Spain to listen, without suspicion, to their councils. If it were deemed expedient to accede to his proposal, and he is right in believing it to possess any peace virtue, it may well stand along side of the measure of this Government, to which, in that view of it, it would prove auxiliary.

There is another aspect of the British proposal in which it is viewed more favourably. The British Minister truly says that the United States cannot allow the occupation of Cuba by either Great Britain or France, and neither of those Powers would acquiesce in the occupation of it by the United States. If the acceptance of it would not (and so we are inclined to think) operate as a new inducement to Spain to put an end to the war, it might have a quieting effect among the great maritime powers themselves, by removing all causes of suspicion on the only subject which, in the existing state of the world, is likely to engage, materially, their solicitude, in regard to their own security. This is what is here understood to be the real object of the proposal. A declaration on the part of the Government of the United States that it will abstain from taking advantage of any of the incidents which may grow out of the present war, to wrest Cuba from Spain, is unnecessary, because their pacific policy, their known moderation, and the very measure which they have, already, voluntarily adopted, to bring about peace, are sufficient guarantees of their forbearance. From the amicable relations which, happily, exist between Great Britain and the United States, and the perfect union in their policy, in respect to the war between Spain and the new States, no apprehension can be felt that Great Britain will entertain views of aggrandizement in regard to Cuba, which could not fail to lead to a rupture with the United States. With respect to France, aware as her ministers must be that neither Great Britain nor the United States could allow her to take possession of Cuba, under any pretext, the hope is indulged that she will equally abstain from a measure, frought with such serious consequences. Considering, however, the distracted condition of Spain, every day becoming worse and worse, and the intimate relations which subsist between the two branches of the House of Bourbon, it must be admitted that there is some cause of apprehension on the side of France. The fact of having given instructions to the Captain General of the French forces in the West Indies,[11] to aid the Governor of Havanna [sic] to quell internal disturbance, proves that the French Government has deliberated on a contingent occupation of Cuba; and possession once gained, under one pretext, would probably be retained under the same pretext or some other. With the view, therefore, of binding France, by some solemn and authentic act, to the same course of forbearance which the United States and Great Britain have mutually prescribed to themselves, the President sees no great objection, at present, to acceding to one or other of the two alternatives contained in Mr. Cannings proposal. As information, however, is shortly expected from Russia, as to the manner in which the Emperor has received the invitation to employ his friendly offices to bring about a peace, no instruction will now be given you, as to the definitive answer to be communicated to the British Government. In the mean time, you are authorized to disclose to it the sentiments and views contained in this dispatch.   I am, with great respect, Sir, Your obedient Servant   H. CLAY.

Copy. DNA, RG59, Dip. Instr., vol. 10, pp. 394-401 (M77, R5). AL draft, in DLC-HC (DNA, M212, R7).   1 That is, 24th.
2 See above, Clay to Middleton, May 10, 1825; Clay to King, May 11, 1825; Clay to Brown, May 13, 1825.   3 Alexander I.
4 The word is "use" in draft version.
5 See above, King to Clay, August 11, 1825, note.
6 See above, Brown to Clay, July 15, 1825, no. 31.
7 The United States.
8 See above, Raguet to Clay, March 11, 1825.
9 The word is "imminent" in draft version.
10 Ferdinand VII.
11 Count Dongelot. See above, King to Clay, August 11, 1825, note.

MISCELLANEOUS LETTERS   October 17, 1825

From JOHN HOLLINS, Baltimore. Sends documents relative to a claim on the French Government, dating from 1803; states that the debt, acknowledged twenty years ago, still is "so very unjustly with held." ALS. DNA, RG76, Misc. Claims, France. Hollins signs as President of the Maryland Insurance Company.

From C[HARLES] J. INGERSOLL, Philadelphia. Acknowledges receipt of Clay's letter of October 12, with enclosure; asserts that "what he [Salmon] complains of . . . , admitting all he states to be fact," has "nothing in it that amounts to breach of law"; and states that Ingersoll, unless "further instructed on the subject," will not attempt to ascertain whether the circumstances complained of actually exist. ALS. DNA, RG59, Misc. Letters (M179, R63).

From JAMES PH. PUGLIA, Germantown, Pennsylvania. Acknowledges receipt of Clay's letter of September 27; declares his determination to lay his case, in the form of a memorial, before Congress; and states that he will soon resume his "former residence" in Philadelphia. ALS. Ibid. Puglia's petition for relief of patent infringement was presented to the House of Representatives on December 22, 1825, but withdrawn on January 10, 1826. U. S. H. of Reps., Journal, 19 Cong., 1 Sess., pp. 82, 138.

From GABRIEL RICHARD, Detroit. Acknowledges receipt of a letter (not found) from D (aniel) Brent relative to the case of John McDonell; asks Clay to put in motion a request that the Governor of Upper Canada inform McDonell "officially of the instructions sent by the british Govt. at home relative to his case" (see above, Rush to Clay, May 12, 1825, note; Smith to Secretary of State, June 15, 1825) ; adds, in a postscript, that, after two months of investigation, the canvassers of votes in the election of a delegate (to Congress from Michigan Territory) have not yet reached a decision. ALS. DNA, RG59, Misc. Letters M179, R63). The election, in which Richard was one of the contestants, was won by Austin E. Wing, of Detroit, a native of Massachusetts, who had lived for a time in Ohio before moving to Michigan. He served in Congress from 1825 to 1829 and from 1831 to 1833, was a member of the State legislature in 1842, and held appointment as United States marshal for the District of Michigan from 1846 to 1849.

APPLICATIONS, RECOMMENDATIONS   October 17, 1825

JOHN G. CAMP, Buffalo, recommends Hezekiah A. Salisbury, editor of the *Buffalo Patriot,* as printer of the laws; states "that his appointment would give Genl Satisfaction to the republicans of this part of the State. . . ." ALS. DNA, RG59, P. and D. of L. Camp, born in Culpeper Couny, Virginia, had been distinguished for his service in the battles of Chippewa and Lundy's Lane, during the War of 1812, and, after leaving the Army with the rank of major in 1815, had settled at Buffalo. Salisbury had established the *Niagara Patriot* at Buffalo in 1818, as a continuation of the *Buffalo Gazette,* of which he had been one of the founders and proprietors since 1811. He did not receive a contract for public printing under the Adams administration.

J[AMES] G. DANA, Frankfort (Kentucky) , solicits, as "a co-proprietor and editor" of the Frankfort *Commentator,* appointment to publish the laws. ALS. *Ibid.* Dana, a lawyer and, from 1834 to 1840, reporter for the Kentucky Court of Appeals, had purchased a half-interest in the *Commentator* in April, 1824. He continued as editor, with but one brief intermission, until the termination of the journal in 1832. He did not at this time receive the contract for publishing the laws, but he was so appointed the following year. Cf. below, Worsley to Clay, December 11, 1826, note.

PETER B. PORTER, Black Rock, recommends the appointment of Hezekiah A. Salisbury, "owner & publisher of the 'Buffalo Patriot,' " as printer of the laws. ALS. DNA, RG59, P. and D. of L.

WILLIAM PRESTON, Philadelphia, solicits commission as midshipman or any equivalent appointment in the Army or Navy; states that he is an orphan, sixteen years old. ALS. DNA, RG59, A. and R. (MR3). Preston, not further identified, received no appointment.

To Amos Kendall

WASHINGTON, 18th Oct. 1825.

Dear Sir: I received your obliging letter of the 4th inst. With respect to what has been or may be said about the desire which I had to engage your services in the Department of State, I should be sorry if it gave you any concern. To me it is utterly indifferent. It is enough for me to know that I was influenced by no improper motive, and that I was guided solely by the consideration that your industry, capacity and integrity might be beneficially employed for the public in that department. To guard against improper suspicions, you will remember that I told you, if you came into it, I did not wish you to enter it until after the close of the late political campaign in Kentucky. I had known you for a long time—from Mrs. Clay, as a member of my family[1]—and personally, as the Editor of the Argus. Although I believed you to be wrong in your State politics, no difference in opinion between us, on that subject, could prevent my making a fair estimate of your endowments.

No change has occurred in the office since my return; and unless a clerkship should be created or become vacant, I do not know that I could offer you any other than that which you thought it your interest to decline. As it was originally made without reference to your agency in K. politics, or to the then state of them, the recent change would have no effect on my wishes to engage you in the public service.

I regret extremely the prospect which you describe, of a renewal, with increased bitterness, of our unhappy local controversy. I think your party is wrong; that they should hasten to forget the past, and unite, for the future, in advancing the true interests of the State, without indulging in unavailing regrets. As to the calumnies of which you and they believe themselves to have been the object, you should despise and outlive them. Besides, no doubt many calumnies have been levelled at individuals of the opposite party, and upon the whole they probably neutralize each other. The causes which led to the ascendancy of your party were, in their nature, temporary, and they have gone by. If you persevere, I have no doubt that the result of the next election will be, to place you in a still smaller minority than you now are. And the very effort which is making to thwart the recent decisive expression of the public will, cannot fail to augment the present majority. I know how a defeated party deludes itself by assigning to sinister causes, rather than to the true one, their loss of, or failure to acquire the ascendancy. It is the same thing every where and in all times with the losing party. A strong illustration of this remark is furnished by the Argus of the 6th instant. You there labor to show that, by a small change of votes, in a few counties, where the majorities of your adversaries happened to be small, you might have prevailed. But, my dear sir, take the opposite side, suppose a small change in some of the counties where your majorities happened to be small;

do you not see how the present number in the H. of R. against you might have been augmented?

As to the intention of some of the relief gentlemen to attack the administration, and especially me, I can only say that it is their clear right to do it, if they please. If, by the allegation that I have interfered and contributed to their defeat, they only mean that my opinion was against them, on the act of the last session, and that I did not conceal my opinion, they are perfectly correct. If they mean any thing else, they err. I certainly wished success to the party which has prevailed on that question. But during my late visit to K. I neither had time nor inclination to do more than express my opinion, which was not very often done. It was very well known before. I count in the relief party, many of my best personal and political friends, and I can never believe that the wish to assail me extends beyond a few, whom I well know. If it is imagined that Gen. Jackson can be elected against Mr. Adams, no calculation, in my humble opinion, will be found to be more erroneous. I believe that, in a contest between those two, (always carrying along that the course of administration shall be what I believe it will be, during the next three years,) Mr. Adams will prevail by a majority of two thirds of the Union. He will succeed, in my judgment, against any competitor; but there is another much more formidable than Gen. Jackson.[2]

In frankly expressing these sentiments, it is not my intention to discourage you from the pursuit of what you may deem to be your duty. I thought they were due to the friendly relations which have subsisted between us. I certainly am anxious to see harmony and concord once more restored to our distracted State; but if a sense of duty impels the combatants to continue the strife, I can only deplore a state of things so inauspicious. At a distance, and full of other cares, I shall look on as a spectator, reserving always the right, upon that and every other human occasion, freely to express my thoughts. I am truly your friend, &c.   H. CLAY.
AMOS KENDALL, ESQ.

Frankfort *Argus of Western America,* July 9, 1828.   1 See above, II, 54n.
2 Possibly DeWitt Clinton. Cf. above, Clay to Crittenden, July 25, 1825; Carroll to Clay, October 4, 1825.

MISCELLANEOUS LETTERS   October 18, 1825

From EDGAR MACON, "St. Augustine East Florida." Requests a copy of charges which, he has heard, have been made against him (as United States attorney for East Florida) "by Judge [Joseph L.] Smith of the Superior court for East Florida." ALS. DNA, RG59, Misc. Letters (M179, R63). Published in Carter (ed.), *Territorial Papers,* XXIII, 344. Macon, of Virginia, had been appointed to this office in December, 1823. Smith, born and trained as a lawyer in Connecticut, had entered the United States Army during the War of 1812 and held the rank of colonel at his discharge in 1821. He had been named to the judgeship in 1823 and served until 1832. From 1838 to 1845 he was Territorial Delegate to Congress. Cf. below, White to Clay, March 18, 1826, note; Clay to Macon, April 6, 1826; Macon to Clay, July 7, 1826, note.

APPLICATIONS, RECOMMENDATIONS   October 18, 1825

BEN[JAMIN] BARTON, DONALD FRASER, JACOB A. BARKER, E[BENEZER] WALDEN, WILLIAM A. MAPLEY, ROSWELL CHAPIN, "Citizens of the State of New York," recommend appointment of Hezekiah A. Salisbury, of the *Buffalo Patriot*, to publish the laws. DS. DNA, RG59, P. and D. of L. Barton and Fraser had served in the United States Army, both entering as residents of New York City and resigning with the rank of major at the close of the War of 1812. Barker and Walden were residents of Genesee County, commissioned as quartermaster and paymaster, respectively, of a militia cavalry brigade organized there in 1822. Chapin had been a major of militia in Madison County, New York, prior to his resignation in 1818. Mapley (the name not clear), not identified.

INSTRUCTIONS AND DISPATCHES   October 19, 1825

To R[ICHARD] C. ANDERSON, JR., Bogotá, no. 2. Transmits "a copy of a letter [not found] from John Lewis Nicklye, of New York," to the State Department, seeking reconsideration by Colombia of a claim, "heretofore rejected" by that Government, in the case of the *Paloma*. Copy. DNA, RG59, Dip. Instr., vol. 10, pp. 401-402 (M77, R5). L draft, with Clay interlineations and endorsement: "Mr. [Linnaeus] Smith will please prepare a letter according to the inclosed, which I believe conforms to the case. I wish the letter to Mr. A. transmitted under cover to Mr. Nicklye   H. C." AEI. DLC-HC (DNA, M212, R7).

From SAMUEL HODGES, JR., "Consulate U. States, Cape de Verd Islands   Villa da Praya   St. Iago." Reports the case of a distressed seaman, who had "shipped on Shares," with only the clothes which he was wearing at the time, and the refusal of Captain Nye, of the *Commodore Rodgers*, New Bedford, to accede to Hodges' request for payment to the man of a sum equal to three months wages for an ordinary seaman; declares that "the Captain deserves to be made an example"; and requests instructions concerning the discharge of seamen employed in the whale fishery on shares. LS. DNA, RG59, Cons. Disp., Santiago, vol. 1 (M-T434, R1) . Received December 16. The skipper was probably Captain Ezra Nye, born at Sandwich, on Cape Cod, later renowned as the commander of trans-Atlantic packets. He subsequently settled in Newark as owner and manager of shipping operations. Robert Greenhalgh Albion, *Square Riggers on Schedule, the New York Sailing Packets to England, France, and the Cotton Ports* (Princeton, 1938), pp. 170, 339.

From JOHN C. JONES, JR., Boston. States that, after prolonged absence, caused by ill health, he will soon return to "the Sandwich [sic] Islands," where he "had resided as Commercial Agent for the United States"; asks if he may again "enter on the duties of that appointment"; and refers to the importance, to American trade and whaling, of a public agent at that location, where the British established a consulate last year. LS. DNA, RG59, Cons. Disp., Honolulu, vol. 1 (M144, R1). Jones, son of John Coffin Jones, had been the United States commercial agent in Hawaii from 1820 until January, 1824, when he had returned to Boston for a visit. On his reappointment to the position, see below, Clay to Jones, October 24, 1825. Despite strong criticism of him by 1827, among missionary and Navy personnel, he retained the office until 1838, when he was recalled at the request of the Hawaiian Government. Harold Whitman Bradley, *The American Frontier in Hawaii; the Pioneers, 1789-1843* . . . (Stanford University, Calif., [1942]) , pp. 89-92, 301-304.

MISCELLANEOUS LETTERS October 19, 1825

To JOHN HOLLINS, "President of the Maryland Insurance Company, Baltimore." Promises attention to his letter of October 17, "at the earliest period of convenience." Copy. DNA, RG59, Dom. Letters, vol. 21, p. 171 (M40, R19).

From JOSEPH SEAWARD, Portsmouth, Virginia. Gives details of the capture, by a Colombian privateer, in August, 1825, of the schooner *Ranger,* of which he was master and part owner; notes that he wrote Beaufort T. Watts at Bogotá, "requesting him to pursue such measures for the recovery" of vessel and cargo "as he might think proper"; expresses a hope that "on A Claim being made on the Colombian government . . . it will not turn a deaf Ear"; describes himself as a native of New Hampshire, a resident of Virginia for twenty-five years, and a seaman for twenty-nine years. ALS. DNA, RG76, Misc. Claims, Colombia. Replying to this letter, on January 19, 1826, Daniel Brent informed Seaward that the case of the *Ranger* would "be duly attended to. . . ." Copy, in DNA, RG59, Dom. Letters, vol. 21, p. 254 (M40, R19). Cf. below, Watts to Clay, January 6, 1826.

To John J. Crittenden

Dear Critten [*sic*] Washington 20h. Oct. 1825.
    The bearer here of Mr. Daniel Dougherty[1] claims to be one of the heirs of Winser Brown,[2] and as such to be entitled to the Lands which Brown was entitled to as an officer in the Revolutionary War. He will carry with him, he tells me, to Kentucky, evidence of his connexion with the decd, and, if necessary, will petition the Legislature to release the forfeiture which may have been incurred by the alienage of the Heirs.[3] A part of the lands remain to be surveyed. He may stand in need of advice, and I therefore take the liberty of recommending him to you for it and for your friendly offices. On seeing him you will perceive that he is one of that description of persons to whom I am sure you will always take pleasure in affording aid. For your professional services he will probably have the means of compensating you.
John J. Crittenden Esqr. I remain Yr's faithfy

AL (signature removed). DLC-John J. Crittenden Papers (DNA, M212, R20).
1 A native of Ireland, naturalized a United States citizen.
2 A native of Ireland, member (1777) of the Williamsburg Lodge of Masons, and a captain of Virginia marines, Brown had served throughout the Revolution. He had entered 4,666⅔ acres of land in Kentucky under military warrant in 1784 and 1785

but, before receiving the patents, had died, childless. Dougherty was his nephew.

3 By act of the Kentucky Legislature on December 20, 1825, Dougherty was granted the lands, except as they might be held, in whole or part, under adverse title and with the further proviso that they must be divided if any other heir "equally or more nearly connected" should appear within ten years. Ky. Gen. Assy., *Acts, 1825-1826,* pp. 93-94.

Check to Daniel Dougherty

20 Oct. 18[25]

Pay to Daniel Dougherty or order Sixty dollars. Cashr. of the Off. of Dt. & Dt. Washington[1]   H CLAY

ADS. DLC-TJC (DNA, M212, R16).   Margin torn.   Endorsed on verso: "Dan Dougherty."   1 Richard Smith.

INSTRUCTIONS AND DISPATCHES   October 20, 1825

From JAMES E. BRICE, Cap Haitien. Reports smallpox raging there. ALS. DNA, RG59, Cons. Disp., Cap Haitien, vol. 5 (M9, R-T5).

From A[LEXANDER] H. EVERETT, Madrid, no. 10. Reports that he has asked "the Minister" (Francisco de Zea Bermudez) about a rumored change of Spanish policy toward the South American States and received a reply "most decidedly in the negative"; that Zea "spoke with so much decision and apparent openness of the probability of reconquering the colonies" that Everett "felt . . . bound to give him credit for sincerity at the expense of his sagacity and good sense"; that Zea, professing to have just heard of the communication by the United States to the Emperor of Russia (above, Clay to Middleton, May 10, 1825), requested such information in this connection as Everett could give him; that, in turn, Everett stated the wish of the United States that the long struggle be ended; and that the Minister then requested Everett to put his views in writing but at the same time declared "the King's mind . . . completely made up beyond the possibility of change." Notes conversations with Frederick (James) Lamb and (Pierre) d'Oubril, the ministers of Great Britain and Russia, relative to the "South American question," and states that he has pointed out to Zea and d'Oubril that England will not interfere in the war, for the longer it continues, "the longer she enjoys a monopoly of the Spanish American market for her fabrics, and the more difficult will Spain find it to recover her natural advantages upon the return of peace." Describes d'Oubril as "somewhat guarded in his language" and willing "to declare merely his own personal opinions and feelings. . . ." Adds: "It is understood however that the influence of the Emperor has been employed in support of the present system, and the general impression which I received from his [d'Oubril's] remarks coincided with this opinion." Comments that "The position of the Minister [Zea] is still extremely critical and the party opposed to him are indefatigable in their labors to effect his removal." LS. DNA, RG59, Dip. Disp., Spain, vol. 25 (M31, R27). Received January 3, 1826. Extract published in *American State Papers, Foreign Relations,* V, 795-97, 867-69.

Lamb, a brother of the essayist William Lamb, was a career diplomat, having served as Secretary of Legation at the Court of the Two Sicilies (1811—Minister Plenipotentiary *ad interim,* 1812) and Vienna (1813) and Minister at Munich (1815-1820). He had become Minister Plenipotentiary at Madrid in February,

1825, and remained there until December, 1827, when he was transferred to Lisbon. He was subsequently Ambassador at Vienna from 1831 until his retirement in 1841. He had been named a member of the Privy Council in 1822; he was created a peer, with the title Baron Beauvale, in 1839; and in 1848 he succeeded to the family estate as third Viscount Melbourne. D'Oubril, not further identified.

On the political position of Zea Bermudez, cf. above, Brown to Clay, March 22, 1825, note; September 19, 1825; below, Everett to Clay, October 26, 1825; Brown to Clay, October 29, 1825; October 30, 1825; Brent to Clay, October 31, 1825.

MISCELLANEOUS LETTERS   October 20, 1825

From EDWARD L. PETTIT, New York. Files a complaint against Lewis Shoemaker, United States commercial agent at Matanzas, but expresses gratitude for aid given to Pettit, when ill, by F. M. Diamond, vice commercial agent at Havana, and A. O. Newton, a United States citizen and merchant at Matanzas. ALS. DNA, RG59, A. and R. (MR1). Endorsed on wrapper by Clay: "Qu. Was he a Seaman? To be laid before the President." Pettit, not further identified.

From NATHANIEL WHEELER, Philadelphia. States that he has "this day presented to the Cashier of the United States Bank the Papers to Proov [sic] the oner [sic] Ship & . . . [his] authority to Receve [sic] the Money awarded them" in the case of the *Minerva* and was informed of a "Small Defishency" in documentation, which he will "be abel [sic] to make up"; requests, in case further proof should be needed, that Clay write him "at Taunton County of Bristol Massachusetts. . . ." ALS. DNA, RG76, Misc. Claims, Colombia. Wheeler not further identified.

In reply, Daniel Brent wrote that he was directed by "the Secretary" to inform Wheeler that "the proceeds of the Bill in the case of the . . . Minerva" would be paid to him upon his "sending to this Department sufficient evidence of . . . [his] authority to receive the money." Copy. DNA, RG59, Dom. Letters, vol. 21, p. 183 (M40, R19).

APPLICATIONS, RECOMMENDATIONS   October 20, 1825

JOHN MOODY, "New Canton, Buckingham County" (Virginia), solicits employment. ALS. DNA, RG59, A. and R. (MR3). Cf. above, Moody to Clay, April 2, 1825.

JAMES NOBLE, Washington, recommends "The Editors of the Indiana Republican printed at Madison" for appointment to publish the laws. ALS. DNA, RG59, P. and D. of L. Cf. above, Arion and Berryman to Clay, September 13, 1825, note.

INSTRUCTIONS AND DISPATCHES   October 21, 1825

From JOHN MULLOWNY, Tangier, no. 40. Reports a decision by Morocco, following a remonstrance by the Spanish consul general and consultation with himself, to receive vessels from Colombia on the same basis as those from any other nation; urges that "some person here" be authorized to negotiate a commercial treaty, the expenses of which "would not exceed thirty thousand dollars journey to Fez included." ALS. DNA, RG59, Cons. Disp., Tangier, vol. 4 (M-T61, R4). Received December 29.

From JOHN RAINALS, Copenhagen. Reports that (John) Connell left yesterday for France and that "The Sweedish men of warr, purchas[ed] for South America, have not yet left" port. ALS. *Ibid.*, Copenhagen, vol. 3 (M-T195, R3). Received April 18, 1826. On the ship transfer, see above, Hughes to Clay, July 8, 1825, note.

MISCELLANEOUS LETTERS   October 21, 1825

From DANIEL SMITH, Harrisonburg. Declines accepting appointment "as Judge of the United States for the Western District of Virginia." ALS. DNA, RG59, Letters of Resig. and Declin.

APPLICATIONS, RECOMMENDATIONS   October 21, 1825

A[LEXANDER] THOMSON, Bedford (Pennsylvania), recommends William Crawford, of Georgetown, for appointment as bearer of dispatches. ALS. DNA, RG59, A. and R. (MR1). Thomson, a lawyer, had held several local offices and was a member of Congress (1825-1826), judge (1827-1841), and professor of law at Marshall College, Lancaster, Pennsylvania.

To Lewis Sanders

Dear Sir   Washn. 22d. Oct. 1825
I recd. your letter on the 8h. instant[1] on the subject of my sheep. If Judge Beatty declines taking them (and I have not heard whether he will accept of an offer that I made of them to him)[2] I will take four dollars specie per head for them, including the Steubenville ewe and her produce at the same price, but including also a pair that I have just purchased from the same place at $100. I will be satisfied to take Mr. Robert Scotts, and Mr. R. Hawes note for the amount payable on the first of July next. Should Mr. Beatty decline the bargain, this letter may be deemed a sufficient authority to Mr. Scott to complete that which I offer above. As to leaving it to men to fix their value, it is useless trouble.

I thank you for the hint about folding the sheep—I had previously directed my overseer to do it. Yr. ob. Servant   H. CLAY
Mr. Lewis Sanders.

ALS. Owned by Miss Anna V. Parker, Ghent, Kentucky.
[1] Not found.   [2] See above, Clay to Beatty, September 24, 1825.

From John H. Pleasants

Dr Sir,   New York Octo. 22d. 1825.
[Reports his arrival "today"; refers to his letters of July 8 (*i.e.*, 7) and August 20 (*i.e.*, 31, 1825).]

Convinced as I am, that my life would have fallen a sacrifice, had I persevered in the voyage, and although too ill at the moment, to exert any agency in the step, I cannot help feeling uneasiness at the impressions the apparent abandonment of my trust, may have made on your mind. This uneasiness is proportioned to the frank confidence with which that trust was conferred. I shall be uneasy until I have the honour of hearing from you, and I entreat Sir, if your engagements will permit, to address a line to me at this place, where I am forced to remain a few days—

I know not on what footing to place my A/c with the Government—whether it will expect me to refund, or feel itself under an obligation to comply with the terms at first understood. This I submit to liberality & justice only observing, that the act of God (for it was scarcely less) ought scarcely to defeat the understanding.[1]

Whilst in London, I was under the necessity of drawing on this place, (Mr King having the goodness to supply my wants) for £50— You have no doubt recd the Draft— If it has been paid, and the Government should not be indebted to me so much, I will refund it to you on my return to Richmond. I know not how to excuse the liberty, but by the old plea of necessity. Should any thing still be considered as due, may I ask that it should be forwarded to this place. It may be proper to state that I was absent from home, since the 19h. April—and that I have already recd. $1946— Hoping that all things have worked prosperously, since the spring, and of having the happiness of seeing you in a few days, I remain Most Resply,   JNO H PLEASANTS.

P. S. I brought out Despatches for the Department of State from Mr King, which I will have the honour to deliver in person—JHP.

ALS. DNA, RG59, Letters from Bearers of Dispatches. An extract, published in *House Reports*, 20 Cong., 1 Sess., no. 259, p. 80.

[1] Pleasants' account, totaling $1940, was approved by Clay, December 7, 1826. It allowed $900 "for voyages out and home"; $247 as traveling expenses between April 19 and May 28, 1825, when he "was seeking from Baltimore to Boston, the means of getting to Buenos Ayres"; $37, for expenses on returning from New York to Richmond; and $756, as a per diem allowance from April 19 to August 22 (1825). Copy, in DNA, RG59, Letters from Bearers of Dispatches.

INSTRUCTIONS AND DISPATCHES   October 22, 1825

To JOHN MULLOWNY, Tangier. States that his expenditures for presents, "at a rate of upwards of $2400" per annum over a period of three years, exceed those of (James) Simpson ($750) and (William) Shaler ($600); requests an explanation; and establishes for future expenditures of this nature a limit of $1000, which is not to be exceeded without prior approval of the Department. Copy. DNA, RG59, Cons. Instr., vol. 2, pp. 369-70 (M78, R2). Simpson, Mullowny's predecessor in Morocco, had been appointed consul for the United States at the port of Gibraltar in 1794 and transferred to Morocco two years later, where he had remained until his death.

From THOMAS L. L. BRENT, Lisbon, no. 10. Transmits copies of correspondence in the case of "Jonathan Chase Master of the american brig Hope's Delight," recently released from imprisonment at Oporto; acknowledges receipt of dispatch of September 13, from the Department of State, concerning the case of the *Osprey;* refers to his own dispatch of July 11; and encloses a copy of his offer of aid to Israel P(emberton) Hutchinson, the agent of the owners. LS. DNA, RG59, Dip. Disp., Portugal, vol. 6 (M43, R5). Received December 28. The accompanying documents indicate that the difficulties of Captain Chase (not further identified) arose from a dispute with a Portuguese passenger, whose smuggling efforts had been thwarted by the Captain. When the false charges leveled at the Captain had been disproved, he had been released, but not before he had been roughly handled by the customs guards.

The dispatch of September 13, written by Daniel Brent, transmitted a copy of a letter "written a long time ago, to General [Henry] Dearborn," to which no reply was ever received from the Legation at Lisbon, and urged attention to the case. Copy. DNA, RG59, Dip. Instr., vol. 10, p. 378 (M77, R5). Hutchinson, of Pennsylvania, had been appointed consul for the United States at Lisbon in 1813 and remained there for thirty years.

APPLICATIONS, RECOMMENDATIONS   October 22, 1825

H[UTCHINS] G. BURTON, Raleigh, recommends Robert Potter for appointment as successor to (William) Miller in Guatemala. ALS. DNA, RG59, A. and R. (MR3). Potter, a young North Carolina lawyer, formerly a midshipman in the United States Navy, did not receive the appointment here recommended. He was later a member of the State legislature (1826, 1828, 1834) and of Congress (1829-1831). In 1835 he moved to Texas, where he became active in the independence movement.

NATHANIEL F. WILLIAMS, Baltimore, recommends Thomas Finley, also of Baltimore, for appointment as Chargé d'Affaires to Guatemala. ALS. *Ibid.* (MR2). Finley (Findley) received no diplomatic appointment but from 1826 until 1835 held the position of Federal marshal in Maryland.

INSTRUCTIONS AND DISPATCHES   October 23, 1825

From CHARLES W. DABNEY, Fayal (Azores). Reports restrictions against employment of Portuguese as seamen on American vessels and against American whalers refreshing along the coast, imposed in retaliation for their introducing tobacco, a contraband article. ALS. DNA, RG59, Cons. Disp., Fayal, vol. 1 (M-T203, R-T1). Received November 30. Date supplied by editors. Dabney, born in Alexandria, then in the District of Columbia, and educated in France and in a Boston counting house, was a merchant, dealing in naval supplies at the Azores. For the past eight years he had been acting as vice consul at Fayal. In 1827 he was appointed consul and held this position for the next twenty years.

To Charlotte Mentelle

Dear Madam.   Washn. 24h. Oct. 1825
    Mrs. Clay has received several kind letters from you for which we are both greatly obliged. Our last affliction has almost over-

whelmed us.[1] We were beginning to be composed, by reflection, by occupations, and by time, as to that which preceded it.[2] But this new, unexpected, and severe blow has opened again all the sources of our grief. The calm self possession with which our poor Susan met her untimely fate, if, in one aspect, it has afforded us consolation, has served, in another, to make us feel more acutely the great value of her whom we have lost. Her last care seemed to be for us and for her children.[3] She knew, by her own feelings, as a mother, what must be ours. Ah! Madam is it not cruel out of six daughters to be deprived of all but one![4] Age, grief and misfortune make us feel a great want, and God alone can supply that.

We are keeping house. Mrs. Clay wishes, as I do, very much for Sally Hall; and we are in some uncertainty about her coming. She would do well I think not to wait for the rise of the river, which is very uncertain. The roads are now good; the Stage makes its day's journey with ease; and if she gets fatigued she could always stop & rest a day or two. There is no danger, and almost always some body travelling in it; the fewer however the better.

Make my respects to your husband.[5] Yr's respectfully   H CLAY
Mrs. C. Mentelle

ALS. Elsie Jackson Kelly Collection, Henry Clay Memorial Foundation, Lexington, Kentucky.   1 The death of Susan Clay Duralde.
2 The death of Eliza Clay.
3 Martin Duralde III and Henry Clay Duralde.
4 In addition to those mentioned above, Henrietta, Lucretia, and Laura had died, only Anne Brown Erwin remained.   5 Augustus W. Mentelle.

From Jesse L. Holman

Honored Sir,   Veraestau[1]   Indiana Oct. 24th. 1825.

Messrs. Gregg & Cully [sic], Editors of the Indiana Palladium at Laurenceburgh,[2] are anxious to obtain the printing of the Laws of the Union. They are young men who are just entering public life, & make fair promise to become useful & respectable: And it would gratify a considerable circle of their friends, as well as be of important Service to them if they could obtain their request. Although I have heretofore refused to interfere in many similar applications, I have readily entered into this, as a suitable opportunity (which I have long desired) of addressing a line to you on a very different Subject; and that is simply to tell you that I am not so ungrateful for past favors as I may have seemed to have been. Although my movements in general, have been too unimportant to attract your attention, yet in the late Presidential Election, when enquiry was all alive, & intensely bent to every minute transaction throughout the Union; I do not suppose that I have escaped your observation.

You have no doubt heard that my name was on the Electoral Ticket for Mr. Adams. Shall I tell you it was placed there, by the friends of Mr. Adams, in the Indiana Legislature, without my knowledge or consent; That I was not apprized of it until after the adjournment of the Legislature, & that I then urged some of its more prominent promoters, to substitute some other name in the place of mine. I gave two principal reasons for this: One was that I had long withdrawn myself from every political contest; & had no wish that my name should be used in any public controversy whatever; the Other reason, & the One on which I principally dwelt, was, that I had received many personal favors from Mr. Clay. That there were but few persons in existence to whom I felt so deeply indebted, & whose kindness at an important period of my life was recollected with the liveliest sensations of gratitude; and therefore I did not wish to be conspicious [sic] in the Election or have my name to appear as one who was opposed to his success. It is unnecessary to detail the reasons that were urged why the ticket should remain as it was— It did so remain— But had no other effect than to make you think of me (If you thought of me at all) that I could soon forget past favors, & ungratefully injure the friend who had confered [sic] them. But you are mistaken— I have a clear recollection of what I was when I entered under your tuition, & of the vast benefit I derived from your instruction, besides a knowledge of the Law. I never review my course of life, & compare my uniform, yet quiet success, with that of my youthful companions, whose prospects were even better than mine, without feeling the weight of my obligations to Henry Clay.— It would be unnecessary to enunciate the reasons why I was in favor of the Election of Mr. Adams. Not one of them was person respect [sic]. One, and a Strong one, was, that I was anxious to see the northern Jealousies quietted [sic]. I also thought that Mr. Adams & Mr. Clay might both succeed to the presidency; but that Mr. Adams was too old to be the successor of Mr. Clay; but that Mr. Clay was not too Old to succeed Mr. Adams. As to the clamor a few noisy politicians have raised against the course you have pursued, it reaches us only as the distant thunder, & dies away among us without an echo. You was [sic] the choice of almost every friend of Friend [sic] of Mr. Adams, & at a future period you would be the first. And notwithstanding the success of Genl. Jackson, in our state;[3] I am well assured that if it had not been for the division between your friends, & those of Mr. Adams, that he would not have succeeded. He had but few influential friends in his favor, & many of them did not wish him elected.

Honored friend of my youth. I do sincerely desire your political prosperity. and I feel that the expression of this desire has nothing sinister in it. nor has it any thing selfish, unless the desire not to be thought ungrateful is selfish. I feel that my own political race is run. I have been for nine years in an office with which I am contented.[4] I have no thought that runs forward to any other. I have none, nor do I expect shortly to have any, who depend on me for public promotion. I not unfrequently second the application of my friends and [acqu]aintance [*sic*], for office & appointment, but I do no[t] [per]mit the desire for their success to take deep [*hold*] of my anxieties. But I am unnecessarily detaining you. If you should think of it, will you remember to Mrs. Clay the uncouth Lad, who from the smile of kindness which played over her features, twenty two years ago first learned the vast difference between refined society, & the rustic scenes to which he had be [*sic*] accustomed. With the highest sentiments of Grateful respect. I remain &c. &c.   JESSE L. HOLMAN

ALS. DNA, RG59, P. and D. of L. Addressed to Clay.
1 The Holman homestead near Aurora.
2 Milton Gregg and David V. Culley had founded the *Indiana Palladium* in January, 1825. Though the journal did receive State Department patronage toward the close of the Adams administration, it was non-partisan until September, 1829, when Gregg sold out and Culley continued it as a Jackson organ. Born and educated as a printer in Pennsylvania, Culley had settled at Elizabethtown, Kentucky, in 1821 and, after several intermediate moves, at Lawrenceburg, Indiana, in 1824. He served in both branches of the Indiana Legislature during the early 1830's and, after disposing of the *Palladium* and removing to Indianapolis in 1835, held the position of register of the land office there from 1836 to 1846. Gregg, meanwhile, had founded the pro-Clay Lawrenceburg *Western Statesman* in 1830, which he relinquished the following year to accept office as sheriff. In 1837 he established the Lawrenceburg *Political Beacon*, which he published as a Whig organ until 1844, when he moved to Madison. He returned to newspaper publication at New Albany in 1852, with acquisition of a journal renamed as the *Tribune,* and continued this venture until at least the end of the decade.   3 See above, III, 889n.
4 See above, II, 347n.

Rental Agreement with Louis Marshall and Others

[October 24, 1825]

It is agreed between Henry Clay of the one part, and Lewis Marshall, James E. Davis and John George Baxter of the other as follows—

The said Clay leases to the said Marshall, Davis and Baxter for the term of three years, begining [*sic*] with the 26th. day of December next and ending with the 25th. day of Decr. 1828, his large Stone building in the lower part of the Town of Lexington called the Tammany Mill, with all the buildings on the lot on which it is situate, including the dwelling houses on the street or Alley leading from Water Street to Watts factory[1]—

In consideration whereof the said Marshall, Davis and Baxter, hereby bind and oblige themselves, their heirs and assigns to pay to the said Clay, his Executors, Administrators, heirs or assigns, the sum of seven hundred and fifty dollars in gold or silver coin of the United States, payable in three equal annual instalments, that is to say, 250$ on the 25th. day of Decr. 1826—250$ on the 25th. day of Decr. 1827 and two hundred and fifty dollars on the 25th. day of December 1828—and to surrender to said Clay, his Exrs. &c. on the said 25th. day of Decr. 1828, the said premises in as good condition as they may be rendered by any repairs or improvements on them during said three years—Natural decay and inevitable accidents only excepted—

It is agreed however, that the said Marshall, Davis and Baxter are to have the priviledge [*sic*] of expending the sum of One hundred and fifty dollars in repairs and improvements on said house and premises, which is to be deducted from the first years rent— But is expressly understood that said repairs and improvements are to be such as will be for the benefit of said premises or said Clay, and not machinery &c. Should said repairs not amount to the sum of One hundred & fifty dollars the said Marshall, Davis & Baxter shall not be allowed more than what they actually amount to— And if they should expend more than the 150$. then the overplus expended shall be on their own account not that of said Clay— In either case they shall satisfy said Clay, that the amount claimed as a deduction from the first years rent, has been expended in repairs and improvements aforesaid [*sic*]—

The right of distress for any of the rent in arrear is reserved to the said Clay—

In witness whereof the parties have hereunto set their hand and seals this 24h. day of October 1825 and signed Duplicates hereof

H. CLAY   ⎫
by ROBT SCOTT ⎬ {Seal}
            ⎭
JAMES E. DAVIS   {Ls}
JOHN GEO BAXTER   {s}
LOUIS MARSHALL   {S}

[Endorsement][2]

Robt. Scott on the part of H. Clay agrees to take back the property in this Lease, on the first of March 1828, the rent for which is to expire at that time without prejudice to the claim of H. Clay for arrearages. to which We hereby give our consent.

23 Feby. 1828   LOUIS MARSHALL
                                      JAMES E DAVIS

ADS by Robert Scott, signed also by Davis, Baxter and Marshall. DLC-TJC (DNA, M212, R16). Baxter, born in Dundee, Scotland, had attained prominence there as a manufacturer of linen and jute bagging before coming to the United States. After first settling at Philadelphia, he had moved to Lexington to engage in manufacturing of hemp. He died before the new factory was well established.

1 Henry Watt's rope walk, on High Street at Locust.
2 ES in Scott's hand.

INSTRUCTIONS AND DISPATCHES   October 24, 1825

To JOHN C. JONES, JR., Boston, Acknowledges receipt of his letter of October 19; states that Jones should consider himself "continued in the Commercial Agency of the United States at the Sandwich Islands, until otherwise advised from this Department." Copy. DNA, RG59, Cons. Instr., vol. 2, p. 370 (M78, R2).

From ALEXANDER BURTON, Cádiz. Reports the departure of troops for Cuba and preparations for another expedition to that island; states that, unless funds can be obtained from "some other power, the expedition in question" will be long delayed. ALS. DNA, RG59, Cons. Disp., Cádiz, vol. 4 (M-T186, R4). Received November 28.

From JAMES MAURY, Liverpool. Cites the inconveniences to American vessels in consequence of "no legal means in this Country for proceeding against a foreign seaman for desertion"; adds that this evil is increasing and requires consideration. ALS. *Ibid.,* Liverpool, vol. 3 (M141, R-T3).

MISCELLANEOUS LETTERS   October 24, 1825

To JOHN STEELE, "Collector of the Customs, Philadelphia." Inquires as to the practice at that port concerning "the collection of the discriminating duties, under the Act of 7 January 1824" (see above, Lorich to Clay, March 16, 1825, note), when vessels of enumerated nations are laden "with other produce than that of the particular Country to which the Vessel belongs." Copy. DNA, RG59, Dom. Letters, vol. 21, p. 173 (M40, R19). Steele, born in Lancaster County, Pennsylvania, was a veteran of the Revolution, had served in the Pennsylvania Senate (1804 and 1805) and, since 1806, had held appointment as collector of the port of Philadelphia. Letters of the same content were sent on this date also to H(enry) A. S. Dearborn and to Jonathan Thompson, collectors of the customs at Philadelphia and New York, respectively. Both copies. *Ibid.,* p. 174.

From JAMES PH. PUGLIA, Germantown. Encloses a paragraph accidentally omitted from his letter of October 17. ALS. DNA, RG59, Misc. Letters (M179, R63).

APPLICATIONS, RECOMMENDATIONS   October 24, 1825

JAMES CARNAHAN, Princeton, New Jersey, recommends William Crawford for appointment as bearer of dispatches. ALS. DNA, RG59, A. and R. (MR1).

L[EWIS] H[AMILTON] REDFIELD, Onondaga, solicits appointment to publish the laws in the *Onondaga Register.* ALS. DNA, RG59, P. and D. of L.

To James Brown

No. 2   James Brown Esquire Envoy Extraordinary
and Minister Plenipotentiary, U. S., to France
Sir,   Department of State   Washington 25 Octr. 1825
    The insurrection of the Blacks in St. Domingo,[1] as you well

know, threw a large portion of the white inhabitants of that Island, who escaped the massacre, into the United States, where many of them have become incorporated in the mass of our Citizens. Their misfortunes and their respectability entitle them to kind consideration. By the late arrangement between Hayti and France, it is understood that 150.000.000 of Franks have been agreed to be paid for the indemnity of the sufferers;[2] and the papers inform us that a respectable Commission has been constituted in France to adjust the claims, and to distribute the indemnity. Applications have been already made,[3] and others will, no doubt, be presented, to this Department, by some of the Emigrants or their descendants for information of what it is incumbent upon them to do to obtain their distributive share of the indemnity which has been so stipulated. It is the purpose of this note to request that you will procure the necessary information, as soon as may be, and communicate it to this Department. It will occur to you to ascertain,

1. What is the requisite proof of the nature and ownership of the property, of which the sufferers were stripped, and its value.

2. What proof is required of the identity of the sufferers.

3. In the event of death, to whom is payment to be made—to the heirs or personal representatives.

4. What proof will be required of succession

5. Where, and how, will payment be made

6. What is the limitation of time, within which claims must be exhibited and established.

What forms are required of authenticating testimony.

Other points may suggest themselves to you, upon your own reflection, or by what may be passing in France, in regard to this matter. The object is to obtain full and explicit information on all questions that may arise, so as to enable the claimants to establish their rights, and secure their just proportions of the indemnity.

Many of the Emigrants or their descendants, in the United States, are believed to be yet languishing in a state of extreme indigence, occasioned by their misfortunes. From the very nature of the calamity, to which they became victims, it can hardly be supposed that they brought off with them, very regular and complete proofs of title to the estates and property of which they were deprived. Of those which they were then able to preserve, time and accident have, subsequently, no doubt, destroyed or impaired many. The deficiency must be supplied, frequently, by oral proof. Under such circumstances, you will suggest to the French Government whether it might not conduce to the fulfilment of the benevolent and just objects which they are supposed to have in view, to establish a commission, in the United States, more convenient to many of the parties interested, before which they might exhibit, and substantiate, their claims; and whether it would not, also, correspond to the same objects that the amount which may be ultimately awarded to claimants, resident in the United States, should be paid here. You are authorized to assure that Government, that the Government of the United States will afford to such a Commission any aid that may be proper to enable it to execute its functions. I am, Sir, Your obedient Servant   H. CLAY.

Copy. DNA, RG59, Dip. Instr., vol. 10, pp. 402-403 (M77, R5). ALI draft, in DLC-HC (DNA, M212, R7).
1 See above, II, 504n.   2 See above, Holden to Clay, July 16, 1825.
3 Cf. above, Clay to Daggett, September 1, 1825.

To James Brown

No. 3   James Brown Esquire, Envoy Extraordinary and
      Minister Plenipotentiary U. S. to France
Sir   Department of State Washington 25. Oct. 1825.

During the last summer, a large French fleet visited the American seas, and the coast of the United States.[1] Its object naturally gave rise to much speculation. Neither here, nor through you at Paris was the Government of the United States made acquainted with the views of that of France in sending out so considerable an armament. The President conceives it due to the friendly relations which happily subsist between the two Nations, and to the frankness by which he wishes all their intercourse to be characterised, that the purpose of any similar movement, hereafter, made in a season of peace, should be communicated to this Government. You will, therefore, inform the French Government of his expectation that such a communication will, in future, be accordingly made. The reasonableness of it, in a time of peace of which France shall enjoy the blessings, must be quite apparent. The United States having, at the present period, constantly to maintain in the Gulf of Mexico, and on the coasts of Cuba and Porto Rico, a naval force, on a service beneficial to all commercial nations,[2] it would appear to be quite reasonable that, if the Commanders of any American Squadron, charged with the duty of suppressing Piracy, should meet with those of a French squadron, the respective objects of both should be known to each. Another consideration to which you will advert, in a friendly manner, is the present condition of the Islands of Cuba and Porto Rico. The views of the Executive of the United States, in regard to them, have been already disclosed to France by you, on the occasion of inviting its cooperation to bring about peace between Spain and her former Colonies, in a spirit of great frankness. It was stated to the French Government that the United States could not see, with indifference, these Islands passing from

Spain to any other European Power; and that, for ourselves, no change was desired in the present political and commercial condition, nor in the possession which Spain has of them.[3] In the same spirit, and with the hope of guarding, beforehand, against any possible difficulties on that subject, that might arise, you will now add, that we could not consent to the occupation of those Islands by any other European Power than Spain, under any contingency whatever. Cherishing no designs on them ourselves, we have a fair claim to an unreserved knowledge of the views of other great maritime Powers in respect to them. If any sensibility should be manifested to what the French Minister may choose to regard as suspicions entertained here of a disposition on the part of France, to indulge a passion of aggrandisement, you may disavow any such suspicions, and say that the President cannot suppose a state of things in which either of the great maritime Powers of Europe, with, or without, the consent of Spain, would feel itself justified to occupy, or attempt the occupation of, Cuba or Porto Rico, without the concurrence, or at least the knowledge of the United States. You may add, if the turn of your communications with the French Minister should seem to make it necessary, that, in the course of the summer rumours reached this Country, not merely of its being the design of the French fleet to take possession of Cuba, but that it had, in fact, taken possession of that Island.[4] If the confidence in the Government of France entertained by that of the United States, could not allow it to credit these rumours, it must be admitted that they derived some countenance from the weakness of Spain, the intimate connexion between that Monarchy and France, and the general ignorance which prevailed as to the ultimate destination and object of a fleet greatly disproportionate, in the extent of its armament, to any of the ordinary purposes of a peaceful commerce

You are at liberty to communicate the subject of this note to the French Government, in conference, or in writing, as you may think most proper; but, in either case, it is the President's wish that it should be done in the most conciliatory and friendly manner.

I am, with great respect, Sir, Your obedient Servant   H. CLAY.

Copy. DNA, RG59, Dip. Instr., vol. 10, pp. 404-407 (M77, R5). AL draft, in DLC-HC (DNA, M212, R7).
[1] See above, Armstrong to Clay, July 4, 10, 1825; Poinsett to Clay, August 17, 1825 (nos. 15 and 16).   [2] See above, III, 337, 338n.
[3] See above, Clay to Brown, May 13, 1825.
[4] The Washington *Daily National Intelligencer,* August 8, 1825, had carried a report, reprinted from the New York *Evening Post,* which, in turn, had attributed the "intelligence" to New Orleans papers, that a treaty had been completed between Spain and France, by which the latter was to occupy Cuba and Puerto Rico. *Niles' Weekly Register,* on August 13, 1825 (XXVIII, 370), had noted that "An impression had recently prevailed in Havana that the island . . . was ceded to France. . . ."

To James Harper

Dear Sir   Washington 25h. Oct. 1825

I received to day your obliging favor of the 12h instant.[1] In relation to Minters debt, for which the office holds a mortgage on the land which I procured from him in exchange,[2] I suppose that I must pay the debt. I will thank you therefore to include the amount of the mortgage debt in my note[3] at you[r] office on its next renewal, or if you prefer it to apply the first funds which you may collect on my account to the paym[t.] of the debt. In either case I should wish to have the mortgage itself assigned to me (without recourse to the Bank) to enable me to protect and defend my title to the Estate[.]

> I am with great regard Yr ob. Servant   H CLAY

Mr. J. Harper.

ALS. Owned by Mrs. W. George Thomas, Charlotte, North Carolina. Margin obscured.   [1] Not found.
[2] See above, Agreement, July 4, 1825.   [3] See above, III, 886.

To James Neale

Mr. James Neale, Baltimore.

Sir,   Department of State, Washington, 25th. Octr. 1825.

In reply to your Letter of the 14th. instant, I have the honour to inform you that about the 10th. April last, Mr. Obregon[1] the Mexican Minister, called at this Department, to request that a notification might be made, through this Government, of the fact of the Blockade, by the Arms of Mexico, of the Castle of San Juan d'Ulloa. He was informed that such a notification from a neutral was not according to the usage of Nations. It is not necessary to the legality of a Blockade, maintained by a competent force, and otherwise conforming to the Law of Nations, that its existence should be promulgated by a neutral. If there be present such a force, rendering entry into the blockaded port dangerous, and a neutral should, notwithstanding, attempt to enter after notice of the blockade, or after being warned off, he will subject himself to all the penal consequences of such indiscretion.

> I am, Sir, Your Obedt. Servt.   H. CLAY.

Copy. DNA, RG59, Dom. Letters, vol. 21, pp. 174-75 (M40, R19).
[1] Pablo Obregón.

DIPLOMATIC NOTES   October 25, 1825

From the BARON DE MAREUIL, Washington. Protests, on two grounds, an award by a Florida court of indemnity of salvage to the American schooner *William*

Henry, which had brought to St. Augustine a part of the cargo of the French ship *La Revanche,* after that vessel had run aground: first, he questions the application of Florida law when the Federal Constitution places admiralty and maritime jurisdiction under Federal courts; and, second, he refers to the operation, along the coast, of "Wreckers," who connive "to prevent those interested from being able, themselves, to discuss the expenses of Salvage." Adds that he has yet received only an acknowledgment (above, May 13) of his letter of May 6, 1825, with a promise of later response. LS, in French, with translation. DNA, RG59, Notes from French Legation, vol. 9 (M53, R7). Received October 27.

MISCELLANEOUS LETTERS   October 25, 1825

To JAMES H. CAUSTEN, Baltimore. Encloses "a copy of the table" requested in Causten's letter of August 29. Copy. DNA, RG59, Dom. Letters, vol. 21, p. 174 (M40, R19).

APPLICATIONS, RECOMMENDATIONS   October 25, 1825

SAMUEL HANNAH, ABEL LOMAX, and CALEB LEWIS, Centerville, "Representatives of Wayne county in the Legislature of Indiana," recommend the Richmond (Indiana) *Public Ledger* as a medium for publication of the laws. ALS by Hannah, signed also by Lomax and Lewis. DNA, RG59, P. and D. of L. Hannah, a Quaker, born in Delaware, had been a pioneer settler of Wayne County and had served in several local political offices before his election to the legislature in 1825. A hotel keeper and merchant, he was appointed postmaster of Centerville in 1825 and removed from that office under the Jackson administration. Lomax served as a member of the Indiana House of Representatives from 1823 to 1828 and as a State Senator from 1829 to 1832. Lewis was a member of the State legislature from 1825 to 1826 and in 1832 and 1838; in 1829 he was commissioned an associate judge for Wayne County.

JAMES MORRISON, Maysville, states that his "son Shederick M. Morrison expresses a desire to become a Pupil of the West Point Milleraty [*sic*] Accadamy [*sic*]"; requests information in this connection; and adds in a postscript: "I know you are generally Immersed in Buisness [*sic*] and at first I. disliked to Call on your agency for such Trifels [*sic*], But Reflecting on your Great Willingness to aid or Premote [*sic*] the Views of Your Friends. I. Concluded to Call On. You." ALS. DNA, RG94, Military Academy, Cadet Applications, 1825-168 (M688, R38). Endorsed by clerk on cover: "Referred to the Secy of War [James Barbour]." James Morrison was a wealthy Maysville merchant. The son Shederick (or Shadrach) has not been further identified; he received no appointment.

WILLIAM L. REANEY, Boston, having been informed that Clay "would shortly leave the seat of Government for Kentucky," takes the liberty of addressing him again in connection with his application for an appointment. ALS. DNA, RG59, A. and R. (MR3).

B[ENJAMIN] D. WRIGHT, Pensacola, states that "The death of A[lbert] J. Clagget[t] Esq District Atty. for the Western District of" Florida has induced him to solicit appointment to that office and, if his application meets favorable response, asks that this letter be considered his resignation as district attorney for the Middle District of Florida. ALS. *Ibid.* (MR4). Published in Carter (ed.), *Territorial Papers,* XXIII, 349-50. Wright, born and educated at Wilkes-Barre, Pennsylvania, had settled at Pensacola as a young man and in 1824 had been appointed district attorney for the Middle District of Florida. Following the death of Claggett from yellow fever at Mobile, Alabama, earlier this month (October, 1825), Wright was transferred to the position in West Florida and reappointed to it in 1830. In 1834 he acquired the *Pensacola Gazette,* which he owned until 1839 and for which he provided editorials as late as 1845. He became a member of the Territorial legislative council in 1830, later a judge of the Superior Court for the Western District, and, in 1857, chief justice of the State.

To Francis Jones

Dear Frank.   Washn. 26 Oct. 25.

Allow me to introduce to your acquaintance and request your kind attentions to Mr. Thomas P. Taul, who will present you this letter. A native of K. where he has qualified himself for the practice of the Law, he goes to Alabama[1] to establish himself in his profession. The indications of usefulness which he has given in his native state have created a strong interest, in which I cordially participate, for his future welfare.

I remain always. Truly Your friend   H. CLAY
F. Jones Esq

ALS. Adams Papers, Letters Received (MR477).
[1] Clay had first written "Tennessee." Thomas Paine Taul, a son of Micah Taul, had received the Master of Arts degree in 1821 and the Bachelor of Laws degree in 1824, both at Transylvania University, and was now moving to Huntsville, Alabama. His parents, however, settled at Winchester, Tennessee, where Thomas was killed a few years later. "Memoirs of Micah Taul," Kentucky State Historical Society, *Register,* XXVII (1929), 507, 517.

To Rufus King

No. 8   Rufus King, Envoy Extraordinary and
Minister Plenipotentiary U. S. London.
Sir,   Department of State, Washington 26 Octr. 1825.

Since the date of my note to you of the 17th. of the current month, your despatch No. 5, under date at London on the 13th. of September, has been received with the accompanying note of Mr. Canning, under date at Storrs, on the 8th. of the same month. It appears from his statement, that the French Minister,[1] after having encouraged the overture of the British Ambassador[2] in a manner which led him to believe that France would willingly concur in the proposed declaration respecting the Spanish islands, has suddenly changed his language, and formally declined to accede to the proposal. Under these circumstances, and without waiting for the desired information from Russia,[3] which is not yet received, it seems to the President to be altogether useless and improper for the Government of the United States to unite with that of Great Britain in repeating the proposal to France. With respect to the signature of such a declaration, by the United States and Great Britain alone, for the reasons which are stated in my note of the 17th. instt., it cannot be necessary. After the friendly and unreserved communications which have passed between the two Governments, on this subject, each must now be considered as much bound to a course of forbearance and abstinence, in regard to Cuba and Porto Rico, as if they had pledged themselves to it by a solemn act.

But supposing the British Ambassador at Paris to have laboured under no misconception as to the encouragement which he supposes Count de Damas to have given, prior to his having formally declined to accede to the British proposal, the motives for obtaining from France some security for the observance of the same course of moderation which the United States and Great Britain have respectively prescribed to themselves, instead of losing any of their original force, have acquired additional strength. I have, therefore, by the direction of the President, prepared an instruction for Mr. Brown,[4] of which a copy is herewith transmitted, to inform the French Government that, under no contingency, with or without the consent of Spain, can the United States agree to the occupation of the islands of Cuba and Porto Rico by France. You are authorized to communicate its contents by reading it to Mr. Canning. If the British Government should direct its Ambassador, at Paris, in like manner, to protest against France, under any circumstances, taking possession of those islands, it can hardly be doubted that, if she really has entertained any designs upon them, they will be abandoned. And the substantial object of the British Government will have been attained, and by means but little varied from those which it had devised. In coming to the determination to cause the above communication to be made to France, through the American Minister, the President has been influenced, in a considerable degree, by a desire to correspond to the wishes of the British Government, which cannot fail to recognize, in that measure, a signal proof of the confidence and friendship of the Government of the United States.

I have the honour to be Your obedient Servant. H. CLAY

LS. NHi-King Papers. Copy, in DNA, RG59, Dip. Instr., vol. 10, pp. 405-407 (M77, R5); ALI draft, in DLC-HC (DNA, M212, R7).
1 Baron de Damas. 2 Lord Granville.
3 Cf. above, Clay to Middleton, May 10, 1825. 4 Above, October 25, 1825.

INSTRUCTIONS AND DISPATCHES October 26, 1825

From A[LEXANDER] H. EVERETT, Madrid, no. 11. Reports "that Mr. Zea Bermudez has been finally compelled to quit his post, and that the Duke del

Infantado has been named his successor"; explains reasons for this alteration in the cabinet and notes the possibility of other changes. LS. DNA, RG59, Dip. Disp., Spain, vol. 25, (M31, R27). Received January 3, 1826. Pedro Alcantara de Toledo, Duke del Infantado, long a favorite of Ferdinand VII, had been one of the Council of Regents in 1823.

From JOHN M. FORBES, Buenos Aires, no. 26. Reports passage by the National Congress of a resolution proclaiming that "the Oriental Province is reincorporated"; notes that this is "equivalent to a declaration of War" against Brazil (cf. above, Forbes to Clay, May 2, 1825); states that the Congress has authorized a "national loan of nine to ten millions of dollars"; and encloses, among other documents, a proposed "new law on our flour trade," more favorable to the United States than any earlier regulation. LS. *Ibid.*, Argentina, vol. 2 (M69, R3). Continued on October 26, 28, 30, 31, and November 5. Received December 23. Published in Espil (comp.), *Once Años en Buenos Aires,* 391-94.

From CONDY RAGUET, Rio de Janeiro. Reports that Luiz Joze de Carvalho e Mello has resigned as Minister of Foreign Affairs, that the title of the Emperor is settled, that the first titles of nobility in Brazil have been conferred, and that the governing regime is stable. Comments that publication of proceedings of the Georgia Legislature has led to "reports of a contemplated dissolution of our Union" (see above, Clay to Southard, July 3, 1825, note). Notes that Thomas B. Tilden, formerly of the United States Navy, has been given a commission in the Brazilian Navy; that a treaty, of which the terms are secret, has been concluded between Great Britain and Brazil; that the case of the *Spermo* has not been decided; and that no damages have yet been awarded in the case of the *Exchange.* Acknowledges receipt of his credentials and letters from the Department dated April 13, 14, 16 (no. 3), and 16 (no. 4). ALS. DNA, RG59, Dip. Disp., Brazil, vol. 4 (M121, R6). Received December 29. Extract published in Manning (arr.), *Diplomatic Correspondence . . . Latin-American Nations,* II, 835-36. On the cases of the *Spermo* and the *Exchange,* see above, Raguet to Secretary of State, March 11, 1825, note. Thomas B. Tilden, of Maryland, had entered the United States Navy as a midshipman in 1815 and, after service for a year and a half as a lieutenant of artillery in the Army during 1820 to 1821, had returned to the Navy as a midshipman from 1822 to 1824. He later (before 1835) became captain of a Baltimore merchant vessel.

Two treaties had been signed between Great Britain and Brazil at Rio de Janeiro on October 18, 1825, one prohibiting Brazilians from engaging in the African slave trade, effective four years after the date of ratification, and the other, a convention of friendship, commerce, and navigation. For the treaties, see *Annual Register, 1825,* pp. 72-80; for comment on the principles incorporated, see below, Raguet to Clay, November 23, 1825; for notice of the British refusal to ratify, see below, Vaughan to Clay, April 12, 1826.

MISCELLANEOUS LETTERS   October 26, 1825

From S[AMUEL] L. S[OUTHARD], Navy Department. Encloses copies of correspondence "relative to the detention of the American brig, Morgiana," in the Canary Islands. Copy. DNA, RG45, Executive Letter-book, vol. 1821-1831, p. 133. The *Morgiana,* not further identified.

From S[AMUEL] L. S[OUTHARD], Navy Department. Acknowledges receipt of

Clay's note of October 11; explains charges against Edwin Welsh; states that it would be impossible to restore him without a trial, which "would be difficult now, if not impracticable." Copy. *Ibid.*

From S[AMUEL] L. S[OUTHARD], Navy Department. Acknowledges receipt of "the letter [not found] of Mr. Cannon referred . . . to this Department" by Clay; states that there is no vacancy in the Marine Corps and that, "when one does arise, . . . there will be difficulty in placing him in it. He wished to be first Lieutenant. This cannot be: appointments are only made to Second Lieutenancies: and for this the age of Col. Cannon is probably an objection. It is besides, the intention of the Executive to make the Officers of this Corps from the graduates at West Point, as far as circumstances will permit." Copy. *Ibid.*, 134. Probably refers to Newton Cannon who had served as a colonel of Tennessee mounted rifles during the War of 1812.

MISCELLANEOUS LETTERS   October 27, 1825

From JOHN STEELE, Collector's Office, Philadelphia. Replies to Clay's letter of October 24 by stating his interpretation of the act of January 7, 1824, to the effect that discriminating duties should be charged on that part of a ship's cargo coming from a country to which such duties should apply. LS. DNA, RG59, Misc. Letters (M179, R63).

APPLICATIONS, RECOMMENDATIONS   October 27, 1825

THOMAS FINLEY, Baltimore, solicits appointment as Chargé to Guatamala. ALS. DNA, RG59, A. and R. (MR2). Cf. above, Williams to Clay, October 22, 1825, note.

EBENEZER HERRICK, Bowdoinham, Maine, recommends, as publisher of the laws, the Portland (Maine) *American Patriot* instead of the Portland *Eastern Argus,* "which was virulent in abusing Mr Adams, and although it now professes no hostility to the administration keeps up an incessant warfare [*sic*] against all its firm and undisguised supporters." ALS. DNA, RG59, P. and D. of L. The *Eastern Argus* retained the patronage for the next Session of Congress, but the *American Patriot* received the contract during the remainder of the administration.

DOUGLASS MAGUIRE, Indianapolis, solicits renewal of contract to publish the laws. Comments: "I am still, as I always have been, your warm and devoted friend, and I hope again to have an opportunity to exert my little influence, through the press and otherwise, towards elevating you to a station to which your talents, patriotism, and public services entitle you." ALS. *Ibid.* On the requested contract, see above, Brent to Douglass and Maguire, April 14, 1825, note.

JAMES NOBLE, Brookville (Indiana), recommends (Edmund S.) Buxton, editor of the Richmond (Indiana) *Public Ledger,* for appointment to publish the laws. ALS. DNA, RG59, P. and D. of L.

E. STEDMAN and others oppose publication of the laws at both New Bern and Washington, North Carolina; request, instead, an appointment at Fayetteville. LS, with 92 signatures. *Ibid.* Not dated and not addressed; filed between items

dated October 27 and 29, 1825. Stedman, not identified. The public printing
was continued in the New Bern *Carolina Sentinel,* a Jackson organ, during the
next Session of Congress but was shifted in 1826 to the Fayetteville *North
Carolina Journal,* also sympathetic to Jackson. No newspaper at Washington,
North Carolina, was listed as holding such a contract, though the *American
Recorder,* of that city, supported Adams. *House Docs.,* 19 Cong., 1 Sess., no. 41
pp. 10, 14; Daniel Miles McFarland, "North Carolina Newspapers, Editors and
Journalistic Politics, 1815-1835," *North Carolina Historical Review,* XXX
(1953), 386, 396-97, 410.

Bank Check to Joseph Somers

28h. Oct. 1825.

Pay to Joseph Somers or order forty-seven dollars.   H CLAY
Cashr. of the Off of Dt. & Dt. Washington[1]

ADS. DLC-TJC (DNA, M212, R16). Endorsed: "Joseph Somers." Somers, not
identified.   [1] Richard Smith.

From Christopher Hughes

Private.   New York. 28th. October. 1825.
My dear Sir: *Friday noon.*
We arrived here today, having sailed from Havre on 27th.
September. We shall repose ourselves a day or two here, and
then proceed for Baltimore, and after I shall have passed a few
days there with my friends, I shall go on to Washington hoping
to find you in good health; and in improved spirits, after the
melancholy event in your family,[1] which came to my knowledge
through the public prints. It is the second affliction of the kind,[2]
that you have suffered since I saw you, and I assure you that I
have partaken sincerely in your and Mrs. Clay's sorrow. I may
speak earnestly on the subject, for we have also had our share
of grief. We lost in 1823, a son and a daughter;[3] and I was met
at Brussels by the mournful news of the sudden death of my good
and pious mother.[4] Thus, one of the chief joys I promised myself
on my return to my native land, the joy of seeing my children in
my mother's arms, is snatched from me.

I have no very interesting political news to give you. I have
written (on board ship) a very hasty and imperfect sketch of my
general observations during the few last months of my residence
there, in the form of a private letter to the president.[5] I enclose it
herein; and I beg to refer you to it; if I were to touch the topics
in this, it would be a mere recapitulation of what I have written
to Mr. Adams. In perusing my letter you will exercise your usual
indulgence, and remember it is the first rough draught and written
on board ship.

Mr. Brown's[6] health had experienced the most extraordinary benefit by his visit to the waters of Savoy; if he could have staid there some 3 weeks longer, his health would have become quite renovated. I received a most friendly letter from him the day before I sailed from Havre.

I write you in the hurry of our arrival, and merely to announce it. You will, therefore, pardon this dull letter.

Sir Charles Bagot charged me with kindest messages for you. He intended to write; but the arrival of two of the English Princes at Brussels took up his time so completely that he had scarcely a moment free.

I found several packages on board the Lewis, to your address, which I took possession of. and forwarded by post.

I shall be very happy to receive a few lines from you at Baltimore; and if you wish me to come to Washington, I shall always be ready to render myself to *your summons* in a few hours after receipt of your letter.

I enclose a despatch for the Baron de Huygens from the Minister of Foreign Affairs,[7] given to me at Brussels. I also send you a letter from Mr. de Conincke in reply to yours,[8] which I had the honor to hand to him on taking possession of my post. I am, my dear sir, truly & devotedly, Your friend   CHRISTOPHER HUGHES.
To. Mr. Clay, Washington.

Copy. OHi.   [1] The death of Susan Clay Duralde.
[2] See above, Clay to Crittenden, August 22, 1825, note.
[3] Not identified.   [4] Margaret Sanderson Hughes.
[5] Hughes to Adams, October 28, 1825 (MHi-Adams Papers [MR472]).
[6] James Brown.   [7] De Conincke.
[8] See above, Clay to Hughes, March 24, 1825, note.

From Lafayette

LAGRANGE, October 28, 1825.

MY DEAR SIR,—I am the more anxiously waiting for the packet of the 1st instant, as an account of your having been sick, since my departure, has appeared in the French papers. Yet there are evident inaccuracies in the report. Now I must hasten these lines to the Cadmus, which sails on the 1st November. I have written to the President,[1] sending him an article of the *Journal des Debats,* which may interest him and you. I also tell him a few words of what I have heard respecting the affairs of Greece, upon which I have seen nothing to alter my opinion. I came directly from Havre to Lagrange, and have been very friendly received by the people on the road, and here, on my arrival. Ministerial and court people have either kept aloof, or acted foolishly to their own damage. I have been only four days in

Paris, to see several friends, and do not intend returning to town
before the first days of January. The mass of the nation is quiet
and industrious, though dissatisfied with the measures of the
Government, and the incroachments of nobles and priests. I found
Mr. Brown[2] much better than I expected, indeed, almost quite
well. Mr. Sheldon[3] is better, also, and has wisely, I think, determined to nurse his health in Paris, rather than go to *ennuyer*
himself in the South, while his time here is usefully employed.
Mr. Somerville[4] has been very sick; I hope he will be soon on his
travels. Present my affectionate respects to Mrs. Clay and family.
Receive those of my children[5] and Le Vasseur.[6]

Colton (ed.), *Private Correspondence of Henry Clay,* 130.
[1] Dated October 27, 1825 (MHi-Adams Papers [MR472]).
[2] James Brown.   [3] Daniel Sheldon.
[4] William C. Somerville.
[5] George Washington Lafayette; Anastasie-Louise-Pauline de Lafayette, the Countess
de La Tour-Maubourg; and Virginie de Lafayette, Mme. Louis de Lasteyrie.
[6] Auguste Levasseur, formerly a colonel in the French army, had been Lafayette's
secretary during the American tour and remained in his employ for two or three
more years. In 1829 Levasseur published at Paris a two-volume account of *Lafayette
en Amerique.* Long identified with French revolutionary activity, Levasseur was
wounded during the uprising of 1830 but recovered and later became French consul
at Trieste.

INSTRUCTIONS AND DISPATCHES   October 28, 1825

From THOMAS L. L. BRENT, Lisbon, no. 11. Reports concern by the King of
Portugal (John VI) whether the appointment of (Frederico) Torlade de
Azambuja as Chargé to the United States will be agreeable to that Government;
expresses Brent's favorable impression of Torlade; summarizes discussion between
Brent and Torlade relative to a possible commercial treaty between their two
countries based upon the provisions of the treaty between the United States
and Britain (above, II, 57-59); and notes that Torlade has drafted a memoir
to his government endorsing such terms. Observes that, since receipt of
dispatches from Brazil following Sir Charles Stuart's arrival there (see above,
Raguet to Clay, July 30, 1825), "great efforts are making to fill up the incomplete
regiments" of the army. LS. DNA, RG59, Dip. Disp., Portugal, vol. 6 (M43,
R5). Received December 28.

From JOSHUA DODGE, Marseilles. Encloses copy of a notification from the local
board of health that the plague, referred to in his letters of July 22 and August
4, "has entirely disappeared." ALS. DNA, RG59, Cons. Disp., Marseilles, vol.
2 (M-T220, R-T2). Received January 4, 1826.

From A[LEXANDER] H. EVERETT, Madrid, no. 12. Encloses copy of a memoir,
"presented to the King [of Spain, Ferdinand VII] by the Danish Minister
Count Dernath (or Vander Naath)," critical of Zea Bermudez; asserts that "If
such a document proceeding from such a source really had any effect in
producing the Minister's removal, the tenure by which he held his office must
have been on all accounts sufficiently feeble." LS. DNA, RG59, Dip. Disp.,
Spain, vol. 25 (M31, R27). Received January 3, 1826.

MISCELLANEOUS LETTERS   October 28, 1825

To ALEXANDER CALDWELL, "Judge of the United States for the Western District of Virga., Wheeling." Forwards commission for this office. Copy. DNA, RG59, Dom. Letters, vol. 21, p. 178 (M40, R19). Cf. above, Zane to Clay, April 5, 1825, note. In his acceptance, dated November 2, Caldwell wrote, to Clay: "I shall ever feel towards yourself, also, grateful recollections of your friendly office in this affair." ALS. DNA, RG59, Acceptances and Orders for Commissions (M-T645, R2).

From JONATHAN THOMPSON, Custom House, New York. Acknowledges receipt of Clay's letter of October 24; states that on that part of cargoes not the produce of enumerated countries an addition of ten per cent is made to the duties collected. LS. DNA, RG59, Misc. Letters (M179, R63).

APPLICATIONS, RECOMMENDATIONS   October 28, 1825

E[DWARD] B. JACKSON, Clarksburg, Virginia, recommends James Pindall for appointment to "the U States Judgeship for Western Virginia." ALS. DNA, RG59, A. and R. (MR1). See above, Jackson to Clay, April 12, 1825, note.

PETER LITTLE, Freedom (Maryland), recommends Thomas Finley for appointment as Chargé at Guatemala. ALS. DNA, RG59, A. and R. (MR2). See above, Williams to Clay, October 22, 1825, note.

From James Brown

Dear Sir,   Paris Octr. 29. 1825

The state of Mr. Sommerville's[1] health has for some days been such as to give us great uneasiness, and his recovery is at this moment exceedingly uncertain. Some few days after his arrival he was so unfortunate as to rupture a blood vessel in his lungs, he was bled very copiously and confined to his bed, and it was hoped that all danger of any immediate unfavorable consequences was over. The complaint however appears to have passed into his stomach of which the irritability became so great that the least and lightest nourishment occasioned and still occasions violent vomiting with loss of blood, and it is seriously apprehended that unless he can be speedily relieved he must sink under his complaint. We all feel a deep interest in his situation, visit him frequently, and endeavor to sustain his spirits which are of course very much depressed at his alarming situation. He is attended by able Physicians but all their remedies have hitherto been ineffectual.

The accounts from Greece continue to be more favorable and we may now consider the fifth Campaign as terminated. The country however has suffered more severely from the invasion of this, than from those of former years, and if friendly powers do not come to the assistance of the Greeks, it is greatly to be feared that the next summer may bring with it a termination of all their hopes of liberty and Independance [*sic*]. It is generally believed that Great Britain will ultimately interfere rather than that the struggle should have this unfortunate issue, but is [*sic*] also thought that to avoid any collision with other powers which might lead to war, she will delay her interference until it shall have become apparent that it is the only means left to save Greece from utter ruin. The friends of the Greeks seem generally to believe that the Squadron under the command of Commodore Rodgers has been sent to assist them, and the French papers are filled with speculations on the terms on which our assistance is to given[*sic*].[2] It is said by some that we wish to make a commercial treaty with Greece, whilst others assign our desire to acquire an Island in the Mediterranean for the accommodation of our vessels of war as the motive of our interference. The better informed and particularly those connected with public affairs treat these as idle rumors, and either beleive [*sic*], or affect to beleive, that the Government of the United States are too prudent to engage in a cause so remote from the usual sphere of their political influence, or to endanger their peace by mingling their interests with those of the Continent of Europe.

It is beleived that the Governments of England & France have, through their ministers at Madrid, very strenuously urged the King to acknowledge the independance of the new Republics, and that the subject has been repeatedly discussed by the Ministry without being brought to any decision— So much care has been taken to prevent the publication of any intelligence in the Spanish papers which could enable the people to see the utter impossibility of conquering those Republics, that the impression is still general that by a vigorous effort the authority of the mother country might be re established and consequently the public mind is not prepared for any recognition of their independance— The party composed of the Ultras, priests, and lower classes, is very powerful, and already much disatisfied [*sic*] with the measures adopted by Mr Zea, and they would avail themselves of the acknowledgement of these Governments as a fresh and powerful means of opposition. I have no reason to doubt that France is in favor of that measure but I have heard it asserted that it meets with considerable opposition from the Ministers of Russia and Prussia. I have had no letters from Mr Everette[3] on that subject, but presume you will be fully informed respecting it by the despatch from him which will go by the Packet which carries this letter.

If the standing of Ministers here is to estimated [*sic*] by what we find in a majority of the public journals or hear in political circles, we should arrive at the conclusion that they could not long continue in place. But when the complaints against them are carefully examined they appear to form no adequate cause for removing them. In making this this [sic] remark I do not look back to the time at which the present chamber of Deputies was elected when it was said that much undue ministerial influence and perhaps even corruption was practised. The administration of the laws for the last twelve months has been such as to furnish fewer causes of disatisfaction than during the same period under any former Ministry. The two principal charges against them are the encouragement given to the Jesuits, and the attempt to convert the public debt from a stock bearing five, to one bearing four per cent interest. The first of these charges in [sic] confined to the liberal papers, the second is common to all the journals of the opposition. It is beleived by many that Mr de Villele has no very strong leaning towards the Jesuits, but that he encourages them, from deference to *higher* authority, and because, pressed by the combined opposition of liberals and Ultras, he stands in need of the support of the Clergy. With respect to the public debt as the stock was redeemable at the pleasure of the Government, it was the right, as well as duty, of the Government to reduce the interest if possible; Mr de Villele beleived he could borrow money at four per cent, and he offered stock irredeemable for a long period at that rate of interest, to those who should chuse to exchange their five per cents for it rather than incur the risk of re imbursement.[4] Very few of the public creditors converted their stocks, the great portion of them retained their five per cents. The four per cents have declined considerably, the fives remain nearly at par. The recognition of the Independance of St Domingo,[5] and the steps taken by Ministers to obtain an acknowledgment of the New Republics, will be popular measures upon which they may sustain themselves at the meeting of the Chambers. The present Ministry are opposed to our claims,[6] and I should be gratified if I could anticipate the appointment of a new Ministry more favorable to them. I do not beleive the Ultra opposition would furnish Ministers of the sentiment we wish, and it is by no means probable that the liberal opposition can gain the ascendancy. If we ever obtain Indemnity for our loss we shall owe our success rather to a change of *circumstances* in the affairs of the two countries than to a change of Ministry. The Indemnities we formerly obtained were procured by the desire on the one hand to acquire territory, and on the other to exchange territory for money. Our claims rest alone on arguments proving them to be just, and these unfortunately have not always their due weight.

Mrs Brown has been very much occupied with Mrs. Clays

commission[7] which is not so easily executed in Paris as our friends at Washington might imagine. You may be grossly imposed on in the articles as well as in the price and therefore much care and attention are necessary. She hopes they will b[e] put on board the vessel which will sail on the 15.

Mrs. Patterson and her sister Miss Caton[8] have been in Ireland for some time— Mrs. B recieved [sic] a letter from the former stating that she would be married on the 29 Inst to the Marquis of Wellesley Lord Lieutant [sic] of Ireland.[9]

Mrs. Brown joins me in respects to Mrs. Clay. I am Dear Sir very truly Your Obedt Servt.   JAMES BROWN
Honb Henry Clay.

ALS. DLC-HC (DNA, M212, R2).   1 William C. Somerville.
2 Rumors had reached western Europe late in September, stating that the American Mediterranean Squadron, under Commodore John Rodgers, had taken possession of the island of Porros and that an American ship of the line was to accompany the Greek fleet "preparing to sail for Alexandria, to watch the motions of the new expedition fitting out there." Washington *Daily National Intelligencer*, October 31, 1825. The latter report probably stemmed from Rodgers' decision to detach an American vessel at Smyrna for the protection of American commercial shipping. *American State Papers, Naval Affairs*, II, 112. See also, above, Clay to Rodgers, September 6, 1825.   3 Alexander H. Everett.
4 Cf. above, Brown to Clay, April 1, 1825, note.
5 See above, Holden to Clay, July 16, 1825; Armstrong to Clay, July 21, 1825.
6 Cf. above, Brown to Clay, June 25, 1825.
7 Cf. above, Brown to Clay, October 13, 1825.
8 Mrs. Robert Patterson; Elizabeth Caton.
9 Richard Colley Wellesley, the Marquis Wellesley, had become Lord Lieutenant of Ireland in 1821.

DIPLOMATIC NOTES   October 29, 1825

From PETER PEDERSEN, Washington. States that, after several conferences with Clay, he "understands it to be the wish of The President, that the negociation be suspended for a few weeks, in order to afford time fully to examine the subject in general, and in particular the principle proposed in the third article of the project [sic] submitted by" Pedersen; wishes to know "the conditions on which the United States can, and are disposed to form a Convention with Denmark taking for basis. . . , the project above alluded to. . . ." AN. DNA, RG11, Records Having General Legal Effect, Unperfected Treaty P. A copy of the "Project," undated and unsigned, containing nine articles, is located in *ibid*. The article referred to provided that vessels of the two signatory powers could, with perfect reciprocity, introduce goods not of their domestic manufacture into each other's ports, free of discriminatory "duties or other charges."

INSTRUCTIONS AND DISPATCHES   October 29, 1825

To THOMAS M. RODNEY, "Commercial Agent U. S. Havana." Encloses papers relative to William Perry; requests information on the steps taken and progress made in connection with this case. Copy. DNA, RG59, Dom. Letters, vol. 21, pp. 179-80 (M40, R19). See above, Perry to Clay, March 25, 1825; below, Rodney to Clay, February 4, 1826.

From RUFUS KING, London, no. 9. Expresses doubt that an early consideration of the disagreement between (George) Jackson and (Langdon) Cheves can be expected (see above, Clay to King, May 10, 1825) — (George) Canning believes that the United States and Great Britain should adjust their differences without referring them to a third power. Reports that Canning is ready to exchange ratifications of the treaty between Great Britain and Colombia (see above, Watts to Clay, May 10, 1825, note), that a Minister from Buenos Aires is expected, that the treaty with Mexico has been returned to that country for correction "in respect to Free Ships" (see above, Poinsett to Clay, May 5, 1825, note), and that England will urge Brazil to accept an invitation "to send a Minister to Panama." Refers to British trade in South America, to the possibility of their negotiating commercial treaties with other Latin American Republics, and to the effect on France of this British policy. LS. DNA, RG59, Dip. Disp., Great Britain, vol. 32 (M30, R28). Received December 8. Extract published in Manning (arr.), Diplomatic Correspondence . . . Latin-American Nations, III, 1572-73.

From JOEL R. POINSETT, Mexico, no. 25. Refers to preparations for an expedition against Cuba; states his opinion "that the attempt will fail and produce only the most disastrous consequences"; expresses fear that "the blacks may be armed . . . by one or both parties" and that the attempt against Cuba may cause Spain to cede the island to France. Discusses difficulties experienced in Mexican waters by certain vessels from the United States and adds "that our vessels are frequently engaged in smuggling along the coast." LS. DNA, RG59, Dip. Disp., Mexico, vol. 1 (M97, R2). Received January 3, 1826. Published in Manning (arr.), Diplomatic Correspondence . . . Latin-American Nations, III, 1640.

MISCELLANEOUS LETTERS   October 29, 1825

From JOHN H. PLEASANTS, New York. States that he is "much obliged . . . for the exCulpation . . . extended," in Clay's letter of October 25 (not found), and adds: "—an exculpation, which however, I had a right to claim from hard necessity." Declares that, in regard to settlement of his accounts, he discards "liberality, and only request[s] that common justice may prevail. . . ." Notes that he has found it "necessary" to return to Richmond "in one of the Packets," rather than by way of Washington, and that he is forwarding (Rufus) King's dispatches through the mail. Offers sympathy in regard to the "heavy calamities," of which he has just heard, that Clay's family has suffered (cf. above, Clay to Crittenden, August 22, 1825, note; Mazureau to Clay, September 19, 1825). Subjoins the following postscript: "Notwithstanding the indulgence which your words import, I cannot but perceive, that a feeling of dissatisfaction at my adventures, is at bottom entertained. If you feel this, others must still more disapprove—and for my own justification and still more yours, I beg your consent to publish such a vindication in Richmond, as the occasion seems to demand—" ALS. DNA, RG59, Letters from Bearers of Dispatches.

APPLICATIONS, RECOMMENDATIONS   October 29, 1825

CLEMENT C. BIDDLE and others, Philadelphia, recommend George Latimer, of Philadelphia, for appointment as consul "at the City of Santo Domingo." DS, with 26 signatures, including those of N. Biddle, Henry Toland, and John

Sergeant. DNA, RG59, A. and R. (MR3). Not dated; enclosed in Latimer to Clay, below, this date. Clement C. Biddle, of Philadelphia, a remote kinsman of Nicholas Biddle, had published in 1824 an annotated edition of Jean Baptiste Say's *Treatise on Political Economy* and was himself influential as a financial expert. In 1834 he became president of the Philadelphia Saving Fund Society, of which he was the principal founder. Latimer, born in Ireland and engaged in mercantile pursuits, did not receive an appointment at this time; but he was subsequently consul for the United States at Mayagues, Puerto Rico, from 1835 to 1839 and at St. John's, Puerto Rico, from 1845 to 1859.

GEORGE BISSETT, St. Francisville, Louisiana, solicits appointment to publish the laws in a new paper, *La Fourche Gazette,* which he is establishing at Donaldsonville, Louisiana; states that *The Asylum,* a paper which he formerly conducted at St. Francisville, had published the laws until last year; notes that *The Asylum* has been discontinued and "the establishment" moved to Donaldsonville. ALS. DNA, RG59, P. and D. of L. Bissett, not further identified.

GEORGE LATIMER, Philadelphia, solicits appointment as consul or commercial agent at the city of Santo Domingo. ALS. DNA, RG59, A. and R. (MR3) .

INSTRUCTIONS AND DISPATCHES　　　　　　October 30, 1825

From JAMES BROWN, Paris, "Private." Reports receipt of information that "Mr Zea has been dismissed from his place as [Spanish] Minister of Foreign Affairs, and the Duke del Infantado appointed as his successor." Recalls that Zea owed his appointment to the "wishes of the great Continental Powers" and notes that his removal "has given a shock to the hopes of the friends of Spain on this Continent." Adds: "In the triumph of the Ultras England and France perceive a postponement of the recognition of the American Republics—France, danger to their troops in Spain and delay in obtaining payment of the money due from her; whilst the Holy Alliance find their plans for tranquilizing the peninsula defeated, and an argument against their intervention furnished by the utter failure of success." ALS. DLC-HC (DNA, M212, R2) . Published in Padgett (ed.) , "Letters from James Brown to Henry Clay," *Louisiana Historical Quarterly,* XXIV (October, 1941) , 973-74.

From A[LEXANDER] H. EVERETT, Madrid, no. 13. Reports issuance by the Department of Justice of an order that the balance of "the six thousand dollars due from the house of Wiseman Gower & Co." be paid but states that further delay may be expected. LS. DNA, RG59, Dip. Disp., Spain, vol. 25 (M31, R27) . See above, Clay to Nelson, April 14, 1825, note; Everett to Clay, September 25, 1825.

MISCELLANEOUS LETTERS　　　　　　　　　October 30, 1825

To TENCH RINGGOLD, marshal, District of Columbia. States that "The Baron Maltitz, the first Secretary of the Russian Legation," has complained of a violation of his "official privileges" in an attempt, by a Georgetown constable, to enter his residence to execute a warrant against a servant; requests Ringgold to prevent "further proceedings to enforce the warrant" until an investigation can determine whether "diplomatic privileges appertain." Copy. DNA, RG59, Dom. Letters, vol. 21, p. 180 (M40, R19). Jean-François-George-Frédéric, Baron de Maltitz, Knight of the Order of Vladimir and of St. Stanislaus of Poland, became Chargé d'Affaires *ad interim* for Russia in the United States from March, 1826, to December, 1827. He was later transferred to the legations at Berlin and London and, finally, served for many years as Minister Plenipotentiary to Holland.

From ROBERT BRECKINRIDGE, Louisville (Kentucky). States that the managers of the Louisville Hospital, erected by legislative act of February 5, 1817, "have progressed so far with the building to accomodate [*sic*] from Sixty to eighty patients" and that "those persons engaged in the navigation on the western waters" have already benefited from its existence; cites limitation of funds for support of the institution; and, in the name of the board of managers, makes application, through Clay to the President, for a portion "of the hospital fund destined for the relief of sick seamen. . . ." ALS. DNA, RG59, Misc. Letters (M179, R63). The act establishing the institution (Ky. Gen. Assy., *Acts, 1817,* pp. 255-58) had called for provision of a hospital to treat "those engaged in navigating the Ohio and Mississippi rivers, [who] . . . owing to the fatigue and exposure incident to long voyages, become sick, and languish at the town of Louisville, where the commerce in which they are engaged, sustains a pause occasioned by the falls of Ohio river. . . ." Popularly known as the Louisville Marine Hospital, it was completed to the designed capacity of 150 by August, 1829. In 1798 Congress had provided for establishment of hospitals for distressed seamen, to be supported by a tax on American vessels returning from foreign ports. An amendment in 1802 had levied a tax on Mississippi River craft for the care of "sick or disabled seamen of the United States" at New Orleans. 1 *U.S. Stat.,* 606 (July 16, 1798); 2 *U.S. Stat.,* 192-93 (May 3, 1802). Congressman Charles A. Wickliffe introduced a resolution in January, 1826, urging a grant of such funds to the hospital, but the measure was tabled. *Register of Debates,* 19 Cong., 1 Sess., 926-27.

From TENCH RINGGOLD, Washington. Acknowledges receipt of Clay's letter (above, this date); states that he will proceed immediately "to George Town to take the measures directed. . . ." ALS. DNA, RG59, Misc. Letters (M179, R63).

INSTRUCTIONS AND DISPATCHES   October 31, 1825

From M[ARTIN] BICKHAM, "Port Louis Isle of France." Reports that, owing to ill health, he will leave the island "in a few months," whereupon his position will become vacant. Notes that the scarcity of American trade renders "it of little Importance for our Government to have an Agent at this Place." ALS. DNA, RG59, Cons. Disp., Port Louis, vol. 1 (M-T118, R-T1). Addressed to Secretary of State; received February 25 (1826). Bickham, born in New Jersey, had been appointed to the post on Mauritius in 1816.

From THOMAS L. L. BRENT, Lisbon. Reports news from Madrid of the removal of Zea Bermudez, with which "It is supposed that France will not be pleased . . . and that England will." LS. DNA, RG59, Dip. Disp., Portugal, vol. 6 (M43, R5). Received December 28.

MISCELLANEOUS LETTERS   October 31, 1825

From JOHN COX, "Mayors Office   George Town." Refers to Clay's "note to Tench Ringgold" (above, October 30); states that he has acted to prevent further proceedings relative to the warrant until notice from Clay; gives "an account of the affair," involving an attack by the Baron de Maltitz's coachman on a young man, which led to issuance of the warrant. LS. DNA, RG59, Misc. Letters (M179, R63). Cox, reared in Baltimore, was a large property owner and merchant in Georgetown. He had been appointed a justice of the peace of Washington County in 1822, which position he retained for over a decade, while, from 1823 to 1845, he also served as mayor.

From JAMES RAY, Newark, Delaware. Requests that the documents in the case of the *James Lawrence* (see above, Ray and others to Clay, May 15, 1825) "be forwarded to our ambassador at Madrid [Alexander H. Everett], with instructions for him to Employ a Law agent, to prosecute the appeal under his orders. . . ." ALS. DNA, RG76, Misc. Claims, Spain.

On November 14 (copyist erroneously dated it as "Feby."), Daniel Brent, "by direction of the Secretary," informed Ray that Obadiah Rich, "now at Madrid," would "be instructed by our Minister there . . . to superintend the prosecution" in Ray's behalf, "of the appeal from Havanna [*sic*] to Madrid, in the case of the James Lawrence"; that Everett would also be instructed to advance the necessary funds; but that before the latter could be done Ray must arrange "re-imbursement." Copy, in DNA, RG59, Dom. Letters, vol. 21, pp. 189-90 (M40, R19).

APPLICATIONS, RECOMMENDATIONS   November, 1825

BENEDICT J. SEMMES, Prince Georges County (Maryland), recommends the bearer, Edward Taylor, for "a Clerkship in some of the Departments of the National Government." ALS. DNA, RG59, A. and R. (M531, R8). Unaddressed. Cf. above, Kent to Clay, October 1, 1825, note. Semmes, a graduate of Baltimore Medical School, practiced medicine and farmed at Piscataway, Maryland. He was a member of the State legislature (1825-1828, 1842, and 1843), at this time speaker of that assembly, and, from 1829 to 1833, a member of Congress.

GEORGE WARNER and others, Baltimore, recommend the *Baltimore Patriot and Mercantile Advertiser* to publish the laws. LS, signed by 80 persons. DNA, RG59, P. and D. of L. Dated: "November 1825." Warner, who had settled in Baltimore around 1775, was prominent in commercial and civic affairs of that city. The journal, published by Isaac Munroe, did not receive the recommended appointment. Munroe, who had earlier edited several Boston newspapers, had become part owner of the Maryland organ in 1814 and after 1817 had continued it alone.

To Charles Hammond

My Dear Sir   (Confidential)   Washn. 31st.[*i.e.,* 1st.] Nov. 1825
    I am glad to be able to tell you that at last circumstances admitted of the appointment of Mr. Caldwell as Judge of the Western District of Virginia[1] and he has been accordingly appointed. The Midshipmans appointment has been also sent to Mr. Ruffin.[2]
    Have you ever seen any thing more supremely ridiculous than the scene at Murfreesboro'— Such an exhibition on the occasion of the resignation of a seat in the Senate![3] It is a miserable compound imitation of the august event at Annapolis, when Washn. resigned the

sword of Liberty,[4] and the late Legislative receptions of La Fayette.[5]
I should like to see the same pen, that so justly criticised the Swartwout letter,[6] employed, on the more fit and fruitful subject, of the
General's address to the assembled wisdom of Tennessee.[7] The
briny tears that stole down the furrowed cheeks of the veteran hero!
The presence of the ladies; the solemnity and imposing character
of the scene; the hero surrounded by his "most intimate acquaintances, his bosom friends and companions in arms." And wherefore
all this solemn mockery? The resignation of a seat in the Senate
of the U.S.! obtained to promote an election to another office,[8] and
given up as soon as the occasion has passed by! Well, the General
having tried to be elected President by going into the Senate, now
means to make the experiment by going out of it. He *resigns* a place,
to which he had been called by the unsoli ited [*sic*] suffrage of the
Legislature, yet he never departs from his maxim neither to seek or
decline public stations! His friends however professed (by what
authority?) when he was elected, that a longer term of service than
one Congress would not be expected or required—would not be
expected or required by whom?

If, during the service in the Senate, which is thus pompously
terminated, any illustrious deeds had been performed—any brilliant schemes of policy, foreign or domestic, had been brought
forward and carried by the persevering eloquence of the Tennessee
Senator, the farce at Murfreesborough might be tolerated. But what
giant footstep has he left in the chamber of that body—what page
in the annals of his Country has he filled by his Legislative exertions? The moving cause of his resignation is stated to be that
he has been *advised* of a resolution of the Legislature (a resolution,
by the bye, that he was no doubt well advised of, before it was
introduced into the Legislature) presenting his name to the American people for their Chief Magistrate. Well; was he not advised
of a similar resolution formerly passed before he accepted the office
of Senator?[9] If its passage now furnishes sufficient cause for giving up
the Commission—ought not its adoption formerly to have prevented his acceptance of it—an acceptance which was attended with
the exclusion of one of the most useful & experienced members
of the Senate?[10]

Being about *again* to retire, he seizes that last occasion to address
some remarks to the Legislature of Tennessee on the subject of an
amendment which it had proposed to the Constitution.[11] And
what is that amendmt.? One that the Legislature was divided about,
and on which therefore the weight of his character & the weight
of his arguments were necessary to ensure its passage? Not at all;
on the contrary, that body was perfectly agreed about it. Why then
argue the matter with them? Undoubtedly not for their benefit, who

did not want the argument, but for that of the good people of the U. States. But he would go further than the Legislature has gone. He would *impose* a provision rendering any member of Congress (who of course as such is an officer under the general Government) ineligible to office under the General Government, during the term for which he is elected and two years thereafter, except in case of judicial office.[12] He would, to take the terms of his proposition as he lays it down, disqualify the member from being a member. But let us suppose that he means, what he certainly has not expressed with any precision, that the member is to be excluded from any other office, issuing from an Executive source. Well why except Judicial offices? Because, he says, no barrier should be interposed in selecting to the bench men of the first talents and integrity. If in the pursuit of the highest attainments, it is desirable, in regard to Judicial offices, to leave the field open, and the sphere of selection as wide as possible, why should not that be done in case of the appointment of Foreign ministers, Secretaries &c &c? The objection is that an influence is exerted on the Legislature by the President. That will equally happen in respect to judicial appointments. And, as to this alleged influence, why there is no doubt that it is mutual, acting and reacting; and both parties again acted upon by the great popular influence, through the medium of periodical elections.

But corruption will become the order of the day; and under the garb of conscientious sacrafices [*sic*] to establish *precedents* for the public good, evils of serious importance to the Republic may arise. Ah! there is the rub. If the general had been elected, all would have been pure. We shd. have heard nothing of corruption. But that any man shd. have thought that it was a dangerous precedent to elect a mere military chieftain sticks in the General's stomach. The Generals desire for the Presidency seems to be increased, as the prospect of obtaining it grows dim— He did not think, at the moment, last winter, when the question was decided, of imputing corruption to Mr. Adams. Then he was among the foremost to congratulate him. Then he wd. not accept a public dinner offered him by his friend Swartwout, lest the public shd. doubt his cordial acquiescence in the result.[13] Now he does not hesitate to insinuate that Mr. Adams descended from independent ground, and degraded himself by intriguing for the Presidency. Now he accepts every where of all the public dinners which may be offered him, even by the most obscure places, whose names are not, and never will be, indicated on the maps of the Country. And before the American public is tranquillized, after the agitations of a violent and warmly contested election, he sanctions a nomination which his friends at least expect will again set this Continent in motion, near four years before the period of decision. So eager is he for the office that, old and infirm as he is, and frail and liable to death as all men are, he bounds forward, over all the contingencies embosomed in three eventful years, and stands, dead or alive, before the American public as a Candidate for the *next* presidency commencing the 4h. day of March in the year of our Lord 1829! And, at the moment, when he thus lends himself to the premature disturbance of public repose, he is playing the affected part of a Cincinnatus by a retirement to the vocation of the plough! This early taking of the field recalls to recollection an anectdote [*sic*]. A french gentleman, a member of a State Legislature, entered in a hurried manner the body, at a moment when another member, at the close of some remarks, was resuming his Seat. The Frenchman immediately rose and said, I second de gentleman's motion. The Speaker told him the gentleman had made no motion— Den, said he, I second de gentleman's motion when he makes one. The legislature of Tennessee second the veteran's motion to be a Candidate, when three years hence, it may be necessary for the American people to recognize the utility of considering who are Candidates & their pretensions.

I send you these hasty observations, provoked by a procedure marked by as manifest a demagogical spirit as was ever displayed. Is it possible that any portion of the people can be deceived—that any should be so blind as not to see though the veil of hypocrecy [*sic*]?

I am as ever faithfully Your friend   H CLAY
C. Hammond Esqr.

ALS. InU. Addressed to Hammond at Cincinnati; "Forwarded by R McClure Wheeling." Richard McClure, a native of Ireland, was postmaster at Wheeling.

1 Alexander Caldwell.   2 Charles K. Ruffin.

3 See above, Carroll to Clay, October 4, 1825, note. On October 14 Jackson had addressed the Tennessee legislators at Murfreesboro, acknowledging their renomination of him (on October 6) for the Presidency, expressing appreciation for their approval of his course "on a late occasion," when he had left the issue of the presidential election "where by the constitution it was placed, free from any attempted controul, or interference," and submitting his letter of resignation as Senator. In the latter document he had explained that when previously his name had been before the nation as a candidate for the Presidency while he yet served in the Senate, he had found the "situation truly delicate," that his enemies could not charge him with "descending from the independent ground then occupied, or with degrading the trust reposed . . . by intriguing for the Presidential chair," but that, having again been presented as a candidate, he wished to be "excused from any further service in the Senate and . . . to retire from a situation where temptation may exist and suspicions arise in relation to the exercise of an influence tending to . . . [his] own aggrandisement." Tenn. Senate, *Journal, 1825*, pp. 118-20, 136.

4 Probably an allusion to the ceremony before the Continental Congress at Annapolis, on December 23, 1783, when Washington resigned his commission as general and commander-in-chief of the Continental Army.

5 See above, III, 815, 853, 868, 893-94n.

6 See above, Clay to Hammond, April 4, 23, 1825.

7 Early in December, 1825, Hammond published such an article over the signature, "Warren." Francis Phelps Weisenburger, "A Life of Charles Hammond, the First Great Journalist of the Old Northwest," *Ohio Archaeological and Historical Quarterly,* XLIII (1934), 379.   8 Cf. above, III, 501.

9 See above, III, 265.   10 John Williams.

11 On the second day of the session, Robert C. Foster, of Davidson County, near Nashville, formerly of Bardstown, Kentucky, Speaker of the Tennessee Senate in 1825,

had introduced a measure requesting that the State's congressional delegation "use their best exertions" to procure adoption of an amendment to the Constitution, "altering the mode of electing a President and Vice President." On October 8 the senate and on October 10 the house of representatives had agreed to appoint a joint committee to draft such a memorial. Tenn. Senate, *Journal, 1825*, pp. 19, 62, 94, 99. The object of the proposal was "to introduce an uniform mode throughout the United States of electing" these officers and, in the words of Foster, "to refer the election of these high and responsible officers immediately to the people, and thereby preclude all idea of fraud and combination in these elections." Quoted in *Washington Gazette*, October 29, 1825.

12 In suggesting, as Clay accurately recounts, this addition to the Tennessee proposal, Jackson argued that such a provision would, "in a considerable degree," free Congress "from that connection with the Executive Department, which at present gives strong ground of apprehension and jealousy on the part of the people." Tenn. Senate, *Journal, 1825*, p. 135. The amendment which the Tennessee Legislature subsequently recommended to Congress included a section providing that "no member of Congress shall be eligible to any office within the gift or nomination of the President, during the period for which he shall have been elected, and for six months thereafter, except appointments in the regular army or navy of the United States." U. S. H. of Reps., *Journal*, 19 Cong., 1 Sess., p. 109 (January 3, 1826).

13 Jackson to Samuel Swartwout and others, February 10, 1825, published in Washington *Daily National Intelligencer*, February 12, 1825.

To Christopher Hughes

My dear Hughes,   Washn. 1st. Nov. 1825.

I recd. your letter of the 28h. Ulto. announcing your arrival at New York. I congratulate you, most cordially, on your return to our Country. I have received several communications from you lately, private and public, under date at different points of Europe—Further notice of them now is not necessary as I shall so soon, I hope, have the gratification of seeing you. I shall not withdraw you, for some time at least, by a summons to this City, from those scenes of grief and of pleasure which await you, at your native place. Nor do I think there is necessity for your hastening hither. Under all circumstances indeed, (perhaps my own peculiar domestic afflictions, of which you appear to be informed, may have too much weight in this opinion) I do not think it advisable for you to come to us until towards the last of the month. The President's recent absence from the seat of Government, and other causes operating at this moment, leave us but little leisure.

I most heartily sympathise with you on the occasion of your losses. But those, of recent occurrence, have been of aged parents,[1] who have only paid, in due season, the common debt. Mine have been of dear children, just risen or rising into majority, concentrating a large share of our hopes and affections, prematurely (if we may be allowed so to think) called from among us—our chief consolation is, that they have been summoned to an eternal bliss, which we believe they merited.   Yrs truly & affectly   H. CLAY
C. Hughes Esqr

ALS. MiU-C. Addressed to Hughes at Baltimore but forwarded to Philadelphia.
1 Christopher Hughes, Sr.; Margaret Sanderson Hughes.

From William R. Dickinson

Dear Sir,—   Steubenville Nov. 1st. 1825
    Immediately upon receiving your order[1] to do so, I went and selected a pair of my finest merinos for you.— I then made arrangements with a Mr. Norris, of this place, (a careful good man[2]) to take them to Maysville.— This was done early in September, and he was prepared to start on the *very first rise* of *the river*.— About the first week in October, I calld [*sic*] upon him (by the bye I saw him very often) when he *assured* me that he would start on a particular day.—*the day was set*.— Confiding fully in this arrangement, I directed the clerk of the Bank, to forward the *bill*[3] to you about the 12 or 15th. of October, and went myself, to Canton, where I remained for nearly three weeks.— On my return, to my great mortification, I found that the sheep were still at my fold, and Mr. Norris at home, alledging that the low state of the river prevented his starting.— The bill too, was beyond my reach, and it only remained for me, to make a candid statement to you, and immediately to return you the money;—and as I intended visiting the city in all this month, I thought that I would wait a few weeks and offer you, personally the proper explanations.— The receipt of your letter of the 25th. Uto.[4] has rendered it necessary for me to write to you immediately.— Indeed I saw an intimation in the papers that you contemplated an immediate visit to the west,[5] in which event, I flattered myself that I should have the satisfaction of seeing you either at this place or at Wheeling.—
    The sheep and the boat and Mr. Norris are still ready to start at a moments warning, and Mr. N— says that he expects to be off in a day or two.— The ram however, as you intimate, will certainly not reach your farm in time—at least, the lambs will come at a very late season of the year.— But if the ewes do not have lambs this year, they will bring much finer lambs next season—
    I hope to see you very soon, and even if the sheep should start, I will, with great cheerfulness, return you the money, inasmuch as that they did not go agreeably to your instructions.— In a word, I shall be governed altogether by your own views—
    I stand reproved for not having advised you of the fact of drawing; —but my dear Sir, it was an intentional omission—; relying upon the confidence which I beleived [*sic*] you would place in me, I thought that the dft. would speak for itself, and that I should, by writing, commit a trespass upon feelings, which I knew to be deeply wounded from recent mournful intelligence.[6]
    I hope, in a week or two to see you, when I will assuredly set the matter right— Mean time, I am with sentiments of the highest respect Your friend & obt. Servt.   W, R, Dickinson

ALS. DLC-HC (DNA, M212, R2). Addressed to Clay.
1 Not found. Cf. above, Clay to Beatty, September 24, 1825.
2 Not further identified.   3 Not found.   4 Not found.
5 Cf. above, Reaney to Clay, October 25, 1825. Newspaper report not found.
6 See above, Clay to Crittenden, August 22, 1825, note; Mazureau to Clay, September 19, 1825.

MISCELLANEOUS LETTERS   November 1, 1825

To HENRY HITCHCOCK, Cahaba. Transmits commission as Federal attorney for the Southern District of Alabama. Copy. DNA, RG59, Dom. Letters, vol. 21, p. 181 (M40, R19). Cf. above, Hall to Clay, August 16, 1825, note.

From JAMES BARBOUR, Department of War. States, in response to a letter, dated October 13 (not found), from (Philander) Chase to Clay, concerning the possibility of obtaining remuneration for the educational expenses "of Six or Eight Indian Youths," that an annual appropriation of $10,000 was provided by act of Congress, March 3, 1819 (3 *U. S. Stat.,* 516-17) "for the Civilization of the Indians"; encloses copies of regulations established under the act; cites two exceptions to the general rule that disbursements are confined to schools in "the Indian Country"; and expresses willingness "to contribute from the Civilization fund, to the Revd. Bishop" an allowance of $100 per annum for each of "Six Indian Youths to be educated at his Seminary." Copy. DNA, RG75, Letters Sent, vol. 2, pp. 219-20. In August, Bishop Chase had promised the Mohawks "to take several of their young men and boys, board and educate them." Chase, *Reminiscences . . . ,* II, 491. The War Department allowed him $100 a year, each, for the expenses of educating six Indians; and in November, 1825, the Bishop brought the boys to his farm at Worthington. Cf. above, Chase to Clay, January 27, 1825, note.

From H[ENRY] A. S. DEARBORN, Custom House, Boston. States, in reply to Clay's letter of October 24, that no occasion has arisen for the collection of discriminating duties under the first section of the act of July 7, 1824, and that "the opinion on . . . the second section" is that an "additional discriminating impost" should be collected. LS. DNA, RG59, Misc. Letters (M179, R63).

APPLICATIONS, RECOMMENDATIONS   November 1, 1825

JAMES DILL, Lawrenceburg, Indiana, recommends appointment of (Milton) Gregg and (David V.) Culley, editors of the *Indiana Palladium,* to publish the laws. States that these young men "most zealously and warmly advocated *Some* of the most prominent members of our present administration." ALS. DNA, RG59, P. and D. of L. See above, Holman to Clay, October 24, 1825, note.

M[ILTON] GREGG and D[AVID] V. CULLEY, Lawrenceburg, Indiana, solicit appointment to publish the laws in the *Indiana Palladium.* ALS. DNA, RG59, P. and D. of L.

ALEXANDER MILLER, Paris (Kentucky), solicits an appointment. "There is no news here butt what the Papers will inform you of— Jacksons freinds [*sic*]—with a number of your old ones is makeing much hub ub about next Election a matter that is 3 years and 6 months off—what a Shame— I combat them with tongue and Pen; why Covet or envy the Gentelmen [*sic*] of his place when he is doeing all, and every thing for the Good an Honour of his Country— the Fact is, that they love *War* and *Blood*—he Loves *Peace*." ALS. DNA, RG59, A. and R. (MR3). Miller, not further identified, received no appointment.

JOHN D. PATTON, Hopkinsville, Kentucky, states that application was made "last Winter" for admission of one of his sons (Alexander W. Patton) "in the Academy at West Point"; adds: "My brother Benjamin . . . intended, when he last saw you to have solicited your aid in procuring his admission; but his extreme indisposition, as he informed me, caused him to forget it— Nature was *then* slumbering to a final repose"; and cites "Major [Robert P.] Henry as a reference for the son. ALS. DNA, RG94, Military Academy, Cadet Applications, 1825-164 (M688, R38). Endorsed by Clay on cover: "Respectfully refered [*sic*] to the Secretary of War [James Barbour], by H. C." Neither John D. nor Alexander W. Patton has been further identified. The young man was rejected in 1825 and again in 1826 in his application for admission to West Point. Benjamin W. Patton had died February 11, 1825.

JAMES RARIDEN, Centerville, Indiana, recommends E (dmund) S. Buxton, editor of the Richmond (Indiana) *Public Ledger,* for appointment to publish the laws. ALS. DNA, RG59, P. and D. of L. Rariden, born at Cynthiana, Kentucky, had studied law in Indiana and had begun practice there in 1820. He had been State prosecuting attorney from 1822 to 1825, a State senator since 1823, and a Clay elector in the presidential campaign of 1824. He was a State senator again in 1829, a member of the State House of Representatives in 1827, 1830, 1832, and 1833, and a member of Congress from 1837 to 1841. On the proposed appointment, see above, Hendricks to Clay, September 21, 1825, note.

J. WINGATE, JR., Portland, Maine, recommends the Portland *American Patriot,* formerly the *Independent Statesman and Maine Republican,* to publish the laws. ALS. P. and D. of L. See above, Herrick to Clay, October 27, 1825, note.

Check to Josiah S. Johnston

2d. Nov. 1825.

Pay to the Honble J. S. Johnston or order the sum of five hundred and eighty eight dollars and 75 Cents.
The Cashr of the Off. of Dt. & Dt. Washn. City[1]   H. CLAY
588.75/100

ADS. DLC-TJC (DNA, M212, R16). Endorsed on verso: "J. S. Johnston."
[1] Richard Smith.

Check to John McLeod

2d. Nov. 1825.

Pay to John McLeod or order (on loan) Two hundred dollars.
Cashr. of the Off. of Dt. & Dt. Washington City[1]   H. CLAY

ADS. DLC-TJC (DNA, M212, R16). Endorsed on verso by McLeod, principal of Central Academy, in Washington, where James Brown Clay was probably now enrolled as a student.   [1] Richard Smith.

Property Deed from Mary O. Russell

[November 2, 1825]

[For the sum of $1,000 in current money of the United States, paid and acknowledged, Mary O. Russell conveys to Henry Clay a tract on the waters of Hickman Creek, containing 50 acres, bounded "Beginning at (A) N 45 E one and two tenth poles from a broken top Elm on the S.W. Side of the Winchester road corner to Richard Downton running N 45 E with the line of a tract of land formerly owned by Thos Wallace purchased by Said Clay of James Minter[1] and now occupied by Nathl. Pettit 186 poles to a hickory Stump corner to John Price thence S 32 1/2 E 53 poles to a Stake near an old Locust Stump thence S 47ıı 36" W 146 8/10 poles to a Stake in the winchester road thence N 76 3/4 W with Said road 53 poles to the Beginning," with appurtenances. General warranty of title. Signature witnessed by Robert Scott and Francis Downing, and the indenture recorded on testimony by the witnesses, November 7, 1825.]

Copy. Fayette County Court, Deed Book 1, pp. 76-77. A survey of this property, dated October 31, 1825, ADS by James Darnaby, surveyor of Fayette County, is located in DLC-TJC (DNA, M212, R16). Cf. above, Memorandum to Scott, July 6, 1825.

[1] See above, Property Deed, July 4, 1825.

DIPLOMATIC NOTES   November 2, 1825

From JOSE MARIA SALAZAR, Washington. States that "the great assembly of the plenipotentiaries of America" is to convene soon in Panama and that Clay has indicated the conditions on which the United States would send representatives (see above, Tudor to Clay, April 12, 1825, note; Clay to Anderson, September 16, 1825) ; extends an invitation, by authority of his government and with the knowledge that similar invitations will be made by the ministers from Mexico and Guatemala (see below, Obregón to Clay, November 3, 1825; Cañaz to Clay, November 14, 1825) ; asserts that the subjects to be discussed there will not tend to violate the neutrality of the United States, that certain matters will concern the belligerents alone, and that others will involve both belligerents and neutrals; cites, as examples, four problems that may be considered: "some principles of international law, the confusion of which have occasioned great evils to humanity," "the best way of resistance to any future colonisation of the European powers on the American continent, and to prevent their interference in the present wars between Spain and her ancient colonies," means for abolition of the African slave trade, and relations with Haiti and "other countries of our hemisphere that in future may find themselves in the same circumstances." LS (accompanied by translation, also LS). DNA, RG59, Notes from Colombian Legation (M51, R2). Translation published in *American State Papers, Foreign Relations,* V, 836-37.

MISCELLANEOUS LETTERS   November 2, 1825

To TENCH RINGGOLD. States that the Baron de Maltitz has given assurance that his servant, accused of breach of peace, will surrender himself to Ringgold at four o'clock this afternoon; requests that Ringgold deliver him to the Mayor of Georgetown "to be dealt with according to law." Copy. DNA, RG59, Dom. Letters, vol. 21, pp. 181-82 (M40, R19). Cf. above, Clay to Ringgold, October 30, 1825; Cox to Clay, October 31, 1825.

From J. BARTLETT, Eastport (Maine). States that, after obtaining through (James) Maury and (Richard) Rush from (William) Huskisson an interpretation of British law exempting from tonnage duties at Canadian ports vessels of the United States carrying only passengers and their baggage, he established steamboat service between Eastport and St. John, New Brunswick; that no orders to this effect were received, however, by the customhouse at St. John; that charges against him for tonnage duties amount to $4,000; and that subsequent inquiry through Maury has brought a reply that Huskisson's explanation, or "indulgence," had been predicated on "some understanding," about which Bartlett knew nothing. Encloses copies of correspondence relative to the case and asks the protection and interposition of the Government. ALS. DNA, RG59, Misc. Letters (M179, R63). Endorsed by Clay on wrapper: "Write to Mr. Bartlett and ask if the $4000 mentd. in his letter have been actually paid by him; and if not whether he is bound & how for its paymt." Answer not found; Bartlett not further identified. Cf. below, Bartlett to Clay, June 5, 1826.

From S[AMUEL] L. S[OUTHARD], Navy Department. Transmits a copy of a letter from Isaac Hull, "relating to the seizure and condemnation of the American Ship China" by Spanish forces at Callao; requests instructions so "Commodore Hull may be advised what course to pursue." Copy. DNA, RG45, Executive Letterbook, vol. 1821-1831, p. 137. See above, Southard to Clay, May 5, 1825.

APPLICATIONS, RECOMMENDATIONS   November 2, 1825

JOHN MOODY, New Canton, Buckingham County, Virginia, again solicits an appointment. ALS. DNA, RG59, A. and R. (MR3). See above, April 2, 1825, note.

C[HARLES] TAIT, Claiborne, Alabama, recommends David R. W. McRae of Alabama, a native of South Carolina, as United States attorney for West Florida. ALS. DNA, RG59, A. and R. (MR5). McRae, not further identified, did not receive appointment.

From James Wolcott, Jr.

Hon. Henry Clay   Southbridge Novr 3d 1825
Dear Sir

[Submits his views on "a further protection on fine cotton goods"; believes that a recommendation to that end by the President would meet favorable response by both houses of Congress; declares: "That stuborn [sic] opposition from the South, and part of the North will never again be witnessed as heretofore"; and argues that "the most sure dependence on a revenue, must be based on the prosperity of the citizens" rather than on the income from import duties.]

Pardon me Sir for taking this liberty in intruding my Opinions on you. Had I not known your perseveran[ce] in the cause of the "American Policy," I would not have troubled you thus. If in the midst of your troubles in your official capacity, you can spare time to write me your views on this subject, you may depend on my Keeping it sacred from the public. I believe you have converted Mr Webster to your opinions on the nation [*sic*] policy. Mr Webster I find by conversing with him, is a great friend to the "American Policy." I am with great respect Yours truly   JAMES WOLCOTT JR

ALS. DNA, RG59, Misc. Letters (M179, R63). The correspondent was probably the son of J. Wolcott, cited above, III, 640n.

DIPLOMATIC NOTES   November 3, 1825

From CHARLES R. VAUGHAN, Washington. Solicits "the interference of the Government of the United States with that of the State of New York in order to procure the arrest of Michael Neilson, a native of Scotland, who has taken refuge in that State after having committed in his own Country, the crime of Forgery." States that he is "well aware" that he is not authorized by any treaty "to call upon the Government of the United States to cause the arrest of a British subject, who may have sought an Asylum in this Country from punishment due to his crimes"; that a New York law, enacted April 5, 1822, authorizes the Governor of that State "to deliver up to Justice" a person charged with certain crimes committed outside the jurisdiction of the United States; that an earlier application, made by the British consul at New York, for Neilson's arrest has not been successful; and that defects in that application are now remedied by the submission of additional documentary proof of the crime and by this formal application of the British Minister through the Department of State. LS. DNA, RG59, Notes from British Legation, vol. 14 (M50, R15). Neilson not further identified.

From PABLO OBREGON, Washington. Invites the United States to send "representatives to the Congress of Panama." Notes that a similar invitation is being extended by the Colombian Minister (see above, Salazar to Clay, November 2, 1825). ALS. DNA, RG59, Notes from Mexican Legation, vol. 1 (M54, R1). Translation published in *American State Papers, Foreign Relations*, V, 836.

MISCELLANEOUS LETTERS   November 3, 1825

From W[ILLIAM] J. COFFEE, "City of New York." Requests Clay to present an enclosed note to the President; solicits Clay's support for Coffee's claim to the premium, offered during the administration of (James) Monroe, for the best design submitted for the pediment of the Capitol. ALS. DNA, RG59, Misc. Letters (M179, R63). Coffee, an English sculptor and painter, had come to the United States in 1816 and for the next decade resided in New York City. From 1827 to 1845 he lived at Albany, where he did several of the bas-reliefs for the city hall. He has not been identified as a designer for the National Capitol.

APPLICATIONS, RECOMMENDATIONS   November 3, 1825

JAMES WILSON, Steubenville (Ohio), solicits reappointment to publish the laws in *The Western Herald and Steubenville Gazette*. ALS. DNA, RG59, P. and D. of L. The contract was continued throughout the Adams administration.

APPLICATIONS, RECOMMENDATIONS   November 4, 1825

HEMAN ALLEN, Valparaiso, states that, about a year ago, he informed the Department that his "salary was inadequate to the necessary expenses of living" there and that he should like an appointment as Minister to Peru, but only if given another outfit. ALS. DNA, RG59, Dip. Disp., Chile, vol. 1 (M-T2, R1). Received March 20, 1826. Allen, remaining in Chile until 1827, did not receive an alternative appointment.

D[AVID] C. PINKHAM, who states that he has "a slight acquaintance" with Clay and has "a short time since removed from Kentucky to this place with an intention of practicing law," seeks appointment as district attorney in the place of Albert J. Claggett, deceased. ALS. DNA, RG59, A. and R. (MR5). Undated; postmarked: "Pensacola Nov 4." Pinkham did not receive the appointment requested. In 1833 he was named judge of Monroe County court, Florida Territory.

JOHN SAXTON, Canton, Ohio, editor of the *Ohio Repository*, seeks appointment to publish the laws. ALS. DNA, RG59, P. and D. of L. Saxton, born in Pennsylvania, had moved in 1815 to Canton, where he had founded and for the next 56 years edited the *Ohio Repository*. A Federalist, later a Whig, and still later a Republican, he did not receive the appointment here requested.

C[ORNELIUS] P. VAN NESS and others, Montpelier, Vermont, recommend appointment of the Montpelier *Vermont Watchman*, edited by E(zekiel) P. Walton, to publish the laws. LS by 18 members of the Vermont State Government. *Ibid.* Born in New Hampshire, Walton had been educated in Vermont and had begun work as an apprentice on the *Vermont Watchman* at its founding in 1807. He became one of the owners of the journal in 1810, sole proprietor in 1816, and remained its editor until shortly before his death in 1855. The journal was designated to publish the laws of the Congress beginning in December, 1825, one of but ten changes in such patronage made at this time.

INSTRUCTIONS AND DISPATCHES   November 5, 1825

From HEMAN ALLEN, Valparaiso, no. 22. Reports an unsuccessful insurrection against the authority of the Director, (Ramón de) Freire, the subsequent dissolution of the "self-constituted" Congress at Santiago (cf. above, Allen to Clay, September 9, 1825), the appointment of "Mr. Campino, a very worthy, good man, as Minister of Foreign Relations," and the banishment of eleven of the leaders of the revolution, whose "concealed object" had been to restore (Bernardo) O'Higgins "to his lost authority." Expresses belief that the changes have resulted in "a better feeling in the government" toward the United States, although "The English interest in Chile, created by mining companies, commercial relations, & intermarrying with the natives, constituting in all a pretty numerous body, and supported by the influence of a strong naval force, is already very great, and seems destined to direct her future course." Encloses a copy of "a reclamation" he has made "in the case of the American Brig, Warrior," and states that "a very early or satisfactory" decision on any claim cannot be expected. Notes the latest information from Peru. Cites seizures by

Chile of foreign vessels and mistreatment of their crews as necessitating an increase of the United States naval force, "should the war continue between Spain and these countries." ALS. DNA, RG59, Dip. Disp., Chile, vol. 1 (M-T2, R1). Extract published in Manning (arr.), *Diplomatic Correspondence . . . Latin-American Nations,* II, 1106-1107.

Joaquín Campino, who had been serving as a member of the Chilean Congress, acted as Foreign Minister only until February, 1826. On March 6, 1828, he became Chile's first Envoy Extraordinary and Minister Plenipotentiary to the United States, where he remained until June, 1829. The enclosed "reclamation," undated and endorsed with the notation that it had not yet been sent because of the "present peculiar state of the government," complains of the treatment accorded the American brig *Warrior* and its officers and crew while docked at Coquimbo, Chile, in 1820 to 1821. Several sailors had been impressed into the Chilean Navy; the mate had been tortured; and the vessel had been searched, her rudder, ballast, long boat, and some of the cargo seized—all on the unproved suspicion that the brig was carrying munitions to the Spanish. Damages demanded for the owner were set at $15,868. The Chilean Government in 1841 awarded $15,000 in settlement of this claim. Miller (ed.), *Treaties. . . ,* IV, 325-28.

From HEMAN ALLEN, Valparaiso, no. 23. Reports receipt of letters from Commodore (Isaac) Hull relative to the Peruvian seizure of the *General Brown;* notes that "every thing is very quiet, both here and at Santiago." ALS. DNA, RG59, Dip. Disp., Chile, vol. 1 (M-T2, R1). On the case of the *General Brown,* see above, Tudor to Clay, June 8, 1825, note.

From SAMUEL LARNED, Santiago de Chile. Transmits "certain publications which have lately made their appearance here," including articles by (Juan) Egaña on the religious and political institutions of the United States; states that he was induced by (Joaquín) Campino and others "to undertake a reply"; and encloses copies of the "two numbers" that he has published. ALS. DNA, RG59, Dip. Disp., Chile, vol. 1 (M-T2, R1). Egaña, born at Lima, Peru, had taught law and theology and practiced law there for five years before moving to Chile in 1810, when that country first established its independence from Spain. He had been elected a representative to the first Congress, had been imprisoned during the period of Spanish reassertion of authority (1814 to 1817), and, after the subsequent Patriot victory, had been active in formulating the new government, presiding at the constitutional convention of 1823 and serving for years as a senator.

From JOHN RODGERS, "U. S. Ship N Carolina Gibraltar Bay." Acknowledges receipt, by the *Brandywine,* of Clay's communication of September 6; reports that, "At the time of quitting the [Greek] Archipelago with the Squadron," he "left the Sloop of War Ontario there for the protection of our commerce"; states his expectation that the vessel will rejoin him about January 1 and that he will receive by her an answer to his letter of September 20 to the Captain Pashaw (Khosref Mehemet—see above, Rodgers to Clay, October 14, 1825). ALS. *Ibid.,* Turkey, vol. 1 (M46, R2). Received December 29.

From GEORGE W. SLACUM, Buenos Aires. Transmits copies of documents relative to the case of the *Henry;* suggests the desirability of a United States naval force in the area, especially as he thinks war will break out soon between the Provinces of Río de la Plata and Brazil. LS. DNA, RG59, Cons. Disp., Buenos Aires, vol. 2 (M70, R3). Received February 13, 1826. The enclosed documents, based upon reports by Buenos Aires boatmen, state that on October 19, while Captain (H. T.) Whittredge was ashore, the *Henry*, "then lying below the outer roads," was boarded by marines from the Brazilian Squadron, the mate was struck "with the flat part of their Swords," the cook was beaten, the water casks and stanchions in the holds were destroyed—"all which was done under the pretence that the Vessel had Arms on board for the Patriots." Upon his return, Captain Whittredge had been ordered to present his papers aboard the Brazilian flagship but had been detained there only briefly. The vessel had subsequently proceeded on her voyage without the filing of an official report by the captain. Enclosures endorsed (AE) by Clay: "To be submitted to the President."

MISCELLANEOUS LETTERS   November 5, 1825

From JOHN C. JONES, [JR.], Boston. Acknowledges receipt of Clay's letter of October 24; states that he will continue as "Agent for the United States at the Sandwich Islands until otherwise advised"; cites the "always heavy" expenditures for "the support of destitute seamen" in those islands; and requests advice concerning the extent to which he is authorized to make advances and how claims are to be adjusted. LS. DNA, RG59, Cons. Disp., Honolulu, vol. 1 (M144, R1). On November 10, Daniel Brent replied, "by direction of the Secretary," that Jones' "own discretion, under the" printed consular instructions is his "best guide" in making disbursements "for the relief of destitute seamen. . . ." Copy, in DNA, RG59, Cons. Instr., vol. 2, p. 372 (M78, R2).

APPLICATIONS, RECOMMENDATIONS   November 5, 1825

DOUGLASS MAGUIRE, Indianapolis, Indiana, recommends Morris Morris as receiver of public moneys, since John Hawkins, previously recommended (above, October 4, 1825), declines applying. Adds: "I write to you . . . because you are the only member of the Cabinet of whom we have much knowledge, or in whose prospects we are very deeply interested. Mr. Morris is an emigrant from that state whose councils you have enlightened, and whose bar you have adorned. He always has been, is now, and in all probability always will be a warm political friend of yours." ALS. DNA, RG59, A. and R. (MR3). Endorsed: "Referred to Secy of Treasury." Morris, who had been a merchant at Carlisle, Kentucky, following the War of 1812, had moved to Indianapolis in October, 1821, and had there become active in politics. He was a representative in the Indiana Legislature in 1826-1827 and for many years State auditor, but he did not receive the appointment here recommended.

JOSEPH M. WHITE, Charlottesville, Virginia, recommends Robert Mitchell of Pensacola as collector of the port and district of Pensacola; requests that no one be named district attorney for West Florida until White can reach Washington and lay recommendations before the President. ALS. *Ibid.* (MR5). See above, Brackenridge to Clay, May 1, 1825, note.

To Charles Hammond

My Dear Sir   Washn. 6h. Nov. 1825
    I received your obliging letter of the 26h. Ulto.[1] I had previously

addressed a letter to you[2] to the care of the Post Master at Wheeling to be forwarded to you at Cincinnati, if you had left that neighbourhood. In that letter I informed you of the appointments of Mr. Caldwell and Mr. Ruffin. And I also suggested the propriety of your writing on the ridiculous farce at Murfreesborough. I am confirmed in the propriety of your doing so by subsequent reflection. It is a fine subject. Such pretensions to virtue and patriotism! The reception of the resignation and nomination, on this side of the mountains, is such as I had expected. All condemn the latter as premature—even Noah and Simpson,[3] the latter having relinquished his paper. The whole scene in Tennessee was got up, no doubt, by the prompting of the General to furnish an occasion for his resignation.

I observe what you say about Jennings.[4] I could wish, for the credit of the Country, that he would not take his seat, but if he does I hope the affair will not be disturbed. I will comply with your request as far as is possible.

I presented your pamphlet[5] to the President

As to the Georgia business[6] (entre nous) we are attempting what you suggest, to re-model the treaty. But suppose the Indians reject all overtures to treat, and refuse to confirm the former treaty, what then is to be done? I confess I see, in that contingency, no way to avoid the agitation of the subject before Congress. I believe Troup's re-election (which from his lean majority is not to be boasted of) in some measure owing to Gaines's want of prudence.[7] The event is of very little importance. Indeed I doubt if his party is not destined to be more favorable to the administration than that of Clarke. Will you be at Columbus this winter? Do you think that the General Assembly would pass a resolution expressive of its disposition to support the present Administration?[8] Is such a resolution expedient? Would it not have an anti-Jackson tendency?

I thank you for your kind condolence on my late affliction.[9] It has been a most heart-rending event, and has put in requisition all my fortitude. However unavailing reason tells us regrets are, our feelings nevertheless are beyond our absolute control.

With great regard I am truly Your friend   H. CLAY
C. Hammond Esqr.

ALS. InU.   1 Not found.
2 Above, November 1, 1825.
3 Mordecai M. Noah; Stephen Simpson, whose paper, the Philadelphia *Columbian Observer*, had ceased publication in July, 1825.
4 David Jennings, who resigned his seat at the close of the next Session of Congress.
5 Not found.
6 See above, Clay to Southard, July 3, 1825, note.
7 See above, Clay to Hammond, September 23, 1825.
8 No such resolution was passed. Hammond declined pressing for one. Cf. Weisen-

burger, "A Life of Charles Hammond. . . ," *Ohio Archaeological and Historical Quarterly*, XLIII (1934), 381.
    9 The death of Susan Clay Duralde.

To Jesse L. Holman

Dear Sir   ' Washington 6h. Nov. 1825
    I received, in due course of the mail, your obliging letter of the 24h. Oct. Your recommendation of Mess. Gregg and Cully Editors of the Indiana Palladium to be designated as printers of the Laws shall have full consideration, when I come to act on that subject. For the friendly sentiments expressed in your letter I am very thankful. I have not been an indifferent spectator of your progress in life, which I have, on the contrary, witnessed with much gratification. As to the part taken by you, in the late presidential election, with which I was acquainted, you would have been unworthy of the esteem which I entertain for you, if you had not have independ ly formed and acted on your own judgment. The reasons which you assign for your preference of an other have great force, and being satisfactory to you, are entirely so to me.
    With my best wishes for your continued prosperity, in which Mrs. Clay cordially joins me, I remain Faithfully your friend and obedient Servant   H. CLAY
The Honble Jesse L. Holman.

    ALS. Owned by Holman Hamilton, Lexington, Kentucky.

APPLICATIONS, RECOMMENDATIONS   November 6, 1825

J[OHN] LEE, "Needwood," recommends William Crawford as bearer of dispatches to Europe. ALS. DNA, RG59, A. and R. (MR1). Lee, born at "Needwood," the family estate near Frederick, Maryland, and educated as a lawyer, had been a member of Congress (1823-1825) and subsequently served in both houses of the Maryland Legislature. On the recommended appointment, see above, Crawford to Clay, October 8, 1825, note.

To [John Quincy Adams]

                                                7h. Nov. [1825]
    Mr. Clay presents his respectful Compliments to the President, and he regrets extremely that late events[1] will not allow him the honor of accepting his invitation to dinner on wednesday next.
The President

    AN. MHi-Adams Papers.
    1 The death of his daughters, Eliza Clay and Susan Clay Duralde.

Check to Pairo and Prout

7 Nov. 1825

Pay to the order of Pairo and Prout Two hundred and ninety eight dollars and 55 Cents.   H CLAY

Cashr. of the Off. of Dt. & Dt. Washington[1]—

298 55/100

ADS. DLC-TJC (M212, R16). Endorsed on verso: "Pairo & Prout." Thomas W. Pairo and Prout, probably William, were partners as stationers and carpet dealers in Washington.   [1] Richard Smith.

To Peter Pedersen

The Chevalier Pederson [sic], Minister Resident from Denmark.

Sir,   Department of State, 7th. Novr. 1825.

I have the honor to acknowledge the receipt of your Note of the 29th. October last, refering [sic] to the project submitted by you of a Commercial Convention between the United States and Denmark and to the conferences, in relation to it, which we have had together.[1] You request, for the information of the Government of Denmark, the views of that of the United States on the subject, and particularly the conditions on which the United States are disposed to form a Convention with Denmark, taking as far as may be practicable the project presented by you as a basis. I proceed to comply with that request.

The United States would have no difficulty in agreeing to the articles proposed by you, with some modifications, and with the addition of some other articles not contained in your project. But your project embraces a principle more extensive than has yet entered into the Commercial policy of the United States, that of allowing the Vessels of the two Countries reciprocally to import any manufactures and productions of the Countries; [sic] the importation of which is allowed by law, at the same rate of tonnage duties, and paying paying [sic] on the Cargo no higher duties of import in the vessels of the one than in those of the other party. To this principle, if it were adopted by all maritime Nations, the United States would be willing to accede; but the principle is one requiring much consideration, when it is proposed to be applied to the Navigation and Commerce of a particular Nation only. It was to give more opportunity for that consideration that I expressed to you a wish to suspend our negotiation for a short time.

If we should happily be able to effect any accomodation [sic] of that point, there would yet remain other arrangements which it is thought should enter into the contemplated Convention, and these I will now particularize. They are.

1. That no higher duties shall be imposed on the productions of one of the two Countries, in the ports of the other, than are imposed on similar productions of any other country.

2. That no prohibition of the produce of one of the two Countries shall be imposed which does not equally extend to all other Countries.

3. Whatever favor may be hereafter granted by either of the two Powers to the Commerce or Navigation of any other Nation, shall be equally extended to the other party, freely, if it was granted without compensation, and upon paying the same equivalent, if an equivalent were given.

4. Consuls to be reciprocally admitted into the ports of the two Countries and their Exequaturs to be granted gratis.

5. When Citizens or Subjects of the one party Die in the Country of the other, their Estate shall not be subject to any droit de detraction, but shall pass to their Successors, free from all duty.

We are desirous also that the Convention should embrace the liberal and humane principles, 1st. to abolish privateering on the Ocean, if War unhappily should break out between the two Countries, and 2dly. that free Ships shall make free Goods, but these would not form an unsuperable [*sic*] obstacle to the conclusion of a Convention.

Having thus complied with your request I take pleasure in adding that the personal esteem which is felt for you would render it highly agreeable that we should be able to bring our negotiation to such a conclusion as would promote the interests of both Countries.

I pray you to accept assurances of the distinguished Consideration entertained for you by Your obedient Servant.   H. CLAY.

Copy. DNA, RG59, Notes to Foreign Legations, vol. 3, pp. 451-52 (M38, R3). ALS draft, in CSmH.

1 An unsigned, undated list, of eleven proposals, possibly in the hand of a State Department clerk, constituting what appears to be an informal American counter-projet of a treaty with Denmark, is located in DNA, RG11, Records Having General Legal Effect, Unperfected Treaty P. Included in it are items 1 and 2 of the "arrangements" here presented by Clay, suggestions conforming to Clay's items 3 and 4, and matters found in both Pedersen's projet and the treaty. It does not include item 5 or Clay's "liberal and humane principles" in regard to privateering and mutual rights. A point-by-point commentary on these proposals, bearing no salutation or address, but signed by Pedersen, October 27, 1825, accompanies the eleven proposals.

From James Erwin

Dr Sir,   Cahauba [*sic*] Nov. 7th. 1825.

I wrote you by last weeks mail informing you of our arrival at this place & the determination of Anne[1] to remain here until Jany. I shall leave here in the morning for N Orleans.

In my last I mentioned to you that the appointment of U States Atto, for this Section of the State was vacant, and that Mr Hitch-cock[2] & others were applicants, I have just learned that a compromise has taken place between Dillet & Rust[3] for the purpose of Securing to the latter the appointment over Mr H, and much to my surprize that Some men of Standing have recommended Rust thirsty to effect Some local interest?—& that Mr Owen & Mr, King[4] who have Set out for Washington intended waiting on the President with those recommendations in behalf of Mr Rust— I before Stated to you that at home "Rust had no character" that is none in his favor, he is what might be properly called a Flippant Lawyer, but his Character has for the last Eight years been so bad as nearly if not entirely until very lately to exclude him from the Society of Gentlemen who regarded their own standing   Nor is he now taken by the hand, But for the purpose of effecting Some party purposes—and that too by the avowed enemies of the Administra-tion, I will venture to Say that altho the appointment of Distt Atto is so responsible a one in a pecuniary point of view & no bonds to be given, that no one of those gentlemen who recommend Mr Rust would trust him for $500— If they would I would not— as to his political importance he has none but the object of Owen & King both of whom are unfriendly to Mr Hitchcock, is to thwart him and to do so will make use of any one,

In my last I detailed to you Some of the late remarks of the Hone, Mr King I find the conversation then related was not the only one of the Kind, Owen is more prudent—but not less willing to pull down both you & Mr Adams—& either of them would be glad to see Mr Adams make such an appointment as Mr Rust—for a more unpopular one could not be made,   the approaching Session of the Legislature of this State is to the people here, one of the most interesting that they'l have for many years—they have all the judges & State officers to reelect & the Seat of Govermt to locate permanently, their College to establish,[5] & all the little factions are on the alert to obtain an advantage, I have no doubt that Mr Kelly[6] (late U S Senator) now a member of the Legislature of this State will introduce Resolutions in favor of Genl, Jackson, Similar to those lately passed by the Legislature of Tennessee, which will pass with great ease, as no one however much opposed to them, will risk his popularity with the people,[7]

On the subject of the appointment of Dist Atto, I have only to add, that if there is no impropriety or rather if you feel no delicacy in presenting the claims of Mr Hitchcock before the President, I should be greatly obliged by your interest in his behalf— inde-pendant [sic] of all feeling arising out of the existing connection existing [*sic*] between him & Me,[8] I can safely say to you, that no man in the State is better qualified to do justice to the appointment and as to character as a lawyer & Gentleman not even his worst enemy could make an objection— But Should there be a single reason, why you should not interfere in this matter, I beg then that you will not do so— But whether Mr H, gets the appointment or not I do sincerely hope that the enemies of Mr Adams, will not so far impose on him as to induce him to appoint Such a man as Rust— I again Say with great Confidence that a more unpopular appointment Could not be made in the State,   Anne joins me in her love to Mrs. Clay & for yourself   Believe me Very Truly   J ERWIN

ALS. DLC-TJC (DNA, M212, R13).
1 Mrs. Erwin. The letter has not been found.
2 Henry Hitchcock.   3 James Dellet; David Rust.
4 George W. Owen (cf. above, Owen to Clay, September 25, 1825); William Rufus de Vane King.
5 The capital of Alabama was shifted in 1826 from Cahaba to Tuscaloosa. The University of Alabama, for which provision had been made by a grant of public lands under the State enabling act of 1819, had been evolving slowly: the school had been chartered in 1820, and sale of lands had been provided for by the legislature of 1822; but the location of the institution was not designated until a site within fifteen miles of Tuscaloosa was called for by act of 1827, and the specific tract was not chosen until the spring of 1828. *Memorial Record of Alabama* . . . (2 vols.; Madison, Wisc., 1893), I, 154-56.   6 William Kelly.
7 Cf. above, Clay to Hammond, November 6, 1825, note. A resolution stating that it was the intention of the members of the Alabama House of Representatives "to support him [Jackson] at the next Presidential election for that important office, by every honorable means in their power," was introduced in the Alabama Legislature on June 8, 1827, by Matthew F. Raney, of Greene County, and passed by a vote of 48 to 10. Ala. H. of Reps., *Journal, 1826-1827*, p. 233. A similar resolution, expressing belief "that it would be to the interest of the United States for him [Jackson] to be elected President for the next presidential term," was adopted in the following session (December 31, 1827), by a vote of 58 to 5. *Ibid., 1827-1828*, p. 183.
8 Hitchcock had married Erwin's sister, Anne, in 1821.

DIPLOMATIC NOTES   November 7, 1825

To the BARON DE MAREUIL. Acknowledges receipt of his note of October 4, "which has been submitted to the President"; states that his note of October 3, 1824, was not answered "in consequence of some conversation" between Clay's predecessor (Adams) and Mareuil, which seemed to make an answer unnecessary, and that, if a written reply is desired, it will be made; notes that the refusal of local officials at Norfolk to aid in the recovery of a deserter was based on their misinterpretation of the Convention of 1822, that their error could have been corrected by resort to the United States courts, and that they have been informed of the incorrectness of their views. Copy. DNA, RG59, Notes to Foreign Legations, vol. 3, pp. 234-35 (M38, R3). ALS draft, in CSmH.

INSTRUCTIONS AND DISPATCHES   November 7, 1825

From ANDREW ARMSTRONG, Port au Prince. Reports arrival of a French frigate with consuls aboard; states that the French treaty has not been concluded and that the ordonnance was apparently accepted only with modifications. ALS.

DNA, RG59, Cons. Disp., Cap Haitien, vol. 5 (M9, R-T5). Cf. above, Armstrong to Clay, October 5, 1825.

MISCELLANEOUS LETTERS   November 7, 1825

To [JOHN E. HOLT,] "The Mayor of Norfolk." Informs him of the complaint of the Baron de Mareuil (above, to Clay, October 4, 1825); states that the President "conceives that the sixth Article of the Convention with France of . . . 1822 comprehends as well deserters from public ships as from Merchant Vessels"; and adds that, "Assuming this to be the meaning of the Treaty," it is "unnecessary to shew that it is the Law of the Land." Copy. DNA, RG59, Dom. Letters, vol. 21, p. 185 (M40, R19). Holt, mayor of Norfolk since 1812, continued in that office until his death in 1832.

To [STEPHEN WRIGHT,] "the Presiding Officer, of Norfolk County Court." "Same Letter, same date, as written to The Mayor of Norfolk. See p. 185." *Ibid.* Wright, a colonel of Virginia militia, in the 1790's, had also been a member of the Virginia House of Delegates.

From THOMAS L. WINTHROP and JAMES LLOYD, Boston. Transmit a letter in corroboration of the existence of "depredations made by the British on the north Eastern frontier of the United States. . . ." LS. DNA, RG59, Misc. Letters (M179, R63). The enclosure, written by Samuel Cook (see below, Clay to Lloyd and Winthrop, December 10, 1825), has not been found; but an extract of a letter from Cook, dated March 25, 1824, relating to the same topic, was enclosed in Clay to Addington, March 27, 1825. Winthrop, born at New London, Connecticut, and graduated from Harvard, was a prominent Boston merchant. Active in politics, he was a member of the Massachusetts Senate and from 1826 to 1832, Lieutenant Governor of that State. Cook was assistant land agent of Maine.

APPLICATIONS, RECOMMENDATIONS   November 7, 1825

ROBERT M. GOODWIN, Savannah, referring to his service as an officer in "the last war" and to his friendship for Clay, seeks appointment as United States marshal for the District of Georgia. ALS. DNA, RG59, A. and R. (MR2). Goodwin, born in Virginia, had served as a lieutenant of infantry in the War of 1812. See below, Goodwin to Clay, February 8, 1826.

THOMAS HOGE, JR., Greenville, Tennessee, solicits appointment to publish the laws in his newspaper, the *American Economist and East Tennessee Statesman.* ALS. DNA, RG59, P. and D. of L. Hoge not further identified; the journal, founded in 1823, was discontinued in 1825.

SAMUEL HOIT, Port Gibson (Mississippi), seeks appointment as a consul. ALS. DNA, RG59, A. and R. (MR2). In March, 1825, Hoit had been appointed collector and inspector for the district of Pearl River, Mississippi, but he did not hold that office in September. He received no other appointment.

B[ETHUEL] F. MORRIS, Indianapolis, recommends John Vawter as marshal of Indiana. ALS. *Ibid.* (MR4). Cf. above, Clay to Parke, March 16, 1825. Morris a banker, was at this time agent of the Indianapolis Capitol Fund and active in civic organizations.

To Albert Gallatin

Albert Gallatin Esqr.　　(Confidential)　　Department of State,
Sir,　　　　　　　　　　　　Washington, 8 November 1825.

The President has determined to accept the invitation, which has been received from several of the American Republics, to cause the United States of America to be represented at the contemplated Congress at Panama,[1] whose deliberations will be occupied with interests of high importance to this hemisphere. He wishes to give to the Mission, which he purposes sending, a distinguished character, and is therefore desirous of availing the public of your services. I am directed by him to ascertain if you are disposed to render them. In the event of your acceptance, Mr. Richard C. Anderson Jr. the Minister of the United States at Colombia will be associated with you, and the rank of both of you will be that of Minister Plenipotentiary and Envoy Extraordinary. As to the time of your departure, should you think proper to accept the appointment, I suppose it can hardly take place earlier than some time about the middle or twentieth of next month.

I am happy to be the organ of this distinguished proof of the confidence of the President in your patriotism, zeal and abilities. I am your obedient Servant.　　　　　　　　　　　　H Clay

LS. NHi-Gallatin Papers (MR13). Copy, in DNA, RG59, Dip. Instr., vol. 10, p. 427 (M77, R5). ALS draft, in DLC-HC (DNA, M212, R2).
1 See above, Salazar to Clay, November 2, 1825; Obregón to Clay, November 3, 1825.

To Joel R. Poinsett

Mr. Poinsett, Minister at Mexico　　Washington 8 Novr. 1825.
My Dr. Sir,

The bearer hereof Mr. Stephen McLellan Staples[1] has been introduced to me this day in a manner that interests me in his prosperity. A Graduate at Bowdoin College,[2] he has since been employed in the instruction of youth, to whose Parents, among the most respectable Citizens of Philadelphia, he has rendered entire satisfaction. He has also published an English and Spanish Grammar,[3] which is well spoken of.　Being about to visit Mexico, I take pleasure in recommending him to your kind offices.—

I am yours faithfully　　　　　　　　　　　　Henry Clay.

Copy. DNA, RG59, Unofficial Letter-Book of H. Clay, 1825-1829, p. 6.
1 Not further identified.
2 Founded in 1794 but not opened to students until 1802.
3 The volume, *Gramática Completa de la Lengua Inglesa, para Uso de los Espanoles; con un Suplemento, que Contiene las Frases Mas Precisas para Romper en una Conversacion, Formas de Documentos Comerciales, y Descripciones de las Ciudades de Filadelfia y de Washington*, had been published at Philadelphia earlier in 1825.

INSTRUCTIONS AND DISPATCHES   November 8, 1825

From JOHN RAINALS, Copenhagen. Refers to his dispatch of October 21; reports that "the contract for the purchase of the 3 ships" has been cancelled; encloses a publication on the subject; and states that American trade to the Baltic Sea has "exceeded that of any former year." ALS. DNA, RG59, Cons. Disp., Copenhagen, vol. 3 (M-T195, R3). On the sale of the vessels, see above, Hughes to Clay, July 8, 1825, note.

APPLICATIONS, RECOMMENDATIONS   November 8, 1825

I[SAAC] Q. LEAKE, Newhope, Bucks County, Pennsylvania, recommends H. A. Salisbury, editor of the Buffalo *Patriot,* to publish the laws. Salisbury enjoys, "personally and politically, the confidence and esteem, of all" Clay's friends "in that quarter." ALS. DNA, RG59, P. and D. of L. See above, Camp to Clay, October 17, 1825, note.

JAMES NOBLE and JOHN TEST, Brookville (Indiana), recommend (Milton) Gregg and (David V.) Culley, editors of the Lawrenceburg *Indiana Palladium,* to publish the laws. ALS by Noble, signed also by Test. DNA, RG59, P. and D. of L. Cf. above, Holman to Clay, October 24, 1825, note.

To Joel R. Poinsett

No. 7   Joel R. Poinsett. Envoy Extraordinary and
Minister Plenipotentiary. U. S. to Mexico
Sir.   Department of State   Washington 9 Nov. 1825.

Since the date of my Letter of the 26th. September last, your despatches to No. 21. have been received. That of the 13th. September. 1825, was received yesterday. They have all been laid before the President, and I shall now make the remarks which appear to be called for by the last, being the only one which seems to require particular notice. In that you state that, in the course of your conferences with the Plenipotentaries of the United Mexican States on the subject of the proposed Commercial Convention, a point of difficulty has arisen which has been agreed to be reserved. The point is, an exception in favour of the American Nations, which were formerly Spanish possessions, to which, on account of the fraternal relations that unite them to the United Mexican States, the latter may grant special privileges which shall not be extended to the dominions and citizens of the United States. The President approves of your refusal to accede to that exception.

The United States have neither desired, nor sought, to obtain for themselves, in their commercial relations with the new States, any privileges which were not common to other nations. They have proposed, and only wished to establish, as the basis of all their Commercial Treaties, those of equality and reciprocity. They can consent to no other. Ready, themselves, to extend to the United Mexican States any favours which they have granted to other nations, the United States feel themselves authorized to demand in this respect, a perfect reciprocity. They could not agree to treat on the principle of a concession to any European Power of Commercial privileges which were denied to them. They would feel even more repugnance to the adoption of such a principle in respect to any American Nations; because, by placing the United States, in some degree, out of the pale of that American System, of which they form no unessential part, it would naturally wound the sensibility of the people of the United States.

As you had not time, at the date of your despatch, to communicate the reasons which were urged in support of this extraordinary exception, they can only be collected from the tenour of the clause inserted in the British Treaty which you have cited. That clause asserts, as the motives for the exception, 1st.—That the new States, in whose favour it is to be applied, were formerly Spanish possessions;— and 2ndly.—That certain fraternal relations unite them to the Mexican States. The validity of neither of these reasons, can be perceived. What is there in the nature of the fact that those Nations were once bound by a common allegiance to Spain, to justify the exception? Can any rule be fairly deduced from a Colonial condition which should govern independent nations, no longer bound by any common tie? Is there not something derogatory from the character of free States, and free men, in seeking to find a rule for their commercial intercourse, in their emancipated condition, from a retrospect of their Colonial State, which was one of dependence and vassalage? What is to be the limit of this principle? If the accident of a Colonial connexion under a common Sovereign is to justify a peculiar rule for the emancipated Colonies, may not that common Sovereign, also, insist, on the ground of ancient relations, upon special privileges? And then it would be incumbent upon the United States to consider if they had not been premature in their recognition of the Independence of the United Mexican States. But if the fact of the Spanish dominion having once stretched over the new States is to create an exception of commercial privileges, in their behalf, the United States, upon a similar ground, have a right to demand the benefit of it. For the same Spanish dominion once, and at no very distant day, extended over the larger part of their territories, and all that part which is conterminous with those of the United Mexican States.

With respect to the second reason deducible from the clause in the British Treaty, there is no statement of the nature of those fraternal relations which we supposed to warrant the exception. Certainly, as between the United Mexican States and the other new Nations carved out of the former Spanish Colonies, none are known to the world which can sanction the exception. The United Mexican States have, it is true, been waging war with Spain, cotemporaneously with the other States, but, hitherto, there has been no co-operation of arms between them. The United Mexican States have, alone, sustained their contest. If the idea of those fraternal relations is to be sought for in the sympathy between the American Belligerents, this sympathy has been equally felt, and constantly expressed, throughout the whole struggle, by the United States. They have not, indeed, taken up arms in support of the independence of the new States; but the neutrality which they have maintained has enabled them more efficaciously to serve the cause of independence, than they could have done by taking part in the war. Had they become a Belligerent, they would probably have drawn into the war, on the other side, parties whose force would have neutralized, if it had not overbalanced, their exertions. By maintaining neutral ground, they have entitled themselves to speak out with effect, and they have, constantly, so spoken, to the Powers of Europe. They [dis]concerted the designs of the European Alliance upon the new States by the uncalculating declarations which they made in the face of the world.[1] They were the first to hasten to acknowledge the Independence of the United Mexican States, and, by their example, drew after them Great Britain.

It has, no doubt, not escaped your observation that, in the case of the Treaty which has been concluded between the United States and the Republic of Colombia,[2] (And of which a printed authentic copy, as it has been ratified by the two Governments, is herewith transmitted) no such exception was set up by that Republic. On the contrary, it is expressly stipulated in the second Article, that the parties "engage mutually, not to grant any particular favour to other Nations in respect of Commerce and Navigation, which shall not, immediately, become common to the other party, who shall enjoy the same, freely, if the concession was freely made, or on allowing the same compensation, if the concession was conditional."

There is a striking inconsistency in the line of policy which the United Mexican States would seem disposed to pursue towards the United States. They would regard these States as an American Nation or not, accordingly as it shall suit their own purposes. In respect to Commerce, they would look upon us as an European Nation, to be excluded from the enjoyment of privileges conceded to other American Nations. But when an attack is imagined to be menaced by Europe upon the Independence of the United Mexican States, then an appeal is made to those fraternal sympathies which are justly supposed to belong to our condition as a member of the American family. No longer than about three months ago, when an invasion by France of the Island of Cuba, was believed at Mexico, the United Mexican Government promptly called upon the Government of the United States, through you, to fulfil [*sic*] the memorable pledge of the President of the United States in his Message to Congress of December 1823.[3] What they would have done, had the contingency happened, may be inferred from a despatch to the American Minister at Paris,[4] a copy of which is herewith sent, which you are authorized to read to the Plenipotentiaries of the United Mexican States. Again, the United Mexican Government has invited that of the United States to be represented at the Congress of Panama, and the President has determined to accept the invitation.[5] Such an invitation has been given to no European Power, and it ought not to have been given to this, if it is not to be considered as one of the American Nations.

The President indulges the confident expectation that, upon reconsideration, the Mexican Government will withdraw the exception. But if it should continue to insist upon it, you will, upon that ground, abstain from concluding any Treaty, and put an end to the negociation. It is deemed better to have no Treaty, and abide by the respective Commercial Laws of the two Countries, than to subscribe to a principle wholly inadmissible, and which, being assented to, in the case of Mexico, might form a precedent to be extended to others of the new States.

I am your obedient Servant   H. CLAY.

Copy. DNA, RG59, Dip. Instr., vol. 10, pp. 407-10 (M77, R5). ALS draft, in DLC-HC (DNA, M212, R7).
[1] Cf. above, Clay to Poinsett, March 26, 1825.
[2] See above, Clay to Salazar, March 21, 1825.
[3] See above, Poinsett to Clay, August 17, 1825.
[4] Above, Clay to Brown, October 25, 1825, no. 3.
[5] Above, Obregón to Clay, November 3, 1825; Clay to Gallatin, November 8, 1825.

From Charles Caldwell

Dear Sir,   Lexington (Ky) November 9th. 1825.

[Encloses letters[1] testifying to "the sterling character and high competencies" of "Major Broom,"[2] whom Caldwell, also, recommends highly for an appointment.]

Confident that although far removed from among us, your good feelings are still with us in the West, allow me to claim your congratulations on the brilliant prospects and flourishing condition of our medical school. The present, although not yet filled, promises to be the largest and finest class we have ever had. Place its minimum at 250 and its maximum between that and 270.[3]

Accept, I pray you, an assurance of the high and sincere estimation with which I have the honour to be, Dear Sir, Your very faithful and Obedient Servant   CH: CALDWELL

ALS. DNA, RG59, A. and R. (MR1). Addressed to Clay at Washington.
[1] Not found.
[2] Thomas Randolph Broom, appointed to the United States Military Academy as a resident of New York and graduated from that institution in 1814, had served as a lieutenant of artillery until November, 1816, when he had resigned. In 1818 he had re-enlisted as a paymaster and served with infantry units until they were disbanded in 1821. He died in Mississippi in 1829.
[3] The enrollment of the Transylvania University Medical Department reached 282 in January, 1826, an increase of 58 over the previous year. "Trustees' Report," January 2, 1828, in Ky. Senate, *Journal, 1827-1828,* p. 371.

From William Creighton, Jr.

Dear Sir.   Chillicothe 9th. Nov. 1825.

Yours of the 8th Ultimo[1] was duly received. It reached me during the Term of our Court when I was deprived of the assistance of my friend Colo. Bond[2] who had not nor has not yet entirely recovered from a severe spell of sickness. At the close of our Term I was hurried off on the Circuit & have just returned— We did not obtain an order at the last Term autherising [*sic*] the present Marshal to make a Deed for the House and lot in New Ark— As this property was devised by Colo. Morrison to a young Lady in Baltimore, we could not obtain the order for the Marshal to make the Deed to her without a Copy. or an extract of Colo. Morrison's will.[3] If you will have the goodness to furnish us with an extract of the Will in relation to the devise in question, the deed can be made directly by the Marshal to the devisee, unless otherwise controuled by the Will.— this matter shall be attended to at the ensuing Term in January.—

Mr. Dun paid me Ten dollars and twenty one cents for you[4]— I have written to Judge Barriere [*sic*] the security of McDonald for whom you appeared and have urged the payment of your fee[5]— I consider the Judge a correct man and expect he will shortly make arrangements to pay—

In consequence of the death of Harvey D Evans the late Clerk of the Circuit & District Courts, who died shortly after the last Term,[6] we are without a Clerk— The office being closed it will not be in my power to examine the bills of costs in the two cases of McDougal and Stansberry but will do so and advise you[7]—

On the demise of H.D Evans the District Judge[8] appointed Colo. Bond Clerk pro tem: he gave Bond and commenced on the duties of his office. when he was requested to desist. by some doubts expressed by Judge Todd[9] in a letter to Judge Byrd as to the powers of the Court to appoint a Clerk in the recess—thus things stand at present— The District Judge will make the appointment at the next Term[10]— Judge Todd, if then alive, will certainly never be in Court again— I regretted extremely that I was absent when you was here— I sympathise most sincerely with you and Mrs. Clay for the double loss you have sustained during the last Season.[11]

I am dear Sir. Your friend   W CREIGHTON JUN
Hon Henry Clay Esqr

ALS. DLC-HC (DNA, M212, R2).   1 Not found.   2 William Key Bond.
3 William Doherty (Dougherty) was the marshal. For the bequest of the Newark property to Esther Morrison Harris, see above, III, 528n.
4 Cf. above, Clay to Dun, September 22, 1825.
5 Case not found. The judge was probably George W. Barrere, a member since 1816 of the Highland County court of common pleas, formerly (1808-1809, 1810-1814) of the Ohio Senate. McDonald (name not clear), not identified.
6 Evans had died in July, 1825.
7 Probably the case of Stephen McDougal and others vs. Alexander Holmes and others and one, or all, of three cases—John Roads, David Beaver, and Ziba Lindley, respectively, vs. J. C. Symmes and W. Stanberry. All these cases had been carried from Licking County to the Ohio Supreme Court at the December term, 1824. Clay did not appear to argue them there. None of the appeals was successful. 1 *Ohio Repts.* 281-317, 376-80.   8 Charles Willing Byrd.
9 Thomas Todd.   10 Bond received the appointment.
11 The deaths of Eliza Clay and Susan Clay Duralde.

From Joseph Vance

Dear Sir   Urbana[1] Nov. 9th. 1825
In the Presidents Message to congress would it not be well to notice some of the important intrests [sic] of the western & southwestern parts of our country; as you know that their [sic] has been much complaint hertofore [sic] of wilful [sic] neglect from that quarter,

The subjects that the people feel the most intrest in at present in the western & southwestern States are the location and extension of the two national roads[2] and a further relief to the Purchassers [sic] of the Publick Lands by the extension of the provisions of the act of May 20,[3] you have no Idea what intrest the People feel on the subject of a further relief relative to the payment of their land debt.

Sir from the sincerity of my heart I condole with you and Mrs. Clay in your late domestic afflictions:[4]— be so good as to give my respects to Mrs. Clay & [. . .][5] and accept for yourself the best wishes of your friend   JOSEPH VANCE
H. Clay

ALS. DNA, RG59, Misc. Letters (M179, R63). Endorsed (AE) by Clay: ". . . To be put in the Presidents box—"   1 Ohio.
2 The Cumberland Road; the road from Washington to New Orleans (see above, Speech, January 17, 1825, note 3; Thornetine to Clay, May 6, 1825).

3 Cf. above, Ewing to Clay, August 6, 1825, note.
4 The death of Eliza Clay and Susan Clay Duralde.
5 Word obscured in binding of MS.

DIPLOMATIC NOTES   November 9, 1825

To the BARON DE MAREUIL. States that, although "no information has yet reached this Department in regard to the French Ship Calypso and the schooner William Henry other than that contained in" Mareuil's notes of May 6 and October 25, Clay has determined without further delay "to make such observations as appear to be called for by the cases of those unfortunate vessels." Without further information, "all that can now be safely said is that the salvage which was actually allowed appears to have been enormous"; but, he points out, the courts of justice are "competent to afford the proper redress," and the owners of the vessels have no claims upon the Government of the United States. With reference "more particularly to the case of the Schooner, the law of Florida, under which the assessment of salvage was made," has been declared unconstitutional by a district court in South Carolina. "If that decision be correct," the owners may recover their property through the courts. Complaints made by United States citizens against that law will probably cause Congress to take it under consideration. Copy. DNA, RG59, Notes to Foreign Legations, vol. 3, pp. 235-36 (M38, R3). ALS draft in CSmH. On Clay's confusion in referring to the *William Henry,* cf. above, Mareuil to Clay, October 25, 1825. Daniel Brent, at the Secretary of State's direction, addressed a letter on November 10, 1825, to Edgar Mason, United States attorney for East Florida, requesting an inquiry and report upon the libel of *La Revanche.* Copy. DNA, RG59, Dom. Letters, vol. 21, pp. 187-88 (M40, R19).

To C[HARLES] R. VAUGHAN. Transmits copies of a letter from (George) Canning to (Richard) Rush (cf. above, Rush to Clay, August 15, 1825) and of one received from (Gabriel) Richard (above, October 17, 1825), relative to "Mr. Macdonald" (John McDonell); requests that appropriate measures for McDonell's relief be adopted. Copy. DNA, RG59, Notes to Foreign Legations, vol. 3, p. 236 (M38, R3). ALI draft, in CSmH. Published in Manning (arr.), *Diplomatic Correspondence . . . Canadian Relations,* II, 69-70.

From [PETER] PEDERSEN, Philadelphia, *"private."* Requests a reply, which he "expected already in the course of last week," to his note of October 29, "as far at least as a decision at this time can be taken"; states that "he is anxious to communicate it as early as possible, to his Govt." in order that an answer may be returned "before the approaching Session of Congress terminates." AN. DNA, RG59, Notes from Danish Legation, vol. 1 (M52, R1). Cf. above, Clay to Pedersen, November 7, 1825.

From PETER PEDERSEN, Philadelphia. States that he has learned from his latest dispatches from Copenhagen that (Christopher) Hughes' request for the admission of an American consul at St. Thomas has been granted and that (Nathan) Levy or another appointee will be "received and recognized" there. ALS. DNA, RG59, Notes from Danish Legation, vol. 1 (M52, R1). Cf. above, Hughes to Clay, August 19, 1825, note.

INSTRUCTIONS AND DISPATCHES   November 9, 1825

To CHARLES D. COXE, "Consul U. S. Tripoli." Encloses commission, printed circular instructions, and blank consular bond. Copy. DNA, RG59, Cons. Instr., vol. 2, p. 371 (M78, R2). Cf. above, Southard to Clay, April 21, 1825, note.

To SAMUEL D. HEAP, "Consul U. S. Tunis." Encloses documents similar to those immediately above. Copy. DNA, RG59, Cons. Instr., vol. 2, p. 371 (M78, R2). Cf. above, Coxe to Secretary of State, April 28, 1825, note.

MISCELLANEOUS LETTERS   November 9, 1825

From THOMAS CROCKER, Boston. States that, upon his departure from the Sandwich Islands he left no agent "as there was no resident who would accept of it that was respectable & responsible, owing to the very frequent & troublesome calls upon him, and being a place destitute of all law as regards the Whites. . . ." ALS. DNA, RG59, Cons. Disp., Honolulu, vol. 1 (M144, R1). Received November 14. John C. Jones, Jr., on January 1, 1824, had appointed Crocker, of Massachusetts, a trader on Oahu, as "Vice Agent for the Commerce and Seamen of the United States at the Sandwich Islands." Cf. above, Jones to Clay, October 19, 1825; Clay to Jones, October 24, 1825.

From CHANDLER PRICE, United States Insurance Office, Philadelphia. Transmits "a Transcript of Spoliations Committed by European & other powers upon property Insured and paid for by this Institution. . . ." LS. DNA, RG76, Misc. Claims, France. Price signs as president of the company. The enclosure, consisting of 8 sheets listing spoliations, from 1807 to 1813, by the British, French, "French at Antwerp," Danish, Haitians, and Spanish, asserts that payment of the claims by the company "has wrested from the Stockholders in Said Institution almost all its earnings for years, and nearly exhausted its original Capital ($400,000) depriving them of any dividend therefrom since the year 1811."

APPLICATIONS, RECOMMENDATIONS   November 9, 1825

SAMUEL HOIT, Port Gibson (Mississippi), repeats solicitation for an appointment, preferably for "one of those at the Barbary States to which is attached a salary." Concludes: "I do think the active part I have always taken in politicks and the public services rendered entitle me to a place. . . ." ALS. DNA, RG59, A. and R. (MR2). See above, Hoit to Clay, November 7, 1825, note.

CHARLES TURELL, Portsmouth, New Hampshire, seeks appointment of his newspaper, the *Commercial Advertiser,* to publish the laws. Refers Clay to "Capt. [Samuel E.] Watson, of the marine corps," with whom he believes Clay to be acquainted. ALS. DNA, RG59, P. and D. of L. Turell, born at Salem, Massachusetts, had published another Portsmouth newspaper from 1813 until the early twenties. He established the *Commercial Advertiser* in 1825 and edited it until 1829, when the journal was discontinued. It did not receive the support here requested. Turell later removed to New York City. Watson, born in Virginia and commissioned a captain of Marines in 1820, was stationed at Portsmouth.

To Samuel Smith

My Dear Sir   Washington 10h. Nov. 1825
I received your favor of the 1st. instant with the letter of Mr.

Dawson inclosed.¹ I have seen the acts of parliament and the Speeches of Mr. Huskisson to which you refer.² The moment I brought myself clearly to understand the operation of the discriminating duties on our British West India trade, I confess that I thought it was our clear interest to abolish them, as you might have inferred from the tenor of the enquiries which I took the liberty to address to you last Spring.³ On that subject I concur entirely with Mr. Dawson, as I do on several other of his opinions expressed in his sensible practical letter. I doubt however whether we can accomplish the object of a mutual abolition of the alien duties but by treaty, so as to guard against the double voyages, which would operate against us. As I shall shortly see you here I will defer, until I have that pleasure, saying more to you at present.

I remain faithfully Your ob. Servant   H. CLAY
The Honble Sam. Smith .

ALS. DLC-Samuel Smith Papers (DNA, M212, R22).
¹ Neither letter has been found; the latter was probably from William Dawson, British consul at Baltimore.
² See above, Rush to Clay, March 26, 1825.   ³ Above, May 9, 1825.

From William Duane

Henry Clay, Esq   (Private)   Phila. 10 Novr. 1825
Sir

I was so unfortunate as not to meet as I wished Mr Anderson¹ on his way thro' this city—and he had sailed the very day I reached N. York with the hope of seeing him. My wish was to send by him, a triplicate of my memorial to the Colombian Government, in which I applied the 10th of March last. for the privilege of opening a canal or Strait between the two Oceans in the Isthmus of Panama;² and to solicit his good offices there in my behalf. I take the liberty to make you acquainted with the fact, because every citizen should I think make known to the government any concerns he may have with other countries; and because being not personally acquainted with Mr Anderson, I wish, if you should deem me worthy, to request your good offices in the prosecution of the design as your Nature may authorise

It is of some moment that this undertaking should be prosecuted by some person from the U. S. for many reasons: there is a British Competitor in the House of Heslop & Co³ of Jamaica, who I learn lately sent Surveyors to the Isthmus, but who were compelled to desist and reembark, which has occured [sic] since the arrival of My Memorial at Bogota

If any Agent should be required for Guatemala or the Isthmus, where the amphyctions are soon to assemble[4] I persuade myself that fitness would not be denied me—and I am sure no man would act with more zeal in any trust   Pardon this freedom of your Obed Ser

WM DUANE

ALS. DLC-HC (DNA, M212, R2).   [1] Richard C. Anderson, Jr.
[2] After surrendering publication of the Philadelphia *Aurora* (above, III, 310n), Duane had toured South America. He now had two volumes in preparation, describing Guatemala and Colombia (see below, Duane to Clay, this date), in the preface to the latter of which he noted that he had "made propositions to affect [*sic*] that long talked of *Strait* of Panama" and that he had arranged for financial support by the house of Goldsmith and other bankers in Rotterdam and London. Duane to Thomas Jefferson, June 20, 1826, in Massachusetts Historical Society, *Proceedings*, Series 2, XX, 386. No further action on the proposal has been found.
[3] Firm headed by Maxwell Hyslop, a merchant of Jamaica friendly with Simón Bolívar since 1814.   [4] See above, Salazar to Clay, November 2, 1825.

DIPLOMATIC NOTES   November 10, 1825

To C[HARLES] R. VAUGHAN. Acknowledges receipt of his note of November 3, a copy of which Clay "will, without delay, transmit . . . to the Governor of New York, who is most competent to decide whether, consistently with the laws of that state, he can cause to be rendered the requisite assistance to arrest the accused and deliver him over, as is desired." Copy. DNA, RG59, Notes to Foreign Legations, vol. 3, p. 236 (M38, R3). Cf. below, Clay to Clinton, November 11, 1825.

INSTRUCTIONS AND DISPATCHES   November 10, 1825

From RICHARD C. ANDERSON, JR., Cartagena, no. 31. Reports his arrival, on November 5, and his intention to "take the earliest conveyance for the seat of Government," probably by steamboat; notes that the country is tranquil and that the vote for Bolívar, in the election now in progress, will probably be unanimous; states that a naval expedition is being fitted out and that no one seems to know its destination, which, however, must be one of Spain's remaining two islands "in the American Seas"; summarizes a conversation with (Pedro) Gual, concerning representation of various countries at the Panama Congress; expresses relief upon finding that the authority given him in Clay's letter of September 16 was rendered unnecessary by (Charles) MacNeal's surrender of his position as vice consul to William Berrien (cf. above, MacNeal to Clay, July 1, 1825), who is serving until the arrival of (John M.) MacPherson. ALS. DNA, RG59, Dip. Disp., Colombia, vol. 3 (M-T33, R3). Received December 12.

From F. M. DIAMOND. Reports the existence of a thirteen-volume digest of all sales and grants of land and town lots, by the King and by local authorities in his name, in the Floridas, compiled by Capt. (Vincente Sebastian) Pintado, who, since he was never paid by the Spanish Government, offers his work for sale to the United States for $6,000. The compilation also includes a digest of old British grants in the Floridas. LS. DNA, RG59, Cons. Disp., Havana, vol. 3 (M-T20, R3). Pintado, who for many years had been surveyor general of West Florida under the Spanish administration, had considered his plans of the province as "his private property" and had taken them with him to Havana upon the departure of the Spanish authorities from the mainland. James H. Forbes to John Quincy Adams, June 25, 1821; Andrew Jackson to Secretary of State, July 30, 1821—in Carter (ed.), *Territorial Papers* . . . , XXII, 94, 152. Both Forbes and Jackson had thought Pintado's work not worth purchasing.

From A[LEXANDER] H. EVERETT, Madrid, no. 14. Transmits a copy of his note to the Duke del Infantado, proposing "a Convention for the arrangement of the respective claims of the two Governments," modeled after that of March 23, 1823, between Spain and England, a copy of which is also enclosed; expresses a fear that the business will move slowly because of the recent change of ministry (see above, Everett to Clay, October 26, 1825) and because "this Government will endeavour to escape from the necessity of paying our demands by resorting to their usual system of delay"; suggests, in that case, "a display of energy" and, if necessary, "an actual resort to reprisals"; advocates, in connection with this and similar cases, that the United States "shew the world that we do not mean to be made in future, as we have been heretofore, victims to the cupidity of every petty state that has a pretext for fitting out a Privateer"; declares "that if we cannot obtain indemnity for past injuries from the Great powers, we may at least secure ourselves from any further prosecution of this system of plunder by those of the second order; and we ought to do it, unless the United States are to become in perpetuity, a sort of general *vache au lait* to the belligerent nations for the time being"; notes that in his communication to the Duke he has agreed, in case Spain admits "our first demands, to allow a compensation for the damages done by Commodore [David] Porter at Fajardo." LS. DNA, RG59, Dip. Disp., Spain, vol. 25 (M31, R27). Received January 13, 1826. On the Fajardo incident, see above, Nelson to Clay, April 6, 1825, note.

From ROBERT M. HARRISON, Antigua. Reports the reception (by local officials) of orders "from the Commissioners of the Customs in England to have all American vessels coming into the Colonial Ports measured to ascertain their Tonnage"; gives a schedule of the tonnage charges imposed "by an act of the assembly of this Island"; and notes that an American vessel that has "paid $200 port charges, will now pay $232." ALS. DNA, RG59, Cons. Disp., Antigua, vol. 1 (M-T327, R1). Received December 20.

MISCELLANEOUS LETTERS   November 10, 1825

To JOHN WILLIAMS. Informs him of the President's wish to appoint him Chargé d'Affaires to Guatemala. Refers to our friendly relations with that Republic, one province of which "offered to unite itself to this Confederacy." Adds: "We wish to give extension and strength to these relations; and great reliance would be placed on your zeal, discretion and patriotism, in accomplishing that object, if you should see fit to accept the appointment." Copy. DNA, RG59, Dip. Instr., vol. 10, p. 415 (M77, R5). ALS draft, in DLC-HC (DNA, M212, R7). Williams, whose letter of acceptance is dated November 25 (ALS. DNA, RG59, Dip. Disp., Central America, vol. 1 [M219, R2]), served as Chargé from December 29, 1825, until December 1, 1826. On the proposal of San Salvador for annexation by the United States, see above, Clay to Miller, April 22, 1825, note.

From WILLIAM DUANE, Philadelphia. Requests the return of "books and maps &c," given to him by Manuel Torres, who, before his death, had borrowed them from Duane for loan to the Department of State. Cites need for these documents to complete preparation of a volume on Colombia; mentions that he has a history of Guatemala ready for publication and comments on the importance to the United States of disseminating fuller knowledge on those countries where "the markets of commerce must continue to augment in an annual duplication of amount for a thousand years." ALS. DNA, RG59, Misc. Letters (M179, R63). Daniel Brent, in an undated note, assured Duane that his letter had not been overlooked but that a search, made at Clay's direction, "for the Books and Maps" had proved unsuccessful. Copy. DNA, RG59, Dom. Letters, vol. 21, p. 192 (M40, R19). Duane later published *A Visit to Colombia, in the Years 1822 & 1823, by Laguayra and Caracas, over the Cordillera to Bogotá, and Thence by the Magdalena to Cartagena* . . . (Philadelphia, 1826) ; the work on Guatemala has not been found.

From ALBERT GALLATIN, Baltimore. Acknowledges receipt of Clay's letter of November 8; declines "with reluctance" accepting "An appointment so honourable"; cites the danger of encountering a tropical climate and his ignorance of the Spanish language. AL draft. NHi-Gallatin Papers (MR13).

APPLICATIONS, RECOMMENDATIONS   November 10, 1825

WILLIAM J. HOBBY, Augusta, Georgia, seeks reappointment for publication of the laws in the Augusta *Chronicle and Advertiser,* with A. H. Pemberton as new owner. ALS. DNA, RG59, P. and D. of L. Hobby had been an editor in Augusta since 1804. The appointment was continued throughout the Adams administration.

W[ILLIAM] RAWLE, Philadelphia, recommends Peter DeHaven, a lawyer, for public employment. ALS. DNA, RG59, A. and R. (MR2). Rawle, born in Philadelphia and educated in New York City and London, where he had emigrated as a Loyalist during the Revolution, had returned to attain prominence as Federal attorney for Pennsylvania (1791-1799), author of a text, *View of the Constitution of the United States* (1825), and of other legal, historical, and literary publications, an active member of various learned societies, and an abolitionist. DeHaven, who had also been a merchant, was not appointed to office.

JAMES BROWN RAY, Indianapolis, recommends (Nathaniel) Bolton and (George) Smith (owners of the Indianapolis *Gazette*) to publish the laws. LS. DNA, RG59, P. and D. of L. Smith, born at Lancaster, Pennsylvania, had moved to Chillicothe, Ohio, and thence in 1820 to Jeffersonville, Indiana, and the following year to Indianapolis, where he had been one of the founders of the Indianapolis *Gazette*. He was a judge of the Marion Circuit Court. Bolton, son-in-law and stepson of Smith, had been born in Chillicothe and moved with the Smiths to Indiana. The partnership was dissolved in 1829 but Bolton continued in journalism until 1841, after which he served as a member of the Indiana Legislature (1843), State librarian, and consul at Geneva, Switzerland (1855-1858). The *Gazette* was not given the requested appointment during the Adams administration.

W[ALTER] SMITH, Georgetown, transmits recommendations (by residents of Baltimore) for William Flemming Taylor as consul at Quilca and Arica. ALS. DNA, RG59, A. and R. (MR4). See above, Barney to Clay, October 6, 1825.

To Albert Gallatin

My dear Sir   (Private and Confidential)   Washington 11h. Nov. 1825
I regret very much that you decide against going to the proposed Congress at Panama.[1] For the public I am sure you have not decided wisely; for yourself it does not belong to me to judge. I think the mission the most important ever sent from this Country, those only excepted which related to its independence, and the termination of the late War. It will have objects which cannot fail to redound to the lasting fame of our negotiators, if they should be accomplished, as I think there is much reason to believe they may be. It's duration will not, I should think, exceed about six months. Every thing that can would be done for your personal accommodation. Thus, a public vessel would be ordered to New Orleans, if you prefered a departure from that port; and the descent to that place in Steam boats is easy, and in the winter would not be disagreeable; and your convenience would be consulted in other respects as far as it was possible consistently with the public interests. In your proposed associate,[2] knowing you both well, I take upon myself to answer for harmony and cordial cooperation.
I will prevail upon the President to suspend, for a day or two, looking out for another, under the hope that, upon reconsideration, you may find the service compatible with your interest and inclination. If you continue to be averse from it, we must reluctantly acquiesce in your final determination. I am faithfully Your's
A. Gallatin Esqr.   H. CLAY

ALS. NHi-Gallatin Papers (MR13).
1 See above, Gallatin to Clay, November 10, 1825.   2 Richard C. Anderson, Jr.

To Joseph Nourse

Joseph Nourse Esquire, Register of the Treasury.
Sir,   Department of State, Washington 11th. Novr. 1825.
I have the honour to transmit, herewith, an Estimate of the expenses at this Department for the year 1826.
I am with great Respect, Sir, Your Obedt. & very humble Servt.
H CLAY.

[Enclosure]   Department of State
                    Estimate of Appropriations for 1826.
Compensation to the Secretary of State ....$ 6000. ,,
Clerks in that Department by Act of April 20th. 1818[1] .... 15,900. ,,
Mechanist at the Patent Office by Act of 26th. May 1824[2] ....   700. ,,
                    Messengers.
Two in the Department ....1,050. ,,
One in the Patent Office by Act of 26 May 1824[3] .... 400. ,,   1,450. ,,

Incidental and Contingent expenses, including
the expenses of printing the Laws and for
extra copying of papers, viz.

Books	2000.	,,
Binding of Books	500.	,,
Stationery and Parchment	1500.	,,
Mediterranean Passports[4]	1500.	,,
Blank personal Passports, Circulars, &c.	1000.	,,
Fuel and Candles	900.	,,
Newspapers for the Office and Agents abroad	500.	,,
Translations of Foreign Languages	350.	,,
Forage for the Messengers horse	200.—	
Expenses in distributing Congressional Documents	300.—	
Wages of a Laborer	300.—	
Miscellanies	1000.—	
Extra Copying of papers	1000.—	

Carried over	$11,050.—	$24,050.—
Amount brought over	$11,050.—	$24,050.—

Printing in Newspapers and in Pamphlets
from the Laws of the First Session of the } 13,500.—
Nineteenth Congress

distribution of the Acts of Congress through- } 3,500.—
out the States & Territories

                                                            28,050.—

T. B. Wait, Balance reported by the Fifth
Auditor, as due him for printing the Journals
of the Federal Convention, and Secret Jour-
nals of the Revolutionary Congress[5] ....   45.—

Salaries of the Ministers of the United-States at
London, Paris, St. Petersburg, and Madrid,[6]
and of Chargé d'Affaires, at Stockholm,[7] in
the Netherlands,[8] and at Lisbon[9] ....   49,500.—

Salaries of Ministers or Chargé d'Affaires, who
have been or may be appointed to the Governments on the Continent of America, viz

Colombia[10]	9,000.—
Buenos Ayres[11]	4,500.—
Chile[12]	9,000.—
Mexico[13]	9,000.—
Guatemala[14]	4,500.—
Brazil[15]	4,500.—
Peru[16]	4,500.—

Outfits of a Chargé d'Affaires at } 9,000 —   54000.—
Peru & Guatemala

Salaries of the Secretaries of Legation	14,000.—
Contingent Expenses of all the Missions abroad	30,000.—
Salaries of Agents of Claims at London and Paris[17]	4,000.—

Carried forward	$203,645.—

Amount brought over	$203,645.—
Salaries of the Commissioner and Arbitrator[18] under the 1st. Article of the Treaty of Ghent; one half the salaries of the Secretary, Clerk and Messengers and half the Contingent expenses of the Commission	12,000.—
Expenses of carrying into effect the 6th. & 7th. Articles of the Treaty of Ghent, including the compensation of the Commissioners,[19] Agents[20] and Surveyors & their contingent expenses	16,000.—
Expenses of Intercourse with the Barbary Powers	30,000.—
Contingent Expenses of Foreign Intercourse	40,000.—
Relief and Protection of distressed American Seamen in Foreign Countries	35,000.—
Dollars	336,645.—

Copy. DNA, RG59, Dom. Letters, vol. 21, pp. 203-205 (M40, R19).

[1] The statute includes payment to the Superintendent of the Patent Office. 3 *U. S. Stat.*, 445.   [2] 4 *U. S. Stat.*, 42.

[3] The statute covers all the messengers. 4 *U. S. Stat.*, 42.

[4] For protection of vessels owned by United States citizens against depredation by the Barbary powers.

[5] *The Journal, Acts and Proceedings of the Convention, Assembled at Philadelphia, Monday, May 14, and Dissolved Monday, September 17, 1787, which Formed the Constitution of the United States* . . . (Boston, 1819) and the *Secret Journals of the Acts and Proceedings of Congress, from the First Meeting Thereof to the Dissolution of the Confederation, by the Adoption of the Constitution of the United States* . . . (Boston, 1820-1821) had been published by Thomas B. Wait, from a compilation of papers in the State Department by John Quincy Adams, at the behest of President James Monroe, in accordance with joint resolutions of Congress, approved March 27, 1818 (3 *U. S. Stat.*, 475), and May 8, 1820 (3 *U. S. Stat.*, 609).

[6] Rufus King; James Brown; Henry Middleton; Alexander H. Everett.

[7] Cf. above, Clay to Somerville, September 6, 1825; below, Clay to Appleton, June 8, 1826.   [8] Christopher Hughes.

[9] Thomas L. L. Brent.   [10] Richard C. Anderson, Jr.

[11] John M. Forbes.   [12] Heman Allen.

[13] Joel R. Poinsett.   [14] John Williams.

[15] Condy Raguet.

[16] Cf. below, Tudor to Clay, May 11, 1826.

[17] Isaac Cox Barnet and Thomas Aspinwall had been designated as agents for claims and for seamen with salary additional to their fees as consuls at Paris and London.

[18] Langdon Cheves; Henry Seawell, of North Carolina, formerly a member of the State legislature (1790's) and judge of the Superior Court (1818-1819), now (1821-1826, 1831-1832) State Senator and (1823-1827) arbitrator under the St. Petersburg Convention, and, by appointment in 1827, joint commissioner for the final settlement under that convention.

[19] Peter B. Porter; Anthony Barclay.

[20] Joseph Delafield; John Hale (not further identified).

From Theodore W. Clay

My dear Father   Lexington Nov. 11th. 1825

I received your's[1] with great concern for the deep distress, in which our great loss[2] must have thrown both yourself & my Mother. I have not the power of deriving any consolation to myself and have not therefore the means of offering you any, whom I would gladly render happy by any sacrifice.in my power. As I advance in years I feel the value of a relation more and more, because they must and should be the best friends. I hope however that you may not suffer your spirits to be too much depressed, for it is an inevitable effect that the health is thereby impaired; and that of yourself & my dear Mother by these repeated shocks is more and more necessary to our happiness.

There is a degree of interest in the Legislative proceedings quite novel: All is however rapt in doubt. Every effort will be made to induce the Senate to acquiesce with the wishes of the public: but it is said not without foundation that they will resist the appeals.[3] The Message of the Gov. has produced very general inquietude & discontent. He has capped the Climax by his bullying, indecent disregard to truth, in the message. By threatening to call out the militia, for what, to suppress the expression of opinion, or the Court of Appeals from holding sessions directed by law.[4] You will percieve [sic] by the prints that one of the most atrocious and unheard of acts of murder was committed a few nights ago on Sol. P Sharpe.[5] Language could not find terms strong enough to condemn it in, nor could the law be too severe in avenging the rights of humanity. He was called to his door by a man passing himself for an old acquaintance and seeking hospitality for the night at 1 o clock, and in the act of confering [sic] the favor, & in the dark the savage stabbed him to the heart— Deplorable is the condition of that country, where it is a mercy to persecute the offenders to the last [recourse] of the law without any exercise of clemency. But the villain has not been discovered, there seems to be no hope for it.[6]

I enclose [sic] W'ffe's separate answer.[7] He seems to throw the case upon the original defect of title. Gen Lytle[8] is in [. . .][9] at this time; We have not yet heard of the Sheep from Steubenville;[10] it is probable they are waiting for water[11] to send them. Mr. Scott however wrote to Jany[12] of Maysville to forward them on their arrival by some safe hands—

AL. DLC-TJC (DNA, M212, R10). Addressed to Henry Clay; endorsed by him on attached sheet. "Theo. W. Clay. {With Mr. Wickliffe's Answer}"

1 Not found.

2 The deaths of Eliza Clay and Susan Clay Duralde.

3 See above, Bodley to Clay, August 23, 1825; Beatty to Clay, September 13, 1825; below, Kendall to Clay, December 25, 1825.

4 Delivered on November 7, the message had treated first "the existing differences in our judiciary, and the encroachments of the Federal tribunals"; the operations of the United States Bank and its branches, which, "exempt from the burthens imposed on the wealth of our own citizens, have proceeded to buy up the real property of the

country, and fill it with tenantry; thus, and by many other means, extending their influence and establishing their power"; the desirability of curtailing "salaries, and other public expenditures," particularly "the salaries now paid to the President and other officers of the Bank of Kentucky, and the Bank of the Commonwealth"; the "extravagant" compensation to the president and some of the professors at Transylvania University, it seeming "that the State has lavished her money for the benefit of the rich, to the exclusion of the poor; and that the only result is to add to the aristocracy of wealth, the advantage of superior knowledge." Desha had argued that "the whole of the Federal Judiciary may be made to bend to the power of the people, and renounce its errors" by the State's prohibiting "the use of her jails for the purpose of imprisoning debtors under an authority unknown to her laws and constitution." He had proposed that the legislature resolve the dissatisfaction expressed by the people against both the former judges and "the present incumbents" by providing for appointment "of an entirely new set of appellate Judges" and pledged himself "to select them equally from the two contending parties." He had urged that the State "go earnestly to work to put into operation a system of Common Schools," a system "projected several years ago" (see above, III, 351n) but "published more as a feint to content the people with large appropriations that were then made to Transylvania, than with any view to carry it into actual operation." The Governor had also recommended "the speedy commencement of a General system of Internal Improvements," particularly the commencement of "two great Turnpike Roads" from Louisville east through Frankfort to Maysville and from Louisville south through the Green River country to Nashville. At the same time he had called for lower taxes and especially for abolition of the head tax. Ky. Senate, *Journal, 1825*, pp. 4-19. The message had not contained a specific threat to call out the militia; but, in referring to the resumption of the sessions of the old Court of Appeals, the Governor had assured the legislature "that painful as it may be, the Executive will not shrink from the performance of that which he conceives himself bound to do by his oath of office and the constitution of his country." *Ibid.*, p. 11. The inference was drawn in conjunction with newspaper controversy relating to the possible use of force. Cf. Frankfort *Argus of Western America*, October 19, 26, November 2, 1825; Lexington *Kentucky Reporter*, October 17, November 14, 1825.

5 See above, I, 777n.

6 On the day this was written Jereboam O. Beauchamp was arrested for the murder.

7 Robert Wickliffe's answer to Clay's bill of complaint, above, *ca.* July 5, 1825, had been filed in Fayette Circuit Court, September 30, 1825. Fayette Circuit Court, File 823.

8 William Lytle.   9 One word illegible.

10 See above, Dickinson to Clay, November 1, 1825.

11 *I.e.,* for the river to rise.

12 Robert Scott; Andrew M. January, who had recently announced a new partnership, with William Huston, Jr., as receivers and forwarders of goods and property.

MISCELLANEOUS LETTERS   November 11, 1825

To DeWitt Clinton, "Governor of New York." Transmits copies of a note and accompanying documents from Charles R. Vaughan (above, November 3, 1825), who seeks "to obtain the arrest of Michael Neilson, a British subject, now a resident or sojourner in the State of New York. . . ." Adds: "Whether the laws of New York admit of the arrest and delivery of the accused as requested by Mr. Vaughan, or not, Your Excellency is most competent to determine. If they do, you will judge how far it may lead to promote the amicable relations which exist between Great Britain and the United States, and the cause of justice, to comply with the request." LS. NcU-William Asbury Whitaker Papers.

From James Brown

Dear Sir,   Paris Novr. 12. 1825

Mrs. Brown has been forced to delay the sending of the articles you ordered[1] longer than she wished as some of them required to be made to order and all selected with much care and attention as to price and quality— The whole are this day sent to the Agent of the Packet Ship Montano consigned to one of the Owners, my friend Mr Isaac Bell Merchant[2] No 72 Greenwich Street New York—and you will find a list of the articles and prices inclosed[3] in order that you may effect Insurance if you think proper and for which you will have time as this letter will be received by the Packet which will sail from Havre on the 15 and the Montano will be delayed until the 25. From Mrs. Brown's reputation for good taste, a reputation which she enjoys even at Paris, and from the attention she has bestowed in the selection, you will I hope have reason to be convinced that the articles are as handsome as could be procured without trangressing [sic] on those limits which a strict attention to œconomy has imposed— The only expences to be added will be the custom house here (very small) the envellope [sic] of trimed [sic] cloth, and the transportation to Havre. These will not in any essential degree vary the sum to be insured.

I have made some enquiries here respecting the sale of a Bill on America, and find the Exchange so high that I cannot prevail on myself to subject you to the expence of it. Indeed if I was sure that the funds which I have ordered to eke out my very inadequate Salary would arrive in safety, I would feel satisfied that the amount paid for these articles should remain in your hands until my return to the United States. At all events I have enough now in my hands to get along until I hear the fate of a Bill which I hope soon to receive from New Orleans, and which in consequence of the numerous failures and wide spread embarrassments has given me some concern— I am very anxious to hear whether my Merchants Wm Kenner & Co[4] have escaped the mania of cotton speculation— I have in their hands independantly [sic] of my last crop fourteen thousand dollars, and should feel very sensibly any accident which might happen to them. I have not heard any thing that can induce a belief that they are in danger but as I know some of the Merchants in New Orleans will suffer severely, I apprehend others may be in some degree involved in their embarrassments.

In my last[5] I mentioned the removal of Mr Zea Bermudez and the appointment of the Duke of Infantado, and promised by this Packet to write you more particularly as to the influence which this change might have on the affairs of Spain— I had prepared a dispatch on that subject when I received the Dispatches of Mr Everett which will go by this packet,[6] and which he was so obliging as leave [sic] open for my perusal. They more than supply the place of a letter from me a great portion of which would necessarily have been composed from reports and conversations upon which implicit reliance cannot be placed.

Poor Mr Sommerville[7] is still confined to his room and is reduced to a very weak state from which it must be some time before he can recover. I think however that his health is in a very small degree improved as he now for the first time in four weeks can bear a little food on his stomach— He begs me to tell you how uneasy he is lest the views of the Government should be in some measure thwarted by his confinement—

Mr. Sheldon[8] who has since April been in a state of health very alarming to himself and his friends, appears to be out of danger, and is now able to attend as usual to the duties of his office— His constitution is however very delicate and nothing but his extreme abstinence and a temporary suspension of his attention to business could have prevented him from sinking into a pulmonary complaint.

My own health continues much better, and will I hope be such as to enable me to pass a tolerable winter here— Mr Connell[9] who has been at Copenhagen and Stockholm—attending to the claims of some of our Merchants will sail in the Montano on the 25 and afford me an opportunity of writing more particularly on the State of our affairs than I can do by this Conveyance— The Ministry[10] are assailed with great violence, and it is thought by many will not be able to retain their places beyond the next session of the Chambers. These will not be convoked before the 15 of February.

I am Dear Sir with great regard Your Most obt Servt.

Honb Henry Clay   JAMES BROWN

ALS. DLC-HC (DNA, M212, R2).
[1] Cf. above, Clay to Brown, September 4, 1825; Brown to Clay, October 13, 29, 1825.
[2] Active in the East India trade.   [3] Not found.
[4] Kenner, who had moved to Louisiana from Caroline County, Virginia, around the turn of the century, had acquired property in New Orleans and, during the early years of American occupation, had become a prosperous merchant. He had been appointed a member of the first legislative council. On the failure of the firm, see below, Brown to Clay, January 30, 1826.
[5] Above, October 30, 1825.
[6] See above, Everett to Clay, October 26, 28, 1825.
[7] William C. Somerville.   [8] Daniel Sheldon.
[9] John Connell.   [10] Headed by the Comte de Villèle.

INSTRUCTIONS AND DISPATCHES   November 12, 1825

From THOMAS L. L. BRENT, Lisbon. Reports the arrival of "A British Ship of war . . . bringing despatches from Sir Charles Stuart"; notes that, although nothing has been published, "it is . . . circulated by the English Ambassador that Sir Charles Stuart has concluded an arrangement that is satisfactory to this government." LS. DNA, RG59, Dip. Disp., Portugal, vol. 6 (M43, R5). Received January 5, 1826. See above, Raguet to Secretary of State, March 11, 1825, note.

From RUFUS KING, London, no. 10. Reports an audience with the King (George IV) and the presentation of his credentials; states that "It was no small satisfaction, that the Envoy of Columbia [*sic*—Manuel José Hurtado] was presented, and delivered his Letter of Credence at the same time"; asserts that "this is a Great Point; and puts an End to difficulties which hitherto for some unknown cause, seem to have stood in the way of the Reception of Ministers from these States." LS. DNA, RG59, Dip. Disp., Great Britain, vol. 32 (M30, R28). Published in Manning (arr.), *Diplomatic Correspondence . . . Latin-American Nations,* III, 1573.

From CONDY RAGUET, Rio de Janeiro, no. 1. Reports that he received, on October 26, a trunk, forwarded by (John M.) Forbes, "containing the several despatches from Your Department No. 1, 2, 3 & 4, of 14', 13 [*i.e.,* 15]₁₁, 16₁₁ & 16₁₁ April last"; that the delay in arrival of his credentials aroused suspicion in Brazil, whose Government, he thinks, "is much hurt at this appearance of indifference towards it"; that he has presented his credentials and has been received by the Emperor (Peter I); that his note to the Brazilian Government relative to a treaty of amity and commerce, proposing "a reciprocal abandonment of discriminating duties," has been declined; and that recent reports have been received of the defeat of Imperial forces in the Banda Oriental and the probability of war with Buenos Aires. ALS. DNA, RG59, Dip. Disp., Brazil, vol. 4 (M121, R6). Received December 28. Extracts published in Manning (arr.), *Diplomatic Correspondence . . . Latin-American Nations,* II, 838-39. Among the enclosures is a journalistic abstract of the commercial treaty between England and Brazil (see above, Raguet to Clay, October 26, 1825). For explanation of the Brazilian annoyance at the delay in presentation of Raguet's credentials, see below, Rebello to Clay, November 26, 1825, note.

MISCELLANEOUS LETTERS   November 12, 1825

To [SAMUEL L.] SOUTHARD. States that "Mrs. [Thomas] Hart [Jr.] of Lexington (K) is very desirous that her son John [S.] to whom the Secy of Navy has been pleased to grant a Mid shipman's warrant [see above, III, 842n] should be ordered into immediate service." AN. DNA, RG45, Misc. Letters Received, vol. 7, p. 31. Endorsed on cover, two lines by different hands: "Give orders & inform Mr Clay—orders to Cyane."

From H[ARVEY] GREGG, Indianapolis. Announces his readiness to depart; asks further instructions. ALS. DNA, RG59, Cons. Disp., Acapulco, vol. 1 (M143, R1). On November 29, Daniel Brent replied that he had been instructed to inform Gregg that he must arrange transportation to his destination at his own expense, that he must request (Joel R.) Poinsett to obtain an exequatur for him, that "no further instructions . . . than those . . . in the printed Pamphlet" are to be given him, and that a "personal passport" would be obtained for him from the Mexican Minister (Pablo Obregón). Copy, in DNA, RG59, Cons. Instr., vol. 2, pp. 373-74 (M78, R2).

APPLICATIONS, RECOMMENDATIONS   November 12, 1825

WILLIAM H. BAYLEY, Georgetown (District of Columbia), notes that he has learned from his mother of Clay's "having expressed a wish to serve" him; solicits, in the name of his widowed mother and two younger brothers, help in procuring a clerkship; states that he understands that Clay will influence some appointments in the Post Office Department. ALS. DNA, RG59, A. and R. (MR1). None of the Bayleys has been identified; no appointment was made.

D. W. AND C[HARLES] W. HUTCHEN, Brookville, Indiana, apply to publish laws in the *Franklin Repository* (late *Brookville Inquirer*). LS. RG59, P. and D. of L. Appointment (re-appointment as to the Hutchens) granted.

[GEORGE] SMITH and [NATHANIEL] BOLTON, Indianapolis, apply to publish laws in the Indianapolis *Gazette*. ALS. *Ibid*. See above, Ray to Clay, November 10, 1825.

SWEETSER AND COMPANY, Baltimore, recommends appointment of a consul at Arica and Quilca; alludes to recent memorial of recommendation (cf. above, Smith to Clay, November 10, 1825). ALS. DNA, RG59, A. and R. (MR3). The firm was probably headed by Seth Sweetser, Jr., not further identified.

APPLICATIONS, RECOMMENDATIONS   November 13, 1825

H[UTCHINS] G. BURTON, Raleigh, transmits recommendations of (Robert) Potter by Leonard Henderson, Cadwallader Jones, Robert A. Jones, and John S. Shepard. ALS. DNA, RG59, A. and R. (MR3). See above, Burton to Clay, October 22, 1825. Henderson, of Williamsboro, North Carolina, had been a judge of the North Carolina Superior Court (1808-1816) and of the State Supreme Court (since 1818, chief justice from 1829 to 1833) and was influential as a teacher of law in his private legal practice. The Jones' were both prominent residents of Halifax. Shepard not identified.

J[AMES] BROWN RAY, "Indiana Executive Department," recommends Abner McCarty as receiver of public moneys. ALS. DNA, RG59, A. and R. (MR3). See above, Lane to Clay, October 1, 1825, note.

To [James Brown]

My dear Sir   Washington 14h. Nov. 1825
   We have recently been the subjects of so much affliction that I have been obliged to suffer my private correspondence to get much in arrear. You will have heard that whilst we were yet suffering under the event at Lebanon,[1] the death of Mrs. Duralde opened anew all our griefs. That melancholy and unexpected event happened on the 18h. of September, with the yellow fever. Her attack was insidious. So little was she or Duralde alarmed by it, that she took no medicine until within about 36 hours of her dissolution, when she was beyond the reach of any. I have never before found all the resources of my fortitude so entirely unavailing. Great as have been the sufferings of Lucretia, on the occasion, the character of her sex or her mind has enabled her to sustain the shock better than I have done. I will pass from this melancholy subject.

I have recd. your several letters of the 26h. August. 13h. and 19h. and 27h. Sept. As to your public affairs, I think you had better not press for a decision, if, as from your last would seem to be probable, the decision will be against the claimants. Our public journals have been a good deal lately attracted to our claims abroad, and the spirit of the Country appears to be awakening to the injustice of which we have been so long the object. The President will take some strong notice of them in his message, at the ensuing Congress; and I should not be surprized if the Nation should think soon of resorting to reprisals. In that case France will probably be selected, as well on account of the justice and magnitude of our claims against her, as because, as an example, she will have most effect— I will send you as soon after the message as my other duties will allow me, a paper which shall speak a corresponding language.[2]

We shall be represented in the Congress at Panama. Without affecting our neutral & pacific relations, other objects of great importance are contemplated.

The Nation appears to be well pleased with the administration. Porter's[3] affair produced some little excitement, but the approbation of the sober and the considerate is general. As to the course of Government with respect to Troup,[4] out of Georgia, there is scarcely a dissentient. Jackson has been nominated in Tennessee for the next presidency;[5] but out of Tennessee every body thinks it premature, and I am deceived if the time and manner of it do not give him the coup de grace—

Our friends in K. generally are well; with the exception of a loss sustained by Mrs Hart[6] in the death of her daughter Louisa, who was married about eighteen months ago to Mr. Taylor[7]—

I will endeavor soon again to write you & more fully.   My respects to Mrs' Brown. Your's faithfully   H. CLAY
P. W. [sic] We have been keeping house about six weeks. We reside in the largest of Forrests two houses which were occupied by De Neuville.[8] The rooms are very good, and sufficient in number for my reduced family.   H C

ALS. DLC-HC (DNA, M212, R2).   1 The death of Eliza Clay.
2 Adams referred to the claims as "indemnity for property taken or destroyed under circumstances of most aggravated and outrageous character" and reported that, despite "continued and earnest appeals," there had been not even an answer from the new French sovereign (Charles X); but he proposed no course of action in reprisal. Richardson (comp.), *A Compilation of the Messages and Papers of the Presidents*, II, 301. For a report of the Cabinet disagreement on Clay's urging of a recommendation that Congress authorize issuance of letters of marque and reprisal, see Adams, *Memoirs*, VII, 60-61.
3 David Porter. See above, Nelson to Clay, April 6, 1825, note; Hammond to Clay, August 31, 1825.
4 George M. Troup. See above, Clay to Southard, July 3, 1825, note.
5 See above, Clay to Hammond, November 6, 1825.
6 Mrs. Thomas Hart, Jr. (née Eleanor Grosh).

To Francisco Dionisio Vives

To His Excellency Don Francisco Dionisio Vives,
Governor and Captain General of Cuba &c. &c. &c.
Sir,　　　　　　　　　　　　　　Department of State. 14. Novr. 1825.

A complaint has been made to this Department of the arrest and detention of J. Baker,[1] mate of the ship Thalia of Philadelphia, by the authorities at the Havanna for an alleged chastisement inflicted by him on John Robinson,[2] Steward of that ship, whilst she was at Sea, some distance from Cuba and of course before she entered the port of the Havanna. Assuming those facts to be true, I cannot doubt that your Excellency, from whom we have had so many proofs of a disposition to cultivate friendly relations with the U. States, will immediately direct the discharge of Mr. Baker. For if they be correctly stated, the alleged offence having been committed out of the jurisdiction of Spain, the tribunal of the Havanna could not rightfully take cognizance of it.

I beg leave to recall to the recollection of your Excellency the cases of the seven American Seamen[3] who, upwards of two years ago, were arrested and imprisoned at the Havanna on the suspicion of their having taken part in the murder of a Spanish soldier. Four of them are understood to be still kept in confinement. Humanity, to say nothing of justice, would seem to require that they should be immediately brought to trial. Your Excellency can appreciate and, I am sure, will sympathise in the feelings of their parents and relations, on account of their protracted imprisonment and the uncertainty of their fate.

I avail myself of the occasion to assure you of the friendly recollection which I cherish of the acquaintance which I had the honor of making with you at Washington, and of my distinguished consideration.　　　　　　　　　　　　　　　　H. CLAY.

Copy. DNA, RG59, Notes to Foreign Legations, vol. 3, p. 237 (M38, R3). See Diamond to Clay, October 8, 1825.
1 Not further identified.　　　　　　2 Not further identified.
3 See above, Perry to Clay, March 25, 1825; Warner to Clay, March 26, 1825; Bruce to Clay, August 26, 1825; Diamond to Clay, October 8, 1825; Clay to Rodney, October 29, 1825; and below, Bruce to Clay, January 21, 1826; Rodney to Clay, December 19, 1825; January 7, 1826; February 4, 1826.

From William Creighton, Jr.

Dear Sir.　　　　　　　　　　　　　　Chillicothe Nov. 14 1825.
We have lately been visited by Genl. Cadwallader & Mr. Thomas D

[*sic*] Cope[1] directors of the Bank of the United States on their way to, and on their return from Cincinnati[2]— They informed me that it was the intention of the Parent Bank to remove this office, and I believe it is in contemplation to remove the Branch from Lexington & probably from Norfolk[3]— How the removal of the Branch from Lexington may affect the Town and that section of the State I cannot say. The removal of the Branch from this place will have a most injurious effect at this time on the Town and a very large district of Country. on that account I have been using all my exertions to get them to stay their hand, at least for a time—

There is not the slightest fault found with the management of the office—independant [*sic*] of the expences and bad debts the office has made a handsome profit to the Bank— Those Gentleman [*sic*] placed the removal on general policy. The three states named have each two Branches, and are less commercial than many of the States where only Branch [*sic*] is located. This may be true, But for the interest of the Western Country they have selected a most unfortunate time to carry their their [*sic*] policy into effect. We have every thing but money. and that is indespensable [*sic*] to take the produce of the Country to Market. If you should feel yourself at liberty to interpose your good offices: to stay the removal for at least two years, when th[is] Country will be releived [*sic*] by the expenditures on the Canal,[4] you would gratify your friends in this part of the State[5]—

You will have seen Governor Desha's communication and the assassination of Sharp[6]—

Genl. Jackson's Grooms have brought on [*sic*] the turf too soon[7] he will be broke down in training— I am dear Sir your friend

Hon. H Clay.   W CREIGHTON JUN

ALS. DLC-HC (DNA, M212, R2). Margin of MS. obscured.

1 Thomas Cadwalader, of Philadelphia, admitted to the Pennsylvania bar in 1801, a lieutenant colonel of cavalry, promoted to brigadier general during the War of 1812 and in 1824 raised to the rank of major general, had been active in projects for civic development. He had been a leader in organizing the Schuylkill Navigation Company in 1815 and had been elected a director of the Bank of the United States in 1823. Thomas Pym Cope, long a successful importer and merchant, had established in 1821 the first regular packet line between Philadelphia and Liverpool. He shared Cadwalader's civic interests, was the founder and first president of the Mercantile Library Company, the first president of the Philadelphia Board of Trade (1832-1854), and an active promoter of the Schuylkill Navigation Company. He had also served in the Pennsylvania Legislature of 1807 and in 1837 became a member of the State constitutional convention.

2 The Cincinnati Branch of the Bank of the United States had been reorganized in May, 1825.

3 The Chillicothe Branch of the Bank of the United States was closed in 1825 but the Lexington and Norfolk offices continued until the winter of 1835-1836.

4 The Ohio to Lake Erie Canal. See above, Stuart to Clay, March 15, 1825, note.

5 No action found.

6 See above, Theodore W. Clay to Henry Clay, November 10, 1825.

7 See above, Clay to Hammond, November 6, 1825, note.

From Albert Gallatin

Dear Sir   Private   Baltimore 14th. Nover. 1825
    No one can be more sensible than I am, both of the importance
of laying the foundation of a permanent friendship between the
United States and our new sister Republics, and of the distinguished
honour conferred on the persons selected to be the Representatives
of our glorious and happy country at the first Congress of the
Independant [sic] powers of this Hemisphere. But without affecting
any false modesty, I cannot perceive that I am peculiarly fitted for
that mission, either by knowledge of the language things or men
of South America, or by being known to them. My personal objection has already been stated: I had none whatever to a sea-voyage
or to embarking from an atlantic port. On the receipt of yr.
friendly letter of the 11th, I had further private enquiries made
from men thoroughly acquainted with the country, as if the object
had been a commercial establishment & without my name being
mentioned. The result of these and the decided opposition I would
have to encounter in my family compel me, though with great
reluctance, to persist in declining the appointment. I will preserve
a grateful sense of your's and the President's favorable disposition
in my favour; and I beg to accept my thanks for your friendly
conduct towards me on this occasion. I remain truly Your's
Honble. H. Clay Washington   ALBERT GALLATIN
The intervening Sunday has delayed my answer one day.

ALS. DLC-HC (DNA, M212, R2). ALI draft, NHi-Gallatin Papers. Cf. above, Clay
to Gallatin, November 8 and 11, 1825; Gallatin to Clay, November 10, 1825.

From John H. Pleasants

My dear Sir,   Richmond Nov. 14h. 1825.
    I did not arrive at this place until last evening, or receive your
favor of the 31st. October[1] until this. This will explain my not
having replied to it sooner. I passed through Washington contrary
to my expectation when I last wrote you[2]— Several reasons prevented me from calling on you— I was with a gentleman who had
left Richmond 6 years ago, a refugee from justice, who was returning by my persuasion, and was unwilling to lose a day; and to say
truth, altho' I did not in the least doubt such a reception as my
feelings desired, yet I should have felt a restraint in your presence,
which I thought it as well to avoid—
    I hope and believe that your apprehensions as to the safety of
the Despatches committed to my care, are groundless. There is
but one possible cause which can have occasioned their loss, and

that my presence could not have averted—namely, the loss of the Ship— If she arrived safely in the La Plata, Mr Forbes[3] undoubtedly got the despatches, for he was the intimate acquaintance and Consignee of the Captain. Under the most favorable circumstances, the Captain did not expect to return to the U. S. sooner than the 20h. November, and as the despatches had to be sent from Buenos Ayres to Rio, it is scarcely time to expect the acknowledgment of their receipt[4]— I mention these facts to relieve your fears for the safety of the papers, and not as aiding in my exculpation— I cannot rest that upon a stronger ground than the great jeopardy in which my life was placed—nor have I the least doubt, that had I proceeded in the unfortunate ship in which I took passage, that my life would have fallen a sacrifice to the horrible privations of air, exercise and the most common necessaries to which I was exposed— I will as soon as may be, forward my vouchers—

I submit with cheerfulness to your opinions about an expose of the reasons which altered my destination. Indeed a desire to vindicate you, from any censure, and to offer myself as a victim, should the *newspapers* require one, alone prompted the proposition made in my former letter— This I am still, and always shall be, ready to do, should it be necessary— To be the cause of uneasiness or reproach to you, would be a return for all your kindness, which I should regret for the rest of my life.

My father[5] is well and presents his sincere respects to you, and his condolence in those afflictions, which he has himself been called upon to feel— I saw Judge Brooke on yesterday, who was just mad [sic] happy by the return of his son in good health.[6]

The question of a senator is agitating the Metropolis here and the State   It is considered important, as indicating the feeling of the State towards the Administration. The violent party are like [sic] to settle down on Giles, who has evinced all the ambition of a youth of 20 to get the situation. It is impossible to say what the result will be— I think myself that he cannot be elected[7]— I remain Dear Sir, Yr most Grateful, and Respectful Friend & Sert.   JNO H PLEASANTS.

ALS. DNA, RG59, Letters from Bearers of Dispatches.
1 Not found.   2 Above, October 29, 1825.
3 John M. Forbes.
4 On December 7, 1825, Daniel Brent wrote Pleasants to inform him that the dispatches entrusted to his care had been delivered to Forbes on August 10. Copy, in DNA, RG59, Dom. Letters, vol. 21, p. 209 (M40, R19).
5 James Pleasants
6 See below, Brooke to Clay, November 27, 1825.
7 *Ibid.*, note.

DIPLOMATIC NOTES   November 14, 1825

From ANTONIO JOSE CANAZ, Washington. Invites the United States to send representatives to the Panama Congress. ALS, in Spanish, translated in State Department file. DNA, RG59, Notes from Central American Legations, vol. 1 (M-T34, R1). Published in Manning (arr.), *Diplomatic Correspondence . . . Latin-American Nations,* II, 883.

INSTRUCTIONS AND DISPATCHES   November 14, 1825

From THOMAS L. L. BRENT, Lisbon. Reports "a decided disappointment among all classes of persons" relative to the treaty between Portugal and Brazil, which, "it is generally supposed," will be ratified tomorrow. LS. DNA, RG59, Dip. Disp., Portugal, vol. 6 (M43, R5). Received January 13, 1826. See above, Raguet to Secretary of State, March 11, 1825, note; Brent to Clay, November 12, 1825.

From RUFUS KING, London, no. 11. Reports an interview, November 8, with the Russian Ambassador, Count Lieven, who read to him Count Nesselrode's reply to Middleton's note founded on Clay's instructions (see above, Clay to Middleton, May 10, 1825; Middleton to Clay, September 8, 1825 (1), note); refers to the ratification of the treaty between Great Britain and Colombia (above, Watts to Clay, May 10, 1825) and to the "decisive importance" of the reception of the Colombian envoy, (Manuel José) Hurtado; states that it "is understood" that envoys from other new states will be recognized; notes that nothing of these matters has appeared in the French or Spanish press. LS. DNA, RG59, Dip. Disp., Great Britain, vol. 32 (M30, R28). Received January 13, 1826. Published in Manning (arr.), *Diplomatic Correspondence . . . Latin-American Nations,* III, 1574-75.

APPLICATIONS, RECOMMENDATIONS   November 14, 1825

THOMAS U. P. CHARLTON, Savannah, recommends Robert M. Goodwin as Federal marshal in that district. ALS. DNA, RG59, A. and R. (MR2). See below, Goodwin to Clay, February 8, 1826.

MORTON A. WARING, Charleston, South Carolina, seeks reappointment as Federal marshal. ALS. DNA, RG59, A. and R. (MR4). Waring held the position from 1813 to 1832.

DIPLOMATIC NOTES   November 15, 1825

From CHARLES R. VAUGHAN, Washington. Transmits a copy of a letter, with enclosures, from Sir Howard Douglas, Lieutenant Governor of New Brunswick; comments: "It appears that two . . . [agents of Massachusetts and Maine] have circulated a notice amongst the Settlers upon the Rivers St John & Madawaska, that they were authorized to execute deeds of conveyance of Lands in those Districts; & the same persons on their Passage through the Settlement of Madawaska, endeavoured to induce the Men belonging to the Militia, not to attend the General Training, asserting, that . . . the Territory which they occupied belonged to the United States"; and states that he is sure Clay "will concur . . . in opinion, that so long as the Question of the Boundary remains in the present undecided State, it will be the duty of our Governments to controul, mutually, any Conduct on the part of their respective Subjects, which is calculated to produce disunion and disagreement—" LS. DNA, RG59,

Notes from British Legation, vol. 14 (M50, R15). Published in Manning (arr.), *Diplomatic Correspondence . . . Canadian Relations,* II, 492-93. In the enclosed letter, Douglas requests Vaughan to demand "that an immediate stop be put to practices which have such a marked tendency to sow dissension, & insubordination, in Settlements long since established by Grant from His Majesty, and considered as subject to the British Crown; & which if persisted in, may lead to serious consequences which it will not be in . . . [his] power to prevent." Cf. above, Clay to Addington, March 27, 1825, note. The land agent of Maine was James Irish and that of Massachusetts, George W. Coffin, the latter in 1829 prominent as a shipowner and merchant of Nantucket.

INSTRUCTIONS AND DISPATCHES   November 15, 1825

To RUFUS KING, no. 9. Refers to an earlier proposal, by King's predecessor, that England cede part of the Island of Abaco to the United States for the site of a lighthouse (cf. above, Rush to Clay, May 12, 1825); to a counter proposal that the British establish in that area the "necessary aids to navigation," provided that United States vessels pay the necessary fees for their upkeep; and to the British promise, never fulfilled, to reduce their proposal to writing. Instructs King to bring this matter again to the attention of the British Government, to explain what the United States has done in establishing lighthouses and other aids to navigation, to state that other lighthouses are contemplated near Cape Florida and Cape Canaveral, and, if the British Government continue to refuse the cession and to insist on participation by the United States in the expenses of building and maintaining lighthouses, "to assure it that the United States will defray such reasonable proportion of the expense, as shall be hereafter mutually agreed upon between the two Governments." Copy. DNA, RG59, Dip. Instr., vol. 10, pp. 412-14 (M77, R5). AL draft, in Clay's hand, in DLC-HC (DNA, M212, R1). Published in *American State Papers, Foreign Relations,* VI, 753-54.

From ALEXANDER BURTON, Cádiz. Notes that the quarantine at Cádiz is suspended from this date until June, "when the usual summer regulations will be again enforced by the French"; that the persons mentioned in his letter of September 28, "together with others," have been sent to Gibraltar to be exchanged; that three people "of this description, natives of the United States," will be sent to France to be turned over to the United States consul "at the Port of their arrival." ALS. DNA, RG59, Cons. Disp., Cádiz, vol. 4 (M-T186, R4). Received December 28.

From JOHN W. PARKER, Amsterdam. Refers to his letter of July 7; states that (George) Lee was released from imprisonment "for a certain Sum, to avoid the payment of which the Ship's agent has again requested . . . [Parker's] interference"; and, in view of the precedent that will be established by the decision of the Government of the Netherlands and of the delicate nature of the case, requests instructions. ALS. *Ibid.,* Amsterdam, vol. 2 (M-T182, R-T2). Received February 14, 1826.

MISCELLANEOUS LETTERS   November 15, 1825

From JOHN DORR, Boston. Acknowledges receipt of Clay's letter of October 15, 1825, sends copies of documents relating to the case of the *Esther,* and expresses gratification for the action being taken. ALS. DNA, RG76, Misc. Claims, Peru.

APPLICATIONS, RECOMMENDATIONS   November 15, 1825

ALEXANDER G. McRAE, Clarksburg (Virginia), seeks reappointment to publish the laws. ALS. DNA, RG59, P. and D. of L. McRae had been a journalist in Clarksburg since 1815 and had founded the Clarksburg *Intelligencer* in 1823; he was reappointed as here requested.

HUGH L. WHITE, Knoxville (Tennessee), recommends reappointment of (Frederick S.) Heiskell and (Hugh) Brown to publish the laws. LS. *Ibid.* Heiskell and Brown, who had founded the *Knoxville Register* in 1816, held the requested appointment throughout the Adams administration.

From Peter B. Porter

Sir,   Troy November 16th. 1825
I presume that you must have made yourself acquainted with the progress of the Commission instituted by the Seventh Article of the Treaty of Ghent for establishing our North Western Boundary; and with the present state of its operations, so far as the same is exhibited by the documents already on file in your Department.

This Commission has, I presume, been already protracted to a period beyond what was originally contemplated by either of the two Goverments [*sic*], and, indeed, beyond what seemed to be required by the importance of the subjects of adjudication. I trust however that the Journal of our proceedings, and other official documents, copies of which will have been transmitted to you before the receipt of this by Mr Delafield the American Agent, will satisfy the President that the delay is not imputable to me, nor to any of the Agents constituting the American part of the Commission; and that it has not been in my power to bring the business to an earlier close, but by a total rupture of the Commission, which would have defeated, at once, all the objects for which it was instituted.

The Journal of our meeting on the 1st. & 2d. of this month will shew that we have adjourned untill may next, /the earliest day at which, in the opinion of Mr Barclay, he could be prepared for a final adjudication/

His refusal to close the Commission a year ago, arose, as I then knew, from an expectation entertained by him that he should be able to establish, as the boundary beyond Lake Superior, a line far to the south of the one which was obviously in contemplation of the Signers of the Treaty of —83. And, with this object in view, he has made a tour himself, during the past Summer, to the North West, accompanied not only by his former Surveyor & Astronomer, but by another British Astronomer of some distinction /Doct. Tiark/[1]

who was sent out by that government for this express purpose. From the informal conversation, however, which I have had with Mr Barclay & Doct Tiark, since their return, I apprehend no serious difficulties in our amicable adjustment of the Boundary at our next meeting. I am, Sir, with great respect, Your Obt. Servt.

Hon. Henry Clay Secretary of State   PETER B. PORTER

ALS. DNA, RG76, Northern Boundary: Treaty of Ghent, Arts. VI and VII, env. 1, folder 1. Cf. above, Delafield to Clay, September 23, 1825.

¹ John Lewis Tiarks, born at Jever, near Wilhelmshaven, and graduated from the University of Göttingen with a degree in mathematics, had emigrated to England to escape conscription under Napoleon and, from 1817 to 1821, had served as British astronomer to the Northeast Boundary Commission. From 1825 to 1826 he was again in America, assigned to locate the most northwesterly point of the Lake of the Woods. He was at the Hague in 1828 to 1829 as an adviser to the arbitration commission studying the boundary and from 1834 to 1835 again in England as an expert on this matter. The remainder of his life was passed in Germany, where he died in 1837.

From Thomas I. Wharton

Dear Sir   Philada. 16 Novr. 1825

Since your appointment to your present elevated station I have not had an opportunity to assure you of the unaltered respect and Continued Confidence with which you are regarded by your friends here. Until very lately I entertained the hope that we should have the pleasure to see you here on your return from Lexington. The duties of your office will I presume detain you all winter in Washington—where I hope in the Course of the Season to pay my respects to you personally And the only regret I shall feel will be your absence from the floor of Congress where you have so often signalized yourself but where I have never had An opportunity of hearing you. Among the interesting Subjects which will probably be discussed there at the next Session is that of the claims upon France & Holland, with regard to which a warm And very natural feeling prevails And the hope seems to be entertained that something more to the purpose will be done by the government.¹

It has struck me that perhaps the Administration might feel itself strengthened if the Attention of Congress were Again called to the subject by memorials from this City and other places And I have thought of obtaining from the merchants here the Agency for their claims both in presenting And urging the memorials upon Congress And in the subsequent Arrangements. If there was reason to beleive [sic] that the government thought it consistent with a due regard to the other interests of the Country to press the matter further, the mercantile interest here would take early measures to forward memorials upon the subject to Congress, And if you can with propriety inform me whether you think Another Application

to Congress proper And likely to be attended with beneficial consequences you will particularly oblige me.

I am not quite clear whether Another subject which I am about
to mention falls within your province—if it does not you will excuse
the application as I am not otherwise interested in it than by a
regard to [*sic*] a very worthy & honorable family nearly related to
mine. A grandson of Mr Rawle[2] of this city of whose eminent
character as a Lawyer & Citizen you have probably heard is An
applicant for the post of Cadet at West Point. He is a remarkably
fine and manly boy, of the best disposition And promise And if the
Appointment Can be obtained for him it will not only be a
gratification And releif [*sic*] to an excellent family recently unfortunate, but a valuable Addition will be made to the stock of
future officers. His name is already on the list, And he is now at
the proper age for admission.

We have lately had the pleasure to see & entertain the President[3]
And I hope it will not be long before the Secretary of State gives
us a similar opportunity. I Am Dr Sir With great respect And
regard Your Friend & Servt.   T. I. WHARTON
Hon: H. Clay Secretary of State &c

ALS. DLC-HC (DNA, M212, R2).
1 Cf. above, Clay to Brown, November 14, 1825.
2 William Rawle (Sr.); grandson not identified.
3 See above, Clay to Adams, September 26, 1825, note.

DIPLOMATIC NOTES   November 16, 1825

From the BARON DE MAREUIL, Washington. Presents two observations relative
to Clay's letter to him of November 7: first, in regard to the conversation
between Adams and himself last year, he remembers only certain difficulties
resulting from division of territories and of jurisdiction for the execution of
Article 6 of the convention, on which the Attorney General was to be consulted,
and he still inquires concerning the result of that consultation in order to
establish complete reciprocity between the two countries; and, second, concerning Clay's reference to the possibility of appeal to the courts, he points out
that between governments the execution of treaties is not subject to judicial
action and that each government must procure in its own territory full execution
of treaty stipulations. LS, in French, translated in State Department file. DNA,
RG59, Notes from French Legation, vol. 9 (M53, R7). Published in *American
State Papers, Foreign Relations*, V, 788-89.

INSTRUCTIONS AND DISPATCHES   November 16, 1825

To JOHN SERGEANT. Same as the letter to Albert Gallatin, November 8, 1825,
"with the following addition at the end of the 1st. paragraph, viz— 'to the 20th
of January, nor your absence from the United States be of longer duration
than six months.'" Note appended to the letter to Gallatin in DNA, RG59,

Dip. Instr., vol. 10, p. 427 (M77, R5). N, in Brent's hand, in DLC-HC (DNA, M212, R7). Sergeant replied, November 19, accepting the appointment. ALS. DNA, RG43, First Panama Congress (M662, R1).

From CHARLES L. BARTLETT, Trinidad. Refers to his letter of April 25; encloses a copy of a letter addressed to him by the Governor of the island (Sir Ralph Woodford), declining to recognize Bartlett as consular agent; requests further instructions; and describes his aid to American seamen at that port. ALS. DNA, RG59, Cons. Disp., Trinidad, vol. 1 (M-T148, R1).

From THOMAS L. L. BRENT, Lisbon. Describes an interview with the King (John VI), who "appeared dejected," expressed "discontent at the Treaty" with Brazil (above, Raguet to Secretary of State, March 11, 1825, note), characterized "the Brazils" as ungrateful, and added "that the british had attended too much to their own interests"; reports that, in answer to an inquiry by the King whether the United States "would be content with what been [sic] done," he stated that acknowledgment of Brazilian independence could be considered only as a wise measure and that in the rest he saw "nothing that might be contrary to the interests of the United States"; states that he has received from the Count of Porto Santo a communication on the subject, which is not being enclosed because of lack of time for copying but will be forwarded within a few days. Encloses a copy of the treaty between Portugal and Brazil. LS. DNA, RG59, Dip. Disp., Portugal, vol. 6 (M43, R5). Received January 14, 1826. António de Saldanha da Gama, Count of Porto Santo, had been governor and captain-general of Maranham (1802) and Angola (1805), a naval officer and member of the Conselho Ultramarino, a representative of Portugal at the Congress of Vienna (1814), envoy to the Court of Madrid in 1820, promoted to ambassador there in 1823, and from February 5, 1825, to July 13, 1826, held the dual position of Minister of State and Foreign Affairs.

From JOHN M. FORBES, Buenos Aires, no. 27. Reports that the prohibition of importation of flour has been abolished, "but the opposition prevailed in raising the duty to three dollars per quintal"; encloses copies of his note to the Minister of State, (Manuel José) García, stating that the law "can in no manner Satisfy the expectations" of the United States, and of the reply; explains his conviction that British influence caused adoption of the high rate of duty; and describes his efforts to obtain official interpretations of two obscure points in the law. Notes receipt by the Government (of Buenos Aires) of communications "from their Ministers or Commissioners near the Deliverer, Bolivar," who promises "efficient Co-operation in Case of need" against Brazil. Discusses "the political Struggle for power" between (Bernardino) Rivadavia and García and the preparations for forming "a permanent Executive and perhaps a written Constitution." States that he has determined to republish there the pamphlet sent to him by (Samuel) Larned (see above, Larned to Clay, November 5, 1825). Notes that the Congress has authorized a loan of $15,000,000, "which, it is expected, will be chiefly negotiated in London. . . ." LS. Ibid., Argentina, vol. 2 (M69, R3). Continued on November 17 and 21, 1825. Received February 16, 1826. Published in Espil (comp.), Once Años en Buenos Aires, 394-98.

From MICHAEL HOGAN. Reports receipt of mail, apparently through mistake, including a commission as consul at St. Iago de Chile (cf. above, Clay to Wynne, April 16, 1825; Wynne to Clay, June 25, 1825, October 4, 1825); recommends that a vice consul be appointed for Coquimbo. ALS. DNA, RG59,

Cons. Disp., Valparaiso, vol. 1 (M146, R1). Hogan, of New York, had been the United States consul at Cork, Ireland, from 1819 to 1823 and from the latter year until his death in 1834 held the post at Valparaiso, Chile.

APPLICATIONS, RECOMMENDATIONS   November 16, 1825

H[UTCHINS] G. BURTON, Raleigh, transmits additional recommendations (for Robert Potter as Chargé d'Affaires at Guatemala). ALS. DNA, RG59, A. and R. (MR3). See above, October 22, 1825.

LIPPINCOTT AND ABBOTT, Edwardsville (Illinois), new editors of the *Spectator,* seek reappointment to publish the laws. ALS. DNA, RG59, P. and D. of L. Lippincott and Abbott not further identified; the appointment was continued in the name of Hooper Warren, who had established the journal in 1819.

Warren, born in New Hampshire, and trained as a printer in Rutland, Vermont, had resided from 1814 to 1817 in Delaware and a few months at Frankfort, Kentucky, and St. Louis, Missouri, before settling in Illinois. In 1827 he established the Springfield *Sangamo Spectator,* which he edited until 1829. Both it and the *Edwardsville Spectator* served as organs to further the political career of Ninian Edwards. From 1829 to 1832 Warren edited a journal in Galena, and subsequently he worked, for short periods, on newspapers in Chicago and Lowell. His later life was spent as a farmer at Henry, in Marshall County.

JOHN B. ROSE, a member of the Indiana Legislature from Union County, recommends the Richmond *Public Ledger* (edited by Edmund S. Buxton and Samuel B. Walling) to publish the laws. ALS. *Ibid.* See above, Hendricks to Clay, September 21, 1825, note.

DIPLOMATIC NOTES   November 17, 1825

From P[ETER] PEDERSEN, Philadelphia. States that he has communicated to his government Clay's letter of November 7, 1825. ALS. DNA, RG59, Notes from Danish Legation, vol. 1 (M52, R1).

INSTRUCTIONS AND DISPATCHES   November 17, 1825

From ROBERT M. HARRISON, Antigua. Refers to his letter of November 10 and encloses a statement of the method by which American vessels are to be measured. ALS. DNA, RG59, Cons. Disp., Antigua, vol. 1 (M-T327, R1). Received December 28.

APPLICATIONS, RECOMMENDATIONS   November 17, 1825

F[RANCIS] W. ARMSTRONG, St. Stephens (Alabama), recommends Henry Hitchcock as district attorney (in Alabama) and strongly opposes David Rust. ALS. DNA, RG59, A. and R. (MR2). Armstrong, born in Virginia and later removed to Tennessee and Alabama, had been appointed marshal for Alabama District in December, 1823. In 1832 he was named agent for the Choctaws west of the Mississippi River and remained in that office for the next decade. On Hitchcock's appointment, see above, Hall to Clay, August 16, 1825, note.

J[OHN] HOLMES and JOHN CHANDLER, Senate Chamber, recommend the Portland, Maine, *Eastern Argus* and the Hallowell, Maine, *American Advocate* to publish the laws. ALS by Holmes, signed also by Chandler. DNA, RG59, P. and D. of L. Chandler, Senator from Maine (1820-1829), was a veteran of the Revolutionary War and the War of 1812 and had served in the legislatures of Massachusetts and Maine. He was later (1829-1837) collector of customs at Portland, Maine. Both the recommended journals were reappointed.

NOAH ZANE and others recommend Robert I. Curtis, editor of the Wheeling *Gazette,* to publish the laws. LS, signed by 12 persons, including A[lexander] Caldwell and John McLure. *Ibid.* Dated by postmark. Curtis had been editor of the journal since 1820; he did not receive the appointment recommended.

INSTRUCTIONS AND DISPATCHES   November 18, 1825

From WILLIAM TAYLOR, Alvarado. Reports the capitulation of the Castle of San Juan de Ulloa (see above, Clay to Poinsett, March 26, 1825, note; below, Poinsett to Clay, November 23, 1825). States that last spring Nathaniel Cox, "U. S. N. Agent," and Samuel Elkins, merchant, both of New Orleans, revoked a power of attorney they had given to (James) Wilkinson, in connection with claims against Mexico, and substituted Taylor and that in September he received from Wilkinson a letter, a copy of which is enclosed, wherein the General's "well known malice prompted him to state that which he knew to be false. . . ." Notes an expectation that "this Port will be closed by order of the Mexican Government, so soon as the merchants can conveniently remove to Vera Cruz." ALS. DNA, RG59, Cons. Disp., Vera Cruz, vol. 1 (M183, R1). Received December 20. Extract published in Manning (arr.), *Diplomatic Correspondence . . . Latin-American Nations,* III, 1643. In the enclosure Wilkinson declares his intention of informing the President that Taylor is "Charged by Several Gentlemen of Alvarado to be a Contrabandist, & Smuggle [*sic*]." Cox had been appointed naval agent for the port of New Orleans in January, 1825. Elkins not further identified.

APPLICATIONS, RECOMMENDATIONS   November 18, 1825

JEREMIAH AUSTILL, Mobile, transmits a petition of the merchants of Mobile recommending appointment of Henry Hitchcock as district attorney for the Southern District of Alabama. ALS. DNA, RG59, A. and R. (M531, R4). Unaddressed. The enclosure, dated November 13, carries 45 signatures. Austill, born in South Carolina and a pioneer settler in Alabama, was clerk of the United States District Court for the Southern District of his adopted State. On the recommended appointment, see above, Hall to Clay, August 16, 1825, note.

O[LIVER] H. SMITH, prosecuting attorney, Third Circuit, Connersville, Fayette County, Indiana, recommends Richmond *Public Ledger* to publish the laws. LS. DNA, RG59, P. and D. of L. Smith had been a member of the Indiana Legislature (1822-1824) and later served in the United States House of Representatives (1827-1829) and Senate (1837-1843). On the result of the recommendation, see above, Hendricks to Clay, September 21, 1825, note.

DANIEL WEBSTER, Boston, recommends Benjamin Gardner, acting consul at Palermo, for appointment as consul. ALS. DNA, RG59, A. and R. (MR2). See below, Blake to Clay, November 19, 1825.

From David Chambers

Hon. H. Clay   Wood Grove,[1] November 19, 1825.

Sir—I had the honor duly to receive yours of the 25th August
last acknowledging mine of the 6th July.[2] I regretted its delay in
reaching you as my chief object was, merely to inform you promptly,
of the *manner* of our canal celebration, the fact of the *presence* of
Governor Clinton,[3] as well as your *own good standing* among us
in contrast with the other eminent men passing in review. I attended the canal celebration partly with the anticipated expectation
of your being a guest, and should have experienced great pleasure
in seeing you at Zanesville, which would have been the case had
you been permitted to accept of the friendly hospitality entertained
towards you by the citizens of that place and vicinity.[4] I however
early anticipated the disappointment of our wishes from causes,
which it was still hoped when you passed here would not have
terminated so fatally.[5] In the heavy losses which your family have
recently sustained[6] I have most sincerely sympathised, and offer
you my most feeling condolence; but for *me* to attempt bringing
you consolation would be idle— May the Almighty dispenser of
good and evil to the sons of men, strengthen and support you in
every trial, and enable you to dis harge [*sic*] every duty incumbent,
either of a private or public character in a manner satisfactory to
yourself and for the promotion of the best interests of all concerned.—

In whatever situation you may be placed politically, I shall be
proud to rank myself as one of your friends and defenders, so long
as you continue to pursue a course not inconsistent with your past
public conduct; And your friends generally in this quarter I am
persuaded will at all times be prompt to act upon such intimations
of public movements as may be calculated to sustain your public
character and public views.—

It is evident that Genl. Jackson will again enter the lists to
compete for the presidential chair at the next election. It is somewhat singular to observe, that Gen. Jackson was elected to the
Senate of the United States, *ostensibly* with a view to *place him on
a footing with his competitors* at the last election. The General
now makes it convenient to *resign* his seat,[7] *because he has again
been brought forward as a candidate!* Few men have be[en] so
fortunate as to have had it in their power to resign at pleasure so
many offices as have been conferred upon this man, and that too
without any injury to the public, or any apparent loss of popularity.—

In conclusion I beg to leave to observe, that if in the course of
public duties you may be called upon to select or mention any

person as suitable or fit for any decent public employment which might be adapted to my limited capacity, you will do me a great kindness to mention me favorably to the President.[8] In making this request I pray you sir not to consider me as approaching you with the importunity of a friend,— But as one who may have some little claim to public employment, from a long and ardent attention to *public affairs,* and a strenuous support of the successive republican Administrations of our Government from the prosperous days of the revered Jefferson up to the present time; and that too perhaps with an earnestness not well adapted to the advancement of my *private* advantage. I am therefore not *above* the convenience which an appointment suited to my capacity might afford. I presume if required, I can receive ample recommendation from the represen- tion [*sic*] from this state in Congress.— Although I possess a respect- able share of popularity among my fellow citizens, I have nevertheless been unsuccessful in two attempts to be returned a representative from this district, owing to local causes, and the unceasing exertions of a small faction in Zanesville headed by our late Marshal,[9] because I had the temerity to do justice to his character, while a represen- tative, at his last application for office. His weight thrown into the scale with that of a few others have been sufficient heretofore to prevent the success of my friends, whose support has been, and would still be strenuously exerted, were I to allow it.

With much respect and sincere regard, I remain sir Yours &c

DAVID CHAMBERS.

ALS. DLC-HC (DNA, M212, R2). Endorsed by Chambers on verso: "Private."
[1] Probably Chambers' farm, near Zanesville, Ohio.
[2] Neither letter has been found.
[3] See above, Toasts and Speech, July 13, 1825, notes.
[4] No invitation has been found.   [5] The illness of Eliza Clay.
[6] The death, also, of Susan Clay Duralde.
[7] See above, Carroll to Clay, October 4, 1825, and note.
[8] Chambers received no Federal appointment.   [9] John Hamm.

INSTRUCTIONS AND DISPATCHES   November 19, 1825

From JOEL R. POINSETT, Mexico, no. 26. Acknowledges receipt of dispatches nos. 4 and 6 (above, September 12, 26, 1825); states that (Daniel) Brent's letter, to which Clay alludes in his no. 6, was not received, and Poinsett knows nothing of the claim of Chouteau and De Mun; reports that the surrender of the Castle (of San Juan de Ulloa) is imminent and that "The Junta for the affairs of Cuba [see above, Poinsett to Clay, September 13, 1825] is dissolved after appointing a permanent commission"; encloses a letter to (Charles J.) Ingersoll, which "will explain the state of the claim of the Assignees of Mr John Coulter." LS. DNA, RG59, Dip. Disp., Mexico, vol. 1 (M97, R2). Received January 3, 1826. On the claim here cited, cf. above, Clay to Poinsett, September 12, 1825.

From THOMAS MILLER, Washington. Requests that steps be taken to procure the attendance of Thomas M. Bailey, of Accomac County, Virginia, before the board of commissioners (under the St. Petersburg Convention). ALS. DNA, RG59, Misc. Letters (M179, R63). In an endorsement, on verso, Clay directs (Daniel) Brent to reply that Bailey has already given a deposition but that he will be sent for if his presence is needed. On April 29, 1825, Daniel Brent had written to Bailey requesting the latter to call on Clay "before he sets out for Kentucky," to discuss Bailey's "observation and recollection of circumstances as to the situation of Slaves, Citizens of the United States, captured by the Enemy during the late war with Great Britain, and which actually were or were supposed to be within the jurisdictional Limits of the United States, when . . . [he was] sent to Tangier Island, at the termination of that war, by direction of President Madison, upon the ratification of the Treaty of Ghent to demand the surrender of such Slaves. . . ." Copy. DNA, RG59, Dom. Letters, vol. 21, pp. 46-47 (M40, R19). Brent also wrote to Miller on November 19, in accordance with the directions of Clay's endorsement. Copy. *Ibid.,* pp. 192-93. Miller, a former resident of Virginia who had moved to Washington in 1820, was a claimant of indemnity for slaves carried off by the British after the War of 1812. Bailey, not further identified.

APPLICATIONS, RECOMMENDATIONS   November 19, 1825

JOSHUA BLAKE, Boston, recommends Benjamin Gardner, a merchant of Palermo, as consul at that port. ALS. DNA, RG59, A. and R. (MR2). Blake was also a merchant. Gardner, born in Massachusetts, was granted an interim appointment to the post later this month, was confirmed in the office on December 19, and retained it until 1837.

From Thomas J. Jennings

Dear Sir,   Paris Tenn. Novr. 20th. 1825.
   When you were last at Lexington I was a student of Transylvania University, and visited you at Ashland. I mention these circumstances lest, from the great number of persons who eagerly sought to be presented to you, on that occasion, you may have forgotten one who can, indeed, claim but a very brief and passing acquaintance with you
   Knowing that you have now but little time to give to letters of this sort, I shall proceed forthwith to what I will candidly confess is my principal object in addressing you at present.
   The office of Post-Master at Jackson, in this District, became vacant a few days ago by the death of the late incumbent.[1] I wish to obtain it, and desire you to make application for it to the Post-Master General.[2] I at first hesitated about the propriety of troubling you in a matter So unimportant as this, but that hesitation was at an end when I reflected, from a knowledge of your character and

feelings, that nothing with you is unimportant by which you can confer a favour on a Kentuckian and a friend.

I left Lexington in July, and after remaining a week or two at my father's[3] in Todd County Ky I came on to the Section of Tennessee which I have chosen for *my home.* While in Todd c'ty, I asked my father what R. P. Henry's constituents thought of his voting, in the House of Representatives, for Genl. Jackson?[4] He replied "We have entire confidence in Majr. Henry's honesty," and as he Says "he thought he was representing our wishes in the vote he gave, although he was mistaken, we forgive him." I was astonished to find your friends here So numerous. I would Scarcely be speaking extravagantly if I were to say they compose one half of the citizens of this county. And I am told they are respectable in numbers, and powerful, when their influence over the people is considered, throughout the Western District. I have two brothers here, the one a lawyer and the other a Physician,[5] who have resided in this country three or four years, and although they are well known to be warm and decided friends of yours, they are as popular as any men of their ages in the District.

You may perhaps have seen Some account of a dinner that was given to Genl. Jackson in this place, a few weeks ago. I'll tell you what it meant. Before the project was announced to the Public, the General's most prominent friends, in this place, called privately on Some of yours and Solicited our concurrence and assistance, agreeing that it should be considered that we were honouring him exclusively as a distinguished military man, and one of the agents of Government in purchasing from the Indians the territory we occupy,[6] and that no unfriendly allusions should be made to the present administration, but particularly, to yourself. Accordingly my brother, D. S. Jennings, who acted by appointment as one of the presiding officers, the General who ordered out the Militia of the County, on the occasion, myself (his aid de camp) and the Colonel[7] who more immediately commanded them, were all known to be opposed to the General's advancement to the Presidency, and friendly to yours. Through men of *these political Sentiments* and with *these views* has Genl. Jackson lately been honoured by the citizens of Paris and Henry County, in the Western District of *Tennessee!*

This new country is rapidly advancing to wealth and influence in the councils of the State. Our Soil is about as well adapted to the culture of Cotton as that of Alabama, and it is populating with Such unexampled rapidity that it is confidently expected that, according to the present rate of apportionment, we will be entitled to five representatives in Congress by the year 1830. It is necessary that the application I have desired you to make for me, should be made immediately, or it can avail me nothing, in as much as the office will certainly be given to Some person or other without delay.[8] Any communication that you or the Post-Master General may address to me on this Subject I would thank you to direct, or have directed, to this place. Present my compliments to Mrs. Clay and Mrs. Erwin.[9] With high respect Your friend

Hon: H. Clay   THOMAS J. JENNINGS

ALS. DLC-HC (DNA, M212, R2). MS. stained. Jennings, a graduate in law from Transylvania University in July, 1825, opened an academy at Paris in December of that year. He has not been further identified.

[1] Samuel Taylor, born in North Carolina, had been appointed a member of the court of pleas and quarter sessions at the organization of Madison County, Tennessee, in 1821 and served as postmaster of Madison Courthouse (renamed Jackson in 1824) from 1822 to 1825.   [2] John McLean.

[3] Probably William Jennings, a veteran of the Revolution and colonel of militia, who had held Federal appointment as an assessor in 1817 and had served in the Kentucky Legislature in 1818.

[4] See above, Kendall to Clay, February 19, 1825, note.

[5] Dudley S. Jennings, the lawyer, not further identified; possibly William R. Jennings, a graduate of the Transylvania Medical Department in 1824.

[6] See above, II, 770n.

[7] The general and colonel of the local militia, not identified.

[8] Robert Johnson (I.) Chester held the office from 1825 to 1833. Chester, who in later life accepted the middle initial "I.," because of common popular error in reading the handwritten signature, had been quartermaster of a Tennessee regiment in the War of 1812 and was a staunch political adherent of Andrew Jackson.

[9] Mrs. James Erwin (Anne Brown Clay).

MISCELLANEOUS LETTERS   November 20, 1825

From JOSEPH HILL CLARK, Havana. States that an expedition sent from Havana to relieve the Castle of San Juan de Ulloa has failed and returned; notes fear of a Mexican attack on Cuba; and reports on the population and economy of the island. ALS. DNA, RG59, Misc. Letters (M179, R63).

APPLICATIONS, RECOMMENDATIONS   November 20, 1825

EDMUND S. BUXTON and SAMUEL B. WALLING, Richmond, Indiana, apply to publish the laws (in Richmond *Public Ledger*). LS. DNA, RG59, P. and D. of L. See above, Hendricks to Clay, September 21, 1825, note.

EDWARD R. GIBSON, Tallahassee, Florida, recommends (David B.) Macomb for appointment as "U. States Attorney for this district." ALS. DNA, RG59, A. and R. (MR5). The appointment was not granted.

J[OHN] SPEED SMITH, Richmond (Kentucky), seeks appointment as "Chargé de Affaires to some subordinate Court" or "Secretary of Legation to a distinguished minister either to France England or Russia." ALS. DNA, RG59, A. and R. (M531, R7). Addressee not named. Smith received no appointment at this time. He was named secretary to the mission to Tacubaya (cf. below, Poinsett to Clay, August 20, 1826, note) in March, 1827, but declined the commission.

INSTRUCTIONS AND DISPATCHES   November 21, 1825

From A[LEXANDER] H. EVERETT, Madrid, no. 15. Transmits a copy of a note
which he has sent to the Duke del Infantado, concerning the admission of a
consul of the United States at Havana; reports a conversation with the Duke,
on this and other matters, which has led Everett to believe that he could obtain
an exequatur for a consul if an appointment were made and the commission
were sent to him, that the Duke is willing to undertake the settlement of
claims by means of "a convention providing for the appointment of Commissioners," that the Duke will receive proposals relative to commercial relations
between Spain and the United States, and that, in regard to the war between
Spain and her former colonies, "there is at present no direct intention in the
[Spanish] Cabinet to change their policy, but . . . there is at least, as much
probability of a recognition now as before the late Ministerial revolution."
States that he will prepare a communication, which the Duke has agreed to
receive, stating the opinion of the United States Government relative to the
conflict between Spain and the former colonies. LS. DNA, RG59, Dip. Disp.,
Spain, vol. 25 (M31, R27). Received March 6, 1826. Published in *American
State Papers, Foreign Relations,* V, 879-80. On the recent change of Spanish
ministry, see above, Everett to Clay, October 26, 1825.

APPLICATIONS, RECOMMENDATIONS   November 21, 1825

PETER LITTLE, Baltimore, introduces William Bose and recommends continuation
of the appointment of the Baltimore *American,* edited by Dobbin, Murphy, and
Bose, to publish the laws. ALS. DNA, RG59, P. and D. of L. Bose, in 1815,
had entered into publication of the *American,* of which his brother-in-law,
George Dobbin, and Thomas Murphy had assumed partial ownership in 1810.
Dobbin had died in 1811 but his son, Bose's nephew, Robert A. Dobbin, had
joined the firm in 1820. Murphy, who had emigrated from Dublin to Baltimore
around 1795, had been apprenticed as a printer. The firm of Dobbin, Murphy,
and Bose continued until 1853, with the younger Dobbin remaining one of
the owners until 1862.

Full Powers to Negotiate a Treaty of Amity and Commerce

[November 22, 1825]
[Henry Clay is granted "full power and authority" to negotiate
with "the Envoy Extraordinary and Minister Plenipotentiary of The
Central Republic of America" (Antonio José Cañaz) a treaty or
convention "relating to the Peace, Friendship, Commerce and
Navigation between the . . . United States and the government
of the said Central Republic. . . ."]

Copy. DNA, RG59, Ceremonial Communications, vol. 2, p. 29.

INSTRUCTIONS AND DISPATCHES   November 22, 1825

To ALEXANDER H. EVERETT, Madrid, no. 3. States that the owners of the

American brig *James Lawrence,* condemned at Havana in September, 1824, have appealed to the Council of the Indies and have requested the President to instruct Everett "to pay some attention to" the matter (see above, Ray and others to Clay, October 31, 1825); notes that "The decision appealed from is most extraordinary, and one altogether inexplicable, but upon the supposition of a want of integrity in the Tribunal which pronounced it" and that "Under the peculiar circumstances of the case, the President is disposed to comply with the request"; instructs Everett to "direct the filing of the Record, and the docketing of the appeal; and, the parties furnishing . . . the means of engaging Counsel," to "employ such as may appear . . . proper, to conduct it to a speedy and successful conclusion." Copy. DNA, RG59, Dip. Instr. vol. 10, pp. 414-15 (M77, R5). ALI draft, in DLC-HC (DNA, M212, R7).

On December 1, Brent acknowledged receipt of a letter from Ray, dated November 29 (not found), and pointed out that the dispatch to Everett, a copy of which had been transmitted to Ray, had been prepared after careful determination "that an opposite course would form a very inconvenient precedent." Everett had accordingly been "instructed to employ Counsel to conduct the appeal to a speedy and successful conclusion upon the parties furnishing him with the means to do so." Copy, in DNA, RG59, Dom. Letters, vol. 21, pp. 201-202 (M40, R19).

MISCELLANEOUS LETTERS   November 22, 1825

From A[BRAHAM] L. SANDS, New York. Calls attention to documents on file in the State Department "relating to a Danish law subjecting foreign inheritors of property in their colonies to a sacrifice of 25 pr Cent. upon its removal"; states that "by a late negociation, British subjects are exempt from the operation of this law"; and suggests that a similar exemption be included in the negotiations between the United States and Denmark. ALS. DNA, RG59, Misc. Letters (M179, R63). Sands signs as "late Capt. U. S. Arty." Endorsed by Clay: "Write to the gentleman within mentd. and let him know that the subject of it will be duly considered in the pending negotiation with Denmark." Sands, a graduate of the United States Military Academy, had resigned from the service in November, 1823. Brent wrote the reply, as directed, on November 29, 1825. Copy. DNA, RG59, Dom. Letters, vol. 21, pp. 198-99 (M40, R19).

APPLICATIONS, RECOMMENDATIONS   November 22, 1825

JAMES DILL, Lawrenceburg, Indiana, seeks an appointment for his son (Alexander H. Dill). ALS. DNA, RG59, A. and R. (MR2). See above, Dill to Clay, October 10, 1825.

JOHN MILLER, Providence, Rhode Island, applies for appointment to print the laws in his publications, the *Manufacturers and Farmers Journal* and the *Independent Inquirer,* both issued at Providence. ALS. DNA, RG59, P. and D. of L. Miller, a justice of the peace of Providence and formerly the publisher of another journal in that city, had been one of the founders in 1820 of the *Manufacturers and Farmers Journal,* a semi-weekly publication. *The Independent Inquirer,* a weekly, had been established in 1823. The *Manufacturers and Farmers Journal* was given a contract to publish the laws of the Congress beginning in 1825.

From Charles King

D Sir New York 23 Novr 1825

You may have heard, or if not, this letter will apprize you that with a view of affecting the nomination of my father when made to the Senate,[1] a scoundrel named Noah, who published a paper in this City, has among other things charged him with having in the year 1786 assented to a proposal to Prince Henry of Prussia to come over & become the Sovereign of this land[2]— the absurdity of the story & the source whence it emanates, could render any contradiction unnecessary, but that some names are vouched that carry weight with them, & particularly that of Mr Barbour— It is said that this gentleman once intimated on the floor of the Senate in my father's presence, that such a proposition had been made, & with his Mr King's Concurrence—and that he was not Contradicted[3]— What color there may be for any report of this kind I dont know— I never heard of it before— but as it is quite improbable that Mr. Barbour Could have made any such statement, and at any rate quite untrue, that my father was, or Could have been, concerned in any such plan, if peradventure any such was Ever entertaine[d,] I am anxious that, the authority which the use of Mr. Secretary Barbour's name may give to this "weak invention of the Enemy" should be withdrawn— Having however no acquaintance with Mr. B. I have ventured so far to tax your friendship, as to request you to ascertain in my name from Mr Barbour whether there is any & what truth in the part ascribed to him, in the Senate, and if there is none, to ask his permission formally to Contradict it—

I hope Mr Barbour will duly appreciate my motives for thus applying thro' you to him, and tho' aware of the reluctance he would very naturally feel to be brought before the public in a matter where he has no Concern, & in which he is introduced without any Consent or privity on his part, I cannot but flatter myself he will so far Consider what is due from a son to the reputation of an absent father, as to Comply with my request—

To you whose friendship I have heretofore so often Experienced, I make no apology for this new tax upon it— Very truly & Sincerely Yours CHAS. KING

Hon: H. Clay

ALS. DLC-HC (DNA, M212, R2).
1 See above, Clay to Strong, March 29, 1825, note.
2 The account, signed "Civis" and published by Mordecai Noah, had been widely circulated by subsequent journalistic discussion. The *Washington Gazette* of November 24, 1825, presented a summary of the publications in a piece signed "Seventy Six," which reiterated the attack upon Rufus King, as being one of "certain members of the congress of 1786," who had conferred with the Baron von Steuben prior to the

latter's transmittal of such a proposal to Prince Henry of Prussia, a brother of
Frederick the Great and a nephew of George I of England. "Seventy Six" quoted
from a letter by Prince Henry, declining the proposition. Cf. Richard Krauel, "Prince
Henry of Prussia and the Regency of the United States, 1786," *American Historical
Review*, XVII (October, 1911), 44-51.

3 James Barbour. See below, Barbour to Clay, November 26, 1825.

Receipt from Thomas Smith

[November 23, 1825]
[Lists weights of ten hogs, totaling 1550 pounds, "received from
Mr. Clay's Overseer,¹ Nov. 23, 1825." Addendum notes that two
hogs, weighing 148 and 150 pounds, were delivered to "Mrs. S.
Hart by Mr. Clay's Overseer Nov 23 1825."]

ADS. DLC-TJC (DNA, M212, R16).   1 John H. Kerr.

INSTRUCTIONS AND DISPATCHES   November 23, 1825

To BENJAMIN GARDNER, "Consul U. S. Palermo." Encloses commission, printed
circular, instructions, and a blank consular bond. Copy. DNA, RG59, Cons.
Instr., vol. 2, p. 373 (M78, R2). See above, Blake to Clay, November 19, 1825.

From JOEL R. POINSETT, Mexico, no. 27. Reports that he has just received
notice that the Mexican "flag floats over the Castle of Ulua"; acknowledges
receipt of Clay's "various despatches up to No 6 inclusive" (September 26,
1825), as well as a letter from (Daniel) Brent "respecting the claim of Messrs.
A. P. Chouteau and Julius De Mun" (see above, Clay to Poinsett, September
26, 1825, note); states that, since Brent's letter was dated May 27, "there must
have been some neglect in forwarding" it; notes that he has also received from
Brent a memorial concerning Mexican duties on cotton goods. LS. DNA,
RG59, Dip. Disp., Mexico, vol. 1 (M97, R2). Received January 3, 1826. In a
proclamation dated November 23, President Guadalupe Victoria confirmed the
news of the fall of the Castle of San Juan de Ulloa and the victory of the
Mexicans at Veracruz. *Niles' Weekly Register*, XXIX (January 28, 1826), 356.

From CONDY RAGUET, Rio de Janeiro, no. 2. Refers to the enclosure in his
dispatch of November 12; now transmits a later issue of the same journal, containing "a copy of an additional treaty between the same two Governments . . .
by which it is stipulated, that the slave trade shall cease on the part of Brasil
after the expiration of four years from the exchange of ratifications"; and
praises the Emperor for "this act of Illuminated and philanthropic policy."
Points out that the commercial treaty, however, contains "doctrines and
principles" to which the United States cannot subscribe; that Great Britain
rejected the treaty with Mexico because it contained "the admission, that the
flag should cover the property"; that Sir Charles Stuart has enlisted the
Brazilian Government "on the European side of the question"; and that the
acceptance by England of "the footing of the most favoured nation *Portugal
excepted*" may have been "influenced in some degree by the design of throwing
obstructions in our way." Sketches his views of the power Great Britain has
achieved over Brazil through the commercial treaty and its probable effects
on United States trade. Expresses a hope that, if he is authorized to negotiate

a treaty of commerce, his instructions will be drafted so as not to recognize Dom Pedro and his dynasty but, rather, to emphasize the sovereignty of the people. States that he sees no gain for the United States in a treaty unless by equalization of duties, for which he sees little chance, and that he hopes his orders will call for his leaving Brazil "in case our reasonable request be not complied with." Reports word of defeat of the Imperial troops in the Banda Oriental, notes a consequent uneasiness in the Government, but asserts that he sees no likelihood of the overthrow of the Emperor. Refers again to the unfavorable publicity given to the action of Georgia against the Federal Government (cf. above, Raguet to Clay, October 26, 1825). ALS. DNA, RG59, Dip. Disp., Brazil, vol. 4 (M121, R6).

APPLICATIONS, RECOMMENDATIONS   November 23, 1825

JOHN BARNEY, Baltimore, recommends Robert M. Goodwin as United States marshal for the District of Georgia. ALS. DNA, RG59, A. and R. (MR2). See above, Goodwin to Clay, November 7, 1825, note.

CHRISTOPHER HUGHES, Washington, also recommends Robert Goodwin, whom Hughes has known since boyhood, as marshal for Georgia. ALS. DNA, RG59, A. and R. (MR2).

H[ENRY] POTTER, Raleigh, recommends his kinsman, Robert Potter, for diplomatic appointment to Guatemala. ALS. *Ibid.* (MR3). Henry Potter, appointed to the Federal judiciary in 1801, was judge for the District of North Carolina for over fifty years. On Robert Potter, see above, Burton to Clay, October 22, 1825.

MISCELLANEOUS LETTERS   November 24, 1825

From DANIEL WYNNE, New York. States that he has been unable to complete arrangements to leave for his consulate and requests an extension of time until spring; expresses hope that the favor may be granted since (Heman) Allen is on the spot. ALS. DNA, RG59, Cons. Disp., Santiago de Cuba (M-T155, R1).

APPLICATIONS, RECOMMENDATIONS   November 24, 1825

WILLIAM A. MENDENHALL, Wilmington, Delaware, applies to publish the laws in his newspaper, the *Wilmingtonian and Delaware Advertiser*. ALS. DNA, RG59, P. and D. of L. Mendenhall, long prominent in Wilmington, received one of the few new contracts for public printing granted by the Adams administration in 1825.

From William Carroll

My dear Sir: Murfreesboro. November 25th. 1825.
    Two days ago on a visit to Nashville I found your esteemed letter of the 21st. of October[1] and thank you Sincerely for the information it contains.

The resignation of General Jackson as a member of the Senate[2] was very unexpected here, though I have no doubt it was resolved upon by him and two or three confidential friends a considerable time ago. A few days before the introduction of the resolutions proposing amendments to the constitution of the United States[3] we had a visit from Major Eaton;[4] and if rumor is to be credited he is their author. This was necessary as a basis upon which the General could found his resignation. But it was further necessary that he should be invited here; and that resolutions should be adopted recommending him as a suitable person for the presidency. All this parade was intended to produce effect throughout the United States, and I know that it was expected by many that his course would be approbated in every quarter. In this however they have been disappointed, for little or no notice is taken of it any where. The resignation, altho written with some degree of caution, is, as I think very injudicious, being at war with all his former declarations, that he would neither seek nor decline Office, and evincing throughout a most unconquerable desire for the presidency. He moreover avows indirectly that he went into the Senate with the view of aiding his election.[5]

Many of the Generals friends were opposed to Judge White[6] as his Successor, prefering [sic] some one who would boldly denounce the acts of the administration, and cling to the General through good and through bad report. Such a person however could not be Selected who had strength enough to defeat Colo. Williams,[7] who would have been a candidate in opposition to any one but Judge White. It was therefore a choice of evils and White was thought to be safer than Williams.

Judge White is certainly one of the first men of our State. All esteem him as an honest and valuable citizen—an able lawyer—an independent and unprejudiced politician. I think he may be calculded [sic] upon, as disposed to do every Justice to the administration.

The conduct of Governor Troup was certainly very highly exceptionable in relation to the Creek treaty.[8] His letters wanted that kind of good temper which should ever characterize Official correspondance [sic]. But, it is said that it was the best method he could adopt to insure his re-election. If that be true it furnishes something like an excuse. How General Gaines could think of entering into a controversy with him,[9] is to me unaccounable [sic]— It was not the purpose for which he was sent to Georgia and the Creek nation—and his letters present very little to recommend them either in matter or manner.

When our legislature acted upon the resolution recommending

General Jackson to the consideration of the American people for the Presidency, Thomas H Fletcher Esquire, author of the political horse race,[10] in a neat little speach [sic] inlisted [sic] under the banners of the General. As he had always been the stedfast [sic] friend of Mr. Crawford,[11] his conversion was looked upon as no ordinary triumph. The truth is, that there was no Sincerity in his conduct. He has ever considered the General as lacking those varied talents which are necessary in the chief Majistrate [sic] of the Union; and his speach was designed for the people, as he intends becoming a candidate for congress in opposition to Mr. Isaacks [sic]. Fletcher is a man of fine genius—of extensive political information, and in every respect qualified to hold a respectable rank in Congress, where it is entirely probable he will be in 1827.[12]

Your old friend Mr. Grundy has consented again to become a candidate for Congress, and I know of no one who can oppose him successfully.[13]

It is understood that there is much solicitude to re-elect Major Eaton to the Senate, his services being of the utmost consequence to the success of General Jackson as is said by his friends. He will be defeated. Opposition can, and will be brought against him, which will most probably beat him two to one.[14]

I think your determination in relation to the public printing in West Tennessee intirely [sic] correct.[15] Were you to bestow all the offices within your gift upon your enemies, they would not forgive you. It is therefore proper that they should feel the weight of your power. I will Just remark, that the *Whig* has a circulation nearly double that of any other paper in the State.

I cannot close this letter without expressing to you, how valuable I have always esteemed your corrispondence [sic], and to assure you, that I shall be happy to hear from you as often as your official duties will permit you to write with convenience. Most Sincerely. Yr. friend.   WM. CARROLL

Hon: Henry Clay   Washington City.

[Marginal note]

P. S. The General Assembly will adjourn ten days hence, after which time I shall be at Nashville.

ALS. DLC-HC (DNA, M212, R2).   1 Not found.
2 See above, Carroll to Clay, October 4, 1825, note.
3 See above, Clay to Hammond, November 1, 1825.
4 John H. Eaton.
5 Jackson stated, in his address to the legislature on October 14, that he had entered the Senate two years before, "not, however, without its being previously professed by . . . friends that a longer term of service than one Congress would neither be required or expected." Washington *Daily National Intelligencer*, November 1, 1825. This arrangement would have permitted his movement from the Senate to the Presidency on March 4, 1825.   6 Hugh L. White.
7 John Williams.

8 See above, Clay to Southard, July 3, 1825, note.

9 See above, Clay to Hammond, September 23, 1825, note.

10 Thomas H. Fletcher, born in Virginia, had settled in Nashville in 1808 and, after failure in the mercantile business during the depression of 1819, had studied law and opened practice in Fayetteville in 1821. He served two terms in the Tennessee Legislature as representative of Franklin County (1825-1826). He had been appointed by Governor Carroll as State attorney general and in February, 1827, was commissioned Federal attorney by President Adams. In the early summer of 1823, he had published in the *Nashville Gazette*, widely copied in other newspapers, including the Lexington *Kentucky Gazette*, July 10, 1823, a sketch, entitled "The Political Horse Race," humorously portraying the characteristics of the various candidates.

11 William H. Crawford.

12 Jacob C. Isacks was re-elected and continued in Congress until 1833; Fletcher was never elected to that body.

13 Grundy ran for Congress in 1827, with the support of Andrew Jackson, in opposition to John Bell, and was defeated. Bell, born near Nashville, had begun the practice of law at Franklin, Tennessee, in 1816, served in the State Senate in 1817, and, returning to Nashville, became a member of the United States House of Representatives from 1827 to 1841, Secretary of War in 1841, United States Senator from 1847 to 1859, and candidate for the Presidency in 1860.

14 Eaton was re-elected, in 1826.

15 On the shifting of the contracts for printing of the laws to the *Jackson Gazette* and the *Nashville Whig*, see above, McLean to Clay, August 30, 1825, note; Carroll to Clay, October 4, 1825, note.

From Lafayette

My dear friend   La Grange November 25h 1825

This letter will find You in the full Occupation of Congressional Business and altho' Your duties as a Speaker are over there will Be enough for the Secretary of State to do. I am ever Anxiously Waiting for News from the U. S. and particulary [sic] from Washington. My American Habits Have Been So Happily Renewed in the Blessed thirteen Month [sic] I Have passed on Your Side of the Atlantic that I Cannot easily Submit to an interruption in those Communications. Let me Hear from You as often as You Can.

You Have But too melancholy Motives to Sympathise with the Cruel Anxiety I Have Had Lately to Experience; one of my Grand daughters, the third daughter of George[1] Has Been on the Eve of death. She is now out of danger. How often and How feelingly I Have thought of You and Mrs Clay You will easily Conceive. I was Gone to town, and expected to See Mr Brown[2] the Next Morning when a Courier, Announcing the dear Girl'[s sit]uation, Recalled me Suddenly to la Grange. I Suppose He Has more than me to write about European politics. indeed the politics of the Republican Hemisphere, untill this is greatly Mended, Appear to me the principal Business of Mankind.

I much wish to know what Answer You Have Had to Your South American and Mexican Communications Respecting the Congress of panama,[3] and who Has Been Sent as minister from the U. S. to that momentous Meeting[4] where His Good and Honest Advice will no doubt prove Highly Useful. they Say the Empire of Brazils Has Been invited also to Send a Minister to panama. I wish it might Be to give don pedro a passport for Europe: for I aprehend [*sic*] this Brazilian Spot will Be a focus of European intrigues untill it Has adopted the Republican form of Government.

While British publications Speak of their Half Recognition of American independence as if no Such feat of liberalism Had Ever Existed Elsewhere, the french Government are wavering Betwen [*sic*] a Sense of public discontent at their Bakwardness [*sic*] and their Ridiculous Notions of Legitimacy, and when Lately they thought of Grasping at Something Like a mezzo termine on the part of Spain they Have Been momentarily discomfited By a Change in the Spanish Ministry.⁵ Such is the diplomacy of Europe, and the fittness [*sic*] to Have An American Era of foreign as well as interior policy. However, an irrestible [*sic*] Current must Soon wash a way those difficulties.

Notwistanding [*sic*] the quarelling [*sic*] Spirit of the Grecian Chiefs, and abuses attending a long interruption of National Government, there is an admirable Heroism in the Resistance of that people and a moral obligation to every liberal man, or body of men to Give them Encouragement and the Assistance which Special Situations Can allow. the British Government is, as Usual, Under a Conflict of interests Opposed to Each other, and wants to obtain, as cheap as possible, the first place in the poor Carrier [*sic*] of European liberalism. while french Committees are Sincere and Eager in their Concern for the Cause of Greece, the Government of the tuileries Holds a Connexion, Most Unpopular in france, with the Egyptian despot.⁶ The Rumour of Very peculiar Acts of Benevolence from the American Squadron and Commodore Rogers in Behalf of the Greeks,⁷ which Has produced No party Complaint that I know of, Has in the Enlightned [*sic*] and liberal part of the World added to the popularity and dignity of the American Name. What Has Really past I do not know, But very much lament the illness of Mr Somerville⁸ which forcibly keeps Him in paris. I Have pressed Him to Come to la Grange to Refitt [*sic*] Himself and from there pursue His journey; But when He will Be able to Support this short Ride to our Country Residence I Cannot Yet Say. He is However a little Better as He Himself writes to me, and you will no doubt get from Him a later and more positive Account.

Present my Affectionate Respects to Mrs Clay, to the president, to Your Colleagues, and all other friends in Washington as well as to their families. George and le Vasseur⁹ Beg to Be Respectfully Remembered. Be So kind as to forward the inclosed letters;

Remember me to Your own family present and absent, and Believe me forever Your Sincere friend   LAFAYETTE

I Have Received Before I left the United States Communications from my old Comrades of the Connecticut and Massachuset [*sic*] Lines intimating the purpose to present Congress, during this Session, with a petition Relative to the Manner in which old Accounts Have Been Settled in their very interesting Claims on their Country's Bounty, and also Respecting to the interpretation Given in 1820 to the pension Law of 1798.[10] At all times I would Have taken the most lively interest in their Behalf, But now loaded as I am with the Munificent Bounty of Congress,[11] I am More than Ever Anxious to Hear they Have Had Cause to Be Satisfied. there are few Survivors; any thing done for them would, I Hope, Be Gratifying to the people, and You know it would Have an excellent effect abroad.

Mr Connel[12] Returns to England By way of liverpool. He will talk with You of Several claims upon Europe, namely that of Antwerpt [*sic*] which He Had Been Commissioned to pursue.[13] I Have Seen Mr and Mme delaRue. they know You are of Opinion that Congress might with all propriety, and without Hurting any [petitioner] instead of taking it for Granted that the president is Entitled to introduce this french claim in the Negotiation, express a positive Vote upon it, and indeed I don't See Any obj[ection to] express what Every one Considers as Being already understood.[14]

Here is a Bundle of letters which with perfect Confidence in Your Godness [*sic*] I Beg You to forward.

[Endorsed at bottom of first page]
Hbl Henry Clay Secretary of State

ALS. DLC-HC (DNA, M212, R2). MS. faded.
1 Clementine Lafayette; George Washington Lafayette.
2 James Brown.
3 See above, Clay to Anderson, September 16, 1825; Salazar to Clay, November 2, 1825; Obregón to Clay, November 3, 1825.
4 See above, Clay to Anderson, September 16, 1825; below, Clay to Anderson, November 25, 1825.
5 See above, Everett to Clay, October 26, 1825.
6 French army officers had been training Egyptian forces since 1819. This program had been re-enforced under arrangements for a French military mission, which arrived at Alexandria in November, 1824, to direct "formation, organization, and instruction of the [Egyptian] troops . . . [and to provide] assistance in naval construction, and assistance in the organization of factories for military purposes." Puryear, *France and the Levant*, 43. The exact relationship of the French Government with this activity is not known, but the provision of supplies for Egyptian naval construction from French naval stores indicates a close connection. Opposition journals of the French press were criticizing the role of the Government in this matter during the winter of 1825-1826. *Ibid.*, 45-48.
7 See above, Brown to Clay, October 29, 1825.
8 William C. Somerville.   9 Auguste Levasseur.
10 See above, II, 876n. Lafayette's third digit is blurred, a correction of a date, probably 1798, which was inapplicable. (The pension act of 1798 related to dependents of service men deceased of wounds received after March 4, 1789. 1 *U. S. Stat.*, 540.)

President Adams. in his message of December 6, 1825, proposed payment of pensions for service in the Revolution, without proof of poverty, but the recommendation was not enacted. Richardson (comp.), *A Compilation of the Messages and Papers of the Presidents. . .* , II, 308.   11 See above, III, 900.
12 John Connell.
13 Cf. above, Kearney to Clay, September 26, 1825. Antwerp was incorporated in the Kingdom of the Netherlands from 1815 to 1830.
14 See above, III, 312, 313n, 498.

DIPLOMATIC NOTES   November 25, 1825

To C[HARLES] R. VAUGHAN. Acknowledges receipt of his note of November 15; states that Clay has "caused the necessary enquiries to be made" and hopes, upon receipt of further information, to be able to give "satisfactory explanations of the transactions to which the Lt. Governor refers." Copy. DNA, RG59, Notes to Foreign Legations, vol. 3, pp. 237-38 (M38, R3). ALS draft, in CSmH. Published in Manning (arr.), *Diplomatic Correspondence . . . Canadian Relations,* II, 70.

INSTRUCTIONS AND DISPATCHES   November 25, 1825

To RICHARD C. ANDERSON, JR., no. 3. Informs him that the President has decided to accept the invitation to be represented at Panama (see above, Clay to Gallatin, November 8, 1825) and that John Sergeant will be his associate; adds: "Of course the whole movement depends upon the concurrence of the Senate in the measure, which is however confidently anticipated." Copy. DNA, RG59, Dip. Instr., vol. 10, pp. 416-17 (M77, R5). ALI draft, in DLC-HC (DNA, M212, R7); LS copy, in OCHP-Whelpley Autographs.

From JOHN MULLOWNY, Tangier, no. 42. States that a treaty between "the United Nations of S. America, and this Power" (Morocco), if considered desirable, could be negotiated by one representative of the six Republics upon payment of about $80,000; adds that, with the consent of the President of the United States, he is willing to "become the Mediator, for this Important purpose." ALS. DNA, RG59, Cons. Disp., Tangier, vol. 4 (M-T61, R4). Received March 4, 1825.

From JOEL R. POINSETT, Mexico, no. 28. States that he has "received and attentively examined" Clay's "instructions, No. 5" (September 24, 1825); expresses regret that the treaty between Mexico and Great Britain preceded his own negotiations; promises "to urge the example of Colombia"; notes that the provision, to which Clay calls attention, concerning duties on imports of manufactures from the United States, has been agreed to by the Mexican plenipotentiaries; states that he will renew negotiations concerning the road and the boundaries. LS. DNA, RG59, Dip. Disp., Mexico, vol. 1 (M97, R2). Received January 3, 1826.

MISCELLANEOUS LETTERS   November 25, 1825

To LEVI LINCOLN, Governor of Massachusetts, Boston. "The same Letter, as written to Govr. Parris, Portland" (below, this date). DNA, RG59, Dom. Letters, vol. 21, p. 197 (M40, R19). Lincoln, brother of Enoch Lincoln, was a

Harvard graduate and a lawyer. He had been a member of the Massachusetts Legislature (1812-1822), Lieutenant Governor of the State, and an associate justice of the State Supreme Court and was Governor from 1825 to 1834. He was a member of Congress (1834-1841), collector of the port of Boston (1841-1843), State Senator (1844-1845), mayor of Worcester (1848), and president of the Worcester County Agricultural Society (1824 to 1852).

To ALBION K. PARRIS, Governor of Maine, Portland. Transmits a copy of the note and enclosures received from the British Minister (above, Vaughan to Clay, November 15, 1825); requests information relative to the matter discussed. Copy. *Ibid.,* pp. 196-97. Parris, whose service in Congress had extended from 1815 to 1818, had been graduated from Dartmouth College and had held several political and judicial offices. He was Governor of Maine from 1822 to 1827, United States Senator (1827-1828), a judge of the State Supreme Court (1828-1836), second comptroller of the United States Treasury (1836-1850), and mayor of Portland (1852).

From AMOS CLARK, Evansville (Indiana). Expresses surprise "at the rect. of a letter from" an agent of the State Department "returning the account of Thomas Evans for public printing and assigning as a reason that a letter had been received from E. Harrison requesting that the account should not be paid to Evans or any one for him." Explains the legal aspects of the case. ALS. DNA, RG59, P. and D. of L. Cf. above, Harrison to Clay, September 16, 1825; October 16, 1825; Clark to Clay, October 12, 1825.

From SAMUEL CURSON, Boston. Mentions that he is "personally known to" Clay and that he made "some communications" (not found) to Clay "on the State of Spanish America in 1822; particularly Peru, where . . . [he] had been long resident. . . ." States that, since he intends sailing to Tampico about December 8, he would be happy to forward letters for the consulate or for (Joel R.) Poinsett. ALS. DNA, RG59, Misc. Letters (M179, R63). Curson not further identified.

From James Barbour

Dear Sir   Washington Novr 26th. 1825

I have read attentively the letter, you presented to me, addressed to you by Mr Charles King.[1] I certainly feel great reluctance to appearing in a news-paper controversy; the more especially as it is the first instance in my life of such an occurrence: Yet, on this occasion I yield to the request of Mr King to state what remains within my recollection of the subject to which he refers.[2] The intervening time since the occurrence & the multiplicity as well as variety of my pursuits have rendered the traces of the transaction somewhat slight. As there was no note taken of the debate at the time I have endeavored to regain its character by reference to the President Mr Gaillard[3]—who says he has not the smallest recollection of any circumstance connected with this subject. Thrown on my own resources I will endeavor to give the most faithful narrative I can—

In the debate which occurred on the revolutionary pension bill Session 17-18- the utmost latitude was indulged—the effects of that revolution on ourselves as well as in the world at large, the progress of political science, the dangers to which our institutions had been Exposed from the termination of the revolution to the adoption of the Constitution &c were largely and freely discussed— Taking an active part in that debate and pursuing the range of discussion I made an allusion to a rumor namely that a wish was beleived [sic] to exist with some politicians to impart a monarchical character to our institutions, and which was said to have been manifested by a proposal of inviting some German prince to the intended American throne— But it was stated as a mere rumor, nor did I point to any particular individual, for none by name had been mentioned to me, that I now recollect— Mr. King[4] who took part in the debate spoke of this rumor as most idle and unfounded—and with asperity at its having been mentioned by me— The remainder of the debate on my part it is not necessary to state, as it went merely to repel the personal remarks of Mr King in a manner which the feelings of the moment as I thought justified. From that day to the recent publications I heard nothing more of the subject— You may use this letter as you please by transmitting it to Mr King, or give it any other direction you may think best[5]— Hon H. Clay   Yours   JAS. BARBOUR

Copy. NHi. Published in King (ed.), *Life and Correspondence of Rufus King*, VI. 645-46.   [1] Above, November 23, 1825.
[2] As early as November 19, Barbour had consulted President Adams on the propriety of publishing a contradiction of the Noah account. Adams, *Memoirs*, VII, 55-56.
[3] John Gaillard.   [4] Rufus King.
[5] This sentence was omitted in the published version.

DIPLOMATIC NOTES   November 26, 1825

From JOSE SILVESTRE REBELLO, Washington. States that he has been instructed by his government to urge that a higher rank be given to the United States diplomatic agent in Brazil so that the Emperor may confer equal rank on his representative at Washington. Cites, as reasons for the proposed change, the flow of communications across Brazil, rather than around the Horn or through the unhealthful Central American states; the probability that commercial relations of the United States with Brazil will continue to flourish, because their products are complementary while the trade of Argentina and Chile will be competitive with that of the United States; and the priority of United States recognition of the independence of Brazil (see above, Clay to Raguet, April 14, 1825, note). LS. DNA, RG59, Notes from Foreign Legations, Brazil, vol. 1 (M49, R1).

INSTRUCTIONS AND DISPATCHES   November 26, 1825

From THOMAS L. L. BRENT, Lisbon, no. 12. Reports that the efforts to fill the regiments, referred to in his dispatch no. 11 (October 28), have ceased; that the treaty between Brazil and Portugal (see above, Raguet to Secretary of State, March 11, 1825, note) has been published; and that he is enclosing a note received from the Count of Porto Santo, relative to the grant of independence to Brazil and the change in the King's title. Describes an audience with the King (John VI) ; comments on a royal decree (enclosed) concerning the title and position of Dom Pedro; notes some opposition to the treaty; and expresses concern for the King's health. LS. DNA, RG59, Dip. Disp., Portugal, vol. 6 (M43, R5) .

MISCELLANEOUS LETTERS   November 26, 1825

From S[AMUEL] L. S[OUTHARD]. Acknowledges receipt of "the letter of Mr. Warfield [not found], submitted by you to this Department, in behalf of Mr. Murphy, an applicant for admission into the Navy"; and states that his name is being placed on file. Copy. DNA, RG45, Executive Letterbook, vol. 1821-1831, p. 147. Warfield and Murphy not identified. See below, Southard to Clay, December 10, 1825.

From WILLIAM WILLIAMS, Saybrook. Inquires whether a person who sells a vessel in a foreign port to an American is required by law to pay into the hands of the consul three months' pay for the crew if "the crew are not discharged but continue on board voluntarily and proceed back to a port in the United States" or "if the seller prefers furnishing his crew with a passage back to the United States, bearing all their expences. . . ." LS. DNA, RG59, Misc. Letters (M179, R63). Williams not further identified. On December 7, 1825, Daniel Brent, at Clay's direction, replied to Williams at "Saybrook, Ms. [*sic*]," that the Department "uniformly declined giving an opinion upon the true construction of a Law of Congress" and, instead, referred him to the relevant statutes. Copy. DNA, RG59, Dom. Letters, vol. 21, pp. 208-209 (M40, R19).

APPLICATIONS, RECOMMENDATIONS   November 26, 1825

WILLIAM H. CAMPBELL, A. WOODWARD, and D[ANDRIDGE] FARISS, Huntsville, Alabama, acting as D. Fariss and Company, apply for appointment to publish the laws in the Huntsville *Southern Advocate and Huntsville Advertiser*. Campbell has replaced H. Orlando Alden in the firm. ALS by Woodward, signed also by Campbell and Fariss. DNA, RG59, P. and D. of L. Campbell, Woodward's law partner, had been born in Tennessee and by 1835 had removed to Talladega, Alabama. The request for a renewal of appointment was granted.

JOHN A. MORTON, JR., New York, urges appointment of Benjamin Gardner as United States consul at Palermo and encloses a memorial (signed by fourteen New York merchants) supporting this recommendation. ALS. DNA, RG59, A. and R. (MR2). See above, Blake to Clay, November 19, 1825, note. Morton not further identified.

HORACE STEELE, Montpelier, Vermont, recommends that the contract for publication of the laws be given to a journal to be established by George Washington Hill and Company, at Montpelier, under the patronage of Hill's brother (Isaac), of Concord, New Hampshire, "well known as a supporter of Govt." Comments that a petition circulated by (Ezekiel P.) Walton, publisher of the Montpelier *Watchman,* who also seeks the appointment, contains an inaccurate statement of the circulation of that paper, which "during the late war . . . *was devoted* to the cause of those opposed to the administration. . . ." ALS. DNA, RG59, P. and D. or L. Steele and George Washington Hill not further identified. Isaac Hill, a native of Massachusetts, was editor of the Concord *New Hampshire Patriot* (1809-1829) and at various times a member of the State legislature (1820-1822, 1826, 1827), second comptroller of the United States Treasury (1829-1830), United States Senator (1831-1836), Governor of New Hampshire (1836-1839), and United States subtreasurer at Boston (1840-1841), On the recommended appointment, cf. above, Van Ness and others to Clay, November 4, 1825, note.

JOHN McKINNEY, JR., Versailles (Kentucky), states that his "friend Mr. William Mayo is anxious to obtain for his son Addison the appointment of Cadet at West point [*sic*]"; and adds: "Mr. Mayo is one of your particular & warm friends. . . ." ALS. DNA, RG94, Military Academy, Cadet Applications, 1825-13 (M688, R36). Postmarked: "Shelbyville K Dec 14." Endorsed on cover (AEI): "Respectfully refered [*sic*] to the Honble Secy. of War. H C." William Mayo was proprietor of a tavern in Versailles. He moved to Shelbyville, Kentucky, about 1846 and, a few years later, to Cooper County, Missouri. His eldest son, Addison, did not enter the Military Academy but, instead, became a doctor and practiced at Versailles until shortly before the Civil War, when he joined the great rush to Colorado.

To Charles King

Dr Sir   Washington 27 Nov. 1825

On the day I received your letter of the 23 inst: I met with Mr. Secretary Barbour, and having conversed with him on the subject of it, I put it into his hands that he might furnish me with such a statement as he deemed proper— The enclosed letter from him to me[1] furnishes that statement— The Notice of that subject by Noah is so far countenanced by this statement, as that it establishes that there was an allusion to it in a debate in the Senate by Mr Barbour and that this allusion occasioned some warm words between him and your father— Indeed the Honble. Secretary told me, that the words which passed were very sharp and personal— But Mr. Noah has no support from this statement of his allegations that the Secretary intended to implicate your father, or that he silently acquiesced in the truth of the Secretary's suggestion— If his letter is published the malignant will seize hold of the fact of the sensibility displayed by your father (as described by Mr B.) as evidence of his conscious participation in the Prussian scheme[2]— I transmit the letter however to you to be disposed of as you may think right— Perhaps it would be better for you in the first instance, simply to aver in some newspaper, 1st. that you have the highest authority for contradicting the allegation that Mr. B. implicated your father—2d that altho' there was an allusion in the Senate to the matter, it was vaguely referred to as a mere rumor—and further that your father promptly and explicitly denied as [*sic*] most idle and unfounded— This may draw from your antagonist further disclosures &c. and in the end you may publish the whole letter if necessary—

I never heard of this Prussian affair before— Upon enquiry I learn that there was during the Revolutionary war, when our affairs were very gloomy, and there was some dissatisfaction with Genl Washington a project on foot to invite the Duke of Brunswick[3] or Prince Henry over to take the Command of our armies, not to make a King of him— And I suspect that matter has been drawn down from '77 to 78 when it occurred to 1786 and confounded with incidents of the latter epoch[4]—

I cannot think there is the smallest danger of [*sic*] your father's nomination passing the Senate[5]— Still it is well to keep a look out & not to indulge in too much confidence.

Who could have communicated to Noah the account of the debate in the Senate? You see that Mr. Gaillard retains no recollection of it— I suspect therefore that the communication must have been made by some bitter & secret enemy—

I have taken pleasure in the agency you have requested of me in this matter & shall be pleased if the letter of Mr Barbour shall prove of any benefit[6]— Yrs faithfully   H. CLAY
C King Esq.

Copy. NHi. Published, in part, in King (ed.), *Life and Correspondence of Rufus King*, VI, 644-45.   1 Above, November 26, 1827.
2 The remainder of this paragraph was omitted from the published version.
3 Ferdinand, Duke of Brunswick, a Prussian field marshal during the Seven Years War, who had retired in 1766, after estrangement from Frederick the Great.
4 The misdating argument had already been presented by King's defenders and had been demolished by "Seventy Six" in the *Washington Gazette*, November 24, 1825. Charles King, however, again raised it in accordance with the suggestion offered by Clay. See King's public letter on "The Hamilton Papers," in Washington *Daily National Intelligencer*, December 8, 1825.
The following paragraph in Clay's letter to King was omitted from the published version.
5 King's nomination was confirmed on December 20, without a recorded division of vote.
6 This paragraph omitted from the printed version.

From Francis T. Brooke

My Dear Sir   Richmd Nov 27h 1825,
I should have written you more frequently if there had been anything in our political world worth communicating, and now I am prompted in some degree by what may Seem a personal rather than of a general Character— what I mean to say to you on the former I beg you to consider as extracted from me by considerations which no one can better appreciate than yourself— my son Robert[1]

who I presented to you last winter by Letter,[2] has returned to the U, S, in fine health and contemplates settling in one of the new States or in one of the Territories with the intention to persue [sic] his profession,   under circumstances [sic] if he can be made useful to the government by any appointment it would be very useful to him to have its countenance,   I am not apprised of any Situation that would accord with his views at present, and my only object in mentioning the Subject to you, is to avail myself of your friendship if anything Should occur by which at the Same time that you fulfill your public duty you may promote his intentions— you saw too little of him last winter to form any opinion of his qualifications, and anything I should Say of them might be attributed to my paternity,   I refer you therefore to my friends Southard & Barbour[3] who know more of him—

when I came here I thought that there was very little doubt that Genl Tucker would be our Senator, Mr Giles efforts to the contrary notwithstanding,   I am Still of opinion that no man in the Eastern portion of the State will be, unless it be Govr Pleasants,   I learn very lately however that there is Strong probability that Mr Randolph has prevailed on Genl Tucker not to permit himself to be named with a view to his own election or that of Genl Floyed, Should this be the case, Pleasants will be the Senator,[4]   I have been much confined by an inflamation [sic] in in [sic] one of my knees though my genl health was never better, or I should have been able to know a little more of the movements of gentlemen here in this matter,   in Some Short time I shall be able to give you more distinct information of the probable event of that contest, you will have Seen by the papers that there is an effort in Virginia to get up an antiadministration party under the pretext of defending State rights and that Mr Giles was to wield the moral force of the State for the attainment of these objects, but it will fail unless I am much in the dark— Your Sincere Friend   F BROOKE

ALS. DLC-HC (DNA, M212, R2). Addressed to Clay.

[1] Robert Spottswood Brooke, born in 1800, had been graduated from the United States Military Academy in 1820 and, resigning his commission shortly thereafter, had been trained as a lawyer. He was a captain in the Virginia militia from 1824 to 1832 and a member of the Virginia House of Delegates, representing Augusta County, from 1832 to 1843. He did not receive a Federal appointment to civil office.

[2] Not found.   [3] Samuel L. Southard; James Barbour.

[4] James Pleasants was not among the nominees in the election by the Virginia Assembly, on December 8, to fill the vacancy occasioned by the resignation of Barbour when he accepted Cabinet appointment. On the first ballot, the vote was 65 for Henry St. George Tucker, 63 for John Randolph, who was Tucker's half brother, 58 for William B. Giles, and 40 for John Floyd. With the last name dropped, the next ballot stood at 87 votes for Tucker, 79 for Randolph, and 60 for Giles. Giles' name was then excluded and the ballots were cast, when Tucker's friends announced that he would not oppose Randolph. After some discussion, it was decided that the count of votes already deposited in the election boxes should be taken. Randolph received 104; Tucker, 80. Garland, Life of John Randolph, II, 239-40.

INSTRUCTIONS AND DISPATCHES   November 27, 1825

From RUFUS KING, London, no. 12. Encloses a copy of his "last Note to the office for Foreign affairs" relative to "the delays of the Mixed Commission at Washington"; encloses also a copy of his note to (George) Canning, transmitting a copy of Clay's instructions of May 10, which King thought proper to communicate *"in Extenso"* at this time, and Canning's reply; reports that "the Envoy of Buenos Ayres [Manuel de Sarratea] has arrived in London, and waits only for the recurrence of a Levee, to be presented to, and recognized by the King." LS. DNA, RG59, Dip. Disp., Great Britain, vol. 32 (M30, R28). Received January 18, 1826.

APPLICATIONS, RECOMMENDATIONS   November 27, 1825

GEORGE I. BROWN, Nicholasville (Kentucky), solicits aid in obtaining "a situation in the Military Acadamy [sic]" for Charles Sturdevant, an orphan, of Nicholasville. ALS. DNA, RG94, Military Academy, Cadet Applications, 1825-161 (M688, R38). Endorsed by Clay on cover: "Respectfully refered [sic] to the Secy of War [James Barbour] H. Clay." Court records on November 21 had noted that young Sturdevant had received no inheritance. Jessamine County Court, Order Book F, 78-79. He did not win consideration for the Military Academy.

To Peter B. Porter

My dear Sir   (Confidential)   Washn. 28h. Nov. 1825

I thank you for your obliging letter from Utica of the 22d. current.[1] The information which it communicates is valuable and the friendly hints will not be gotten [sic].

Mr. Clinton[2] is, & has always been, well understood by me, and *now* is by Mr. Adams also. You are mistaken however in supposing that any systematic exertion has been made by Mr. Adams to conciliate him. Mr. Adams thought that some expression was due to the State of N. York, and Mr. Clinton was offered the appointment to England.[3] In afterwards appointing Mr. King,[4] Mr. C. I have reason to believe was much dissatisfied. With respect to the appointment of a Western Judge,[5] it was a selection made by Mr. Adams not upon the strength of Mr. Clinton's recommendation alone, but upon that of others also.

The maxim of the present Administration is to abstain from identifying itself particularly with any of the local parties that happen to divide a State. Its appointments must, however, necessarily be made from some of them; but it is a great error to infer from a particular or even several appointments being made from a certain party that the general administration has lent itself to its views. However, I should be glad if you would tell me frankly on what the belief is founded of a subserviency here to Mr. Clinton.

We may at least undeceive the public, in that respect, in future.

The Admon continues to act in perfect harmony. It is also daily acquiring additional strength, and conciliating the public confidence The exposition, in the message,[6] of our public affairs will be very satisfactory. The President, with my hearty concurrence, has decided that we shall be represented at Panama.[7] Of course however our peace or neutrality is not to be affected by it.

I recd your report.[8] The President expressed himself entirely satisfied with the reasons which induced you to acquiesce in the postponement until May. We both think that the harmony among the Commrs, and the prospect of a successful termination of their labors fully compensate for any incidental delay which has arisen. I remain faithfully Your friend   H. CLAY
Genl. P. B. Porter.

ALS. NBuHi.
[1] Not found. The letter related to politics, "expressing his surprise at . . . [Adams'] complacency towards the New York Clintonians against whom the recent elections to the Legislature have turned," and his belief that Judge (Ambrose) Spencer would not be the Senator. Adams, *Memoirs*, VII, 66.
[2] DeWitt Clinton.
[3] See above, Stuart to Clay, March 15, 1825.
[4] Rufus King.
[5] Alfred Conkling. For reference to his appointment as "Judge of the Western district of New York," see Adams, *Memoirs*, VII, 83.
[6] The President's annual message to Congress, December 6, 1825.
[7] See above, Tudor to Clay, April 12, 1825, note; Clay to Gallatin, November 8, 1825.
[8] Above, Porter to Clay, November 16, 1825.

From Francis P. Blair

My dear Sir   Frankfort Nov. 28 1825
I recd. your letter on the subject of Kentucky politics written in Sept. last.[1] I immediately answered it, but as I had then recently sent you a letter on White's account[2] I feared I should be considered troublesome, & did not send my reply— To tell you the truth I was not very well prepared to decide upon what I should do & did not know well what to say— I could not think of abandoning my party,[3] if they were disposed to acquiesce in public sentiment as I understood it; & as I conscientiously beleived [sic] that the country was anxious to get rid of both sets of Judges & to compose a mixed tribunal I urged it upon those who had influence & the proposal was formally made in the Governors Message.[4] As the senate stands unshaken with regard to the repeal of the late law, a reconciliation, & compromise has at length become a subject of serious consideration on both sides, & the leaders in the Legislature Crittenden & Hardin on one side, & McAfee Haskin & Ewing[5] on the other are at the moment engaged in drawing up preliminaries

which I trust will terminate in a peace— I am a little afraid that
the preponderance of the *old court* party in the Legislature will
be urged as a strong circumstance to sacrifice my pretensions to the
clerkship,[6] if the compromise should be effected (*as it will be, if
at all,*) on terms of equality in other respects— My side have I know
resolved not to give me up but if I find that there is no other
practicable means of giving peace to the country, I have taken a
secret resolution to yield my prospects of better fortune, rather
than keep up the state of distraction which now exists— I take it
however to be a hard alternative— Swigert[7] is my Junior every
way—is young—hearty—independant [*sic*] in his means, & without a
family— My condition is (you know) the reverse of this, but
reverses seem to belong to my fortunes & I must learn to bear them—

From your letter I fear Gratz[8] has been a solicitor with you for
me— If he has been, I assure you that his solicitation was wholly
unbidden & unexpected— I have always known that there was no
appointment at Washington to which I was equal that was equal
to my necessities— Nothing therefore was more distant from my
hopes than a place there—

I have turned my eyes towards Florida as a position where I
might probably better my condition & where the climate promises
advantages to a pulmonary constitution— My first thought is for
the welfare of my family & I feel that I could undergo any labor
to raise them to a moderate independance— You have I know
from your elevation a much wider horizon than I have, & a mind
that sees things however far off with distinctness— You know me,
& my condition— Let me therefore ask your advice— It is somewhat late in life to be transplanted to a new Country, but I think
that such places present facilities to persons situated as I am &
I think it probable that I might succeed in the profession I studied
early in life,[9] & to which my employments have constantly drawn
my attention— But I am conscious that I am not the best Judge
of this matter— I ask your advice therefore from no idle motive—
I would not trouble you with impertinence— I ask your advice
because I know you will give it frankly without respect to any
consideration but my real interests—

I will send you a reply I wrote hastily a day or two before the
session in answer to the demand of the old Court on me for the
papers[10]— It was at first as badly printed, as written, & I have been
at the pains to have it reprinted so as to take off some of the
defects, with a view to send some abroad to let our neighbors see
that our pretensions are not so wholly unfounded as is generally
imagined— You must pardon me that I have availed my self of
your arguments on a particular point on this controversy[11]— Your

Opinion on the main question has done us much harm, & what I have taken from you is but in the way of reprisal— What you said as advice to me & my party in Opposition to *the compromise* in your letter, I sedulously concealed, because I thought it would do me harm if known to one side, & would not be advantageous to you if known to the other— So with Mrs B.'s advice & my own Opinion in support it [*sic*], I resolved to make a secret of your views but your Opinion on this subject has escaped through other Channels, & if the treaty fails I fear it will be somewhat attributable to the Judgment you have given on the matter[12]—

[. . .][13] Novr. I interrupted my letter in the hope of convey[ing] ce[rta]in intelligence with regard to the end of our controversies— A committee of the senate addressed both sets of Judges desiring them to resign, that a new court might be formed out of both, & the contest about constitionality [*sic*] quieted in that way— The new court complied—the old court refused— The breach seems to widen; the friends of both courts being confirmed in their different purposes by the acts of the other— The compromise is gone for the present.[14]

The Committee of courts of Justice called me before them this morning to answer on oath for the felonies & misdemeanors I am charged withal, in taking the papers from the proper office & refusing to yeild [*sic*] them to the Old Court according to order— I answered all interrogatories without reserve & told them they should not have the papers— The Old court next will lay its commands on me in the way of compulsion— I shall also give them the Spartan's answer when his arms were demanded— "Come & take them" I shall stand a siege, & hope before all is is [*sic*] over to capitulate on honorable terms, & get a fair compromise[15]— Notwithstanding things have gone so far I beleive I stand well with my old friends, & trust that I shall lose nothing of your esteem & affection because I do not desert   Yr Friend   F. P. Blair

ALS. DLC-HC (DNA, M212, R2). Addressed to Clay. MS. torn.
1 Not found.
2 Above, August 30, 1825.
3 The friends of the new Court.
4 See above, Theodore W. Clay to Clay, November 11, 1825, note.
5 John J. Crittenden; Benjamin Hardin; Robert B. McAfee; Joseph Haskin; Young Ewing. McAfee and Haskin were both of Mercer County, Haskin representing that county in the State House of Representatives in 1825, 1826, 1831, 1833, 1843, and 1844. McAfee, a lawyer and a veteran of the War of 1812, had been elected to the lower house of the State Assembly in 1819, had held office as lieutenant governor from 1820 to 1824, and now presided over the State Senate. He returned to the legislature in 1831-1832 and 1841 and served as United States Chargé d'Affaires at Colombia from 1833 to 1837.
6 On his appointment, see above, Blair to Clay, February 11, 1825.
7 Jacob Swigert.
8 Benjamin Gratz. No recommendation found.
9 See above, III, 10n.

10 Addressed to "Messrs. Mills, Boyle and Owsley" and published in the Frankfort *Argus of Western America,* November 16, 23, 1825. Blair rejected the demand of the old court for restoration of the court records (see above, Blair to Clay, March 7, 1825, note), on the ground that, until legislative action reversed the law establishing the new court, the latter remained the duly constituted judicial authority of the State.

11 Noting that the old court judges had conceded the power of the legislature to appoint additional jurists, Blair argued that the designation of one of the latter as "Chief Justice" and the others as "1st, 2d and 3d associate Justices," when others already bore these titles, did not affect their power. "Here," he continued, "you must not understand me as urging my own arguments. I do but urge those of some of the ablest individuals who advocate your pretensions. I myself heard them advanced by the most illustrious citizen of our state, who at the same time declared that they had been suggested by the head of the Judiciary—by chief Justice Marshall himself." Frankfort *Argus of Western America,* November 23, 1825.

12 See above, Clay to Kendall, October 18, 1825; below, Clay to Hammond, December 10, 1825.   13 MS. torn, date missing.

14 See below, Kendall to Clay, December 25, 1825, note.

15 Blair continued his refusal to surrender the records until requested by law to do so; and since the requisite legislation was not passed, the old court suspended further action against him.

INSTRUCTIONS AND DISPATCHES   November 28, 1825

From JAMES BROWN, Paris, no. 37. Encloses copies of an exchange of letters with the Baron de Damas; notes that "the French Government still insists that all the questions of controversy between the two nations shall be embraced in the same negociation"; concludes "that no disposition is felt at this time, to do justice to the claimants." LS. DNA, RG59, Dip. Disp., France, vol. 22 (M34, R25). Received January 13, 1826. Cf. above, Brown to Clay, September 24, 27, 1825.

From DAVID OFFLEY, Smyrna. Reports that "His Excellency Hassan Pacha commanding here" has informed him that "the Ottoman Porte" is disappointed that "an ambassador has not been sent by our Government to Constantinople," that he informed the Pacha that the United States could accept only most favored nation treatment, and that the Pacha replied that the United States would have no difficulty in obtaining from the Porte such treatment, although nations already enjoying trade privileges "would naturally use all their endeavours to prevent the Americans participating therein. . . ." States that "the well known high standing of this Pacha with his Goverment [*sic*]" and the favorable impression made by the American squadron (under John Rodgers) "in this quarter" induces him to make this report. Comments on the treatment accorded several American merchant vessels which have entered Turkish ports in this vicinity, notes that Commodore Rodgers "found the American Trade and Citizens in the enjoyment of especial favor and protection from the authorities of this place. . . ," and requests that his (Offley's) "Compensation . . . be made equal to that of other Consuls in Turkish Ports." LS. DNA, RG59, Dip. Disp., Turkey, vol. 1, part 1 (M46, R2). Endorsed by Clay: ". . . To be submitted to the President." The same letter, dated November 25, 1825, was published in *House Docs.,* 22 Cong., 1 Sess., no. 250, pp. 51-52. Cf. above, Clay to Rodgers, September 6, 1825, note. Offley, born in Pennsylvania, held official rank as only a commercial agent until 1832, when he was formally accredited as consul. He continued in that post until his death in 1838.

From WILLIAM C. SOMERVILLE, St. Cloud, *"Private* No. 1." Discusses the state of his health and his intention to leave Paris about December 10 to continue his journey to Greece. ALS. DNA, RG59, Dip. Disp., Sweden and Norway, vol. 4 (M45, R5). Received January 13, 1826.

From BEAUFORT T. WATTS, Quinta de Bolívar, no. 4. Encloses copies of his correspondence with (Pedro) Gual and his successor as Secretary of Foreign Affairs, (Joseph R.) Revenga, relative "to the mistake that was committed in the Department of State, in transcribing the documents relating to the Schooner Josephine, & of the condemnation of the Cargo of the Schooner Mechanic"; states that the balance in the case of the *Josephine* will be recovered but that Colombian officials are convinced that the cargo of the *Mechanic* was Spanish. Reports that Colombia is tranquil, that Bolívar will return from Peru, by way of Panama, in the spring, that the Provinces of Upper Peru have become the Republic of Bolívar, and that elections now in progress in Colombia will result in the choice of Bolívar for President. ALS. *Ibid.,* Colombia, vol. 3 (M-T33, R3). On the case of the *Josephine,* see above, Clay to Anderson, September 16, 1825; on the *Mechanic,* see above, Anderson to Secretary of State, March 18, 1825, note. On Revenga's temporary appointment as Secretary of Foreign Affairs, see below, Salazar to Clay, January 6, 1826.

MISCELLANEOUS LETTERS   November 28, 1825

From MATTHEW SWAN, Baltimore. Conveys his speculations concerning European politics; warns of the possibility of a British army in Mexico. ALS. DNA, RG59, Misc. Letters (M179, R63). Swan, not further identified.

APPLICATIONS, RECOMMENDATIONS   November 28, 1825

NICHOLAS DAVIS, Cahaba (Alabama), encloses a recommendation, signed by 51 of the 64 members of the State House of Representatives and by 18 of the 21 State senators, for appointment of William Crawford as Federal district judge in Alabama. ALS. DNA, RG59, A. and R. (MR1). A copy of this recommendation was transmitted to Clay by Davis on December 2. ALS. *Ibid.* On the appointment, see above, Owen to Clay, September 25, 1825, note.

JOHN EWING, Vincennes (Indiana), recommends John W. Osborn, editor of the Terre Haute *Western Register and Terre Haute Advertiser,* to publish the laws. ALS. DNA, RG59, P. and D. of L. Ewing, born in Ireland and educated at Baltimore, Maryland, had settled in 1813 at Vincennes, where he engaged in commerce, established a newspaper, served as associate judge of Knox County Circuit Court (1816 to 1820), and at this time (1825 to 1833) was a member of the State Senate. He later, as a Whig supporter, became a member of Congress (1833-1835, 1837-1839) and returned to the State Senate (1842-1844). Osborn had been born and educated in New Brunswick but, imbued with republican ideals, had joined the American forces in the War of 1812 and subsequently settled in western New York. He had edited several newspapers in the latter area before moving in 1817 to Vincennes, Indiana, and establishing another journal. In 1823 he removed to Terre Haute and founded the *Western Register and Terre Haute Advertiser,* a reformist paper, opposing slavery and supporting public education and prohibition. In later life he returned repeatedly to newspaper publication, notably as a farm journalist and temperance advocate. He became State printer for Indiana in 1841 but did not receive the Federal appointment here recommended.

William Hunter, Providence, Rhode Island, requests that his name be submitted to the President as an applicant for the position of district attorney; explains that he has not solicited the usual recommendations because he is "perhaps too well known at Washington and to no individual more than to" Clay; and, "anticipating . . . naught but good" from the administration, pledges his support. Extends congratulations to Clay that he holds "so deservedly and with such prevalent approbation . . . [his] present elevated Station. . . ." ALS. DNA, RG59, A. and R. (MR1). Hunter, of Newport, Rhode Island, who had been graduated from Rhode Island College (Brown University) and trained in law at the Inner Temple, London, had been a member of the State legislature (1797-1811) and of the United States Senate (1811-1821). He was now again a member of the Rhode Island Legislature (1822-1826) and later became United States Chargé (1834-1841) and Minister (1841-1843) to Brazil. He did not receive the appointment here solicited.

Abraham Markle, Markles Mills, Indiana, recommends John W. Osborn, editor of the Terre Haute *Western Register,* to publish the laws. ALS. DNA, RG59, P. and D. of L. Markle, of Fort Harrison, on the east edge of North Terre Haute, had been one of the founders of Terre Haute. On the proposed appointment, see above, Ewing to Clay, this date.

Philip S. Markley, Norristown (Pennsylvania), recommends the Philadelphia *Democratic Press* to publish the laws. ALS. DNA, RG59, P. and D. of L. The journal was given the contract, one of the few new appointments of this sort made by the Adams administration.

H[erman] J. Redfield, LeRoy, Genesee County, New York, recalls that he formerly recommended (Oran) Follett as publisher of the laws and asks that his contract be renewed, despite the application made by Redfield's brother, Lewis H. ALS. *Ibid.* Herman J. Redfield was a State senator. On the subject of the printing contract, cf. above, Oran Follett to Clay, June 24, 1825; Frederick Follett to Clay, July 9, 1825; Hayden to Clay, August 27, 1825, note.

Albert H. Tracy, Buffalo, recommends the *Buffalo Journal,* published by D(avid) M. Day, in place of the (Batavia *Spirit of the*) *Times,* as printer of the laws. ALS. DNA, RG59, P. and D. of L. Day had been one of the founders of the journal, in 1815. He did not receive the appointment now requested.

Check to Joseph King and Company

29h. Nov. 1825

Pay to Joseph King & Co. or order sixty one dollars and 25 Cents. Cashr. of the Off. of Dt. & Dt. Washn. City.[1]   H. Clay

ADS. DLC-TJC (DNA, M212, R16). Endorsed by payee on verso. King sold firewood (perhaps also other fuel or lumber products) in Washington.
[1] Richard Smith.

DIPLOMATIC NOTES   November 29, 1825

From Hilario de Rivas y Salmon, Philadelphia. Refers to his note of September 22; claims to have confirmation of rumors that an expedition is in preparation against Cuba and Puerto Rico; notes the construction of warships in the United

States for Mexico and South American governments; and argues that the exportation of such vessels is illegal. ALS. DNA, RG59, Notes from Spanish Legation, vol. 8 (M59, R11).

INSTRUCTIONS AND DISPATCHES   November 29, 1825

From JOHN M. FORBES, Buenos Aires, no. 28. Reports an interview with (Manuel José) García, who disclaimed authorization of a privateer engaged in piratical activities; encloses copies of correspondence formally stating this position; and advises publication of this disclaimer in the United States, as a warning to "our Countrymen of the imminent danger they incur in entering into any belligerent enterprise" under commissions of former authorities of the Banda Oriental. In reply to an inquiry by Forbes, García explained that the tax, levied in lieu of military service, on "foreign artificers and mechanics," was general in application, with no "exemption in favour of the English" under the recent treaty (see above, Raguet to Clay, March 11, 1825, note); whereupon Forbes asserted the American preference for "a general and frank declaration of reciprocal rights and privileges" rather than "the detailed stipulations of a treaty." Notes that García favors "Dr. Dn. Manuel Moreno" for appointment as Chargé d'Affaires to the United States, that "elections for doubling the present number of representatives in Congress are now taking place," and that the issue of federal as opposed to centralized government is being discussed. Observes that while "Bolivar is disposed to aid these Provinces against Brazil," the leaders of Buenos Aires are fearful "of the influence which such a Co-operation would give to the Liberator. . . ." War preparations by the Emperor (Peter I) are known, but "It is confidently believed . . . that these efforts will prove the dying agony of the Brazilian Power in this quarter"; reports on December 14 "give the opinion that Sir Charles Stuart will effectually mediate, and that peace will result." Explains that he has had reprinted and distributed "here, in its original language, and . . . through the provinces and to Chile and Peru" the newspaper accounts of Lafayette's departure (from the United States, above, Clay to Somerville, September 6, 1825), "As this was the closing scene of a grand, national representation . . . exhibiting the most exalted feelings, honourable to both the parties, and calculated to excite an extensive and lively political and moral influence. . . ." States that he has been notified that the "late law respecting flour" (above, Forbes to Clay, November 16, 1825) will be placed in full operation on January 1. Discusses outrages committed at Tucumán by La Madrid, who on November 26 declared himself Governor of the Province and arrested all members of the governing junta and Secretary Paz. LS. DNA, RG59, Dip. Disp., Argentina, vol. 2 (M69, R3). Parts of letter dated December 7, 10, 11, 14. Published in Espil (comp.), *Once Años en Buenos Aires*, 398-402. Extracts published in Manning (arr.), *Diplomatic Correspondence . . . Latin-American Nations*, I, 651-53.

Manuel Moreno, born in Buenos Aires, had been named first secretary of a mission to Great Britain in 1811 but, following his return in 1815, had edited a journal critical of the government and had been forced into exile in the United States from around 1817 to 1821. Subsequently he had been elected a deputy to the representative assembly of Buenos Aires, 1821 to 1826, and, in the latter year, a member of the Constitutional Congress. In April, 1826, he was named Minister Plenipotentiary to the United States; he was transferred to the embassy at London in 1828 and from 1835 to 1837 again assigned to the United States.

Gregoria Aráoz de La Madrid, a colonel of the army, had been sent to

Cumuná to raise forces with which to oppose Brazil but, instead, had fomented revolution against the local leaders, notably Dr. Juan Bautista Paz, who were supporting the central government. La Madrid assumed the office of provisional governor of the province in 1825 and again in 1826. An opponent of a unitarian government, he headed in 1840 a coalition of the interior provinces in revolt against the federalized State, was defeated, and fled to Chile.

Paz had been lieutenant governor of the province in 1813 and returned to office as provisional governor in 1829, 1834, and 1835.

MISCELLANEOUS LETTERS   November 29, 1825

From WILLIAM P. DUVAL, "Middle Florida Tallahassee." Calls "attention, to the Wreckers on the Florida Keys, and the evils that have, for a long time, and yet continue, to distress the Commerce of the United States on this coast." Cites judicial decisions declaring unconstitutional the "Wrecking law" enacted by "The Legislative Council of Florida" (see above, Henry to Clay, April 6, 1825, note); estimates "that there is annually wrecked on the Florida Coast, property to the value of $500:000"; refers to activities of vessels "little better than Pirates and Smugglers . . . engaged in smuggling and Wrecking"; and suggests the appointment of "a Judge to reside on some of the Keys, or at Tampa Bay, who should have jurisdiction of all such cases," the licensing of wreckers, the designation of a port to which "all Wrecked property on the coast should be carried for adjudication," the careful selection of revenue officers for that area, and the exercise of "The utmost attention and vigilence [sic] . . . over this coast. . . ." Carter (ed.), *Territorial Papers,* XXIII, 363-65. Endorsed: ". . . . This letter is respectfully referred to the Judiciary Committee of the H of R. by direction of the Sec: of State, with a request that it may be returned."

From ROBERT TILLOTSON, New York. Acknowledges receipt of Clay's letter (above, October 12, 1825) enclosing a copy of one from (Hilario de Rivas y) Salmon; admits "that ships intended from their structure, for warlike pourposes [sic], are now building in this City" but sees no authority, under the act of Congress of April 20, 1818 (see above, II, 492-507n), to seize them; and states that "the utmost that can be done, under this act, will be done by the Collector who under the 10 Sec, will require Bonds from the present owners." ALS. DNA, RG59, Misc. Letters (M179, R63).

APPLICATIONS, RECOMMENDATIONS   November 29, 1825

THOMAS H. BLAKE, WILLIAM C. LINTON, and MOSES TABBS, Terre Haute (Indiana), recommend that the *Western Register and Terre Haute Advertiser,* edited by John W. Osborn, be authorized to publish the laws. ALS by Blake, signed also by Linton and Tabbs. DNA, RG59, P. and D. of L. Linton not further identified. Tabbs, a lawyer of Vincennes, had been associated with Osborn and others in a test case against slavery, won before the Indiana Supreme Court in 1820 (1 Blackford 60). On the recommended appointment, see above, Ewing to Clay, November 28, 1825.

CHARLES ELDRIDGE, East Greenwich (Rhode Island) recommends Richard W(ood) Greene for appointment as United States attorney in Rhode Island. ALS. DNA, RG59, A. and R. (MR2). Eldridge not further identified. Greene, born in Rhode Island, educated at Brown University, and in 1816 admitted to practice of law in Massachusetts and Rhode Island, was appointed to the office here recommended and held it from 1824 to 1845. He then served two years in the State legislature and from 1848 to 1854 as chief justice of the State.

ORAN FOLLETT, Batavia (New York), encloses a letter from Redfield (to Clay, November 28, 1825) and requests appointment of Frederick Follett to publish the laws. Asserts: "As a member of the Legislature of the state, *in 1824,* I feel as tho' I had some small claim to consideration from the present administration." ALS. DNA, RG59, P. and D. of L. See above, Evans and others to Clay, June 25, 1825, note.

To Francis T. Brooke

My dear Sir   (Confidential)   Washington 30h. Nov. 1825

I recd. this morning your favor of the 27h. instant. Altho'. my personal knowledge of your son is limited, I have very favorable impressions of him, derived through several channels and particularly from Mr Southard.[1] I shall, therefore, as well on that account, as from other considerations, take particular pleasure in endeavoring to promote your and his wishes. At present there is nothing that I know of worthy of acceptance in the Territories. The office of Atto. in one of the districts of Florida is vacant, but a person has been fixed upon to fill it.[2] As it regards appointments in any State it is extremely difficult, if not altogether wrong and impracticable to Send a person from one into another State. If therefore he means to Settle in one of the new States, his settlement must precede his appointmt. to any office, if there be any to which he can be appointed. As to Territorial appointments it is otherwise. Previous settlement is not indispensible, though even there it is advisable. I pray you to keep me informed of his movements and wishes. And it will be well also to correspond with Barbour[3] and Southard.

If Virginia is to designate a Senator upon the principle of opposition to the administration, let that Senator be Wm. B. Giles. He would be a real friend 'though a nominal enemy— I mean that his indiscretions, always great, and now greater than ever, would benefit more than his hostility would injure. But I should hope that no such principle would govern the choice. I should be delighted to see Govr. Pleasants here, or Genl. Tucker, or Mr. C. Johnson.[4] Of the latter I know personally but little, but the accounts I have always had of him are highly favorable. It is of no great consequence, in respect to the success or movement of the Admon, who may be sent. The judgment which the public will form of it depends upon its measures. And one Senator out of 48 cannot, in that view of the matter, be very essential. You will hear with pleasure that our harmony, in the cabinet, continues without the slightest interruption, and that we have daily testimonies of increased strength and confidence.

The President has acceded to the wishes of several of the new American Republics that the U. States shd. be represented at Panama.[5] Our friends need have no fears of our contracting there unnecessary or onerous engagements, or menacing the peace or neutrality of the Country.

There is a treaty now going on in this City with the Creeks with prospects of a successful issue.[6] Yours faithfully & respectfy

The Honble F Brooke   H CLAY

ALS. NcD.   1 Samuel L. Southard.
2 See above, Wright to Clay, October 25, 1825, note.
3 James Barbour.
4 James Pleasants; Henry St. George Tucker; Chapman Johnson. On the result of the election, see above, Brooke to Clay, November 27, 1825, note.
5 See above, Clay to Gallatin, November 8, 1825; below, Clay to Obregón and Clay to Cañaz, both this date.
6 See above, Clay to Southard, July 3, 1825, note; Clay to Hammond, November 6, 1825.

To Pablo Obregón

Don Pablo Obregon, Envoy Extraordinary and Minister Plenipotentiary from Mexico.

Sir,   Department of State, Washington, 30 Novr. 1825.

I have the honour to acknowledge the receipt of your official note of the third instant, communicating a formal invitation from the Government of the United States of Mexico to that of the United States to send deputies to the contemplated Congress at Panama, and particularizing several subjects which your Government conceives may be proper for the consideration of that Congress; and I have laid your note before the President of the United States.

When, at your instance, during the last spring, I had the honour of receiving you at the Department of State, and conferring with you verbally in regard to the proposed Congress, and to the friendly wish entertained by your Government, that ours should be represented at it,[1] I stated to you, by the direction of the President, that it appeared to him to be necessary, before the assembling of such a Congress, to settle between the different powers to be represented several preliminary points, such as the subjects to which the attention of the Congress should be directed; the substance and the form of the powers to be given to the respective representatives; and the mode of organizing the Congress; and that if these points should be satisfactorily arranged, the President would be disposed to accept, in behalf of the United States, the invitation with which you were provisionally charged.

In your note there is not recognized so exact a compliance with the conditions on which the President expressed his willingness that the United States should be represented at Panama, as could have been desired. It would have been perhaps better if there had been a full understanding between all the American Powers, who may assemble by their representatives, of the precise questions on which they are to deliberate, and that some other matters respecting the powers of the deputies and the organization of the Congress should have been distinctly arranged prior to the opening of its deliberations. But as the want of the adjustment of these preliminaries, if it should occasion any inconvenience, could be only productive of some delay, the President has determined, at once, to manifest the sensibility of the United States to whatever concerns the prosperity of the American hemisphere and to the friendly motives which have actuated your Government in transmitting the invitation which you have communicated. He has therefore resolved, should the Senate of the United States, now expected to assemble in a few days, give their advice and consent, to send Commissioners to the Congress at Panama. Whilst they will not be authorized to enter upon any deliberations or to concur in any acts inconsistent with the present neutral position of the United States, and its obligations, they will be fully empowered and instructed upon all questions, likely to arise in the Congress, on subjects in which the nations of America have a common interest. All unnecessary delay will be avoided in the departure of these Commissioners from the United States for the point of their destination.

I avail myself of the occasion to offer you assurances of my distinguished consideration.   H. CLAY

Copy. DNA, RG59, Notes to Foreign Legations, vol. 3, pp. 238-39 (M38, R3). A duplicate of this letter was sent to José Maria Salazar. Both letters were published in *American State Papers, Foreign Relations*, V, 837-38.

1 See above, Tudor to Clay, April 12, 1825, note.

From Samuel Eddy

Dear Sir,   Providence Novr. 30. 1825.

As the time will soon arrive when printers of the laws in the several States will be appointed, will you excuse me for saying a word on that subject, in relation to the printing in this State. From conversation which I had with you, a short time before I left Washington, I have encouraged the Editors of the Patriot,[1] in this town, to expect a continuance of the public patronage. The laws have been published in this paper, ever since the republican party came into power in 1801. Indeed it is the only paper, in this part of the State, which has supported that party. This it did, boldly and manfully, in the worst of times, when it required no little strength of nerve to face the opposition. In this town the wealth and influence has always been federal, and its power was exercised with an unsparing hand in those trying times— Efforts I presume will be made by my successor[2] to procure the printing for the Manufacturers Journal,[3] which *affects* to consider itself republican, but has *always* opposed the republican party, and whose object has been to break us in pieces. This however it cannot effect. This paper supported my Successor, than whom there was never, in this State, a more bitter enemy to the republican party, both State and United States. Could I persuade myself that a Republican administration, would prefer its enemies to its friends, other circumstances being equal, I might add that the Providence Patriot has a more extensive circulation than any other paper in the State. And I will further add that I shall be much gratified, should your opinion coincide with mine, that this paper ought still to be preferred.[4]

If I can at any time, communicate any information, in relation to matters and things here, I will with pleasure do it, in candour and sincerity, if it will be acceptable. As three of our delegation are new members,[5] I could say a word on that subject, but perhaps it might be considered invidious and I therefore forbear. I am with the most Sincere Respect Your friend and Servant

Hon. Henry Clay   Secry. of State.   SAMUEL EDDY

ALS. DLC-HC (DNA, M212, R2).
[1] Cf. above, Jones and Simons to Clay, September 12, 1825.
[2] Tristam Burges, Providence lawyer, was a member of the United States House of Representatives from 1825 to 1835.
[3] That is, *Manufacturers and Farmers Journal.*
[4] Both journals received contracts for publishing the laws of the new Congress.
[5] In addition to Burges, the new members included Dutee J. Pearce, in the House, and Asher Robbins, who was chosen to fill the vacancy in the Senate caused by the resignation, October 31, 1825, of James De Wolf.

DIPLOMATIC NOTES   November 30, 1825

To ANTONIO JOSE CANAZ, Washington. Acknowledges receipt of his "official note of the 14th. instant" and states that the United States "will be represented at the Congress if the Senate of the U. States should so advise and consent." Copy. DNA, RG59, Notes to Foreign Legations, vol. 3, p. 239 (M38, R3). ALI draft, in CSmH. Published in *American State Papers, Foreign Relations,* V, 839.

INSTRUCTIONS AND DISPATCHES   November 30, 1825

To PAYTON GAY, "Consul U. S. Island of Teneriffe." Encloses commission, printed circular instructions, and a blank consular bond. Copy. DNA, RG59, Cons. Instr., vol. 2, p. 375 (M78, R2). Gay, of Massachusetts, had been replaced at Teneriffe by 1835 but received appointment early in 1837 as consul at Campeche, Mexico, and, from 1837 to 1840, held the same office at Martinique.

MISCELLANEOUS LETTERS   November 30, 1825

To WILLIAM B. ROCHESTER, "Confidential." Tenders to him by authorization
of the President, "the appointment of Secretary of the Legation" which will
represent the United States at the Panama Congress; states that "The duration
of the service abroad will not be shorter than six months, and may be much
longer." Copy. DNA, RG59, Dip. Instr., vol. 10, p. 417 (M77, R5). ALI draft,
in DLC-HC (DNA, M212, R7). Rochester replied, December 8, accepting the
appointment. ALS. DNA, RG43, First Panama Congress (M662, R1).

APPLICATIONS, RECOMMENDATIONS   November 30, 1825

JOHN C. ANDREWS, Pittsburgh, asks reappointment of his journal, the *Statesman*,
to publish the laws. ALS. DNA, RG59, P. and D. of L. Andrews had been,
from August, 1819, to October, 1820, one of the publishers of the Chillicothe,
Ohio, *Weekly Recorder;* in 1824 he and P. C. M. Andrews had taken over
proprietorship of the Pittsburgh *Statesman,* which retained the contract to
publish the laws throughout the Adams administration.

RICHARD W. GREENE, Providence (Rhode Island), asks appointment as "U. S.
Attorney for this District." ALS. DNA, RG59, A. and R. (MR2). See above,
Eldridge to Clay, November 29, 1825, note.

W. S. THOMAS, Louisville, Kentucky, seeks an appointment, possibly as consul
to one of the new republics. Mentions "the Small acquantance [*sic*]" he has
with Clay, "Which Occured [*sic*] at . . . [his] last visit to this place. . . ," and
his own "decided" advocacy of Clay "On the Ocasion [*sic*] of the Presidential
Ellection [*sic*]." Comments: "My tallents [*sic*] are of Moderate grade— Yet I
have not past [*sic*] the verge of acquirement—" Postscript states that (John)
Rowan and (Thomas Hart) Benton have been "written to." ALS. DNA, RG59,
A. and R. (MR4). Thomas, an exchange broker in the 1830's, received no
appointment.

CHARLES PEN[DLETO]N TUTT, Washington, seeks appointment to a civil office of
rank equivalent to navy agent. ALS. DNA, RG59, A. and R. (MR4). Tutt, of
"Locust Hill," Loudoun County, Virginia, a veteran of the War of 1812 and
a large plantation owner, received no appointment under the Adams administration but was named navy agent at Pensacola, Florida, in 1830 and remained
there for several years.

To Josephus B. Stuart

Dear Sir   Washington 1st. Decr. 1825
   I recd. your letter of the 26h. instant [*sic*][1] requesting my opinion
whether the Govt. of Mexico would probably sell the province of
Texas with or without the jurisdiction. I am not able to give you
any satisfactory opinion. I should hardly think however that they
would alienate the jurisdiction. Further; there is a negotiation
pending on the subject of the boundary between the U. States
and Mexico which,[2] whilst it continues, ought to prevent any
American Citizen from interfering.

I presume the President will notice the subject of Internal [Improveme]nts in his Message;[3] but, from the character of that paper, he can hardly enter into any detailed notice of particular projects, except it be those which are in a progress of execution.

I ha[ve la]tely recd. a letter from our friend Genl. Porter,[4] dated since the message from him which you kindly communicate, and for which I thank you. Yr's faithfully & respectfully   H. CLAY
Dr. J. B. Stuart.

ALS. NcD.   1 Not found.
2 See above, Poinsett to Clay, November 25, 1825.
3 In the annual message of December 6, 1825, Adams confined his discussion of internal improvements, in the traditional sense of the phrase, to a report of the surveys conducted under the act of April 30, 1824 (above, III, 633n) and the progress made under previous legislation for extending the Cumberland Road (above, Speech, January 17, 1825, note), building new roads through the territories (above, Clay to Poinsett, March 26, 1825, note), confirming State laws incorporating the Chesapeake and Ohio Canal Company (4 U. S. Stat., 101-102, March 3, 1825), and constructing lighthouses and harbor improvements. But Adams expressed a major enlargement of the conception of internal improvements when he recommended public support for programs of geographic exploration and of research on astronomic phenomena. In the latter connection he referred to (George Washington's) earlier proposal for establishment of a national university and deplored the lack of any astronomical observatories, "lighthouses of the skies," in the American hemisphere. Richardson (comp.), Messages and Papers of the Presidents, II, 306-308, 311-14.
4 Cf. above, Clay to Porter, November 28, 1825.

From Christopher Hughes

My dear Sir,   Private.   Baltimore, December 1st. 1825.
I dare say, with your usual mercy, you gave me a dab of Lynch Law, for my rapid retreat from Washington. The fact is I was seized with a most ardent inclination to kiss my wife; (I mean, my children![1]) & as Mr. Johnson was already involved in a sort of arrangement to go to Coll. Monroe's, with Mr. Graham,[2] on the Saturday, (& not on the Friday,) I came home, urged by my marital, (I mean my paternal,) anxieties; intending to go back to Washington, in the Saturday's morning stage, in time to join him & Mr. Graham! Proof—I routed up all General Smith's[3] horse, & went up to the Stage office, on Saturday morning!—I reached there, at 6; but unfortunately, on getting there, I found that the 5 oClock Stage, dont go at Six; & so I lost my passage & my morning's nap! Now, there was no object in going on a later stage; for I should have arrived at Washington, too late; yet by way of palliating my error between 5. & 6, oClock Stage, the fact is, the 8 oClock Stage, does go at 9! Thus the advertisement lieth; but why should I trouble you, with this horary nonsense?— I hope, as you did with Edward, the Confessor, (Wier)[4] you have pronounced the short word "forgive," & there is an end of it.—

I enclose a letter[5] giving the last news of Mr. Connell.[6] I have understood that Mr. Walsh[7] gave all the credit of the Swedish liquidation to Mr. Connell, in his paper![8] I am quite sure, that poor Mr. Connell would feel himself quite grieved, if he knew, that this had been done; for I verily believe his sense of obligation to me, to be of the most conscientious & friendly nature; but we will let that pass.—

I have just received a letter dated Stockholm 30 Septr. 1825.— It says — — — "It is now asserted, that no sales of our remaining men of war at Carlscrona, will take place! The Russian Minister, Count Suchtelen,[9] who went in great haste from hence to Christiania, (where the king[10] is) & who is back again, is said to have effected this final decision!— The Argus (a very able paper, & in opposition) which took up this matter, has been prosecuted; but will probably be acquitted by the jury, which is to decide on the case."

This extract, applies to the *last* sale made by the king of Sweden of 2 frigates & a 74, to the Goldsmidts of London, for the Mexican Government![11] The Emperor of Russia[12] interposed, & asked it as a mark of personal friendship from the King of Sweden, as well as a proof of H. M.s continuance in *"good principles,"* that the King would cancel *this* bargain. The King consented—provided, the Emperor would engage to make King Ferdinand[13] pay the penalty of 20,000 £ Stg., forfeited in case of either party violating the bond of sale!— The first Sale of men of War, (applying to 1. 74, & 1. frigate;) had been carried into effect, & the Ships delivered over to the purchasers; I saw them riding at anchor, at Elsinore, in July; & I hope they will soon be heard of, blockading St. Juan d'Ulloa![14]—

Make my homage to Mrs. Clay; the ottoman is making & I hope it will succeed; the columns are also in work; but you must not expect *them* to be ornamental; they are meant merely as firm stands for Lamps, & to economize space; I have ordered them to be painted a lead colour, so as to be as little en *evidence,* as possible! if you do not like the colour, you can let me know, what Mrs. Clay does like, & it can be changed! As to the glasses, I have had a person scouring (not *glasses,* but *shops;*) for them, & I do not think a match can be found! if found, the 2 dozen shall be sent to Washington, if not, I sha'ant [*sic*] break either the glass you gave me, or my own heart, for I think the glass pattern detestable! I beg your pardon for so thinking, or rather, for so saying. My sincere apologies to Mr. Johnson, if you please; & my prostrations to Mrs. Johnson, if she please! I should like to be *co-terminous* to you all; but I suppose Yr excellency thinks Baltimore the best perch for Yr. devoted Servant   C HUGHES

N.B. Will you do me the favour to send the bundle of letters I left with you, in an envelope, addressed to Doctor Watkins.[15] You will vy much oblige yrs. respectfuly [*sic*]   C H

Henry Clay Esqr Washington.

ALS. DLC-HC (DNA, M212, R2).   1 Charles J. and Margaret S. Hughes.
2 Probably Josiah S. Johnston; James Monroe; George Graham.
3 Samuel Smith.   4 Edward Wyer.   5 Not found.
6 John Connell.   7 Robert Walsh, Jr.
8 Philadelphia *National Gazette and Literary Register.* Cf. above, Clay to Smith,
October 12, 1825.   9 Count Jan Pieter Suchtelen.
10 Charles XIV.
11 See above, Hughes to Clay, July 8, 1825, note.
12 Alexander I.   13 Ferdinand VII of Spain.
14 See above, Clay to Poinsett, March 26, 1825, note.
15 Tobias Watkins.

INSTRUCTIONS AND DISPATCHES   December 1, 1825

From M[ARTIN] BICKHAM, "Isle of France." Reports that he has appointed
Prosper Froberville "to act as Consular Agent for the United States until further
orders"; adds that "Mr. Froberville is a native of this Island, a Gentleman of
Handsome Property, of a Highly Respectable Character"; and recommends
him for appointment if the government wishes to have a consul or agent there.
ALS. DNA, RG59, Cons. Disp., Port Louis, vol. 1 (M-T118, R-T1). Addressed
to Secretary of State; received April 12, 1826. Froberville continued in the post
for nearly a decade.

From JOEL R. POINSETT, Mexico, no. 29. Reports that acting in conformity
with Clay's instructions relative to excessively high duties on cotton goods
manufactured in the United States (above, March 26, 1825), he learned that in
November, 1824, customs officials at Alvarado had "suddenly increased the
valuation of that description of goods nearly one hundred per cent: But, that
on the injustice of this measure being represented to the government here, the
valuation was reduced to its former standard in January 1825." States that his
representation to the Mexican Government in the case of Taylor, Sicard and
Company (see above, Poinsett to Clay, July 18, 1825) "was promptly attended
to"; that at the time he had been unaware of the existence of other claims,
which have since come to his attention; and that he has addressed a note in
this connection to "the Secretary of State and foreign Relations" (Sebastián
Camacho). Encloses a copy of a letter written by (José Ignacio) Esteva, Secretary
of the Treasury, to his government concerning "Consular regulations which were
onerous to our trade," which Poinsett thinks will be acted upon. LS. DNA,
Dip. Disp., Mexico, vol. 1 (M94, R2). Received January 14, 1826.

APPLICATIONS, RECOMMENDATIONS   December 1, 1825

DOBBINS, MURPHY, AND BOSE, Baltimore, seeks continuance of appointment as
publisher of the laws, in the Baltimore *American and Commercial Daily
Advertiser.* ALS. DNA, RG59, P. and D. of L. Endorsed (ES) by members of
the Maryland congressional delegation (Samuel Smith, Peter Little, John Barney,
George E. Mitchell, Joseph Kent, and Thomas Contee Worthington), who
recommend renewal of the appointment.

DIPLOMATIC NOTES   December 2, 1825

From the BARON DE MAREUIL, Washington. Reports delay and irregularity in
the arrival of mail sent him from France by way of New York. Noting that all
the packets in service between the two countries belong to the United States,

he offers to enter into any kind of agreement with Clay to expedite the passage of mail between the two countries. LS in French, with translation in State Department file. DNA, RG59, Notes from French Legation, vol. 9 (M53, R7).

From CHARLES R. VAUGHAN, Washington. Refers to his note of November 15; now lays before Clay copies of two grants of land, "in the British Settlement of Madawaska," made by agents of Maine and Masachusetts, "in virtue of certain Resolutions of the Legislatures of" those two states; and repeats his "request, that this conduct may be disavowed, & discountenanced by the Government of the United States." LS. DNA, RG59, Notes from British Legation, vol. 14 (M50, R15). Published in Manning (arr.), *Diplomatic Correspondence . . . Canadian Relations*, II, 493-95.

INSTRUCTIONS AND DISPATCHES   December 2, 1825

From HEMAN ALLEN, Valparaiso, no. 24. Transmits a copy of part of his letter to Commodore (Isaac) Hull, in answer to an inquiry concerning the case of the *General Brown*. Also encloses copies of his correspondence with the Chilean Government relative to the claim of the representatives of John Campbell; states that his efforts in regard to all claims have proved unavailing. Reports that an expedition against Chiloé "went to sea" on November 27, "commanded by the Director [Ramón de Freire] in person." ALS. DNA, RG59, Dip. Disp., Chile, vol. 1 (M-T2, R1). Received April 20, 1826. Enclosures reveal that the claim here mentioned was for the liquidation of the account of Campbell, a citizen of the United States, who had died in the service of the Chilean Navy. The Chiloé Archipelago, a large island together with some sixty smaller ones, off the coast of Chile, remained in Royalist hands. The expedition here mentioned was successful in the battles of Pudeto and Bella Vista, and the defenders capitulated January 15, 1826.

From A[LEXANDER] H. EVERETT, Madrid, no. 16. Reports that, during a personal interview, he handed to the Duke del Infantado a copy of the article of the treaty under which the United States claims the right to have a consul at Havana (cf. above, Clay to Everett, April 27, 1825, note 15) and, although the Duke "could not deny that it was explicit and obligatory," he refused to give a decisive answer, on the ground that he needed time to inform himself further. Comments that, in regard to claims, the Duke's "system of defence" consists "in pleading an entire and complete ignorance of the whole business" and his questions "shewed but too plainly that his ignorance was far from being pretended." Encloses, among other documents, "a project of a Convention," which Everett has drawn up and presented to the Duke "In order to convey to him some general notions of the nature of the question in dispute." States that (Frederick James) Lamb (the British Minister to Spain) has communicated to the Spanish Government a copy of the treaty between Portugal and Brazil (above, Raguet to Secretary of State, March 11, 1825, note), with a request that Spain "recognise the new Empire," and that Lamb has promised to support a note which Everett has "thought of addressing . . . to the Minister [the Duke] upon the subject of recognition of the new States. . . ." LS. *Ibid.*, Spain, vol. 25 (M31, R27). Received March 6, 1825. Among the enclosures are copies of a letter from John Mullowny to Everett, November 10, relative to the presence of a Colombian sloop of war in the Bay of Tangier (cf. above, Mullowny to Clay, October 21, 1825), and of Everett's note to the Duke del Infantado, November 24, concerning the actions of the Spanish consul at Boston

(Ramunda Chacon—see above, Jones to Clay, March 28, 1825). On Everett's contemplated note to Spain, see below, January 27, 1826.

From JOEL R. POINSETT, Mexico, no. 30. Reports that, "after the surrender of the Castle of Ulloa" (see above, Poinsett to Clay, November 23, 1825), the Cabinet of Mexico proposed to the Congress of that Republic an expedition against Cuba and that "yesterday" the proposal was defeated in the House of Representatives. Notes that during the debate on this matter, in secret session of the House, "the secretary of war [Manuel Gómez Pedraza] urged the necessity of getting rid of at least six thousand men and a number of officers whose presence he considered dangerous to the liberties and peace of the republic." LS, in code, deciphered in State Department file. DNA, RG59, Dip. Disp., Mexico, vol. 1 (M97, R2).

APPLICATIONS, RECOMMENDATIONS   December 2, 1825

NICHOLAS BROWN, EDWARD CARRINGTON, THOMAS P. IVES, and NATHANIEL SEARLE, Providence, recommend Richard W. Greene as district attorney for Rhode Island. LS. DNA, RG59, A. and R. (MR2). The first three correspondents were prominent merchants; the last, a well-known lawyer. Brown and Ives, brothers-in-law, were partners in the firm Brown and Ives, active in manufacturing, banking, and insurance as well as maritime enterprise. On Greene's appointment, see above, Eldridge to Clay, November 29, 1825, note.

WILLIAM MAYO expresses a wish to obtain for his son, Addison, an appointment to the United States Military Academy; observes that "it is said that he is a boy of Capacity and understands Geography, Arithmatick, &. Grammer and a tolerable spattering of Lattin"; and requests Clay to write him at Shelbyville (Kentucky). ALS. DNA, RG94, Military Academy, Cadet Applications, 1823-13 (M688, R36). Cf. above, McKinney to Clay, November 26, 1825.

INSTRUCTIONS AND DISPATCHES   December 3, 1825

From THOMAS L. L. BRENT, Lisbon. Reports the King (John VI) "out of danger and recovering rapidly" and notes the expectation that he will "be able to return to Lisbon in three weeks." ALS. DNA, RG59, Dip. Disp., Portugal, vol. 6 (M43, R5). Received February 7, 1826. Cf. above, Brent to Clay, November 26, 1825.

MISCELLANEOUS LETTERS   December 3, 1825

From ROSEWELL SALTONSTALL, New York. Requests "aid in the Amount of Four Hundred or Five Hundred Dollars" to enable him to perfect an invention based on his discovery of the principle of perpetual motion. ALS. DNA, RG59, Misc. Letters (M179, R63). Enclosed in a letter to Samuel L. Southard, also of this date, in which Saltonstall complains that he has already forwarded "Letters and a Petition for aid" (not found), without, however, being able to "extort a Single answer from the Honbl H Clay." He adds that he has also "addressed the President on this subject. . . ." The letter to Southard is endorsed: "Respectfully referred to the Secty. of State. S. L. S. 5 Decr 1825." Saltonstall not further identified. See below, Clay to Southard, December 6, 1825.

From CHARLES SAVAGE, New York. Announces his intention to depart for Guatemala in ten days. ALS. DNA, RG59, Cons. Disp., Guatemala, vol. 1 (M-T337, R1). Received December 6.

On December 10, Daniel Brent replied, "by direction of the Secretary," that Clay "has no commands at present for that part of the world." Copy, in DNA, RG59, Cons. Instr., vol. 2, p. 376 (M78, R2).

From THOMAS SKIDMORE, New York. Asserts that "there are . . . but *two* great objects" that "might come before" the Panama Congress: "1st., a general confederacy of all the American governments for the purpose of *self defence,* against any aggressions which may be made on them or any of them, by the Monarchs of Europe:—and second—*the cutting a magnificent canal thro' Darien, at the joint expence of the Confederation."* Advocates construction, through territory purchased by "the Confederacy" for that purpose, of a canal large enough to accommodate "the heaviest ship that floats, or that the wants of mankind may require to float"; protection of that canal by forts, armies, and squadrons; and division of toll revenues, above the expenses for "defense and preservation," among the members of the confederation. ALS. DLC-HC (DNA, M212, R2). Skidmore, born in Connecticut and experienced as a teacher in New Jersey, Virginia, and North Carolina, had settled in New York in 1821 and worked as a machinist and inventor. At this time a Clay supporter, he became one of the founders of the New York Working Men's Party in 1829. He published *The Rights of Man to Property! Being a Proposition to Make It Equal among the Adults of the Present Generation; and to Provide for Its Equal Transmission to Every Individual of Each Succeeding Generation, on Arriving at the Age of Maturity* . . . (New York, 1829). When the Working Men's Party failed to support these radical views, he organized his followers as a separate Poor Man's Party, which was badly defeated in the New York election of 1830. Skidmore then turned to journalism but died in 1832.

APPLICATIONS, RECOMMENDATIONS   December 3, 1825

N[ATHANIEL] HUNTINGTON, Markles Mills (Indiana), recommends appointment of John W. Osborn to publish the laws. ALS. DNA, RG59, P. and D. of L. Date illegible; postmarked December 3. Huntington, born in Connecticut, was postmaster at Markles Mills. On the appointment of Osborn, see above, Ewing to Clay, November 28, 1825, note.

THOMAS MCGIFFIN, Washington, Pennsylvania, recommends Peter DeHaven for an appointment. ALS. DNA, RG59, A. and R. (MR2). See above, Rawle to Clay, November 10, 1825, note.

NATHANIEL F. WILLIAMS, Baltimore, forwards a memorial (possibly above, Warner and others to Clay, November, 1825) recommending the *Baltimore Patriot* to publish the laws. Speaks of the journal's support for "that Administration it has so essentially contributed to build up." ALS. DNA, RG59, P. and D. of L.

A. AND H. WILSON, Wilmington, Delaware, note transfer to them of the Wilmington *American Watchman* and request continuation of that journal's appointment to publish the laws. ALS. *Ibid.* The Wilsons have not been further identified. The contract was renewed.

Convention with Central American Federation

December 5, 1825

[This "general Convention of Peace, Friendship, Commerce and Navigation" provides a mutual agreement "not to grant any particular favour to other nations in respect of commerce and navigation, which shall not immediately become common to the other party, who shall enjoy the same freely, if the concession was freely made, or on allowing the same compensation, if the concession was conditional" (Article 2); undertakes to place the commerce of the two nations on a basis of "equality and reciprocity," permitting citizens of each to frequent all the coasts of the other, to reside and trade there, and to "enjoy all the rights, privileges and exemptions in navigation and commerce, which native Citizens do or shall enjoy," but not to participate in the coasting trade (Article 3); states that "whatever kind of produce, manufacture or merchandize of any foreign county can be . . . lawfully imported . . . in their own vessels" may be also imported in vessels of the other, without "higher or other duties, upon the tonnage of the vessel, or her cargo. . . , whether the importation be made in vessels of the one country or of the other," and "whatever may be lawfully exported or re-exported from the one country, in its own vessels, to any foreign country, may, in like manner, be exported or re-exported in the vessels of the other country," with "the same bounties, duties and drawbacks" to "be allowed and collected" (Article 4). No higher duties or charges and no restrictions shall be imposed upon the importations into or exportations from either country "than are or shall be payable on the like articles being the produce or manufactures of any other foreign country" (Article 5).

[Additional articles forbid embargo or detention of vessels or cargoes "for any military expedition, . . . [or] for any public or private purpose whatever, without allowing to those interested a sufficient indemnification" (Article 7) and provide for restoration of property seized by pirates (Article 9), relief of shipwrecked seamen (Article 10), release of the effects of deceased citizens of the signatories (Article 11), "judicial recourse, on the same terms which are usual and customary with the natives or Citizens of the Country in which they may be" (Article 12), and freedom of religious belief so long as respect is shown to "the laws and established usages of the country" (Article 13).

[Articles 14, 15, and 17 assert the principle "that free ships shall also give freedom to goods. . . , contraband goods being always excepted," and provided also that the rule shall apply only with respect to the goods and persons of parties accepting this principle and to shipments not directed to "places which are at that time besieged or blockaded." Article 16 defines contraband as "materials manufactured, prepared, and formed, expressly to make war. . . ." A blockade is stated to be limited to those places "which are actually attacked by a belligerent force capable of preventing the entry of the neutral." It is further stipulated that no citizen of the contracting parties shall "accept a Commission, or letter of marque, for the purpose of assisting or co-operating hostilely" with the enemy of either against the other (Article 24). Succeeding clauses provide for the mutual protection of citizens and their property "If, by any fatality which cannot be expected, and which God forbid, the two contracting parties should be engaged in a war with each other. . . ."

[Diplomatic and consular officials are to be exchanged with "all the rights, prerogatives, and immunities" extended to those of the most favored nation (Articles 27 and 28); deserters from public or private vessels are to be surrendered upon the submission of public documents in substantiation of such charge before competent authorities (Article 31); and the contracting powers further "agree, as soon hereafter as circumstances will permit them, to form a Consular Convention" which shall more fully elaborate the powers and immunities of consular personnel (Article 32). The present treaty is to remain in force for twelve years from the date of exchange of ratifications in so far as it relates to commercial clauses and in perpetuity so far as it relates to "peace and friendship" (Article 33). The "ratifications shall be exchanged in the City of Guatemala within eight months from the date of signature hereof. . . ."]

Miller (ed.), *Treaties. . . ,* III, 209-33. The Convention was approved unanimously by the United States Senate, on December 29, 1825. U. S. Sen., *Executive Journal,* III, 468. On the exchange of ratifications, see below, Williams to Clay, August 3, 1826.

INSTRUCTIONS AND DISPATCHES   December 5, 1825

From F. M. DIAMOND, Havana. Reports that the Mexican brig of war *Victoria* has entered the harbor of Havana, under a flag of truce, bringing the remnant of the garrison of the Castle of San Juan de Ulloa. ALS. DNA, RG59, Cons. Disp., Havana, vol. 3 (M-T20, R3). See above, Poinsett to Clay, November 23, 1825.

From RUFUS KING, London, no. 13. Notes receipt from (Henry) Middleton of "a Copy of Count Nesselrodes reply to the letter of Mr Middleton" (see above, Middleton to Clay, September 8, 1825 [1], note) comments that "There can be no doubt that the cause of South America makes a favorable progress, and that it cannot be much longer Baffled"; encloses a copy of his note to the

Foreign Office in the case of Jordine. LS. DNA, RG59, Dip. Disp., Great
Britain, vol. 32 (M30, R28). Received January 15, 1826. Extract published in
Manning (arr.), *Diplomatic Correspondence . . . Latin-American Nations,* III,
1575-76. King's note to George Canning, dated December 5, 1825, requested
restoration to Jordine of some papers seized by a British naval officer. A
report of the case has not been found.

From BEAUFORT T. WATTS, "Quinta de Bolivar." Transmits copies of his
correspondence with (Joseph R.) Revenga "in relation to the Capture, and
condemnation, of the American Brig Cygnet and her Cargo" by Colombian
authorities at Rio La Hacha; reports that "A restitution in the Case of the
Josephine, will doubtless be made," but in the case of the *Mechanic* the
Colombian Government maintains "that the Condemnation of the Cargo was
correct." Notes receipt of a letter from (Richard C.) Anderson (Jr.), who
will probably "reach Bogota by the 25th. Inst." ALS. DNA, RG59, Dip. Disp.,
Colombia, vol. 3 (M-T33, R3). Received February 13, 1826. The enclosures
reveal that the *Cygnet,* of Bath, Maine, had been charged with carrying
contraband. No action on the claim has been found. On the case of the
Josephine, see above, Clay to Anderson, September 16, 1825; on that involving
the *Mechanic,* see above, Gracie to Clay, March 25, 1825, note.

MISCELLANEOUS LETTERS   December 5, 1825

From JOHN BINNS, Philadelphia. Acknowledges receipt of "authority and
instruction relative to printing the laws of the United States. . . ." ALS. DNA,
RG59, P. and D. of L.

APPLICATIONS, RECOMMENDATIONS   December 5, 1825

JOHN BLAIR, SAM HOUSTON, ROBERT ALLEN, JAMES K. POLK, J[AMES] C. MITCHELL,
JOHN H. MARABLE, J[ACOB] C. ISACKS, Washington City, recommend that A(bram)
P. Maury, Nashville, be continued as publisher of the laws. LS. DNA, RG59,
P. and D. of L. Cf. above, Carroll to Clay, October 4, 1825, note. Allen, of
Carthage, Tennessee, Congressman from 1819 to 1827, had been born in
Virginia, studied law, and moved, in 1804, to Tennessee, where he engaged in
business and served as clerk of Smith County. He had been an officer under
Andrew Jackson during the War of 1812.

C[HARLES] TAIT, Claiborne, Alabama, recommends appointment of William
Crawford as district judge in Alabama. LS. DNA, RG59, A. and R. (MR1).
See above, Owen to Clay, September 25, 1825, note.

To Samuel L. Southard

6h. Decr. 1825

Mr. Clay presents his respects to the Honble Secy of the Navy,
and he sends him a letter from young Murphy,[1] the applicant for
a Midshipman's place, to enable the Honble Secy to judge of
his capacity.

The letter from N. York sent to the Department of State by

Mr. Southard[2] is from a deranged person, who has been writing all the past summer & autumn letters which would make a volume—

AN. CtHi.
[1] See above, Southard to Clay, November 26, 1825; below, Southard to Clay, December 10, 1825.
[2] Above, Saltonstall to Clay, December 3, 1825.

DIPLOMATIC NOTES   December 6, 1825

To [JOSE SILVESTRE] REBELLO. Acknowledges receipt of his note of November 28 (*i. e.*, 26); states that Clay has submitted it to the President, who directs a reply "that a consideration shall be given to the wishes" of Rebello's government. Copy. DNA, RG59, Notes to Foreign Legations, vol. 3, pp. 239-40 (M38, R3). ALS draft, in CSmH.

MISCELLANEOUS LETTERS   December 6, 1825

From LEVI LINCOLN, Worcester, Massachusetts. Replies to Clay's note of November 25 by referring to the official report to himself from George W. Coffin, land agent of Massachusetts, a copy of which was recently transmitted to the President of the United States. Under resolutions of February 16 and June 11 of this year the Massachusetts Legislature has directed the land agent, in conjunction with his counterpart for the State of Maine (James Irish), "forthwith to take effectual measures to ascertain the extent of the depredations committed on the lands belonging to this Commonwealth and the State of Maine, by whom the same have been committed, and under what authority, if any, such depredations have been made, and all other facts necessary to bring the Offenders to justice— Also to make and execute good and sufficient deeds conveying to the Settlers on the Undivided public lands on the St Johns [*sic*] and Madawaska Rivers in actual possession. . . , their Heirs or Assigns One Hundred Acres each, of the land by them possessed, to include their improvements, on their paying to said Agents for the use of the Commonwealth five Dollars each, and the expence [*sic*] of surveying the same. And also, to sell the timber on such of the undivided public lands as lie contiguous to and near to the waters of the River St Johns, in all cases where such sale, will in the opinion of the land Agent promote the interests of this Commonwealth." Asserts that, unless Coffin "has transcended his authority, in which he would not be justified, but which from his known character for intelligence and discretion" is unlikely, "the British Government can have no just cause of complaint against his proceedings." Cites "the occurrence of the present misunderstanding, as an additional motive for pressing to obtain a speedy Establishment of the true line of division between the British Provinces and the United States" and stresses the "serious prejudice to the interests of the States of Massachusetts and Maine" inherent in the discouragement to settlement of the lands by the persistence of the British claim to the territory in "an undefined extent." LS. DNA, RG76, Northeast Boundary: Misc. Papers. Published in *House Docs.*, 20 Cong., 2 Sess., no. 90, pp. 15-16.

From JOHN R. THOMSON, Philadelphia. Submits resignation of his commission as United States consul at Canton. ALS. DNA, RG59, Cons. Disp., Canton, vol. 1 (M101, R1).

TRISTAM BURGES, Washington City, recommends Richard W. Greene as district attorney for Rhode Island and John Miller, proprietor of the Providence (Rhode Island) *Manufacturers Journal,* as publisher of the laws. ALS. DNA, RG59, A. and R. (MR2). On the Greene appointment, see above, Eldridge to Clay, November 29, 1825, note; on that of Miller, see above, Miller to Clay, November 22, 1825.

JOHN M. SNOWDEN, Pittsburgh, seeks appointment to publish the laws in the *Pittsburgh Mercury,* which, he states, "has from the commencement been the steady and unwearied advocate of the American System." ALS. DNA, RG59, P. and D. of L. Snowden, born in Philadelphia and apprenticed to Mathew Carey, had published journals at Chambersburg and Greensburg, Pennsylvania, before purchasing the *Pittsburgh Mercury* in 1812. He was mayor of Pittsburgh from 1825 to 1827 and an associate judge of Allegheny County from 1840 until his death in 1845. The *Pittsburgh Mercury,* which was not during the Adams administration named an organ for publication of the laws, had been strongly pro-Jackson as early as 1824.

JAMES B. THOMAS, Frederick (Maryland), applies for "a situation" in Clay's office; expresses belief that Clay knew his father, Samuel; gives Thomas C. Worthington as a reference. ALS. DNA, RG59, A. and R. (MR4). Neither Thomas has been identified; the younger received no appointment.

DANIEL WEBSTER, "H. R." (Washington), "Private," recommends appointment of Richard W. Greene. ALS. *Ibid.* (MR2). See above, Eldridge to Clay, November 29, 1825, note.

To Thomas B. Robertson

Thomas B. Robertson Esq N. Orleans   (Confidential)
Sir.   Department of State   Washington, 7 December 1825
    The very great interest which the United States have in the future fortunes of Cuba, and the present dangers to which that Island is exposed, from foreign attack, as well as from internal commotion, render it expedient that this Government should have some confidential Agent on the spot, who can communicate, from time to time, whatever may be likely to affect its condition. The President entertaining an high opinion of your prudence, patriotism and ability, is desirous of availing the public of your services on this occasion; and I have been directed by him to propose the Commission to you. If you should determine to to [*sic*] accept it, you will be pleased to proceed, without unnecessary delay, from New Orleans to the Havanna. It is deemed best that your Agency should not be publicly known, as by keeping it secret, you will be more able to penetrate the views and designs of parties and persons, and collect that information which we desire to possess. But a Commission is, nevertheless, herewith transmitted, to be used, if

necessary, for the protection or safety of your person, or in any emergency in which it may appear to you to be proper to exhibit it. And a Cypher is likewise sent, with directions for its use, to be employed in your despatches whenever you may deem it advisable.

The objects to which you will particularly direct your attention, and on which it is desirable to obtain all the information that may be practicable, are,

1st. The state of the population of the Island, exhibiting the relative numbers of the various Castes, their dispositions towards each other, education intelligence, &c.

2nd. The condition of its agriculture, extent of its foreign Commerce, and proportion of good land yet waste, and in cultivation.

3rd. The state of political parties in the Island, their views with regard to a continuation of the existing connexion with Spain, or in favour of Independence, or towards the new American Republics; and especially, whether a preference exists, and on what account, for one of those Republics, and an aversion towards another of them. We have understood here, that a party in the Island is anxious that it should be connected with Mexico, and that a great repugnance exists among the inhabitants, to any connexion with Colombia.

4th. What are the Spanish means of resisting an attack should one be made by the combined or separate forces of Colombia and the United Mexican States? Would they find any succour or co-operation in the Island, and to what probable extent?

In particularizing these objects, it is not intended to exclude others which may present themselves to you. On the contrary, the President desires any sort of information which may tend to the formation of a correct estimate of the value of the Island, its resources, natural and artificial, its capacity to maintain its independence, or to resist any foreign attack with which it may be menaced, and the dispositions and wishes of its inhabitants in respect to the continuance of its Colonial condition, to independence, or to a connexion with any, and which, of the new Republics.

The design of your Agency being exclusively that of collecting and transmitting information to this Government, you will keep yourself aloof from and entirely unconnected with, any of the parties within the Island. It does not enter into the policy or views of the Government of the United States to give any Stimulus or countenance to insurrectionary movements, if such be contemplated, by any portion of the inhabitants. Our position, being that of peace with Spain, and neutrality in the existing war between her and the new American Republics, fixes our duties in reference to any commotions which may be either meditated, or, in fact, may arise in the Island. And if they should happen to be of a character, or to take a turn, which would require of the United States, from the relations in which they stand to the Island, to interpose their power, it will be time enough for the Government here, to consider, and decide, the nature of their intervention, when the exigency arises.

Your allowance will be at the rate of four thousand five hundred dollars per annum, to commence from the time of your departure from New Orleans, for Cuba. As to the duration of the service, no time can be prescribed for it, at present. It will last until the occasion which has suggested it shall cease. If you should determine to accept the appointment, as its duties will be incompatible with the performance of those of Judge of the United States for the Louisiana District, the President expects you will resign the latter office, some time prior to your leaving the United States.

I am your obedient Servant   H. CLAY.

Copy. DNA, RG59, Dip. Instr., vol. 10, pp. 418-20 (M77, R5). ALS draft, in DLC-HC (DNA, M212, R7). Cf. above, Clay to Adams, October 3, 1825.

From Christopher Hughes

Sir   Private!   Baltimore 7, December 1825.
[Encloses two letters addressed to himself, one relating to the heavy expenses of sending dispatches through the mails, on which Hughes elaborates, and the other recommending sale of the American Hotel at the Hague.[1]] A power might be sent to Messrs. Willinks to sell the Hotel; though, perhaps it may be as well, to defer it until I return; (in April, or May:) so that I may take some order, in the matter, & see the best & most made of it! I have never been at the Hague; (for neither you, or Mr. Adams, would let me go there from Ghent; I suppose, you always contemplated sending me there at some later period:) but of course, I shall be there; & you shall see, that I can do a piece of common business, with tolerable discretion, if you decide on leaving the sale of the hotel to be controlled & managed by Sir, your very obdt. Servt.   C. HUGHES
To Mr. Clay, Washington.

ALS. DNA, RG59, Dip. Disp., Sweden and Norway, vol. 4 (M45, R5).
[1] Cf. above, Willink and Van Staphorst to Clay, September 13, 1825.

INSTRUCTIONS AND DISPATCHES   December 7, 1825

From ROBERT MONROE HARRISON, Antigua. Expostulates against the employment of foreign seamen by masters of American vessels and "the indiscriminate manner of granting protections to the seamen of all nations who may apply for them"; notes the impossibility in Antigua of forcing deserters from American vessels to return to service; and cites the case of an American brig, recently condemned there, the crew of which included only two citizens of the United States although all members were so listed in the "Role de Equipage." ALS. DNA, RG59, Cons. Disp., Antigua, vol. 1 (M-T327, R1). Received January 8, 1826.

From WILLIAM TAYLOR, Alvarado. Reports disposition of the garrison after surrender of (the Castle of San Juan de) Ulloa. ALS. *Ibid.,* Veracruz, vol. 1 (M183, R1). Published in Manning (arr.), *Diplomatic Correspondence . . . Latin-American Nations,* III, 1644-45. See above, Poinsett to Clay, November 23, 1825.

MISCELLANEOUS LETTERS December 7, 1825

From JOSEPH HILL CLARK, Havana. Reports the arrival of a Mexican warship, bringing Spanish officials from the Castle of San Juan de Ulloa (see above, Poinsett to Clay, November 23, 1825), and a decision reached "Last evening" by officers of the Cuban Government "to send by a fast sailing vessel to Cadiz" news of the surrender and a recommendation, as the only alternative to losing Cuba, that Spain recognize the independence of South America. Notes a belief that "the crisis is not far off" and that "the fate of the Castle will hasten it." ALS. DNA, RG59, Misc. Letters (M179, R63). Received December 24.

From W[ILLIAM] J. COFFEE, New York City. Refers to his former letter (above, November 3, 1825), to which he has had no response, and again asks Clay's intercession. ALS. *Ibid.* On December 10, 1825, Daniel Brent, at the direction of the Secretary (of State), acknowledged receipt of both of Coffee's letters and assured him "that no time was lost" in submitting the first appeal to the President. Copy. DNA, RG59, Dom. Letters, vol. 21, p. 210 (M40, R19).

APPLICATIONS, RECOMMENDATIONS December 7, 1825

ATHANASIUS FORD, Washington, solicits a clerkship in the State Department; states that he served nearly nine years "in a similar situation in the Pay Dept." ALS. DNA, RG59, A. and R. (MR1). Ford, a native of Maryland, had been employed in the office of the Paymaster General of the War Department until 1821. He was hired by the State Department on a temporary basis in 1826 and 1827.

SAM HOUSTON, Washington City, encloses "a recommendation of several members of Congress from Tennessee" (above, Blair and others to Clay, December 5, 1825) supporting A(bram) P. Maury to publish the laws. ALS. DNA, RG59, P. and D. of L.

CHRISTOPHER HUGHES, Baltimore, recommends James Williams as "Register, or Receiver, of Land office of East Florida. . . ." ALS. DNA, RG59, A. and R. (MR1). See above, Williams to Clay, March 10, 1825, note.

JOHN PITMAN, Providence, Rhode Island, recommends Richard W. Greene as district attorney for Rhode Island. ALS. DNA, RG59, A. and R. (MR2). See above, Eldridge to Clay, November 29, 1825, note. Pitman, born in Providence, graduated from Brown University, and in 1806 admitted to the bar in New York City, had shortly thereafter resided briefly in Kentucky. From 1812 to 1816 he had practiced at Salem, Massachusetts, and from 1816 to 1820, at Portsmouth, New Hampshire. He had returned to Providence in 1820 as United States attorney for the District of Rhode Island and four years later had been named Federal judge.

INSTRUCTIONS AND DISPATCHES December 8, 1825

From ROBERT MONROE HARRISON, Antigua. States that he has, "more than once," addressed the Department of State "relative to the custom of exacting full tonnage mony [*sic*] upon American vessels putting into this Port in distress, and condemned as unseaworthy &c.," and that he has "remonstrated to the principal officer of His Majestys Customs"; but the practice continues. ALS. DNA, RG59, Cons. Disp., Antigua, vol. 1 (M-T327, R1). Received January 8, 1826.

MISCELLANEOUS LETTERS December 8, 1825

From WILLIAM WILSON AND SONS, Baltimore. Inquires whether "the case of the Ship Harriot of Baltimore" is included in the claims recently presented to the Danish Government; presents a statement of the case, growing out of the seizure, by a Danish privateer in 1809, of the *Harriot,* bound for the port of Stavanger, in Norway. ALS. DNA, RG59, Misc. Letters (M179, R63). On December 10, 1825, Daniel Brent replied, at the direction of the Secretary of State, that the demands of American citizens recently urged upon Denmark (see above, Clay to Hughes, March 24, 1825) had "embraced the claims generally . . . without allusion to any particular one. . . ." Copy. DNA, RG59, Dom. Letters, vol. 21, p. 210 (M40, R19). The damages in the case of the *Harriot,* amounting to nearly $52,000, were filed in Clay's report, below, January 31, 1827, and encompassed in the settlement under a convention between the United States and Denmark, signed March 28, 1830. Miller (ed.), *Treaties. . . ,* III, 531-40. The firm, William Wilson and Sons, Baltimore shipping merchants, antedated the Revolutionary War.

APPLICATIONS, RECOMMENDATIONS December 8, 1825

CHAPMAN COLEMAN, Frankfort (Kentucky), cites an application made by Newton Loughery "through the Honble James Clarke for a situation for a brother of his, Ardevan Loughery, in the National School at West Point"; notes that the applicant "was raised in Woodford [County] where the procurement of the situation for him would meet with the warmest approbation"; and solicits Clay's "aid in effecting this object. . . ." ALS. DNA, RG94, Military Academy, Cadet Applications, 1825-67 (M688, R37). Newton Loughery had held local offices, as deputy sheriff and tax commissioner, since 1818. Ardevan Loughery was admitted to the Military Academy in 1827 but failed to complete the course.

PETER LITTLE, Washington, transmits the application of the editors of the Baltimore *American,* with a recommendation signed by "all the Democratic Republican [*sic*] from Md. except Mr. [Edward] Lloyd (he is not in Town)," for continuation of the appointment of that journal to publish the laws. ALS. DNA, RG59, P. and D. of L. See above, Dobbin, Murphy, and Bose to Clay, December 1, 1825.

CHARLES SHALER, Pittsburgh, Pennsylvania, urges reappointment, as marshal of the Western District of Pennsylvania, of Hugh Davis, "a gentleman who stands high in the estimation of the Democratic party." ALS. DNA, RG59, A. and R. (MR2). Shaler, born in Connecticut and educated at Yale, had been admitted to the bar of Ohio in 1809 and to that of Pennsylvania in 1813. From 1818 to 1821 he had been recorder of the Pittsburgh mayor's court, and from 1824 to 1835 he was a judge of common pleas. He thereafter served as associate judge of the county district court (1841-1844) and United States district attorney for Western Pennsylvania (1853-1858). Davis, born in Pennsylvania, had been appointed marshal in 1822 and was re-appointed later in December, 1825. From 1838 to 1840 he was an associate justice of Allegheny County court.

JOSEPH M. WHITE, Washington, endorses appointment of Benjamin D. Wright as district attorney of West Florida and recommends either Adam Gordon, of Tallahassee, or John W. Overton, of Tennessee, for appointment to "the other office." ALS. *Ibid.* Later in the month Gordon, prosecuting attorney of Escambia County court, was appointed district attorney for Middle Florida, the position from which Wright was transferred. Gordon resigned the office at the end of 1826, because of the inconvenience of the duty so far from his home in Pensacola, and in 1828 was appointed marshal of West Florida. Removed from office in 1829 because of his anti-Jackson views, he again received Federal appointment in 1834 as United States attorney for the Southern District of Florida, and in 1842, as collector and inspector of customs for Key West.

To Joel R. Poinsett

No. 8   Joel R. Poinsett, Envoy Extraordinary
and Minister Plenipotentiary, U. S. to Mexico.
Sir   Department of State   Washington 9th. December 1825
   Your despatch No. 22, under date the 28th. September 1825, is this day received. By mine of the 9th. Ultimo. you will have learnt that the President approves of your rejection of the exception in the proposed commercial Treaty, which the Mexican Government insists upon making, of favours in behalf of the new Governments established within what was formerly Spanish territory; and that you are instructed to break off the negociation, rather than accede to that exception. It is, therefore, seen with regret, that the Mexican Government perseveres in an exception which is so inadmissible. On the 5th. Instant, a Treaty of Peace, Amity, Commerce and Navigation was concluded and signed here with the Central Republic, which will be submitted to the Senate for its advice and consent in a day or two.[1] This treaty embraces the same Articles as that which we have made with Colombia,[2] and three others (one, a modification of a similar Article in that Treaty, and two new ones) of which copies are herewith sent. It contains no exception

of favours to any of the American Republics, carved out of former Spanish Territory. On the contrary, no such pretension was ever advanced, in the progress of the negociation. It has been brought forward by no American Power but Mexico. The Treaty with the Republic of the Centre is characterised by the greatest liberality, and by a true American spirit. And it expressly provides that whatever favours shall be granted to any foreign Power (of course, American, as well as European) by either of the high contracting parties, shall extend to, and be enjoyed by, the other.

Our information here, in regard to the Treaty negociated by Great Britain with Mexico,[3] is, that the objection taken to it in England was that it embraced the principle that Free Ships should make Free Goods, to which Great Britain is not prepared to subscribe.   I am your obedient Servant   H. CLAY.

Copy. DNA, RG59, Dip. Instr., vol. 10, pp. 420-21 (M77, R5). ALI draft, in DLC-HC (DNA, M212, R7). Endorsement by Clay on draft copy: "Memo. made 31 Mar. 1826. This despatch was overlooked when my report to the President, in pursuance of a call of the H[ouse]. R[epresentatives] of the 29h. inst. [cf. below, Clay to Adams, April 3, 1826] was made, and was not recollected or seen by me until this day. H. C."
1 See above, Treaty, December 5, 1825.
2 See above, Clay to Salazar, March 21, 1825.
3 See above, Poinsett to Clay, May 5, 1825, note; King to Clay, October 29, 1825.

From W[illiam] B. Blackburn

Dear Clay   Frankfort December 9th 1825
A youth of the Name of Ardevan Laughrey[1] is verry [sic] anxious to get a Situation in the scholl [sic] at west point   The application will be made by our representative James Clarke   if you can be of any service to him it will be a favour well bestowed as he is every way worthy;

The Legislature will I fear do nothing with the Judge Question[2] we This day Elected James Davidson of Lincoln Treasurer[3] J H Holman. Public printer[4] John J Marshall president of the Commonwealths Bank & a Majority of the directors old Court Men[5]—

Your Mother[6] & all Friends are Well   we have had no rain since May last worth naming But as yet we have had no Cold weather   Present my best love to Mrsts Clay & the children & Except [sic] for yourself assurances of my highest esteem
                                             W B BLACKBURN

ALS. DNA, RG94, Military Academy, Cadet Applications, 1825-67 (M688, R37). Endorsed by Clay on cover: ". . . Respectfully refered [sic] to the Secy of War. H. C."
1 Loughery.   2 Cf. below, Kendall to Clay, December 25, 1825.
3 Davidson, a pioneer resident of Lincoln County, veteran of the War of 1812, and member of the Kentucky Senate (1818-1826), remained in the position of State Treasurer until 1848.
4 Jacob H. Holeman had held the contract as State printer from 1822 to 1824, now

regained it for the next three legislative sessions, and again won the appointment in 1830-1831 and 1835-1836.

5 Cf. above, Blair to Clay, August 30, 1825, note.   6 Elizabeth Clay Watkins.

From Daniel J. Caswell

Honble. Henry Clay   Cincinnati Decr 9th. 1825
Dear Sir

[Recommends Thomas Douglas for appointment as district attorney in Florida.] I hope you will pardon this interference— Although our acquaintance was Short, to me it was Interesting, and the few Days Spent with us in Cincinnati[1] will long be Remembered as Days of "*Good feeling*"— I will not however presume upon that acquaintance as an apology for asking your interference in favor of a friend, but must Refer to a principle fundamental in a Government like ours "That each and every Citizen of this Republic has a Right to make known his wishes and wants to those who preside over the Destiny of our common country"—

We are anxious to hear the progress of things at Washington— It is Rumored that an organized opposition will be got up to the Administration, but who is to Lead is not Distinctly understood— Genl[n] Jacksons *Modest pretensions* I suppose must not be overlooked   I hope the Survivors of your interesting family are in health, please present my compliments to them, and accept for yourself assurances of the Highest Respect of your Obt. Servt.

DANIEL J. CASWELL

ALS. DNA, RG59, A. and R. (MR2). Caswell was a Lawrenceburg, Indiana, lawyer.
1 See above, Toasts and Speech, July 13, 1825.

From Charles King

My Dear Sir   (private)   New York 9 Decr. 1825
You will have seen the use made by me of Mr Secretary Barbour's letter[1]— It has had the effect of putting an End Completely to the vile calumny— I beg you will offer my thanks to him for having thus enabled me to vindicate my father's name—

I see by the Message[2] that the U.S. are to be represented at Panama— A very clever young man of this City Mr Wm. Beach Lawrence[3] of good Education, and property, & Conversant with the French and Spanish languages, would like very much to be Employed as a Secretary of the legation or Commission— His Studies and qualifications fit him for the place, his connections in this City are numerous & highly respectable, and they would be gratified as well as himself by Such an appointment— My interest in him arises from his having married a Sister of my deCeased wife[4]—and from the acquaintance & respect which I have with & for his good qualities— Can any thing be done for him? Write me Confidentially about it.

If you Can find time occasionally to let me hear from you during the Sitting of Congress, especially relative to matters, which do not always appear on the surface, but which nevertheless you may with propriety inform me of, I shall feel much obliged, & will always receive any such information, as you may direct, Either in strict Confidence, or to be used at pleasure— In great haste, but with great regard Believe me Always Your   CHAS. KING
Hon: H. Clay

ALS. DLC-HC (DNA, M212, R2).
[1] Above, Barbour to Clay, November 26, 1825. In a public letter under the heading "The Hamilton Papers," in the Washington *Daily National Intelligencer*, December 8, 1825, King had asserted that he held "the authority of Mr. Secretary Barbour himself" for revealing the details as disclosed in the latter's letter. The Barbour statement does not appear to have been published at that time.
[2] The annual message of December 6, 1825, had publicly announced the decision expressed in Clay to Gallatin, November 8, 1825; Clay to Obregón, November 30, 1825; Clay to Cañaz, November 30, 1825, and in intervening diplomatic and personal correspondence.
[3] Born in New York in 1800, young Lawrence had been educated in law at Litchfield, Connecticut, had travelled in Europe from 1821 to 1823, and had entered the practice of his profession in New York. He was appointed Secretary of Legation in London in 1826 and raised to the rank of Chargé there in 1827. Returning to New York shortly thereafter, he resumed his profession and attained note in the field of commercial and international law. In 1851 he was elected Lieutenant Governor of Rhode Island and the following year served as acting Governor.
[4] King had married, in 1810, Eliza, daughter of Archibald Gracie. Mrs. King, whose sister, Esther, had married Lawrence in 1821, had died in 1823.

INSTRUCTIONS AND DISPATCHES   December 9, 1825

From JOSHUA BOND, Montevideo. Reports receipt of his commission as consul and provisional authorization to perform the duties of his office "until the *Exequatur* of the Imperial government shall be received from Rio de Janeiro." Adds that he intends visiting Buenos Aires and that his brother, Dr. James Bond, will act as vice consul in his absence. ALS. DNA, RG59, Cons. Disp., Montevideo, vol. 1 (M71, R1). Received April 22, 1826.

APPLICATIONS, RECOMMENDATIONS   December 9, 1825

SAM HOUSTON, Washington, recommends reappointment of Heiskell and Brown, Knoxville, Tennessee, to publish the laws. ALS. DNA, RG59, P. and D. of L. See above, White to Clay, November 15, 1825, note.

JOHN L. LAWRENCE, New York, recommends William Beach Lawrence for appointment as "Secretary of the Legation, or Commission to be Sent to Panama." ALS. DNA, RG59, A. and R. (MR3). Cf. above, King to Clay, this date, note. The Lawrences were collaterally related.

BENJAMIN HAMMETT NORTON, editor of the Hartford, Connecticut, *Times and*

Weekly Advertiser, seeks appointment to publish the laws. ALS. DNA, RG59, P. and D. of L. The contract, instead, was given to another Hartford journal.

H[ENRY] WHEATON, New York, urges appointment of William Beach Lawrence as "Secretary to the proposed mission to the Congress of Panama." ALS. DNA, RG59, A. and R. (MR3). See above, King to Clay, this date, note.

To Charles Hammond

My dear Sir   Washington 10h. Decr. 1825

I duly recd. your obliging letter of the 20h. Ulto.[1] Public opinion appears to be more than usually united in the condemnation of late events at Murfreesborough.[2] Some of the Generals friends here have been obliged to reprehend them.

Matters look favorably here, especially in the H. of R. The demonstrations so far are very good. I believe the great mass of the American public is satisfied with the past, and sanguine as to the future. Some individuals, however have great bitterness, and there is a full proportion of them in Congress. We shall see how they will conduct themselves in the progress of the Session.

The U. States are now treating here with the C. Indians. The object of the Executive is to put aside the objectionable treaty by a new one, which shall be free from the defects of the old, and which shall at the same time secure whatever was supposed to be obtained by the former one for Georgia. But we are by no means assured of success.[3] To set aside the old treaty simply, without doing any thing else, in the new one, I apprehend could hardly be justified. The Indians would of course eagerly agree to such an annulment.

I will not trouble you with K. affairs. They render me sick almost when I think of them. I cannot agree with you in thinking that the Judicial question presents a case for compromise. When both the Constitution and the people, to whom each party appealed, are on one side, I think the minority ought to yield; and it will yield, or be beaten further at the next election than it was at the last.[4]

C. Hammond Esqr.   Yr's faithfully   H. CLAY

ALS. InU.   [1] Not found.
[2] See above, Clay to Hammond, November 1, 1825, note.
[3] See above, Clay to Southard, July 3, 1825, note; Clay to Hammond, November 6, 1825. On December 22 President Adams devoted a Cabinet meeting to the matter. Reporting the discussion, he noted that Secretary James Barbour proposed "incorporating the Indians within the States of the Union—ceasing to make treaties with them at all, but considering them as altogether subject to our laws." Adams cited constitutional objections to this approach. Clay, Adams noted, believed the Barbour approach "impracticable; that it was impossible to civilize Indians; that there never was a full-blooded Indian who took to civilization. It was not in their nature. He [Clay] believed they were destined to extinction, and, although he would never use or countenance inhumanity towards them, he did not think them, as a race, worth preserving. He considered them as essentially inferior to the Anglo-Saxon race, which were now taking their place on this continent. They were not an improvable breed, and their disappearance from the human family will be no great loss to the world."

In point of fact they were rapidly disappearing, and he did not believe that in fifty years from this time there would be any of them left." Adams, *Memoirs*, VII, 89-90.
4 See above, III, 902n; Bodley to Clay, August 23, 1825; Beatty to Clay, September 13, 1825; Clay to Kendall, October 18, 1825; Theodore W. Clay to Henry Clay, November 11, 1825; Blair to Clay, November 28, 1825; below, Kendall to Clay, December 25, 1825.

From William Creighton, Jr.

Dear Sir.   Chillicothe 10 Decr. 1825

Yours of the 23d November[1] was received on my return from the Circuit. An extract from the Will of Colo. Morrison will be necessary to enable me to obtain an order of the Court to authorise the present Marshal to make a Deed for the House and lot in New Ark[2]— Please enclose it to me before the ensuing January Term. It has been intimated to me that an attempt will be made this winter by the Post-Master Genl. and his Brother in the House of Representatives[3] to have a Brother[4] of theirs, at present keeper of the Penitentiary in this State appointed Marshal in the room of Colo. Doherty whose Term of office will expire I believe in February. Which your friends here most ardently hope will not be done. Colo. Doherty is the best officer we have ever had, faithfull in the discharge of his duties, a high minded honorable man, and justly a great favourite with the Court and Bar.—

I rejoice to hear that the President has determined to accept the invitation of the Southren [*sic*] Republics and have this Government represented at Panama.[5]

As our old acquaintance Doctor Gaul [*sic*][6] Secretary of State of Columbia has been appointed to represent that Republic It has occurred to me with great force. That our Government ought to follow the example, If the office of Secretary of State could remain vacant until your return— There are many high considerations for this Measure, provided it would not deprive you of your present situation which the Western people would not consent to—

I shall visit Columbus the last of this Month. In the mean time the Presidents Message will be in the hands of the Members.[7] I can then feel the representatives on the subject of the resolutions spoken of[8] and if the measure can be carried, with a good degree of unanimity it will be done. I am dear Sir. Your friend

H. Clay Esqr.   W CREIGHTON JUN

ALS. DLC-HC (DNA, M212, R2).   1 Not found.
2 Cf. above, Creighton to Clay, November 9, 1825.
3 John McLean; William McLean.
4 Nathaniel McLean, two years younger than John, had been born in New Jersey and during childhood had resided in Jessamine and Mason Counties of Kentucky. He had been one of the proprietors of the Lebanon *Western Star* from 1810 to 1814, had represented Warren County in the Ohio House of Representatives (1817-1818) and the Ohio Senate (1819-1823), and had been an Adams elector, from Franklin

County, Ohio, in 1824. He did not receive the position as marshal, the incumbent, William Doherty, being reappointed. Nathaniel McLean much later was named an Indian agent.

5 See above, Clay to Cañaz, November 30, 1825; Clay to Obregón, November 30, 1825.

6 Pedro Gual, whose appointment as Colombia's "Minister to the Assembly of the American States, about to meet at Panama," had been reported in the Washington *Daily National Intelligencer,* November 28, 1825.

7 Of the Ohio Legislature.

8 Cf. above, Clay to Hammond, November 6, 1825.

From Lafayette

Paris december 10h 1825

Altho' No direct information from You, My dear friend, Has Confirmed the fatal report Communicated to me, for the first time by Mr Brown and Your Sister,[1] I But too well know I Have Again to Sympathise With you in a Most Heavy Calamity. I Have also to Mourn for Myself. it Was impossible to Have formed an acquaintance With the Most Valuable daughter you Have lately lost,[2] to Have Been favoured With Her friendly Welcome and affectionate attentions Without feeling a deep and lively personal Regret. I Condole Most tenderly and Mournfully With You, My dear friend, With Mrs Clay, and the Whole family So Cruelly Visited of late, and Want Words to Express what I feel on the Lamentable occasion.

A Similar kind of Misfortune Has Been Very Near attending me. My grand daughter Clementine, the Youngest daughter of George[3] Has passed Several days in an Hopeless State; she is Now Recovering. I Was then thinking of a former altho' a late loss. far Was I from Suspecting What New Blow Had fallen upon You.

I Have No Heart to talk with You of other Matters. the president Will Receive a letter from Me. My Son and le Vasseur[4] share in My Sad feelings and Beg to Be Remembered. Most affectionately Your Sympathising friend   LAFAYETTE

I Have writen [*sic*] to the president that Mr Somerville[5] Expected to proceed Slowly towards its [*sic*] destination; Mr Brown Whom I Have just Now Seen Gives me a Much More Sad Account than what I Had Received from poor Somerville Himself.

Hble Henry Clay &c.

ALS. DLC-HC (DNA, M212, R2).   1 Mr. and Mrs. James Brown.
2 Susan Clay Duralde. Cf. above, Lafayette to Clay, November 25, 1825.
3 George Washington Lafayette.   4 Auguste Levasseur.
5 William C. Somerville.

DIPLOMATIC NOTES   December 10, 1825

To [C. D. E. J. BANGEMAN] HUYGENS. Notes that the United States and the Kingdom of the Netherlands profess to act toward one another, "in regard to navigation, upon the basis of perfect reciprocity and equality"; cites correspondence between (Alexander H.) Everett and officials of the latter government concerning discrimination in Dutch ports in favor of Dutch vessels; inquires whether the discrimination has been ended; and states that "It will afford the President much satisfaction to find" that it will not be his duty, under terms of the act of January 7, 1824 (see above, Lorich to Clay, March 16, 1825, note) "to withdraw from Dutch vessels the privileges which they enjoy in the ports of the United States equal with their own vessels." Copy. DNA, RG59, Notes to Foreign Legations, vol. 3, pp. 240-41 (M38, R3). ALS draft, in CSmH. Published in *American State Papers, Foreign Relations,* VI, 374-75.

INSTRUCTIONS AND DISPATCHES   December 10, 1825

From HARRIS E. FUDGER, Santa Marta (Colombia). Reports "the present sickly state of Rio Hacha," which is located in his consular district, and information "that the fever had attacked the crews in the vessels in port." States that he will go there, if necessary, to protect American property. ALS. DNA, RG59, Cons. Disp., Santa Marta, vol. 1 (M-T427, R1). Received January 21, 1826.

MISCELLANEOUS LETTERS   December 10, 1825

To [SAM] HOUSTON. States that, prior to receipt of Houston's note of December 7, "the Nashville Whig, the Knoxville Register and the Jackson Gazette had been designated as the three papers to publish the Laws in Tennessee, and an authority for that purpose had been transmitted to their respective Editors." Copy. DNA, RG59, Dom. Letters, vol. 21, pp. 211-12 (M40, R19).

To [JAMES] LLOYD and [THOMAS L.] WINTHROP. Acknowledges receipt of their note of November 7, "with the Letter enclosed from Saml. Cook," which will "be put on file in the Department of State, according to their request." Copy. *Ibid.,* 212.

From TENCH RINGGOLD, "Marshals Off D Ca." States that he has in hand a writ in the case of "the United States against William McGunty alias John McNulty" for assault on Enoch Brian, constable of the County of Washington, committed before McNulty entered his present employment as coachman of the Dutch Minister (C. D. E. J. Bangeman Huygens). Requests Clay's advice relative to serving the writ. ALS. DNA, RG59, Misc. Letters (M179, R63). Endorsed by Clay: "Write to the Marshall [*sic*] that there is no legal obstacle to the service of the writ but that   [*sic*]." On the same day Daniel Brent informed Ringgold "that the writ may be served elsewhere than on the Premises of the Minister, . . . or at any time and place other than that in which the Coachman may be employed in the service of the Minister." Copy. DNA, RG59, Dom. Letters, vol. 21, pp. 210-11 (M40, R19).

From S[AMUEL] L. S[OUTHARD], "Navy Department." Acknowledges receipt of Clay's note of December 6 and expresses "regret that the State of the Service will not, at this time, permit the Appointment of young murphy [*sic*]." Copy. DNA, RG45, Executive Letterbook, vol. 1821-1831, p. 151.

From JOSEPH M. WHITE, Washington. States that he has received complaints that the marshal at St. Augustine (Waters Smith) will not allow the sheriff to confine prisoners in a public building there; requests that orders be issued from the State Department "requiring the Marshal to do so. . . ." ALS. DNA, RG59, Misc. Letters (M179, R63). Published in Carter (ed.), *Territorial Papers*, XXIII, 378.

APPLICATIONS, RECOMMENDATIONS   December 10, 1825

JAMES BARRON, "Navy Yard   Gosport," recommends Thomas Gatewood for appointment to "the Collectorship of this port." ALS. DNA, RG59, A. and R. (MR2). In May, 1824, Gatewood, born in Virginia, had been appointed naval officer for Norfolk, in which post he remained for over twenty years.

JAMES ROBERTSON, Petersburg (Virginia), applies for transfer from the position of collector at Petersburg, Virginia, to the same office at Norfolk; suggests that he may be remembered as a member of the (Virginia) Senate when Clay was "in Richmond a few years ago" (see above, III, 158-71). ALS. DNA, RG59, A. and R. (MR3). Endorsed (AEI and AES): "Refered [*sic*] respectfully to the Secy of the Treasury. HC   Respectfully submitted to the President   R. Rush   Dec. 13. 1825." Robertson had been appointed to the Petersburg collectorship in 1824 and held it until 1830.

APPLICATIONS, RECOMMENDATIONS   December 11, 1825

JOHN PEGRAM, Richmond (Virginia), recommends Dr. Samuel Colton for appointment as collector at Norfolk. ALS. DNA, RG59, A. and R. (MR1). Pegram, former member of the Virginia Legislature (1797-1801, 1804-1808, 1813-1815) and of Congress (1818-1819), a militia officer during the War of 1812, was now (since 1821) United States marshal for the Eastern District of Virginia. On Colton, see below, Pleasants to Clay, December 12, 1825. He did not receive appointment.

To James Brown

My dear Sir   Washn. 12h. Decr. 1825
   You will receive the President's Message[1] through the public prints. Every where North of this place it has been received with acquiescence, or with applause. What has been its reception, South and West of us, we have not yet heard, with the exception of Richmond. There it is said to have produced great and unfavorable sensation and to have contributed to the event, which has just occurred, in the election of Mr. John Randolph. Its doctrines on Internal improvements[2] &c have given the offence in the antient dominion; but that very cause must have an opposite and friendly effect almost every where else. My belief is that upon the whole it will be very popular.
   There are elements which, if they possessed any principle of cohesion, might create a strong opposition. I think they cannot combine, and that the administration, which has undoubtedly

gained much strength, in the recess of Congress, will possess all the power and influence which the Executive ought to enjoy.

The labors of my office are very great; and one of the effects is that I write few and short letters to friends. I mentioned in my last that some notice would probably be taken in the message of our claims on France.[3] That has been done and I shall follow it up by an official letter into which I shall endeavor to infuse some force. It may be the Spring before I shall send it. In the mean time, I think you had better not press the affair unless something decidedly favorable occurs.

I have heard from Russia, in respect to the invocation made to her in behalf of peace between Spain and the Colonies.[4] The appeal has had all the effect I expected, and I have no doubt that the good offices of the Emperor[5] will be (if they have not been already) employed on the side of peace. Whether they will be successful or not, I am inexpressibly delighted with the good effect of our effort with the Emperor. It was emphatically *my* own measure (sanctioned by the President) and Mr. G. Canning confidently predicted its failure.[6] It is true that affairs in Spain, for the moment, do not look favorable to peace. But the change of ministry itself[7] is not unlikely the consequence of the change in the views of the Allies—I mean that the King of Spain,[8] finding no longer countenance from the Allies, in the further prosecution of the War, has resorted to the desperate expedient of throwing himself upon the mad councils of the ultras. And the change which has just happened, you know, may be immediately followed by another. Things have now become there as bad as they can be, and then (according to old Genl. Scott[9]) reform may be anticipated.

I recd. your letters of the 29h. & 30h. Oct. Mrs. Clay is thankful for her sister's attention to her Commission. The articles will arrive in due time; for, as you may well suppose, we are in no state of feeling for seeing or entertaining much company.[10]

All are well in K. according to my last accounts.   Public matters there are are [*sic*] as bad as they can be short of civil war.[11] My respects to Mrs. Brown.   Yr's faithfully   H. CLAY
James Brown Esq.

P.S. The Senate to day elected Lowrie[12] from Pennsa. their Secretary.   H C.

ALS. KyLxT-Haupt Collection.   1 Of December 6, 1825.
2 See above, Clay to Stuart, December 1, 1825, note.
3 Above, November 14, 1825.
4 See above, Middleton to Clay, September 8, 1825.
5 Alexander I.
6 Cf. above, King to Clay, September 18, 1825.
7 See above, Brown to Clay, October 30, 1825.
8 Ferdinand VII.   9 Charles Scott.

10 Cf. above, Clay to Crittenden, August 22, 1825; Mazureau to Clay, September 19, 1825.
11 Cf. above, Clay to Hammond, December 10, 1825.
12 Walter Lowrie.

From James Brown

Dear Sir,   Paris Decr. 12. 1825

I have had nothing from you of a later date than the 9th. of October,[1] and as your health was then extremely delicate, I have been apprehensive that the painful event of which you soon afterwards received intelligence[2] has increased your indisposition and prevented you from writing to me. We have for some days waited for the arrival of the Packet of the 15 Ulto. by which we expected to hear from you but from the prevalence of eastwardly winds we have been disappointed.

In my last Dispatch[3] which went by the Packet sailing from Havre on the 1st. you will find the Answer of the Minister of Foreign Affairs to my letter of the 22 Octr. 1824. The intimation which it gives that the Royal Government is under no obligation to repair injuries done by the government of Napoleon, seemed to require some notice in order that my silence might not be considered as an acquiescence in the doctrine, and therefore I considered it my duty to remark upon it in a very summary way. On the same day on which I received this answer, a letter from Mr Appleton[4] was placed in my hands, informing me, that the Neapolitain [*sic*] Government had insisted that France had rejected our claims upon the ground of the irresponsibility of the present, for the Acts of the former Government, and had suspended their conferences with him, until the fact could be ascertained by writing to their Ambassador at Paris. I was induced by this circumstance to suspect that the Minister of foreign affairs had modified his answer with some view to the wishes of the Neapolitain Government— As our Government had in strong terms expressed its determination not to admit the construction placed by France on the 8 Art of the Treaty, it would have been sufficient to defeat our claims to have merely insisted upon that construction without alluding to the other objection— The introduction of it in answer to my letter would therefore seem to have been in compliance with the wishes of Naples and in order to fortify that Government in its ground for rejecting our Claims against it— I fear Mr Appleton will be as unsuccessful there as Mr Gallatin[5] and myself have been here. I have many reasons for apprehending that my residence here will be rendered unpleasant in consequence of the state in which this and other matters may place the relations of the two Governments.

You need not be told that the visit of Gen Lafayette and the use made of it by the opposition papers here have excited some feeling. Nor need I say that our institutions are not greatly admired by the Courts of Europe which attribute to them all the revolutions which have appeared within the last fifty years. My situation has required, and I have observed, the greatest possible circumspection, not in my conversation only, but also in my intercourse with society. Genl Lafayette is the only *liberal* with whom I have associated since my arrival in France, and I have carefully abstained from taking any part in the politics of the Nation.

In the funeral of Genl Foy[6] a distinguished orator of the opposition the liberals have had an opportunity of expressing their feelings and they have made all they could out of it— The body was followed to the grave by more than one hundred thousand persons and nearly half a Million of francs have been subscribed for the support of his family and for the erection of his monument. A triumph has been obtained by that party in the acquittal of the Constitutionel and Courier[7] two of the most prominent of the opposition Journals which were prosecuted for publications tending to bring disgrace on the Religion of the State. The decision of the Court dismissed the prosecution on the ground that the attacks were directed, not against the religion of the State, but against the Jesuits, who had entered France and established themselves contrary to law and whose doctrines were hostile to the rights of the Crown and to the established religion— The conduct of the Judges on this occasion has been very much applauded, as the Jesuits although very unpopular had been encouraged by *some* persons of great influence and were rapidly increasing in wealth and number—

Mr Somerville[8] is yet in Paris and I fear will never leave it— His Physician considers his case as one admitting but little room for hope and indeed his appearance but too fully confirms the opinion— His stomach and lungs are diseased and he is subject to constant fevers and a distressing cough— I called on him yesterday and found him so unconscious of his danger that he was actually contracting for a Carriage to convey him to Nice and from thence to Italy. I see him every day and shall do all I can to smooth the few days which remain to him. As it is *possible* and barely possible that he may recover, perhaps it might be useless to afflict his relations by giving them this account of his situation— I fear they will soon receive accounts that he exists no longer. Should he persist in his intention of leaving Paris, I will as delicately as possible suggest to him the propriety of placing his *papers* with some person who in case of accidents on the road would prevent them from falling into improper hands. In case he should recover and be disposed to travel *further*[9] they can be sent to him—

The last accounts from Greece leave very little room for hope that it will hold out many weeks longer. Capt Rodgers writes to Capt Morris[10] that their affairs appear desperate. The reinforcements, so long expected have arrived at Navarino— Accounts vary as to the number, some making it amount to above 9,000 whilst others represent it as not exceeding 4,500 troops part of which is composed of Cavalry. It does not appear probable that the Greeks will receive aid from any other power and they want money, credit, and men to enable them to repel this formidable force.[11] Commodore Rodgers will pass the winter at Mahon,[12] and has ordered Captain Read[13] to take the command of the Constitution, Capt McDonough[14] having expressed his wish to return to the United States.

I shall write you on the 25— Mrs Brown is in good health and writes to her sister.[15] Yours truly   J. BROWN

Mr Sheldon's[16] recovery has been so complete that it leaves some room to hope that Mr Somerville may survive his attack. He has made an effort and written to some of his friends— His fever is more moderate since the last two or three days.
Honble Henry Clay Secy of State

ALS. DLC-HC (DNA, M212, R2).   1 Not found.
2 The death of Susan Clay Duralde.
3 Above, November 28, 1825.   4 John J. Appleton.
5 See above, III, 155n.
6 Maximilien-Sébastien Foy, educated at the artillery school at La Fère, had become famous not only for his valor and skill as a military leader at Flanders (1791-1792), in the Swiss campaign of 1798, in the Peninsular War (1808-1814), and at Waterloo (1815), but also for his courage in expressing political principles opposed to the Radicals during the French Revolution, against Napoleon's imperial ambitions, and, as a member of the Chamber of Deputies from 1819 to 1825, against the conservatives under the Bourbon Restoration.
7 Paris *Constitutionnel;* Paris *Courrier-Francais.*
8 William C. Somerville.
9 Cf. above, Clay to Somerville, September 6, 1825.
10 John Rodgers; Charles Morris.
11 Cf. above, Moore to Clay, May 31, 1825, note. Additional Egyptian forces had sailed in mid-October as reinforcements for this position, which remained under Turkish-Egyptian control and a base for their Greek operations until 1827.
12 Cf. above, Rich to Clay, August 22, 1825.
13 George Campbell Read, a native of Ireland, who had entered the United States Navy in 1804 and had served throughout the War of 1812, had received his captaincy in 1825. He commanded the *Constitution* from 1826 to 1832 and the *Constellation* from 1832 to 1843 in the Mediterranean Squadron and, at the head of a small squadron in the Far East from 1838 to 1840, attained distinction for landing men at Sumatra in protest against plundering of a Yankee schooner. From 1846 to 1849 he commanded the African Squadron, and from 1853 to 1855, the Philadelphia Navy Yard.
14 Thomas Macdonough, who died at sea en route.
15 Mrs. Clay.   16 Daniel Sheldon.

From John P. Erwin

Dear Sir   Nashville 12 Decr. 1825.

I wrote a few lines on the 8th. designing to Say more another time— I consider myself flattered by an intimation that my communications afford some information worthy of notice[1]—and so long as I am enabled to furnish any thing which can be deemed equivalent to the time required to read it, I shall with much pleasure continue to keep you advised of the State of the war in this quarter of these U. S.— The "demonstration" made at Murfreesboro,[2] altho gotten up with deliberation, viz—(as much of it as belongs to the men who contrived it) & designed no doubt for effect, has fallen lifeless on the public attention, exciting only here, & there, a feint at adulation from his friends—the criticism of neutrals, & derision of opponents— Even here there seems to be somewhat of chagrin & disappointment— It begins to be whispered among his friends, that the game is up; the time gone by—& an effort to produce division & excitement three years hence, is considered almost hopeless—

It was expected, that Mr C— & New York could be enlisted under his banners But it seems that Mr C— is at present in a minority at home—& has enough to do, to take care of himself[3]— From present appearances I am of the opinion that the next three years will present no serious struggle, & that Mr. A— will sit quietly in the Presidential chair, the usual term.—

You will have seen in the Whig,[4] the proceedings of our Legislature up to its close— A violent effort was made to put down Mr Yeatman's Bank[5]— We think the Old Genl.[6] wished it done, Mr Y— being the son in law of a man[7] he very much disliked— He had spoken in that way to his friends previous to the meeting of the Legislature— Mr. Grundy[8] also had some agency in the attempt— they were however all defeated by the ability of Fletcher Gibbs,[9] & the zealous cooperation of Govr. Carroll[10]—who is very powerful with the Legislature—   The friends of Colo. Williams are gratified at the notice taken of him by the Government[11]—it has also excited some of the illiberality of his opponents— They call him the head of the *radicals*—& term it buying up— It will evidently create some degree of interest in favor of the Presidt. with a very respectable portion of this State—for Colo. Ws. is considered generally as having been badly treated by Jackson— He is spoken of for Govr.— & should he on his return from Guatemala, be disposed to offer, will be elected[12]—

I said something in a former letter relative to my friend Judge White— His letter to the Legislature accepting the appointment of Senator, was rather a draw back, upon the estimation in which he is universally held in this State— Altho it was perhaps designed for, & perhaps was very well adapted to the temperature of Tennessee[13]— He is an able man, & an honest man—has a good deal of temper—no great dislike to fame—& a great partiality for his friends—

Govr. Carroll, will at the next election afford to Mr Eaton an opportunity of retiring to private life—& if Judge White should occupy any other Station, Colo Ws.[14] can again be elected Senator—

Much is said here about the contemplated National Road[15]— There is Some dissatisfaction at the hasty manner in which one mile has been surveyed—& it is said that Va. No. C. &c are to have the Road—"for and in consideration of." &c— I hope our people will make the discovery ere long, that they have almost no Representation in Congress—& also, (as I said to them in my Whig last Spring)—that we will get along better by pursuing a mild, & rational, course towards, "the powers that be" whether of our choice, or not.—

I hope my Radical brother in Law from No. C.[16] will carry himself straight, during this Session— I think he is at heart very decidedly with you— He was opposed partly on that ground in his recent election— He an & [sic] old Mr Macon[17] are the high priests in No. C—

James[18] writes me from N Orls. 26 Novr. that he would remain there until 1 of Jany. —then go to Cahawba & take his wife with him back again to N Orls.— She is now at Cahawba, in good health, when last I heard from there— I believe he designs making his permanent summer residence in Tennessee—on Duck River, where my father[19] resides—50 miles So. of this towards Huntsville— He is to become the purchaser of the Whig Establishment, in order to place it under my Control—my own poverty and embarrassment not allowing me to do so— *Norvell* the Proprietor was about to sell to Hunt, formerly of Lexington[20]—thro the machinations of Grundy & others, who dislike the space occupied by me before the public—& in order to defeat their plans, & retain the power of aiding my friends, & watching the progress of Error, &c I had to procure a purchaser— I do not design to have it generally understood who is the purchaser— It will be conducted by me in behalf of the proprietor— I design to pursue a very mild, & conciliatory course—& not furnish the enemy with the materials with which to annoy me— As to Genl. J— I shall not know much of him as a Candidate for Pres dt.

Should any thing occur to you as coming within my range, so as to promote your interests—7 yrs. hence—You have only to suggest in what manner I can make it available—

I wish it were the fashion of the day for the Pres dt. & Secry. to make a Southern Tour[21]— There would be made many Converts to the true faith, by such a mission—

My best wishes to Mrs. Clay. & family   Very respectfully

J. P. ERWIN

ALS. DLC-HC (DNA, M212, R2).
[1] Neither Erwin's letter nor Clay's reply has been found.
[2] See above, Clay to Hammond, November 1, 1825.
[3] DeWitt Clinton had been re-elected Governor by a small majority in the fall of 1825; but his supporters had been badly defeated, principally by the "Bucktails," or Van Buren faction, in the struggle for control of the legislature.
[4] The *Nashville Whig*.
[5] Early in the 1820's, Thomas Yeatman had initiated a private banking business, issuing notes without a State charter. Jackson's supporters during the legislative session of 1825 had proposed a bill to outlaw private banking. Charles G. Sellers, Jr., "Banking and Politics in Jackson's Tennessee, 1817-1827," *Mississippi Valley Historical Review*, XLI (June, 1954), 77-78.
[6] Andrew Jackson.   [7] Andrew Erwin.
[8] Felix Grundy.
[9] Thomas H. Fletcher and George W. Gibbs. The latter, a general of militia, was for many years a lawyer of Davidson County; he later retired to a farm near the site of Union City, Tennessee.   [10] William Carroll.
[11] See above, Clay to Williams, November 10, 1825; Williams to Clay, November 25, 1825.
[12] Williams, instead, ran for the State Senate, was elected, and served in the sessions of 1827 and 1828.
[13] Hugh L. White had spoken of the flattery in being "thought of as the successor of such a man [Jackson]. . . ." Tenn. H. of Reps., *Journal, 1825*, 278-79.
[14] Williams. On these political eventualities, see above, Carroll to Clay, October 4, 1825, note.
[15] See above, Speech, January 17, 1825; Thornetine to Clay, May 6, 1825, note.
[16] Lewis Williams, whose sister, Frances Lanier Williams, had married Erwin.
[17] Nathaniel Macon.   [18] James Erwin.
[19] Andrew Erwin.   [20] Joseph Norvell; William Gibbes Hunt.
[21] Cf. above, II, 701n.

DIPLOMATIC NOTES   December 12, 1825

To the BARON [DURAND] DE MAREUIL. Acknowledges receipt of his note of December 2; encloses a copy of a letter from the Postmaster General (John McLean—letter not found) which exonerates "the post office department . . . from any charge of neglect or infidelity in the transmission of letters and papers confided to its care"; notes that "The Post master General thinks that in some instances there may have been carelessness or neglect in the transfer of letters and papers from the vessel bringing them from foreign ports to the post office"; and states that instructions will be given for increased vigilance. Clay believes that "the number of miscarriages of letters and papers cannot be very great," since those addressed to his department arrive punctually and no complaint has been received from "any other foreign minister. . . ." Inquires: "May not those to which you refer have proceeded from a want of attention on the road in the carriage of your letters from Paris to Havre?" Copy. DNA, RG59, Notes to Foreign Legations, vol. 3, p. 242 (M38, R3).

From [C. D. E. J. BANGEMAN] HUYGENS, Washington. Acknowledges receipt of Clay's note of December 10 and states that he has asked his government for instructions on the matter discussed. ANS, in French with translation in State

Department file. DNA, RG59, Notes from Netherlands Legation, vol. 1 (M56, R1). Published in *American State Papers, Foreign Relations*, VI, 375.

From L[EWIS CHARLES] LEDERER, Newburgh (New York). Explains the basis for the imposition from January 1, 1824, of discriminatory tonnage duties on all foreign vessels entering Austrian ports; states that all governments were apprized of Austrian willingness to modify and abolish these duties "whenever Similar restrictions on Austrian vessels Should be modified and abolished in Such Countries"; and notes that the difficulty with application of the reciprocity offered by the act of Congress of March 3, 1815 (see above, Clay to Forbes, April 14, 1825, note) is that the United States still levies a 10 percent duty on the importation of goods not the produce of the country whose vessels bring them. ALS. DNA, RG59, Notes from Austrian Legation, vol. 1 (M48, R1). Lederer was consul general at New York for Austria and Tuscany from 1820 to 1838.

INSTRUCTIONS AND DISPATCHES December 12, 1825

From ALEXANDER H. EVERETT, Madrid, no. 17. Reports an interview with the Duke del Infantado, who had not yet "given any particular attention to our affairs," but who said, however, that the demand for a consul at Havana "appeared to be well founded, and that he thought that the King would accede to it; but that the measure when adopted would probably be general." Notes that the Duke has not yet mentioned the subject to the King (Ferdinand VII). States that the Russian Emperor (Alexander I), in reply to a Spanish request for a loan, has answered affirmatively, on condition that other parties to the (Holy) Alliance join him "and that Spain herself . . . offer some appearance of proceeding upon a settled and consistent plan of Government." Acknowledges receipt a few days ago from (Rufus) King, of a copy of the instructions to Middleton on Spanish America (above, May 10, 1825), which, Everett declares, "came very opportunely while I was engaged in preparing the note which I intend to address to this Govt upon the same subject." LS. DNA, RG59, Dip. Disp., Spain, vol. 25 (M31, R27). Extract published in *American State Papers, Foreign Relations*, V, 880.

From GEORGE W. SLACUM, Buenos Aires. Reports, as "a direct and wilful violation of the laws of the United States for the protection of American Seamen," the case of two men from the ship *Clara*, of Baltimore, whom the master, John Jones, has put ashore and refuses to allow on board again; cites this as an example of an evil attending the traffic in old ships, sold to be broken up, while their crews are left stranded; and suggests that "The prosecution of captain Jones, and the publication of the decision in the case, will . . . have a good effect." ALS. DNA, RG59, Cons. Disp., Buenos Aires, vol. 2 (M70, R3). Received February 17, 1825.

MISCELLANEOUS LETTERS December 12, 1825

To AUGUSTUS B. WOODWARD, Tallahassee, *"Private."* Transmits letters "left at or sent here" for Woodward and notes receipt of "several others, addressed to General La Fayette and others, to be forwarded." Daniel Brent, "directed by the Secretary," now intimates "that as the forwarding of private Letters thro' this Department to persons abroad, as well as in this Country, has become a very troublesome office to it, in repugnance, too, to Law, and to the disadvantage of the Revenue," Clay has "determined that the practice should no longer be tolerated, unless the Letters . . . are known to be of a scrictly [*sic*] official character, and appertain to concerns under the direction of the Department of State. . . ." Copy. DNA, RG59, Dom. Letters, vol. 21, pp. 213-14 (M40, R19).

From [GEORGE W. SLACUM], Buenos Aires. Refutes charges which, he understands, have been made against him in "a remonstrance or some such thing [not found] . . . got up in this place by a few captains of Vessels. . . ." AL (part of document, including signature, missing). DNA, RG59, A. and R. (MR2). Endorsed in strange hand on last page: "Anon. 1825–S." Received February 18, 1826.

From S[AMUEL] L. S[OUTHARD], Navy Department. Transmits a copy of a letter from Isaac Hull, "together with the protest, and other papers, relating to the Seizure & condemnation of the American Ship General Carrington." Copy. DNA, RG45, Executive Letterbook, vol. 1821-1831, p. 151. The *General Carrington,* owned by Edward Carrington and Company, of Providence, who also owned four-fifths of her cargo—in all, valued at $100,000—had been seized and condemned in the summer of 1824, by Royalist forces in the port of Quilca, Peru, on charges that it had delivered firearms and powder to the Patriots at Coquimbo.

APPLICATIONS, RECOMMENDATIONS   December 12, 1825

JOHN H. PLEASANTS, Richmond (Virginia), recommends Dr. Samuel Colton, "a member of the Executive Council of Virginia," for appointment as collector at Norfolk; states that "Dr Colton in capacity of Surgeon, rendered services for three years during the last War— He is a decided friend to the present Administration, having been in favor of Mr Adams from the beginning. . . ." ALS. DNA, RG59, A. and R. (MR1). See above, Pegram to Clay, December 11, 1825, note.

G[ULIAN] C. VERPLANCK, Washington, recommends William Beach Lawrence for appointment "to fill the secretaryship of the Legation or Commission to Panama." ALS. DNA, RG59, A. and R. (MR3). Dated "Monday evening." Verplanck, a member of Congress from 1825 to 1833, had been born in New York City in 1786, had been graduated from Columbia College, had studied law, and in 1807 had been admitted to the bar. He had joined his cousin, Johnston Verplanck and others in founding the New York *American,* had sat in the New York Assembly (1820, 1821, 1822), and had been, from 1821 to 1824, a professor in the Episcopal General Theological Seminary in New York. As editor and author he published essays and other works on politics, religion, history, and literature. He was a member of the New York Senate, 1838-1841, and was active in civic affairs until his death, in 1870.

DANIEL WEBSTER, "H. R.," transmits documents "in connection with the application of Richard W. Greene for appointment as district attorney for Rhode Island." Comments: "You will understand, that I take no undue interest in the matter, but am only willing to speak well of a deserving & respectable man." ALS. *Ibid.* See above, Eldridge to Clay, November 29, 1825, note.

To Lafayette

My dear General   Washington 13 Decr. 1825
    I learnt with much pleasure, from under your proper hand, in
your obliging letter of the 28h. October, by the Cadmus, that you
were reposing at Lagrange, in the bosom of your affectionate family
and friends. There, you know, I wish you to be, as your friend
Washington was at Mount Vernon, when he left the Presidency,
retired from the bustling world, a calm spectator, rather than an
active participator, of its numerous vexations and cares.
    We traced you across the Ocean, somewhat alarmed for your
safety by reports unfavorable to the Brandywine which returned
to us.[1] We witnessed and shared in the emotions of your joyous
meeting with your children and friends at Havre, and pursued
you thence by Rouen to your own residence, the incidents which
occurred on the journey not escaping our notice.[2] You have not
been troubled, as I imagined you would not be, by the Government
of France, although it is evident from your treatment by some of
its functionaries that they have no friendly feelings towards you.
    Since you left us but little has occurred here to interest you. The
Session of Congress has commenced, under auspices as favorable
to the administration as could be expected. Among the elements,
disposed to opposition, there is a great want of cohesion. I do not
apprehend that we shall have more than a salutary opposition.
The President's message will have reached you, through the public
prints, before this letter arrives. You will observe that the mission
to Panama is announced.[3] I regret that Mr. Gallatin declined
accepting it.[4] His place is supplied by Mr. John Sergeant of
Philadelphia, who will be associated with our minister at Bogota,[5]
and those two will represent the U. States at the first Congress
of the American Nations. With what satisfaction, my dear General,
must you contemplate that event, in which you have had so great
an agency! Several of the new Republics have suggested that the
affairs of Hayti should be considered at Panama with a view to
the establishment of an uniform rule to be observed towards it by
the American powers.[6] The perpetual grant of exclusive commercial
privileges which that island has made to France[7] will affect the
question of the recognition of its Independence.
    You have inspired us with fresh hopes about Greece. We began
to despair, and I own that my fears are still great. We cannot
see the events of the late campaign clearly. Without foreign
succour, with her intestine divisions, and the infidelity of her
chiefs, do you think it possible that she can continue to maintain

a contest in which the inequality of numbers is so much against her?

I am glad to be able to quiet your friendly solicitude about my health. It was never better than it is now and has been for some weeks past. Another and a severe affliction in my family,[8] after you left us, added much to my griefs and contributed to impair my health.

Mrs. Clay joins me in affectionate remembrance to you, and I pray you to communicate my friendly regards to your son and to Col. LaVasseur[9]— With never ceasing wishes for your happiness I remain Cordially & faithfully Your friend   H CLAY
Genl. La Fayette

ALS. NNPM.
[1] The Washington *Daily National Intelligencer,* on October 28, 1825, had reprinted from the Philadelphia *Democratic Press* a report that the *Brandywine,* when only a few days at sea, had been found to have eight feet of water in her hold, where caulking had washed out. The same account had reported the death of "several hands." *Niles' Weekly Register,* XXIX (November 5, 12, 1825), 146-48, 161, attributed the rumors to partisan criticism of Secretary of the Navy Samuel L. Southard and minimized the extent of the damage found in the vessel's *"upper-works."*
[2] Enthusiastic crowds had welcomed Lafayette at Havre and Rouen; but at the latter place the populace, gathered beneath a balcony on which Lafayette had appeared, was attacked by *gendarmerie* and a detachment of the Royal Guard with drawn sabres. Several persons were wounded and many arrested on charges of rioting. *Niles' Weekly Register,* XXIX (December 3, 1825), 213, reporting a Paris dispatch dated October 10.
[3] See above, King to Clay, December 9, 1825.
[4] See above, Gallatin to Clay, November 10, 14, 1825.
[5] Richard C. Anderson, Jr.
[6] Cf. above, Salazar to Clay, November 2, 1825.
[7] See above, Armstrong to Clay, October 12, 1825.
[8] The death of Susan Clay Duralde.
[9] George Washington Lafayette; Auguste Levasseur.

From Francis T. Brooke

My Dear Sir   Richmd Decmr 13 1825
There is nothing passing here of more interest than what you see in the newspapers. The Sensation produced by the message[1] is Subsiding, its effect conduced very much to elect Mr. Randolph[2] as Govr Pleasants[3] would not permit himself to be named much of the interest in the choice was lost.— the immediate object of this letter is to recommend to you Doctor Colton[4] a member of the executive Council here—he is a gentleman of unblemished integrity of good abilities comes from the neighbourhood of Norfolk and wishes to be appointed a collector at that place— although that appointment belongs to the Treasury, yet you may render him a Service for which you will have his gratefull acknowledgements and the thanks of your friend   FRANCIS BROOKE

ALS. DNA, RG59, A. and R. (MR1). Addressed to Clay.
1 President Adams' message to Congress, December 6, 1825.
2 John Randolph. Cf. above, Brooke to Clay, November 27, 1825.
3 James Pleasants.   4 Samuel Colton.

INSTRUCTIONS AND DISPATCHES   December 13, 1825

From AL[EXANDER] McRAE, London. States that he has not "for many months" thought he could add to information received by Clay through regular channels "concerning the wishes and the views of European Governments in regard to the independence of South America . . ."; congratulates him now "on the certain success" of the "valiant struggles of our patriotic neighbours"; and reports that his own belief that England did not "favor the independence of South America" has been confirmed by a "note of March 25, to the Spanish Minister, the Chevalier de los Rios," in which (George) Canning said: "The separation of the Spanish Colonies from Spain, has been neither our work nor our wish. Events in which the British Government had no participation, decided that separation, which we are still of opinion might have been averted, if our Counsels had been listened to in time." Referring to the "graceless act of recognition," by Great Britain, of some of the new Republics, McRae warns that many Englishmen and "the public Prints, are boasting that this Government took the lead in establishing the independence of South America" and that these "pretensions" will "be impudently asserted hereafter before the Governments of South America, in support of claims to peculiar advantages, which the ambition or cupidity of this Government may prompt it to seek. . . ." Deplores the extravagant praise bestowed by (Simón) Bolívar on Britain for her recognition of Colombia, the "seeming propensity on the part of our neighbours to prefer the friendship of Britain to that of all other nations"; and the "obsequiousness" of certain representatives of Latin America at the British Court. Postscript adds that (Rufus) King's health has improved, that a memorandum on Greece is enclosed with this letter, and that he hopes for an announcement soon that Lord (Thomas) Cochrane, now in France, "is at Sea actually embarked in the service of the Greeks." ALS. DNA, RG59, Dip. Disp., Special Agents, vol. 9 (M37, R9). Received February 19, 1826. McRae, a Richmond lawyer, former member of the Virginia House of Delegates (1803-1804) and Council (1805), and in 1808 Lieutenant Governor of that State, had been appointed in December, 1823, as a secret agent to report upon the pro-ceedings of a congress of European states expected to discuss Spain's relation-ship to her American colonies. His assignment had been terminated under a letter from the State Department dated August 6, 1824, and received by McRae on October 31, 1824. For the letter cited from Canning to Los Rios, March 25, 1825, see [Great Britain] Foreign Office, *British and Foreign State Papers, 1824-1825* (London, 1826), pp. 909-15.

MISCELLANEOUS LETTERS   December 13, 1825

To [RICHARD RUSH]. Encloses an extract of a letter (not found) relating to a complaint by the French Minister (above, Mareuil to Clay, December 2, 1825), in which the Postmaster General attributes "some want of attention . . . in the transfer of Letters from Vessels arriving from Foreign Countries to the Post-Office." Clay suggests the propriety of investigating the possibility of neglect in the office of the collector of New York (Jonathan Thompson). Copy. DNA, RG59, Dom. Letters, vol. 21, p. 246 (M40, R19).

From BORIE AND LAGUERENNE, Philadelphia. Complains of a regulation, imposed by the vice consul of Mexico at Philadelphia (Henry B. Chew), requiring "that a certificate [sic] from his office should be attached to each 'invoice of every shipper for all goods shipped in any vessel proceeding from this port to any port in Mexico,'" and requests Clay to ascertain from the Mexican Minister (Pablo Obregón) whether the regulation results from a decree of the Mexican Government or merely from the policy of the vice consul. LS. DNA, RG59, Misc. Letters (M179, R63). On December 20, Daniel Brent, by Clay's direction, informed Borie and Laguerenne that the Secretary had "lost no time in taking the steps which seemed . . . required in regard to the Mexican Vice-Consul at Philadelphia. . . ." DNA, RG59, Dom. Letters, vol. 21, p. 222 (M40, R19). Chew, not further identified.

APPLICATIONS, RECOMMENDATIONS   December 13, 1825

JONATHAN ELLIOTT, Washington, solicits appointment "to print the pamphlet edition of the Laws for the Dept. of State that may be passed at the present session of Congress, of 11,000 copies. . . ." ALS. DNA, RG59, P. and D. of L. Cf. above, Colvin to Clay, September 21, 1825, note.

JOHN McLEAN (Washington) transmits a letter, from A(ugustus) B. Woodward to McLean, dated November 18, 1825, recommending (David B.) Macomb for appointment as United States attorney for East Florida. ALS. DNA, RG59, A. and R. (MR5). See above, Gibson to Clay, November 20, 1825, note.

AL[EXANDER] McRAE, London, seeks temporary appointment to some agency in Europe. Notes that he will remain there some months longer, on private business. ALS. DNA, RG59, Dip. Disp., Special Agents, vol. 9 (M37, R9). Received February 19, 1826. Endorsed: "Private." McRae received no further appointment.

SAMUEL L. SOUTHARD, Navy Department, transmits letter of recommendation from Edward Carrington in favor of Richard W. Greene as Federal district attorney, for the District of Rhode Island. LS. DNA, RG59, A. and R. (MR2). See above, Eldridge to Clay, November 29, 1825, note.

To Samuel L. Southard

Dear Sir   14 Decr. 1825
    I thank you for the opportunity afforded me of perusing Capt. Morris s[1] letter, which is returned. I have one, under the same date, from La Fayette at Lagrange[2] which I would send for your perusal, if it contained any thing interesting.   Yr's faithfully   H CLAY
Honble Mr. Southard.

ALS. NjP-Samuel L. Southard Papers.   [1] Charles Morris.
[2] Above, October 28, 1825.

MISCELLANEOUS LETTERS   December 14, 1825

From S[AMUEL] L. S[OUTHARD], Navy Department. Transmits copies of a letter from Commodore (Isaac) Hull and a decree of the Government of Peru; requests that instructions to Hull, if considered desirable in this connection, be provided soon. LS. DNA, RG59, Misc. Letters (M179, R63). See above, Tudor to Secretary of State, April 22, 1825, note; Allen to Clay, September 16, 19, 1825, notes; below, Clay to Hull, December 20, 1825.

From S[AMUEL] L. S[OUTHARD], Navy Department. Encloses a copy of a letter (not found) from Commodore Isaac Hull, regarding the *General Brown.* Copy. LS. DNA, RG59, Misc. Letters (M179, R63). See above, Allen to Clay, November 5, 1825, note.

From STEPHEN TWYCROSS "of Brig Belvidere," Wilmington, North Carolina. Complains of extortion by the American vice consul at the Island of St. Thomas. ALS. DNA, RG59, Misc. Letters (M179, R63). Dated December, 1825; postmarked December 14. Endorsed by Clay: ". . . Who is he." Twycross not further identified. Stephen Cabot, formerly of Boston, at this time a merchant at St. Thomas, had held the office of vice consul since July, 1824.

APPLICATIONS, RECOMMENDATIONS   December 14, 1825

SILAS BROWN, Jackson, Mississippi, reports sale of the Jackson *Southern Luminary* to Peter Isler and requests that the appointment to publish the laws be "made this year in his name." ALS. DNA, RG59, P. and D. of L. Brown, who had been assessor and collector of Monroe County, Mississippi, in 1821, had acquired the Jackson *Pearl River Gazette* in 1824 and renamed it the *Southern Luminary.* Postmaster of Jackson from 1825 to 1827 and prominent as a physician of that community, he served as a member of the State House of Representatives in 1828 and later as State treasurer. Isler, a printer, formerly of Winchester, Virginia (1804), Bardstown, Kentucky (1806-1811), and Natchez, Mississippi (1812-1819), had held the contract for Mississippi State printing from 1823 to 1825, when he lost it to Brown. Following Isler's purchase of the *Southern Luminary,* the latter organ was merged with his *State Gazette* as the *State Journal,* which again acquired the State contract and also received appointment for publishing the Federal laws.

A[NDREW] R. GOVAN, House of Representatives, encloses a letter from a person unknown to Govan but recommended by "a particular friend." ALS. DNA, RG59, A. and R. (MR2). Endorsed by a clerk: "Encloses Samuel Hoit's letter Soliciting Office." Further endorsed by Clay: "Mr. [Daniel] Brent will return the enclosed, and inform Mr. Govan that Mr. Hoit's name is on file." Govan, from South Carolina, was a member of the House from 1822 to 1827. In 1828 he moved to Mississippi, where he spent the remainder of his life as a planter. On December 19, Brent executed Clay's direction. Copy, in DNA, RG59, Dom. Letters, vol. 21, p. 218 (M40, R19).

WILLIAM R. KING and G[EORGE] W. OWEN, "Washington City," recommend the appointment of James Dellet as "District Judge for the State of Alabama." ALS by King, signed also by Owen. DNA, RG59, A. and R. (MR2).

To [John Quincy Adams]

15th Decr 1825

Mr. Clay has the honor to accept the invitation of Mr. and Mrs. Adams to dinner on tuesday next. Mrs. Clay regrets that she feels herself obliged to decline the honor of dining with them at the same time, which was intended her—

AN. MHi-Adams Papers.

To Levi Lincoln

His Excellency, Levi Lincoln, Governor of Massachusetts.

Sir,   Department of State, 15th. Decr. 1825.

I have the honour by the direction of the President, to acknowledge the receipt of your Letter, addressed to him on the 26th. ultimo,[1] transmitting a Copy of the report of the Land Agent of the Commonwealth of Massachusetts; and to assure you of the anxious desire of the Government of the United-States to make a satisfactory arrangement with that of Great Britain of our North Eastern Boundary. No time will be unnecessarily lost in bringing the negotiation to a final conclusion. In the mean time, it is desirable that each party, governed by a spirit of moderation, should refrain from the adoption of any measures which may tend to give just, inquietude to the other. It would perhaps be best for neither to do any act which would change the state of the question as it existed when the Commission under the Treaty of Ghent was constituted.[2] If one attempt to strengthen his pretensions by the exercise of acts of Sovereignty or ownership over parts of the disputed Territory, which were then waste and uninhabited, the other will resort to the same expedient; and the collisions, which would inevitably follow, would place both parties in a state less propitious to an amicable settlement of the difference. It was under this view of the propriety of mutual forbearance that, when, in the course of the last Spring statements were received, at this Department, of depredations committed, under color of British authority, within the limits of the State of Maine, as claimed by us, I addressed a note to the British Chargé d'Affaire [sic] near this Government remonstrating against those depredations.[3] It appears from the above report of your Commissioner, and from other sources of information, that our remonstrance has had the desired effect; that the Governor of the adjoining British Province[4] has been directed, by proper authority to discontinue granting licences [sic] to cut Timber; and that he has accordingly discontinued. The President wishes that this conciliatory course on the part of Great Britain should be reciprocated by us, and I am therefore directed by him respectfully to suggest to Your Excellency the propriety of its being observed by the Government of Massachusetts.

I seize the occasion to renew to Your Excellency assurances of my respectful consideration.   H. CLAY.

Copy. DNA, RG59, Dom. Letters, vol. 21, pp. 215-16 (M40, R19). A similar letter was addressed this same date to Albion K. Parris. See below, Clay to Vaughan, January 18, 1826.   1 Cf. above, Lincoln to Clay, December 6, 1825.
2 See above, I, 1006.   3 Above, Clay to Addington, March 27, 1825.
4 Sir Howard Douglas.

To Samuel L. Southard

15 Decr. 1825

H. CLAY requests the favor of the Company of Mr. Southard at Dinner on Wednesday next at five o'clock

An answer is respectfully solicited.

AN, partially printed. NjP-Samuel L. Southard Papers. Addressed to Southard.

From Ninian Edwards

Dear Sir,   (Confidential)   Belleville Illinois December 15th 1825

A long absence from home prevented my receiving your very kind letter[1] for several weeks after its arrival at this place, and has delayed, until this time, my acknowledgements for the friendly disposition it evinces—

I discover in it however, an additional reason for making my controversy with Mr Crawford[2] better understood than it has been— You think I was injudicious "in the time & manner of exhibiting my charges against him," which proves to me that you are wholly unapprized of the necessity under which I acted— Whatever may be thought of the manner of my repelling his attack, I had no choice as to the time, and therefore am not blameable [sic] for not selecting a period more propitious to the object— I was apprized by the most *undoubted* authority from Virginia, in the summer of 1823, of an intention to attack me at the succeeding session of Congress, though, at that time, I had no suspicion of the grounds on which I was to be attacked. But it was Mr Crawford's object to fix a charge of perjury on me, in regard to the famous letter of the Receiver at Edwardsville[3]— You would be astonished to find that, that very letter had been seen in the Treasury Department— And it is known to two of the Senators and one member of the House of Representatives (one of whom is an efficient & devoted friend of yours) that I could have established this fact, if I could have reconciled it to myself to betray a confidential communication— This I presume you will yet ascertain before very long— Who then could blame me for repelling such an unprincipled & malignant attack upon my reputation? No man— no not all the men in the world, could have dissuaded me from it— I should dispise [sic] myself, if any hopes of office or emolument could have induced me to hesitate— I freely confess however, that I think I could have managed the thing much better, if I had not been taken so much by surprise— And had not my health put it out of my power to return to the Senate, all the clamours that were, or could have been raised, should not have prevented my reviving the controversy at the succeeding session in a new shape— I however should not, at this time, have adverted to this subject, were I not under an impression, that your memory retains a remark I once made to you, and that you have mistakenly applied it to the charges I exhibited against Mr Crawford— I said, or intimated to you, that I could exhibit a case against him which in my opinion merited impeachment— Had I been a member of the House of representatives I should have exhibited it— But this case was not even adverted to in my memorial— I however offered to lay it before the committee—and if I shall here after have occasion to do so, you will see that I shall make out a case that it will be difficult to meet & that cannot be fairly met with success— The publication of my book has been so long, and to me so unexpectedly delayed, for the want of about two or three documents from Washington, which I have not yet been able to obtain that I do not know whether I shall publish it at all; unless it shall be called forth by new persecutions on the part of Mr Crawfords [sic] or his friends— His sit[ua]tion greatly abates my disposition to defend myself by reviving any controversy with him—and as I have not made up my mind to enter again on the Arena of politics, or to take any part whatever in the political struggles there are to ensue, I am inclined to content my self with leaving in the hands of my children the means of defending my reputation against any charges that may grow out of that controversy (Mr Nobles testimony however always excepted)[4]—

With respect to my claim to compensation for my services as superintendent of the U.S. Saline,[5] your remarks are so unexpected to me that though, not in the least dissatisfied with you on that account, I feel excessively mortified at the suspicion they create that you have considered me as exhibiting this claim in consequence of my having to refund money to the Govt— You are certainly one of the last men in the world from whom I should have feared that by postponing my claim (which I did in consequence of the relation in which I stood to Mr Crawford & the late President[6]) I should either weaken it; or subject it to the quieting influence of a kind of statute of limitations. And I must be permitted to say that instead of establishing a new & dangerous precedent (which you seem to suppose) by paying me what my services justly merit, it would be in direct violation of a multitude of precedents that are within my own knowledge to refuse to pay me on account of the lapse of time that has intervened since those services were performed. If I mistake not you yourself once appealed to me, at Mr Wirts in a case of your own, not at all dissimilar in principle[7]—and I doubt very much whether the President himself has not had accounts settled by one administration for services performed under a previous one.[8] I have been repaid by one administration money that I had advanced for the govt several years before under a previous administration—and in the latter part of Mr Monroes administration was paid for extra services performed in the early part of Mr Madisons, which had not been previously demanded because I did not stand in need of the money. This is not at all extraordinary in my case, for it may be seen that I often advanced considerable sums of money out of my own pocket to the Govt, and that even my salary as Govr[9] remained undrawn for a very unusual length of time—

The services for which I claim compensation were not terminated till after Mr Monroes administration had commenced—and without precedent, how does the case stand on principle— If there had been a regular sala[ry] attached to the office of superintendant [*sic*] of the Saline, no lapse of time wou[ld] have barred my demand for it, so neither should it bar my right to whatever the services I performed ex equo & bono entitle me to— I can see no difficulty in the case, the records show that I performed the services and have never been paid for them— The precedents that show me entitled to pay for those extra services are innumerable, allowances then made, or now made for extra services, are suffi[ci]ent to show that the sum I charge is extremely reasonable reasonable [*sic*]— I however, am willing to take whatever the President may choose to allow me— But I shall think it extremely hard, and it is impossible that I should be satisfied, to get nothing— I never had a thought of abandoning the claim, and were I now upon my oath I would swear that I firmly beleive [*sic*] I was out of pocket at least $200 a year by that business in the actual expences it produced. I have however said more than I intended, my object in referring to this subject was merely to assure you, that if you have, for a moment, entertained the injurious thought of me, which gives me my present uneasiness, it is in my power to show by my correspondence with Mr Tiffin[10] as Commissioner of the Genl Land Office (who considered me entitled to compensation) that it is not just— I know too well the importance of your time to wish to draw you into any correspondence on this subject. As I do not write to you officially I have written with all the freedom which the nature of our present correspondence, I hope will be considered as justifying— As I *never will give up* this claim I will thank you to deliver the statement I inclosed to you to Mr Cook[11] that he may present it for official decision as soon as possible. I will be *Amy* Dar[din][12] with it—if necessary— Very respectfully Yrs Hon: H. Clay.   NINIAN EDWARDS

ALS. DLC-HC (DNA, M212, R2). Right side of two MS. pages obscured.
1 Not found.   2See above, III, 187n, 744n-45n.
3 During his appearances before committees of the House of Representatives on February 13, 1823, and in the spring of 1824, Edwards had claimed that Benjamin Stephenson, receiver of public moneys at the Edwardsville Land Office and also president of the Bank of Edwardsville, had written a letter in his presence on October 12, 1819, addressed to the Secretary of the Treasury (Crawford), speaking of past difficulties of the bank and of apprehension regarding its prospects, expressing unwillingness to make further deposits of public funds without instruction from the Secretary, and enclosing a copy of a communication published by Edwards, announcing his resignation from the directorship of the bank. Edwards contended that he had advised the receiver to withhold deposits of Government money from the bank until he received further orders from the Secretary of the Treasury and that Stephenson later asserted that he had been directed to continue the deposits. Crawford, in his letter of March 22, 1824, had stated that no such letter from the receiver and no record of an answer directing continuation of the deposits could be found in the files of the Treasury Department. *House Docs.*, 18 Cong., 1 Sess., no. 140, p. 3; *House Repts.*, 18 Cong, 1 Sess., no. 133, p. 113 *et passim*. The Bank of Edwardsville had subsequently failed; and when the existence of Edwards' warning communications was denied, his earlier efforts to obtain deposit of the public moneys for the bank engendered criticism.
4 See above, Edwards to Clay, July 18, 1825, note. No book appears to have been published, but an "address" (not found) in reply to Noble's testimony is supposed to have been issued later in this month. For extensive quotations from the latter, see Ninian W[irt] Edwards, *History of Illinois from 1778 to 1833; and Life and Times of Ninian Edwards* (Springfield, 1870), 137-46.
5 See above, Edwards to Clay, July 18, 1825.   6 James Monroe.
7 Cf. above, III, 54-55 and note, 59-60, 188-89, 258.
8 See above, III, 190n.   9 Of Illinois Territory.
10 Edward Tiffin.   11 Daniel P. Cook.
12 Mecklenburg County, Virginia, widow, whose claim for a blooded stallion impressed by officers during the Revolutionary War was presented to Congress annually from 1796 to 1815 before she was finally awarded payment.

From David Fullerton

Hone. Henry Clay   Green Castle Pa. Decr. 15th. 1825
Dear Sir

[Refers to the letter in his behalf addressed to Clay by Joseph Bard[1] and states that, although he has become a candidate for sheriff, he would prefer an appointment at Washington.]

I See General Jackson is Looking forward to the presidential Chair and I think as Anxious to obtain it, as Ever a hungry fish was to Catch a fly— I think the general desserves [sic] well of his Country—but I do hope he never will be president of the United States, for reasons which long Er'e this have forceably Operated on your mind he has been a Successfull [*sic*] Commander—but it requires quite different talents from those the Genl. possesses to make a good president. Jefferson, Madison, & Monroe, made good presidents, but from the Knowledge I have of Any of those Gentlemen I think they would have made poor Generals—

Wishing you health and happiness, I am Dear Sir Your friend & Humbe Servt   DAVID FULLERTON

ALS. DNA, RG59, A. and R. (MR2).   [1] Above, Bard to Clay, March 15, 1825.

From James Harper

H. Clay Esqr   Office B.U States Lexington Decr. 15th. 1825
Dear Sir

I have received your favour of 2d Inst. enclosing Mr. Bryans letter[1]— A few days after he had wrote to you he called at the Bank and Showed me a copy of his letter & on a reexamination of the papers[2] I found that I was wrong in computing the interest from 11h. October 1824 and that it should be as stated by him from 8h. Decr. 1824— I was led into this error by the agreement for extending the time of payment which bears the former date & contains a provision that the interest shall be paid annually on the 11h. October— I then informed Mr. Bryan that there was no difference in our views except as to the small allowance of interest on the $1150[3] for the time that payment was anticipated— Mr B. is expected in daily to pay the interest—

We have received $65 6/100 exclusive of $27 19/100 costs, (through the Office at Louisville) for ballance of R Breckenridges debt assigned by you[4]— this added to former payment of $565 50/100 is according to our estimate about $10. too much, but we have put the whole to your credit, leaving it for future correction, if, as we suppose, Mr B. has overpaid that Sum.

I should have acknowledged the receipt of your letter of 23 [*i.e.,* 25] Octr. before this, but was waiting to inform you of the payment of Bryans interest of which I was in daily expectation— On consideration I think it best to let Minters Note remain in its suspended state and apply the first monies recd. on your account (after paying discounts on your own Note) to its extinguishment— the applications shall be made as the monies are deposited to your credit so that no interest shall be improperly charged against you— please let me know whether this course is approved by you.—

Since the late extraordinary message of Govr. Desha to our Legislature[5] I have several times been on the point of addressing a letter to Mr. Biddle[6] soliciting an inquiry into my conduct, but have still postponed it as I thought the result of the investigation of the matter by the Legislature might be a sufficient contradiction[7]—

Such charges coming from so high authority are certainly calculated to produce a belief abroad, that the Officers here & particularly myself (who it is Said in a late publication of some leading relief Gentlemen[8] *rules* the Board) have been guilty of some very indiscreet interferences in electioneering matters whereby the Bank & its interests have been unnecessarily brought into conflict with the State authority—

I think that a Sufficient portion of my conduct has passed under your observation & that you are well enough acquainted with my habits & disposition to exculpate me from this charge and I will thank you to avail yourself of any opportunity you may have of speaking to Mr. Biddle, (who will no doubt be at Washington this Winter) on the Subject—

We have no local news of any interest— I am with much respect Yr Obt. Servt.   J HARPER Cashr

ALS. DLC-TJC (DNA, M212, R13).
[1] Daniel Bryan. Neither letter has been found.
[2] Cf. above, III, 72, 296-98, 872, 892n.
[3] See above, III, 872.   [4] Cf. above, II, 888; III, 346.
[5] See above, T. W. Clay to H. Clay, November 10, 1825, note.
[6] Nicholas Biddle.

[7] Replying to a series of resolutions adopted by the Kentucky House of Representatives, which requested that he communicate, with other information, "any evidence he may possess, to establish the charge contained in his message, that the Bank of the United States had controlled many of our citizens, as their tenants in the exercise of their right of suffrage. . . ," Governor Desha on December 14 had delivered a lengthy indictment of the activities of the branches of the bank in Kentucky, of Clay for his relationship to the legal actions brought by the bank, and of members of the legislature whom the Governor considered tools of the bank. The following day the house referred the statement to the Committee for Courts of Justice, which on December 19 submitted a report pointing to the limited number of debtors who had been foreclosed by the bank and noting the bank's expressed desire to avoid acquisition of landed holdings and its efforts to effect alternative adjustments. The committee found that there were, among the tenants on bank property, only "about 75 or 80 apparently free white males, qualified as voters of this Commonwealth," that no more than about 25 lived in any one county, and that, "So far as the committee can ascertain, a majority of the tenants of the Bank are believed to have voted against what his Excellency seems to consider the interest of that corporation. . . ." Observing, however, that there was considerable dissatisfaction because branches of the bank had been established in the State, the committee recommended that Kentucky's Senators be instructed and her Representatives be requested "to use their best exertions to procure" a constitutional amendment "to preclude the Congress from locating or giving authority to locate any bank, or branches thereof, in any State in this Union, without the express consent of the Legislature thereof, previously had." The report was tabled and was not again taken up before adjournment of the Session. Ky. H. of Reps., *Journal, 1825,* 56-58, 299-338, 379-95.

[8] Not found.

DIPLOMATIC NOTES   December 15, 1825

To HILARIO DE RIVAS Y SALMON. States that investigation by law officers at Philadelphia and New York, ordered after receipt of Salmon's letter of September 22, shows no violation of law but that the President, anxious to afford proof of the "earnest desire" of the United States "scrupulously to fulfil all of its neutral duties," had sent, before receipt of the note of November 29, instructions to require bond of owners of vessels "said to be fitting out . . . for belligerent purposes." Copy. DNA, RG59, Notes to Foreign Legations, vol. 3, p. 243 (M38, R3). Published in Manning (arr.), *Diplomatic Correspondence . . . Latin-American Nations*, I, 263. See above, Ingersoll to Clay, October 17, 1825; Tillotson to Clay, November 29, 1825.

MISCELLANEOUS LETTERS December 15, 1825

From C[HURCHILL] C. CAMBRELENG, Washington. Encloses documents "relating to the case of the Spermo seized at Pernambuco" (see above, Raguet to Clay, March 11, 1825); requests that American "agents there will be instructed to furnish such aid as may be compatible with the duties of the Govt. of the U. States and the rights of its Citizens." ALS. DNA, RG76, Misc. Claims, Brazil.

From AARON HOBART, "House Reps." Requests a copy of papers relative to the claim of the Weymouth Importing Company, of Massachusetts, in the case of the ship *Commerce,* taken into Corfu by a Russian brig in 1807 and there condemned as lawful prize. ALS. DNA, RG59, Misc. Letters (M179, R63). Endorsed by Clay: "Mr. Brent will have the papers desired prepared." Hobart, a Representative from Massachusetts (1820-1827), had been graduated from Brown University, had studied law, and had served in the State legislature (house, 1814; senate, 1819). He was later a member of the Executive Council of Massachusetts (1827-1831) and probate judge (1843-1858). Eliphalet Loud and Samuel Bailey were partners in the Weymouth, Massachusetts, concern. In 1807 the *Commerce,* en route to Lisbon with a cargo of wheat under contract held by a Leghorn merchant, had been forced to attempt a landing at Corfu for repairs. Seized offshore by a Russian gunboat, the vessel had been condemned by a prize court at Corfu. Under an agreement dated March 17, 1828, with the Russian Government, the Weymouth Importing Company was awarded 50,000 rubles (about $10,000) in compensation. Miller (ed.), *Treaties . . .* , III, 421-25.

On December 17, 1825, Daniel Brent, "by direction of the Secretary," acknowledged receipt of Hobart's letter but reported that the statement wanted could not be found in the files of the State Department. Brent surmised that it had been "communicated by Mr. [Levett] Harris directly to our Legation at St. Petersburg, and not to this Department." Copy. DNA, RG59, Dom. Letters, vol. 21, p. 218 (M40, R19).

From J[OSEPH] LAWRENCE, "Congress Hall." Encloses a paper, given him by John Brady, a lawyer of Washington, Pennsylvania, relative to a claim of the nature of those "assumed by the Government of the U. S. when it purchased Louisiana. . . ." ALS. DNA, RG59, Misc. Letters (M179, R63). Lawrence, a Pennsylvania Congressman (1825-1829, 1841-1842), served in the State legislature (1818-1824, 1834-1836) and was State treasurer (1837). Under the terms of a convention accompanying the Louisiana Purchase Treaty, the United States had agreed to assume the "debts due by France to citizens of the United States contracted before" September 30, 1800, with six per cent interest, these obligations being "for Supplies [*sic*] for embargoes and prizes made at Sea in which the appeal has been properly lodged within the time mentioned in the . . .

Convention 8th Vendemaire ninth year (30th Septr 1800)." Miller (ed.), *Treaties* . . . , II, 517-18. (The French version inserts a comma, as, *"fournitures, embargoes et prises. . . ."*)

On December 19, Daniel Brent, at Clay's direction, returned the memorandum, "purporting to be a claim of John Moore against this Government, for the amount, with a small deduction, of two Bills on the Government of New Orleans, which are presumed to have been drawn as long ago as April 1803. . . ." Since the account was "unaccompanied by any explanatory document," it was inadmissible. Copy. DNA, RG59, Dom. Letters, vol. 21, p. 219 (M40, R19). Moore may have been the native of Virginia, born in 1788, who by 1813 had developed a sugar plantation on the Bayou Teche of Louisiana, was now a member of the Louisiana House of Representatives (1825 to 1834), and later became a Whig member of Congress (1840-1843, 1851-1853).

From GABRIEL MOORE, "House of Representatives." Informs Clay, at the request of the editors of the Huntsville *Alabama Republican,* of changes in title and ownership of that paper. Now the (Huntsville) *Southern Advocate and Huntsville Advertiser,* it is owned by (Dandridge) Fariss, ... Alsop, (A.) Woodward, and (William H.) Campbell, under the firm name D. Fariss and Company. ALS. DNA, RG59, P. and D. of L.   Alsop, not identified. Cf. above, Campbell and others to Clay, November 26, 1825.

From GEORGE PETER, "Congress Hall." Encloses a letter and requests Clay to furnish him "with the information asked." ALS. DNA, RG59, Misc. Letters (M179, R63). Cf. below, Clay to Peter, December 16, 1825.

From ROBERT TILLOTSON, New York. Reports that one of the vessels mentioned by (Hilario de Rivas y) Salmon, "a ship pierced for 64 guns, owned by Mr. Henry Eckford . . . , called the South America," is preparing to sail with complete armament on board; states that he does not know her destination; and asks whether she is subject to forfeiture or whether the neutrality act of April 20, 1818, will be executed by requiring bond. ALS. DNA, RG59, Misc. Letters (M179, R63). Answer not found. The vessel ultimately sailed for Cartagena. Cf. *Niles' Weekly Register,* XXX (May 13, 1826), 200.

From JOHN WURTS (Washington). Encloses papers forwarded to him by Borie and Laguerenne to be transmitted to Clay (above, December 13, 1825). ALS. DNA, RG59, Misc. Letters. Undated; the covering letter, from Borie and Laguerenne to Wurts, is dated December 13. Wurts, a Philadelphia lawyer, native of New Jersey, graduate of Princeton, and former Pennsylvania legislator, was a member of Congress from 1825 to 1827. He became a United States district attorney (1827-1831), member of the Philadelphia City Council, and president of the Delaware and Hudson Canal Company (1831-1858).

On December 19, Daniel Brent, at Clay's direction, replied that a strong remonstrance had been addressed to the Mexican Minister in the United States, "upon the practice in the Mexican Vice-Consular Office at Philadelphia, complained of by Messrs. Borie & Languerenne [*sic*]," and that, if necessary, this action would probably be followed "by a direct remonstrance to the Government of Mexico, thro' our Minister in that Country." Copy. DNA, RG59, Dom. Letters, vol. 21, p. 219 (M40, R19).

APPLICATIONS, RECOMMENDATIONS   December 15, 1825

MYRON HOLLEY, Lyons, Wayne County, New York, refers to the letter from (Peter B.) Porter to Clay "Last winter" (cf. above, III, 904-905) ; notes that "That application was not successful, but" has been renewed; solicits Clay's aid; and states that he believes several congressmen from New York will favor the "petition." ALS. DNA, RG94, U. S. Military Academy, Cadet Applications, 1824/324.

THOMAS NEWTON, House of Representatives, transmits letters just received "under cover of one addressed to" him. ALS. DNA, RG59, A. and R. (MR1). Endorsed: "Encloses Letters recommendatory of persons, as Collector of Customs   Norfolk." The enclosures include Pegram to Clay, December 11, and Pleasants to Clay, December 12, 1825.

B[ARTLETT] YANCY and H[UTCHINS] G. BURTON, Raleigh, North Carolina, recommend, for a consular appointment, John G. A. Williamson, of Person County, a young man between twenty and thirty years of age. ALS by Yancy, signed also by Burton. DNA, RG59, A. and R. (MR1). Williamson was appointed consul to La Guaira, Colombia, in 1826 and in 1835 was raised to the position of Chargé d'Affaires in Venezuela.

From George McClure

Dear Sir   Bath 16th. Decr, 1825

Mr, Woods[1] informs me that my son George W.— name was placed on the books of the late Secretary of War[2] with an assurance that this Year he should receive a Warrant as a Cadet to West point— The present Secretary[3] may not be acquainted with this fact, will therefore esteem it a favour if You will be pleased to mention the subject to the Secretary at War, as my Son is verry [sic] anxious to receive a Military education,[4]   You will pardon me for troubling You on this occasion, as I am sensible that the ardous [sic] duties of Your Office leaves You but little spare time to attend to such matters,

I have written to Mr, Porter[5] our member in Congress on the subject, but as he is an entire stranger at Washington, I cannot expect that he can have much influence with the chief of the War department—

I perceive that Genl. Jackson is determined to put in his claim for the Presidency in due season,   He has truly overshot the mark this time, in his address of resignation of his Seat in the Senate[6] he has exposed himself to much obliquay [sic], so much so, that his bosom *friend George Kramer*[7] cannot redeem him from merited censure, there is but one opinion about his views, motives, & conduct amongst the People in this region—

I cannot well describe the politics of New York, the parties are composed of a hetoragenous [sic] mass, and both sides claims [sic] the ascendancy,   Our great *Champion* of internal improvements[8] is labouring hard to reach Washington City at the end of three Years, which he is to effect through the medium of the N. York & *Ohio Canal*,[9]   His political career so far, has been a serious [*sic*] of ups & downs, of prosperity and adversity,   The foolish and indiscreet conduct of the Republican[s] of this State in opposing the Electoral bill[10] and other popular measures raised Mr. Clinton, but those things are almost forgotten, and a Union of the great republican family of this State will be effected and *Mr. C,s* Federal friends will be left in the minority,   The friends of Mr. Clinton at the late Election used the utmost exertion to carry the Genl. Ticket systom [*sic*] for the Election of Electors of P. & V P, but the District Systom prevailed by a handsome majority without any exertion— It would be verry desireable [*sic*] if Congress would take up this subject and adopt the District systom throughout the Union—

I have Just received the Presidents message[11] and I have read it with pleasure to the end, but at the same time was extremely mortified in not finding a single line on the subject of our Manufactures,   If his object in recommending the construction of Canals though [*sic*] every section of the Union is to facilitate the transportation of foreign fabricks to the Exclusion of our own, then I should be no advocate for Canals, but perhaps I do not do the President justice,   Yet I think if he had the subject at heart his mouth an [*sic*] pen would declare it—

I am Dr. Sir Your friend & Servt.—   GEO, MC,CLURE— Honl. H. Clay—

ALS. DNA, RG94, U. S. Military Academy, Cadet Applications, 1826/130. Endorsed by Clay: ". . . Refered [*sic*] to the Honble Secy. of War, with the particular recommendation of H. C."   1 William Woods.
2 John C. Calhoun.   3 James Barbour.
4 The young man was appointed to the Military Academy in 1826, was brevetted a second lieutenant in 1830, and remained in the Army until his death four years later.
5 Timothy H. Porter, of Olean, a lawyer, born in Connecticut, had served in local legal and judicial offices and in the State legislature (1816, 1817, and 1823). After one term in Congress (1825-1827), he returned to the practice of law and was again a member of the New York Senate (1828-1831) and Assembly (1838 and 1840).
6 See above, Carroll to Clay, October 4, 1825, note.
7 *I.e.*, Kremer.   8 DeWitt Clinton.
9 Cf. above, Toasts, July 13, 1825.   10 See above, III, 476, 477n.
11 Cf. above, Clay to Stuart, December 1, 1825.

Check to William Worthington

16 Decr. 1825
Pay to William Worthington or order ninety five dollars.
$95—   H. CLAY
Cashr. of the Off. of Dt. & Dt. Washn.[1]

ADS. DLC-TJC (DNA, M212, R16). Endorsed on verso: "W. Worthington." Worthington not identified.   1 Richard Smith.

INSTRUCTIONS AND DISPATCHES   December 16, 1825

From JOEL R. POINSETT, Mexico, no. 31. Transmits "the official notice of the blockade of San Juan de Ulúa being raised" and notes that "the port of Vera Cruz is now open to our commerce and is in every respect more advantageous than that of Alvarado." States that he does "not know all the objections made by Mr. [George] Canning" to the proposed British treaty with Mexico but is "credibly informed, that the exception, made in favor of the States formerly Spanish Colonies, is among the principal." That being true, Poinsett expects less difficulty on that point when his own negotiations are resumed. Adds: "I have communicated to this Government such parts of your instructions to our Envoy at the court of St. Petersburg [above, Clay to Middleton, May 10, 1825] as I thought likely to produce a favorable effect." LS. DNA, RG59, Dip. Disp., Mexico, vol. 1 (M97, R2). Received January 21, 1826.

MISCELLANEOUS LETTERS   December 16, 1825

To [GEORGE] PETER. Returns "the letter of Mr. Morse, on the subject of which no information is possessed at the Department of State, other than that" obtained from the newspapers, which state that a commission is to be formed in France to decide upon indemnities "to the sufferers at St. Domingo." Adds that (James) Brown has been requested to supply information for the use of claimants. Copy. DNA, RG59, Dom. Letters, vol. 21, p. 216 (M40, R19). See above, Peter to Clay, December 15, 1825; Clay to Brown, October 25, 1825 (Instructions no. 2). Morse not identified.

From A. MEWHALL, PHILIP GREELY, HEZ[EKIAH] WINSLOW, JACOB KNIGHT, and CHARLES FOX, Portland (Maine). The signers, "a Committee of the Merchants and Ship Owners of the port of Portland State of Maine," complain of excessive fees, charged by agents of the Spanish consul at Boston (Ramundo Chacon), on vessels departing for Cuba. ALS by Fox, signed also by the others. DNA, RG59, Misc. Letters (M179, R63). Winslow was a lumber merchant; the others not identified.

APPLICATIONS, RECOMMENDATIONS   December 16, 1825

WILLIAM P. DUVAL, Tallahassee, recommends Col. Abraham Bellamy for appointment as United States attorney for the Western District of Florida. ALS. DNA, RG59, A. and R. (MR5). Bellamy, a native of South Carolina, had come to Jacksonville, Florida, in 1822, the first lawyer to settle in that community. He had been a member of the Territorial Legislative Council since 1824 and later became clerk (1827) and president (1831) of that body. He did not receive the requested appointment. By 1829 he had established residence as a planter in Jefferson County.

P[ELEG] SPRAGUE, "House of Representatives," recommends continuation of the appointment of the Hallowell (Maine) *American Advocate and Kennebec Advertiser* to publish the laws. ALS. DNA, RG59, P. and D. of L. Born in Massachusetts, educated at Harvard and the Litchfield Law School, Sprague had moved to Maine in 1815. He had been a member of the State legislature in 1821 and 1822 and was a member of the United States House of Representatives from

1825 to 1829 and of the United States Senate from 1829 to 1835. He removed to Boston and from 1841 to 1865 served as United States district judge of Massachusetts. The requested contract for public printing was granted and retained throughout the Adams administration.

MISCELLANEOUS LETTERS   December 17, 1825

From WILLIAM P. DUVAL, Tallahassee. Encloses a copy of a letter to the President and solicits Clay's "interference" in his behalf. States that the health of his son, who has acted as his clerk for over a year, has been injured by the work and the young man "has not been able to render much assistance for two weeks past." ALS. DNA, RG59, Misc. Letters (M179, R63). Published in Carter (ed.), *Territorial Papers*, XXIII, 388-89. In the enclosure, dated December 16, Duval requests authorization to employ a clerk in the executive office of the Territory. Which of Duval's four sons acted as his clerk has not been identified.

APPLICATIONS, RECOMMENDATIONS   December 17, 1825

JOHN HAY, "Bruce Town," Frederick County, Virginia, asks for appointment to a clerkship in the (State) Department. Writes: "Although thirty Years have elapsed, since I had the pleasure of seeing you, yet a Hope is indulged, that when you recognize in my Signature, the Name of an Associate, & Companion of your Youth, you will not deem any Apology necessary, for the freedom of this Communication." Extends congratulations upon Clay's "accession to the Cabinet"; expresses "unfeigned pleasure" at seeing him "entered upon the Threshold of that Reward, which in our beloved Country, is reserved for the virtuous Patriot, & enlightened Statesman"; and wishes that Clay "may live, to be invested with its highest Gift, & enjoy, amidst the Cares of State, the inestimable Consolation, of an approving Conscience. . . ." ALS. DNA, RG59, A. and R. (MR2). Hay did not receive a Federal appointment but in 1836 was named a justice of Clarke County, Virginia, was thereupon elected clerk of the court, and served in that capacity until 1852.

ROBERT Y. HAYNE, J[AMES] HAMILTON, JR., GEORGE McDUFFIE, A[NDREW] R. GOVAN, and WILLIAM DRAYTON, Washington City, express opposition to any change which would remove the contract for printing of the laws from John N. Cardozo, owner and editor of the Charleston, South Carolina, *Southern Patriot*. LS. DNA, RG59, Misc. Letters (M179, R63). Cardozo (not further identified) had acquired the journal around 1822. On the change of appointment, cf. below, Haig to Clay, December 19, 1825.

MARSHALL, SPALDING, AND HUNT, Rochester, solicit appointment of their journal, the new Rochester *Album,* to publish the laws; state that their application will be supported by "Mr Sibley, late editor of the [Rochester] *Monroe Republican.*" ALS. DNA, RG59, P. and D. of L. Endorsed by Clay: ". . . . Query has the Monroe Republican been discontd?" The correspondents have not been individually identified.

Accompanying this letter in the State Department files is a communication dated December 22, 1825, from Derick Sibley to "Hon. Francis Johnson Member of Congress Washington," transmitting the application.

The printing contract for the Nineteenth Congress, Second Session, was given to Edwin Scrantom, a native of Connecticut, reared in Rochester, who had become editor of the *Monroe Republican* in the summer of 1824. Cf. above, Sibley to Clay, February 25, 1825; below, Scrantom to Clay, November 9, 1826, note.

[SIMRI] ROSE and [MATTHEW] ROBERTSON, "Publishers of the Georgia Messenger," Macon, Georgia, solicit appointment to publish the laws. ALS. DNA, RG59, P. and D. of L. Robertson, founder of the journal in March, 1823, had taken Rose into partnership the following August. Born in Connecticut and trained as a printer in New York, the latter remained as editor of the *Messenger* into the 1850's.

To Christopher Hughes

My dear Hughes   Washington 18h. Decr. 1825
    I was prevented, by causes which it would be needless to state, from answering your obliging letter of the   instant[1] (the date is not very legible) until today. My answer will arrive too late to assist you, in the consideration of the new honors which are tendered to you, which I regret the less because, from certain signs in your letter, I think you were already prepared to make the decision which became you. The place of Governor of Maryland is highly respectable, and several gentlemen (Dr. Kent[2] &c) have been solicited to occupy it. It does not suit you *yet*. It belongs to a later period of your life. You should shed a few more of your follies, in foreign parts, (can you bear such democratic frankness?) and retire on the Governorship of Md. at Annapolis, some twenty years hence, cum otiam [*sic*] &c &c.
    I am curious to see the Ottomans[3] and anxious to see the Governor, that was to have been, of Md.
    The inclosed[4] speaks for itself. I beg you not to measure the extent of my friendship by the length of my letters. Yr's Cordially
C. Hughes Esq.   H. CLAY

ALS. MiU-C.   1 Not found.
2 Joseph Kent was elected to the office on January 2, 1826, by joint ballot of the two houses of the general assembly.
3 Cf. above, Hughes to Clay, December 1, 1825.
4 Not found.

INSTRUCTIONS AND DISPATCHES   December 18, 1825

From HENRY MIDDLETON, St. Petersburg, no. 51. Encloses a note from Count Nesselrode giving details of the illness and death of Alexander I; discusses the question of succession; notes that Grand Duke Nicholas has sworn allegiance to his brother, Grand Duke Constantine, who is absent at Warsaw. ALS. DNA, RG59, Dip. Disp., Russia (M35, R10). Dated December 6/18, 1825. Received March 18, 1826. The Grand Duke Constantine Pavlovich had been designated by Emperor Paul I to supplant the eldest son, Alexander, as his successor; but when Alexander was placed upon the throne after his father's murder, the czarevich had accepted the situation, had ultimately settled in Poland, and in 1822 had renounced claim to the throne. When Alexander's death on December 1 was announced, the Grand Duke Nicholas declared his loyalty to Constantine; but the latter refused to return to St. Petersburg and, instead, took an oath to support Nicholas. For accounts of the "Decembrist" uprising in connection with these events, see below, Middleton to Clay, January 2, 7, 1826.

From R[ichard] Douglas

Hon Henry Clay   Chillicothe Decer 19—1825.
Dear Sir
     [Recommends his brother, Charles Douglas, for a diplomatic or consular appointment "near one of the Southern Republics."][1]
     Our Nashville journey, terminated at Cincinnati. After a delay of two weeks by sickness, Mrs. Ds[2] Physicians advised her decidedly to return— Although we were thus casually denied the pleasure of an acquaintance with your Lexington friends through the medium of your letters,[3] yet I can assure you—My Dear Sir—that the favor will not on that account be the less appreciated.—
     A retrospect of your detention at Lebanon,[4] leads us to *remember you in tears*.— The Poets tell us, that although the Grecian Parents ceased, perpetually to bewail the departure of the lovely Sisters, yet they could not desist from uttering their tender complaints.
     The Administration appear (to my mind) *"venturing upon wisdom"*[5] with great boldness— This is as it should be— The stand is worthy of this mighty age: Its spirit has gone forth "conquering, and to conquer",—and *thou also* "wilt not suffer *its feet* to be moved."—
     Of the character of "The Message"—it appears to me the first among that class of papers which have been, and still are, identifying the literature with the Glory of this—*Great Nation*.—Were a hasty description of it called for, nothing could more fitly occur than the well known verse of Sir John Denham—
          Though deep—yet clear—Though gentle, yet not dull.
          Strong, without rage; without oerflowing—full.[6]
     Very Respectfully—Your sincere Friend.   R. Douglas.—

ALS. DNA, RG59, A. and R. (MR2).
1 See above, King to Clay, June 22, 1825, note.
2 Not further identified.   3 Not found.
4 See above, Clay to Crittenden, July 25, August 22, 1825.
5 See above, Clay to Stuart, December 1, 1825, note.
6 From "Cooper's Hill," first published at London in 1642; but the apostrophe to the Thames River, here quoted, was not included until the printing of 1655.

DIPLOMATIC NOTES   December 19, 1825

To the Baron de Mareuil. States, in reply to Mareuil's note of November 16, that the instances of desertion of sailors from vessels of either the United States or France in the ports of the other country "cannot be so numerous as to require the establishment of any new tribunals or the creation of any new officials to enforce the provisions of the sixth article of the Convention"; denies that the American form of government presents any enforcement difficulties; asserts that "both nations contemplated, at the time of contracting, the actual forms of their respective Governments"; and points out that the sixth article of the Convention "expressly refers itself to judicial means for its execution." Copy. DNA, RG59, Notes to Foreign Legations, vol. 3, pp. 243-44 (M38, R3). ALI draft, in CSmH.

INSTRUCTIONS AND DISPATCHES December 19, 1825

From T[HOMAS] M. RODNEY, Havana. States that he has secured the release of two of the seven American seamen imprisoned in Havana (see above, Perry to Clay, March 25, 1825; Warner to Clay, March 26, 1825; Bruce to Clay, August 26, 1825; Diamond to Clay, October 8, 1825; Clay to Rodney, October 29, 1825; Clay to Vives, November 14, 1825) and that the remainder are still in prison; reports the arrival of a long-expected Spanish expedition; and notes that the United States sloop *Hornet* and schooner *Shark* are also in port. LS. DNA, RG59, Cons. Disp., Havana (M-T20, R3).

MISCELLANEOUS LETTERS December 19, 1825

To R[OBERT] Y. HAYNE and others. States that, prior to receipt of their letter of December 17, the Charleston *City Gazette (and Commercial Daily Advertiser)* had been selected to publish the laws. Copy. DNA, RG59, Dom. Letters, vol. 21, p. 221 (M40, R19). Cf. below, Haig to Clay, this date.

From DEWITT CLINTON, Albany. Acknowledges receipt of Clay's letter of November 11; declares that, if the laws of New York permitted, he would be glad to comply with (Charles R.) Vaughan's request; encloses copies of two opinions of the New York attorney general (Samuel A. Talcott) which have led Clinton to decline to act in a prior, similar case; and notes that the extradition law of his State, enacted after the Governor of Canada some years past acceded to a request to deliver up a fugitive charged with forgery in New York, is operative only with regard to fugitives from the neighboring British provinces. ALS. DNA, RG59, Misc. Letters (M179, R63).

From JAMES HAIG, Charleston, South Carolina. Acknowledges, with thanks, Clay's letter (not found) informing him "of the selection of the City Gazette for the publication of the Laws &c of Congress." LS. DNA, RG59, P. and D. of L. Haig, not further identified. This contract represented one of the ten changes made in the first year of the Adams administration.

From JOHN H. HOUSTON, Washington. Requests that the American Minister at Paris (James Brown) be asked to obtain documents from the archives of the commissioners appointed by France under the Louisiana Purchase treaty, in relation to the claim of "The late Com. [Thomas] Truxton." States that this claim had been rejected by the commissioners, but the claimants may "petition our own Government for relief." ALS. DNA, RG76, Misc. Claims, France. Houston has not been identified.

From ISRAEL THORNDIKE, Boston. Transmits a copy of his letter of March 13, 1825; notes that he has received no information from (Henry) Middleton; asks what more should be "done to bring the business to a close." Adds that he has asked (Daniel) Webster "to cooperate in any measures which may be deemed advisable." LS. DNA, RG76, Misc. Claims, Russia.

APPLICATIONS, RECOMMENDATIONS   December 19, 1825

W[ILLIAM] H. HARRISON, WILLIAM HENDRICKS, JOHN TEST, R[ATLIFF] BOON, J[ONATHAN] JENNINGS, JAMES FINDLAY, and JAMES NOBLE, Washington, recommend Thomas Douglas for appointment as district attorney in Florida. ALS by Hendricks, signed also by the others. DNA, RG59, A. and R. (MR2). Published in Carter (ed.), *Territorial Papers,* XXIII, 390. See above, Gregg to Clay, April 6, 1825.

JONATHAN JENNINGS, "House of Reps.," transmits letters (above, Rawle to Clay, November 10, 1825; McGiffen to Clay, December 3, 1825) forwarded to him "for presentation," recommending an appointment of Peter De Haven, whom Jennings endorses as "an estimable and highly deserving gentleman. . . ." ALS. DNA, RG59, A. and R. (MR2).

JAMES NOBLE, Washington, recommends appointment of Thomas Douglas. ALS. DNA, RG59, A. and R. (MR2). See above, Harrison and others to Clay, this date; Gregg to Clay, April 6, 1825.

ROMULUS M. SAUNDERS, "Repres. Hall," encloses a letter received "from the young gentleman [John G. A. Williamson] . . . mentioned" to Clay "some days since"; states that Saunders thinks, after enquiry of (Benjamin W.) Crowninshield, that the consulship at Canton "would *not* suit Mr. Williamson"; encloses the recommendation from Yancey and Burton (above, December 15, 1825). ALS. DNA, RG59, A. and R. (MR1).

C[HARLES] YANCY, Richmond (Virginia), a candidate for the collectorship at Norfolk, seeks Clay's support. While not personally acquainted with him, Yancy recalls an observation of his brother, Joel, of Kentucky: "If You ever Want any thing That Henry Clay Can do, write, or see him—& If he is Satisfied, he will be up to the Hob. for You." Concludes with the statement: "I am Your friend Among Your Enemies." ALS. *Ibid.* (MR4). Charles Yancy, born in Albemarle County, Virginia, had been a State senator in 1805 and a member of the House of Delegates in 1820, in the latter role serving as a prominent supporter of James Monroe. He did not receive the desired appointment as collector.

To John Quincy Adams

Department of State. 20 Decemr. 1825.
To the President of the United States.
Sir, Agreeably to your direction, that a statement should be presented to you of what passed in the Department of State with the Ministers of the Republics of Colombia, Mexico and central

America, in respect to the invitation to the U. States to be represented in the Congress at Panama, I have the honour now to report,

That during the last spring, I held separate conferences, on the same day, with the respective Ministers of Mexico and Colombia,[1] at their request, in the course of which each of them verbally stated that his Government was desirous that the U. States should be represented at the proposed Congress; and that he was instructed to communicate an invitation to their Government to send representatives to it. But that as his Government did not know whether it would or would not be agreeable to the U. States to receive such an invitation, and as it did not wish to occasion any embarrassment, he was charged informally to enquire, previous to the delivery of the invitation whether it would be accepted if given by both of the Republics of Mexico and Colombia. It was also stated by each of those ministers that his Government did not expect that the U. States would change their present neutral policy, nor was it desired that they should take part in such of the deliberations of the proposed Congress as might relate to the prosecution of the present War.

Having laid before you what transpired at these conferences, I received about a week after they had been held, your direction to inform the Ministers of Mexico and Colombia and I accordingly did inform them,[2] that their communication was received with due sensibility to the friendly consideration of the U. States by which it had been dictated, that, of course, they could not make themselves a party to the existing War with Spain, nor to councils for deliberating on the means of its further prosecution; that the President believed such a congress as was proposed might be highly useful in settling several important disputed questions of public Law and in arranging other matters of deep interest to the American Continent, and stregnthening [sic] the friendship and amicable intercourse between the American powers; that before such a Congress however assembled, it appeared to him to be expedient to adjust between the different powers to be represented, several preliminary points, such as the subjects, to which the Attention of the Congress was to be directed; the nature and the form of the powers to be given to the diplomatic Agents who were to compose it and the mode of its organization and action. If these preliminary points could be arranged in a manner satisfactory to the United States, the Ministers from Colombia and Mexico were informed that the President thought the U. States ought to be represented at Panama. Each of those Ministers undertook to transmit to his Government the answer which was thus given.— In this posture the affair remained until the letters were received which accompany this report, from the Ministers of the Republics of Mexico and

Colombia, under date of the 3rd and the 2d of November. To both of those letters that same answer was returned, in official notes[3] a copy of one (of) [sic] which is with this report.

The first and only communication from the Minister of the Republic of Central America to this Department in regard to the Congress at Panama is contained in his official note, a copy of which together with a copy of the answer[4] which was returned, by your directions, will be found along with this report. All which is respectfully submitted.— I have the honor to be with great Respect your obedient servant—   H. CLAY.

Copy. DNA, RG59, Report Books, vol. 4, pp. 112-13. President Adams communicated this letter and the accompanying documents to the United States Senate December 26, 1825. *American State Papers, Foreign Relations,* V, 834-39.
[1] Pablo Obregón; José Maria Salazar. See above, Tudor to Clay, April 12, 1825, note.
[2] Perhaps orally; no documents found.
[3] See above, Clay to Obregón, November 30, 1825, and note.
[4] See above, Cañaz to Clay, November 14, 1825; Clay to Cañaz, November 30, 1825.

To Isaac Hull

To Captain Isaac Hull.
Sir.   Department of State Washington, 20. December, 1825
Your Letter under date the 22nd. August last, addressed to the Secretary of the Navy, and transmitting a Decree, purporting to have been issued on the 17th. of April last, by the Republic of Peru,[1] having been submitted to the President, I have now the honour of addressing you, by his direction.

That Decree is levelled against property belonging to Spanish subjects or of Spanish origin, which it subjects to seizure and condemnation within the territory of the Republic. The second article of the Decree declares that "all vessels which may be found with Spanish property of any kind, shall be declared lawful prize by the competent Tribunals." And by the third Article, the owner-ship of the property is infered [sic], and determined, to be Spanish, from the fact of its Spanish origin, no matter what sales or transfers of it may have been made subsequently to its production or fabrication. Considered as a mere municipal regulation, to be enforced only within the jurisdictional limits of the Republic of Peru, this Decree must be regarded as one of great rigour. Its operation in accomplishing its proposed object, that of punishing, or subduing, the obstinacy of Spain, in uselessly prolonging the war, must be inconsiderable; whilst the amount of the vexation and injustice which it inflicts upon innocent neutrals, is very great. Viewing it in this light, the President indulges the expectation that, upon reconsideration, the Peruvian Republic will annul the

Decree. But if they adhere to it, as a municipal regulation, the opposition which Foreign Nations are authorized to make to it, is limited to remonstrance, or to the adoption of countervailing regulations.

If, as the words above quoted of the second Article, may be interpreted, it was intended to carry the Decree into effect beyond the jurisdictional limits of the Republic, and to seize at sea, and condemn, as lawful prize, vessels which may have on board Spanish property of any kind, other rights and duties will accrue to Foreign Nations. Although the clause referred to, is ambiguous, the President cannot allow himself to believe that it was intended to give it this extended scope. Such an ex-territorial application of the Decree would be without countenance in the principles of the public Law, or in the practice of Nations, except in the instances of the memorable British Orders in Council and French Decrees, promulgated during the reign of Bonaparte,[2] and which were condemned by the cotemporaneous judgment of the impartial world, and were not attempted to be justified by either of those Powers, but upon notions of retaliation. To guard, however, against any misconception of the true import of the Decree, you are directed to ascertain whether it is intended to enforce it beyond the jurisdiction of the Republic. In that case, you will notify the Government of Peru that you are instructed to resist its execution on vessels of the United States; and you will, accordingly, resist its execution against any vessels of the United States beyond the Peruvian jurisdiction, and afford to those vessels all the protection of which the force at your disposal will admit. In performing this duty, you will consider yourself authorized not only to defend any American vessel whose capture, in virtue of that decree, shall be attempted in your presence, or within the reach of your power, beyond the Peruvian jurisdiction, but you will re-capture any vessel of the United States, seized under that decree, at any time before it is actually carried within that jurisdiction.

I am, with great respect, Your obedient Servant   H. CLAY.

Copy. DNA, RG59, Dip. Instr., vol. 10, pp. 421-22 (M77, R5).
[1] See above, Tudor to Clay, April 22, 1825, note; Southard to Clay, December 14, 1825.   [2] See above, I, 276n, 526n.

To José Maria Salazar

Don José Maria Salazar, Envoy Extraordinary and
Minister Plenipotentiary from Colombia.
Sir,   Department of State, Washington, 20 Decr. 1825.
During the last Spring I had the honor to state to you that the

Government of the United States had addressed that of Russia with the view of engaging the employment of its friendly offices to bring about a peace, if possible, between Spain and the new American Republics, founded upon the basis of their independence; and the despatch from this Department to the American Minister at St. Petersburg,[1] having that object, was read to you. I have now the satisfaction to state that it appears, by late advices just received from St Petersburg that this appeal to the Emperor of Russia has not been without good effect; and that there is reason to believe that he is now exerting his friendly endeavours to put an end to the war.[2] The first would be naturally directed to his Allies, between whom and His Imperial Majesty it was desirable that there should be, on that interesting subject, concurrence of opinion and concert in action. Our information from Europe authorizes the belief that all the great powers are now favourably inclined towards peace, and that separately or conjointly, they will give pacific counsels to Spain.[3] When all the difficulties exterior to Spain, in the way of peace, are overcome, the hope is confidently indulged that those within the Peninsula cannot long withstand the general wish. But some time is necessary for the operation of these exertions to terminate the war, and to ascertain their effect upon the Spanish Government. Under these circumstances the President believes that a suspension, for a limited time, of the sailing of the Expedition against Cuba or Porto Rico, which is understood to be fitting out at Carthagena, or of any other expedition which may be contemplated against either of those Islands by Colombia or Mexico, would have a salutary influence on the great work of peace.[4] Such a suspension would afford time to ascertain if Spain, resisting the powerful motives which unite themselves on the side of peace, obstinately resolves upon a protraction of the war. The suspension is due to the enlightened intentions of the Emperor of Russia, upon which it could not fail to have the happiest effect. It would also postpone, if not forever render unnecessary, all consideration which other powers may, by an irresistable sense of their essential interests, be called upon to entertain of their duties, in the event of the contemplated invasion of those islands, and of other contingencies which may accompany or follow it. I am directed, therefore, by the President to request that you will forthwith communicate the views here disclosed to the Government of the Republic of Colombia, which he hopes will see the expediency, in the actual posture of affairs, of forbearing to attack those islands until a sufficient time has elapsed to ascertain the result of the pacific efforts which the great powers are believed to be now making on Spain.

I seize with pleasure, the occasion, to renew to you assurances of my distinguished consideration.   H. CLAY

Copy. DNA, RG59, Notes to Foreign Legations, vol. 3, pp. 245-46 (M38, R3). A letter of the same wording was addressed to Pablo Obregón, this date. For Clay's role in initiating this correspondence, see Adams, *Memoirs,* V, 88.

1 Above, Clay to Middleton, May 10, 1825.

2 See above, Middleton to Clay, September 8, 1825; but cf. above, Middleton to Clay, December 18, 1825.

3 See above, Brown to Clay, September 13, 19, October 29, 1825.

4 See above, Poinsett to Clay, June 15, August 5, 21, September 13, 1825; Watts to Clay, June 30, 1825; Anderson to Clay, November 10, 1825; Salmon to Clay, November 29, 1825.

DIPLOMATIC NOTES   December 20, 1825

To the Baron [LEWIS CHARLES] LEDERER. Acknowledges receipt of his letter of December 12; states that if the Congress, which now has the subject of navigation under consideration, approves removal of remaining restrictions, as the President recommended in his recent message, a convention between the two governments would become necessary and its conclusion would be facilitated if the Emperor of Austria would empower some person to negotiate in this country. Copy. DNA, RG59, Notes to Foreign Legations, vol. 3, p. 245 (M38, R3). ALI draft, in CSmH. In his annual message of December 6, President Adams had urged legislation to extend the provisions of the act of January 7, 1824 (see above, Lorich to Clay, March 16, 1825, note), so as to lift discriminating duties upon importation from the designated countries "of all articles of merchandise not prohibited, of what country soever they may be the produce or manufacture." Richardson, *A Compilation of the Messages and Papers of the Presidents. . . ,* II, 301. Such a proposal was submitted by Clay to James Lloyd, Chairman of the Senate Committee on Commerce (below, December 21, 1825), and by that committee reported to the Senate on January 25, 1826. The measure passed the Senate but was not acted upon by the House of Representatives. A bill with the same wording was finally enacted on May 24, 1828 (4 *U. S. Stat.,* 308-309), and Austria was brought under its application by Presidential proclamation of June 3, 1829 (*ibid.,* 814).

To PABLO OBREGON. Inquires whether the regulations promulgated by Henry B. Chew, Mexican vice consul at Philadelphia, rest on competent authority and are to be enforced in Mexican ports; points to the objectionable features; and expresses a hope that Chew will be directed to modify them. Copy. DNA, RG59, Notes to Foreign Legations, vol. 3, pp. 244-45 (M38, R3). AL draft, in CSmH. See above, Borie and Laguerenne to Clay, December 13, 1825.

INSTRUCTIONS AND DISPATCHES   December 20, 1825

From THOMAS APPLETON, Leghorn. States that he has been requested by Francisco Grilli, an Italian chemist residing in Leghorn, to communicate to the United States information of a process by which iron is made rust-proof. Grilli has patented his discovery, useful in the protection of firearms and in shipbuilding, and expects the Government of the United States to make an offer for the use of it. ALS. DNA, RG59, Cons. Disp., Leghorn, vol. 2 (M-T214, R2). Received April 8. Appleton, of Massachusetts, had been named American consul at Leghorn in 1798 and held the position until 1840.

MISCELLANEOUS LETTERS   December 20, 1825

To C[HURCHILL] C. CAMBRELENG. States that (Condy) Raguet "was instructed, as far back as the 16th. of April last, to afford any Official aid in his power to the Owners of the Spermo, in the recovery of their property" and that no information has been received "as to the effect of his interposition." Copy. DNA, RG59, Dom. Letters, vol. 21, p. 222 (M40, R19). See above, Raguet to Secretary of State, March 11, 1825, note.

To ALFRED CONKLING, "Judge of the United States for the Northern District of New York, Canajoharie." Encloses commission for this office. LS. NUtHi. Copy, in DNA, RG59, Dom. Letters, vol. 21, p. 222 (M40, R19). Conkling's appointment had received Senate approval on December 14. Receipt of the commission was acknowledged by Conkling to Clay, December 26, 1825. ALS. DNA, RG59, Acceptances and Orders for Commissions (M-T645, R2).

To [SAMUEL L.] SOUTHARD. Inquires, "at the instance of a Committee of the Senate," whether Dr. (Samuel D.) Heap has resigned "his commission of Navy Surgeon." AN. DNA, RG45, Misc. Letters, p. 141. Cf. below, Southard to Clay, this date.

From BORIE AND LAGUERENNE, Philadelphia. Encloses a newspaper clipping containing a public protest of the Philadelphia merchants against the regulations enforced by the Mexican vice consul (Henry B. Chew), who has told "Mr. Borie" that (Pablo) Obregón by letter recommended that Chew take no notice of the complaints. LS. DNA, RG59, Misc. Letters (M179, R63).

From SAMUEL L. SOUTHARD, Navy Department. In answer to Clay's note of this date, transmits a copy of a letter to Dr. (Samuel D.) Heap, who has not replied. LS. *Ibid.* The enclosure requests Heap's resignation as a Navy surgeon if he accepts an appointment from the State Department. Cf. above, Clay to Heap, November 9, 1825.

APPLICATIONS, RECOMMENDATIONS   December 20, 1825

PETER ISLER, Jackson, Mississippi, reports the purchase of the Jackson *Southern Luminary* from Silas Brown and solicits continuation of the appointment of that paper to publish the laws. ALS. DNA, RG59, P. and D. of L. See above, Brown to Clay, December 14, 1825, note.

C[HRISTOPHER] RANKIN, Washington, recommends William Crawford for appointment to "the office he solicits." ALS. DNA, RG59, A. and R. (MR1). See above, Owen to Clay, September 25, 1825, note.

To ....

Dr Sir   Washington 21st. Decr. 1825

I return the papers the perusal of which you have been good enough to allow me. They contain the first intimation I have received of any intention, on the part of the British Government, to suspend the intercourse between the British American Colonies and this Country, and I can not but think that there is some misconception about the matter. Yr's respectfully   H. CLAY

ALS. MH. Cf. below, Clay to Cambreleng, December 25, 1825; Clay to Gallatin, June 19, 1826; Gallatin to Clay, August 19, 1826, note.

DIPLOMATIC NOTES   December 21, 1825

From CHARLES R. VAUGHAN, Washington. Transmits copies of an act of Parliament of June (27), 1825, "entitled, 'an Act to repeal the several laws relating to the performance of Quarantine, and to make other provisions in lieu thereof,'" (6 *Geo. IV*, c. 78) and of an order in council "in furtherance of the Act of Parliament." LS. DNA, RG59, Notes from Foreign Legations, Great Britain, vol. 14 (M50, R15). Dated: "Decr. 1825." Received December 21.

From CHARLES R. VAUGHAN, Washington. States that, following representations by (Richard) Rush, shortly before his departure from England, "the Tonnage duty levied under the Order in Council of the 21st. of July 1823, upon American Ships entering the Ports of . . . [British] Colonies in the West Indies and British North America," worked hardship on "American Steam Vessels carrying Passengers and Baggage only, and Vessels in Ballast" (see above, Rush to Clay, March 5, 1825, note), orders were given "not to demand those duties from American Vessels so circumstanced; but certainly in the full persuasion that the same rule would be observed towards British Vessels of the like description, in the Ports of the United States"; declares that "representations recently received by the Board of Trade" indicate "that such reciprocity does not prevail"; and reports that he has been instructed to inform the American Government that Great Britain will "be compelled" to withdraw its indulgence unless the expectation of reciprocal treatment "shall be realized." Requests an answer "with as little delay as possible. . . ." LS. *Ibid.* Dated: "Decr. 1825." Received December 21. Published in Manning (arr.), *Diplomatic Correspondence . . . Canadian Relations,* II, 496. Cf. above, Bartlett to Clay, November 2, 1825.

INSTRUCTIONS AND DISPATCHES   December 21, 1825

To THOMAS L. L. BRENT, Lisbon, no. 3. Transmit a memorial submitted to the President by the owners of the cargo of the brig *Osprey;* refers to Brent's dispatch no. 9 (above, July 11, 1825), relative to this case, and suggests "an earnest and fresh appeal to" the "justice and good faith" of the Portuguese Government to bring about a settlement. Copy. DNA, RG59, Dip. Instr., vol. 10, p. 423 (M77, R5). L draft, in Daniel Brent's hand, in DLC-HC (DNA, M212, R7).

From JAMES BROWN, Paris, no. 38. Reports information received in Paris of the death of Alexander I, speculation concerning the succession to the throne, and fluctuation of the stock market. LS. DNA, RG59, Dip. Disp., France, vol. 22 (M34, R25). Received February 16, 1826. See above, Middletoii to Clay, December 18, 1825, note.

From RUFUS KING, London, no. 14. Reports a meeting of British financiers to discuss a possible stoppage of specie payment by the Bank of England and a resort to issuing of paper money; notes that "The Money Confidence of the Country . . . has given way"; states that the death of the Emperor of Russia, "and perhaps a disputed succession" (see above, Middleton to Clay, December 18, 1825, note), has "left all in confusion in the North, and upon the Continent." Comments on "a manifest feverishness and impatience in South America." Predicts that, "If the Black Sea comes into the White, England Must Make War to oppose it—this will be the beginning of New troubles in Europe." Acknowledges receipt of Clay's dispatches numbered 7, 8, and 9 (October 17, 26, 29, 1825) and Clay's dispatch no. 3 to James Brown (October 25, 1825). LS. DNA, RG59, Dip. Disp., vol. 32 (M30, R28). Received February 7, 1826. Extract published in Manning (arr.), *Diplomatic Correspondence . . . Latin-American Nations,* III, 1576. The expression, "White Sea," was applied to both the Sea of Marmora and the Mediterranean. Allusion was here made to the possibility of active intervention by Russia to support the Greek revolt against Turkey.

From HENRY MIDDLETON, St. Petersburg, no. 52. Reports that, in conformity with Clay's instructions of April 25, he has twice urged Count Nesselrode to lay before the Emperor the correspondence between Clay and Tuyll of April (1)9 and 22; encloses a copy of a letter from Nesselrode in reply to an inquiry directed to him after the death of the Emperor (Alexander I). ALS. DNA, RG59, Dip. Disp., Russia, vol. 10 (M35, R10). Received March 18, 1826. In the enclosure Nesselrode states that he did not lay the matter before the Emperor and must now await "the orders of the new Sovereign."

MISCELLANEOUS LETTERS   December 21, 1825

To [JAMES] LLOYD. Encloses "the project of An Act in addition to An Act entitled 'An Act concerning Discriminating Duties of Tonnage and Impost'." Copy. DNA, RG59, Report Books, vol. 4, pp. 113-14. The wording of the enclosed proposal is the same as that later reported by the Senate Committee on Commerce (see above, Clay to Lederer, December 20, 1825, note).

To [RICHARD RUSH]. Transmits "a Note just received from the British Minister" (Vaughan to Clay, this date) and inquires whether "the American tonnage duty is levied on British Steam Vessels, arriving in the ports of the United States, with passengers and baggage only and in ballast." Copy. DNA, RG59; Dom. Letters, vol. 21, p. 225 (M40, R19).

From J[OHN] ADAMS, JR. States that "The President requests that all resolutions from either House of Congress, as soon as acted upon by the Departments may be returned to him." Requests the return of "that . . . sent to the Department confirming the appointment of Mr. (Alfred) Conkling of N— Y—" ALS. DNA, RG59, Misc. Letters (M179, R63). Young Adams (1803-1834), second son of John Quincy Adams, served as his father's secretary. On the Conkling appointment, see above, Clay to Conkling, December 20, 1825, note.

From RICHARD RUSH, Treasury Department. Transmits, in reply to Clay's letter of December 13, a copy of a letter from the collector of New York (Jonathan Thompson), written in answer to a request for explanations relative to the complaint of the French Minister. LS. DNA, RG59, Misc. Letters (M179, R63).

MISCELLANEOUS LETTERS   December 22, 1825

From LEVI LINCOLN, "Executive Department of Massachusetts, Worcester, Mass."
Acknowledges receipt of Clay's letter of December 15; states that he will bring
the subject again to the attention of the legislature, soon to reassemble; and
requests that assurance be given the President "that no steps are in contemplation, which can in any degree tend to produce further excitement on the part
of the British, in the neighborhood of the lands, or to embarrass the Government of the United States, in their endeavors to obtain a satisfactory arrangement with that of Great Britain, in the establishment of the true line of our
North eastern boundary—" ALS. DNA, RG76, Northeast Boundary, Misc. Papers,
env. 4, item 4. Published in *House Docs.*, 20 Cong., 2 Sess., no. 90, pp. 17-18.

From JOHN WURTS, Washington. Transmits a communication (probably above,
December 20) from Borie and Laguerenne. ALS. DNA, RG59, Misc. Letters
(M179, R63).

APPLICATIONS, RECOMMENDATIONS   December 22, 1825

WILLIAM SMITH, "House of Reps.," recommends the appointment of J(oseph)
F. Caldwell, editor of the Lewisburg *Palladium of Virginia*, to publish the laws.
ALS. DNA, RG59, P. and D. of L. Smith, a native of Virginia, had served in
the State House of Delegates in 1782 and was a member of Congress from 1821
to 1827. Caldwell, a printer by trade, after working on other journals at Winchester and Fincastle, Virginia, had founded the· *Palladium* in November, 1823,
and published it until 1830, or later. In 1826 he acquired the contract to carry
the mail from Lewisburg to Big Sandy and, about the same time, joined with a
partner to operate a stagecoach line from Lewisburg to Charleston; but he did
not receive the desired appointment to publish the laws.

JOHN TALIAFERRO, Washington, recommends Edward T. Tayloe, of Virginia,
who "is now along with Mr. [Joel R.] Poinset [sic]," as "Secretary of Legation,
to be attached to the contemplated mission to Panama." ALS. DNA, RG59, A.
and R. (MR4). Edward Thornton Tayloe, son of Colonel John Tayloe, had
been graduated from Harvard University in 1823. The young man, who had
accompanied Poinsett to Mexico in the spring as private secretary without
remuneration, was named Secretary of Legation to Colombia in 1828. Replaced
by the Jackson administration the following year, Tayloe spent the remainder
of his life as a plantation owner in Virginia.

INSTRUCTIONS AND DISPATCHES   December 23, 1825

From JAMES BROWN, Paris, no. 39. Acknowledges receipt, on December 16, of
Clay's dispatches no. 2 and no. 3 (October 25); states that the vessels composing
the French fleet in the West Indies during the past summer were assembled to
make a demonstration to induce the Haitian Government to accept the terms
offered by France (see above, Holden to Clay, July 16, 1825, note); explains
that the secrecy of orders to the fleet accounts for his "inability to give . . . due
notice of the expedition and of its objects." Notes that he will make to the
Minister of Foreign Affairs (the Baron de Damas) the communication Clay
directs, that he has already stated the American position concerning Cuba and

Puerto Rico, "that the policy of England on that point corresponds with that of the United States," and that it is hardly possible that France will attempt to acquire either island. LS. DNA, RG59, Dip. Disp., France, vol. 22 (M34, R25). Received February 16, 1826. Extract published in Manning (arr.), *Diplomatic Correspondence . . . Latin-American Nations,* II, 1416-17.

From CONDY RAGUET, Rio de Janeiro, no. 3. Reports that a defeat of the Brazilian Army in the Banda Oriental has eventuated in the incorporation of that province with "The Republick of the United Provinces of the River Plate," in a Brazilian blockade of the ports of the United Provinces, and in a formal declaration of war. Expresses a fear of violations of neutral rights as well as of great loss to the commerce of the United States, cites the case of the *Spermo* (above, Raguet to Secretary of State, March 11, 1825, note) as an example of the disregard for neutral rights to be expected in this contest, and declares that a United States naval force in the area "is absolutely essential for the protection of our citizens and commerce. . . ." Notes changes in the Ministry of Brazil, that a treaty between France and Brazil, under negotiation, has not been concluded, and that the Empress has given birth to a son. Encloses copies of various documents, including the Brazilian proclamation of blockade and a statement by Raguet to the Brazilian Government "upon the doctrine of blockades, as maintained by the United States." ALS. DNA, RG59, Dip. Disp., Brazil, vol. 4 (M212, R6). Published in *American State Papers, Foreign Relations,* VI, 1022-23. The Empress of Brazil was Maria Leopoldina Josepha Carolina, daughter of Francis I, Emperor of Austria. Her son ascended the throne as Peter II, Emperor of Brazil, in 1831 and ruled until 1889, when he was overthrown. On the Brazilian treaty with France, see below, Raguet to Clay, January 17, 1826, note.

MISCELLANEOUS LETTERS   December 23, 1825

From JOHN FORSYTH, "Committee of Foreign Relations H. of R." Requests, on behalf of the committee, copies "of the Statement presented in October 1809 to the Russian Govt. by Levett Harris Consul Genl. of the United States of the claims of the owners of the ship Commerce . . . , also the answer of the Russian Govt. to the reclamations of our ministers in favor of the owners of said Vessels [*sic*]." ALS. DNA, RG59, Misc. Letters (M179, R63). Published in *American State Papers, Foreign Relations,* V, 785. Cf. above, Hobart to Clay, December 15, 1825, note.

APPLICATIONS, RECOMMENDATIONS   December 23, 1825

THOMAS CORWIN, Lebanon (Ohio), states that, in accordance with a suggestion made by Clay when in Lebanon last summer, (William) Miner is about to forward papers in application for a clerkship in the State Department. Refers to the recommendation signed by Corwin and others, (above) July 16, 1825. ALS. DNA, RG59, A. and R. (MR3).

WILLIAM L. REANEY, Boston, solicits appointment to the Boston customs service, "should the Agency in Porto Rico have been disposed of"; adds that he would be willing "to go to any part of the world in the Country's service. . . ." ALS. *Ibid.* Cf. above, Van Ness to Clay, September 7, 1825, note.

From J[ames] B[rown]

My dear Sir   Paris Decr. 24. 1825.

I was highly gratified by having received from you a letter of the 15 ulto[1] in which as you have not complained of ill health, you have left me to infer that you are well. I was afraid that the weak state in which you found yourself on your return from the West, followed by heart rending calamities, and irritated by the incessant calls of business might have overpowered you and deprived your own immediate family of a head, but also your dependant [sic] relations of a friend and kind protector. I am happy to learn that Mrs. Clay had met the shafts of misfortunes [sic] with her accustomed fortitude, and hope that in the sympathy of kind friends and neighbors, and in domestic cares, her mind will gradually resume its accustomed elasticity and cheerfulness.

I regret as much as any one the obstacles which have been thrown in the way of our claims as well here as in other places. As the French Government yet offers to treat on them in connexion with the treaty we are saved from the mortification which would have followed a direct refusal to settle them   You seem to think that strong measures will probably be adopted by Congress and intimate the possibility that reprisals may be made upon France. I think it may well be doubted whether the present moment would be the one which we ought to select even were things in other respects such as would recommend that measure. Although England has believed it to be her interest to separate herself on some points of policy from the Holy Alliance yet I am very far from feeling any great confidence in her friendship for the United States— It is obvious too that she dreads a war, and is using all the means in her power to maintain friendly relations with the Continental powers. At no period have the sovereigns of Europe appeared more anxious to cement their friendship and to bind more closely their engagements to give material support than at the present time— The shock occasioned by the death of the Emperor Alexander and the sollicitude [sic] evinced as to the policy which Constantine[2] may pursue manifest an anxiety that the bonds of the Holy Alliance should remain unbroken— In one sentiment they all appear to unite a dislike for free institutions and as they consider the United States as at the head of them they would do all in their power to mar our prosperity and retard our growth— If we take any step to make any reprisals on France we may expect from all the other powers of the Continent if not open hostilities, at least enmity and any indirect assistance which they can give to France. The French navy is already strong in its number of vessels of war; and sailors will be furnished from every quarter— From the sixty millions already appropriated to the navy, this Country is enabled to send out a very formidable armament without adding a single sous [*sic*] to the public burthens. Privateering too would be commenced on an extensive scale, and the Capitans [*sic*] and seamen of every Country would be found embarked in it— England, our commercial rival, would see this state of things with indifference if not with pleasure and the consequences of it would be such as we ought seriously to reflect on before we take any measure which may lead to hostilities. By waiting some time we take the chances of a rupture among the Allied powers. In that event we may be felt has [*sic*] throwing our weight in favor of one of the Contending parties— In maritime operations of a hostile character, the French have less to fear as to their commerce than ourselves, and they have no exposed positions which we Could take or even seriously menace— If we do not mean to *strike* we ought to avoid threats which can only excite bad feelings without producing any favorable effect on our negociations— I confess my own opinion is that however provoking this conduct may be considered we ought to bear it a little longer in order as well to gain strength ourselves and to wait for more favorable circumstances, an event which I think by no means improbable or very distant—

Mr. Somerville[3] continues to decline and although he yet speaks of going to the South of France yet I greatly fear he will never leave Paris. The last accounts from Greece still leave some room for hope that they may hold out this winter. The death of Alexander and the hope it may inspire of aid from Russia may encouarge them to persevere in defending themselves themselves [*sic*] to the last extremity—

The Chambers will meet on the 30 of January and the strength of the present Ministry will be tried. It is said that upon Mr de Villeles offering his resignation to the King he expressed his determination not to change his Ministers so long as they were supported by Majorities in the two Chambers. The majority in favor of Ministers in the Chamber of Deputies is certain   in the House of Peers it is doubtful. It has been the practice to confer the Peerage on Ministers who have lost their places, and as the changes in the Ministry have been very frequent since the restoration, the number of Ex-Ministers in that house is considerable— These are generally in the opposition and many of them have great weight from their virtues and Talents—

The belief gains ground that the Emperor Constantine will pursue a different course in relation to Turkey from that followed by his predecessor. I am not sure that his doing so would be considered as a cause of war by all the other powers. England would I be-leive [*sic*] strengthen herself in the Mediterranean and remain at peace. A few weeks will throw some light on this subject, and you will hear from me.

As Mr King[4] transacted business last week at the foreign Affairs [*sic*] I hope his health has improved—

Mrs. B joins in afte. salutations to Mrs. C.   Yours truly.   J. B.

ALS. DLC-HC (DNA, M212, R2).   [1] *I.e.*, November 14, 1825.
[2] Cf. above, Middleton to Clay, December 18, 1825, note.
[3] William C. Somerville.   [4] Rufus King.

DIPLOMATIC NOTES   December 24, 1825

To [C. D. E. J. BANGEMAN] HUYGENS. Acknowledges receipt of his note of De-cember 12; expresses surprise that he has "no instructions on the subject of the inequality of duties"; and states that the President will defer action under the legislation referred to in Clay's last note (above, December 10) until Bangeman Huygens receives an answer to his inquiry. Copy. DNA, RG59, Notes to Foreign Legations, vol. 3, pp. 246-47 (M38, R3). ALI draft, in CSmH. Published in *American State Papers, Foreign Relations*, VI, 375-76.

From the BARON DE MAREUIL, Washington. Expresses regret that the Federal Government has found no means of ensuring reciprocity in the application of Article 6 of the Convention of 1822, relative to deserters; notes disagreement on the meaning of the convention and the failure of Clay's assurances of No-vember 7 (above) to prevent a new refusal by the Mayor of Norfolk (of whose letter, of December 16, to Mareuil a copy is enclosed) ; states that in this case, as well as in those referred to in his letter of November 17, he finds it im-possible to admit that the consul must address himself to the United States court; argues that the consul can only make his representation to the minister of his country, who in turn should approach the Federal Government, and that, if the cabinet cannot regulate the conduct of magistrates, it is the duty of the Federal Government to seek judgment from the courts; and appeals again, through Clay, to the justice of the President for the full execution of the en-gagements between France and the United States. LS. DNA, RG59, Notes from French Legation, vol. 9 (M53, R7). See above, Clay to Mareuil, December 19, 1825.

From FR[ANCIS]CO DION[ISI]O VIVES, Havana. Replies, to Clay's "agreeable letter of the 14th. of November last, . . . that J. Baker, Mate of the American vessel Thalia who was put in prison in this city, has been set at liberty by the competent tribunal which has heard his cause; and that the seven sailors . . . have been acquitted. . . ." Congratulates Clay upon his "new office" and ex-presses "friendship and high consideration" for him. LS, with translation. DNA, RG76, Records re French Spoliations.

MISCELLANEOUS LETTERS   December 24, 1825

To SAMUEL L. SOUTHARD. States, in reply to Southard's letter (below) of this date, that Dr. S(amuel) D. Heap's resignation should be accepted. ALS. DNA, RG45, Misc. Letters Received, 1825, vol. 7, p. 156.

To SAMUEL L. SOUTHARD, Secretary of the Navy. States "observations and orders to be communicated to Captain Hull," concerning his actions in response to the Peruvian decree "issued on the 17th. of April last." LS. *Ibid.,* p. 158. After the introductory paragraph, the text of the document differs from that published above, Clay to Hull, December 20, 1825, only in accordance with the role of Southard as intermediary in transmitting the orders.

From H[UTCHINS] G. BURTON, Raleigh (North Carolina). Requests transmittal of a letter of thanks to Lord Teignmouth, president of the British Bible Society, for Bibles, in various languages, presented to the University of North Carolina. ALS. DNA, RG59, Misc. Letters (M179, R63). John Shore, 1st Baron Teignmouth, had served nearly thirty years as an administrator of the East India Company in India (as governor general, 1793-1798). In 1807 he had been appointed a member of the Privy Council and of the colonial Board of Control, but his interests during his later life centered upon religious and philanthropic activities. He had been elected in 1804 as the first president of the British and Foreign Bible Society and retained that office until his death in 1834.

From EDGAR MACON, "Gadsby's Hotel Washington." States that he has learned, since arriving in Washington, that Judge (Joseph L.) Smith has dismissed him from the office of United States attorney for East Florida and has appointed a replacement; inquires whether he is still regarded, by the State Department, as the incumbent and asks immediate notification if it be thought proper to suspend him; requests an investigation into his official conduct; and reveals that the object of his presence in Washington is to prefer charges against Smith. ALS. DNA, RG59, Misc. Letters (M179, R63). Published in Carter (ed.), *Territorial Papers,* XXIII, 392-93. Around 1819 John Gadsby had moved from Baltimore to Washington, where he now operated a hotel at Pennsylvania Avenue and Nineteenth Street. On the issue of Macon's dismissal, see below, Clay to Macon, April 6, 1826; Macon to Clay, April 8, 25, 1826.

From SAMUEL L. SOUTHARD, Navy Department. Encloses a copy of a letter from Dr. S(amuel) D. Heap and inquires whether Heap's resignation should be accepted. LS. DNA, RG59, Misc. Letters (M179, R63). In the enclosure Heap states his intention of accepting the appointment offered him by the State Department and, in case the Senate refuses to confirm that appointment so long as he holds a commission in the Navy, requests that this letter be considered his resignation of that commission. Cf. above, Coxe to Secretary of State, April 28, 1825, note; Southard to Clay, December 20, 1825, note.

APPLICATIONS, RECOMMENDATIONS   December 24, 1825

W[ILLIAM] S. YOUNG, Washington, recommends appointment of William R. Abbott, editor of the Henderson (Kentucky) *Columbian,* to publish the laws. ALS. DNA, RG59, P. and D. of L. Young, a native of Nelson County, Kentucky, a graduate of Jefferson Seminary (one of the institutions later merged to form the University of Louisville), and a physician, had settled at Elizabethtown, Kentucky, in 1814. He was elected to two successive terms in Congress and served from 1825 until his death in 1827. Abbott had begun publication of the

Columbian at Henderson in 1822 and remained identified with its management until some time after 1830, when it was merged under new identification. He did not receive the appointment here requested.

To Churchill C. Cambreleng

The Hon. C. C. Cambreling [*sic*], H. R.
Sir,   Department of State, December 25th. 1825.
I have perused the Letter which you left with me, and which is herewith returned, respecting the construction put at Halifax upon the late British Act of Parliament opening the trade and intercourse between the British American Colonies and foreign Countries. And I have also examined the Acts of Parliament of the 4th. and 5th. Geo: the 4-th, referred to in the fifth Section of the above mentioned Act.[1] The result is a belief that the Halifax construction is not that which was intended by the British Government, or, if it be, that it was designed by an order in Council to except the trade and intercourse with the United States from the operation of the Act when so interpreted. I should strongly incline to think, but for the opposite view entertained at Halifax, that the Act to regulate the trade of the British possessions abroad, passed in July last, did not intend to disturb or affect the trade between the British American Colonies and the United States, but meant to leave that trade on the footing which it was put by the aforesaid Act of the 4th. Geo: the 4th. and the subsequent Act of indemnity of the 5th. Geo: the 4th..

That the British Government did not look forward to such an operation of the Act of Parliament, as is about to be enforced at Halifax, I think clear from the following considerations.
1st. It would be inconsistent with professions made by that Government to this, and with negociations between the two Governments contemplated if not yet resumed.
2d. No notification has been given at Washington, or at London, of such a purpose as that which, for the first time, is indicated at Halifax.
3d. The British Minister here[2] is unadvised by his Government of any intention to close the Colonial Ports against our Vessels, and
4th. No information has been received here from any British Colonial port, except Halifax, of such intention.

If the Halifax construction be correct, I am persuaded that the British Government must have intended to have created an exception to our trade, by an order in Council, which had not arrived at the date of the last advices from Halifax.

If I am right in that conjecture, the order may yet reach that place before, or a few days after, the day fixed (the 5th. of January next) for the commencement of the Act.

I am Your Obedient Servant,   H. CLAY.

Copy. DNA, RG59, Dom. Letters, vol. 21, pp. 342-43. On the outcome of the Halifax action, here discussed, see below, Vaughan to Clay, February 18, 1826. On the broader question, the effect of the British legislation of July, 1825, see below, Gallatin to Clay, August 19, 1826; Clay to Gallatin, October 12, 1826; Gallatin to Clay, November 8, 1826.

1 See above, Rush to Secretary of State, March 26, 1825, note. The fifth section of the act of July 5, 1825, provided that nothing in that legislation should "extend to repeal or in any way alter or affect" the act of 4 *Geo. IV*, "intituled, *An Act to authorize His Majesty, under certain Circumstances, to regulate the Duties and Drawbacks on Goods imported or exported in Foreign Vessels, and to exempt certain Foreign Vessels from Pilotage*," or the act of 5 *Geo. IV*, "among other Things, to amend the last mentioned Act, and that all Trade and Intercourse between the *British* Possessions and all Foreign Countries shall be subject to the Powers granted to His Majesty by those Acts." The relevant act of 4 *Geo. IV* was c. 77, enacted July 18, 1823, which authorized either the removal of duties and drawbacks or the imposition of discriminating charges in relation to foreign shipping, dependent upon the reciprocal policies of the respective nations concerning shipments in British vessels. The relevant act of 5 *Geo. IV* was c. 1, enacted March 5, 1824, which had given statutory authority to the British Order in Council levying a tonnage duty upon vessels of the United States entering British American or West Indies colonies "equal (as nearly as may be) to the Difference between the Tonnage Duty payable by Vessels of the United States, and the higher Tonnage Duty payable by *British* Vessels entering any of the Ports of the said United States from any Ports of His Majesty's Dominions in *America* or the *West Indies*. . . ." It had also authorized imposition of additional tonnage duties to countervail such differences and the removal of duties when proof was provided that British vessels were accorded "no other or higher Tonnage Duties on their Entrance into the Ports of such Foreign Country. . . ."

2 Charles R. Vaughan.

From Amos Kendall

Dear Sir,   Franklin Cty Ky Dec. 25th 1825

Some months ago the account of the Editors of the Argus against your department for publishing the Acts of Congress passed at their last session, was forwarded, and no return has ever been received. Will you have the goodness to enquire of your clerks whether it was ever received and whether an answer was returned.[1]

Our Legislature has had a short and boisterous session. As you will see, they have done nothing to allay our judicial troubles, and we have the prospect of another severe contest.[2] It is fortunate that they have postponed the Congressional election one year.[3] It will measurably prevent the presidential question being thrown into this controversy.

You will have seen, that Mr. Crittenden offered resolutions approving of your course; but he never called them up. I have no doubt they would have passed, but not without powerful opposition.[4] I thought it imprudent to offer them.

The defeat of David White by Marshall[5] has produced a strong sensation here. It was thought that your friends would support him.

I think you will see him beat Crittenden for the Legislature next year.[6]

I am about to marry and settle down here at my mills.[7] You have my most hearty thanks for the place you have offered me,[8] and I should have accepted it with much pleasure, had the salary been adequate. At this moment, no consideration would induce me to leave Kentucky. I feel that I have a duty to perform to myself and my principles, which it would be criminal to abandon. I am preparing to perform it with entire self devotion. But it is the last effort of the kind I will ever make, unless I change my determination. I long for a quiet and peaceful life, and after August next I intend to seek it.

It is with concern I was lately informed that your health is bad. I hope it is not such as to endanger you.

Give my best remembrances to Mrs. Clay. I sympathize with her most sincerely for the loss of her children.[9]

If you have leisure, it would give me pleasure to hear from you occasionally.   Your friend   AMOS KENDALL

ALS. DLC-HC (DNA, M212, R2). Addressed to Clay.
[1] A letter with a draft in payment for running a special advertisement had been sent to Kendall by W(illiam) Browne on August 31, 1825. This settlement may have occasioned confusion relative to payment for the larger account, which was finally transmitted by Browne on January 7, 1826. Copies of both letters in DNA, RG59, Dom. Letters, vol. 2, pp. 140, 238-39 (M40, R19).
[2] The legislature had adjourned on December 21, two days after the house of representatives by a vote of 52 to 36 had rejected a motion to give second reading to a proposal, approved in the senate by a vote of 22 to 14, designed as a compromise of the court controversy (cf. above, Blair to Clay, November 28, 1825). The measure had provided for repeal of the act of 1824 reorganizing the court of appeals (see above, III, 902n) and for establishment of still another new court, to consist initially of six members but ultimately of four as vacancies should reduce the number. It had been intended that the bench would thus be composed of both the old and the new court judges. Ky. H. of Reps., *Journal, 1825*, pp. 401-402; Lexington *Kentucky Reporter*, January 2, 1826, reprinting item from Frankfort *Commentator*. See also below, Blair to Clay, January 4, 1826, note.
[3] By act approved December 21. Ky. Gen. Assy., *Acts, 1825*, pp. 139-40.
[4] See below, Crittenden to Clay, December 26, 1825.
[5] See above, Blair to Clay, August 30, 1825, note.
[6] Both White (who received more votes than Crittenden) and Crittenden were defeated in that election.
[7] Kendall and Jane Kyle, of Georgetown, Kentucky, were married January 5, 1826.
[8] Cf. above, Kendall to Clay, October 4, 1825; Clay to Kendall, October 18, 1825.
[9] Eliza Clay; Susan Clay Duralde.

INSTRUCTIONS AND DISPATCHES   December 25, 1825

From JOHN M. FORBES, Buenos Aires, no. 29. Reports the Brazilian declaration of war "against this Province" (cf. above, Raguet to Clay, December 23, 1825); requests instructions relating to the effect of the Brazilian blockade on American vessels; states that he has warned citizens of the United States against military service under foreign flags; notes the struggle among local political rivals and the financial crisis faced by the national bank; predicts, on the basis of the failure of mining ventures in which Englishmen have invested, "that mutual distrust will Soon Succeed the honey moon which has so long existed between England and this Country"; and refers to a proclamation and letters indicating that Bolívar will "resign the Supreme Executive Government of Lower Peru" and devote himself to completing "the organization of that of *Bolivia.*" LS. DNA, RG59, Dip. Disp., Argentina, vol. 2 (M69, R3). Continued on December 26, 29, 31, 1825, and January 3, 9, 24, 27, 1826. Received April 11, 1826. Published in Espil (comp.), *Once Años en Buenos Aires,* 403-11.

From RUFUS KING, London, no. 15. Refers to a communication from (Joel R.) Poinsett concerning French intrigue in Mexico (see above, Poinsett to Clay, September 22, 1825), which (George) Canning characterized, in an interview with King, as "without foundation, and without credit." Reports that Canning observed that Nesselrode's reply to (Henry) Middleton (see above, Middleton to Clay, September 8, 1825) "was of the Draft of the Emperor" (Alexander I) and gave less credit to it than Middleton had ascribed. Notes that Canning believes the death of the Emperor (see above, Middleton to Clay, December 18, 1825, note) has produced "a Mighty change" on which it is useless to speculate until Constantine's views become known. States that Canning considers Clay's "Dispatches, concerning our past correspondence . . . [see above, Clay to King, October 17, 26, 1825] and the Instructions to Mr. [James] Brown of 25 October" satisfactory and promised to send a courier to the British Ambassador (Lord Granville) at Paris with "Instructions to act in Conformity with the opinion contained in the Note, to be delivered by Mr. Brown to the French Government." Informed that (Henry U.) Addington has been named to replace Stratford Canning as (William) Huskisson's colleague in discussions "respecting the Colonial Trade, and other Matters, left unfinished," King reminds Clay that he has "neither Powers nor Instructions" in this regard. Acknowledges receipt of Clay's "Despatches up to No 9 [November 15, 1825], with the exception of No. 4 [August 31, 1825], which has not come to hand." Encloses a copy of a note to Canning relative to "the Mixed Commission at Washington." LS. DNA, RG59, Dip. Disp., Great Britain, vol. 32 (M30, R28). Extract published in Manning (arr.), *Diplomatic Correspondence . . . Latin-American Nations,* III, 1576-77. Received February 14, 1826.

From JOHN RODGERS, "U. S. SHIP N CAROLINA PORT MAHON." Encloses a copy of a letter received from (David) Offley, United States consul at Smyrna, which corroborates the information given in Rodgers' letter to Clay of October 14; states that he will be at Gibraltar with his squadron about April 1 "in readiness to execute any further commands"; and, for recent information concerning "the political relations of Greece," refers Clay to the report of Captain (John B.) Nicholson, which has been sent to (Samuel L.) Southard. ALS. DNA, RG59, Dip. Disp., Turkey, vol. 1, part 1 (M46, R2). Nicholson, a native of Virginia, had been commissioned in 1817 as "Master Commandant" of the sloop *Ontario,* assigned to the Mediterranean Squadron. He was not formally raised to the rank of captain until 1828 and subsequently attained that of commodore.

MISCELLANEOUS LETTERS   December 25, 1825

From JARED SPARKS, Boston. Transmits a letter from William Shaler to Clay (above, May 25, 1825) and inquires whether Clay has any objection to publication of extracts from Shaler's consular journal. ALS. DNA, RG59, Misc. Letters (M179, R63). Sparks, born in Connecticut and graduated from Harvard University, had been a Unitarian minister from 1819 to 1823, serving as chaplain in the United States House of Representatives the last year, and then had acquired the *North American Review,* which he edited until 1829. Continuing active in journalistic and literary affairs and as a public lecturer, he became professor of ancient and modern languages at Harvard in 1838 and the following year organized there the first department of history in an American university. From 1849 to 1853 he was president of Harvard. He published extensively as a biographer and as a compiler of manuscripts. Sparks appears to have acted as Shaler's agent in arranging for publication of the latter's book. On December 31, 1825, Daniel Brent, at Clay's direction, answered Sparks' letter by granting Shaler the desired permission to use "the letters in question" and to publish "any part of his Official Journal," but noting that the Department has no record of "any Letter from the President to the Dey" in 1816 and stating that "a transcript of it [if available] would be very acceptable to this Department." Copy. DNA, RG59, Dom. Letters, vol. 21, pp. 234-35 (M40, R19).

To John A. King

Dear Sir   (Private and inofficial)   Washington 26h. Decr. 1825

I transmit you herewith two letters written by Mr. Geo. H. Norton[1] to Robert S. Rose esquire respecting a peerage and estate to which Mr. Norton believes or hopes himself entitled. My object in sending them to you is to request that you will obtain such information as you can and transmit it to me. This I presume you may do, without much trouble.

I also send herewith a letter from a friend of mine at Chillicothe (Mr. Creighton)[2] inclosing a note on a British officer. The letter explains its object. If you can, *without subjecting yourself or me to any expence,* have it collected or put it in a train of collection, you will oblige me.

Others will have informed you that, after making various demonstrations of a disposition to defeat the nomination both of your father and yourself, it has been approved by the Senate with scarcely any shew of opposition.[3]   I am with great respect Your ob. servant

John A. King Esqr.

AL (signature removed). NHi.
[1] Probably George Hatley Norton, of Virginia, the nephew of George, Wilson Cary, Philip Norborne, and John Nicholas. The Norton family had been prominent merchants of London, England, and Yorktown, Virginia, in the eighteenth century.
[2] William Creighton, Jr. The letter has not been found.
[3] The nominations of both had been confirmed, on December 20, without recorded vote.

To Henry Middleton

No. 2. Henry Middleton, Envoy Extraordinary, and
Minister Plenipotentiary, U. S. St. Petersburg.

Sir.   Department of State Washington 26 Decr. 1825.

Your despatches, Nos. 48 and 49,[1] have been duly received and submitted to the President. He sees, with much satisfaction, that the appeal which has been made, through you, to the Emperor of Russia, to employ his friendly offices in the endeavor to bring about a peace between Spain and the new American Republics, has not been without favourable effect. Considering the intimate and friendly relations which exist between the Emperor and his Allies, it was, perhaps, not to be expected that, previous to consultations with them, language more explicit should be held than that which is contained in Count Nesselrode's Note. Although very guarded, it authorizes the belief that the preponderating influence of Russia has been thrown into the scale of peace. Notwithstanding predictions of a contrary result, confidently made by Mr. Secretary Canning,[2] this decision of the Emperor corresponds with the anticipations which have been constantly entertained here ever since the President resolved to invoke his intervention. It affords strong evidence, both of his humanity and his enlightened judgement. All events out of Spain, seem now to unite in this tendency towards peace; and the fall of the Castle of San Juan d' Ulloa, which capitulated on the 18th. day of last month,[3] cannot fail to have a powerful effect within that Kingdom. We are informed that when information of it reached the Havanna [sic], it produced great and general sensation; and that the local Government immediately despatched a fast sailing vessel to Cadiz to communicate the event, and in its name, to implore the King immediately to terminate the war, and acknowledge the new Republics, as the only means left of preserving Cuba to the Monarchy.[4]

In considering what further measures could be adopted by this Government to second the pacific exertions which, it is not doubted, the Emperor is now employing, it has appeared to the President that a suspension of any military expedition which both, or either, of the Republics of Colombia and Mexico may be preparing against Cuba and Porto Rico, might have a good auxiliary influence. Such a suspension indeed, seemed, [sic] to be due to the friendly purposes of the Emperor. I have, accordingly, addressed official Notes to the Ministers of those Republics, accredited here, recommending it to their Governments;[5] an extract from one of which (the other being, substantially, the same) is herewith transmitted. You will observe it intimated in those notes, that other Governments may feel themselves urged by a sense of their interests and duties, to interpose, in the event of an invasion of the Islands, or of contingencies which may accompany or follow it. On this subject, it is proper that we should be perfectly understood by Russia. For ourselves, we desire no change in the possession of Cuba, as has been heretofore stated.[6] We cannot allow a transfer of the Island to any European Power.

But if Spain should refuse to conclude a peace, and obstinately resolve on continuing the war, although we do not desire that either Colombia or Mexico should acquire the Island of Cuba, the President cannot see any justifiable ground on which we can forcibly interfere. Upon the hypothesis of an unnecessary protraction of the war, imputable to Spain, it is evident that Cuba will be her only point d'appui in this hemisphere. How can we interpose, on that supposition, against the party clearly having right on his side, in order to restrain or defeat a lawful operation of war? If the war against the Islands should be conducted by those Republics in a desolating manner; if, contrary to all expectation, they should put arms in the hands of one race of the inhabitants, to destroy the lives of another; if, in short, they should countenance and encourage excesses and examples, the contagion of which, from our neighbourhood, would be dangerous to our quiet and safety, the Government of the United States might feel itself called upon to interpose its power. But, it is not apprehended that any of those contingencies will arise, and consequently, it is most probable that the United States, should the war continue, will remain, hereafter, as they have been, heretofore, neutral observers of the progress of its events.

You will be pleased to communicate the contents of this despatch to the Russian Government. And as, from the very nature of the object which has induced the President to recommend to the Governments of Colombia and Mexico a suspension of their expeditions against the Spanish Islands, no definite time could be suggested for the duration of that suspension, if it should be acceded to, it must be allowed, on all hands, that it ought not to be unnecessarily protracted. Therefore, you will represent to the Government of Russia, the expediency of obtaining a decision from Spain as early as possible, in respect to its disposition to conclude a peace.

I am your obedient Servant   H. CLAY.

Copy. DNA, RG59, Dip. Instr., vol. 10, pp. 424-26. (M77, R5). ALI draft, in DLC-HC (DNA, M212, R7).   1 Above, July 27, September 8, 1825.
2 Cf. above, King to Clay, August 9, September 18, 1825.
3 See above, Clay to Poinsett, March 26, 1825, note.
4 See above, Clark to Clay, December 7, 1825.
5 See above, Clay to Salazar, December 20, 1825.
6 See above, Clay to Middleton, May 10, 1825.

Check to William J. Stone

26 Decr. 1825

Pay to William J. Stone or order fifteen dollars and eighteen Cents. Cashr. of the Off. of Dt. & Dt. Washington[1]   H. CLAY

ADS. DLC-TJC (DNA, M212, R16). Endorsed on verso by Stone, a Washington engraver and stationer.   1 Richard Smith.

From John J. Crittenden

Dr Sir,   Frankfort Decr. 26th 1825

In sitting down to write to you I really feel all the consciousness of an offender against the rules of good correspondence, if
not of good manners— It is an offence, however, which in our instance, so evidently carries its own punishment with it, & I am myself so much the looser [*sic*] by it, that I do not feel that I deserve
to undergo a much greater penance.

Our Legislature has adjourned, & we have failed in all our great
objects, & in those measures that were necessary to tranquilise the
country[1]— All our proceedings have been made known to you
through the public prints— The end of all is that we are in a state
approaching more nearly than ever to Anarchy— We have made
"confusion worse confounded"— The obstinacy & perverseness of
the Governor[2] & a few Senators have defeated the public Will, &
prevented the restoration of order & constitutional government.
We look with confidence to the people, & trust the next election will
place it beyond the power of a factious administration to do much
more mischief, or much longer to continue the distractions of the
country. We, (the majority of the House of representatives) have
not perhaps in all things, acted most forbearingly or prudently, but
upon the whole we think ourselves well prepared for the ensuing
political campaign— I shall engage in it with infinite reluctance,
but there seems to be no alternative— If Desha & his party should
succeed, I do not really think I could endure to live under their
domination. I do not permit myself to beleive [*sic*] such an event
probable.

I introduced into the House of representatives some resolutions
expressive of our undiminished confidence in you &c and of our
acquiescence in the election of Mr. Adams & our sanguine hopes of
a wise administration &c[3]   About the time I intended to call them
up, the House occupied by our representatives took fire & was burned
down, and the remainder of the session was such a scene of hurry
& confusion, that there was no suitable opportunity of acting upon
them[4]— I did not wish moreover to make these resolutions a criterion for the division of our State parties, & I found that every
means had been used upon the members of the relief party, to make
them beleive that the interest of their party required them to vote
against the resolutions— And many good men would have done so,
under these excitements and artifices, & to have promoted other
factious & factitious purposes — I have no doubt but that the resolutions would have been carried, and in our house certainly by a
considerable majority, but the division that would have existed,

would have done you & Mr. Adams injustice, as it would have proceeded principally from the factitious considerations growing out
of our State politicks, & not from any opposition to the resolutions
taken abstractedly.

Your best friends here under these circumstances, thought it best
to defer the resolutions untill the next session, when we hope for
a representation less entangled by sinister artifices, & more truely
[*sic*] speaking the sentiments of the country—

There is no doubt a disposition here, & that patronised by our
Govnr. as I beleive, to raise the standard of Genl Jackson, against
you & the administration.— The object of it is not so much, as I
think, to help Jackson, as it is to recruit the ranks of the relief party
& to sustain if possible the governor & his faction. They feel their
situation to be hazardous in the extreme, if not desperate, & they
are willing to draw aid from any quarter— And they can think of
no other resource— It will fail them, & in my judgment they will
prejudice Jackson.

The Presidents message[5] has been read here with very general
approbation and applause— There are some cavillers of the school
alluded to above— But I have only heard their criticisms mentioned, to be derided, & the message praised.

Accept my best wishes for your health & fame   Yr Friend
Hon: H Clay Secty: State   J J CRITTENDEN

ALS. NcD.
[1] See above, Kendall to Clay, December 25, 1825.
[2] Joseph Desha.
[3] Presented on December 3, the proposed resolutions had also stated that the General
Assembly of Kentucky regarded "with indignation, the aspersions against the character and conduct of their distinguished fellow-citizen, HENRY CLAY. . . ." Ky. H. of
Reps., *Journal, 1825*, p. 225.
[4] Following the destruction of the Kentucky State House, in November, 1824 (see
above, III, 878, 879n, 881n), the house of representatives had met in a Frankfort
church until that building, too, had burned, on December 12, 1825.
[5] The annual message of December 5, 1825.

From John and James Williams

The Honble. Henry Clay   Balto. 26 Decr. 1825.
Sir

Above we hand you a a [*sic*] receipt for One Sofa and four Columns[1] shipped per Sloop Brothers Captn. Moffitt by order of Christopher Hughs [*sic*] Esqr, which we hope you will receive safe—

We are very respectfully Sir Your most obdt Servts.

JNO & JAS WILLIAMS

ES. DLC-TJC (DNA, M212, R13). Endorsement on receipt, from John Moffitt to
John and James Williams, Baltimore, December 24, 1825. The Williamses were a

mercantile firm of Baltimore. Moffitt was master of vessels sailing from Havre-de-
Grace or Baltimore for over a quarter of a century.
  1 Cf. above, Hughes to Clay, December 1, 1825; Clay to Hughes, December 18, 1825.

DIPLOMATIC NOTES   December 26, 1825

To the BARON DE TUYLL. Transmits, according to promise of "Saturday last,"
an extract from Clay's note of December 20 to the Colombian Minister (José
Maria Salazar). Adds that "A similar note was, at the same time addressed to the
Mexican Minister" (Pablo Obregón). DNA, RG59, Notes to Foreign Legations,
vol. 3, p. 247 (M38, R3). ALI draft, in CSmH. Published in Manning (arr.),
Diplomatic Correspondence . . . Latin-American Nations, I, 264-65.

From the BARON DE TUYLL, Washington, "Confidential." Acknowledges "receipt
of the important paper" promised him on Saturday. LS. DNA, RG59, Notes
from Russian Legation, vol. 1 (M39, R1).

INSTRUCTIONS AND DISPATCHES   December 26, 1825

From HENRY MIDDLETON, St. Petersburg, no. 53. Encloses two "papers" from
Count Nesselrode; notes some discontent among "the Guards at the proposed
change in the Succession." Middleton thinks the matter "will be settled without
much disturbance." ALS. DNA, RG59, Dip. Disp., Russia (M35, R10). Dated
December 14/26, 1825. Received March 18, 1826. The enclosures include a copy
of a note from Nesselrode to Middleton and a copy, transmitted therewith, of a
"SUPPLEMENT EXTRAORDINAIRE" of the "JOURNAL DE ST. PETERSBOURG,"
announcing Constantine's renunciation of the right of succession to the imperial
throne and the accession of Nicholas as Emperor. See above, Middleton to Clay,
December 18, 1825, note.

MISCELLANEOUS LETTERS   December 26, 1825

From BORIE AND LAGUERENNE, Philadelphia. Refer to their letter of December
13 to Clay; express disappointment in not having, because of the absence of
the Mexican Minister from Washington, "something certain & official" to report
to their friends in Alvarado; state that the threat of interruption of navigation
of the Delaware River by ice has caused them to send their vessel to Alvarado and
to submit, under protest enclosed herewith, "to the Mexican Consul's Certificates"; and list in a postscript other vessels which have sailed from Philadelphia for Alvarado or Veracruz, on which the vice consul has collected
$50 to $60 and obtained information advantageous to his own shipments of
goods. LS. DNA, RG59, Cons. Disp., Veracruz, vol. 1 (M183, R1).

From JOSEPH C. MORGAN, Philadelphia. Requests aid in collecting from the
Government of the Netherlands on bills of exchange drawn by S. H. Van Kempen,
deceased, former consul of the Netherlands at Tripoli, the bills having been
protested for non-acceptance by the Government of the Netherlands and, after
successive endorsements, now being held by Morgan. States that the Government
of the Netherlands has already been informed, by John Quincy Adams, when
Secretary of State, of this demand. ALS. DNA, RG59, Misc. Letters (M179,
R63). Morgan, not identified. On December 31, Daniel Brent, at Clay's direction,

informed Morgan that (Christopher) Hughes would be given instructions to prosecute the claim. Copy. DNA, RG59, Dom. Letters, vol. 21, p. 233 (M40, R19).

From ALBION K. PARRIS, "State of Maine. Executive Department, Portland." Replies to Clay's letter of November 25 by transmitting copies of a resolution of the Maine Legislature "respecting the settlers on St. John and Madaweska Rivers, under which the Agent of this State acted," of a resolution of the Massachusetts Legislature "respecting the same," and of "the Report of the Land Agent of Maine, detailing particularly the transactions of the two Agents [James Irish and George W. Coffin] under" these resolutions. LS. DNA, RG76, Northeast Boundary, Misc. Papers, env. 4.

From BUSHROD WASHINGTON, "Mount Vernon." Requests Clay to forward, "by the first safe conveyance to Paris," a book containing copies of (George) Washington's letters to Lafayette. ALS. DNA, RG59, Misc. Letters (M179, R63).

APPLICATIONS, RECOMMENDATIONS   December 26, 1825

L[EMUEL] SAWYER, Washington, recommends appointment of James Wills, editor of the Edenton, North Carolina, *Gazette,* to publish the laws. ALS. DNA, RG59, P. and D. of L. Wills had been a journalist at Edenton since before the turn of the century; he did not receive the appointment requested.

DIPLOMATIC NOTES   December 27, 1825

From C. D. E. J. BANGEMAN HUYGENS, Washington. Acknowledges receipt of Clay's note of December 24, which he will hasten to transmit to his government. ANS, in French, with translation in State Department file. DNA, RG59, Notes from Netherlands Legation, vol. 1 (M56, R1):

From C. D. E. J. BANGEMAN HUYGENS, Washington. Protests against the detention of a Dutch ship by the marine court of New York, which required the ship's master to defend himself against the complaints of one of his crew, and against the refusal of local officials there to accede to the captain's request for the arrest and return of deserters; cites the failure of authorities in American ports, visited during the summer by two vessels of the Dutch Royal Marine, to arrest deserters; and demands "the adoption of a system," in regard to deserters and to differences among crews, "analogous to that . . . followed in the Netherlands." ANS, in French, with translation in State Department file. *Ibid.* Published in *American State Papers, Foreign Relations,* V, 799-800. Cf. below, Clay to Forsyth, January 17, 1826, note.

MISCELLANEOUS LETTERS   December 27, 1825

To JOHN FORSYTH, "Chairman of the Committee of foreign Relations of the H. of R. of the U. S." States, in reply to Forsyth's letter of December 23, that the statement referred to has not been found in the letters of Levett Harris to the State Department, that Harris probably sent a transcript to the United States Legation at St. Petersburg and not to the Department, that both (George W.) Campbell and his predecessor (as Minister to Russia), (John Quincy) Adams, had presented notes to the Russian Government relative to the claim of the Weymouth Importing Company, and that no answer was received. Copy. DNA, RG59, Report Book, vol. 4, pp. 114-15. Published in *American State Papers, Foreign Relations,* V, 785.

From S[AMUEL] L. S[OUTHARD], Navy Department. Encloses a copy of a letter addressed this day to S(amuel) D. Heap. LS. DNA, RG59, Misc. Letters (M179, R63). The enclosure is an acceptance of Heap's resignation.

DIPLOMATIC NOTES   December 28, 1825

From JOSE SILVESTRE REBELLO, Washington. Announces the signing, on August 29, of a treaty of peace and alliance between Brazil and Portugal and encloses a copy of the treaty. LS, in Portuguese, with translation in State Department file. DNA, RG59, Notes from Brazilian Legation, vol. 1 (M49, R1). Translation published in Manning (arr.), *Diplomatic Correspondence . . . Latin-American Nations,* II, 840. See above, Raguet to Secretary of State, March 11, 1825, note.

INSTRUCTIONS AND DISPATCHES   December 28, 1825

From JAMES BROWN, Paris, no. 40. Acknowledges receipt, on December 16, of Clay's "No. 2" (October 25, 1825); states that a commission has been created to propose the manner in which claims should be made and "the principles and mode" of paying them and that Clay's questions cannot be answered precisely until the commission reports and a law shall have been enacted; encloses a letter from S. Wante, "Director of the Bureau of the St. Domingo indemnities," replying to certain questions Brown has submitted to him; and transmits also "copies of the rules laid down by the commission. . . ." LS. DNA, RG59, Dip. Disp., France, vol. 22 (M34, R25). Received February 16, 1826. Published in Washington *Daily National Intelligencer,* February 25, 1826. Charles Peter Stephen Wante, the merchant formerly of Baltimore, had moved to Santo Domingo around 1802.

MISCELLANEOUS LETTERS   December 28, 1825

To VICTOR DuPONT. Announces his appointment and the forwarding of his commission as a director of the Bank of the United States. Copy. DNA, RG59, Dom. Letters, vol. 21, p. 230 (M40, R19). A circular of this text was addressed on this date also to Manuel Eyre, Joseph W. Patterson, and Campbell P. White. DuPont and White were new appointees at this time; the others were being reappointed. White, a native of Ireland, who had emigrated to the United States in 1816 and engaged in mercantile activities, was a prominent New York political leader. He served in Congress as a Jacksonian Democrat from 1829 to 1835.

By letter to Clay, on January 3, 1826, Patterson declined the reappointment, ALS, in DNA, RG59, Letters of Resig. and Declin.

From JOHN WURTS, Washington. Transmits a letter from Borie and Laguerenne (above, December 26, 1825). ALS. DNA, RG59, Cons. Disp., Veracruz, vol. 1 (M183, R1).

ADDIN LEWIS, "Collector's Office, Mobile," recommends the appointment of William Crawford as judge for the District of Alabama. LS. DNA, RG59, A. and R. (MR1). See above, Owen to Clay, September 25, 1825, note.

To Henry B. Bascom

My dear Sir   Washington 29h. Decr. 1825
    I have received your very kind letter of the 24h. inst.[1] from Wheeling, as I always receive your favors, with unaffected satisfaction. The pleasure of our existence and of our pursuits depends much upon the interest which other beings around us, constituted like ourselves, take in us. That which you have constantly, and in a way so obliging and friendly, expressed in whatever concerns me, has been a source of peculiar gratification. I am rejoiced to hear that your health is good. Long may you enjoy that great blessing! My own is not bad. During some weeks past it has been better than at any time since the last adjournment of Congress.
    Of the manner in which I shall acquit myself, in my present station, the public must decide. My zeal for its service is unabated, and it will occasionally have some evidences to enable it to decide upon the amount of capacity which I exert in my new career. If I am to believe those who have opportunities of judging me, my friends will not hereafter be, as I trust heretofore they have not been, ashamed of me.
    I learn from several competent quarters that you are doing well at Pittsburg. So you will continue to do if the prayers can prevail of   Your faithful friend   H. CLAY
The Revd. H. B. Bascom.

ALS. NHi.   [1] Not found.

To James Taylor

My dear Sir   Washn. 29 Decr. 1825
    I recd. your friendly letter of the 17h. inst.[1] and thank you for your kind condolence on the occasion of our late severe losses.[2] Mr. Bibbs[3] conduct in again dismissing the suit of the U.S. agt. you[4] is most strange. You have certainly been much harrassed, even if the claim agt. you were perfectly just.
    I observe what you say in recommendation of Mr. W. D. Adison.[5] I shall be happy if those considerations, which must always be weighed, shall admit of the gratification of your wishes. I need

not say that with me your recommendation will have much influence.

Poor Todd![6] I am prepared to hear the saddest news of him. He will leave few so good, none better, behind him.

My best respects and those of Mrs. Clay to Mrs. T.[7] and our congratulations to you both on the increase of your grand children. I am Cordially & faithfly Yr friend   H CLAY
Genl. J. Taylor.

ALS. KyHi.   [1] Not found.
[2] The deaths of Eliza Clay and Susan Clay Duralde.
[3] George M. Bibb.
[4] Cf. above, III, 69-70. In October, 1823, and November, 1825, the suit had been again continued. On March 2, 1833, after five non-suits had been suffered by the Government, Taylor obtained passage of legislation to compel a settlement of accounts (6 *U. S. Stat.*, 540-41), under which adjustment Taylor's debt was reduced to $5,309.34. The following year he sought another bill to allow him one and a half per cent commission on the sums he had disbursed, that is, on $1,122,340. A Senate committee reported favorably at that Session, but no action was taken upon it; committees of the House in 1840 and the Senate in 1843 subsequently rejected the renewal of Taylor's petition. *Senate Docs.*, 23 Cong., 1 Sess., no. 107; 27 Cong., 3 Sess., no. 110; *House Repts.*, 26 Cong., 1 Sess., no. 422.
[5] Not identified.   [6] Thomas Todd.
[7] In 1795 Taylor had married a widow, Keturah Moss Leitch.

From William Bullitt

The Honl Henry Clay   New Orleans 29h. December 1825
Dear Sir

I did hope that my letter enclosing the strong and honorable recommendation for the appointment of Naval Officer would have been worthy of an answer[1]— The very act of asking your support implied that you had my good wishes and little Support—you will be pleased to deliver the recommendation to my friend the Honl J S. Johnston when convenient—

I need not say to you that the very hasty appointment of Mr Cruzat[2] thro the improper influence of Mr W L. Brent has given a great deal of surprise and dissatisfaction, you have no doubt been informed of it by Others— I hope never to be under the disagreeable necessity to trouble you or Our worthy president again for an appointment— Respectfully your Huml St.   WM. BULLITT

ALS. DNA, RG59, Misc. Letters (M179, R63).
[1] Cf. above, Bullitt to Clay, May 26, 29, 1825. The recommendation, not found.
[2] Cf. above, Derbigny to Clay, May 28, 1825, note.

From Richard Rush

My dear Sir.   Washington Dec 29. 1825
The petition of the sugar refiners has been referred to me, as you will see by the enclosed papers.[1] Certainly, this forms no good

reason why *I* should refer it to *you*, except that your past kindness is leading me to fresh encroachments. I well know how multiplied, and constant, and harrassing, are your labours, and I do not want you even to open the papers, but as you may find it possible to snatch a quarter of an hour within a fortnight to come, or as much longer as you chuse; and on no account whatever to trouble yourself by putting pen to paper upon the subject. But your mind, I know, will act upon it at once, and I shall greatly value your conclusions as you may be able to impart them to me at intervals when we may be together.

The Treasury Report[2] seems, as far as I learn, to have been tolerably well received, so far; confirming what you were good enough to say of it at the Russian Ministers.[3] Whatever little merit it may be thought to have, I shall certainly always continue to declare belongs to you more than to me. It was you who strengthened me in the sentiments I had, enlarging some and correcting others; it was you who encouraged me to throw them upon congress and the country in the manner I pursued; and, more than all it was you who suggested to me the propositions with which it concludes. Left to myself I should have struck into a path much less judicious.

Permit me, my dear Sir, to subscribe myself Your attached,
Mr Clay.   R. RUSH.

ALS. DLC-HC (DNA, M212, R2).
[1] Not found. The petition was probably from the sugar refiners of Baltimore. The Committee of Ways and Means of the House of Representatives, acting upon such a memorial, reported a bill on January 31, 1826, to allow an additional drawback on sugar refined in the United States and exported. U. S. H. of Reps., *Journal*, 19 Cong., 1 Sess., p. 209. No action was taken upon the proposal by the Nineteenth Congress.
[2] The *Letter from the Secretary of the Treasury, Enclosing His Annual Report on the State of the Finances of the United States* (*Senate Docs.*, 19 Cong, 1 Sess., no. 6) had been submitted to Congress on December 22. In it Rush had cited the very large proportion of exports and imports carried in American vessels, despite the "footing of equality, as to duties, and charges of whatever kind, in our ports," which was applicable to "the vessels of those foreign nations with which the United States have the most extensive commercial intercourse. . . ." This situation, he contended, served "to show how the efficient protection extended to it [American shipping] by the early laws of Congress, succeeded in establishing it in a manner to meet and overcome all competition." He had then called attention to the increasing value of exports of American domestic manufactures, which he attributed to the "new tariff" (see above, III, 756n); and noted that the effect of that legislation, while yet not fully known, had "not been to diminish the general aggregate of the Foreign trade of the Country." The concluding half-dozen pages constituted a declaration of the nature of the development of manufacturing and a recommendation for higher tariff rates on "fine quality" cotton.   [3] The Baron de Tuyll.

DIPLOMATIC NOTES   December 29, 1825

To CHARLES R. VAUGHAN. Transmits a letter, "just received from the Governor of New York," with its enclosures (above, Clinton to Clay, December 19, 1825), "respecting the case of Michael Neilson." Copy. DNA, RG59, Notes to Foreign Legations, vol. 3, p. 247 (M38, R3). ALI draft, in CSmH.

INSTRUCTIONS AND DISPATCHES   December 29, 1825

To WILLIAM SHALER, "Consul General of U. S.   Algiers." Notes that, in consequence of increasing contacts of the United States with the Levant and the need for trustworthy persons, acquainted with the Turkish and Arabic languages, in the public service, the President has decided to place "a mid-shipman or some other youth with each of our Consuls near the four Barbary powers, to be instructed, under the superintendance [*sic*] of the Consul in those languages"; states that William B. Hodgson, employed as translator by the State Department "for some time past," has been selected for Shaler's consulate for a term of three years; suggests that Hodgson also be taught the French language; notes that the young man will be sent out by a public vessel and will be paid at the rate of $600 per year; authorizes Shaler, in case Hodgson "conducts himself unworthily," to return him to the United States; and, in a postscript dated February 3, 1826, adds that in the absence of public trans-portation Hodgson will engage passage in a private vessel. Copy. DNA, RG59, Cons. Instr., vol. 2 (M78, R2). Hodgson, born in Virginia, had received the M. A. degree from the College of New Jersey (Princeton) in April, 1824. He was appointed in 1832 as dragoman to the United States Legation at Turkey.

From WILLIAM C. SOMERVILLE, Paris, "Private." States that, though still weak after an illness of over two months, he believes he will "be able in a day or two" to begin his "journey to the South." ALS. DNA, RG59, Dip. Disp., Sweden and Norway, vol. 4 (M45, R5). Received February 16, 1826.

MISCELLANEOUS LETTERS   December 29, 1825

To DeWITT CLINTON. Expresses an intention to "lose no time in communica-ting to the British Minister Clinton's letter of December 19, with its enclosures. Copy. DNA, RG59, Dom. Letters, vol. 21, p. 231 (M40, R17). Cf. above, Clay to Vaughan, this date.

From H[UTCHINS] G. BURTON, Raleigh. Calls attention to a representation, recently made to him, "that the United States has no Consul or commercial representative at Kingston in Jamaica— And that for want of one our Citizens frequently sustain loss & Inconvenience." Adds that "our commercial inter-course with that place will probably increase." ALS. DNA, RG59, Misc. Letters (M179, R63). See below, Clay to Burton, January 3, 1826.

APPLICATIONS, RECOMMENDATIONS   December 29, 1825

THOMAS W. COBB, "Senate Chamber," encloses a letter (not identified) for Clay's consideration; states that the paper mentioned in it "circulates principally in the Western Counties of the state." AN. DNA, RG59, P. and D. of L. See below, Clay to Cobb, December 30, 1825.

From Christopher Hughes

Private!   Washington; December 30th. 1825.
My dear Mr. Clay!
    As you were charged with functions distinct from those of the

Foreign Department, during almost *all* of the time of my absence from home, I feel a strong, & I hope an excusable wish, to present to you a condensed view of my official acts, which will prove *zeal*, at least, if they do not claim to be called *services!*

[Beginning with his arrival in Sweden in 1817, Hughes sketches in eight manuscript pages, his successes as a diplomat. He claims to have prevailed on the Swedish Government to relax, in favor of Americans, the rule that no foreigner could enter the country "without a Passport from the Capitol"; to have "restored order to the Consular affairs" of the United States in Sweden; to have obtained for American merchants, without concessions in return, special privileges in bringing into the country "West Indian & South American produce" and "in getting the toleration continued" despite opposition from Swedish ship owners; to have procured from the King special advantages in the ports of Norway; to have obtained admission of the right of the United States "to have a consul at St. Bartholomews"; to have made possible (John) Connell's "liquidation of the Stralsund claims";[1] to have saved "In many *particular* cases" large sums of money to Americans ignorant of Swedish "Custom-house-usages"; and to have procured "a considerable mitigation in" the application of Danish quarantine regulations upon American Baltic trade.]

In political communications & information, I believe I have not been behind others, in zeal or Success! Mr. Monroe & Mr. Adams have had the kindness to say so! And I trust that in a general sense, the *renown* of the Country has suffered nothing, wherever I am known in Europe, by its representation having been confided to Your true & devoted Friend   C. HUGHES

Excuse the blunders & the liberty! I have two other topics; but I'll talk of them! I have written enough!

ALS. DLC-HC (DNA, M212, R2).
[1] See above, Hughes to Secretary of State, March 19, 1825, note; Hughes to Clay, June 21, July 15, 1825.

DIPLOMATIC NOTES   December 30, 1825

From JOSE MARIA SALAZAR, New York. Acknowledges receipt of Clay's note of December 20; conveys the gratitude of the Colombian Government, which has been informed of the instructions to the American Minister at St. Petersburg (above, Clay to Middleton, May 10, 1825); states that he will transmit to his government the wishes of the President of the United States for a suspension of the invasion of Cuba and Puerto Rico pending the outcome of the mediation of the great powers with Spain; professes to have no knowledge, from any source, of an expedition being prepared at Cartagena; points out that, in view of the augmentation of Spanish forces in Cuba and Puerto Rico, Colombia has cause for alarm and that Colombian preparations for defense are a necessary consequence of Spain's prolongation of the war and the refusal of European powers to recognize the independence of the new Republics. Suggests that to many it would appear unreasonable to renounce a chance to end the war and dictate a peace advantageous "del sistema Americano" in the expulsion of a European nation from Cuba and Puerto Rico, which, considering the condition of Spain, could fall into the hands of a European great power; remarks that it is unreasonable to expect Colombia to continue inaction in the face of the heavy expenses of maintaining defenses against possible attack by Spain; states that Colombia has long postponed action against these islands, awaiting a favorable moment for concerted action with her allies; and concludes by declaring that, if the matter is not settled by the forces of Colombia and Mexico, the future of the islands must be decided by the Panama Congress, which gives time for the result of mediation by the Russian Emperor to be known. LS, in Spanish, with translation in State Department file. DNA, RG59, Notes from Colombian Legation, vol. 1, pt. 2 (M51, R2). Published in *American State Papers, Foreign Relations,* V, 856-57.

INSTRUCTIONS AND DISPATCHES   December 30, 1825

To RICHARD C. ANDERSON (JR). Instructs him to inform the Colombian Government immediately of the purpose of the letter to Salazar (above, December 20, 1825), "of which a copy is enclosed," and to "further the object of it . . . by direct and friendly explanations . . . upon the subject." Transmits also copies of Nesselrode's answer to Middleton's dispatch "inviting the Emperor to cooperate in the work of peace" and two letters from Middleton (above, July 27, September 8, 1825, and note). States that "The Baron de Tuyll, the Russian minister accredited here in an interview . . . had with him agreeably to instructions received by him from St. Petersburg corroborates and supports the views which Mr. Middleton presents of the effect of the appeal to the Emperor of Russia." Further instructs him to use "the papers and facts now communicated" to bring a suspension of any expedition being prepared against Cuba and Puerto Rico. Copy. DNA, RG59, Dip. Instr., vol. 10, pp. 426-27 (M77, R5). LI draft, partially written by Clay, in DLC-HC (DNA, M212, R7). A similar letter, adapted for reference to the Mexican Government and enclosing a copy of the letter to Obregón (above, December 20, 1825), was addressed on the same day to Joel R. Poinsett.

MISCELLANEOUS LETTERS   December 30, 1825

To THOMAS W. COBB, "in Senate." Replies to Cobb's "Note of yesterday" by stating that no change has been made "in the printers designated in Georgia to publish the Laws"; adds that an application from Macon, "in behalf of the Georgia Messenger," was received after the selection had been made and is on file; returns the enclosure sent by Cobb. Copy. DNA, RG59, Dom. Letters, vol. 21, pp. 232-33 (M40, R19).

From BRITTON EVANS, Philadelphia. States that the Lafayette Institute, an organization of which he is president, has been formed in Philadelphia; that the body has no desire to violate the Constitution and laws of the United States, but that its intention is "to proceed to Greece to aid the Greeks by . . . advice or otherwise if necessary"; inquires whether the United States would be willing "to aid the emigration of a number of individuals to Greece." ALS. DNA,

RG59, Misc. Letters (M179, R63). Evans, born in Pennsylvania, had served as a lieutenant in the War of 1812, had re-enlisted in the Army after the war, and had been honorably discharged with the rank of first lieutenant in 1821. He later served in both the Seminole War in Florida and the Mexican War and retained a life-long interest in the issue of Greek independence. Lafayette Institute not further identified.

From EDWARD EVERETT, Washington. Lists the documents wanted in "the Call for papers relative to French spoliations between 1793 & 1800." ALS. *Ibid.* On April 20, 1824, the House of Representatives had adopted a motion calling upon the President to communicate the correspondence between the United States and France relating to those spoliations and to the claims of France upon the United States "for not complying with the treaties of alliance and commerce of February 6, 1778." *Annals of Cong.,* 13 Cong., 1 Sess., pp. 2431, 2457. Cf. below, Clay to Adams, May 20, 1826.

From EDWARD EVERETT, Washington. Inquires, as Chairman of the Library Committee, House of Representatives, how many copies of documents are distributed by the Department of State under "the Joint Resolution Approved December 27, 1813 (See Laws U. S. Vol. IV, p. 712 [3 *U. S. Stat.,* 140-41])." ALS. DNA, RG59, Misc. Letters (M179, R63).

From LEWIS WILLIAMS, "Committee Room." On behalf of the Committee on Claims (of the House of Representatives), refers to Clay the case of Moritz Furst and requests a search in the files of Clay's Department "for the authority given to Mr. [Thomas] Appleton to employ an artist for the mint of the United States, and for any papers that may refer to the employment of . . . Furst." If no information is available, asks that Clay write Appleton at Leghorn for a deposition relative to the employment of Furst and "authority for so doing—" ALS. *Ibid.* Furst, a Hungarian engraver of dies for coins and medals, had purportedly been induced by the United States consul at Leghorn in 1807 to come to Philadelphia as die-sinker at the mint. He had prepared dies for numerous Congressional medals awarded during the War of 1812 and had conducted a private business in Philadelphia from 1808 to 1820. Fielding, *Dictionary of American Painters, Sculptors and Engravers,* p. 131.

APPLICATIONS, RECOMMENDATIONS   December 30, 1825

HUGH NELSON recommends for appointment as porter, George Colston, "a coloured man, in Washington," who had accompanied Nelson to Spain. ALS. DNA, RG59, A. and R. (MR1). Colston, a free Negro, not further identified.

INSTRUCTIONS AND DISPATCHES   December 31, 1825

From CONDY RAGUET, Rio de Janeiro. Encloses copies of his correspondence with the Government of Brazil, not already forwarded with his letter of December 13, from the date of his reception as Chargé; remarks that he has had no reply to his note relative to the case of the *Spermo* (see above, Raguet to Secretary of State, March 11, 1825, note) and that personal inquiries have yielded no information concerning "Tobias Madden, of whose impressment in August 1824, there can be no doubt. . . ." ALS. DNA, RG59, Dip. Disp., Brazil, vol.

4 (M121, R6). Received March 30, 1826. In one of the enclosures, to the Minister of Foreign Affairs (the Viscount of St. Amaro), December 10, Raguet refers to his note of August 12, 1824, on the impressment of Madden. St. Amaro, formerly Counsellor of State, had been named Minister of Foreign Affairs on November 22, 1825, but resigned on January 18, 1826, and shortly thereafter became president of the Senate.

MISCELLANEOUS LETTERS   December 31, 1825

From SAMUEL L. SOUTHARD, Navy Department. Requests, "for the House of Representatives," translations of papers transmitted with Clay's note to the Navy Department (to Southard), May 6, 1825, and subsequently returned to the State Department. ALS. DNA, RG59, Misc. Letters (M179, R63). Endorsed by Clay on wrapper: "Mr. [Daniel] Brent will be pleased to have them prepared."

APPLICATIONS, RECOMMENDATIONS   December 31, 1825

JOHN GRAEFF, JR., Washington, solicits employment in copying, "out of Office," for the State Department. ALS. DNA, RG59, A. and R. (MR2). Graeff, not further identified, received payment during October and November, 1826, from State Department contingency funds for arranging and labelling "old papers." *House Repts.*, 20 Cong., 1 Sess., no. 226, pp. 47, 52-54. Cf. below, Hemphill and others to Clay, May 4, 1826.

JONATHAN PRESCOTT HALL, New York, recommends John (H.) Grosvenor, of Pomfret, Connecticut, for appointment as consul at Canton, where he now resides. ALS. DNA, RG59, A. and R. (MR1). Hall, born in Connecticut and graduated from Yale, was now practicing law in New York and from 1831 to 1833 published the two-volume *Reports of Cases in the Superior Court of the City of New York, 1828-'29*. Later active as a Whig politician, he became Federal district attorney for the Southern District of New York in 1850. Grosvenor, also a native of Connecticut, was appointed to the Canton consulate and served until his removal in 1835.

INDEX